THE
SCOTS
DIALECT
DICTIONARY

THE
SCOTS
DIALECT
DICTIONARY

Compiled by
Alexander Warrack, MA

WAVERLEY
BOOKS

This edition published 2006 by Waverley Books Ltd
First published 2000

© 2000, 2006 Waverley Books Ltd,
New Lanark, Scotland

Compiled by Alexander Warrack, MA,
with an introduction by William Grant, MA

ISBN 10: 1 902407 35 0
ISBN 13: 978 1 902407 35 7

Printed and bound in Poland by OZGraf S.A.

POLSKABOOK

Introduction to the First Edition

By William Grant

Angles and Anglian

The Angles were one of the Teutonic tribes that invaded Britain in the fifth and sixth centuries of our era. They settled along the eastern seaboard, and for a time were able to establish something like a political unity between the Humber and the Forth. Such was the prestige of the Anglian name that the terms 'England' and 'English' came to signify in politics and literature the ideal unity of the Teutonic people in South Britain. In the eighth century Anglian learning and culture were famed throughout Europe, and Caedmon, the poet, and Bede, the historian, are names that still recall to the modern Englishman the ancient glory of the race. Internal dissension and the fierce onslaught of the Danes overthrew this early English state at the end of the eighth century and swept away nearly every trace of its literature. The West Saxon kingdom succeeded to its political influence, and West Saxon writers in a long series of literary works give us a perfect picture of their own language. But the old Anglian speech is known directly to us only by the runic inscriptions of the Bewcastle and Ruthwell crosses, the death-bed verses of Bede, and a fragment of Caedmon. Until the thirteenth century we get only some scanty glimpses of the language in a few glosses of Latin ecclesiastical works, in some charters, and in the laws of the four boroughs, Berewic, Rokisburg, Edinburg, and Strevelin. About the year 1275 appeared a work called *Cursor Mundi*, whose author lived near Durham. Early in the fourteenth century Richard Hampole wrote *The Pricks of Conscience*, near Doncaster in Yorkshire; and towards 1375 John Barbour, Archdeacon of St Machar, Aberdeen, produced his great epic of *The Brus*. In these three works the language is identical, and it is the same dialect into which the Latin laws of the early Scottish kings were translated in the fourteenth and fifteenth centuries. It is quite different from the language used in contemporary literature in the middle and south of England; and even with the scanty relics that we have of an older period, we can say that the tongue of Barbour and of Hampole, of Aberdeen and York, is the lineal descendant of the speech of Bede and Caedmon.

Inglis

Up till the beginning of the sixteenth century, the Scots called their language Inglis, which is the northern form of the primitive 'Angelisc'. Contemporary literature makes this quite clear. Barbour (*Brus* iv, 252), in translating a Latin sentence, says:

Rex ruet in bello, tumulique carebit honore.
This wes the spek he maid perfay
And is in *Inglis* for to say:
The King sall fall in the fichting
And sall fale honor of erding.*

Gawin Douglas (*c*.1475–1522) is the first writer of importance to use 'Scottis' as a term for his 'tongue materne'. Yet Lyndsay in his panegyric on Douglas writes:

Allace for one quhilk lamp wes of this land
Of eloquence the flowand balmy strand
And in our *Inglis* Rethorik the rose.*

Scots and Scottis

A glance at history will explain this curious mixture of names. The original Scots belonged to the Goidelic branch of the Celts. From their home in the north of Ireland, they crossed over to the west coast of which is now called Scotland, and gradually gained an ascendancy in the country north of the Firths of Forth and Clyde. In 843 AD their king, Kenneth Macalpin, was recognized as ruler over all this district, the original inhabitants, commonly known as Picts, henceforth constituting with the invaders a single nation. Whatever the language of the Picts may have been, that of the Scottish kingdom was Gaelic. But the Scottish kings were not content with their northern domain, and soon the British kingdom of Strathclyde, speaking Welsh, another Celtic language, came under their protection. Then Edinburgh, the great Anglian citadel, looking out on the Scottish sea, was ceded to the northern conquerors. Shortly after 970 AD, Kenneth III, King of the Scots, came into possession of the Lothians, and one of the conditions of his occupation was that he should permit the province the use of its own laws and customs and Anglian speech. Henceforth we have a Scottish dynasty ruling over an English-speaking folk, and adopting the language and customs of its new subjects. We can easily believe that many Scots would object to the anglicizing of their kings; but the fall of Macbeth marked the triumph of the new

* Quoted by Sir James Murray in *The Scottish Dialect of the Southern Counties*.

order of things, and henceforward the kings are Scottish only in name. According to Bede, colonies of Angles had tried to settle in the land of the Picts before 685, but the defeat of Ecgfrith in that year, in the battle of Nechtansmere, probably led to their expulsion. An any rate, in 1074, when Margaret, queen of Malcolm Canmore, in her zeal for Church reform, called a meeting of the clergy, she found that they understood nothing but Gaelic. Before the death of Alexander III, in 1286, the Anglian speech had crept northward along the coast to the Moray Firth, and apparently also was paramount in that part of the west which lies to the south of the Firth of Clyde, except in Galloway and South Ayrshire. The War of Independence separated definitely the two divisions of Anglia, and the Cheviots became a national boundary; but the language of the Scottish court was still called Inglis, and John of Fordoun, writing about 1400 AD, tells us that the people occupying the coast and the Lowlands speak a Teutonic tongue, and the people of the Highlands and Islands use the Scottish language. Later on, Gaelic was contemptuously styled Yrisch or Ersch, and as national pride demanded a separate name for the national language, the old Inglis tongue of the Lowlands began to arrogate to itself the title of Scottish.

Early Scots

The Scottish language in the modern sense thus has its root in the Anglian of ancient Northumbria. Its subsequent history has been described as covering three periods – viz. Early, Middle and Late Scots. Our national literature may properly be said to begin with Barbour's *Brus* (*c*.1375). In the early period we might place also Wyntoun's *Cronykil* and Blind Harry's *Wallace*, the second of which takes us to the middle of the fifteenth century. We must not, however, forget that, so far as the language is concerned, Early Scots is more a convenient than an absolutely correct term, as it properly indicates a regional division of late Anglian.

Middle Scots

Political conditions after the War of Independence began to effect a cleavage in the language spoken on the two sides of the Cheviots. The speech of London and Oxford, the centres of political authority and of learning, gradually supplanted the old dialect of the northeastern counties of England as a literary medium. While the Anglian of Northumberland was being degraded to that of a humble patois, that of the Scottish area was flourishing round the court at Edinburgh and the University of St Andrews with all the dignity of national life. This second or middle period, dating from about 1450 AD to 1603 AD, was adorned by a galaxy of brilliant writers, of whom the most distinguished were Douglas, Dunbar, Henryson, Lyndsay, Scott and Montgomerie. The spelling of the writers of this period points to a great change in pronunciation, which was most probably the result of the natural tendencies of development in the language itself. We notice a great influx of Latin and

French words; and the study of Chaucer and his followers has also a certain influence on the vocabulary and grammar.

Causes of decadence of Scots

Political and social events combined to increase the influence of the South upon the northern speech. The reformers in Scotland looked for sympathy to their co-religionists in England. A large section of the people turned their eyes from 'la belle France' to regard more favourably their 'auld enemy of England'. In their communications with Englishmen they tried to efface the differences between the two forms of speech, and this was done mostly by giving up what was distinctively Scottish. The Catholic party actually taunted their opponents for their anglicizing tendencies, and the language of the later works of Knox seems to justify their reproach. But at least three things rendered the fall of Scots inevitable as the complete expression of national life. The first was the failure of the Reformers to give the people a vernacular translation of the Bible, and the consequent adoption of a version that was couched in the language of Chaucer, Wycliffe and Tyndale. The second cause was the Union of the Crowns in 1603; and the third was the giant growth of Elizabethan literature. The great mass of the people were trained through their religious exercises to regard the speech of the south as the most dignified vehicle for serious discussion, and poets and scholars writing in English thereby secured a wider audience and a greater name. After the Union, James VI wrote his *Counterblast to Tobacco* (1604) in the language of his new subjects; and his fellow-countrymen and contemporaries, Drummond of Hawthornden, Ayton, Stirling, all are distinguished as English and not as Scottish authors. The nobles and gentry who went to the court at London began to send their sons to be educated at the great English schools, and thus an indelible brand of gentility was given to the softer language of the south. In Sir John Sinclair's *Statistical Account of Scotland*, vol. ii, published in the end of the eighteenth century, is a report by the Rev. Mr Auld upon the parish of Mauchline. 'In this parish,' he says, 'the Scots dialect is the language spoken, but is gradually *improving*.' The single word 'improving' suggests at once the attitude of the superior person towards the vernacular and the causes that were at work in destroying the purity of the dialect. For two hundred years the nation went to school in England, and Scots was disused as the medium for communicating the higher thought of the race. The language has thus been excluded from the general trend of our modern European culture, and can never regain what it has lost.

Late Scots

We give the name of Late Scots to the period dating from 1603 till the present time. During the seventeenth century we see the language gradually discarded for all forms of literature except the lyrical. Even in this department the relics are few, which fact may be due to the absorption of the people in political and religious questions and the stern discipline of the clergy, who frowned on such manifestations of the natural man as the profane ballad and the jovial song. The mighty river is reduced to a trickling rill, on which float such leaves of poetry as 'The Life and Death of Habbie Simson' (by Sempill), 'Maggie Lauder', 'Hardyknute' (by Lady Wardlaw), 'Werena my Heart Licht I wad Dee' (by Lady Grizel Baillie). These and a few more compositions kept up the tradition of lyrical verse until the revival of interest in Scottish literature which is associated with the names of Ramsay, Fergusson, Burns and Scott. The last named introduced the vernacular with great effect into the dialogue of his novels, and he has had a host of imitators down to the present, such as Galt, Macdonald, Stevenson, Barrie, Crockett. If we compare their language with Middle Scots, we find that a large number of old words have been lost, or replaced by English forms, though the reprinting of old ballads and songs by Ramsay and others led to the revival of a few. Even in the lyrical sphere, where we would expect something different, the proportion of purely Scottish words is surprisingly small. In four of Burns's poems, 'A Man's a Man for a' that', 'Duncan Gray', 'Auld Lang Syne', 'The Death of Poor Mailie' – containing in all 873 words – Murray counts 152 only as altogether un-English – i.e. 17.88 per cent. When writers in Scottish dialect attempt a serious subject in prose or verse, they have recourse to English, sometimes concealing the fact from themselves and their readers by using characteristic Scottish spellings, such as the dropping of *d*, *g*, or *ll* at the end of words.

Dialect in Late Scots

Late Scottish writers differ from their predecessors in having no spoken standard on which to model themselves. For some time they continued to follow the old spelling, which represented, in a rough way, the speech of the court in the sixteenth century; but they were not uninfluenced by southern models. There was not much inconvenience for writers who used Central Scots, because their dialect was so closely akin to the old standard speech. But those hailing from the north-east of Scotland were very soon compelled to seek a spelling that would convey better to their readers their manner of speech. The peculiarities of the 'Broad Buchan' had been parodied as early as 1692 in Pitcairne's *Satire of the Assembly or Scottish Reformation*. Laird Littlewit is made to use such Aberdeen pronunciations as 'keerates', 'deen', 'seen', 'seeth', 'jeedge', 'fat', 'fan', for 'curates', 'done', 'soon', 'sooth', 'judge', 'what', 'when'. In the eighteenth century, dialect crops up in words, rhymes and occasional spellings in such works as *Ajax, his Speech to the Grecian Knabbs*, by Robert Forbes, and Ross's *Helenore*; but the best attempt in more modern times to represent dialect in literature is the famous northern classic of *Johnny Gibb o' Gushetneuk*.

Origin of Dialects

Although dialects do not begin to appear in Scots literature till after the Union of the Crowns, they must have existed in the mouth of the people from remote times. The dialect of the southern counties (Roxburgh, Selkirk, East and Central Dumfries) is probably the most direct descendant of the old Anglian speech. Its phonetic system would seem to indicate this, as well as the fact that the Teutonic colonists there made a more thorough clearance of the British than in the east and north. The Lothians, on the other hand, was long the debatable land of Angle, Briton and Scot, and had finally to accept a royal dynasty and train of nobles of Scottish blood and speech. Although the Angles imposed their language on the newcomers, it is very probable that the common speech was affected by the Celtic dialects (Welsh and Gaelic) with which it came into contact. Here, perhaps, we have the beginning of dialectal differences that were ultimately to distinguish Scots from northern English. In any case, this Lothian dialect spoken at the court of the Scottish kings spread, with the extension of their power, along the east coast to Caithness, and to the west country south of the Firth of Clyde, as far as the Solway. It would supplant Welsh in Strathclyde; Gaelic in Galloway and South Ayrshire; Gaelic and Pictish north of the Forth and Tay; Scandinavian in some parts, and Flemish in others. In each district it would be modified in pronunciation, vocabulary and intonation by the language to which it succeeded. Wherever, in Modern Scots, we have marked dialectal characteristics we may be fairly certain that we are dealing with racial conditions different from other parts of Scotland.

Standard Scots contains very little trace of dialect

The old standard Scots was founded, then, on a regional dialect – viz. the Lothian, as spoken at the court and the university. As the standard form of speech, it would be slow to record the changes going on in the popular dialects, and very sensitive to such literary influences as Latin, French and southern English. It would thus contain many elements that would appear but sparsely in the local dialects. In the artificial Scots of the literature of the middle period we may look in vain for the dialectal differences that undoubtedly existed in provincial speech.

I Vowel Distinctions

After these general observations we proceed now to a more detailed account of the outstanding vowel and consonant distinctions between Scots and Standard English, taking Old English as our basis of comparison for the vowels. Old English *a* (as in father) has now in Scots an *eh* sound, and in English an *oh* sound.

	Old English	Scots	Modern English
A (1)	lad	lade	load
	ham	hame	home
	ta	tae	toe
	mar	mair	more

Old English *aw* becomes *a* generally in Modern Scots; but in the central dialects a sound like the vowel in Modern English 'hall' is developed.

A (2)   raw   ra   row

       sawan   sa   sow

An *ai* and *ay* spelling occurs very often in words in class A (1). Its explanation is curious. *Ay, ey, ai, ei* were used at first to indicate diphthongs, which subsequently became single long sounds. Then the *i* or *y* began to be used as a mark of length and was joined to most of the vowels. Hence, when we do not know the origin of a word, it may be difficult to determine whether we have originally a simple vowel or diphthong. Examples of such spellings are:

Scots	Modern English
dede, deid	dead
chese, cheys	choose
flude, fluid	flood
gude, guid	good
mast, maist	most

B   Old English long *u* (pronounced as in English 'food') remains in Scots but is diphthongized in Modern English.

Old English	Scots	Modern English
mus	moose	mouse
hus	hoose	house
cu	coo	cow
scur	shoor	shower
	showre	
	schour	

The only exception to this is in the southern counties, where final *u* is diphthongized. *ou* and *ow* were very often written for this sound to distinguish it from the French value of *u* (e.g. in 'cure'), and here again it is often difficult to decide from the spelling whether we are dealing with an original vowel or diphthong.

Old English long *o* becomes *oo* in Modern English, but has a peculiar development in Scots, where the sound is brought to the front of the mouth, and in some districts the lip-rounding is lost. In its rounded form the sound resembles sometimes the French *eu* in 'peu' and sometimes *u* in 'lune'. Romance words like 'cure', 'sure', 'suit' fall into this class. The theory that this sound was introduced into Scotland through our close connection with France is phonetically absurd.

Old English	Scots	Modern English
C (1) mona	muin	moon
stol	stuil	stool
god	guid	good

When a back or guttural consonant follows this sound, an *i* or *y* often develops before the vowel, which may be, according to the district, *oo, ui,* or *u* – e.g.:

Old English	Scots	Modern English
C (2) boc	beuk (buik)	book
hoc	heuk	hook

D   Old English short *o* in closed syllables becomes *a* regularly in Modern Scots when preceded or followed by a lip consonant, like *p, b, f, w*. 'Crop', 'drop', 'world', 'top', 'croft', 'loft' become 'crap',

'drap', 'warl', etc.

The Old English short *u* vowel (as in Standard English 'foot') is changed in Scots into the vowel we hear in 'but'. In this respect our language agrees with Standard English and differs from most of the English dialects, where 'soom' and 'coom' stand for 'some' and 'come'. In Scots there are a considerable number of words where this Old English *u*, generally before a nasal consonant, becomes some variety of the *i* vowel in 'hit'.

E	Old English	Scots	Modern English
	sumor	simmer	summer
	sunne	sin	sun
	sunu	sin	son
	dunn	din	dun
	knutu	nit	nut

F   The Old English *i* sound (as in Modern English 'hit') has suffered some modification in the Scots dialects. It assumes one or more of three variants similar to the vowels in the Standard English words 'fell', 'hut', 'arise'. This vowel was often written in Middle Scots with a *y* symbol, as in 'hym', 'bytten', 'nevyr' (never). After *w* it was very generally the sound in 'hut' – e.g. 'will', 'win', 'whin' becomes 'wull', 'wun', 'whun'. Apparent exceptions to the general tendencies of development given above are accounted for as analytical formations, shortenings, importations from allied dialects (or changes due to the influence of contiguous sounds).

II Consonantal Distinctions

The following are the most marked of the consonantal peculiarities of Scots:

(1) *r* is always a strong tongue trill, except in Celtic areas (as in Caithness), where the point of the tongue is often retracted in the production of the sound.

(2) *l* is generally the same as in English, though the guttural variety is often heard in conjunction with back consonants, as in 'muckle gowk', 'clock'. The so-called liquid *l*, formed with the middle of the tongue, is believed to have existed in Middle Scots, and was indicated by the spelling *lz*. This symbol z was confused with *z* and *y*, and hence we have such spellings as 'spulzie', 'spulzie', 'spulyie', 'spuillie'. Sir James Murray believes that the old liquid sound survives in some words in the southern counties. In proper names the book-spelling 'Dalzell' has led to a new pronunciation. *l*, preceded by a back vowel, developed in early times into a vowel sound, especially when followed by a consonant in the same syllable. In the case of *ol*, a diphthong is the result in Modern Scots, but the old *al* and *ul* are now mostly represented by a single vowel.

	Scots	Modern English
(3)	smout	smolt
	cout	colt
	ha'	hall
	sma'	small

sta'	stall
skouk	skulk
fu'	full
pu'	pull

(4) Liquid *n* was written *nz*, and has a similar history to that of liquid *l*. Its modern descendant is *ng* (as in 'sing'), as in 'Bluidy Mackingie', 'Menzies', and in 'spaingie' (Indian cane), or 'nyie', as in 'Cockenzie', although in proper names the polite pronunciation takes the sound of *z*.

(5) *ng* in the middle of a word is a simple sound – no *g* sound follows it; hence we say – 'sing-l', 'lang-er', 'hung-ry', just as in Standard English we pronounce 'sing-er'. Before *th* and in the ending *ing*, *ng* is replaced by *n*, as 'lenth', 'strenth', 'runnin', etc.

(6) The Scots dialects all retain the old guttural sound *ch*, *gh*, which has been lost in Modern English, as in 'loch', 'lach' (laugh), 'saugh' (a willow). The digraph *ch* is used also for the double sound in the beginning of 'chin'. This sound at the end of a word is sometimes very conveniently written *tch*.

(7) The *wh* sound in 'why' is never replaced by *w*, as in southern English. 'While' and 'wile', 'where' and 'wear', 'whin' and 'win' are still distinct words to the ear of an educated Scot. The old spelling of *wh* was *quh* and *qwh*, as in 'quhilk', 'quha', for 'which' and 'who'. *qu* stands for *kw*, as in 'quene' (queen) and 'quair'.

(8) Until very recently *w* was heard pronounced before *r*, as in 'wricht' (wheelwright), 'wrang', 'wratch' (wretch). *w* is replaced by a vowel in 'ouk', 'oo', 'soom', 'soop', 'sook', for 'week', 'wool', 'swim', 'sweep', 'swick' (deceive).

(9) The sound of *f* is kept in the plural in words like 'wives', 'lives', etc. Final *v* and *th* are often absorbed by a preceding vowel, as in 'loo', 'pree', 'lea', 'mou', 'unco' (very and strange), for 'luve', 'prove', 'leave', 'mouth', 'uncouth'. Final *th* in ordinals becomes *t*, as 'fift', 'tent', for 'fifth' and 'tenth'.

(10) *sh* is frequently used for *s*, as in 'vessel', 'officer', 'notice', 'mince', 'sew' (shoo). The reverse process is seen in 'wuss' (wish), 'buss' (bush), 'ase' (ash), 'sall' (shall). In words like measure and pleasure the sound is *z* instead of *sh*.

(11) The second consonant is dropped regularly in *mb*, *pt*, *kt*, as in 'tumble', 'fumble', 'except', 'respect', which become 'tum-l', 'fum-l', 'excep' and 'respec'. In many districts also final *d* disappears in *nd* and *ld*, as 'lan(d)', 'han(d)', 'aul(d)' (old), 'baul(d)' (bold), 'taul(d)' (told).

(12) *k* used to be heard everywhere in 'knee', 'knife', 'knock' (the clock), etc. Hard *c* and *g* are retained in such words as 'brig', 'seg', 'kirk', 'birk', 'sclate', 'scleyce', 'skelf', 'skimles', for 'bridge', 'sedge', 'church', 'birch', 'slate', 'slice', 'shelf', 'shambles'.

(13) The termination *ed* (part participle and adjectival) is very generally changed into *it*, as 'waggit', 'raggit', 'crabbit', 'jaggit', etc.

(14) Very often a Scots word shows a curious transposition of consonants as compared with the English.

Scots	English
croods, cruds	curds
corse (place-name)	cross
fiedle	field
wardle	world
roobrub	rhubarb
wrat	wart
kerses	cresses

Mid-Lowland Dialect

In addition to these characteristics of Scots pronunciation, the central dialects have a vowel resembling the vowel in Standard English 'law', in such words as 'half', 'land', 'wall', 'salt', 'walk'. The exact distribution of this sound is not known, but it does not occur in the South Lowland, nor is it heard in the northern area. In the west, especially in South Ayrshire, there seems to be a tendency to unround the *ui* vowel, and one hears a sound like the *i* in 'hit' or the *eh* in 'fate'. A peculiarity of central speech is a curious catch in the voice before certain consonants – e.g. *t*, *p*, hard *c*, and often *n*. It is very strong in the Glasgow district, and frequently takes the place of the following consonant in careless speech. 'Down the water' becomes 'Doon the wa'er'.

The South Lowland

In the South Lowland, which has been minutely described by Sir James Murray, there is a great variety of diphthongs. Old English *u* (*see* class B) when final becomes a diphthong very nearly the same as that in Standard English. Sir James Murray spells it *uw*, as 'cuw' (cow). Words like 'sea', 'me', 'we', 'he', 'dee' (die) are all diphthongized into 'sey', 'mey', 'wey', etc. South Lowland 'Yuw an' mey 'll gang owre the deyke an' puy a pey' becomes in Central Scottish 'Yoo an mee 'll gyang uwr the duyke an' poo a pee' (Murray's spelling). Words like 'bore', 'fore', 'sole', 'foal', which have an *o* sound in other parts of Scotland, have a diphthong written *uo* in this dialect – viz. 'buore', 'fuore', etc. Where there is an *eh* sound in the rest of Scotland, we have here a diphthong which sounds like the *i* of 'it', followed by an *uh*. Sir James Murray writes it *ea*, as 'neame', 'deale', 'teale' (from Old English open *d*), for 'name', 'dale', 'tale'; and 'leade', 'measte', 'cleathe' (for Old English *a*, *see* class A), for 'load', 'most', 'cloth'. When the diphthongs *uo* and *ea* occur in the beginning of a word or preceded by *h*, the first develops into *wu* and the second into *ye*.

South Lowland	Modern English
wurtshet	orchard
hwull	hole
hwup	hope
wuppen	open
yek	oak
yet	oat
yecker	acre

hyel	whole
hyem	home

Other Scots dialects have examples of a similar development, but in none has it been carried out so consistently as in the south. The South Lowland is, lastly, distinguished from the Central Scots by its broad pronunciation of the vowel in 'men', so that it sounds like the South English *a* in 'man'. Hence Pen-chrise-en (a hill in Teviotdale) seems in Border speech to be pronounced as 'P*a*n, chrise-p*a*n' and a 'penny' becomes a 'panny'.

Between the North and Mid-Lowland

In Forfarshire and Kincardine we are in the borderland between north and south. *f* begins to take the place of initial *wh*, but only in the pronominal words 'who', 'when', 'where', 'what', 'whose', 'which', 'whether'. In its vowel system, this debatable land retains the southern *ui* in words like 'guid' but rejects the *aw* vowel in 'ha'' (hall), etc. The boundary between the north and south for the *ui* vowel is said to run between Mount Battock and Skateraw on the coast of Kincardine. Dr Craigie has noted that a line drawn due north from Buddon Ness marks a division between those who say 'red heds' (west) and those who say 'reed heeds' (east).

Mid-North Lowland

North of the *ui* line all the words of the C (1) class have the sound of *ee* (or *wee* after a back consonant), as 'meen', 'steel', 'gweed', for 'moon', 'stool', 'good'. An unexpected diphthong occurs in many words, as 'weyme', 'weyte', 'speyk', 'weyve', 'greyt', 'queyle', 'queyte', 'jeyl', for 'womb', 'wot', 'speak', 'weave', 'great', 'coal', 'coat', 'jail'. In Aberdeenshire and on the Banffshire coast words like 'bone', 'stone', 'one' (Old English a + n) become 'been', 'steen', 'een'.

In this Mid-North Lowland, initial *wh* becomes *f* in all words. 'Fa fuppit the fulpie?' means 'Who whipped the wehlp?' *wr* becomes *vr*, as 'Ye vratch, yee've vrutten that a' vrang,' 'You wretch, you've written that all wrong.' In some words a *v* is heard instead of an older *w*, as 'schav', 'snav', 'lavyer', 'yave' – i.e. 'sow', 'snow', 'lawyer', 'owe'. In the eastern parts of this district *d* replaces Standard English *th* before the termination *er*, as 'fader', 'midder', 'breeder', 'the tane and the tidder' – i.e. 'father', 'mother', 'brother', 'the one and the other'. A *y* sound is frequently developed, especially before a vowel which precedes a back consonant, as 'kyaks', 'byak', 'nyakit', 'tyangs', 'gyang', for 'cakes', 'bake', 'naked', 'tongs', 'go'. Some have found in this evidence of Scandinavian influence.

The Northern North Lowland

The Northern North Lowland (Caithness) closely resembles the last named. The *ui* vowel, however, after *g* or *k*, never becomes *wee*. Hence 'geed', 'keet', 'skeels' stand for 'gweed' (good), 'kweet' (ankle), 'skweels' (disease of the mouth in horses). Before *r* this same vowel *ui* has the value of *yoo*, as 'myoor',

'pyoor', for 'moor', 'poor'. This pronunciation is also prevalent in the western part of Mid-North Lowland. The *oo* vowel in 'hoose' seems also to be pronounced farther forward in the mouth. Initial *th* is dropped in the pronominal words 'the', 'this', 'that', 'they', 'them', 'there', 'then'; *r* is pronounced without a trill and with a retraction of the tongue. In some consonants – e.g. *t*, *d* – the tongue is thrust forward on to the teeth. This dialect still retains the distinction between the present participle and the gerundive – e.g.:

He's fond o' gutter*in* aboot.

He's aye gutter*an* aboot.

Initial *ch* becomes *sh*, as 'shair', 'shylder', for 'chair', 'children'. The ending *et* becomes *ad*, and *ock* becomes *ag*, as 'lempad', 'wifag', 'bairnag', for 'limpet', 'wifock', 'bairnie'. Standard English *ed* does not change to *it* as elsewhere – hence 'crabbed', not 'crabbit'. Norwegian and Gaelic have contributed very largely to the vocabulary of this dialect. The part played by each language in forming the present variety of Lowland speech is still a matter for scholarly investigation.

A Dialect Intermediate between Mid-North and Northern North Lowland

The dialect of the fishing villages in the Black Isle (Avoch, Rosemarkie and Cromarty) seems to resemble that of Caithness. I have noticed the following features in Avoch:

(1) *wh* is dropped in 'who', 'whose', 'what', 'where' – e.g. 'A sa me deet?' = 'Who saw me do it?', 'At a bots that?' or, 'Az is that bot?' = 'Whose boat is it?', 'At ein wuz it?' = 'Which one was it?'

(2) 'Thoo' and 'thee' are still used in conversation for 'ye' and 'you'. 'Ar thoo gaein, byoch?' = 'Where are you going, boy?'

(3) The aspirate is dropped or prefixed contrary to standard use. 'An', 'botuk', 'heilus', 'Enderetta', 'ad', 'esp', for 'hand', 'boathook', 'alehouse', 'Henrietta', 'hold', 'hasp'; and 'hegg', 'Hannie', 'happle' for 'egg', 'Annie' and 'apple'. This peculiarity was noted by Dr Gregor in the Banffshire fishing villages and has been reported also for Futty, Aberdeen.

(4) A diphthong is heard in words like (1) 'pear', 'swear', 'tear', 'wear', and (2) 'ale', 'shame', 'home', 'bone', 'stone', which are pronounced 'sweyr', 'teyr', etc.

The Insular Lowland

The distinguishing mark of the Insular Division is the use of *d* or *t* for *th*, as in 'dat', 'de', 'dem', 'dis', 'strent', 'tink', 'tree', for 'that', 'the', 'them', 'this', 'strength', 'think', 'three'. According to Ellis, initial *ch* becomes *sh* in Shetland only. We note the same peculiarity in Caithness, the Black Isle and Chirnside in Berwick. *wh* does not appear as *f* in this division, nor is the *ui* vowel (e.g. 'guid', 'mune') unrounded. In this respect the Insular Dialects fall into line with the Central. Lowland Scots has been acquired only in recent times by the islanders and has incorporated thousands of Norse words. The thorough examination of these dialects, in which Dr Jakobsen of Copenhagen University has been engaged for fifteen years, may enable us to identify and estimate the influence of Norse in other districts. The problem is often complicated by the fact that some Scandinavian communities (e.g. in Caithness) have passed through the Gaelic stage before acquiring Anglian. If we add that there are at least two forms of Scandinavian and various sub-dialects, it will be seen that the complete investigation of the patois of a fishing village may afford ample scope for the highest scholarship.

The present volume will be of great value to those who cannot easily get access to larger works; and as a concise record of Scottish words in use since c.1650, it will be a handy book of reference to all engaged in Scottish Dialect study.

List of Abbreviations used in this Dictionary

adj	adjective
adv	adverb
aux	auxiliary
comb	combination
conj	conjunction
excl	exclamation
int	interjection
n	noun
neg	negative
phr, phrs	phrase, phrases
pl	plural
poss	possessive
ppl	participle
ppl adj	participial adjective
pref	prefix
prep	preposition
pret	preterite, perfect tense
pron	pronoun
(qv)	cross reference
refl pron	reflexive pronoun
suff	suffix
v	verb

A

a¹ *prep in comp* on.
a² *v* have.
a³ *pron* I.
a⁴ *int* ah! eh!
a⁵, **aa** *n* an island.
a' *adj* **1** all. **2** every.
aa¹ *v* **1** owning. **2** possessed of.
aa² *v* to owe.
aad *v* owed.
aal *same as* **auld**.
aan, aand *v* owing.
a'ane *n* **1** everybody. **2** quite the same thing.
aar¹ *same as* **arn**.
aar² *same as* **arr**.
Aaron's beard *n* **1** St John's wort. **2** the *Linaria cymbalana*. **3** the *Orchis nascula*.
Aaron's rod *n* mullein.
aava *int* an exclamation of banter or contradiction.
aave *n* a spoon net or scummer (qv) used in herring fishing.
aback *adv* **1** aloof. **2** away. **3** (*of time*) ago.—*v* to keep or hold back.
abaid *v* abode.
abaisin, abasin *n* ill-treatment by word or deed.
abaisit *adj* **1** abashed. **2** confounded. **3** ill-treated.
abaw *v* to suffer for.
abb *n* the weft.
abbey laird *n* a bankrupt who fled for sanctuary to Holyrood precincts.
abee *adv phr* **let-abee 1** to let alone. **2** not to mention.—*n* forbearance.
abeech *same as* **abeigh**.
abeen *same as* **aboon**.
abefoir *adv* formerly.
abeigh *adv* **1** aloof. **2** at a distance.
abeis *prep* in comparison with.
aben *adv* in the parlour.
Aberdeen-awa *adv* in or near Aberdeen.—*adj* native of or hailing from Aberdeen.
abidden *v* **1** did abide. **2** dwelt.
a-biel *adv* in shelter.
abies *same as* **abeis**.
†abigent *n* forcible driving away in theft.
ability *n* wealth.
abin *same as* **aboon**.
abit *conj phr* yes! but.
ablach, ablack *n* **1** a dwarf. **2** an insignificant worthless person. **3** a particle fragment.—*adj* incapable.
able¹ *adj* **1** substantial. **2** well-to-do. **3** fit. **4** liable.
able², **ables** *adv* **1** perhaps. **2** possibly.
ableeze *adv* ablaze.
ables *same as* **able**².
able-sea *adv* it may be so.
ablich *same as* **ablach**.
ablins *same as* **aiblins**.
ablow *prep* below.
a'body *n* everybody.
aboil *adv* in or to a boiling state.
abok *n* a talkative forward child.
aboon *adv* **1** above. **2** overhead.—*prep* **1** beyond. **2** superior to. **3** more than.
aboot¹ *adv* **1** into the bargain. **2** to boot.
aboot² *prep* about.—*adv* **1** alternately. **2** about. **3** out of the way.
aboot with *phr* upsides with.
aboulziement *same as* **abuliement**.
above *prep* **1** in addition to. **2** after.
abraid *adv* abroad.

abraidit *adj* (*used of a carpenter's whetstone*) too smooth to sharpen tools.
abrede, abreed, abreid *v* **1** to publish. **2** to spread abroad.—*adv* **1** in breadth. **2** in pieces. **3** asunder. **4** to the winds. **5** abroad.
abroad *adv* **1** out of doors. **2** away from home.
absient *n* an absentee.
abstinence *n* **1** a truce. **2** cessation of hostilities. **3** a fast. **4** a time of fasting.
abstract *adj* **1** apart. **2** withdrawn from.—*v* **1** to withdraw a person. **2** to withdraw from considering. **3** to withhold.
abstractness *n* aloofness.
abstraklous *adj* **1** cross-grained. **2** bad-tempered. **3** obstreperous.
abuliement *n* **1** dress. **2** cloth. **3** habiliment.
abune *same as* **aboon**.
aby *v* **1** to pay smartly for. **2** to suffer for. **3** to expiate. **4** to atone.
abye *adv* **1** ago. **2** past.
acamie, acamy *adj* small, diminutive.—*n* anything diminutive.
acause *conj* because.
accable *v* to overthrow.
accedent *n* **1** an accession. **2** a casual payment.
accept *v* to welcome.
access *n* **1** accession. **2** being accessory to.
accidence *n* **1** an accident. **2** a slip, as of memory.
accidently *adv* accidentally.
acclame *v* to claim, put in a claim.
accomie, accumie *n* **1** latten. **2** a mixed metal. **3** a trumpet made of accomie.
accomie-pen *n* a metallic pencil for writing on a tablet.
accomie-spoons *n* spoons made of accomie (qv).
accompt *n and v* account.
accost *v* to court, pay addresses.
accrese *v* to accrue.
accudom't *adj* settled down upon.
ace¹ *same as* **ase**.
ace² *n* **1** the smallest division of a thing. **2** a particle.
ace o' picks *n* the ace of spades.
ach *int* an exclamation of impatience.
achan *same as* **auchan**.
ache *v* to cause to ache.
achen *n* a marine bivalve used for bait.
acher *n* an ear of corn.
acherspire *v* to germinate.—*n* the sprouting of malt.
ack *n* an act.—*v* **1** to act. **2** to enact.
ackadent *n* **1** whisky. **2** an ardent spirit resembling rum.
ackavity *n* whisky.
acker, ackre *n* an acre.—*v* **1** to pay at a fixed rate per acre. **2** to pay at this rate harvest labourers.
acker-dale *adj* divided into single acres or small portions.
ackran, ackrin *n* the harvesting of grain crops at so much per acre.
ackrer *n* one who harvests crops at so much per acre.
ackward *adj* **1** backward. **2** back-handed.
a-clatter *adv* **1** in a talkative or gossipy way. **2** in a clattering, chattering way. **3** noisily.
aclite, aclyte *adv* **1** awry. **2** to one side. **3** out of joint.
acquaintancy *n* acquaintance.
acquant, acquaint *adj* acquainted.
acqueesh *same as* **atweesh**.
†acquent *same as* **acquant**.
acquit *adj* acquitted.
acre *same as* **acker**.
acre-braid *n* an acre.
acrer *n* a very small proprietor.
acrerer *n* an acrer (qv).

act *v* **1** with oneself to come under legal obligation to do or not do certain things. **2** to enter in a court book.

action-sermon *n* the sermon preceding the celebration of the Lord's Supper intended to stir up thanksgiving.

actual *adj* (*of a minister*) in full orders.

adaes *n* difficulties.

adap *v* to adapt.

addebted *adj* indebted.

addebtor *n* a debtor.

adder-bead *n* a stone supposed to be formed by adders.

adder-bell *n* the dragon-fly.

adder-cap *n* the dragon-fly.

adderlin *n* a young adder.

adder-stane *n* an adder-bead (qv).

addikit *v, adj* addicted.

addiscinse *same as* **audiscence**.

addle *n* **1** foul and putrid water. **2** the urine of cattle.—*adj* **1** rotten. **2** putrid. **3** foul.—*v* to water plants with liquid manure from a byre.

addle-dub *n* a pool of putrid water.

adee *same as* **ado**.

adew *adj* **1** gone. **2** departed.

adhibit *v* (*used of faith*) to place it in one.

adidst *same as* **adist**.

adience *n* **1** room. **2** space. **3** scope.

adiest *same as* **adist**.

adill *same as* **addle**.

adist *prep* on this side of.

adjournal *n* the record of sentences passed in a law court.

adminicle *n* **1** a writing, etc, tending to establish the existence or terms of a lost deed. **2** collateral proof.

adminiculate *v* to support by adminicle (qv).

admirality *n* admiralty.

admiration *n* a wonder, marvel.

admire *v* to wonder, marvel.

ado *v* to do.—*n* **1** stir. **2** excitement. **3** (*in pl*) difficulties. **4** a pretence.

adone *int* **1** cease. **2** leave off.

adow *adj* worth.

adrad *adj* **1** afraid. **2** in dread.

adreich *adv* **1** behind. **2** at a distance.

adulterate *adj* (*used of money*) forged, false.

advent *n* interest or other money payable in advance.

advertish *v* **1** to advertise. **2** to warn.

advise *v* **1** to deliberate judicially with a view to judgment. **2** to seek advice. **3** to purpose, be of a mind to.

advisement *n* **1** advice. **2** counsel.

advocate¹ *v* to order or allow an appeal from an inferior to a superior court.

advocate *n* the Scottish equivalent of English barrister.

advocation *n* the granting of such an appeal.

adwang *adj* **1** tiresome. **2** oppressive.

adzoons *int* an exclamation of surprise, etc.

ae a'e *adj* **1** one. **2** only (*used intensively with superlatives*).

ae ae *adj phr.*one only.

ae-beast-tree *n* a swingletree for a single horse ploughing.

a'een *n* **1** everybody. **2** quite the same thing, all one.

aefald, aefauld *n* a single fold.—*adj* **1** guileless. **2** honest. **3** simple. **4** sincere.

aefaldness *n* **1** singleness of heart. **2** uprightness. **3** sincerity.

ae-fur *adj* having all the soil turned one way by the plough.

ae-fur-land *n* steep land ploughed in only one direction.

ae-haun't *adj* **1** single-handed. **2** with one hand.

aem *n* **1** vapour. **2** hot air. **3** warm glow from a fire.

aen *same as* **ane**.

ae-pointit-girse *n* sedge grass.

aesome *adj* **1** single. **2** solitary. **3** lonely. **4** (*used of husband and wife*) in harmony, at one.

aesomeness *n* loneliness.

aet *v* to eat.

afald *same as* **aefald**.

afeared *adj* afraid.

aff *adv* **1** off. **2** past. **3** beyond.—*prep* **1** out of. **2** from. **3** from the direction of.—*adj* deranged mentally.—*v* to go or run off.

aff-book *adv* **1** extempore. **2** without notes or book.

aff-brack *n* **1** a break-off. **2** any part disrupted from the whole.

aff-cast *n* **1** a castaway. **2** anything cast off.

aff-come *n* **1** issue. **2** escape. **3** an evasion. **4** an apology. **5** excuse.

affect *v* (*used of lands*) to burden them.

affeiring *adj* **1** appertaining to. **2** proportionate.

aff-fain' *n* **1** a scrap. **2** a dropping. **3** a perquisite. **4** a decline. **5** a falling off. **6** a person or thing that falls off or away from. **7** off-scouring.

aff-fall *n* **1** a scrap. **2** a piece fallen off.

aff-fend *v* to ward off.

aff-gain *same as* **aff-going**.

aff-gang *n* outlet.

aff-ganging *adj* (*used of a tenant*) leaving one's farm.—*n* the proportion of crop due to such a tenant by his successor.

aff-gate *n* an outlet or market for goods.

aff-go *n* **1** a start. **2** beginning.

aff-going *n* **1** outset. **2** departure. **3** death.

aff-han' *adv* **1** instantly. **2** on the spur of the moment. **3** extempore.—*adj* **1** plain-spoken. **2** blunt. **3** plain.

aff-handit *adj* written or done on the spur of the moment.

affidat *ppl adj* affianced.

affin-hand *adj and adv* aff-han' (qv).

aff-lat *n* **1** an outlet. **2** any outlet for water at a roadside. **3** a great show-off. **4** a temporary respite from work. **5** a short holiday.

aff-loof, -lufe *adv* **1** off-hand. **2** extempore. **3** without premeditation. **4** from memory. **5** without book or notes.

affordell *adj* **1** alive. **2** yet remaining.

aff-put, aff-pit *n* **1** delay. **2** an evasion. **3** pretence for delay. **4** a makeshift. **5** one who delays.

aff-putting *adj* **1** loitering. **2** trifling. **3** procrastinating.

affrichten *v* to affright.

affront *v* to disgrace, put to shame.—*n* **1** disgrace. **2** shame.

affrontedly *adv* **1** with a bold shameless front. **2** shamelessly.

affrontless *adj* **1** shameless. **2** past feeling.

aff-set *n* **1** dismission. **2** dismissal. **3** an excuse. **4** pretence. **5** what flatters or becomes a person or thing. **6** an ornament. **7** recommendation. **8** outset. **9** delay. **10** hindrance. **11** illness.

aff-side *n* **1** the farther side. **2** the off-side.

aff-tak *n* **1** a piece of waggery. **2** chaff. **3** a wag. **4** a mimic. **5** one who turns another to ridicule.

aff-takin' *adj* **1** poking fun. **2** taking off in ridicule.

affward *adv* **1** away. **2** off.

afiel' *adv* **1** abroad. **2** in the fields. **3** from home.

afire *adv* on fire.

afit, a-fit *adv* afoot.

aflat *adv* flat.

aflaught *adv* lying flat.

afley *v* **1** to dismay, discomfit. **2** to frighten.

aflocht, aflought *adj* **1** agitated. **2** fluttered, flustered.

afoord *v* to afford.

afore *adv* in front.—*prep* before.—*conj* ere.

afore-fit *adv* **1** indiscriminately. **2** without any exception.

afore-hand *adv* beforehand.

afore-lang *adv* shortly, erelong.

afore-syne *adv* **1** formerly. **2** previously.

afore-the-stern *n* a large sleeping bunk in a fishing boat.

afouth *adv* **1** enough. **2** in plenty. **3** in numbers.

afrist *adv* **1** on credit. **2** in a state of delay.

aft *adv* **1** oft. **2** often.

aft-crap *n* **1** stubble grass. **2** aftermath.— *v* to take two successive similar crops from the same field.

aften *adv* often.

after *prep* **1** courting. **2** in pursuit of. **3** past.—*adv* **1** afterwards.

2 left over. **3** denotes an action just about to take place or one that has just taken place.

after ane *adj* **1** alike. **2** uniform.—*adv* similarly.

aftercast *n* **1** consequence. **2** result.

afterclap *n* **1** disastrous result. **2** evil issue.

aftercome *n* consequence.

aftergait *adj* **1** proper. **2** seemly. **3** moderate. **4** tolerable.

aftergang *v* **1** to follow. **2** to go after.

afterheid *n* grass in the stubble after harvest.

afterhin', afterhend *adv* **1** afterwards. **2** behind.

afterings *n* **1** the remainder. **2** surplus. **3** the last milk drawn from a cow. **4** consequences.

after ither *adj* resembling each other.—*v* to follow each other in succession

afternoon *n* afternoon refreshment.

aftershot *n* the last whisky that comes from the still.

afterstang *n* the pain that follows certain pleasures.

aftersupper *n* the time between supper and bedtime.

afterwald *n* the outfield (qv) part of a farm.

aftwhiles *adv* **1** often. **2** ofttimes.

afward *same as* **affward**.

again *prep* **1** against. **2** averse or opposed to. **3** before. **4** in time for.—*adv* at another indefinite time. *conj.* **1** by the time that. **2** until.

again-call *v* **1** to recall. **2** gainsay.

again-calling *n* revocation.

again-give *v* to restore.

again-say *v* to recall.

against *conj* **1** in readiness for. **2** before.

agait *adv* **1** astir. **2** afoot. **3** on the road. **4** away. **5** at a distance. **6** astray. **7** at a loss.

agaitward *adv* **1** on the way. **2** on the road. **3** on the way towards.

agane *adv* ago.

agate[1] *n* a glass marble of variegated colour.

agate[2] *same as* **agait**.

a' gates *adv* **1** everywhere. **2** in all directions. **3** all ways.

agatting *v* gathering together.

agaun *adv* agoing.

agee *adj* **1** awry. **2** crooked. **3** ajar. **4** off one's balance.— *adv* aside.

agent *n* one's lawyer, solicitor, etc.—*v* **1** to act as such. **2** to manage.

agenter *n* **1** an agent. **2** solicitor.

aggrege, aggrage *v* **1** to aggravate. **2** to enhance. **3** to increase.

aggress *v* to assail.

agitate *v* to discuss thoroughly.

agitation *n* **1** a heated discussion. **2** a debate.

aglee, agley, aglie, agly *adv* **1** off the straight. **2** obliquely. **3** amiss. **4** in an immoral direction. **5** unsuccessfully after all scheming.

agog *adv* **1** adrift, to the winds. **2** loose.

agone *adv* ago.

agonizing *v, adj* suffering the death throes.

agree *v* **1** agree with. **2** agree to. **3** (*with* **with**) to like an article of food, to partake of it without subsequent discomfort. **4** to settle business. **5** to reconcile.

agreeable *adj* **1** willing. **2** compliant. **3** kind. **4** obliging. **5** (*with* **to**) in accordance with.

agreeance *n* **1** agreement. **2** harmony.

agroof, agrouf, agrufe *adv* **1** on one's belly. **2** prone. **3** grovelling.

agrue *adv* in a shudder.

agyaun *v* agoing.

ahame *adv* **1** at home. **2** within doors.

ahan *n* **1** a horse. **2** a cow a year old.

ahechie *int* an exclamation of ludicrous contempt.

ahin, ahint, ahent *prep* **1** behind. **2** after. **3** at the back of.—*adv* **1** late. **2** behind in time. **3** behindhand. **4** backward. **5** in error. **6** in debt. **7** in arrear.

a-hishi-baw *n* a lullaby.

ahomel *same as* **awhummel**.

ah-wa *int* an exclamation of surprise, contempt, etc.

aiblach *same as* **ablach**.

aiblins *adv* **1** perhaps. **2** possibly.

aich *n* an echo.—*v* to echo.

aichan *same as* **achen**.

aicher *n* **1** an ear of barley. **2** a head of oats or barley.

aicherd *adj* (*used of grain*) eared.

aicht[1] *same as* **aucht**[4].

aicht[2] *same as* **aucht**[3].

aichus *n* a heavy fall causing strong respiration.

aiderin *conj and adv* either.

aidle *same as* **addle**.

aidle-hole *n* a hole to receive addle (qv).

aifer *n* ground exhalations on a warm day.

aifrins *n* the last milk drawn from a cow, afterings.

aifter *adj, adv and prep* after.

aifterhin *adv* afterwards.

aifternune *n* afternoon.

aiftland *same as* **aith**.

aig *v* to work persistently and eagerly.

aigar, aiger *n* grain dried very much in a pot before being ground in a hand-mill.

aigar-brose *n* brose (qv) made with aigar-meal (qv).

aigar-meal *n* **1** the meal of aigar (qv). **2** a mixture of oatmeal and peasemeal.

aigh *v* to owe.

aighins *n* **1** debt. **2** correction for faults.

aight *same as* **aucht**[3].

aiglet *n* **1** a tagged bootlace. **2** a jewel in a cap.

aigre *adj* sour.

aik *n* an oak.

aiken[1] *adj* oaken.

aiken[2] *same as* **achen**.

Aiken Drum *n* the name of an unprepossessing but beneficent brownie (qv).

aiker[1] *same as* **acker**.

aiker[2] *n* the break or movement made in the water by a fish swimming rapidly.

aiker-braid *n* the breadth of an acre.

aikerit *same as* **aicherd**.

aikle guineas *n* children's name for small flat pieces of shells bleached by the sea.

aikle *n* a molar tooth.

aikraw *n* the pitted warty lichen.

aik-snag *n* the broken bough of an oak.

all *v* **1** to affect with pain. **2** to be unwell or suffering in body. **3** to have something amiss. **4** (*with* **at**) to be dissatisfied with. **5** to hinder, prevent.—*n* an illness, ailment.

aile *same as* **aisle**[1].

allickey *same as* **allekay**.

ailing *n* **1** sickness. **2** ailment.

ailis, ailiss *n* a large glowing fire.

Ailsa cock, ~ parrot *n* the puffin.

aim *n* **1** a blast of hot air. **2** vapour.

ain[1] *adj* own.

ain[2] *v* **1** to own. **2** to acknowledge.

aince, aincin *adv* once.

ainlie *adj* **1** familiar. **2** friendly.

ains, ainse *same as* **aince**.

ainsel' *n* own self.

air[1] *n* **1** a small quantity of anything. **2** a pinch of snuff. **3** a whiff. **4** a taste.—*v* to taste.

air[2] *n* **1** a sandbank. **2** a beach.

air[3] *n* an oar.

air[4] *adj* early.—*adv* long since.

air[5] *v* **1** to fan. **2** to take off the chill, etc.

air[6], **aire** *n* an itinerant court of justice.

airch[1] *n* **1** an arch. **2** an aim.—*v* **1** to aim. **2** to let fly a missile.

airch[2] *same as* **argh**.

aircher *n* a marksman.

air-cock *n* a weathercock.

airel *n* **1** a pipe made from a reed. **2** a wind instrument. **3** (*in pl*) musical tones of any kind.

aires *n* heirs.
airgh *adj* hollow needing to be made up to level.
airgh *same as* **argh**.
air-goat *n* the snipe.
airie *n* **1** hill pasture. **2** an opening in the hills. **3** a summer residence for a herdsman, a sheilin (qv).
airish *adj* chilly.
airle, airl-penny *same as* **arles-penny**.
airles *same as* **arles**.
airm *n* an arm.
airm-cheer *n* an armchair.
airn *n* **1** iron. **2** (*in pl*) fetters.—*v* to iron.
airness *n* earliness.
airn-sauled *adj* iron-hearted.
airny *adj* hard or strong as iron.
air-oe *n* a great-grandchild.
air-up *adj* early up.
airt[1] *n* **1** the quarter of the heavens. **2** point of compass. **3** the direction of the wind. **4** a direction. **5** way.—*v* **1** (*used of the wind*) to blow from a certain quarter. **2** to urge onward. **3** to incite to mischief. **4** to irritate. **5** to point out the way to a place. **6** to direct. **7** to turn in a certain direction. **8** to tend towards. **9** to aim at. **10** to find out, discover.
airt[2] *n* art.
airt[3] *n* an evil or artful design.
airtan *n* **1** direction. **2** the placing towards a point of the compass.
airt-an'-pairt *adj* **1** accessory to. **2** aiding and abetting.
airter *n* an inciter.
airth *same as* **airt**[1].
airtie *adj* **1** artful. **2** dexterous. **3** ingenious.
airtily *adv* artfully.
airtiness *n* artfulness.
airy *adj* **1** showy. **2** pretentious. **3** conceited.
air-yesterday *n* the day before yesterday.
air-yestreen *n* the night before last.
aise *same as* **ase**.
aise-backet *n* a wooden box for holding or carrying ashes.
aise-midden *n* an ashpit.
aishan *n* **1** stock. **2** brood. **3** family. **4** a term of contempt.
aishin, aisin *n* the eaves of a house.
aislar *n* ashlar.
aislar-bank *n* a reddish bank with projecting rocks in a perpendicular form resembling ashlar-work.
aisle[1] *n* **1** a passage between pews. **2** a projection from the body of a church. **3** a wing of a transept. **4** an enclosed and burial place adjoining a church but not part of it. **5** a mausoleum.
aisle[2] *v* **1** to dry in the sun. **2** to dry on the surface.—*n* **1** drying by the sun. **2** the first process of drying linen.
aisle-tooth *n* a molar tooth.
ait[1] *n* **1** a custom. **2** a bad habit.
ait[2] *n* **1** an eating. **2** a feed. **3** a feast.
aiten[1] *adj* oaten.
aiten[2] *n* a partridge.
aiten[3] *n* **1** a giant. **2** a hobgoblin.
aiten[4] *n* the juniper.
ait-farle *n* the quarter of a circular oatcake.
aith[1] *n* an oath.
aith[2] *n* the infield (qv) part of a farm made to bear oats after barley without fresh manure.
aith[3] *adj* easy.
'aith *n* faith.—*int* faith!
aither[1] *v* to weave straw or coir ropes on the thatch of a stack or roof.
aither[2] *n* an adder.
aither[3] *adj, pron and conj* either.
aitherens *adv and conj* either.
aitherins *n* ropes woven crosswise on thatch.
aitherns *conj* **1** either. **2** rather.
aitliff-crap *n* the crop after barley.
aitnach *n* **1** the juniper. **2** (*in pl*) juniper berries.
aitseed *n* oat-sowing and its season.

aiven *adj and adv* even.
aiver[1] *same as* **aver**[1].
aiver[2] *sameas* **aver**[2].
aiverie *adj* very hungry.
aiverin *same as* **averin**.
aivering *adj* eager for hungering.
aivis *n* an unprofitable job.
aivrin *n* the larboard.
aixies *n* **1** the access of an ague. **2** hysterics.
aixtree *n* an axletree.
aize *n* a large glowing fire.
aizle *n* **1** a hot ember. **2** a live coal.
aizle-tooth *same as* **aisle-tooth**.
ajee *same as* **agee**.
alabast-beer *n* a superior kind of beer.
alacampine *n* **1** elecampane. **2** a coarse candy.
alagust *n* suspicion.
alaigh *adv* below, as to situation relative to another place.
alakanee *int* alas!
alake, alacke *int* alas!
alamod *n* a fashionable kind of cloth.
alane *adj* alone.
alanerlie *same as* **allanerly**.
alaney *adj* alone.
alang *adv and prep* along.
alavolee *same as* **allavolie**.
albuist *conj* **1** though. **2** albeit.
ald *same as* **auld**.
ale-brewin *n in phr.* **a sma' ale-brewin'** courting with a view to marriage.
alee *adv* to the leeward.
aleen *adj* alone.
alelladay *int* an exclamation of grief.
alenth *adv* in the direction of the length.
ale-saps *n* wheaten bread boiled in beer.
aless *conj* unless.
algates *adv* **1** in every way. **2** by all means. **3** however. **4** at all events.
alicht *v* to alight.
alicreesh *n* **1** liquorice. **2** black sugar.
aliftin *adj* unable to rise from weakness.
alikay *same as* **allekay**.
aliment *n* **1** parochial relief to paupers. **2** sum given by law for support of a wife or child in cases of separation, etc, or of an illegitimate child in cases of affiliation.—*v* **1** to pay such aliment. **2** to maintain support.
alis *int* a sudden cry of pain.
alist *adv in phr* **come alist 1** to recover from faintness or decay. **2** to revive. **3** to recover from a swoon.—*adj* alive.
alkin' *adj* of every kind.
allagrugous *adj* **1** grim. **2** ghastly. **3** discontented-looking.
allagust *same as* **alagust**.
allakey *same as* **allekay**.
allanerly *adj* **1** sole. **2** alone.—*adv* **1** solely. **2** exclusively. **3** quite alone.
allanhawk *n* **1** the great northern diver. **2** Richardson's skua.
allar *n* the alder.
allars *n* **1** garden walks. **2** alleys like garden walks.
allavolie, alle-volie *adj* **1** giddy. **2** volatile.—*adv* at random.
alleadgance *n* an allegation.
allege *v* to confirm.
allegiance *n* allegation.
allekay *n* the bridegroom's man and messenger at a wedding.
allemand *v* to conduct or escort in a formal manner.
aller *n* the alder.
allerish *adj* **1** weird. **2** uncanny. **3** surly. **4** (*of weather*) chilly. **5** (*of a sore or wound*) painful. **6** fretted.
alleviation *n* palliation of an offence.
all-heal *n* the mistletoe.
allicomgreenyie *n* a girls' game like 'drop handkerchief'.

allister *adj* **1** sane. **2** *compos mentis*. **3** all astir.
allo *same as* **alow**[1].
allocate *v* **1** to apportion the sums due by each landholder in a parish in an augmentation of a parish minister's stipend. **2** to assign seats in a parish church.
all one's lane *phr* quite alone.
alloo *v* **1** to allow. **2** to order.
all out[1] *adv* **1** in a great degree. **2** beyond comparison.
all out[2] *adj* **1** mistaken. **2** disappointed.—*adv* too late.
all over *prep* over and above.
allow *v* **1** to order. **2** to approve of. **3** to oblige.—*n* the way in which trees were made to fall when cut down.
allowance *n* approbation
allure *n* **1** a lure. **2** an attraction. **3** an inducement.
allutterly, alluterlie *adv* wholly, completely.
allycriesh *same as* **alicreesh**.
alm *same as* **aum**.
almanie-whistle *n* a small flageolet used by children.
almery *same as* **aumrie**.
almous *n* **1** alms. **2** a dole. **3** a meritorious act.
almous dish *n* a beggar's dish for alms.
alona *n* a term of endearment.
alonely *adv* **1** only. **2** solely.
alow[1] *adv and prep* below.
alow[2], **alowe** *adv* on fire, ablaze.
alpuist *same as* **albuist**.
alrich, alrisch *adj* **1** weird. **2** unearthly.
alry *adj* **1** weird. **2** unearthly.
alse[1] *adv* else.
alse[2] *conj* as.
alshin, alson *n* a shoemaker's awl.
alshinder *n* the horse-parsley.
alter *n* **1** a change. **2** a change of weather.
alterchange *v* to exchange.
alunt *adv* ablaze, aflame.
alutterly *same as* **allutterly**.
alvertly *adv* utterly.
always[1] *adv* still.
always[2] *conj* notwithstanding, although.
amains o' *phr* **1** getting even with one. **2** getting the advantage or upper hand over one.
amains o' *in phr* **teen amains o' 1** taken in hand. **2** apprehended and dealt with.
amaist *adv* almost.
amand *n* a penalty.
amang *prep* **1** among. **2** in. **3** into. **4** together with.
amang hands *phr* **1** in the meantime. **2** at hand. **3** in process. **4** among other things.
amangs *prep* amongst.
amaton *n* **1** a thin bony person. **2** an opprobrious term.
a-maugres *adv* in spite of.
ambry *same as* **aumrie**.
amel *n* enamel.
amerciate *v* to amerce.
amers *n* embers.
amind *adj* of a mind.
amission *n* **1** loss. **2** forfeiture.
amit *v* **1** to lose. **2** (*a legal term*) to forfeit.
amitan *n* **1** a weak foolish person. **2** one given to excess of anger.
ammel *n* a swingletree.
ammer goose *n* the great northern diver or ember goose.
amo' *prep* among.
amond, amon't *phr* among it.
amove, amow *v* **1** to vex. **2** to move to anger. **3** to rouse.
amplefeyst *n* **1** a fit of the sulks or spleen. **2** needless talk.
amplush *v* to nonplus in argument.
amry *same as* **aumrie**.
amshach *n* **1** an accident. **2** a misfortune.
amshack *n*. **1** a noose. **2** a fastening.
amuve *same as* **amove**.
an[1] *adj* equal. **2** the same.
an[2] *prep* **1** before. **2** ere. **3** by the time of.
an[3] *conj* **1** if. **2** although.

an' *conj* and.
'an *conj* than.
an' a' *phr* **1** et cetera. **2** and everything else. **3** also.
ana, anay *n* a river island, a holm.
analie *v* to alienate property.
analier *n* one who alienates property.
anam *n* **1** a spectre. **2** a ghost.
anan *int* an interrogative exclamation: 'What did you say?'
anatomy *n* **1** a skeleton. **2** a thin bony person. **3** a term of contempt for a man.
ance *adv* once.
anchor stock *same as* **anker stock**.
ancient *adj* **1** (*used of children*) staid, demure. **2** precocious.
ancientary *n* **1** antiquity. **2** precociousness in children.
anciety *n* antiquity.
ancleth *n* an ankle.
and *conj* if.
Andirmess, Andirmas *n* St Andrew's Day, 30 November.
andlet *n* **1** a very small ring. **2** a mail.
Andrea Ferrara *n* a basket-hilted Highland broadsword.
ane *adj* one.—*n* a single person or thing.
aneath *prep and adv* **1** beneath. **2** under.
anee *int* an exclamation of sorrow.
ane-e'ed *adj* one-eyed.
anent, anenst *prep* **1** opposite to. **2** in front of. **3** over against. **4** side by side with. **5** about. **6** concerning. **7** in competition with.
anerly *adv* **1** alone. **2** singly.—*adj* **1** single. **2** solitary. **3** given to solitude.
Anermas *same as* **Andirmess**.
anery *n* a children's term in a counting-out game.
anes *adv* once.
ane's errand *n* **1** an exclusive errand. **2** express purpose.
aneth *same as* **aneath**.
aneuch, aneugh *adj* (*used of quantity*) enough.—*adv* sufficiently.
anevval *adj* lying on the back.
anew[1] *adj* (*used of numbers*) enough.
anew[2] *prep and adv* **1** below. **2** beneath.
anger *v* **1** to become angry. **2** to grieve.—*n* **1** grief. **2** what causes anger.
angersome *adj* **1** annoying. **2** provoking. **3** vexatious.
angleberry *n* an excrescence on the feet of sheep and cattle.
angry *adj* (*used of a sore*) inflamed.
angry teeth *n* the fragment of a rainbow appearing on the horizon and when seen in the north or east indicating bad weather.
anidder *adj* another.
anie *n* a little one.
aniest[1] *prep* **1** near. **2** next to.
aniest[2] *prep* on this side of.
animose *adj* **1** hearty. **2** spontaneous.
animositie *n* **1** hardihood. **2** firmness. **3** courage.
anist[1] *same as* **aniest**[1].
anist[2] *same as* **aniest**[2].
anither *adj and pron* another.
anker *n* **1** a liquid measure of about four gallons used by smugglers for convenience of carriage on horseback. **2** a dry measure for the firlot (qv) for measuring potatoes.
ankerly *adv* unwillingly.
anker stock *n* a large oblong rye loaf, sometimes one of wheat.
ann *n* a half-year's stipend legally due to a deceased parish minister's heirs over and above what was due to him at the date of his death in his incumbency.
annal *n* yearly income produce or groundrent.
annat *n* half-year's stipend due as ann (qv).
anno *v* to keep a boat's head to the wind while fishing with rod or line.
annosman *n* the man who annos a boat. *See* **anno**.
annoy *n* annoyance.
annual *n* **1** annual feu duty. **2** annual income or interest.

annual-rent *n* yearly interest.
annuity *n* yearly house-rent.
anonder, anoner *same as* **anunder.**
anower *prep* in or into and over.—*adv* **1** within. **2** under.
anse *conj* **1** else. **2** otherwise.
answer *v* **1** to supply with sufficient funds from a distance. **2** (*of a colour*) to suit, become.
anter *v* **1** to venture. **2** to chance. **3** to wander. **4** to saunter.
antercast *n* **1** a misfortune. **2** an accident. **3** mischance.
anterin *adj* **1** wandering. **2** occasional. **3** meeting occasionally.—*n* an occasional meeting or thing, etc.
anthony-over *n* the game of throwing a ball over a house from the one party to the other.
antic *n* **1** an oddity. **2** an eccentric person. **3** a spectacle. **4** (*in pl*) odd ways, dress tricks.
anti-lifters *n* a name given to those who objected to the minister at the Communion lifting the bread before the thanksgiving. *See* **lifter.**
antle *v* **1** to keep harping on a grievance. **2** to go on faultfinding, complaining or grumbling.
Antonmas *n* St Anthony's Day, 17 January NS, 29 January OS.
antrin *same as* **anterin.**
anunder *adv* beneath.— *prep* underneath.
anwell *same as* **annual.**
a' oot *same as* **all out**².
a' owre *same as* **all over.**
apen *v* to open.—*adj* open.
apen-furth *n* **1** the free air. **2** an open exposure.
apenin *n* **1** a gap. **2** opening.
apenly *adv* openly.
apert *adj* **1** open. **2** manifest. **3** avowed.
apery *n* scandalous imitation of what is sacred.
apiece, apiest *conj* although.
aplace *adv* **1** in this place. **2** here.
aploch *n* **1** a dwarf. **2** carrion. **3** a remnant. **4** (*in pl*) corners of cornfields or of meadows left un–mowed for the supposed benefit of the warlocks, to keep their favour.
apo', apon *prep* upon.
apotheck *n* **1** a lot. **2** a collection. **3** concern.
appeal *v* to challenge to a duel.
appell *v* to cease to rain.
appety *n* appetite.
apple-glory *n* apple-blossom.
apple-ringie *n* southernwood.
apple rose *n Rosa villosa.*
apport *v* **1** to bring. **2** to conduce.
approve *v* to bring proof.
approven *adj* approved.
appryse *v* to value for distraint.
apprysing *n* **1** the act of valuing for distraint. **2** such a valuation
April-gowk *n* April fool.
apron *n* the abdomen of a crab.
apurpose *adv* **1** intentionally. **2** expressly.
aqua, aquavitae *n* **1** whisky. **2** spirits.
aquavity-hoose *n* a tavern in which spirits are sold.
aqueesh *same as* **atweesh.**
ar *same as* **air**⁴.
arage *same as* **average.**
arase *v* arose.
arbres *n* an arrangement of trees marking distances in the game of the mall.
arch¹ *same as* **airch**¹.
arch² *same as* **argh.**
archer *n* one who throws.
archilagh, archilowe *n* the return which a guest who has been treated makes to the tavern company who were hosts.
archness *same as* **arghness.**
ardent *n* whisky.
are *same as* **air**⁴.
ared *v* to erase, remove.
arend *v* (*used of a horse*) to rear.

argh *adj* **1** timorous. **2** apprehensive. **3** hesitating. **4** reluctant. **5** scanty. **6** insufficient.—*adv* **1** scarcely. **2** insufficiently.—*v* **1** to be timid. **2** to hesitate.
arghness *n* **1** shyness. **2** timidity. **3** awe. **4** reluctance.
argie *v* **1** to argue. **2** to wrangle.—*n* an assertion in a dispute.
argie-bargie *n* **1** a contention. **2** a quarrel.—*v* to contend.
argie-bargiement *n* **1** wrangling. **2** contention.
argie-, argey-reerie *n* **1** a wrangle. **2** a scolding.
argle-bargle *v* to bandy words, cavil, dispute.
argle-bargler *n* a caviller, a contentious person.
argle-bargling, ~-barging *n* cavilling, contention.
argol-bargol *same as* **argle-bargle.**
argol-bargolous *adj* **1** quarrelsome. **2** contentious about trifles.
argoseen *n* the lamprey.
argufy *v* **1** to argue. **2** to signify matter.
argument *n* the subject of a Latin version or piece of English dictated at school to be turned into Latin.
arguy-barguy *same as* **argie-bargie.**
arguy-barguying *n* contention.
aricht *adv* **1** rightly. **2** aright.
Arinffew *n* the old name of Renfrew.
ark¹ *n* a large wooden chest for holding meal flour, etc.
ark² *n* the masonry in which the water wheel of a mill moves.
ark³ *n* a formation of clouds supposed to resemble Noah's ark.
ark-bane *n* the bone called the *os pubis.*
arle *v* **1** to give an earnest of any kind. **2** to pay money to confirm a bargain. **3** to engage for service by payment of a coin as earnest of wages. **4** to beat severely.
arles *n* **1** money paid as an earnest. **2** money given to a servant on engagement. **3** one's deserts. **4** a thrashing.
arles-penny, arle-penny *n* **1** an earnest. **2** the pledge token. **3** a coin given on engaging a servant.
arlich, arlitsh *adj* **1** sore. **2** fretted. **3** painful.
arling *n* the giving of arles (qv).
arm *v* **1** to give one's arm to. **2** to walk arm-in-arm.
arm-lang *adj* **1** as long as the arm. **2** prolix.
armless *adj* unarmed.
arn¹ *n* the alder.
arn² *n* the awn of wheat or barley.
arnet, arnit, arnot *n* a shrimp.
arnot, arnut *n* the pignut or earthnut.—*phr* **lea arnot** a stone lying in a field.
arns *n* a low-lying marsh.
a-road *adv* **1** here and there. **2** in disorder.
aron *n* the *Arum maculatum* or wakerobin, cuckoo's pint.
arr *n* **1** a scar left by a wound or sore. **2** the mark of smallpox. **3** a grudge. **4** ill-feeling.
arrage *same as* **average.**
arran-ake *n* the red-throated diver.
arras, arres *n* **1** the angular edge of anything, of a stone. **2** the tips of the little ridges laid by the plough.
arrayed *adj* (*used of a mare*) in season.
arred *adj* **1** marked by smallpox. **2** scarred.
arrisat *n* an ancient dress of Hebridean women.
arrow *same as* **argh.**
arse *n* **1** the backside or bottom of a person. **2** the rump of an animal. **3** the bottom or hinder part of anything.—*v* **1** to move backwards. **2** push back. **3** to balk, defeat. **4** to back out of a promise, engagement, etc. **5** to shuffle.
arse-bare *adj* with bare buttocks.
arse-burd *n* **1** the backboard of a cart. **2** a tailboard.
arse-cockle *n* a hot pimple on any part of the body.
arselins *adv* backwards.
arselins-coup *n* the act of falling backwards on the hams.
arset, arset-back *adv* backwards.
arse-verse *n* a spell on the side of a house to ward off fire.
arsin *n* shuffling.
art and part *phr* aiding and abetting.
artful *adj* **1** skilled in one's art or craft. **2** expert.
artificial *n* artificial manure in contrast to farm dung.
artval-, arvil-supper *n* the supper given after a funeral.

arty *adj* **1** artful. **2** dexterous. **2** ingenious.
as[1] *adv* how.
as[2] *conj* **1** than. **2** as if (*used to express the superlative degree when occurring between an adjective and its immediate repetition*).
asclent *same as* **asklent**.
ascrive *v* to ascribe.
ase *n* ashes.
ase backet *n* a wooden box for removing ashes.
ase hole *n* a hole beneath or in front of the grate or out-of-doors to receive ashes.
ase midden *n* an ash heap.
ase packad *n* a box to contain ashes.
ase pit *n* an ash pit.
ase puckle *n* a spark from the fire.
ashad *same as* **ashet**.
ashen *adj* belonging to or consisting of ash trees.
ashet *n* a large flat oval dish on which a joint is placed on the table.
ash-gray *adj* grey as ashes.
ashie-pattle *n* **1** a neglected child. **2** a dirty child or animal that lies about the hearth.
ashie-pet *n.* **1** an ashie-pattle (qv). **2** an idle slattern. **3** a kitchen drudge.
ashiler *n* ashlar.
ash, ashen-keys *n* the seed vessels of the ash.
aside *prep* **1** beside. **2** near to. **3** compared with.
asil *same as* **aisle-tooth**.
ask[1] *n* a newt.
ask[2] *n* **1** a chain for fastening cattle in the stall. **2** the stake to which they are fastened.
ask[3] *v* **1** to publish the banns of marriage. **2** (*with* out) (*used of a child*) to ask permission to leave school for a few minutes.
asking *n* **1** a petition, request. **2** the price asked.
asklent *adv* **1** aslant. **2** obliquely. **3** dishonourably.—*prep* across.
askoy *adv* **1** asquint. **2** askew.
asled *adv* aslant.
a-slew *adv* aslant.
aslin-tooth *same as* **aisle-tooth**.
asloap *adv* **1** aslant. **2** on the slope.
a-slype *adv* aslant.
asol *same as* **aisle**[2].
asoond *same as* **aswoon**.
aspait *adv* in flood, in spate.
aspar *adv* **1** wide apart. **2** in a state of opposition
ass *same as* **ase**.
assal-, assle-tooth *same as* **aisle-tooth**.
assassinat, assassinite *n* an assassin.
asseer *v* to assure.
assie *adj* abounding in ashes.
assie-pet *same as* **ashie-pet**.
assignay *n* an assignee.
assilag *n* the storm-petrel.
assiltree *n* an axletree.
assize *v* to try by jury.—*n* **1** a jury. **2** a tax. **3** a measure of fourteen gallons.
assize fish *n* so many fish from each boat for liberty of anchorage, etc.
assize-herring *n* **1** herring duty. **2** a royalty on herring fishing.
assizer *n* a juryman.
assoilyie, assoilzie *v* to acquit, absolve.
assort *v* **1** to dress up. **2** to overdress.
assuess *v* to accustom.
assy-pet, assy-pod *same as* **ashie-pet**.
assyser *n* a juryman.
assyth *v* **1** to make compensation. **2** to satisfy for injury.
assythement *n* **1** legal compensation. **2** atonement.
asteep *adv* in steep, in a soaking condition.
asteer *adv* **1** astir. **2** in confusion or bustle out of doors.
asterne *same as* **austern**.
astid *adv* instead of.

astit, astid *adv* **1** as soon. **2** rather. **3** as well as.
astraying *adj* **1** straying. **2** wandering.
astren *same as* **austern**.
astrick *v* to astrict.
astride-leg *adv* astride.
astrologian *n* an astronomer.
astruct *v* to prove or confirm by investigation.
aswaip *adv* aslant.
aswim *adv* **1** afloat. **2** covered with water. **3** in a swim.
aswoon *adv* in a swoon.
asyle *n* **1** an asylum. **2** a sanctuary.
at[1] *prep* **1** used of feeling towards a person. **2** with. **3** towards. **4** (*with* himself) in full possession of one's mind, etc.
at[2] *pron* **1** who. **2** whom. **3** which. **4** that. **5** (*with a poss pron*) whose.
'at *conj* that.
ata *adv* (*used after a negative*) at all, in the least degree.
atap *adv* atop.
at a will *phr* to one's utmost wish.
atchison *n* a copper coin washed with silver, worth eight pennies Scots or two-thirds of an English penny.
ate-meat *n* an idler who lives upon others.
ather *adj and conj* either.
ather *n* an adder.
ather-bill *same as* **adder-bell**.
ather-cap *same as* **adder-cap**.
athil *n* **1** a noble. **2** a prince.
athin *prep and adv* within.
a'thing *phr* (*used in playing marbles*) a claim for every advantage.
athis'd *adv* on this side.
athol-brose *n* a mixture of whisky and honey.
athoot *prep* without.—*adv* outside.—*conj* unless.
athort *adv* **1** across. **2** far and wide. **3** abroad.—*prep* **1** across. **2** over. **3** through. **4** athwart. **5** along.
athraw *adv* **1** awry. **2** off the straight. **3** acrosswise.
a-tift *adv* on the alert.
atlon *n* **1** family. **2** stock. **3** brood (*used contemptuously*).
atomie, atomy *same as* **anatomy**.
at one'd alone *phr* by oneself, alone.
atour, at-owre *prep* **1** across. **2** over. **3** 'outover', in spite of.—*adv* **1** over and above. **2** besides. **3** moreover. **4** at a distance away.
atry *same as* **attery**.
attact *v* to attack.
attamie *same as* **anatomy**.
atter *n* **1** poison. **2** purulent matter. **3** proud flesh. **4** ill-nature.
attercap *n* **1** a spider. **2** an irascible person.
attery *adj* **1** purulent. **2** fretful. **3** irascible. **4** grim. **5** virulent. **6** quarrelsome. **7** irritable.
attle *v* **1** to intend. **2** to aim at.—*n* **1** an aim. **2** an attempt.
attour *adv* **1** out of the way. **2** over and above.—*v* to get out of the way.
attrie *same as* **attery**.
a-tune *adv* in tune, in harmony.
atwa *adv* in two.
atweel *adv* **1** indeed. **2** truly. **3** of course.
atween *prep* between.
atweesh, atweesht *prep* between.
atwixt *prep* between, betwixt.
auch *same as* **argh**.
auchan *n* a species of pear.
auchimuty *adj* **1** mean. **2** paltry.
auchindoras *n* a large thorn tree at the end of a house.
auchlet *n* a measure of meal, the eighth part of a boll.
aucht[1] *adj* eight.
aucht[2] *v* ought.
aucht[3], **aught** *v* **1** to own. **2** to possess. **3** to owe, to be indebted to.
aucht[4], **aught** *v* possessed of.
aucht[5], **aught** *n* **1** property. **2** possession. **3** applied often contemptuously to persons. **4** opinion. **5** judgment.

aucht⁶ *n* **1** duty. **2** place. **3** office.
aucht⁷ *pron* anything.—*n* **1** importance. **2** moment.
aucht-day *n* a common daily occurrence.
auchtigen, auchtikin *n* the eighth-part of a barrel or half a 'firkin'.
auchtlins, aughtlins *adv* in any or the least degree.
auchtsome *adj* consisting of eight persons, etc.
audie *n* **1** a careless or stupid fellow. **2** a simpleton.
audiscence *n* **1** audience. **2** hearing. **3** attention.
augh *int* an exclamation of disgust or impatience.
aughimuty *same as* **auchimuty**.
aught-pairt *n* an eighth.
auld, aul' *adj* **1** old. **2** eldest. **3** stale. **4** in arrears. **5** usual. **6** unreasonable. **7** great. **8** fine. **9** (*used jocularly of the devil with the following names*) A' Ill Thing, Ane, Bobby, Bogie, Bo-ho, Boy, Carle, Chap, Chiel, Clootie, Donald, Fellow, Hangie, Harry, Hornie, Mahoun, Man, Neil, Nick, Nickey, Nickie Ben, Roughy, Sandy, Saunders, Smith, Sooty, Thief, Waghorn, Whaup-neb.
auld-aunty *n* a grand-aunt.
auld-boy *n* an old man with youthful propensities, etc.
aul'-da *n* a grandfather.
auld coomey *n* a name for the devil.
auld-day *n* an idle day after feasting or hard drinking.
auld-fangle *adj* old-fashioned.
auld-farrant *adj* **1** old-fashioned. **2** precocious.—*n* an old head on young shoulders.
auld-fashiontness *n* childish precocity.
auld-father *n* a grandfather.
auld fowk *adj* **1** elderly people. **2** the parents of bride and bridegroom.
auld gibbie *n* the common cod.
auld-headed *adj* **1** sagacious. **2** shrewd.
auld kirk *n* **1** the Established Church of Scotland. **2** whisky.
auld langsyne *n* **1** old days of long ago. **2** old friendship.
Auld Licht *adj* conservative in theology and church practices.—*n* a member of the Secession Church.
auldlike *adj* old-looking.
auld-man's beard *n* the wild clematis.
auld man's bell *n* the bluebell.
auld-man's fauld *n* a portion of ground set apart for the devil.
auld-man's milk *n* a potation of milk and whisky or rum.
auld mischanter *n* a name for the devil.
auld-mither *n* a grandmother.
auld-mou'd *adj* sagacious in speech.
auldness *n* **1** oldness. **2** age.
auldrife, auldruff *adj* of the old style.
auld shanks, ~ shanky *n* death.
auld son *n* the eldest son.
auld sough *n* an habitual cant or whine.
auld threep *n* **1** a legend. **2** tradition. **3** an old superstition.
auld uncle *n* a granduncle.
auld-warld, ~-wardle *adj* **1** ancient. **2** old-fashioned.
auld wecht *n* more than one's fair share of brains.
auld wife *n* **1** an old woman. **2** a great talker. **3** a chimney cowl.
auld wife's necessary *n* a tinderbox.
auld woman *n* a chimney cowl.
auld word *n* a proverb, saw.
auld-young *adj* middle-aged.
Auld Yule, Aul' Eel *n* Christmas (OS).
aum *n* alum.—*v* **1** to dress leather or paper with alum. **2** to thrash or beat soundly.
auman *n* a sound thrashing.
aumer *n* an ember.
aumeril *n* **1** a stupid unmethodical person. **2** a mongrel dog.
aumitant *same as* **amaton**.
aum-leather *n* white leather.
aumous *same as* **almous**.
aum-paper *n* paper soaked in a solution of alum and water and used as tinder.
aumrie *n* **1** a cupboard. **2** a pantry. **3** a stupid person.

aumus *ame as* **almous**.
aun *n* due.—*adj* owing.
aunch *adj* empty.
auncient *same as* **ancient**.
auner *n* an owner.
aunter *same as* **anter**.
aunterens *adv* **1** occasionally. **2** perhaps.
auntern *same as* **anterin**.
aunterous *adj* adventurous.
aunty *n* **1** an aunt. **2** a loose woman. **3** a female brothel-keeper. **4** the bottle (qv). **5** a debauch.
aur *same as* **arr**.
aurea *n* area.
aurgle-bargle *same as* **argle-bargle**.
aurnit *same as* **arnot**.
aurrie *n* **1** a passage in a church. **2** the unseated area in a church before the introduction of fixed pews.
ause *same as* **ase**.
austern *adj* **1** austere in looks. **2** frightful or ghastly in appearance.
austrous *adj* **1** frightful. **2** ghastly.
author *n* **1** ancestor. **2** predecessor. **3** one who transfers property to another. **4** an informant. **5** authority for a statement.
auwis-bore *n* a knot-hole in a board.
aux *same as* **ax**.
aux-bit *n* a V-shaped nick cut out of the hinder part of a sheep's ear.
auze *n* a blazing, glowing fire.
ava *adv* **1** at all. **2** of all.
ava *same as* **awa**.
avail *n* **1** value. **2** worth. **3** property. **4** means.
aval¹ *n* **1** helplessness. **2** a helpless condition. **3** prostration.—*adj* **1** helpless. **2** prostrate. **3** lying on the back and unable to move.—*adv* **1** helplessly. **2** in a helpless condition.
aval² *same as* **awald**¹.
aval-broth *n* second day's broth.
aval-land *n* land laid down to be cropped.
aval-moon *n* the moon lying on its back.
aval-thrawn *adj* **1** overthrown. **2** cast prostrate.
avant curriers *n* the advanced guard of an army.
avayle *v* **1** to unveil. **2** to doff.
ave *n* the bucket of a millwheel.
avel *same as* **awald**¹.
aver¹ *n* **1** a beast of burden. **2** a cart-horse. **3** an old, out-worn, worthless animal. **4** a stupid person.
aver² *n* a gelded goat.
average *n* service of tenants to landlords in men, horses and carts.
Averile *n* April.
averin, averan *n* the cloudberry.
avil *same as* **awald**¹.
avise *n* **1** advice. **2** counsel.—*v* **1** to inform, make aware. **2** to deliberate judicially with a view to giving a decision
avizandum *n* judicial consideration before giving judgment.
avoke *v* **1** to call away. **2** to keep on.
avow *int* an exclamation of sorrow, alas!
avowe *n* **1** a declaration. **2** a discovery. **3** an avowal.
aw¹ *adj* all.
aw² *pron* I.
aw³ *v, adj* **1** owning. **2** owing.
awa *int* exclamation of banter or contradiction.
awa' *adv* **1** away. **2** along. **3** forward. **4** off. **5** in the state of death. **6** dead, departed. **7** in a reduced state of health. **8** in a decline. **9** in a swoon.
awa-gain, ~-gaun *adj* **1** outgoing. **2** departing.—*n* **1** departure. **2** death.
awald¹, **awal** *n* **1** the second of two crops of corn. **2** a field lying the second year without being cropped. **3** lea of the second year that has not been sown with artificial grasses.—*adj* **1** belonging to the second crop after lea. **2** (*of land*) laid down to be cropped.

awald², **awalt** *adj* (*used of a sheep or other animal*) lying on its back and unable to rise.

awald-, **awal-aits** *n* the second crop of oats after grass.

awald-, **awal-crap** *n* the second crop after grass.

awald-, **awal-infield** *n* the second crop after bear.

awald-, **awal-land** *n* ground under a second crop.

award, **awart** *same as* **awald**².

award-crap *n* a crop of corn after several others in succession.

awastle *adv* 1 to the westward of. 2 at a distance.

awat¹ *adv* 1 indeed. 2 truly.

awat² *same as* **awald**².

awat-crap *n* the crop produced from ground so ploughed.

awat fu' weel *phr* adding emphasis to what has just been said.

away-taking *n* abduction.

awbund, **awbun'** *adj* 1 under restraint. 2 submissive to authority. 3 reverential.

aw'd *pron with v* I would.

awe *v* 1 to own. 2 to owe.

aweband *n* 1 a band or rope for fastening cattle to the stake. 2 a person who inspires reverence. 3 a check, restraint.— *v* to bind with an aweband.

awee *n* 1 a little time. 2 a little of anything.

aweel *int.* ah well! well then! well well!

aweel-a-wat *adv* assuredly.

aweers *adv* 1 on the point of. 2 about to. 3 within a little of.

aweil *int* ah well!

awell *same as* **aweel**.

awelt, **awelled** *same as* **awald**².

awerin *n* harvesting at so much per acre.

awes *n* 1 (*used of a windmill*) the sails or shafts. 2 (*of a millwheel*) the buckets or floats.

awesome *adj* 1 awful. 2 awe-inspiring. 3 appalling.—*adv* 1 very. 2 extremely.

awfae *adj* awful.—*adv* very.

awfall *same as* **aefald**.

awfulsome *adj* 1 awful. 2 dreadful.

awfy *same as* **awfae**.

a'where *adv* everywhere.

a-whilt *adv* in a state of perturbation.

a-whummel *adv* upside-down, bottom upwards.

a-wid *adj* 1 eager. 2 anxious. 3 longing for.

a-will *adv* 1 of one's own accord. 2 of itself.

awin *adj* 1 own. 2 proper.

awin *v* owing.

awis *adv* certainly.

awittens *adv* unwittingly.

awkart *prep* athwart.

awkir *n* 1 a bit. 2 piece. 3 fragment.

awkward-crap *same as* **award-crap**.

awl *n in phr* **pack one's awls**, **stick one's awls in the wall** to give anything up as a bad business.

aw'll *pron with v* I will, I shall.

awm *same as* **aum**.

aw'm *pron with v* I am.

awmous *same as* **almous**.

awmrie *same as* **aumrie**.

awn¹ *v* owing.

awn² *v* to own, acknowledge.

awn³ *same as* **ain**¹.

awner *n* owner.

awnie *adj* (*used of barley or wheat*) having awns or beards.

aworth *adj* (*used of time*) long enough to be worth counting.

awowe *same as* **avow**.

awp *n* the curlew.

Awprile *n* April.

awpron *n* an apron.

awrige *n* 1 the angular points above the level of a ploughed field into which the seed falls. 2 the edge of a stone beam. 3 the edge of anything.

aws *same as* **awes**.

aw'se *pron with v* I shall.

awsk *same as* **ask**¹.

awsum *adj* frightful.

awte *n* 1 the direction in which a stone or piece of wood splits. 2 the grain. 3 a flaw in a stone.

awtus *n* 1 a dwarf. 2 anything diminutive.

aw've *pron with v* I have.

a'wye an' athort *adv* in every direction.

awyte *pron with v* I wot (qv), I warrant.—*adv* assuredly.

awytens *same as* **awittens**.

ax *v* to ask.

axes¹ *n* 1 business with. 2 a right to meddle with.

axes² *n* 1 an ague fit. 2 aches. 3 pains. 4 hysterics.

axle-tooth *same as* **aisle-tooth**.

axtree *n* 1 an axle tree. 2 an axle.

ay *int* an exclamation of surprise or wonder.

ay-de-mi *int* an exclamation of regret, pity, sorrow, etc.

ayden *adj* diligent, industrious.

aye¹ *adv* 1 always. 2 continually. 3 still.

aye² *adv* 1 yea. 2 yes.

ayehae *int* an exclamation of approval.

ayen *n* 1 a beast of the herd of one year old. 2 a year-old child.

aye sure *adv* surely.

ayler *n* an elder.

aynd *n* breath.—*v* to whisper.

aynoo *adv* just now.

ayoke *adv* in the yoke for ploughing, carting, etc.

ayon *prep* beyond.

a' yonner *phr* quite sane, in possession of one's senses.

ayont *prep* 1 beyond. 2 in excess of. 3 after. 4 later than.—*adv* farther beyond.

B

b' *prep* by.

ba' *n* a ball.

baa¹ *v* 1 to cry like a calf. 2 to bleat like a sheep.—*n* 1 a calf's cry. 2 a sheep's bleat.

baa² *same as* **baw**².

baach *same as* **bauch**¹.

baachle *same as* **bauchle**¹.

baak *same as* **balk**¹.

baak ropes *n* the ropes on the upper edge of a drift net.

baal *adj* bold.

baal fire *same as* **bale-fire**.

baass *adj* (*used of potatoes*) hollow in the heart.

bab¹ *n* 1 a nosegay. 2 a tassel. 3 a knot of ribbons. 4 a bunch of grass, corn, etc, growing above the rest.—*v* to grow in luxuriant patches.

bab² *n* 1 a slight blow. 2 a taunt, gibe. 3 a scolding. 4 a curtain lecture.

bab³ *n* the smartest, sprightliest or best-looking lad or lass in a company.

bab⁴ *v* 1 to bob. 2 to move up and down quickly. 3 to dance. 4 to pop in and out. 5 to curtsey. 6 to move quickly.—*n* 1 a dance. 2 a quick motion. 3 a curtsey. 4 a bow.

bab⁵ *v* to close, shut.

bab⁶ *v* to fish for eels with worsted.

ba'-baises *same as* **ball-baises**.

bab-at-the-bowster *n* 1 an old Scottish dance, winding up festive gatherings. 2 a children's singing game, played with a cushion or handkerchief.

babbanqua *n* a quaking bog.

babber *same as* **bobber**.

babbis *v* to scoff, gibe.

babbity-bowster *same as* **bab-at-the-bowster**.

babble *adj* half-witted.—*n* (*in pl*) 1 foolish nonsense. 2 nonsense that may be truth in reality.

babbs *n* particles of loose skin on the face when the beard has not been shaved for two or three days.

babby *n* a baby.

babie *n* a halfpenny.

babie clouts *n* baby's napkins or clothes.

babie-pickle *n* the small grain lying in the bosom of a lower one, at the top of a stalk of oats.

babret *same as* **back-bread**.

Bacchus' oil *n* spirituous liquor.

bach *int* an exclamation of disgust.

bachelor-coal *n* dead coal that does not burn but only turns white.

bachie *same as* **batchie**[1].

bachille, bachelle *n* a pendicle or small piece of arable land.

bachle *n* **1** an old, worn or twisted shoe. **2** a person or thing of no account. **3** a bungle. **4** a butt. **5** a clumsy person.—*v* **1** to distort. **2** to shamble. **3** to wear shoes out of shape. **4** to walk loosely or in slippers.

bachram, bachrim *n* **1** an adhesive spot of dirt. **2** cow dung, used as fuel or left to dry where it fell.

back[1] *n* **1** a wooden vessel for carrying peat, coal, etc. **2** a brewer's large cooling vat. **3** a vessel or board for kneading dough.

back[2] *n* an instrument for toasting bread.

back[3] *n* **1** back premises or yard. **2** the outermost board from a sawn tree. **3** a body of supporters. **4** a backing. **5** used of one who has changed his or her occupation or mode of living or has seen better days. **6** also of anything worn out. **7** a refusal. **8** repulse.

back[4] *v* **1** to mount a horse. **2** to move a horse backwards. **3** to carry on one's back. **4** to address a letter. **5** to endorse a bill. **6** to place at the back of.

back[5] *adj* **1** (*of crops*) late. **2** backward.—*adv* **1** behindhand. **2** late.

back-a-back *adv* back to back.

back-aboot *adj* **1** lonely. **2** out-of-the-way. **3** remote.

back-an'-face *adv* completely.

back-an'-fore, --forrit *adv* backwards and forwards.

back-an-side *adv* completely.

back-answer *n* a reply, retort.

back-at-the-wa' *phr* **1** unfortunate. **2** in trouble. **3** at extremity.

backband[1] *n* the chain or strap passing over the cart or carriage saddle and holding up the shafts.

backband[2] *n* a bond that nullifies or modifies a former one entered into for a special and temporary purpose.

back-bid *v* to bid at a sale simply to raise the price.

back-bind *n* the backband (qv) of a cart saddle, etc.

back-birn *n* a load on the back.

back-bit *n* a nick on the back part of a sheep's ear.

back-bond *same as* **backband**.

back-bone-links *n* **1** the vertebrae. **2** the spine.

back-bread *n* a baking or kneading trough.

back-breed, --breeth *n* **1** the breadth of the back. **2** a fall or throw on the back.

back-burd *n* **1** the larboard of a boat. **2** the hind board of a cart.

back-burden *n* a burden on the back. —*v* to burden the back, weigh down.

back-ca' *n* **1** a recall. **2** a relapse. **3** a driving back. **4** a misfortune.

back-cast *n* **1** a retrospect. **2** a review. **3** a relapse. **4** a misfortune.—*adj* retrospective.

back-chap *n* a back-stroke.

back-come *n* a return.—*v* **1** to return. **2** (*used of food*) to repeat in eructation.

back-coming *n* return.

back-creel *n* a fishwife's creel (qv).

back-door *n* the movable hinder board of a cart, etc.

back-door-trot *n* diarrhoea.

back-draught *n* the convulsive gasp of a child with whooping-cough.

back-drawer *n* **1** an apostate. **2** one who recedes from his former profession or course.

backend *n* **1** the close of a season or of the year, autumn, winter. **2** the outlying part of a parish or district. **3** the place where mine rubbish is cast.

backet *n* **1** a box or trough of wood to carry fuel, ashes etc. **2** a small wooden box with a perforated sloping lid, kept near the kitchen fireplace, for holding salt.

backet-stane *n* a stone on which the sautbacket (qv) rested.

back-fa' *n* **1** the side sluice of a mill lade or pond where the water runs off when a mill is not going. **2** a fall backwards. **3** a relapse. **4** a fall on one's back, a somersault.

back-faulds *n* fields at the back of, or at a distance from, a farmhouse.

back-fear *n* an object of fear from behind.

back-feast *n* the groomsman's return feast for the wedding feast given by the bride's friends.

back-fire *n in phr* **to gyang back-fire** (*used of grazing cattle*) to fall off in condition through the failure of grass.

back-friend *n* **1** one who seconds or abets another. **2** a secret enemy. **3** a place of strength behind an army.

backfu' *n* as much as can be carried on the back.

back-gain *n* **1** a relapse. **2** decline. **3** consumption.—*adj* **1** receding. **2** not healthy or prosperous.

backgane *adj* **1** ill-grown. **2** not thriven in health or business.

back-gangin' *ppl adj* **1** back-going. **2** not thriving.

back-gate *n* **1** a back-road. **2** cunning. **3** immoral conduct.

back-half *n* the worse or latter half of an article.

backhander *n* **1** a blow with the back of the hand. **2** a sarcastic retort. **3** an indirect snub.

back-hand o' the wa' *n* **1** the other side of a wall. **2** the outside of a room.

back-hap *v* to draw back from an agreement.

back-hash *n* ill-natured, abusive talk. —*v* to scold vigorously.

back-het *adj* (*used of food*) twice heated or cooked.

back-hicht *n* high excitement, great anger.—*adv* as high as the ceiling.

backie[1] *n* a lift or hoist on the back.

backie[2] *n* the bat.

backie[3] *same as* **baikie**[2].

backie[4] *same as* **baikie**[1].

backie-bird *n* the bat.

backin *n* the day after a wedding.

backin'[1] *n* **1** a body of followers. **2** support.

backin'[2] *n* the direction on a letter.

backins *n* the refuse of flax, wool, etc, used for coarser stuffs.

backin' turf *n* **1** the turf laid on a low cottage fire at bedtime to keep it alive till morning. **2** one placed against the back of the fireplace, in putting on a new turf fire, to support the side turfs.

backit dyke *n* a stone fence backed up with earth on the inner side.

backjar *n* **1** a sly, ill-natured objection or opposition. **2** an artful evasion. **3** a reverse.

backjaw *n* **1** mutual bad language. **2** altercation.—*v* **1** to retort abusive language. **2** to altercate.

back-land *n* a house or building lying back from the street.

back-letter *n* a letter that virtually qualifies one previously given that was written to serve a purpose.

back-lick *n* a back-blow.

backlins *adv* **1** backwards. **2** back.

back-load, --loaden *v* **1** to overload a cart or a horse. **2** to burden heavily.

back-look *n* a retrospect, review, the act of reviewing. **2** a record of the past.

back-lying *adj* in arrear.—*n* (*in pl*) arrears of rent, etc.

backman *n* **1** a follower in war. **2** a henchman.

back-out-owre *adv* **1** backwards. **2** back to a place in order to return thence. **3** back. **4** away from.

back-owre *adv* **1** behind. **2** far back.—*prep* from the back of.

back-rans *adv* backwards.

back-rape *n* the band over the horse's back in the plough, supporting the traces.

back-rent *n* a mode of fixing the rent of a farm, by which the tenant was always three terms in arrears.

back-roup *v* to bid at an auction simply to raise prices.

backs *same as* **backins**.

back-seam *n* a seam up the back.

backset *n* **1** a check, a reverse, a relapse. **2** a sub-lease. **3** compensation.

backset *v* to weary, to disgust.

back-sey *n* the sirloin.

backside *n* **1** the rear. **2** the side of an object which is farthest from the speaker. **3** back premises of house, etc. **4** the posterior, buttocks.

backspang *n* **1** an unsettling, underhand trick. **2** a retreat from a bargain. **3** a reverse, a recoil. **4** a back current. **5** a retort on a person after a contested affair has seemed settled.

back-spare, ~-spaiver *n* the back cleft or opening of breeches.

back-spaul, ~-spauld *n* **1** the back of the shoulder. **2** the hindleg.

back-speir, ~-speer, ~-spear *v* **1** to trace back a report to its source, if possible. **2** to cross-examine, cross-question.

back-speirer, ~-spearer *n* a cross-examiner.

back-spoken *adj* contradictory, gainsaying.

back-sprent *n* **1** the backbone. **2** a spring or catch.

back-stane *n* a stone at the back of a fireplace.

back stool *n* **1** a stool with a back. **2** a rough chair made of rungs.

backtalk *n* **1** contradiction. **2** saucy replies to a superior.

back-thought *n* reflection.

back-trace *v* to investigate past events.

back-tread *n* retrogression.

backtrees *n* the joists in a cot house, etc.

back-turn *n* a relapse.

backwardlies *adv* backwards.

backwater *n* **1** too much water in a mill lade, hindering the revolution of the millwheel. **2** tears.

back-widdie, ~-woodie *n* the band or chain over a cart saddle, supporting the shafts.

backwuth *adv* backwards.

back yett *n* a back gate.

bacon ham *n* the ham of a pig, as distinguished from a mutton ham.

bad[1] *adj* **1** ill. **2** sick.

bad[2] *v* **1** bade. **2** did bid.

bad bread *n in phr* **be in bad bread 1** to be in danger or poverty. **2** to be at enmity with.

badder *same as* **bather**.

badderin' breet *n* one who delights to tease.

badderlocks *n* an edible seaweed resembling the hart's-tongue fern.

badders, baddords *n* low raillery.

baddock the fry of the coalfish.

bade *v* did bide.

badge *n* a large, ill-shaped bundle.

badger *v* to beat.

badgeran *n* a beating.

badger-reeshil *n* a severe blow.

badling *n* a worthless person.

badlins *adj* **1** out of health. **2** poorly.

badly *adj* sick, unwell.

badman *n* a child's name for the devil.

badminnie, bad money *n* **1** the baldmoney. **2** gentian.

baddock *n* **1** the common skua. **2** the Arctic gull.

bad place *n* a child's name for hell.

badrons, badrans *same as* **baudrons**.

bad use *v* to use badly, abuse.

bae *same as* **baa**[1]

bae-wae *adj* out of sorts, not very well.

baff *n* **1** a blow, a buffet. **2** a shot. **3** a thud. **4** a jog with the elbow.—*v* **1** to beat. **2** to buffet. **3** to strike the ground with the sole of the club head in playing golf.

baffin *n* a soft, stupid person.

baffle *n* **1** a trifle. **2** a thing of no value. **3** nonsense. **4** a sheet of scroll paper on which schoolboys sketched mathematical diagrams or mensuration plans. **5** a portfolio.

baffy *same as* **buffie**.

bafle *n* **1** a check. **2** a snub.

bag *n* **1** a sack. **2** the stomach. **3** a playful or reproachful designation of a child.—*v* **1** to swell, bulge. **2** to cram the stomach. **3** to dismiss from employment. **4** to jilt in love.

bagaty *n* the female of the lump or sea owl.

bagenin *n* rough and sometimes indecent horseplay at harvest time.

baggage[1] *n* rubbish.

baggage[2] *n* **1** a strumpet. **2** an opprobrious epithet applied to women and children.

bagged *adj* **1** having a big belly. **2** pregnant. **3** corpulent.

baggie[1] *n* **1** the belly. **2** a corpulent person.

baggie[2] *n* the purple-top Swedish turnip.

baggie[3] *n* a large minnow.

baggie-mennon a large minnow.

bagging time *n* baiting time.

baggit[1] *n* **1** a contemptuous name for a child. **2** an insignificant little person. **3** a feeble sheep.

baggit[2] *same as* **bagged**.

baggity *adj* greedy.

bagglers *n* the fry of trout.

baggy *adj* blistered.

baghash *same as* **backhash**.

baglin *n* **1** a misgrown child. **2** a puny child with a big belly. **3** a term of abuse.

bag-mennon *same as* **bag-mennon**.

bagnet, bagonet *n* a bayonet.

bag-rape *n* a straw rope used in fastening the thatch of a roof or stack.

bagrel *n* **1** a minnow. **2** a person or animal corpulent and misgrown otherwise. **3** a child. **4** a silly person.—*adj* puny and plump.

bagrie *n* trash.

bags *n* the entrails.

bagwame *n* a silly, gluttonous fellow.

bai *same as* **baa**[1].

baible *v* **1** to tipple. **2** to drink carelessly so as to spill. **3** to drink as a child.

baich, baichie *n* a child (*used with some contempt*).

baichie *v* to cough.

baid *v* did bide.

baigie *same as* **baggie**[2].

baigle[1] *n* **1** an odd figure. **2** a sight. **3** a fright.

baigle[2] *v* **1** to run or walk with short steps, as a child. **2** to walk slowly, as if weary.

baiglet *same as* **baiklet**.

baignet, baiginet *same as* **bagnet**.

baik *same as* **bake**.

baik-bred, ~-brod *same as* **back-bread**.

baiken *n* **1** a burden of skins. **2** a sort of flap.

baikie[1] *n* **1** the stake to which cattle are bound in the stall. **2** a piece of wood with rope attached to tie up cattle to the stake. **3** the stake or peg of a tether.

baikie[2] *n* a square wooden vessel used for carrying fuel, ashes, etc, feeding cattle and washing dishes.

baikiefu' *n* the fill of a baikie (qv).

baikins *n* **1** a beating. **2** drubbing.

baiklet *n* **1** an under waistcoat or flannel shirt worn next to the skin. **2** a semmit (qv). **3** a binder (qv). **4** a piece of dress, linen or woollen, formerly worn above a young child's shirt.

bail[1] *v* (*with* **up**) to tie up.—*n* a call to cows to stand still.

bail[2] *v* to guarantee, warrant.

bailch *same as* **bilch**[1].

bailie, baillie *n* **1** a farm steward. **2** a man or boy in charge of the cows on a farm. **3** a city magistrate.

bailierie, bailliary *n* **1** the office of a bailiff of a lord of regality. **2** the extent of his jurisdiction in a barony.

ba'in' *n* a football match.
bain[1] *n* a bone.
bain[2] *n* **1** a bucket. **2** a washtub.
baingle *n* an abusive term applied to a woman.
bainie *adj* bony.
baird[1] *v* to caparison.
baird[2] *n* a beard.—*v* to rub with the beard.
bairdie[1] *n* the loach.
bairdie [2]*n* the whitethroat.
bairdie[3] *n* the three-spined stickleback.
bairdie[4] *n* **1** a large jar. **2** a greybeard (qv) for holding spirits, etc.
bairdie-loach, ~-lowrie *n* the loach.
bairdy *adj* belonging to the beard.
bairge[1] *n* **1** the voice loudly used. **2** one who uses his or her voice loudly.—*v* **1** to raise the voice loudly. **2** to scold, abuse, bully.
bairge[2] *n* an affected, bobbing walk.—*v* **1** to walk with a jerking spring upwards. **2** to strut.
bairge board *n* **1** a barge board. **2** a board at the gable of a building, hiding the timbers of the roof.
bairn *n* **1** a child. **2** a weak-minded or childish person, irrespective of age.
bairn-clouts *n* dolls' clothes.
bairned *adj* in a state of dotage.
bairn-folk *n* children.
bairnie *n* a little child.—*adj* **1** childish. **2** silly.
bairnie o' the e'e *phr* the pupil of the eye.
bairnish *adj* **1** childish. **2** silly.
bairnless *adj* childless.
bairnlike *adj* **1** like a child. **2** childish. **3** weak-minded.
bairnliness *n* childishness.
bairnly *adj* childish.
bairnly-like *adj* childish.
bairn's bairn *n* a grandchild.
bairn's bargain *n* **1** a bargain that may be easily broken. **2** a mutual agreement to overlook anything unpleasant in the past between two persons or parties.
bairn's fee *n* a nursemaid's wages.
bairn's pan *n* a small pan for preparing a child's food.
bairns' part o' gear *phr* that part of a man's personal estate to which his children succeed.
bairn's piece *n* biscuit, cake, cheese, etc, given in connection with the birth or baptism of an infant.
bairns' play *n* **1** children's sports. **2** a matter easily performed.
bairn-stooth, ~-stowth *n* the stealing of children by fairies.
bairn's woman *n* a dry-nurse.
bairn-time, ~-teme *n* **1** the time during which a woman bears children. **2** a woman's whole birth of children. **3** childhood.
baise[1] *n* **1** haste. **2** expedition.—*v* to move or walk with energy.
baise[2] *v* to persuade, to coax.
baise[3] *same as* **baiss**[2].
baise[4], **baiss** *adj* **1** ashamed. **2** sad, sorrowful.
baisler *n* a bachelor of arts.
baiss[1] *v* **1** to beat, drub. **2** to baste.
baiss[2] *v* **1** to sew slightly. **2** to sew with long stitches or in a loose, careless manner. **3** to baste in sewing.
baissie *same as* **bassie**[2].
baissing *n* a drubbing.
baissing *n* a slight sewing.
baissing thread *n* basting-thread.
baist[1] *adj* great.
baist[2] *adj* **1** apprehensive. **2** afraid.
baist[3] *v* **1** to beat, strike. **2** to baste. **3** to defeat, overcome.—*n* **1** one who is struck by others, especially in children's play. **2** one who is defeated.
baister *n* a boy's challenge to his companions to a daring or difficult feat.
baistin *n* a drubbing.
bait[1] *n* the grain or cleavage of wood or stone.

bait[2] *n* the lye in which skins are steeped.—*v* to steep and soften skins in a lye of hens' or pigeons' dung to clean them before tanning.
bait[3] *v* **1** bit. **2** did bite.
bait[4] *n* a mash of oats, etc, for a horse.
baitchil *v* to beat soundly.
baiten *v, adj* **1** bitten. **2** eaten.
baith *adj and pron* both.
baitie-bummil *same as* **batie-bum**.
bait-pick *n* a spud for removing limpets for bait.
bait pot *n* a large pot for cooking food for horses, etc.
baittle *same as* **battle**[1].
bait-troch *n* a trough in a stall for feeding horses.
bait-yaud *n* a woman who gathers bait for fishermen.
baivee[1] *same as* **bevie**[1].
baivee[2] *n* a kind of whiting.
baivenjar *n* **1** a ragamuffin. **2** tatterdemalion.
baiver *v* **1** to gad about. **2** to run after shows, etc.
baiver *same as* **bever**.
baivie *n* **1** a bevy. **2** a large collection. **3** a large family. **4** a covey of partridges.
baivie *same as* **bevie**[1].
bajan *same as* **bejan**.
bake *n* a small biscuit.—*v* to knead dough or paste.
bake-brod *same as* **back-bread**.
bake-byord *same as* **back-bread**.
bakement *n* bakemeat.
baken *v, adj* baked.
baker-legs *n* knock-knees
bakie[1] *n* a kind of peat, kneaded or baked from the wet dross or dust of peats.
bakie[2] *same as* **baikie**[1].
bakie-bird *same as* **backie**[2].
baking-case *n* a kneading trough.
bakin-lotch *n* a species of bread.
bakster *n* the one of two bakers who kneads dough.
balaloo *n* **1** a lullaby. **2** sleep.
bala-pat *n* a pot in a farmhouse for the family, but not for the reapers, in harvest.
balax *n* a hatchet.
bald *same as* **bauld**[1].
balderry, baldeirie, baldberry *n* **1** the female handed orchid, *O. maculata*. **2** the *O. latifolia*, formerly used in love potions.
baldie-worrie *n* an artichoke.
bale *n* **1** a blaze. **2** a bonfire.
baleen, balene *n* whalebone.
bale-fire *n* **1** any large fire. **2** a bonfire.
balillalee *same as* **balaloo**.
balk[1] *n* **1** a ridge in ploughing. **2** a pathway through a cornfield. **3** the first two furrows in ploughing a field, laid facing each other. **4** a strip of ground untilled, serving as a boundary. **5** a beam or rafter. **6** the beam of a pair of scales. **7** a hen roost. **8** (*in pl*) the gallery of a church.
balk[2] *v* **1** to miss accidentally a strip of ground in ploughing, sowing or reaping. **2** to secure a cow's head during milking. **3** to shy at an obstacle. **4** to be restive.
balk and burral *n* a ridge raised very high by the plough and a barren space of nearly the same extent alternately.
balk-height *adv* as high as the balk (qv) or ceiling.
balkie[1] *n* a narrow strip of land separating two farms.
balkie[2] *same as* **baikie**[1].
balksome *adj* (*of a horse*) restive, given to shying.
ball[1] *n* **1** the calf of the leg. **2** the palm of the hand. **3** a globular sweetmeat.
ball[2] *n* **1** a bustle. **2** disturbance. **3** uproar.—*v* to behave in a disorderly way.
ball[3] *n* a spree.
ball[4] *n* **1** a parcel. **2** abundle. **3** a bale.
ball[5] *v* to pelt, throw at.
ball[6] *v* to play at football.
ball[7] *v* **1** (*used of snow*) to gather in lumps. **2** to stick to the feet.
ballan, ballant *n* **1** a ballad. **2** a song.

ballant-bodice *n* a leather bodice formerly worn by women.
ball-baises *n* a game of ball.
ball-clay *n* very adhesive clay.
ballerny *n* exaggeration in narrative, 'drawing the long bow'.
ball-fire *same as* **balefire**.
ballfuff *n in phr* **back o' ballfuff** an unknown distance.
balliillilly, --loo, --low *same as* **balaloo**.
balling[1] *n* pelting.
balling[2] *n* frequenting balls.
ballion[1] *n* **1** a knapsack. **2** a tinker's tool box. **3** any box that can be borne on the back.
ballion[2] *n* a supernumerary reaper who assists any who fall behind on their 'rig'.
ballish *n* ballast.
balloch[1] *adj* **1** slow. **2** unwilling. **3** strong. **4** plump.—*n* a short, plump person.
balloch[2] *n* a narrow mountain pass.
ballop, ballup *n* the old-fashioned flap in the forepart of trousers.
bally *n* a milk pail.
bally-cog *n* a milk pail with a handle.
balm *v* to soothe, ease, assuage.
balne *n* a bath.
balow, baloo *int* a nursery exclamation hush!—*n same as* **balaloo**.
balter *n* a sudden bolt or start upwards.
bam *n* **1** a joke. **2** trick. **3** a hoax.—*v* to hoax, play a trick.
bambaze *v* **1** to confuse, puzzle. **2** to bewilder. **3** to bamboozle.
bambling *adj* **1** awkwardly made. **2** clumsy.
bamboozle *v* **1** to handle roughly. **2** to affront.
bamf *v* **1** to stump. **2** to toss or stumble about.
bamling, bammeling *adj* **1** awkward. **2** clumsy.
ba' money *n* money demanded from a wedding party to buy a football.
bampot *n* **1** a crazy person. **2** an idiot.
bamullo *n in phr* **gar ane lauch, sing** *or* **dance bamullo** to make one change one's mirth into sorrow.
ban[1] *v* **1** to curse, swear. **2** to abuse, scold. **3** to use the devil's name as an intensive or expletive.
ban[2] *v* bound.
ban' *same as* **band**[1].
band[1] *n* **1** twine. **2** a rope or chain for tying cattle. **2** a straw or hay rope for tying thatch. **3** twisted straw for tying sheaves. **4** a hinge. **5** a narrow, flat strip of iron with a loop at the end, fixed in a door, to receive an iron hook fixed on the doorpost. **6** the hairband once worn by women. **7** a choir. **8** a bond. **9** covenant. **10** agreement. **11** a binding stone inserted in a wall. **12** a brace or couple of things. **13** a number of things fixed on a string. **14** the bond of marriage.
band[2] *n* the ridge of a small hill.
band[3] *v* bound.
bandalier *n* a bandoleer.
bander *n* one who enters into a bond or covenant.
bandie[1] *n* the stickleback.
bandie[2] *n* a stick hooked at one end, used in a boy's game played with a nacket (qv).
bandless *adj* **1** without bonds. **2** altogether abandoned to evil.
bandlessly *adv* regardlessly.
bandlessness *n* abandonment to evil.
bandrums *same as* **baudrons**.
bandsman *n* a binder of sheaves.
bandstane *n* a large binding stone in a wall, used for stability.
bandster *n* a binder of sheaves.
band-string *n* **1** a string across the breast for ornamental tying. **2** a kind of long-shaped confection.
bandwin *n* a band of six or eight reapers served by one bandster (qv).
bandwin rig *n* a ridge wide enough to contain a bandwin (qv).

bandy *adj* **1** impudent. **2** obstinate.
bane[1] *n in phr* **king of bane** *or* **king of the bean** a character in the Christmas gambols, the person who got that part of a divided cake which contained a bean.
bane[2] *n* **1** bone. **2** (*in pl*) the substantial portion of anything. **3** the mechanism. **4** a skeleton.—*adj* made of bone.
bane[3] *adj* **1** ready. **2** prepared.
bane[4] *n* **1** poison. **2** envy. **3** malice.
baned *adj* **1** evil-disposed. **2** envious.
bane-dry *adj* thoroughly dry.
bane dyke *n in phr* **gane to the bane dyke 1** reduced to skin and bone. **2** fit only for the dyke (qv) where the bones of dead horses lie.
banefire *n* a bonfire.
bane-headit *adj* (*of a staff*) having a bone handle.
bane-idle *adj* thoroughly idle, bone lazy.
baneless *adj* insipid, without pith.
bane-mill *n* a mill for crushing or grinding bones.
bane-prickle *n* the stickleback.
banes-breaking *n* a bloody quarrel.
banff-baillies *n* white, snowy-looking clouds on the horizon, betokening foul weather.
bang[1] *n* **1** a blow. **2** onslaught. **3** an act of haste. **4** impetuosity. **5** a fit of temper. **6** a huff.
bang[2] *n* **1** a crowd. **2** a large number.
bang[3] *v* **1** to change places with impetus. **2** to beat, knock. **3** to throw or thrust violently. **4** to overcome. **5** to excel, outdo, surpass. **6** to push off with salmon-fishing boats without having seen fish in the river.
bang[4] *adj* **1** vehement. **2** agile. **3** strong.—*adv* **1** quite. **2** suddenly.
bang-beggar, --the-beggar *n* **1** a constable. **2** a cudgel.
bang-dollop *n* the whole number.
banged *adj* under the influence of drink.
bangie[1] *n* a policeman.
bangie[2] *adj* **1** huffy. **2** irritable.
banging *n* **1** a beating. **2** a defeat.
bangister-swipe *v* to cozen artfully.
bangistry *same as* **bangstrie**.
bangnue *n* much ado about nothing.
bang-rape *n* a rope with noose, used by thieves to carry off corn or hay.
bangrel, bangree *n* an ill-natured, ungovernable woman.
bangsome *adj* quarrelsome.
bangster *n* **1** a bully. **2** a braggart. **3** a victor. **4** a loose woman.—*adj* **1** rough. **2** violent.
bangstership *n* **1** force. **2** violence.
bangstrie *n* violence to person or property.
bangyal *n* **1** a bundle. **2** a slovenly fellow. **3** a crowd of people.—*v* **1** to crowd. **2** to move in a confused crowd.
bangyalin' *n* act of crowding.
banjie *n* **1** a great number. **2** a disorderly mob.
bank[1] *n* the place in a peat moss whence peats are cut. **2** the part of a mine above ground.
bank[2] *n* a public proclamation.
bank[3] *v* to save and put by money.
bank-dollar *n* a species of dollar, ten of which equalled ten ordinary dollars plus £1 Scots.
banker[1] *n* the bench or table on which a mason rests the stone he is working.—*v* to place a stone in position on the banker.
banke[2] *n* a bench-cloth or carpet.
banker[3] *n* one who buys corn sold by auction.
bankerup *adj* bankrupt.
banking-crop *n* corp bought or sold by auction.
bank-rape *v* to become bankrupt.
bankrout *n* a bankrupt.
banks *n* **1** precipitous rocks or crags near the sea. **2** the seashore.
bankset *adj* full of little eminences.
bankster *same as* **bangster**.
bankstership *n* **1** force. **2** violence.
bannag *n* **1** a white trout. **2** a sea trout.

banna-rack *n* the frame before which bannocks are put to be toasted when taken off the girdle (qv).
bannet *same as* **bonnet**.
bannet-fire *n* a punishment inflicted by boys on a companion with their caps, similar to running the gauntlet.
bannet-fluke *n* the turbot.
banniel *same as* **bangyal**.
bannock *n* **1** a thick, round, flat cake, generally of oatmeal, baked on a girdle (qv). **2** a small quantity of oatmeal, as a perquisite, due to the servants of a mill, owing to thirlage (qv).
bannock-chower *n* a bannock-eater.
Bannock Even *n* Shrove Tuesday.
bannock-fed *adj* fed chiefly on bannocks.
bannock-fluke *n* the turbot.
bannock-hive *n* **1** corpulence owing to plentiful eating. **2** a corpulent person.
bannock stick *n* a rolling-pin for bannocks.
banquier *n* a banker.
bansel *n* what is given for good luck.
banstickle *n* the stickleback or minnow.
banters *n* **1** rebukes. **2** admonitions.
bantin, banton *n* a bantam.
banty *n* a bantam.
banty *n* **1** a stickeback. **2** a minnow.
banyel *same as* **bangyal**.
bap *n* **1** a small, flat, diamond-shaped breakfast roll. **2** a thick cake of bread baked in an oven. **3** a blow, a thump.
bapper *n* a baker.
bapp-nose *n* a nose threatening to meet the chin.
bapteeze *v* to baptise.
bapteezement *n* baptism.
bar¹ *n* **1** a flail, the 'swing' of a flail. **2** a tollbar. **3** an obstacle.
bar² *same as* **barrie**.
bar³ *n* **1** a joke. **2** a game. **3** a matter of joking.
bar⁴ *same as* **bear**¹.
bar⁵ *v* **1** to swing a flail. **2** to thresh.
bar⁶ *v* **1** to exclude, shut out. **2** to except.
bar-bannock *n* a barley-meal bannock.
barbar *n* a barbarian.
barbarize, barbaze *v* to act as a barber.
barber *n* what is best or excellent of its kind.
barber-eel *n* the viviparous blenny.
barbet *n* an arrow.
barbour, barbourize *v* to act as a barber.
bar-bread *n* barley-bread.
barbulie *same as* **barbulyie**.
barbulyie, barbulzie *n* **1** perplexity. **2** quandary.—*v* to perplex.
Barchan's Day *n* 21 June.
bard¹ *n* **1** a scold. **2** a bold, noisy woman.
bard² *v* to caparison.
bardach, bardoch *adj* **1** bold. **2** fearless.
bardie¹ *n* a gelded cat.
bardie² *n* **1** a minor poet. **2** a humble bard.
bardily *adv* **1** boldly. **2** fearlessly. **3** pertly.
bardiness *n* **1** forwardness. **2** pertness in conversation.
bardish *adj* **1** rude. **2** insolent.
bardizan *n* a bartizan.
bard's croft *n* the piece of land on the property of a chief hereditarily appropriated to the family bard.
bardy *adj* **1** bold. **2** fierce. **3** turbulent. **4** pert. **5** shameless. **6** insolent.—*v* **1** to vituperate. **2** to bandy words with.
bare *adj* **1** plain. **2** unadorned. **3** mere. **4** meagre. **5** hard up, poor. **6** (*used of soil*) poor.—*v* to remove surface soil for what lies beneath.
bare-back *n* a species of fluke.
barefit *adj* barefooted.
barefit-broth, ~-kail *n* broth made with butter and vegetables without meat.
barelies *adv* **1** barely. **2** scarcely. **3** hardly.
bareman *n* a bankrupt who has given all up to his creditors.

bare-naked *adj* quite naked.
bare-powed *adj* bareheaded.
barescrape *n* very poor land yielding little return for labour.
barfit *same as* **barefit**.
bar-for-bar *n* a rhyming game.
bargain-bide *v* to take one's own way, being under no obligation to others and quite able to act for oneself.
bargane, bargain *n* **1** contention. **2** controversy.—*v* to contend, fight.
bargain-gud *n* a kind of pear.
bargain-tacker *n* a foreman undertaking work in a section of a lead-mine.
bargle *n* a squabble.—*v* **1** to wrangle. **2** to bandy words.
bark¹ *n* **1** the skin. **2** cuticle.—*v* **1** to excoriate. **2** to strip a tree of bark. **3** to tan leather, nets, etc. **4** to clot. **5** to besmear. **6** to encrust on the skin.
bark² *v* to give a hard, rapid cough.
barken *v* **1** to become clotted, encrusted or hardened on the skin, etc. **2** to tan. **3** to stiffen anything, as with blood, mire, etc.
barker *n* a tanner.
barking and fleeing *phr* (said of propert) prodigally wasted, so as to lead to bankruptcy.
barla-fummil *n* a cry for truce by one who has fallen in fighting or wrestling.
barley *int* a cry for truce in a children's game.
barley-bing *n* a heap of barley.
barley box *n* **1** a small cylindrical box formerly used by farmers to carry samples of grain. **2** a toy for children.
barley-breaks, barla-bracks *n* a stackyard game of tig.
barley-bree, ~-brie, ~-broo *n* **1** malt liquor. **2** whisky.
barley-corn *n* a species of grain. *See* **John Barleycorn**.
barley-cream *n* whisky.
barley-doons *n* the place for playing at barley-breaks (qv).
barley-fetterer *n* an implement for removing the awns of barley.
barley-fever *n* illness owing to hard drinking.
barley-hood *n* a fit of drunken, angry passion.
barley Jock *n* whisky.
barley-joice *n* **1** malt liquor. **2** whisky.
barley-kail *n* barley-broth.
barley-, barlaw-men *same as* **burlaw**.
barley-oats *n* early white oats with short grains.
barley-pickle *n* **1** a grain of barley. **2** the topmost grain on an ear of barley.
barley-sick *adj* sick from excessive drinking.
barley-unction *n* **1** malt liquor. **2** whisky.
barlic-, barlik-hood *same as* **barley-hood**.
barm¹ *n* a peculiar kind of dance.
barm² *n* **1** yeast. **2** froth. **3** nonsense. **4** foolish talk.—*v* **1** (*used of the mind*) to work. **2** to fret. **3** to mix wort with barley to cause fermentation. **4** (*used of money*) to grow with interest.
barman *n* **1** a thresher. **2** a user of a flail.
barming *n* interest accruing.
barmkin *n* **1** a barbican. **2** the outermost fortification of a wall. **3** the parapet of a bridge.
barmskin *n* a leather apron worn by tanners and curriers.
barmy *adj* **1** volatile. **2** flighty. **3** passionate. **4** irascible.
barmy-brained *adj* **1** foolish. **2** giddy.
barmy-faced *adj* wearing a silly expression.
barmy scones *n* scones levigated with barm (qv).
barnacles *n* spectacles, eyeglasses.
barnage *n* **1** a military company. **2** army followers.
barn bole *n* an aperture in a barn wall.
barne *same as* **bairn**.
barn fan *n* a winnowing fan.
barnheid *n* childhood.
barnman *n* **1** one who labours in the barn. **2** a thresher with a flail.
barnman's jig *n* a thresher's dance.
barn's-breaking *n* **1** a mischievous action. **2** an idle frolic.
barnyard *n* a stackyard adjoining the barn.

barnyard beauty *n* a buxom rustic beauty.
baron bailie *n* the deputy of the baron in a burgh of barony.
barr¹ *n* a kind of fishing fly.
barr² *n* **1** a ridge of a hill. **2** a large hill.
barrace, barras *n* tournament-lists.
barragon *n* **1** a cloth used for cloaks. **2** a rich cloth imported from Italy.
barras *n* a wire fireguard.
barras-door *n* a door made of equidistant bars of wood.
bar-reet *same as* **bear-reet**.
barreis *same as* **barrace**.
barrel *n* **1** the belly of a horse. **2** the barrel-shaped part of a loom.
barrel-briestit *adj* corpulent.
barrel-briestit stays *n* corsets for pigeon-breasted women.
barrel-fevers *n* disorders of the body through excessive drinking.
barrel-gird *n* **1** the hoop of a barrel. **2** the name given to a thin horse with projecting ribs.
barrelled *adj* (*of a cow*) having its belly filled with grass and like a barrel.
barrie¹ *n* **1** an infant's flannel swaddling cloth. **2** a woman's petticoat.
barrie² *adj* excellent, very fine.
barrier *n* a thresher.
barrow¹ *v* to carry in a wheelbarrow or in a sedan chair.
barrow² *v* to borrow.
barrowman *n* **1** a mason's labourer who carries stone, mortar, etc, on a hand-barrow. **2** a lame beggar, formerly carried from farm to farm in a barrow.
barrow-steel *n* **1** equal cooperation. **2** drawing well together.
barrow-tram *n* **1** the shaft of a wheelbarrow. **2** a raw-boned, awkward-looking person. **3** a muscular arm or leg.
barry¹, **barrie** *v* to thresh corn.
barry² *n* a barrow.
bars¹ *n* a grate.
bars² *n* **1** a schoolboys' game. **2** prisoner's base.
bar-seed *same as* **bear-seed**.
barsk *same as* **bask**.
barst *v* burst.
bar-stane *n* one of the upright stones in a fireplace to which the bars of a grate are fixed.
bartice *n* a brattice.
Bartle Day *n* St Bartholomew's Day, 24 August.
Bartle-fair *n* a fair held on St Bartholomew's Day.
barty *n* a boy's name for a bartizan.
bar-yauven *n* a spike surrounding barley, thrown off while the grain is being threshed and very dangerous to the eyes.
baser *n* a bass singer.
bash¹ *n* **1** a heavy blow. **2** a dint.—*v* **1** to beat, to crush, smash. **2** to bruise, dint. **3** (*with* **up**) to bend the point of an iron instrument inwards.
bash² *v* to abash.
bash³ *n* a term of contempt.
bash hat *n* a soft hat.
bashle *v* to shamble.
bashlebands *n* bands to keep up shoe heels.
ba' siller *n* pence given to children at a wedding.
bask *adj* **1** dry. **2** withering. **3** bitter. **4** harsh to the taste.
basket-hinger *n* the gold-crested wren.
basle *v* to talk ignorantly or at random.—*n* idle talking.
basnet *n* a helmet.
ba' speil *n* a game of football.
bass *n* **1** a door mat. **2** the soft fibres composing a bird's nest. **2** a workman's tool basket. **3** a straw horse collar. **4** a table mat to protect a table from hot dishes. **5** the best or inner bark of a tree.
bass-bottomed *adj* (*used of chairs*) having the seat made of rushes or of bass (qv).
bass-cock *n* the puffin.
bassen'd, bassand, bassent *same as* **bausand**.
basser-, bass-goose *n* the gannet.

bassie¹ *same as* **bawsie**.
bassie² *n* a large wooden basin or bowl, frequently used for carrying and mixing oatmeal in baking.
bassin *n* **1** a church offertory plate. **2** a kirk basin (qv).
bassle *v* **1** to struggle. **2** to wallow.
bassonet *same as* **basnet**.
ba'-stane *n* a testicle.
bastardrie *n* illegitimacy.
bastardy *n* the property of an illegimate person.
bastel chamber *n* a chamber in a border fortress.
bastert *adj* bastard, illegitimate.
basties, bastish *adj* **1** coarse, hard, bound, as applied to soil. **2** obstinate of temper.
bastile, bastle *n* a fortress, principally used for prisoners.
bastiment *n* **1** a building. **2** pile. **3** structure.
bastle house *n* a fortified house.
bastoun *n* a cudgel.
bastous *same as* **basties**.
bat¹ *conj* but.
bat² *n* a staple or loop of iron.
bat³ *n* **1** a smart blow. **2** a stroke of work. **3** condition. **4** state of health.
bat⁴ *n* a bundle of straw or rushes.
bat⁵ *n* **1** a holm. **2** a river island. **3** low-lying land overflowed at spring tides and floods.
bat⁶ *v* **1** to hit. **2** to press or beat down with a spade. **3** to thresh by striking sheaves against a stone, etc. **4** (*used of mistletoe, ivy, etc*) to cling to a tree, grow on a tree.
batch¹ *n* a bachelor.
batch² *n* **1** a crew. **2** a gang. **3** a set number. **4** a baking. **5** a clump.
batch bread *n* bread made of common flour.
batch day *n* baking day.
batchie ¹*n* a bachelor.
batchie² *n* **1** a card game. **2** the male loser in the game.
batch-loaf *n* a loaf of batch bread (qv).
bate¹ *v* **1** to cease. **2** to reduce the price.
bate² *v* did beat.
bate³ *v* did bite.
bateable land *n* the debatable land on the borders of Scotland and England.
bath *v* to give or take a bath.
bather *v* to bother, pester.—*n* **1** a bother. **2** a troublesome person.
batherlocks *same as* **badderlocks**.
batherment *n* **1** bother. **2** trouble.
bathie *same as* **bothie**.
batie¹ *n* **1** a large dog of any species. **2** a hare. **3** a term of contempt for a man.
batie² *adj* **1** round. **2** plump.
batie-bum, ~-bummil *n* **1** a simpleton. **2** a fool.
bating *prep* **1** excepting. **2** except.
baton *n* an instrument for beating mortar.
batridge *n* the lace or band for tying up the fold of a cocked hat.
batrons *same as* **baudrons**.
bats, batts *n* **1** a disease in horses or dogs caused by small worms or the botfly. **2** the colic.
batt *n* *in phr* **keep one at the batt** to keep one steady.
batted *adj* hardened.
batter¹ *n* **1** paste. **2** weaver's and shoemaker's paste.—*v* **1** to fasten with or apply adhesive paste. **2** (*with* **up**) to clout, patch shoes, etc.
batter² *n* a heavy blow.—*v* to give repeated blows.
batter³ *n* **1** the slope or inclination of a wall, embankment, etc. **2** a spree or drinking bout.—*v* to build a sloping wall, etc.
batter⁴ *n* the cover of a book.
battered¹ *adj* (*of a book*) provided with covers or boards. **2** (*of fish*) covered with a batter.
battered² *adj* pasted and posted on a board or wall.
batter horn *n* a horn for holding shoemaker's paste.
batterification *n* battery, assault.
battle¹ *adj* **1** fat. **2** thickset. **3** (*of soil*) rich, fertile.

battle² *n* a bundle or bottle of straw.—*v* to put straw into bottles.

battock *n* **1** a tuft of grass. **2** a spot of gravel or ground of any kind surrounded by water. **3** flat ground by a river-side.

batton *v* to cudgel.

battoon *n* a general's baton.

baub *n* beat of a drum.

baubee *same as* **bawbee**.

bauch¹ *adj* **1** disagreeable to the taste, etc. **2** not good. **3** insufficient. **4** incapable. **5** indifferent. **6** timid, sheepish, shy. **7** tired-out. **8** (*of ice*) partially thawing.—*v* to make one look sheepish.

bauch² *v* to speak loudly and noisily.

bauch³ *adj* dull, lifeless.

bauchle¹ *v* **1** to shamble. **2** to wear shoes out of shape. **3** to distort. **4** to treat contemptuously. **5** to make of little or no account. **6** to jilt.—*n* **1** an old shoe. **2** a slipper that is down-at-heel. **3** a person or thing of nought. **4** a laughing stock. **5** a clumsy person.

bauchle² *n* **1** the upright front of a peat barrow. **2** one of two pieces of wood fixed on the sides of a cart to extend the surface.

bauchling *n* **1** scorning. **2** rallying. **3** taunting.

bauchly *adv* **1** sorrily. **2** indifferently.

bauchness *n* **1** slowness from timidity. **2** want. **3** defect of every kind.

bauckie *same as* **backie**².

baud¹ *n* a mass of furze, broom, etc, growing together thickly.

baud² *v* bade.

baudminnie *n* a plant with the medicinal virtue of savin.

baudrons *n* **1** a kindly designation of a cat. **2** puss.

bauf *v* to make a clattering noise with shoes or clogs in walking.

baugh¹ *v* to look or be confused, sheepish, put out.

baugh² *same as* **bauch**¹.

baughed *adj* **1** confounded. **2** made to look sheepish.

baughle *same as* **bauchle**¹.

baughling *same as* **bauchling**.

bauk¹ *same as* **balk**¹.

bauk², **baulk** *same as* **balk**².

bauk³ *n* **1** a weighing machine. **2** one hanging from the batiks or rafters. **3** *in phr* **to deal the bauk with one** to settle a matter with one, come to terms.

bauk⁴ *n* **1** a footpath or narrow road through a field. **2** a march between two estates.

bauken *n* the bat.

bauk-heicht *same as* **balk-height**.

baukie¹ *ame as* **baikie**¹.

baukie² *n* **1** the razorbill or auk. **2** the black guillemot.

baukie³ *n* the bat.

baukie⁴, **baukie-up** *same as* **backie**¹.

baukin *n* **1** a hobgoblin. **2** a supernatural appearance.

bauld¹ *adj* **1** bold. **2** keen. **3** pungent. **4** fiery-tempered. **5** harsh. **6** stormy. **7** (*used of a fire*) great, strong.—*v* to kindle or blow up a fire.

bauld² *adj* bald.

bauld-daur *adj* bold and daring.

baulie-loo *same as* **balaloo**.

baulkie *same as* **balkie**¹.

baumy *adj* balmy.

baun *same as* **band**¹.

baur *same as* **bar**³.

baurdy *same as* **bardy**.

bausand, bausent, bauson, bausond *adj* (*of animals*) having a white spot or streak on the face.

bausand-faced *adj* streaked with white on the face.

bausy *adj* **1** large. **2** corpulent. **3** coarse.—*n* a big, fat person or animal.

bauthrin *adj* **1** bustling. **2** fluttering.

bauthrin *same as* **baudrons**.

bautie *adj* guileful.

bauty *same as* **batie**¹.

bavard *adj* **1** worn-out. **2** bankrupt.

bavarie, bavarra *n* **1** a greatcoat. **2** a disguise.

baver *same as* **bever**.

baw¹ *n* **1** a ball. **2** the ball of the leg.

baw² *v* to lull asleep.—*n in phr* **beddie baw** a child's cradle or bed.

bawaw¹ *n* a scornful side glance.

bawaw² *n* a ludicrous term for a child.

bawbee *n* **1** a halfpenny. **2** (*in pl*) money. **3** a dowry.

bawbee-dragon *n* a boy's cheap kite.

bawbee-elder *n* an elder who merely takes up church collections.

bawbee-jo *n* a lover hired to walk with a girl for a shilling or so.

Bawbee-Kirk *n* the Free Church of Scotland.

bawbee-row *n* a halfpenny roll.

bawbee-whistle *n* a halfpenny whistle.

bawb net *n* a bonnet, now illegal in salmon fishing.

bawbreck *same as* **back-bread**.

bawbrie *n* **1** a broil. **2** great noise.

bawburd *same as* **back-bread**.

bawd *n* a hare.

bawd-bree *n* hare soup.

bawd-skin *n* a hare's skin.

bawk¹ *same as* **balk**¹.

bawk² *same as* **balk**².

bawm *n* a silly person.

bawsie *n* **1** a horse with white on its face. **2** an old horse.

bawsint *same as* **bausand**.

bawsy-broon *n* **1** a brownie (qv). **2** a hobgoblin.

bawty *n* **1** a dog. **2** a hare.

baxter *n* a baker.

baxter-chap *n* a baker's man or boy.

bay¹ *v* **1** to weep loudly. **2** to raise the voice loudly. —*n* the voice raised loudly.

bay² *n* unseemly mass.

bay³ *n* the sound of birds' notes.

bayed *adj* bent or giving way in the middle.

baze, baize *n* a state of bewilderment.—*v* **1** to bewilder. **2** to daze.

bazed *adj* **1** stung by insects. **2** stupefied. **3** stupid.

bazil *n* **1** a drunkard. **2** a sot.

bazzle *v* **1** to rush about. **2** to bustle.

be¹ *v* **1** to pay for. **2** to be at the cost of.

be² *prep* **1** by. **2** in comparison with. **3** towards.—*conj* than.

bead¹ *n* a ring of people hastily formed on any pressing business.—*v* to form such a ring of people.

bead² *n* a glass of spirits.

bead house *n* an almshouse.

bead-lambs *n* part of the mounting of a silk loom.

beagle¹ *n* a sheriff's officer.

beagle² *n* **1** an oddly dressed figure. **2** a person bespattered with mud.

beagle³ *n* a duck.

beak¹ *v* **1** to cry loudly. **2** to roar, bellow like a bull.

beak² *n* **1** the nose. **2** the face.—*v* **1** to kiss. **2** to bill. **3** to attack with the bill.

beak³ *same as* **beek**¹.

beal¹ *v* **1** to fester, suppurate. **2** to swell with pain or remorse.

beal² *n* a narrow mountain pass.

bealing *n* **1** a festering sore. **2** a boil.—*adj* festering, suppurating.

beam¹ *v* to warm a teapot before use.

beam² *v* to soak the staves of a leaking tub, barrel, etc, in order to stop leakage.

beam³ *n* the chief support of a plough.

beamfill *v* **1** to fill up spaces in the walls of a house after the beams are placed. **2** to fill up completely.

beamfilling *n* chips of brick and stone used to beamfill (qv) the walls of a house.

beamfilt *adj* indulged.

beamfull *adj* full to overflowing.

beam-shin'd *adj* having the shinbone rising with a curve.

beam-traddle *n* the treadle of a weaver's beam.
beamy *adj* beaming, glittering.
bean[1] *same as* **bein**[2].
bean[2] *n* advantage.
bean-hool *n* a bean pod.
bean-shaup *n* an empty bean pod.
bean-swaup *n* 1 a bean pod. 2 a thing or person of no value or strength.
bear[1] *n* four-rowed barley.
bear[2] *v* to go to a length.
bear barrel *n* 1 whisky. 2 a festival celebrating the stooking of the bear. *See* **stook**.
bear-buntling *n* a bird like a thrush, haunting especially growing bear.
bear-curn *n* a handmill or quern (qv) for husking bear.
beard *same as* **baird**[2].
bearder *n* one who rubs with the beard.
beardie[1] *n* rubbing a man's beard on a child's face in sport.
beardie[2] *same as* **bairdie**[4].
beardie[3] *n* 1 the three-spined stickleback. 2 the loach.
beardie[4] *n* the whitethroat.
beardie-lotch, --lowrie *n* the loach.
beardly *same as* **buirdly**.
beardy-land *n* the part of the face and throat on which the beard grows.
beardoc *n* the loach.
bearers *n* legs.
bear-feys *n* land set apart for barley.
bearge *v* to persist in clamorous repetition.
bear-land *n* land set apart for barley.
bear-lave *n* ground the first year after a crop of barley.
bear-meal-raik *n* a fruitless errand.
bear-meal-wife *n* a woman who cannot pay her debts.
bear-mell *n* an implement for beating the husks off barley.
bear-pundlar *n* an instrument for weighing barley.
bear-reet *n* 1 land that has borne a crop of barley in the previous year. 2 the first crop after bear.
bear's-ears *n* the auricula.
bear-seed *n* 1 barley. 2 the time of sowing barley or of preparing the ground for it.
bear-seed-bird *n* the yellow wagtail.
bear-stane *n* a hollow stone anciently used for husking bear or barley.
beas' *n* 1 beasts. 2 lice.
beast[1] *same as* **baist**[3].
beast[2] *n* 1 a horse, cow, ox or sheep. 2 a louse. 3 the devil. 4 any animal but man.
beastie *n* (*diminutive of* **beast**) used to express sympathy or affection.
beastie milk *same as* **beest milk**.
beastie-milk cheese *n* a cheese made of beest milk (qv).
beat[1] *n* 1 a stroke, blow, contusion. 2 what beats or puzzles one.
beat[2] *same as* **beet**[1].
beat[3] *v* to bruise the feet in walking.—*n* a bruise.
beat-the-badger *n* an old game used in Fife.
beat-to-chucks *phr* to surpass utterly.
beattocks *n* mashed potatoes.
beaufit *n* a side table set apart for wine, glasses, etc, a buffet.
beautiful *adj* delicious.
beaver[1] *n* a top hat.
beaver[2] *n* a schoolboy's term for his lunch.
beb *v* 1 to drink immoderately. 2 to swill.
bebbing-full *adj* (*used of the tide*) high, full.
bebble *v* 1 to sip. 2 to tipple. 3 to drink carelessly.
bebbs *same as* **babbs**.
beblacken, beblaiken *n* to calumniate boldly.
becam *v* became.
because *n* a cause.
bechance *v* to happen by chance.
bechle *n* a settled cough.—*v* to cough.
becht *same as* **bicht**.
becht *v*, *adj* tied.

beck[1] *n* a brook.
beck[2] *n* the call of the grouse.
beck[3] *n* 1 a curtsey. 2 obeisance.—*v* 1 to curtsey. 2 to cringe. 3 to do obeisance. 4 (*used of a horse*) to jerk the head.
beck and boo *v* to curry favour.
becklet *same as* **baiklet**.
bed[1] *n* 1 a woman's confinement. 2 litter for animals.—*v* 1 to go or put to bed. 2 to give litter to animals. 3 to lay a stone evenly. 4 to plant in flowerbeds.
bed[2] *v* stayed, abode.
bedboard *n* the board in front of a box bed (qv).
bed-bound *adj* bedridden.
bed-cronie *n* a bedfellow.
beddal *n* a bedridden person.
beddall, beddell *n* a licensed beggar.
beddie *n* a small bed.
beddie-ba' *n* a child's cradle or cot.
bedding *n* 1 litter for horses or cattle. 2 an old wedding custom of putting the bride and bridegroom to bed.
beddit *adj* 1 gone to bed. 2 put to bed.
beddle[1] *same as* **beddal**.
beddle[2] *n* a beadle.
beddy *adj* 1 greedy. 2 covetous of trifles. 3 conceited. 4 self-sufficient.
be deein' *v* to have patience, wait.
bedeen, bedien *adv* 1 immediately. 2 forthwith. 3 often used as an expletive or as a rhyme word to eke out a line.
bede house *n* an almshouse.
bedeman *n* 1 a resident in an almshouse. 2 a pauper who formerly received the king's annual bounty, with a blue coat and badge.
bederal *same as* **bedral**.
bed-evil *n* sickness confining one to bed.
bedfast *adj* bedridden.
bedfellow *n* a spouse.
bedgown *n* a woman's short, cotton working jacket.
bedicht *v* to wipe.
bedink *v* 1 to dress out smartly. 2 to bedizen.
bedirtin *adj* soiled with excrement.
bedler *n* a beadle.
bedoitrify *v* to stupefy.
bedown *prep* down.—*adj* downwards.
bed-plaid *n* a blanket.
bedraigle *v* to bedraggle.
bedral, bedrel *n* a church beadle, bellman and sexton in one.
bedrel, bedral *n* 1 a bedridden person. 2 a helpless cripple.—*adj* bedridden.
bedrite *v* 1 to soil with excrement. 2 to bedirt.
bedritten *same as* **bedirtin**.
beds *n* the game of hopscotch.
bedshank *n* buttermilk.
bedstock *n* the front bar of wood in a bed.
bedstone *n* 1 the nether millstone. 2 the piece of stone or slate used in the game of beds (qv).
bedunder *v* 1 to stupefy. 2 confound.
bee[1] *n* 1 a metal ring. 2 a ferrule for implements, axles, etc.
bee[2] *n* the hollow between the ribs and hipbone of a horse.
bee-ale *n* mead made from refuse honey.
be-east *adv* eastwards.
bee-baw-babbety *n* a game.
bee-bike *n* a wild bees' nest.
bee-bread *n* a mixture of pollen and honey, the food of the bees' larvae.
beed[1] *n* delay.
beed[2] *v* must, had to (used of moral or logical necessity).
beef-boat *n* a pickling tub or barrel.
beef bree *n* beef tea.
beef brewis *n* beef broth.
beef brose *n* brose (qv) made with the skimmings of beef broth.
beefer *n* an ox or cow fed for the butcher.

beefy *adj* **1** fat. **2** pursy. **3** short and stout. **4** (*used of oxen*) yielding good and abundant beef.—*n* a nickname for a short and stout person.

beegle *same as* **beagle**¹.

bee-headit *adj* **1** hare-brained. **2** flighty. **3** eccentric. **4** excitable.

bee-in-the-bonnet *n* **1** an eccentric. **2** a flighty person.

beek¹ *v* **1** to warm before the fire. **2** to make warm. **3** to bask in the sun or warmth of a fire. **4** (*of the sun*) to shine brightly. **5** to add fuel to fire.—*n* **1** what warms. **2** basking in the sun or warmth of a fire.

beek² *v* to bathe, foment.

beel¹ *v* (*used of cattle*) to collect them at night to a spot suitable for their spending the night in the open.—*n* a place where cattle are so collected.

beel² *same as* **bield**.

beel³ *same as* **beal**¹.

beeld *n* an image.

beeld *same as* **bield**.

beeldy *same as* **bieldy**.

beem *same as* **beam**².

been *same as* **bane**².

beene *v* to steep a tub when its staves have shrunk.

beenge *v* **1** to bow. **2** to cringe, fawn.

beenmost *same as* **bunemost**.

beeny *adj* **1** bony. **2** full of bones.

beer *n* a drinking bout.

beerach *n* a cord fastening a cow's tail to her leg during milking.

beeran *n* a small trout.

beerial *n* a funeral, burial.

beerlin *same as* **berlin**.

beerly *adj* stalwart.

beer-mell *n* a mell (qv) for pounding barley.

beery *v* to bury.

bees *n* **1** a state of confusion. **2** muddle. **3** light-headedness. **4** fuddle.

bee-scap, ~-skep *n* a beehive.

beesnin *n* milk drawn from a cow newly calved.

beest¹ *v* had to, was compelled to.

beest² *n* the milk of a cow newly calved.

beest³ *v* to have to pay at a card game.

beest ~, beesting cheese *n* cheese made from coagulated beest (qv).

beest milk *n* the milk of a cow newly calved.

beestone *n* the stone on which a hive rests.

bee's-wisp *n* a wild bee's nest on the surface of the ground.

beet¹ *v* to tie up flax in sheaves or bundles.—*n* a sheaf or bundle of flax prepared for the mill.

beet² *v* **1** to kindle or mend a fire. **2** to rouse or kindle a passion. **3** to repair. **4** to praise. **5** to blazon. **6** to supply. **7** to prevent waste by addition. **8** to soothe, mitigate.—*n* **1** an addition. **2** a supply. **3** (*in pl*) needful things.

beet³ *n* a boot.

beet⁴ *v* **1** had to, was compelled.

beet⁵ *n* what is given along with an article exchanged for another to equalize the exchange.

beetikin *n* a hobnailed boot.

beetin band *n* the strap that binds a bundle of flax.

beetle¹ *v* **1** to beat with a beetle. **2** to pound. **3** to mash.—*n* a flat piece of wood used by dyers and washerwomen.

beetle² *v* **1** to project. **2** to grow long and sharp.

beetle³ *same as* **bietle**.

beetle-bee *n* **1** a flying beetle. **2** a humming beetle.

beetle-hicht *n* the height of a beetle.

beetling stone *n* the stone on which clothes are beetled. *See* **beetle**¹.

beetl't-taties, ~-praties *n* mashed potatoes.

beet-master, ~-mister *n* a person or thing helpful in emergency.

beeton *n* in phr **burdie-beeton** a fondling term for a little child.

beetraw *n* beetroot.

beezin-ticht *adj* clean-swept.

befa' *v* to befall.

beff¹ *n* a stupid person.

beff² *same as* **baff**.

beff³ *n* **1** fat. **2** a swelling, as when the face is swollen by a blow.

beffan, beffin *same as* **baffin**.

beflude *v* to flood.

beflum *v* to befool by cajolery.—*n* idle, nonsensical, wheedling talk.

befong *n* a kind of handkerchief and its material.

before *adv* (*of a watch or clock*) fast.—*conj* rather than.

befreen *v* to befriend.

beft *v* **1** to beat. **2** to strike.

befyle *v* to soil, defile.

begairied *adj* **1** bespattered. **2** bedaubed. **3** variegated.

begairies *n* ornamental stripes of cloth on garments.

begarie, begarrie *v* **1** to variegate. **2** to bespatter, besmear.

begarred *adj* **1** variegated. **2** covered with filth. **3** bespattered with mud.

begeck, begeik *v* **1** to deceive. **2** to jilt. **3** to disappoint.—*n* **1** a trick. **2** disappointment.

beges *adv* **1** by chance. **2** at random.

begg *n* **1** barley. **2** bigg.

beggar *v* used as a quasi-imprecation.—*n* a term of reproach or familiar address.

beggar-bolts *n* **1** darts. **2** missiles of stone.

beggar's bed *n* a bed allotted to beggars in a barn.

beggar's brown *n* light-brown snuff made from tobacco stems.

beggar's plaits *n* wrinkles or creases in garments as if slept in.

begging weed *n* a beggar's garb.

begin *v* to say grace before a meal.

begink *same as* **begunk**.

beglammer *v* **1** to bewitch. **2** to deceive. **3** to hoodwink.

beglaum *v* to bewitch.

begnet *same as* **bagnet**.

bego *int* used as an expletive or oath.

begoud, begouth *v* began.

begowk, begouk *v* **1** to trick, befool. **2** to jilt.—*n* **1** a trick. **2** jilting.

begowker *n* a deceiver.

begoyt *adj* foolish.

begrat, begratten, begritten *adj* **1** tear-stained. **2** disfigured with weeping.

begrudge *v* **1** to regret. **2** to ill-wish.—*n* suspicion.

begrutten *same as* **begrat**.

beguid *same as* **begoud**.

beguile *v* **1** to deprive by a trick. **2** to lead into error. **3** to disappoint.—*n* **1** a trick. **2** disappointment.

begullion *n* a glamour deceiving the eyes.

begunk *n* **1** a trick. **2** misfortune. **3** unlooked for disappointment. **4** jilting.—*v* **1** to cheat. **2** to jilt. **3** to play a trick. **4** to disappoint.

begyke *same as* **begeck**.

begyte *v* to cheat.

behad *v* **1** to stop, wait. **2** to hold, maintain, hold as certain.

behadden, behadin *v, adj* **1** held or kept back. **2** indebted. **3** obliged.

behald, behaud *v* **1** to behold. **2** to wait. **3** to delay. **4** to permit. **5** to connive at. **6** to watch. **7** to scrutinize. **8** to view with jealousy or suspicion. **9** to recognize.—*n* **1** recognition. **2** notice.

behan, b'han *adj* by-hand, over and done.

behand *adv* in phr **come weel behand** to manage well.

behauden *same as* **behadden**.

beheef *n* behoof.

beheeld *v* **1** beheld. **2** waited to see what would happen. *See* **behald**.

behinds *n* the posterior.

behint, behin' *adv* **1** late. **2** too late. **3** in arrears of work, payment or fulfilment. **4** (*used of a clock or watch*) slow.—*prep* behind.

beho *same as* **boho**¹.
behold *same as* **behald**.
beholden *same as* **behadden**.
behoove, behove *v* to be obliged.—*n* behoof.
behouchie *n* the backside, bottom.
beigh *v* to cough.
beik¹ *same as* **bike**¹.
beik² *same as* **beek**¹.
beik³ *same as* **beak**².
beikat *n* a male salmon.
beil, beill *same as* **beal**¹.
beild¹ *same as* **beeld**¹.
beild² *same as* **bield**.
beildless *adj* unsheltered.
beiling *n* suppuration.
bein¹ *same as* **bane**².
bein² *adj* **1** well-to-do. **2** comfortable. **3** eager. **4** (*of a house or cask*) thoroughly dry, watertight.—*adv* comfortably.
beine *v* to warm a teapot before using it.
being¹*n* **1** livelihood. **2** means of subsistence.
being² *n* the beach of the seashore.
beinge *same as* **beenge**.
beinless *adj* comfortless.
bein-like *adj* in apparent comfort and wellbeing.
beinly *adv* **1** comfortably. **2** happily. **3** prosperously.
beinness *n* **1** comfort. **2** prosperity. **3** moderate wealth.
beirtree *n* the bier on which a corpse is carried to the grave.
beis¹ *prep* **1** in comparison with. **2** in addition to.
beis² *v 3rd per sing pres subj of* be.
beisand *adj* **1** quite at a loss. **2** stupefied. **3** benumbed.
beist ~, beistie milk *same as* **beest milk**.
beit *same as* **beet**².
beiting band *same as* **beetin band**.
beizless *adj* extreme.—*adv* extremely.
bejan *n* a first year's student at a Scottish university.—*v* to initiate a new shearer in the harvest field by bumping his posterior on a stone.
beke *same as* **beek**¹.
belaired *adj* stuck fast in mud, etc.
belaubir *v* to belabour.
belaw *prep and adv* below.
belay *v* to overcome.
belbevar *v* **1** to puzzle. **2** to perplex. **3** to be unable to decide.
belch *n* **1** a very fat person or animal. **2** a brat of a child.
beld *adj* bald.—*v* **1** to make bald. **2** to become bald.
beldness *n* baldness.
belicket *n in phrs* **deil-belicket, fient-belicket** absolutely nothing.
belike *adj* **1** probable. **2** likely.—*adv* probably.
belie *same as* **belive**.
belirt *v* **1** to jilt. **2** to beguile, deceive.
belive *adv* **1** speedily. **2** immediately. **3** soon.
belks *n* the stems of seaweed, formerly used in making kelp.
bell¹ *n* **1** the top of a hill. **2** the highest part of a slope. **3** a bellman. **4** a town crier with a bell.—*v* to advertise by means of a bellman.
bell² *n* a bubble.—*v* **1** to bubble. **2** to swell out.
bell³ *n* a blaze or white mark on a horse's face.
bell⁴ *n* the blossom of a plant.
bell⁵ *same as* **beld**.
bella *n* a bonfire.
bellam *same as* **bellum**.
bellandine *n* a broil, squabble.
bell'd-wadder *n* a bellwether.
beller *v* to bubble up.
bell-groat *n* a bellman's fee for ringing.
bell-heather *n* the cross-leaved heather.
bell house *n* a church tower, belfry.
belli-bucht *n* a hollow in a hill transverse to the slope.
bellicon *n* a blusterer.
bellie-mantie *n* blindman's buff.
belli-hooin' *n* riotousness.

bellisand *adj* **1** elegant. **2** of imposing appearance.
bell-kite *n* the bald coot.
bell money *n* money demanded by children at a house in which there is a wedding.
belloch¹ *v* **1** to bellow. **2** to cry loudly, roar.—*n* a roar, bellow.
belloch² *same as* **balloch**².
bellonie *n* a brawling, noisy woman.
bell-penny *n* money laid past to provide for one's funeral.
bell-pow *n* a bald head.
bellraive *v* **1** to rove about. **2** to be unsteady. **3** to act on impulse.
bellringer *n* the long-tailed titmouse.
bellstring *n* a bell rope.
bell't *same as* **beld**.
belltime *n* the time when church bells begin to toll for service.
bell'tness *n* baldness.
bellum *n* **1** force. **2** impetus. **3** a stroke. **4** a blow. **5** a blast.
bellums *n* a boys' game.
bellware *n* seaweed, of which kelp was made.
bellwaver *v* **1** to straggle. **2** to stroll. **3** (*used of the mind*) to fluctuate, be inconstant. **4** to tell a story incoherently.
bellwavering *n* **1** fluttering. **2** rambling.
bellweed *n* bellware.
belly¹ *v* **1** to eat or drink voraciously. **2** to stuff the belly.
belly² *v* **1** to bellow. **2** to weep loudly.
belly-blind, *adj* quite blind.—*n* blindman's buff.
belly-flaught *adv* **1** headlong. **2** hastily. **3** face down. **4** flat-forward. **5** overhead in skinning an animal.
belly-flaughtered *adj* thrown flat on the ground.
belly-god *n* a glutton.
belly-gourdon, --gut, --hudroun *n* a glutton.
belly-rack *n* **1** gormandizing. **2** good things to eat.
belly-rive *n* **1** a great feast. **2** a social gathering.
belly-thraw *n* a colic.
belly-timber *n* **1** food. **2** provisions.
below *v* to demean.
belsh *same as* **belch**.
belshach *n* **1** a contemptuous designation of a child. **2** a brat. *See* **belch**.
belshie *adj* short and fat. *See* **belch**.
belstracht *adv* headlong, prostrate.
belt¹ *n* the bolt of a door.
belt² *n* a narrow plantation.
belt³ *v* **1** to flog. **2** to scourge.
belt⁴ *v* to come forward with a sudden spring.
belt⁵ *v* to gird as an honorary distinction.
Beltane *n* **1** 1 May OS and NS. **2** sometimes 3 May and Whitsunday. **3** a festival formerly kept by herds and young people on 1 May and 21 June.
belted plaid *n* a Highlander's full military dress plaid.
belter *n* **1** a heavy blow, a succession of blows. **2** bickering.
beltie¹ *n* a small, narrow plantation.
beltie² *n* a water hen.
Belting *same as* **Beltane**.
bely *v* to besiege.
belyve *same as* **belive**.
bemang *v* **1** to hurt, injure. **2** to maul.
bemean *v* to degrade, to lower oneself.
bement *v* to render demented.
bemmle *n* **1** an ill-made man. **2** an ungainly walker.
ben¹ *n* a hill, mountain.
ben² *n* the supply of empty coal tubs.
ben³ *n* a small species of salmon.
ben⁴ *adv* **1** in, inside, within. **2** in or into the parlour. **3** in toward the speaker.—*prep* in, within.—*n* an inner room, a parlour.
ben⁵ *v* to bend.
ben-a-hoose *adj* belonging to the parlour or the best room.—*adv* in the parlour.
ben-a-hoose breakfast *n phr* breakfast for the farmer's family in the parlour.

ben-a-hoose breid *n phr* an oatcake of finer quality for use in a farmer's parlour.

ben-a-hoose woman, ~ umman *n phr* a parlourmaid.

bench *n* a plate rack.

bend[1] *n* strong thick leather for the soles of boots or shoes.

bend[2] *n* **1** a piece of bent iron plate going over the back of the last horse at plough. **2** (*in pl*) the complete furniture of a peat horse.—*v* to adjust on a horse the harness for panniers.

bend[3] *n* **1** a foolish, foppish fellow. **2** a heavy drinker. **3** a draught of liquor.—*v* **1** to drink hard or greedily. **2** to drink heavily.

bend[4] *n* a bound, spring, leap.—*v* to bound, spring.

bend[5] *n* **1** a muffler. **2** a kerchief. **3** a cowl.

bend[6] *v* to cock a gun.

bend[7] *v* (*with* **up**) to embolden.

bend[8] *adj* bold.—*adv* bravely.

bender *same as* **bend**[3].

bendit *adj* crouching, ready to spring.

bend-leather *n* thick leather for soling boots and shoes.

bend up *v* to bear up.

bene *same as* **bein**[2].

benefit *n* farm servant's wages so far as paid in kind.

benefit-man *n* a farm servant paid partly in kind.

ben-end *n* **1** the better room in a two-roomed house. **2** the best part of anything.

benew *adv* beneath.

bengie *n* a penalty exacted by harvesters from a visitor to the field, either in money or in the infliction of bumping on the stubble.—*v* to inflict the penalty of bumping. *See* **bump**[1].

bengiel *same as* **bangyal**.

ben-hoose *n* the inner or principal room.

ben-inno *adv* **1** to within. **2** towards the speaker in a room.

benjamine *n* benzoin.

benjel *same as* **bangyal**.

benk *same as* **bink**[1].

benlin *n* a long, light stone, slung in the loops of straw ropes on a thatched or turfed roof.

benlins *adv* towards the interior of a house.

benmost *adj* inmost, farthest ben (qv).

benicht *v* to stay in another's house until after midnight.

benn *same as* **bend**[5].

bennel *n* **1** long, reedy grass, growing in stagnant waters. **2** (*in pl*) mats made of bennel and used as cottage partitions and ceilings. **3** dry, withered weeds gathered for burning.

bennels *n* the seed of flax.

benner *adj* inner.

benner gowan *n* **1** the mountain daisy. **2** the garden feverfew.

bennermost *adj* innermost.

benorth *adv* to the northward of.

bense *n* **1** a violent movement. **2** a blow, spring, strong push. **3** vigour, energy.—*v* **1** to walk or move violently. **2** to bounce.—*adv* violently.

bensel *n* (*used of cloth*) tear and wear.

benshee *n* a banshee.

bensie *v* to strike vigorously.

bensil, bensell *v* **1** to beat. **2** to bang.—*n* **1** a heavy blow. **2** a violent or sudden movement. **3** violence of storm, etc. **4** a severe rebuke. **5** a place exposed to the violence of the storm.

bensing *n* the showing of great vigour in walking, working, etc.—*ppl adj* **1** bouncing, vigorous. **2** (*used of a bow*) full bent.

bensome *adj* quarrelsome.

bent *n* **1** coarse grass growing near the sea or on moorland. **2** common hair grass. **3** the open field. **4** a sandy knoll covered with bent. **5** the slope or hollow of a hill.

bent dues *n* a levy formerly exacted from scholars for playing on the links on half-holidays.

ben-the-hoose *adv* in the parlour.—*n* the best or inner part of a house.

bentiness *n* the state of being covered with bent (qv).

bent moss *n* soil composed of hard moss covered thickly with bent (qv).

bent silver *n* blessed money claimed on a saint's day.

benty *adj* covered with bent grass.

benty bows *n* bandy-legs.

benward *adv* inward, forward.

benweed, benwood *n* the common ragwort.

benwuth *same as* **benward**.

benzel *same as* **bangyal**.

beowld *same as* **beuld**.

berge, berje *same as* **bairge**[1].

berjer *n* a female scold.

berlin *n* a sort of galley, a half-decked rowing boat.

bern windlin *n* a kiss given in the corner of a barn.

berry[1] *n* **1** the grain of corn. **2** a gooseberry.

berry[2] *n in phr* **no' the berry** a bad character, not the thing.

berry[3] *v* **1** to beat, to cudgel. **2** to thresh corn.

berry-barn *n* the third finger.

berry-heather *n* the crowberry.

berthinsek *n* a law by which no man was to be capitally punished for stealing a calf or sheep or as much meat as he could carry on his back in a sack.

bervie, bervie-haddock *n* a haddock split and smoke-dried.

besaunt *v* **1** to canonize. **2** to repute as very holy.

beseek, beseik *v* to beseech.

beseene *adj* **1** conversant with. **2** skilled in. **3** provided, furnished with.

beset *v* to become.

besetment *n* a besetting weakness, trouble or sin.

beshachil *v* **1** to crook. **2** to deviate from the straight.

beshacht *adj* **1** not straight. **2** tattered, dirty.

besides *prep* in comparison with.

beslabber *v* **1** to eat slovenly. **2** to besmear in eating or drinking.

besle *v* to talk much at random and ignorantly.—*n* idle talk.

besmarten *v* to make smart, neat.

besmiacher *v* to besmear.

besmotter *v* **1** to smear or daub with muck, etc. **2** to be-spatter, foul.

besna *v neg* be not.

besnang *v* to crush, batter, beat in.

besom *n* **1** a loose or slovenly woman. **2** a term of contempt applied to a women.

besom-clean *adj* **1** clean only on the surface. **2** clean by sweeping though not by washing.

besom-shank *n* the handle of a besom.

besouth *adv* to the southward of.

bess[1] *same as* **baiss**[2].

bess[2] *n* **1** a boys' school game with bat and ball. **2** baseball.

bessy *n* **1** an ill-mannered, romping or bad-tempered woman or girl. **2** a light-headed girl.

bessy-lorch *n* the loach.

best[1] *v* to excel, to get the better of one.—*adj* better.

best[2] *n* a beast.

best-aucht *n* the best thing of a kind that one possesses.

best-cheip, ~-cheap *adj* the best for the money.

bestial *n* the livestock on a farm.

best-like *adj* best-looking.

best maid *n* a bridesmaid.

best man *n* a bridegroom's supporter.

best respects *n* intimate friends.

besturted *v, adj* startled, alarmed.

besweik, beswik *v* **1** to allure. **2** to cheat, deceive.

bet[1] *v* **1** to beat. **2** to defeat.—*v* did beat.

bet[2] *v* to assuage, mitigate.

bet[3] *v* did bite.

betake, betack *v* **1** to inflict. **2** to hand over. **3** to resort. **4** to recover. **5** to take over.

betaucht *v* committed, delivered up. *See* **beteach**.

betchell *v* to beat.

betchellin' *n* a drubbing.

beteach *v* 1 to deliver up. 2 to entrust. 3 to recommend to.

beteach us *phr* 1 have a care of us. 2 give us understanding.

bethank *n* 1 thanks. 2 indebtedness.

bethankit *int* God be thanked!—*n* grace after meat.

betheikit *v, adj* thatched.

betheral, bethral *same as* bedral.

bethout *prep and adv* without.

betid, beted *v* befell.

betimes *adv* 1 occasionally, at times. 2 by and by.

bet-lick *n* the conquering blow.

betoggit *v, adj* 1 covered. 2 burdened.

betooch, betootch *v* to commit, entrust. *See* beteach.

betooch-us-to *int* alas! commend us to (God)! have a care of us!

better *v* to improve in health.—*n* the best.—*adj* 1 greater, more, higher in price. 2 recovered from illness.—*adv* 1 repeatedly. 2 with renewed efforts.

better-cheap *adv* cheaper, at a less price.

better-gates *adv* in a better way or manner.

better-like *adj* 1 better-looking. 2 looking better (in health, etc).

betterlins *adv* better.

bettermer *n* the better or upper classes.

betterness *n* improvement in health.

betters *n in phr* ten betters ten times better.

better side *n* what is more or older than.

better sort *n* the upper classes.

bettle *n* a blow, a stroke.

betuik *v* betook.

between-hands *adv* at intervals.

between-the-lights *phr* twilight.

between two minds *phr* undecided.

betweesh *prep* between.

betwixt and between *phr* 1 neither one thing nor another. 2 intermediate.

beuch *n* 1 the bow of a boat or ship. 2 a person, an individual person. 3 a bough. 4 a limb.

beuchel *v* 1 to shamble. 2 to walk feebly with short steps.—*n* a little, weak, crooked creature.

beugle-backit *adj* crook-backed.

beuk¹ *same as* book.

beuk² *v* baked.

beuk³ *v* (*used of cattle*) to grow fat, take on flesh.

beukin' *n* the handing in of banns of marriage for proclamation.

beukin' nicht *n* the evening when names are beukit for marriage banns. *See* book.

beuk-lare, ~-lear *same as* book-lare.

beuk-lared, ~-lear'd *same as* book-lared.

beukworm *n* a bookworm.

beuld *adj* bow-legged.

beust *n* 1 grass two years old. 2 grass withered from standing through the winter.

beusty *adj* 1 (*used of grass*) dry. 2 half-withered.

beuter *n* the bittern.

bevel *n* 1 a strong thrust. 2 a heavy blow.

bever *v* 1 to shake, quiver. 2 to tremble from age, infirmity, fright or cold.

beverage, beveridge *n* 1 a fine in money, kisses or drink, demanded of anyone on the first wearing of new clothes. 2 the first kiss given to a newly married bride by the bridegroom. 3 a hansel (qv).—*v* to hansel (qv).

bevie¹ *n* a large fire.

bevie² *n* a jog, push.

bevil *v* 1 to manage. 2 to arrange.

bevil-edge *n* the edge of a sharp tool, sloping towards the point.

bevir horse *n* a lean horse, one worn-out with age or hard work.

bevver *same as* bever.

bewaur *v* to beware.

bewave *v* 1 to lay in wait for. 2 to overcome by mean strategem.

bewest *adv* to the west of.

bewiddied *adj* bewildered.

bewild *same as* bewill.

bewill *v* to cause to go astray.

bewith *n* a temporary substitute or makeshift.

bewk *v* baked.

bewter *same as* beuter

bey *n* a room of a cottage or house.

beychel *n* a small, agile person.

beylie *n* a bailie.

beyont *adv* 1 yonder, beyond. 2 beyond all things. 3 over and above.—*prep* beyond.—*n* a place or district supposed to be beyond ken.

beyon'-the-beyont *phr* 1 quite incredible. 2 quite out of the way.

beysand *same as* beisand.

beyzless *same as* beizless.

bezle *same as* besle.

biach *n* a familiar term of address, often used to children.

bias *adv* very.

bib¹ *n* the stomach.

bib², bibble *v* to tipple.

bibble¹ *same as* bubble.

bibble² *n* nonsense.

bibbles *n* nasal mucus.

bibblie *same as* bubbly.

bibblie-gauger *n* the nose.

bible *n* 1 a book of any kind. 2 a large quarto or folio volume.

bibliothecar *n* a librarian.

bibliotheck *n* a library.

bicht *n* 1 anything folded or doubled. 2 the loop in a rope. 3 a measure of the length of a coil of fishing line. 4 a bay, creek.

bick¹ *v in phr* bick and birr to cry as grouse.

bick² *n* 1 bitch. 2 a sluttish woman.

bicker ¹*v* 1 to pelt with stones. 2 to strike repeatedly. 3 to move quickly and noisily. 4 to ripple. 5 to indulge in rough or indelicate horseplay.—*n* 1 a scrimmage. 2 a stone-fight. 3 a rapid and noisy movement. 4 a rough, stupid and noisy person.

bicker² *n* 1 a wooden beaker or drinking cup. 2 a porridge dish. 3 a bowl. 4 a small wooden vessel with one of the staves prolonged as a handle. 5 a mess of porridge or brose in a bicker.

bicker ³ *n* a droll fellow.

bicker-cut *n* hair-cutting by means of a bowl placed on the head.

bickerfu' *n* a bowlful.

bickerin' *n* 1 indelicate toying. 2 quarrelling.

bicker-joy *n* the joy of a carouse.

bicker raid *n* a harvest frolic in which a young man threw down a girl and the other harvesters covered them with their bickers.

bid *v* 1 to desire, wish. 2 to invite to a wedding or funeral.

biddableness *n* docility, compliance.

biddably *adv* obediently, meekly.

biddenable *adj* obedient, docile.

bidding *n* an invitation.

bide *v* 1 (*used of persons*) to wait, remain, tarry. 2 dwell, live. 3 (*of things*) to remain, continue. 4 to await. 5 to tolerate. 6 to be the better of. 7 to receive, require.—*n* pain, suffering.

bide by *v* to adhere to, maintain.

bidie-in *n* a person with whom one lives and with whom one has a sexual relationship but to whom one is not married.

biding *n* 1 endurance, enduring. 2 (*in pl*) sufferings.

biel', bield *same as* beeld.

bield, biel *v* 1 to shelter, protect. 2 to take shelter.—*n* 1 a shelter, refuge. 2 a home, house. 3 anything that shelters or shades.

bielding *n* 1 shelter. 2 protection.

bieldy, biely *adj* **1** furnishing shelter. **2** snug.
bien *same as* **bein**².
bier¹ *v* to roar as a bull.—*n* **1** a shout. **2** a complaint.
bier² *n* twenty threads in the breadth of a web.
bierling *same as* **berlin**.
bierly *adj* big, burly.
biets *same as* **beest**².
bietle *v* **1** to amend, recover health. **2** (*used of a crop*) to improve.
biffy *n* a nickname for a short, pursy fellow. *See* **beefy**.
big¹ *adj* **1** pregnant, gravid. **2** haughty. **3** consequential.
big², **bigg** *v* **1** to build. **2** to build a nest.
big coat *n* a greatcoat.
big end *n* the greater part.
bigent *same as* **bejan**.
bigger *n* a builder.
biggie, biggin *n* a linen cap or coif.
biggin *n* **1** a building. **2** a house. **3** a cottage. **4** the act of building.
biggit *adj* **1** built. **2** grown. **3** wealthy.
biggit-land *n* land built on.
biggit-wa's *n* **1** buildings. **2** houses.
biggle *v* to separate grain from the straw by shaking it.
biggonet *n* a linen cap or coif.
bighornie *n* the devil.
bightsom *adj* having an air of ease combined with activity.
bigly *adj* **1** pleasant. **2** commodious.
big mavis *n* the mistle thrush.
big miss *n* a great loss by death or by the departure of a friend.
bigness *n* size, bulk.
bignet *same as* **bagnet**.
big on, ~ upon *v* to fall upon, attack.
big-ox-eye *n* the great titmouse.
bigsie *adj* **1** rather large. **2** proud, conceited (used contemptuously).
big up *v* **1** to confirm in an opinion. **2** to devote oneself to an opinion, idea, purpose or person.
bike¹ *n* **1** a nest of wild bees. **2** a swarm. **3** a habitation. **4** an assembly of people. **5** a windfall, unexpected luck. **6** an erection shaped like a beehive for preserving grain.—*v* **1** to swarm like bees. **2** to assemble, crowd.
bike² *n* the hook of the crook from which pots hang over a fire in cooking.
biking *n* **1** a hive. **2** a swarm.
bikker *same as* **bukkar**.
bilbie *n* **1** a residence. **2** shelter.
bilch¹ *n* **1** a fat, short person or animal. **2** a monster. **3** a brat. **4** a little, crooked, insignificant person.
bilch² *v* to limp, halt.
bilcher *n* one who limps.
bilder *n* a scab.
bile¹ *n* **1** a boil. **2** *in phr* **bile in the stomach** a bilious attack.
bile² *n* **1** the heating of corn stacks. **2** boiling point. —*v* to boil.
biler *n* **1** a boiler. **2** a kettle.
bilf¹ *n* **1** a contemptuous designation of a pursy person. **2** a monster.
bilf² *n* a blunt stroke.
bilfert *n* **1** an overgrown lad. **2** a stout or fat person.
bilgate *n* **1** a bout, a go.
bilget¹ *n* a projection to support a shelf, etc.—*adj* bulging, jutting out.
bilget² *n* a billet for a soldiers' quarters.
bill¹ *n* a letter, a missive.—*v* **1** to register. **2** to indict.
bill² *n* a bull.
billatory *n* a restless bull.
bill-blo *n* a bull.
billibue *n* a hullabaloo.
billie *same as* **billy**¹.
billie-dawkus *n* a leader, chief manager, principal actor.
bill-jock *n* a bull.

billseag *n* an old, castrated bull.
bill-sweater *n* a moneylender.
billy¹ *n* **1** a young fellow. **2** a comrade. **3** a brother. **4** a lover. **5** a boy.
billy² *n* the golden warbler.
billy³ *same as* **belly**².
billy-bentie *n* a smart, roguish boy.
billy-blin *n* a benevolent sprite, a brownie (qv).
billy-blind *n* **1** blindman's buff. **2** the person blindfolded in the game.
billy-blinder *n* **1** the person who hoodwinks another in the game of blindman's buff. **2** an imposture, a blind.
billy-fairplay *n* a game of chance, common at village fairs.
billyhood *n* brotherhood.
billy-play-fair tummlin' tans *n phr* riddles for riddling coals.
billy-whitethroat *n* the golden warbler.
bilsh *same as* **bilch**¹.
bilshie *adj* **1** short and stout. **2** plump and thriving.
bilt¹ *n* a short, thickset person.
bilt² *n* a blow.
bilt³ *n* a limp.—*v* **1** to limp. **2** to walk with crutches.
bilter *n* a child.
biltie *adj* **1** thickset. **2** clubbish. **3** clumsy.
biltieness *n* clumsiness.
bilting *v, adj* moving like a short, thickset person.
bim *n* to hum, to buzz.—*n* the act of humming or buzzing.
bimmer *n* anything that hums or buzzes.
bin¹ *same as* **ben**¹.
bin² *n* key, mood, humour.
bin³, **binn** *v* to bind.
bin⁴ *v* to move or run swiftly.
bin⁵ *v* to curse (*imperative used as an imprecation*).
bind¹ *n* **1** capacity, ability. **2** sense.
bind² *v* **1** to tie sheaves in harvesting. **2** to restrain.
binder *n* **1** one who ties sheaves at harvest. **2** a strip of cloth put round cheese when taken from the chessel (qv). **3** the bandage wound round a newborn child. **4** the bandage wound round a woman after parturition. **5** a large stone built in a wall to give solidity.
binding bouse *n* a treat at the signing by master and man of the engagement for service.
bindle *n* a cord or rope of hemp or straw for tying or binding.
bindpock *n* a niggard.
bindweed *n* the ragwort.
bindwood *n* ivy.
bine *same as* **boyne**.
bing¹ *n* **1** a crowd. **2** a heap, pile. **3** a heap of waste from mine workings.—*v* **1** to pile. **2** to accumulate.
bing² *v* to go.
bing³ *n* a bin or box for corn, wine, etc.
bing⁴ *same as* **being**.
binge *same as* **beenge**.
bingly *adv* comfortably.
binjel *same as* **banyal**.
bink¹ *n* **1** a large shelf. **2** a plate rack. **3** a bench. **4** a bank. **5** a ledge in a cliff. **6** a peat bank. **7** a wasps' or wild bees' nest. **8** a small heap of clay, mortar, etc. **9** a raised built part, or a large stone, at each side of a fire with a kind of grate resting on the pair.
bink² *n* a crease, a fold.
bink³ *v* **1** to bend down. **2** to lean forward awkwardly. **3** to curtsy. **4** to press down. **5** to destroy the shape of shoes.—*n* a bending movement.
binkart *n* a pile of stones, dirt, etc.
binked shoes *n* **1** shoes full of creases and bends. **2** shoes down at the heels.
binker *v* to pile up in a heap.—*n* a heap of stones, dirt, etc.
binkie *adj* **1** gaudy. **2** trimly dressed.
bink-side *n* the side of a long seat near the fire in a country house.
binn¹ *same as* **bind**¹.
binn² *same as* **boon**².

binna[1] v be not.

binna[2], **binnae** prep except, save.

binne n a temporary enclosure for preserving grain.

binner adj more comfortable. See **bein**[2].

binner v 1 to move swiftly. 2 to rush. 3 to work with a dash. 4 to cause a whirring or humming sound, to buzz.— n 1 a quick movement, noisy dash. 2 a sounding blow. 3 a quantity of work done. 4 the boiling point. 5 a state of excitement. —adv noisily and forcibly.

binnins n the chains, etc, by which cattle are tied up in the byre (qv).

binster n one who ties sheaves in harvesting.

bin up v to bind a cow to her stall.

bir same as **birr**.

birbeck n the call of the moorcock or grouse.

bird n 1 a young bird. 2 a damsel. 3 offspring of quadrupeds, in particular of the fox. 4 a grouse. 5 a partridge. 6 also applied to man or woman in ironic familiarity.

bird-and-joe adv cheek-by-jowl, like Darby and Joan.

bird-mouthed, **~-mou'd** adj 1 unwilling to speak out. 2 mealy-mouthed. 3 tender in finding fault.

bird's-nest n the wild carrot.

birk[1] n a piece of round timber laid horizontally in roof-making, over which the rafters were laid loose.

birk[2] n the birch tree.

birk[3] same as **birkie**.

birk[4] v 1 to give a tart answer. 2 to converse in a lively or cutting way. 3 (with **up**) to brisk up, cheer up.

birken adj 1 abounding in birches. 2 made of birch.—n a birch tree.

birkenshaw n a small wood of birch trees, etc.

birkie[1] adj abounding in birches.

birkie[2] n 1 a lively, smart youth. 2 a designation of a person of any age.—adj 1 lively, smart. 2 spirited in speech and action.

birkie[3] n the card game beggar-my-neighbour.

birk knowe n a knoll covered with birches.

birl v 1 to revolve with a whirring sound. 2 to twirl round. 3 to spin. 4 to cause to sound. 5 to move quickly, hurry along. 6 to spend money freely in drink or gaming. 7 to pour out liquor. 8 to ply with drink. 9 to drink hard. 10 to carouse.—n 1 a brisk dance. 2 a whirring sound. 3 the sound of a coin flung on a table.

birley oats same as **barley oats**.

birlie, birlin n 1 a loaf of bread. 2 a small cake of barley or oatmeal.

birlie-, birlaw-court same as **burlaw**.

birlie-man n a member of a burlaw (qv).

birlin same as **berlin**.

birling n 1 a feast, a carousel. 2 a drinking match in which the drink is clubbed for. 3 a whirring noise. 4 a noisy, rapid revolution of a wheel.

birn[1] n 1 a burden. 2 a load carried on the back.

birn[2] n the labia pudenda of a cow.

birn[3] n 1 a burnt mark on a sheep's nose for identification. 2 a scorched stem of burnt heather.—v to burn.—phr **skin and birn** the whole of anything or any number.

birn[4] n dry, heathery pasture for the summering of lambs after weaning.—v to put lambs on a poor, dry pasture.

birney adj 1 sturdy. 2 muscular, brawny. 3 rough.

birnman n the man who carried grain to a mill and carried back the meal.

birny adj 1 covered with charred stems of heather. 2 having rough or stunted stems. 3 (of the temper) crusty, sour, irascible.

birr n 1 force. 2 impetus, energy. 3 violence. 4 passion. 5 a rapid, whirling motion. 6 a whirring noise.—v 1 to move rapidly, bustle. 2 to act with energy. 3 to whir. 4 to be in a turmoil or confusion.

birrel n a ring for a staff.

birringly adv with vigour, energetically.

birrit, birritie n 1 the hedge sparrow. 2 the willow warbler.

birr up v to prick up the ears.

birs n the gadfly.

birse[1] n 1 a bristle. 2 hair. 3 a plume of hair or bristles. 4 a bristle attached to the end of shoemakers' or saddlers' waxed thread. 5 temper, anger. —v to bristle, to get suddenly angry.

birse[2] n 1 a bruise, contusion. 2 pressure, a squeeze.—v to bruise, crush, squeeze, force, press.

birse[3], **birze** n 1 a push. 2 help in pushing. 3 pecuniary help.

birsie adj 1 pushing, forward. 2 bristly. 3 hot-tempered, passionate. 4 keen, sharp.—n a pert, forward child.

birsk n gristle, cartilage.

birsle v 1 to scorch, toast, parch. 2 to crackle with heat.— n a thorough warming.

birslin' adj drying, scorching.—n a scorching.

birst n a small, impudent person.

birst n 1 a difficulty, emergency, battle. 2 brunt. 3 burst. 4 over-exertion causing injury. 5 convulsive weeping.—v 1 to over-exert injuriously. 2 to burst. 3 to burst into tears.

birstle[1] same as **birsle**.

birstle[2] n a bristle.

birsy[1] same as **birsie**.

birsy[2] n a nickname for a pig.

birth n a berth, office, situation.

birth brief n evidence of birth, a birth certificate.

birth grun n one's birthplace.

birthy adj prolific, productive.

birze same as **birse**[3].

biscuit n a small round cake of flour.

bishop n 1 a cantankerous, ill-natured boy. 2 the great northern diver. 3 a second-hand horseshoe. 4 an implement for packing and pressing soil round a post or levelling a causeway.—v to beat down soil or stones with a bishop.

bishop's foot n a taste of burning in food.

bishop weed n the goutweed.

bisket n brisket, the breast.

bisse v to buzz, to make a hissing noise.—n 1 a buzz. 2 a hissing noise. 3 a bustle.

bissom same as **besom**.

bit[1] n 1 a morsel of food. 2 food. 3 a piece of money. 4 a place, position, station. 5 a short distance or time. 6 a crisis, point. 7 the nick of time. 8 the hinge of an argument, the conclusion aimed at or reached. 10 an ear mark for sheep or cattle.—v to cut an ear mark.—adj 1 small. 2 puny (used contemptuously or endearingly).

bit[2] v had to.

bit[3] n a blow, a stroke.

bit[4] conj, prep and adv but.

bitch[1] n a term of contempt applied to a man.

bitch[2] n the cheating of a landlord by a moonlight flittin (qv).

bitch-fou, ~-fu', ~-full adj 1 beastly drunk. 2 (used of liquors) filling the containing vessels full.

bite n 1 a mouthful. 2 a little food. 3 pasturage. 4 a hoax. 5 a taunt, scoff. 6 a disappointment in love.—v 1 to smart, tingle. 2 to sting. 3 to take food.

bite and brat n food and clothing.

bite and buffet phr food and blows.

bite and drap phr something to eat and drink.

bite and soup, sup phr something to eat.

bited v, adj bitten.

bitle same as **bittle**.

bittag same as **bittock**.

bitter adj spiteful.

bitter-bank, bitterle n the sand martin.

bitterness n bitter, stormy weather.

bittie n a little bit.

bittle n 1 a beetle. 2 a leg.—v to beat with a beetle.

bittlins n the battlements of any old building.

bittock n 1 a little bit. 2 a short distance.

bizz v 1 to hiss, as water on hot iron. 2 to hiss like an adder. 3 to buzz. 4 to frizzle. 5 to fuss about.—n 1 a buzz. 2 a bustle. 3 a state of tousled hair. 4 the startling or pricking (qv) of cattle in hot weather. **5** the hissing noise of water on hot iron. **6** *in phr* **say bizz to one** to be more than a match for one.—*int* an exclamation of derision.

bizzan *n* a multitude, a confused crowd.

bizzard-gled *n* a hawk.

bizzel *n* a hoop or ring round the end of any tube.

bizzie *n* a stall in a cattle shed.

bizzy *adj* **1** busy. **2** bustling. **3** officious, meddling.

blaad *same as* **blad**⁴.

blaadin *n* a blow.

blaadit *adj* weakly.

blaathrie *same as* **blawthirie**.

blaavin *v, adj* **1** blowing, puffing. **2** boasting.

blab¹ *same as* **blob**.

blab² *n* **1** a gossip, a telltale.

blab³ *v* **1** to tipple. **2** to slobber in drinking.—*n* **1** a quantity of liquor. **2** a gurgling noise in drinking or taking semiliquid food.

blabban *n* the act of drinking with a gurgling noise.

blabber¹ *n* a tippler.

blabber² *v* **1** to babble. **2** to speak indistinctly.

blabber³ *v* **1** to drink much and often. **2** to make a gurgling noise in drinking or supping.—*n* **1** a quantity of strong drink. **2** a gurgling noise with the lips in drinking or supping.

blabberin *n* the act of making a gurgling noise in drinking, etc.

black *v* **1** to blacken. **2** to put a thing in black and white by writing it. **3** to grow black. **4** to scold. **5** to defame, slander.—*n* **1** a scoundrel, blackguard. **2** smut in wheat. **3** a mild imprecation. **4** a contemptuous designation for a puny, insignificant person.—*adj* **1** dark in complexion. **2** grimy. **3** (*of the weather*) overcast, foul. **4** sad, melancholy. **5** extreme, dead.—*adv* quite, thoroughly.

black airn *n* malleable iron, in contrast to tin.

black-aviced, -avized *adj* of dark, swarthy complexion.

blackball *v* to scold, abuse.

black-bean *adj* unlucky.

black-belickit *n* absolutely nothing.

blackberry *n* the crowberry.

black-bide *same as* **blackboyd**.

black-bitch *n* a bag clandestinely attached to a hole in the mill spout to abstract some of the meal running down the spout.

black-blutter *n* a blackberry, a bramble.

black-bonnet *n* **1** an elder of the Church. **2** the black-headed bunting.

black-boo *n* a nursery bogy.

blackboyd *n* a blackberry.

black bun *n* a cake made of a thick pastry casing and a rich fruit cake mixture, particularly associated with Hogmanay (qv).

black-burning *adj* causing intense blushing or shame.

black-cap *n* the core-tit.

black-clock *n* **1** a cockroach. **2** a black beetle.

black-coaly-head *n* the reed bunting.

blackcoat *n* a minister of religion.

blackcock *n in phr* **make a blackcock of one** to shoot one.

black-cork *n* porter.

black cow *same as* **black ox**.

black-crap *n* **1** a crop of beans or peas. **2** a crop that is always green.

black-doctor *n* a leech.

black-doggie *n* a variety of the game 'drop the handkerchief'.

black-dooker *n* the cormorant.

blackening *n* the black that affects iron moulders injuriously.

black-fasting *adj* practising severe fasting.

blackfish *n* **1** newly spawned fish. **2** a salmon after spawning.

black-fisher *n* **1** a night poacher of fish. **2** a fisher of blackfish (qv).

black-fishing *n* fishing illegally for salmon at night or for blackfish.

blackfit *n* a lovers' go-between, a matchmaker.

black frost *n* hard frost without rime or snow.

black-fyse *adj* of swarthy complexion.

blackgang *adj* blackguardly.

blackguard *n* black-rappee (qv) snuff, 'Irish blackguard'.

blackhead *n* the laughing gull.

black-headed tomtit *n* the great tit.

black hole *n* **1** prison. **2** a police cell.

black hudie *n* **1** the black-headed bunting. **2** the core-head or reed bunting.

blackie *n* a blackbird.

blackie *n* **1** a bee. **2** a kind of wild bee.

blackit *adj* looking as if stained with blacking.

blackjack *n* a dark-coloured sweetmeat made of sugar or treacle and spice.

black-keel *n* plumbago.

blackleg¹ *n* a workman who works for a master whose men are on strike.

blackleg² *n* a disease of cattle.

blackleg³ *same as* **blackfit**.

blacklie *adj* **1** ill-coloured. **2** dirty. **3** badly washed. **4** dark with threatening clouds.

blackman *n* **1** a nursery bogy. **2** liquorice.

black martin *n* the swift.

blackmill *n* a water mill with one wheel.

black money *n* forged copper coinage.

blackneb *n* **1** a person disaffected toward government. **2** a carrion crow. **3** a 'blackleg' workman.

black-nebbit *adj* **1** having a black bill. **2** disaffected toward government.

blacknebbit crow *n* the carrion crow.

black oil *n* oil made from the haddock and other fish.

black o' the e'e *n phr* the apple of the eye.

black ox *n* **1** a misfortune. **2** a bereavement. **3** a great calamity.

black ox-eye *n* the cole titmouse.

black Peter *n* **1** a portmanteau. **2** a lamp in which the pith of rushes served as the wick.

black pishminnie *n* a black ant.

black quarter *n* a disease of cattle.

black rappee *n* a kind of snuff.

blacks *n* **1** black clothes. **2** mourning garments.

black saxpence *n* the devil's sixpence, supposed to be received as pledge of engagement to be his, soul and body, and reputed, if kept constantly in the pocket, to have always another sixpence along with it, however much is spent.

black-sole *n* a lovers' go-between.

black spats *n* irons on the legs.

black-spaul, ~-spauld *n* pleurisy in cattle, especially calves.

black starling *n* the starling.

black stool *n* the stool of repentance for offenders doing public penance.

black-strap *n* **1** weak treacle beer. **2** a contemptuous name for porter.

black swift *n* the swift.

black-tang *n* the ore-weed, seaweed.

black-toed gull *n* Richardson's skua.

black victual *n* peas and beans.

black-wamed *adj* having a black belly.

black ward *n* servitude to a servant.

black weather *n* rainy weather.

black wet *n* rain as distinguished from snow.

black wine *n* dark-coloured, in contrast to white wine.

black winter *n* the last cartload of grain brought from the harvest field.

black wood *n* ebony.

blad¹ *v* to take long steps, treading heavily.—*n* **1** a long and heavy step in walking. **2** a person walking with long and heavy step.

blad² *n* **1** a large portion of anything. **2** a leaf. **3** a specimen. **4** a fragment. **5** a portfolio. **6** a blotting pad.

blad³ *n* a person of weak, soft constitution, from rapid overgrowth.

blad⁴ *n* **1** a slap, blow. **2** a squall. **3** a heavy fall of rain. **4** a dirty spot. **5** a discoloration.—*v* **1** to slap, strike, thrust violently. **2** (*used of wind and rain*) to beat against, to drive in gusts. **3** to spoil. **4** to injure. **5** to soil. **6** to abuse, defame.

bladderdash *n* nonsense.

bladderskate *same as* **blatherskite**.

bladdin *adj* breezy, gusty.—*n* a spoiling, destruction.

bladdo, bladdoch *same as* **bleddoch**.

bladdy *adj* **1** gusty. **2** unsettled.

blade *same as* **blad⁴**.

blade *n* a cabbage or kail (qv) leaf.—*v* to take the outer leaves off cabbages.

blad haet *n* absolutely nothing.

bladie *adj* full of large, broad leaves growing from the stem.

bladrock *n* a talkative, silly fellow.

bladry *same as* **blaidry**.

blads and dawds *n phr* large leaves of greens boiled whole in broth.

blae¹ *adj* **1** bluish. **2** livid. **3** lead-coloured. **4** disappointed. **5** blank as with disappointment. **6** bleak, cold.—*v* to numb.

blae² *v* **1** to bleat as a lamb. **2** to cry as a child.—*n* a loud bleat.

blae³ *n* **1** a hard blue clay. **2** (*in pl*) laminae of this clay.

blae⁴ *n* (*in pl*) the rough parts of wood left in consequence of boring or sawing.

blaeberry *n* the bilberry.

blae-bows *n* the flower of the flax.

blaeflummery *n* nonsense, vain imaginations.

blaelike *adj* livid, pale.

blaeness *n* lividness.

blaese *n* the bilberry.

blaewort *n* **1** the blue cornflower. **2** the round-leaved bellflower.

blaff *n* a blow.—*v* to bang or hit.

blaffart *n* a blow.

blaffen *n* loose flakes or laminae of a stone.

blaflum *n* **1** nonsense, idle talk, a hoax. **2** a pompous, empty-headed person. **3** a gewgaw.—*v* to coax, cajole, deceive, play upon.

blaick¹ *n* a scoundrel.

blaick², blaik *v* to puzzle, mystify, baffle.—*n* a puzzle.

blaidry *n* **1** nonsense, foolish talk, blethers. **2** phlegm coughed up. **3** empty parade. **4** unmerited applause.

blaids *n* a disease acompanied by pustular eruptions.

blaiker *n* **1** a challenge to a feat of daring. **2** a puzzle.

blain¹ *n* **1** a fault. **2** a blemish. **3** a scar. **3** discoloration of skin after a sore.

blain² *n* **1** a bare place in a field where grain has not sprung. **2** a blank, a vacancy.—*v* **1** (*used of a field*) to be covered with blank spaces. **2** (*of grain*) to have no kernel.

blainag *n* a small pustule, a pimple.

blainch *v* to cleanse.

blaink *same as* **blink¹**.

blains *n* empty grain.

blainy *adj* **1** full of blains (qv). **2** (*used of a potato patch*) in which frequent gaps occur. **3** (*of seeds*) that have not germinated.

blair¹ *v* to dry by exposure to drought.—*n* that part of flax which is used in manufacture, after being steeped and laid out to dry.

blair² *same as* **blare**.

blair³ *same as* **blear**.

blairin *n* the ground on which flax is dried or where peats are spread to dry.

blairney *n* blarney, silly talk.

blais'd *same as* **blased**.

blaise *n* the particles of wood scooped out by a wimble in boring.

blaister *v* to blow with violence.

blait¹ *adj* naked, bare.

blait² *same as* **blate**.

blaith *adj* blithe, glad.

blaitie-bum *n* **1** a lazy fellow,. **2** a simpleton. **2** a sheepish fellow.

blaitly *adv* bashfully.

blait-mouit *adj* **1** bashful, sheepish. **2** shy in speaking.

blaize *n* a blow.

blakwak *n* the bittern.

blamefull *adj* blameworthy.

blan *v* ceased, caused to cease.

blanch *n* a flash or sudden blaze.

blanded-bear *same as* **blendit-bear**.

blander *v* **1** to scatter sparingly. **2** to sow thinly. **3** to babble, spread a report or calumny. **4** to exaggerate or misstate.

bland-hoe *same as* **blind-hoe**.

blandish *n* the grain left uncut by careless reapers in the furrows during a kemp (qv) or struggle to be first done.

blandish *n* flattery.

blandrin *n* a scanty diffusion, a withholding of sufficient seed.

blane *same as* **blain¹**.

blanket *n* a form of the game hie-spy.

blanket-bay *n* bed.

blanket-heezie *n* one who tosses another in a blanket.

blardit *adj* **1** short-winded. **2** broken-winded.

blare *v* **1** to bleat. **2** to cry out.—*n* **1** the bleat of a sheep or goat. **2** a cry. **3** noisy scolding.

blarn *v* to employ blarney or flattery.

blart *v* to fall flat in the mud.—*n* the sound of such a fall.

blased *adj* (*used of milk*) turned sour.

blash *n* **1** a splash or dash of liquid, mud, etc. **2** a heavy shower of rain. **3** too much water for the purpose of diluting. **4** a deluge.—*v* **1** to drench, soak, deluge. **2** to splash liquid or mud about by spilling it or treading in it. **3** to rain heavily and noisily. **4** to drink to excess.

blashy *adj* **1** rainy, wet, gusty. **2** weak, watery.

blasnit *adj* hairless.

blast *n* **1** a whiff of the pipe. **2** a sudden illness. **3** a chill. **4** a stroke. **5** a brag, boast.—*v* **1** to pant. **2** to smoke tobacco. **3** to play the bagpipes. **4** to brag. **5** to use big words or strong language. **6** to have a stroke of paralysis.

blaster *n* **1** a boaster. **2** one who exaggerates. **3** one who blasts stones.

blastie¹ *n* **1** a shrivelled dwarfish person. **2** an ill-tempered or unmanageable child. **3** a term of contempt.

blastie² *adj* **1** gusty, blustering. **2** puffing, panting.

blasting *n* **1** the cow quake (qv) or inflated stomach of cows. **2** the cold easterly wind that causes the disease.

blastit *adj* paralysed, having a shock of paralysis.

blatant *adj* bellowing like a calf.

blate *adj* **1** shy. **2** bashful. **3** timid. **4** sheepish. **5** simple. **6** dull, unpromising. **7** (*of crops*) backward.

blately *adj* (*of rain*) soft, gentle.—*adv* bashfully.

blateness *n* shyness.

blather *same as* **blether**.

blatherskite *n* **1** a babbler. **2** a foolish talker. **3** nonsense.

blatherumskite *n* a blatherskite (qv).

blathrie *adj* nonsensical, foolish.

blatter¹ *v* **1** to rattle. **2** to make a rattling sound. **3** to beat on with force and noise like hail. **4** to dash noisily. **5** to make a disturbance. **6** to talk loudly and noisily.—*n* **1** a rattling sound. **2** a hailstorm. **3** a noisy dash or blast. **4** loud, forcible, noisy talk.

blatter² *v* (*of breath or life*) to flutter, flicker.

blaud¹ *same as* **blad⁴**.

blaud² *n* **1** a large piece or fragment. **2** a large leaf of cabbage or kail (qv). **3** a portfolio.

blaudie *same as* **bladie.**

blaugh *adj* bluish or sickly in colour.

blauve *v* to blow.

blauven *v, adj* blown.
blaver *same as* **blawort**.
blaw[1] *n* a blow, a stroke.
blaw[2] *v* **1** to blow. **2** to breathe. **3** to publish. **4** to brag. **5** to exaggerate from ostentation. **6** to whisper in the ear, flatter, coax, wheedle. **7** to puff-up. **8** to huff in the game of draughts. **9** to scold. **10** to pull at a drinking vessel. **11** to smoke a pipe. **12** to play the bagpipe, etc.—*n* **1** a blast, gust. **2** the direction of the wind. **3** a tune on any wind instrument. **4** a boast. **5** a lie from ostentation. **6** a smoke. **7** a whiff of a pipe. **8** a pull at a drinking vessel. **9** a jorum of liquor.
blaw[3] *n* a blossom, a bloom.—*v* to blossom, to flower.
blawart *same as* **blawort**.
blawerts *n* a blacksmith's bellows.
blawflum *same as* **blaflum**.
blaw-i'-my-lug *n phr* **1** flattery. **2** a flatterer.
blawing-girss *n* the blue mountain grass.
blawn-cod *n* a split cod, half-dried.
blawn-drink *n* the remainder of drink in a glass of which one or more have partaken and which has frequently been breathed on.
blawn-win' *n* broken wind in a horse.
blawort, blawirt *n* **1** the harebell. **2** the corn bluebottle.
blaw-out *n* **1** a good meal. **2** a drinking bout. **3** a great display or feast.
blawp *v* to belch, heave up water.—*n* watery matter gathered under the skin.
blawstick *n* a tube used as a bellows.
blawthir *n* wet weather.
blawthrie *adj* very wet.
blay *same as* **blae**[4]
blaze[1] *same as* **bleeze**[4].
blaze[2] *n* **1** alum ore. **2** a substance lying above coal.
blaze[3] *n* **1** the torch used in salmon spearing. **2** a sudden blast of dry wind.
blazed *same as* **bleezed**.
blazin' chield *n* a braggart.
blazing-fou' *adj* uproariously drunk.
blaznicks *n* large and showy ornaments.
bleach *v* **1** to strike. **2** to fall flat.—*n* **1** a blow. **2** a fall.—*adv* **1** violently. **2** with a heavy blow.
bleacher *n* a severe blow.
bleaching *n* **1** a beating. **2** a beating about.
bleak-bleak *n* the cry of the hare.
blear *n* **1** anything dimming the sight. **2** (*in pl*) tears or their traces.—*v* **1** to dim the vision. **2** to deceive by flattery.
bleared *adj* **1** (*of milk, etc*) thin and bluish in colour. **2** skimmed.
blearie *adj* **1** dim of sight. **2** watery-eyed.
bleart *same as* **blearie**.
blease *v* to bleach.
bleat *same as* **blate**.
bleater *n* the cocksnipe.
bleather *same as* **blether**[1].
bleatly *adv* timidly.
bleb *n* **1** a bubble. **2** a small blister or pustule. **3** a drop. **4** (*in pl*) a children's skin eruption.—*v* **1** to spot. **2** to slobber. **3** to sip. **4** to tipple.
blebber *same as* **blabber**.
blebbit *adj* **1** blurred. **2** besmeared.
bleck[1] *n* **1** a challenge to a feat. **2** a baffle at any feat. **3** a nonplus in an argument or examination. **4** as a school term, thus: 'if A be below B in the class and during B's absence gets farther up in the class than B, B is said to have a "bleck" upon A and takes place of him when he gets next to him'.—*v* **1** to baffle. **2** to surpass. **3** to nonplus or overcome in an argument. **4** to puzzle.
bleck[2] *adj* black.—*n* **1** blacking. **2** smut. **3** a black person.—*v* **1** to blacken. **2** to apply blacking. **3** to defame.
bledd *n* **1** a blade. **2** a leaf.
bledder[1] *n* a bladder.
bledder[2] *same as* **blether**[1].

bledderin *n* boastful talking.
bleddin' *adj* (*used of snowflakes*) falling.
bleddoch *n* buttermilk.
blee *n* complexion.
bleech[1] *same as* **bleach**.
bleech[2] *v* **1** to blanch. **2** to bleach.
bleed *n* blood.—*v* **1** to shed blood. **2** (*used of corn*) to yield well when threshed.
bleeder *n* corn yielding well when threshed.
bleed-raing *v* to become bloodshot.
bleedy *adj* bloody.
bleem *n* **1** the potato plant. **2** its stalk.
bleer *v* **1** to blear. **2** to make the eyes water. **3** to bedim the eyes with rheum or tears.—*n* **1** what dims the sight. **2** a trace of weeping.
bleerit *adj* dim-sighted.
bleery[1] *adj* **1** dim-sighted. **2** watery-eyed.
bleery[2] *adj* (*used of liquor*) weak, thin.—*n* **1** thin, poor gruel, soup, etc. **2** boiled oatmeal and buttermilk, with the addition of a piece of butter.
bleese *same as* **bleeze**[4].
bleet *v* to bellow.
bleetly *same as* **blately**.
bleevit *n* a blow.
bleeze[1] *n* the rough parts of wood left after boring or sawing.
bleeze[2] *n* a smart blow with the fist.—*v in phr* **to let breeze at one** to strike one.
bleeze[3] *v* to turn slightly sour.
bleeze[4], **bleese** *v* **1** to blaze. **2** to flare up. **3** to get angry. **4** to spread news or scandal. **5** to defame. **6** to boast. **7** to bluster.—*n* **1** a rage, passion. **2** a rapid growth. **3** a fire of furze, straw, etc. **4** a sudden blast of dry wind.
bleezed *adj* **1** muddled. **2** at the state of intoxication when the face reddens or is flushed. **3** ruffled. **4** fretted.
bleeze money *n* a gratuity formerly given by scholars to their master at Candlemas when the one who gave most was proclaimed king or queen and had to entertain the whole school.
bleezie *n* a small blaze.
bleffart *n* **1** a squall, storm, hurricane. **2** a sudden and violent snowstorm. **3** the blow of a calamity. **4** a stroke.—*v* to bluster as the wind.
bleflum *same as* **blaflum**.
bleflummery *n* vain imaginations.
bleib *same as* **bleb**.
bleid *n* blood.
bleir *v* to asperse, cast aspersions, calumniate.
bleirie *n* a lie, a fabrication.
bleirie *same as* **bleery**[2].
bleis *n* the river-fish bleak, *Leuciscus alburnus*.
bleize *same as* **bleeze**[4].
blellum *n* an idle, talking fellow.
blench[1] *v* to blanch, turn pale.
blench[2] *v* (*used of milk*) to turn sour.
blenched *adj* (*used of milk*) a little sour.
blench-lippit *adj* having a white mouth.
blendit-bear *n* bear mixed with barley.
blenk *same as* **blink**[2].
blenshaw *n* a drink composed of meal, milk, water, etc.
blent *v* **1** (*used of the sun*) to shine after the sky has been overcast. **2** (*of fire*) to flash.
blenter *n* **1** a boisterous, intermittent wind. **2** a gust. **3** a flat stroke, a strong, sharp blow.—*v* **1** to rush, make haste. **2** to strike with a strong, sharp blow.
blentering *same as* **blinterin'**.
blephum *same as* **blaflum**.
blet *n* a large fragment.
blether[1] *v* **1** to speak indistinctly. **2** to stammer. **3** to talk nonsense. **4** to prattle, chatter.—*n* **1** nonsense, foolish talk. **2** a windbag, a talkative person, a foolish talker.
blether[2] *same as* **bledder**[1].
bletheration *n* foolish talk.
bletherbag *n* a fluent, foolish talker.

bletherer *n* a foolish talker.
blether-headed *adj* **1** foolish. **2** noisy.
bletherie *n* **1** foolishness. **2** deception.
bletherin *n* **1** loud, foolish talking. **2** stammering.
blett *v* bleated.
bleuchan *n* a small salt-water fish of some kind.
blevit *n* a blow.
blewder *n* a hurricane.
blewdery *adj* tempestuous.
blewart *same as* **blawort**.
blew-spot *n* a blue spot on the body, regarded as a witch mark (qv).
blib *n* (*used of tea, etc*) a weak, watery portion.
blibbans *n* **1** strips of soft, slimy matter. **2** seaweed on rocks at ebb tide. **3** large shreds of greens or cabbage put into broth.
blibe *n* **1** a stroke. **2** the mark of a blow.
blicham *n* a contemptuous designation of a person.
blichan, blichen *n* **1** a small person. **2** a lean, worn-out animal. **3** a lively, showy youth. **4** a harum-scarum fellow. **5** a worthless person. **6** a term of contempt.
blicher *n* a spare portion.
blicht *v* to blight.—*n* a blight.
blichtnin *v, adj* blighting.
blicker *n* a boaster, a braggart.
blide *adj* blithe, glad.
bliers *n* the eyelashes.
bliffart, bliffert *same as* **bleffart**.
blighan *same as* **blichan**.
blighten *v* to blight.
blin[1], **blind** *v* **1** to cease, desist. **2** to stop, cause to stop.— *n* **1** delay, hindrance. **2** a rest, a pause. **3** deceit.
blin[2] *adj* blind.—*v* **1** to blind. **2** to close the eyes in sleep.— *n* a little sleep.
blind-barnie *n* blindman's buff.
blind-bell *n* a game in which all the players were blindfolded except one, who bore a bell that he rang while endeavouring to escape being caught by the others.
blind-bitch *n* a bag formerly used by millers.
blind-brose *n* brose (qv) without butter.
blind-champ *n* a cruel pastime of boys, who, when blindfolded, turn round and try to crush eggs from a harried bird's nest laid on the ground.
blind coal *n* a kind of coal that gives no flame.
blind dorbie *n* the purple sandpiper.
blind-, blin'-drift *n* **1** heavily driving snow. **2** a blinding, drifting snow.
blind-, blin'-drunk *adj* unable to see properly from drink.
blind-fair *adj* like an albino.
blindfish *n* the lesser spotted dogfish.
blind-, blin'-fou *adj* unable to see properly from drink.
blind harry *n* blindman's buff.
blind-hoe *n* the rabbitfish.
blind-hoy *v* (*used of boys*) to exchange articles, such as knives, by blin'-hooie (qv).
blindlins *adv* **1** blindly. **2** blindfolded.
blind lump *n* a boil that does not come to a head.
blindman's-ball, ~-bellows, ~-e'en *n* the common puffball or devil's snuffbox.
blind-palmie, ~-pawmie *n* blindman's buff.
blinds *n* the pogge or miller's thumb.
blind-staff, ~-stem *n* the boys' game of blind-champ (qv).
blindstam *n* **1** a method of sewing a patch on a boot upper. **2** used figuratively for blind, captious or arbitrary criticism.
blind tam *n* a bundle of rags made up as a child, carried by beggars.
blind window *n* an imitation window in a wall.
blin' hooie *n* an exchange of two articles by boys, each of whom holds his own concealed in the closed hand until the exchange is made.
blink[1] *n* **1** a gleam, a ray. **2** the least glimmer. **3** a glance, a glimpse, a wink. **4** a moment. **5** sunshine between two showers. **6** a jilting, 'the slip'.

blink[2] *v* **1** to shine, gleam. **2** to twinkle, glimmer, flicker. **3** to take a hasty glance. **4** to wink, cause to wink. **5** to look with pleasure or fondness. **6** to ignore, evade. **7** to jilt, deceive. **8** to bewitch, 'overlook', exercise an evil influence. **9** to turn anything sour. **10** to spoil.
blinker *n* **1** a smart, attractive girl. **2** used also contemptuously. **3** a star. **4** a poser. **5** a conclusive argument or blow. **6** the eye. **7** a blear-eyed person. **8** a person blind of one eye. **9** a near-sighted person. **10** (*in pl*) eyelids.
blinkit *adj* **1** bewitched. **2** soured, spoiled. **3** half-drunk.
blinkit milk *n* sour milk.
blinlins *same as* **blindlins**.
blinner *v* to move the eyelids like one with weak sight.
blint *v* to shed a feeble or glimmering light.
blinter[1] *v* **1** to shine with a feeble, unsteady light. **2** to flicker. **3** to blink. **4** to look at with weak eyes. **5** to see obscurely.—*n* **1** a feeble light. **2** a person with weak eyes.
blinter[2] *same as* **blenter**.
blinteran[1] *n* a beating.
blinteran[2] *n* the act of looking with the eyelids nearly closed.
blinterer *n* a person with weak eyes.
blinterin' *adj* **1** having weak eyes. **2** near-sighted. **3** blundering.
blipe *n* a stroke, a blow.
blipe *n* a shred of skin when it peels off.
blirt *v* **1** to burst into tears, to weep. **2** to rain or snow.—*n* **1** a burst of weeping. **2** a storm of wind and rain. **3** a cold drift of snow.—*adj* **1** bleared. **2** pale with fear. **3** on the verge of tears.
blirted *adj* tear-stained, swollen with weeping.
blirtie, blirty *adj* **1** (*of weather*) changeable, squally. **2** cheerless.
blirtin'-fu', ~-fow *adj* maudlin in drink.
blirty-eild *n* extreme old age, in which tears trickle as if one were weeping.
bliry *n* the exterior of a mare's uterus.
blissing *n* increase of property.
blithe *adj* cheerful, merry, glad.—*adv* cheerfully, merrily.
blithely *adv* **1** cheerfully. **2** gladly.
blithemeat *n* food, bread and cheese, partaken of by visitors at the birth of a child.
blithen *v* to gladden.
blitheness *n* gladness, gaiety, cheerfulness.
blithesome *adj* merry, cheerful, happy, jolly.
blitter *same as* **bleater**.
blitter-blatter *n* a rattling, irregular noise.
blizzen *v* to parch, dry up and wither.
blob *n* **1** a bubble. **2** a blister. **3** a drop or splash of liquid. **4** a small patch of colour. **5** a blur. **6** the honey bag of a bee. **7** a large gooseberry.—*v* **1** to gather in drops. **2** to weep. **3** to bubble. **4** to blister. **5** to rob a bee of its honey bag. **6** to plunder. **7** to blot. **8** to blur.
blobb *n* a gooseberry.
blobby *adj* **1** containing or causing bubbles. **2** very rainy.
blocher *v* to make a rough noise in coughing from phlegm.
block *v* **1** to bargain. **2** to exchange. **3** to plan, to devise.— *n* **1** a scheme. **2** a bargain. **3** an exchange. **4** an agreement. **5** a honorarium.
blockan *n* the young coalfish.
block, hammer and nails *n phr* a boys' rough game of bumping.
blockie *n* a small cod.
blockin' ale *n* drink taken at the conclusion of a bargain.
bloichum *n* a person troubled by a cough.
bloik *n* mischief.
bloisent *adj* **1** bloated. **2** (*used of the face*) red, swollen, whether by weather or intemperance.
bloit *n* diarrhoea.
blood *v* **1** to bleed. **2** to let blood.—*n* **1** bloodshed. **2** effusion of blood.
blood-friend *n* a blood relation.
blood-grass *n* a disease of cattle, bloody urine.
blood-run *same as* **bluid-run**.

blood tongue *n* the goosegrass.
blood wit, ~-wite *same as* **bluid-wyte**
bloody bells, ~ fingers *n* the foxglove.
bloody jaudie *n* a bloody pudding (qv).
bloody pudding *n* a black pudding of blood, suet, onions and pepper in part of a sheep or ox gut.
bloody scones *n* scones made with the blood which formerly was drawn from farm cattle.
bloom *n* the efflorescent crystallization on the outside of thoroughly dried fishes.
bloomer *n* a schoolgirl's headdress or bonnet.
bloom-fell *n* yellow clover, the bird's trefoil.
bloomy *adj* **1** blooming. **2** having many blooms.
blort *v* (*used of a horse*) to snort.
bloss *n* a term of endearment applied to a buxom young woman.
blost *v* **1** to blow up. **2** to pant. **3** to boast. **4** to bluster.—*n* **1** an explosion. **2** a whiff of a pipe. **3** a brag, a boast. **4** a boasting narration, an ostentation person.
blot *v* to nonplus, to puzzle.
blots *n* **1** water for washing clothes. **2** soapsuds, dirty water.
blot sheet *n* blotting paper.
blotty o *n* a schoolboy's slate game.
bloust *same as* **blost**.
blout *n* **1** the bursting of a storm. **2** a sudden fall of rain, snow or hail, with wind. **3** a sudden and noisy eruption of liquid matter. **4** foul water thrown from washing tubs.—*v* (*used of liquids*) to belch or rush out with force.
blouter *same as* **blewder**.
bloutering *v, adj* boasting, bragging.
blow *same as* **blaw**².
blower *n* a boaster, exaggerator.
blowing *n* **1** flattery. **2** boasting.
blown *adj* (*used of fish*) dried by wind without salt.
blown-cod *n* a split cod half-dried.
blown fish *n* fish wind-dried without salt.
blown-skate *n* skate dried without salt by pressure and exposure to the wind.
blow-out *n* **1** a great display. **2** a festive occasion. **3** a drinking bout.
blowt *v* to belch forth.—*n* **1** an outburst of liquid. **2** *in phr* **windy blowts** flatus.
blowthir *v* **1** (*used of a large body*) to plunge with great force. **2** to blunder.—*n* **1** the plunge of a heavy body. **2** a blow. **3** a big, stupid person. **4** a sudden gust of wind. **5** exposure to a storm.
blowthirin *n* the act of plunging.—*adj* **1** blundering, stupid. **2** gusty, stormy.
blow-up *v* **1** to mislead, delude. **2** (*used of a cow*) to swell with flatus.
blowy *adj* gusty, blustering, windy.
blub *v* to cry, weep.
blubbert, blubbit *adj* tear-stained, disfigured by weeping.
bluchan *same of* **bleuchan**.
bluchtan, bluchton *n* a piece of the hollow stem of the mugwort, used as a popgun.
bludder¹ *v* to make a noise in the mouth or throat in swallowing any liquid.
bludder² *v* **1** to blot or disfigure any writing. **2** to disfigure the face in any way. **3** to besmear with blood, mud, tears. **4** to disfigure in a moral sense. **5** to exhibit in an unfair point of view.—*n* **1** mud. **2** any dirty or disgusting liquid or semiliquid substance. **3** wet weather. **4** a spell of foul weather.
blude *same as* **blood**.
bludker cake *n* a cake mixed with hog's blood, eaten on Easter Sunday, called also redemption or ransom cake.
blue¹ *n* whisky.
blue² *adj* (*used of the weather*) chill, frosty.—*adv* used as an intensive.
blue³ *n* **1** quality, condition. **2** a bad state of matters.
blue-bannet *n* the blue titmouse.

blue-bell *n* the harebell.
blue blanket *n* the banner of the Edinburgh craftsmen.
blue-blaver *n* the bellflower or wild blue campanula.
blue-bonnet¹ *n* **1** the devil's bit, the flower of *Scabiosa succisa*. **2** the mountain centaury. **3** the blue-cap or titmouse.
blue-bonnet² *n* **1** a man's blue cap. **2** a Scotsman.
blue bore *n* a rift or opening in the clouds.
blue-cap *n* the blue titmouse.
blue-day *n* **1** a day which is bleak and frosty. **2** a day of uproar or disturbance.
blue-fly *n* **1** a bluebottle. **2** a flesh-fly.
blue-gled *n* the hen harrier.
blue-gown *n* a king's pensioner, who wore a blue gown with a badge on it and was licensed to beg.
blue grass *n* the name given to various sedges, especially the carnation grass.
blue-hap *n* the blue titmouse.
blue-hawk *n* **1** the sparrowhawk. **2** the hen harrier.
blue-jay *n* the jay.
blue-kite *n* the hen harrier.
blue-lit *n* blue dye.
blue-maa *n* the common gull.
blue-merlin *n* the sparrowhawk.
blue mogganer *n* a jocular designation of a native of Peterhead, from the wearing of coarse blue stockings over boots.
blue-mooled *adj* (*used of cheese*) blue-mouldy.
blue nappy *n* whisky.
blue ox-eye *n* the blue titmouse.
blues *n* delirium tremens.
blue seams *n* an emissary of the law.
blue seggin *n* **1** the blue flower-de-luce. **2** the stinking iris.
blue sickness *n* a kind of rot in sheep.
blue sleeves *n* the hen harrier.
blue spald *n* a disease of cattle.
blue sparrow *n* the hedge sparrow.
bluester *n* **1** a blusterer. **2** one who uses bullying speech.
bluestone *n* sulphate of copper.
blue thread *n* whisky.
blue tom *n* the hedge sparrow.
blue yaup *n* the fieldfare.
bluff *n* **1** a credulous person. **2** a trick, cheat.
bluffert *same as* **bleffart**.
bluffet *n* a blow, a buffet.
bluffle-headed *adj* **1** having a large head. **2** stupid-looking.
bluid *same as* **blood**.
bluid-run *adj* bloodshot.
bluid wyte *n* a fine paid for effusion of blood.
bluidy *adj* bloody.
bluidy alley *n* a boy's marble used for pitching and often painted with blue and red lines.
bluidy-fingers *n* the foxglove.
bluifs *n* clumsy shoes or slippers made of selvedges.
bluist *same as* **blost**.
bluit *n* a skate.
bluiter¹ *n* **1** a coarse, clumsy, inconsiderate, blundering fellow. **2** a rumbling noise.—*v* **1** to blurt. **2** to make a rumbling noise. **3** to obliterate. **4** to work clumsily. **5** to spoil work in the doing of it. **6** to overdilute with water. **7** to splutter.
bluiter² *n* **1** mud. **2** any dirty stuff. **3** a dirty, slovenly person.—*v* to besmear with mud etc.
bluiter³ *v* to talk foolishly.—*n* **1** a great talker. **2** a boaster.
bluiterin *adj* clumsy.
blume *v* to blossom.
blumf *n* a dull, stupid fellow.
blunk¹ *n* coarse cotton or linen for printing.
blunk² *n* **1** a small block of wood or stone. **2** a dull, lifeless person.
blunk³ *v* **1** to bungle. **2** to spoil a thing. **3** to mismanage. **4** to injure mischievously.

blunkart *n* **1** a small block of wood or stone. **2** a thickset person. **3** a stupid person.

blunker[1] *n* one who prints cloth.

blunker[2] *n* a bungler.

blunkit *adj* pale.

blunner *same as* **blunther**.

blunnerboar *n* a blundering fool.

blunt *n* a stupid fellow.

blunther *v* **1** to blunder. **2** to move clumsily and noisily. **2** to stumble. **3** to make a noise.—*n* a loud noise, as of stumbling.

bluntie *n* **1** a stupid fellow. **2** a sniveller.

blunyierd *n* **1** an old gun. **2** any old rusty weapon.

blup *n* **1** a misfortune or mistake from lack of foresight. **2** one who makes an awkward appearance.

blupt *adj* suffering misfortune from lack of foresight.

blush *v* to chafe the skin so as to cause a tumour or blister, to blister.—*n* **1** a blister. **2** a boil.

blushin, blushion, blushon *n* **1** a blister or boil on hands or feet. **2** a pustule full of matter.

bluster *v* to disfigure in writing.

blusterous *adj* (*of weather*) boisterous, blustering.

blute[1] *n* a bad or foolish action.

blute[2] *n* a sudden burst of sound.

bluter *same as* **bluiter**[3].

bluther[1] *same as* **bludder**[1].

bluther[2] *same as* **bludder**[2].

bluthrie[1] *adj* wet, stormy.

bluthrie[2] *n* **1** phlegm. **2** frothy, incoherent, flatulent discourse.

bluthrie *n* **1** thin porridge. **2** water gruel.

blutter[1] *same as* **bludder**[1].

blutter[2], **blutter**[3] *same as* **bluiter**[2], **bluiter**[3].

blutter[4] *n* **1** a term of reproach. **2** one who has not the power of retention.

blyave, blyaave *v* **1** to blow, pant. **2** to fire a gun. **3** to boast.

blybe[1] *v* to drink much and often.—*n* **1** a large quantity of liquor. **2** a drunkard.

blybe[2] *same as* **blibe**.

blyber *v* to drink hard.

blyberin *n* hard drinking.

blybin *n* the act of drinking spirits.

blype *same as* **blipe**.

blyte *n* a flying shower.

blyter *same as* **bluiter**[2].

blythe *same as* **blithe**.

bo[1] *n* a louse.

bo[2] *n* a submerged rock.

bo[3] *n* **1** a hobgoblin. **2** a bugbear. **3** an object of terror.

bo[4] *int* an exclamation meant to frighten or surprise.

bo[5] *v* **1** to talk noisily. **2** (*used of cattle*) to low.

boag *v* (*used of a shoemaker*) to go out to work in the house of his customers.

boak *same as* **boke**.

boakie *n* **1** a bogle. **2** a bugbear. **3** a hobgoblin. **4** a scarecrow. **5** an oddly-dressed person. **6** dried nasal mucus.

boal *n* **1** a small square aperture in a wall for light or air. **2** a similar recess in a wall for holding small articles. **3** a small doorless cupboard.

board[1] *n* **1** a table. **2** a tailor's table. **3** a parochial board. **4** parish relief.

board[2] *v* to become intimate with.

board-cloth *n* a tablecloth.

board-end *n* the table end.

board head *n* the head of the table.

boardly *adj same as* **buirdly**.

boardtrees *n* the plank on which a corpse is stretched.

board wages *n* the money paid by a person for his board.

boar's ears *n* the auricula.

boas *same as* **boss**[1].

boast *v* to threaten.—*n* a threat, a scolding.

boat *v* **1** to take boat. **2** to carry in a boat.—*n* **1** a barrel or

tub to hold meal or meat. **2** a pickling tub. **3** a small vessel for serving melted butter. **4** a wooden skimming dish.

boatie *n* **1** a yawl, small boat. **2** a ferryman.

boat's draw *n* the furrow made by a boat's keel when launched or drawn ashore.

boat stick *n* **1** the pole of a boat. **2** the mast of a small sailing boat.

boatswain *n* a sailor's name for the skua and other birds with pointed tails.

bob[1], **bobb** *same as* **bab**[1].

bob[2] *n* a gust, blast.

bob[3] *same as* **bab**[2].

bob[4] *same as* **bab**[4].

bob[5] *same as* **bab**[3].

bob *n* a fishing float.

bobantilter *n* **1** any dangling piece of dress. **2** a pendant. **3** an icicle.

bobber *n* **1** the hook used in fly-fishing, as distinguished from the trailer (qv), a fishing float. **2** a poacher who catches salmon with the illegal bobnet.

bobbin[1] *n* a weaver's quill.

bobbin[2] *n* the seed pod of birch.

bobbinjohn *n* a tin cylinder perforated at one end for sowing by hand turnip seed where it has failed in the drills.

bobbinqua *same as* **babbanqua**.

bobbins *n* **1** the wild arum. **2** the water lily, *Nymphaea alba*. **3** the bunch of edible ligaments attached to the stalk of the badderlocks seaweed.

bobbin wheel *n* **1** a wheel used in filling 'bobbins'. **2** the wheel of time with its revolutions and changes.

bobbit *adj* **1** ornamented with tassels. **2** uneven of surface.

bobble *n* a slovenly fellow.

bobby[1] *n* **1** a grandfather. **2** a policeman.

bobby[2] *n* **1** the robin. **2** the devil.

bobnet *n* an illegal fixed fishing net.

bob-robin *n* the robin.

bobs *n* loose cash.

boch *n* **1** a child's plaything. **2** an untidy or disagreeable woman.

bochars and stars *n* the prickly-headed carex.

bocht[1] *v, adj* bought.

bocht[2] *v in phr* **he bocht aboot him** he offended another so as to lead to retaliation.

bock *same as* **boke**.

bockie *n* a bugbear.

bo-cow *n* **1** a scarecrow. **2** a bugbear.

bod[1] *n* **1** a dwarf. **2** a person of small size. **3** a creature. **4** a person.

bod[2] *n* **1** a personal invitation. **2** a price bidden or asked.

bod[3] *n in phr* **new boa, new shod** afresh, with renewed effort.

bodach[1] *n* **1** an old man. **2** a spectre, hobgoblin. **3** a diminutive person. **4** a person. **5** a name of the devil.

bodach[2] *n* the small-ringed seal.

bodden *v, adj* forced on one.

boddle *n* **1** a copper coin, value one-sixth of an English penny or of two pennies Scots. **2** anything of trifling value.

boddle-pieces *n* small coins.

boddle-, bodle-pin *n* a large pin for fastening clothes together.

boddom *n* **1** bottom. **2** the seat of the human body, buttocks. **3** the sole of a shoe.

boddom-lyer *n* a large trout that keeps to the bottom of a pool.

boddom room *n* a sitting for one person in a church pew.

boddum *same as* **bodom**.

bode[1] *n* a portent.—*v* **1** to foretell, portend. **2** to expect, look for. **3** to desire. **4** to betoken, signify.

bode[2] *n* **1** a bid, a price asked or offered at a sale. **2** an invitation.—*v* **1** to bid at a sale. **2** to offer a price. **3** to offer with insistence. **4** to promise, proffer.

bode[3] *v* abode.

bodeable *adj* marketable.

bodement *n* a foreboding.
boden, bodden *adj* 1 arrayed. 2 prepared. 3 furnished with, equipped with.
bodeword *n* a portent, an ominous prediction regarding a person or family.
bodgel *n* a little man.
bodie, boddie *same as* **body**.
bodily *adv* entirely, completely.
bodin *same as* **boden**.
boding *v, adj* 1 desiring. 2 striving.
bodle *same as* **boddle**.
bodom *n* 1 a tub. 2 a barrel. 3 a ship.
bodsie *n* a nickname for a short, thickset person.
bodword *same as* **bodeword**.
body *n* 1 a person, anyone. 2 an inferior. 3 a puny person. 4 a term of contempt.
body-claes *n* wearing apparel.
body-like *adv* with the whole bodily faculties complete.
bofft *adj* (*of standing grain*) suffering from ravages of birds and from a long and wet harvest.
bog[1] *v* 1 to stick in the mire or bog. 2 to confuse, befog. 3 to dumfound. 4 to entangle oneself inextricably in an argument or dispute. 5 to flow as from a bog. 6 (*used of pus*) to flow or ooze from a festering sore.
bog[2] *n* a bug.
bog[3] *v* to go out working at so much a day.
bogan *same as* **boggan**.
bog-bean *n* the common trefoil.
bog-blitter, ~-blutter, ~-bumper, ~-drum *n* the bittern.
boggan, boggen *n* 1 a boil. 2 a tumour. 3 a large pimple filled with white matter, chiefly appearing between the fingers of children in spring.
boggart *n* a bugbear.
boggie *n* a designation of a displaced priest who married people contrary to canon laws, though not to nature's laws.—*adj* plotting in secret.
boggle *v* 1 to perplex, baffle. 2 to quake as a bog. 3 to take fright, shy.—*n* 1 a fright, fear, scruple. 2 a bogle (qv).
bog-gled *n* 1 the moor-buzzard. 2 the marsh harper.
bogglie *adj* quaking like a bog.
bog hay *n* hay grown on marshy, uncultivated ground.
bog-hyacinth *n* the orchis Adam and Eve.
bogie *n* 1 a bogle, an apparition. 2 a scarecrow. 3 a craze, infatuation. 4 a hobby. 5 a name for the devil.
bogie-keek *n* bo-peep.
bogle[1] *n* 1 an apparition, a ghost. 2 a scarecrow. 3 a game of hide-and-seek.
bogle[2] *n* a supper cake eaten in Shetland on Bogle Day (qv).
bogle[3] *v* 1 to bewitch. 2 to bamboozle. 3 to terrify.
bogle-, bogill-about-the-bush *n phr* 1 the game of hide-and-seek. 2 circumvention.
bogle-about-the-stacks *n phr* the game of hide-and-seek played in a full stackyard.
bogle-bo *n* 1 a hobgoblin. 2 a pettish humour. 3 any object of terror.
bogle-catch-the-fairy *n phr* the game of 'hide-and-seek'.
Bogle Day *n* 29 March.
bogle-rad *adj* afraid of ghosts.
boglesome *adj* 1 shy. 2 skittish.
bogle wark *n* the matter of ghostly action.
boglie *adj* haunted by hobgoblins.
bognut *n* the marsh trefoil.
bog-reed *n* a reed pipe.
bog-sclent *v* to avoid fighting, to abscond on the day of battle.—*n* a coward.
bog-shaivelt *adj* knocked out of shape.
bog-spavin *n* wind gall, a soft swelling on a horse's leg.
bogstalker *n* an idle, lounging, stupid fellow.
boguish *adj* (*of land*) soft, spongy.
bog-war *n* tangles and other seaweeds with balls or bladders on the fronds.
boho[1] *n* a laughing stock
boho[2] *n* a name for the devil.

boich *v* to cough with difficulty.—*n* a short, difficult cough.
boicher *n* one having a short, difficult cough.
boichin *n* a continuance of coughing with difficulty.
boid *n* a blackberry.
boikin *n* the piece of beef called the brisket.
boikin *n* a bodkin.
boil[1] *n* the bole or trunk of a tree.
boil[2] *n* 1 meat for boiling in contrast to meat for roasting. 2 the boiling-point.—*v* 1 to well up. 2 (*with* **out**) to waste in boiling.
boiler *n* a large cast-iron kettle.
boil house *n* an outhouse where food for cattle is steamed or boiled.
boiling *adj* in a towering passion.—*n* 1 enough for boiling at a time. 2 the whole quantity, party, etc.
boilled *adj* profusely decked.
boin *same as* **boyne**.
boir *n* an aperture.
boisert *n* a louse.
boist[1] *same as* **buist**[1].
boist[2] *same as* **boast**.
boistart *adj* boisterous.
boit *n* 1 a cask or tub for pickling beef, etc. 2 a butt.
boke *v* 1 to retch, vomit, belch. 2 to object to.—*n* 1 a belch, vomiting. 2 a drinking to the extent of vomiting.
bokie *same as* **boakie**.
bokie-blindie *n* blindman's buff.
bokin *n* a bodkin.
bold *same as* **bauld**[1].
bolden *v* 1 to take courage, put on a bold face. 2 to swell with pride, wrath, etc.
boldie *n* the chaffinch.
boldin *same as* **bowden**[2].
bole *same as* **boal**.
bole-hole *n* a small opening in the wall of a barn, stable or cowhouse for light and ventilation, etc.
bole-window *n* 1 a small window with one pane of glass. 2 the window of a small recess.
bolgan *same as* **boggan**.
bolgan leaves *n* the nipplewort.
boll-kail *same as* **bow-kail**.
boll[1] *n* 1 an old Scotch dry measure, not exceeding six bushels. 2 six bushels of barley or oats. 3 four bushels of wheat, beans and peas.
boll[2] *n* a flash of lightning.
bolster *n* the part of a mill in which the axletree moves.
bomacie *n* a thunderstorm.
bomariskie *n* 1 a herb, the roots of which taste exactly like liquorice. 2 a restharrow.
bombard *n* a cannon.
bombard-shot *n* cannon shot.
bombass, bombaze *same as* **bumbaze**.
bombell[1] *v* 1 to read in a low, indistinct voice. 2 to weep.
bombell[2] *same as* **bumble**.
bomf *n* a bump, shake.
bomill *n* a cooper's tool.
bommle *same as* **bumble**.
bomulloch *n in phr* **gar ane lauch bomulloch** to make one's mirth turn to sorrow.
bon[1] *adj* 1 gratuitous. 2 begged, borrowed.
bon[2] *n* humour, mood.
bon accord *n* 1 amity, agreement. 2 the city of Aberdeen. 3 that city's motto.
bonage *same as* **bondage**.
bonally, bonaillie *n* 1 farewell. 2 good speed. 3 a farewell feast.
bona magna *n* a kind of plum.
bon-companion *n* a boon companion.
bon-criteon *n* the pear called bon Chrêtien.
bond *v* to mortgage.—*n* a mortgage.—*adj* conjoined in a bond or written obligation.
bondage *n* the services due by a tenant to a proprietor, or by a cottager to a farmer, on whose farm he dwells.

bondage hook *n* a tenant bound to reap for his landlord in harvest.

bondage peats *n* peats that a tenant is bound to supply to his landlord.

bondager *n* a female worker provided by a cottager when he undertakes to work for a farmer.

bone-dry *adj* very dry, as dry as a bone.

bonefire *n* a bonfire.

bone-lazy *n* thoroughly lazy.

boneless *adj* 1 without pith or substance. 2 insipid.

bones-breaking *n* 1 a fight, scrimmage. 2 a bloody quarrel.

bone-shanks *n* death represented as a skeleton with a scythe.

bone-, bon-wark, ~-wrak *n* 1 rheumatic pains. 2 aching of the bones.

bongrace *n* 1 a woman's large linen or cotton bonnet. 2 a large straw bonnet.

bonnack *n* a thick, flat and round cake, a bannock.

bonnage *same as* **bondage**.

bonnar *n* 1 a bond. 2 a mortgagee.

bonnet[1] *n* a man's cap.

bonnet[2] *n* 1 a person who bids for his own goods at a sale. 2 one who is employed by the owner to bid for him.

bonnet-ba' *n* a boys' game played with their caps and a ball.

bonnet-fecht *n* a boys' fight with their caps as weapons.

bonnet-fire *n* a penalty inflicted by boys on one who breaks the rules of the game.

bonnetie[1] *n* the game of bonnet-ba (qv).

bonnetie[2] *n* the little grebe.

bonnet laird *n* 1 a yeoman, one who farms his own land. 2 one who farmed land as tenant, in its natural state and at a nominal rent, for a long lease, sometimes of 99 years.

bonnet lug *n* the ear that is more visible when the cap is worn on one side of the head.

bonnet-man *n* a ploughman.

bonnet piece *n* a gold coin of James V, who is represented on it wearing a bonnet.

bonnilie *adv* beautifully.

bonnivochil *n* the great northern diver.

bonnock *n* 1 a sort of cake. 2 a bannock.

bonny[1] *n* a small quantity of anything.

bonny[2], **bonnie** *adj* 1 beautiful, pretty. 2 handsome, fine, attractive. 3 goodly. 4 (*of a wound*) healthy. 5 also used ironically.—*adv* prettily, finely, well.

bonny die *n* a trinket, a toy.

bonny-fyd *adj* bona-fide.

bonnylike *adj* good to look at, fine to appearance.

bonnyness *n* beauty.

bonny penny *n* a goodly sum of money.

bonny sair *n* a healthy sore.

bonn-wallies, ~-wawlies *n* gewgaws, trinkets.

bonny wee *n* a good while.

bonoch *n* a binding for a cow's hindleg during milking.

bonour *same as* **bonnar**.

bonspeil, bonspiel *n* 1 a contest or match, at curling especially. 2 a match at any game on a large scale.

bonxie *n* the common skua.

boo[1] *n* 1 a manor house. 2 a farmhouse. 3 a village.

boo[2] *same as* **bo**[3].

boo[3] *n* a bull.

boo[4] *v* to bow, to bend.—*n* a bow, etc.

boo[5] *same as* **bo**[5].

booby[1] *n* the lowest in a class of children at school.

booby[2] *adj* shy, bashful.

bood *v* had to, behoved.

bood be *n* a necessary obligation.

boodie[1] *n* dried nasal mucus.

boodie[2] *n* 1 a ghost, hobgoblin. 2 a small and unattractive person, a dwarf.

boodie-bo *n* 1 a bugbear. 2 an object of dread or terror.

boof, booff *v* to strike with the hand, causing a hollow sound.—*n* 1 the sound thus produced. 2 such a stroke.

boofin *n* a clumsy person.

boogers *same as* **bougars**.

boo-hoo *int* an exclamation of derision with outshot lips.—*n* 1 a cry of derision. 2 an outburst of weeping.—*v* 1 to show contempt in cries of derision. 2 to weep noisily.

booin'[1] *n* disorderly shouting 'boo!'.

booin'[2] *n* 1 bowing. 2 cringing.

booit *same as* **bouet**.

book *n* the Bible.—*v* to record the names of a couple for proclamation of banns of marriage.

booking[1] *n* 1 the act of recording names for proclamation of banns. 2 the feast formerly held on that occasion.

booking[2] *n* 1 a peculiar tenure of lands in Paisley. 2 a holding under this tenure.

booking night *n* the night on which parties were booked for proclamation of banns of marriage. *See* **book**.

bookit *v, adj* booked for proclamation of marriage banns. *See* **book**.

book-lare, ~-lear *n* 1 education. 2 knowledge gained from books.

book-lared *adj* 1 educated. 2 learned.

book-leernt *adj* 1 educated. 2 learned.

bool[1] *n* 1 a boy's marble. 2 a large round stone. 3 a bowler's bowl.

bool[2] *n* 1 the curved handle of a bucket, kettle, cup, jug. 2 the bow of a key, scissors, shears. 3 anything curved or circular. 4 a pothook. 5 an iron movable handle for lifting a pot by the ears on and off the fire. 6 (*in pl*) the rims of spectacles.

bool[3] *n* 1 a term of contempt for an old man. 2 a thickset man or boy.

bool[4] *v* 1 to weep in childish fashion. 2 to drawl in singing.

boo-lady *n* a cow.

bool-backit *same as* **bowlie-backit**.

bool-bag *n* a boy's bag for carrying marbles.

booled-oars *n* oars strengthened with wood towards the handles.

booler *n* a large marble for throwing.

bool-fit *n* a crooked, deformed foot.

bool-horned *adj* 1 perverse. 2 headstrong.

boolie *same as* **bowlie**.

boolie-back *n* 1 a bent back. 2 a humpback.

boolie-backit *same as* **bowlie-backit**.

boolyie *n* 1 a loud, threatening noise, like a bull's bellow. 2 perplexity.

boom *v* (*of a flying beetle*) to make a booming sound.

boo-man *n* the cattleman on a large farm.

boon[1] *n* the core and worthless part of a stalk of flax.

boon[2] *n* a band of reapers or turf-cutters.

boon[3] *adv and prep* above.

boon-dinner *n* the dinner given in the harvest field to the reapers.

booner *adj* upper.

boonermoat *adj* uppermost.

boon-hook *n* the harvest work that a tenant was bound to give to his landlord.

boonmost *adj* uppermost.

boor, boore *v* to bore.

boorach *same as* **bourach**[2].

boord[1] *v* to board, to stay with.—*n* a board.

boord[2] *v* to split a stratified stone.

boordly *same as* **buirdly**.

boorichy *n* a small cluster, heap or crowd. *See* **bourach**.

booriek *same as* **bourach**[1].

boortree *same as* **bourtree**.

boos *n* the shoulders of a horse.

boosam *adj* busy, bustling.

boosan *n* moving about, bustling.

booscht *n* a little, talkative person.

boose[1] *n* 1 a cow's stall. 2 a crib.—*v* to enclose in a stall.

boose[2] *n* 1 force, energy. 2 a bounce.—*v* 1 to push. 2 to bounce. 3 to bustle about. 4 to be violently active.

boose[3] *n* an exclamation expressing a rushing sound of water, blood, etc.

booshty *same as* **buisty**.

boosin *adj* active, bouncing.

boost[1] *same as* **buist**[2].

boost[2] *v* **1** to shoo off. **2** to guide in a particular direction.

boost[3] *same as* **buist**[1].

boost[4] *same as* **buist**[3].

boosum *adj* **1** pliant. **2** blithe.

boot[1] *n* an instrument of torture for the leg, formerly used in Scotland.

boot[2] *same as* **bout**[5].

boot[3] *v* **1** must. **2** ought.

boot[4] *n* what is given into the bargain or to equalize an exchange.—*v* to divide.

boo't *adj* bent.

boot-catcher *n* a servant who removed a person's boots for cleaning.

boot-dighter *n* the boot-cleaner.

boo-teind *n* a tithe of the produce or value of cows.

booth-meal, ~-mail *n* shop rent.

bootikin *n* **1** a small boot. **2** (*in pl*) the boot (qv) as an instrument of torture for crushing the leg.

booting *n* booty, prize.

bootsna *v neg* matters not.

booty[1] *n* a disease of growing wheat in spring.

booty[2] *n in phr* **play booty** to play the cheat.

bootyer *same as* **byoutour**.

booze *n* **1** intoxicating liquor. **2** a carouse.

boozer *n* a a hard drinker, fuddler, a sot.

boozy[1] *same as* **bouzy**[2].

boozy[2] *adj* **1** tipsy, drunk. **2** fond of drink.

boozy[3] *same as* **bouzy**[1].

bor *n* a hole.

borag *n* **1** a bradawl. **2** a pointed iron heated for boring.

boral, borale *n* **1** a wimble. **2** a borer, an end of which is placed on the breast.

boral-hole *n* a hole made by a wimble.

boraltree *n* the handle of a wimble.

bord *n* **1** a broad hem or welt. **2** a ruffle, frill. **3** (*used of a woman's cap*) the border or the band in front.—*v* to provide an edge or border.

bordel, bordel house *n* a brothel.

bore *n* **1** a crevice, chink, hole. **2** a break in the clouds. **3** a teat. **4** a turning over of a new leaf in conduct. **5** (*in curling*) a passage between two guarding stones. **6** (*in cricket*) the passage of the ball between two fielders.—*v* to sew.

bore-awl *n* a shoemaker's awl.

bore-iron *n* an instrument for boring holes.

borel, borell *same as* **boral**.

boreman *n* a smith who wields the sledgehammer.

bore's-ears *same as* **boar's ears**.

bore-staff *n* part of a loom which deals with the tension of the web.

bore-staff-cord *n* a smooth cord regulating by pulley and lever the tension of the web.

boretree *same as* **bourtree**.

borie *n* a clear opening of the sky in wet weather.

born-days *n* lifetime.

born-deevil *n* a downright blackguard.

borne-doon *adj* depressed in mind, health or outward circumstances.

born-head[1] *n* **1** a young precocious fellow. **2** a very foolish person.

born-head[2] *adv* **1** straightforward, impetuously. **2** headlong.—*adj* furious, impetuous.

born-mad *n* furious.

boroughmonger *n* a rabbit.

borough-, borough's-town *n* a burgh.

borough laird *n* the owner of house property in a burgh.

borra, borrach *same as* **bourach**.

borrach *same as* **bourach**[2].

borral *n* the elder tree.

borrel[1] *adj* rough, rude, clownish.

borrel[2] *same as* **boral**.

borrow[1] *n* a burgh or town.

borrow[2] *n* **1** a pledge, a surety. **2** anything borrowed.—*v* **1** to be surety for. **2** to ransom. **3** to give security to. **4** to urge one to drink, to pledge one in liquor.

borrow-flag *n* the burgh standard with the town's arms.

borrowing days *n* the last three days of March, OS.

borrow land *n* a land (qv) or tenement in a burgh.

borrow mail *n* annual tribute formerly paid to the king by a burgh in return for certain privileges.

borrowstoun *n* **1** a royal burgh. **2** a borough town.

borthel *same as* **bordel**.

bose *same as* **boss**[2].

bosh *v* to talk nonsense.

bosie *n* the bosom.

boskill *n* an opening in the middle of a stack of corn, made by pieces of wood fastened on the top, a boss kiln.

bosky *adj* **1** the worse for drink. **2** wild, unfrequented.

bosness *n* (*of stone*) friableness, tendency to moulder.

bosom faulds *n* a woman's breasts.

boss[1] *n* a frame of wood on a staddle.

boss[2] *n* **1** anything hollow. **2** a despicable, worthless person.—*adj* **1** hollow, empty. **2** hungry. **3** weak. **4** emaciated. **5** ignorant. **6** poor, despicable, worthless. **7** pretentious. **8** applied to a recess or bay window.

boss[3] *n* a small cask.

boss[4] *n* **1** a bunch or tuft of grass. **2** a round projecting mass. **3** the front of the body from chest to loins.

bossie[1] *same as* **bassie**[2].

bossie[2] *n* a metal button used in the game of buttons, got from naval or military uniorms or livery servants' coats.

bossin *n* a ventilating opening in a corn stack.

bossness *n* **1** hollowness. **2** emptiness from lack of food.

bost *same as* **boast**.

Botang *n* Botany Bay.

bote *n* **1** help. **2** advantage. **3** compensation.

botheration *int* used as an expletive.

botherment *n* **1** trouble. **2** perplexity.

bothersome *adj* troublesome.

bothie, bothy *n* a cottage in common for farm servants.

bothie-man *n* a farm servant living in a bothie (qv).

bothier *n* a bothie-man (qv).

bothom *same as* **bodum**.

botion *n* a botch, bungle.

botkin *n* a bodkin.

bottle *n* **1** a bottle of medicine. **2** the contents of a bottle.

bottle *v* to bundle up hay or straw for fodder.

bottle-crony *n* a boon companion.

bottle-nose *n* the 'ca'ing' whale.

bottle-screw *n* corkscrew.

bottling *n* **1** a festivity. **2** a gathering of friends invited to a wedding.

bottom *n* the breech, the backside.

bottomer *n* one who attends to the bottom of a pit shaft.

bottom room *n* **1** a seat for one in a church pew. **2** as much room as a person requires in sitting.

bottom runner *n* the boards between the stern boards of a boat.

bottrel *adj* thickset, dwarfish.—*n* a thickset, dwarfish person.

bou *v* to bow, bend.

bouat *same as* **bowet**.

boubie *same as* **booby**.

bouch *n* a coward, a sneak.— *v* **1** to pilfer in a sneaking way. **2** to plagiarize.

boucht[1] *n* **1** a curvature, bend. **2** the hollow of the elbow or knee. **3** a coil of fishing line, a fishing line of 50 to 55 fathoms. **4** a bay, bight.—*v* **1** to fold down. **2** to enclose in a loop.

boucht[2] *n* **1** a fold for sheep or cattle. **2** a milking pen for ewes. **3** a house for folding sheep at night. **4** a large, square church pew.—*v* **1** to fold or pen cattle, etc. **2** to fence in, enclose for shelter.

boucht curd *n* sheep droppings that fall into the milk pail.

bouchting blanket *n* a small blanket laid across a feather bed, with the ends tucked in on both sides.

bouchting time *n* the time for milking ewes.
boucht-knot *n* **1** a running knot. **2** one made with doubled cord.
boucht-seat *n* **1** a large, square church pew. **2** a pew with a table.
boud *v* had to.
bouden *same as* **bowden**.
bouet *same as* **bowet**.
bouff¹ *same as* **booff**.
bouff² *v* **1** to bark like a large dog. **2** to cough noisily. **3** to burst out laughing.—*n* **1** a loud bark. **2** a noisy cough. **3** a dog. **4** nonsense.
bouff³ *n* a stupid, blundering fellow.
bouffie *n* a dog's short bark.
bouffin¹ *n* continued coughing.—*adj* given to barking.
bouffin² *n* (*used rather contemptuously*) a big, stout person.
boug *n* a child's name for the stomach or belly.
bougars *n* the rafters or cross-spars of the roof of a house on which wattlings were placed.
bougar-stakes *n* the lower part of the rafters, in old houses, resting on the ground.
bougar sticks *n* strong pieces of wood fixed to the rafters by wooden pins.
bouger *n* the puffin.
bought *same as* **boucht**.
boughtie *n* a twig.
bougie *n* a sheepskin bag.
bougies *n* **1** boxes. **2** coffins.
bougil *n* **1** cockcrow. **2** the crow of a cock.
bouguie *n* a posy, nosegay, bouquet.
bouk¹ *n* **1** the whole body. **2** size, quantity, bulk.—*v* **1** to make bulk. **2** to pack in (small) compass.
bouk² *n* a lye made of cow dung and stale urine or soapy water in which foul linen was steeped in order to its being cleansed or whitened.—*v* to steep foul linen in such a lye.
bouk³ *same as* **boke**.
boukie *same as* **bouky**.
bouking *n* the quantity of clothes steeped for washing at a time.
bouking-, boukit-washing *n* the great annual washing of family linen by means of the bouk (qv) or lye of cow dung, etc.
boukit *adj* **1** large, bulky. **2** swollen. **3** corpulent. **4** pregnant.
bouksome *adj* **1** bulky, of large size. **2** pregnant. **3** morally great.
bouky *adj* **1** bulky. **2** obese. **3** well-attended. **4** numerous.
boul¹ *n* a contemptuous expression applied to a person.
boul² *same as* **bool²**.
boulden *same as* **bowden**.
boulder *same as* **bowder**.
boulder stane *n* a paving stone.
boule *n* **1** a gap, break. **2** an opening in the clouds betokening fine weather.
boules *n* marbles.
boul-horned *same as* **bool-horned**.
boullin'-maill *n* a charge for playing bowls on a green.
boult claith *n* a bolting cloth for sifting flour.
bouman *n* a tenant who takes stock from his landlord and shares with him the profit.
boun¹ *v* **1** to make ready, prepare. **2** to dress. **3** to betake oneself to a place. **4** to go.
boun² *adj* **1** ready, prepared. **2** bound for.
bouncer *n* a lively person.
bouncie *n* a slight bounce.
bouncing *adj* **1** lively. **2** vigorous.
bouncy *same as* **bouncing**.
bound¹ *n* **1** a district. **2** a boundary. **3** limit or size of the body.
bound² *adj* sure, certain.
bounder *v* to limit, set boundaries to.
bound out *v* to swell out, to enlarge.

bound-road *n* **1** a fenced road. **2** a boundary road. **3** a frontier.
bount *v* to spring.
bountie-shoes *n* shoes given as part of a servant's wages.
bountith, bounteth *n* **1** something given in reward for service, over and above wages. **2** a bounty, a bonus.
bountree, bountry *same as* **bourtree**.
bountree-berries *n* elderberries.
bountree-gun *n* an elderwood popgun.
bourach¹ *n* **1** a mound. **2** a heap of stones. **3** a small cairn. **4** a confused heap. **5** a cluster, ring or crowd of people and things. **6** a hut of loose stones. **7** a shepherd's hut. **8** a house that children build in play. **9** a knoll. **10** an enclosure.—*v* **1** to enclose, encircle. **2** to crowd together in a mass or ring or confusedly.
bourach² *n* a band put round a cow's hindlegs at milking time.
bourbee *n* the spotted whistlefish.
bourd¹ *v* **1** to jest. **2** to dally.—*n* a jest, joke.
bourd² *n* an encounter, fight.
bourd³ *v* **1** to meddle with. **2** to contend.
bourding *n* jesting.
bourie *n* **1** a rabbit's burrow. **2** a fox's den.
bournie *n* a small bourne.
bouroch, boutock *same as* **bourach¹**.
bourriau, bourrier *n* an executioner.
bourtree *n* the elder tree.
bouse *same as* **booze**.
bouser *same as* **boozer**.
boushty *same as* **buisty**.
boussie *same as* **boussie²**.
boust *same as* **buist³**.
bousteous *same as* **busteous**.
bouster *same as* **bowster**.
bousterous *adj* boisterous.
boustrously *adv* boisterously.
bousum *adj* merry.
bousy¹ *same as* **boozy¹**.
bousy², bousy³ *same as* **bouzy¹**, **bouzy²**.
bousy-like *adj* apparently distended or big.
bout¹ *prep* without.
bout *n* **1** every two turns with the plough. **2** the extent of land mown by a labourer moving straightforward. **3** the amount of thread wound on a clew while held in the same position. **4** the corn and hay cut by a scythe and lying in rows. **5** a swath of grass. **6** an attack of illness.
bout² *v* **1** to bolt, spring, leap. **2** to rise quickly from beneath a surface.—*n* **1** a bolt into or out of a room, etc. **2** the act of coming upon by surprise.
bout³ *n* a roll of cloth, etc, of 28 ells.
bout⁴ *v* to sift flour through a fine sieve or cloth.—*n* a sieve.
boutch *v* to botch, bungle.
bout-claith *n* cloth of a thin texture.
boutefeu *n* **1** an incendiary. **2** one who adds fuel to fire.
boutent *adj* (*used of cattle*) swollen up after eating wet clover.
bout-gang *n* the space gone over or the work done with one sharpening of a scythe in harvesting.
bout-gate *n* **1** a bout-gang (qv). **2** a roundabout way. **3** an underhand means. **4** a deceitful course.
boutger *same as* **byoutour**.
bouting *n* a bout-gang (qv).
bouvrage *n* drink, beverage.
bouzy¹ *adj* **1** bushy, wooded. **2** bushy in appearance. **3** umbrageous.
bouzy² *adj* **1** big, swelling, distended. **2** fat, overgrown. **3** of a jolly and good-humoured appearance.
bow¹ *same as* **boll**.
bow² *n* the boll containing flax seed.
bow *n* **1** the arch of a bridge. **2** the curve of a street. **3** the wooden yoke for attaching oxen to the plough. **4** a fiddler. **5** the semicircular handle of a pail, pot, etc. **6** (*in pl*) sugar tongs.—*v* to curve, bend.

bow³ *n* **1** a field for cows. **2** a cattle fold. **3** a house. **4** the principal farmhouse on an estate.

bow⁴ *n* **1** a fisherman's buoy. **2** the iron which passes through the lead stone from which the hooks hang.—*v* **1** to buoy up. **2** to affix buoys to fishing lines.

bow⁵ *v in phr* **bow an e'e** to close an eye, to sleep.

bowater *n* a night poacher of salmon, who uses a torch or lantern.

bow brig *n* a one-arched bridge.

bowd *n* a breaker, a billow.

bow'd *adj* crooked.

bowden¹ *v* **1** to fill. **2** to burden. **3** to create flatulent distention. **4** (*used of cattle*) to swell from overeating. **5** to swell with wrath or courage.

bowden² *adj* **1** swollen heavy. **2** burdened. **3** provided.

bowder *n* a great squall, blast, a heavy storm of wind and rain.

bowdie-leggit *adj* having bow legs.

bowding *n* swelling.

bowel hive *n* an inflammation of the bowels in children.

bowel-hive grass *n* the field lady's mantle, said to be effective in children's bowel hive (qv).

bowen *n* **1** a broad, shallow dish made of staves, for holding milk, etc. **2** a washing tub.

bower¹ *n* **1** an inner room, a parlour. **2** a boudoir.

bower² *n* a bow-maker.

bower³ *n* the manager of a dairy on a dairy-farm.

bowerique *n* a small bower or parlour.

bower-woman *n* a lady's maid.

bowet *n* **1** a hand lantern. **2** the moon.

bowet-licht *n* lantern light.

bowfarts *n in phr* **in the bowfarts** on the back and unable to rise.

bowff *same as* **bouff²**.

bowff *same as* **booff**.

bowfit-steel *n* a buffet stool.

bowg *n* a child's belly.

bowger *n* the puffin.

bow-han' *n* **1** a fiddler. **2** style of fiddling. **3** a fiddler's right hand.

bow-houghed *adj* **1** bow-legged. **2** bow-thighed.

bow-houghs *n* crooked legs or thighs.

bowie *n* **1** a small barrel or cask open at one end. **2** a tub. **3** a milk pail. **4** a water bucket or pail with a bow handle. **5** a wooden vessel with staves and hoops for holding milk, porridge, brose, broth, etc.

bowiefu' *n* the fill of a bowie (qv).

bowing *n* **1** a holding or lease of a grass farm and its livestock. **2** the management of a dairy on a dairy farm.

bowing chaffs *n* distortion of the face by grimaces.

bowk¹ *same as* **boke**.

bowk² *same as* **bouk¹**.

bow kail, ~ caill *n* cabbage.

bow keg *n* a small keg used as a buoy for fishing lines.

bowl¹ *v* to boil.

bowl² *v* to crook.

bowled-like *adj* **1** crooked-like. **2** with the appearance of being bowed.

bow-leggit *adj* having bandy legs.

bowler *n* a kettle, a boiler.

bowlie *adj* crooked, bent.—*n* a contemptuous name for a bow-legged person.

bowlie-backit *adj* **1** round-shouldered. **2** hump-backed.

bowl-man *n* a male hawker of crockery.

bowlochs *n* **1** the ragweed. **2** the mugwort.

bowltest *adj* the most bent or crooked.

bowl-wife *n* a female hawker of crockery.

bowman *n* a cottager, a ploughman, a cattleman, on a farm.

bown *same as* **boun¹**.

bow-pot *n* a nosegay, bouquet.

bowrach¹ *same as* **bourach¹**.

bowrack², bowrick, bowrock *same as* **bourach²**.

bowrad *n* a fatal encounter.

bow-ribbed *adj* bent in the ribs or spars.

bowrow *n* the row of a boat from one buoy to another when a line breaks and the fisherman seeks to haul it from the other end.

bows *n* **1** a severe punishment. **2** *in phr* **through the bows** said of one who misbehaves and suffers punishment.

bow-sail, -sele *n* a piece of heavy wire or curved iron rod going round a cow's neck and, with the ends clasped together with a piece of iron, attached to a rope or chain and used for binding her to the stall.

bowsan *adj* very big.

bow-saw *n* a flexible, narrow-bladed saw fixed in a bow-shaped frame, for cutting.

bowse¹ *n* a bowsie for frightening children. *See* **bowsie⁴**.

bowse² *v* to rush like the wind.

bowse³ *v* to bouse, pull hard in tacking.

bowset *n in phr* **bowset and down the middle** a country dance.

bowsey *n* nasal excrement.

bowsie¹ *same as* **bouzy¹**.

bowsie² *adj* curved like a bow.—*n* a contemptuous name for a crooked person.

bowsie³ *same as* **bouzy²**.

bowsie⁴ *n* a huge, misshapen, hairy monster, used to frighten children.

bowsprit *n* the nose.

bowster *n* a bolster.

bow-stock *n* a cabbage.

bowt¹ *n* **1** a bolt. **2** a thunderbolt. **3** an iron rod.

bowt² *v* **1** to spring up or away. **2** to bolt.

bowt³ *n* as much worsted as is wound upon a clew while it is held in one position.

bowt⁴ *n* a roll of cloth.

bow't *adj* **1** bowed, bent. **2** crooked.

bowting claith *n* cloth of fine texture.

bowt o' nittin *n phr* a roll of tape.

bow tow *n* a buoy rope.

bow-wow *v* **1** to scare. **2** to frighten by barking. **3** to bully, cheat.—*n* a threat.—*adj* captious, snarling.

bowze *same as* **booze**.

bowzelly¹ *same as* **bouzy¹**.

bowzelly² *v* to frighten children.

box¹ *n* **1** the poor's fund in each parish, as formerly supplied by church collections, fines, etc. **2** the fund of a guild, benefit or friendly society. **3** a precentor's desk.

box² *v* to panel walls with wood, to wainscot, to wall in with wood.

box³ *v* (*of cattle*) to strike, gore or push with the head.

box and dice *n phr* **1** the sum total, everything. **2** the whole collection.

box barrow *n* a wheelbarrow with wooden sides.

box bed *n* **1** a bed with wooden sides and top and two sliding or hinged panels for doors. **2** a folding bed in the form of a chest of drawers.

box drain *n* a drain laid carefully with stones.

boxed *adj* sheltered, walled in.

box-feeding *n* the method of feeding sheep in sheds, etc.

boxie vrack *n* the seaweed *Fucus pixidatus*.

boxing *n* wainscotting.

boxings *n* the coarse offal of grain after the bran is taken off.

box kirn *n* a box churn.

box ladder *n* a ladder-shaped staircase in which each step forms part of a sloping box, as it were.

box-master *n* the treasurer of a town's fund or of any guild, benefit society, etc.

box seat *n* a square pew in church.

boy *n* **1** a male person of any age and condition, if unmarried and residing in the parental home. **2** a smart, clever, capable fellow (*used in derision as well as praise*).

boyd *same as* **boid**.

boyne, boyen *n* **1** a broad, flat dish for holding milk. **2** a tub. **3** a washing tub.

boynfu' *n* the fill of a boyne (qv).

boysteous *same as* **busteous**.

boytach n 1 a bunch, a bundle. 2 a small, dumpy animal.
boytoch adj bad at walking from stoutness.
bra same as **brae**.
bra' same as **braw**.
braad n a sharp pull to hook a fish.—v to give such a pull.
braal n a fragment.
brabblach n refuse.
brace n 1 a chimneypiece. 2 a chimney of straw and clay.
  3 the projection of the wall into a room, in which the
  chimney is placed. 4 a bit of wall in the middle of a Caithness kitchen floor against which the fire was placed.
brace-brod n a chimney board.
bracel same as **brachle**.
brace-piece n a chimneypiece.
brachan same as **brochan**.
brachle v to advance hastily and noisily.
brachton n a term of contempt.
brack[1] v to break.—n 1 a break, breach. 2 breaking waves.
  3 a large number.
brack[2] n 1 a strip of untilled land lying between two plots
  of land. 2 a tract of barren ground in or near a township.
brack[3] n 1 a sudden fall of earth or snow on a slope. 2 a
  flood from a thaw. 3 a sudden and heavy fall of rain.
brack[4] n very salt liquid or half-liquid food.
bracken, brachen n the female fern.
bracken clock n the small, brightly coloured chafer.
bracking adj abounding in brackens.
brackit same as **brockit**.
bracks n a disease of sheep, braxy (qv).
bracksy n (of sheep) suffering from bracks (qv).
brad n an opprobrious epithet applied to an old man.
braddan n a salmon.
brade[1] same as **braid**[1].
brade[2] same as **braid**[2].
brae n 1 a declivity, hillside,. 2 a steep road. 3 a knoll. 4 a
  hill. 5 the bank of a river. 6 the upper part of a country.
brae-face n the front or slope of a hill.
brae-hag, ~-hauld n the overhanging bank of a stream.
brae head n the top of a brae (qv).
braeie adj 1 hilly. 2 sloping.
brae-laird n a landowner on the southern slope of the Gram-
  pians.
brae-man n a dweller on the southern slope of the Gram-
  pians.
braengel same as **brangle**.
braeset adj full of braes. See **brae**.
brae-shot n 1 a quantity of earth fallen from a slope. 2 a
  large sum of money which one unexpectedly inherits.
braeside n a hillside.
brag v 1 to challenge to a feat. 2 to defy. 3 to reproach.—n
  a boast.
braggand, braggie, braggy adj 1 boastful. 2 bombastic.
braggir n 1 a coarse seaweed. 2 the broad leaves of marine
  algae.
bragwort n 1 mead. 2 honey and ale fermented together.
braichum n 1 a horse collar. 2 any untidy or clumsy piece
  of dress, especially anything wrapped round the neck.
braichum up v to wrap up untidily for protection against
  the weather.—n the act of doing so.
braid[1] n the cry of a newborn child.
braid[2] v (used of members of the same stock or family) to
  resemble, to take after.
braid[3] adj 1 broad. 2 having a strong dialect language or
  accent.—adv 1 broadly. 2 without reserve.—n breadth.
braidband n corn spread out unbound on the 'band'.—
  adv (with **fa'**) said of a woman who does not resist improper toying.
braidcast n sowing with the hand.—adj (used of seed) scattered over the whole surface, broadcast.
braid letter n 1 a letter on a broadsheet. 2 a long letter.
braid lining n a peculiar kind of soft woollen cloth.
braidness n breadth.
braidsome adj rather broad.
braidways adv broadside, on one's breadth.

braig v to brag, boast.
braiggle n an old and dangerously rickety article.
braik[1] same as **brake**[1].
braik[2] n 1 an internal mortification. 2 a disease among
  sheep, braxy (qv).—v to belch up wind from the stomach.
braik[3] same as **brake**[4].
braiken n a bracken.
braik-fur same as **break-fur**.
braikit same as **brockit**.
brain n 1 spirit, mettle. 2 a severe injury.—adj furious raging.—v 1 to hurt severely. 2 to stun by an injury to the
  head.
brainbox n the skull.
braindge, brainge v 1 to plunge rashly forward. 2 to dash
  carelessly towards. 3 to bustle about noisily in a fit of
  temper. 4 to use violence, to dash in pieces. 5 to vibrate.
  6 to show excitement.—n 1 a forward dash or plunge. 2
  bustling, angry haste. 3 a fit of temper.
brainding v, adj striving to be first on the harvest field.
brainger n 1 one who rushes forward. 2 a formidable
  foe.
brainin n a severe injury.
brainish adj 1 hot-headed. 2 high-spirited. 3 delirious.
brain-mad adj 1 determined. 2 keenly bent on. 3 hurried
  on with the greatest impetuosity. 4 mad.
brainpan n the skull.
brain-wud adj 1 mad. 2 acting with fury or intense impetuosity.
brainy adj 1 unmanageable. 2 high-mettled, spirited. 3
  lively.
brainyell, brainzel v 1 to rush headlong. 2 to break forth
  violently. 3 to brangle (qv), to storm, rave.—n the act of
  rushing forward or doing anything carelessly or violently.
braird n 1 the first sprouting of young grain, turnips, etc. 2
  a young, growing fellow.—v to germinate, to sprout above
  ground.
brairded-dyke n a fence made of thorn, furze, etc.
brairdie adj abounding with braird (qv).
brairds n 1 the coarsest sort of flax. 2 the short 'tow' drawn
  out straight in carding it. 3 the best part of flax after a
  second heckling.
braisant adj 1 brazened. 2 impudent, bold, hardened,
  shameless.
braise n 1 the roach. 2 a fish of the genus *Pagrus vulgaris*.
braissil v to work hurriedly.—n 1 a rush start. 2 (in pl) fits
  and starts.
braist v to burst.
braithel n a wedding.
braithel-ale n ale drunk at a wedding.
braize same as **broose**.
brak v 1 to break. 2 to become bankrupt. 3 to express great
  sorrow. 4 with **out**, to block out roughly.—n 1 the break-
  ing-up. 2 breach. 3 noise. 4 uproar.—adj broken.
brak-back n the harvest moon as entailing heavy labour.
brake[1] n 1 a toothed instrument for dressing flax or hemp.
  2 a heavy harrow for clodbreaking.—v to treat land with
  such a harrow.
brake[2] n a considerable number.
brake[3] n a bracken.
brake[4] v to puke, to retch.
brakeseugh n a disease of sheep, braxy (qv).
brakin n 1 chastisement. 2 a severe whipping.
brakkins, braks n 1 the remains of a feast. 2 broken meats.
brallion n an unwieldy person or animal.
bramlin, brammel-worn, brammin n a red and yellow
  worm found in old dunghills, used as bait for freshwater
  fish.
bramskin n a tanner's leather apron.
bran[1] same as **brawn**[1].
bran[2] adv quite, entirely.
bran' n a brand.
brancher n 1 a young bird unable to fly. 2 a young crow
  leaving the nest for branches.

brand[1] *n* **1** a glowing cinder. **2** a burning peat. **3** a worthless person.

brand[2] *same as* **brawn**[1].

branded *adj* brindled.

branden *adj* grilled.

brander *n* **1** a gridiron. **2** a trestle, the support of a scaffold. **3** a grating for the mouth of a drain or sewer.—*v* **1** to broil or bake on a brander. **2** to be broiled. **3** to form a foundation in building, as for a ceiling or a scaffold.

brander bannock *n* a bannock (qv) fired on a brander (qv).

brandered *adj* **1** cooked on a brander (qv). **2** (*used of ceilings*) having a framework as well as joists.

brandering *n* **1** scaffolding. **2** framework for panelling. **3** cooking on a brander (qv).

brandie *adj* brindled.—*n* a brindled cow.

brandied *adj* brindled.

brandling worm *same as* **bramlin**.

brandraucht, brandreth *n* a brander (qv).

brandstickle *n* the stickleback.

brandy cellars *n* underground places for storing smuggled brandy.

brandy cleek *n* palsy in the leg from hard drinking.

brandy holes *n* brandy cellars (qv).

brandy wine *n* brandy.

bran'er *n* a brander.

brang *v* brought.

brange *same as* **braindge**.

branglant *adj* brandishing.

brangle *v* **1** to brandish. **2** to vibrate, shake. **3** to entangle, confuse. **4** to throw into doubt. **5** to cast doubt upon.—*n* **1** a tangle. **2** a confused crowd.

branglement *n* **1** confusion. **2** perplexity.

brangler *n* a quarrelsome, wrangling person.

branit *adj* brindled.

brank[1] *v* **1** to bridle or restrain.—a sort of bridle or halter for horses or cows when at grass or tethered. **2** (*in pl*) a bridle for scolds, witches, etc. **3** the mumps.

brank[2] *v* **1** to hold the head erect in a constrained or affected manner. **2** to bridle up. **3** to prance. **4** to trip. **5** to toss the head. **6** to deck, dress up.—*n* **1** a prance. **2** a toss of the head, a caper.

brankie *adj* finely dressed, gaudy, pranked-up.

brankin, branken *adj* **1** lively, gay. **2** showy, ostentatious. **2** prancing.

brankit *adj* vain, puffed-up.

brankless *adj* unrestrained.

brank-new *adj* quite new.

branks *v* **1** to put on the branks. **2** to halter, bridle. *See* **brank**[1].

branlie, branlin *n* the samlet or parr.

brann *same as* **brawn**[2].

brannie *same as* **brandie**.

brannit, bran'it *same as* **branded**.

brannock *n* a young salmon.

branstickle *same as* **brandstickle**.

brash[1] *n* **1** a sudden gust, shower or thunder peal. **2** a short turn at work. **3** a short but severe attack of illness. **4** an effort. **5** an attack.—*v* **1** to assault, bruise. **2** to break bones. **3** to belch acrid liquid into the mouth.

brash[2] *n* broken bits, fragments, pieces.

brash[3] *v* to rush headlong.

brash bread *n* bread made from a mixture of oats and rye.

brashloch *n* **1** rubbish. **2** a mixed crop of oats and rye or of barley and rye.

brashnoch *n* the wild mustard.

brashy *adj* **1** weak. **2** of delicate constitution. **3** subject to frequent ailments.

brashy *adj* **1** noisy. **2** stormy. **3** rugged.

brass *n* **1** money. **2** effrontery.

brassle *same as* **braissil**.

brassy *n* a golf-club shod with brass on the sole.

brassy *n* the fish wrasse.

brast *v* burst.

brastle *n* **1** a push. **2** an encounter. **3** a wrestle.

brat[1] *n* **1** clothing in general. **2** a child's pinafore. **3** a coarse kind of apron. **4** a bib. **5** a rag. **6** scum, floatings of whey. **7** the glazed skin of porridge or flummery.

brat[2] *n* a cloth put on a ewe to prevent copulation. —*v* to cover the hinder part of a ewe.

brat[3] *n* a child (used in contempt or disparagement).

bratch *n* a bitch hound.

bratchel *n* a heap of flax husks set on fire.

bratchet, bratchart *n* **1** a pert, mischievous child. **2** a silly person. **3** a true lover.

bratchie *n* India-rubber.

brath *v* to plait straw ropes on the thatch of a stack or house.

brathins *n* the cross-ropes on the thatch of a stack or house.

bratt *same as* **brat**[1].

brattice, brattish *n* a wooden partition between rooms.

brattie *n* **1** a small apron. **2** a shepherd's plaid.

brattie string *n* an apron string.

bratting *v, adj* covering a ewe with a cloth to prevent copulation.

brattle *n* **1** a loud, clattering noise. **2** the crash of thunder or of a storm. **3** a sudden start. **4** a short race. **5** a noisy fray.—*v* **1** to make a loud rattling or crashing sound. **2** to run quickly, to hurry. **3** (*used of a stream*) to flow tumultuously and noisily. **4** to peal as thunder.

bratty *adj* ragged.

braucht *v* brought.

braughtin *n* green cheese parings or wrought curd, kneaded with butter or suet and broiled in the frying pan.

braul *v* to shake.

braun *same as* **brawn**[2].

brauner *n* a gelt pig.

brauny *same as* **brandie**.

brave *adj* **1** handsome. **2** goodly, fine. **3** used also ironically. **4** considerable, great.—*adv* capitally, in first-rate style.

brave and *adv phr* very, exceedingly.

bravelies *adv* very well, finely, prosperously.

bravely *adv* **1** very well, satisfactorily. **2** prosperously. **3** in good health.

braverie *n* **1** a bravado. **2** show, splendour. **3** fine clothes, showy dress. **4** fine or ornate language.

bravity *n* **1** courage, bravery. **2** fine show, display, finery.

bravoora *n* a mad-like degree of irritation or fury in man and beast.

braw *adj* **1** fine. **2** smartly or brightly dressed. **3** handsome. **4** pleasant, agreeable. **5** worthy, excellent. **6** very good, surpassing in any respect. **7** stout, able-bodied.—*n* **1** (*in pl*) fine clothes. **2** wedding clothes.

braw and *adv phr* very, exceedingly.

brawchton *n* anything weighty or unwieldy.

brawd *n* a large,clumsy article.

brawl *v* to gallop.

brawlies, brawlins *adv* **1** well, finely. **2** in good health, fairly well.

brawlins *n* the trailing strawberry tree or bearberry.

brawly *adv* **1** well, finely. **2** in good health.—*adj* grand, splendid.

brawn[1] *n* the calf of the leg.

brawn[2] *n* a boar pig.

brawn-burdened *adj* having sturdy calves or legs.

brawner *n* a gelt boar.

brawnit *adj* brindled.

brawny *adj* brindled.—*n* **1** a brindled bull, cow or ox. **2** a name given to such an animal.

brawsome *adj* **1** rather braw (qv). **2** comely.

braw-warld *adj* showy, gaudy.

braxiea *n* brown-spotted marbles for playing.

braxy *n* **1** an internal inflammation in sheep. **2** a sheep that has died of braxy or other natural death. **3** the flesh of such sheep. **4** diseased mutton. **5** food of any kind.

bray *v* **1** to press, squeeze. **2** to shove, push.—*n* a squeeze.

bray *same as* **brae**.

brayie *same as* **braeie**.

braze *same as* **braise**.

brazed *adj* **1** brazened. **2** hardened to effrontery.

breach *n* broken water on the seashore.

bread[1] *n* **1** a roll. **2** a loaf. **3** oatcake.

bread[2] *same as* **braid**[3].

breadberry *n* children's pap.

bread kit *n* a kit in which fishermen carry provisions to sea.

breadlings *adv* with the flat side of a sword, etc.

bread-meal *n* a flour of peas and barley.

bread-morning *n* **1** bread that a labourer takes with him when going to work in the morning. **2** a morning snack or piece (qv).

bread spaad *n* an iron spattle for turning bread on the gridiron.

breadth *n* a row of potatoes, etc.

bread-turner *n* a wooden spattle for turning bannocks on the gridiron.

break[1] *n* **1** a piece of ground broken up. **2** a division of land on a farm. **3** a furrow in ploughing. **4** a breach. **5** the breaking wave on the shore. **6** a heavy fall of rain or snow. **7** a large harrow. **8** a hollow in a hill. **9** an instrument for taking the rind off flax. **10** the turning point of a road or hill. **11** failure, bankruptcy.

break[2] *n* a large number, a crowd.

break[3] *v* **1** to prepare land for cultivation or for a particular crop in rotation. **2** to become bankrupt. **3** to cut up, carve. **4** to burgle. **5** to open a full bottle. **6** to begin spending. **7** to change money. **8** to set out or run off briskly. **9** to defeat. **10** to cause a breach of the peace. **11** to begin to use a store of food, etc. **12** to disappoint, deny, refuse. **13** to sell by retail. **14** to break the skin, abrade. **15** to spread manure. **16** to lower prices or wages. **17** (*used of milk*) to curdle. **18** (*of sheep or cattle*) to break fences or stray. **19** to trample down and destroy crops.—*n* defeat.

break an egg *phr* to strike one curling stone with another with just force enough to crack an egg on contact.

break-back *n* the harvest moon, so called by harvest labourers because of the additional work it entails.

break bread *v* **1** to taste food, to breakfast. **2** to deprive one of means of subsistence.

break breath *v* to utter a sound.

break down *v* (*of the weather*) to become wet or stormy.

breaker *n* **1** one who carves a fowl or cuts up a carcass. **2** a retailer, one who sells goods in small quantities. **3** a large, hard marble for throwing. **4** a red-clay marble.

break-faith *adj* perfidious, treacherous.

break-fur *v* to plough roughly so as to lay the upturned furrow over the uncut furrow.—*n* such rough ploughing.

break-heart *n* heartbreak.

breaking bread on the bride's head *phr* breaking the infar (qv) cake on the bride's head as she crosses the threshold of her new home.

breaking of bread *n* **1** breakfast. **2** the spoiling of one's prospects.

breakings *n* the remains of a feast, broken meats.

break off *v* **1** a type-casting term. **2** to discharge wind from the stomach.

break-off *n* the turning point of a road or hill.

break one's day *phr* **1** to take a holiday or part of one. **2** to interrupt one's daily work.

break out *v* **1** to bring new ground under cultivation. **2** (*of the skin*) to have a rash, sores, etc.

break out fine *phr* (*used of the weather*) to clear up.

breakshough *n* dysentery in sheep.

break-the-barn *n* a child's name for one of the fingers.

break the ground *phr* to open a grave.

break the weather *v* to bring about a change in the weather, said of a cat washing its face with its paws.

break up *v* **1** (*of the weather*) to change. **2** to open an ecclesiastical meeting with a sermon. **3** to break into, as a burglar.

break upon *v* **1** to change money. **2** to draw on one's savings, etc.

break with the full hand *phr* to make a fraudulent bankruptcy.

breard, breards *same as* **braird, brairds**.

breast[1] *n* **1** the front, the forepart. **2** the part of a peat moss from which peats are cut. **3** a step or layer in a manure heap. **4** *in phr* **in a breast** abreast, side by side.

breast[2] *v* **1** to mount a horse, wall, etc, by applying one's breast to it. **2** to get up. **3** to spring up or forward. **4** to cut peats horizontally. **5** to overcome a difficulty. **6** to swallow an affront. **7** to believe a wonder. **8** (*used of a bride and bridegroom*) to face the minister at a marriage.

breast beam *n* a beam in a handloom, reaching up to the weaver's breast.

breast bore *n* a wimble.

breast knot *n* a knot of ribbons worn on the breast.

breast peat *n* a peat formed by a horizontal push of the spade into the perpendicular face of the moss.

breast spade *n* a peat spade pushed forward with the breast.

breastwoodie *n* the harness round the breast of a horse.

breath *n* **1** opinion. **2** sentiments, tendency of thought. **3** a moment.

breath bellows *n* the lungs.

breathe *v* to give a horse time to recover breath.

breathin' *n* an instant of time.

brecham, brechan, brechom *same as* **braichum**.

brechan *n* a Highland plaid.

brechin *n* **1** *same as* **britchin**. **2** *in phr* **hang in the brechin** to lag behind.

breck[1] *n* barren ground in or near a township.

breck[2] *v* **1** to break. **2** to become insolvent.

breckan *n* **1** a brake. **2** a fern.

brecks *n* a piece of cloth sewn across the tail of a ewe and extending about six inches down the hips on each side.

breckshaw *same as* **breakshough**.

bred *n* **1** a board, plank. **2** the lid of a pot or pan. **3** the board of a book. **4** the offertory plate.

breder *n* brethren.

bree[1] *n* **1** liquor, whisky, ale, etc. **2** moisture of any kind. **3** water in which any article of food is boiled, broth, soup, gravy, sauce, juice.—*v* **1** to pour water on articles of food to be boiled. **2** to drain solids that have been boiled. **3** to brew.

bree[2] *n* **1** a disturbance, fuss, hurry. **2** bustle. **3** the brunt.

bree[3] *n* **1** the brow. **2** the eyebrow.

bree[4] *v* to spring past a person.

breears *n* the eyelashes.

breech *v* **1** to flog on the breech. **2** to tuck the skirts above the knee. **3** to put in trousers. *See* **breek**.

breed[1] *v* to educate, train, bring up.—*n* a brood, a litter.

breed[2] *same as* **bread**[1].

breed[3] *same as* **braid**[2].

breed[4] *n* breadth.

breeder *n* **1** brethren. **2** brother.

breeding *n* **1** education. **2** good breeding.

breeds *n* the pancreas.

breef *n* an irresistible spell.

breeghle *v* **1** to waddle and bustle about work, like a small person. **2** to do little work.—*v* with a great fuss.

breeghlin *n* motion with much bustle and little result.

breeid *n* **1** a curch. **2** a fine linen handkerchief worn by married women on their heads with a flap hanging down their backs, peculiar to the Hebrides.

breeirs *same as* **breears**.

breek *n* **1** the leg of a trouser. **2** (*in pl*) trousers, breeches.—*v* **1** to put into breeches. **2** to don the trousers. **3** (*used of female labourers*) to tuck up the skirts to facilitate working in rainy weather. **4** to flog.

breekband *v* **1** to lay hold of the band of the breeches. **2** to wrestle.

breekbandit *n* a wrestling match.

breek-brother *n* a rival in love.

breekens *n* breeches.

breek-folk *n* the male sex.

breekies[1] *n* a young boy's breeches.

breekies[2] *n* the half-grown roe of the haddock.

breek-knees *n* knee breeches.

breeklan *ppl adj* shabby in appearance, in person or in dress.

breekless *adj* without breeches, wearing a kilt.

breek-pouch *n* trouser pocket.

breekum *n* 1 a person of short stature. 2 (*in pl*) knee breeches. 3 short trousers or breeches.

breekumstoich *n* a short, thick child in breeks. *See* **breek**.

breekum trullie *n* 1 one whose breeches do not fit. 2 a very little boy too young to wear breeches.

breel *v* 1 to move rapidly. 2 to make a noise. 3 to reel.

breelish *n* whisky in its strong ale stage.

breells *n* 1 spectacles. 2 double-jointed spectacles. 3 eyeglasses.

breem[1] *n* broom.

breem[2] *adj* 1 keen, fierce. 2 violent. 3 bleak.

breem[3] *same as* **brim**[1].

breenge *same as* **braindge**.

breenging *n* a severe beating, an assault.

breenje *same as* **braindge**.

breer[1], **breerd** *same as* **braird**.

breer[2] *n* a briar.

breerie *same as* **briary**.

breers *n* 1 the eyelashes. 2 *in phr* **draw the breers owre ane's een** to hoodwink one.

brees *same as* **broose**.

breese[1] *n* 1 sandstone chippings. 2 crushed sandstone for strewing on the floor.

breese[2] *v* to bruise.—*n* a bruise.

breese[3] *v* 1 to come on in a hurry.—*n* 1 a broil. 2 a blow, stroke.

breese[4] *n* 1 brose. 2 porridge made with various ingredients.

breeshle, breesil *v* 1 to come on in a hurry. 2 to rustle.—*n* 1 a hurried advance. 2 an onset. 3 a rapid descent.

breest[1] *same as* **breast**[1].

breest[2] *same as* **breast**[2].

breet *n* a brute, contemptuously applied to a person.

breeth *n* breadth.

breether *n* 1 a brother. 2 brethren.

breether *n* corn in the seed leaf.—*v* to germinate.

breetner *n* an energetic worker.

breeze[1], **breeze**[2], **breeze**[3] *same as* **breese**[1], **breese**[2], **breese**[3].

breggan *n* an iron collar, for the neck of offenders, fastened by a chain to a wall.

bregwort *same as* **bragwort**.

breid[1] *same as* **bread**.

breid[2] *same as* **breed**[1].

breid[3] *same as* **braid**[2].

breid[4] *same as* **braid**[3].

breid roller *n* a roller for flattening oatcakes or scones in baking.

breif *same as* **brief**.

brein *same as* **brien**.

breinge *same as* **braindge**.

breird *same as* **braird**.

breird *n* 1 the surface. 2 the top.

breist, breistie *n* the breast.

breme *n* broom.

breme-buss *same as* **broom-buss**.

brenn *v* to burn.

brent[1] *v, adj* burned.

brent[2] *adj* 1 steep, difficult to ascend. 2 (*used of the forehead*) lofty, unwrinkled. 3 straight, direct.—*adv* directly, clearly.

brent[3] *v* to dart or spring suddenly and violently or fearlessly.—*n* a sudden spring or bound.—*adv* with a spring or bound.

brent[4] *n* spring (of the year).—*adj* relating to the spring.

brent[5] *n* a doorpost.

brent-brow *n* a smooth, high forehead.

brent-browed *adj* forward, impudent.

brent-fir *n* fir or pine dug out of bogs.

brenth *n* breadth.

brent-new *adj* 1 quite new. 2 spick and span.

brenty *adj* smooth, unwrinkled.

bress[1] *n* brass.

bress[2] *n* 1 the chimneypiece. 2 the back of the fireplace.

bressie *same as* **brassy**.

brest *v* to burst.

bretchin *n* a horse's breeching.

brether, brethir *n* brothers, brethren.

breuk *same as* **bruick**.

breuk *n* the mark on the knees of a broken-kneed horse.

breukie *n* a cant name for a smith's bellows.

brevity *same as* **bravity**.

brew[1] *n* soup, broth.

brew[2] *same as* **broo**[2].

brew[3] *v* 1 to suspect. 2 to fear future evil. 3 to meditate mischief.

brew-creesh, ~-tailon, ~-tauch *n* a duty paid formerly to a landlord for liberty to brew.

brewis *n* broth, pottage.

brewster-wife *n* a female publican.

brey *v* to frighten.

briary *adj* 1 prickly, thorny. 2 sharp, clever. 3 bold. 4 restless.

brichen *n* breeches.

brichten *v* to brighten.

bricht *adj* bright.

brichten *v* to brighten.

brichtie, bricht-lintie *n* the chaffinch.

brick[1] *n* an oblong loaf of bread of various sizes.

brick[2] *n* 1 a breach. 2 a distinct portion of land.

bricker *n* a boy's marble made of brick clay, a large marble.

brickit *same as* **brockit**.

brickle *same as* **bruckle**.

bridder *same as* **brither**.

bridal bread *n* bread broken over a bride's head and scrambled for, after the marriage.

bridal potion *n* a drink formerly given at the bedding of the bride and bridegroom.

bridal-wife *n* a newly married wife.

briddell *n* a wedding.

bride bed *n* the bridal bed.

bride bun *n* a wedding cake, formerly broken over the bride's head.

bride day *n* the wedding day.

briddell *same as* **braithel**.

bride's knots *n* ribbons worn at a wedding.

bride's pie *n* a pie of which the contents were contributed by neighbours and which served as a bride cake at penny weddings.

bride stool *n* the pew in the church reserved for those who were to be married.

bridie *n* a beef or mutton pie with gravy in it.

bridle *n* 1 the head of a plough. 2 the piece of iron fastened to the end of the beam of a plough, to which the harness is attached.—*v* 1 to modify. 2 to rope a stack, thatch a roof.

bridle renzie *n* a bridle rein.

bridling ropes *n* ropes that hold down the thatch of a stack, etc.

bridstell *n* the seat occupied by bride and bridegroom before the beginning of the marriage service.

brie[1] *n in phr* **spoil the brie** to upset the apple cart.

brie[2] *v* to crush, pound.—*n* crushed sandstone for floors, etc.

brie[3] *same as* **bree**[3].

brief[1] *n* 1 a spell, a charm. 2 a certificate, as of birth.

brief[2] *adj* 1 keen, clever, apt. 2 busy, bustling.

brien *v* to roar, bellow.

brier *n* an eyelash.

brier-blade *n* the sprouting blade.

brierd, brier *same as* **braird**.
briest *v* to breast.—*n* a breast.
briestone *n* sandstone or freestone for rubbing on a door-step, etc.
brig *n* a bridge.—*v* to bridge.
brigancie *n* **1** robbery, spoliation. **2** brigandage.
briganer, brigander *n* **1** a robber, brigand. **2** a rough, rude, boisterous person.
briggie stones *n* a pavement of flagstones.
bril *n* the merry-thought of a fowl.
brilch *n* a short, thickset, impudent person.
briler *n* a particular kind of large marble.
brim¹ *v* (*of swine*) to lie in heat, to copulate.—*adj* in heat.—*n* a harlot, a trull.
brim² *adj* bleak, exposed to the weather.
brime *n* **1** brine, pickle. **2** salt.
brimful *adj* full of sorrow or anger.
brimming *adj* (*used of a sow*) in heat.
brimstane *n* **1** sulphur. **2** a term of abuse.
brin, brinn *n* a ray, flash, beam.—*v* to burn.
brindal, brindal-brass, brindle *n* cash, money.
bringle-brangle *n* a very confused bustle.
brink *n* a river's bank.
brinkie, brinkum *n* a comely and lively person.
brinkie-brow *n* a nursery term for the forehead.
brinnage *n* the brunt of a fight.
brinth *same as* **brenth**.
brise *same as* **brize**.
brisken *v* to refresh, make or become livelier.
briskie, brisk-finch *n* the chaffinch.
brisky *adj* brisk.
briss *same as* **brize**.
brissal *adj* brittle.
brissel-cock *n* the turkey cock.
brissle *same as* **birsle**.
bristow *n* **1** a white crystal set in a ring. **2** a Bristol diamond.
brit *n* a brute.
britchin *n* the portion of harness that passes round the hinder-part of a horse in shafts.
brithell *same as* **braithel**.
brither *n* brother.—*v* **1** to match, pair. **2** to initiate into a society or guild. **3** (*with* **down**) to accompany in being swallowed.
brither-bairn *n* a cousin, an uncle's child.
brither-dochter *n* a niece, a brother's daughter.
brither-sin *n* a nephew, a brother's son.
brittle *v* to render friable.—*adj* **1** shaky. **2** on the verge of bankruptcy. **3** difficult. **4** ticklish.
brittle-brattle *same as* **brattle**.
brize, brizz *v* to bruise, crush, squeeze.—*n* force, pressure.
brizel'd *adj* bruised.
broach¹ *n* a clasp.
broach² *n* a flagon or tankard.
broach³ *n* **1** a spit. **2** the spindle or reel on which newly spun yarn is wound. **3** yarn so wound. **4** a narrow, pointed iron chisel for hewing stones.—*v* to rough-hew.
broadband *adj* spread out as a sheaf in the band, openly exposed.
broad-lipped *adj* (*used of a hat*) broad-brimmed.
broad-meal *n* barley meal.
broadside *n* **1** in *phr* **at a broadside** suddenly. **2** unawares.
broadsome *adj* broad.
broak *same as* **brook³**.
broakie *same as* **brookie**.
broakit *same as* **brookit**.
broakitness *n* the condition of being brookit (qv).
broath *same as* **broth**.
broble *n* a sharp-pointed piece of wood to keep horses apart in ploughing.
broch¹ *n* a narrow piece of wood or metal to support a stomacher.
broch² *n* a prehistoric structure, in shape a circular tower, supposed to be Pictish.
broch³ *n* **1** a halo round the sun or moon. **2** the circle round the tee in a curling rink.
broch⁴ *same as* **brugh²**.
broch⁵ *same as* **brock²**.
broch⁶ *n* an apron.
brochan *n* water gruel, thin porridge made of oatmeal, butter and honey.
broch an' haimil *same as* **brogh and hammel**.
broch-dweller *n* **1** a dweller in a broch. **2** a Pict. *See* **broch²**.
broche *same as* **broach³**.
brochle *adj* lazy, indolent.—*n* a lazy fellow.
brocht *v* brought.
brock¹ *n* **1** a badger. **2** an opprobrious epithet applied to a person.
brock² *n* **1** a scrap of food. **2** broken meats. **3** rubbish, refuse, remnants. **4** grass and bits of straw shaken out of corn after threshing.—*v* to eat or crumble anything to shreds or small pieces.
brock³ *v* **1** to work unskilfully. **2** to waste cloth in cutting.—*n* **1** work ill-done. **2** an unskilful worker.
brockage *n* fragments of crockery, biscuits, furniture, etc.
brockan *n* **1** unskilful working. **2** the wasting of cloth in cutting out.
brockit *adj* **1** variegated. **2** with black and white stripes or spots.
brocklie *same as* **bruckly**.
brock-skin *n* a badger's skin.
brod¹ *n* **1** a board. **2** a shutter. **3** the lid of a pot or kettle. **4** the cover or board of a book. **5** the offertory plate at the church door. **6** a piece of wood sprinkled with rough sand, used for whetting a scythe.—*v* **1** to cover with a lid. **2** to put the lid on a pot, etc.
brod² *n* **1** a goad. **2** a short nail, a brad. **3** a thorn, prickle. **4** a stroke, stab or push with a pointed instrument. **5** a nudge, poke.—*v* **1** to goad, prick, pierce. **2** to jog. **3** to poke.
brod³ *n* brood, breed.
brod⁴ *adj* (*used of the hair*) braided.
broddit-staff *n* **1** a pikestaff. **2** a staff with a sharp point.
broddy *adj* (*used of a sow*) with a litter of pigs.
brodequin *n* a half-boot.
brod-hen *n* a brood hen, a sitting hen.
brodie *n* the fry of the rock tangle or kettle codling.
brodmil *n* a brood.
brod-mother *n* **1** a brood hen. **2** the mother of a family.
brod's-mother *n* a brood hen.
broe *same as* **broo¹**.
brog¹ *n* a coarse shoe, a brogue.
brog² *n* **1** a brad-awl. **2** a boring instrument. **3** a thrust with a stick, etc. **4** a sprig-bit. **5** a poke with a boring instrument.—*v* **1** to prick, pierce. **2** to goad. **3** to incite.
brogan *n* a coarse, light kind of shoe, made of horse leather.
broggit-staff *same as* **broddit-staff**.
brogglie *adj* (*used of a road*) awkward and dangerous for a rider.
broggle¹, brogle *v* to prick.—*n* a vain effort to strike with a pointed instrument.
broggle², brogle *v* **1** to bungle, 'botch'. **2** to cobble shoes, to vamp.—*n* a bungler.
broggler¹ *n* one who fails to strike with a pointed instrument.
broggler² *n* **1** a bad tradesman. **2** a bungler.
brogh *same as* **brugh²**.
brogh and hammel, ~-hammer *phr* **1** proof, evidence. **2** legal security. **3** proof of legal possession.
brogue *n* a trick, an off-take.
brogue-shod *adj* wearing brogues.
brogwort *same as* **bragwort**.
broigh, broich *v* to pant and sweat profusely.—*n* a state of violent perspiration and panting.
broil *v* to be very warm and perspire profusely.—*n* a state of heat and perspiration.

broilerie, broillerie n 1 a state of contention. 2 a struggle, broil.

broilyie v to parboil and then roast on a gridiron.

broizle v to press, crush to atoms.

brok, broke same as **brock**².

broked same as **brockit**.

broken adj 1 bankrupt. 2 curdled. 3 churned. 4 outlawed. 5 vagabond.

broken bottle n a bottle of which the contents have been broken upon.

broken men n 1 outlaws. 2 robbers. 3 men separated from their clans through crime, etc.

broken-up v, adj 1 begun upon. 2 broken upon.

broker n a male flirt.

broll n a drinking pot.

brollochan n a bivalve used for bait.

bron n 1 a brand or peat for burning, used as a torch or as a signal. 2 a glowing cinder.

bronse, bronze v to overheat oneself in a strong sun or too near a hot fire.

broo¹ n 1 broth. 2 juice. 3 liquor. 4 snow water.

broo² n 1 inclination, liking. 2 good opinion.

broo³ n 1 the brow. 2 the part of a moss out of which peats are cut.

broo n 1 bureau. 2 Labour Exchange Office. 3 unemployment office. 4 unemployment benefit.

broo-creesh same as **brewcreesh**.

brood n 1 a young child. 2 the youngest child of a family. 3 a goose that has hatched goslings.

broodent adj 1 (used of a child) petted, spoilt. 2 cross.

broody adj 1 prolific. 2 having a brood. 3 fruitful, fecund.

broofle same as **bruffle**.

brook¹ n a heap, gathering or drift of seaware, driven ashore.

brook² v 1 to use, possess, enjoy. 2 to bear a name. 3 to grace, become.

brook³ v 1 to soil with soot. 2 to dirty. 3 to become spotted, streaked.—n soot adhering to pots, kettles, etc.

brook⁴ v broke

brookable adj tolerable, bearable.

brookie adj smutty, grimy, sooty, dirty.—n 1 a person whose face is smeared with dirt. 2 a blacksmith. 3 a cow with white hair on her face. 4 a child whose face is streaked with dirt.

brookie-face n 1 a person with a face streaked with dirt. 2 a blacksmith.

brookie-faced adj sooty, smutty, having a dirty face.

brookit, brookt adj 1 streaked with grime. 2 soiled with tears, etc. 3 (of cattle, sheep, etc) speckled, streaked with black and white on the face, etc.

broo-lan' n steep ground.

broom v to signal by a broom how many whales are taken.

broom buss n 1 a broom bush. 2 a simpleton.

broom cow n a broom or heather bush used to sweep in curling.

broom deevil, ~ dog n an instrument for grubbing up broom, furze, etc.

broom-thackit adj 1 thatched with broom. 2 covered with broom.

broon adj brown.—n porter ale. See **brown**.

broonie¹, **broonie**² same as **brownie**¹, **brownie**².

broo o' maut n whisky.

broo-talloun, ~-tauch same as **brew-creesh**.

broose n a race on horseback at a country wedding, from the church or the bride's house to the bridegroom's house.

broost n 1 a violent forward motion. 2 a spring.

broostle n 1 a state of great bustle. 2 an impetuous forward movement.—v 1 to be in a great bustle about little, to be in a great hurry. 2 to perspire.

brooze v to browse.

broozle¹ v to perspire greatly from exertion.

broozle² same as **broizle**.

brose¹ v to toil arduously.

brose² n 1 oatmeal or peasemeal mixed with boiling water, milk, colewort or the skimmed fat of soup, etc. 2 porridge. 3 any ordinary article of food. 4 a meal.

brose caup n 1 the wooden cup in which the ploughman made his brose. 2 the ploughman himself.

brose-fed adj fed on brose.

brose meal n meal of peas much parched, of which brose was made.

brose time n suppertime.

brosilie adv in an inactive manner, sluggishly.

brosiness n 1 semifluidity. 2 softness and consequent inactivity.

brosy, brosey adj 1 semifluid. 2 soft, inactive. 3 bedaubed with brose. 4 stout. 5 well-fed.—n a very fat person.

brosy-airt adj fat, inactive, heavy.

brosy-faced adj having a fat, flaccid face.

brosy-heidit adj fat, inactive, stupid.

brosy-mou'd adj fat, stupid, slow of speech.

brot¹ n a name for the Pleiades.

brot² same as **brat**¹.

brot³ n a tangle, muddle, bungle.—v 1 to entangle. 2 to quilt over. 2 to cobble. 3 to darn clumsily.

brot⁴, **brotach** n a quilted cloth or covering used to keep the back of a horse from being ruffled by the shimach (qv), or straw mat, on which the panniers are hung, being fastened to a packsaddle.

brotag n the caterpillar of the drinker moth or of the tiger moth.

brotch v to plait straw ropes round a corn stack.

brotch same as **broach**¹.

brotekin same as **brodequin**.

broth n in phr **a broth of a sweat** a violent perspiration.— v to be in a state of perspiration.

brother v 1 to inure, accustom, often by rough usage. 2 to initiate into a guild or citizenship, often by ludicrous means.—n 1 inurement. 2 rough usage. 3 exposure to rough weather.

brotherin n 1 rough usage. 2 initiation, proper and formal, or ludicrous.

brottlet n a small coverlet.

brotty adj ragged.

brough¹ same as **broch**³

brough² same as **brugh**².

broughan same as **brochan**.

brouk same as **brook**³.

brow¹ n 1 a hill, a steep slope. 2 a peat breast.—v 1 to force. 2 to browbeat.

brow² same as **broo**².

brow³ adj 1 gentle. 2 unselfish. 3 loved for such qualities.

browden v 1 to be fond of, warmly attached. 2 to be set upon. 3 to pet, pamper.—adj 1 fond of, warmly attached. 2 petted.

browdened, browdent adj 1 pampered. 2 arrayed, decked.

browhead n the forehead.

browl n a gnarled limb of a tree.

browlies same as **brawlies**.

browls n bits of dry wood gathered for burning

browly same as **brawly**.

brown n ale or porter.—adj 1 (used of soup) rich with animal juice. 2 discontented. 3 indifferent.

brown-bill n a brown-painted halberd formerly borne by foot soldiers and watchmen.

brown cow n a liquor jar.

brown cow's lick n hair on a child's head standing almost erect and resembling the marks cattle make on their skins by licking them.

brown gled n the hen harrier.

brownie¹ n a benevolent household sprite.

brownie² n a kind of wild bee.

brownie-bae n a benevolent brownie.

brownie's stone n an altar dedicated to a brownie. See **brownie**¹.

brown-janet n 1 a knapsack. 2 a musket.

brown-leamer n a nut ripe and ready to fall from the husk.

brown-swallow n the swift.
brown-yogle n the short-eared owl.
browst n **1** a brewing, what is brewed at a time. **2** an opportunity for drinking. **3** a booze. **4** the consequences of one's own acts. **5** urine.
browster n a brewer.
browster-wife n an ale-wife.
browten same as **browden**.
broylie same as **bruilyie**.
broyliement n a commotion.
brub v to check, restrain, oppress.
bruch¹ same as **broch³**
bruch² same as **brugh²**.
bruch³ same as **broch²**.
brucher same as **brugher**.
bruchle v (with up) to muffle or wrap up a person untidily.—n a wrapping up.
bruchman n a burgher, citizen.
bruchty adj dirty, soot-begrimed.
bruck¹ same as **brock²**.
bruck² same as **brook²**.
bruck³ same as **brook³**.
bruckie same as **brookie**.
bruckit same as **brockit**.
bruckle adj **1** fragile, brittle, friable. **2** uncertain, not to be relied on.—v to crumble away.
bruckleness n the state of being bruckle (qv).
bruckles n **1** the prickly-head carex. **2** the bent grass.
bruckly adj **1** brittle. **2** (used of the weather) uncertain, changeable.—adv in a brittle manner or state.
brude n a brood.
brudy, bruddy adj prolific.
brue same as **broo¹**.
bruff v to clothe thickly.
bruffle v **1** to be in a great hurry. **2** to toil and moil. **3** to be overheated by exertion or excitement. **4** to work clumsily.—n **1** impetuous haste. **2** a bungler, botcher.
brugh¹ same as **broch³**
brugh² n a town, burgh.
brugh and hammer same as **brogh and hammel**.
brugher n a curling stone lying within the circle round the tee.
brughle same as **bruffle**.
brughtin, brughtin cake n green cheese parings or wrought curd, kneaded with butter or suet, broiled in a frying pan and eaten with bread.
brughtins n an oatcake or bannock toasted, crumbled down, put into a pot over the fire with butter and made into a sort of porridge for shepherds at the Lammas feast.
bruick n **1** a boil. **2** a tumour.
bruick-boil n a swelling of the glands under the arm.
bruik¹ v to stitch, embroider.
bruik², bruick same as **brook²**.
bruil, bruillie same as **bruilyie**.
bruilyie,¹ bruilzie v **1** to fight. **2** to get engaged in a broil.—n **1** a quarrel. **2** a disturbance. **3** a broil.
bruilyie² v **1** to broil. **2** to heat. **3** to be in a ferment.
bruind same as **brund²**.
bruise v to jam, squeeze.
bruistle, bruizle same as **broostle**.
bruize v **1** to bruise. **2** to squeeze
bruke same as **brook²**.
bruk-kneed adj broken-kneed.
brulie same as **bruilyie¹**.
brulyie¹, brulye, brulzie same as **bruilyie¹**.
brulyie² same as **bruilyie²**.
brulyiement n **1** a disturbance, a broil. **2** commotion.
brumble v to make a hollow, murmuring sound, as rushing water.
brume n the broom.
brummel¹, brummle n the blackberry, bramble.
brummel² same as **brumble**.
brummin ame as **brimming**.
brumple n the viviparous blenny.

brumstane n brimstone.
brumstane-candle n a match made of brimstone and paper to suffocate bees.
brun n the brow of a hill.
brund¹ n a vestige, portion.
brund v **1** to flash. **2** to emit sparks. **3** to see stars owing to a heavy blow on the head. **4** (used of the eye) to sparkle, to glance. **5** to be angry.—n **1** a brand for burning. **2** a spark of fire.
brung v brought.
brungle n **1** a job, trick. **2** a knavish piece of business.
brunstane same as **brumstane**.
brunstickle n the stickleback.
brunt¹ v burned.— adj **1** burnt. **2** (used of a curling stone) illegally touched or played. **3** taken in in a bargain. **4** cheated. **5** tricked.
brunt² adj keen, eager, ardent.
brunt³ v to bear the brunt of.
brunt-crust n a played-out person.
bruntie n a blacksmith.
bruntlin n a burnt moor.—adj belonging to a burnt moor.
bruse¹ same as **broose**.
bruse² n a brew house.
brush n **1** vigorous exercise of any kind. **2** a determined effort for a short time. **3** a struggle, tussle.
brush² v to beat, thrash.
brush³ v (with up) to smarten, titivate.
brushie adj **1** smartly dressed. **2** fond of clothes.
bruskness n **1** brusqueness. **2** freedom of speech or manner.
brussen v burst.
brussle same as **broostle**.
brust v to burst.
brusten v burst.
brustle¹ same as **birsle**
brustle² same as **broostle**.
brutch same as **broach³**.
brutify v to make a beast of oneself.
brye n powdered sandstone, used for scouring.
brylies same as **brawlins**.
brym adj **1** grim. **2** fierce.
bryttle v to cut up or carve venison.
bu¹ same as **bo³**.
bu² same as **boo³**.
bu³ same as **bo⁵**.
buat same as **bowet**.
bub n a blast, a gust.
bubbies, bubies n the breasts.
bubblan n tippling, toping.
bubble v **1** to discharge nasal mucus. **2** to snivel, blubber, weep.—n (in pl) nasal mucus, snot.
bubbly adj **1** dirty, tear-stained. **2** snotty.
bubbly-jock n a turkey cock.
bubbly-nosed adj having a dirty, snotty nose.
buccar same as **bukkar**.
buchan-sergeant n a skim-milk cheese.
buchan-vittal n **1** meal consisting of two-thirds oats and one-third barley. **2** a person on whom no reliance can be placed.
bucharet n the swift.
bucht same as **boucht**.
buchted adj **1** enclosed. **2** sheltered.
bucht flake n a hurdle at the entrance to a sheep pen.
buck¹ n **1** the body. **2** the carcass of an animal.
buck² n the beech tree.
buck³ v to butt, push.—adv vigorously, with force.
buck⁴ v **1** (of water) to gush out, pour forth. **2** to gurgle when poured from a strait-necked bottle.
buck⁵ same as **bouk²**.
buck⁶ n the sound made by a stone falling into water.—v to gulp in swallowing.
buck⁷ n **1** walking over the same ground repeatedly. **2** crowding.—v **1** to walk on the same ground repeatedly. **2** to crowd. **3** to walk with stately step.

buckalee *n* a call to negligent herd boys who allow the cows to eat the corn: 'buckalee, buckalo, buckabonnie, buckabo: a fine bait among the corn—what for no'?'

buckan *n* the act of walking or crowding.

buck and crune *phr* to show extreme solicitude to possess anything.

buckartie-boo *v* to coo as a pigeon.

buckaw *n* the short game which concludes a curling match or bonspiel.

buck-bean *same as* bogbean.

buck-beard *n* a hard, whitish moss found growing on rocks, often in the shape of a wine glass or inverted cone.

bucker¹ *v* 1 to rustle. 2 to wear rich, rustling clothes. 3 to move or work fussily or awkwardly. —*n* 1 the rustling of paper, silk, etc. 2 noisy bustle. 3 annoyance. 4 an awkward, noisy person.

bucker² *n* a name given in the west of Scotland to a species of whale.

bucker³ *n* 1 a native of Buckie in Banffshire. 2 a person from the south coast of the Moray Firth. 3 a boat of a special build used on the Moray Firth coast.

bucker⁴ *v* 1 to bother, worry about. 2 to suffer pain.

buckerin *n* 1 rustling. 2 fuss.—*adj* fussy, awkward.

bucket *n* a cant name for a glass of spirits.

bucketie *n* weavers' paste.

buckie¹ *n* 1 the sea snail or its shell. 2 any spiral shell. 3 a periwinkle. 4 a trifle of no value.

buckie² *n* a child's rattle made of rushes.

buckie³ *n* the fruit of the wild rose.

buckie⁴ *n* a smart blow or push.—*v* 1 to strike or push roughly. 2 to walk hurriedly.—*adv* violently.

buckie⁵ *n* 1 a refractory person. 2 a mischievous boy.

buckie⁶ *n* the hindquarters of a hare.

buckiean *n* the act of striking.—*adj* pushing, bouncing.

buckie-berries *n* the fruit of the wild rose.

buckie-brier *n* the wild rose.

buckie-brow *n* a projecting or beetling brow.

buckie-faalie, --faulie *n* the primrose.

buckie-ingram *n* the crab.

buckie-man *n* a seller of periwinkles.

buckie-prin *n* a periwinkle.

buckie-ruff *n* 1 a wild, giddy boy. 2 a romping girl.

buckie-tyauve *n* 1 a struggle. 2 a good-humoured struggle or wrestling match.

bucking *n* the sound of water escaping through a narrow neck.

bucking basket *n* 1 a clothes basket. 2 a buck basket.

buckise *n* a smart stroke.—*v* to beat with smart strokes.

buckle¹ *n* a tussle, a pretended struggle.—*v* 1 to wrap in or round. 2 to bandage. 3 to secure, mend. 4 to marry. 5 to join in marriage. 6 to bend, twist, warp. 7 to quarrel, struggle. 8 to attack. 9 to meddle with. 10 to apply oneself to work.

buckle² *n* a curl, curliness.

buckle³ *n in phr* up-i'-the-buckle used of one rising in the social scale.

buckle-beggar, buckle-the-beggars *n* 1 one who marries persons clandestinely or in an irregular fashion. 2 a hedge parson. 3 a Gretna Green parson.

buckle-horned *adj* perverse, headstrong, obstinate.

buckle't *v, adj* dressed.

buckle to *v* 1 to set to work. 2 to join in marriage.

buckle with *v* 1 to assail, grapple with. 2 to have the worst in an argument. 3 to be engaged in a business so as to be at a loss to finish it.

buckling *n* 1 a fight. 2 a grappling in a fight.

bucksturdie *adj* obstinate.

bucky *n* the sluice of a millpond.

bud¹ *n* a bribe.—*v* to bribe.

bud², bude *v* must, had to.

bud-be *n* a necessary duty devolving on anyone.

budden *v* bidden, invited.

budder *v* to trouble, bother.

buddy *n* a pet designation of a little child.

bude *same as* bud².

budget *n* a workman's wallet.

budna *v* must not, could not, might not. See bud².

bue *same as* bo⁵.

buff¹ *v* 1 to beat, buffet. 2 to strike with a soft substance. 3 to emit a dull, soporific sound. 4 to thresh corn. 5 to half-thresh grain. 6 to lose by a bargain.—*n* 1 a blow, buffet. 2 a blow in challenge to fight. 3 any dull, soporific sound. 4 the sound of a blow with a soft substance or of anything that falls.

buff² *same as* bouff².

buff³ *n* (*of time*) a while.

buff⁴ *n* the skin.

buff⁵ *v* (*used of herrings*) to steep salted herrings in water and hang them up.

buff⁶ *n* 1 a puff or blast of wind. 2 a fuss, outcry. 3 an ado.

buffer *n* 1 a dolt. 2 a fellow. 3 (*used half-contemptuously*) a chap.

buffet *v in phr* buffet the boar a boys' game.

buffets *n* a swelling in the glands of the neck, mumps.

buffet stool *n* a stool with sides, like a square table with leaves folded down.

buffie, buffle *adj* 1 fat, chubby. 2 pursed. 3 shaggy, dishevelled.

buffle¹ *same as* buffie.

buffle² *v* 1 to confuse, perplex. 2 to baffle.

buffle-headit *adj* 1 large-headed. 2 dull of comprehension.

bufflin' *adj* 1 (*of boys*) wandering, unsettled. 2 roving.

buff nor sty *phr* 1 nothing whatever. 2 not the smallest part.

buft *adj* 1 (*of standing corn*) having the ears eaten by birds or shaken by wind or wasted by a prolonged harvest. 2 shorn. 3 half-shorn.

bug¹ *v* built. See big².

bug² *n in phr* let bug to tell, to divulge.

bugaboo *n* a hobgoblin.

bugars *same as* bougars.

bugelet-horn *n* a bugle.

bugge *n* a bogey, bugbear.

buggen built. See big².

bugger, buggar *v* to imprecate in vile language.—*n* a contemptuous term used in vile imprecation.

buggery *n in phr* play buggery to play mischief.

buggid *v* built.

buggle *n* a bog, morass.

bught *same as* boucht.

bughted glade *n* a winding glade.

bugle *v* 1 (*of bulls*) to bellow. 2 (*of cocks*) to crow.—*n* a cock's crow.

buick *v* curtsied.

buide *v* must, had to.

buik¹ *same as* bouk¹.

buik² *same as* beuk².

buik³ *same as* book.

buik⁴ *v* curtsied.

buikie *n* a booklet.

buik-lare *same as* book-lare.

buik-leared *same as* book-leared.

buiksome *adj* large.

build *v* to pile or stack sheaves or peats.

builyie *n* a quandary, perplexity.

buind *n* a band of reapers or peat-cutters.

buird *n* a board.

buirdly *adj* stalwart, goodly, fine-looking, well-made.

buise¹ *same as* boose¹.

buise² *n in phr* shoot the buise to be hanged.

buist¹ *n* 1 a box, chest. 2 a coffin. 3 a large meal chest. 4 a receptacle. 5 the match for a firelock. 6 a thick or gross object. 7 stays. 8 a bodice.—*v* to enclose.

buist² *same as* boost¹.

buist³ *v* to mark cattle and sheep with tar, to brand.—*n* 1 a branding iron, an instrument for marking sheep. 2 a tar mark of ownership on sheep or cattle.

buist⁴ *n* a football.

buisting iron *n* the instrument used in marking sheep, etc.
buist-maker *n* a coffin-maker.
buisty *n* **1** a bed. **2** a nest. **3** an animal's lair.
buit[1] *same as* **buist**[1].
buit[2] *n* a boot.
buith *n* a booth.
buittle *v* to walk ungracefully, taking short, bouncing steps.
bukat *same as* **beikat**.
buke[1] *same as* **beuk**[2].
buke[2] *same as* **bouk**.
buke[3] *same as* **book**.
bukk *v* to incite, instigate.
bukkar *n* a large, heavy-armed lugger used in smuggling.
bukker *n* vexation, annoyance.
bukow *n* anything that scares.
bulb, bulboch *n* a disease of sheep, causing them to drink until they swell and burst.
bulch *same as* **bilch**.
bulder *n* **1** a loud gurgling noise. **2** a bellowing.—*v* **1** to make a gurgling sound as of water rushing to and fro in the cavity of a rock or passing through a narrow pipe which emits an echo. **2** to gush out. **3** to bellow.
bule[1] *same as* **bool**[4].
bule[2] *same as* **bool**[2].
bulf, bulfart *n* **1** a fat, pursy person. **2** a fat child.
bulfie *adj* **1** dull, stupid.—*n* a stout, fat boy. **2** used as a nickname for such a boy.
bulfin *n* a very stout person.
Bulgan's Day *n* 4 July, the feast of St Martin. *See* **Bullion's Day**.
bulger *n* a boy's large marble.
bulk *v* to play marbles.
bulker *n* the puffin.
bulkie[1] *n* a game in which marbles are placed in a row and each player has two chances.
bulkie[2] *n* a policeman.
bulkish *adj* bulky.
bull[1] *n* the bar or beam of a harrow.
bull[2] *n in phr* **the black bull of Norroway** an imaginary monster.—*v* **1** (*of a cow*) to desire the bull. **2** to serve a cow. **3** (*with* **in**) to swallow hastily.
bulla *n* **1** a brother. **2** a comrade.
bullace *n* an axe.
bullament *same as* **bulyiement**.
bullax *n* a hatchet.
bullax-wright *n* a clumsy, unskilful wright.
bull-beef *n in phr* **as proud as bull-beef** proud, conceited.
bull-beggar *n* a scarecrow.
bull-daisy *n* a wild orchis.
buller *same as* **bulder**.
bullet *n* a boulder.
bullets *n* the game of bowls.
bullet-stane *n* a round stone, used as a bullet for throwing along the highway in the game of 'lang bullet'.
bull-fit *n* **1** a swift. **2** a martin.
bull-french *n* a bullfinch.
bull-head *n* a tadpole.
bullie[1] *n* the bullfinch.
bullie[2] *v* to speak, call or weep loudly.—*n* a loud cry, weeping, roaring.
bullie[3] *n* a boys' fight.
bulliean *n* a loud raising of the voice.
bullie stick *n* a stick used in a bullie.
bulligrubs *n* a colic.
bulliheisle, bulliheizilie, bulliehislee *n* **1** a boys' game, in which it is attempted to throw on the ground all the boys standing close in a line. **2** a scramble. **3** a squabble.
Bullion's Day *n* 4 July, the translation of St Martin.
bullister *n* **1** a sloe bush. **2** the wild plum.
bulliwan *n* the stalk of a dock.
bull-maill *n* fee for the service of a bull.
bull-neck *n* an onion that does not bulb but grows like a leek.
bull of the bog *n* the bittern.

bull-reel *n* a reel danced by men alone.
bull's bags *n* any tuberous orchis supposed to be aphrodisiac.
bull-seg[1] *n* any tuberous orchis.
bull-seg[2] *n* **1** a bulrush. **2** the great cat-tail.
bull-segg *n* a castrated bull.
bull's grass *n* the goosegrass.
bull's head *n* an ancient signal of execution brought in at a feast.
bull stirk *n* a young bull.
bully *same as* **bullie**[2].
bullyrag *v* **1** to scold vigorously. **2** to hector. **3** to haggle. **4** to wrangle.
bullyraggle *n* a noisy, abusive wrangle.
bully-war *n* a boys' game in which, from a certain line, they seek to dislodge with pebbles the top stone of a conical heap of stones of a gradually lessening size without dislodging any of these.
bulmie *n* any large edible root.
bulrash *n* a bulrush.
bult *v* **1** to push violently, jolt. **2** to butt.
bultin' *adj* (*used of a cow*) apt to butt.
bulty *adj* bulky, large.
bulwand *n* **1** the bulrush. **2** the common mugwort.
bulwaver *same as* **bellwaver**.
bulyiement *n* **1** clothing, habiliments. **2** odds and ends.
bulyon *n* a crowd, a collection
bum[1] *n* the bottom.
bum[2] *n* a term of contempt for a big, dirty, lazy woman.
bum[3] *v* **1** to hum like a top. **2** to buzz like a bee, etc. **3** to spin a top, to make it hum. **4** to drone, to make a sound like the bagpipe or big bass fiddle. **5** to be glad. **6** to sing. **7** to read in a droning, indistinct manner. **8** to sing or play badly. **9** to cry, to weep.—*n* **1** the hum of bees, tops, etc. **2** the hum of conversation. **3** the noise in a busy street. **4** an indistinct or droning reader. **5** a singer or player without taste or skill.
bum[4] *v* **1** to strike, knock. **2** to throw away carelessly.
bu-man *n* **1** a nursery bogey. **2** a hobgoblin. **3** the devil.
bumbaze *v* to confound, bewilder, stupefy.
bumbee *n* a humblebee or bumblebee.
bumbee-byke *n* a nest of bumbees.
bumbee-looking *adj* looking like a bumbee.
bumbeleery-buzz *n* a sound made by children, when they see cows taking fright, to incite them to greater speed.
bumble *same as* **bummil**.
bumble-kite *n* a blackberry.
bum-bumming *n* a continuous humming sound.
bum-clock *n* a humming, flying beetle.
bumfle *n* a large pucker.—*v* to pucker.
bumfly *n* a stout, pursy person.
bum fodder *n* toilet paper.
bum leather *n* the skin of the buttocks.
bumler, bummeler *n* a bungler.
bumlick *n* anything round and full like a turnip.
bumling *n* the humming noise of a bee.
bumlock, bumlack *n* **1** a small, prominent, shapeless stone. **2** anything that endangers one's falling or stumbling.
bummack *n* the brewing of malt to be drunk at once at a merrymaking.
bumman, bumming *n* **1** reading or talking in a drawling, indistinct manner. **2** singing or playing badly.— *adj* **1** weeping, given to weeping. **2** chicken-hearted, cowardly.
bummer[1] *n* **1** a blundering, drawling reader. **2** a bad singer or player on an instrument. **3** a managing, officious person. **4** a headman, manager. **5** one given to weeping.
bummer[2] *n* **1** a bumblebee. **2** a bluebottle fly. **3** any buzzing insect. **4** a great boaster. **5** an empty, foolish talker. **6** a thin piece of serrated wood attached to a string, used by children swinging it to give out a booming sound. **7** a boy's peg-top that bums loudly when spinning. *See* **bum**[3].
bummie *n* **1** a stupid fellow, fool. **2** a bumblebee.
bummie-bee *n* a bumblebee.
bummil, bummle *v* **1** to bungle. **2** to read or sing indistinctly

and badly. **3** to bustle about, work busily. **4** to weep, blubber.—*n* **1** a wild bee. **2** a drone. **4** an idle fellow. **5** a bungler. **6** a clumsy, heavy person. **7** clumsy work. **8** low, blundering reading. **9** one who reads, sings or plays without skill or taste.

bumming duff *n* a tambourine.

bummler *n* a bungler, blunderer.

bump[1] *n* **1** a stroke. **2** a swelling caused by a blow or fall.—*v* to initiate into burgess-ship, etc, by bumping a person's buttocks against a stone or post. *See* **burgess**.

bump[2] *v* to boom like a bittern.

bumper *v* **1** to fill to the brim. **2** to drink healths in a bumper.

bumphle *same as* **bumfle**.

bum pipe *n* the dandelion.

bumplefeist *n* **1** a sulky humour. **2** a fit of spleen.

bumpy *n* the buttocks.

bumpy coat, ~ jacket *n* one reaching only to the buttocks.

bumshot *adj* said of those whose plot gives way with them.

bum-speal *n* a speal (qv) of wood, notched on both sides, with a string at the end for whirling round in the air.

bum-whush *n* **1** perdition, ruin. **2** annihilation. **3** obscurity.

bun[1] *n* a cake baked with flour, dried fruits and spices, used about the New Year and known also as **sweetie loaf**.

bun[2] *same as* **boon**[1].

bun[3] *n* **1** a rabbit. **2** the tail of a rabbit, the seat, the posterior.

bun[4] *n* a large cask in which water is carted from a distance.

bun[5]**, bund** *v, adj* bound.

bun-briest *n* a wooden bed.

bunce *n* **1** a schoolboy's claim to the half of anything he finds. **2** a bonus, dividend.

bunch[1] *n* an awkward-looking woman or girl.

bunch[2] *v* (*used of squat or corpulent persons*) to hobble, walk clumsily.—*n* **1** a blow, push, punch. **2** the line from which a start in a race is made. **3** the point from which one jumps in leapfrog.

bunching *adj* **1** showy in dress or manner. **2** of an imposing appearance.

bunder *n* **1** a bang. **2** a sudden, heavy fall. **2** a battering sound.

bundle *v* **1** to sleep together without undressing in the same bed or couch, an old form of courting. **2** to live in concubinage.

bundling *n* the practice of sweethearts sleeping together in their clothes.

bund-sack *n* a person engaged or under promise of marriage.

bundweed, bunweed *n* the ragweed.

bune *same as* **boon**[1].

bunemost *same as* **boonmost**.

buner *same as* **booner**.

bunewand *n* **1** the cow parsnip. **2** the dock.

bung[1] *adj* tipsy, fuddled.—*v* to make tipsy.

bung[2] *v* **1** to throw with force. **2** to get in a passion. **3** to bang. **4** to walk quickly and proudly. **5** to incur displeasure. **6** to sulk and refuse to speak. **7** (*with* **out**) to rush or burst forth.—*n* **1** a blow, crash, bang. **2** bad temper, a pet. **3** offence.

bung[3] *v* to emit a booming or twanging sound, as when a stone is slung.—*n* **1** the sound thus made. **2** the act of slinging a stone.

bung[4] *n* an old, worn-out horse.

bung[5] *n* the instep of a shoe.

bung-fu' *adj* quite intoxicated.

bungie *same as* **bungy**.

bung-tap *n* a humming top.

bungy[1] *adj* petulant, testy, huffy.

bungy[2] *adj* **1** tipsy, fuddled. **2** full to the bung.

bunjel *same as* **bangyal**.

bunk *same as* **benk**.

bunker[1]**, bunkart** *n* **1** an earthen seat in the fields. **2** a roadside bank. **3** a large heap of stones, etc. **4** the desk of a

schoolmaster or precentor. **5** an inequality in the surface of ice. **6** a small sandpit.

bunker[2] *n* a country dance.

bunkert *same as* **bunker**[1].

bunkle *n* a stranger.

bunn *v* bound.

bunnel, bunnle *n* **1** ragwort. **2** cow parsnip.

bunnerts *n* cow parsnip.

bunnet *n* a boy's cap.

bunshie *adj* fat, plump.

bunsucken *adj* (*used of a farm*) bound to have all the corn grown on it ground at a particular mill.

bunt[1] *n* the tail of a horse or rabbit.

bunt[2] *v* **1** to hurry, run away. **2** to provide for, look after, attend. **3** to forage.

buntin *adj* short and thick, plump.—*n* **1** a short, thickset person. **2** a dwarf. **3** a bantam.

buntin-crab *n* a crab-apple.

bunting-lark *n* the common or corn bunting.

buntlin[1] *n* **1** the blackbird. **2** the corn bunting.

buntlin[2] *same as* **buntin**.

buntling *n* a banding.

buntling-lark *n* the corn bunting.

bunty *n* a cock or hen without a tail.

bunwand *same as* **bunewand**.

bunweed *same as* **bundweed**.

bunyel *same as* **bangyal**.

bunyoch *n* diarrhoea.

buoy *v* (*used of smells*) to rise up, swell up.

bur[1] *n* a fir cone.

bur[2] *same as* **burr**[2].

burble[1] *v* **1** to purl. **2** to bubble or boil up, like water from a spring.—*n* **1** a 'bell' or bubble on water. **2** purling, a purl.

burble[2] *n* perplexity, trouble, disorder.—*v* to perplex, trouble.

burble-headed *adj* stupid, confused.

burd[1] *n* a table.

burd[2] *n* **1** a maiden. **2** a young lady.

burd[3] *n* **1** offspring, in a bad sense. **2** an unweaned seal.

burd alane *adj* quite alone.—*n* the only surviving child of a family.

burden *n* the drone of a bagpipe.

burdenable *adj* burdensome.

burden-camer *n* a carrier of wood.

burdenous *adj* burdened.

burdie *n* **1** a small bird. **2** a term of endearment or of irony, used to a young man or woman.

burdie house *n* in phr **gang to burdie house** used by old people to those with whose conduct or language they are, or pretend to be, displeased.

burdinseck *same as* **berthinsek**.

burdit *adj* (*used of stone*) split into laminae.

burdliness *n* stateliness.

burdly *same as* **buirdly**.

burd-mou'd *adj* **1** unwilling to scold. **2** gentle in fault-finding.

burdocken *n* the burdock.

burdoun *same as* **burden**.

bure[1] *n* a loose woman.

bure[2] *v* bore.

bouregh *v* to crowd together.

burger *n* a burgher.

burgess *v* in riding the marches of a burgh, to make burgesses by bumping them on a stone. *See* **bump**[1].

burges-thread *n* flaxen thread.

burg-hall *n* a town-hall.

burgher *n* a member of the Secession Church who upheld the lawfulness of the burgess oath.

burg of ice *n* whalefishers' name for an icefield afloat.

burgonet *same as* **biggonet**.

burg-toon *n* a burgh.

burial boding *n* a death warning.

burial bread *n* cakes, etc, partaken at a funeral.

burian *n* **1** a mound, tumulus. **2** a kind of fortification. **3** a prehistoric camp.

buried *adj* obsolete.

burio, burrio *same as* **bourriau.**

burlaw *n* a court of neighbours in a district to settle local disputes, etc.

burlaw baillie *n* the officer of the burlaw court.

burley-bracks *same as* **barley-breaks.**

burley-whush *n* an obsolete game of ball.

burlins *n* bread burned in the oven in baking.

burly¹ *n* a crowd, a tumult.

burly² *adj* thick, rough, strong.

burly baillie *n* the officer of the burlaw court. *See* **burlaw.**

burly-headit *adj* of rough appearance.

burly-man *n* a member of the burlaw court. *See* **burlaw.**

burly twine *n* strong, coarse twine, somewhat thicker than pack thread.

burn¹ *n* **1** a brook, a small river. **2** water from a fountain or well. **3** water used in brewing. **4** the brew itself. **5** urine.

burn² *v* **1** to deceive. **2** to cheat in a bargain. **3** to suffer in any effort. **4** to derange the game of curling by improper interference.

burn-airn *n* a branding-iron.

burn-becker *n* **1** the water ouzel. **2** the water wagtail.

burn-blade *n* a large, broad-leaved plant growing on the banks of burns. *See* **burn¹.**

burnbrae *n* a slope with a burn (qv) at its foot.

burnewin *n* a blacksmith.

burn-grain *n* a small burn (qv) flowing into a larger one.

burnie-baker *same as* **burnbecker.**

burning beauty *n* a very beautiful person.

burning-water *n* marine phosphorescence.

burnist *v, adj* **1** burnished, polished. **2** decorated.

burn-sae *n* a water butt carried by two persons on a pole resting on their shoulders.

burnside *n* ground at the side of a burn (qv).

burn-the-water *phr* to leister (qv) salmon by torchlight.

burn-the-wind *same as* **burnewin.**

burnt-nebbit, ~-tae'd *adj* (*used of a tawse* (qv)) having the ends hardened in the fire.

burnwood *n* firewood.

burr¹ *n* **1** a stout, strong, thickset person of stubborn temper. **2** the sea urchin.

burr² *n* **1** the tongue of a shoe. **2** the edge of the upper leather.

burr³ *v* to make a whirring sound in the throat in pronouncing the letter 'r'.

burrach'd *adj* enclosed, encircled. *See* **bourach¹.**

burran¹ *n* the act of sounding the letter 'r' in the throat.

burran² *n* a badger.

burrel¹ *n* a barrel.

burrel² *n* a hollow piece of wood used in twisting ropes.

burrel-ley, ~-rig *n* land of an inferior kind where there was only a narrow ridge ploughed and a large strip of barren land lay between every ridge.

burreo-like *a* like an executioner. *See* **bourriau.**

burrian *n* the red-throated diver.

burrie *v* **1** to push roughly. **2** to crowd confusedly and violently. **2** to overpower in working or in striving at work.—*n* **1** crowding. **2** a rough push. **3** a children's game.—*adv* roughly.

burroch *same as* **bourach².**

burrochit *adj* restrained.

burrochless *adj* **1** wild. **2** intractable. **3** without restraint.

burrow *n* a burgh.

burrows *n* security.

burry *adj* full of burs.

bursar *n* one who holds a scholarship at school or college.

bursary *n* a scholarship at school or college.

bursen *adj* **1** dainty or fussy about food, as if already surfeited. **2** burst. **3** breathless. **4** panting from overexertion. **5** overpowered by fatigue.

bursen-belch *n* a person breathless from corpulence.

bursen-kirn *n* such a laborious harvest that all the grain is not cut before sunset.

burss-money *n* a bursary (qv).

burst *v* **1** to overfeed. **2** to fill to excess. **3** to be breathless, overheated and exhausted from great exertion.—*n* **1** injury from over-exertion. **2** an outburst of drinking. **3** a company or detachment forming part of a moving or mobbing crowd.

bursted-churn *n* a bursen-kirn (qv).

bursted *adj* **1** burst. **2** breathless from exertion, overfatigue.

burstin *n* grain dried over the fire.

burth¹ *n* a counter-current in a bay, caused by the tidal current outside.

burth² *n* birth.

burthen *n* a stone in curling so retarded by touching another as to become harmless.

bur-thristle *n* the spear-thistle.

burying *n* a funeral.

bus *n* a call to cattle to stand still in the stall.

buse *same as* **boose.**

buse-airn *n* a marking iron for sheep.

bush¹ *v* **1** to sheathe. **2** to enclose in a metal case. **3** to fit a metal lining to a cylindrical body, to put on an iron ring or bush.—*n* a ring inserted to prevent the effect of friction.

bush² *v* to place bushes on fields to prevent poachers from netting partridges.

bush³ *v* to burst or gush out.

bush⁴ *v* **1** to move about briskly. **2** to tidy up.

bush⁵ *int* expressive of a rushing sound, as of water rushing out.

bushel *n* a small pond, a dam made in a gutter to intercept water.

bushel breeks *n* wide, baggy trousers.

busheries *n* clumps of bushes.

bush rope *n* the rope to which the nets of a drift are attached.

busht *same as* **buist¹.**

bushty *same as* **buisty.**

busk *v* **1** to make ready. **2** to dress, deck, adorn. **3** to dress flies for fishing.—*n* dress, decoration.

busker *n* one who dresses another.

buskie¹ *adj* fond of dress, smart.

buskie² *adj* bushy.

buskin *n* dressing.

buskry *n* dress, decoration.

buss¹ *n* **1** a bush. **2** straw, etc, used as litter for animals or material for birds' nests. **3** a sunken rock on which at very low tides seaweed is visible, like a bush. **4** a clump or tussock of rushes, etc. **5** a pouting or sulking mouth.

buss² *v* **1** to dress. **2** to dress hooks.

buss³ *n* cant name for a bursary (qv) or scholarship.

bussard *n* a class of carnations.

bussie *adj* bushy.

bussin *n* a linen cap or hood worn by old women.

bussing *n* covering.

bussle *n* bustle.

buss-sparrow *n* the hedge sparrow.

buss-taps *n in phr* **gang o'er the busstaps** to behave extravagantly.

bussy, buzzy *adj* busy.

bust¹ *v* to powder, to dust with flour.

bust² *v* to beat.

bust³ *same as* **buist¹.**

bust⁴ *same as* **boose¹.**

bust⁵ *same as* **buist³.**

bust⁶ *same as* **boost¹.**

busteous *adj* **1** boisterous, powerful. **2** fierce, terrible.

bustiam, bustian, bustine, bustin *n* **1** fustian. **2** a cotton fabric used for waistcoats.

bustle *v* to toast.

bustuous, bustyious *same as* **busteous.**

but¹ *prep* without, outside.—*adv* out, outside of, in the outer room or kitchen.—*n* the outer room or kitchen of a two-roomed cottage.—*adj* **1** outer, outside. **2** pertaining to the but or kitchen of a cottage.

but² *n* **1** an impediment. **2** an 'if'.

but³ *conj* **1** unless, nothing but. **2** except, save only. —*adv* **1** verily, certainly. **2** used redundantly for emphasis.

but⁴ *v* must, had to.

but-a-hoose *n* the kitchen end of a house.

but and *phr* **1** besides. **2** as well as. **3** and also.

but and a ben *n* a two-roomed cottage.

but and ben *adv* **1** from the but (qv) of a house to the ben (qv), and vice versa. **2** backwards and forwards.

butch *v* **1** to act as butcher, to be a butcher. **2** to kill for the market.

buter *n* the bittern.

but gif, but gin *conj* but if.

but-hoose *n* the kitchen, the outer room.

butt¹ *n* **1** ground set apart for archery. **2** the distance between a player and the goal or target in playing marbles, etc.

butt² *n* **1** a piece of ground which in ploughing does not form a proper ridge but is excluded as an angle. **2** a small piece of land disjoined from adjacent lands.

butt³ *n* the bottom of a sheaf or stack.

butt⁴ *n* the part of tanned hides of horses which is under the crupper.

butt⁵ *v* (*used in curling*) to drive at one or more stones lying near the tee so as to remove them.

butten *prep* without.

butter *v* to coax, flatter.—*n* flattery, fulsome praise.

butter-and-bear-caff *n phr* gross flattery.

butter-bake *n* a biscuit made with butter.

butter boat *n* a small table dish for serving melted butter.

butter-brughtins *n* an oatcake or bannock toasted, crumbled down, cooked in a pot with butter and made into a sort of porridge. *See* **brughtins**.

butter-clocks *n* small pieces of butter floating on the top of milk.

butter crock *n* a butter jar.

butter-dock *n* the broad-leaved dock.

butterfish *n* a species of the blenny.

butter-groat *n* a farmer's wife's perquisite of butter money.

butterie *adj* (*used of the tongue*) plausible, flattering for selfish ends.

butter-luck *n* an expression used as a charm in butter-making.

buttermilk-gled *n* a bird of the falcon tribe.

butter-saps *n* oatcake or wheaten bread soaked in melted butter and sugar.

butter-wife *n* a woman who sells butter.

buttery *n* a butterfly.

buttery-fingers *n* a person who lets things slip from the fingers.

Buttery Willie Collie *n* an old nickname for an undergraduate of Aberdeen University, especially in the first session, when his scarlet gown was new.

buttle *same as* **battle².**

buttlins *same as* **bittlins.**

buttock *n* **1** the remainder, end. **2** the bottom.

buttock-mail *n* the fine formerly imposed by a kirk session in a case of fornication.

button *n* (*in pl*) the boys' game played with buttons aimed at a mote.

button-mouse *n* small fieldmouse.

button-mule *n* a mould for a button.

buttons and buttonholes *adv phr* entirely, completely.

buttony *n* a children's game in which the players, with eyes shut and palms open, guess who has received a button from another player who passes along the line in which they stand.

butt'rie *same as* **buttery.**

butts *n* (*used of children*) intimate companions.

butty *n* **1** an intimate companion. **2** a fellow worker.

butwards *adv* towards the but (qv) of a cottage or the outer part of a room.

bus *v* to hurry, bustle.

buy *v* in *phr* **buy a broom** to take out a warrant.

buzzard *n* a bluebottle.

buzzard-hawk *n* the buzzard.

buzzle *v* (*used of grain crops*) to rustle when touched in the stook (qv), indicating readiness to be carted home.—*n* the rustling sound emitted by a sheaf ready for the stack.

buzzy *same as* **bussy.**

by¹ *prep* **1** beyond. **2** by the side of. **3** judging from. **4** relating to. **5** in comparison with. **6** from. **7** against, except. **8** out of. **9** besides, over and above.

by² *conj* by the time that.

by³, bye *adj* **1** lonely, out-of-the-way. **2** (*in combination with* **up, down, in, near, out, owre**) denoting locality not far off. **3** past. **4** done for. **5** finished off.—*adv* aside, out of the way.

byaak *v* to bake.

byach *int* a meaningless exclamation.

byass *n* bias.

byauch *n* any small living creature.

byauk *same as* **byaak.**

by-bit *n* **1** an extra bit. **2** a snack between meals.

by-blow *n* an illegitimate child.

by-board *n* a side table, a sideboard.

by-body *n* one who procrastinates.

by-comin' *n* passing by.

by-common *adj* extraordinary, out of the common.—*adv* extraordinarily.

by-courting *n* courting on the sly.

by-east *adv* towards the east.

bye-attour *conj* moreover.

bye-days *n* former days.

byehand *adv* over, past.

byeless *adv* unusually, extraordinarily.

by-end *n* **1** a sinister end. **2** a side issue.

byes *same as* **by's.**

by-gaein, ~-ganging, ~-gawn *n* **1** passing by. **2** (*with* **in**) incidentally.

bygane *n* the past.—*adj* past, gone by.

by-gate *n* a byway.

by-hands *adj* **1** casual, accidental. **2** underhand, devious.—*adv* **1** finished, settled. **2** over.

by himself *phr* out of his mind.

by-hours *n* **1** extra time, odd hours. **2** time not allotted to regular work. **3** overtime. **4** leisure hours.

bykat *same as* **beikat.**

byke¹ *same as* **bike¹.**

byke² *n* the nose, the beak.

byke³ *same as* **bike².**

byke⁴ *v* to weep, whine, sob.

byle *n* a boil.

bynall *n* a tall, lame person.

by-name *n* a nickname, sobriquet.

by-neuk *n* an out-of-the-way corner.

by-ocht *adj* used of something almost impossible or inconceivable.

by one's sell *phr* distracted, demented.

by-ordinar' *adj* out of the common.—*adv* extraordinarily.

byous *adj* extraordinary, remarkable.—*adv* very, in a great degree.

byouslie *adv* **1** uncommonly, extraordinarily, remarkably. **2** very.

byoutour *n* a gormandizer, a glutton.

byowtifu' *adj* beautiful.

byowty *n* beauty.

by-pit *n* **1** a makeshift. **2** a slight repast between mealtimes. **3** a pretence. **4** one who procrastinates. **5** a pretender.

by-pitting *adj* **1** procrastinating. **2** pretending.

by random *adv* at random.

byre *n* a cowhouse.

byre-man n the man who attends to farm cattle.

byre time n the time for bringing cows to the byre (qv) for milking etc.

byre-woman n the woman who attends to the cows on a farm.

byruns n arrears.

by's, by'se prep 1 compared with. 2 besides, in addition to.

bysenful adj disgusting.

bysenless adj worthless, shameless.

by-set n a substitute.

by-shot n one who is set aside for an old maid.

by-spell, byspale n 1 one who has become a byword for anything remarkable. 2 an illegitimate child.—adv exceedingly, remarkably.

byssum same as **besom**.

by-stand n a standby.

by-start n a bastard.

by-start-born adj illegitimate.

by-table n a side table, a sideboard.

by-time n extra or leisure time, odd hours.

by-token phr an expression introducing a confirmatory statement.

by-whiles adv now and then, at times.

byword n a proverb, a proverbial saying.

C

ca n a mountain pass, a defile.

ca'[1] n quick, oppressive breathing.

ca'[2] n 1 a call. 2 a summons by voice or instrument. 3 a whistle, pipe. 4 occasion, need, obligation. 5 a passing visit. 6 the right to call on the next performer. 7 the sound of the sea before or after a storm. 8 the call to die. 9 an invitation to be minister of a particular congregation.—v 1 to call, name. 2 to abuse, scold, call names. 3 (with **again**) to contradict, retort. 4 (with **for** or **with**) to pay a visit.

ca'[3] v 1 to drive cattle, vehicles, tools, machinery, etc. 2 to hammer, knock. 3 to overturn. 4 to move rapidly. 5 to submit to be driven. 6 (with **about**) to spread a report, etc.—n a knock. 1 (of water) the motion of waves as driven by the wind. 2 a walk for cattle, a district in which cattle pasture. 3 a drove of sheep. 4 a strip of ground left open for cattle going to a common pasture.

ca'[4] v to calve.—n 1 a calf. 2 a silly, foolish person.

caa'[1] same as **ca'**[2].

caa'[2] same as **ca'**[3].

caaing n 1 the driving of whales into shallow water. 2 a drove of whales. See **ca'**[3].

caaing-whale n the Delphinus deductor.

caak v 1 to cackle as a hen. 2 to talk noisily.

caar same as **car**[3].

caar cake same as **car cake**.

caa-tee n a great disturbance, a driving together, or to and fro, of people.

cab v 1 to pilfer. 2 to snatch by underhand means.

cabal same as **cabble**.

cabarr n a lighter.

cabback n a cheese.

cabbage-daisy n the globeflower.

cabbage-fauld n a place where cabbage is grown.

cabber n an old lean horse.

cabbie n a box made of laths, which claps close to a horse's side and is narrow at the top to prevent the corn in it from being spilled.

cabble n 1 a violent dispute.—v 1 to quarrel. 2 to dispute. 3 to find fault with.

cabbrach adj 1 rapacious. 2 lean.—n 1 lean meat. 2 meat unfit for use. 3 a disagreeable person as to temper and manners. 4 a big, uncouth, greedy person.

cabbrach, cabrach-sweetie n a box on the ears.

cabelow n salted fish.

caber, cabre[1] n 1 a large, heavy pole for tossing at athletic contests. 2 a beam. 3 a rafter. 4 a large stick. 5 (in pl) the small wood laid on the rafters under the roofing. 6 the transverse beams on a kiln, on which grain is laid for drying. 7 the thinnings of young plantations.

cabre[2] same as **cabber**.

cabroch, cabrach same as **cabbrach**.

cache v to shake, knock about.—n a shake, jog.

cack v (used of children) to void excrement.—n human excrement.

cacker n 1 the calker of a horseshoe. 2 the iron shod of a clog or shoe.

cackie v to cack (qv).—n (in pl) human excrement.

cacuana n ipecacuana.

ca'd[1] v called.

ca'd[2] v 1 drove. 2 driven.

caddel n caudle, a warm drink.

caddie n 1 a cadet. 2 an errand boy. 3 a street porter. 4 a young fellow. 5 a golfer's attendant.

caddis n 1 shreds. 2 rags. 3 cotton wool. 4 surgeon's lint. 5 a pledget.

caddle[1] n 1 a set of four cherry stones in the game of papes (qv). 2 a couple of cherry stones.

caddle[2] v to move violently.—n a disordered, broken mass.—adv in a disordered, broken mass.

cadge[1] v 1 to shake roughly. 2 to knock about.—n a shake, jog.

cadge[2] v to carry.

cadgell v to carry roughly.—n a wanton fellow, a rake.

cadger n 1 a carrier. 2 a person of disagreeable temper.

cadger-like adj like a carrier.

cadger-pownie n a huckster's pony.

cadgie, cadgey adj 1 merry, sportive. 2 wanton. 3 in good spirits. 4 kind and hospitable.—adv gaily, happily, cheerfully.

cadgily adv gaily, merrily, happily.

cadgin adj having a jolting motion.—n the act of being jolted.

cadgy adj jolting.

cadie[1] same as **caddie**.

cadie[2] n a hat.

cadie[3] n a tea caddy.

cadis same as **caddis**.

caducity n (used as a legal term) the falling of a feu (qv) to a superior in irritancy.

caern n a very small quantity, a curn (qv).

caew v 1 to knead dough. 2 to mix clay, etc.

ca'f same as **calf**[2]

caff[1] n chaff.

caff[2] v to buy. See **caft**.

caff bed n 1 a chaff bed. 2 a mattress filled with chaff.

cafle same as **cavel**[3].

ca'f's lick n a lock of hair rising up on the head.

caft v bought. See **caff**.

ca'f-ward n an enclosure for calves.

cag[1] n a keg.

cag[2] v to annoy, vex, offend, grieve.

cagey, cagie same as **cadgie**.

cagily same as **cadgily**.

cahow, cahoo int the call of those who hide themselves to the seeker in the game of hide-and-seek, to let him or her know to begin the search. —n the game of hide-and-seek.

cahute n the cabin of a ship.

caib n iron used in making a spade or any such tool.

caich v to jolt.

caidge v to wanton.

caidgie same as **cadgie**.

caidgieness n 1 wantonness. 2 gaiety. 3 sportiveness. 4 affectionate kindness.

caif adj 1 tame. 2 familiar.

caige same as **caidge**.

caigh n in phr **caigh and care** every kind of anxiety.

caik n a stitch or sharp pain in the side.

caikal n a hungry worm supposed to lodge in the intestine and produce a voracious appetite.

caikie n 1 a gawky. 2 a foolish, silly person.

caikle v 1 to cackle. 2 to chuckle. 3 to recover one's spirits. 4 to become eager.—n 1 a chuckle. 2 noisy laughter. 3 loud chatter. 4 idle, foolish talk. 5 cackle.

cail n colewort.

cailleach, cailliach n an old woman.

caim same as **cam**.

caime n a comb.

cain[1] n 1 the cheese made by a farmer during the season. 2 300 stones of cheese.

cain[2] n 1 part or whole of a rent paid in kind by a farmer. 2 a penalty.

Cain-and-Abel n the *Orchis latifolia.*

cain-bairn n a child supposed to be paid as tribute to the fairies or to the devil.

cain cock, ~ fowl, ~ hen n a fowl given in part-payment of rent.

cain rent n the rent or part of it paid in kind.

caip same as **cape**[1].

caipe v to caper.—n a caper.

caipercaillie same as **capercailzie**.

caipstane same as **capestane**.

cair[1] v 1 to toss to and fro. 2 to stir about. 3 to mix. 4 to rake from the bottom the thickest of soup, etc. 5 to try to catch by raking from the bottom. 6 to handle overmuch. 7 to search for among dust, ashes, etc.—n 1 the act of extracting the thickest of soup, etc, at the bottom of a dish. 2 much handling.

cair[2] adj 1 left. 2 left-handed.

cairban n the basking shark.

cair-cleuck n the left hand.

caird[1] n 1 a travelling tinker. 2 a gipsy, tramp. 3 a sturdy beggar.

caird[2] n 1 a calling card. 2 a photograph of card-size. 3 a playing card.

caird[3] v 1 to card wool. 2 to scold, abuse.—n 1 a comb for dressing wool, made of wires set in leather. 2 a rude, scolding person.

cairder[1] n a card-player.

cairder[2] n a wool-carder.

cardin'-mill n a carding mill.

cairdy n a wool-carder.

cair-handit adj left-handed.

cairie n the motion of the clouds in stormy weather.

cairlin same as **carlin**.

cairn n 1 a loose pile of stones. 2 a conical heap of stones. 3 a tumulus. 4 a ruined building. 5 a heap of rubbish. 6 a high hill.

cairn-tangle n the fingered fucus, sea girdle.

cairn-tombed adj (used of a chieftain) buried under a cairn (qv).

cairny adj abounding in cairns.

cairriet adj 1 carried. 2 light-headed. 3 excited. 4 flighty. 5 flirting.

cairt[1] n a cart.

cairt[2], **cairte** same as **caird**[2].

cairter[1] n a carter.

cairter[2] n a card-player.

cairts n a game of cards.

cairt-sheuch n a cart track or rut.

cait same as **cate**.

caithie n a large-headed fish, *Lophius piscatorum.*

caition same as **caution**.

caiver v 1 to waver in mind. 2 to be incoherent.

cake n 1 a thin, hard cake of oatmeal. 2 oilcake for feeding cattle.

caker n a stroke on the palm of the hand from the tawse (qv).

cakker n 1 the hinder part of a horseshoe sharpened and turned downwards to prevent slipping. 2 the iron rim or plate on a wooden clog or shoe heel.

calamy, calomy n calomel.

calavin n a lead pencil.

calaw n 1 the pintail-duck. 2 the long-tailed duck.

calchen n a square wooden frame, like a gridiron, in which fir candles were dried in the chimney.

cald adj 1 cold. 2 dry in manner, unkind, repellent.—n a cold.

caldrife adj 1 giving the sensation of cold, chilly. 2 susceptible to cold. 3 indifferent, cool, reserved. 4 (used of a sermon or a preacher) not interesting, delivered in a cold fashion, not rousing.

calender n a mangle.

caley n gossip, chat.

calf[1] same as **colf**.

calf[2] n 1 a simpleton. 2 a stupid, silly person. 3 a term of ridicule.

calf-country, ~-ground n native place.

calf-drukken adj as fond as calves of drinking milk.

calfin same as **colfin**.

calf-lea n infield ground, one year under natural grass.

calf-reed n rennet.

calf-skins n 1 the sea ruffled by the wind in occasional spots. 2 'cat's paws'.

calf-sod n sward bearing fine grass.

calf stick n a stick for driving cattle or calves.

calf-ward n a small enclosure for feeding calves.

calimanco n calamanco.

calk same as **cauk**.

calker same as **cauker**.

call same as **ca'**[2]

callack n a young girl.

callan, callant n 1 a stripling, a lad, a term of affection. 2 a girl (rarely).

calledin-o'-the-blade n phr a slight shower which cools and refreshes grass.

caller, callour adj 1 fresh, not stale, newly caught or gathered, in proper season. 2 cool, refreshing, bracing.—v 1 to cool, freshen, refresh.

callet n a prostitute, concubine.

callet[1] n a woman's cap without a border.

callet[2] n the head.

callevine n a lead pencil.

callion n anything old and ugly.

call-me-to-you n phr the heart's-ease.

callot same as **callet**.

calloused adj callous, hard-hearted.

call-the-guse n a kind of game.

calm[1] adj (used of ice) smooth, even.

calm[2] same as **caulm**[1].

calmes n the small cords through which the warp is passed in the loom.

calm sough n silence, quietness, saying little.

calourie n cockweed.

calsay n the causeway, street.

calsay-paiker n a street-walker.

calse maill n 1 road-money. 2 tolls.

calsh adj same as **calshie**.

calshes n a slip-dress buttoned behind and forming jacket and trousers for young boys and vest and trousers for older ones.

calshie, calshich adj crabbed, ill-humoured, rude.

calumnie v to calumniate.

calver n a cow in calf or that has calved.

cam[1] n a small peninsula terminating on the beach and connected with the cliff by a narrow, low isthmus.

cam[2] v came.

cam[3] n whitening.—v to whiten a hearth.

camack *same as* **cammock**.
camaled *adj* (*used of a scythe*) turned on the edge.
cambie leaf *n* the white water lily, *Nymphaea alba*.
camble *v* **1** to prate saucily. **2** to scold, bully.
camblet *n* camlet.
Cambuslang marble *n* a calcareous stratum near Rutherglen and Cambuslang.
camdootshie *adj* sagacious.
camdui *n* a species of trout.
came *n* **1** a honeycomb. **2** a comb.
camel's-hair *n* the vertebral ligament.
cameral¹ *n* a spawned haddock.
cameral², cameril *n* a large, ill-shaped, awkward person.
camerick *n* cambric.
camester *n* a wool-comber.
camla-like *adj* sullen, surly.
cammag *n* a short staff with a crooked head.
cammas *n* a coarse cloth.
cammel *n* a crooked piece of wood used as a hook for hanging things on.
cammelt *adj* crooked.
cammeril *n* a butcher's gambrel.
cammock, cammok, cammon *n* **1** a curved stick used in playing hockey or shinty. **2** the game of shinty.
camovine, camowyne *n* camomile.
camp¹ *n* a heap of potatoes, turnips, etc, covered with earth through winter.
camp² *adj* brisk, active, spirited.—*n* a romp.—*v* **1** to play the romp. **2** to contend. **3** to strive to outstrip in the harvest field.
campagne, campaine *adj* suited or belonging to the country.
campaine hat *n* a hat for country wear.
campaine shoes *n* shoes for country wear.
campaine wig *n* a wig for country wear.
campesce *same as* **compesce**.
campruly *adj* quarrelsome.
campsho *adj* distorted, crooked.
campy *adj* spirited.—*n* a smart young fellow.
camrel *n* a butcher's gambrel.
camshach *adj* **1** crooked, distorted. **2** cross-grained, ill-tempered. **3** stern-faced. **4** unlucky.
camshachle, camschacle, camshacle *v* **1** to distort, pull askew. **2** to upset. **3** disorder.—*adj* **1** involved, intricate. **2** confused.
camshack *same as* **camshach**.
camshak-kair *n* an unlucky concern.
camshauchle, camshaucle *v* **1** to distort. **2** to be angry. **3** to be difficult to repeat. **4** to walk inactively or lamely.
camsheuch, camschol *same as* **camshach**.
camstane *n* **1** common compact limestone. **2** indurated white clay. **3** pipeclay, whitening. **4** coarse fuller's earth.
camstairical *adj* camstairy (qv).
cainstairiness *n* obstinacy, perversity.
camstairy, camstairie, camstairy, camsteary, camsteerie, camsteery, camsterie, camstrary *adj* wild, unmanageable, obstinate, riotous.—*n* an obstinate, unmanageable person.
camstrudgeous *adj* wild, unmanageable, camstairy (qv).
can¹ *n* **1** a cup. **2** a broken piece of earthenware.
can² *n* **1** skill, knowledge. **2** ability. **3** cleverness. **4** intuitive knowledge
canage *n* payment of cain-duty. *See* **cain²**.
canailyie, canalyie *n* a rabble, a mob.
cancer¹ *n* the red campion.
cancer² *n* the burying beetle.
canch *n* a breadth of digging land.
candavaig *n* **1** a foul salmon that has lain in fresh water till summer, without going to the sea. **2** a peculiar species of salmon.
candel-bend *n* very thick sole-leather used for ploughmen's boots, such as was picked and tanned at Kendal.
candle, can'le *n in phr* **can'le and castock** a turnip lantern with a face formed by blacking on the outside.

candle coal *n* **1** parrot coal. **2** a piece of splint coal put on a cottage fire to give light to spin by.
candle doup *n* a candle end.
candle fir *n* bog fir or moss-fallen fir, split and used for candles.
candle futtle, ~ gullie *n* a large knife for splitting up bog fir for candles.
Candlemas, Can'lemas *n* Scottish quarter day, 2 February.
Candlemas ba' *n* a football match played at Candlemas.
Candlemas bleeze *n* **1** a gift formerly made by pupils to their schoolmaster at Candlemas. **2** a bonfire on the evening of 2 February.
Candlemas crown *n* a badge of distinction formerly given at some schools to the pupil giving the highest gratuity to the master at Candlemas.
Candlemas king, ~ queen *n* the boy and the girl giving the highest gratuity to the schoolmaster.
Candlemas offering *n* the gift formerly made by pupils to their teacher at Candlemas.
Candlemas silver *n* the Candlemas offering.
candle shears *n* a pair of snuffers.
candle whittle *n* a candle futtle (qv).
candy-broad sugar *n* lump sugar.
candy glue *n* candy made from treacle, etc, well boiled.
candyman *n* a seller or hawker of candy.
candy rock *n* candy in blocks or stalks.
cane *same as* **cain²**.
canech *same as* **cannagh**.
cangle *v* **1** to quarrel, wrangle. **2** to bandy words. **3** to cavil. **4** to find fault with. **5** to show displeasure. **6** to haggle.
cangler *n* a jangler, a caviller.
cangling *n* altercation, quarrelling.
canker *v* **1** to fret, become peevish or ill-humoured. **2** to put into a bad temper. **3** to render cross, to sour. **4** (*of plants*) to be covered with blight. **5** (*of the weather*) to become stormy.—*n* bad temper. **6** a corroding care.
canker-nail *n* a painful slip of flesh at the base of a finger-nail.
cankersome *adj* cross-grained, bad-tempered.
cankert, cankered *adj* **1** cross, ill-humoured, fretful. **2** (*of a sore*) inflamed, festered. **3** (*of the weather*) threatening, gusty.
cankert-leukin *adj* (*of a sore*) **1** inflamed, painful. **2** (*of persons*) having a sour, unkind expression. **3** (*of weather*) threatening, lowering.
cankert-like *adj* **1** cross-looking. **2** threatening in appearance.
cankertly *adv* ill-naturedly, crossly.
cankery *adj* **1** bad-tempered. **2** eating like a cancer.
cankling *adj* quarrelsome, wrangling.
cankrif *adj* cankering.
cank'rous *adj* sore, painful.
cankry *same as* **cankery**.
canlie *n* a boys' game, of the nature of chase or tig.
cann *same as* **can²**.
canna¹, cannae *v neg* cannot.
canna², cannach *n* the cotton grass.
canna-down *n* the cotton grass.
cannagh *n* the pip in fowls.
cannalye *same as* **canailyie**.
cannas, cannes *n* **1** coarse canvas. **2** sailcloth, the sail of a ship. **3** a coarse sheet used for keeping grain from falling to the ground when winnowed in a sieve.
cannas-braid *n* the breadth of such a sheet.
canneca *n* the woodworm.
cannel¹ *n* the sloping edge of an axe or chisel.—*v* **1** to bevel the edge of a knife, etc. **2** to chamfer.
cannel² *n* cinnamon.
cannel³ *n* a candle.
cannel water *n* cinnamon water.
canniburr, canniber *n* the sea urchin.
cannie *same as* **canny**.
cannie nail *n* the nail that holds the cart body to the axle.

cannies *same as* **cannas**.

cannily *adv* cautiously, craftily, skilfully, gently, frugally, quietly, easily.

canniness *n* the possession of canny qualities. *See* **canny**.

cannon nail *n* the cannie nail.

canny, cannie *adj* **1** cautious, prudent, shrewd. **2** artful, crafty, dexterous. **3** careful, frugal, sparing in the use of. **4** moderate in charges, conduct, spirit. **5** not extortionate, hard or exacting. **6** gentle, useful, beneficial. **7** handy, expert, skilful in midwifery. **8** gentle in using the hands or the tongue. **9** soft, easy, slow in action or motion. **10** safe, not dangerous. **11** composed, deliberate, not flustered. **12** not difficult of execution. **13** snug, comfortable, cosy. **14** fortunate, lucky, of good omen, from a superstitious point of view. **15** favourable. **16** endowed with supposed supernatural knowledge or magical skill. **17** good, worthy, douce (qv). **18** convenient, well-fitted. **19** comely, agreeable, pleasant. **20** used as a general term of affection, goodwill and approbation.—*adv* **1** cautiously. **2** gently.

cannyca *same as* **canneca**.

canny moment *n* the moment of birth.

canny nannie *n* a kind of bumblebee.

canny noo *int* take it easy!

canny wife *n* a midwife.

canny wyes *adv* cannily. *See* **canny**.

canopy *n* a sofa, couch.

canse *v* to speak pertly and conceitedly.

canshie *adj* cross, ill-humoured.

cansie *adj* pert, speaking from self-conceit.

cant[1] *v* **1** to sing. **2** to speak in recitative. **3** to talk cheerfully, gossip.—*n* **1** gossip, tattle. **2** speaking in recitative.

cant[2] *n* a jerk, a turn to one side.—*v* **1** to set a stone on edge. **2** to upset.

cant[3] *v* to canter.

cant[4] *n* an illusion.

cant[5] *n* **1** a trick, a bad habit. **2** a custom.

cant[6] *n* a little rise of rocky ground on a highway.

cantation *n* talk, conversation.

canter *n* a plausible beggar.

cantily *adv* cheerfully, merrily.

canting *n* a sale by auction.

cantle[1] *n* **1** a triangular piece. **2** a slice. **3** the leg of a lamb or other young animal. **4** the crown of the head.

cantle[2] *v* **1** to tilt up, to fall over. **2** to set aloft, to perch up. **3** (*with* **up**) to brighten up. **4** to recover health or spirits.

cantlin *n* **1** a corner. **2** the chine of a cask or adze.

canton *n* an angle.—*v* to divide, distribute.

cantraip, cantrip *n* **1** a magic spell, incantation, charm. **2** witch's trick. **3** any trick, frolic, piece of mischief.—*adj* magical, witch-like.

cantraps *n* caltrops.

cant-robin *n* the dwarf wild rose, with white flowers.

canty[1] *adj* **1** lively. **2** pleasant, cheerful. **3** small and neat. **4** in good health.—*adv* contentedly, merrily.

canty[2] *n* a hole in the game of kypes (qv) played with marbles.

canty-smatchet *n* a louse.

canvas *v* to ponder, think over.

canyel *v* **1** to jolt. **2** to cause a jolt.—*n* **1** a jolt. **2** jolting.

cap[1] *n* **1** the comb of wild bees. **2** the top put on a beehive in order to get the combs.

cap[2] *n* a wooden cup or bowl.

cap[3] *v* **1** to outdo, crown, surpass. **2** to take off the hat or cap in saluting. **3** to confer a degree at a Scottish university.—*n* the lifting of the cap in saluting.

cap[4] *v* **1** to seize by violence what belongs to another. **2** to act piratically or as a privateer.

cap[5] *v* **1** to bulge. **2** to twist, warp.

cap[6] *v* to take possession of anything used in play out of season.

cap ale *n* a beer between table beer and ale.

cap ambry *n* a cupboard for holding small wooden cups.

cap and knee *phr* humbly and gratefully.

cape[1] *n* **1** the highest part of anything. **2** coping of a wall or house.—*v* to put on the cover of a roof or wall.

cape[2] *same as* **cap**[4].

caped *adj* (*of a ship*) taken by a pirate.

caper[1] *n* **1** a captor, one who takes a prize. **2** a privateer, a pirate.

caper[2] *n* a piece of buttered oatcake with a slice of cheese on it.

caper[3] *v* to frisk, dance.

capercailzie *n* the wood grouse or mountain cock.

caperer *n* bread, butter and cheese toasted together.

caperilla, caperoilie *n* the heath pea.

caper-lintie *n* the whitethroat.

capernodgus *adj* discontented.

capernoited *adj* **1** peevish, irritable. **2** under the influence of drink. **3** imbecile. **4** whimsical.

capernoitet-looking *adj* peevish-looking.

capernoitetness *n* perversity, obstinacy.

capernoitie[1] *n* the head.

capernoitie[2] *adj* peevish.

capernuted *same as* **capernoited**.

capernuitie *same as* **capernoited**.

caperonish *adj* (*used of food*) good, excellent, first-rate.

capes *n* **1** grains of corn to which the chaff adheres after threshing. **2** grain insufficiently ground or where the shell remains with part of the grain. **3** flakes of meal which come from the mill when the grain has not been properly dried.

capestane *n* **1** a copestone. **2** a remediless calamity.

capey-dykey *n* a game of marbles.

cap-full *n* the fourth of a peck.

capidocious *adj* capital, first-rate.

caple-dosie *n* a hairy cap.

caple-hole *n* the game of marbles, kypes (qv).

capilation *n* **1** drugget. **2** a cheap and light stuff.

capilow *v* to outdo another in reaping.

caping *n* privateering.

capitane *n* captain.

cap-neb *n* an iron plate on the toe of a boot.

capon *n* in phr **a crail capon** a dried haddock.

cap out *v* to drink to the bottom.—*n* the act of so drinking.

capper[1] *n* **1** a cup-bearer. **2** a turner of wooden bowls or caps. *See* **cap**[2].

capper[2] *n* copper.

capper[3] *n* a spider.

capper[4] *n* part of a shoemaker's tools for toe caps, etc.

capper[5] *v* **1** to seize ships, privateer. **2** to lay hold of forcibly.—*n* a privateer.

capper[6] *n* a late riser, one who has to make the best of what remains in the porridge cap at breakfast. *See* **cap**[2].

cappernishious *adj* **1** short-tempered. **2** perpetually fault-finding.

capper-nosed *adj* having a copper-coloured nose.

cappid *adj* **1** fickle. **2** flighty. **3** whimsical.

cappie *n* a beer between ale and table beer, drunk out of caps. *See* **cap**[2].

capple[1] *adj* **1** cup-shaped. **2** hollow.

capple[2] *n* **1** a small cap. **2** a drinking cup.

capple[3] *adj* given to warping, like green wood.

capple-out *n* **1** deep drinking. **2** drinking to the bottom.

cappilow *same as* **capilow**.

cappin *n* the leather or wood band through which the middle band of a flail passes.

cappit[1] *adj* twisted, bent, warped.

cappit[2] *adj* **1** crabbed, ill-humoured. **2** quarrelsome. **3** short-tempered.

caprowsy *n* a short cloak with a hood.

cap-sheaf *n* **1** a sheaf covering a stook (qv) in wet weather. **2** straw forming the top of a thatched rick or roof. **3** the finishing touch.

capshon *n* a windfall, prize.

capstane *n* copestone.

cap-stride *v* **1** to forestall another in drinking as the cap goes round (*see* **cap**[2]). **2** to cheat.

captain *n* the grey gurnard.

caption *n* **1** arrest, apprehension. **2** *in phr* **horning and caption** an order requiring a debtor to pay his debt on pain of being declared a rebel. **3** a lucky, valuable or serviceable acquisition. **4** a windfall.

captivity *n* waste, destruction.

car¹ *n* calves.

car² *n* **1** a sledge. **2** a cart wanting wheels, ledges, sides and front.

car³ *adj* **1** left, left-handed. **2** sinister. **3** fatal.

carameile *n* the root of the heath-pea.

carb¹ *v* to cavil, carp.—*n* cavilling, carping, dissatisfaction.

carb² *n* a raw-boned, loquacious woman.

carberry *v* to wrangle, to argue perversely.

carbin¹ *same as* **cairban**.

carbin² *adj* fretful, peevish.

carble *v* **1** to cavil, carp, show dissatisfaction. **2** to be captious.

carbling *n* a wrangling.

car-, care cake *n* a small cake, baked with eggs, eaten on Fastern's E'en.

carcant *n* a garland of flowers for the neck.

carcase, carcatch *n* the trunk of the human body.

carcidge *n* a carcass.

car-cleugh *n* the left hand.

carcudeuch *same as* **curcuddoch**.

card¹, **card**² *same as* **caird**², **caird**³.

cardecue *n* a silver coin.

carder *n* a card-player.

carding *n* a scolding.

carding *n* card-playing.

cardow *same as* **curdow**.

cardower *n* a mender of old clothes.

cardin *n* a rare trout found in Loch Leven.

care *same as* **cair**¹.

care² *v* **1** to care for, regard. **2** (*with neg*) to have no objection. **3** (*with neg and* **by**) to be indifferent, to take no interest in.

care³ *n* **1** *in phr* **care's my case** woeful is my plight. **2** *phr* **to take care of** to refuse.

care-bed *n* a bed of suffering.

care-bed-lair *n* **1** a bed of suffering. **2** a disconsolate situation.

careerin *adv* **1** swiftly. **2** cheerfully.

careful *adj* careworn.

care-weeds *n* mourning garb.

carf *n* **1** a cut in timber for the insertion of another piece of wood. **2** the incision made by an axe or a saw.

carfin *n* the basking shark.

carfuddle *v* **1** to discompose. **2** to rumple.

carfuffle¹ *same as* **curfuffle**.

carfuffle² *n* a contemptuous designation of a person.

carfumish *n* **1** to diffuse a very bad smell. **2** to overpower by a bad smell.

cargliff *same as* **curglaff**.

carhail *v* to hail in a bantering manner.

car-handed *adj* left-handed.

carie *adj* **1** soft, pliable. **2** lazy.

carin' *adj* causing care or pain.

cark *v* **1** to fret. **2** to complain peevishly.

carket *n* a garland of flowers worn as a necklace.

carknet *n* a carcanet, a necklace.

carking *adj* anxious, fretting.

carl¹, **carle** *n* **1** a man. **2** a clown, boor in manners, a churl. **3** an old man.

carl², **carle** *n* **1** a carol. **2** a gift to carol-singers at Christmas. **3** a licentious song.

carl-again *v* to resist, to return a stroke, to retort. —*n* **1** a retort. **2** the return of a stroke. **3** tit for tat.

carlage *same as* **carlish**.

carl-and-cavel *phr* **1** honest man and rogue. **2** all without distinction.

carl-cat *n* a tom cat.

carl-crab *n* the male of the black-clawed crab.

carl-doddy *n* **1** a stalk of ribgrass. **2** the greater plantain. **3** a term of endearment.

carle *n* a tall rustic candlestick.

carled *adj* (*used of a bitch*) served by a dog.

carl-gropus *n* a stupid person.

carl-hemp *n* **1** the largest stalk of hemp. **2** mental vigour, firmness.

carlie *n* **1** a little man. **2** a precocious boy.

carlin, carline *n* **1** an old woman. **2** a shrew, hag. **3** a witch. **4** a man, an old man. **5** the last handful of corn cut in a field, when it is not shorn before Hallowmas.

carling *n* the name of a fish, perhaps the pogge.

carlin'-heather *n* fine-leaved heath, bell heather.

carlin's *n* brown peas boiled or broiled, eaten on the fifth Sunday in Lent.

Carlin's E'en *n* the last night of the year.

carlin'-spurs *n* needle furze or petty whin.

Carlin Sunday *n* the fifth Sunday in Lent, Passion Sunday.

carlin-teuch *adj* sturdy, tough as an old wife.

carlish, carlitch *adj* **1** churlish, boorish. **2** rustic, clownish.

carl-tangle *n* a large, long tangle with tree-like roots.

carl-wife *n* a man who concerns himself with household matters.

carmalade *adj* sick, diseased.

carmele *n* the root of the heath pea.

carmovine *same as* **camovine**.

carmud *same as* **curmud**.

carmudgelt *adj* made soft by lightning.

carmudgeon *n* **1** a curmudgeon. **2** a forward child.

carnaptious *same as* **curnaptious**.

carnawin *same as* **curnawing**.

carneed *n* a pig.

carnock pear *n* a kind of pear.

carn-tangle *same as* **cairn-tangle**.

carnwath, carnwath-like *adj* **1** awkward-looking. **2** boorish. **3** rustic.—*adv* out of line.

Carol-ewyn *n* the last night of the year, when young people go from door to door carol-singing.

caroline hat *n* a black hat, fashionable towards the end of the 17th century.

carp *v* **1** to talk. **2** to recite as a minstrel, sing.

car-pawed *adj* left-handed.

carpets *n* carpet slippers or shoes.

carrant *same as* **courant**.

carreen *v* to lean to one side.

carr gate *n* a road across steep rocks.

carribine *n* a carbine.

carrick¹ *n* **1** the game of shinty or hockey. **2** the ball played with.

carrick² *n* a crag.

carrickin' *n* a gathering of herd boys to play shinty at Lammas, 1 August.

carrie *n* a two-wheeled barrow.

carried *adj* **1** light-headed, delirious. **2** conceited.

carrie-elt *n* a thick, badly baked oat bannock.

carrier *n* *in phr* **come back with the blind carrier** to return, if ever, after a very long time.

carrion *n* a term of reproach to a person.

carrion-corp *n* a dead body.

carris *n* flummery.

carritch *v* to catechize.—*n* **1** a catechism. **2** (*in pl*) the Shorter Catechism. **3** reproof. **4** scolding.

carritch'd *adj* taught the Shorter Catechism.

carrot-pow *n* a head of red hair.

carry¹ *adj* left, as opposed to right.

carry ²*adj* (*used of oatmeal*) badly baked.

carry³ *v* (*used of land*) to provide food for farm stock.—*n* **1** the bulk or weight of a burden, what is carried. **2** the motion of wind-driven clouds. **3** the sky. **4** the distance anything is carried.

carry coals *v phr* to submit to indignity.

carrying on n **1** unseemly behaviour. **2** undue familiarity.

carry-my-lady-to-London n a children's game.

carry on v **1** to behave strangely or improperly. **2** to do or to speak anything at a great rate. **3** to flirt. **4** to scold continuously.—n **1** proceedings. **2** flirtation. **3** unbecoming behaviour. **4** fuss.

carry-out n **1** alcohol purchased from licensed premises for drinking elsewhere. **2** food bought from a restaurant, etc, for consumption off the premises.

carry-warry n **1** a charivari. **2** a burlesque serenade.

carry-wattle n a general 'scrimmage' or wordy conflict.

carsackie n **1** a workman's coarse apron. **2** a woman's bedgown or loose working dress.

car-saddle n the small saddle on the back of a carriage horse to support the shafts.

carse[1] n the watercress.

carse[2], **carse-land** n a stretch of flat, fertile land near a river.

carseese v **1** to examine strictly, catechize. **2** to reprove.— n **1** a reproof. **2** a strict examination

car-sham-ye int an exclamation in the game of shinty when one of the players strikes the ball with the club in his left hand.

carsons[1] n the lady's mantle.

carsons[2] n pl the watercress.

carstang n the shaft of a cart.

cart n a map, chart.

cart-aver n a carthorse.

carte n a playing card.

Carters'-play n a yearly procession of the Carters' Society.

cart gate n a cart road.

carthanum n the carthamine or safflower.

cartie n a small cart.

cartil n a cartload.

cartouch n **1** jacket worn by women when working. **2** a little frock for a girl.

cartow n **1** a great cannon. **2** a battering piece.

cart-piece n an ancient kind of ordnance.

cart-tram n the shaft of a cart.

carvey, carvie n **1** caraway. **2** a confection containing caraway.

carvey seed n caraway seed.

carvey sweetie n caraway coated with sugar.

ca's[1] v calls.

ca's[2] v drives.

case[1] n shape, repair, size.—v to shut up, confine.

case[2] n phr **case-alike 1** all the same. **2** lest, in case.

caseable, casable adj **1** natural. **2** naturally belonging to a particular case. **3** possible.

casements n carpenters' planes called hollows and rounds.

caserrin n **1** a crook-handled spade, used by Highlanders. **2** a kind of foot plough.

cashhornie n a game played with clubs by two opposite parties, who each try to drive a ball into a hole belonging to their antagonists.

cashie[1] adj **1** delicate. **2** easily tired. **3** soft, flabby, spongy. **4** luxuriant, succulent. **5** of rapid growth.

cashie[2] adj **1** talkative. **2** forward.

cashle v to squabble.—n a squabble.

cashlick adj careless, regardless.

caspicaws, caspie-laws, caspitaws n an obsolete instrument of torture.

cass v (a legal term) to annul, make void, repeal.

cassedone n chalcedony.

cassen v cast.

cast[1] n **1** a twist. **2** opportunity, a turn, event. **3** lot, fate, chance. **4** a casual lift, ride or help on a journey. **5** help, assistance. **6** the cutting of a certain quantity of peats. **7** a swarm of bees. **8** a handful of herrings, haddocks, oysters, etc, four in number. **9** a district, tract of country. **10** the direction in which one travels. **11** appearance, style, slight likeness. **12** a degree. **13** touch, little. **14** a throw of a fishing line. **15** the earth thrown up by moles, etc.

16 an earthen mound as fence or boundary. **17** (of scales) the turn. **18** some mental power.

cast[2] v **1** to put on, scatter, sprinkle. **2** to toss the head. **3** to throw on the back. **4** to thwart, defeat. **5** to condemn in an action at law. **6** (used of clothes) to throw off, discard. **7** (of hair, teeth, etc) to shed, cast off. **8** (of cows) to abort. **9** (of soil) to bear crops that do not ripen. **10** (of bees) to swarm. **11** (of colour) to fade, become pale. **12** to vomit. **13** to dig, or cut, and cast up with a spade. **14** to add up, compute. **15** to estimate the quantity of grain in a stack by counting the sheaves. **16** to ponder, consider. **17** to warp, twist. **18** to coat with lime or plaster. **19** to tie a knot. **20** (used of clouds or sky) to clear after rain or at dawn, to gather, to threaten rain. **21** to beat up eggs for puddings, etc, to drop their whites into water for divination. **22** to foretell events, divine. **23** (with about) to plan, look about for, manage, arrange for. **24** (with at) to spurn. **25** to object to, find fault with. **26** (with by) to make oneself ill. **27** (with out) to quarrel. **28** (with up) to call to remembrance and upbraid for some past fault, misfortune, etc. **29** to throw up scum. **30** to discontinue, renounce. **31** to occur, to come accidentally in one's way, turn up. **32** to befall. **33** to vomit.

cast[3] v, adj **1** prematurely born, aborted. **2** rejected as faulty. **3** worthless, inadmissible.

castan n the estimating of the quantity of grain in a stack.

castawa' n a person or thing neglected or rejected as useless.

cast-by n what is thrown aside as unserviceable.

casten v, adj **1** (used of meat, etc) spoilt, worthless. **2** thrown aside.

casten-awa' n anything thrown away as worthless.

caster n a peat-cutter.

caster hat n a beaver hat.

cast-ewe n a ewe not fit for breeding.

casting[1] adj applied to land on which crops fail to ripen.

casting[2] n **1** rough-casting. **2** the swarming of bees. **3** a quantity of peats. **4** the cutting of peats.

casting-out n a quarrel.

castings n cast-off clothes.

casting stone n the stone by which a setline is cast into a river.

casting-up n taunting, recalling the past, reminding unpleasantly.

castle n four cherry stones in the game of paips (qv).

castle-waird n castle defence.

cast line n a fishing line.

castock n the stem of colewort or cabbage.

cast-of-corn n as many oats as a kiln will dry at a time, perhaps six bushels.

cast-out n a quarrel.

cast-up n **1** a taunt. **2** an unpleasant reminder. **3** a reproach.

cast weeds n perennial weeds growing on beanstalks.

casual adj accidental from mistake or ignorance.

casualty n an incidental payment or duty.

cat n **1** a ball or piece of wood used in certain games. **2** the stick used to strike the cat in such games. **3** soft clay mixed with straw, used in building mud walls and thrust between the laths and the walls. **4** a handful of straw or reaped grain simply laid on the ground. **5** a small piece of rag rolled up and put between the handle of a pot and the hook that suspends it over the fire in order to raise the pot a little. **6** a small lump of manure.—v to toss or strike a ball or cat with the hand or a light bat in certain games.

ca't[1] v **1** drove. **2** driven.

ca't[2] v called.

cat and clay n a method of building mud in walls, etc, by thrusting soft clay mixed with straw between the laths and the walls and afterwards daubing or plastering it.

cat-and-dog n a boys' game played by three.

cat-and-dog-hole n the hole towards which the cat (qv) is thrown in the game of cat-and-dog.

catastrophes *n* fragments, pieces.

catband *n* **1** an iron bar or band for securing a door or gate, hooked into a staple at one end and locked at the other. **2** a strong hook fixed to the wall and inside a door or gate to keep it shut. **3** a chain across a street for defence in war.

cat-bar *n* a bar that fastens that half of a door which does not contain the lock.

cat-beds *n* a children's game, played with pieces of turf.

catch *n* **1** an acquisition. **2** a most eligible husband or wife, a good matrimonial match. **3** a knack, the trick of a thing. **4** a sudden pain or stitch. **5** the sneck (qv) of a door, etc. **6** a stumble. **7** a sudden surprise.

catched *v* caught.

catch-honours *n* a card game.

catchie[1] *adj* **1** merry, jocund. **2** attracting one's interest, liking, etc.

catchie[2] *n* a mason's small hammer for pinning walls.

catch match *n* a match of great advantage to one side.

catch-rogue *n* goosegrass.

catcht *v* caught.

catch-the-lang-tens *n* a card game.

catch-the-plack *n* money-grubbing.

catch-the-salmon *n* a boys' game, played with a piece of rope.

catch-the-ten *n* a card game.

catch-the-thief *n* a constable.

catchy *adj* **1** disposed to take unfair advantage. **2** quick at taking the catch. **3** uncertain, unsettled. **4** irritable. **5** ready to take offence.

cate *v* (*used of cats*) to desire the male.

catechis *n* **1** a catechism. **2** the Shorter Catechism.

category *n* a list or class of accused persons.

cater[1] *n* money, cash.

cater[2] *v* (*used of cats*) to desire the male.

cateran *n* a Highland robber or freebooter.

catfish *n* the sea wolf, the sea cat.

cat-gull *n* the herring gull.

cat-gut *n* sea laces.

cath *v* to drive or toss a ball by striking it with the hand or a light club or bat.

cat-harrow *n* in phr **draw the cat-harrow** (*used of persons*) to quarrel among themselves, thwart each other.

cathead band *n* a coarse ironstone.

cat-heather *n* a species of heather growing in separate upright stalks with flowers at the top.

cathel *n* **1** caudle. **2** a hot-pot of ale, sugar and eggs.

cathel nail *n* the nail by which the body of a cart is fixed to the axle.

ca'-the-shuttle *n* a weaver.

cat-hole *n* **1** a loophole or narrow opening in the wall of a barn to give cats admission and exit. **2** a niche in the wall in which small articles are deposited.

ca'-through *n* **1** great energy. **2** an uproar.

cat-hud *n* a large stone at the back of the fire on a cottage hearth.

catill, cattil *v* to thrust the fingers forcibly under the ears, as a cruel punishment.—*n* the act of inflicting such.

cat-in-clover *n* bird's-foot trefoil.

cat-in-the-barrel *n* a barbarous game formerly played at Kelso once a year.

cat-in-the-hole *n* a boys' game.

cat-kindness *n* cupboard love.

catling *n* catgut, a fiddle-string.

catloup *n* **1** a short distance. **2** a moment of time.

catmaw *n* **1** a somersault. **2** in phr **tumble the catmaw** to turn topsy-turvy.—*adv* **1** (*used of the eyes*) turned upward. **2** heels over head.

catogle *n* the great horned owl.

catribat *v* **1** to contend. **2** to quarrel.

catrick *n* **1** a supposed disease of the roots of the fingers from too frequent handling of cats. **2** a cataract supposed to affect the eyes of the first person who meets a cat that has leapt over a dead body.

catridge, catrons *n* a diminutive person fond of women.

cat's-carriage *n* a seat formed by two persons crossing their hands, on which to place a third.

cat's-cradle *n* a plaything of twine on the fingers of one person transferred to those of another.

cat's hair *n* **1** the down on an unfledged bird. **2** the down on the face of a boy before a beard grows. **3** thin hair growing on the bodies of persons in bad health. **4** the cirrus and cirrostratus clouds.

catsherd *n* cataract.

cat siller *n* mica.

cat's-lug *n* *Auricula ursi*.

cat's-stairs *n* a child's toy made of thread, etc, and so disposed by the hand as to fall down like steps of a stair or twisted into the shape of stairs.

cats'-tails *n* hare's-tail rush, cotton grass.

catstanes *n* the upright stones that support a grate on either side.

cat-steps *n* the projections of the stones in the slanting part of a gable.

cat-strand *n* a very small stream.

cat-tails *same as* **cats'-tails**.

catten-clover *same as* **cat-in-clover**.

catter[1] *n* money, cash.

catter[2] *same as* **catrick**.

catterbatch *n* a broil, quarrel.

catterbatter *v* to wrangle good-humouredly.

catterthraw *n* a fit of rebellious ill-temper.

catter-wier *adj* **1** snappish. **2** surly. **3** churlish.—*n* an ill-tempered person.

catter-wurr *same as* **catter-wier**.

catter-wower *v* to caterwaul.—*n* a caterwaul.

cattie-and-doggie *n* the game of cat-and-dog (qv).

cattie-bargle, ~-bargie *n* a noisy, angry quarrel among children.

cattie-wurrie *v* to dispute noisily and violently.—*n* **1** a violent dispute. **2** a noisy, angry quarrel among children.

cattie-wurriein *n* a continuous violent disputing. —*adj* peevish.

cattle *n* lice, fleas, etc, used contemptuously of persons.

cattle close *n* a farm cattle yard.

cattle creep *n* a low arch or gangway to enable cattle to pass under or over a railway.

cattleman *n* a servant in charge of the cattle on a farm.

cattle raik *n* a common, or extensive pasturage, where cattle feed at large.

cat-wa' *n* a stone wall dividing a cottage into two rooms.

cat-whins *n* the needle furze.

cat-witted, ~-wutted *adj* **1** harebrained. **2** savage in temper.

catyogle *same as* **catogle**.

caudebec hat *n* a woollen French hat.

cauder *n* money.

caudron *n* a caldron.

cauf[1] *n* **1** a calf. **2** a fool.

cauf[2] *n* chaff.

cauf-grun *n* one's native place.

caugle *n* four cherry stones in the game of 'paips' (qv).

cauk[1] *n* chalk.—*v* **1** to draw with chalk. **2** to mark down a debt.

cauk[2] *n* cark.

cauk[3] *n* the point turned down on a horseshoe.—*v* to turn down the ends and toes of horseshoes.

cauk[4] *v* to demand payment for what is due or is marked as a debt.

cauker[1] *n* **1** the hind-part of a horseshoe sharpened and turned down. **2** the iron rim or plate on a clog or shoe heel.

cauker[2] *n* **1** a bumper. **2** a drink of spirits.

caul[1], **cauld** *n* **1** a dam head. **2** a weir on a river to divert water into a mill lade.

caul[2], **cauld** *v* (*used of a river bank*) to lay a bed of loose stones from the channel of the river backwards, as far as necessary, to defend the land from the inroads of the water.

caul³, cauld *n* a cold.—*adj* cold.

caul cap *n* an old woman's cap of triangular shape.

cauld *adj* cold.

cauld-bark *n* a coffin, grave.

cauld-casten-tee *adj* **1** lifeless, dull. **2** insipid.

cauld coal *n in phr* **to blew a cauld coal** to engage in unpromising work, to undergo failure or loss.

cauld comfort *n* inhospitableness, poor entertainment.

cauld kail het again *n phr* **1** broth warmed up again. **2** a sermon preached twice to the same audience. **3** a broken-off love affair renewed. **4** an insipid repetition of anything.

cauld-like *adj* (*of the weather*) likely to be cold.

cauldness *n* coldness.

cauldrid *adj* chilling.

cauldrife *same as* **caldrife**.

cauld seed *n* late peas.

cauld steer *n* sour milk or cold water and meal stirred together.

cauld straik *n* a dram (qv) of raw spirits.

cauld win' *n* little encouragement.

cauld winter *n* the last load of corn brought from the field to the stack yard.

cauler, caullerr *same as* **caller**.

cauliflower *n* the head on ale.

caulk *same as* **cauk¹**.

caulker¹ *same as* **cauker¹**.

caulker² *same as* **cauker²**.

caulm¹ *n* **1** a mould, frame. **2** a bullet mould. **3** (*in pl*) course of framing or construction.

caulm² *adj* **1** calm. **2** smooth, even.

caulms *n* the small cords through which the warp is passed in the loom, the heddles (qv).

caum¹ *n* slate pencil.—*v* to whiten a hearth with camstane (qv).

caum² *same as* **caulm¹**.

caum³ *adj* **1** calm. **2** smooth.

caumshell *n* a piece of white shell, or bony matter, in shape not unlike a lady's slipper, frequently found on the seashore.

caumstane *same as* **camstane**.

ca' up *n* a thorough, overhauling search.

caup¹ *n* blackmail paid by private men to thieves.

caup² *n* a wooden drinking vessel.

caup³ *same as* **cap³**.

caup⁴ *n* the shell of a snail.

cauped *adj* bulging, bending in curves.

caup-snail *n* the snail inhabiting the black shell, common among old gardens and castles.

cauppie *n* **1** a small wooden drinking vessel. **2** a small wooden porringer.

caur¹, caure *same as* **car¹**.

caur², caurry *same as* **car³**.

caurry-, caur-handed *adj* left-handed.

cause *conj* because.

cause *n* **1** sake. **2** trial in a court. **3** *in phr* **hour of cause** the time of a trial, in inferior courts, formerly from 10 a.m. to 12 noon.

causey, caussey *n* a causeway, street.—*v* to pave.

causey-clash *n* street gossip.

causey-clothes *n* dress in which one may appear in public.

causey-crown *n* the middle or highest part of the road.

causey-dancer *n* a gadabout, one who is continually on the street.

causeyer *n* a pavior, one who makes a causey (qv).

causey-faced *adj* brazen-faced, unashamed.

causey-raker *n* a street-sweeper, a scavenger.

causey-stanes *n* cobblestones, pavingstones.

causey-tales *n* common news, street news.

causey-talk *n* street gossip.

causey-webs *n in phr* **to make causey-webs** to neglect one's work and idle in the streets.

caution *n* **1** security, guarantee. **2** a surety.—*v* **1** to be surety. **2** to wager. **3** to guarantee, warrant.

cautioner *n* a surety for another.

cautionry *n* suretyship.

cautionry-bond *n* a bond in security.

cautious *adj* **1** unassuming, quiet. **2** kindly, obliging.

cauts *n* the tremulous appearance near the surface of the ground in hot sunshine.

cave¹ *same as* **cavie¹**.

cave² *n* a deficiency in intelligence.

cave³ *v* **1** to push. **2** to drive backward and forward. **3** to toss. **4** to toss the head haughtily or awkwardly. **5** to rear and plunge. **6** to topple over. **7** to climb a steep wall, etc. **8** to walk awkwardly. **9** to tread heavily, as in mud or from fatigue. **10** to separate grain from broken straw, after threshing. **11** to separate corn from chaff. —*n* **1** a stroke, a push. **2** a toss of the head, forelegs or hands.

cave⁴ *v* to live in a cave. **2** to dwell.

cavee *same as* **cavy**.

cavel¹ *n* a low fellow.

cavel² *same as* **cavil**.

cavel³ *n* **1** a lot. **2** a share. **3** lot, fate, destiny. **4** a division or share by lot. **5** a rig (qv) of growing corn on the run-rig (qv) system. **6** a rod, pole, long staff.—*v* to divide by lot.

cavelling *n* the division by lot.

caver *n* a gentle breeze moving the water slightly.

cavie¹ *n* **1** a hen coop. **2** the lower part of a cupboard or meat press.

cavie² *v* **1** to rear, prance. **2** to toss the head. **3** to walk with an airy or affected step.

cavied *v, adj* cooped up.

cavie-keek-bo'in *phr* courting near the aumrie-cavie (qv).

cavil *n* a wrangle, quarrel.—*v* **1** to argue, quarrel. **2** to scold.

cavings *n* the short, broken straw from which the grain has been separated after threshing.

cavy *n* **1** perturbation of mind. **2** a state of commotion.

caw *same as* **ca'**.

caw-again *v* to contradict.

cawaw'd *adj* **1** fatigued. **2** wearied to disgust.

cawdah *n* lint.

cawdebink hat *same as* **caudebec hat**.

cawdy *same as* **caddie**.

cawer *n* a driver.

cawk *same as* **cauk**.

cawker *same as* **cauker**.

cawlie *same as* **coulie**.

cawmer *v* to calm, quiet.

cawmril *same as* **cameral¹**.

cawnle licht *n* candlelight.

cawn aoul *n* a cunning person.

cawper *n* bargain, profit, advantage.

cawr *same as* **car³**.

cawsay, cawsey *same as* **causey**.

cazzie *n* a sack or net made of straw twisted and plaited.

cazzie chair *n* an easy chair made of straw twisted and plaited.

cea *n* a small tub.

cedent *n* (*a legal term*) one who cedes or yields to another or executes a bond of resignation.

ceety-fowk *n* citizens, dwellers in a city.

cell *n* a chain for fastening a cow in a stall.

censor *n* one who calls the roll of students at the University and of the scholars of the Grammar School at Aberdeen.

censure *v* to take toll of.

cep, ceps, cept *prep* except, but.—*conj* except, unless, but.

cepin *conj* excepting.

cert *n in phr* **for cert** beyond a doubt.

certainly *adv* accurately, correctly.

certaint *adj* certain, sure.

certes, certis, certies, certie, certy *adv* of a truth, certainly.—*n in phr* **my certie** by my troth, take my word for it.

certify *v* to warn of legal consequences of disobedience, etc.

certiorate *v* (*used as a legal term*) to certify.

cese *n* **1** a tax, rate. **2** a local tax. **3** a pest.

cess money *n* money paid in rates or taxes.

chack[1] *n* **1** a slight and hasty refreshment, a snack. **2** a slight bruise or knock.—*v* **1** to cut or bruise suddenly. **2** to prick. **3** to cause moral pain. **4** to lay hold of anything quickly, so as to gash it with the teeth.

chack[2] *v* **1** to clack, make a clicking or clinking noise. **2** (*of the teeth*) to chatter with cold or fright.

chack[3] *n* the wheatear.

chack[4] *v* to check, squeeze.—*n* a check, squeeze.

chack[5] *n* **1** a rut in a road. **2** a wheel track.

chack[6] *adj* of a check pattern.

chack-a-pudding *n* a selfish person who always seizes what is best at meals.

chackart, chackert *n* **1** the stonechat. **2** the whinchat. **3** the wheatear. **4** a term of endearment or of affectionate reproach.

chacker *adj* (*used of tartans*) checked.

chackie[1] *n* a striped cotton bag for carrying a ploughman's clean clothes, etc.

chackie[2] *n* the stonechat.

chackie[3] *adj* **1** unequal. **2** full of ruts. **3** gravelly.

chackie[4] *adj* (*perhaps*) dimpled.

chackie-mill *n* the deathwatch.

chackit *adj* **1** checkered. **2** of a check pattern. **3** chequered.

chack-lowrie *n* mashed cabbage mixed with barley broth.

chack-purse *n* a sporran.

chack-reel *n* **1** the common reel for winding yarn, with a check. **2** a clicking noise, when a cut of yarn has been wound on it.

chad *n* **1** compacted gravel. **2** small stones forming a river bed. **3** a rough mixture of earth and stones, quarry refuse.

chaddy *adj* gravelly.

chaep, chaip *adj* cheap.

chaet *v* to cheat.—*n* a cheat.

chaetry *n* cheating.

cha'fause *v* (*perhaps*) to suffer.

chaff[1] *v* **1** to chew. **2** to eat.

chaff[2] *v* to chatter, be loquacious.

chaff[3] *v* **1** to chafe, rub. **2** to fret, be angry.—*n* **1** a rage. **2** ill-humour.

chaff-blades *same as* **chaft-blades**.

chaffer[1] *n* the round-lipped whale.

chaffer[2] *n* a chafing dish.

chaffie *n* the chaffinch.

chaffle *v* to chaffer, higgle.

chaffrie *n* refuse, rubbish.

chaft *n* **1** the jaw, jawbone. **2** (*in pl*) chops, cheeks.

chaft-blades *n* jaws, jawbones.

chaft-talk *n* prattle, idle talk.

chaft-tooth *n* a jaw-tooth, molar.

chain-drapper *n* a cheap jeweller who frequents fairs and professes to give great bargains to his own loss and to the advantage of his customers.

chainge *v* to change.

chaip[1] *same as* **chape**[2].

chaip[2] *v* to ask the price of an article on sale.—*n* purchase, bargain.

chaipin *n* inquiry as to the price of an article.

chair-haffets *n* the upright sides of a high-backed easy chair.

chaise *v* to drive fast in a wheeled conveyance.

chaistain *n* a chestnut.

chaistifie *same as* **chastify**.

chait *v* to cheat.

chak *same as* **chack**[1].

chak *same as* **chack**[5].

chalder *n* a measure of grain, nearly eight quarters.

chalk heugh *n* a chalk quarry.

challenge *v* to rate, scold.—*n* summons to death.

chalmer *same as* **chamber**.

chalmer-chield *n* a valet or groom of the chambers.

chalmer-glew *n* secret wantonness.

chalmerie *n* a small chamber.

chalmer o' deis *n* **1** a parlour. **2** the best bedroom.

cham *v* to chew.

chamber *n* **1** a room. **2** any upper room. **3** the farm servants' sleeping room, formerly above the stable or partitioned off from it. **4** a bedroom. **5** the police court. **6** the magistrate's room.—*v* **1** to closet. **2** to shut up, confine, restrain. **3** to be chary of.

chamber bed *n* the bed in the best bedroom.

chambered *adj* **1** closeted. **2** shut up.

chambradeese *same as* **chalmer o' deis**.

chamer *n* a chamber.

chamie *n* the game of shinty or hockey.

chammer *v* to silence.

champ[1] *n* stamp, quality, kind.

champ[2] *n* **1** a mire. **2** ground trodden and mashed by the feet of animals.—*v* **1** to chop. **2** to mash. **3** to crush, bruise.

champ[3] *n* **1** the figure raised on diaper, silk, etc. **2** tapestry.

champart *n* **1** field rent. **2** rent in kind.

champers, champies *n* mashed potatoes.

champion *adj* **1** first-rate. **2** very good. **3** in fine health.

champit *adj* (*used of patterns or figures*) raised on a ground.

chance *v* **1** to risk. **2** to give the chance.

chance-bairn *n* an illegitimate child.

chancellor *n* the foreman of a jury.

chancer *n* a brass button, gilded and lettered.

chance time *n* odd times.

chancler *n* **1** a chancellor. **2** foreman of a jury.

chancy *adj* **1** lucky, auspicious, presaging good fortune. **2** fortunate, happy. **3** safe to deal or meddle with (*generally with negative*).

chandler *n* a candlestick.

chandler-chafts *n* **1** lantern-jaws. **2** a meagre visage.

chandler-pins *n in phr* **be a' on chandler-pins 1** to be particularly precise or nice in speech. **2** to speak fine English.

chang *n* a loud, confused noise, like that of a flock of geese.

change *n* **1** the custom of one who buys from particular persons or shops. **2** a small inn, a tavern, alehouse. **3** (*in pl*) underlinen.—*v* **1** (*used of milk*) to turn sour. **2** (*of meat, etc*) to decompose. **3** to exchange. **4** to substitute, as fairies were supposed to do with children. **5** (*with* **self**) to change one's clothes.

change-house *n* an alehouse, tavern.

change-house-keeper, change-keeper *n* **1** a tavern-keeper. **2** the landlord of a small inn.

change-seats-the-king-is-coming *n* a children's game.

change-wife *n* a female tavern-keeper.

changy *adj* fickle, given to change.

chanler *same as* **chandler**.

channel *n* gravel from the channel of a river.—*v* **1** to play at curling. **2** to cover with gravel, to spread gravel.

channelly *adj* gravelly, shingly.

channel stane *n* a curling stone.

channer[1], **channers** *n* gravel.

channer[2] *v* **1** to scold fretfully. **2** to grumble.—*n* **1** strife. **2** querulousness.

channery *adj* gravelly.

channery-, chanry-kirk *n* a canonry church, a church of the canons.

chanrock *n* a channel of round stones.

chant *v* **1** to speak much pertly. **2** to speak with a strange accent or with an English accent.—*n* **1** pert language. **2** a person given to pert language.

chanter *n* the fingering part of a bagpipe.

chanter-horn *n* a shepherd's pipe or reed.

chanticleer *n* the fish dragonet.

chantie-beak *n* a chatterbox.

chanting *adj* loquacious, pert.

chantin' thing *n* an impertinent young person.

chanty *n* 1 a chamber pot. 2 a kind of flat-topped spinning top.

chap[1] *n* 1 a fellow. 2 a person. 3 used humorously of a woman. 4 (*with* **auld**) the devil.

chap[2] *v* 1 to strike a bargain. 2 to choose, fix upon. —*n in phr* **chap and choice** a great variety to choose from.

chap[3] *v* 1 to knock. 2 to strike. 3 to hammer. 4 to rap. 5 (*used of a clock*) to strike. 6 to chop, pound, bruise, break in pieces. 7 to step, walk. 8 (*with* **hands**) to clasp in betrothing or bargaining. 9 (*with* **out**) to call a person out by tapping at a window. 10 (*with* **yont**) to get out of the way.—*n* 1 a knock, stroke, blow with a hammer. 2 a tap. 3 (*used of drought*) a long period. 4 the noise breaking waves on a pebbly beach.

chap[4] *n* the jaw, the cheek.

chap[5] *n* a shop.

chape *v* to escape.

chapel-folk *n* Episcopalians.

chapin *same as* **chappin**.

chapling *n* (*of a guild or craft*) the loss of individual votes of members at an election who go with the majority.

chapman's drouth *n* hunger and thirst.

chap-mill *n* clappers.

chappan *n* 1 tall of stature. 2 clever. 3 lusty.

chapper[1] *n* a door knocker.

chapper[2] *n* a blacksmith's man who wields the sledgehammer.

chapper[3] *n* a beetle for mashing potatoes, etc.

chappie[1] *n* a little fellow.

chappie[2] *n* a name given to a ghost, from its frequent knockings.

chappin *n* 1 a chopine. 2 a dry or liquid measure, nearly an English quart.

chappin' hammer *n* a stone-breaker's hammer.

chappin' knife *n* a butcher's knife or cleaver.

chappin' stick *n* any instrument or weapon used for striking with.

chappit tatties *n* mashed potatoes.

chaps me *int* an exclamation when one person claims a share in anything found by two or more persons in company or when he chooses a particular article.

chaps ye *int* an exclamation used by a person at once accepting an offer or bargain.

chapterly *adv* (*used of the meeting of a presbytery*) when all the members are present.

char'd *n* a leaning place.

chare *n* 1 care, charge. 2 a ward, one under a guardian.

charet *n* a chariot.

char-filler *n* a blast-furnace worker.

charge *n* expense, cost.

chargeable *adj* costly, expensive.

chariot *n* a urinal or chamber pot.

charitcher *n* the Shorter Catechism.

chark *v* 1 to make a grating noise, as teeth in biting any gritty substance. 2 to make a grinding, grunting noise. 3 to be continually complaining, to be querulous. 4 (*of a bird*) to repeat a melancholy call. 5 to chirp as a cricket.

charker *n* a cricket.

charlie-mufti *n* the whitethroat.

charnle ~, charnal pins *n* 1 the pins on which the hinges of machinery turn. 2 *in phr* **to miss one's charnle pins** to be unable to stand straight through intoxication.

charter *v* to hand down to one's posterity.

chaser *n* a ram with only one testicle.

chass window *n* a sash window.

chasten *same as* **chaistain**.

chastify *v* to chastise, castigate.

chastise *v* to abridge.

chat[1] *n* 1 chatter, talkativeness. 2 pert language.

chat[2] *n* a lunch, slight refreshment.

chat[3] *n* 1 an opprobrious epithet addressed to a child. 2 a chit.

chat[4] *n* the gallows.

chat[5] *v* 1 to bruise slightly. 2 to chafe, rub.

chat[6] *n* a call to swine.

chat-dinner *n* a little bit of dinner.

chatter[1] *v* 1 to divide a thing by causing many fractions. 2 to shatter. 3 to break suddenly into small pieces. 4 to tear, bruise.—*n* 1 a bruise. 2 the act of shattering.

chatter[2] *v* to rattle.

chattering bit, ~ piece *n* a piece of oatcake eaten on leaving the water after bathing in the open air.

chat-maet *n* a litle food.

chattle *v* 1 to nibble, chew, chew feebly. 2 to eat as a lamb or a young child.

chatty-puss *n* a call to a cat.

chaudmallet, chaudmelle *n* 1 a sudden broil or quarrel. 2 a blow, a beating. 3 homicide in a passion.

chauffer *n* a person of bad disposition.

chauks *n* a sluice.

chaum *v* 1 to chew voraciously. 2 to eat up.

chaumer *same as* **chamber**.

chaumerie *n*, a small chamber.

chauner *same as* **channer**.

chaunter *same as* **chanter**.

chaup[1] *same as* **chap**[2].

chaup[2] *same as* **chap**[3].

chaut *v* 1 to chew feebly. 2 to chew with a crackling-sound.

chauther *same as* **chalder**.

chauttle *same as* **chattle**.

chauve *adj* 1 (*used of cattle*) having white hair pretty equally mixed with black. 2 (*of a swarthy person*) pale.

chaveling *n* a spokeshave.

chaw *v* 1 to chew. 2 to fret or cut by attrition. 3 to vex, provoke. 4 to be sulky. 5 feel annoyed.—*n* 1 a mouthful. 2 a quid of tobacco. 3 a bitter and envious disappointment which shows itself in face and eyes. 4 (*with* **words**) to speak indistinctly. 5 (*with* **upon**) to brood upon, think over.

chawchling *adj* eating like a swine.

cheap *adj phr* **cheap o't** thoroughly deserving of it, serves one right.

cheap-good *adj* cheap.—*n* a good bargain.

chearer *n* a glass of toddy.

cheat[1] *same as* **cheet**.

cheat[2] *v* to deceive, mistake (*used impersonally or in passive*).

cheatery, cheatry *n* cheating, fraud, deception.—*adj* fraudful, deceitful, false.

cheats *n* the sweetbread.

cheat-the-wuddy *n* a gallows knave, one who deserves to be hanged.

check[1] *same as* **chack**[3].

check[2] *same as* **chack**[1].

check[3] *n* a door key.

check-reel *same as* **chack-reel**.

check-spail *same as* **cheek-spool**.

check-weigher *n* the man who checks the weight of coal on the surface.

cheek *v* (*with* **in with**) 1 to flatter, curry favour. 2 (*with* **up**) to use insolent language. 3 (*with* **up till**) to court, to make love to.—*n* 1 the side of a place, post, door or fire. 2 a doorpost. 3 a gatepost. 4 the side of a loaf of bread. 5 impertinence.

cheek-aside *adv* 1 on the side of the cheek. 2 beside the cheek.

cheek-atone *n* a curling stone played so as to lie alongside another.

cheek-blade *n* the cheekbone.

cheekbone, ~rack *n* the bridle of the twelve-oxen plough.

cheek-for-chow *adv* side by side, close together.

cheek-haffit *n* the side of the face or head.

cheekie *adj* 1 full of cunning. 2 forward, impertinent.

cheekie-for-chowie *n* a dainty made of oatmeal, butter and sugar.

cheekie-, cheek-for-chowie *adv* side by side.

cheek-spool *n* **1** a box on the ear. **2** a blow on the cheek.

cheekyside *same as* **cheek-aside**

cheel, cheelie *same as* **chield**.

cheemist *n* a chemist, druggist.

cheen *v* to chain.—*n* a chain.

cheenge *v* to change. *cf* change.

cheeny *n* **1** china. **2** a boys' china marble.

cheep *n* **1** a chirp, cry of a young bird. **2** a creak, faint noise. **3** a soft or light kiss. **4** a word, hint, least mention.—*v* **1** to chirp, cry like a young bird. **2** to squeak like a mouse or rat. **3** to creak like a shoe or door. **4** to speak feebly or quietly. **5** to make a slight sound. **6** to disclose a secret. **7** to tell only a little. **8** (*of grain*) to begin to sprout in malting.

cheepart *n* **1** the meadow pipit. **2** a small person with a shrill voice.

cheeper *n* **1** a half-fledged bird, a young grouse or partridge. **2** a silent kiss. **3** the cricket. **4** the bog iris.

cheepers *n* creaking shoes.

cheer *n* a chair.

cheery-pyke *n* (*generally with a negative*) anything pleasant to the taste or feeling.

cheese *n* **1** the receptacle of the thistle, *Carduus lanecolatus*. **2** *in phr* **not to say cheese** to say nothing.

cheese-breaker *n* a curd crusher.

cheese-brizer *n* a cheese press.

cheese-drainer *n* a vessel for draining whey from the curd.

cheese ford *n* a cheese press.

cheese hake, ~ rack *n* a frame for drying cheese.

cheese loft *n* an upper room in a dairy reserved for the storing and ripening of cheese newly made.

cheese set *n* a cheese press.

cheese stane *n* a large, heavy stone, worked with a screw, for pressing cheese.

cheese tub, ~ vat *n* a tub for pressing cheese.

cheet *n* **1** a call to cats. **2** a cat.

cheetie *n* **1** a call to cats. **2** pussy.

cheetie-bautherin *n* a cat. *See* **baudrons**.

cheetie-pussy *n* a cat.

cheetle *v* to chirp, pipe, warble.

cheik *n* a brass button.

cheim *v* **1** to divide equally. **2** to cut down the backbone of an animal equally.

cheip *same as* **cheep**.

cheir *v* **1** to cut. **2** to wound.

cheirs *n* scissors.

cheitle *same as* **cheetle**.

chenyie *n* a chain.

cheritable *adj* charitable.

cherity *n* charity.

cherk *same as* **chirk**.

cherry *n* a red worsted knob on the top of a man's bonnet.

chesbow *n* the poppy.

chess[1] *n* the sash or frame of a window.

chess[2] *n* **1** the quarter or smaller division of an apple or pear cut regular into pieces. **2** the pith of an orange.

chess *n* **1** a strap. **2** a hawk's jess.

chessart, chessirt *n* a tub for pressing cheese.

chessel, chessil *same as* **cheswell**.

chessford *n* a chessart (qv).

chest *n* **1** a large box for holding meal, bread, etc. **2** a coffin.—*v* to put into a coffin

chester barley, ~ bear *n* a coarse barley with four rows on each head.

chesting *n* the ceremony of putting a corpse into the coffin, the coffining.

cheswell *n* a cheese press or vat.—*v* to press cheese in a vat.

chettoun *n* the setting of a precious stone.

cheugh-jean *n* a jujube.

chevalier *n* a favourite son.

cheveron *n* a kid glove.

chew[1] *v* to stew.

chew[2] *int* a call to a dog to get out of the way or of reproof.

chice *n* choice.

chick[1] *int* a call to chickens, etc.

chick[2] *n* **1** a tick. **2** a beat.—*v* to tick, make a clicking noise.

chickenweed, ~wort *n* chickweed.

chicker *v* to cluck as a hen.

chickmarly *n* a hen grey and black.

chickstane *n* the wheatear.

chide *n* a chiding, scolding.

chief *adj* intimate, friendly.

chield, chiel *n* **1** a child. **2** a fellow. **3** a man. **4** a son. **5** a daughter. **6** a young man or woman, a stripling. **7** a valet, a servant. **8** a term of fondness or intimacy.

chiel nor (or) chare *phr* **1** kith nor (or) kin. **2** belongings, relations.

chier *same as* **cheir**.

chiff[1] *v* to spit, making a noise or puff with the lips.

chiff[2] *v* to fray out at the ends of a garment.

chiffer-oot *n* one who bears a name tabooed among fishermen of the northeast of Scotland.

chilcorn *n* a blackhead on the face.

childer *n* children.

chill-cauld *adj* nearly frozen.

chilpie, chilpy *adj* **1** chilly. **2** chilled.

chim[1] *v* to take by small portions.

chim[2] *n* a friend, a chum.

chimbla, chimblay *n* a chimney.

chim-cham *v* to talk in a long-winded, undecided way.

chimins *n* furmenty.

chimla, chimley *n* a chimney.

chimla brace *n* **1** the mantelpiece. **2** the beam supporting cat and clay chimneys in cottages.

chimla can *n* a chimney pot.

chimla cheek *n* **1** the fireside. **2** the side of the grate. **3** an insertion to lessen the size of the grate.

chimla end *n* the wall of a room where the fireplace is.

chimla heid *n* a chimney top.

chimla lug *n* the fireside.

chimla nook *n* the fireside or a corner near it.

chimla ribs *n* the bars of a grate.

chimney *n* **1** a grate, fireplace. **2** the fire.

chin *n* a primitive knocker, being a metal boss fixed on the doorpost and struck by anyone wishing admittance.

china *n* a boys' painted marble.

chin cloth *n* a kind of mask for the lower part of the face.

chine *n* that part of the staves of a barrel which projects beyond the head.

chingle *n* **1** gravel free from dirt. **2** sea gravel, shingle.

chingly, chingily *adj* gravelly, shingly.

chink *n* money, cash.

chink *n* the reed bunting.

chinkie *n* the chin.

chinlie *same as* **chingly**.

chintie-chin *n* a long chin, a projecting chin.

chip[1] *v* **1** to chop, cut with an axe. **2** (*of seeds, buds, etc*) to burst, sprout, germinate. **3** (*of young birds*) to begin to crack the shell, to prepare for necessary flight. **4** to be in the early stage of pregnancy. **5** (*of ale*) to begin to ferment in the vat.

chip[2] *n* beaver for hats.

chip hat *n* a beaver hat.

chippey-holey *n* a game of marbles in which the chippy was used.

chippie-burdie *n* a promise made to pacify a child.

chippit *adj* touched with liquor.

chippy *n* a boy's large, hard marble.

chirk *v* **1** to emit a grating sound. **2** to creak, squeak. **3** to grind with the teeth, to gnaw.—*n* a grating sound, a sound made by the teeth when rubbed together or by one hard body rubbing against another.

chirking *adj* shifty, tricky.

chirkle *v* to grind the teeth.

chirl *v* **1** to chirp, warble merrily. **2** to whistle shrilly. **3** to emit a low, melancholy sound, as birds do in winter or before a storm. **4** to laugh immoderately.—*n* **1** a low, melancholy sound. **2** chirping.

chirle[1] *n* **1** a double chin. **2** the wattles or barbs of a cock.

chirle[2], **chirlie** *n* a**1** small piece of anything edible. **2** a piece of coal of intermediate size between the largest and small coal used in smithies.

chirlie *adj* **1** well-shaped. **2** of a handy size. **3** suitable, handy for use.

chirm[1] *n* **1** the note or song of a bird. **2** a low, murmuring, mournful conversation.—*v* **1** to chirp, sing. **2** to make a low, melancholy note, as a bird before a storm. **3** to warble, croon, hum. **4** to murmur, fret, complain.

chirm[2] *n* **1** a small or undeveloped thing. **2** (*in pl*) the early shoots of grass.

chirm[3] *v* to argue a point that has been settled.

chirnells *n* small hard swellings in the neck-glands of young people.

chirper *n* the cricket.

chirple *v* to twitter as a swallow.—*n* a twittering note.

chirr *same as* **churr**.

chirt[1] *v* to make a grating noise with the teeth.—*n* a grating noise.

chirt[2] *v* **1** to squirt with the teeth. **2** to press, squeeze. **3** to press out. **4** to act in a gripping manner. **5** to practise extortion.—*n* **1** a squeeze. **2** a squirt. **3** a small quantity.

chirt[3] *v* to press hard at stool.

chirt[4] *v* to restrain laughter.

chirurgeon *n* a surgeon.

chirurgerie *n* surgery.

chisell *same as* **cheswell**.

chiskin *n* the wheatear.

chislet *adj* engraved.

chisp *n* a gap in the woof of cloth.

chissat *same as* **chessart**.

chit[1] *n* a small bit of bread or of any kind of food.

chit[2] *same as* **cheet**.

chits *same as* **cheats**.

chitter *v* **1** to tremble. **2** to shiver from cold. **3** (*of the teeth*) to chatter. **4** to twitter. **5** to chirp.—*n* **1** a fragment. **2** a piece broken by a fall.

chitter-chatter *n* **1** foolish talk. **2** the chattering of the teeth from cold.—*v* **1** to chatter. **2** to talk foolishly.—*adv* in a chattering fashion.

chitterie-chatterie *n* a piece of bread eaten immediately after bathing.

chittering *n* talking, chattering.

chittering bit, ~ chow, ~ piece *n* a piece of bread eaten immediately after bathing in the open air.

chitterling *n* an old-fashioned shirt frill.

chittery *n* **1** small, backward fruit. **2** small, bad potatoes.

chittle *v* to eat corn from the ear, to pull off the husks with the teeth.

chittle *v* to warble, to chatter, to twitter, chirp.

chittler *n* a small bird of the titmouse species.

chitty-face *n* **1** a thin, pinched or childish face. **2** one who has a thin face.

chiver *v* to shiver.

chivery ~, chivering chow *n* a piece of bread eaten just after bathing.

chize *same as* **chice**.

chizer *n* a chooser.

chizors *n* scissors.

chizzard, chizzat, chizat *same as* **chessart**.

chizzel *same as* **cheswell**.

chizzel *v* to cheat.

chizzy *n* a chosen article.

choak *v* **1** to stifle. **2** to check. **3** to choke.

choalt *n* a foster brother.

chock *n* the croup.

choffer *n* a chafing dish.

choice, choise *v* to choose.

choiced *v* chose.

choisen *v* chosen.

choke-a-block *adv* quite full, chock-full.

chokeband *n* a leather band for fastening the bridle round the jaws of a horse.

choke rope *n* a rope used to clear the throat of a cow that chokes in eating turnips.

chol *n* the jowl.

choller, choler *n* **1** a double chin. **2** the flesh covering the jaw of man or beast, when fat and hanging. **3** (*in pl*) the gills of a fish.

choo *int* a call to silence a dog.

chookie *n* a chicken, hen, etc.—*int* a call to fowls.

chool *same as* **chowl**.

choop *n* the fruit of the wild briar.

choosed *v* chose.

choowow *v* **1** to grudge. **2** grumble.

choowowing *n* grumbling.

chop[1] *n* a shop.

chop[2] *v* to go on, proceed.

chop[3] *n* a crack.

chops me *same as* **chaps me**.

chore *same as* **core**.

chork *same as* **chirk**.

chorp *v* (*used of shoes*) to creak or squeak when there is water in them.

chouk *n* **1** the jaw, cheek, neck. **2** a gland of the throat.

choup[1] *same as* **choop**.

choup[2] *n* in phr* **tak choup for a cheenge** take a dish of want for a change of diet.

chouskie *n* a knave.

chow[1] *same as* **chaw**

chow[2] *n* **1** the wooden ball used in shinty (qv). **2** the game of shinty. **3** a bullet head.

chow[3] *same as* **chol**.

chow'd mouse *n* **1** a worn-out person. **2** one who is unwell after a night's debauch.

chowks *n* **1** the jaws. **2** the throat. **3** the neck glands.

chowl *v* **1** to distort the face. **2** to whine. **3** to emit a mournful cry.—*n* **1** a mournful cry. **2** a whine.

chows *n* a small coal used in forges.

chowtle *v* to chew feebly, like a child or old person.

choyse *v* to choose.

chraisy *n* a cap or bonnet covering the head and the back of a woman's neck.

Christendie *n* Christendom.

christening bit *n* a piece of bread, of cheese and of gingerbread given to the first person met by those carrying the child to be baptised.

Christenmas *n* Christmas.

Christmas flower *n* black hellebore.

chub *n* a chubby child.

chuck[1] *int* a call to fowls.—*n* **1** chicken. **2** a term of endearment.

chuck[2] *n* **1** a pebble. **2** a boys' marble. **3** a game played with pebbles or shells.

chuck[3] *v* to toss or throw anything smartly from the hand.

chucken *n* a chicken.

chucken-heartit *adj* faint-hearted.

chucket *n* the blackbird.

chuckie *n* a hen, a chicken.—*int* a call to fowls.

chuckie-stane *n* **1** a small pebble. **2** a small fragment of quartz, etc, as in the crop of hens. **3** (*in pl*) a girls' game with small pebbles.

chuckle *v* to nurse, look after children.

chuckle-head *n* a stupid person, a dolt.

chucks[1] *n* the game of chuckie-stanes (qv).

chucks[2] *n* lumps of oatmeal in porridge.

chue down *int* a call to a dog to keep quiet.

chuffie *adj* **1** fat. **2** chubby of cheek.

chuiffie-cheekit *adj* fat-faced.

chuffie-cheeks *n* a fat-faced child.

chug *v* **1** to tug at an elastic substance. **2** to pull, jerk.

chuist *v* chose.

chuller *same as* **choller**.

chum *n* **1** food, provisions. **2** chump (qv).

chumla *n* a chimney.

chump *n* **1** a short, fat person. **2** a sharp blow. **3** the head.
chun *n* the sprout of grain or potatoes.—*v* **1** (*of potatoes*) to sprout. **2** to nip off the shoots to prevent sprouting.
chunner *same as* **channer**[2].
chunnering *n* grumbling.
church-and-mice *n* a children's game.
churl *same as* **chirl**.
churm *same as* **chirm**.
churnels *n* small, hard swellings in the neck glands of children.
churn staff *n* the staff fitted for working in the old-fashioned churn.
churr *v* **1** to chirp, twitter. **2** to coo, to murmur. **3** to call as a moorcock, partridge, etc.—*n* the call of a partridge, etc.
churr-muffit *n* the whitethroat.
churr-owl *n* the nightjar.
chuttle *same as* **chowtle**.
chye *n* the chaffinch.
chymy *n* chemistry.
chyne *n* a chain.
chynge *v* to change.
ciel, cielery *n* ceiling.
cinder *n* spirits mixed with water, tea, etc.
circumduce *v* (*a legal term*) to declare time elapsed for introducing evidence.
circumjack *v* **1** to enfold closely. **2** to correspond with, agree to.
cirssen *v* to baptise.
cit *n* the civet.
civileer *n* an inquisitor formerly appointed by the town council and kirk session of Glasgow to apprehend persons taking a walk on the Sabbath.
civils *n* civil matters as distinguished from criminal.
claaick *n* **1** the state of having all the corn on a farm reaped but not led to the stack yard. **2** the harvest home.
claaick sheaf *n* the last handful of corn cut down by the reapers.
claaick supper *n* the feast formerly given on the cutting down of the corn but latterly when the crop is stacked.
claams *n* a shoemaker's pincers.
claar *n* a large wooden vessel.
clabber *n* **1** soft, sticky mud. **2** mud on a roadway. **3** mire. **4** a handful, a dollop.—*v* to cover with mud or dirt.
clabby *adj* sticky.
clachan *n* **1** a hamlet, village, containing a church. **2** a village alehouse.
clachan-howdie *n* a village midwife.
clach-coal *n* candle or parrot coal.
clacher *same as* **claucher**.
clack[1] *n* **1** the clapper of a mill. **2** the noise made by hens, etc. **3** noisy talk. **4** slander or impertinent talk. **5** gossip. **6** a female scandalmonger, gossip. —*v* **1** to cackle like a hen, etc. **2** to cry incessantly or clamorously. **3** to clatter, resound, echo. **4** to chatter, talk gossip or scandal.
clack[2] *n* a kind of toffee or treacle candy.
clacken *n* a wooden hand bat or racket, used by the boys of the Edinburgh Academy and High School.
clacker *same as* **claucher**.
clacking *n* **1** talking. **2** gossip.
clackrie *n* talk, gossip, chatter.
clad *adj* **1** thickly covered, thronged. **2** accompanied, attended by.
cladach *n* talk.
clade *v* to clothe.
claes *n* clothes.
claes beetle *n* a mallet for beating clothes in washing.
claft *n* the cleft or part of a tree where the branches separate.
claffie *adj* disordered, dishevelled.—*n* a slattern.
clag *v* **1** to clog, cover with mud, glue, etc. **2** to dirty, bemire. **3** (*used of a lubricant*) to thicken.—*n* **1** clay, mud, etc, adhering to shoes, skirts, etc. **2** an encumbrance, burden. **3** fault, imputation of blame. **4** a mess of food.
claggie[1], **claggim** *n* a sticky sweetmeat made of treacle.

claggie[2] *adj* **1** glutinous. **2** adhesive. **3** spotted with mire. **4** miry.
clagginess *n* adhesiveness in moist, miry soils, substances, etc.
claggock *n* **1** a draggle-tail. **2** a dirty wench.
claghan *same as* **clachan**.
clagher *same as* **claucher**.
claich *v* **1** to besmear. **2** to work a viscous or semiliquid stuff in a disgusting fashion. **3** to walk in mud or wet soil in a disgusting fashion. **4** to expectorate greatly, to clear one's throat.—*n* the act of besmearing or working viscous stuff in a dirty way.
claichie *adj* viscous, sticky, messy.
claiching *ppl adj* untidy, dirty, unskilful, messy.
claid *v, adj* covered, clothed.
claik[1] *n* the teredo or shipworm.
claik[2] *same as* **claich**.
claik[3] *v* **1** to cluck, cackle like a hen. **2** to cry clamorously. **3** to talk much in a trivial way. **4** to tattle, carry tales.—*n* **1** the cackle of a hen. **2** an idle or false report. **3** a woman addicted to talking.
claik[4], **claik goose** *n* the barnacle goose.
claik-eaten *adj* bored by the shipworm.
claikie *adj* adhesive, sticky.
claiking *v, n* **1** gossiping. **2** (*used of crows*) cawing.
claikrie *n* tattling, gossiping.
claip *n* the clapper of a mill.
claiperdin *n* a gossip.
clair *v* to search by raking or scratching.—*adj* **1** distinct, exact. **2** ready, prepared. **3** confident, certain. **4** (*of a lesson*) repeated without mistake.
clairach *same as* **clorach**.
clairshach, clairshoe *n* a harp.
clairt *same as* **clart**.
clairty *same as* **clarty**.
claish *n* clothes.
claister *n* **1** any sticky compound. **2** a person bedaubed with mud or clay.—*v* to bedaub, plaster.
claith *n* **1** cloth. **2** *phr* **lang in the claith** long in the dead clothes, long dead and buried.
claithe *v* to clothe.
claithing *n* clothes, clothing.
claith-like *adj* comfortably clothed.
claithman *n* a clothier, a woollen draper.
claiver *same as* **claver**.
clake[1] *same as* **claik**[4].
clake[2] *same as* **clack**[1].
clam[1] *adj* mean, low (*a schoolboys' word*).
clam[2] *n* a scallop shell.
clam[3] *v* climbed.
clam[4] *v* to grope at, grasp ineffectually.—*n* (*in pl*) **1** an instrument for weighing gold, like a forceps. **2** a vice or pincers used by saddlers and shoemakers. **3** nippers used by farriers for castration of animals and by shipwrights for drawing strong nails.
clam[5] *v* **1** to besmear, daub. **2** to stop a hole with an adhesive substance.—*adj* moist, clammy, sticky.
clamb *v* climbed.
clamehewit, clamiehewit, clamahouit *n* **1** a stroke, blow. **2** a drubbing. **3** a misfortune.
clamersum *adj* clamorous.
clamjamfry, clamjamphrey *n* **1** a company of people. **2** a mob. **3** a vulgar crowd. **4** the riffraff. **5** trumpery, odds and ends. **6** nonsensical talk.—*v* to crowd, to fill with a rabble.
clammer *v* to clamber, climb.
clammersome, clamoursome *adj* clamorous.
clammyhewit *same as* **clamehewit**.
clamp[1] *n* a small heap of peats.—*v* **1** to put peats in clamps. **2** to heap up potatoes, turnips, etc, in a mound.
clamp[2] *n* an iron brace to strengthen masonry.—*v* to hoop or brace with iron.
clamp[3] *n* a patch.—*v* to patch clothes.
clamp[4] *v* **1** to make a noise with the shoes in walking. **2** to

walk with a heavy and noisy tread. **3** to crowd things together noisily. **4** to walk on ice with clamps on the shoes.—*n* **1** a noisy blow or stroke. **2** a heavy footstep or noisy tread. **3** a piece of spiked iron fastened to the sole of the shoe by a strap across the instep, worn by curlers on the ice.

clamper[1] *v* **1** to patch, mend or make clumsily. **2** to patch up accusations industriously.—*n* **1** a piece of metal with which a vessel is mended. **2** the vessel thus mended. **3** arguments formerly answered. **4** a patched-up handle for crimination.

clamper[2] *v* **1** to make a clattering noise in walking. **2** to crowd things together noisily.—*n* a stout, heavy shoe.

clampe[3] *v* to fight a thing out.

clamps *n* claws, pincers used for castrating animals.

clampet *n* **1** a piece of iron worn on the shoes by curlers on the ice. **2** the guard of a sword handle.

clamph *same as* **clomph**.

clampher *v* to litter, strew in confusion.

clamp-kill *n* a kiln built of sods, for burning lime.

clamsh *n* a piece of wood with which a thing is clumsily mended.—*v* to splice two pieces of wood together.

clam shell *n* **1** a scallop shell. **2** (*in pl*) wild sounds supposed to be made by goblins in the air.

clan *n* a coterie, group, class, set of people.

clanch *n* an unmannerly person who eats like a pig.

clangle *n* a slight clang.

clanglumshous *adj* sulky.

clanjamph, clanjamfry, clanjamphries *same as* **clamjamfry**.

clank *v* **1** to strike with noise. **2** to thrash. **3** to seat oneself noisily and violently. **4** to take hold of noisily and violently.—*n* **1** a hasty catch. **2** a sounding noise. **3** a severe blow. **4** chatter.

clankum-bell *n* a bellman.

clankum-jankum *n* the noisy working of a pump handle.

clanter *n* the noise made by walking in a house with clogs.

clap *v* **1** to press down. **2** to sit or lie down. **3** to crouch. **4** to lie flat. **5** to place down or on hastily. **6** to pat, fondle. **7** to smooth with a flat implement. **8** to slam. **9** to beat the arms for warmth. **10** to strike with a noise. **11** to adhere. **12** to halt, tarry. **13** (*with* **down**) to write down. **14** (*with* **to**) to shut. **15** (*with* **up**) to imprison—*n* **1** a stroke. **2** the tongue of a bell. **3** the clapper of a mill. **4** a heavy fall. **5** the sound of a heavy fall. **6** a watchman's or town-crier's rattle. **7** a night-watchman's pole for rousing sleepers in the morning by knocking on their windows. **8** a moment.

clapdock breeches *n* breeches tightly made round the breech.

clap door *n* **1** the lower half of a door divided in the middle. **2** a trap door.

clapman *n* a public crier.

clap mill *n* clappers used like castanets. *See* **clappers**.

clapper *n* **1** a wooden rattle for scaring birds. **2** a door knocker. **3** a watchman's rattle. **4** a talkative person's tongue. **5** a talkative person. **6** a sharp, rattling noise. **7** the device in a mill for shaking the hopper so as to move the grain down to the millstones.—*v* to make a rattling noise.

clapper *n* a rabbit's hole.

clapperclash *n* gossip.

clapperclaw *v* **1** to strike a blow, as a spider at a fly. **2** to scratch in fighting.

clapperdin *n* a gossip.

clappers *n* two pieces of wood or bones used like castanets.

clapper stick *n* the clapper (qv) of a mill.

clappertie-clink *n* the sound of a the clapper (qv) of a mill.

clappit *adj* **1** (*used of a horse*) shrunk in the flesh after great fatigue. **2** flabby.

clappit-leukin *adj* thin or twisted in appearance.

clappity *adj* talkative.

clark *same as* **clerk**.

clark-plays *same as* **clerk-plays**.

clarried *adj* besmeared with mud.

clarsach *n* the old harp.

clart *n* **1** a spot of dirt, mud. **2** any dirty, defiling substance. **3** any sticky substance. **4** a dirty, slovenly woman. **5** a worthless article or person. **6** any large, awkward, dirty thing—*v* **1** to daub, smear with mud or dirt. **2** to work in a sloppy fashion. **3** to be employed in dirty, messy work. **4** to nurse a child to an excessive degree with little good effect.

clarty *adj* **1** dirty, sticky, filthy. **2** muddy. **3** miry.—*v* to dirty, befoul.

clash[1] *n* **1** the sound made by a heavy blow or fall, a blow, slap. **2** a heavy fall. **3** a quantity of moist or soft substance thrown at an object. **4** a heap of any heterogeneous substances, a mess. **5** a large quantity of anything. **6** a sudden shock. **7** a dash. **8** the throwing of a soft body. **9** something learned or repeated by rote. **10** gossip, tittle-tattle. **11** tale-bearing. **12** a tale-bearer, a great talker. **13** news.—*v* **1** to slam, bang, shut violently. **2** to slap with the open hand or something soft. **3** to pelt, throw mud or water, etc. **4** to gossip, tattle, tell tales. **5** (*with* **up**) to cause one object to adhere to another by mortar, etc.—*adv* with a clashing sound.

clash[2] *n* a cavity of considerable extent on the acclivity of a hill.

clashach *n* a lump of soft stuff.

clash-bag *n* **1** a tale-bearer, a great talker. **2** a bundle of scandal, gossip. **3** a person full of low, mean stories.

clasher *n* a tattler, tale-bearer.

clashing *n* **1** gossip, scandal. **2** a meeting for gossip.—*adj* given to tattling.

clash-ma-clavers, clash-ma-claters *n* **1** low, idle, scandalous tales. **2** silly talk.

clash-market *n* **1** a tattler, a scandalmonger. **2** one greatly given to gossip.

clash-piet, ~-pyot *n* a telltale, scandalmonger.

claspin *n* **1** a clasp. **2** a bracelet.

clasps *n* an inflammation of the termination of the sublingual gland, a disease of horses, caused by eating bearded forage.

clat[1] *n* **1** a clod of earth, turf, etc. **2** cow dung. **3** moist, wet earth. **4** a mess, a muddle.—*v* to bedaub, dirty, make a mess.

clat[2] *v* to prattle, chaster.

clat[3] *n* **1** a clutch. **2** a grasping hand. **3** an instrument for raking together dirt, mud, dung or for clearing the bars of a furnace of slag, cinders, ashes. **4** a hoe. **5** raking together property. **6** what is scraped together by niggardliness. **7** dirt, mud, dung, etc, as gathered in heaps. **8** a gathering of rags. **9** a handful.—*v* **1** to rake together. **2** to scrape together. **3** to accumulate by extortion. **4** to clean out a dish, pot or pan with a spoon. **5** to scratch.

clatch[1] *n* a brood of chickens or ducklings.

clatch[2] *n* **1** a mess, slop. **2** mire, dung, etc, raked together in heaps. **3** any soft substance thrown in order to daub. **4** any work done carelessly, a clumsily made article. **5** a fat, clumsy woman. **6** a slut. **7** a very loquacious woman.—*v* **1** to daub with lime. **2** to close up with any adhesive substance. **3** to finish work carelessly and hurriedly.

clatch[3] *n* **1** a slap with the palm of the hand. **2** the noise of the collision of soft bodies or of a heavy fall.

clatch[4] *n* a clutch, a sudden grasp at anything.

clatchin *n* **1** a brood of chickens or ducklings. **2** a setting of eggs.

clate *same as* **clat**[1].

clats *n* layers of 'cat and clay', the materials of which a mud-walled cottage is constructed.

clatt *same as* **clat**[1].

clatter *n* **1** noisy talk, chatter, familiar conversation. **2** gossip. **3** a chatterer, a gossip. **4** news, idle rumour.—*v* **1** to work noisily. **2** to chatter, talk fast or familiarly. **3** to gossip.

clatterbags *n* a chatterer, a tale-bearer.

clatter-bane *n* a bone supposed humorously to move when one chatters.

clatter-banes *n* bones used as castanets.

clatterbus *n* a gossip.

clatterer *n* a chatterer, a tale-bearer.

clatter goose *n* the brent goose.

clatter-malloch *n* meadow trefoil.

clattern *n* a tattler, babbler, a gossip.

clatter-strap *n* a noisy, chattering person.

clatter-traps *n* articles, goods for sale.

clatter-vengeance *n* one who talks with a vengeance.

clattie *adj* 1 nasty. 2 dirty, muddy. 3 obscene.

clattilie *adv* 1 nastily. 2 dirtily. 3 obscenely.

clattiness *n* 1 nastiness. 2 obscenity.

clatts *n* cards for teasing wool.

clauber *same as* **clabber**.

claucher *v* 1 to use both hands and feet in rising to stand or walk. 2 (*with* **up**) to snatch up. 3 (*with* **to**) to move forward to an object feebly from old age.

claucht, claught *v* to lay hold of forcibly and suddenly, to clutch.—*v* clutched, caught.—*n* 1 a sudden and forcible catch, a clutch, a grasp. 2 a handful. 3 a blow in clutching.

clauer *same as* **claur**.

clauick *same as* **claaick**.

claum¹ *same as* **clam**⁴.

claum² *same as* **clam**⁵.

claumy *adj* 1 clammy. 2 viscous.

claur *v* to clutch.

claurt¹ *n* 1 a clutch, grasp. 2 a scratch.

claurt² *v* to scrape together.—*n* what is so scraped.

claut *same as* **clat**³.

clautch *same as* **clatch**⁴

claut hook *n* a gaff or clip for landing salmon.

clautie scone *n* 1 coarse bread made of oatmeal and yeast. 2 a cake carelessly baked and fired.

clauts *n* cards for teasing wool.

claver¹ *n* clover.

claver² *v* 1 to talk idly or foolishly. 2 to chat, gossip. —*n* 1 one who talks foolishly. 2 (*generally in pl*) idle talk, gossip.

claverer *n* 1 a chatterer. 2 a gossip.

clavie *n* a tar barrel, within which is fixed a fir prop, surmounted by the staves of a herring cask, burned at Burghead on New Year's Eve to secure a good year's fishing.

claw¹ *n* 1 finger, hand. 2 clutch. 3 a scratch. 4 an iron spoon for scraping a baking board.—*v* 1 to scratch, tear with the claws. 2 to clutch. 3 to snatch up. 4 to paw, handle, fondle. 5 to scrape. 6 to hit. 7 to do anything smartly. 8 (*with* **aff**) to eat rapidly and voraciously.

claw² *n* a clause.

claw³ *n* a greatly perplexed, excited or frenzied state.

clawback *n* a flatterer.

claw-hammer coat *n* a swallow-tail coat.

clawscrunt *n* an old tree against which cattle rub themselves.

clay *v* 1 to stop a hole with clay or any viscous or adhesive substance. 2 (*with* **up**) (*of the eyes*) to bung up or blind in boxing.—*n* 1 a boys' clay marble. 2 the body, the flesh. 3 the grave.

clay-biggin *n* a cottage built of clay and wood.

clay-cauld *adj* quite cold, lifeless.

clayer, clayey *n* a boy's clay marble.

clay-hallan *n* a thin partition wall in a cottage.

clayock *same as* **claaick**.

clead *same as* **cleed**.

cleadfu' *adj* handsomely dressed.

cleading *same* as **cleeding**.

clean¹ *v* 1 to clear land of weeds, etc. 2 to clear, remove.

clean² *n* the after-birth of a cow or sheep.

clean³ *adj* 1 neat, well-made, shapely. 2 free from weeds. 3 (*of grain*) properly winnowed.—*adv* altogether, entirely.

clean-dakeith for *adj* too clever for.

clean-fittet *adj* having neat feet.

clean-fung *adv* cleverly.

clean muck *n* nothing but muck.

cleanse *v* to acquit, absolve.

clean-shankit *adj* having neat, well-shaped legs.

cleansing *n* the afterbirth of cows, sheep, etc.

clean town *n* a farm which all the servants leave together at one term.

clear¹ *adj* 1 certain, sure, determined. 2 ready, prepared. 3 free from punishment.—*adv* certainly, confidently.

clear² *v* 1 to search by raking or scratching. 2 to pay off in full.—*n* (*with* **the**) whisky.

clearer *n* a water insect with two rows of legs, found in quarry holes.

clear-headed *adj* bald-headed.

clearing *n* (*generally in pl*) 1 a scolding. 2 a beating.

clear kelty aff *v phr* to empty one's glass.

clear-lowing *adj* brightly burning.

clear o' the warld *phr* free of debt, able to pay one's way.

cleary *adj* (*perhaps*) shrill, sharp.

cleave *v* 1 (*with* **candles**) to make candles of bog fir. 2 (*with* **down**) to plough to the outside and from the middle ridge.

cleaving *n* the fork of the human body.

cleck¹ *same as* **claik**.

cleck² *v* 1 to hatch, bring forth. 2 to invent. 3 a setting of eggs.

cleck³ *v* to gossip, be talkative.—*n* idle, pert chatter.

clecker *n* a sitting hen.

cleckie *adj* prolific.

cleckin¹ *adj* gossiping, loquacious.

cleckin² *n* a brood, litter, family.

cleckin brod, ~ bred *n* a board for striking with at handball.

cleckin hen *n* a sitting hen.

cleckin stane *n* any stone that separates into small parts by exposure to the atmosphere.

cleckin time *n* 1 hatching time. 2 the time of birth.

cleckit *adj* 1 hatched, born. 2 *in phr* **ill-cleckit** misbegotten, base-born.

cled *adj* clad, clothed.

cled-bow *n* a heaped boll.

cled-score *n* twenty-one to the score.

cleed *v* 1 to clothe. 2 to cover over with a protection, to shelter, to heap.—*n* 1 an article of clothing. 2 dress.

cleeding *n* 1 clothes. 2 a suit of clothes. 3 a covering of deal boards. 4 the outer casing of a cylinder pipe or boiler. 5 the cover of a threshing-mill drum.

cleek¹ *v* 1 to seize with the claws, to clutch. 2 to grab, to snatch hastily, roughly or eagerly. 3 to hook, catch up by a hook, fasten on a hook. 4 to hook arms, walk arm in arm. 5 to attach oneself to, unite with. 6 to marry. 7 to cheat.—*n* 1 a clutch. 2 the arm. 3 a hook on which to hang pots over the fire. 4 a shepherd's crook. 5 a salmon gaff. 6 an inclination to cheat, a fraudulent disposition.

cleek² *n* 1 a small catch designed to fall into the notch of a wheel. 2 the latch of a door or gate.—*v* (*used of tooth and pinion*) to click.

cleek-anchor *n* a hook anchor of a boat.

cleek-hours *n* the keeping of horses in the harvest field yoked for ten hours a day.

cleek-in-the-back *n* 1 lumbago. 2 rheumatism.

cleeks *n* cramp in the legs of horses.

cleekum *n* a pastoral crook.

cleeky *n* a staff or stick with a crooked end.—*adj* 1 ready to snatch advantage. 2 inclined to cheat.

cleepie *n* 1 a severe blow. 2 a contusion. 3 a blow on the head.

cleer *v* to clear.—*adj* bright, shining.

cleesh¹ *n* a large mass of any semiliquid substance.

cleesh² *v* to repeat any idle story.

cleeshach *n* 1 the soft part of an animal's frame. 2 the fat or entrails of slaughtered animals. 3 a stout, unhealthy, dirty-looking woman.

cleester *n* a clyster.
cleet *same as* **clet**.
cleethe *v* to clothe.
cleetit *adj* **1** emaciated. **2** lank. **3** in a state of decay.
clevin *same as* **cleaving**.
cleg *n* **1** a gadfly, horsefly. **2** a prick, sting.
cleid *same as* **cleed**.
cleidach *same as* **clydigh**.
cleighin *n* something comparatively light.
cleik[1] *same as* **cleek**[1].
cleik[2] *adj* lively, agile, fleet.
cleipy *same as* **clypie**.
cleiro *n* **1** a sharp noise. **2** a shrill sound.
cleish *v* to whip, lash.—*n* **1** a whip. **2** a lash from a whip.
cleitach *same as* **clydigh**.
cleitch *n* a hard, heavy fall.
clekan-wittit *adj* childish, feeble-minded.
clekin *same as* **clacken**.
clem[1] *adj* **1** mean, low. **2** untrustworthy. **3** curious, singular.
clem[2] *v* to stop a hole by compression or by clay, mortar, etc.
clench[1] *same as* **clinch**.
clench[2] *v* to clutch with the hands.
clenchie-fit *n* a club foot.
clenge *v* **1** to cleanse. **2** to exculpate, to prove innocent.
clep[1] *v* to call, name.—*n* a citation in criminal cases.
clep[2] *n* an iron hook on which a pot is hung over the fire.
clep[3] *v* to walk or move like a crab.
clep[4] *same as* **clype**[1].
clepie *same as* **clypie**.
clepped *adj* **1** web-footed. **2** with the fingers webbed.
clepping *n* tale-telling.
clepshears *same as* **clipshears**.
clerk *n* a scholar.—*v* **1** to write, indite, compose. **2** to act as an amanuensis.—*adj* learned, scholarly.
clerk-curate *n* a priest.
clerk-plays *n* theatrical representations of scriptural subjects.
clert *same as* **clart**.
clet, clett *n* a rock or cliff in the sea broken off from adjoining rocks on the shore.
cleuch[1] *adj* **1** clever. **2** dexterous, light-fingered. **3** inclined to take advantage. **4** niggardly.
cleuch[2] *n* **1** a ravine. **2** a narrow glen. **3** a deep wooded valley. **4** a coal pit.
cleuch-brae *n* **1** a cliff overhanging a ravine. **2** the slope of a cleuch.
cleuchten *n* a flat-lying ridge.
cleugh *same as* **cleuch**[2].
cleuk *n* **1** a hand. **2** a claw. **3** a paw. **4** a clutch, grasp, hold.—*v* **1** to seize. **2** to scratch with the claws. **3** to grip, clutch.
cleurach *same as* **clorach**.
clev *v* to reel up a fishing handline after use.
clever[1] *v* **1** to climb, to scramble. **2** to hurry, to make haste, look sharp.
clever[2] *adj* **1** good, well-behaved. **2** eloquent, fluent of speech. **3** able. **4** quick, speedy.
cleverality *n* ability, cleverness.
clew[1] *n* **1** *in phr* **the winding of the clew** a Hallowe'en ceremony to ascertain one's future spouse. **2** wealth amassed.
clew[2] *v* clawed.
clibber *n* a wooden saddle, a packsaddle.
clichen *n* something comparatively very light.
click[1] *n* **1** a moment of time. **2** a latch of a door or gate. **3** the tick of a clock.—*v* to tick as a clock, etc.
click[2] *v* **1** to seize, catch up hastily, grab. **2** to steal.
click-clack *n* uninterrupted loquacity.
clickett-staff *n* a hooked staff.
click-for-clack *adv* with ceaseless talk.
clicking *n* ticking.
clicky *same as* **cleeky**.

clicky-staff *n* a hooked staff.
clidyoch *n* the gravel bed of a river.
clien *n* a small heap of stones.
cliers *n* **1** a disease affecting the throat of a cow. **2** thick saliva that obstructs the windpipe.
clift *n* **1** a cleft. **2** the fork of the legs. **3** a piece of ground separated from the rest.
cliftie[1] *adj* **1** clever. **2** (*applied to a horse of light make and good action*) fleet. **3** (*used of fuel*) easily kindled and burning brightly.
cliftie[2] *adj* rugged, with clefts and fissures in ground.
cliftin' *n* a cleft of a rock.
cliftiness *n* the quality of being easily kindled and burning brightly.
clim *v* to climb.—*n* a climb.
clime *n* *in phr* **heeze up to the climes** to extol to the skies.
climmer *n* a climber.
climp[1] *v* **1** to hook. **2** to take hold of suddenly. **3** to pilfer.
climp[2] *v* to limp, to halt.
climpet *n* a sharp-pointed rock.
climpie *n* a lame person.
climpy *adj* thievish, inclined to purloin.
clinch *v* **1** to limp, to halt. **2** to feign lameness.—*n* a halt, a limp.
clincher *n* a lame or halt person.
cling[1] *v* (*used of vessels made with staves*) to shrink with heat,
cling[2] *n* diarrhoea in sheep.
cling-and-clang *n* the clinking of glasses, etc.
clink[1] *n* **1** a sharp metallic sound or ring. **2** a chime. **3** stroke of a bell. **4** a smart, resounding blow. **5** rhyme, jingling metre. **6** a woman telltale. **7** money, cash, coin. **8** an instant, a moment. —*v* **1** to chink, jingle. **2** to beat, thrash. **3** (*used of verses*) to rhyme, go well together. **4** to compose. **5** to move with a clinking sound. **6** to walk briskly. **7** to do anything smartly or unexpectedly. **8** to spread scandal. **9** to fly as a rumour. **10** (*with* **up**) to seize forcibly and quickly. **11** (*with* **out**) to die.
clink[2] *v* **1** to hammer, to weld by hammering, to clinch. **2** to mend, patch clothes. **3** to hold to an agreement. **4** to jot down in writing.
clink[3] *adj* alert.
clink-and-clank *n* the clinking of glasses, etc.
clinker[1] *n* a telltale.
clinker[2] *n* anything large or good of its kind.
clinkers *n* broken pieces of rock.
clinkie *adj* noisy.
clinking[1] *adj* **1** jerking. **2** (*used of coin*) jingling, chinking. **3** (*of verses*) rhyming, jingling.
clinking[2] *n* a beating, a thrashing.
clinkit *adj* **1** struck. **2** mended. **3** clasped. **4** riveted.
clink-knock *v* to rhyme easily and readily.
clink-nail *n* a nail that is clinched or riveted.
clinkum *n* a ringer of a church bell or of a town bell.
clinkum-bell *n* a church- or town-bell ringer.
clinkum-clankum *n* a rattling sound in which a metallic sound predominates.
clinkum-jankum *n* a creaking, rattling sound, as when water is drawn from a well into a bucket by a pump.
clinkum-toll *n* the ringing of a bell.
clint *n* **1** a rocky cliff. **2** a projecting rock or ledge. **3** flinty or hard rock. **4** a hard, tough stone used in curling and first played off.
clinted *adj* (*used of sheep*) caught among cliffs by leaping down to a ledge from which ascent is impossible by leaping back.
clinter *n* the player of a clint (qv) in curling.
clintin' *n* a cleft of a rock.
clinty *adj* hard, flinty.
clip[1] *n* **1** the foal of a mare. **2** an unbroken colt.
clip[2] *n* **1** a gaff for landing fish. **2** an instrument for lifting a pot from the fire. **3** one for carrying a barrel, etc,

between two persons. **4** a pincer-shaped wooden imple- ment for weeding out thistles. **5** an instrument like tongs, with long wooden handles, formerly used to catch dogs intruding into a church.—*v* **1** to gaff a salmon or other fish. **2** to catch and hold a dog in a clip.

clip³ *v* **1** to embrace, clasp with the arms. **2** (*used of a mus-ket ball*) to pass quite close to, whiz past almost touch-ing one.

clip⁴ *v* **1** to cut horses' rough winter coats. **2** to shear sheep. **3** to cut short, curtail, lessen. **4** to speak indistinctly. **5** to speak affected English—*n* **1** a newly shorn sheep. **2** the yearly sheep-shearing. **3** the amount of wool shorn yearly. **4** a smart cuff or blow. **5** (*with* **the**) the very thing.

clip⁵ *n* a wild, romping, pert girl.

clip-clouts *n* a sharp-tongued person.—*v* **1** to argue or speak snappishly. **2** to talk sharply about little or noth-ing.

clipe¹ *v* to scratch with the nails.—*n* a scratch made by the nails.

clipe², **clipe³**, **clipe⁴** *same as* **clype¹**, **clype²**, **clype³**.

clipfast *n* a pert, impudent girl.

clip house *n* the house formerly set apart for defacing or clipping false coins.

clipie *same as* **clypie**.

clipmalabor *n.* **1** a girl who does as little work as possible. **2** an impudent girl.

clipock *n* a fall.

clippart¹ *n* a shorn sheep.

clippart² *n* a talkative woman.

clipper¹ *n* a sheep-shearer.

clipper² *n* anything first-rate of its kind.

clipper-clapper *n* the sound of a revolving millwheel or clapper.

clipperty-clap *n* clipper-clapper (qv).

clippet *adj* (*used of language*) affected, indistinct from mincing one's words.

clippie *n* **1** a young person wearing too neatly cut clothes. **2** a talkative woman.—*adj* sharp of speech, snappish, pert.

clippie *n* a shorn sheep.

clippin' *n* sheep-shearing.

clippinet *n* an impudent girl, a talkative woman.

clipping house *n* the house for clipping false coin.

clippin' time *n* the nick of time.

clippock *n* a sharp-tongued person.

clippy *n* a greedy, grasping person.

clips¹ *n* **1** shears. **2** snuffers.

clips² *n* stories, false tales.

clipshears *n* the earwig.

clipwit *adj* biting or shrewd of speech.—*n* a sharp-tongued, quick-witted speaker.

clire *same as* **clyer**.

clired *adj* having tumours in the flesh.

clish *v* to repeat an idle story.

clish-clash *n* **1** idle talk. **2** rumour. **3** scandal.

clish-for-clash *n* ceaseless talking.

clish-ma-clash *n* **1** idle talk. **2** gossip.

clish-ma-clashin' *adj* gossiping

clish-ma-claver *n* **1** idle talk. **2** gossip. **3** false or scandal-ous reports.—*v* to indulge in idle talk, gossip, etc.

clite¹ *same as* **cloit¹**.

clite² *adj* splay-footed.

clitie *n* the fall of a child.

clitter-clatter *n* **1** a sharp, clattering noise. **2** a succession of rattling sounds. **3** chatter, idle talk, noisy talk.—*v* **1** to make a sharp, rattling noise. **2** to walk or run with sharp, noisy steps. **3** to talk a great deal noisily.—*adv* with a succession of rattling sounds.

clitter-clatterin' *n* **1** idle talk. **2** the act of gossiping.—*adj* given to gossip.

clivace *n* a hook for catching the buckets in which coals were drawn up from the pit.

clivver *n* clover.

clivvie *n* **1** a cleft in the branch of a tree. **2** an artificial cleft in a piece of wood for holding a rush light

cloa *n* coarse woollen cloth made in the Isle of Skye.

cloan *n* a large, round mass of dirt.

clobber *same as* **clabber**.

clobber-hoy *n* a dirty walker, one who becomes muddy in walking.

clobbery *adj* dirty, muddy.

clocaleddy *same as* **clock-leddie**.

cloch *v* to cough frequently and feebly.

clocharch *n* the wheatear.

clocharet, clochret *n* the stonechat.

clocher *v* to cough with much expectoration, wheeze.—*n* a wheezing in the throat or chest with much mucus.

clocherin *n* **1** mucous ronchus. **2** the sound of coughing.—*adj* wheezing.

clock¹ *v* **1** to cluck. **2** to hatch, sit on eggs. **3** to call chick-ens together.—*n* **1** the condition of a hen when she wishes to sit on eggs. **2** a hen's call to her chickens.

clock² *n* a beetle.

clock-bee *n* a flying beetle.

clocker *n* a sitting hen.

clockiedow *n* the river pearl oyster or horse mussel.

clockin' *n* a hearty welcome.

clocking *n* **1** the act of hatching or desiring to sit on eggs. **2** the disposition or wish to marry. **3** inclination to wan-tonness.

clocking hen *n* **1** a brooding or sitting hen. **2** a woman capable of bearing children. **3** a sum of money at interest in a bank.

clocking time *n* **1** the time for hatching. **2** the time of child-bearing. **3** pregnancy.

clock-leddie *n* the ladybird.

clocks *same as* **clouks**.

clocksie, clocksey *adj* vivacious.

clod¹ *v* (*of crows*) to dart up and down in flying.

clod² *n* **1** a clew of yarn, etc. **2** a ball of twisted straw rope.

clod³ *n* a small halfpenny loaf or bap (qv) made of coarse, brownish flour.

clod⁴ *n* a single peat or piece of peat.—*v* **1** to throw as a clod. **2** to pelt with clods. **3** to fling, dash. **4** to throw or pile up peats in building a stack. **5** to break clods on land.

cloddan *n* flying up and down rapidly.

clodder *n* the person who throws up peats to the builder of the stack.

cloddoch *n* a small heap of stones.

cloddy *adj* full of clods.

clod-fire *n* a peat fire.

clod-mell *n* a wooden mallet for breaking clods.

clod-shod *adj* (*used of a ploughman, etc*) having the boots weighted with adhering soil.

clod-thumper *n* a heavy roller for crushing clods on land.

cloff *n* **1** a fissure, crevice. **2** a cleft between two hills. **3** the fork or cleft of a tree where a branch joins the trunk.

cloffin¹ *n* the act of sitting idly by the fire.

cloffin² *n* the noise made by a loose shoe on man or beast.

clog *n* **1** a small, short log. **2** a short cut of a tree. **3** a thick piece of timber.—*v* to burden an estate.

clogger *n* a maker of wooden shoes.

cloggie *n* a wearer of wooden shoes.

cloich *n* **1** a place of shelter. **2** the cavity of a rock where one may elude search.

cloik *v* to cluck.

cloit¹ *v* **1** to fall heavily down suddenly. **2** to bump down smartly. **3** to squat down.—*n* a hard and sudden fall.—*adv* suddenly, with a bump.

cloit² *n* **1** a heavy burden. **2** a clown. **3** a stupid, inactive fellow.

cloit³ *n* an afternoon nap, siesta.

cloiter *v* **1** to do dirty work. **2** to handle liquid in a careless or slovenly way.—*n* the act of working carelessly or dirt-ily among liquids or wet substances.

cloitery *adj* **1** dirty. **2** messy. **3** sticky.—*n* **1** dirty, messy work. **2** filth. **3** offal.

cloitery-maid *n* a female servant whose work it was to carry off filth or rubbish.

cloitery-market *n* an Edinburgh market where the offal of animals was sold.

cloitery-wife *n* a woman who cleans and sells tripe, etc.

clokie-doo *same as* **clockiedow**.

clok-leddy *same as* **clockleddie**.

clomb *v* climbed.

clomph *v* **1** to walk in a dull, heavy manner. **2** to walk in shoes too large or loose.

cloo¹ *n* a scraper of heavy sheet-iron, riveted on to an ox hoof, used for scraping scalded pigs.

cloo² *n* **1** a ball of worsted. **2** a ball of straw rope.

clood *n* a cloud.

clook *same as* **cleuk**.

cloor *same as* **clour**.

cloose *same as* **clouse**.

clooster *n* **1** a cluster. **2** a group. **3** a collection or bunch of various things. **4** a miscellaneous heap. **5** a mass of wet or sticky stuff, mud, etc.—*v* to besmear, to clot.

cloot¹ *n* **1** a division of the hoof of cattle, sheep, pigs, etc. **2** the hoof, foot. **3** (*in pl*) the devil.

cloot², cloot³ *same as* **clout¹**, **clout²**.

clooter *n* the noise made by a badly delivered curling stone.

clootie, clootie-ben *n* the devil.

clootie's craft *n* the devil's croft, the goodman's field (qv), a small portion of land set apart for the devil and left untilled.

clooty *same as* **clouty**.

clorach *v* **1** to do domestic work dirtily and untidily. **2** to expectorate greatly. **3** to sit lazily over a fire, as if in bad health. **4** to coddle a sick child or animal by overnursing.—*n* **1** a mass of liquid or semiliquid substance. **2** ill-cooked or ill-served food.

clort *same as* **clart**.

clortin *n* **1** a besmearing. **2** (*with* **on**) a thick besmearing.

clorty *same as* **clarty**.

close¹ *n* **1** enclosed land. **2** a farmyard. **3** a narrow alley. **4** a blind alley.

close² *adj* **1** constant. **2** regular. **3** reticent. **4** (*of weather*) oppressive. **5** (*of evening*) dusky. **6** foggy. **7** (*of a fog*) thick.—*adv* constantly, regularly.

close³ *v* to breathe with difficulty from cold, etc.

close bed *n* a panelled bedstead with wooden hinged or sliding doors, a box bed (qv).

close cart *n* **1** a farm cart. **2** a covered ammunition cart.

closeevie *n* **1** a collection, lot, number. **2** *in phr* **the haill closeevie** the whole lot or collection.

close fit *n* the lower or inner end of a close (qv) or alley.

close head *n* the entrance or mouth of a close, opening on a street.

close mouth *n* the principal entrance to a close (qv).

close-nieved *adj* close-fisted.

closer *n* **1** a conclusive argument or blow. **2** the act of shutting-up.

close-sichtit *adj* **1** near-sighted. **2** short-sighted.

close-thonged *adj* tightly laced.

closhach, closhich *n* **1** a large mass or handful of a semiliquid substance. **2** a handful. **3** a gathering. **4** money saved. **5** a person lying in a heap. **6** a dead body.

closing *n* a difficulty in breathing from cold, asthma, etc.

closs *n* **1** a close (qv). **2** a lane. **3** a passage through a house.

clossach *same as* **closhach**.

closter *n* a cloister.

clotch *v* to walk heavily, move awkwardly.—*n* **1** a clumsy, awkward person. **2** anything worn-done. **3** a person with a broken constitution. **4** a bungler.

clotch *v* to sit lazily.

clotchy *adj* liable to colds.

clothes-press *n* a wardrobe.

cloth-rund *n* a washer of cloth on the spindle of a roving box, between the lifter plate and roving.

cloth-runds *n* selvedges of cloth.

clotter *v* to clot, congeal.

clotterit, clottert *adj* clotted.

cloudberry *n* the ground mulberry.

cloudy *adj* threatening, perilous.

cloughret *n* the stonechat.

clouk *v* to cluck as a hen.

clouks *n* the refuse of grain after sifting in a riddle.

cloup *n* curve or bend in a stick.

cloupie *n* a walking stick with the head bent in a semicircle.

cloupit *adj* (*used of a walking stick*) having the head curved.

clour *v* to strike, indent, batter, beat.—*n* **1** a blow. **2** an indentation. **3** a lump caused by a blow.

clouring *n* a beating.

clouse *n* a sluice.

clout¹ *v* to beat, strike with the hands.—*n* **1** a blow, slap, box on the ear. **2** a heavy fall.—*phr* **fa' clout** to fall on the ground with force.

clout² *v* to patch, mend, repair.—*n* **1** a patch. **2** a rag, a shred of cloth. **3** a cloth used for household purposes. **4** a sail of a boat. **5** a garment. **6** an infant's napkin. **7** (*in pl*) clothes, ragged clothes. **8** *phr* **as white's a clout** very pale.

clouted *v, adj* **1** dressed. **2** clothed. **3** patched.

clouter¹ *n* the noise made by a badly delivered curling stone.

clouter² *v* **1** to to walk noisily. **2** to work in a dirty fashion.

clouty *adj* **1** ragged, patched. **2** made of cloth clippings.

clove *n* an instrument used in preparing flax by which those shows are removed which have not been taken off at the scutch mill (qv). **3** (*used of a mill*) that which removes the bridgeheads. **4** (*in pl*) an implement of wood, closing like a vice, in which carpenters fix their saws to sharpen them. —*v* to separate lint from the stalk.

clover sick *adj* used of land on which clover has been grown too often to support it further.

clow¹, clowe *n* **1** a clove. **2** one of the laminae of a head of garlic. **3** the clove pink.

clow² *v* to beat down.

clow³ *v* to eat or sup greedily.

clow⁴ *n* a sluice.

clow⁵ *n* a small bar of wood on a screw pivot, fixed to a door to prevent it from being opened.

clow-July flower *n* the clove pink, clove gillyflower.

clowk *n* the gurgling in the neck of a bottle while its contents are being poured out.—*v* **1** to gurgle when liquid is poured from a full bottle. **2** to whip up eggs.

clown *v, adj* cloven.

clowns *n* the butterwort.

clowr *same as* **clour**.

clowse *same as* **clow⁴**.

clowtter *v* **1** to work dirtily. **2** to do dirty work.

cloyte *same as* **cloit¹**.

club *n* **1** a golf or shinty club. **2** a club-shaped knot in which men's hair was formerly dressed. **3** finger and toe (qv) in turnips.—*v* (*used of turnips, cabbage, etc*) **1** to be diseased with finger-and-toe (qv) or bulbous malformation. **2** to dress or wear the hair in a club.

clubber *same as* **clibber**.

clubbish *adj* clumsy, heavy, disproportionately made.

clubbock *n* the spotted blenny.

club-fitted *adj* **1** having the feet turned too much inward. **2** having deformed feet. **3** club-footed.

clubsides you *int phr* used by boys at shinty when a player strikes from the wrong side.

club-tae'd *adj* club-footed.

clucking *same as* **clocking**.

clud *n* **1** a cluster, crowd. **2** a cloud.

cluddock *n* a dry, shingly bed at the side of a stream.

cluddy *adj* cloudy.

clud-fawer *n* a bastard child, one fallen from the clouds.

cludgie *n* a lavatory, a toilet.

clue *v* clawed, scratched.

cluf *n* **1** a hoof. **2** a claw.

cluff *v* to cuff, slap.—*n* a cuff, slap.

cluggie *same as* **cloggie**.

clugston *n* an obsolete amusement among farmers.

cluif *same as* **cluf**.

cluik *v* **1** to grip. **2** to scratch.—*n* **1** the hand. **2** a claw, paw. **3** a clutch. *cf* cleuk.

cluish *v* **1** gossiped. **2** slapped. **3** slammed. *See* **clash**¹.

cluit *same as* **cloot**¹.

cluke *same as* **cleuk**.

clukny *n* **1** a hen. **2** a term of contempt for a person.

clum *v* climbed.

clumber *v* to daub, as with clay.

clump *n* **1** a heavy, unwieldy person. **2** the noise of a heavy shoe or footfall. **3** a thud, a heavy blow. —*v* to walk or tread heavily.

clumper *n* (*in pl*) **1** shapeless blocks of stone scattered on the ground. **2** thick, heavy shoes or clogs.—*v* to make a noise in walking, as with heavy or loose shoes.

clumsey *adj* (*used of a meat bone*) having meat adhering to it.

clunch *n* a lump, a mass, a hunch.

clung *v*, *adj* shrunken, empty from want of food, hungry.

clunk *v* to emit a hollow, interrupted sound, like liquid issuing from a bottle or narrow orifice.—*n* **1** a hollow sound as of a fall. **2** the sound of a cork being drawn, of a liquid coming from a bottle or narrow orifice or of a pebble falling perpendicularly from a height into smooth and deep water. **3** a draught, what is swallowed at a gulp. **4** the call of a hen to her chickens when she has found food for them.

clunkart *n* **1** a very large piece of anything. **2** a large hump or bump on the body. **3** a stout, dumpy person or child.

clunker *n* **1** a tumour. **2** a bump. **3** a good big glassful. **4** (*in pl*) dirt hardened in clots, tendering a road, pavement or floor uneven. **5** inequalities in a road, etc, caused by frost.

clunkerd *adj* (*used of a road or floor*) overlaid with clots of indurated dirt.

clunkert *same as* **clunkart**.

clunkertonie *n* a jellyfish, medusa.

cluph *n* an idle, trifling creature.

cluphin *v*, *adj* spending time idly and in a slovenly way.

clure *same as* **clour**.

clushach *same as* **closhach**.

clushan *n* cow dung as it drops in a small heap.

clushet¹ *n* **1** the udder of a cow. **2** the stomach of a sow.

clushet² *n* one in charge of a cow house.

clute *same as* **cloot**¹.

clute *same as* **clout**².

cluther¹ *v* to conceal, to cover, huddle up.

cluther² *same as* **clutter**.

clutie *same as* **clootie**.

clutter *n* **1** a disorderly heap. **2** a piece of bad stone building. **3** noise, commotion, bustle.—*v* to do anything in an awkward or dirty way of working.

clyack *same as* **claaick**.

clyack dish *n* meal and ale, a mixture of home-brewed ale and oatmeal, with a little whisky stirred into it, forming the chief dish at the harvest home.

clyack horn *n* a drinking horn used at the harvest home.

clyack sheaf *n* the last sheaf shorn at harvest.

clyauk *same as* **clack**².

clydigh *v* **1** to talk in a strange tongue, especially Gaelic. **2** to talk inarticulately, chatter as a child. —*n* talk, discourse.

clydyock *same as* **clidyoch**.

clyer *n* **1** a gland formed in the fat of beef or mutton. **2** a hard substance formed on the liver or iungs of animals. **3** (*in pl*) a disease affecting the throat of a cow.

clypach *v* **1** to work dirtily and in slovenly fashion. **2** to walk in a dirty and ungraceful fashion. **3** to hang wet, loose and dishevelled. **4** to gossip, to speak much and loudly.—*n* **1** a large, wet mass of anything semiliquid. **2** a hanging wet mass. **3** work done dirtily among semiliquid substances. **4** walking ungracefully. **5** a heavy

fall on wet ground. **6** a dirty, uncomely and disagreeable person. **7** gossip, one who gossips.—*adv* flatly, heavily, with noise.

clype¹ *v* to tell tales, gossip.—*n* **1** a telltale. **2** idle tales.

clype² *v* **1** to walk over wet ground in a slovenly fashion. **2** to act as a drudge.—*n* **1** work done in a dirty manner. **2** a clot, a confused, wet mass. **3** a drudge. **4** an ugly, ill-shaped fellow.

clype³ *v* to fall.—*n* a fall.—*adv* flat, heavily, with noise.

clyper *n* a telltale.

clypie *n* **1** a telltale.—*adj* **1** gossiping. **2** loquacious. **3** tattling.

clypie-clash-pyet *n* a chattering telltale.

clypin' thing *n* a tale-bearer.

clypit *adj* (*used of clothes*) loose, ill-made, badly fitting.

clypock *same as* **clypach**.

clyre *same as* **clyer**.

clystre *v* to besmear.—*n* a mass of semiliquid stuff.

clytach¹ *v* to walk or work dirtily.—*n* a mass of semiliquid stuff.

clytach² *same as* **clydigh**.

clyte¹ *n* a mass of liquid or semiliquid stuff.

clyte² *same as* **cloit**¹.

clyter¹ *v* **1** to walk ungracefully. **2** *with* **over** to overnurse. **3** to gossip. **4** to speak a strange tongue.—*n* **1** an ungraceful walk, as over wet ground. **2** gossiping. **3** speaking and speech in a strange tongue.—*adv* **1** with ungraceful step. **2** with force.

clyter² *same as* **cloiter**.

clyteran *n* **1** the hum of many people speaking. **2** overnursing.

clytie lass *n* the servant girl who carries out house filth, etc.

clytrie *same as* **cloitery**.

clytrie maid *same as* **cloitery maid**.

clytrie market *same as* **cloitery market**.

clytrie wife *same as* **cloitery wife**.

co¹ *same as* **cove**.

co² *v* quoth.

coach *v* to drive in a coach.

coachbell *n* an earwig.

coact *v* forced, constrained.

coag¹ *v* to shear and so save the neck wool of sheep sometime before the regular sheepshearing.

coag² *n* a wooden vessel for holding porridge, milk, etc.

coal *n* a red-hot cinder.

coal-and-candlelight *n* the long-tailed duck.

coal grieve *n* a coal overseer.

coal gum *n* coal dust.

coal heugh *n* a coal pit.

coal hood, ~ hoodie, ~ hooden *n* **1** the reed bunting. **2** the blackcap. **3** the British cole-titmouse.

coalmie *n* the full-grown coalfish.

coalsay *n* the coalfish, the saith.

coal scoop *n* a coal scuttle.

coal stalk *n* a vegetable impression found on stones in coal mines.

coal-stealer-rake *n* a thief, a vagabond.

coalyer *n* a collier.

coaly hood *same as* **coal hood**.

coan *same as* **cown**.

coarctat *v* coerced, restrained.

coarse *adj* **1** (*used of the weather*) rough, stormy. **2** rough, brutal.

coaster *n* a resident along the coast of Caithness, south of Wick.

coat *n* a petticoat.

coat-and-bit *phr* clothes and food.

coatie *n* **1** a child's coat. **2** a child's petticoat.

coats *n* refuse of threshed corn, beans, etc, given to horses.

cob¹ *v* to shear the wool off a ewe's udder.

cob² *n* the husk of a pea.

cob³ *n* a kind of coin.

cob⁴ *v* to beat one on the backside.—*n* a blow.

cobble[1] *v* to bungle.—*n* a tangle, confusion.
cobble[2] *same as* **coble**[4].
cobbler *n* a bungler.
coble[1] *n* **1** a short, flat-bottomed boat, used in salmon fishings and in ferries. **2** a deckless fishing boat with sharp bow, flat, sloping stern and without a keel, used on the northeast coast.
coble[2] *n* a place for steeping malt.—*v* to steep malt for brewing.
coble[3] *n* a square pew in a church.
coble[4] *n* a pond for cattle, etc, to drink at.
coble[5] *v* **1** to rock. **2** to undulate, be unsteady. **3** to see-saw.—*n* **1** a rocking motion. **2** a seesaw. **3** playing at seesaw.
cobleing *n* steeping malt.
cobletehow-mutch *n* (*perhaps*) a cap ironed or dressed fancifully.
coblie[1] *adj* **1** shaky. **2** liable to rock or undulate.
coblie[2] *n* a small pond.
cob-selbow *n* a young shoot from onions of the second year's growth.
cobworm *n* the larva of the cockchafer.
cochbell *same as* **coachbell**.
cock[1] *n* **1** a brisk, smart fellow. **2** a familiar term of address. **3** a boys' game, 'rexa-boxa-king'. **4** the tee of a curling rink.
cock[2] *n* **1** a cap, a headdress. **2** an upward turn or tilt. **3** a brickwork projection in steps to receive a piece of timber.—*v* **1** to swagger, show off. **2** to hold erect, prick up. **3** to lift up threateningly. **4** to throw up to a high or inaccessible place. **5** to stick a hat or cap jauntily on one side of the head. **6** to mount an offender on another's back for a flogging. **7** to make a false shot, miss. **8** to go back from a bargain. **9** (*with* **up**, *used contemptuously*) giving to anyone what he does not deserve or to one who is too ambitious. **10** to indulge, pamper needlessly.
cock[3] *adj* fuddled.
cock-a-bendy *n* **1** a sprightly boy. **2** an instrument for twisting ropes, consisting of a hollow piece of wood, through which runs a pin that, being turned, twists the rope.
cock-able *adj* **1** of age. **2** of the age of puberty.
cock-a-breekie *n* a person of small stature.
cock-a-hoop *adj* intoxicated.—*n* a bumper.
cockalane, cockaland *n* **1** a comic representation. **2** a satire. **3** an imperfect writing. **4** an infamous libel. **5** a pasquinade.
cock-a-leekie *n* soup made of a fowl boiled with leeks.
cockalorum-like *adj* foolish, absurd.
cock-and-key *n* a stopcock.
cock-and-pail *n* a spigot and faucet.
cockandy *n* the puffin.
cock-a-pentie *n* one whose pride makes him or her live above his or her income.
cock-a-ridy *v* (*of a child*) to ride on the shoulders with a leg on each side of the person carrying.
cock-a-roora-koo *n* the sound of cockcrowing.
cockats *n* a scolding.
cockawinie *v* to ride on the shoulders of another.
cock-bead plane *n* a plane for making a moulding that projects above the common surface of the timber.
cock-bird height *n* **1** tallness equal to that of a male chicken. **2** infancy. **3** elevation of spirits.
cock-bird high *adj* youthful, very young.
cock-brain *n* a weak brain.
cock-bree cock-a-leekie (qv)
cock-crow kail *n* broth heated a second time.
cocked *v, adj* **1** containing sperm. **2** (*with* **up**) conceited. **3** (*with* **up with**) overindulged.
cockee *n* the circle round the tee towards which curling stones must be played.
cocker[1] *n* the sperm of an egg.
cocker[2] *n* a dram of whisky.
cocker[3] *v* **1** to be tottering, unsteady. **2** to put in an insecure place.

cocker[4] *v* to fondle, indulge, pamper.
cocker-de-cosie, ~-de-hoy *v* to sit or ride astride on the shoulders of a person.
cockerie *adj* unsteady in position, likely to tumble.
cockerieness *n* **1** insecurity of position. **2** instability.
cockernonie *n* **1** the gathering of a woman's hair into a snood or fillet. **2** anything small, neat and old-fashioned.
cookernonied *adj* having the hair dressed in a cockernonie (qv).
cockersum *adj* unsteady, threatening to tumble.
cockertie-hooie *n* carrying a boy astride the neck.
cockerty *adj* unstable, shaky.
cock-fechtin *n* cock-fighting.
cock-fight *n* a boys' game played by two hopping on one leg and butting each other with their shoulders until one lets down his leg.
cock-head *n* the herb all-heal or woundwort.
cock-headed *adj* **1** vain, conceited. **2** whimsical.
cockie *adj* **1** vain. **2** affecting airs of importance.
cockie-bendie *n* **1** the cone of the fir tree. **2** the large conical bud of the plane tree.
cockie-breekie *adv in phr* **ride cockie-breekie** to sit or ride astride on the shoulders of a person.
cockie-dandie *n* **1** a bantam cock. **2** a pert, forward youngster.
cockie-leekie *n* soup made from a fowl boiled with leeks.
cockie-leerie *n* **1** a cock, chanticleer. **2** the sound of a cock crowing.
cockie-loorie *n* **1** a children's name for any showy artificial flower or bright-coloured thing with which they play. **2** a knot of ribbon or other bright-coloured thing.
cockie-ridie-rousie, ~-rosie *n* **1** a game of children in which one rides on another's shoulders. **2** a punishment inflicted by children on each other.
cockin' *n* a cock fight.
cockin *n* the sperm of an egg.
cock-laird *n* **1** a small landholder who cultivates his own estate. **2** a yeoman.
cockle[1] *v* **1** to crow like a cock. **2** to cackle like a hen.
cockle[2] *v* to totter, be unstable.
cockle[3] *v* to cuckold.
cockle[4] *v* to mark the cogs of a mill before cutting off the ends of them, so that the whole may preserve the circular form.—*n* the instrument used in marking the cogs of a mill.
cockle[5] *v* (*with* **up**) to become better in health or spirits.
cockle-brained *adj* whimsical, eccentric.
cockle-cutit *adj* having bad ankles, so that the feet seem twisted away from them, lying outwards.
cockle-headed *adj* **1** whimsical. **2** eccentric.
cockler *n* one who cuckolds a husband.
cockloft, ~laft *n* **1** the space between the uppermost ceiling and the roof. **2** the highest gallery in a church.
cockman *n* a sentinel.
cock-melder *n* the last melder (qv) or grinding of a year's grain.
cock-my-fud *n* rum shrub.
cocknee stones *n* the echinus or buttonstone.
cock o'crowdie *n phr* a term of commendation.
cock o' pluck *n phr* a brave fellow.
cock o' the midden *n phr* the master, superior, one who has it all his own way.
cock o' the North *n* a name given to the dukes of Gordon.
cock-paddle *n* the lumpfish.
cock-picket *adj* pecked or dabbled in by poultry.
cock-raw *adj* sparingly roasted or boiled.
cockrel *n* **1** a cockerel. **2** a young male raven.
cock rose *n* a wild poppy with a red flower.
cock's-caim *n* meadow pink or cuckooflower.
cock's-comb *n* adder's-tongue.
cock's-eye *n* a halo that appears round the moon and indicates stormy weather.
cock's-foot, cock's-foot grass *n* the dewgrass.
cock-shilfa *n* the male chaffinch.

cocksie *adj* affecting airs of importance.

cock's-odin, ~-hoddin *n* a boys' game of hide-and-seek.

cock stool, ~-stule *n* **1** the cuckstool. **2** the pillory.

cockstride *n* **1** a short distance. **2** used figuratively of the lengthening of days. **3** a boys' game.

cock-up *n* **1** a towering headdress formerly worn by women. **2** a hat or cap turned up in front.

cocky *n* **1** a brisk, smart young fellow. **2** a friendly term of address.—*adj* **1** pert, saucy. **2** conceited. **3** elated.

coclico *adj* red, purple.

cod[1] *n* **1** a pillow. **2** a cushion. **3** a kind of riding pad.

cod[2] *v* (*with* out) (*used of grain*) to separate easily from the husk.

cod[3] *v* to sham, hoax, humbug.

cod[4] *n* the penis.

cod[5] *v* **1** in *phr* **cod pease** to pilfer peas. **2** to steal.

cod bait *n* **1** the strawworm. **2** the caddis worm.

codber *n* a pillowslip.

cod-crune, ~-croonin' *n* a curtain lecture.

coddle[1] *v* to embrace, cuddle.—*n* an embrace, a cuddle.

coddle[2] *v* to roast apples before the fire.

codgebell *same as* coachbell.

codger *n* a fellow, a character.

codgie *adj* **1** comfortable, cosy. **2** in fair health.

cod-hule *n* a pillowslip.

codle *v* to make grain fly out of the husk by a stroke.

codlick, codlock *n* the spotted gunnel.

codlins-and-cream *n* the great hairy willowherb.

codroch *adj* **1** rustic, clownish. **2** dirty, slovenly, nasty.

codrugh *adj* **1** chilly, cold. **2** cauldrife (qv).

codslip, codware *n* a pillowslip.

co'er *v* to cover.

cofe *n* a bargain, a barter.

coff *v* to buy, barter, to procure.

coffee, coffe *n* **1** a beating. **2** a quid pro quo.

coffer *n* a legacy of wealth, a fortune.

coff-fronted *adj* (*used of a bed*) half-shuttered, comparatively open.

coffin clock *n* a grandfather clock.

coffin cough *n* a cough that threatens to end fatally.

coffining *n* the ceremony of putting a corpse into the coffin.

cog[1] *v* **1** to steady anything shaky by wedging it. **2** to scotch a wheel.—*n* a wedge or support for a wheel, etc.

cog[2] *n* **1** a wooden vessel for holding milk, ale, porridge, broth, etc. **2** a pail. **3** a measure, the fourth part of a peck. **4** liquor.—*v* to empty into, or fill, a cog.

cog-and-soup *n* some food and drink.

cog-boine *n* a small wooden trough, a tub.

cog-fu' *n* the fill of a cog (qv).

cogg *n* a flat surface not lying horizontally.

coggie, coggun *n* a small cog (qv).

cogging *adj* given to drink.

coggle[1] *v* to prop, support.

coggle[2] *v* to shake, to move unsteadily.

cogglety *adj* shaky, insecure, not steady.

cogglety-carry *n* the game of see-saw.

cogglin *n* a prop, a support.

coggling-like *adj* looking unsteady.

coggly *adj* **1** unsteady, unstable. **2** apt to be overset.

cog-hand *n* the left hand.

coghle *v* to wheeze, as from cold or asthma.

coghling *adj* husky, wheezing.

cogie *n* a small cog (qv).

cogill *n* **1** the fill of a cog (qv). **2** the fourth part of a peck.

coglan-tree *same as* **covin-tree**[2].

cogle *same as* **coggle**[2].

cognosce *v* **1** (*a legal term*) to inquire, investigate, with a view to judgment. **2** to scrutinize the character of a person or state of a thing in order to make a decision or regulation of procedure. **3** to pronounce a decision as the result of investigation. **4** to pronounce a person to be an idiot or insane by the verdict of an inquest. **5** to survey lands in order to make a division of property.

cognost *v* to sit close together and plan in secrecy some harmless mischief.

cognostin *n* sitting in secret conference.

cogster *n* the person who, in swingling flax, first breaks it with a swing bat and then throws it to another.

cogue *n* a small wooden dish for holding porridge, etc.

cog-wame *n* a protuberant belly.

cog-wymed *adj* corpulent, portly.

cohow *same as* **cahow**.

coil[1] *n* an instrument formerly used in boring for coal.

coil[2] *v* **1** to enfold in a coil. **2** to ensnare.

coil[3] *n* noisy disturbance, fuss, stir.

coil[4]**, coile** *n* a haycock.—*v* to put hay in cocks.

coil-heuch *n* a coal pit.

coinyel *v* **1** to agitate, as in churning milk. **2** to injure a liquid by too much shaking.

coinyelling *n* a shaking.

coist *same as* **cost**.

coit *v* to play at curling.

coject *v* **1** to agree. **2** to fit.

cok *v* to cock, erect.

cokaddy *same as* **cookuddy**.

cokeweed *n* cockweed.

col-candlewick *n* the long-tailed duck.

cold *adj* (*used of land*) stiff and holding moisture. —*n* a cold, a chill.

colded *adj* suffering from cold.

coldie *n* the long-tailed duck.

Coldingham-packmen *n* cumulus clouds in the north or east on fine summer afternoons.

cole[1] *n* a haycock.

cole[2] *n* money.

cole hood, ~ hooding *same as* **coal hood**.

cole hough, ~ heugh *n* a coal pit.

colemie *same as* **coalmie**.

colf *v* **1** to stuff. **2** to stop a hole. **3** to stop a leak. **4** to wad a gun. **5** to caulk a ship.—*n* **1** wadding for guns. **2** the act of stuffing. **3** the material used for stuffing a hole.

colfin *v* to stuff, to colf (qv).—*n* wadding for guns.

colibrand *n* a contemptuous name for a blacksmith.

colin-blackhead *n* the reed bunting.

colk *n* the eider duck.

coll[1] *n* the hog score (qv) in a curling rink.

coll[2] *v* **1** to cut. **2** to clip. **3** to snuff a candle.

coll[3] *n* a haycock.—*v* to put hay into cocks.

collady stone *same as* **cow-lady stone**.

collation *v* **1** to collate. **2** to partake of a collation.

colleague *same as* **collogue**.

colleck *v* **1** to collect. **2** to recollect, think.

colled *adj* **1** cut. **2** shaped, fashioned.

college *v* to educate at a college.

college-fee *n* a schoolmaster's fee.

collegener, colliginer *n* a collegian, a student at college.

collie[1]**, colley**[1] *n* **1** a lounger. **2** one who hunts for a dinner. **3** one who dogs another constantly. **4** a great admirer.

collie[2]**, colley**[2] *v* **1** to abash. **2** to silence in an argument. **3** to domineer over. **4** to bewilder, entangle. **5** to wrangle, quarrel. **6** to attack.

collie[3]**, colley**[3] *v* **1** to yield in a contest. **2** to knock under.

collie-buckie *n* a pickaback.

colliebuction *n* a noisy quarrel, a wrangle, disturbance.

collier *n* the black-dolphin, an insect injurious to growing beans.

collieshangie *n* **1** an uproar, squabble. **2** loud, earnest or gossiping talk. **3** a ring of plaited grass or straw through which a lappet of a woman's dress or fold of a man's coat is clandestinely thrust to excite ridicule.—*v* to wrangle, fight.

collinhood *n* wild poppy.

collocan-gull *n* the black-headed gull.

collogue *v* **1** to conspire, plot together for mischief. **2** to talk confidentially.—*n* **1** collusion. **2** a conversation, a confidential chat.

colloguin' *v, adj* scheming, plotting.—*n* a plot, conspiracy.

colloguy *same as* **collogue**.

collop *n* **1** a portion. **2** a thin slice of meat.

collop-tongs *n* tongs for roasting slices of meat.

colly *n* the hog score (qv) in a curling rink.

colly-tyke *n* a dog of any kind.

coloured knittings *n* red tape, tape used by lawyers.

colpindach *same as* **cowpendoch**.

colsie *adj* comfortable, cosy, snug.

comamie *n* a young coalfish.

comb *n* a coalfish of the fifth year.

comball *v* **1** to meet together for amusement. **2** to plot together, cabal.—*n* a company of plotters, a cabal.

combie *n* a small comb.

comble-stane *n* the top stone of a heap.

Comb's Mas *n* St Columba's Mass, Whitsunday.

comburgess *n* a fellow citizen.

combustion *n* a fierce, hot wrangle.

come[1] *v* **1** to sprout, spring, germinate. **2** to sprout at the lower end in the process of malting grain. **3** (*with* **of** *or* **on**) to become of, happen to.—*n* **1** growth. **2** the act of vegetation.

come[2] *n* a crook, bend, curve.

come[3] *v, adj* born, descended from.

come about, ~ about again *phr* to recover from an illness.—*n* a call to a horse in a stall to move to one side.

come above *phr* to recover, get over.

come after *phr* to woo, court.

come-again *n* **1** a severe scolding. **2** a kiss at the close of a dance.

come-against *adj* repulsive.

come-and-be-kissed *n* a garden flower, (*perhaps*) the viola tricolor.

come and gang *phr* give and take.

come at *phr* **1** come to. **2** to strike, assault.

come-a'thegither *adj* quite sane.

come-ather, ~-ether *n* a call to a horse to turn to the left.

come athort *phr* to strike across or athwart.

come away *phr* **1** (*used of seed*) to germinate. **2** to come along.

come back *phr* to regain consciousness.

come by *phr* **1** to obtain. **2** to meet with an accident.

come crack for crack *phr* to give a sound whipping.

come doon *phr* **1** to lower a price. **2** to become bankrupt. **3** (*used of a river*) to be in flood.

come doon upon *phr* to scold, reprove.

come doon with *phr* pay down.

come gude for *phr* be security for.

come hame *phr* to be born.

come in *phr* **1** to shrink in size or measurement. **2** to come to be of use.

come inowre *phr* to come in towards the speaker.

come-keik *n* a novelty.

comeling *n* a strange animal that attaches itself to a person or place.

comely[1] *adj* **1** reverent. **2** well-behaved.

comely[2] *n* a term of endearment applied to a child.

come-of-will *n* **1** an illegitimate child. **2** anything that comes or grows accidentally. **3** a newcomer.

come on *phr* **1** to thrive, grow, succeed. **2** to get on, manage. **3** to rain. **4** to follow on.

come on ahin *phr* **1** to retaliate. **2** to interfere with another secretly and unfairly in bargaining. **3** to become surety for.

come one's ways *phr* to come along.

come out *phr* to widen, expand.

come-out-awa *n* a swindler.

come outowre *phr* **1** to strike. **2** to come out of. **3** to come towards the speaker.

come over once *phr* to have little experience.

come owre[1] *phr* **1** to cajole, coax successfully. **2** to outwit. **3** to happen. **4** to overtake. **5** to repeat what one has been told in confidence. **6** to strike, assault.

come owre[2] *n* a call to a horse to move to one side of the stall.

comer, comere *same as* **cummer**[2].

comerade *v* to meet for social gossip.—*n* a meeting for social gossip.

comeradin *n* the habit of visiting, day after day, with little interruption.

come round *phr* **1** to recover consciousness. **2** to recover from an illness. **3** to be reconciled. **4** to cajole. **5** to regain lost temper.

come speed *phr* to thrive, prosper.

comestable *adj* **1** eatable. **2** fit for food.

come thrift *phr* to thrive, prosper.

come through *phr* to recover from an illness.

come time *adv* by-and-by.

come to *phr* **1** to recover consciousness. **2** to become reconciled, come up to. **3** to happen. **4** to recover from bad temper. **5** to yield or agree to a proposal, etc. **6** to rise to a state of honour.

come together *phr* to be married.

come to milk *phr* (*of cows*) to give milk after calving.

come to oneself *phr* to perish, die, become useless.

come to one's time *phr* (*used of a woman*) to be confined.

come-to-pass *n* an event that comes to pass.

come to the bile *phr* to begin to boil.

come to the door *phr* (*used of a knock*) to sound on the door.

come to with *phr* to overtake.

come up *n* a call to a horse to start or to go faster.

come upon with *phr* to strike, assault, with.

comfarant-like *adj* decent, becoming.

comflek *v* to reflect.

comfort, comfer-knit-bane *n* the plant *Symphytum tuberosum*.

comical-tommy *n* **1** a game of chance. **2** billy-fairplay (qv).

cominie *same as* **comamie**.

commandement *n* a command, mandate, commandment.

commanding *adj* (*of pain*) severe, disabling.

commands *n* the Decalogue.

commend *n* commendation.

commer *same as* **cummer**[2].

commerce *n* intercourse, communication, dealings with.—*v* to have to do with.

commission *n* the quarterly meeting of the General Assemblies for specific business.

comitt *ppl* committed.

commodity *n* **1** a measure. **2** a considerable quantity.

common *n* **1** an obligation. **2** indebtedness. **3** what is common or usual.—*v* **1** to arrange. **2** to agree in bargaining.—*adv* commonly.

common corn *n* oats in which each grain hangs singly on the stalk.

common debtor *n* (*a legal term*) one in whose favour a fund is held by trustees.

common good *n* **1** the funds of a royal burgh. **2** a town or village common.

commonty *n* **1** a common. **2** the right of common pasturage. **2** the commonalty.

commune *v* **1** to arrange. **2** to agree in a bargain.

communer *n* a party to an agreement.

commuve *v* **1** to bring into a state of commotion. **2** to perturb. **3** to offend, displease. **4** to move.

commy *n* a common clay marble.

comorade *n* a comrade.

comp *n* company.

compack *n* a compact.

companion *n* a low fellow.

companionry *n* companionship, fellowship.

compear *v* to appear before a court in answer to a citation.

compearance *n* appearance before a court in answer to a citation.

compengon *n* a companion.

compesce *v* **1** to restrain, keep under. **2** to assuage.

compleen *v* **1** to complain. **2** to ail. **3** to feel unwell and express it.

compleit *v* to pay arrears in full.

complext *adj* complex.

complice *n* an accomplice.

compliment *n* a present, gift.—*v* to make a present of.

complimental *adj* **1** complimentary. **2** expressive of courtesy.

complouther, complouter, comploutre, complowther, compluther *v* **1** to agree. **2** to mix. **3** to work together. **4** to comply. **5** to suit, fit, answer an end proposed.—*n* **1** a mixture. **2** a mess, confusion. **3** an entanglement. **4** a mistake.

comply *v* to bring about, accomplish.

compone *v* **1** to compose. **2** to settle. **3** to compound.

composity *n* **1** composure. **2** self-possession.

compost *n (used of a person)* a mixed character, compound.

comprisement *n* **1** the valuation of timber in farm buildings at a change of tenancy. **2** the values ascertained in comprising.

compromit *v* **1** to promise jointly. **2** to compromise.—*n* a compromise.

compryse, comprise *v* **1** to attach for debt legally. **2** to value the timber in farm buildings at a change of tenancy.

compryser *n* the person who attaches the estate of another for debt.

comprysing *n* attachment for debt.

compt[1] *n* company.

compt[2] *v* **1** to account for. **2** to count. **3** to justify.—*n* an account, a reckoning.

compt[3] *adj* neat in dress.

comptable *adj* accountable for.

comthankfow *adj* thankful, grateful.

compting *n* counting.

con[1] *n* a squirrel.

con[2] *v in phr* **con thanks** to return thanks.

conceit[1], **concait** *n* **1** a fancy ornament. **2** a knick-knack. **3** neatness. **4** good taste. **5** an opinion. **6** a fancy. **7** a liking. **8** an eccentric or oddly dressed person.—*v* to imagine, fancy, think.

conceit[2] *n* **1** the object of one's particular fancy or love. **2** a chosen sweetheart.

conceit net *n* a fixed net enclosing a portion of a river or estuary.

conceity *adj* **1** conceited, vain. **2** witty, appropriate.

concerns *n* relations by blood or affinity.

conclude *v* **1** to decide. **2** to prove valid or sufficient.

concluding *adj* conclusive.

concos-mancos *adj* of sound mind, compos mentis.

concurrans *n* occurrence.

concurse *n* **1** concurrence. **2** co-operation.

concussion *n* **1** coercion. **2** the forcible exaction of money, extortion.

condemn *v* to block up entrance and exit.

condescend *v* **1** *(a legal term)* to state one's case specifically. **2** to particularize. **3** to agree.

condescendence *n* a detailed statement of one's case.

condiddle *v* to make away with, filch.

condie *same as* **cundy**.

conding *adj* condign.

condingly *adv* agreeably, lovingly.

conduce *v* **1** to hire. **2** to bargain, deal. **3** to agree, arrange.

conducer *n* a hirer.

conduction *n* **1** hiring. **2** the hiring of troops.

condumacity *n* contumacy.

cone *n* butcher meat.

confab *v* to confabulate.—*n* a confabulation.

confabble *n* a confabulation.

confeerin, confeirin *adj* corresponding to, accordant with.—*conj* considering.

confeese *v* to confuse.

confeesed-like *adj* looking confused.

conference *n* analogy, agreement.

confess *v* **1** *(used of a bottle)* to be drained to the last drop by pouring or dripping. **2** to bring up the contents of the stomach.

confident *adj* trustworthy.

confine *n* **1** confinement. **2** an enclosure.

confirm *v* to fall in with an agreement.

confit *n* a comfit.

confloption *n* panic, flurry, fluster.

confoon' *v* to confound.

confoondedest *adj* most confounded.

conform *adj* conformable.—*adv* conformably.

conformity *n* a concession, consent.

confort *v* to comfort.—*n* a comfort.

congee *n* a bow, a flattering obeisance.—*v* to bow, salute.

congey *n* leave, permission.

congou-bree *n* tea.

congree *v* to agree.

conjee *same as* **congee**.

conjugality *n* conjugal union.

conjunck *adj* conjunct, conjoined.

conjured *adj* perjured.

con-kind *n* all kinds or sorts.

connach[1] *n* a fatal distemper of cows.

connach[2] *v* **1** to waste, destroy, trample on, spoil. **2** to consume carelessly.—*n* **1** an unskilful worker. **2** a waster of food, etc. **3** work badly done, spoilt.

connachin *n* overcareful nursing.—*adj* lazy, clumsy at work, from fondness for good living.

connagh *same as* **cannagh**.

conneck *v* to connect.

connect *adj* connected, consecutive.

connie *n* a rabbit, coney.

connoch *same as* **connach**.

connoch worm *n* a caterpillar lurking in grass and causing disease to cows.

connyshonie *n* **1** a silly, gossiping conversation. **2** a whispered conversation.

conquess, conquest *v* **1** to acquire otherwise than by inheritance. **2** to conquer.—*n* acquired possessions, personal acquisition, in contrast to inheritance.

consate *same as* **conceit**.

conscienceable *adj* conscionable, according to conscience.

conscious *adj* privy to.

consequentially *adv* consequently.

consolement *n* consolation.

constable *n* a large drinking vessel, to be drained by one in a company who has drunk less than the rest or otherwise has transgressed the rules of the company.

constancy *n in phr* **for a constancy** continually, always.

constant *adj* evident, manifest.

constitute *v* to open an ecclesiastical court with prayer.

construct *v* to construe.

consume *v* to nullify, neutralize.

consuming *adj* wasteful, not economical.

consumpt *n* consumption, phthisis.

consumption dyke *n* a temporary wall of stones which have been cleared off land.

cont *n* estimation.

contain *v* to restrain oneself.

conteena *v* to continue.

contend *v* to contend for.

contens *n in phr* **by my contens** used as an oath.

content *v in phr* **content and pay 1** to satisfy a creditor. **2** to pay up in full.

conter *v* to contradict, thwart, run counter to.—*n* **1** a reverse of fortune, a cross, trial. **2** the contrary, the opposite. **3** *(in pl)* a state of opposition. —*prep* against.—*adv* in opposition to.—*adj* contrary, opposite.

contermashious, contermaushus *same as* **contramashous**.

conter-poison *n* an antidote to poison.

conter-tree *n* a crossbar of wood or stick attached by a rope to a door and resting on the wall at each side in order to keep the door shut from without.

conthankfow *adj* grateful.

con thanks *see* **con**[2].

contingency *n* **1** contiguity. **2** close relationship. **3** connection.

contingent *n* one near in blood.

continuation *n* prorogation.

continue *v* to delay, postpone, prorogue.

contra[1] *n* the country.

contra[2] *same as* **conter**.

contrack *v* **1** to contract. **2** to betroth. **3** to give in the names of a couple for the proclamation of their banns.—*n* **1** a formal betrothal before witnesses. **2** an application to the session clerk of a parish to register the names of a couple for proclamation of their banns.

contract night *n* Saturday night, when names were generally given in for proclamation of banns.

contradict *v* to object to.

contrair *adj* contrary, opposite.—*n* the contrary, the opposite.—*phr* against.—*v* to oppose.

contrairisum *adj* perverse, froward.

contrairy *adj* **1** contrary, adverse. **2** perverse, stubborn.—*adv* in opposition to.

contramashous, contramacious, contramawcious *adj* **1** self-willed. **2** obstinate. **3** rebellious.

contrecoup *n* **1** opposition. **2** pursuit of an object.

contrepoise *v* to counteract.

contrive *v* to design.

contumace, contumasse *v* **1** to act contumaciously. **2** to pronounce one to be contumacious.

contumax *adj* contumacious.

convell *v* to refute.

convene[1], **conveen** *v* **1** to assemble, meet together. **2** to cite to a court.—*n* **1** a gathering. **2** a convention.

convene[2], **conveane** *v* to agree.

convene[3] *n* convenience.

conveniable *adj* accessible, convenient.

conveniency *n* expediency.

covenient *adj* near, contiguous.

conventicular *n* an attender of conventicles.

conversation, conversation lozenge *n* a flat lozenge of various shapes, printed with a motto or short sentence.

convey *v* **1** to escort, accompany, courteously or in kindness. **2** to confer an office.

conveyancy *n* a legal conveyance.

convocate *v* to call to arms.

conivocation *n* an assembly of men to arms.

convoy *v* **1** to escort. **2** to see a person home. **3** to accompany part of the way. **4** to convey. **5** to manage, see a business through.—*n* **1** a personal escorting. **2** a marriage company going to meet and escort the bride. **3** mode or channel of conveyance. **4** skilful management. **5** painstaking action. **6** successful accomplishment.

convoyance *n* **1** management. **2** finesse.

cony *n* cognac.

coo[1] *n* a pigeon's call.

coo[2] *n* a cow.

cooard *n* a coward.

cooch *same as* **couch**.

coocher *same as* **coucher**.

cood[1] *same as* **cude**[2].

cood[2] *n* the cud.

coodie *same as* **cootie**[1].

cooer *same as* **coor**[1].

coof *n* **1** a fool, simpleton. **2** a man who interferes with domestic work.

coofish *adj* bashful, awkward.

coog *n* a boys' game, the same as cahow (qv).

cooie *same as* **cowie**[1].

cook[1] *v* **1** to manage. **2** to arrange so as to gain one's end.

cook[2] *v* **1** to appear and disappear by fits. **2** to hide oneself.

cook[3] *v* to imitate the call of the cuckoo.

cooke *n* **1** a big draught of liquid. **2** a mouthful.—*v* to take a long draught of liquid.

cookie *n* **1** a small plain bun. **2** a bath bun.

cookie-shine *n* a tea-party.

cookit *adj* **1** hidden. **2** secluded.

cook stool *n* a cucking stool.

cookuddy *n* **1** a dance performed by children in a crouching posture. **2** *phr* **dance cookuddy** to perform antics.

cool[1] *same as* **cowl**.

cool[2] *n* a certain quantity of any soft mess, as porridge.

coolie *n* **1** a raised peak in the centre of the foam on home-brewed ale. **2** a nightcap.

coolin *n* **1** a West Highland New-Year's Eve sport. **2** the principal actor in the game.

cooling stone *n* a large stone in or near a school on which a boy who has been breeched (qv) is set to cool his posterior.

coolriff *same as* **cauldrife**.

cool-the-loom *n* **1** an indifferent worker. **2** a lazy person.

cooly *same as* **cully**.

coolyshangie *same as* **collieshangie**.

coom[1] *n* **1** the wooden frame used in building a bridge. **2** a coffin lid.

coom[2] *n* **1** coal dust. **2** peat dust. **3** very small coal used in smithies. **4** the dust of grain. **5** soot. **6** dirt.—*v* to blacken, begrime.

coomb[1] *n* **1** the bosom of a hill having a semicircular form. **2** a hollow in a mountainside.

coomb[2] *n* **1** a tub. **2** a cistern.

coom-ceiled *adj* (*used of a garret*) having the ceiling sloping or arched.

coo-me-doo *n* a term of endearment.

Coomey *n* (*with* **Auld**) a name for the Devil.

coomy *adj* **1** grimy. **2** begrimed with coom. *See* **coomb**[2].

coonchie *n* a hunchback.

coonjer *v* **1** to give a drubbing. **2** to scold. **3** to frighten. **4** to conquer. **5** to tame.—*n in pl* a scolding.

coonjerin *n* **1** a drubbing. **2** a scolding.

coont *same as* **count**.

coonter *n* **1** one who does counts. **2** a shop counter.

coony[1] *same as* **cunzie**.

coony[2], **coonyie** *n* **1** a corner. **2** a coign.

coop[1] *v* to catch in traps.

coop[2] *same as* **coup**[5].

coop[3] *n* a small heap.

coop[4] *v* to hoop, bind with hoops.

cooper[1] *n* a horse imperfectly gelded.

cooper[2] *v* to tinker up.

cooperman *v* to play into each other's hands unjustly.

cooper o' Stobo *phr* one who excels another in any particular line.

coopin *same as* **cowpon**.

coor[1] *v* **1** to cower, squat down. **2** to hide, keep still in a place. **3** to bend, submit. **4** to lower, droop.

coor[2] *v* **1** to cover. **2** to recover.

coordie *same as* **cowardie**.

coordie-lick *same as* **cowardie-blow**.

coordie-smit *same as* **cowardie-smit**.

coorie *v* to cower, crouch, stoop down.

coorse[1] *adj* coarse.

coorse[2] *n* course.

coort *v* to court.

coorter *n* a courter.

cooser *n* **1** a stallion. **2** a stout, vulgar fellow. **3** a libertine.

coo-sharn *n* cows' dung.

coosie *n* a challenge to a feat of daring, dexterity or difficulty.

coost[1] *n* condition of body.

coost[2] *v* cast.

coosten *v* cast.

coot[1] *n* the guillemot.

coot[2] *same as* **cuit**.

cootcher *v* to parcel out.

cooted *adj* having ankles. *See* **cuit**.

cooter[1] *same as* **cuiter**.

cooter[2] *v* to sew carelessly.

cooth[1] *n* a young coalfish.
cooth[2] *same as* **couth**[2].
coothie *same as* **couthie**.
cootie[1] *n* **1** a small wooden bowl or basin. **2** a bucket-shaped barrel. **3** a wooden chamber pot in nursery use.
cootie[2] *adj* (*used of fowls*) having the legs covered with feathers.
cootikins *same as* **cuitikins**.
cootle *same as* **cuitle**.
cootrie *n* the puffin.
cope[1] *n* a coffin.
cope[2] *n* the vault of heaven.
coper *same as* **couper**.
cophouse *n* a house or room for keeping cups.
copy *n* a copybook.
coranich *n* a Highland dirge.
corback *n* the roof of a house.
corban *n* a basket.
corbandie *n in phr* **there comes in corbandie** used of a plausible hypothesis which is opposed by some great difficulty that occurs.
corbie *n* **1** a raven. **2** a crow.—*v* to speak in a harsh, guttural manner.
corbie aits *n* a species of black oats.
corbie craw *n* **1** a raven. **2** the carrion crow.
corbie messenger *n* a messenger who returns either not at all or too late.
corbie steps *n* the projections on the slanting part of a gable resembling steps.
corcolit *same as* **corkie-lit**.
corcuddoch, corcudoch *same as* **curcuddock**.
cord *v* to accord, be in accord.
cordain *same as* **cordowan**.
cordet *adj* (*used of a baking roller*) ridged, as if with cords.
cordevan *same as* **cordowan**.
cordiner, cordiwaner *n* **1** a cordwainer. **2** a shoemaker.
cordisidron *n* lemon or citron peel.
cordon *n* a band, wreath.
cordowan *n* **1** Spanish leather. **2** sealskin used as leather, tanned horseskin.
cords *n* a contraction of the muscles of the neck, a disease of horses.
cordy *n* a familiar designation of a shoe maker.
core[1] *n* the heart.
core[2] *n* **1** a choir, company of singers or musicians. **2** a convivial company. **4** friendly terms.
corf house *n* a house or shed for curing salmon, etc, and for keeping nets in the close season.
corft *adj* **1** (*used of salmon and other fish*) cured, salted. **2** boiled with salt and water.
corianders *n* coriander seeds covered with sugar and used as sweets.
corie *v* to curry leather.
corier *n* a currier.
cork[1] *n* **1** an overseer. **2** a master tradesman. **3** an employer. **4** applied by weavers to the manufacturers' agents and by journeymen tailors to their masters.
cork[2] *v phr* **cork the bottle** to throw a pebble up so as to fall perpendicularly into a pond or river with a plop.
cork-coom *n* burnt cork.
corker, corker-pin *n* **1** a very large pin. **2** a corking pin.
corkie[1] *n* a species of lichen used for dyeing.
corkie[2] *n* **1** the largest kind of pin. **2** a bodkin pin. **3** corking pin.
corkie-lit, corklit *n* a purple dye made from the lichen corkie (qv).
corkin-preen *n* a corking pin.
corkir *n* the lichen corkie (qv) used for dyeing.
cork-swollen *adj* beery.
corky *adj* **1** airy, brisk. **2** flighty, frivolous. **3** drunk.
corky-headit *adj* light-headed, giddy.
corky-noddle *n* a light-headed person.
cormeille *n* the bitter vetch.
cormes *n* sorb-apples.

cormundum *v* **1** to confess a fault. **2** to sue for peace. **3** to own oneself vanquished.
corn[1] *n* **1** oats. **2** a single grain of anything, such as sand, pellets, etc. **3** a small quantity of anything. —*v* **1** to feed with oats. **2** to exhilarate with liquor. **3** to sprinkle meat with salt, to pickle. **4** (*used of cereals*) to fill out, yield much good grain.
corn[2] *n* a circular stone for grinding malt, etc, a quern (qv).
corn ark *n* a stable corn bin.
corn-baby *n* a bunch of oats in the ear, as an ornament.
corn cart *n* an open-spoked cart.
corn-cauger *n* a corn-carrier.
corn-clock *n* a beetle found among corn.
corncraik, ~craker *n* **1** the landrail. **2** a hand rattle. **3** a child's rattle.
corned *adj* **1** fed, provisioned. **2** slightly drunk. **3** salted, pickled.
cornel *n* a colonel.
corner[1] *n in phr* **put one to a corner** to take precedence or authority in a house.
corner[2] *v* (*used of grain*) to fill out.
corners-change-corners *n* **1** a game. **2** *phr* **play corners-change-corners** to play fast and loose.
cornet *n* a scarf anciently worn by doctors or professors as part of their academic costume.
corn fatt *n* a corn chest.
corn harp *n* a wire implement for freeing grain from seeds of weeds.
corn head *n* the end pickle on a stalk of oats.
cornief *n* cats' excrement.
corning *n* **1** a feed of oats. **2** food, provision.
cornish *n* a cornice.
corn kist *n* a stable corn bin.
corn knot *n* the knot of the band which ties up the sheaf.
corn loft *n* a granary.
corn-mou *n* **1** a stack of corn. **2** the place where corn is stacked.
cornoy *n* sorrow, trouble.
corn-pickle *n* an ear of corn, a very small quantity of corn.
corn pipe *n* **1** a reed or whistle, with a horn affixed by the tip. **2** a toy music pipe made from a corn stalk.
corn-rig *n* a ridge of growing corn.
corn-scrack, ~-skraugh *n* the landrail.
corn-stook *n* a shock of corn.
corn-waters *n* distilled spirits.
corny *adj* **1** fruitful, prolific. **2** abounding in grain.
cornyard *n* the stack yard.
corny-skraugh *same as* **cornscrack**.
corny-wark *n* food made of grain.
coronoy *same as* **cornoy**.
corp *n* a corpse.
corp-candle *n* a will-o'-the-wisp.
corphed *same as* **corft**.
corpie *n* a child's corpse.
corplar *n* a corporal.
corp-lifter *n* a body-snatcher.
corpse *n* a living body.
corpse-chesting *n* the placing of the corpse in the coffin.
corpse sheet *n* a shroud, winding sheet.
corp-snapper *n* a body-snatcher.
corpus *n* the body of a man or animal.
corrach, corrack *n* a pannier, a basket.
correck *adj* **1** correct. **2** upright, steady, of good character.
correctory *adj* **1** correcting. **2** explanatory.
correnoy *n* **1** a disturbance in the bowels. **2** a rumbling noise in the belly.
corrie *v* **1** (*with* **on**) to hold exclusive intimate correspondence in a low sort of way. **2** to gossip together.
corrieneuchin *adj* conversing intimately, talking together.
corrock *same as* **icorrach**.
corruption *n* bad temper, 'bile'.
corrybuction *n* a dense crowd of people moving to and fro and rendering a passage through difficult.
corrydander *n* the coriander plant. See **corianders**.

cors, corse, corss *n* **1** a cross. **2** a marketplace. **3** the signal formerly sent round for assembling the Orcadians. **4** a piece of silver money which bore a cross.—*v* **1** to cross, pass over. **2** to thwart.

corsicrown *n* a game, with a square figure divided by four lines crossing each other on the crown or centre, played by two with three men each.

corsy-belly *n* a child's first shirt.

corter *n* **1** a quarter. **2** a quarter of oatcake.

cosey *n* a woollen cravat.

cosh[1] *adj* **1** neat, snug, comfortable. **2** quiet, uninterrupted. **3** familiar, friendly. **4** loyal. **5** smart. **6** brisk. **7** vivacious. **8** happy.

cosh[2] *adj* with a hollow beneath, over a hollow.

coshly *adv* neatly, comfortably, briskly.

cosie *same as* **cazzie**.

cose *v* to exchange, barter.—*n* a bargain, exchange.

coss a doe *phr* to exchange one piece of bread for another.

coss-blade, cost-blade *n* the costmary, an aromatic plant with yellow flowers growing in umbels on the top of the stalks.

cossnent *n* **1** working for wages without victuals. **2** *in phr* **work black cossnent** to work without meat or wages.

cost *n* **1** duty paid in kind, as distinguished from that paid in money. **2** the board, etc, given to a servant instead of money. **3** meal and malt, a feu duty paid in meal and malt.

costard *n* the head.

coster *n* a piece of arable land.

cot *v* **1** to cohabit. **2** to live together in a small cottage.

cote *n* a house or cottage of humble construction.

coteral *n* an elastic piece of thin split iron, put through a bolt to prevent it from losing hold, as the end opens after passing through the orifice.

cotham *v* **1** to satisfy with food. **2** to eat to excess.

cothaman *n* a surfeit.

cothie *same as* **couthie**.

cothie-guckie, ~-juke *n* a snug, cosy shelter.

cothiely *adv* snugly.

cothroch *v* **1** to work or to cook in a dirty, disgusting manner. **2** to overnurse. **3** to handle too much.

cothrochie *adj* **1** fond of good eating. **2** making much ado about cooking.

cothrochin *adj* dirty and unskilful.

cothrugh *same as* **codroch**.

cotlander *n* a cottager who keeps a horse to plough his croft.

cotman *n* a farm cottager.

cottar, cotter *n* the inhabitant of a cothouse or cottage.

cottar-body *n* a cottager.

cottar-folk *n* cottagers.

cottar house *n* a farm labourer's house.

cottar-man *n* a cottager.

cottar's-ha' *n* a peasant's cottage.

cottar-toun *n* a hamlet inhabited by cottagers dependent for work on the neighbouring farms.

cottar-wark *n* stipulated work done by the cottagers for the farmer on whose ground they dwell.

cotter[1] *v* (*used of eggs*) to fry them with butter, stirring them round until they are cooked.

cotter[2] *v* to grow potatoes by giving seed, manure and culture for the use of the land.

cotter[3] *v* to potter about.—*n* unskilful working.

cotter[4] *v* to live together in fellowship.

cotterie *n* **1** a cottar's holding. **2** his provision of a house.

cottie *same as* **coatie**.

cotton[1] *v* **1** to take a liking to. **2** to make oneself agreeable to.

cotton[2] *n* a village of cottagers who work on neighbouring farms.

cottonial *adj* cotton-like.

cotton weavry *n* cotton-weaving.

cotton-winsey *n* a material made of cotton and wool.

couch *v* **1** to sleep. **2** (*used of dogs*) to be sulky, unyielding.—*n* a dog's kennel.

coucher *v* **1** to bow down, crouch. **2** to do in a trial of strength what another cannot.—*n* a coward.

coucher's blow *n* **1** the blow given by a mean and cowardly fellow before he gives up. **2** the last blow to which a coward submits.

couda *v* could have.

coudie *adj* **1** affable, familiar, loving. **2** comfortable. **3** pleasant to the ear. **4** ominous of evil.

coudle *v* to float as a feather, alternately rising and sinking with the waves.

couf *same as* **coof**.

coug *n* **1** a small wooden vessel with hoops. **2** a boat.

cougher *v* to continue coughing.

couk[1] *v* to retch.

couk[2], **couk**[3] *same as* **cook**[1], **cook**[2].

coukie *same as* **cookie**.

coul, coulie[1] *same as* **cowl**.

coulie[2] *n* **1** a boy. **2** a contemptuous designation of a man. **3** a boy's cap.

coulter *n* **1** a nose. **2** the appendage to a turkey cock's bill.

coulter-neb *n* the puffin.

coulter-nebbit *adj* long-nosed.

coum *same as* **coom**[2].

coumit bed *n* a bed formed of deals on all sides except the front, which is hung with a curtain.

coummie-edge *n* an edge of bad, ill-polished steel.

coun *same as* **cown**.

council house *n* the town hall.

council post *n* a special messenger, such as formerly bore messages from the Lords of the Council.

counger, counjer *same as* **coonjer**.

count *v* **1** to practise arithmetic. **2** to settle accounts.—*n* **1** calculation. **2** a sum in arithmetic.

count-book *n* **1** an account book. **2** a textbook of arithmetic.

counter *n* a person learning arithmetic, an arithmetician.

countercheck, ~check plane *n* a tool for working out the groove that unites the two sashes of a window.—*v* in the middle.

counter-coup *v* **1** to overcome, surmount. **2** to repulse. **3** to overturn. **4** to destroy.

counter-louper *n* **1** a draper's assistant. **2** a shopman.

counting *n* **1** arithmetic. **2** the yearly settlement between landlord and tenant.

counting-dram *n* the dram of spirits given after a settlement of accounts.

count-kin-with *phr* **1** to compare one's pedigree with another's. **2** to claim blood relationship with.

country *n* **1** a quarter, region. **2** the people of a district.

country-keeper *n* one employed in a district to apprehend delinquents.

coup[1] *n* a cup or bowl.

coup[2] *v* **1** to exchange, barter. **2** to expose to sale. **3** to deal, traffic.—*n* **1** a good bargain. **2** anything bought below its real value.

coup[3] *n* **1** a company of people. **2** a quantity of things.

coup[4] *v* **1** to capsize, tilt. **2** to tumble. **3** to become bankrupt. **4** to empty by overturning. **5** to turn the scale. **6** to drink off. **7** to bend, submit.—*n* **1** a tip cart. **2** a fall, upset. **3** a sudden break in a stratum of coal. **4** a place for emptying cartloads of earth, ashes, rubbish, etc.

coup[5] *n* a box cart, with closed ends and sides.

coup[6] *same as* **coop**[1].

coup aff *v* to fall off.

coupal *n* a disease of sheep, causing lameness.

coup and creel *phr* entirely.

coup cart *n* a box cart that tilts up.

coup carts *phr* to turn heels over head.

coupe-jarret *n* one who hamstrings another.

couper *n* **1** a dealer. **2** a horse- or cattle-dealer.

couper-word *n* the first word in demanding boot (qv) in a bargain.

coupin *same as* **coupon**.
coupit *adj* confined to bed by illness.
couple *n* a rafter.—*v* **1** to marry. **2** to mate.
couple-baulk,-beak *n* **1** a rafter, beam. **2** the collar-beam of a roof.
couple-hicht *adj* in great excitement or anger.
couple nail *n* a rafter nail.
couple-yill *n* drink given to carpenters on putting up the couples in a new house. *See* **couple**.
coupon *n* **1** a piece. **2** a portion of a body that has been quartered.
coup over *v* **1** to fall asleep. **2** to be confined in childbed.
coup over the creels *phr* to come to grief, make a mess of.
coup the cart *phr* get the better of, be done with.
coup the crans *phr* to overthrow, get the better of.
coup the creels *phr* **1** to fall, turn head over heels. **2** to die. **3** to bring forth an illegitimate child.
coup the harrows *phr* to overthrow.
coup-the-ladle *n* the game of seesaw.
cour[1] *same as* **coor**[1].
cour[2] *same as* **coor**[2].
cour[3] *v* to fold.
courage bag *n* the scrotum.
courant *n* **1** a running and violent dance. **2** a great fuss. **3** a scolding.
courch *same as* **curch**[1].
courchieff *n* a covering for a woman's head.
courers *n* covers.
courie[1] *adj* timid.
courie[2] *same as* **currie**.
courple *n* a crupper.
court *n* the lawn or grass plot about a house.
court-day *n* rent day.
courtin *n* a farm straw yard.
courtiser *n* one who holds property by right of courtesy.
couser *same as* **cooser**.
cousin-red *n* kinship, consanguinity.
coust *same as* **cost**.
cout[1] *n* **1** a young horse. **2** a term of contempt applied to a man.
cout[2] *n* a hard-twisted handkerchief used in the game of craw (qv).
coutch *v* to lay out land in a proper and convenient division among joint proprietors.—*n* **1** a portion of land held in one lot and not in runrig (qv). **2** *in phr* **coutch by cavel** to divide land by lots.
coutchack *n* **1** a blazing fire. **2** the clearest part of a fire.
coutcher *same as* **coucher**.
couter *n* a coulter.
cout-evil *n* strangles in young horses.
couth[1] *v* could.
couth[2] *adj* **1** pleasant, kind, affable. **2** comfortable, snug.— *n* kindness.
couthie *adj* **1** kind, pleasant, agreeable, affable. **2** tender, sympathetic. **3** snug, comfortable. **4** well-to-do.—*adv* affectionately.
couthily *adv* kindly.
couthiness *n* friendliness, familiarity.
couthless *adj* cold, unkind.
couthy-like *adj* having the appearance of kindness.
coutribat *n* a tumult.
coutter *n* a sort of decanter for holding wine.
coutterthirl *n* the vacuity between the coulter and the ploughshare.
cove *n* **1** a cave, cavern. **2** a sea cave with a narrow entrance.
covenant *n* wages without food.
covenanter *n* a whisky jar.
cover[1] *n* stock, property, etc, convertible into cash.
cover[2] *n* a good crop covering the ground.
covetise *n* covetousness.
covetta *n* a plane used for moulding framed work.
covine[1] *n* fraud, artifice.

covine[2] *n* a company or division of witches, consisting of thirteen.
covin-tree *n* a large tree in front of an old mansion house where the laird met his visitors.
cow[1] *n* **1** a twig of a shrub. **2** a bush. **3** a besom of broom. **4** a birch for whipping. **5** fuel for a temporary fire.
cow[2] *n* **1** a goblin, sprite. **2** an apparition. **3** scarecrow.
cow[3] *v* **1** to rate, upbraid. **2** to scold an equal or superior. **3** to snub. **4** to surpass, beat, outdo.—*n* **1** a fright. **2** a coward. **3** a frightful object.
cow[4] *v* **1** to cut, crop, clip short, prune. **2** to crop, browse.— *n* **1** a clipping, polling. **2** the act of pruning.
cow[5] *n* a rude shed over the mouth of a coal pit.
cowan[1] *n* a fishing boat.
cowan[2] *n* **1** a mason who builds drystone dykes or walls without mortar. **2** a term of contempt for a mason who has not been regularly apprenticed. **3** one who is not a Freemason.
cowaner *n* a cowan mason.
cowardie[1] *v* to surpass in athletics.
cowardie[2] *n* a coward.
cowardie-blow, ~-lick, ~-smit *n* a blow given as a challenge to fight.
cowardly-blow *n* a blow given as a challenge to fight.
cow baillie *n* a cattleman on a farm.
cow beast *n* a cow, an ox.
cowble *v* (*used of ice*) to undulate. *See* **coble**.
cow byre *n* a cow house.
cow cakes *n* wild parsnip.
cow carl *n* **1** a bugbear. **2** one who uses intimidation.
cow cloos *n* the common trefoil.
cow clushern *n* cow's dung as it drops in a heap.
cow-couper *n* cow-dealer.
cow cracker *n* the bladder campion.
cow craik *n* a mist with an easterly wind.
cowd *v* **1** to float slowly, moving on slight waves. **2** to swim.—*n* **1** a gentle, rocking motion. **2** a pleasant sail. **3** a swim.
cowda, cowdach *same as* **cowdy**.
cowder *n* a boat that sails pleasantly.
cowdie *adj* pleasant, kindly, cheerful.
cowdle *v* to float, move with the motion of the waves.
cow doctor *n* a veterinary surgeon.
cowdrum *n* **1** a beating. **2** a severe scolding.
cowdy *n* a **1** little cow. **2** a hornless cow. **3** a heifer.
cowe[1] *same as* **cow**[1].
cowe[2], **cowe**[3] *same as* **cow**[3], **cow**[4].
cowe'en-, cowen-elders *n* cormorants.
cowen *same as* **cowan**.
cower *same as* **coor**.
cowery *same as* **coorie**.
cowey *same as* **cowie**[1].
cow-feeder *n* a dairyman who keeps cows and retails milk.
cowfish *n* any large, oval shellfish.
cow gang *n* a cow's walk.
cow grass *n* the common purple clover.
cow-heave *n* the colt's-foot.
cowhow *n* a state of excitement, a hubbub, much ado.
cow hubby *n* a cowherd.
cowie[1] *n* **1** a hornless cow. **2** a small cow. **3** the seal.
cowie[2] *adj* odd, queer.
cowie[3] *adv* very, exceedingly.
cow-ill *n* any disease of cows.
cowin' *n* **1** a fright, **2** an alarm. **3** a snubbing.
cowin's *n* what is cut or broken off.
cowit *adj* **1** closely cropped or polled. **2** with short and thin hair.
cowk *v* to retch, strain, vomit.—*n* a belch, a vomit.
cowl *n* **1** a nightcap. **2** a close cap worn indoors.
cowlady stone *n* a kind of quartz.
cowl-headed *adj* wearing a nightcap.
cowlick *same as* **cow's lick**.
cowlie[1] *same as* **cowl**.
cowlie[2] *n* **1** a man who picks up a girl on the street. **2** a rogue, fellow. **3** a boy. **4** a term of contempt.

cowll n a fellow, cowlie (qv).
cow mack n the bladder campion.
cowman n a name for the devil.
cown v (used of children) to cry, weep aloud.
cowp[1] n a basket for catching fish.
cowp[2] same as **coup**[3].
cowp[3] same as **coup**[2].
cowp[4] same as **coup**[4].
cowpendoch n a young cow.
cowper same as **couper**.
cowper-justice n 1 trying a man after execution. 2 Jeddart justice (qv).
cowpers n part of the mounting of a weaver's loom.
cow plat n cow dung dropped in the fields.
cowpon n 1 a shred, fragment. 2 (in pl) shivers, bits.
cow quake n 1 a cattle disease caused by cold weather. 2 the cold easterly wind in May that produces the disease.
cowr[1] same as **coor**[1].
cowr[2] same as **cower**[2].
cow's backrin n cow dung dropped in the fields.
cow's-band n the band binding the cow to the stake, given in pledge for borrowed money.
cowschot, cowshot same as **cushat**.
cow sharn n cow dung.
cow shite n a contemptible person.
cowshot n a kind of marl, brown and grey.
cowshus, cowshious adj cautious.
cowslem n the evening star.
cow's-lick n an upstanding lock of hair.
cow's-mouth n the cowslip.
cow's-thumb n 1 a small distance. 2 a hair's-breadth.
cowstick n lunar caustic.
cowt[1] n 1 a colt. 2 a rough, clumsy fellow, lout.
cowt[2] v 1 to colt. 2 to beat, thrash.—n a cudgel, rung, strong stick.
cow-the-cady, ~-cuddy phr to surpass, outdo.
cow-the-gowan phr n a fleet horse.—v to outdo, excel.
cow tushlach n cow dung.
cowzie adj 1 boisterous. 2 terrific.
cox v 1 to coax. 2 to persuade.
coxy[1] adj conceited, coxcombical.
coxy[2] adj coaxing.
coy n a heifer.
coy-duck n a decoy.
cozin n a cousin.
crab[1] n 1 a sour, disagreeable person. 2 a crab apple.—v to put out of temper, fret.
crab[2] n a kerb.
crabbit-like adj looking cross-grained.
crabbitly adv 1 crossly. 2 peevishly. 3 morosely.
crabbitness n 1 crossness. 2 bad temper.
crab-craigs n rocks on which crabs are caught.
crabfish n a crab.
crab-grained adj cross-grained, ill-tempered.
crab-stane same as **crib-stane**.
crack n 1 a sudden, loud crash. 2 a thunder peal. 3 an instant. 4 a blow. 5 a boast, brag. 6 conversation, gossip. 7 a tale, story. 8 a lie. 9 a good talker, a gossip.—v 1 to become bankrupt. 2 to strike a sharp blow. 3 to strike a match. 4 to brag, boast. 5 to chat, gossip. 6 (with up) to extol, praise.—adj crack-brained.
crack a spunk phr to strike a match.
cracker n 1 a boaster. 2 a great talker. 3 a gossip. 4 the small cord at the end of a whip. 5 a manifest exaggeration. 6 an astounding statement.
crackerheads n the roots of tangles, the vesicles of which crack.
crackers n 1 castanets. 2 bones or pieces of wood used as castanets.
cracket[1] n a small wooden stool.
cracket[2] n the cricket.
crack-hemp n a gallows bird.
crackie, crackie stool n a low, three-legged stool with a small hole in the middle of the seat for lifting it.

crackin' bout n a bout of gossip.
cracking of the herrings phr a loud sound like a pistol crack, after which the herrings leave a place.
crackings n a dish made of the strainings of suet or lard, mixed with oatmeal and browned over the fire.
crackling n tallow refuse.
crackling biscuit n a biscuit made for dogs from the refuse of fat used in making margarine.
crackling-cheese n refuse tallow pressed into the form of cheese for feeding dogs or poultry.
crackly adj brittle.
crack-massie n 1 a boaster. 2 boasting.
cracknut n a hazelnut.
cracks n news.
cracksie adj 1 talkative. 2 newsy.
crack-tryst n one who fails to keep an engagement to meet.
crack-wittet adj silly.
cracky[1] adj 1 talkative. 2 affable.
cracky[2] adj silly, cracked, of weak mind.
cradden, cradeuch n 1 a dwarf. 2 a diminutive person.
cradle n a frame for carrying glass.—v to lie still in the cradle.
cradle chimlay n a large, oblong cottage grate, open on all sides.
cradle-end n the beginning.
cradley-ba n 1 a cradle. 2 a lullaby.
craem same as **crame**.
craft[1] n a craftsman.
craft[2] n a croft.
craft-crammed adj stuffed with learning.
crafter n a crofter.
craftily adv skilfully, cleverly.
craggin n a jar, a pitcher.
craich same as **creagh**.
craickle n a hoarse, croaking sound.
craid n yellow clover.
craig[1] v 1 to creak. 2 to make a harsh noise.
craig[2] n a crag, a rocky place.
craig[3] n the neck, throat.—v to drink, swallow.
craig-agee adj wry-necked.
craig-bane n the collarbone.
craig-cloth n a neckcloth, cravat.
craiged adj pertaining to the neck or throat.
craig-fluke n the rock flounder.
craig-herring n the allice shad.
craighle v to cough huskily or hard.—n a short, dry cough.
craigie n 1 the throat. 2 a long-necked bottle.
craigie-heron n the heron.
craig-lug n 1 the point of a rock. 2 a sharp-pointed rock.
craig's close n the throat.
craig-sitting n a seat on the rocks for fishing.
craigsman n one who climbs sea cliffs for sea fowl or their eggs.
craig's naigie n the throat.
craigstane n a seat on the rocks for sea fishing.
craigy adj rocky.
craik[1] n 1 the landrail. 2 a child's toy rattle.
craik[2] v 1 to croak. 2 to cry out harshly. 3 to murmur. 4 to whine for anything.—n 1 a croaking cry, grumbling. 2 the cry of a hen after laying.
craik[3] n 1 a gossip. 2 ill-natured talk. 3 telling tales.
craik[4] v to creak, as a door hinge.
craiker n the landrail.
crail-capon n a dried haddock.
craim same as **crame**.
crainroch same as **cranreuch**.
craise, craize same as **craze**.
crait n a crate for holding window glass.
craitur n a creature.
craive same as **cruive**.
crake same as **craik**.
cram v to gorge.
cramasie, cramasye same as **cramoisie**.

crambo-clink, ~-jingle, ~-jink *n* rhyme, doggerel verse.
crame *n* 1 a merchant's booth. 2 a stall for sale of goods in a street or in a market. 3 merchandise. —*v* to hawk goods.
cramer *n* a pedlar, hawker.
crame-ware *n* articles sold at a stall or booth.
crame-wife *n* a female stall-holder at markets or fairs.
cramoisie, cramosie *n* 1 crimson. 2 crimson cloth.
cramp *n* an iron sheet, indented to grip the ice, on which the curler stands to throw his stones.—*v* to contract.—*adj* 1 confined. 2 difficult to decipher or understand.
cramp-bit *n* a spiked iron strapped to the shoe by curlers to prevent slipping.
cramp-hand *n* a cramped style of handwriting.—*adj* not easily deciphered.
crampit, crampet *n* 1 an iron with small spikes, worn on the curler's foot to keep him from slipping. 2 a cramping iron. 3 the cramp iron of a scabbard. 4 the guard of a sword handle. 5 the iron shod of a staff. 6 an iron runner of a sledge. 7 a spike driven into a wall to support something.
cramp-speech *n* a set speech in Latin, formerly made by an advocate on his entry at the Scottish Bar.
cramp word *n* a word difficult to pronounce or understand.
cran[1] *n* a measure of herrings taken from the net, averaging 750.
cran[2] *n* 1 an iron tripod for supporting a pot on a hearth fire. 2 an iron instrument, laid across the fire, reaching from the front to the back of the grate, to support a pot or kettle. 3 a bent tap.
cran[3] *n* 1 the crane. 2 the heron. 3 the swift.
cran[4] *same as* **crang**.
cranachan *n* a kind of creamy desert.
cranberry *n* 1 the cowberry. 2 the bearberry.
crance[1] *n* a crack or chink in a wall, through which wind blows.
crance[2] *n* a chaplet.
cranch *v* to crush, crunch, grind with the teeth.—*n* a crush, a crunch, grinding with the teeth.
cran-craig *n* one who has a long neck.
cran-craigie, ~-craigit *adj* long-necked.
crancreugh *same as* **cranreuch**.
crancrums *n* things hard to be understood.
crancum *n* a prank, trick.
crandruch *same as* **cranreuch**.
crane *n* the tap of a gaslight or of a barrel.
craneberry *n* the cranberry.
cranes *n* stilts.
crane-swallow *n* the swift.
crang *n* a carcass, dead body.
cran-hooks *n* the hooks for lifting barrels by their chines.
cranie *n* a small person
cranie-wee *adj* very small.
crank[1] *n* 1 an iron attached to the feet in curling, to prevent the player from slipping on the ice. 2 a difficult point. 3 an effort to overcome a difficulty.—*adj* 1 twisted, distorted. 2 ill-balanced. 3 infirm, sick. 4 impossible to get on with or manage. 5 hard, difficult, curious, not easy to understand.
crank[2] *n* 1 a harsh, creaking noise. 2 the noise of an ungreased wheel. 3 inharmonious verse.
crank[3] *v* to shackle a horse.
crankous *adj* fretful, captious.
cranks *n* the crooked windings of a river or stream.
cranky *adj* 1 ailing, sickly. 2 irritable.
crannach *n* porridge.
crannie[1] *n* the little finger.
crannie[2] *n* 1 a square or oblong aperture in the wall of a house. 2 a bole, a bore.
crannie bore, ~ hole *n* a chink, crevice.
crannied *adj* pent up.
crannie-doodlie, ~-wannie *n* the little finger.
cranreuch, cranreuth *n* hoarfrost, rime.
craurochie *adj* rimy, abounding with hoarfrost.

cranshach, cranshak, cranshank *n* 1 a cripple. 2 a deformed person.
crany, crany-wany *same as* **crannie**[1].
crap[1] *n* 1 a bird's crop. 2 the throat. 3 the stomach. 4 the highest part of anything. 5 (*of whey*) the thick part that rises to the surface. 6 the stilts of a plough. 7 the horizon. 6 the cone of a fir tree.—*v* 1 to top. 2 to keep to the top.
crap[2] *v* 1 to fill. 2 to stuff.
crap[3] *v* crept.
crap[4] *v* 1 to crop. 2 to lop. 3 to gather flowers. 4 to yield a crop. 5 to cut the hair closely.—*n* 1 a crop, produce of the fields, of lambs, of wool, etc. 2 a close cutting of the hair.
crap[5] *n* the quantity of grain put at one time on a kiln to be dried.
crap and root *phr* 1 entirely. 2 from top to bottom.
crapfu' *n* a full crop or maw.
crapin *same as* **crappin**.
crapland *n* land under crop.
crap o' the causey *n* the crown or raised middle of the causeway.
crap o' the wa' *n* the highest part of an inside wall.
crap o' the water *n* the first water taken from a well after midnight of 31 December, supposed to bring good luck for the new year.
crappet *adj* crop-eared.
crappie[1] *adj* (*used of cereals*) bearing well, having large ears.
crappie[2] *n* 1 the crop. 2 the throat.
crappin[1] *n* 1 a bird's crop. 2 the stomach.
crappin[2] *n* 1 carping. 2 asking troublesome questions.
crappin-, crappit-head *n* the head of a cod or haddock stuffed with a mixture of oatmeal, suet, onions and pepper.
crapple-mapple *n* ale.
craps *n* 1 runches. 2 the seed pods of runches or wild mustard.
crasie *n* a woman's cotton sunbonnet.
crat *adj* puny, feeble.—*n* 1 a weak child. 2 a person of weak stomach.
crater *n* 1 the centre. 2 the vortex.
cratur *n* 1 a creature. 2 whisky.
craug *same as* **craig**[3].
crauk *same as* **craik**[2].
craundroch *same as* **cranreuch**.
craup *v* crept.
crave[1] *v* 1 to demand payment, dun for a debt. 2 to long for food and drink. 3 to go about begging.
crave[2] *same as* **cruive**.
craver *n* 1 a creditor, a dun. 2 a note demanding payment of a debt.
craving *n* 1 dunning. 2 hunger, from want of food or from cold.
craving card *n* a begging letter.
craving extracts *phr* asking extracts of minutes of an inferior church court in an appeal to a higher.
craw[1] *n* 1 the rook. 2 the carrion crow. 3 the hooded crow. 4 a strong craving for drink. 3 a children's game.—*v* 1 to caw. 2 to croak.
craw[2] *n* the crop of a bird.
craw[3] *n* a pen, a pigsty.
craw[4] *v* 1 to crow like a cock. 2 to boast, brag.—*n* 1 the crow of a cock. 2 a brag, boast. 3 a shout, noise as of children at play.
craw-berry, ~-croup *n* the crowberry.
craw-bogle, ~-deil *n* a scarecrow.
craw-day *n* the mornings dawn.
crawdoun *n* a coward.
craw-dulse *n* an edible fringed fucus.
craw-feet *n* wrinkles round the eyes.
craw-flee *n* a boys' game.
craw-flower *n* 1 the wild hyacinth. 2 the ranunculus.
craw-foot[1] *n* the ranunculus, crowfoot.

craw-foot² *n* a caltrop.

craw head *n* the chimney head

crawl *v* (*used of insects*) to swarm, infest, abound.

craw-maa *n* the kittiwake.

craw-mill *n* a large rattle for frightening crows.

craw-plantin *n* a rookery.

craw-pockies *n* the eggs of sharks, skate and dogfish.

craw-prod *n* a pin fixed on the top of a gable to which the ropes fastening the roof of a cottage are tied.

craw-road *n* the direct way, as the crow flies.

craws *n in phr* **wae's my craws!** woe's my heart!

craws' bridal, ~ court, ~ marriage *n* a large gathering of crows.

craws' nest *n* a robbers' den.

craw's-purse *n* the ovarium of a skate.

craws'-siller *n* mica.

craw-steppit *adj* having craw steps (qv).

craw steps *n* a set of projecting steps on the gables of the roofs of old houses.

Craw Sunday *n* the first Sunday in March, on which crows were supposed to begin to build nests.

craw-tae *n* **1** the wild hyacinth. **2** the ranunculus or crowfoot. **3** a wrinkle about the eye.

crawtaes *n* caltrops.

crawtt *n* a small, insignificant person.

cray *n* a hutch, a coop.

craze *v* **1** to weaken, wear out, be ready to fall in pieces. **2** to creak, groan. **3** to distract, to madden.—*n* **1** a crack, blow. **2** a measure of wrong-headedness, dotage. **3** foolish or inordinate fondness.

craziness *n* physical weakness.

crazy¹ *same as* **chraisy**.

crazy² *adj* **1** rickety. **2** dilapidated. **3** tumbledown. **4** infirm, weak.

creagh *n* **1** a Highland raid. **2** prey, booty.

cream *same as* **crame**.

creamer *same as* **cramer**.

creamerie *n* **1** merchandise. **2** goods sold by a pedlar.

cream of the well *n* the first water drawn from a well on New Year's Day.

cream-ware *same as* **crame-ware**.

cream-wife *same as* **crame-wife**.

crear *n* a kind of lighter or barque.

creash *same as* **creesh**.

creast *v* to worry or tear in pieces with the mouth.

creature *n* **1** whisky. **2** a term of contempt or pity.

credit *n* approbation, approval.

credulity *n* belief.

cree¹ *n* **1** a pen. **2** sty. **3** fold.

cree² *v* to meddle with.

creech *n* a declivity encumbered with large stones.

creed *n* **1** a severe rebuke, lecture. **2** a piece of one's mind. **3** an adage, saying.

creek *n in phr* **creek o' day** daybreak.

creekle *v* to tremble, shake in feebleness.

creeks *n in phr* **creeks and comers** nooks and corners.

creeks *n* traps, snares.

creel¹ *n* **1** a state of perplexity, stupefaction or madness. **2** the stomach.—*v* (*with* **eggs**) to meddle with.

creel² *adj* **1** worth preserving. **2** worth house room.

creel-fu' *n* a basketful.

creel house *n* a cottage of wattle or wickerwork.

creelie *n* a small creel.

creeling *n* an obsolete marriage custom on the second day of the wedding.

creen *v* **1** to hum, sing in a low, plaintive style, croon. **2** to whine.

creenge *v* to cringe.

creenie *same as* **crannie**¹.

creenie-cranie *n* the little finger.

creep *v* **1** (*used of a child*) to crawl on all fours. **2** (*of the flesh*) to shudder or shiver from cold or fear. —*n* **1** a crawl. **2** a shiver from cold or fear.

creep-at-even *n* one who courts under cloud of night.

creeper *n* **1** a grapnel. **2** (*in pl*) dragging tackle used by smugglers to catch and raise to the surface kegs that had been sunk at the approach of a revenue cutter. **3** the sensation of creeping or shivering.

creepie¹ *n* **1** a grapnel. **2** a child at the creeping stage.—*adj* having a sensation of creeping.

creepie² *n* a bed.

creepie³, **creepie stool** *n* **1** a low stool. **2** a child's stool. **3** a milking stool. **4** any small stool. **5** the stool of repentance.

creepie chair *n* **1** a low chair. **2** the stool of repentance for public penitents.

creep in *v* to shorten, to grow short, shrink, contract.

creeping-bur *n* the club moss.

creeping-seefer *n* the ivy-leaved toadflax.

creeping-wheat grass *n* couchgrass.

creepit *v* crept.

creep out *v* to lengthen, grow long.

creep over *v* to swarm with insects, vermin, etc.

creep together *v* to marry.

creepy *n* the hedge sparrow.

creese *n* a crisis.

creesh *n* **1** grease, fat, oil. **2** a blow, thrashing.—*v* **1** to grease, lubricate. **2** to thrash, beat. **3** (*with* **loof**) to bribe.

creeshie *adj* greasy, oily.—*n* **1** a greasing. **2** sometimes used of a big pinch of snuff.

creeshiness *n* greasiness.

creeshing *n* a beating.

creeshless *adj* lean, without fat.

creest *v* to raise the head, crest.

creesty *adj* forward, precocious.

creeze *n* a crisis.

creighle *same as* **craighle**.

creil *n* a creel.

creish *same as* **creesh**.

creist *same as* **cryste**.

cresie, cresie-jean *same as* **chraisy**.

crespeis, crespie *n* **1** a grampus. **2** a small whale.

cress *v* **1** to crease. **2** to rumple.—*n* **1** a crease. **2** a rumple.

cressy *adj* abounding in cress.

crested-doucker *n* the great crested grebe.

crettur *n* a creature.

creuk *n* **1** a hook on which a gate hangs. **2** a hook and chain for hanging pots, etc, over a fire. **3** anything crooked. **4** a scheme, device. **5** the turn of a stream. **6** a misfortune, trial, cross. **7** a limp, halt.—*adj* awry, crooked.—*v* **1** to bend, bow. **2** to limp.

creuzie¹ *same as* **crusie**.

creuzie² *n* a flat hat worn by women.

crevice, crevise, crevish *n* the rack above the manger in a stable.

crevish *n* the crayfish.

cre-waw *n* a jackdaw's cry.

crewe *same as* **crue**.

crewells *same as* **cruels**.

creyst *same as* **cryste**.

creyt *n* a species of polypody fern.

criauve *v* to crow.

crib¹ *n* **1** a bicker of porridge. **2** food.

crib² *n* a reel for winding yarn.

crib³ *n* a coop, a pen.

crib⁴ *n* **1** a curb. **2** the kerbstone.—*v* to curb, check.

cribbie *n* the quantity of yarn reeled on a crib.

crib-biter *n* a horse that gnaws the manger and sucks in wind.

crib-stane *n* a kerbstone.

crick-crack *n* a talk, a chat.

cricke *same as* **crike**.

cricket *n* the grasshopper.

cricklet *n* **1** the smallest of a litter. **2** the weakest nestling.

crickly *adj* small, puny.

cried-fair *n* a market or fair, of which time and place have been proclaimed some time before and which is therefore well attended.

criesh *same as* **creesh**.

criest *same as* **creest**.

criftens, crifty *int* an exclamation of surprise.

crike *n* **1** a species of tick infesting the human body. **2** a louse.

crile *n* **1** a dwarf. **2** a child who does not thrive.

cril't *adj* unthriven, stunted.

crim *v* to purse up the mouth.

criminals *n* criminal matters, in contrast to civil.

crim-mou't *adj* **1** having the mouth pursed up or deeply sunk in the face. **2** proud, conceited.

crimp[1] *adj* **1** crisp. **2** hard, difficult.

crimp[2] *adj* **1** short of measure. **2** scarce.

crimp[3] *v* to pucker.

crimpet *n* a crumpet.

crimping-pin *n* an instrument for puckering the border of a woman's cap.

crinch *v* **1** to grind with the teeth. **2** to masticate hard and brittle substances, as biscuits, unboiled vegetables or unripe fruit.—*n* a small bit or morsel.

crine *v* **1** to shrivel. **2** to shrink in cooking. **3** to dry up from exposure. **4** to grow small through old age, etc.

cringe *v* to tremble for one's safety.

crinkams *n* twists and turns.

crinkie-winkie *n* a contention.

crinkling *adj* (*used of a cough*) hard, dry, rustling.

crinky *n* an iron rod with a hook at the end.

crinsh *same as* **crinch**.

cripple *v* **1** to walk lame. **2** to hobble. **3** to struggle lamely.

cripple-dick *n* a lame person.

cripple-goat *n* the last cut handful of corn, sent as a trophy by a farmer to his neighbour who is still busy cutting corn.

cripple-justice *n* a person lame yet proud of personal appearance.

cripple men *n* oatcakes toasted before a fire.

crise *same as* **creese**.

crisp *v* to crackle, as ground under the feet in a slight frost.

Cristendie *n* Christendom.

cristing *n* a christening.

crittle *same as* **crottle**.

crittly *adj* friable, crumbly.

criv, crive *same as* **cruive**.

criv't *adj* used of one who is unable to leave his home for a time.

cro[1] *n* a cattle disease affecting the limbs.

cro[2] *n* compensation made for the slaughter of a man, according to his rank.

croachle *same as* **craighle**.

croagh *v* to strangle.

croak[1] *same as* **crock**[2].

croak[2] *v* to crow like a child. **2** to die.

crocanition *same as* **crockanition**.

croch *v* to make a noise in the throat, as if from cold or weak lungs.

crochet *n* the end of a curb chain.

crochle *n* (*in pl*) a disease in the hindlegs of cattle, rendering them lame.—*v* to limp, be a cripple.

crochle-girs *n* the self-heal plant, believed to produce the disease of crochles. *See* **crochle**.

crochlet *adj* having the limbs twisted by rheumatism, etc.

crock[1] *n* **1** a large earthenware jar for holding butter, sugar, salt, etc. **2** a fragment of earthenware.

crock[2], **crock-yow** *n* an old ewe, one too old for breeding.

crock[3] *v* to crouch, cower.

crock[4] *v* to kill.

crock[5] *v* **1** to croak. **2** (*used of the bowels*) to rumble.

crockanition *n* **1** shivers, bits. **2** destruction. **3** smash.

crockats *n* **1** ruffles, neck ornaments. **2** curls, tresses.

crocker *n* a species of boys' marble.

crockie *same as* **crackie**.

crof, croft *n* a temporary shed variously used during the fishing season.

croft[1] *n in phr* **the goodman's croft** a small piece of land left untilled and dedicated to the devil.

croft[2] *same as* **crof**.

croft[3] *n* a crop.

crofthead *n* the end of the croft or small field adjoining the dwelling house.

croftie *n* a small croft.

crofting *n* **1** the state of land constantly in crop. **2** the land thus cropped.

croftland *n* land of superior quality, kept constantly manured and under crop.

croft-rig *n* a croft ridge or field.

crog[1] *n* a milk bowl.

crog[2] *n* **1** a paw. **2** a large hand.

crogan[1] *n* paws.

crogan[2] *n* a milk bowl.

croggie *n* a small jar

croichle[1] *same as* **crochle**.

croighle, croichle[2] *same as* **craighle**.

croighlin *n* dry, hard coughing.

croil *n* **1** a frail person or animal. **2** one broken down from age or use. **3** a dwarf, a stunted person or animal.

crointer *n* the grey gurnard.

croise[1] *n* **1** to burn with a mark. **2** to brand with a cross.

croise[2] *v* **1** to gossip. **2** to talk much about little. **3** to whine in sympathy. **4** to use flattering talk. **5** to whine.—*n* **1** flattery. **2** a flatterer.

croishtarish *n* the fiery cross as a war signal.

croittoch *n* a lameness in cattle's hoofs.

croittoch'd *adj* suffering from croittoch (qv).

crok[1] *n* a dwarf.

crok[2] *v* **1** to suffer decay from age. **2** to die.

crok[3] *same as* **crock**.

crok[4] *same as* **crog**[1].

croke[5] *same as* **croak**[2].

crokets *n* ruffles. *cf* crockats.

crokonition, crockonition, crokynition *same as* **crockanition**.

croll *n* **1** a pause. **2** respite. **3** time for reflection.

crom *v* **1** to bend. **2** to double.—*n* a bend.—*adj* bent.

cromack, cromag *n* the hand with the fingertips and thumb brought together.

cromag's-fu *n* the quantity lifted with the fingers and thumb brought together.

crombie's-punch *n* grog, half-water, half-whisky.

cromie *n* a cow with crumpled horns.

cronach *n* a Highland dirge.

cronachie *n* a child's name for the little finger.

cronaching *v, adj* gossiping, tattling.

crone *same as* **croon**.

cronnie *n* a crony.

crony *n* a potato.

crony-hill *n* a potato field.

croo[1] *same as* **cro**[2].

croo[2] *v* to coo, as a pigeon.

croo[3] *same as* **crue**.

croo[4] *v* to hide by crouching.

croobacks *n* panniers worn by horses in mountainous districts for carrying grain, peat, etc.

crood[1] *v* **1** to coo, as a pigeon. **2** to croak, as a frog. **3** to groan, complain.

crood[2] *n* curd.

crood[3] *v* to crowd.—*n* a crowd.

crooden-doo *n* a wood pigeon.

crooding-doo *n* **1** a wood pigeon. **2** a term of endearment.

croodle[1] *v* **1** to huddle together for warmth or protection. **2** to crouch, cower, stoop down.—*n* a heap, a collection.

croodle[2] *v* **1** to coo like a dove. **2** to purr as a cat. **3** to hum a song.

croodling-doo *n* **1** a wood pigeon. **2** a term of endearment.

crook[1] *v* to halt in walking.—*n* a halt, limp.

crook[2] *n* **1** the iron hook on which a gate or door is hung. **2** the iron hook and chain on which pots, kettles, etc, are hung over the fire. **3** the fireside. **4** anything bent. **5** a device. **6** a bend in a river. **7** a trial or cross in one's lot.

8 a mark cut out in a sheep's ear.—*adj* twisted, awry.—*v* to bend, to bow, to twist.

crookal *adj* pertaining to a crook or cooking vessel. *See* **crook**².

crookal band *n* the chain by which the crook is suspended over the fire. *See* **crook**².

crook-and-the-links *n* pothooks or suspenders.

crooked *adj* **1** deformed, crippled. **2** cross, crabbed.

crooked mouth *n* a species of flounder.

crooked-whittle *n* a reaping hook.

crookie *n* a sixpence.

crook-liver *n* a disease of calves causing inflammation of the intestines.

crook-saddle *n* a saddle for bearing panniers or creels.

crooks and bands *n* the hinges and iron braces of a door.

crook-shell *n* a hook for suspending a pot, etc, over a fire.

crook studie, ~ tree *n* a crossbeam or iron bar in a chimney from which the crook hangs.

crook-yowe *n* a ewe too old for breeding.

croon¹ *v* **1** (*used of cattle*) to low. **2** to roar in a menacing tone like an angry bull. **3** to sing softly, hum, murmur. **4** to make a low, monotonous sound. **5** to purr like a cat. **6** to wail, lament. **7** to mutter a prayer. **8** to sing a tune in a low tone. **9** to use many words in a wheedling way. **10** to hobnob.—*n* **1** the lowing of cattle. **2** a low murmuring sound. **3** the purr of a cat. **4** a mournful song, wail, lament.

croon² *v* **1** to crown. **2** to top, excel.—*n* **1** the top of anything. **2** a crown. **3** the top balk in supporting the roof in a coal pit. **4** the head. **5** that part in deciduous vegetables from which new shoots spring.

croon³ *n in phr* **kaim one's croon** to tear one's hair.

croonach, crooner *n* the grey gurnard.

crooning *n* **1** the bellowing of a bull. **2** a murmuring sound.

croonle *n* the croonach (qv).

croon-piece *n* the upper of the two main crossbeams that tie the rafters in the timbering of a house roof.

croop *same as* **croup**.

croose *same as* **crouse**.

croot¹ *n* **1** a puny, feeble child. **2** the smallest pig of a litter. **3** the youngest bird of a brood.

croot² *same as* **crout**.

crootle *n* a heap.

crootles *n* a nickname for a small and ill-proportioned person.

crootlie *adj* short-legged in proportion to the body.

crootling *v, adj* hunched up, crouching, cowering over. *See* **croodle**¹.

croove *n* a sort of basket for catching fish.

croovie *n* a little snug hut or den

croovie skool *n* a small or snug cottage schoolhouse.

croozumit *n* **1** a puny person. **2** one worn with age. **3** a hermit, one living alone.

crop¹ *same as* **crap**⁴.

crop² *n* a potato stem.

cropen, croppen *v, adj* **1** crept. **2** contracted, shrunken.

cropped-head *same as* **crappin-head**.

cropper *n* that which yields a crop.

cropt *n* a crop.

crose *v* **1** to whine in sympathy. **2** to speak in a whining, flattering voice, to gossip. **3** to magnify trifles.—*n* **1** flattery. **2** expression of sympathy. **3** a flatterer.

croser *n* one given to flattery.

crosle *v* to settle down gently to nestle.

crospunk *n* the Molucca bean, drifted to the shores of some of the Western Isles.

cross *n* **1** the obverse side of a coin bearing a cross. **2** a pile of stones on a hill top.—*v* **1** to brand with the mark of the cross. **2** (*used of the hand of a clock*) to approach a certain point.—*adj* contrary, untoward, wrong, inconvenient.—*adv* **1** crossly. **2** untowardly.

cross-and-pile *n* coin, money.

cross-braces *n* leather supports for the body of a carriage.

cross-brath'd *adj* braided across.

crossfish, ~fit *n* the starfish.

cross-ful *adj* cross-tempered.

crossie-croon-shillin' *phr* a coin over which cows were first milked after calving to protect them from the evil eye and every evil cantrip.

crosslet *n* a crucifix, small cross.

crossmark *n* a person scarred by burning.

cross-nook *v* **1** to check, restrain. **2** to sit close into the neuks. **3** to make room for another person at the fire. *See* **neuk**.

cross nor pile *n* no money whatever.

cross-roupin' *n* a sale by auction at the public cross.

cross-skeppack *n* the game of cross-tig (qv).

cross-speir *v* to cross-examine.

cross-stick-war *n* cudgelling.

cross-tig *n* a variety of the game of chase or tig.

crotal, crottle *n* a lichen, used for dyeing reddish-brown.

crotal-coat *n* **1** a coat of the colour of crotal (qv). **2** a term of contempt.

crottle *n* a crumb, fragment of any hard body.

crottlie *adj* covered with lichen.

crouchie *adj* humped, having a hunch on the back. —*n* a hunchback.

croud *same as* **crood**¹.

croude *n* a fiddle.

croudle *same as* **croodle**².

crouds *n* curds. *See* **crud**.

croun *same as* **croon**.

croup¹ *v* **1** to croak as a raven, frog, etc. **2** to speak hoarsely. **3** to growl. **4** to grumble. **5** (*of the bowels*) to rumble from flatulence. **6** to speak in a whining or wheedling way, to flatter.—*n* **1** a croak. **2** flattery.

croup² *n* a berry.

croup³ *v* to stoop, bend, crouch.—*n* the slope of a hill.

croupie, croupie-craw *n* the raven.

croupit *adj* crabbed.

croupy *adj* hoarse.

crouse *adj* **1** brisk, lively, cheerful. **2** bold, keen. **3** conceited, elated. **4** cosy, comfortable.—*adv* briskly, proudly, conceitedly.

crousely, crously *adv* **1** proudly, confidently, boldly. **2** briskly, merrily, eagerly.

crouseness *n* boldness, forwardness, conceit, apparent courage.

crousie *adv* briskly, merrily, eagerly.

crousy *adj* brisk, crouse (qv).

crout *v* **1** to croak, make a hoarse noise. **2** to coo. **3** (*used of the bowels*) to rumble.

crow *same as* **craw**⁴.

crowder *n* **1** a constant attendant. **2** a diligent frequenter.

crowdie *same as* **crowdy**.

crowdle¹ *v* to crawl as a crab.

crowdle², **crowdle**³ *same as* **croodle**¹, **croodle**².

crowdy *n* **1** meal and cold water, forming a gruel. **2** porridge. **3** a mixture of pure curd with butter. **4** a kind of soft cheese. **5** food in general.

crowdy-butter *n* a mixture of curds and butter.

crowdy-meal *n* **1** milk and meal boiled together. **2** milk porridge.

crowdy-mowdy *n* milk porridge.

crowdy time *n* mealtime.

crowl¹ *n* **1** a dwarf. **2** a stunted, deformed person or child.

crowl² *v* **1** to crawl, creep. **2** to crouch, cower.

crowly *adj* **1** lame. **2** crawling in walk.

crown *n* the head.

crownary, crownry *n* the office of crowner. *See* **crowner**².

crowner¹ *same as* **crooner**.

crowner² *n* a commander of troops raised in a county.

crownfull *n* a certain quality of herrings.

crowp *same as* **croup**¹.

crow-toe *same as* **crae-tae**.

croy¹ *n* compensation made by workmen in some factories for the shortcomings of any of their number.

croy² *n* **1** a semicircular pen on a beach for catching fish. **2**

a mound or quay projecting into a river to break the force of the stream.

croyd *n* yellow clover.

croydie *adj* covered with clover.

croyl *n* a dwarf.

croyn *same as* **crine**.

croze[1] *same as* **crose**.

croze[2] *v* to speak with a weak, shaky voice like an aged person.

crozie *adj* fawning, wheedling.

crub[1] *n* a crib for cattle.—*v* to curb, restrain, confine.

crub[2] *n* the curb of a bridle.

cruban *n* a disease of cows produced by hard grass, scarcity of pasture and severe sucking of their calves.

cruban *n* a term of contempt for a tippler.

cruban *n* a wooden pannier for a horse's back.

crubbin' *n* a snub.

crubbit *adj* cribbed, pinched for room, confined.

crubs *n* the framework within which a millstone revolves.

cruchlin *n* a dry, husky cough.

cruck *same as* **crook**.

cruckie *same as* **crookie**.

crud *n* curd.

cruddle, crudle *v* to coagulate, curdle, congeal.

cruddy *adj* **1** curdled. **2** containing curds.

cruddy-butter *same as* **crowdy-butter**.

cruden *n* a crab.

crue *n* **1** a sheep pen, a small fold. **2** a hovel.

crue-herring *n* the shad.

cruels *n* scrofula.

cruet *n* **1** a water bottle. **2** a small decanter.

cruety *adj* vinegarish, sour-tempered.

crufe *n* a pen for cattle.

cruggles *n* a disease of young cattle, causing convulsive movements of the limbs.

cruick, cruik *same as* **crook**[2].

cruik-studie *n* an anvil with projecting horn for bending horseshoes.

cruise, cruisie *same as* **crusie**.

cruisken *n* a measure of whisky.

cruit *same as* **croot**[1].

cruittie *n* a measure of beer.

cruive *n* **1** a pen for livestock. **2** a pigsty. **3** a cabin, hovel. **4** a cottage garden. **5** an apparatus and method of catching salmon in a river or sea beach.—*v* **1** to shut up in a cruive. **2** to shut up.

cruizey, cruizie, cruizy *same as* **crusie**.

cruke[1] *same as* **crook**[1].

cruke[2] *n* **1** the winding of a river. **2** the space enclosed on one side by the windings of a river.

crulge *n* a confused coalition, conjunction or heap. —*v* to contract, draw together, crouch.

crull *v* **1** to contract, draw oneself together. **2** to stoop, cower.—*n* a confused heap.

crulzie *v* to crouch, cower.

crum *n* **1** a crumb. **2** a small portion of anything, as paper.

crumby *same as* **crummie**.

crumch *n* a small piece.

crumchick *n* a very small piece.

crumchickie *n* a very, very small piece.

crumle *v* **1** to crumble.—*n* a crumb, a broken piece. **2** (*in pl*) broken meats.

crumlick *n* a very small piece, a crumb.

crumlickie *n* an extremely small piece.

crummet *adj* with crooked horns.

crummie *n* **1** a cow with crooked horns. **2** a name for a cow.

crummie's-punch *same as* **crombie's punch**.

crummie-staff, ~-stick *n* a staff with crooked handle, used by boys herding cattle.

crummilt *adj* **1** crooked, crumpled. **2** bent spirally, twisted.

crummock[1] *n* **1** a short staff with crooked head. **2** a name for a cow.

crummock[2], **crumock** *n* the plant skirret.

crummy *n* a crumb, a very small portion, a particle.

crump[1] *v* to smack, knock.—*n* a smart blow.

crump[2] *adj* **1** crisp, brittle. **2** crumbling. **3** friable. —*v* **1** to crunch with the teeth anything hard or brittle. **2** to emit a crackling sound, like ice or snow when trodden on. **3** to boast noisily, brag.

crumpie *n* a crisp oatcake.—*adj* (*of bread*) hard, brittle, crisp.

crumping *adj* crackling, noisy.

crunch *same as* **crinch**.

crune *same as* **croon**[1].

cruner *same as* **crooner**.

crunkle *v* **1** to crease, rumple. **2** to shrivel, contract. **3** to wrinkle with cold.—*n* **1** a crease, wrinkle. **2** a crackle as of crumpling paper.

crunkly *adj* **1** shrivelled, shrunken. **2** rough, as with frost or ice. **3** rough of character.

crunt *n* **1** a blow with a cudgel. **2** a smart blow on the head.—*v* to strike the head with a weapon.

cruppen *v* crept.

cruppen thegether *phr* used of one bowed by age or shrunken with cold.

cruppocks *n* crisp oatcakes.

cruse *same as* **crouse**.

crushie *n* **1** a familiar name for a shepherd's dog. **2** a collie.

crusie, crusy, cruzy *n* **1** a small, old-fashioned open lamp, in which the pith of rushes was burned with animal oil. **2** a triangular iron candlestick, with one or more sockets to hold candles. **3** a crucible or hollow piece of iron for melting metals.

crusie-gabbit *adj* (*used of a dog*) having a mouth like a crusie (qv), sharp-pointed.

crusil *v* to contract the body in sitting.

crut *n* a short person.

crutch *n* the pommel of a woman's saddle.

crutch phrase *n* a phrase like 'as it were' or 'so to say', which gives a speaker time to think what comes next.

crute *same as* **croot**[1].

crutlachin *v*, *adj* conversing in a silly, tattling way.

cruttlins *n* the refuse of soft food.

cruve *same as* **cruive**.

cry *n* **1** a call, summons, shout. **2** a musical sound. **3** (*in pl*) the proclamation of banns of marriage. —*v* **1** to call. **2** to summons. **3** to proclaim, publish in the streets. **4** to publish banns of marriage. **5** (*used of a woman*) to cry in travail. **6** to speak, talk, make a sound.

cry doon *phr* to depreciate, decry.

cry in *phr* **1** to invite to enter. **2** to make a passing call.

cryin' *n* **1** proclamation of banns. **2** a woman's confinement. **3** a feast given to neighbours shortly after a woman's confinement.

cryin' bannock *n* a special cake eaten at the feast held on the birth of a child.

cryin' cheese, ~ kebbuck *n* cheese given to neighbours and visitors on the occasion of the birth of a child.

cryin' fever *n* a raving, raging fever.

cryin'-out *n* **1** an outcry. **2** misfortune, calamity.

cryin' pipes *n* little straw pipes through which children make a noise.

cryin' siller *n* the fee paid for proclamation of banns.

cryin' wife *n* a woman in travail.

cryle *same as* **crile**.

cryne *same as* **crine**.

crynet *adj* stunted in growth.

cryrste *n* a diminutive, talkative person.

cubb *n* a droll fellow.

cubbag *n* a small hand basket, made of leather and narrow at the bottom.

cubbirt *n* a cupboard.

cubby-hole *n* a dog hutch.

cubicular *n* a page of the bedchamber.

cuckie *same as* **cookie**.

cucking *n* the sound made by the cuckoo.

cuckold *n in phr* **cuckold's cut** *or* **slice** the first or uppermost slice of a loaf of bread.
cuckold carlie *n* an old cuckold.
cuckoo *v* to harp on a subject, say the same thing over and over again.
cuckoo's meat, cuckoo sorrel *n* the wood sorrel.
cuckoo's spittens, ~ spittle *n* a froth discharged by the young froghoppers or frogflies.
cuck-stule *n* **1** the cucking stool. **2** a pillory.
cucuddy *n* a children's game in which they sit on their hams and hop round.
cud[1] *v* to chew the cud.
cud[2] *n* **1** a tub. **2** a wooden chamber pot.
cud[3] *n* a cudgel.—*v* to cudgel.
cud[4] *n* **1** an ass. **2** an inferior.
cud[5] *n* an untruthful young man.
cud[6] *v* could.
cudd *n* a donkey.
cuddeigh *same as* **cudeigh**.
cuddem *same as* **cuddum**[2].
cudden *same as* **cuddin**.
cudderie *same as* **cutherie**.
cuddie[1] *same as* **cuddin**.
cuddie[2] *n* a small basket made of straw.
cuddie[3] *n* **1** a street gutter. **2** a conduit. **3** an overflow connection between a canal and a river.
cuddie[4] *same as* **cucuddy**.
cuddie *n* **1** a donkey. **2** a horse.
cuddin *n* the coalfish from a year old till full-grown.
cudding *n* the char.
cuddle *v* **1** to nestle for warmth or shelter. **2** to sleep, lie down to sleep. **3** to crouch, to sit over. **4** to approach a person flatteringly. **5** (*used of lovers*) to talk in soft tones, fondle. **6** to coax, entice. **7** (*of marbles*) to get the pitcher to lie as near the ring as possible.—*n* **1** a very close intimacy. **2** conversation in low or soft tones.
cuddle-muddlin, cuddle-muddle *n* a low, muttered conversation.
cuddler *n* **1** a bedfellow. **2** a nestling. **3** a fondling.
cuddlie *n* whispering among a number of people.
cuddlin *n* **1** close intimacy. **2** whispered conversation.
cuddly *n* a nursery word for bed.
cuddoch, cuddock *same as* **cuttoch**.
cuddom *same as* **cuddum**[2].
cud-doos *n* eider ducks, St Cuthbert's pigeons.
cuddum[1] *n* **1** substance. **2** the largest share.
cuddum[2] *v* **1** to tame. **2** to domesticate.—*adj* tame, broken-in.
cuddumin' siller *n* money given to a shepherd for special attention to a beast newly joined to his herd or drove.
cuddum o' tait *n* the custom of giving a newly-bought horse part of a handful of unthreshed straw as it enters the new stable and putting the remainder above the stable door, the idea being that the horse, when at liberty outside, will remember and return to finish the straw.
cuddy *n* **1** a simpleton. **2** a stupid or half-witted person.
cuddy-and-the-powks *n* a boys' game.
cuddy-back *n* a ride on someone's back and shoulders.
cuddy-block *n* a blockhead.
cuddy cairt *n* a donkey cart.
cuddy door *n* the opening in the gable of a byre (qv) for carrying out the dung.
cuddy heel *n* an iron heel on a boot.
cuddy-loup *n* a boys' game.
cuddy rung *n* a cudgel.
cuddy-wanter *n* one on the outlook for a donkey.
cude[1] *n* the cud.
cude[2] *adj* **1** harebrained. **2** appearing deranged or greatly alarmed.
cude[3] *n* a small tub.
cude[4] *n* a face cloth for a child at baptism.
cudeigh, cudeich *n* **1** a bribe. **2** a clandestine gift. **3** a present in addition to wages.

cudger, cudgie *n* a blow given by one boy to another as a challenge to fight.
cudie *n* a small tub.
cudiegh *same as* **cudeigh**.
cudroch-chiel *n* a timid, worthless youth.
cudum *same as* **cuddum**[1].
cudynch *n* **1** an ass. **2** a sorry animal.
cue[1] *v* to fuddle.
cue[2] *n* humour, temper.
cuer *n* one who intoxicates others.
cufe *same as* **coof**.
cuff[1] *n* **1** the scruff of the neck. **2** the nape.
cuff[2] *n* **1** an old man. **2** contemptuous term for one.
cuff[3] *v* to winnow corn, etc, for the first time.
cuffet *n* **1** a blow, buffet. **2** (*in pl*) a boys' game.
cuffle *adj* chubby.
cuffin riddle *n* the riddle used in the first winnowing of cereals.
cuffock *n* a mode of winding up a worsted clew.
cufie, cuffie *v* to surpass, outstrip.—*n* the act by which one is surpassed.
cugg *v* to prop up.
cuggly *adj* unsteady, shaky.
cuid *same as* **cude**[4].
cuide *same as* **cude**[2].
cuif *same as* **coof**.
cuil *adj* cool.—*v* to cool.
cuilzie *same as* **culyie**.
cuinyie, cuinzie *same as* **cunzie**.
cuinyie-hoose *n* the mint house.
cuirie *n* a stable, mews.
cuisse-madame *n* the French jargonelle.
cuisser *same as* **cooser**.
cuissen *v* cast.
cuist[1] *v* cast.
cuist[2] *same as* **coost**[1].
cuisten cast.
cuit[1] *n* an ankle.
cuit[2] *v* to play at curling.
cuitchen *v* caught.
cuiter *v* **1** to talk in a low and confidential tone. **2** to fondle. **3** to coax, wheedle. **4** to cocker, fuss over, to manage one adroitly. **5** to set on one's feet. **6** to restore to health. **7** to patch, mend, put to rights. **8** to work in a trifling way.
cuiterer *n* a coaxer, flatterer.
cuitie boyn *n* a small tub for washing the feet and holding as much water as will cover the cults or ankles.
cuitikins *n* **1** gaiters. **2** leggings.
cuiting *n* a covering, coverlet.
cuitle, cuittle *v* **1** to wheedle, coax, flatter, to fuss over. **2** to tickle. **3** to flirt. **4** (*with* **in with**) to gain friendship or affection. **5** (*with* **up**) to wheedle successfully.—*adj* difficult, ticklish.
cuitling *n* a flatterer, wheedler.
cuittie *n* **1** bowl of liquor. **2** a measure of beer or spirits.
cule *v* to cool.—*adj* cool.
cule-an'-sup *n* a state of poverty.
cules *n* the buttocks.
cule-the-lume *n* a person very indolent at his or her work.
culf *same as* **colf**.
cull[1] *n* a fool, dupe, stupid fellow.
cull[2] *n* a lump of hard food.
cullage *n* the distinctive marks of sex.
Cullen skink *n* a kind of thick soup made from smoked haddock.
culliebuction *same as* **colliebuction**.
cullion *n* **1** a poltroon. **2** a base fellow. **2** a person of disagreeable temper and manners.
cullionly *adv* rascally.
cullionry *n* cowardice, roguery.
cullishangy *same as* **collieshangie**.
culls *n* the testicles of the ram.
cully *same as* **culyie**.
cullyeon *same as* **cullion**.

cully-haikie *same as* **curry-haikie**.
culm *n* **1** the slack of anthracite coal used in lime-burning. **2** coal dust. **3** peat dust.
culpable homicide *n* the Scottish equivalent of the crime known as manslaughter in England.
culrach *n* surety, security.
culravage *n* a disorderly mob.
culroun *n* a scamp, rascal.
culsh *n* a big, disagreeable person.
cultie *n* **1** a young colt. **2** a nimble-footed animal. **3** (*in pl*) the feet.
culyeon *same as* **cullion**.
culyie, culye, culzie *v* **1** to befool, dupe.—*n* a flatterer. **2** flattery.
cum[1] *v* to come.
cum[2] *n* a crook, bend, curve.
cum[3], **cumb** *n* **1** a tub. **2** a cistern. **3** a large ladle for bailing out a boat.
cumallee *n* the king's signal in the game of King of Cantelon.
cumber *same as* **cummer**[1].
cumbered *adj* (*used of the hands*) benumbed, stiff with cold.
cumbluff *adj* stupefied.
cumlin *n* an animal that comes and attaches itself voluntarily to a person or place.
cummer[1] *v* **1** to cumber.—*n* **1** cumbrance. **2** an encumbrance.
cummer[2] *n* **1** a gossip, godmother. **2** a midwife. **3** a girl, young woman. **4** a contemptuous designation for a woman, old or young. **5** a supposed witch.—*v* to meet for a gossip.
cummer-fialls *n* an entertainment formerly given on recovery from childbirth.
cummerlyke *adj* like cummers or gossips. *See* **cummer**[2].
cummer-room *v* to appear as an intruder.—*n* an encumbrance.
cummer-skolls *n* entertainment given to visitors on occasion of a child's birth.
cumming *n* a vessel for holding wort.
cummock *n* the restharrow.
cummock *n* a short staff with curved head.
cummudge *adj* snug, cosy, comfortable.
cum-out-awa' *n* a swindler.
cumplouter *same as* **complouther**.
cumsiled *adj* (*used of small houses*) ceiled with wood, partly on the rafters and collars.
cumstroun *adj* dangerous.
cun[1] *v* **1** to learn, to know. **2** to taste, to test by tasting.
cun[2] *v* **1** *in phr* **cun thanks** to give thanks. **2** to feel grateful.
cundy *n* **1** a covered drain. **2** a concealed hole, an apartment. **3** the hole covered by a grating for receiving dirty water for the common sewer. **4** a small drain crossing a roadway.
cundy-hole *n* a conduit, as one across a road.
cungle *n* a rumpus, quarrel.
cuningar *n* a rabbit warren.
cunjer *same as* **coonjer**.
cunjert *adj* **1** overawed. **2** subdued to obedience, etc. **3** tamed. **4** conquered.
cunnach *same as* **cannagh**.
cunner *v* to scold.—*n* a scolding, reproof.
cunniack *n* a chamber pot.
cunning *adj* **1** skilful, expert. **2** difficult to find.
cunster *n* a taster, who tested officially the quality of liquor sold in a burgh.
cuntack *n* the fish fatherlasher.
cunyie *same as* **cunzie**.
cunyie-mirk *n* a very snug situation.
cunzie, cunyie *n* money, coin.—*v* to coin, to mint.
cup *n* **1** a small thick biscuit, slightly hollow in the middle. **2** a kind of fishing net or trap.
Cupar *n* *in phr* **he that will to Cupar maun to Cupar** a wilful man must have his way.

Cupar justice *n* **1** judgment after execution. **2** Jeddart justice (qv).
cuplins *n* the length between the tops of the shoulderblades and the tops of the hip joints.
cup-moss *n* a name given to the lichen, *tartareus*.
cupper *n* a toper, tippler.
cuppil, cupple *same as* **couple**.
cupplin *n* the lower part of the backbone.
curach *same as* **currach**.
curbawdy *n* active courtship.
curch[1] *n* **1** a woman's cap or headdress. **2** a kerchief.
curch[2] *v* to bend, to curtsy.
curchie *n* a curtsy.—*v* to curtsy.
curcuddie, curcuddock *same as* **cucuddy**.
curcuddock, curcuddoch, curcudynch, curcoddoch *adj* **1** sitting close together in a friendly manner. **2** cordial, intimate, kindly, fond.—*v* **1** to whisper or talk intimately together. **2** to sit closely and cosily together.
curdie[1] *n* a small bit of curd.
curdie[2] *n* a farthing.
curdoo, curdow *n* the cooing sound of pigeons.—*v* to make love.
curdooer *same as* **curdower**.
cur doon *v* **1** to cower under danger. **2** to lie down in a cramped position.
curdow[1] *same as* **curdoo**.
curdow[2] *v* to patch, mend, sew clumsily.
curdower *n* **1** one who works at any trade within a burgh of which he is not a free man. **2** a tailor or sempstress who goes from house to house to mend old clothes.
curdy-butter *same as* **crowdy-butter**.
cureckity coo *v* **1** to coo. **2** to make love to.
curfuffle *v* to rumple, ruffle, dishevel, discompose.—*n* a ruffling, tremor, fuss, agitation, dishevelment
curfumish *same as* **carfumish**.
curgellit *adj* shocked by seeing or hearing anything horrible.
curglaff, curgloff *n* the shock felt in bathing at the first plunge into cold water.
curhung *n* a slide on ice on one's bottom.
curious *adj* **1** careful, particular. **2** anxious, eager. **3** fond.
curiously *adv* carefully.
curjute *v* **1** to overwhelm, overthrow. **2** to overcome with strong drink.
curkling *n* the sound emitted by the quail.
curl-doddy *n* **1** the cone of a pine or fir tree. **2** curled cabbage. **3** natural clover. **4** ribgrass.
curled mill *n* a snuffbox made of the tip of a horn.
curlie-doddie *n* **1** blue sacaious. **2** the daisy. **3** a kind of sugar plum.
curlie-fuffs *n* false hair worn by women to make up deficiencies.
curlie-pow *n* **1** a curly head. **2** a curly-headed boy.
curlies *n* **1** curled colewort. **2** curly kale (qv).
curlie-wurlie *n* a fantastic figure or ornament on stone, etc.
curlippie *v* to steal slyly.
curluns *n* the earthnut, pignut.
curly *n* **1** a curly head. **2** a curly-headed boy.
curly-andrew *n* sugared coriander seed.
curly-head-a-craw *adv* topsy-turvy.
curly kale *n* curled colewort.
curly-murchy[1] *n* the female nymphae, etc.
curly-murchy[2] *adj* churlish and ungrateful.
curly-murly nightcap *n* the monkshood.
curly plant *n* curly kale (qv).
curmow *n* an accompaniment, an escort.
curmud *adj* **1** cordial, intimate, neighbourly. **2** snug, comfortable.—*v* to sit close, to be very intimate.
curmudge *n* a mean fellow, a curmudgeon.
curmudgeous *adj* mean, niggardly.
curmudlie *n* close contact, pressure. *See* **curmud**.
curmur *n* the purring of a cat.

curmurrin *n* **1** a low, rumbling sound, a murmuring. **2** a source of grumbling.

curn[1] *n* **1** a grain or particle of corn. **2** a quantity of indefinite size or number. **3** a party, band, assembly. **4** a small price.—*adv* in small pieces.

curn[2] *n* a handmill.—*v* to grind.

curnab *v* to pilfer, seize.

curnaptious *adj* cross, ready to take offence, irritable.

curnawin' *n* the sensation of hunger.

curneedy *n* a pig.

curney *n* a small quantity of anything.

curnie[1] *adj* **1** full of grains. **2** knotted, candied.

curnie[2] *n* nursery term for the little finger.

curnie[3] *n* a small quantity.

curnie-wurnie *n* the little finger, a nursery term.

curnoitted *adj* peevish.

curpal, curple *n* a crupper.

curpin, curpan, curpen, curpon *n* **1** a crupper. **2** the back. **3** the backbone. **4** the buttocks. **5** the rump of a fowl.

curple-gawt *adj* (*used of a horse*) galled by the crupper under the tail.

curr[1] *v* **1** to coo. **2** to purr.—*n* **1** a whisper. **2** a rumour.

curr[2] *v* **1** to cower, crouch. **2** to squat.

curr[3] *v* **1** to move a thing by touching it slightly with anything pointed. **2** (*with* **at**) to attempt such a movement.—*n* such a touch.

currach[1], **currack** *n* **1** a wickerwork pannier. **2** a small cart made of twigs.

currach[2] *n* a small boat or skiff.

currack[1] *n* a sea tangle.

currack[2] *same as* **currach**[1].

currack[3] *n* a person of stubborn temper.

currag[1] *n* the forefinger.

currag[2] *same as* **currach**[2].

curran[1] *n* a small quantity.

curran[2] *n* a currant.

curran-petris *n* the wild carrot.

currant-bun *n* a large Christmas bun, consisting mainly of dried fruits and spices, a sweetie-loaf (qv).

currbawty *n* the art of seeking a quarrel.

current *n* every single peck, as multure (qv) for so many ground at a mill, so that the 17th current is every 17th peck.

curriched *adj* **1** made of wickerwork. **2** covered with hides. *See* **currach**[1].

currie[1] *n* a small stool.

currie[2] *n* a deep pool or recess in a river, where fish hide.

currieboram *n* a crowd of living creatures.

curriebuction, currybuckshon *n* a confused gathering that is quarrelsome or dangerous.

curriebushel *n* a confused crowd of people.

curriehunkers *n* the hams, the hams in a crouching posture.

curriemudge, curriemudgel *v* to beat good-naturedly.

curriemushel *n* a confused crowd of people.

currie wirrie, ~ wurrie *n* a violent dispute.—*adv* violently disputing.—*v* to dispute violently.

currie-wurriein' *n* a prolonged violent dispute.—*adv* peevish, fretful.

currit *v* (*used of a vehicle*) to run smoothly.

currivell *v* to squabble noisily.—*n* a noisy squabble.

curroch *n* a wickerwork pannier.

currock *same as* **currach**[2].

currock-cross't *adj* bound to a currach.

curroo *v* to coo.

currough *same as* **currach**[2].

currough *n* a cairn, a heap of stones.

currove *v* to coo.

curry-haikie *n* the lifting and carrying of a tired child.

curry-shang *n* a broil, an uproar.

cursackie *n* a long, coarse smock worn by workers over their clothes.

cursaddle *n* the small saddle on a carriage horse.

curse *n in phr* **the curse o' Scotland** the nine of diamonds in a pack of cards.

curseese *v* to catechize, scold, reprove.

curshe *same as* **curch**[1].

cursour *n* a stallion.

curst *adj* ill-tempered.

curstness *n* crabbedness, ill-temper.

curtle *n* a sluttish girl.

curtoush *n* a woman's 'short gown'.

curtsey *n* a woman's cap.

curtshy *v* to curtsy.

curunddoch *n* a dance play among children.

curwurring *n* a rambling, murmuring.

cush *int* an exclamation of surprise.

cushat, cushet, cushat-doo *n* **1** the wood pigeon. **2** the wild pigeon. **3** the stock dove.

cushie[1], **cushie-bonnie** *int* a milkmaid's call to a cow.

cushie[2], **cushey, cushie-, cushey-doo, cushy** *same as* **cushat**.

cushineel *n* cochineal.

cushlan *n* a gentle sliding down.—*n* a gentle sliding down.

cushle *v* to slide down gently.—*n* a gentle sliding down.

cushle-mushle *n* a hubbub, confused muttering and movement.

cussels *n* the viviparous blenny.

cusser *same as* **cooser**.

cussit *n* a small chest.

custen *v* cast.

custoc, custock *n* the stem of a cabbage, etc.

customary weaver *n* one who weaves for private customers.

customer *n* the lessee of burgh customs and dues.

customer wark *n* weaving or work done for private customers.

custril *n* a sort of fool or silly fellow.

custroune *n* a vagabond, cad.—*adj* **1** caddish. **2** low-born.

cut[1] *v* **1** to castrate. **2** to spay. **3** to thrash with a whip.—*n* **1** a blow with a whip. **2** appetite. **3** grass, hay or corn to be reaped. **4** an artificial watercourse. **5** an excavation or cutting. **6** a piece of cloth of varying length, cut from the warp. **7** a measure of yarn, the 12th of a hank. **8** temper, mood.

cut[2] *n* a lot.—*v* to decide by lot.

cut[3] *v* to run quickly, hasten away.

cutchack *same as* **coutchack**.

cutcher *same as* **coucher**.

cutchick *same as* **coutchack**.

cutchie *n* kitchen.

cutchin *adj* cowardly, knocking under.—*n* a coward.

cute *same as* **cuit**.

cutekins *same as* **cuitikins**.

cuter *same as* **cuiter**.

cuterer *n* a flatterer.

cut-fingered *adj* **1** (*used of gloves*) with the fingers cut short. **2** abrupt, curt, giving or getting short answers. **3** leaving a company abruptly.

cuth *n* a coalfish not fully grown.

Cuthbert's beads, St *n* portions of the jointed stems of fossil encrinites common in mountain limestone.

cutherie, cuthrie *adj* **1** chilly. **2** susceptible to cold.

cuthie *same as* **couthie**.

cuthil *same as* **cutle**[1].

cutie stane *n* a curling stone.

cutikins *same as* **cuitikins**.

cutit *adj* having ankles.

cutle[1] *v* to carry corn from one position to a more convenient one, from a distant to a nearer field. —*n* corn carried and set up in another place.

cutle[2] *same as* **cuitle**.

cutling *n* **1** a flatterer. **2** flattery.

cut-luggit *adj* crop-eared (*used contemptuously*).

cut-lugs *n* a crop-eared horse.

cut-pock, ~-pyock *n* the stomach of a fish or of a person.

cutt *n* a term of reproach.

cuttay *n* a term of reproach for a girl.

cutter[1] *n* **1** a mowing machine. **2** a reaping machine.
cutter[2] *n* a small whisky bottle.
cutthroat *n* a kind of sweetmeat.
cut-throat *n* **1** a dark lantern. **2** the name formerly given to a piece of ordnance.
cuttie[1] *n* a hare.
cuttie[2] *v* to eat greedily.
cuttie[3] *n* a horse or mare two years old.
cuttie[4] *n* **1** the black guillemot. **2** the razorbill.
cuttie[5] *same as* **cutty**[2].
cuttie-boyn *same as* **cuitie-boyn**.
cuttie-brown *n* a horse crop-eared or, perhaps, docked in the tail.
cuttie-clap *n* a hare's form.
cuttie-free *adj* able to take food.
cuttiein *n* the act of eating greedily.
cuttie-rung *n* a crupper for a horse wearing a packsaddle.
cuttie's fud *n* a hare's tail.
cuttikins *same as* **cuitikins**.
cutting-off *n* excommunication.
cutting-off-piece *n* the feast of harvest home.
cuttings *n* encouragement, countenance.
cuttit *adj* **1** abrupt, rude, snappish. **2** offended. **3** laconic.
cuttitly *adv* **1** abruptly. **2** laconically. **3** tartly.
cuttle[1] *same as* **cutle**[1].
cuttle[2] *v* to sharpen.
cuttle[3] *v* to smile or laugh in a suppressed way.
cuttoch *same as* **cuddoch**.
cuttum rung *n* that part of the piece of wood (which keeps back the sunks used for a saddle) that goes under the horse's tail.
cutty[1] *n* the wren.
cutty[2] *adj* **1** short, cut short. **2** diminutive. **3** short-tempered, hasty.—*n* **1** a short clay pipe. **2** a short-handled horn spoon. **3** a small knife. **4** a short, stumpy girl. **5** a worthless woman. **6** a rompish child. **7**—*v* to sup with a spoon.
cutty[3] *n* a short, three-legged stool.
cutty[4] *n* a small, thick cake of oatmeal, with a hole in the middle.

cutty basket *n* a basket for holding horn spoons.
cutty clay *n* a short clay pipe.
cutty-full *n* a small measure full.
cutty glies, ~ glier *n* a short, squat flirt.
cutty gun *n* a short tobacco pipe.
cutty-hunker dance *n* an old burlesque dance, performed by mendicants.
cutty knife *n* a small knife.
cutty-mun *n* **1** *in phr* **cutty-mun and tree-ladle** the supposed name of an old tune. **2** used of one who swings on the gallows.
cutty pipe *n* a short tobacco pipe.
cutty quean *n* a worthless woman.
cutty queen *n* the wren.
cutty sark *n* **1** part of a woman's underlinen cut short. **2** a worthless woman.
cutty spune *n* a short-handled horn spoon.
cutty stool *n* **1** a short three-legged stool. **2** the stool of repentance, on which offenders formerly sat in church.
cutty stoup *n* **1** a small drinking vessel. **2** a quartern measure.
cutty-wren *n* the wren.
cutwiddie, cutwuddie *n* the bar of a plough or harrow to which the traces are attached.
cutworm *n* **1** a white grub that destroys vegetables by cutting through the stem. **2** a person with destructive tendencies.
cuve *n* a tub.
cuz *adj* close.—*adv* closely.
cwaw *phr* come away!
cweef *n* a trick, catch.
cweelie off *v* to wheedle out of.
cyclops *n* a name given to a tawse (qv) from its having a large hole or eye in its head.
cyle *n* a beam, rafter.
cymar *n* a shroud.
cypher-man *n* **1** a diminutive man. **2** a person good for little. **3** a loafer. **4** a lazy, drunken rascal. **5** a 'cypher'.
cyprus-cat *n* a cat of three colours, black, brown and white.
cythe *v* **1** to make known. **2** to become known.—*n* appearance.

D

da[1] *n* a child's name for father.
da[2], **daa** *same as* **daw**[1].
daach *same as* **daugh**[1].
daachter *n* a daughter.
daad *same as* **dad**[3].
daak[1] *v* **1** to doze for a short time. **2** (*of bad weather*) to abate for a short time.—*n* a lull in bad weather.
daak[2] *adj* dark and dull.
daaken *same as* **dawken**.
daakenin *same as* **dawkenin'**.
daar *adj* dear.
daart *v* to raise the price of anything.
daat *same as* **daut**.
daatie *same as* **dautie**.
dab[1] *v* **1** to give a slight stroke. **2** to strike with a sharp or pointed weapon. **3** to prick. **4** to peck like a bird. **5** to press or put smartly down. **6** to dip into.—*n* **1** a blow or slap. **2** a thrust, poke, peck. **3** a small quantity of anything.—*adv* with force, violently, sharply.
dab[2] *v in phr* **1 let dab** to hint, give sign, tell, divulge a secret. **2 let dab at** to snatch at.
dab[3] *v* to daub.
dab[4] *n* an expert, an adept.
dabach[1] *v* to thrust, prod.—*n* a blow, a thrust.—*adv* sharply, with force.
dabach[2] *n* an expert, an adept.
dabber *v* **1** to stupefy one with rapid talk. **2** to confound. **3** to jar. **4** to wrangle.—*n* a wrangle.
dabberin *n* continued wrangling.—*adj* quarrelsome.

dabbich *v* **1** to seize. **2** to peck.
dabbies *n* **1** *in phr* **holy dabbies** cakes of shortbread, formerly used in Galloway instead of plain bread at the Lord's Supper. **2** a sort of cake baked with butter, called petticoat tails.
dabbin *n* the act of pecking, pricking, pushing or pressing.
dabble[1] *same as* **daibble**[1].
dabble[2] *v* to chew.
dabble[3] *v* **1** to wrangle. **2** to stupefy with talk.
dabble[4] *v* to compel one to work in wet weather.
dabble-dock *n* **1** the last candle made at a dipping. **2** a person with wet, dripping clothes.
dabblet *adj* employed at work not conducive to tidiness.
dabbril *n* a woman slovenly at work and heartless in manner.
daberlick, daberlack *n* **1** a long seaweed, bladderlock (qv). **2** any wet strap of cloth or leather. **3** the hair of the head, hanging in long, lank, tangled locks. **3** (*used contemptuously*) a long, lanky person.
dablet *n* an imp, a little devil.
dabrich *adj* lewd, lustful.
dabster *n* a proficient, an expert.
daccle *same as* **dackle**.
dacent *adj* decent.
dachan *n* a puny, dwarfish creature.
dachle *same as* **dackle**.
dachter *n* a daughter.
dacker *v* **1** to saunter idly, stroll leisurely, jog. **2** to go about in feeble health. **3** to continue on, continue irresolutely.

4 to peddle, barter. **5** to dispose in an orderly way. **6** to lay out a dead body. **7** to search, examine. **8** to inquire after stolen or smuggled goods. **9** to wrangle, challenge. **10** to engage. **11** to trifle at work.—*n* **1** a stroll, a short walk. **2** a wrangle, struggle.—*adj* (*used of the weather*) uncertain, unsettled.

dackle *v* **1** to hesitate. **2** to lessen speed.—*n* **1** a state of suspense, hesitation. **2** a pause. **3** the abating of heat as a fire fades.

dacklie *adj* **1** swarthy. **2** pale, sickly in appearance.

dacklin[1] *n* a slight shower.

dacklin[2] *adj* **1** in a state of doubt. **2** slow, dilatory.

dacre *v* to inflict corporal punishment.

dad[1] *n* a pet name for father.

dad[2] *same as* **daud**[1].

dad[3] *v* **1** to strike, thrash. **2** to dash, drive forcibly. **3** to bespatter. **4** to pelt. **5** to wander about. **6** to knock. **7** to abuse. **8** to fall with force. **9** (*with* **about**) to dash or drive about a district. **10** (*with* **aff**) to shake off. **11** (*with* **down**) to fall down, knock down.—*n* **1** a dash. **2** a violent blow. **3** a sudden thrust with violence. **4** the clapping of hands in applause. **5** a heavy fall.

dad[4] *same as* **daddit**.

dad a bit *phr* not a bit, devil a bit.

dadd *n* father.

daddin *n* **1** rough usage. **2** knocking, striking. **3** knocking about, wandering.—*adj* (*used of wind or rain*) beating, driving.

daddins *n* a beating.

daddit *adj* **1** beaten. **2** dashed. **3** knocked about.

daddle *same as* **daidle**[1].

daddle, daddlie *same as* **daidle**[2].

Daddy Cloots *n* the devil.

daddy-da *n* a child's name for father.

dadge *n* a bannock.

dadgeon weaver, ~ wabster *n* **1** a linen weaver. **2** one who weaves for private customers.

dadjell *v* to stroll, saunter.

dadle *same as* **daiddle**[2].

dae *v* to do.—*aux v* do.

daevle *n* devil.

daff *v* **1** to be foolish. **2** to sport. **3** to jest. **4** to talk nonsense. **5** to flirt. **6** to romp. **7** to toy amorously.

daffadile *n* **1** a daffodil. **2** a silly, flashy woman. **3** an effeminate or delicate man.

daffer *n* **1** merriment. **2** one who daffs. *See* **daff**.

daffery *n* **1** gaiety. **2** sportiveness. **3** folly.

daffin *n* **1** sport. **2** folly. **3** idle waste of time in foolish talk. **4** loose talk. **5** dallying. **6** matrimonial intercourse.

daffing green *n* a village green where games are played or young people meet to daff (qv).

daffins[1] *n* daffodils.

daffins[2] *n* the small cords by which herring nets are fastened to the rope on their upper edge.

daffodil, daffodilly *n* **1** a silly, flashy woman. **2** an effeminate or delicate man.

daft *adj* **1** mentally deranged. **2** delirious. **3** silly, foolish. **4** giddy, thoughtless. **5** innocently merry. **6** excessively merry. **7** playful. **8** extremely fond of and eager to obtain. **9** doting.

daft-days *n* the holidays at Christmas and the New Year.

daftish *adj* **1** rather daft (qv). **2** mentally slow. **3** stupid.

daft-like *adj* **1** giddy. **2** foolish. **3** thoughtless. **4** dull-witted. **5** absurd. **6** reckless. **7** mad. **8** eccentric in appearance.

daftly *adv* **1** foolishly. **2** merrily. **3** madly.

daftness *n* **1** foolishness. **2** fatuousness. **3** light-headedness.

daftrie *n* **1** merriment, sportiveness. **2** folly.

dafty *n* **1** a half-witted person. **2** a nickname applied to such a person.

dag[1] *n* **1** a drizzling rain. **2** a heavy shower. **3** a fog, a mist.—*v* **1** to drizzle, rain gently. **2** to be foggy.

dag[2], **dagg** *v* **1** to shoot, let fly. **2** to stab.—*n* a gun, a pistol.

dag[3] *v* to confound, used as an imprecation.

dag-daw *n* the jackdaw.

dag-durk *n* a dirk for stabbing.

dage *n* **1** a slut, trollop. **2** a dirty, mismanaging woman.

dagg *n* a cut of earth.

daggered *adj* (*used of lightning*) forked.

daggin *same as* **dagone**.

daggined *adj*dashed.—*adv* used as a very strong intensive.

daggle[1] *v* **1** to fall in torrents. **2** to drizzle, rain continuously.

daggle[2] *v* **1** to knock about. **2** to dangle, trail. **3** to lounge.

daggler *n* **1** a lounger. **2** an idler.

daggy *adj* drizzling, misty, rainy.

dagh *same as* **daich**.

dag-head, ~-man *n* the hammer or the dog-head of a gun or pistol.

dagone *v* **1** to confound, dash, used as an imprecation. **2** to use freely the expletive dagone (qv).

dagont *n* an expletive.—*adv* used as a very strong intensive.

dahie *adj* (*used of weather*) warm, misty, muggy.

dai *same as* **dey**[1].

daible[1] *v* **1** to wash slightly. **2** to dabble. **3** to drink in a slovenly fashion.—*n* a slight washing.

daible[2] *v* **1** to walk like a child. **2** to go about feebly.

daicent *adj* decent.

daich *adj* soft, flabby.—*n* **1** dough. **2** food for poultry.

daichy *adj* **1** soft, flabby. **2** doughy. **3** spiritless, cowardly. **4** used of rich ground.

daickle *same as* **dackle**.

daiddie *n* father.

daidle[1] *n* **1** a pinafore. **2** a large bib,.

daidle[2] *v* **1** to dawdle. **2** to trifle. **3** to saunter. **4** to tipple. **5** to bedaub oneself in eating or in walking. **6** to fondle a child.—*n* a ramble.

daidler *n* a trifler.

daidley *adj* dawdling.

daidlie *n* **1** a pinafore. **2** a bib.

daidlin *adj* **1** silly. **2** mean-spirited. **3** cowardly. **4** trifling.

daigh *same as* **daich**.

daighie[1] *same as* **daich**.

daighie[2] *n* a simpleton.

daighiness *n* **1** flabbiness. **2** the state of being daighie (qv).

daigle *same as* **daggle**[1].

daik[1] *v* **1** to smooth down. **2** to moisten, soak.—*n* a smooth down.

daik[2] *v* to deck.

daiken *n* a decade.

daiker[1] *same as* **dacker**.

daiker[2] *v* to dress, deck.

daikins *int* an exclamation of surprise.

daikit *adj* used, put to use.

dail[1] *n* a field.

dail[2], **daill** *n* **1** a deal of something. **2** a number of persons. **3** a part, portion. **4** value.

dail[3] *n* **1** a deal board. **2** a stretching board for a corpse.

dail[4] *n* a ewe fattened for the butcher.

dail[5] *n* **1** grief. **2** evil.

daill *n* **1** interference. **2** interest. **3** dealing. **4** management.

daily-day *adv* every day, continually.

daily-dud *n* a dish clout.

dailygone *same as* **dayligaun**.

daime-and-laive *phr* **1** great plenty. **2** wasteful extravagance.

daimen *adj* occasional, rare.—*adv* now and then.

daimen icker *n* an ear of corn met with occasionally.

daimis *v* to stun.

daine *adj* **1** gentle, modest. **2** lowly.

dainshoch *adj* nice, dainty, squeamish.

dainta, daintis *int* no matter! it is of no consequence.

daintess *n* **1** a dainty, a delicacy. **2** a rarity.

daintie *n* affection.

daintith, dainteth *n* a dainty, a delicacy.

dainty adj **1** (used of things) large. **2** (of children, etc) plump, thriving. **3** comely. **4** pleasant, good-natured. **5** worthy, excellent. **6** liberal. **7** used ironically for scanty.

dainty wheen n a good many.

dair same as **dere**².

dair away phr (used of sheep) to wander, roam from their usual pasture.

dairg same as **darg**¹.

dairgie same as **dirgie**.

dais, daiss n **1** a wooden settle or sofa, convertible into a table, bed or seat. **2** a bench of stone or turf at a cottage door. **3** a bench seat. **4** a church pew.

daise v **1** to stun, stupefy with drink. **2** to benumb. **3** to wither. **4** to rot.—n **1** the powder or that part of a stone which is bruised by the stroke of a chisel or pickaxe. **2** anything that so injures wood, clothes, etc, as to spoil or rot them.

daised adj (used of wood, plants, etc) spoiled, withered, rotten.

daisie adj **1** (used of the weather) cold, damp, raw. **2** sunless. **3** chilling.

daising n a disease of sheep, called also pining and vanquish.

daisy adj **1** covered with daisies. **2** remarkable. **3** darling.

daiver v **1** to stun, confound, used as an imprecation. **2** to wander aimlessly. **3** to wander in mind. **4** to tarry. **5** to be benumbed, become stiff with cold.—n a stunning blow.

daivered adj **1** fatigued. **2** stupid. **3** confused.

daivilie adv spiritlessly, listlessly.

daize, daizie same as **daise**.

dajon-wabster same as **dadgeon-weaver**.

daker, dakker same as **dacker**.

daldoo n a great noise, a hubbub.

daldrum n **1** a foolish fancy. **2** mental confusion.

dale¹ same as **dail**³.

dale² same as **daill**.

dale³ same as **dell**¹.

dale-land n the lower and arable ground of a district.

dale-lander, ~-man n an inhabitant of the lower ground or dale-land (qv).

dalgan n the stick used in binding sheaves.

dalk n **1** varieties of slate clay. **2** common clay. **3** a coalminer's term.

dall¹ n a large cake of sawdust and cow dung, formerly used by the poor as fuel.

dall² n a sloven.

dall³ same as **doll**¹.

dallion n a person with large, ill-fitting clothes or with an awkward gait.

dallish adj slovenly.

dalloch n a flat piece of rich land.

dallop n a steep shank (qv) or glen, where two haughs are exactly opposite to each other.

dallow v to dig with a spade, delve.

dally¹ n the stick sometimes used in binding sheaves.

dally² same as **dolly**.

dalt n a foster child.

dam¹ n **1** the water confined by a dam or barrier, a mill-pond. **2** (used of children) the quantity of urine discharged at a time. **3** a mill lade.

dam² n a mother, woman.

dam³ n a piece or man in the game of draughts.

dam⁴ n the damson plum.

damack, damackie n a girl, a young woman.

damage n **1** legal damages. **2** cost, expense.

damas n damask.

damasee n the damson or damask plum.

damborded adj (of a checked pattern) crossed like a dambrod (qv).

dambrod n a draughtboard.—adj checked like a dambrod.

dam dyke n the wall of a millpond, etc.

dame n **1** the mistress of a house. **2** a farmer's wife. **3** a mother. **4** a young, unmarried woman. **5** a damsel.

dam-e'e n the outlet of a millpond.

dam head n the upper embankment of a millpond.

damishell n a damsel.

dammer¹ n **1** a miner. **2** one who constructs dams.

dammer² v to astonish, confuse, astound.

dammertit adj stupid.

dammin' and lavin' phr fish-poaching by damming and diverting the course of a stream and then laving out the water.

damming and loving phr preferring a sure though small gain to the prospect of a greater with uncertainty.

dammish v **1** to stun, stupefy. **2** to bruise the surface of fruit. **3** to injure, damage. **4** used as an expletive.

dammishment n damage, injury.

dammit adj stunned.

damnage, dampnage n injury, damage.

damnation n judicial condemnation.

damnify v to damage, injure by loss.

damp¹ n coal-pit gas.

damp² n **1** rain. **2** low spirits.—adj downcast, damped.—v to throw down, fell.

dams n the game of draughts.

damsel n the damson plum.

dan n a respectful term of address.

dance n a needless, hurried or exasperating hunt for a person or thing.

dance-in-my-lufe n a very diminutive person.

dancing v in phr **send one dancing** to send one quickly.

dancing-mad adj in a towering passion.

dandalie same as **dandillie**.

dander¹ n **1** temper, anger. **2** spirit.

dander² v **1** to stroll, saunter. **2** to trifle.—n a stroll.

danderer n **1** a saunterer. **2** a habitual saunterer.

dandering v, adj **1** vibrating, resounding. **2** emitting an unequal sound.

dandering-Kate n the stone-bore or stone-orpine.

danders n **1** smithy-fire refuse. **2** clinkers, slag.

dandgell n **1** a large, thick topcoat. **2** a clumsy person with large, ill-fitting clothes.

dandiefechun n a stroke, a hollow blow on any part of the body.

dandies, dandie-han'-lin' n a handline for catching herring or mackerel from a boat or ship sailing at a moderate rate.

dandillie, dandily adj **1** celebrated for beauty. **2** spoilt by admiration.—n **1** a fondling. **2** a woman who makes too much of herself.

dandillie chain n a chain made by children of dandelion stems for play or ornament.

dandrum n a whim, freak.

dandy, dandie n **1** an elegant woman. **2** a distinguished or prominent person. **3** a female paramour.—adj **1** fine. **2** elegant.—phr **the dandy** the very thing, the fashion, just what is wanted.

dane v done.

daner same as **dander**².

dang¹ beat, drove. See **ding**².

dang² v **1** to throw violently, knock, bang. **2** to drive.

dang³ v used as an imprecation for damn.

dangerous adj dangerously ill.

dangle v **1** to swing, vibrate. **2** to throb, tingle. **3** to quiver with pain.

danglers n the weights of a clock.

dank-will n a will-o'-the-wisp.

dannar'd same as **donnert**.

danner same as **dander**².

danners same as **danders**.

dannle same as **dangle**.

dant v **1** to daunt. **2** to be afraid.

danton same as **daunton**.

danyel v **1** to dangle. **2** to jolt while driving on a rough road.

dapperpy adj diapered, used of variegated woollen cloth.

dapse v to choose, fix upon.

darden n a dry, soft wind.

dardum same as **dirdum**.

dare¹ v to challenge, defy.—n a challenge.

dare[2] *v* **1** to be afraid, shrink in fear. **2** to crouch, lie hid. **3** to terrify, stupefy.—*n* a feeling of fear or awe.

daredeviltry *n* a daredevil spirit.

dare-the-deil *n* **1** a daredevil. **2** one who fears nothing and will attempt anything.

darg[1], **dargue** *n* **1** a day's work. **2** work done in a day. **3** work, whether done in a day or not. **4** a set task. **5** a quantity of land.—*v* **1** to work by the day. **2** to toil.

darg[2] *n* the noise made by a spade in soft earth.

darg-days *n* days of work given as part of a farmer's or cottager's rent.

darger *n* a day-labourer.

darging *n* **1** a day-labourer's work. **2** hard, plodding toil. **3** unskilled labour.

dark[1] *n* a day's work.

dark[2] *v* **1** to grow dark. **2** to cloud with evil. **3** to hide, take shelter.

dark-benichtit *adj* overtaken by darkness.

darken *v in phr* **darken one's door** to enter one's house.

darkening *n* twilight, dusk.

darket *adj* dull, down-hearted.

darkle *v* **1** to darken suddenly in alternation with a gleam of light. **2** to be momentarily obscured.

darklins *adv* **1** darkly. **2** in the dark.

darksome *adj* melancholy, dismal.

darle *n* **1** a bit of bread or of anything. **2** a portion.

darloch *n* **1** a bundle. **2** a valise. **3** a sheaf of arrows.

darlock *n* a large piece of anything solid.

darn[1] *v* **1** to hide, conceal. **2** to hearken stealthily. **3** to loiter at work. **4** to think, muse. **5** (*with* **behind**) to fall back.

darn[2] *v* used in imprecation for damn.

darn[3] *n* a disease of cattle, supposed to be caused by eating the wood anemone.

darn[4] *v* **1** to stuff a hole. **2** to zigzag like a drunk man on a street.

darna *same as* **daurna**.

darr *v* (*used of a blow*) to fall, alight.

darra *n* **1** a handline for catching large fish. **2** the hooks and sinkers attached to the line.

darra-shaft *n* **1** the frame on which the darra (qv) is kept. **2** the darra (qv) itself.

darsna *v* durst not.

dar't *v* dared.

dash[1] *v* **1** to abash, dismay, confuse. **2** to show off. **3** to flourish in writing. **4** to erase, strike out. **5** used in imprecation.—*n* **1** a display. **2** a flourish in writing. **3** (*of rain*) a sudden fall.

dash[2] *n* a hat, a cap.

dashelled *v*, *adj* beaten and wasted by weather,

dashie *adj* making a great show.

dashing *n* a disappointment.

dashy-looking *adj* smart, well-dressed.

dask *n* **1** a desk. **2** a precentor's desk.

dass *n* **1** the portion of a haystack cut off with a hay knife. **2** the corn left in a barn after part is removed. **3** a stratum of stones. **4** a layer in a mass slowly built up. **5** a small landing place. **6** a step.

datch *v* to jog, shake.

datchel-like *adj* having a dangling appearance.

datchie *adj* **1** (*used of the intellect*) penetrating. **2** sly, cunning, crafty. **3** hidden, secret.

datchle *v* **1** to waddle. **2** to walk carelessly, with ill-fitting clothes.

date *n in phr* **gi'e date and gree** to give the preference.

daub[1] *same as* **dab**[1].

daub[2] *same as* **dab**[4].

double[1] *v* **1** to thrust. **2** to work into. **3** to dibble.

double[2] *v* to dabble.

dauch *n* a soft, black substance, composed chiefly of clay, mica and coal dust.

dauchle *same as* **dackle**.

dauchy *adj* (*a curling term, used of the ice*) wet, sloppy, rendering play difficult.

daud[1] *n* a large piece.

daud[2] *same as* **dad**[3].

daudnel *adj* shabby in appearance.

daug *same as* **dag**[1].

daugeon *n* fellow, person.

daugh[1] *n* a measure of land, estimated to yield 48 bolls.

daugh[2] *v* had ability, was able.

daugh[3] *n* a very heavy dew or drizzling rain.—*v* to moisten, bedew.

daught[1] *v* was able. *See* **dow**[2].

daught[2] *n* **1** taste. **2** effluvium.

dauk[1] *adj* stupid, doltish.

dauk[2] *n* clay used for making firebricks.

dauk[3] *adj* dark, murky.

dauk[4] *v* to drizzle.—a drizzling rain.

dauky *adj* moist, damp.

daul'd *adj* **1** fagged, worn-out. **2** depressed.

dauldness *n* low spirits.

dauldrums *same as* **doldrum**.

dauler *n* a supine, delicate person.

dault *same as* **dalt**.

daumer *v* **1** to stun, stupefy. **2** to knock about. **3** to bewilder.—*n* a stunning blow.

daumert *adj* bewildered, sleepy, silly.

daunder, dauner *same as* **dander**[2].

daunders *same as* **danders**.

daunt *same as* **dant**.

daunting *adj* **1** ominous,. **2** discouraging.

dauntingly *adv* courageously.

daunton *v* **1** to terrify, subdue. **2** to depress. **3** to awe.

daupet *adj* **1** silly, stupid. **2** inactive. **3** unconcerned. **4** mentally weak.

daupit-blind *adj* stupid and blind.

daur *same as* **dare**.

dauredna *v neg* dared not.

daurg, daurk *same as* **darg**[1].

daurin' *adj* **1** (*used of beard or whiskers*) very big, bushy. **2** bold, venturesome.

daurken *v* to grow dark.

daurna *v neg* dare not.

daurnin *n* a thrashing, knocking about.

daurt *v* dared.

daur upon *phr* to affect, impress.

daut *v* to fondle, dote upon, make much of.—*n* **1** a caress. **2** a pat fondly given.

dautie *n* **1** a darling. **2** a dear. **3** a sweetheart.

dauting *n* **1** a caress. **2** petting. **3** fondling.

dautit *adj* **1** fondled, petted. **2** spoiled by overpetting.

dave *same as* **deave**[2].

davel *same as* **devel**.

davelin *n* the flat planks on the centres for supporting the arch stones of bridges while building.

daver *same as* **daiver**.

daverer *n* a shuffler.

davering *adj* riding or walking in a dazed condition.

daver't *same as* **daivered**.

davie-drap *n* (*perhaps*) the cuckoo-grass or chimney sweeps.

daviely *same as* **daivilie**.

davoch *n* an ancient measure of land, averaging 416 acres.

Davy *n* Sir Humphrey Davy's safety lamp.

daw[1] *n* **1** a lazy, good-for-nothing person. **2** a sluggard. **3** an untidy woman or housewife. **4** a slattern. **5** a trull.

daw[2] *n* **1** fire clay found on coal. **2** a cake of cow dung and coal dust used as fuel.

daw[3] *n* an atom, particle, jot.

daw[4] *v* dawn.—*v* to dawn.

dawch *v* **1** to moisten with dew. **2** to damp.—*n* a heavy dew or drizzling rain.

dawd[1] *same as* **daud**[1].

dawd[2] *same as* **dad**[3].

dawdge *n* a tatterdemalion, ragged fellow.

dawdie *adj* slovenly, sluttish, dowdy.

dawdle *n* a lazy, indolent person.—*v* **1** to be indolent. **2** to mess, bedabble.—*adv* indolently.

dawdry *adj* slovenly, untidy.

dawds and blawds *n* **1** kail blades (qv), boiled whole and eaten with bannocks. **2** the greatest abundance.

dawfish *n* the lesser dogfish.

dawghie *same as* **dawkie**.

dawing *n* the dawn.

dawk *same as* **dauk**⁴.

dawken *v* to dawn.

dawkenin' *n* the dawn.

dawkie *same as* **dawky**.

dawless *same as* **dowless**.

dawlie *same as* **dowly**.

dawmer *same as* **daumer**.

dawner *same as* **dander**².

dawpit *adj* having lost mental vigour.

dawsie *adj* constitutionally stupid or inactive.

dawt *same as* **daut**.

dawtie¹ *same as* **dautie**.

dawtie² *n* a schoolboy's favourite companion.

day-aboot *n phr* **1** alternate days. **2** an equal footing. **3** tit for tat.

day an' daily *phr* every day.

day an' way o't *phr* **1** self-support. **2** daily payment of one's way.

day-darger *n* a day-labourer.

day-daw, ~-dawin *n* the dawn.

day-level *n* a mine bored to some point lower than the workings, to which the water was carried by gravitation.

dayligaun *n* twilight.

day-lily *n* the asphodel.

day-nettle *n* **1** the dead-nettle. **2** a whitlow, a gathering on the finger.

days *n* (*a curling term*) *in phr* **gi'e him days** do everything right to keep the stone running.

day-set *n* nightfall.

day-sky *n* **1** daylight. **2** daybreak. **3** the appearance of the sky at daybreak or twilight.

daze *same as* **daise**.

dazed *adj* stupid, foolish-looking.

dazie *same as* **daisie**.

dazzle *v* to daze, stupefy.

dazzly *adj* dazzling.

deacon *n* **1** a head workman. **2** a master or chairman of a trade guild. **3** an adept, expert, proficient.

deaconry *n* **1** the office of a deacon (qv). **2** a trade guild under a deacon (qv).

dead¹ *same as* **dad**³.

dead² *adj* **1** exact. **2** stagnant. **3** flat. **4** stale. **5** unprofitable, yielding no interest. **6** (*of bowls, quoits, etc*) equidistant from the tee.—*n* **1** death. **2** the cause of death, a mortal injury or sickness. **3** (*in pl*) quoits, bowls, etc, equidistant from the tee. **4** coarse soil from the bottom of a ditch.—*adv* quite, exceedingly.

deadal *n* death.

dead and gone *phr* dead and buried.

dead-auld *adj* extremely old.

dead bell *n* **1** the passing bell. **2** the funeral bell. **3** singing in the ears as an omen of death.

dead candle *n* phosphorescent light, will-o'-the-wisp, as an omen of death.

dead chack¹ *n* the sound made by a woodworm in houses, regarded as an omen of death.

dead chack² *n* the dinner formerly prepared for the magistrates of a burgh after a public execution.

dead-chap *n* a sharp stroke heard as an omen of death.

dead chest *n* a coffin.

dead claes *n* a shroud, winding sheet.

dead days *n* the days during which a corpse remained unburied and no ploughing or opening of the earth was allowed on a farm.

dead-deaf *adj* quite deaf.

dead-deal, ~-dale *n* the board used for measuring and lifting a corpse.

dead-dole *n* a dole formerly given at a funeral.

dead-dour *adj* utterly immovable.

dead-drap *n* a drop of water falling heavily and at intervals on a floor, as an omen of death.

dead gown *n* **1** a winding sheet. **2** a part of the dead claes (qv).

dead hole *n* the grave.

dead house *n* **1** a mortuary. **2** a grave.

dead-ill *n* **1** a mortal illness. **2** a deadly hurt, a fatal injury.—*adj* sick with a mortal illness.

deadily *n* a boys' game, when one with clasped hands has to run and catch others.

dead kist *n* a coffin.

dead-knack *n* a stroke as of a switch upon the door or bed, the cause of which is unknown, as an omen of death.

dead knell *n* a death knell.

dead-licht *n* **1** phosphorescence supposed to appear in graveyards. **2** the ignis fatuus.

dead-lift *n* **1** help at a pinch. **2** a difficulty. **3** a dilemma. **4** a crisis.

dead-looks *n* signs on the face of the nearness of death.

dead-lown *adj* (*used of the atmosphere*) in a dead calm, quite still.

deadly *adj* death-like, lifeless.

deadman's-bell *n* the passing-bell.

deadman's creesh *n* the water hemlock.

deadman's-paps *n* the starfish *Alcyonium digitatum*.

deadman's-sneeshin *n* the dust of the common puffball.

deadmen's-bells *n* the purple foxglove.

dead-nip *n* **1** a blue mark on the body ascribed to necromancy and regarded as ominous. **2** a sudden and effectual check to one.

dead-picture *n* an exact likeness.

dead-rattle, ~-ruckle *n* the sound made by a dying person.

dead-set *n* the fixed expression of the eye in death. —*adj* quite determined on.

dead sheet, ~ shroud *n* a death shroud.

dead spale *n* the grease of a candle that falls over the edge in a semicircular form, called a winding sheet, and is regarded as a premonition of death.

dead-swap *n* a sharp stroke, supposed to be ominous of death.

dead-sweer, ~-swear *adj* **1** utterly lazy. **2** extremely unwilling.

dead-thraw *n* **1** the death throes. **2** *phr* **in the deid-thraw** (*used of fish*) not fresh. **3** (*of things cooked*) neither hot nor cold when served.

dead-watch *n* the deathwatch or dead chack (qv), a ticking thought to presage death.

deaf *adj* **1** (*used of grain*) having lost the power to germinate. **2** (*of shell and kernelled fruit*) empty, without a kernel. **3** (*of soil*) flat.

deaf-nit *n* a woman without money.

deaister *same as* **doister**.

deal¹ *n* **1** a periodic dole. **2** the time at which it is given.

deal², **deal**³ *same as* **dail**¹, **dail**².

deam *n* a young woman.

deamie *n* a girl.

dean *n* **1** a deep wooded valley. **2** a small valley. **3** a hollow where the ground slopes on both sides.

dear be here, dear keep's, dear kens, dear knows, dear sake *int* various exclamations of surprise, sorrow, pity, etc.

dearie *n* a sweetheart, a darling.

dear-meal cart *n* a farmer's vehicle that came into use when high war prices were got in the early part of the 19th century.

dearsome *adj* costly.

dearth *v* to raise the price of anything.

dearth cap *n* a name given in the Carse of Gowrie to a fungus resembling a cup, containing a number of seeds, supposed to have got its name from the notion that it gave supply in a time of dearth.

dearthful *adj* expensive, of high price.

dear year *n* a year of great scarcity in the beginning of the 19th century.

deas *same as* **dais**.

deasie *same as* **daisie**.

deasil, deasoil *n* walk or movement with the sun from east to west.

death *n in phr* **be going to death with a thing** to be quite positive and sure about it.

death-candle *n* a corpse-candle.

death-chap *n* a knocking ominous of death.

death-deal *n* a stretching board for a corpse.

death-dwam *n* a death swoon or faint.

deathful *adj* death-dealing.

death hamper *n* a long basket made of rushes, used for funerals formerly in some parts of the Highlands.

death-ill *n* a mortal illness.

deathin *n* the water hemlock.

death-ruckle *n* the death rattle.

death sang *n* a banshee's song, supposed to portend death.

death-shank *n* a thin leg like that of a dead person.

death-shut *adj* closed in death.

death's-mailin *n* a burial ground.

death-sough *n* the last breath of a dying person.

death-swap *n* a knock betokening the nearness of death.

death-trouble *n* a mortal illness.

death-weed *n* a shroud.

death yirm *n* the phlegm that causes the death rattle.

deave[1] *v* **1** to deafen, stun with noise. **2** to worry, bother.

deave[2] *v* (*used of pain*) to mitigate, lessen, deaden.

deaven *same as* **deave**[1].

deavesome *adj* deafening.

deaving *n* deafening noise.

deaw *v* to drizzle.

debait[1] *v* **1** to cease eating after having had enough. **2** to cease.

debait[2], **debate** *n* a fight, struggle for existence, etc.

debaitless *adj* **1** without spirit or energy to struggle. **2** feckless. **3** helpless.

debateable *adj* **1** able to shift for oneself. **2** energetic.

debateable land *n* the border between England and Scotland, formerly much fought over.

debaurd *n* departure from the right way.—*v* to go beyond proper bounds or to excess.

debaush *same as* **debosh**.

debitor *n* debtor.

debord *n* excess.—*v* to go beyond bounds or to excess.

debording *n* excess.

debosh *n* **1** excessive indulgence. **2** extravagance, waste. **3** a debauch. **4** one who overindulges himself.—*v* to indulge oneself to excess.

deboshed *adj* debauched, worthless.

deboshing *adj* **1** wasteful. **2** given over to excessive indulgence.

deboshrie *n* a debauch, waste, excessive indulgence.

debout *v* to thrust from.

debritch *n* debris.

debt *n in phr* **come in the debt** to break, destroy, make an end of.

debtfull *adj* due, indebted.

debuck *v* **1** to prevent any design from being carried through. **2** used chiefly in the game of nine-pins.

debuction *n* the loss of thirteen to a player at nine-pins if he knocks down more pins than make up the number required in the game.

deburse *v* to disburse.

debursing *n* disbursement.

debush*same as* **debosh**.

debute *v* to make one's debut.

debushens *n* dismissal from a situation, etc.

decanter *n* a jug.

decay *n* consumption, a decline.

decedent *n* one who demits an office.

deceive *n* a deception.

deceiverie *n* a habit or course of deception.

decency *n* a respectable way of living.

decent *adj* **1** satisfactory for one's position, etc. **2** tolerable, good enough.

decern *v* to adjudge, decree, determine.

decerniture *n* a decree or judgment of court.

dech *v* to build with turfs.

dechlit *adj* wearied.

deck buirds *n* the bulwarks of a ship.

declarator *n* **1** a legal or authentic declaration. **2** an action with that object.

declinable *adj* (*used of a witness*) who may be rejected as incompetent.

declination *n* a courteous refusal.

declinature *n* an act declining the jurisdiction of a judge or court.

decline *n* **1** consumption, phthisis. **2** the end.

decoir, decore *v* to decorate, adorn.

decorement, decorament *n* decoration.

decourt *v* to dismiss from court.

decreet *n* **1** a decree. **2** final judicial sentence.

decript *adj* decrepit.

dede *same as* **deed**[1].

dee[1] *v* to die.

dee[2] *same as* **dey**[1].

dee[3] *v* to do.

deeble *v* to dibble.—*n* a dibble.

deece *same as* **dais**.

deed[1] *adj* dead.

deed[2] *n in phr* **by** or **upo' my deed** surely, certainly.—*int* **1** an exclamation of confirmation or interrogation. **2** indeed!

dee'd *v* did.

deed-doer *n* the doer of a deed, perpetrator.

deeder *n* a doer.

deedin *v* to deaden.

deeding *n* the act of making a deed or contract.

deedle[1] *same as* **dead-ill**.

deedle[2] *v* **1** to dandle, as an infant. **2** to train an infant. **3** to sing in a low tone, hum an air without the words.

deedle-doodle *n* **1** a meaningless song. **2** a badly played tune.

deedley-dumplin' *n* a term of endearment to an infant.

deed-linnings *n* dead clothes.

deeds *n* coarse soil or gravel taken from the bottom of a ditch.

deeds I, ~ aye *phr* yes, indeed!

deedy, deedie *adj* **1** given to doing. **2** *generally in phr* **ill-deedie'** mischievous.

dee-er *n* a doer.

deef *adj* deaf.

deefen *v* to deafen.

deek *v* to spy out, descry.

deem[1] *same as* **deam**.

deem[2] *v* **1** to judge. **2** to estimate. **3** to doom.

deemer *n* one who forms an estimate of another's conduct or intentions.

deemes, deemas *n* a great sum.—*adj* great.—*adv* exceedingly.

deemie *same as* **deamie**.

deemous *adv* very, exceedingly.

deemster *n* **1** a judge. **2** the official of a court who used to proclaim formally its sentence on the prisoner at the bar.

deen[1] *same as* **doon**[2].

deen[2] *v, adj* done.

deen out *adj* exhausted.

deep *adj* clever, crafty.—*n* the deepest part of a river, the channel.

deep-draucht *n* a crafty circumvention.

deep-drauchtit *adj* designing, artful.

deepen *v* to take soundings.

deepens *n* depth.

deepin *n* a fishing net.

deepin-weaver *n* a net-weaver.

deeply-sworn *adj* solemnly sworn.
deepooperit *adj* **1** weak, worn-out in body or mind. **2** impoverished.
deep-sea buckie *n* the *Murex corneus*.
deep-sea crab *n* the spider crab.
deer, deer's-hair *n* the heath club moss.
deece *same as* **dais**.
deester *n* a doer, agent.
dee't *v* died.
deeve *same as* **deave**.
deevil *n* the devil, a devil.
deevilick, deeviluck *n* a little imp or devil.
deevilish *adj* extraordinary, wonderful, supernatural.—*adv* used intensively.
deevilment *n* roguery, the spirit of mischief.
deeze *same as* **daise**.
defaisance *n* defeasance.
defait, defeat *adj* **1** defeated. **2** exhausted by sickness or fatigue.
defalk *v* **1** to resign a claim. **2** to do without payment. **3** to deduct.
defalt *v* to adjudge as culpable.
defame *v* to report guilty.
defeekulty *n* difficulty.
defence *n* confidence in possessing the means of defence.
defend *v* **1** to ward off, keep off a blow. **2** to forbid. **3** to prevent.
defendant *adj in phr* **degrees defendant** the forbidden degrees.
defenn *n* dirt.
defett *same as* **defait**.
deficient *adj* failing in duty.
deforce *n* **1** deforcement. **2** violent ejection or seizure.
deforcer *n* a ravisher, one who commits rape.
deform *n* a deformed person.
defraud *n* a fraud, the act of defrauding.
deft *adj* bold.
deftly *adv* **1** fitly, properly. **2** handsomely.
deg[1] *v* **1** to strike smartly with a sharp-pointed weapon. **2** to pierce or indent with a sharp-pointed instrument.—*n* **1** a sharp blow or stroke. **2** the hole or indentation made by a pointed instrument.—*adv* slap, bang.
deg[2] *same as* **dag**[2].
degener *v* to degenerate.
degs *n* rags, tatters.
degust *n* disgust.
dei *same as* **dey**[1].
deid *n* **1** death. **2** pestilence.—*adj* dead.
deid-day *n* a calm, dull winter day.
deid's pairt *n* that portion of his or her movable estate which a person deceased had a right to dispose of before death in whatsoever way he or she pleased.
deid-wed *n* a mortgage.
deigh *v* to build with turfs.
deighle *n* a simpleton.
deil *n* devil.
deil a bit *phr* **1** nothing at all. **2** not at all.
deil a mony *phr* not many.
deil-be-lickit *phr* nothing at all.
deil-blaw-lickit *phr* nothing at all.
deil fitchit *phr* an emphatic kind of negation.
deil gin *phr* would to the devil that.
deil haet *phr* nothing at all.
deil-in-a-bush *n* the herb paris.
deil-in-the-bush *n* love-in-a-mist, *Nigella damascena*.
deil-ma-care *adj* utterly careless.—*adv* no matter.
deil-mak-matter *adj* careless.—*adv* no matter.
deil-o'-me *phr* **1** not I. **2** never for my part.
deil-perlicket *phr* nothing at all.
deilry *n* devilry.
deil's apple-rennie *n* the wild camomile.
deil's apple trees *n* the sun-spurge.
deil's barley *n* the crimson stonecrop.
deil's beef-tub *n* a roaring linn.

deil's bird *n* the magpie.
deil's bit *n* the blue scabious.
deil's books *n* playing cards.
deil's buckie *n* **1** an imp. **2** a mischievous youth.
deil's butterfly *n* the tortoiseshell butterfly.
deil's cup *n* strong drink.
deil's darning-needle *n* **1** the dragonfly. **2** the shepherd's needle.
deil's dirt *n* asafoetida.
deil's dizzen *n* thirteen.
deil's dog *n* any strange black dog met at night.
deil's dung *n* asafoetida.
deil's elshin *n* the shepherd's needle.
deil's-gut *n* the wild convolvulus.
deil's guts *n* various species of Cuscuta.
deil's kirnstaff *n* the petty spurge, the sun-spurge.
deil's limb *n* **1** an imp. **2** a tiresome or troublesome youth.
deil's mark *n* marks crescent-wise arranged on the lower part of a pig's foreleg.
deil's metal *n* mercury.
deil's milk *n* the white milky sap of the dandelion and other plants.
deil's milk-plant *n* the dandelion.
deil speed one *phr* a form of imprecation.
deil's pet *n* **1** an imp. **2** a mischievous youth.
deil's picturebooks, ~ painted books *n* playing cards.
deil's pots and pans *n* holes in the bed of a stream, caused by stones carried down and boiling in flood time.
deil's putting stones *n* perched boulders.
deil's snuffbox *n* the common puffball.
deil's sowen-bowie *n* a children's game.
deil's spadefu's *n* natural heaps or hummocks of sand or gravel.
deil's specs *n* 'cup and ring' marks.
deil's spoons *n* **1** the water plantain. **2** the broad-leaved bindweed.
deil's toddy *n* punch made with hot whisky instead of water.
deil's wind *n* a winnowing machine.
deil-tak-him *n* the yellowhammer.
deir *same as* **deer**[1].
deis *same as* **dais**.
deisheal *same as* **deasil**.
dejeune *n* breakfast.
del' *v* to dig with a spade, delve.
delash *v* to discharge, let fly.
delator *n* an informer, accuser.
delaverly *same as* **deliverly**.
deleer, deleir, deler, delier *v* **1** to intoxicate. **2** to render delirious.
deleerin' *adj* maddening.
deleerit *adj* gone mad, out of one's senses.
deleeritness *n* **1** madness. **2** delirium.
delf *n* **1** a pit, a quarry. **2** the mark of an animal's foot in soft ground. **3** a sod or cut turf. **4** a large space cut into turfs. **5** a peat hag.—*v* to cut mould, clay, etc, in large lumps.
delf house *n* a pottery.
delfin *adj* made of earthenware.
delf-ware *n* earthenware, crockery.
delgin *n* the stick used in binding sheaves.
delicate *n* **1** a delicacy, a dainty. **2** a luxury.
delicht *v* to delight.
delichtsome *adj* delightful.
del'in' *v* delving.
delict *n* a misdemeanour.
deliverly *adv* **1** nimbly. **2** continually.
dell[1] *n* the goal in boys' games.
dell[2] *v* to dig, labour with a spade, delve.
delt *v* **1** to fondle, treat or spoil with great kindness. **2** to delight in. **3** to toy amorously.
del't *v* delved.
delting *v, adj* spoiling with kindness.
deltit[1] *v, adj* **1** spoiled with kindness. **2** treated with great care. **3** petted.

deltit *v, adj* **1** hid from public view. **2** used of the retired habits of one devoted to a literary life.

delve *v* **1** to hide. **2** to insert. **3** to work hard, drudge.

dem *v* **1** to dam water. **2** to stop the inrush of flood water.

demauns *n* demands for one's services, skill, etc.

demean, demaine, demane, demayne *v* **1** to treat anyone in a particular way. **2** to illtreat. **3** to punish by cutting off a hand.

demeans *n* lands, demesnes.

demelle *n* a rencontre.

demellit *v, adj* hurt, injured.

demellitie *n* **1** a hurt. **2** the effects of a dispute.

demember *v* to deprive of a bodily member.

demembration *n* **1** mutilation. **2** the act of demembering.

dementation *n* a state of derangement.

dementit *adj* **1** distracted, crazy. **2** stupid, nonsensical.

dem-fow *adj* quite full.

demit *v* **1** to dismiss. **2** to permit to go.

demity *n* dimity.

demmish *same as* **dammish**.

demous *adj* great.

demple *n* a potato dibble.

dempster *same as* **deemster**.

demur *n* a plight.

demurr *n* a demurrer.

den *n* **1** a glen, dell, ravine. **2** the home in children's games. **3** the forecastle of a decked fishing boat. **4** the place where the scythe is laid into the sned.—*v* **1** to hide, lurk in a den. **2** to run to cover.

den-fire *n* the fire in a decked fishing boat.

dengle *same as* **dangle**.

denk *same as* **dink**².

denner *n* **1** dinner. **2** *phr* **little denner** a meal taken before the usual breakfast by those who rise earlier than usual.—*v* to have or give dinner.

denner piece *n* a worker's lunch, a substitute for dinner at home.

dennle *same as* **dangle**.

denrick *n* a smoke board for a chimney.

densaix *n* a Danish axe, a Lochaber axe.

denshauch *adj* **1** hard to please. **2** fussy as to food.

den-stair *n* the stair in a decked fishing boat.

dent¹, **denta** *n* affection, regard.

dent² *n* a tough clay, soft claystone.

dented *adj* tainted by damp.

dentelion *n* dandelion.

dentice *same as* **daintess**.

dentis *int* **1** just so. **2** very well. **3** no matter. **4** an expression of indifference.

denty *same as* **dainty**.

denty-lion *n* dandelion.

denum *v* **1** to confound, used as an imprecation. **2** to stupefy by much talking.

denumm't *adj* confounded.

deny *v* to refuse, decline.

depairt *v* **1** to die. **2** to part, divide.

depart *n* departure.

departal *n* **1** death. **2** *phr* **take one's departal** to die.

departure *n* death.

depauper *v* to impoverish.

deplorat *adj* deplorable.

depone *v* **1** to deposit. **2** to depose, give evidence as witness.

deponent *n* a witness.

depositat *v* to lay aside.

depurse *v* to disburse.

depursement *n* disbursement.

deputation *n* the act or deed of appointing a deputy.

depute *n* a deputy.—*adj* deputed.

deray¹ *n* **1** disorder, uproar. **2** a festive crowd. **3** boisterous mirth.

deray² *v* to rout, drive away.

derb *n* common marble.

dere¹ *v* **1** to terrify. **2** to fear.

dere² *v* to affect, make an impression.—*n* injury.

deregles *n* **1** loose habits, irregularities. **2** deceptions, fraudulent informations.

derf, derff *adj* **1** bold, vigorous. **2** unbending. **3** sullen, taciturn. **4** massive, capable of giving a severe blow. **5** hard, cruel.

derfly *adv* boldly, fiercely, vigorously.

dergy *same as* **dirgie**.

derision *n* a practical joke.

derk *adj* dark.

derkening *n* twilight.

derl *n* **1** a broken piece of bread, cake, etc. **2** a rag.

dern¹ *v* **1** to hide. **2** to listen. **3** to loiter at work. **4** to muse, to think. **5** (*with* **behind**) to fall back.—*adj* secret, obscure. **6** dark, dreary, lonely, dismal.—*n* darkness, secrecy.

dern² *adj* **1** bold, daring. **2** fierce, wild.—*adv* **1** boldly. **2** fiercely.

dern³ *v* to darn.

derril *same as* **derl**.

derrin *n* a broad, thick cake or loaf of oat or barley meal or of the flour of pease and barley mixed, baked in an oven or on a hearth covered with hot ashes.

dert *v, adj* frightened, terrified.

descrive *v* to describe.

descriver *n* describer.

designed *adj* disposed, inclined.

desk *n* **1** a precentor's desk. **2** the name formerly given to that part of a church, near the pulpit, where baptism was administered.

desperate *adj* **1** irreclaimable, very bad. **2** great, excessive.—*adv* exceedingly, beyond measure.

desperation *n in phr* **like desperation** as if in despair.

despite *v* to be filled with indignation.

dess *same as* **dais**.

destinate *v* to design.

destructionfu' *adj* **1** destructive. **2** wasteful.

detfall *adj* **1** due. **2** obligatory.

detort *v* **1** to distort. **2** to turn aside in retorting.

deuch *n* a drink, a draught.

deuch-an-dorach *n* **1** a stirrup cup. **2** stark love and kindness.

deug *n* a tall, tough man.

deugind *adj* **1** wilful, obstinate. **2** litigious.

deugle *n* anything long and tough.

deugs *n* **1** rags. **2** shreds.

deuk¹ *n* a duck.

deuk² *n* a cover, shelter.

deuk³ *n* a duke.

deuk-dub *n* a duck pond.

deukie *n* a duckling.

deuks' faul *n* a dilemma.

deule-weeds *n* mourning weeds.

dev *v aux* do.

devall, devaill, devaul, devawl, devald, devalve, devauld *v* **1** to descend, to fall. **2** to halt, cease.—*n* **1** a sunk fence. **2** an inclined plane for a waterfall. **3** a pause. **4** cessation.

devalling, devalving *n* cessation, stop.

devan *n* a large piece of turf or sod.

deve *same as* **deave**¹.

devel *v* **1** to stun with a blow, maul. **2** to fall heavily.—*n* a stunning blow.

develer *n* **1** a first-rate boxer. **2** a dexterous young fellow.

dever *same as* **daiver**.

devilan *n* an insane person.

devilick, devilock *same as* **deevilick**.

devilish *same as* **deevilish**.

devilment *n* wickedness.

devilry *n* communication with the devil.

deviltry *n* **1** mischief, devilry, wickedness. **2** communication with the devil, witchcraft.

devle, devvel *same as* **devel**.

devol *v* to deviate.

dew *n* whisky.—*v* to rain slightly.
dew-cup *n* the ladies' mantle.
dew-droukit *adj* drenched with dew.
dewgs *same as* **deugs**.
dewpiece *n* a little food taken early in the morning by a servant or worker before the regular breakfast.
dew-wat *adj* dewy, wet with dew.
dey[1] *n* **1** a dairymaid. **2** a person in charge of a dairy, male or female.
dey[2] *n* a child's name for father.
deyken *same as* **deacon**.
deyvle *v* to use the word devil profanely.
diacle *n* the compass used in a fishing boat.
diagram *n* the scale of working drawn up for each driver or fireman by the railway companies.
dial cock *n* the style or gnomon of a sundial.
dib *same as* **dub**.
dibber-dabber *n* **1** an uproar, wrangle. **2** a confused purposeless discussion.—*v* **1** to wrangle. **2** to wriggle in argument.
dibber-derry *n* a confused discussion.
dibble-dabble *n* uproar accompanied with violence.—*v* to wrangle.
dibbler *n* a large wooden platter.
diblet *n* *in phr* **neither dish nor diblet** no table dishes whatever.
dice *n* a small square or diamond shape.—*phr* **box and dice** the whole concern.—*v* **1** to sew a wavy pattern near the border of a garment. **2** to weave in figures resembling dice. **3** to do anything quickly and neatly.
dice-board *n* a draughtboard or chessboard.
dichel, dichal *n* **1** a bad scrape, a pickle. **2** (*in pl*) a scolding, drubbing.
dichens *n* a beating, punishment.
dichling *n* a beating, drubbing.
dicht *v* **1** to dress food. **2** to wipe, to clean. **3** to dry by rubbing. **4** to sift grain. **5** to handle a subject. **6** to drub, beat. **7** to dress oneself. **8** to prepare for use. **9** to put in order, tidy.—*n* **1** a wipe, a clean. **2** a blow, beating.
dichter *n* a winnower of grain.
dichtings *n* **1** refuse. **2** the refuse of grain.
dichty *adj* dirty, foul.
dickie *n* filth, ordure.—*adj* dirty.
dickies *same as* **dixie**.
dicky[1] *n* the hedge sparrow.
dicky[2] *n* *in phr* **up to dicky** tiptop, up to date.
dict *v* to dictate.
dictionar *n* a dictionary.
diddle[1] *v* **1** to shake, jog. **2** to move like a dwarf. **3** to keep time with the feet to a tune. **4** to jog up and down. **5** to dance or walk with short, quick steps. **6** to sway to and fro. **7** to dandle, as one does a child. **8** to sing dance tunes to any jingle or without words.—*n* **1** a shake, a jog. **2** a jingle of music.
diddle[2] *n* a swindle, fraud.
diddle[3] *same as* **deedle**[2].
diddle[4] *v* **1** to busy oneself with trifles. **2** to show great energy with little result.—*n* **1** trifling activity. **2** a dawdler.
diddler[1] *n* a trickster, a cheat.
diddler[2] *n* a dawdler.
diddler[3] *n* a person who can hum a tune for others to dance to.
diddle-um-dird *n* one who vainly tries to walk neatly and primly.
diddling[1] *n* **1** fiddling. **2** keeping time with the feet. **3** dandling.
diddling[2] *adj* **1** apparently busy. **2** untrustworthy.
die *n* a toy, plaything, gewgaw.
died *n* a meal, diet.
diel *same as* **deil**.
dien-done *adj* quite done.
diet *n* **1** an excursion, journey. **2** the meeting of an ecclesiastical assembly. **3** the fixed day for holding a market. **4** the stated time of public worship, etc.
diet book *n* a diary.
diet-loaf *n* a large sponge cake.
diet time *n* mealtime.
diffame *v* to defame.
differ[1] *v* **1** to separate, cause difference between.—*n* difference, a misunderstanding.
differ[2] *v* to defer, yield to.
difference *v* to differentiate.
differr *v* to delay, procrastinate.
difficil *adj* **1** difficult. **2** reluctant.
difficult *v* **1** to perplex. **2** to render difficult.
diffide *v* to distrust.
digaal *n* **1** a bad scrape. **2** an awkward fix.
dig-for-silver *n* a children's singing game.
diggot *n* a contemptuous name given to a child, implying some dishonourable action.
dight[1] *adv* **1** properly, fitly. **2** readily. **3** freely.
dight[2] *same as* **dicht**.
dighter *same as* **dichter**.
digne *adj* worthy.
dignities *n* dignitaries.
dignosce *v* to distinguish.
dike *n* **1** a wall. **2** a vein of whinstone traversing coal strata. **3** a causeway or track. **4** a fault or fissure in the stratum.—*v* **1** to dig, to pick with a pickaxe, etc. **2** to build a dike. **3** to fence in with a dike.—*phr* **dike in hauld** to enclose within walls or ramparts.
dike-end *n* a dike (qv) built on the ebb shore, running seaward, to cut off access to the arable land through the ebb and thus prevent cattle from trespassing.
dike-hopper *n* the wheatear.
dike-king *n* the game of rax, as played by boys.
dike-louper *n* **1** an animal given to leaping fences. **2** an immoral person, a transgressor.
dike-loupin' *adj* **1** fence-breaking, that cannot be kept within fences. **2** loose, immoral.
dike-queen *n* the game of rax as played by girls.
diker *n* a builder of dikes. *See* **dike**.
dike-sheugh *n* a narrow trench or ditch alongside a dike (qv).
dike tip *n* the top of a dike (qv).
dikie *n* **1** a low wall, a small ditch. **2** *in phr* **loup the dikie** to die.
dilate *v* to accuse.
dilator *n* an informer, accuser.
dilature *n* legal postponement, delay.
dilder *v* **1** to shake, jerk. **2** to dribble, ooze, trickle. **3** to glide. **4** to trifle, waste time, work carelessly. —*n* a smart jerk, a jolt.
dildermot *n* an obstacle, a great difficulty.
diled *same as* **doilt**.
dileer *same as* **deleer**.
dileerious *adj* extremely foolish.
dilet, dylet *adj* used of one whose life is burdensome and miserable from hard work or ill-treatment or one who has a worn and weary look.
diligence *n* **1** a writ of execution. **2** a warrant to enforce the attendance of witnesses or the production of documents.
dilip *n* a legacy.
dill[1] *v* **1** to conceal. **2** to calm. **3** to assuage, remove. **4** (*with* **down**) to subside, die down.
dill[2] *v* to flap, shake loosely.
dillagate *n* a delicacy, a dainty.
dillow *n* a noisy quarrel.
dilly, dilly-castle *n* a boys' name for a sandcastle on which they stand till it is washed away.
dilly-dally *n* an indolent woman.
dilly-daw *n* one who is slow and slovenly.
dilmont *n* a two-year-old wedder.
dilp *n* **1** a trollop, a thriftless housewife. **2** a heavy, lumpish person.—*v* **1** to walk with long steps. **2** to stalk.
dilse *n* dulse, an edible seaweed.

dilser n the rock- or fieldlark.
dilt same as **delt**.
dim n midsummer twilight between sunset and sunrise.
dimit v 1 to pass into. 2 to terminate.
diment same as **dinmont**.
dimirrities n details, points.
dimple v 1 to indent, make an impression. 2 to dibble. 3 (used of a stream) to ripple, not to flow still or sluggishly.—n a dibble.
dimsome adj (used of colours) somewhat dim.
din[1] n 1 report, fame. 2 loud talking.
din[2] adj dun, dingy, sallow.—n a dun colour.
din[3] v done.
dince v to dance.
dindee same as **dundee**.
dindlin n a tingling.
dine n dinner.
ding[1] adj worthy.
ding[2] v 1 to smash, beat to powder. 2 to overcome. 3 to excel. 4 to discourage, vex. 5 to drive. 6 to dash down. 7 to cut bark in short pieces for the tanner. 8 (of rain) to fall heavily or continuously. —n a blow.
ding[3] v used imprecatively.
ding-dang adv 1 in rapid succession. 2 ding-dong. 3 pell-mell, helter-skelter.—n noise, clatter, confusion.
dinge v to indent, bruise.—n an indentation, a bruise.
dinging n a beating.
dinging on v raining heavily.
dingle[1] v to jingle.
dingle[2] v to draw together.—n the state of being drawn together, a group, gathering.
dingle[3] v 1 to dangle. 2 to vibrate, resound, tremble. 3 to tingle, thrill.
dingle-dangle adv swaying to and fro or from side to side.
dingle-dousie, ~-douzie n 1 a stick ignited at one end, swung about by a child in play. 2 a jack-in-the-box.
dingle't adj stupid, stupefied.
ding-me-yavel phr lay me flat, used as an expletive.
dink[1] n a dint, indentation, bruise.—v to sit down with a bang.
dink[2] adj 1 neat, finely dressed. 2 dainty, nice, squeamish.—v to deck, adorn, dress up.
dinkie adj neat, trim.
dinkly adv neatly.
dinle v 1 to shake, vibrate, tremble. 2 to tingle with cold or pain. 3 to cause to shake.—n 1 vibration. 2 a thrilling blow, a tingling sensation. 3 a slight sprain. 4 a vague report. 5 a slight noise.
dinlin' adj rattling.—n a tingling sensation.
din-luggit adj having dun-coloured ears.
dinmont n a wedder from the first to the second shearing.
dinna-, dinnae v neg do not.
dinnagilt v judged.
dinna gude adj worthless morally.—n a disreputable person past all hope of doing good.
dinnel, dinnle same as **dinle**.
dinnen skate n the young of the fish Raia batis.
dinner v to dine.
dinness n sallowness.
dinnous adj noisy.
dint[1] n 1 a blow, shock, impression. 2 a momentary opportunity.—v (used of fairies) to injure cattle, elf-shoot.
dint[2] same as **dent**[1].
dint[3] n a fancy or liking for a person or thing.
dintle n a thin species of leather.
diocy n a diocese.
dip n a fluid for dipping sheep to kill vermin.—v 1 to dip sheep in that fluid. 2 to sit down. 3 (with in) to join at intervals in a conversation. 4 (with upon or on) to deal with, discuss. 5 to concern, approximate to.
dipin n 1 part of a herring net. 2 the bag of a salmon net.
diploma n a scolding dismissal.
dippen n the stairs at a riverside.
dipper n a Baptist.

dipping n a mixture of boiled oil and grease used by curriers to soften leather.
dippit n a tippet.
dipthaery n diphtheria.
dird n 1 a blow, onslaught. 2 an achievement.—v 1 to beat, thump. 2 to dump. 3 to dash.—adv with violence, heavily.
dirder n a driver, whipper-in, dog-breaker.
dirdoose v to hurt, to thump.
dirdum, dirdom, dirdrim n 1 a tumult. 2 damage. 3 passion, ill- humour. 4 a great noise. 5 a noisy sport. 6 severe scolding. 7 blame. 8 a stroke, blow. 9 a squabble. 10 a scolding woman. 11 a woman who has been jilted. 12 (in pl) ridicule. 13 disgustful slanderings. 14 twinges of conscience.
dirdum-dardum n an expression of contempt for an action.
dirdum-kick n a person who walks with a fanciful or affected gait.
dirdy-lochrag, dirdy-wachle n the lizard.
direck v to direct.—adv directly.
direction book n a book of household recipes for cooking, etc.
dirgie, dirige n. 1 a funeral feast. 2 a dirge.
dirk[1] same as **durk**[2].
dirk[2] v to grope in utter darkness.—adj dark.
dirk[3] v to bungle, blunder.
dirl n 1 a tremulous stroke. 2 a sharp stroke. 3 a blow. 4 a vibration. 5 a vibrating sound. 6 a thrill. 7 anxious haste, hurry. 8 a twinge of conscience. 9 a thrilling pleasure or pain of body or mind.—v 1 to pierce, drill. 2 to tingle, thrill. 3 to emit a tingling sound. 4 to move with the wind. 5 to vibrate noisily. 6 to produce loud vibrations. 7 to rattle. 8 to move briskly.
dirler[1] n a vibrating stick that strikes the large bolter of a mill.
dirler[2] n one who can make things move briskly.
dirr[1] adj 1 torpid, benumbed. 2 insensible, destitute of physical or moral feeling.—v 1 to be benumbed. 2 to deaden pain by narcotics.
dirr[2] n a loud noise.
dirray same as **deray**[1].
dirry n tobacco ash.
dirt n a term of contempt, used for worthless persons or things or troublesome children.
dirtbee n the yellow fly that haunts dunghills.
dirten adj 1 fouled with excrement. 2 dirtied. 3 miry, mean, contemptible.
dirten-allan n the Arctic gull, Richardson's skua.
dirten-gab n a foul-mouthed person.
dirtenly adv in a dirty way.
dirt-fear n great, excessive fear affecting the intestines.
dirt-feared adj in excessive fear.
dirt-flee n 1 the yellow fly that haunts dunghills. 2 a young woman who, after having long remained single from pride, at last makes a low marriage.
dirt-fleyed adj in excessive fear.
dirt-haste n extreme haste, as if the power of retention were lost.
dirt house n 1 a close stool. 2 a privy.
dirtrie n. despicable, good-for-nothing people.
dirty adj 1 (used of weather) wet, stormy. 2 (of land) infested with weeds. 3 mean, contemptible, paltry.
dirty-allan n Richardson's skua.
dirty-coal n pure coal mixed with shale, stones, etc.
dirty-drinker n one who drinks alone and for the love of drinking.
dis v does.
disabeels n dishabille.
disabeeze, disabuse v 1 to misuse, abuse. 2 to mar, spoil.—n a stir, disturbance.
disabil n 1 dishabille. 2 untidiness.
disadvise v to advise against.
disagreeance n disagreement.

disaguise *v* to disguise.
disassent *v* **1** to dissent. **2** disapprove.
disaster *v* **1** to injure seriously. **2** to disgust.—*n* disgust.
disbust *n* an uproar, broil.
discerne *same as* **decerne**.
dischairge *v* to forbid, prohibit, charge not to do.
dischanter *n* a disenchanter.
disclamation *n* **1** disclaiming one as the superior of lands. **2** refusing the duty which is the condition of tenure. **3** repudiation.
discomfish *v* to discomfit, defeat.
discomfist *v*, *adj* overcome.
discomfit *v* to put to inconvenience.
disconform, disconformed *adj* not conformable.
discontent *adj* discontented.
discontigue *adj* not contiguous.
disconvenience *n* an inconvenience.—*v* to inconvenience.
disconvenient *adj* inconvenient.
discoursy *adj* conversable.
discover *v* **1** to uncover. **2** to take off one's hat.
discreet *adj* civil, obliging, courteous, polite.
discreetness *n* politeness, civility.
discretion *n* courtesy, hospitality.
discuss *v* to fight with a man-of-war.
disdoing *adj* not thriving.
diseirish *v* **1** to disinherit, cast off. **2** to put in disorder through officious or improper meddling.
disformed *adj* deformed.
disfriendship *n* animosity, disaffection.
disgeest, disgest *n* digestion.—*v* to digest.
disgeester *n* **1** digestion. **2** the stomach.
disgushle *v* **1** to distort by rheumatism, etc. **2** to warp by the action of heat.
dish[1] *v* **1** to make the spokes of a wheel lie obliquely towards the axle. **2** (*used of a horse*) to splay the forefeet in running. **3** to outwit, get the better of. **4** (*with* **out**) to serve a dish.
dish[2] *v* to push or thrust with horns, butt.
dish[3] *v* to rain heavily.
dishabilitate *v* to incapacitate legally.
dishabilitation *n* the act of rendering a child incapable of succeeding to a father's estate, titles, etc.
dishalago *same as* **dishilago**.
dishaloof *n* a game of children and young people, played by placing hand above hand on a table and removing in succession the lowermost and placing it on the uppermost.
dishaunt *v* to cease to frequent, to forsake.
dishaunter *n* **1** a non-attender. **2** a non-frequenter of church, etc.
dish-browed *adj* having a flat or hollow brow.
dish cloot *n* a cloth for washing dishes.
dishealth *n* bad health.
disheart *v* to dishearten.
disheartsum *adj* disheartening, saddening.
disherys, disherish *same as* **diseirish**.
dish-faced *adj* having a flat or hollow face.
dishilago *n* tussilago, colt's-foot.
dishings *n* a beating.
dishle *same as* **dissle**[1].
dishman *n* a male hawker of crockery.
dish nap *n* a small tub for washing dishes.
dishort *n* **1** a deficiency, loss. **2** a disappointment. **3** an inconvenience. **4** a disadvantage. **5** mischief.
dish o' want *phr* no food at all.
dish-wash *n* **1** dishwater. **2** thin, poor soup.
dishy-lagy *same as* **dishilago**.
disjasket *adj* **1** forlorn, dejected. **2** broken down. **3** exhausted.
disjeest *n* digestion.—*v* to digest.
disjeune, disjune, disjoon *same as* **dejeune**.
disk *n* **1** a half-crown. **2** a piece of money.
dislade *v* to unload.
disload, disloaden *v* to unload.
dislock *v* to dislocate.

disna *v neg* does not.
disobedient *n* a disobedient person.
disobligation *n* a disobliging action.
dispach *v* to drive out of.
disparage *n* disparity of rank.
dispard, dispart, dispert *adj* **1** keen. **2** violent, incensed. **3** excessive.—*adv* excessively.
disparple *v* **1** to scatter. **2** to be scattered. **3** to divide.
displenish *v* **1** to disfurnish. **2** to sell off goods, stock, etc, on leaving a farm.
displenishing sale *n* a sale by auction of stock, implements, etc, on a farm.
displinis *n* a displenishing sale.
dispone *v* **1** to convey to another in legal form. **2** to dispose. **3** to dispose of.
disponee *n* the person to whom property is legally conveyed.
disponer *n* the person who dispones property.
dispose *n* disposal.—*v* **1** (*with* **upon**) to dispose of. **2** to deal with.
disposition *n* **1** a legal conveyance, a formal disposal of property. **2** deposition, forfeiture.
dispurse *n* to disburse.
dispute *v* to refuse.
disremember *v* to forget.
disrespeckit *adj* unnoticed, neglected.
dissipate *v* to disperse a gathering.
dissle[1] *v* to drizzle.—*n* **1** a drizzle. **2** wetness on standing corn, the effect of a slight rain.
dissle[2] *n* an attack.—*v* to run, move.
dist[1] *n* **1** dust. **2** the husk of grain.
dist[2] *adv* just.
distan *v* to distinguish.
distance *n* difference, distinction.
distant *adj* distinct.
distinct *adj* definite, not discursive.
distract *v* **1** to go distracted. **2** to become mad.
distrenzie, distrinzie *v* to distrain.
distressed *adj* **1** ill. **2** disordered.
distriction *n* distraint.
distrubil *v* to disturb.
disty *adj* dusty.
disty-melder *same as* **dusty-melder**.
dit[1], **ditt**[1] *v* to indulge, fondle, make much of.
dit[2], **ditt**[2] *v* **1** to close up, shut up. **2** to shut the mouth.
ditch *v* to clean out a ditch.
dite *v* **1** to indite, compose. **2** to dictate to an amanuensis. **3** to point out as duty.
ditement *n* anything indited or dictated by another.
diting *n* composition, inditing, writing.
ditt *same as* **dit**.
dittay, ditty *n* **1** an indictment, legal accusation. **2** a scolding.
ditty[1] *n* a story.
ditty[2] *same as* **dittay**.
ditty[3] *v* to write ditties.
ditty-gifted *adj* having the gift of composing ditties.
div *v aux* do.
divan[1] *n* a large piece of turf or sod.
divan[2] *n* a small wild plum or kind of sloe.
divauld *v* to cease.
dive[1] *n* putrid moisture from the mouth, etc, of a person after death.
dive[2] *same as* **deave**[1].
dive[3] *v* to plunge, hurry forward.
diven't *v neg* don't, do not?
diver[1] *same as* **dyvour**.
diver[2] *n* **1** the pochard. **2** the goldeneye.
divert *n* **1** an amusement, diversion. **2** a diverting person.—*v* **1** to go out of one's way. **2** to separate, live apart. **3** to depart. **4** to amuse.
divet *same as* **divot**.
divider *n* a soup-ladle.
dividual *adj* individual, particular, identical, precise.

divie-goo *n* the black-backed gull.
diving-duck *n* the pochard, the goldeneye.
divna *v neg* do not.
divinin' *v neg* do not?
divor *same as* **dyvour**.
divot *n* **1** a thin, flat piece of sod, used as thatch. **2** a lump. **3** a clumsy, irregular mass of anything. **4** a short, thick, stout person. **5** a sod used as fuel. **6** a broad, flat neck-tie.—*v* **1** to cut divots. **2** to cover with divots.
divot-cast *n* as much land as one divot can be cut on.
divot-dyke *n* a turf dike (qv) or wall.
divoted *adj* made or covered with divots.
divot-happit *adj* thatched or covered with divots.
divot house, ~ hut *n* a turf-covered house or hut.
divoting *n* cutting divots.
divot-seat *n* a seat made of divots.
dixie *n* a severe scolding.—*v* to scold severely.
dixie-fixie *n* a state of confinement in prison or in the stocks.
dixiein *n* a severe scolding.
dizen'd *adj* bedizened.
dizzen *n* **1** a dozen. **2** as much yarn as a woman might spin in a day or a dozen cuts.
dizzy *adj* bemused, fuddled.
do *v* **1** to suffice. **2** to have the effect of, cause.—*n* a swindle.
doach, doagh *n* a salmon weir or cruive.
doak *v* to dock.
doaver *same as* **dover**.
dob¹ *n* the razorfish.
dob² *v* **1** to peck as a bird. **2** to prick.—*n* **1** a prick. **2** a bird's peck.
dobbie¹, dobie *n* **1** a fool, booby, clown. **2** a dunce.
dobbie² *adj* prickly.
docas *same as* **docus¹**.
doce down *v* to pitch down, pay down.
doch-an-dorris *n* the stirrup cup, parting glass.
docher *n* **1** fatigue, strain. **2** injury. **3** deduction.
dochle *n* a dull, heavy person.
dochlin *adj* soft, silly, foolish.
docht *v* **1** could. **2** availed.—*n* power, ability.
dochter *n* a daughter.
dochterlie *adj* becoming a daughter.
dochtless *same as* **douchtless**.
dochtna *v neg* could not.
dochty *adj* **1** strong, powerful. **2** assuming. **3** malapert.
dochy *same as* **dauchy**.
dock *v* **1** to deck, to make oneself look attractive. **2** to shorten a baby's clothes. **3** to abridge. **4** to lessen wages or price. **5** to cut the hair. **6** to flog on the breech. **7** to walk with short steps or in a conceited fashion.—*n* **1** a cutting of the hair. **2** the breech. **3** the peg of a top.
docken *n* **1** the dock. **2** anything worthless.
docker *same as* **dacker**.
docket *adj* showing an unusually short temper.
docketie *adj* short, round and jolly.
dockie *n* a bad humour.
dockit *adj* (*used of words*) clipped, minced.
dockle *v* **1** to flog on the hips. **2** to punish.
dockus *same as* **docus²**.
docky *n* a neat little person taking short steps.—*v* to move with short steps.
docky-doon *n* help in descending from a vehicle.
doctor *n* an assistant master in a high school.—*v* **1** to kill. **2** to do one's business successfully.
doctor-student *n* a medical student.
doctory *n* doctoring.
docus¹ *n* a stupid fellow.
docus² *n* anything very short.
dod¹, dodd *n* **1** a slight fit of ill-temper. **2** (*in pl*) the sulks.—*v* to sulk.
Dod² *n* euphemism for God, in exclamation.
Dod³ *n* a familiar form of George.
dod⁴ *n* a soft, reddish marble.
dodd¹ *same as* **dod¹**.

dodd² *v* to be, or be made, hornless.
dodd³ *n* a bare, round hill or fell.
dodd⁴ *v* **1** to jog. **2** to jolt in trotting.
dodder *v* **1** to shake, tremble. **2** to potter about, dawdle.
doddered *adj* decayed.
dodderment *n* one's deserts, recompense.
doddit *adj* hornless.
doddle¹ *v* **1** to walk feebly, toddle. **2** (*with* **about**) to wag, to move from side to side.
doddle² *same as* **deedle²**.
doddy¹, doddie *adj* **1** hornless. **2** bald.—*n* a hornless cow or ox.
doddy² *adj* **1** sulky. **2** surly. **3** peevish. **4** pettish.
Doddy³ *n* a familiar form of George.
doddy-mitten *n* a worsted glove without separate divisions for the four fingers.
dode *n* a slow person.
dodge¹ *n* a large cut or slice of food.
dodge² *v* to jog, trudge along.
dodgel¹ *v* **1** to walk infirmly, hobble. **2** to jog on.
dodgel² *n* **1** a large piece, a lump. **2** a lumpish person.
dodgel-hem *n* **1** the hem made by sewing down the edges of two pieces of cloth which have been run up in a seam. **2** a splay hem.
dodger *n* a slow, easy-going person.
dodgie *adj* thin-skinned, irritable.
dodgill-~, dodjell-reepan *n* the meadow rocket, supposed to produce love.
dodle *v* to trouble, bother.
dod-lip *n* a pouting lip.
dodrum *n* a whim, fancy.
dodsake *int* for God's sake.
doe *n* **1** the wooden ball used in shinty or hockey. **2** a boy's large marble.
doeler *same as* **dollar**.
doer *n* a legal agent, steward, factor to a landlord.
dofart *same as* **dowfart**.
dog¹ *n* **1** a sawyer's implement to hold timber together. **2** an iron implement, hook-shaped, for lifting stones. **3** the trigger or hammer of a pistol. **4** a blacksmith's lever used in horseshoeing, etc. **5** a name given to various atmospheric appearances. **6** a dogfish. **7** used in exclamations and mild oaths.
dog² *v* (*with* **up**) to wrangle, threaten to fight.
dog-a-bit *n* a mild oath.
dog-dirder *n* a caretaker of dogs.
dog-dirt *n* ruin, bankruptcy.
dog-dollar *n* a coin worth £2, 18s. Scots.
dog-drave, ~-drive, ~-driving *n* ruin, bankruptcy.
dog-drug *n* ruinous circumstances.
dog-foolie *n* a sea bird.
dogger *n* a coarse ironstone.
doggerlone *n* wreck, ruin.
doggie-hillag *n* a small hillock with long grass.
doggies *n* a child's feet.
doggindales *n* clouds of mist clinging to hillsides, betokening southerly winds.
doggle, dogle *n* a boys' common marble.
doghead *n* **1** the hammer of a firelock. **2** the part of the lock that holds the flint.
dog-hip, ~-hippin *n* the fruit of the dog rose.
dog-hole *n* an opening at the foot of a house wall to give the dogs access.
dog-hook *n* an instrument of sawyers, etc, for holding timber together or moving heavy logs.
dog-ling *n* a young ling or cod.
dog-luggit *adj* dog-eared.
dog-nashicks *n* a species of gallnut on the leaves of the trailing willow.
dogont *same as* **dagont**.
dog-rowan *n* the berry of the red elder.
dog-rowan tree *n* the red elder.
dog-rung *n* one of the spars connecting the stilts (qv) of a plough.

dog's camovyne *n* weak-scented feverfew.

dog's drift *n* ruin.

dog's gowan *n* weak-scented feverfew.

dog's helper *n* a person of mean appearance.

dog's lug *n* a dog's-ear in a book.

dog's lugs *n* the foxglove.

dog's ont *same as* **dagont**.

dog's paise *n* the lady's fingers.

dog's siller *n* **1** the yellow rattle or cock's-comb. **2** its seed vessels.

dog's tansy *n* the silverweed.

dog-sure *adj* quite certain.

dog's wages *n* food alone as wages for service.

dog-thick *adj* very intimate.

dog-tired *adj* very tired.

dogtrot *n* a jog trot, a steady pace.

dog-winkle *n* the shellfish *Purpura lapillus*.

doichle *n* a dull, stupid person.—*v* to walk in a dreamy, stupid state.

doid *same as* **doit**³.

doighlin *n* a drubbing.

doil *n* a piece of anything, as bread.

doilt *adj* **1** stupid. **2** crazed, confused.—*n* a foolish man.

doing *v phr* **be doing 1** to maintain the status quo. **2** to make no change in one's procedure. **3** to be content with. **4** to bear with.

doing *n* a friendly party or entertainment.

doingless *adj* lazy, inactive.

doing-off, ~-up *n* **1** a scolding. **2** a clearance of scores.

doish, doisht *n* a heavy blow, thump.

doist *n* **1** a sudden and noisy fall. **2** the noise made by it.

doister *n* **1** a hurricane. **2** storm from the sea. **3** a strong, steady breeze.

doistert *adj* **1** confused. **2** overwhelmed with surprise.

doit¹ *n* **1** an obsolete copper coin of the value of one-twelfth of a penny sterling. **2** a trifle, money. **3** a small share or piece. **4** a mite.

doit² *n* a species of rye-grass.

doit³ *n* **1** a fool, a numskull.—*v* to grow feeble in mind. **2** to walk stupidly, blunder along. **3** to stupefy, puzzle.—*adj* stupid, mazed.

doited *adj* **1** foolish, childish. **2** stupefied. **3** in one's dotage.

doitelt *adj* enfeebled.

doiter *v* **1** to walk as if stupefied or indolent. **2** to walk feebly or totter from old age. **3** to be in one's dotage. **4** to become superannuated.

doitered *adj* **1** confused. **2** stupid, imbecile.

doitrified *adj* dazed, stupefied.

doken *same as* **docken**.

dolbert *same as* **dulbart**.

doldie *n* a big, fat, clumsy person.

doldrum *n* **1** low spirits and ill-temper. **2** anything very big.

dole¹ *n* **1** fraud. **2** a design to circumvent. **3** malice.

dole² *same as* **dool**⁵.

dole³ *same as* **doxy**.

dole-bread *n* bread given as a dole.

dole-day *n* the day for serving with doles.

doleful *adj* troublesome, vexatious.

doler *same as* **dollar**.

doless *same as* **dowless**.

dolf *adj* **1** dull, melancholy. **2** frivolous.

doll¹ *n* **1** a smartly dressed young woman. **2** a term of affection. **3** the harvest maiden.

doll² *n* pigeons' dung.

doll³ *n* **1** a dole. **2** a large lump of anything.

dollar *n* **1** a five-shilling piece. **2** a small, thick biscuit. **3** a boys' large marble, three or four times larger than an ordinary one. **4** (*in pl*) money.

dollar-bake *n* a small, thick biscuit of the circumference of a crown piece.

doll in *n phr* a call used by children to enter school.

dollop *n* **1** a lump, a large piece. **2** the lot.

doll-wean *n* a doll.

dolly¹ *n* a silly, dressy woman.—*adj* silly, dressy.

dolly² *n* an old-fashioned iron oil lamp.

dolly³ *same as* **dowie**.

dolly oil *n* **1** oil used for burning in a dolly (qv). **2** oil of any kind.

dolp *same as* **doup**.

doltard *n* **1** a dolt. **2** a dull, stupid fellow.

dolver *n* **1** anything large. **2** a large apple. **3** a large marble.

domage *n* damage.

dome *n* a dwelling place of any kind.

domeror *n* a madman.

domicil *n* household articles, excluding clothing.

dominie *n* **1** a slightly contemptuous name for a minister. **2** a schoolmaster.

don¹ *n* **1** an adept, proficient. **2** a favourite, a leading spirit. **3** an intimate acquaintance.

don² *n* a gift.

do-nae-better *n* a substitute, when one can find nothing better.

do-nae-gude *n* **1** one likely to do no good. **2** a thoroughly worthless person.

donal'-blue *n* the jellyfish.

donald *n* a glass of spirits.

donald *n* the last small stack brought from the field to the cornyard.

donar *same as* **donner**.

donator *n* one who received an escheat.

doncie *same as* **donsie**¹.

done *v, adj* **1** outwitted. **2** exhausted, tired. **3** worn-out with fatigue, illness, old age, etc.

donel *same as* **donald**.

dong-ding *adv* ding-dong.

donie *n* a hare.

donkey-beast *n* a donkey.

donn'd *adj* fond, greatly attached.

donner, donnar, donnor *v* to stupefy, stun.

donner-bee *n* a bumblebee, drum-bee.

donnering *adj* walking stupidly.

donnert *adj* **1** in dotage. **2** stupid, dazed.—*n* a blockhead, fool.

donnertness *n* stupidity.

donnery *n* a clothes moth.

donnot, donnat, donot *n* a good-for-nothing person.

donsie¹ *n* a stupid, lubberly fellow.—*adj* **1** unlucky. **2** weak. **3** sickly. **4** dull, stupid, dunce-like, dreamy. **5** depressed.

donsie² *adj* **1** neat, trim. **2** affectedly neat. **3** selfimportant. **4** saucy, restive. **5** testy.

donsielie *adj* in poor health.

dontibour *n* a courtesan.

doo¹ *n* **1** a dove. **2** a term of endearment.

doo² *n* **1** an infant. **2** a child's doll.

doobie *same as* **dobbie**¹.

dooble *adj* double.

doocot *n* a dovecot.

doocot hole *n* a pigeonhole.

doock *same as* **douk**³.

doodle¹ *same as* **deedle**².

doodle² *v* to drone on the bagpipe.

doodlie *n* a nursery name for the little finger.

doof *n* a stupid fellow.—*v* to render stupid.

dooff *same as* **dowff**.

dooffart, doofert *same as* **dowfart**.

dook¹ *n* **1** a stout peg or wedge driven into a plastered wall to hold a nail, etc. **2** the bung of a cask. —*v* **1** to bung a cask. **2** to drive home a dook.

dook² *n* an inclined road or dip in a mine.

dook³ *same as* **douk**².

dooket *n* a dovecot.

dookie *n* a Baptist.

dookin'-pool *n* a pond for ducking witches, etc.

dool¹ *n* a blow with a flat surface.—*v* to beat, thrash.

dool² *n* **1** the den or goal in a game. **2** a boundary mark in an unenclosed field.—*v* (*with* **off**) to fix the boundaries.

dool³ *same as* **doll**³.

dool⁴ *n* an iron spike for keeping the joints of boards together in laying a floor.

dool⁵ *n* **1** sorrow, grief, misfortune. **2** mourning weeds. **3** sombre hangings.—*adj* sorrowful, mournful.

dool-a-nee *int* alas!

dool-charged *adj* sorrow-charged.

dool-ding *n* the mournful knell of the passing bell.

dooless *same as* **dowless**.

doolful *adj* **1** sad, sorrowful. **2** troublesome, annoying.

dool-hill *n* a hill formerly occupied by a castle or place of refuge.

doolie¹ *adj* **1** sorrowful, gloomy. **2** solitary.

doolie² *n* **1** a hobgoblin, spectre. **2** a scarecrow.

doolie-doomster *n* a spectre.

doolies *n* a boy's marbles.

doolie-yates *n* ghost-haunted gates.

dool-like *adj* having the appearance of sorrow.

doolloup *n* a steep glen in which two haughs are exactly opposite each other. *See* **haugh**.

doolsome *adj* sad, sorrowful.

dool-string *n* a long string worn on the hat as a sign of mourning.

dool-tree¹ *n* **1** a gallows. **2** a tree or post on which evildoers were hanged in the exercise of the power of pit and gallows (qv).

dool-tree² *n* a tree that marks the goal in playing ball.

dool-weeds *n* mourning garb.

doolzie *n* a frolicsome, thoughtless woman.

doom-hour *n* **1** the last hour. **2** the hour of doom.

doomie *n* a mischievous sprite.

dooming *n* **1** sentence, judgment. **2** destiny.

dooms *adj* great.—*adv* extremely, exceedingly.—*n* a great sum.

dooms-earneat *adj* in dead earnest.

doomster *n* **1** the official who formerly pronounced the death sentence in a criminal court. **2** a judge.

doon¹ *n* **1** the goal in a game. **2** the place used for playing it.

doon² *adv* extremely.

doon³ *adj* done, worn-out.

doon⁴ *prep* down.—*adj* **1** down. **2** laid down, sown, fixed down. **3** confined to bed by illness. **4** knocked down. **5** far gone in drinking, drunk. —*adv* **1** down. **2** in reduction of rent, price. **3** in payment of cash instead of credit.—*v* **1** to upset. **2** to overthrow. **3** to throw in wrestling. **4** to fell, knock down. **5** (*with* **take**) to dilute spirits, etc, by adding water, etc.

doona *v neg* do not.

doon-bearing *n* **1** oppression. **2** the pain or signs of approaching parturition.

doon-brae *adv* downwards.

doon-broo *n* a frown.

doon-bye *adv* down below, down yonder.

doon-casting *adj* **1** grieved, sorrowful. **2** pressing. —*n* depression.

doon-come *n* **1** a heavy fall of rain, snow. **2** a descent, fall in the market, means or social position.

doon-comin' *n* a heavy fall of rain etc.

doon-cryin' *n* disparagement, depreciation.—*adj* disparaging, deprecatory.

doon-ding *n* a heavy fall of rain, snow, sleet.

doon-drag *n* **1** what keeps a person down in the world. **2** a dead weight. **3** a sin or weakness that acts as a drag. **4** a person who is a grief or disgrace to his family.—*v* to pull down.

doon-draucht *n* **1** a gust of wind sending smoke down a chimney. **2** any thing or person that is a reproach or a moral deadweight.

doon-draw¹ *same as* **doon-drag**.

doon-draw² *n* to launch a boat.

doon-drawin' *n* a feast at Beltane on launching a fishing boat for the fishing.

doon-drug *same as* **doon-drag**.

doone *n* **1** a hill fort. **2** a mound.

doon-efter *adj* following downwards.

dooner *adj* lower, nearer the bottom.

doonermaist *adj* lowest, farthest down.

doonfa' *n* **1** a fall of rain, snow. **2** a slope. **3** descent of food, etc, in swallowing. **4** low ground at a mountain foot to where sheep retire in winter. **5** a reverse, misfortune.

doon-gang *n* used of a person who has a very large appetite.

doon-had *n* **1** hindrance, drawback, check. **2** what represses growth, etc.

doon-hadden *adj* repressed, kept in check, kept down.

doon-haddin' *adj* repressing, oppressive, holding down.

doon-head *n* a grudge, pique.

doon-head-clock *n* the dandelion.

doon-hill *n* a castle or refuge on a hill.

doon-lay *n* a heavy fall of snow, etc.

doon-leuk *n* **1** a frowning face. **2** disapproval, displeasure.

doon-leuking *adj* **1** supercilious, condescending. **2** morose-looking.

doon-lie *n* a grave, a resting place.

doonlins *adv* very, in a great degree.

doon-looking *adj* unable or unwilling to look one in the face.

doon-lying *n* a woman's confinement.

doonmaist *adj* lowermost.

doon-moo't *adj* melancholy, in low spirits, down in the mouth.

doon-pour *n* a heavy fall of rain.

doon-proud *adj* very proud.

doon-richteous *adj* downright.

doons *adv* extremely.

doon-seat *n* a settlement as to situation.

doon-set¹, **~-sit** *n* **1** a settlement, provision, especially in marriage. **2** a location, a home in marriage.

doon-set² *n* **1** any work that depresses or overpowers. **2** *same as* **doon-come**. **3** a scolding that silences.

doon-sett *n* a downward stroke.

doon-setter *n* something that settles an argument.

doon-sinking *n* **1** the sun setting. **2** depression, melancholy.

doonsins *adv* very, exceedingly.

doon-sitting *n* **1** a sitting down to drink. **2** a drinking bout. **3** a sederunt or session of a church court. **4** a settlement. **5** a location. **6** a home or settlement in marriage.

doon-stroy *v* to destroy.

doon-sway *n* a downward impetus or direction.

doon-tak *n* anything enfeebling the body or mind.

doon-takin *n* reduction in price.

doon-the-brae *phr* towards the grave.

doon-through *adv* in the low or flat country.

doon-throw *v* to upset, overthrow.

doon-toon *n* down the village.

doon-weicht *n* overweight.

doonwith *adv* downwards.—*n* a declivity.—*adj* downward.

doon-worth *n* a declivity.

doop *same as* **doup**.

door *same as* **dour**¹.

doorband *n* **1** a door hinge. **2** the iron band by which a hinge is fixed to the door.

door-board *n* the panel of a door.

door-cheek *n* **1** a doorpost. **2** a threshold.

door-crook *n* a door-hinge.

door-deaf *adj* very deaf, deaf as a doornail.

door-drink *n* a stirrup cup.

door head *n* the lintel of a door.

doorie *n* a game of marbles, played against a wooden door.

door-lan *n* a plot of ground near a door.

door-nail-deafness *n* stone-deafness.

door-neighbour *n* a next-door neighbour.

door-sill *n* a threshold.

door-sneck *n* a door latch.
door-stand *n* a doorstep.
doorstane *n* the flagstone at the threshold of a door.
doorstep *n* the landing place at a door.
door-stoop *n* a doorpost.
doo's cleckin *n* a family of two.
doose *same as* **douce**[1].
doosey *n* a punishment among men and boys by bumping the posteriors on the ground.
doosh *v* to butt.
doosht *n* **1** a soft, heavy blow. **2** a heavy fall or throw. **3** a rough shake. **4** a push from side to side.—*v* **1** to strike with a soft, heavy blow. **2** to bump. **3** to throw in a violent, careless manner.
dooshtin *n* a beating.
doosil *v* to beat, thump.—*n* a thump, blow.
doot *v* to doubt.
dootious *adj* cherishing an unpleasant conviction.
dootsome *adj* **1** doubtful, uncertain. **2** apprehensive.
doozil *n* **1** an uncomely woman. **2** a lusty child.
doozy *adj* uncomely. **2** unpleasant.
dorbel *n* anything unseemly in appearance.
dorbie[1] *n* a stonemason, hewer or builder.
dorbie[2] *adj* **1** sickly, weakly. **2** soft. **3** sleepy. **4** lazy.
dorbie[3] *n* the red-backed sandpiper, the dunlin.
dorbie-brither *n* a fellow stonemason.
dorbie's knock *n* a peculiar knock, as a Freemason's signal.
dordermeat *n* a bannock or piece of oatcake formerly given to farm servants after loosing the plough, between dinner and supper.
dore-cheek *n* a doorpost.
doreneed *n* the youngest pig of a litter.
dorestane *n* a threshold stone.
dorlach[1], **dorloch** *same as* **darloch**.
dorlach[2] *n* **1** a short sword. **2** a dagger.
dorlack *same as* **darlock**.
dorle *same as* **darle**.
dorn *n* diaper.
dornel *n* a horse-dealers' name for the fundament of a horse.
dornell *n* darnel.
dornick, dornock *n* **1** linen cloth, formerly made at Tournay, for table use. **2** diaper.
dornicle *n* the viviparous blenny.
Dornoch-law *n* **1** execution before trial. **2** summary justice.
dornton, dorntor *same as* **dortor**.
doroty *same as* **dorrity**.
dorra *n* a net fixed to a hoop of wood or iron, used for catching crabs.
dorrity *n* **1** a doll. **2** a tiny woman. **3** the name Dorothy.
dort *n* a pet, sulks.—*v* **1** to sulk, to become pettish. **2** (*with* **at**) to overnurse.—*adj* sulky, pettish.
dortilie *adv* saucily, pettishly.
dorting *n* sulkiness.
dortor *n* **1** a slight repast. **2** food taken between meals. *See* **dordermeat**.
dortor *same as* **dortour**.
dortour, dortor *n* **1** a bedchamber, dormitory. **2** a sleeping draught taken at bedtime.
dorts *n* a slight repast.
dorty *adj* **1** spoilt, pettish. **2** proud, haughty, conceited. **3** ailing, always weak. **4** (*used of plants*) difficult to rear except in certain soils.
dorty-pouch *n* a saucy person.
dose[1] *v* to drug, stupefy.—*n* a large quantity.
dose[2] *same as* **doze**[1].
dose[3] *n* an allowance of bread.
dosen *same as* **dozen**[2].
dosie *n* a small dose.
doss[1] *n* a tobacco pouch.
doss[2] *v* **1** (*with* **down**) to throw oneself down. **2** to sit down violently. **3** to pay down smartly.
doss[3] *v* **1** (*with* **about**) to go about one's business prop-

erly. **2** to do neatly, exactly. **3** (*with* **up**, **off**) to trim, adorn.—*n* **1** an ornament. **2** a bow or circular bunch of ribbons.—*adj* neat, spruce.
dossach *v* (*with* **with**) **1** to treat, nurse tenderly. **2** to overnurse. **3** to gain, win.—*n* overtender nursing.
dossan *n* the forelock.
dossick *n* a small truss or bundle.
dossie[1] *n* a small heap.
dossie[2] *n* a neat, well-dressed person.—*adj* well-dressed.
dossie[3] *v* **1** (*with* **down**) to pay or throw down money in payment. **2** to toss down.
dossins *n* human ordure.
dosslie *adv* with neatness and simplicity combined.
dossness *n* neatness.
dost up *v*, *adj* neatly dressed.
dot *n* **1** a diminutive person or thing. **2** walking with short, quick steps. **3** a short sleep.—*v* **1** to walk with short, quick steps. **2** to fall into a short sleep.
dot and go one *phr* the walk of a lame person whose legs are not equal.
dotch *v* to dangle.
dote[1] *same as* **doit**[1].
dote[2] *n* **1** a dowry. **2** an endowment.—*v* **1** to endow. **2** to give as a salary.
dother *same as* **dochter**.
dotrified *same as* **doitrified**.
dotter *same as* **doiter**.
dottered *adj* doting in old age.
dotterel *n* a silly person, a dotard.
dottet *adj* stupefied.
dottie *same as* **doiter**.
dottle[1], **dottal, dottel** *n* **1** a small particle. **2** a plug, a stopper. **3** the unconsumed tobacco remaining in a pipe. **4** the core of a boil.
dottle[2] *n* a fool, dotard.—*adj* **1** silly, crazy, in dotage. **2** of weak intellect. **3** stupid from drink.—*v* **1** to be in dotage. **2** to become crazy. **3** to hobble from age and infirmity. **4** to walk with short, quick steps.
dottle-trot *n* **1** the quick, short step of an old man. **2** the old man's walk.
dotty *adj* **1** imbecile, half-witted. **2** in dotage.
doubie *same as* **dobbie**[1].
double *adj* (*used of a letter of the alphabet*) capital. —*n* a duplicate, a copy.—*v* **1** to make a copy. **2** to repeat. **3** to clench the fists.
double-breasted *adj* (*used of a word*) long, not easily understood.
double-down-come *n* a mode of measuring yarn by a reel (qv).
double-horsed *adj* (*used of a horse*) carrying two persons on its back.
double-sib *adj* related both by father and mother.
doublet *n* **1** a sleeved jacket or waistcoat. **2** (*in pl*) clothes in general.
doubt *v* **1** to apprehend or expect with a measure of certainty. **2** to suspect. **3** to have an unpleasant conviction.
douce[1] *adj* **1** gentle, kind, pleasant. **2** sedate, sober-minded, grave. **3** respectable. **4** prudent. **5** modest, virtuous. **6** tidy, neat, soft, soothing. **7** not giddy or frivolous.
douce[2] *same as* **douse**[1].
douce-gaun *adj* prudent, circumspect.
douce-like *adj* quiet, respectable in appearance.
douce-looking *adj* grave-looking, of quiet, sober appearance.
doucely *adv* **1** sweetly, gently, kindly. **2** quietly, sedately, soberly.
douceness *n* the quality of being douce (qv).
doucht[1] *same as* **dought**[1].
doucht[2] *v* was able, could.
douchtless *adj* weak, feeble.
douchty *adj* **1** doughty. **2** vigorous of body. **3** used ironically of deeds that promise much and perform little.
doud *n* a woman's cap with a caul.

douden *n* a dry, soft wind.
doudle[1] *n* the root of the common reed grass.
doudle[2] *same as* **deedle**[2].
doudle[3] *same as* **doodle**[2].
doudler, doudlar *n* the roots of the bog-bean.
douf *same as* **dowf**.
douff *same as* **dowff**.
douffert *same as* **dowfart**.
douffie *same as* **dowffie**.
doufness *n* dullness, melancholy.
douf on *v* to continue in a dull, slumbering state.
dough *n* a dirty, useless, untidy person.
dought[1] *n* **1** strength, might, ability, power. **2** a deed. **3** a stroke, a blow.
dought[2] *v* **1** could. **2** was able.
doughtless *adj* weak, worthless, pithless.
doughty *adj* **1** strong, powerful, stout. **2** malapert. **3** saucy.
doughy *adj* **1** half-baked. **2** foolish. **3** cowardly.
douhale *n* an easy-going fellow, one who does not object to being regarded as a fool.
douk[1] *n* a wooden wedge driven into a wall.
douk[2] *v* **1** to duck. **2** to plunge or dip into water. **3** to bathe. **4** to dive.—*n* **1** a dive, a bathe. **2** the condition of being drenched with rain. **3** as much ink as a pen takes up.
douk[3] *n* duck, sailcloth.
douk[4] *v* **1** to bow the head or body hastily in obeisance. **2** to incline the head for any purpose in an unseemly way. **3** to duck so as to avoid suddenly.
douker, doucker *n* **1** a diving bird. **2** the tufted duck. **3** the pochard. **4** the goldeneye. **5** the didapper. **6** a bather.
douket *n* a dovecot.
doukie *n* a Baptist.
doukin *n* a ducking, drenching.
douking stool *n* the cucking stool.
doul'd *adj* fatigued.
doule *n* a fool.
doulie *same as* **doolie**[2].
domineer *v* **1** to stupefy, pester with much talk. **2** to weary.
doun *same as* **doon**[4].
douna *v neg* **1** cannot. **2** dare not.
doun-draugh *n* overburdening weight, oppression.
douner *same as* **donner**.
doung *v* to dash.
dounnins *adv* a little way downwards.
doun-pouthered *adj* reduced to powder.
dounwith *adv* downwards.
doup *n* **1** the bottom or end of anything, as an egg, candle, day, etc. **2** the breech or buttocks. **3** a moment. **4** a cavity.—*v* **1** to dump, thump. **2** to thump or bump the posterior. **3** to stoop, incline the head or body downwards. **4** (*used of night*) to descend. **5** (*of the weather*) to become gloomy.
doup-scour *n* a fall on the buttocks.
doup-scud *adv* with a heavy fall on the buttocks.
doup-skelper *n* **1** one who beats the buttocks. **2** a schoolmaster.
doup-wark *n* work at the bottom of a weaving machine.
dour, doure *adj* **1** hard, stern, stiff. **2** sullen, sulky. **3** stubborn, unyielding. **4** (*used of weather, etc*) severe, hard. **5** (*of soil*) barren, stiff to work. **6** (*of ice*) rough. **7** (*of a task, etc*) difficult to accomplish. **8** slow in learning, backward.
dour *same as* **dover**.
dourdon *n* appearance.
dourie *n* a dowry.
dourin *adj* dozing, slumbering.
dourlach *same as* **darloch**.
dourly *adv* pertinaciously, stubbornly.
dourness *n* **1** obstinacy, stubbornness. **2** melancholy, gloom. **3** severity.
dour-seed *n* a species of oats, slow in ripening.
douse[1] *v* **1** to strike, knock. **2** to strike a ball out of play. **3** to extinguish. **4** to throw down with a bang, to pay down money.—*n* a blow. **5** a dull, heavy blow. **6** the sound of such a blow.

douse[2] *same as* **douce**[1].
doush *n* **1** a douche. **2** a dash of water.—*v* **1** to duck, plunge. **2** to dash water.
dousht *same as* **doosht**.
douss *same as* **douse**[1].
doussle *v* to beat soundly.
dout[1] *v* to doubt.
dout[2] *same as* **doit**[1].
douth[1] *adj* **1** dull, dispirited, melancholy. **2** gloomy, causing melancholy.
douth[2] *adj* snug, comfortable, in easy circumstances.
douth[3] *n* shelter.
douthless *adj* **1** weak. **2** helpless.
doutish *adj* doubtful.
doutless *adv* doubtless.
doutsum *same as* **dootsome**.
douzie *n* a light of any kind, a spark.
dove *v* **1** to be half-asleep. **2** to be in a doting, foolish state.
dove-dock *n* the tussilago or colt's-foot.
dovened *adj* **1** benumbed with cold. **2** deafened with noise.
dover *v* **1** to fall into a light slumber, to be half-asleep, doze. **2** to stun, stupefy.—*n* **1** a light slumber. **3** semi-consciousness. **4** a faint, swoon.
dovering *adj* occasional, rare.
dovie *adj* stupid, apparently weak-minded.—*n* a stupid person, an imbecile.
dow[1] *n* **1** a dove. **2** a term of endearment.
dow[2] *v* **1** to be able to. **2** (*with neg*) to be reluctant to do. **3** to thrive, do well.—*n* worth, value.
dow[3] *v* **1** to betake oneself. **2** to hasten.
dow[4] *v* **1** to wither, decay. **2** to grow stale or putrid. **3** to doze, fall into a sleepy state. **4** to trifle with, perform carelessly.—*adj* doleful, gloomy.—*n* the fading of a leaf, etc.
dowatty *n* a silly, foolish person.
dowbart *same as* **dulbart**.
dowbreck *n* a species of fish.
dowcht *v* could.
dow-cot *n* a dovecot.
dowd *n* a woman's dress cap with a caul.
dow'd[1] *v* could.
dow'd[2] *adj* **1** not fresh, pithless. **2** (*used of water, etc*) flat, dead. **3** (*of meat*) lukewarm, not properly hot.
dowden *v* to toss about with the wind.
dow'd fish *n* fish that has been drying for a day or two.
dowdie *adj* fading, withering.
dowdies *n* a child's feet.
dowdy *n* an old woman.
dowf *adj* **1** melancholy, gloomy. **2** hollow. **3** silly. **4** inactive. **5** rotten. **6** dull to the eye, hazy. **7** unfeeling. **8** worthless, paltry. **9** infertile.—*n* a dull, heavy person, a fool.—*v* **1** to render stupid. **2** to become dull.
dowfart *n* a dull, stupid fellow, a duffer.—*adj* **1** dull, stupid. **2** inefficient, spiritless. **3** dumpish.
dowff *v* to strike a dull, heavy blow.—*n* a dull, heavy blow.
dowffie *adj* **1** low-spirited, melancholy. **2** dull, inactive. **3** stupid. **4** shy.
dowffy-hearted *adj* lacking courage.
dowf-like *adj* gloomy-looking.
dowfness *n* melancholy, sadness.
dowie *adj* **1** sad, mournful, dismal. **2** inclined to decay. **3** languid, weak, ailing.—*adv* sadly, wearily.
dowie-like *adj* sad-looking, sorrowful.
dowiely *adv* sadly, wearily.—*adj* **1** sad. **2** depressing
dowieness *n* sadness.
dowiesome *adj* sad, rather melancholy.
dowiewise *adj* sad, sorrowful.
dowilie *same as* **dowiely**.
dowk *same as* **douk**[2].
dowl[1] *same as* **doll**[3].
dowl[2] *v* **1** to weary, to fatigue. **2** to depress.
dowl-cap *v* to cover the head by drawing anything over it.
dowless *adj* **1** lazy, without energy. **2** helpless. **3** unthrifty, unprosperous. **4** unhealthy.

dowlie-horn *n* a horn that hangs down in cattle.
dowlie-horned *adj* with drooping horns.
dowly *adv* **1** dully, sluggishly, feebly. **2** sadly.
down *same as* **doon**⁴.
downa *v neg* cannot, lack inclination.
downa-do *n* exhaustion of age.
downans *n* green hillocks.
down-sinking *n* sinking of heart.
dowp *same as* **doup**.
dowre *same as* **dour**¹.
dox *n* a sweetheart.
doxie *adj* lazy, slow, restive.
doxy *n* **1** a sweetheart. **2** a wench.
doyce, doyse *v* to give a dull, heavy blow.—*n* **1** a dull, heavy blow. **2** the flat sound caused by the fall of a heavy body.
doychle *n* **1** a dull, stupid person. **2** a sloven.—*v* to walk in a dull, dreamy state.
doyloch *n* a crazy person.
doyst *v* **1** to fall with a heavy sound. **2** to throw down.—*n* a sudden fall, the noise made by falling.
doyte *same as* **doit**³.
doze¹ *v* **1** to spin a top so rapidly that it seems motionless. **2** to spin round rapidly.
doze² *n* **1** a dose. **2** as much as one takes of liquor at a time.
doze³ *v* (*used of straw, hay, wood*) to become spoiled by fungus growths.
doze-brown *adj* **1** snuff-coloured. **2** fox-coloured.
dozed *adj* (*used of wood*) decayed, unsound.
dozen¹ *n* **1** *in phr* **a baker's dozen** thirteen. **2** *in phr* **a fisher's dozen** twenty.
dozen² *v* **1** to benumb, stupefy, daze. **2** to become torpid. **3** to be impotent. **4** to become spiritless. **5** (*used as an imprecation*) to damn.
dozent *adj* **1** benumbed. **2** sleepy. **3** stupid. **4** impotent. **5** spiritless.
dozing-tap *n* a spinning top.
draa *v* to draw.
draan *v, adj* drawn.
draatch *v* to be slow in movement or action.
drabble¹, **drable** *v* **1** to make wet or dirty. **2** to slobber. **3** to draggle. **4** to besmear.—*n* **1** a slattern. **2** a person of dirty habits. **3** (*in pl*) food dropped on clothes while eating. **4** spots of dirt.
drabble² *n* **1** a small quantity of liquid or semiliquid stuff. **2** inferior food.
drabblich *n* inferior food.
drabbly *adj* **1** (*used of the weather*) wet. **2** (*of soil*) muddy. **3** spotted with drabbles.—*n* a child's bib.
drabloch *n* refuse, trash, applied to very small potatoes and bad butcher meat.
drachle *same as* **draggle**.
drachling *adj* lazy, easy-going.
dracht *n* a draught, load, freight.
drachted *adj* designing, crafty.
drack *same as* **drawk**.
draed *v, adj* dreaded.
draff-cheap *adj* very low in price.
draff-pock *n* **1** a sack for carrying draff or grain. **2** an imperfection, a flaw. **3** a term of reproach.
draff-sack *n* **1** a sack for holding grain or draff. **2** a lazy glutton.
draffy *adj* **1** used of draff. **2** of inferior quality, applied to liquor brewed from draff.
draft *n* **1** animals selected from a herd, etc. **2** a picture.—*v* to select animals from a herd, etc.
draft ewe *n* a ewe withdrawn from the flock as one of the best or as past breeding.
draft gimmer *n* a gimmer put aside as unfit for breeding.
drag *n* a toil, hindrance, encumbrance.
dragen *n* sweets, comfits.
draggle *v* **1** to soak or soil with rain, etc. **2** to straggle, drag slowly on. **3** to moisten meal, flour, etc. —*n* **1** a

wet, muddy condition, a soaking with rain or mud. **2** an untidy person. **3** a feeble, ill-conditioned person. **4** a slow person, a laggard.
dragon *n* a boy's kite, made generally of paper.
dragouner *n* a dragoon.
drag-tae *n* a rake.
draible *same as* **drabble**.
draibly *same as* **drabbly**.
draich, draick *n* a lazy, lumpish, useless person.
draicky *adj* slow, spiritless, lazy.
draidgie *same as* **dirgie**.
draig *n* **1** a dirty, low-lying place. **2** an untidy, disordered place.
draighie *same as* **draich**.
draigie *same as* **dirgie**.
draigle¹ *same as* **draggle**.
draigle² *a* small quantity.
draigled, draiglit *adj* **1** dirty, splashed with mud. **2** (*used of a stook* (qv)) soaked with rain.
draiglers *n* the invaders in the game of het rows and butter-baiks.
draigle-tail *n* a trailing, mud-bespattered skirt.—*adj* splashed with mud.
draiglin *n* a small quantity.
draiglin *n* **1** a soaking with rain or mud. **2** a wet, dirty condition.
draigly *adj* dragging the feet wearily.
draigon *same as* **dragon**.
draik¹ *same as* **draig**.
draik², **drake** *same as* **drawk**.
drain *n* **1** a drop. **2** a small quantity of liquor.
dram¹ *n* a glass of whisky.—*v* to drink, tipple.
dram² *adj* **1** indifferent, cool. **2** melancholy.
dramach *same as* **drammach**.
dram-drinking *n* tippling.
dram-glass *n* a wine glass used for whisky, etc.
dram-hearted *adj* depressed, melancholy.
drammach *n* a mixture of raw meal and water.
dramming *n* tippling.
drammlichs *n* small pieces of oatmeal leaven adhering to a bowl or kneading board.
drammock *same as* **drammach**.
dram-shop *n* a public house.
drandering *n* the chorus of a song.
drangle *v* to dawdle, loiter, linger.
drant *v* **1** to drawl. **2** to drone. **3** to pass time slowly.—*n* a slow, drawling tone.
drap¹ *n* **1** a drop. **2** a small quantity of liquid. **3** a sugar plum. **4** a small shot. **5** a weight of nearly 10 ounces.—*v* **1** to drop. **2** to fall. **3** to die. **4** to rain slightly. **5** (*used of animals*) to give birth to young.
drap² *n* a thick woollen cloth used for cloaks, coats, etc.
drap awa' *phr* to die in succession.
drap-glasses *phr* to drop the white of an egg into a glass of water and from the shape it assumes to predict the future, a custom on Fastern's Eve.
drap o' dew *n* a little whisky.
drappie *n* **1** a little drop or quantity. **2** (*with* **the**) drink, whisky.
drappikie *n* **1** a very small quantity of liquid. **2** the usual modicum of liquor.
drappings *n* droppings.
drappit *v, adj* **1** dropped here and there. **2** occasional.
drappit eggs *n* eggs dropped into a pan to be cooked or fried.
drappit scones *n* scones made like pancakes.
drap-ripe *adj* **1** dead-ripe. **2** quite ready.
drap's bluid *phr* related by blood.
draptaberrie *n* cloth made at Berry, in France.
dratch *v* to linger.
drate voided excrement. *See* **drite**.
draucht¹, **draught**¹ *n* **1** convulsive breathing. **2** a load to be carried or drawn. **3** what is carted at a time. **4** a plan, scheme, policy, design. **5** a lineament of the face. **6** a

method of producing a fancy design from plain healds in weaving. **7** light grain blown away in winnowing. **8** the entrails of a wolf or sheep.—*v* to breathe convulsively.

draucht², **draught²** *n* **1** a money draft. **2** a sketch. **3** a photograph.—*v* **1** to draft (qv) from a flock. **2** to draw.

draucht³, **draught³** *n* **1** a ditch as a farm boundary. **2** the land enclosed within such a ditch.

drauchtet *adj* (*used of a horse or ox*) trained to draw a plough, etc.

draucht ewe *n* a ewe picked out for fattening or selling if fat.

drauchtiness *n* artfulness, craftiness.

drauchty *adj* **1** designing. **2** artful. **3** crafty. **4** capable of artfulness.

drauk *same as* **drawk**.

drauky *adj* (*used of the weather*) damp, wet.

draunt *same as* **drant**.

drave¹ *n* **1** a drove of sheep or cattle. **2** a shoal of fishes. **3** a draught of herrings. **4** a crowd of people.

drave² *v* drove.

draw *v* **1** to drag. **2** to get on together, agree. **3** to withdraw. **4** to cart. **5** (*in curling*) to make a careful shot. **6** to select animals from a herd or flock. **7** to let off water from a millpond, etc. **8** to extract the entrails of poultry or game. **9** to draw straw for thatching. **10** to filter through or ooze. **11** to infer, conclude.—*n* **1** a tug, wrench. **2** a carefully played shot in curling. **3** a short smoke of tobacco. **4** a draught of air.

draw a leg *phr* to fool or trick.

draw aside with *phr* to frequent, consort with.

drawback *n* a hindrance, obstruction.

drawboy *n* a boy formerly employed by weavers to pull the cords of their harness.

draw cuts *phr* to cast lots with various lengths of paper slips, etc.

drawers' head *n* the top of a chest of drawers.

drawing *n* **1** dragging or pulling girls about in a romp. **2** making a careful shot in curling.

drawing the sweertree *n* a tug of war with a swingletree.

drawk *v* to drench, soak.—*n* damp, wet weather.

drawky *adj* (*used of the weather*) wet, drizzly, rainy.

drawl *v* to be slow in action.

drawlie *adj* slow of movement, slovenly.

draw-ling *n* **1** bog cotton or moss crop. **2** the tufted club rush.

draw-moss *n* bog cotton, the sheathed cotton sedge.

draw my leg *n* one who takes advantage of another or seeks to make fun of him or her.

drawnt *same as* **drant**.

draw the table *phr* to clear the table.

draw til, ~ to *v* **1** to come to regard with interest or affection. **2** to incline to. **3** to give signs of approaching rain, etc. **4** to take a seat at table.

draw up *v* **1** to increase a bid or offer. **2** to court. **3** to come together in marriage.

dread *v* **1** to look forward with anxiety. **2** to suspect.—*n* suspicion.

dreader *n* **1** a suspicious person, one given to suspicion. **2** terror.—*v* to fear.

dreadour *n* fear, dread.—*v* to fear, dread.

dream *n in phr* **in a widden dream** in a dazed condition, under momentary excitement.

dream-fleyed *adj* scared by dreams.

dreaming bread, ~ cake *n* bride's cake or christening cake, pieces of which are laid under the pillow to be dreamt on.

drean *n* the branch of a bramble.

drear *n* dreariness.

drearisome *adj* dreary, wearisome, lonely.

drearisomeness *n* loneliness.

dreck *n* **1** a dirty, low-lying place. **2** an untidy state.

dreddour, dreder *same as* **dreadour**.

dredge, dredge box *n* a dredger for sprinkling flour, pepper, etc.

dredgie *same as* **dirgie**.

dree *v* **1** to endure, suffer, undergo. **2** to bear pain, burden, etc. **3** to last, endure. **4** to suffer from anxiety.—*n* **1** suffering. **2** a protracted, tiresome tune or song.

dreech *same as* **dreich²**.

dreed *v* to dread.—*n* **1** dread. **2** what one dreads.

dreedle *same as* **driddle**.

dreeful *adj* sad, foreboding.

dreegh¹ *same as* **droich**.

dreegh² *same as* **dreich²**.

dreek *same as* **dreich²**.

dreel *v* **1** to drill. **2** to move or run quickly. **3** (*used of a spinning wheel, etc*) to rotate quickly, to work quickly and smoothly. **4** to scold, reprove smartly.—*n* **1** a swift, violent motion. **2** energy. **3** rapid movement. **4** work speedily got through. **5** (*of wind*) a hurricane. **6** a spell of stormy weather. **7** a scolding. **8** a drill.

dreeling *n* **1** swift and smooth motion. **2** a severe scolding.

dreen *v, adj* driven.

dreep¹ *v* **1** to drip, drop slowly. **2** to cause to drip. **3** to drain a bottle, etc. **4** to drop, descend perpendicularly, to let oneself down. **5** to walk slowly. **6** to do anything slowly and dully.—*n* **1** a dripping condition. **2** a ditch. **3** a drip. **4** dripping from a roast. **5** the eaves, the spot where eave drops fall.

dreep² *n* a humiliating disappointment.

dreep³ *n* **1** a term used in the game of marbles. **2** *in phr* **play dreep** to play for stakes.

dreepend *n* **1** dripping from a roast. **2** perquisites. **3** a fat income or living.

dreepie *adj* (*used of the weather*) dripping, wet.

dreeping *n* **1** a dripping, drop, dreg. **2** drink, liquor.

dreeping roast *n* a constant good income, a fat living with perquisites.

dreeping-wet *adj* soaked to the skin, very wet.

dreeple *v* to trickle, fall in drops.—*n* a dribble.—*v* **1** to drizzle. **2** to tipple.—*n* a drop, small quantity of liquid.

dreeplick, dreeplickie *n* a very small quantity of liquid.

dreet *same as* **drite**.

dreetle *v* to fall in drops or in small quantities.—*n* a small quantity of anything.

dreetlick, dreetlickie *n* very small quantity of any liquid.

dreetling *adj* slow, without energy.

dreeve *v* drove.

dreg¹ *n* a drag, brake.—*v* to drag.

dreg² *same as* **dirgie**.

dreg³ *n* **1** a very small quantity of spirits. **2** the refuse of the still from distilleries. **3** brewers' grains.

dreg-boat *n* **1** a boat or punt carrying a dredger or carrying away dredgings. **2** a track or canal boat drawn by a horse.

dreggle *same as* **draigle**.

dreggle *n* a small drop of any liquid.

dregg-salt *n* refuse salt.

dreggy *adj* **1** consisting of dreg (qv). **2** turbid.

dregie, dregy *same as* **dirgie**.

dregle *same as* **draigle**.

dreg-pot *n* a teapot.

dreg-tow *n* the rope attached to a dredging machine.

dreich¹ *same as* **droich**.

dreich², dreigh *adj* **1** slow. **2** tedious. **3** persistent, continuous. **4** tardy, dilatory. **5** slow in paying, beginning, ending, moving, etc. **6** close-fisted, hard in bargaining. **7** dreary. **8** dull. **9** wearisome. **10** *in phrs* **dreich i' the draw**, **dreich o' drawin** slow to act.

dreichlie *adv* slowly.

dreichness *n* **1** slowness. **2** tedium.

dreik *n* excrement.

dreip *same as* **dreep¹**.

dreipie *n* an inactive female.

dremur't *v, adj* **1** downcast. **2** dejected, rendered demure. *See* **drummure**.

dress *v* **1** to iron linen, clothes. **2** to scold, thrash. **3** to manure land. **4** to clean, rub down a horse. **5** to winnow grain.

dresser head *n* **1** the rack or shelf of a kitchen dresser. **2** the top of a kitchen dresser.

dressing *n* **1** weavers' paste. **2** a scolding, drubbing.

dret *n* voided excrement.—*v* to excrete.

dretch *v* **1** to go heavily and unwillingly. **2** to loiter, dawdle.

drib¹ *n* **1** a drop, small quantity of liquid. **2** a drizzling rain. **3** slaver. **4** (*in pl*) dregs.—*v* **1** to drip. **2** to draw the last milk from a cow.

drib² *v* **1** to beat, scold, punish. **2** to drub.

dribbing *n* a beating, a scolding.

dribbings *n* the last milk drawn from a cow.

dribbit *n* a small quantity of anything.

dribble *v* **1** to drizzle. **2** to tipple.—*n* **1** a drop, small quantity of liquid. **2** drizzling rain. **3** (*in pl*) dregs.

dribble-beards *n* long strips of cabbage in broth.

dribbler *n* a tippler.

dribblick, dribblickie *n* a very small quantity of liquid.

dribbling *n* **1** the dropping of liquid. **2** (*in pl*) the dregs or droppings of a liquid. **3** the last milk drawn from a cow. —*v, adj* **1** tippling. **2** drizzling.

dribloch *n* **1** a small quantity of anything. **2** a trifle. **3** a thing of no value.

dribs *n* dribblings

dridder *same as* **dreddour**.

driddle *v* **1** to dawdle, to potter about a thing. **2** to let fall in small quantities, to spill carelessly. **3** to urinate in small quantities.

driddler *n* an idler at his work, loiterer.

driddles *n* **1** the buttocks. **2** the intestines of an animal slain for food.

driddlins *n* meal forming small lumps in water.

drider *same as* **dreadour**.

drie *same as* **dree**.

driech *same as* **dreich**².

drieshach *n* **1** a bright, blazing fire. **2** the red glow of a peat fire.

drieve *v* drove.

driffle *n* **1** a drizzling rain. **2** a short period of storm. **3** a scolding. **4** anything that urges one to action. **5** a large quantity of work done speedily. —*v* to drizzle.

driffling *n* small rain.

drift *n* **1** a drove of cattle, etc. **2** a flock of birds. **3** snow, etc, driven by wind. **4** a set of fishing nets. **5** delay.—*v* **1** to delay, put off. **2** to let anything slide gently through the fingers. **3** (*used of snow*) to be driven by the wind. **4** *phr* **drift time** to put off time.

drifter *n* a steam trawler.

driftline *n* a rope to which smuggled kegs of spirit were attached and sunk a few feet below the surface of the sea by sufficient weights.

drifty *adj* abounding in driving snow.

drill *same as* **dreel**.

drily *adj* (*used of the weather*) fine, not rainy.

drimuck *same as* **drammach**.

dring¹ *v* **1** to roll, drive forward. **2** to press tightly, to suffocate by strangling.—*n* a close-fisted person, a miser.

dring², **dringe** *v* **1** to linger, loiter. **2** to sing slowly and lugubriously. **3** (*used of a kettle*) to sound before boiling.—*n* the noise of a kettle before boiling.—*adj* dilatory, slow.

dringing *n* suffocation by strangulation.

dringing *v, adj* dawdling.

dringle *v* to be slow, dilatory.

drink¹ *v* **1** (*with* in) to shrink, become shorter, used of the shortening day. **2** (*with* out) to drink off. **3** (*with* one) to drink a health.

drink² *n* a lanky, overgrown person.

drink-siller *n* **1** drink-money. **2** a perquisite, tip, used figuratively.

drinking-sowens *n* flummery (qv), thin enough for drinking, generally with treacle or sugar and butter as a relish.

drins *n* drops of water.

drint *v* (*used of birds*) **1** to sing. **2** to chirp.

dripple *same as* **dreeple**.

drite *v* to void excrement.—*n* excrement.

drither *same as* **dreadour**.

drive *n* **1** (*used of time*) to delay, prolong. **2** to hurry. **3** to throw with force. **4** to pile up in a heap. **5** to float ashore.—*n* **1** a push, shove. **2** a heavy blow.

driver *n* a curling stone forcibly driven.

drizzen *v* **1** to low plaintively, as a cow or ox. **2** to grumble, as a sluggard over his work.—*n* the low, plaintive sound of a cow wanting food.

drizzle, drizel *v* **1** to let fall slowly in small quantities. **2** to walk slowly.—*n* the scanty water in a stream that does not seem to run.

drizzling *n* slaver.

drob *v* to prick with a needle, thorn, etc.—*n* a thorn, prickle.

droch *same as* **droich**.

drochle¹ *v* **1** to walk with short, uneven steps. **2** to stagger. **3** to dawdle.

drochle² *n* a puny person.

drochle³ *n* a short, stout person.

drochlin *adj* **1** puny. **2** lazy. **3** wheezing.—*n* a staggering.

drocht *n* **1** a drought. **2** thirst. **3** dryness.

drod¹ *n* a short, thick, clubbish person.

drod² *n* a rough candle-holder used in visiting farm offices at night.

droddum, drodum *n* the breech.

droddum-skelpin' *n* and *adj* whipping on the breech.

droddy bottle *n* a private bottle into which the liquor formerly given profusely at funerals instead of being consumed at the service could be poured to be taken home or taken outside.

drodge *v* to do servile work, drudge.—*n* a person always behind with his or her work.

drodlich *n* a useless mass.

drods *n* **1** the pet. **2** ill-humour.

drog¹ *n* a drug.—*v* **1** to drug. **2** to take drugs.

drog² *n* a buoy attached to the end of a harpoon line, when the whale runs it out.

drogat, drogget, droggit, drogit *n* **1** a coarse woollen cloth used for women's gowns. **2** a cloth made of a mixture of flax and wool.

drogester *n* a druggist.

droggie, droggist *n* a druggist.

droghle *same as* **drochle**.

droghlin *same as* **drochlin**.

drogue *same as* **drog**¹.

droich *n* **1** a dwarf. **2** a short, unwieldy person.

droichan *n* **1** any small living animal. **2** a term of reproach.

droichle *n* a stout, dumpy person or animal.

droichy *adj* dwarfish.

droke *same as* **drouk**.

drokin *n* a drenching.

droll *n* **1** a droll person. **2** humour, oddity, eccentricity. **3** a droll story or saying.—*v* to joke.—*adj* unusual, strange.

drollich *n* a short, strange-looking woman.

drollity *n* **1** a curiosity. **2** a curio. **3** an unusual thing.

dronach *n* penalty.

drone¹ *n* **1** a dull, drawling speaker. **2** the lowest boy in a class at school. **3** the low plaintive sound made by a hungry cow. **4** the bass pipe of a bagpipe.—*v* **1** to drawl. **2** to sing in a low, monotonous voice. **3** to play the bagpipe. **4** (*used of a cow*) to moan plaintively.

drone² *n* the breech, backside.

drone-brat *n* an apron formerly worn behind.

droner *n* **1** a player on the bagpipe. **2** a bumblebee.

drony *adj* slow, sluggish.—*v* to doze, slumber.

droochle *v* to drench.

droochlet-like *adj* looking as if drenched.

droog¹ *v* to tug, drag at.—*n* a rough pull.

droog², **droogle** *v* to do dirty, heavy work.

drook *same as* **drouk**.

drookit-oxter *n* a good dowry.

drool v to trill, cry mournfully.

droon v to drown.

droonyie v to moan, complain mournfully.—n **1** a droning song. **2** the moaning of cattle. **3** the wail of a child when ceasing to cry.

droop adj **1** dripping. **2** dropping. **3** drooping.

droopit adj **1** weakly, infirm. **2** drooping.

droop-rumplet adj (used of horses) drooping at the crupper.

drooth same as **drouth**.

dropper n a sudden disappointment.

dropping, droppy adj (used of the weather) showery, wet.

drop-ripe adj **1** dead-ripe. **2** quite prepared.

dross n coal or peat dust.

drossy adj (of a gross habit) indicating an unwholesome temperament or a bad constitution.

drotch v to dangle.

drotchell n **1** an idle wench. **2** a sluggard.

drotes n a derisive term for uppish yeomen.

drouble v to bellow, as the hart for the doe.

droud n **1** a cod fish. **2** a herring hake. **3** a heavy, lumpish person. **4** a worthless female. **5** a wattled sort of box for catching herrings.

drouk v to drench, soak.—n **1** a drenching, soaking, a soaked condition. **2** oatmeal mixed with water.

droukitness n the state of being drenched.

drouky adj wet, drenching.

droul n in phr **in dust and droul** in dust and ashes.

droup-rumpl't same as **droop-rumplet**.

drouth n **1** drought. **2** a period of fine, drying weather. **3** thirst, dryness. **4** a thirsty person. **5** a drunkard, a tippler.

drouthielie adv thirstily.

drouthiesome adj given to drink.

drouthiesomeness n addiction to drink.

drouthy adj **1** thirsty. **2** dry, parching. **3** craving for drink.— n **1** a thirsty person. **2** a heavy drinker.

drove¹ v **1** to drive cattle and sheep. **2** to come in droves.— n a road used for driving cattle.

drove² n a broad chisel, the broadest iron used by masons in hewing stones.—v **1** to hew stones for building by means of a drove. **2** to drive horizontal lines on the face of the stone with a drove.

drove road n one of a number of tracks over which cattle or sheep were driven from the Highlands to markets in the the Lowlands or in England.

drove-sail n a sail hanging under water to hinder the too rapid motion of a dogger when fishing.

droving n cattle-driving.

drow¹ n **1** a fit of illness. **2** a swoon. **3** a qualm of anxiety.

drow² n **1** a cold, damp mist. **2** a cloud, shower, squall. **3** a haar (qv).—v (with **on**) to gather in a thick, wet mist.

drow³ n **1** a melancholy sound. **2** a wail. **3** the distant noise of breaking waves.

drow⁴ n a very small quantity of fluid, a drop.

drowie adj moist, misty.

drown v **1** to dilute with too much water, etc. **2** to flood. **3** to be drowned. **4** used in expletives or as a strong appeal.

drowper n one who gives way to dejection.

drowsying n sleepiness, drowsiness.

drowth same as **drouth**.

drub¹ v to beat the ground, trudge, tramp.

drub² v to scold.

drubbing n a scolding.

drubbly adj **1** muddy. **2** turbid. **3** dark.

drucht n **1** drought. **2** a season of drought.

druchty adj (used of the weather) droughty, drying. —n dry weather.

drucken v drunk, having drunk.—adj drunken.

drucken-bite n food of a kind to encourage drinking liquor.

drucken-groat n **1** a fine for drunkenness. **2** money paid for drink at a penny wedding. **3** a tippler's expenditure for drink.

druckensum adj **1** drunken. **2** given to drink.

drudging box n a flour box, dredger.

druffy adj **1** dull, downcast. **2** dispirited.

drug n a tug, a violent pull.—v to pull, tug.—adj **1** slow, dull, dragging heavily. **2** (used of ice) moist, not keen, making curling stones go heavily.

drug-saw n a cross-cut saw.

druidle, druitle same as **druttle**.

druin same as **drune**.

druitlin' n dawdling, wasting time.

druken, drukken same as drucken.

drule¹ n the goal which players strive to reach.

drule² n **1** a sluggard, a lazy person. **2** a stupid person.

drulie adj **1** muddy. **2** thick. **3** muddled.

drulie-heidit adj **1** thick-headed. **2** muddled in the head.

drulled adj **1** stupid. **2** clumsy.

drult same as **drulled**.

drum¹ n the drum-shaped part of a threshing mill. —v **1** to repeat monotonously. **2** to pore over wearily.

drum² n a knoll, ridge, hill.

drum³ same as **dram²**.

drumble¹, drumle v **1** to make muddy. **2** to raise disturbance. **3** to confuse. **4** to bedim.—n mud, etc, raised by troubling water, etc.

drumble² v **1** to move sluggishly. **2** to murmur, to maunder.

drumbling adj **1** muddy. **2** turbid.

drumlie-droits, --drutshocks n blackberries.

drumlieness n **1** muddiness. **2** confusion. **3** obscurity.

drumly adj **1** thick. **2** turbid. **3** muddy. **4** gloomy. **5** confused as to mind. **6** troubled. **7** sullen.

drumly-voiced adj rough-, hoarse-voiced.

drum-major n a virago, a masculine woman.

drummel same as **drumble¹**.

drummel'd v, adj stupefied, muddled.

drummock same as **drammach**.

drummoolich adj melancholy, in low spirits.

drummure adj **1** demure. **2** grave, serious. **3** sad

drummy land n wet land of gentle curve and with a sub-soil of till.

drums n curved wet lands.

drumshorlin adj sulky, pettish.

drumster n a drummer.

drune n **1** the murmuring sound made by cattle. **2** a slow, drawling tune. **3** the termination of child's crying after a whipping.—v **1** to low in a hollow or depressed tone. **2** to complain.

drunk n **1** a drinking bout. **2** a drunk person.

drunken adj shrunken.

drunken-fu' adj quite drunk.

drunkensome adj given to drinking.

drunkilie adv merrily, as with drink.

drunt¹ n ill-humour, a pet, sulk.—v to sulk.

drunt² same as **drant**.

drunyie same as **drune**.

drury n a dowry.

druschoch n **1** any liquid food of a heterogeneous composition and nauseous appearance. **2** a compound drink. **3** a mixture of various drugs.

drush n **1** dross, scum, refuse. **2** fragments. **3** peat dust. **4** peat broken small.—v **1** to crush, crumble. **2** to spoil. **3** to go wrong.

drussie adj drowsy.

drute n a lazy, slovenly, unfeeling person.

druther same as **dreadour**.

drutle v (used of a horse or dog) to stop frequently on its way to eject a small quantity of dung.

druttle v **1** to be slow in movement. **2** to dawdle. **3** to waste time.—n a useless, good-for-nothing person.

dry adj **1** thirsty. **2** (used of a cow) having ceased to give milk. **3** reserved and stiff in manner, not affable.—n **1** a division in a stone where it can be parted. **2** a flaw.—v to make cows go dry.

dry-braxy n inflammation in the bowels of sheep.

dry-darn n costiveness in cattle.

dry dyke *n* a wall built wthout mortar.
dry-dyker *n* a builder of dry dykes.
dry-farrand *adj* frigid in manner, not affable.
dry-gair-flow *n* the place where two hills meet and form a bosom.
dry-goose *n* a handful of the finest meal pressed very close together, dipped in water and then roasted.
dry-haired *adj* cold in manner, not affable.
dry-handed *adj* without weapons.
drylander *n* one who lives on dry land, neither aquatic nor amphibious.
dryland sailor *n* a sham sailor, a tramp professing to be a sailor.
dry-like *adv* **1** with some reserve. **2** without frankness.
dryll *v* to waste time.
dry lodgings *n* lodgings without board.
dry-mou'd *adj* not drinking while others drink.
dry multures *n* corn paid to a mill whether the payer grinds at it or not.
dryness *n* **1** reserve in manner. **2** want of affection. **3** a coolness between friends.
dry nieves *n* bare hands in fisticuffs.
dry seat *n* a close stool.
dry siller *n* **1** hard cash, ready money. **2** money laid past.
drysome *adj* **1** tasteless. **2** insipid. **3** tedious. **4** uninteresting.
drystane dyke *n* a wall built without mortar.
dryster *n* one who has charge of drying grain in a kiln or cloth at a bleach field.
dry stool *n* a close stool.
dry talk *n* an agreement made without drinking and therefore not binding.
dryte *same as* **drite**.
dry tea *n* tea without bread, etc.
dryward *adj* **1** rather dry. **2** dull, prosy.
duan *n* **1** the division of a poem, a canto. **2** poem, song.
dub *n* **1** a small pool of water. **2** a puddle. **3** a gutter. **4** (*in pl*) mud.—*v* to cover with mud, bedaub.
dubback *n* a game at marbles in which the pitcher is forcibly thrown at the others.
dubbin *n* a mixture of tallow and oil for softening leather and preventing boots, etc, from getting wet.
dubbit *adj* mud-stained.
dubble *n* mud, dirt, etc.
dubby *adj* **1** abounding in puddles. **2** muddy, wet, dirty.
dubie *adj* doubtful.
dubish *adj* suspicious, jealous.
dub-skelper *n* **1** one who goes his way regardless of mud and puddles. **2** a rambling fellow. **3** used ludicrously of a young bank clerk whose duty it is to run about giving notice that bills are due.
dub-water *n* muddy water, water from a puddle.
ducadoon *n* a ducatoon, worth £3, 10s. Scots.
duchal *n* an act of gormandizing.
duchas *n* **1** the ancestral seat. **2** the holding of land in one's birthplace or family estate.
ducht, dught *v* could.
duchtna *v neg* could not.
duchty *same as* **dochty**.
duck[1] *n* a term of endearment.
duck[2] *n* **1** a young people's game in which they try to knock off a small stone, or the duck, placed on a larger. **2** the boy in charge of the small stone.
duck dub *n* a duck pool.
ducker *n* the cormorant.
duckie *same as* **duck**[2].
duck-your-head *n* a boys' game.
dud[1] *n* a hare.
dud[2] *n* **1** a rag. **2** a soft, spiritless person. **3** (*in pl*) clothes. **4** dirty, shabby clothes.
dudder *v* **1** to shake, quiver, as a sail in the wind. **2** (*of the wind*) to be boisterous.
dudderon *n* **1** a person in rags. **2** a slut, sloven, lazy person.

duddie *n* a dish turned out of solid wood, with two ears and generally of octagonal form on the brim.
duddieheid *adj* wearing a short shawl round the head.
duddies *n* **1** rags. **2** garments.
duddiness *n* raggedness.
Duddingston-dinner *n* a sheep's head and haggis.
duddrie *n* a quarrel, wrangle.
duddry *adj* **1** disorderly. **2** rough, ill-shaken together.
duddy[1] *adj* ragged.
duddy[2] *same as* **doddy**[1].
dudgeon *n* a short clay pipe.
due *adj* indebted, owing.—*v* to owe money.
dufe[1], **duff**[1] *same as* **dowff**.
dufe[2], **duff**[2] *n* **1** dough. **2** the soft or spongy part of a loaf, cheese, turnip, etc. **3** a soft, spongy peat. **4** a blow with a soft body. **5** a hollow-sounding body. **6** a soft, silly fellow. **7** dry, decomposed moss used as litter.
duff *same as* **dufe**.
duffart, duffer *same as* **dowfart**.
duffie[1] *adj* blunt, round-pointed.
duffie[2] *adj* **1** soft, spongy. **2** foolish. **2** cowardly.
duffie *v* to lay a bottle on its side for a time, when its contents have been poured out, that it may be drained of what remains.
duffiness *n* sponginess.
duffing bout *n* a thumping, beating.
duff-mould *n* dry, decomposed peat, used as litter.
duff's luck *n* some special good fortune.
duffy *adj* **1** powdery, used of coal that crumbles when struck by the poker. **2** soft, spongy. **3** stupid.—*n* a soft, silly fellow.
dugget *n* cloth thickened and toughened by shrinking.
dugind *adj* wilful, obstinate.
dugon *n* contemptuous expression for a poor, weak fellow.
duil *same as* **dool**[5].
duke[1] *n* a duck.
duke[2] *same as* **douk**[2].
duke-ma-lordie *n* a nobleman.
dukery-packery *n* trickery.
duke's-meat *n* the lesser duckweed.
dulbart *n* **1** a heavy, stupid person. **2** a blockhead.
dulder *n* anything large.
dulderdum *adj* **1** confused by argument. **2** in a stupor.
duldie *n* **1** anything large. **2** a large piece of bread, meat, etc.
dule *same as* **dool**.
dulenee *int* alas!
duless *same as* **dowless**.
dule-tree *same as* **dool-tree**.
dulget *n* a small bundle or lump.
dull *adj* deaf, hard of hearing.—*v* (*with* **down**) to pass out of mind or memory.
dullion *n* **1** a large piece. **2** a large, thick bannock of oat or barley meal.
dullyeart *adj* of a dirty, dull colour.
dulse *v* to make dim.—*adj* dull, heavy.
dulse-man *n* a male seller of dulse.
dulser-wife *n* a dulse-gatherer or seller. **2** an untidy woman.
dulshet *same as* **dulget**.
dult, dults *n* a dolt, dunce.
dultish *adj* stupid, doltish.
dumb *adj* (*used of windows*) built up and painted outside to resemble glazed windows.
Dumbarton-youth *n* a person over thirty-six years of age, generally applied to a woman.
dumb-chaser *n* an imperfectly developed ram.
dumfooert *adj* bewildered, speechless
dumbfounder, dumfooner, ~founer, ~funer *v* **1** to dumfound, stun, stupefy by a blow or an argument. **2** to amaze.
dumbfoundered *v, adj* amazed, perplexed.
dumbfounderedly *adv* amazedly, in perplexity.
dumbfounderment *n* amazement, bewilderment, confusion.
dumbie *same as* **dummy**.

dumbnut *n* a nut with no kernel.
dumb-swaul *n* a long, noiseless sea swell in calm, windless weather.
dumfoutter, dumfouther *v* 1 to bewilder. 2 to tease, make game of, annoy.
dummart *n* a blockhead.
dummy *n* 1 a dumb person. 2 one who is speechless. 3 a deaf mute.
dum-ned *n* a hard, continuous step in walking.
dump *v* 1 to set down heavily. 2 to throw down violently. 3 to thump, beat, kick. 4 to walk heavily, stump with short steps. 5 to strike with a marble the knuckles of the loser. 6 to depress the spirits.—*n* 1 a game of marbles played with holes in the ground. 2 a stroke on the knuckles with marbles. 3 a game in which the winner dumps the loser's knuckles. 4 a place in which rubbish, etc, is shot. 5 a blow, a bump. 6 a fit of the dumps.
dumpage *adj* 1 sad, melancholy. 2 *same as* **dumpish** (qv).
dumpeesed, dumpest *adj* stupid, dull, spiritless.
dumph *n* a dull, stupid person.—*adj* dull, stupid.
dumpiness *n* 1 the state of being short and thick. 2 shortness.
dumpish *v* to depress, make despondent.
dumple[1] *n* 1 a quantity, bundle. 2 a lump.
dumple[2] *n* a breakage.
dumpling *n* 1 a lump of oatmeal and suet boiled in broth. 2 a type of rich boiled fruit pudding, often wrapped in a cloth while cooking and called a **clootie dumpling**.
dumps[1] *n* mournful tunes.
dumps[2] *n* a series of bangs on the back, one for each year of life, administered to a child by schoolmates on the occasion of his or her birthday.
dumpy *n* a short, thickset person.—*adj* (*used of cloth*) coarse and thick.
dumscum *n* a children's game, like beds.
dum-tam *n* a bunch of clothes on a beggar's back under his coat.
dun[1] *n* 1 a hill. 2 a hill fort.
dun[2] *v* 1 to beat, thump. 2 to stun with noise.
Dunbar-wedder *n* a salted herring.
dun bird *n* the female pochard.
dunch[1] *v* 1 to push, jog, bump, knock about. 2 to butt with the head.—*n* 1 a thrust, nudge, bump. 2 a butt, push, a knock-down blow by a bull.
dunch[2] *n* 1 a bundle or truss of rags, straw, etc. 2 one who is short and thick.
dunchin'-bull *n* a hornless bull that butts with its head.
dunchy *adj* short, squat.
dunckle, duncle *same as* **dunkle**.
dundee, dundeerie *n* a great noise of people quarrelling in earnest or in fun.
dunder *v* to rumble, give a thundering, reverberating sound.—*n* 1 a loud noise like thunder. 2 a reverberation.
dunder-clunk *n* a big, stupid person.
dunderhead *n* a blockhead.
dunderheaded *adj* dull, stupid.
dundiefeckan *same as* **dandiefechun**.
dune *v, adj* 1 done. 2 exhausted.
dung *v, adj* 1 beaten, defeated. 2 overcome with fatigue. 3 dejected.
dung a-smash *adj* beaten to powder.
dung-by *adj* confined by illness.
dunge *v* 1 to nudge. 2 to push. 3 to butt.
dungel *n* a blow.
dungeon *n in phr* **dungeon of wit** a profound intellect.
dungflee *n* a fly that feeds on excrement.
duniwassal, dunniewassal *n* 1 a Highland gentleman. 2 used contemptuously of the lower class of farmers.
dunk *adj* damp.—*n* a mouldy dampness.
dunkle *n* 1 a dint caused by a blow or fall. 2 a dimple.—*v* 1 to indent, make a hollow or depression, to damage by dinting. 2 to injure one's character.
dunner *same as* **dunder**.
dunnerhead *same as* **dunderhead**.

dunnerheadit *same as* **dunderheaded**.
dunnerin *n* 1 a loud, thundering sound. 2 a reverberating sound.
dunnerin brae *n* a brae (qv) that gives forth a rumbling sound when a vehicle drives over it.
dunnie *n* a mischievous sprite.
dunniewassal *same as* **duniwassal**.
dunsch[1], **dunsh, dunse** *same as* **dunch**[1].
dunsch[2] *same as* **dunch**[2]
dunshach *n* 1 a heavy, soft blow. 2 a big, untidy bundle.
dunsheugh *n* a nudge.
dunshing *n* the act of pushing, nudging, butting.
dunt[1] *n* 1 a heavy blow or knock. 2 a blow causing a dull sound. 3 the sound of a hard body falling. 4 a heavy fall. 5 a thump. 6 throb, palpitation of the heart. 7 a gibe. 8 a slanderous lie.—*v* 1 to beat. 2 to fall heavily. 3 to throb, palpitate. 4 (*with* out) to drive out with repeated strokes. 5 to settle a question or dispute. 6 to indent by striking. 7 to shake together the contents of a sack, etc, by striking it on the ground.—*phr* **done and duntit on** quite done for.
dunt[2] *n* a large piece of anything.
dunt-about *n* 1 a piece of wood driven about at shinty or like games. 2 anything knocked about in common use as of little value. 3 a servant who is roughly treated and is driven about from one piece of work to another.
dunter[1] *n* a porpoise.
dunter[2] *n* a fuller of blankets, cloth, etc.
dunter goose *n* the eider-duck.
dunting *n* a continuous beating, causing a hollow sound.
dunting-case *n* a prostitute.
dunty *n* a doxy (qv), paramour.
dunyel *v* to jolt with a hollow sound.
dunze *adv* extremely.
duosie *adj* obedient, docile.
duplickin *n* a duplicate.
duply *n* a defender's rejoinder to a pursuer's reply. —*v* to make a rejoinder.
durdam,-den,-don,-drum,-dum *same as* **dirdum**.
dure[1] *n* a door.
dure[2] *same as* **dour**[1].
durg *same as* **darg**[1].
durgin, durgon *n* a big, ill-tempered person.
durgy *adj* 1 thick, gross. 2 short, thickset.
durk[1] *n* a dagger, dirk.—*v* 1 to stab with a dagger. 2 to spoil, ruin.
durk[2] *n* 1 a short, thickset person. 2 anything short, thick and strong.—*adj* thickset, strongly made.
durken on *v* to become discouraged.
durkin *n* 1 a short, thickset person. 2 anything short, thick and strong.
durnal *v* (*used of the cheeks*) to move when a flabby person runs or walks very fast.
durr *same as* **dirr**[1].
durs *v* dared.
dursie *adj* 1 obdurate. 2 hard-hearted.
dush *v* 1 to move with force and speed. 2 to butt, push forcibly, thrust. 3 to strike.—*n* a blow, push, stroke.
dushill *n* an untidy female worker.—*v* to disgust with slovenliness.
dusht[1] *same as* **doosht**.
dusht[2] *adj* 1 struck dumb, silenced. 2 silent.
dusk *v* to dim, shadow, darken.
dusk-maill *n* peat rent.
dust *n* 1 chaff. 2 husks of oats. 3 blacksmiths' small coal. 4 a disturbance, uproar. 5 money.—*v* 1 to beat, thrash. 2 to raise a disturbance.
dustyfoot, dustifit *n* 1 a homeless tramp. 2 a pedlar.
dusty-melder, ~-meiller *n* 1 the last meal made from the crop of one year. 2 the end of life. 3 the last child born in a family.
dusty-miller *n* the common auricula.
dut *n* a stupid fellow.
dutch *n* tobacco from Holland.

Dutch admiral *n* a kind of garden flower.

Dutch-plaise *n* the fish, *Pleuronectes platessa*.

Dutch-pound *n* a weight of 28 ounces.

Dutch-splay *n* a hem seam, one side of which alone is sewn.

dute, dutt *v* to doze, slumber.

duthe *adj* 1 substantial. 2 efficient. 3 nourishing.

duty multure *n* a yearly duty paid to the landlord in money or grain whether the tenant ground his corn at the mill or not.

dux *n* the pupil who achieves the greatest academic success in a school or class.

duxy *same as* **doxie**.

dwab *adj* feeble.

dwable, dwabil *adj* 1 flexible, limber. 2 weak, feeble. 3 loose, shaky.—*n* 1 a weak, overgrown person. 2 anything long, flexible and so weak.—*v* to walk feebly or with faltering steps.

dwably *adj* feeble, shaky, infirm.

dwadle *v* 1 to dawdle, lounge. 2 to waste time.

dwaffil *adj* 1 weak, pliable. 2 not stiff or firm.

dwaible *same as* **dwable**.

dwaibly *same as* **dwably**.

dwall *v* to dwell.

dwallion *n* a dwelling.

dwam, dwalm *n* a swoon, qualm, fit of illness.—*v* 1 to faint, fall ill. 2 to decline in health.

dwaminess *n* faintness.

dwaming *n* the fading of light.

dwaming fit *n* a fainting fit.

dwamish *adj* faint, like to faint.

dwamle, dwamel *v* to faint, to look like fainting. —*n* a short swoon, a fit of illness.

dwamlock *n* a very sickly person.

dwamy[1] *adj* 1 like to faint. 2 languid, sickly.

dwamy[2] *v* 1 to oppress with labour, harass, overcome. 2 to toil. 3 to bear or draw a load unequally.—*n* 1 oppressive toil. 2 a rough shake or throw. 3 a large iron lever or turnkey for raising stones or screwing nuts for bolts. 4 a stout bar of wood used by carters for tightening ropes. 5 (*in pl*) transverse pieces of wood between joists to strengthen a floor and prevent swinging.

dwannie *adj* weak, sickly.

dwaub *n* a feeble person.

dwaum, dwawm *same as* **dwam**.

dweable *same as* **dwable**.

dwebble, dweble, dweeble, dwebel *same as* **dwable**.

dwibly *same as* **dwably**.

dwine *v* 1 to waste away, languish, decline in health. 2 to fade away, decay, gradually disappear. 3 to cause to consume or dwindle, used in imprecations.—*n* 1 a decline. 2 the waning of the moon.

dwingle *v* to loiter, tarry.

dwining *n* 1 a wasting illness, consumption. 2 a fading, dwindling. 3 the waning of the moon.

dwinnil *v* 1 to dwindle. 2 to pine away. 3 to waste gradually. 4 to degenerate. 5 (*with* **out**) to cozen, deprive of by cheating, etc.

dwiny *adj* 1 puny, sickly. 2 ill-thriven.

dwybal, dwyble *same as* **dwable**.

dwybe *same as* **dwaub**.

dwyne *same as* **dwine**.

dyb *same as* **dub**.

dyed-i'-the-woo *phr* naturally clever.

dyester *same as* **dyster**.

dyet[1] *n* a meal, diet.

dyet[2] *same as* **diet**.

dyke *same as* **dike**.

dyke-slouch, ~-sheuch *n* a ditch or open drain at the bottom of a dike (qv).

dykey *n* a game of marbles.

dyled, dylt *same as* **doilt**.

dymmond *same as* **dinmont**.

dyn *n* din.

dyoch *n* a drink.

dyod *same as* **dod**[2].

dyow *n* dew.

dyper *v* 1 to decorate, adorn. 2 to dress well or beautifully.

dyrll *same as* **dirl**.

dyse *int* used as an imprecation for damn.

dyst *same as* **doist**.

dyster *same as* **doister**.

dyster *n* a dyer.

dyte *same as* **doit**.

dytit *same as* **doited**.

dytter *same as* **doiter**.

dyuck *n* a duck.

dyvour, dyver, dyvor *n* 1 a debtor, bankrupt, ne'er-do-weel. 2 a restless, troublesome person.—*v* to impoverish, make bankrupt.

dyvour's hose *n* stockings of different colours, formerly worn by those guilty of fraudulent bankruptcy.

E

e' *pron* you.

ea *adj* one.

each[1] *n* a horse.

each[2] *n* an adze.

eag *v* 1 to egg on. 2 to incite to mischief.

eak *same as* **eik**.

ealie *int* alas! an exclamation of woe.

ealins *same as* **eeldins**.

eam *same as* **eme**.

ean[1] *adj* one.

ean[2] *n* a one-year-old horse.

eanarnich *n* 1 a strong soup. 2 flesh juice.

eance *adv* once.

eand *v* to breathe.—*n* breath.

ear[1] *n* a kidney.

ear[2] *v* to plough or till land.

ear[3] *adv* early.

'ear-aul *n* a yearling heifer.

eard *n* 1 earth. 2 unploughed land. 3 one ploughing or furrow.—*v* 1 to bury. 2 to cover with earth for protection against frost, etc. 3 to knock violently to the ground.

eard bark *n* the roots of tormentil, used for tanning.

eard-din *n* 1 thunder. 2 thunder in the earth. 3 an earthquake.

eard-drift *n* snow or hail driven off from the surface of the earth by the force of the wind.

eard-eldin *n* fuel of peat or earth.

eard-fast *adj* deep-rooted in the earth.—*n* a stone or boulder firmly fixed in the earth

eard house *n* a subterraneous house of dug stones, roofed with large stones.

eard hunger *n* 1 eagerness for land. 2 the eagerness for food sometimes shown by the dying.

eard-hungry *adj* ravenously hungry.

eard meal *n* churchyard soil.

eard swine *n* a frightful beast supposed to haunt graveyards and batten on corpses.

eard-titling *n* the meadow pipit.

earest *adv* especially.

eariewig *n* an earwig

earl *v* to fix a bargain or engagement by paying an earnest.

earl-duck *n* the red-breasted merganser.

ear-leather *n* the loin strap, passing through the crupper and over the kidneys of a horse.

ear-leather-pin *n* an iron pin for fastening the chain by which a horse draws a cart.

earm *v* **1** to whine, complain fretfully. **2** to chirp as a bird.

earn[1] *n* the eagle.

earn[2] *v* **1** to coagulate. **2** to curdle milk with rennet, etc.

earn-bleater, ~-bliter *n* **1** the snipe. **2** the curlew.

earnest *n* a game of marbles in which they are staked.

earning *n* rennet.

earnin' grass *n* the common butterwort.

ear-nit *n* the pignut.

earock *n* a hen of the first year.

earth *n* one ploughing of land.—*v* to protect with earth.

earthlins *adv* **1** earthwards. **2** along the ground.

ease *v* to slacken, abate.—*n* (*with* **up**) a hoist, a lifting up.

easedom *n* relief from pain, comfort.

easel *same as* **eassel**.

easenent *n* a motion of the bowels, an evacuation.

easening *adj* feeling desire. *See* **eassin**.

easer *n* maple wood.

easing *n* **1** the eaves of a house. **2** the part of a stack where it begins to taper.

easing-butt *n* a water butt into which the droppings from the easing (qv) are led.

easing-drap *n* **1** the protection of a house roof that carries off the drops. **2** the dropping water from a roof after rain.

easing-gang *n* a course of sheaves projecting a little at the easing (qv) of a stack, to keep the rain from getting in.

easing water *n* water draining from the easing (qv) of a house.

easle *n* the eaves of a house.

eassel, eassil, eassilt *adv* eastwards, in an easterly direction.—*adj* easterly.

easselward *adv* towards the east.

eassin *v* **1** (*used of a cow*) to desire the bull. **2** to desire strongly.

eassint *adj* having taken the bull.

east-bye *adv* eastward.

easter *adj* eastern, towards the east.—*n* the east wind.

easter-side *n* the eastern side.

eastie-wastie *n* a vacillating person.

eastilt *adv* eastward.

eastin *same as* **eisin**.

eastland *n* the countries bordering on the Baltic. —*adj* belonging to the east.

eastle *adv* eastward.

eastlin *adj* easterly, east.

eastlins *adv* eastward.

eastning-wort *n* scabious.

easy *adj* **1** supple, free from stiffness. **2** moderate in price.—*adv* easily.

easy-oasy *same as* **easy-osy**.

easy-osy, ~-ozy *adj* easy-going.—*n* an easy-going person.

eat[1] *v* to taste.—*n* **1** the act of eating. **2** a feed, a feast. **3** taste.

eat[2] *v in phr* **eat oneself** to be much vexed.

eatche *same as* **each**[2].

eated, eatit *v* ate.

eaten and spued *phr* used of an unhealthy, dyspeptic person.

eaten corn *n* growing corn partly eaten by trespassing domestic animals.

eather *n* heather.

eatin *n* the juniper.

eattocks *n* dainties, sweets.

eave *n* the nave of a cart or carriage wheel.

eazle *same as* **easle**.

ebb *adj* **1** (*used of vessels and their liquid contents*) shallow, not deep. **2** near the surface, not deep in the ground.—*n* the foreshore, the part of the beach between high and low tide.

ebb-bait *n* shellfish used by fishermen as bait.

ebb-fur *n* **1** a shallow furrow. **2** a method of ploughing down rye sown over dung.

ebb-land *n* shallow soil.

ebb-minded *adj* shallow, frivolous.

ebb-mother *n* the last of the ebb tide.

ebbness *n* shallowness.

ebb-sleeper *n* the dunlin.

ebbstone *n* a rock exposed at ebb tide.

eccle grass *n* the butterwort.

ech, echay *int* an exclamation of wistfulness or longing.

echie nor ochie *phr* absolutely nothing.

ech nor och *phr* not the smallest word or sound, neither one thing nor another.

echo-stone *n* a black, hard stone, full of holes and making them of a sound-returning nature.

echt[1] *v* owning, possessed of.

echt[2] *n* eight.

eckle-feckle *adj* **1** cheerful, merry. **2** possessing a shrewd judgment.

edder[1] *n* an adder.

edder[2] *conj* either.

edder[3] *same as* **ether**[1].

edder[4] *n* **1** an animal's udder. **2** a woman's breast.

edderin *same as* **etherin**.

edderins, edderins, edderon *conj* **1** either. **2** rather.

eddikat *adj* educated.

edge *n* **1** the ridge of a hill. **2** the summit of a range of hills. **3** the highest part of a large, moorish and elevated tract of ground which may lie between two streams.

edgie *v* to be alert or quick in action.—*adj* **1** eager. **2** clever. **3** quick-tempered, easily irritated.

Edinburgh rock *n* a kind of sweet consisting of light, hard sticks in a range of colours and flavours, made from sugar, water and cream of tartar.

ediwut *n* **1** an idiot. **2** a simpleton.

ee *pron* you.

e'e *n* **1** an eye. **2** an orifice for the passage or outflow of water. **3** an opening into a coal shaft. **4** a regard, liking. **5** desire, craving. **6** a darling, chief delight.—*v* **1** to eye. **2** (*used of liquids*) to ooze, well up.

eean *same as* **ean**.

e'ebree, e'ebroo *n* the eyebrow.

eebrek-crap *n* the third crop after lea.

eechie *n in phr* **eechie nor ochie, eechie or nochy** not a sound, nothing at all.

eeck *same as* **eik**[2].

eediwut *n* **1** an idiot. **2** a simpleton.

eedle-deedle *adj* easy-going in business, etc.—*n* **1** a man of little enterprise or energy. **2** an easy-going person. **3** a daydreamer.

eedle-doddle *same as* **eedle-deedle**.

e'e-feast *n* **1** a rarity. **2** what excites wonder. **3** a satisfying glance that gratifies curiosity.

eeghie nor oghie *phr* neither one thing nor another.

eejit *n* an idiot, a fool.

eek[1] *same as* **eik**[2].

eek[2] *same as* **eik**[1].

eekfow, eekfull *adj* **1** blithe. **2** affable. **3** just, equal. —*n* a match, an equal.

eeksy-peeksy, eeksie-peeksie *adj* **1** equal, exactly equal. **2** alike.

eel[1] *adj* (*used of cows*) ceasing to give milk.

eel[2] *n in phr* **nine e'ed eel** the lamprey.

eel[3] *n* oil.

Eel *n* Yule, Christmas.

eelans *same as* **eeldins**.

eelat *n* the fish myxine or glutinous hag.

eel-backit *adj* (*used of a horse*) having a dark stripe along the back.

eel-beds *n* the water crowfoot.

eeldins *n* equals in age.

eel-dolly *n* an old-fashioned oil lamp, a crusie.

eel-drowner *n* one who is not clever or capable of performing a difficult task.

Eel E'en *n* Christmas Eve.

eelie[1] *v* **1** to ail. **2** (*with* **away**) to dwindle.

eelie² *adj* oily.—*n* 1 oil. 2 a glazed earthenware marble.
eelie-dolly *n* an eel dolly (qv).
eelie-lamp *n* an oil lamp.
eelist *n* a desire to possess something not easily obtained.
e'e-list *n* 1 an eyesore. 2 defect. 3 a break in a page. 4 a legal imperfection. 5 a flaw, offence. 6 a cause of regret.
eel-pout *n* the viviparous blenny.
eel-tows *n* lines laid inshore to catch eels for bait.
eely *same as* ely.
eem *same as* eme.
eemock, eemuch *n* the ant.
eemor *n* humour.
eemost, eemist *adj* uppermost.
een¹ *adj and n* one.
een² *n* an oven
e'en¹ *n* eyes.
e'en² *n* even, evening.
e'en³ *adv* 1 even, even so. 2 nevertheless.
eenach *n* the natural grease of wool.
e'enbright *adj* shining, luminous.
eence *adv* once.
e'end *adj* even, straight.
eenerie *n* a child's word in counting-out rhymes.
e'en-holes *n* eye sockets.
eenil *same as* eyndill.
eenin *n* evening.
eenkin *n* kith and kin.
eenlins *same as* eeldins.
e'enow, e'ennow, e'enoo *adv* 1 just now. 2 shortly.
eens *adv* even as.
e'enshanks *n* an evening meal.
eent *adv* 'even it', used for emphasis.
eer *n* 1 colour, tinge. 2 an iron stain on linen.
eeram *n* a boat song, a rowing song.
eeran *same as* erran'.
eerie *adj* 1 apprehensive. 2 afraid of ghosts, etc. 3 dismal, dull, gloomy. 4 weird, uncanny. 5 haunted by ghosts, etc. 6 awe-inspiring. 7 dreary.
eerieful *adj* foreboding evil, uncanny.
eerielike *adj* appearing like what causes fear.
eeriely *adv* dismally, forebodingly.
eerieness *n* fear excited by the idea of an apparition.
eeries and orries *phr* 1 particulars, details. 2 ins and outs.
eeriesome *adj* 1 dull, sad. 2 ghostly, weird.
eeriesomeness *n* apprehensiveness of ghosts, etc.
e'erly *same as* everly.
eerock *same as* earock.
e'erthestreen *n* the night before yesternight.
eese *n* use.—*v* to use.
eesefu' *adj* useful.
eeseless *adj* useless.
eeset, eezet *adj* used, accustomed.
e'esicht *n* vision, eyesight.
eesk *v* 1 to hiccup. 2 to heave at the stomach. 3 to cough up.—*n* a hiccup.
e'esome *adj* attractive, gratifying to the eye.
e'estane *n* a perforated pebble, supposed to heal eye diseases.
e'estick *n* 1 something that fixes the eye. 2 a rarity, dainty.
e'e-string *n* an eyelid.
eeswall *adj* usual.
e'e-sweet *adj* 1 beautiful. 2 acceptable.
eet *n* a custom, a bad habit.
eeth *same as* eith.
eetim *n* 1 an item. 2 a puny creature.
eetion *n* a living creature.
eetnoch *n* a moss-grown, precipitous rock.
eettie *n* *in phr* eettie ottie for a tottie where shall this boy go? etc a boys' game.
eevenoo *adj* very hungry.
eever *adj* (*used of places*) upper, higher, over.
eevery *adj* hungry.
e'e-winkers *n* the eyelashes.
eezin *same as* easing.
efauld *adj* 1 upright, honest. 2 guileless.

eff-crap *v* to after-crop, to take two successive crops of the same kind from a field.
eff-~, eft-crop *n* 1 stubble grass. 2 aftermath.
effect *v* 1 (*used of money*) to secure, recover payment. 2 (*of lands*) to make them bear the burden of repayment of money with which they have been burdened.—*n pl* produce of anything sold or of money invested.
effeir¹ *n* 1 pomp and circumstance. 2 what is fitting. 3 bearing. 4 garb, panoply.
effeir² *v* 1 to pertain to. 2 to fall to by right. 3 to be proportionate to.
effrayit *adj* afraid.
effront *v* to affront, put out of countenance.
efter *prep* after.—*adv* afterwards.
efter an' a' *phr* after all.
efter-hend, ~-hin' *prep* after.—*adv* afterwards.
efterin *prep* after.
eftername *n* a surname.
efternune, efternin *n* afternoon.
eftersting *n* 1 the after-sting, the pain that follows certain pleasures. 2 contrition. *See* afterstang.
efterwal *n* 1 leavings, refuse. 2 soil rendered useless for cultivation.
eft stool *n* a newt or lizard stool.
egal *adj* equal.
ege *same as* edge.
egeall *same as* egal.
egg *v* to incite.
egg-bed *n* 1 the ovarium of a fowl. 2 (*used of the brain*) where thought arises in the mind.
egg-doup *n* 1 the lower end of an egg. 2 a woman's cap with oval back.
egg-doupit *adj* shaped like the end of an egg.
egger, egges *n* grain very much dried in a pot, for grinding in a quern (*qv*).
eggie *n* a small bird's egg.
eggle *v* 1 to egg on. 2 to incite to mischief or evil.
egg taggle *n* 1 wasting time in bad company. 2 immodest conduct.
eghin and owin *phr* humming and hawing.
eght *v* owning, possessed of.
egsome *adj* pushing, forward.
Egypt-~, Egyptian-herring *n* the saury pike.
Egyptian *n* 1 a gypsy, vagabond. 2 a sturdy beggar.
Egyptian band *n* gypsies.
eicen *v* (*used of a cow*) to desire the bull.
eidence *n* 1 industry. 2 diligence.
eident *adj* 1 industrious. 2 diligent. 3 steady, continuous. 4 attentive.
eidently *adv* 1 diligently. 2 attentively.
eidi-streen *n* the night before last night.
eidi-yesterday *n* the day before yesterday.
eight-part *n* an eighth.
eightpence drink *n* a very strong ale.
eightsome *adj* consisting of eight persons.—*n* a company or family of eight.
eightsome reel *n* a reel with eight dancers.
eik¹ *n* 1 the natural grease of wool. 2 liniment used in greasing sheep.
eik² *v* 1 to add. 2 to increase, supplement. 3 to subjoin.—*n* 1 an addition. 2 an addition to a glass of whisky, etc. 3 an addition to a beehive.—*adv* in addition to, besides, also.
eikend *n* the short chain attaching the traces to the swingletrees of a plough.
eik-name *n* 1 a name used among fishing folk to distinguish those who bear the same names. 2 a nickname.
eikrie *n* an addition to support or prolong anything.
eild¹ *adj* applicable to a cow that has ceased to give milk.
eild² *n* 1 age. 2 old age. 3 an old person.—*adj* aged, old.—*v* to grow old.
eilden *same as* elding.
eildins, eillins *same as* eeldins.
eildron *adj* unearthly, uncanny, weird, eldritch.

eill *adj* (*used of cows*) not giving milk.

ein' *v* to end, come to a close.

ein, eind *v* **1** to breathe. **2** to whisper. **3** to devise. **4** to make an appointment to meet.—*n* breath.

eindill, eindle *v* (*used of a woman*) to be jealous of her husband's fidelity.

eindling *adj* jealous.

eindown *adv* thoroughly.—*adj* **1** downright. **2** thoroughly honest. **3** plain, without reserve.

einel *v* to be jealous. *See* **eindill**.

eir *n* fear.

eirack *same as* **earock**.

eird *same as* **eard**.

eirne *same as* **ern**.

eiry *same as* **eerie**.

eisin[1] *same as* **eassin**.

eisin[2] *same as* **easing**.

eisning *n* **1** a strong desire or longing. **2** the copulation of a cow and a bull.

eissel *same as* **eassel**.

eistack *same as* **eestick**.

eistit *adv* rather.

eitch *same as* **each**[2].

eith *adj* easy.—*adv* easily.

eitheren *n* a straw rope for fastening the thatch of a stack, etc.

eitherens *same as* **edderins**.

eith-kent *adj* easily known or recognized.

eithly *adv* easily.

eiz *n* the eaves of a house

eizel[1] *n* an ass, a donkey.

eizel[2] *same as* **eyzle**.

eizen *same as* **easing**.

eke[1] *v* **1** to egg on, to incite. **2** to incite to mischief.

eke[2] *same as* **eik**[2].

elbock, elbuck *n* the elbow.—*v* to raise oneself on the elbows.

elbow chair *n* an armchair.

elbow-grease *n* snuff, brown rappee.

elbowit grass *n* the fox-tail grass.

elder[1] *n* an ordained member of the Presbyterian Church who has certain official duties.

elder[2] *n in phr* **elders o' Cowend [Colvend]** cormorants.

elderen, elderin, eldern *adj* elderly.

elder's hours *phr* respectable hours.

elding *n* fuel of any kind.

elding-docken *n* the water dock.

eldren, eldrin *adj* elderly.

eldrish, elrish *same as* **eldritch**.

eldritch, eldrich, eldricht *adj* **1** unearthly, ghostly, uncanny. **2** ghastly, frightful. **3** (*of a sore or wound*) painful, fretting. **4** (*of the weather*) chill. **5** surly in temper and manners.

eleck *v* to elect, choose.

eleid *same as* **elide**.

element *n* the sky.

elenge *adj* foreign.

elevener *n* a labourer's luncheon about 11 o'clock a.m.

eleven-hours *n* a slight refreshment about 11 o'clock a.m.

elf *n* a term of contempt or opprobrium.

elf-bore *n* a hole in a piece of wood, out of which a knot has been driven or has dropped.

elf-cups *n* small stones perforated by friction of a waterfall, supposed to be the work of fairies, often nailed over a stable door to protect horses from being elf-shot (qv).

elf-door *n* the opening in an elf-ring (qv) by which the fairies were supposed to enter.

elfer-stone *n* a chipped flint, believed to possess magical properties.

elf-girse *n* grass given to cattle supposed to have been hurt by fairies.

elf-hill *n* a fairy knoll.

elfin *n* **1** elf-land. **2** Hades.

elf-mill *n* the death watch.

elf-ring *n* a fairy circle within which elves were supposed to dance, etc, generally in old pasture.

elf-shoot *v* **1** to bewitch. **2** to shoot with an elf-arrow (qv).

elf-shot *n* **1** a flint arrowhead. **2** a disease or injury to persons or cattle, credited to fairy malice. **3** the lady's mantle.—*adj* shot or injured by fairies.

elfstone *n* a flint arrowhead.

elf-switches *n* **1** elf-locks. **2** tangled locks of hair.

elgins *n* the water dock.

elide *v* **1** (*used as a legal term*) to quash, annul. **2** to evade the force or authority of.

elison *same as* **elsin**.

ell[1] *adj* not giving milk.

ell[2] *n* a measure of length: the Scotch ell = 37.0578 inches, the plaiden ell = 38.416 inches.

ellan *n* a very small island in a river.

eller *n* the alder.

ellerisch *adj* unearthly.

ellieson *n* shoemaker's awl.

ellinge *same as* **elenge**.

ellion *same as* **elding**.

ell stick *n* **1** an ell measure. **2** a measuring rod.

ellwand *n* **1** an ell measure. **2** a measuring rod. **3** a standard.

ellwand of stars *n* **1** the three stars in the northern constellation of Lyra. **2** the king's *or* lady's ellwand the stars of Orion's belt.

elne *n* an ell.

elocate *adj* (*a legal term, used of a woman*) betrothed or wedded.

elore *int* alas! woe is me!

elrick, elricht, elritch *same as* **eldritch**.

else *adv* **1** otherwise. **2** at another time, already.—*phr* **or else no** an expression of contempt.

elsin, elshin *n* a shoemaker's awl.

elsin blade *n* an awl.

elsin box *n* a box for holding awls.

elsin-heft *n* **1** the handle of an awl. **2** a jar-gonelle pear, as resembling the heft of an awl.

elson, elsyn *same as* **elsin**.

elt *v* **1** to mix meal and water. **2** to knead dough. **3** to injure by constant or rough handling. **4** to toil or slave at working the ground. **5** to meddle with. **6** to bemire.—*n* dough. **2** (*with* **carrie**) a thick, ill-baked cake. **3** (*with* **muckle**) a stout, clumsy woman.

elvant, elvint *same as* **ellwand**.

ely *v* to disappear, vanish gradually or one by one.

elyer *n* an elder.

elymosinar *n* an almoner.

embase *v* to debase money.

ember *n* the great northern diver or ember goose.

embezill *v* to injure, to damage.

embezilment *n* injury, damage.

eme *n* **1** a maternal uncle. **2** a familiar friend.

emerant *n* an emerald.

emergent *n* anything that emerges.

emerteen *n* an ant.

emm *n* an uncle.

emmack *same as* **eemock**.

emmers *n* embers, red-hot ashes.

emmis *adj* **1** variable. **2** insecure, unsteady. **3** (*used of the weather*) gloomy.

emmle-deug, emmel-dyug *n* **1** butchers' offal, scrap or paring of carcass. **2** a piece of anything loose and flying. **3** a tatter fluttering from a dress.

emmock, emmot, emock *same as* **eemock**.

emmot-pile *n* an ant heap.

empanell *v* **1** to accuse, charge. **2** (*used as a legal term*) to put at the bar.

empesch *v* to hinder.

enact *v* **1** to bind oneself. **2** to put oneself under legal obligations.

enanteen *n* an ant.

enaunter *conj* lest.

end[1] *v* **1** to breathe. **2** to whisper.—*n* breath.

end[2] *n* **1** a room in a cottage. **2** a parlour. **3** the end of a room. **4** a shoemaker's waxed thread. **5** a unit of play in a curling match. **6** the finishing game of a rink contest in curling. **7** a use.—*v* **1** to set on end. **2** to kill.

endie *adj* **1** attached to one's own interests. **2** selfish. **3** scheming. **4** fertile in expedients. **5** shuffling, shifty.

ending stroke *n* **1** a death blow. **2** a finishing stroke.

endlang *prep* alongside of.—*adv* **1** at full length, lengthwise, along. **2** from end to end. **3** continuously.—*v* to harrow a ploughed field from end to end.—*n* full length.

endlangin *n* harrowing a field along the furrows.

endlangwyse *adv* lengthwise.

endless *adj* **1** long-winded. **2** pertinacious.

end-pickle *n* a head of corn.

endrift *n* snow driven by the wind.

end's errand *n* an exclusive errand, express purpose.

endurable *adj* lasting, enduring.

endurement *n* endurance.

endways *adv* **1** forward, onward. **2** well on. **3** successfully.

endwye *n* headway, progress.

ene *same as* **e'en**.

enel sheet *n* a winding sheet.

enemy *n* **1** the devil. **2** a person of evil disposition. **3** an ant.

eneuch, eneugh *n and adj* enough.

enew *same as* **enow**.

engage *v* to attract.

engine, engyne *n* **1** genius. **2** intellect. **3** disposition, character.

English *n* English, in contrast to Gaelic.

English and Scots *n* a children's game.

Englisher *n* an Englishman.

English weight *n* avoirdupois weight.

engrage *v* **1** to irritate. **2** to aggravate by irony.

engross *v* **1** to swallow up entire. **2** to render a woman pregnant.

enixe *adj* express.

enkerloch *adj* having a difficult temper.

enlang *same as* **endlang**.

enlarger *n* an expositor, one who enlarges in preaching.

enlicht *v* to enlighten.

enlighten *v* to fill or flood with light.

enner *adj* **1** nether. **2** inferior in place.

ennermair *adj* with greater inferiority in place.

ennermaist *adj* nethermost.

enorme *adj* **1** enormous. **2** horrid.

enow[1] *adj* **1** enough. **2** sufficient in number.

enow[2], **enoo** *same as* **eenow**.

enquire for *v* to inquire after.

ens, ense *conj* else.—*adv* otherwise.

ensigneer *n* an ensign (officer).

entering *adj* favourable for beginning or entering on.

entertain *v* **1** to welcome. **2** to pay for the support of.

entitule *v* to entitle, to have as a title.

entramells *n* **1** bondage. **2** prisoners of war.

entry *n* **1** an alley or narrow passage between two houses. **2** a passage or door which gives access to a place. **3** a house lobby.

entry mouth *n* the entrance of a close (qv) or narrow passage.

enuch *adj* enough.

enveigh *v* to inveigh.

envy-fow, --fu' *adj* **1** envious. **2** full of malice.

enze *same as* **ens**.

ephesian *n* a pheasant.

epicacco *n* ipecacuanha.

epie *n* a blow with a sword.

Episcolaupian, Episcopian *n* an Episcopalian.

eppersynd *n* the sign &, ampersand.

equal-aqual *adj* **1** equally balanced. **2** exactly alike or equal. **3** upside with.—*n* exact equality.—*v* **1** to make all equal. **2** to balance.

equals-aquals *adv* on a strict equality.

equiable *adj* equable.

equipage *n* utensils of all kinds, as of glass, china, earthenware.

erack *same as* **earock**.

erch *adj* timorous, shy.—*adv* nearly.—*v* to hesitate.

erchin *n* a hedgehog.

erd *same as* **eard**.

erd and stane *n* a mode of symbolical investiture with land in ownership.

ere *adj* early.—*prep* before.—*conj* **1** previous to. **2** rather than.

ereck *v* to erect.—*adj* erect.

ere-fernyear *n* the year before last.

erethestreen *n* the evening before last.

erf *adj* shy.—*adv* scarcely.—*v* to hesitate.

ergane *ppl* overflowing.

ergh[1] *adj* half-boiled.

ergh[2] *adj* **1** timorous. **2** scrupulous. **3** shy.—*adv* nearly, scarcely.—*v* to hesitate, to be shy.

erle *v* to give an earnest.—*n* (*in pl*) an earnest or instalment of wages for service.

erlish *same as* **eldritch**.

ermit *n* an earwig.

ern[1] *v* (*used of the eye*) to be wet, to water.

ern[2] *n* iron.

ern[3] *n* the eagle, erne.

ern-bleater *n* the snipe.

ern-fern *n* the brake-fern.

ernistfull *adj* eager; ardent.

ernit *n* the pignut.

ern tings *n* iron tongs.

erock *same as* **earock**.

erp *v* **1** to grumble. **2** to repine.

errack *same as* **earock**.

erran' *n* **1** an errand. **2** a message or parcel, etc, for delivery. **3** (*in pl*) marketings, shoppings and articles then bought.

errand-bairn *n* a child messenger.

errie *adj* **1** uncanny. **2** superstitiously gloomy.

erruction *n* a rumpus, a violent outbreak.

erse *n* the backside.

ersit *adj* perverse, contrary.

erst *adv* in the first place.

ert *v* **1** to urge on, incite. **2** to irritate.

erthlins *same as* **earthlins**.

ertienig *adj* **1** ingenious. **2** capable of laying plans.

erudition *n* civility, respect, courtesy.

erumption *n* an outburst, rumpus.

ery, erie *same as* **eerie**.

escape *n* **1** an omission, an oversight. **2** an offence.

esk[1] *n* a newt.

esk[2] *v* **1** to hiccup. **2** to cough up.—*n* a hiccup.

Eskdale souple *n* a broadsword, a two-handed sword.

esplin *n* a stripling, a youth.

ess[1], **esse** *n* **1** an S-shaped hook or link for traces, etc. **2** the ends of a curb chain.

ess[2] *v* (*used by some schoolboys*) to save part of one's allowance of bread in order to pay one's debt.

essael *pron* himself.

essart *adj* perverse, crooked.

ess-cock *n* the dipper.

esscock *n* a hot pimple on any part of the body

essel *n* a red-hot cinder, an ember.

essis *n* ornaments of jewellery in the shape of the letter S.

essonyie, essoinzie *v* to excuse oneself for absence from a law court.—*n* such an excuse for absence.

est *n* a nest.

estalment *n* an instalment.

estit *adv* as soon, rather.

estlar *n* **1** ashlar. **2** hewn or polished stone.

estlins *adv* rather.

eterie *adj* **1** (*used of the weather*) keen, bitter. **2** ill-tempered. **3** hot-headed. **4** angry-looking.

eth *same as* **eith**.

ether[1] *v* to twist ropes of straw round a stack.—*n* a twig, switch.

ether[2] *n* an adder.

ether[3] *adj, pron and conj* either.

ethercap *n* **1** a spider. **2** an ill-humoured person. **3** a hot-tempered person.

etherins[1], **etheran** *conj* either.—*adv* rather.

etherins[2], **etheran** *n* the cross-rope of a thatched roof or stack.

ether-stane *n* an adder-bead.

ethik *adj* delicate.

etion *n* **1** kindred. **2** genealogy. **3** descent.

etnach *n* juniper.—*adj* **1** of juniper. **2** of juniper wood.

ett *n* a custom, habit, generally in a bad sense.

etten[1] *v, adj* eaten.

etten[2] *adj* peevish.

etter *v* to fester.

ettercap *n* **1** a spider. **2** an ant. **3** an irascible, captious, malignant person.

etterlin *n* a cow that has a calf when only two years old.

ettersome *adj* **1** agressive. **2** bitterly cold.

ettery *adj* hot-tempered.

ettin, etin *n* a giant.

ettle *v* **1** to intend, purpose. **2** to take aim. **3** to direct one's course towards. **4** to attempt. **5** to struggle, make an effort. **6** to make ready. **7** to hanker after, to be eager to do or begin. **8** to suppose, guess, reckon, count on.—*n* **1** an intent, aim. **2** effort, attempt. **3** chance. **4** a mark.

ettler *n* one who ettles. *See* **ettle**.

ettling *n* effort, endeavour.—*adj* ambitious, pushing.

euk *v* to itch.

eul-cruke, ~-cruik *n* an oil jar.

evacuate *v* to nullify, set aside, neutralize.

evanish *v* to vanish, disappear quite.

evasion *n* a way or means of escape from danger.

eveat *same as* **evite**.

eve-~, evil-eel *n* the conger eel.

eveleit, evelit *same as* **evleit**.

even *v* **1** to compare. **2** to level down, demean. **3** to suggest as a suitable person to marry. **4** to impute, hint, charge with. **5** to think entitled to.—*n* (*in pl*) equals, quits.

even and eyn *phr* in good earnest.

evendoun *adj* **1** perpendicular. **2** honest, downright. **3** direct, without reserve or qualification. **4** mere, sheer. **5** habitual, confirmed. **6** (*of rain*) very heavy and straight down.—*adv* thoroughly, completely.

even-en-ways *adv* **1** straight on. **2** continuously.

even-hands *adv* on an equality.—*n* an equal bargain.

evenliness *n* equanimity, composure.

evenly *adj* (*of ground, etc*) smooth, level.

evenner *n* a weaver's implement for spreading yarn on the beam.

even-noo, eve'noo *same as* **e'enow**.

even on *adv* continuously.

even out *adv* loudly.

evens *n in phr* **at evens wi' the warld** solvent, paying one's way.

even-up back *n in phr* **to keep an even-up back** to keep straight.

ever[1] *v* to nauseate.

ever[2] *adj* (*used of places*) upper, over.

ever alack *int* alas!

ever and on *adv* continually.

everilk *adj* **1** each. **2** every.

everilk-on, ~-one *phr* each single one, every individual one.

everlasting *adv* continually.

everly *adv* **1** continually. **2** perpetually.

ever now *adv* just now.

everochs *n* the cloudberry.

every[1] *adj* both, each of two.

every[2] *adj* hungry.

every[3] *int* the call of a boy playing at marbles for liberty to play in any position he chose.

eve-, ever-, ere-yesterday *n* the day before yesterday.

eve-, ever-, ere-yestreen *n* the night before yesternight.

evict *v* to dispossess legally of property, used not of the person but of the property.

evident *n* **1** a title deed. **2** documentary proof.

evil-headit *adj* (*used of an ox or bull*) prone to butt.

evil-man *n* the devil.

evil-money *n* false coin.

evite *v* **1** to avoid, shun. **2** to evade. **3** to escape.

evleit *adj* **1** prompt, active. **2** ready, willing. **3** sprightly, cheerful. **4** handsome.

evrie *same as* **every**.

ew *n* a yew.

ewden-drift *n* drifted snow.

ewder[1] *n* **1** a disagreeable smell. **2** the steam of a boiling pot. **3** the odour of anything burning. **4** dust. **5** the dust of flax. **6** a collection of small particles.

ewder[2] *n* a blaze.

ewdroch, ewdruch *same as* **ewder**[1].

ewe *n* **1** a stupid, easy-going person. **2** the cone of a fir, larch, etc.

ewe-bucht, ~-bught *n* **1** a sheep pen. **2** a place where ewes are milked.

ewe-gowan *n* the common daisy.

ewe-hogg *n* a ewe at the stage next to a lamb's.

e-wel *int* indeed! really!

ewe-milker *n* one who milks ewes.

ewendrie *n* **1** the refuse of oats after winnowing. **2** weak grain.

ewer *n* the udder of a cow, sheep, etc.

ewer-locks *n* the wool round a sheep's udder, removed near lambing time.

ewest *adj* **1** most contiguous. **2** nearest.

e-whow *int* an exclamation of grief, surprise or alarm.

ewie *n* **1** a young ewe. **2** a small fir cone.

ewindrift *same as* **ewden-drift**.

ewk *same as* **euk**.

ewous *adj* contiguous.

exack[1] *v* to exact.

exack[2] *adj* exact.—*adv* exactly.

exact *adj* expert.—*adv* **1** exactly. **2** straitly.

exactable *adj* exigible.

examine *n* an examination.

excamb, excambie *v* to exchange lands.

excambion *n* an exchange of lands.

exceppins *prep* except.

excresce *n* **1** overpayment. **2** overplus in value.

excrescence *n* a surplus.

exeem, exeme *v* to exempt.

exem *v* to examine.

exemmin *n* an examination.—*v* to examine.

exemp *n* exemption.—*adj* exempt.

exemplar *adj* exemplary.

exemplarly *adv* for example.

exerce *v* to exercise.

exercise *v* **1** to conduct family worship. **2** to expound Scripture at a meeting of presbytery.—*n* family worship. **2** the presbyterial exposition. **3** a part of a divinity student's trials (qv) for licence to preach. **4** a name for a presbytery.

exercise and additions *n* an exposition, paraphrase and application of a passage, in the original, of Scripture, delivered by a student of divinity or by members of a presbytery in rotation.

exercising *n* public worship.

exheredate *v* **1** to disinherit. **2** to deprive of an inheritance, a legal term.

exhibition *n in phr* **raise an exhibition** to call for the production of writs.

exhort *n* **1** an address. **2** an exhortation.

exhoust *v* to exhaust.—*adj* exhausted.

exies *n* **1** hysterics. **2** an access of ague.

exigent *n* an exigency, an emergency.
exle *n* an axle.
exoner *v* **1** (*used as a legal term*) to relieve from a burden. **2** to exonerate from responsibility, trusteeship, etc.
exorbitant *adj* **1** extreme. **2** extravagant.
expectancy *n* the state of being an expectant (qv).
expectant *n* a divinity student preparing for a licence to preach.
expede *v* to expedite, despatch.
experimented *adj* experienced.
expone *v* **1** to explain, expound. **2** to expose. **3** to represent, characterize.
express *n* a special errand.
extenuate *v* (*used of the body*) to become thin, slender.
exterics *n* hysterics.
exterordinar *adj* extraordinary.—*adv* extraordinarily.
extinguish *v* (*used of a debt*) to pay off gradually.
extort *v* to practise extortion on one.
extortion *n* an exorbitant price.—*v* to charge exorbitantly.
extranean *adj* coming from a distance.—*n* **1** a scholar coming to the higher classes of Aberdeen Grammar School from another school for special drill in classics. **2** an outsider. **3** one not of the family.
extraordinar, exterordinar *adj* extraordinary.—*n* (*in pl*) unusual occurrences.—*adv* extraordinarily.

extravage *v* **1** to wander about. **2** to wander in discourse. **3** to speak incoherently. **4** to enlarge in speaking.
extree, extra *n* an axle.
ey[1] *n* an island.
ey[2] *adv* always.
eydent *adj* industrious, diligent.
eydi-yesterday *n* the day before yesterday.
eydi-yestreen *n* the night before last night.
eye-last, ~-list *same as* **e'e-list**.
eyen *n* eyes.
eye-sweet *adj* pleasing to the eye.
eye-winker *n* an eyelid, an eyelash.
eyn[1] *n* an end.—*v* to end.
eyn[2] *n* an oven.
eynd *v* **1** to breathe. **2** to whisper.—*n* a breath.
eyndill *same as* **eindill**.
eyndling *same as* **eindling**.
eyn't *v, adj* ended.
eyven *adv* even.
eyzle *n* **1** a live coal. **2** a hot ember.
eyzly *adj* red, fiery.
eyzly-ete't *adj* fiery-eyed.
ezar *n* maplewood.—*adj* of or belonging to the maple.
ezin *same as* **easing**.
ezle *same as* **eyzle**.

F

fa[1] *pron* who.
fa[2] *v* to become, to suit, used impersonally.
fa' *n* **1** a fall. **2** a fall of rain or snow. **3** a trap, snare. **4** a lot, fortune, lot, what befalls one. **5** a share, portion.—*v* **1** to fall. **2** (*used of the sea*) to grow calm. **3** (*of lime*) to become powdery. **4** to befall. **5** to change into. **6** to become pregnant. **7** to fall to one's duty. **8** to excel, win. **9** to fail. **10** to put up. **11** to take in hand.
faad *v* fell.
faags *int* faith!
fa'ahint *v* to fall behind, into arrears of rent, work, etc.
faal *n* a fold.—*v* **1** to fold. **2** to bend.
fa'an *v, adj* fallen.
faang *n* an unpleasant person.
faar'd *same as* **faured**.
fa' awa' *v* to waste away.
fab[1] *v* to trick, cheat.—*n* a trick, cheat.
fab[2] *n* **1** a fob. **2** a small pocket. **3** a tobacco pouch.
fabala *n* **1** a trimming of a petticoat. **2** a flounce, a furbelow.
fabric *n* a person, animal or thing of big, clumsy appearance.
fa' by *v* **1** to be sick. **2** to be in childbed.
fac *same as* **fack**.
face *n* the edge of any sharp instrument.
faceable *adj* **1** fit to be seen, pretty. **2** likely to be true.
face o'clay *phr* any living person.
face-plate *n* the face.
face-the-clarts *n* **1** a low, plausible sneak. **2** a mean, grovelling fellow.
face-wise *adj* facing.
facherie *same as* **fasherie**.
facht *same as* **fecht**.
facie *adj* **1** bold, fearless. **2** insolent, impudent.
fack *n* fact, truth, reality.—*int* indeed! really!
faction *n* the name formerly given to a bench in the Aberdeen Grammar School.
factor *n* **1** the manager of a landed property, who lets farms, collects rents and pays wages. **2** a person legally appointed to manage sequestrated property.—*v* to act as factor.
factorship, factory *n* **1** the office of factor (qv). **2** agency.
faddom *v* **1** to fathom. **2** to measure. **3** to encompass with the arms.

fade *n* a director in sports, etc.
fader *n* father.
faderil *n* **1** the loose end of anything. **2** (*in pl*) apparatus.
fadge[1] *n* a faggot, bundle of sticks.
fadge[2] *n* **1** a fat, clumsy woman. **2** a short, thickset person.
fadge[3] *n* **1** a large, flat loaf or bannock. **2** a flat wheaten loaf.
fadle *v* to walk clumsily, waddle.
fadmell *same as* **fodmell**.
fae[1] *pron* who.
fae[2] *n* foe.
fae[3] *prep* from, away from.
fae[4] *n* faith.
faedom *n* witchcraft.
faegit *adj* fagged.
fael *same as* **fail**[1].
faem *same as* **foam**.
fa'en *adj* fallen.
faerdy *same as* **feerdy**.
faert[1] *same as* **fierd**.
faert[2] *adj* afraid.
faffer *n* **1** a flapper. **2** a fan.
fag *n* **1** a sheep-louse or tick. **2** (*in pl*) lousiness in sheep.
faggald, fagald *n* a bundle of heath or twigs bound with straw ropes, a faggot.
faggie *adj* fatiguing, tiring.
fag-ma-fuff *n* a garrulous old woman.
fagot, faggot *n* **1** a slattern. **2** a stout person.
fagsum *adj* wearisome, tiring.
fagsumness *n* tiresomeness.
faick[1] *same as* **faik**[3].
faick[2], **faicks** *int* faith!
faid *n* a director of sports.
faidle *same as* **fadle**.
faighlochs *n* sorry workers doing little.
faigs *int* an exclamation of surprise, faith!
faik[1] *n* truth.—*int* in truth!
faik[2] *v* **1** to fondle. **2** to tuck up. **3** to caress.—*n* **1** a plaid. **2** a fold, ply. **3** the part of a full sack drawn together for tying. **4** a stratum of stone in a quarry.
faik[3] *v* **1** to lower a price. **2** to excuse. **3** to reduce, abate a claim. **4** to let go unpunished.

faik[4] *v* **1** to fail from weariness. **2** to stop, intermit. —*n* a failure.

faik[5] *same as* **fake**[2].

faik[6] *n* the razorbill.

faikie *n* a plaid.

faikins, faickens *n* truth, used in mild oaths.

faikit *adj* wearied out.

faiks *same as* **faix**.

fail[1]**, faill, faile** *n* **1** a sward. **2** a flat sod of turf. **3** turf.

fail[2] *v* **1** to break down in health. **2** to grow weak. —*adj* frail, weak.—*n* decline.

fail-caster *n* one who cuts fails. *See* **fail**[1].

fail-delf *n* the place from which fails have been dug.

fail-dyke *n* a wall built of fails.

fail-housie *n* a small house built with fails.

fail-roofed *adj* roofed with fails.

fail-wa' *n* a house or hut wall built of turf.

failyie, failzie *v* to fail.—*n* failure, default, penalty for breach of bargain.

faim *n* foam, froth.

faimily *n* a family.

faimish *v* to famish.

fa'in *v* **1** to shrink in. **2** to subside.

fain[1] *adj* **1** eager, anxious. **2** fond, affectionate. **3** in love.— *adv* fondly.

fain[2] *adj* **1** (*used of grain in the field*) not thoroughly dry so as to be stacked. **2** (*of meal*) of bad quality, made of grain not ripe enough.

fainfu' *adj* affectionate, kind, loving.

fainly *adj* **1** pleasant, gladsome. **2** welcome. **3** amiable, affectionate.—*adv* **1** gladly. **2** eagerly, excitedly. **3** fondly, lovingly.

fainness *n* **1** gladness. **2** desire. **3** liking. **4** fondness, love, affection.

faint[1] *same as* **fient**[1].

faint[2] *v* **1** to enfeeble. **2** to make faint.

faintly *adj* weak, faint.

faints *n* **1** low wines. **2** inferior spirits.

fainty-grund *n* ground, in passing over which it is deemed necessary to have a bit of bread in one's pocket to prevent fainting.

faiple *n* **1** anything loose and flaccid hanging from the nose. **2** a turkey's crest or comb when elated. **3** the under-lip of men and beasts when it hangs down large and loose.

fair[1] *n* a gift from a fair, a fairing.—*v* to treat at a fair.

fair[2] *adj* **1** plausible. **2** pleasant. **3** clean, tidy, set in order. **4** likely, having a good chance. **5** complete, utter.—*adv* **1** quite, completely, thoroughly. **2** exactly. **3** very.—*v* (*used of the weather*) to become fine, clear up.

fair[3] *same as* **fare**[2].

Fair, the *n* the name given to the last fortnight in July in the Glasgow area, the part of the summer when working people traditionally go on holiday.

fair-ba's *n* fair play.

fair-ca'in *n* address, skill, care.—*adj* plausible, smooth-tongued.

faird[1] *n* **1** stir, bustle. **2** a violent onset, a wrangle. —*v* to bustle. **2** to wrangle.

faird[2] *same as* **fard**[1].

fairdie *adj* **1** passionate. **2** irascible. **3** clever, handy.

fairding *n* **1** painting. **2** embellishment.

fair fa'[1] *phr* good luck to, an expression of good wishes.

fair-fa'[2] *v* to wrestle.—*n* a wrestling match.

fair-faced *adj* of plausible or deceitful appearance.

fair-fa'in *n* a wrestling.

fair fa'ma sel' *phr* used of one who boasts of his success.

fair-farand *adj* good to look at but hurtful.

fair-fashioned, ~-fassint *adj* **1** apparently, but not really, civil. **2** fair-seeming, plausible.

fair-faughlit *same as* **forfaughlit**.

fair fa' ye *int* good luck to you!

fairfle *n* an eruption of the skin.

fairflitten *same as* **forflitten**.

fair-flutter *same as* **forfluther**.

fair-foil *n* fairies.

fair-foor-, ~-four-, ~-fur-days *n* broad daylight.

fair-furth, fair-furth-the-gate *phr* straightforward, honest.

fair-ga'en *adj* (*used of an invalid*) likely to recover.

fair grass *n* **1** the goosegrass. **2** the buttercup.

fair-gude-day *n* good morning.

fair-gude-e'en *n* good evening.

fair-hair *n* the tendon of the neck of cattle or sheep.

fair hornie *n* fair play.

fairin[1] *n* **1** a gingerbread fairing. **2** a present bought at a fair. **3** a drubbing, deserts. **4** holding a fair.

fairin[2] *same as* **faring**.

fairish *adj* tolerably good.—*adv* fairly.

fairlaithie *same as* **forlaithie**.

fairleens, fairlins *adv* almost, not quite.

fairley *same as* **ferly**.

fairly *adv* **1** quite. **2** certainly, surely.

fairly fu' *same as* **ferly full**.

fairm *n* a farm.—*v* to farm.

fairmaist *adj* foremost.

fairney cloots *n* the small horny substance above the hoofs, where the pastern of a horse lies, but said to be found only in sheep or goats.

fairney~~, fairn-tickles *same as* **fern-tickles**.

Fairntosh *n* peat-reek whisky formerly distilled at Ferintosh in Ross-shire.

fairn year *same as* **fern year**.

fairock *n* a mock sun.

fair-ower, ~-owre *adv* in exact exchange.

fairscomfisht *same as* **forscomfisht**.

fair-strae-death *n* a natural death in bed.

fairt *adj* afraid.

fair trade *n* smuggling.

fairy dart *n* a flint arrowhead.

fairy green *n* a small circle of darker green grass in meadows, etc, supposed to be the fairies' dancing ground.

fairy hammer *n* a stone hatchet.

fairy hillock *n* a verdant knoll, supposed to have been the dwelling or the dancing place of fairies.

fairy knowe *n* a fairy hillock (qv).

fairy rade *n* the fairies' expedition to where they held their great annual banquet on 1 May.

fairy ring *n* a fairy green (qv).

faise[1] *same as* **fease**[1].

faise[2] *same as* **fease**[2].

faishochs *same as* **faighlochs**.

faisins *n* stringy parts of cloth, resembling lint, applied to a wound.

faist *adj* fast.

fait[1] *adj* **1** fit. **2** clever. **3** neat, tidy.—*n* an achievement.

fait[2] *n* in phr **to lose fait of** to lose one's good opinion of.

faitchen *v* fetched.

faith *int* an exclamation indeed! truly!

faitha *int* by my faith!

faith and troth *phr* by my faith and truth!

faither *n* father.

faix *n* a mild expletive, faith.—*int* faith!

faizart *n* **1** a hermaphrodite of the hen tribe. **2** a puny young man of feminine appearance. **3** an impudent or shameless person.

faize *same as* **fease**[2].

faizing *n* the stringy parts of cloth when the woof is rubbed out from the warp.

faizle *v* to flatter, coax.

fak *same as* **fack**.

fake[1] *n* a sight, a vision.

fake[2] *n* the strand of a rope.

fakes *same as* **faix**.

falcage *n* the right of mowing.

fald[1] *same as* **fauld**[1].

fald[2] *n* **1** a fold. **2** a curve.—*v* **1** to fold. **2** to bend. **3** to enfold. **4** to bow.

fald dyke *n* a turf wall round a sheep-fold.
falderal, faldaral *n* **1** a gewgaw, useless ornament. **2** an idle fancy. **3** a trifling excuse. **4** a pedantic, giddy person. **5** (*in pl*) odds and ends, trifles.—*v* **1** to make trifling excuses. **2** to behave in a pedantic, giddy way.
fale *same as* **fail**¹.
falk *n* the razorbill.
Falkland-bred *adj* **1** bred at court. **2** courtly. **3** polished.
fall¹ *n* **1** scrap. **2** offal.
fall² *same as* **fa'**.
fall³ *n* a measure of six ells square, a perch.
fallall *n* a**1** superfluous article of dress or part of dress, superficial ornament of women's dress. **2** a gewgaw, trumpery ornament. **3** a kickshaw, needless dainty.
fallauge, falawdge *adj* lavish, profuse.
fall-board *n* the hinged wooden shutter of an unglazed window.
fall-cap *n* a stuff cap worn by a child to protect the head in falling.
fallen-star *n* **1** the sea nettle. **2** (*in pl*) the jelly tremella, a gelatinous plant found in pastures, etc, after rain.
falling nieve *n* a method of cheating at marbles.
falling sickness *n* epilepsy.
falloch *n* a large lump, heap, piece of eatables or of anything lumpish or weighty.—*adj* thick, bulky.
fallow¹ *n* **1** a fellow. **2** a match.
fallow² *v* to follow
fallow break *n* land under grass for two years and then ploughed up.
fallow-chat *n* the wheatear.
falsary *n* **1** a liar, a false witness. **2** a cheat. **3** a forger.
falser *n* a user of false weights, etc.
falset *n* **1** falsehood. **2** dishonesty.
false-tastedly *adv* in false or bad taste.
falten *n* a fillet.
faltive *adj* faulty.
fame¹ *n* **1** common report. **2** country gossip.—*v* to publish, proclaim.
fame² *n* **1** foam, a film of anything floating on another. **2** a rage, passion. **3** an angry flush.—*v* to be in a rage.
famh, famhphear *n* **1** a small, noxious beast. **2** a monster. **3** a cruel, mischievous person.
family duty *n* family worship.
famous *adj* **1** of good character. **2** well reported of.
fan¹ *adv* when.
fan² *n* fanners for winnowing.
fan', fand *v*, *adj* found.
fancy *v* to care for, fall in love with.—*n* affection, liking.
fand *n* a bow, knot.
fane¹ *same as* **fain**².
fane² *n* an elf, fairy.
fanerels *n* anything loose or flapping.
fang *v* **1** to clutch, grasp. **2** to steal. **3** to fill a pump with water to make it work properly.—*n* **1** a trap, a tight corner. **2** the act of thieving. **3** spoil, booty, anything stolen. **4** a catch in buying. **5** a cheap bargain. **6** a heavy burden in the hands or arms. **7** a claw, hook, talon. **8** a thief, scamp. **9** a term of contempt. **10** a lout. **11** the coil of a rope, the thong of a whip. **12** the grip or power of suction in a pump. **13** a large lump cut from something.
fanglet *v*, *adj* fashioned.
fank¹ *n* **1** an enclosure. **2** a sheep cot, a pen for cattle at night.—*v* to fold or pen sheep or cattle.
fank² *n* **1** a coil, noose. **2** a tangle. **3** a coil of ropes. —*v* **1** to coil a rope. **2** to twist. **3** to entangle the feet. **4** to hinder.
fank day *n* the day on which sheep were clipped.
fankle *v* **1** to entangle, twist. **2** to knot. **3** to coil, wind. **4** to disorder, complicate.—*n* an entanglement.
fant *v* to faint.
fantoosh *adj* **1** flashy, showy. **2** fashionable
fa' o' *v* to abate.
fa' o'er *v* **1** to fall asleep. **2** (*used of a woman*) to be confined.
faple *same as* **faiple**.

far¹ *adv* **1** where? **2** whither?
far² *adv* greatly, much.—*n* **1** a degree. **2** the greater part.—*adj* **1** difficult. **2** *in phr* **far to seek** not easy to find.
farack *n* a small mark on the skin.
far aff *adj* distantly related.
farand *adj* seeming.
farand-man *n* **1** a stranger, traveller. **2** a merchant-stranger.
far-awa *adj* **1** (*used of relationship*) distant. **2** (*of time or place*) remote, distant.—*n* abroad, foreign parts.
far-awa-screed *n* a letter or news from abroad.
far-ben *adj* **1** in high favour. **2** in one's good graces. **3** intimate. **4** advanced.
far-by *adv* far past, beyond.—*prep* quite beyond.
farcie *adj* righteous.
far-come *adj* **1** foreign, at a distance. **2** distantly related.
farcost *n* a trading vessel.
fard *v* **1** to paint. **2** to embellish.—*n* **1** paint. **2** embellishment.
far'd *same as* **faured**.
fard *n* **1** a bustle, stir. **2** a violent onset.
fardel¹ *n* a quantity, a lot.
fardel² *same as* **fordal**.
farden, fardin *n* a farthing.
farder *adj* farther.—*adv* further, farther.—*v* to further.
fardest *adj and adv* furthermost, farthest.
farding *n* **1** painting. **2** embellishment.
fardingale *n* **1** a farthingale. **2** a crinoline.
fardle *same as* **farle**.
fare¹ *same as* **fair**¹.
fare² *v* **1** to entertain with food. **2** to serve with food.
farer *adj* further, farther.
farest *adj* furthermost, farthest.
fareway *n* the passage or channel in a river or the sea for a ship, etc.
fareweel *n* farewell.
far-hie-an-atour *phr* at a considerable distance.
farie *n* **1** a stir, bustle. **2** *phr* **fiery-farie** a great hubbub.
faring *n* food, fare.
farkage *n* **1** a confused bundle of things. **2** a mass of cordage entangled beyond unravelling.
far-keeker *n* the eye.
far-kent *adj* widely known.
farle *n* **1** a quarter segment of oatcake. **2** a cake.
far-leukit *adj* far-seeing, prudent, penetrating.
farley, farlie *same as* **ferly**.
farlin *n* the box or trough out of which the gutters take the herrings.
farm *n* **1** rent. **2** part of farm rent paid in grain or meal.
farm meal *n* rent paid in oatmeal.
farm steading *n* a farmstead.
farm town *n* a farmhouse and buildings.
farn-year *same as* **fernyear**.
farouchie *adj* ferocious, savage, cruel.
far-out *adj* distantly related.
far-ower *adv* too, far too.
farra *same as* **farrow**.
farrach, farrich, farroch *n* **1** force, strength, energy. **2** managing faculty. **3** ability.
farrachie *adj* strong, able, energetic.
farran *adj* starboard.
farrand, farrant, farren *adj* **1** fashioned. **2** seeming. **3** mannered. **4** sagacious. **5** well-behaved.
farrel *same as* **farle**.
farrer *adj* further, farther.
farres *n* **1** boundaries. **2** ridges marked out by the plough.
farrest *adj* furthermost, farthest.
farrow *adj* **1** (*used of a cow*) not with calf. **2** not yielding milk.
farry *v* **1** to farrow. **2** to bring forth pigs.
far-seen *adj* **1** learned, well-instructed. **2** penetrating. **3** prudent.
farshach *n* the greater black-headed gull.
farthel *same as* **farle**.

farthing-compliment *n* a worthless compliment.
far-through *adj* very weak, near death.
far to the fore *phr* much to be preferred to.
far-yaud *n* a shepherd's cry to his dog.
fas *same as* **fass**.
fa-say *n* a sham, pretence.
fascal *n* a straw mat used to screen from draughts.
fascious *same as* **fashious**.
fash *v* **1** to trouble, inconvenience, vex, worry with importunity. **2** to weary. **3** to vex oneself, be annoyed.—*n* **1** trouble, care, annoyance, vexation. **2** labour. **3** a troublesome person. **4** one who molests, etc.—*phr* **fash one's beard, head, noddle** or **thumb**, to trouble or vex oneself.
fashery *n* trouble, worry, annoyance, vexation.
fashion *n* *in phr* **for the fashion** for appearance' sake.
make a fashion to make a show or pretence.
fashioned *adj* **1** fashionable, in the fashion. **2** conditioned.
fashionless *adj* out of fashion.
fashious, fashous *adj* **1** troublesome, vexatious. **2** not easily pleased.
fashiousness *n* troublesomeness.
fashrie *same as* **fashery**.
faskidar *n* the northern gull.
fass *n* **1** a knot, bunch. **2** a truss of straw, etc.
fassag *n* a straw hassock as a seat for a child or, when broad and thin, for backs of horses.
fassint *v*, *adj* fashioned.
fassit *v*, *adj* knotted.
fasson, fassin *n* fashion.
fast *adj* **1** busily engaged with. **2** trustworthy. **3** firm. **4** very near or intimate. **5** forward. **6** irascible.
fast and snell *phr* straightforward, in a straight line, briskly and without deviatnon.
Fasten, Fasten's E'en *n* Shrove Tuesday.
Faster-~, Fastern's Eve *n* Shrove Tuesday.
fasting-spittle *n* a fasting man's saliva, as a supposed cure for ringworm.
Fastren's Eve *n* Shrove Tuesday.
fat[1] *adj* what.
fat[2] *adj* **1** thriving, prosperous. **2** (*used of soil*) rich, fertile.
fat-a-feck *adj* (*used of the weather*) favourable, seasonable.
fatality *n* **1** fate. **2** a fatal defect.
fatch[1] *v* to fetch.
fatch[2] *same as* **fotch**[1].
fatch[3] *n* *in phr* **at the fatch** toiling, drudging.
fatch-pleugh *same as* **fotch-plough**.
father *n* *in phr* **father and son** a boys' game.
father-better *adj* surpassing one's father.
father-brother *n* a paternal uncle.
father-in-law *n* a step-father.
father's-fiddle *n* a boys' game.
father-sister *n* a paternal aunt.
father-waur *adj* worse than one's father.
fathom *v* **1** to grasp or hold in one's arms. **2** to measure by the outstretched arms.
fathoming a rick, ~ stack *phr* a Hallowe'en ceremony of measuring a stack with outstretched arms thrice against the sun, when the last fathom would show the apparition of the future husband or wife.
fa' throw *v* **1** to bungle. **2** to cease working through sloth or carelessness.
fa' till *v* **1** to attack. **2** to begin to eat.
fatna *adj* what sort of a.
fat-reck *int* who cares?—*conj* notwithstanding.
fat-recks *int* an exclamation of surprise.
fatten *adj* what sort of?
fattenin' and battenin' *phr* a toast of a child's fattening and thriving, given at its baptism in private, when bread, cheese and whisky customarily were partaken of.
fatter *v* to thresh the awns of barley.
fatter, fattera *adj* what sort of?.
fattrils, fattrels *n* **1** folds, puckerings. **2** ribbon ends. **3**

ornaments of a woman's dress.
fauce *same as* **fause**.
fauch[1] *n* **1** fallow ground. **2** land ploughed at Martinmas for a green crop the next year.—*adj* fallow.—*v* **1** to fallow. **2** to beat soundly. **3** to rub vigorously.
fauch[2] *same as* **faugh**[1].
fauchentulie *n* a contentious argument.—*v* to contend in argument.
faucht *n* a fight, struggle.—*v* did fight, fought.
fauchten *v* fought.
fauconless *adj* without strength.
faucumtulies *n* fowls, etc, paid as cain (qv) or part of rent, to a landlord.
faud *n* a fold.—*v* **1** to fold. **2** to bow. **3** *in phr* **faud the houchs** to sit down.
faugh[1] *adj* **1** dun. **2** fallow-coloured. **3** pale-red.
faugh[2] *same as* **fauch**[1].
faugh-blue *adj* bleached blue.
faughin *n* **1** a tearing up, ploughing. **2** a constant rubbing. **3** a beating.
faugh-riggs *n* fallow ground.
faughs *n* a division of land, not manured, but prepared for a crop by a slight fallowing.
faught[1] *v* did beat.
faught[2] *v* fought.—*n* a fight, struggle.
faul[1] *n* a halo round the moon, indicating a fall of rain.
faul[2] *same as* **fauld**[1].
faul[3] *same as* **fauld**[2].
fauld[1] *n* a sheepfold.—*v* to put sheep in a fold.
fauld[2] *n* **1** a fold. **2** a curve.—*v* to fold.
fauld[3] *n* a section of a farm manured by folding sheep or cattle on it.
fauld-dyke *n* the wall of a sheepfold.
faulderall *n* a gewgaw.
faulding *n* a sheepfold.
faulding slap *n* the gate or opening of a sheepfold.
faulies *n* the faulds of a farm. *See* **fauld**[3].
faulter *n* hesitation.
faun *v* found.
faung *same as* **fang**.
faup *n* the curlew.
fa' upon *v* **1** to pilfer. **2** to tamper with.
faur[1] *adv* **1** where. **2** whither.
faur[2] *same as* **far**[1].
faured, faurd *adj* favoured, featured.
faurer *adv* further, farther.
faurest *adj* furthermost, farthest.
fauron *adv* whereupon.
faur-on *adj* **1** nearly drunk. **2** near death.
fauschious *same as* **fashious**.
fause *adj* false.—*v* to coax, cajole.
fause-face *n* **1** a mask. **2** a deceitful person. **3** a hypocrite.
fause house *n* a vacant space in a stack for ventilation.
fause-loon *n* a traitor.—*adj* traitorous.
fause-tail *n* a braid of hair.
faust *adj* **1** favoured, featured. **2** mannered.
faut[1], **faute** *n* **1** a fault. **2** blame. **3** injury. **4** defect, want. **5** negligence.—*v* **1** to find fault with, blame. **2** to reprove.
faut[2] *same as* **fa', faw**[1].
fauter, fautor *n* **1** an offender. **2** a guilty person.
faut-free *adj* **1** blameless. **2** sound, not defective.
fautie *n* a slight fault.
fautifu' *adj* **1** fault-finding. **2** not easy to please.
fautless *adj* faultless.
fauty *adj* **1** faulty. **2** guilty. **3** unsound.
favour *n* **1** countenance, complexion, appearance. **2** (*in pl*) favour.—*v* to resemble in feature or appearance.
favoured *same as* **faured**.
faw[1] *v* **1** to fall. **2** to befall. **3** to obtain a share.—*n* **1** a fall. **2** a share. **3** a lot. **4** a trap.
faw[2] *same as* **faugh**[1].
fa' wi' *v* to go to waste or ruin.
fawn *n* **1** a white spot on moorish or mossy ground. **2** a rough, wet place on a hill.

fawn *v* **1** to caress, fondle. **2** to fawn upon.

fawsont *adj* honest, becoming, seemly.

fay[1] *n* faith.

fay[2] *same as* **fey**[2].

faze *same as* **fease**[1].

fead *n* **1** feud, quarrel. **2** hatred. **3** a cause of quarrel. **4** an enemy.

feake *same as* **faik**[2].

feal[1] *adj* **1** faithful, loyal. **2** just, fair.

feal[2] *same as* **fail**[1].

feal[3] *same as* **feil**[1].

feam *same as* **fame**[2].

fear[1] *same as* **fere**[1].

fear[2] *n* a fright.—*v* to frighten, scare.

fear[3] *same as* **fear**[3].

fearder *adj* more afraid.

feared *adj* **1** afraid. **2** (*with* for) afraid of.

fear-fangit *adj* panic-stricken, seized with fear.

fearfu' *adj* **1** easily frightened. **2** of very large quantity or dimension.—*adv* exceedingly, extraordinarily.

fearie[1] *adj* afraid.

fearie[2] *adj* sturdy.

fearn *same as* **fern**.

fear-nothing *n* a rough cloth overcoat, a dreadnought.

fearn-owl *n* the nightjar.

fears *same as* **fiars**.

fearsome *adj* **1** terrifying, fearful, awful. **2** timid, frightened.

fearsome-like *adj* frightful, fearful.

fearsome-looking *adj* frightful-looking, of terrifying appearance.

fearsomely *adv* frightfully, dreadfully.

feart *same as* **feared**.

feart-like *adj* like one afraid, frightened.

fease[1] *v* **1** to drive. **2** to drive out. **3** to disturb, annoy.—*n* annoyance, inconvenience.

fease[2] *v* **1** to screw, twist. **2** (*used of cloth*) to fray out. **3** (*of a sharp instrument*) to have the edge turned. **4** to rub hard. **5** to work briskly.

fesaible *same as* **faceable**.

feat *adj* **1** fitting, fitted, suitable. **2** clever, smart. **3** dexterous. **4** tidy, neat. **5** pretty.—*adv* **1** dexterously. **2** prettily.—*v* **1** to dress neatly. **2** to qualify. **3** to prepare.

feather *n* part of a peat-cutting spade at right angles with the broadest part.—*v* **1** (*used of a bird*) to get feathers, to fly. **2** to beat, chastise. **3** to fall foul of.

feather-cling *n* a disease affecting black cattle.

feathered *adj* (*used of cattle*) marked with a feather for identification.

feather-lock *n* a lock, the end of whose spring resembles the hairs of a feather.

feather-wheelie *n* the feverfew.

featless *adj* feeble.

featly *adv* **1** cleverly, smartly. **2** prettily. **3** neatly.

featour *n* a transgressor, evildoer.

feat-peak *n* a neat top or finish to a stack, headdress, etc.

feauk *n* a plaid.

feaze *same as* **fease**[2].

Feberwarry, Februar *n* February.

fechen, fechin *v* fought.

fechie-lechie *adj* **1** insipid, tasteless. **2** diminutive in size. **3** inactive.

fecht *v* **1** to fight. **2** to struggle. **3** to harass.—*n* **1** a fight. **2** a struggle for a living, etc. **3** hard work.

fechter *n* **1** a fighter. **2** (*in pl*) stalks of the ribgrass, which children use in a sort of mimic battle as weapons.

fechtie *n* a fighter.

fechtin' cock *n* a cock trained to cockfighting.

feck[1] *n* **1** value, worth. **2** the majority, the bulk. **3** abundance, quantity.—*adj* strong, vigorous.

feck[2] *same as* **fike**[1].

feck[3] *n* **1** familiar intercourse. **2** affection, esteem.

feck[4] *v* to attain by dishonourable means, to steal.

fecket *n* **1** a waistcoat, underjacket. **2** a shirt.

feck-fack *same as* **fike-fack**.

feck-fow *same as* **feckfu'**.

feck-fow-like *adj* **1** apparently wealthy. **2** capable-looking.

feckfu' *adj* **1** wealthy, of substance. **2** capable, full of resource. **3** powerful, able. **4** stout.

feckfully *adv* **1** efficiently. **2** powerfully.

feckle *n* trouble, anxiety.

feckless *adj* **1** weak, feeble, impotent. **2** incapable, incompetent, not resourceful. **3** awkward, unhandy. **4** spiritless, weak in mind or resolution. **5** of little or no value, profitless. **6** trifling. **7** pithless, tasteless. **8** poor, poverty-stricken.—*n* the poor, the weak, the unhandy.

fecklessly *adv* **1** weakly. **2** incompetently. **2** irresponsibly.

fecklessness *n* **1** weakness. **2** incompetence. **3** worthlessness.

fecklins[1] *adj* **1** physically weak. **2** spiritless. **3** irresponsible. **4** worthless.

fecklins[2] *adv* **1** mostly,chiefly. **2** almost.

fecklish *same as* **feckless**.

feckly *adv* for the most part, mainly.

fecks *int* faith!

fecky *adj* gaudy.

fect *same as* **feck**[1].

fectfully *same as* **feckfully**.

fedam *same as* **feydom**.

fedder *same as* **feather**.

fede *n* a feud, enmity.

fed-gang *n* a low, narrow chest, extending along a wooden bed and serving as a step to enter it.

fedmart *n* **1** an ox fattened for killing at Martinmas. **2** used also figuratively for one whose prosperity paves the way for his destruction.

fedmel, fedmal, fedmill *adj* **1** fattened. **2** gluttonous. **3** fat and lazy.

fedmit *n* a glutton.—*adj* gluttonous.

fee[1] *same as* **fey**[2].

fee[2] *n* **1** salary. **2** a servant's wages, recompense.—*v* **1** to engage for wages, hire oneself. **2** to hire servants.

feech *int* an exclamation of disgust.

feechie *same as* **feeshie**.

feed *v* to supply a mill or machine with material. —*n* food, fodder, for cattle, etc.

fee'd *v, adj* engaged for service.

feeder *n* **1** an ox being fattened for the market. **2** one who supplies a mill or machine with material. **3** one who supplies balls, cherry stones, etc, in various games. **4** one who fattens cattle for the butcher.

feeding storm *n* an increasing fall of snow which threatens to continue long.

feeding mairt *n* a bullock fattened for winter provision.

feedle *n* a field.

feedlie *n* a small field.

feedom *same as* **feydom**.

feedow *n* the store of cherry stones from which children furnish their castles of pips.

feegarie *same as* **fleegarie**.

feegh *int* an exclamation of disgust.

feegur *n* a figure.

feeing *n* engaging as servants.

feeing fair, ~ market *n* a hiring fair or market for farm servants.

feek-fike *same as* **fike-fack**.

feel[1] *v* **1** to smell. **2** to taste. **3** to understand, comprehend.

feel[2] *n* a fool.—*adj* foolish.

feel[3], **feele** *same as* **feil**[1].

feeless *adj* without wages or recognized worth.

feelimageeries *n* gewgaws, knick-knacks, useless trifles.

feelin'-hairted *adj* tender- or kind-hearted.

feelless *adj* **1** without feeling or sensation. **2** insensible.

feem[1] *v* to lie by, in the game of marbles.

feem[2] *same as* **fame**[2].

feeneekin *n* **1** a small person. **2** a person of a tart or finical disposition.

feenichin *adj* **1** foppish. **2** fantastical. **3** finical.

feent *same as* **fient**.

feer[1] *v* **1** to draw the first furrow in ploughing. **2** to mark out the riggs before ploughing the whole field.

feer[2] *same as* **fier**[1].

feer[3] *same as* **fere**[1].

feer[4] *same as* **fere**[4].

feerach[1] *same as* **farrach**.

feerach[2] *same as* **foorich**.

feerachin *adj* bustling, agitated.—*n* a bustling, confused state.

feerdy *adj* **1** strong, able-bodied. **2** hale and hearty. —*n* a person of good constitution.

feerdy-limbed *adj* stalwart, having sturdy limbs.

feer for feer *phr* an equal match.

feerich[1] *same as* **farrach**.

feerich[2] *same as* **foorich**.

feerichin *adj* bustling.

feene *adj* **1** clever. **2** active. **3** nimble.

feerie *adj* **1** in poor health. **2** looking weakly.

feerilie *adv* nimbly, cleverly.

feering *n* the furrow drawn out to mark the riggs before ploughing the whole field.

feering furrow *n* the feering (qv).

feerious *adj* **1** furious. **2** exceeding.—*adv* (*used intensively*) exceedingly.

feerly *same as* **ferely**.

feeroch[1] *same as* **farrach**.

feeroch[2] *same as* **foorich**.

feerochrie[1] *same as* **farrach**.

feerochrie[2] *same as* **foorich**.

feerrich *same as* **foorich**.

feers *same as* **fiars**.

Feersday *n* Thursday.

feery *n* **1** tumult, bustle, confusion. **2** rage, passion.

feery-fary *n* **1** a great hubbub. **2** an angry tumult.

feery o' the feet *phr* active in moving the feet.

feese[1] *same as* **fease**[1].

feese[2] *same as* **fease**[2].

feese[3] *v* to saunter about a spot.

feese[4] *v* fetched.

feesh *v* fetched.

feeshie *int* an exclamation keeping or bringing an opponent to a point, used in boys' fights and games.

feesic *n* physic.

feess *v* fetched.

feesyhant *n* a pheasant.

feet *n* (*in curling*) an acceleration of a stone by sweeping before it.

feet-ale *n* drink after a cattle sale, paid by the seller.

feet-fa'in' *n* the period of childbirth.

feeth, feeth net *n* a fixed net stretching across a river.

feeties *n* **1** a child's feet. **2** small feet.

feeting *n* running.

feets *n* **1** *in phr* **fit-out-o'-the-feets** a designation given to one who betrays a genuine spirit of contradiction. **2** one who will not keep his feet out of the theets or traces.

feetsides *n* ropes used for chains, fixed to the haims and to the swingletree in ploughing.

feet up *int* a call to a stumbling horse.

feet-washing *n* **1** the custom of washing the feet of a bride or a bridegroom the night before marriage. **2** the night before marriage.

feeze *same as* **fease**[2].

feeze about *v* **1** to hang about, to keep near a place. **2** to potter or shuffle about. **3** to turn round.

feeze into *v* to ingratiate oneself, to worm into confidence.

feeze-nail *n* a screw nail.

feeze off *v* to unscrew.

feeze on *v* to screw.

feeze-pin *n* a screw pin.

feeze up *v* **1** to flatter. **2** to work up into a passion.

feezing *n* **1** a continuance of hard rubbing. **2** briskness in working. **3** (*in pl*) the stringy parts of cloth when the woof is rubbed out from the warp.

feff *n* a stench, bad odour.

feft *adj* **1** put in legal possession. **2** claimed by right or long possession.

feftment *n* enfeoffment.

feg[1] *n* **1** a thing of no value. **2** a fig.

feg[2] *v* **1** to propel a marble with the thumb from the middle of the second finger curved. **2** to knock off a marble lying close to another.

feghie-lechie *same as* **fechie-lechie**.

fegrim *n* **1** a whim. **2** finery.

fegs *n* faith.—*int* truly! used in mild oaths and exclamations of surprise.

feich *same as* **feigh**.

feid *n* **1** feud, enmity. **2** a cause of quarrel. **3** an enemy.

feidom *n* enmity.

feigh *int* fie! an exclamation of disgust.

feighing *v* uttering exclamations of disgust.

feight *same as* **fecht**.

feignyie *v* **1** to feign, pretend. **2** to forge.

feik *same as* **fike**[1].

feike *v* **1** to screw. **2** to force. **3** to abate a legal due under pressure.

feik-fak *same as* **fike-fack**.

feil[1] *adj* **1** comfortable, snug. **2** soft, smooth. **3** silky to the touch.

feil[2] *adj* many.

feil[3] *same as* **fail**[1].

feil[4] *adv* **1** very. **2** exceedingly.

feil-beg *n* a fillibeg.

feim *same as* **fame**[2].

feint, feind *same as* **fient**.

feinyie, feinzie *v* **1** to feign. **2** to forge.

feir[1] *same as* **feer**[1].

feir[2] *same as* **fier**[1].

feir[3] *same as* **fere**[1].

feir[4] *n* military equipment.

feirdy *same as* **feerdy**.

feirie *same as* **feerie**.

feiroch[1] *same as* **farrach**.

feiroch[2] *same as* **foorich**.

feish *v* fetched.

feist[1] *n* a noiseless breaking of wind.

feist[2] *v* to exert oneself with difficulty and little effect.—*n* **1** exertion with little effect. **2** a weak person.

feit *same as* **feat**.

feith *same as* **feeth**.

fek *same as* **feck**.

fell[1] *n* the cuticle immediately above the flesh.

fell[2] *n* **1** a fairly level field on the top or side of a hill. **2** untilled ground or ground unfit for pasture, lying high.

fell[3] *v* **1** to stun. **2** to kill. **3** to injure severely or fatally. **4** to surpass, beat. **5** to cast out a net from a boat. **6** to befall, happen.—*n* **1** lot, destiny. **2** a knock-down blow.

fell[4] *adj* **1** keen, pungent, tasty. **2** eager, desirous, energetic, sharp, intelligent. **3** severe, cutting. **4** strong, valiant, vigorous. **5** grave, serious, weighty. **6** strange, unusual. **7** great, very large. —*adv* exceedingly, used as an intensive.

fell[5] *same as* **fail**[1].

fell[6] *n* a large quantity.

fell-bloom *n* the birds' trefoil, yellow clover.

fell-down *n* a fight, struggle.

felled *adj* **1** overcome with surprise. **2** prostrate with illness.

felled-~, fell't-sick *adj* extremely sick, so as to be unable to stir.

fellenly *adv* vigorously. **2** effectively.

fellill, fellin *n* a disease affecting the skin of cattle.

fellin[1] *same as* **fellill**.

fellin[2], **fellon** *adv* **1** pretty. **2** very. **3** wonderfully.

fellon[1] *same as* **fellin**.

fellon[2], **felon** *n* a whitlow.

fellon-, fellin-grass *n* the plant *Angelica sylvestris*.

fell-rot *n* a disease of sheep, affecting the skin.
fell well *adv* very well.
felt[1] *n* **1** creeping wheat-grass, couchgrass. **2** a thick growth of weeds.—*v* to become matted or entangled.
felt[2], **feltie** *n* the missel-thrush.
felt[3] *n* the disease of the stone.
felter *v* **1** to encumber, cling about. **2** to weave cloth faultily. **3** to filter, fall in drops.—*n* a fault in weaving, a knot.
felt-~, felty-gravel *n* the disease of the sandy gravel.
feltifare *n* the redshank.
feltiflyer *n* the fieldfare.
felt-marshal *n* a provost marshal.
femlans *n* the remains of a feast.
femmel *v* to select the best, rejecting the remainder as refuse.
femmil *adj* **1** well-knit, athletic. **2** active, agile.—*n* strength, stamina.
fen' *same as* **fend**.
fence *v* **1** to protect from, defend. **2** to open formally an assembly or law court. **3** to warn off, debar from the Lord's Table unworthy communicants.—*n* **1** the act of fencing a court. **2** a prohibition. **3** security.
fence-fed *adj* stall-fed, well-nourished.
fence-louper *n* **1** an animal that leaps over bounds or fences in a field. **2** an intractable person. **3** one who goes beyond bounds.
fencer *n* **1** a pugilist. **2** anyone who fights with his fists.
fencible *adj* capable of bearing arms to defend the country.—*n* (*in pl*) **1** militia. **2** persons capable of bearing arms.
fencing *n* the warning addressed to intending communicants before the administration of our Lord's Supper.
fencing prayer *n* prayer in connection with the fencing of the tables.
fend *v* **1** to defend, shelter, guard. **2** to ward off, turn aside. **3** to work hard for a livelihood, to struggle. **4** to make shift, provide for. **5** to fare, get on. **6** to support life, exist. **7** to manage, provide subsistence.—*n* **1** a defence, protection. **2** an attempt, endeavour. **3** a struggle for existence. **4** provision, food. **5** a makeshift.
fend-cauld *n* what wards off the cold.
fend-fou *adj* resourceful, good at finding expedients.
fendie, fendy *adj* **1** economical. **2** resourceful. **3** handy. **4** buoyant. **5** healthy.
fending *n* **1** means of subsistence, livelihood. **2** management, providence.
fendless *adj* **1** shiftless. **2** without energy. **3** weak, without body or flavour.
fenester *n* **1** a window. **2** a casement.
fengie *v* to feign.
fenniegreg *n* fenugreek.
fennin *same as* **fending**.
fenny *same as* **fendie**.
fensible *adj* well fenced.
fent *n* **1** an opening or slit in a sleeve, shirt, coat or petticoat. **2** (*in pl*) remnants of cloth sewed together.
fent-piece *n* a piece of cloth sewed to the upper end of a fent (qv) to prevent its tearing.
Fenwick twist *n* a twist given in delivering a curling stone, introduced first and practised more generally by the curlers of Fenwick in Ayrshire.
fenzie *same as* **feignyie**.
fercost *same as* **farcost**.
ferd *n* force.
ferdilest *adj* strongest, stoutest.
ferdin *same as* **fardin**.
ferdy *same as* **feerdy**.
fere *n* **1** a friend, comrade. **2** a spouse. **3** an equal, match.
fere[1] *n* a company, a troop.
fere[2] *n* a puny, dwarfish person.
fere[3] *adj* **1** strong, sturdy, entire. **2** *phr* **hale and fere** thoroughly healthy, whole and entire.
ferely *adv* vigorously.
feriat *adj* observed as a festival.

ferie *same as* **feery**.
ferie-fary *n* bustle, stir, disorder.
feriness *n* adhesiveness, consolidation.
Ferintosh *n* peat-reek whisky distilled at Ferintosh in Ross-shire.
feritie *n* violence.
ferkishin *n* **1** a crowd. **2** a large quantity.
ferle *same as* **farle**.
ferly *adj* strange, wonderful.—*n* **1** a wonder. **2** a novelty. **3** a curio, a curiosity. **4** used contemptuously for a sight, spectacle. **5** (*in pl*) show things of a place.—*v* to wonder, be surprised at.
ferly-full *adj* **1** astonished. **2** filled with wonder.
ferly-, ferlie-troke *n* a strange, miscellaneous stock of goods.
ferm[1] *n* prepared gut as the string of a fiddle, etc.
ferm[2], **ferme** *n* **1** a farm. **2** farm rent.
ferme-meal *n* meal paid as rent.
fermentated *adj* (*used of the stomach*) distended owing to the fermenting of its contents.
fern *same as* **ferm**[1].
fernent *same as* **forenent**.
ferner *n* **1** a remote, indefinite period. **2** a time or date that may never arrive.—*adv* never.
ferniegreg *n* fenugreek.
fer-nothing *same as* **fear-nothing**.
fern storm *n* rain caused by the burning of fern or heather.
fern-tickled *adj* freckled.
fern-tickles *n* freckles.
ferny-buss *n* a clump of ferns.
fern-year, ~-yer *n* **1** the last or past year. **2** a time that may never come.
ferny-hirst *n* a fern-clad hill.
ferny-, ferni-tickle *n* a freckle.
fern-zear, ~-zeer, ~-zier *n* fern-year (qv).
ferra *same as* **farrow**.
ferrichie *adj* strong, robust.
ferrick *same as* **fairock**.
ferrow *same as* **farrow**
ferry *v* to bring forth young.—*adj* not in calf, farrow.
ferry-louper *n* **1** a settler from Scotland in Orkney. **2** one not a native of Orkney.
fersell, fershell *adj* bustling, energetic.—*v* **1** to fuss about. **2** to rustle, bustle.
fersie *n* the farcy.
ferss, fers *adj* fierce.—*adv* fiercely.
ferter[1] *n* a fairy.
ferter[2], **fertor, fertour** *n* a casket, a coffin.
ferter-like *adj* **1** seeming ready for the coffin. **2** death-like.
ferture *n* wrack and ruin.
ferven' *adv* eagerly, readily, fervently.
fesart *same as* **faizart**.
fesh[1] *v* to fetch.
fesh[2] *same as* **fash**.
feshen *v* fetched.
fesil *same as* **fissle**.
fes'n *v* to fasten.
fess *v* to fetch.
fessen *v* to fasten.—*v* fetched.
fess't, fest *adj and adv* fast.
fest *n* a feast, festival.
festen *v* to fasten, to bind.
Festeren's ~, Festren's Eve *same as* **Faster Eve**.
festy-cook *n* new-ground meal made into a ball and baked among the burning seeds in a kiln or mill.
fetch *v* **1** to draw a long breath, gasp. **2** to pull by fits and starts. **3** to strike a blow. **4** to arrive at. **5** to catch sight of.—*n* **1** a trick, stratagem. **2** a long, deep breath, as of one dying. **3** a tug. **4** a jerk.
fetching *n* **1** a long, deep breath. **2** a gasping for breath.
feth *n* faith.—*int* faith!
fether *n* father.
fetherfewie *n* feverfew.
fethir *same as* **feather**.

fett *same as* **feat**.

fettle *n* **1** state, condition. **2** temper, humour. **3** energy, power. **4** order, repair. **5** faculty or capacity of speech, movement, etc.—*v* **1** to repair, put in good order. **2** to attend to animals. **3** to dress, put on clothes. **4** to trim up. **5** to beat, settle. **6** to set about or to work. **7** to manage.—*adj* **1** trim. **2** well made. **3** in good condition.

fettle *n* **1** a rope or strap by which a creel can be carried on the back, leaving the arms free. **2** a handle of straw or rope on the side of a large basket or creel.—*v* **1** to wind a band or rope round anything. **2** to fasten a fettle to a creel.

feu[1] *n* land held in perpetuity or for 99 years, generally, in payment of a yearly rent.—*v* **1** to let out land in feu. **2** to take land in feu.

feu[2] *same as* **few**[2].

feuach *n* a very short, light crop of grass or grain.

feuar *n* one who takes land in feu (qv), generally for building.

feuch[1] *int* an exclamation of disgust.

feuch[2] *same as* **feugh**[1]

feuch[3] *same as* **feugh**[2].

feuchin *same as* **feughen**.

feuchin up *n* a sound beating.

feuchit *n* a sounding blow.

feuchter *same as* **feughter**.

feu duty, ~ ferme *n* the yearly rent of a feu (qv).

feug *n* a sharp and sudden blow.

feuggil *n* a small twisted bundle of hay, straw, rags, etc, for stopping a hole.

feuggle *v* to beat soundly

feugglin' *n* a beating.

feugh[1] *v* to smoke.—*n* a short smoke.

feugh[2] *n* **1** a sounding blow. **2** a sharp and sudden blow. **3** a rush, a rushing sound.—*v* **1** to work hard. **2** (*with* **up**) to beat soundly.

feughen *v* fought.

feughin up *n* a sound beating.

feught *v* fought.

feughter *n* a sudden, slight fall of snow.

feurd *n* a ford.

feure *n* a furrow.

fever *v* to become excited.

fever-foullie *n* the feverfew.

fever-largie, ~-largin *n* laziness, idleness.

fever-wheelie *n* the feverfew.

few[1] *adj in phr* **a few broth, etc** a small quantity of broth, etc.

few[2] *v* **1** to show promise or aptitude. **2** to make a good beginning.

fewe *adj* fallow.

fewgie *v* to manipulate cleverly or artfully.

fews *n* the house-leek.

fey[1] *n* a small field or croft.

fey[2] *adj* **1** doomed to calamity or death. **2** acting unnaturally, as if under doom. **3** (*of grain*) decayed, reduced in substance.—*n* the warning or predestination or presage of calamity or doom. —*v* **1** to be mad. **2** to act unnaturally and so presage death.

fey-crop *n* a crop more than usually large, portending the owner's death.

feydom *n* a presentiment of calamity or death.

feyk *same as* **fike**[1].

fey-land *n* **1** the portion of a farm formerly getting all the farmyard dung and being constantly cropped. **2** the best land on the farm.

fey-like *adj* as if fey (qv) or doomed.

feyness *n* **1** the state of being fey (qv). **2** a wraith, a spectral likeness.

fey-taiken *n* a presentiment betokening or presaging death.

feyther *n* father.

fial[1] *n* one who receives wages.

fial[2] *n* **1** one who has the reversion of property. **2** one who holds land in fee.

fiars *n* the prices of grain legally fixed for the year in each county.

fiarter *n* **1** a term of disrespect. **2** an untidy person.

fib *v* to fight as a pugilists.

fibsch *n* a big person of disagreeable temper.

ficher *v* **1** to work slowly and awkwardly. **2** to fumble, trifle, fidget.—*n* **1** slow, awkward work. **2** toying, fumbling. **3** a fumbler, a person slow and awkward at work.

ficherin' *n* trifling, idling, fidgeting.

fichil *n* a challenge to a difficult feat.

fichil-pins *same as* **fickle-pins**.

fick-fack[1] *n* **1** the ligament running along the vertebrae of the back. **2** the tendon of the neck.

fick-fack[2],**-fyke** *same as* **fike-fack**.

fickle *v* **1** to puzzle, entangle. **2** to cause to fidget. **3** to do what others cannot do.—*adj* **1** unsafe. **2** treacherous. **3** ticklish.

fickle-pins *n* a game in which a number of rings are taken off a double wire united at both ends.

fickly *adj* puzzling.

ficks *n* a disease of sheep.

fid *v* **1** to move up and down or from side to side. **2** to wag like a rabbit's tail.—*n* a small wooden chisel for splicing ropes.

fidder[1] *conj* whether.

fidder[2] *v* to move like a hawk when it wishes to remain stationary over a place or like a bird in the nest over her young.

fidder[3] *same as* **fudder**.

fiddle[1] *v* **1** to dawdle, trifle. **2** to walk with short, quick steps.

fiddle[2] *n* the proper or correct thing.

fiddle-diddle *n* **1** the music of the fiddle. **2** the movements of a fiddler's arm in playing.

fiddle-doup *n* a term of contempt.

fiddle-faddle *n* **1** nonsense, fancifulness. **2** whim, trifle.— *v* to trifle, dawdle.

fiddle-fike *n* **1** a troublesome peculiarity of conduct. **2** an overpunctilious person. **3** a trifler.

fiddle-ma-fyke *n* a silly, fastidious person.

fiddler *n* the common sandpiper.

fiddler's news *phr* stale news.

fiddltie-fa *n* **1** a trifling excuse. **2** hesitancy.—*v* **1** to hesitate. **2** to make much ado about nothing.

fidel-didel *same as* **fiddle-diddle**.

fidge *v* **1** to fidget, move restlessly, kick with the feet. **2** to be anxious, to worry. **3** to be eager.—*n* **1** a fidget, twitch. **2** a shrug.

fidge-fain, ~-fu' fain *v* to be eager with restlessness.

fidgie[1] *same as* **fugie**.

fidgie[2] *n* a mealy pudding.

fidgin *n* **1** fidgeting. **2** uneasiness.

fidgy *adj* restless, fidgety.

fidjie-fiz *n* the crowberry.

fie *same as* **fey**[2].

fiedle *same as* **feedle**.

fief *same as* **feff**.

fief-like *adj* malodorous.

fie-gae-to *n* a great bustle.

fiel[1] *adv* very.

fiel[2] *v* **1** to feel. **2** to understand.

field *v* to sink a margin round a panel of wood.

fieldert *adv* towards the fields, abroad.

fieldfare *n* the mistle thrush.

field-gear *n* gala attire.

fielding-plane *n* the plane used in sinking a margin round a panel of wood.

field-man *n* a peasant.

fieldwart *adv* towards the fields, abroad.

field-wench *n* a female fieldworker.

fieldy *n* the hedge sparrow.

fien *n* a fiend.

fienden *n* the devil.

fient, fiend *n* **1** devil, the fiend. **2** used in negations as an oath or exclamation like 'devil a'.

fient-a-bit, ~-flee, ~-gear, ~-hair, ~-hait *phrs* nothing at all, not at all.
fient-a-fear *phr* no fear!
fient ane *phr* not one.
fient ane o' me, fient o' me *phr* **1** not I for my part. **2** by no means I.
fient-ma-care *phr* no matter.
fient-perlicket *phr* nothing at all.
fier[1] *n* **1** a standard of any kind. **2** a tall, lanky person.
fier[2] *same as* **fere**[1].
fier[3] *same as* **fere**[4].
fier[4] *v* to draw the first furrow in ploughing.
fiercelings, fiercelins *adv* **1** fiercely, with violence. **2** in haste.—*adj* fierce, violent.
fiercie *n* the farcy.
fierd *n* afaert.
fierdy *same as* **feerdy**.
fieroch *same as* **foorich**.
Fiersday *n* Thursday.
fiery, fierie *same as* **feery**.
fiery-bron *n* a blazing peat or brand used for signalling, as a torch.
fiery-fary *same as* **feery-fary**.
fiery-flaw *n* the stingray.
fiery-stick *n* stern reality, dead earnest.
fiery-tangs *n* **1** a crab. **2** a lobster.
fiery-water *n* marine phosphorescence.
fiery-wud *adj* **1** eager, keen. **2** quite mad.
fiese-wilk *n* the striated whelk.
fifer *n* a boys' marble, soft and of a dull brown colour.
fifish *adj* **1** rather eccentric. **2** weak in mind or deranged.
fifishness *n* eccentricity. **2** lack of saneness.
fifteen *n in phr* **the fifteen 1** the judges of the Court of Session, before the reduction of their number. **2** the Rebellion of 1715.
fig *n* **1** a metal vest button, used in the game of buttons. **2** a thing of little value.
fige *same as* fidge.
fig-fag *same as* **fick-fack**[1].
figgle *same as* **feuggil**.
figgle-faggle *n* **1** silly or trifling conduct. **2** ludicrous or unbecoming conduct.
figgle-faggler *n* one who destroys good morals.
figgleligee *adj* **1** finical, foppish. **2** ostentatiously polite.
fight *v* **1** to struggle. **2** to harass.—*n* effort, struggle.
figmalirie *n* a whim, a whigmaleerie (qv).
figure *v* **1** to do arithmetic. **2** to count.
figuring *n* arithmetic.
fike[1] *v* **1** to fidget, move restlessly. **2** to fuss over trifles. **3** to vex oneself. **4** to trouble, make uneasy. **5** to flirt, dally with a woman. **6** to shrug.—*n* **1** a restless motion, a fidget. **2** bustle, fuss. **3** trouble, care, worry. **4** dalliance, flirtation. **5** a whim, freak. **6** a fancy article, a gewgaw.
fike[2] *n* burnt leather.
fike-fack *n* **1** a troublesome, finicking job. **2** needless stir. **3** (*in pl*) minute pieces of work, causing great trouble. **4** little troublesome peculiarities of temper. **5** nonsense.— *v* to trifle away time.
fike-ma-facks *n* **1** nonsense. **2** silly trifling sayings.
fikery *n* **1** fussiness. **2** worry about trifles or troubles.
fiket *adj* **1** fidgety. **2** difficult to please, fastidious.
fikiness *n* agitation.
fiking *n* trouble, effort.—*adj* troublesome, bustling.
fiking-fain *adj* restlessly eager.
fik-ma-fyke *n* **1** a silly, unsettled creature. **2** one busied with nonentities and trifles.
fiky *adj* **1** troublesome, fidgety, fastidious, worrying over trifles, punctilious. **2** itchy. **3** restive.
filbow *n* a thump, a thwack.
filch *same as* **filsch**[1].
filchan *n* **1** a confused, dirty mass. **2** (*in pl*) rags patched or fastened together. **3** the attire of a travelling beggar.
file[1] *n* class or rank in society.

file[2] *v* **1** to defile, soil. **2** to disorder. **3** to accuse. **4** to condemn.
file[3] *conj* as long as.—*n* **1** a while. **2** (*in pl*) now and then.
filement *n* **1** obloquy. **2** moral filth.
filie *n* a little while.
filik *n* a little while.
filing *n* the act of soiling.
filjit *n* **1** a disreputable vagabond. **2** a tramp.
filk *pron* which.
fill[1] *pron* which.
fill[2] *v* **1** to hold a lease of a farm. **2** to fill bobbins with yarn.—*n* anything that fills, as a fill of tobacco or of a pipe, etc.
fill[3] *adv* while.—*prep* until.
fillad *n* a thigh.
fill and fetch mair *phr* **1** riotous prodigality. **2** a continuous bout of drinking.
filler *n* a funnel for filling bottles, etc, with liquid.
fill-fou *n* as much liquor as makes one quite drunk.
fillbeg, filabey, filibeg, filipeg, fillabeg *n* the short kilt worn by Highlanders.
fillies *n* felloes, fellies.
fillister *n* the plane used for making the outer part of a window sash fit for receiving glass.
fillock *n* a filly or young mare.
filly-tails *n* fleecy cirrus clouds.
filock *n* a little while.
filp[1] *n* a person of disagreeable temper.
filp[2] *n* a fall off one's feet.
filrey *adj* fussy, troublesome about trifles.
filsch[1]**, filsh** *n* **1** grass or weeds covering a field, especially when under crop. **2** a long, lean, lank person or child. **3** a term of contempt, generally applied to a man. **4** a bad character. **5** a detested person.
filsch[2] *n* a thump, a blow.
filsch[3]**, filsh** *adj* **1** empty, hungry. **2** faint.—*v* **1** to faint. **2** to flinch.
filsched-up *adj* filschy (qv).
filschy *adj* (*used of a sheaf*) swelled up with weeds or natural grass.
filsh *v* to filch, procure by stealth.
filshens *n* tattered garments
filter *same as* **felter**.
fimmer *v* to move the feet quickly in walking or in dancing gracefully.
fin[1] *adv* when.
fin[2] *n* basalt, whinstone.
fin'[1] *n* **1** humour, vein. **2** temper. **3** eagerness. **4** anger.
fin'[2] *v* **1** to find. **2** to feel, have a sensation of. **3** to feel, grope, search. **4** to provide, supply.—*n* feel, sensation, feeling.
Findhorn haddock *n* a haddock split and cured by smoking, so called from Findhorn in Morayshire.
finding *n* searching, feeling, groping.
findle *n* **1** anything found. **2** the act of finding. **3** treasure-trove.
Findon haddock *same as* **finnan haddie**.
findrum *same as* **Findhorn haddock**.
findrum speldin' *n* a small haddock, split and dried in the sun until hard and tough.
findsily *adj* clever or apt to find.
findy *adj* **1** full, substantial, solid. **2** supporting.
fine *adj* **1** docile, well-behaved, agreeable. **2** very well. **3** in good health or spirits. **4** prosperous.—*adv* **1** very much. **2** perfectly. **3** finely. **4** prosperously.—*v* to free wool from the coarse parts.
fine and *phr* very.
fineer *v* to veneer.
fine-lever *n* a levier of fines.
finely *adv* perfectly, quite well, used of convalescence.
fineries *n* delicacies, dainties.
finever *adv* whenever.
Fingauls *n* a name formerly given to inhabitants of the south end of Kirkmaiden parish in Wigtownshire.
finger *v* (*in weaving*) to work the flowers on a web.

finger-and-toe *n* a disease of turnips.

finger-brod *n* the part of a fiddle grasped by the left hand.

fingerer *n* the boy or girl who fingers on a web. *See* **finger**.

finger-fed *adj* delicately reared, pampered.

finger-full *n* a pinch, very small quantity.

fingering *n* fine worsted, spun from combed wool on the small wheel.

fingering breid *n* a better quality of oatcake, finely baked and toasted, thin and brittle, for a farmer's own table.

fingerings *n* a coarse, slight, woollen cloth.

finger-neb *n* a fingertip.

finger o' scorn *phr* a contemptible fellow.

fingroms *same as* **fingerings**.

fingted *n* a bandaged finger.

finnack, finnock *n* a white trout, in colour and shape like a salmon.

Finnan haddie *n* a haddock, split and cured with smoke, so called from the village of Findon in Kincardineshire.

finner *same as* **finnack**.

finnie¹ *n* a salmon not a year old.

finnie² *same as* **findy**.

finnie³ *n* sensation, the feeling imparted by a thing.

finnin *same as* **fienden**.

finnisin, finnison *n* **1** anxious expectation. **2** earnest desire.—*adj* eager, very desirous.

fin'sily *same as* **findsily**.

fint *same as* **fient**.

fintock *n* the cloudberry.

fintram *same as* **Findhorn haddock**.

finzach *n* the knotgrass.

fipple *same as* **faiple**.

fir *n* a pine-torch, firwood used as a candle.

firach *n* **1** a fire. **2** a fluster. **3** a fit of fiery temper.

fir-candle *n* **1** a torch. **2** firwood used as a candle.

fir-dale *n* a plank of fir.

fire *n* **1** fuel. **2** a light to a pipe. **3** a smithy spark, especially when it strikes the eyeball. **3** marine phosphorescence. **4** carburetted hydrogen in coalmines. **5** sheet lightning. **6** the sultriness preceding a thunderstorm.—*v* **1** to bake or toast bread. **2** to discharge any missile. **1** to cauterize. **2** to inflame or irritate the skin. **3** to warm. **4** to scorch grass or grain by lightning or hot, dry winds. **5** to light up. **6** to brighten up. **7** to spoil milk in sultry weather.

fire and tow *phr* an irascible person.

fire-bit, ~-burn *n* marine phosphorescence.

fire-cheek *n* the fireside.

fire-cross *n* the fiery cross.

fired *adj* **1** (*used of the skin*) irritated. **2** (*of milk*) tasting ill from sultry weather.

fire-dairt *n* lightning.

fire-drum *n* a drum beaten as an alarm of fire.

fire-edge *n* the first eagerness or heat.

fire-en' *n* **1** the fireplace. **2** the end of a room where the fireplace is.

fire-engines *n* cannon, guns, pistols, etc.

fire-fang, ~-fangit *adj* **1** (*of cheese*) spoiled by too much heat before drying. **2** (*of manure*) spoiled by over-fermentation. **3** (*of food*) scorched.

fire-fanging *n* the effect of too much heat on cheese, dung, etc.

fire-fangitness *n* the state of being fire-fangit. *See* **firefang**.

fire-flaught *n* a flash of lightning.

fire-flaw *n* the stingray.

fire house *n* **1** the kitchen of a two-roomed cottage. **2** a house in which there is at least one fireplace.

fire-hung *adj* hanging over the fire.

fire-kettle *n* a pot for holding fire in a fishing boat.

fire-kindling *n* a house-warming entertainment.

fire-levin *n* lightning.

fire-lug *n* the side of the fireplace.

fire-penny *n* a charge for use of flint and steel, paid in kind.

fire room *n* **1** the sitting room of a cotter family. **2** a room with a fireplace.

fire-shool *n* a fire shovel.

fire-slaught *n* lightning.

fire-spang *n* a quick-tempered person.

fire-tail, fire-tail-bob *n* the redstart.

fir-ewe *n* a fir cone used as a child's plaything.

fire-wheel *n* a St Catherine's wheel.

fireworks *n* firearms.

fir-fecket *n* a coffin.

fir-futtle *n* a large knife for cutting fir-candles. *See* **fir-candle**.

fir-gown *n* a coffin.

firie *same as* **feery**.

firie-farry *same as* **feery-fary**.

firing-girdle *n* a baking-griddle.

fir-jacket *n* a coffin.

firk *v* **1** to poke, rummage among. **2** to pilfer.

firl¹ *v* to measure corn.

firl² *n* a ferrule.

firiot *n* **1** a corn measure of varying capacity. **2** a large quantity. **3** a quarter of a boll.

firmance *n* **1** stability. **2** imprisonment.

firnackit *same as* **fornackit**.

firnie *n* a quarrel, broil.

firple *v* to whimper.—*n* the under-lip.

firrating *n* **1** a kind of tape, galloon. **2** a shoelace.

firry *same as* **feery**.

firrystoich *n* **1** a bustle. **2** a broil. **3** a fight.

firsle *v* **1** to bustle about. **2** to rustle.

first¹ *adj* next, ensuing.

first² *same as* **frist**.

firsten *adj* first.

firstend *n* the first payment of interest or a due.

first-foot, ~-fit *n* **1** the first person met on certain special occasions. **2** the first person met with on New Year's Day.—*v* to act as, or be, a first-foot.

first-footer *n* a first-foot (qv).

firstlin' *adj* first, earliest.

firstlins *adv* first, at first.

firth *n* **1** a place on a moor where peats for fuel could be cut. **2** a small wood. **3** an arm of the sea, especially one that is the estuary of a river.

firtig *v* to fatigue.

firtigesom *adj* fatiguing.

firwood *n* bogwood, formerly used for candles.

fir-yowe *same as* **fir-ewe**.

fiscal *n* the public prosecutor in criminal cases, the procurator fiscal.

fish¹ *v* to strive, try hard.

fish² *v* to splice, to fasten a piece of wood on a mast, etc, to strengthen it.

fish carle *n* a fisherman.

fish currie *n* any deep hole or recess in a river where fishes hide.

fisherland *n* land on the seashore used by fishermen to dry fish, spread nets, etc.

fish garth *n* an enclosure of stakes and wattles for catching fish in a river.

fish gouries *n* fish garbage.

fish-hake *n* **1** a weight anchoring a fishing line or net. **2** a triangular framework of wood for drying fish before cooking.

fish-, fishing hawk *n* the osprey.

fishick *n* the brown whistlefish.

fishing wand *n* a fishing rod.

fish rig *n* the backbone of a fish.

fish staff *n* a large iron hook with wooden handle for striking into the fish and lifting them into the boat.

fisk *n* **1** the Exchequer. **2** the Treasury.

fisle *same as* **fissle**.

fison *same as* **fushion**.

fissen *same as* **fushion**.

fissenless *same as* **fushionless**.

fissle, fissil *v* **1** to rustle. **2** to make a rustling, whistling sound, to whistle. **3** to cause to rustle. **4** to fidget. **5** to bustle about.—*n* **1** a whistling sound. **2** fussy compliments. **3** a fuss, bustle.

fissle-fisslin' *n* a faint rustling sound.

fissling *n* **1** a rustle. **2** a whistling. **3** the sound of wind in the keyhole.

fist *v* to grasp with the hand.

fist-foundered *adj* knocked down with the fists.

fistle *same as* **fissle**.

fisty *n* a left-handed person.

fit[1] *n* **1** the foot. **2** speed. **3** the lower part. **4** a footstep.—*v* **1** to go afoot. **2** to dance. **3** to kick. **4** to put a new foot to a stocking. **5** to add up, balance or adjust accounts.

fit[2] *adj* **1** able, capable. **2** inclined. **3** matching. **4** on the point of, ready. **5** in vigorous health.—*v* **1** to set up a mast. **2** to become, suit. **3** to provide what is fitting or supply what one wants. **4** to please.

fit[3] *n* **1** a whit. **2** a bit. **3** an action.

fit[4] *n* a custom, habit.

fit-ba' *n* a football.

fitband *n* **1** a halter for the feet. **2** a company of infantry.

fit-board, ~-brod *n* a footrest, a footstool.

fit-braid, ~-breeth *n* a foot-breadth.

fitch *v* **1** to move a thing slightly from its place. **2** to lift and lay down again. **3** to touch frequently. **4** (*used of a louse*) to crawl. **5** to fidget. **6** to move at the game of draughts.—*n* **1** a slight change of place. **2** a move in the game of draughts.

fitchie *same as* **fidgie**[2]

fit-dint *n* a footprint.

fite[1] *v* to cut, whittle.

fite[2] *adj* white.

fite-breid *n* loaf bread.

fit-eitch *n* a foot adze.

fit-fall *n* a grown-up lamb.

fit-feal *n* the skin of a lamb between castration and weaning.

fit-for-fit *phr* **1** very exactly. **2** step for step.

fit-gang *n* **1** as much ground as one can walk on. **2** a long, narrow chest extending alongside a wooden bed.

fither *adv, conj, pron* whether.

fithit *int* an exclamation of confirmation of one's saying.

fitless *adj* feeble on one's feet, apt to stumble.

fitless-cock *n* **1** a cake of lard and oatmeal boiled in broth. **2** a sodden bannock, usually made at Shrovetide.

fit-lickin' *adj* cringing, fawning.

fitlin *n* a loose bar to place the feet against in rowing.

fit-nowt *n* the hindmost pair of a team of oxen.

fitocks *n* large peats or sods, used for 'resting' a fire through the night.

fit-pad *n* a footpath.

fit peat *n* peat cut with the foot pressing on the peat spade.

fit rig *n* the ridge of land at the lower end of a field on which the horses and plough turn.

fit road *n* a footpath through enclosed lands.

fit rot *n* the foot rot in sheep.

fits *n in phr* **the fits and the fors o't** the whys and the wherefores of it, all about it.

fit-shakin' *n* a dance, a ball.

fit-side *adj* **1** on an equal footing. **2** upsides with, revenged upon.—*adv* step for step.—*n* (*in pl*) ropes, used for chains, attached to the haims and to the swingletree (qv) in ploughing.

fit-soam *n* an iron chain extending from the muzzle of the plough and fixed to the yoke of the oxen next the plough.

fitsole *n* the foot.

fitstap *n* a footstep.

fitsted, ~-stead *n* a footprint.

fitstool *n* the face of the earth, God's footstool.

fitter *v* **1** to patter or make a noise with the feet. **2** to potter about. **3** to totter in walking. **4** to injure by frequent treading. **5** to fumble. **6** to knock unsteadily.

fittering *n* fidgeting, fumbling.

fit-the-gutter *n* a low, loose slipper.

fittie[1] *n* a term of endearment addressed to a shepherd's dog.

fittie[2] *adj* having good feet, safe enough to walk with.

fittie[3] *adj* **1** expeditious. **2** neat, trim.

fittie[4] *n* **1** a short stocking. **2** a person with deformed feet. **3** a mud-stained foot.

fittie[5] *n* an imaginary person of a very useless nature.

fittie-fies *n* quirks, quibbles.

fittie-lan' *n* the near horse of the last pair in a plough, which walks on the unploughed land.

fitting[1] *n* **1** footing. **2** the footing of a stocking.

fitting[2] *n* training, preparation.

fitting-ale *n* a feast given by parents when their child begins to walk.

fittings *n* **1** peats set on end to dry. **2** (*in sing*) the setting of peats on end to dry.

fittininment *n* **1** concern, interest. **2** a good footing with a person.

fittocks *n* the feet of stockings cut off and worn as shoes.

fit-tree *n* the treadle of a spinning wheel.

fit-washing *same as* **feet-washing**.

fit-weary *adj* with weary feet.

fit-yoke *n* the hindermost pair of a team of oxen.

fiumart *same as* **foumart**.

five-sax *phr* five or six.

fivesome *n* a set of five, five together.

fivey *n* a game played with five small stones.

fivver *n* a fever.

fivvert *adj* fevered.

fix-fax *same as* **fike-fack**.

fizenwill *n* part of a gun belonging to the doghead.

fizz *n* **1** a blaze. **2** stir, bustle, fuss, commotion.—*v* **1** to make a spluttering sound. **2** to fuss, bustle about. **3** to rage.

fizzen, fizen *same as* **fushion**.

fizzenless *same as* **fushionless**.

fizzer *n* **1** any thing or person first-rate or excellent. **2** a puzzling question.

flaacht *n* a peat spade.

flab[1] *n* a mushroom.

flab[2] *n* a large, showy article.

flabby *adj* ostentatious, showy, foppish.

flabrigast *v* **1** to flabbergast. **2** to boast, brag.

flabrigastit *adj* **1** flabbergasted. **2** worn out with exertion, extremely fatigued.

flach *v* did fly, flew.

flachan *n* a flake of snow.

flacht *same as* **flaught**.

flachter *same as* **flaughter**.

flachter-golak *n* an earwig.

flachter-spade *same as* **flauchter-spade**.

flack[1] *n* a square plaid.

flack[2] *v* to hang loosely.

flacket *n* a small spirit flask.

flad *n* a piece, portion, slice.

fladge *n* **1** a flake, a large piece. **2** anything broad. **3** a broad-bottomed person.

flae[1] *same as* **flay**.

flae[2] *n* a flea.

flae[3] *same as* **fley**.

flaeie *adj* abounding in fleas.

flaesick *n* a blazing spark from a wood fire.

flaff *v* **1** to flutter, fly about, flap, wave. **2** to flap the wings. **3** (*used of the wind*) to blow in gusts. **4** to fan, blow up. **5** to go off, as gunpowder, to shoot forth.—*n* **1** a flutter of the wings. **2** a fop, one who flutters about. **3** a sudden gust of wind, a flash. **4** an instant. **5** a light blow, fillip. **6** a buffet.

flaffer[1] *v* **1** to flutter. **2** to move with a rustling, awkward motion.—*n* **1** a wing. **2** a fluttering motion. **3** a pound note.

flaffer[2] *n* a duckling, fledged over the body but as yet without quill-feathers.

flafferie *adj* light, easily compressible.

flaffin' *n* 1 a fluttering of the wings. 2 a flapping. 3 fluttering of the heart, palpitation. 4 any very light body. 5 a flake of any kind.—*adj* puffing, suddenly shooting out.

flag[1] *n* 1 a piece of green sward cut or pared off. 2 a large sod, placed at the back of a fire. 3 (*in pl*) a side pavement paved with flagstones.

flag[2] *n* a flake of snow.—*v* to snow in flakes.

flag[3] *n* a contemptuous name for a woman, a slut.

flagarie *same as* fleegarie.

flagartie *adj* squally, stormy.

flagaryin' *n* busying oneself about trifles of dress.

flaggid *n* a flogging.

flaght *same as* flaught[2].

flagirt *n* 1 a flapping, flaunting thing. 2 used as a term of reproach.

flagon bun *n* a bun baked in a can among hot water.

flagrum *n* a blow, thump.

flag-side *n in phr* the flag-side of a split haddock the side without the bone.

flaich *same as* flae[2]

flaik *same as* flack[1].

flaik-stand *n* 1 a refrigerator. 2 the cooling vessel through which the pipes pass in distilling.

flail *n* a tall, ungainly person.—*v* to beat, thump.

flailer *n* 1 a conclusive argument or blow. 2 a difficult question. 3 a thresher with the flail.

flain *same as* flane.

flainen *same as* flannen.

flaip *same as* flap.

flaiper[1] *same as* flapper.

flaiper[2] *n* a person foolish in dress and manners.—*v* to flaunt in foolish clothes.

flair[1] *n* the skate.

flair[2], flair[3] *same as* flare[1], flare[2].

flairach *n* a giddy person who talks much in a shrill voice and makes a great ado about little.—*v* to act as a flairach.

flairdy *v* 1 to coax, cajole, wheedle. 2 to flatter.

flairy *same as* flare[3].

flaisick *n* a spark shot out from burning wood

flait, flaite, flaitte *v* scolded.

flaither *v* to use wheedling or fawning language.

flake[1] *n* 1 a hurdle for penning sheep on a turnip field or cattle, etc., at a show. 2 a hurdle used as a gate or to close a gap in a fence. 3 a frame above the chimneypiece for holding a gun. 4 (*in pl*) temporary sheep pens.

flake[2] *n* a ray, a flash.

flaket *same as* flacket.

flam[1] *n* 1 a humbug, fabrication. 2 flattery, cajolery.—*v* to flatter, humbug.

flam[2] *n* pancake.

flam[3] *same as* flann.

flamb, flam *v* 1 to baste roasting meat. 2 to besmear oneself while eating.

flamboy *n* a flambeau, a torch.

flame[1] *n* 1 a fit of hot anger. 2 a species of carnation. 3 a sweetheart.—*v* 1 (*used of a flag*) to float gallantly in the wind. 2 1 (*of an author*) to become famous.

flame[2], flamm *same as* flamb.

flamfoo *n* 1 a gaudy ornament or frippery in a woman's dress. 2 a gaudily-dressed woman. 3 a woman fond of dress.

flaming *adj* shining out, egregious.

flamming *adj* (*used of oars*) dipping in and out of the water.

flamp *adj* 1 inactive. 2 in a state of lassitude.

flan[1] *adj* shallow, flat.

flan[2] *same as* flann.

flanch *same as* flansch.

Flanderkin *n* a Fleming, a native of Flanders.

flane *n* an arrow.

flang *v* flung.

flann, flan *n* 1 a sudden blast of wind off the land. 2 a

sudden down draught in a chimney.—*v* to be squally, gusty.

flannen *n* flannel.—*adj* made of flannel.

flanninette *n* flannelette.—*adj* made of flannelette.

flanny *adj* gusty, squally.

flansh *v* to flatter, wheedle.—*n* a flatterer. 2 a hypocrite.

flanter *v* 1 to waver. 2 to be slightly delirious. 3 to quiver in agitation. 4 to flinch, falter in speaking. 5 to prevaricate, equivocate.

flanty *adj* 1 eccentric, capricious. 2 flighty, unsteady.

flap *v* 1 to come or strike upon suddenly. 2 to flop, fall suddenly. 3 to fly, to turn inside out.—*n* 1 a blow caused by a fall and producing a dull, flat sound. 2 a fall on to a soft substance. 3 a slice. 4 a smart blow with anything flat.

flapdawdron *n* a tall, ill-dressed person.

flapper *n* 1 a heavy resounding fall. 2 a bird just able to fly.—*v* to flap, flutter.

flapper-bags *n* the burdock.

flare[1] *n* a floor.

flare[2] *v* to coax.—*n* cajolery, flattery.

flash[1] *v* 1 to spend lavishly. 2 to lash.

flash[2] *n* a depository for timber.

flashy-fiery *adj* flashing like fire.

flasicks *n* atoms, small pieces.

flass *n* a flask.

flast *v* to boast, brag.

flat *n* 1 a saucer. 2 a cake of cow dung. 3 low, level ground.—*v* to flatten.

flatch *v* 1 to flatten. 2 to lay over, fold down. 3 to knock down. 4 to walk clumsily.

flate[1] *v* scolded. *See* flite.

flate[2] *n* 1 a straw mat under a horse's saddle to prevent chafing. 2 one used as a draught screen or as an inner door.

flate[3] *n* a hurdle.

flat in the fore *phr* having the stomach empty, hungry.

flatlins, flatlines *adv* 1 flat. 2 with the flat side of anything.

flatter *v* to float.

flatterin' Friday *n* a fine Friday during a time of wet, supposed to indicate more wet weather.

flauf *same as* flaff.

flaught[1], flaucht, flauch, flauchten, flaughen *n* 1 a flake of snow. 2 a lock of hair. 3 a handful of wool before it is carded. 4 a roll of wool carded and ready for spinning. 5 a hide, skin. 6 a bunch, a piece cut off from a larger portion. 7 a flash, gleam. 8 a gust of wind. 9 a cloud of smoke from a chimney at either end. 10 a stream of vapour. 11 (*used of land*) a division, a croft.—*v* 1 to card wool into thin flakes. 2 to weave. 3 to pare turf, etc. 4 to strip off the skin or hide. 5 to mix, mingle. 6 to pilfer straw, hay, etc, in handfuls.

flaught[2], flaucht *n* 1 a spreading or a flapping of wings. 2 hurry, bustle, flutter. 3 sudden fright. 4 a number of birds on the wing. 5 (*used of aviation*) flight.—*v* 1 to flutter. 2 to palpitate. 3 to tremble. 4 (*used of aviation*) to fly.—*adv* 1 with wings outspread. 2 at full length. 3 with great eagerness.

flaught-bred *adv* 1 at full length. 2 with great eagerness.

flaughter[1] *n* 1 a skinner. 2 a carder of wool.

flaughter[2] *n* 1 a man who cuts peats with a flaughter spade (qv). 2 a thin turf pared from the ground.—*v* to pare off turf from the ground.

flaughter[3] *v* 1 to flutter as a bird. 2 to flicker, waver, move hither and thither aimlessly. 3 to flurry, alarm, frighten.—*n* a flutter, fluttering motion.

flaughter[4] *v* to fell, prostrate.—*n* 1 a heavy fall. 2 a knockdown blow.

flaughterer *n* one who cuts peats with a flaughter spade (qv).

flaughter-fail, ~-feal *n* a long turf or peat.

flaughterin' *n* 1 a light shining fitfully, a flickering. 2 a fluttering, quivering, palpitation.

flaughter spade *n* 1 a two-handed spade for cutting turfs,

sods and peats. **2** a boys' game, called also the **salmon loup**.

flaughts, flauchts *n* instruments used in carding wool.

flaune *n* a pancake.

flaunter *same as* **flanter**.

flaunty *same as* **flanty**.

flaur *n* a strong smell or flavour.

flaurie *n* a drizzle.

flaver *n* the grey-bearded oat.

flaw[1] *n* **1** a storm of snow. **2** rage, passion. **3** (*in pl*) snowflakes.

flaw[2] *n in phr* **fire-flaw** the stingray.

flaw[3] *n* **1** an extent of land under grass. **2** a broad ridge.

flaw[4] *n* a lie, a fib.—*v* **1** to lie. **2** (*with* **awa**) to exaggerate in narration. **3** to cheat, defraud.

flaw[5] *n* the point of a horse nail, broken off by the smith, after it has passed through the hoof.

flaw[6] *v* **1** fled. **2** flew.

flaw[7] *n* **1** a thin layer of turf or peat cut for fuel. **2** the place in a moss where peats are spread to dry.—*v* to cut or pare peat moss.

flaw[8] *n* **1** a failure, blunder. **2** an injury, accident.

flawkit *adj* (*used of cattle*) white in the flanks.

flawmont *n* a narrative, story.

flaw moss *n* a moss on which peats are spread to dry.

flawn *same as* **flaune**.

flaw-peat *n* soft, light, spongy peat.

flay[1] *v* to pare the turf off grass or mossland.—*n* a skin.

flay[2] *same as* **flae**[2].

flay-a-louse *n* **1** a skinflint. **2** a very mean person.

flaze *v* **1** (*used of cloth*) to fray out, ravel out. **2** (*of a sharp instrument*) to turn its edge.

flea[1] *v* to flay.

flea[2] *v* to free from fleas.

flea[3] *same as* **flee**[2].

fleach *same as* **flech**[1].

flea'd *adj* frightened.

fleaks *n* fissures between the strata of a rock.

flea-luggit *adj* harebrained, unsettled.

fleasocks *n* wood shavings.

flea-sticker *n* a tailor.

fleat[1] *n* a thick mat under a saddle to prevent chafing.

fleat[2] *v* scolded. *See* **flite**.

flech[1] *n* **1** a flea. **2** a little, frivolous, light-headed person.—*v* to free from fleas.

flech[2] *v* **1** to beat soundly. **2** to fall upon. **3** to scold.

flechan, flechin *n* **1** a small quantity or sprinkling of anything. **2** a particle. **3** a flake of snow.

flechter *same as* **flaughter**[2].

flechts *n* **1** the forked parts of a spinning wheel in which the teeth are set. **2** the part of the fanners of a winnowing machine that raises the wind.

flechy *adj* swarming with fleas.

fleck *same as* **flech**[1].

fleck *n* **1** a flake of snow. **2** a flake. **3** a variety of carnation.—*v* to spot, bespatter.

fleckert *adj* **1** flecked, dappled. **2** torn, mangled.

fleckie *n* **1** a speckled cow. **2** a pet name for such a cow.

fleckit[1] *same as* **flacket**.

fleckit[2] *adj* (*used of the sky*) dappled with clouds.

fleckit-fever *n* spotted fever.

fled *adj* fugitive.

flee[1] *same as* **fly**.

flee[2] *n* **1** a fly. **2** a whit, jot. **3** a fit of passion or temper.—*v* **1** to fly as a bird. **2** to fall into a passion.

flee-about *n* **1** a gadabout. **2** a flighty person.

flee-cap *n* a headdress formerly worn by elderly women, formed by two conjoined crescents standing out by means of wire from a cushion on which the hair was dressed.

flee-catcher *n* a kind of glazed hat or cap.

fleech[1] *v* **1** to flatter, fawn. **2** to coax, cajole. **3** to beseech, importune. **4** to beguile.—*n* flattery.

fleech[2] *v* (*used of a carpenter*) to shave off spills in planing wood.

fleecher *v* to flutter.

fleeching *n* flattery, cajolery.—*adj* **1** (*used of the weather*) falsely assuming a favourable appearance. **2** flattering, deceitful.

fleechingly *adv* flatteringly.

fleed[1] *n* a head ridge on which the plough is turned.

fleed[2] *n* a flood.

flee'd frightened.

fleefu' *adj* fearful. *See* **fley**.

fleeg *same as* **fleg**[2].

fleegarie, fleegerie *n* **1** a vagary, whim. **2** finery, frippery. **3** a gewgaw. **4** a fastidious person, one fond of trifles, etc.

fleegarying *adj* busying oneself about trifling articles of dress.

fleegest *n* a paper flycatcher.

fleegirt *n* a small quantity of anything.

flee-haunted *adj* haunted by flies.

fleein' *adj* very drunk.

fleeing[1] *adj* flying.

fleeing[2] *n* fly-fishing.

fleeing adder *n* the dragonfly.

fleeing buss *n* a whip-bush on fire.

fleeing dragon *n* **1** the dragonfly. **2** a paper kite.

fleeing merchant *n* a pedlar, travelling merchant.

fleeing passion *n* a towering passion.

fleeing pinner *n* a headdress with the ends of the lappets flying loose.

fleeing tailor *n* a travelling tailor.

fleeing washerwoman *n* a travelling washer-woman.

fleeing yett *n* an unlatched gate.

fleem[1] *n* a veterinary lances, a fleam.

fleem[2] *v* **1** to scare. **2** to banish.

fleenge *v* **1** to plunge. **2** to flounder.

fleeock *n* a small fly.

fleep *same as* **flup**[1].

fleer[1] *v* **1** to ogle. **2** to make a wry face. **3** to whimper. **4** to jeer, mock.—*n* **1** a scornful laugh. **2** a jeer. **3** mockery.

fleer[2] *v* to floor.—*n* a floor.

fleerish *same as* **flairach**.

fleeringly *adv* mockingly.

fleensh *n* a piece of steel for lighting tinder or match-paper on a flint.

fleerish *v* to embroider with floral designs, etc.

fleesh[1] *n* **1** fleece. **2** *in phr* **a fleesh o' beasts** any number of cattle bought or sold at one time by a farmer.—*v* to fleece.

fleesh[2] *n* attack, assault, onset.

fleesome, fleesum *adj* frightful.

fleesomelie *adv* frightfully.

fleesomeness *n* frightfulness.

flee's-wing *n* a particle, atom, the least.

fleet[1] *same as* **flit**.

fleet[2] *v* **1** to flow. **2** to float.—*n* **1** a number of fishing lines or nets. **2** the overflow of water. **3** a flat bog or swamp, out of which water flows from the hills.

fleetch *same as* **fleech**[1].

fleet dyke *n* a dyke for preventing inundation.

fleeter[1] *n* a utensil for skimming broth, etc, in cooking.

fleeter[2] *n* a bumper.

fleetfu' *adj* fleeting.

fleetins *same as* **float-whey**.

fleet water *n* water which overflows ground.

flee-up *n* a flighty, irascible person.

flee-up-i'-the-air *phr* a contemptuous phrase for a person of light build or no weight.

fleg[1] *n* **1** a stroke, a random blow. **2** a kick. **3** a fit of temper. **4** an exaggeration. **5** a lie.—*v* to kick.

fleg[2], **flegg** *v* **1** to frighten, frighten away. **2** to take fright.—*n* a fright, scare.

fleg[3] *v* **1** to flutter, fly from place to place. **2** to walk with a swinging step.

flegarie *same as* **fleegarie**.

fleggar *n* **1** an exaggerator. **2** a liar.—*v* to kick.

fleggin *n* a lazy, lying fellow who goes from door to door.
flegging *adj* timid.
flegh *same as* **flech**¹.
fleghings *n* the dust caused by flax-dressing.
flegmagearie *n* a whim, fancy.
flegmaleeries *n* needless finery, frippery.
fleia *n* a landing net used by fowlers in Skye.
fleighter *same as* **flaughter**².
fleighterin *n* 1 a fluttering. 2 palpitation.
fleip *same as* **flipe**¹.
fleir *same as* **fleer**¹.
fleit¹, **fleid** *adj* frightened. *See* **fley**.
fleit² *same as* **fleet**².
fleitch *same as* **fleech**¹.
fleitness *n* fear, fright.
flem, fleme *same as* **fleem**².
flemens-firth *n* an asylum for outlaws.
flench¹ *v* to flinch, yield.
flench² *v* 1 to slice the blubber from a whale's body. 2 to flense.
flench-gut *n* 1 blubber laid out in long slices. 2 the part of the hold into which it is thrown before being barrelled up.
flender *same as* **flinder**.
flenis *n* fragments.
fleock *same as* **fleeock**.
flep *same as* **flap**.
flesh *v* to shave off the flesh on the underside of a hide in the process of tanning.—*n* butcher's meat.
flesh-and-blood *n* the bloodroot or tormentil.
flesh-and-fell *phr* the whole carcass and skin.
flesh-boat *n* a meat tub.
fleshing *n* the business of a butcher.
flet¹, **flett** *n* 1 a house. 2 the inner part of a house. 3 a flat, a storey of a house.
flet² *same as* **fleat**¹.
flet³, **flett** *same as* **flat**.
flet⁴ *v* did scold. *See* **flyte**.
flether *same as* **flaither**.
flett¹ *same as* **flet**¹.
flett² *same as* **flat**.
fleuchan, flewchan *same as* **flechan**.
fleuk¹ *same as* **fluke**³.
fleuk² *same as* **fluke**².
fleume *same as* **flume**.
fleunkie *n* a flunkey.
fleup *v* to dance without lifting the feet.—*n* (*in pl*) broad feet.
fleurie *n* the ace of spades.
fleuwn *v* 1 fled. 2 flown.
flew *n* a horn, a trumpet.
flewat, flewet *n* 1 smart blow. 2 a blow with the back of the hand.
flews *n* a sluice, used in irrigation.
fley *v* 1 to frighten, scare. 2 to put to flight. 3 to be afraid. 4 to warm slightly, take the chill off.—*n* 1 a fright. 2 fear.
fleyit, fleyt *adj* 1 timorous. 2 shy. 2 abashed.
fleyr *same as* **fleer**¹.
fleysome *same as* **fleesome**.
flich *v* to fly.
flichan¹ *n* 1 a sudden glow of heat. 2 a sudden surprise, a fright.
flichan² *same as* **flechan**.
flicher¹ *v* 1 to flutter. 2 to hover, flap the wings. 3 to flirt, giggle, titter. 4 to coax.—*n* 1 a rustle, flutter. 2 a giggle. 3 a giggler.
flicher² *n* a sprinkling.
flicht¹ *n* 1 a small spot of dirt among food. 2 a snowflake.
flicht² *v* 1 to fluctuate. 2 to flutter. 3 to make a great show.—*n* 1 flight. 2 the part of a spinning wheel which twists the thread and, by means of a tooth, guides it to the pirn. 3 the part of a winnowing machine that raises the wind.
flichtened *adj* flecked, sprinkled with.

flichter *v* 1 to flutter. 2 to flap the wings. 3 to move quiveringly in the air. 4 to run with outspread arms. 5 to startle, alarm. 6 to throb, palpitate. 7 to pinion, bind.—*n* 1 a flutter. 2 a flicker. 3 a throb. 4 a great number of small objects flying in the air. 5 a snowflake. 6 the flicht of a winnowing machine.
flichteriff *n* unsteadiness.—*adj* 1 unsteady. 2 fickle, flighty.
flichtering *adj* 1 fluttering. 2 throbbing. 3 unsteady, changing.—*n* a fluttering, flickering, palpitation.
flichtering-fain *adj* throbbing with happiness.
flichter-lichtie *n* a light-headed, unsteady person.
flichtersome *adj* unsteady, whimsical.
flichtery *adj* flighty, fickle.
flichtfu' *adj* fluttering, flickering.
flichtmafleathers *n* articles of adornment, finery, frippery, trifles.
flichtrife *same as* **flichteriff**.
flichtriveness *n* fickleness, flightiness.
flichty *adj* flighty.
flick¹ *n* a small quantity, a modicum, a touch.
flick² *n* a flitch of bacon.
flicker *v* 1 to whirl. 2 to hover. 3 to titter. 4 (*with* **at**) to make light of.—*n* 1 a rustle. 2 a giggle.
flick-pie *n* a suet pudding.
flied *adj* frightened.
fliep *n* a fool.
fliet *n* a flute.
flighan *same as* **flechan**.
flight *same as* **flite**.
flighter¹ *v* to pinion, bind.
flighter² *v* to flutter.—*n* a flighty woman.
flighty *adj* hasty, quick.
fligmagary *n* a whim.
flim *n* 1 an illusion. 2 a whim.
flim-flae *n* 1 flattering speech. 2 a compliment.
flim-flam *n* nonsense.
flimrikin *same as* **flinderkin**.
flinch¹ *same as* **flench**².
flinch² *v* to coax, flatter.
flinder¹ *n* 1 a splinter. 2 a fragment.—*v* to break in pieces.
flinder² *v* (*used of cattle*) to break loose and scamper about.
flinderkin *n* 1 a weak person. 2 a flimsy article. 2 a thin garment.
flindrikin *adj* flirting.
flin'er *n* a splinter.
fling *v* 1 (*used of a horse*) to kick, strike with the hind feet, to throw its rider. 2 to throw in wrestling. 3 to jilt, disappoint, cheat. 4 to reject, throw over. 5 to dance vigorously, caper. 6 to beat, thresh grain. 7 to go off at a tangent in a fit of ill-humour. 8 to go at hastily and forcibly.—*n* 1 a dance, the Highland fling. 2 the act of flinging. 3 a sudden and hasty movement. 4 a rebuff, rejection. 5 a stroke, blow. 6 a disappointment, a disappointment in love. 7 a fit of ill-humour. 8 the knack of using a tool or working properly. 9 gait, style of walking. 10 the act of kicking, dancing, etc.
fling-bag *n* a bag for the shoulder.
flinger *n* 1 a dancer. 2 a kicking horse.
flinging tree *n* 1 a flail, the lower part of a flail. 2 a piece of timber hung as a partition between two horses in a stable. 3 the pole of a carriage. 4 a swingletree.
fling-stick *n* a rowly-powly (qv) man who frequents fairs.
fling-strings *n in phr* **tak' the flingstrings** to lose one's temper, become restive.
flinner *same as* **flinder**¹.
flinrickin, flinriken *same as* **flinderkin**.
flint-specks *n* flint-glass spectacles.
flip *n* the flap of a saddle.
flipe¹ *v* 1 to strip, tear off. 2 to fleece. 3 to turn up or down, fold back. 4 (*used of a stocking*) to turn it partially inside out.—*n* 1 the folded back edge of a knitted woollen cowl or night-cap. 2 a fold, flap. 3 a thin piece of skin. 4 a contemptuous name for a person, a fellow.

flipe² *same as* **flap**.
flipe wool *n* skin wool.
flipin *v, adj* looking absurd.
flipper *v* to move the hands in walking.
flird¹ *n* **1** a thin piece of anything. **2** anything thin, insufficient or threadbare. **3** vain finery.
flird² *n* a sneer, a gibe.
flird³ *v* **1** to flaunt, flutter, flounce. **2** to move about from place to place restlessly.—*n* a foolish, trifling, fickle person.
flirdach *n* a light and cheery person
flirdie *adj* giddy, unsettled.
flirdin'-aboot *adj* **1** unsettled, restless. **2** skittish.
flirdoch *n* **1** a flirt. **2** a foolish trifler.—*v* to flirt.
flirdome *n* affectation, ostentation, pretence.
flirn *v* to twist, distort.
flirr¹ *v* to gnash.
flirr² *v* **1** to fly out in a passion upon one. **2** to flare up. **3** to interrupt rudely.
flirry *n* a blossom.
flirt *v* to take short, swift flights.
flisk *v* **1** to whisk. **2** to move quickly hither and thither. **3** to frisk, to be restive under the yoke. **4** to make restless, uneasy. **5** to displease, fret. **6** to switch.—*n* **1** a swift movement. **2** a whim. **3** a caper. **4** a trifling, skipping person. **5** a moment.
fliskie *n* a frolicsome girl, a 'romp.'—*adj* skittish, lively, frisky, restive.
fliskmahaigo *n* a fliskmahoy (qv).
fliskmahoy *n* **1** a giddy, ostentatious person. **2** a giddy, gawky girl.
flist¹ *n* **1** a flash, a slight explosion, as of gunpowder or of air confined in a bottle when the cork is drawn. **2** an explosion of temper. **3** a flash of wit, etc. **4** a keen, smart stroke, a fillip. **5** a flying shower of snow, a squall. **6** a small quantity of gunpowder exploded.—*v* **1** to make a slight explosion. **2** to flare up, explode in passion. **3** to snap the fingers. **4** to rain and blow at the same time.
flist² *n* **1** a boast. **2** a fib. **3** one who boasts or fibs.—*v* **1** to boast. **2** to fib.
flisterin' *adj* **1** flustering. **2** flighty.
flistert *v, adj* flustered, flushed.
flistin *n* a slight shower.
flisty *adj* **1** irascible, passionate. **2** stormy, squally.
flit *v* **1** to remove, transport, shift, change. **2** to remove from one house to another. **3** to assist one in moving. **4** to cause one to remove. **5** to shift a tethered animal from one place in a field to another. **6** to pass away, depart, die. **7** to leave, quit.—*n* a change of residence.
flitch¹ *v* to move or flit.
flitch² *same as* **fleech**.
flitcher *v* to flutter like young nestlings when their dam approaches.—*n* (*in pl*) light flying flakes.
flitchers *n* the men used in playing the game of corsiecrown (qv).
flite *v* **1** to scold, chide. **2** to flout, jeer. **3** to quarrel, wrangle. **4** to reprimand.—*n* **1** a scolding. **2** a gibe. **3** a scolding match, wrangle. **4** a bully.
flitepock *n* a double chin.
fliter *n* a scold, one given to scolding.
flitfold *n* a movable sheepfold.
flither *same as* **flitter**.
fliting *n* **1** a scolding. **2** the act of scolding.
fliting bridle *n* the branks (qv), a bridle put on scolding women as a punishment.
fliting-free *adj* at liberty to scold without retort or being scolded.
fliting-hot *adj* hot with scolding.
fliting match *n* a scolding match.
flitten *v* removed. *See* **flit**.
flitter *v* **1** to flutter, shake. **2** to bustle.—*n* **1** a flutter. **2** stir, fluster.
flittering *n* a shaking.
flitters *n* **1** splinters. **2** rags, tatters.

flitting *n* **1** a removal to another house. **2** the furniture removed thither. **3** the decay of seed that does not come to maturity.
flitting chack, ~ shack *n* a vibrating sound.
flitting day *n* the removal term day.
flitting feast *n* an entertainment when the mother, after child-bearing, came to the fire and resumed her household duties.
flix *n* a flux.
fliz *v in phr* **let fliz** to let fly at or strike an opponent.
floam *same as* **flume**.
floame, floamie *n* a large or broad piece of anything.
floan *v* **1** (*used of women*) to show attachment or court regard indiscreetly. **2** to go about idly. **3** to fawn. **4** to hang over the fire.—*n* a lazy, untidy person, especially a woman.
float *n* **1** the act of floating. **2** the scum of a boiling broth pot. **3** a fleet. **4** a timber raft for conveyance down a river.—*v* to pilot a timber raft down a river.
float *n* the strip of a ploughed field between two open furrows three poles or so in breadth.
floater *n* one who pilots or floats a timber raft.
floathing *n* a thin layer or stratum.
floating *adj* vacillating, undecided.
float o'feet *n* the fat of boiled legs of oxen.
float-whey *n* the small curdled particles floating in whey.
flobby *adj* (*used of clouds*) large and heavy, indicating rain.
flocht *see* **flaught**².
flochter *same as* **flaughter**¹.
flochterin *same as* **flaughterin'**.
flochtersome *adj* easily elated or fluttered under impulse of joy.
flochtrous *adj* flurried. **2** terrified.
flochtry *adj* **1** flurried, confused. **2** terrified. **3** alarming.
flochty *adj* unsteady, whimsical, volatile.
flockmele *adv* in flocks.
flock-raik *n* a range of pasture for a flock of sheep.
flodden *v, adj* flooded.
flodge *n* a big, fat, awkward person.—*v* to hobble, walk clumsily.
floe *same as* **flow**¹.
flog *n* a flogging.
floggan *v, adj* walking fast.
floichen *same as* **flechan**.
floisterin' *n* hurry, bustle, confusion.
floit *n* a petted person.
flone *same as* **floan**.
flonkie *n* a flunkey.
flood *n* the sea.
floody *adj* flooding, flooded.
flooency *n* influenza.
flooer *v* to flower.—*n* a flower.
flook *same as* **fluke**.
flook-mou'd *adj* having a crooked mouth.
floonge *v* **1** to fawn as a dog. **2** to flatter.
floop *same as* **flup**¹.
floor *n* **1** a portable threshing floor. **2** the sea bottom. **3** a house.—*v* **1** to bring forward an argument. **2** to table a motion.
floorbands *n* the bands that secure the bottom boards of a boat to the keel.
floor head *n* the surface of a floor.
floorstane *n* the hearthstone.
flor, flore *v* **1** to strut about as if vain of one's clothes. **2** to cut a dash. **3** to live extravagantly. **4** to flourish about.
Florence *n* Florence wine.
florentine *n* a kind of pie.
florie *adj* **1** vain, volatile. **2** conceited. **3** dashing, flashy.—*v* to cut a dash.
florier *n* a dashing, extravagant person.
floring *adj* lavish of time, money, dress, foppery.
flory, florrie *v* to cut a dash, flourish about.—*n* **1** a dressy, showy person. **2** a vain, empty fellow.
flory-heckles *n* an empty-headed fop.

flosh n 1 a swamp. 2 a body of standing water overgrown with reeds, weeds, etc.
floshan n a shallow puddle of water.
flosk n the cuttlefish, sea sleeve or ankerfish.
floss n 1 the common rush. 2 the leaves of the red canary grass. 3 material made from the common rush by shaking out the pith.
flossie cap n a cap made of rushes.
flossy adj 1 reedy. 2 covered with reeds or rushes.
flot same as **float**.
flotch¹ same as **flodge**.
flotch² v to weep, sob.
flotter v 1 to float. 2 to wet, to splash.
flottins, flot-whey same as **float-whey**.
flought same as **flaught**².
floughter same as **flaughter**².
floughterty adj flighty.
floughtrous adj alarmed.
flouncing v, adj (used of trees in a gale) tossing to and fro. 2 (of a sail) flapping.
flounge n 1 the act of plunging or floundering in water. 2 the act of flouncing.
flour-bread n wheaten bread.
flour'd same as **flowered**.
flourish¹, **flourice** n a steel for striking fire from flint to kindle match-paper.
flourish² n blossom.—v to cut a dash, make a fine display.
flourished adj covered with blossom.
flouse same as **flaze**.
flouster v to fluster.—n a fluster.
floustering n flurry.
flow¹ n 1 a bog, morass. 2 quicksand. 3 the sea, a sea basin.
flow² n a chimney cowl, open at one side and turning with the wind to prevent smoke.
flow³, **flowe** n 1 a jot, a particle. 2 a small quantity of meal, etc.
flow⁴ v to exaggerate a story.—n an exaggerated story.
flowan n a small portion of meal, flour, flax, etc.
Flow Country n an area of peat bogs and moorland in Caithness and Sutherland.
flow dyke n 1 a drain along the banks of a river. 2 a wall or bank to prevent a river from overflowing.
flower n 1 a nosegay. 2 an edge tool used in cleaning laths.—v to embroider floral and other designs on muslin, etc.
flower bab n a bunch of flowers, a bouquet.
flower basket n an arrangement for growing flowers in beds on a lawn.
flowered adj (used of sheep) scabby and losing their wool.
flowerer n one who flowers muslin, etc. See **flower**.
flowerie n the ace of spades.
flowering n 1 floral embroidery. 2 the act of flowering muslin.
flowff same as **flaff**.
flowin'-ee n a hole in a drinking vessel beyond which it could not be filled.
flow-moss n 1 a very wet, spongy moss. 2 a moving bog.
flown adj muddled, overcome with drink.
flownie n a small portion of any light or dusty substance, as of meal, thrown on a draught of water.—adj 1 downy. 2 trifling, without substance. 3 frivolous.
flowther same as **fluther**².
flowy adj (used of peat) light, spongy.
flozen v 1 to cause to swell. 2 to become swollen.
flozent-up adj fat and flabby.
fluchan same as **flechan**.
flucht v 1 to agitate, flutter, frighten. 2 to make a great show. 3 to flirt.—n a bustling, bouncing, flashy person.
fluchter v to make a great fuss or talking.
fludder same as **fluther**.
flude n flood.—v to flood.
fluet same as **flewat**.
fluff¹ n 1 a flap of the wings. 2 a slight puff or gust. 3 a

slight explosion.—v 1 to puff, blow out. 2 to flap.—adv with a puff.
fluff² n a sea anemone.
fluff³ v to disappoint.
fluffer v 1 to disconcert. 2 to agitate. 3 to flutter. 4 to palpitate. 5 to move excitedly.—n 1 palpitation. 2 mental agitation. 3 a quick vibration and its sound. 4 (in pl) loose leaves, fragments.
fluff-gib n an explosion of gunpowder.
flught same as **flucht**.
flughter same as **fluchter**.
fluir n the floor.
fluish same as **flush**.
fluk n a flux.
fluke¹ n a parasitic insect in the liver of sheep.
fluke² n diarrhoea.
fluke³ n a flounder.
fluke⁴ n a duck's bill.
fluke-mow'd adj having a crooked mouth like a flounder's.
flum n flattery.
flume n phlegm.
flumgummery n 1 fussy ceremony. 2 senseless display in trifles.
flummery¹ n 1 needless show. 2 useless ornaments. 3 flattery.
flummery² n a pudding of oatmeal, eaten cold.
flunge v 1 to skip. 2 to caper.
flunkey-chap n a waiter, servant.
flunkey-craft n the trade of a manservant.
flunkey-lord n a lord in waiting.
flup¹ n 1 an awkward and foolish person. 2 a person of clumsy appearance.—adj awkward.
flup² n sleet.
flure n the floor.
fluris fever n scarlet fever.
flurish same as **flourish**².
flurr v (used of spray) to lie scattered.
flurrikin adj speaking in a flurry.
flurrish v to blossom.—n a blossom.
flush v 1 (used of water) to run fast and full. 2 to bud, blossom.—n 1 a sudden rise in a stream. 2 a run of water. 3 a farm watering place. 4 a marshy place, a surface-drained place after peats have been cut. 5 snow thawing, slush. 6 a superabundance, a surfeit. 7 a rich and rapid growth of grass. 8 blossoms etc. 9 a large flow of milk from cows.
flushy adj (used of ice on the surface of a lake) thawing.
fluster v to be in a bustle.
flutch n an inactive person.
flutchy adj inactive.
fluther¹ v to pretend great regard.
fluther² v 1 to flutter. 2 to confuse, agitate. 3 to overflow.—n 1 a hurry, bustle. 2 an abundance creating confusion. 3 a rising of a river. 4 (used of snow) a thick driving.
fluthers¹ n 1 loose flakes of a stone. 2 laminae of a stone.
fluthers² n frippery attached to a woman's dress
fluthery adj 1 flabby, soft. 2 boggy, marshy.
flutteration n 1 frivolity. 1 unsettlement.
flutter-baw n a puffball.
fluze same as **flaze**.
fly¹ same as **fley**.
fly² adj 1 sly. 2 smart.
fly³ same as **flee**².
flyam n a large seaweed tangle growing round the shore.
flyave n 1 a flake. 2 a thin stratum of rock.—v to take or come off in flakes.
fly-cap same as **flee-cap**.
fly cup n a secret or surreptitious cup of tea, one taken on the sly.
flye v to frighten.
flyer same as **fleer**¹.
flyfe n a fit, a turn.
flyker same as **flicher**².
flyndrig n 1 an impudent woman. 2 a deceiver.—v to deceive, beguile.

flype[1] *same as* **flipe**.
flype[2] *n* a lout, stupid fellow.
flypeshard *v* to castrate.
flypin' *adj* looking abashed, shamefaced.
flyrd *same as* **flird**[3].
flyre *v* **1** to gibe. **2** to ogle. **3** to look surly. **4** to go about complaining. **5** to whine, whimper.
flyre-up *v* **1** to flare up. **2** to break into passion.—*n* a great display.
flyte *same as* **flite**.
flyte-poke *n* a double chin.
foal[1] *n* **1** a cake or bannock. **2** any soft, thick bread.
foal[2] *v* (*used jocularly of a horse*) to throw its rider.
foal's-fit *n* the mucus hanging from a child's nose.
foam *n* **1** a state of great heat and perspiration. **2** a great rage.—*v* **1** to stream out, bubble up. **2** to be very heated. **3** to rage.
foaming-drunk *adj* excessively or raging drunk.
foarrie *adj* (*used of a cow*) not in calf, but giving no milk.
fob *v* **1** to breathe hard, pant. **2** to sigh. **3** to catch the breath.
fochel *same as* **foichal**[1].
fochen, fochten *v, adj* **1** fought. **2** exhausted, distressed. *See* **fecht**.
focht *v* fought.
fochtin-milk *n* buttermilk.
fock *same as* **fowk**.
fodder-door *n* a barn- or straw-house door.
foddering *n* **1** fodder. **2** provisions.
fode *v* fed.
fodge *n* **1** a fat, squat person. **2** one with chubby cheeks.
fodgel *adj* **1** fat. **2** squat, plump.—*n* **1** a fat, good-humoured person. **2** a fat, thriving person or animal.—*v* **1** to prosper, thrive. **2** to waddle, as a fat, clumsy person.
fodgie *adj* fat and squat.
fodmell *n* a weight of lead, 70 lb.
fodyell *same as* **fodgel**.
fodyellin *adj* waddling.
fog[1] *n* moss.—*v* **1** to become moss-covered. **2** to acquire wealth. **3** to furnish, supply.
fog[2] *v* to eat heartily.
fog-clad *adj* moss-covered.
fogel *same as* **fodgel**.
fogget *v* **1** moss-covered. **2** furnished, supplied.
foggie[1], **fogie** *n* **1** an invalid or garrison soldier. **2** an old fellow.
foggie[2], **foggie-bee** *n* a small, yellow humblebee.
foggie-bummer, ~-toddler *same as* **foggie**[2].
fogging-ewes *n* old ewes past bearing.
foggy[1] *adj* **1** mossy, spongy. **2** sapless.
foggy[2] *adj* **1** dull. **2** lumpish. **3** mentally in a fog.
foggy peat *n* a fibrous, soft surface peat.
foggy rose *n* a moss rose.
fog house *n* a summerhouse lined with moss.
fog moss *n* tall grass used as fodder.
fog-theekit *adj* moss-covered.
fog turf *n* mossy turf.
foichal *n* **1** a cant term for a girl from sixteen to twenty years of age. **2** a little, thickset child. **3** a small, weak person trying to grapple with his work but unable to do it.—*v* to do anything with difficulty or unskilfully through weakness.
foichel *same as* **fychell**.
foichlin' *n* unskilful working through weakness.
foigil *n* **1** a bundle of yarn, straw, etc. **2** a tangle, confused mass.
foigilled *adj* tangled, in a lump, ravelled.
foilzie *n* foil, gold leaf.
foison *same as* **fushion**.
foisonach *n* waste straw, dried grass and like refuse.
foisonless *same as* **fushionless**
foisonlessness *n* the condition of being fushionless (qv).
foistering, foishtering, foistring *n* **1** hurry, disorder. **2** slovenly, scamped work.

foistest *adj* next of age.
foiter *v* to puzzle.—*n* **1** a puzzle. **2** a difficulty. **3** a muddle.
fold *same as* **fauld**[2].
foldings *n* wrappers, used in that part of the dress which involves the posteriors.
fole *same as* **foal**[1].
folla *same as* **follow**[1].
follieshat *n* the jellyfish.
follifil *same as* **folly-fool**.
follo *same as* **follow**[2].
follow[1] *n* a fellow.
follow[2], **folloo** *v* to court.
follow-Dick *n* a servile follower.
follower *n* a young animal following its mother.
following *n* a doctor's regular patients.
folly *n* a useless or foolish or too costly building.
folly-foo *adj* very foolish.
folm[1] *n* **1** (*used of the weather*) a long spell of mist, etc. **2** a volume of rolling cloud.
folm[2] *v* to turn upside-down, overturn.—*n* anything that upsets the stomach.
folp *n* **1** a whelp. **2** a term of contempt.—*v* **1** to whelp. **2** to give birth to.
fond *adj* **1** glad, happy. **2** anxious, eager.
fondament *n* **1** a foundation. **2** fundamental fact or truth.
fond-like *adj* doting.—*adv* affectionately.
fondness *n* gladness.
fone *n* foes.
fonned *adj* prepared.
foo *same as* **fou**.
fooanever *adv* however.
foochtir *n* **1** confusion. **2** a fussy, muddling style of working. **3** an unmethodical worker.—*v* to work awkwardly, fussily or unmethodically.
foodge *same as* **fouge**.
foodjie *same as* **fugie**.
fooever *conj and adv* however.
foof[1] *n* a stench.
foof[2] *int* an exclamation of impatience, disgust, etc.
foogie, foogee, foojie *same as* **fugie**.
foogie-lick *same as* **fugie-blow**.
fool[1] *adj* foolish, silly.—*v* to play truant.
fool[2] *adj* foul.
fool[3] *n* a fowl.
foolage *adj* foolish.
fool-body *n* **1** an idiot. **2** a simpleton, a foolish person.
fool-folk *n* fools, foolish persons.
foolie[1] *n* a leaf.
foolie[2] *n in phr* **foolie, foolie** a children's game.
foolies *n* a mountebank's tricks.
fool-like *adj* foolish.
fool's parsley *n* the lesser hemlock.
fool's stones *n* the male and female orchis, *Orchis morio*.
fool-thing *n* a silly, foolish girl or woman.
fool-tongit *adj* foolish-speaking.
foolyery *n* leaved work. *See* **foilzie**.
foolyie *same as* **foilzie**
foomart, foomert *same as* **foumart**.
foon[1] *v, adj* found.
foon[2], **foond** *v* to found.—*n* a foundation.
foondit *same as* **foundit**
fooner *same as* **founder**.
foongan, foonyiean *n* **1** the fawning of a dog. **2** flattery.
foonge, foonyie *v* **1** to fawn as a dog. **2** to flatter.
foor *v* fared, travelled.
foord *v* to ford.
foor-days *adv* late in the afternoon.
foorich, foorigh, fooroch *n* **1** bustle. **2** a state of agitation. **3** a rage, a person of bustling manners. **4** ability, energy.—*v* **1** to hurry, bustle. **2** to work in a flurried manner.
foorichan *n* a state of bustle or confusion.
fooriochie, foorioghie *adj* **1** hasty. **2** passionate. **3** feeble.

foorochie *adj* bustling.
Foorsday *n* Thursday.
foose *same as* **fouse**.
foosht, foost *n* **1** anything useless or needless, lying by or stored up. **2** a dirty fellow, one who breaks wind.—*v* **1** to be mouldy, to decay. **2** to smell foul. **3** to break wind behind. **4** to store up, hoard.
fooshtie *same as* **fousty**.
fooshtit *adj* fussy, musty.
foosht-ye-may-caw *same as* **fousticat**.
foost, foostin *n* a sickness, nausea.
foosticate *same as* **fousticat**.
foosty *same as* **fousty**.
foosum *adj* dirty
foosumness *n* dirtiness.
foot *v* **1** to travel or go on foot. **2** to dance. **3** to knit a new foot to an old stocking. **4** (*used of a horse*) to kick. **5** to set peats on end to dry on the moss. —*n* **1** speed, rate of going. **2** the lower part of a street, town, etc. **3** (*in pl*) the acceleration of a curling stone by sweeping in front of it. **4** progress. **5** ability to walk or run.
foot-ale *n* **1** a feast given to her gossips by a woman recovered from child-bearing. **2** drink given by the seller to the buyer at a cattle fair. *See* **gossip**.
foot-an'-a-half *phr* a boys' game like leapfrog.
footch *int* hush!
footer[1], **footre** *n* a term of greatest contempt.—*v* **1** to ridicule. **2** to disapprove. **3** to hinder.
footer[2] *v* **1** to work hastily, unskilfully and in a manner that calls for contempt. **3** to fuss about, fiddle with.—*n* **1** bungle. **2** confusion. **3** a bungler, a silly, useless person.
footer[3] *n* activity, successful exertion.
footer-footer *v* **1** to strut like a peacock. **2** to walk affectedly.
footerin *n* awkward, hasty working.—*adj* clumsy, unskilful.
footh *same as* **fouth**.
footilie *adv* **1** meanly. **2** obscenely.
footiness *n* **1** meanness. **2** obscenity.
footing *n* **1** entrance money or something paid by way of it as a fine. **2** putting new feet to old stockings. **3** (*in pl*) small heaps of peat set on end to dry.
footing ale *n* an entertainment given by parents when a child begins to walk.
footith *n* **1** a bustle. **2** a riot. **3** an awkward predicament.
footlad *n* a footboy.
footman *n* **1** a pedestrian. **2** a foot passenger. **3** a metal stand for holding a kettle before the fire.
footpad *n* a footpath.
foot peat *n* a peat cut vertically by the cutter pressing the spade down with his foot.
foot soam *n* an iron chain eight or ten feet long, extending from the muzzle of the plough and fixed to the yoke of the oxen next the plough.
footy *same as* **foutie**.
fooze *same as* **foose**.
foozle *v* **1** to fuss. **2** to palaver.
fopperies *n* delusions, false miracles, etc.
for *prep* **1** (*with vb* **to be**) to desire, incline to, purpose. **2** (*with vb* **to go**) understood, expresses motion to a place. **3** (*with vbs of* asking *and* fearing) as to, regarding. **4** in the direction of. **5** for want of. **6** on account of. **7** as to, so far as regards. **8** by. **9** of.—*conj* **1** because. **2** lest. **3** until.—*n* a wherefore.
for a *phr* **1** what a! **2** as a.
for-a-be *conj* notwithstanding.
forage *v* to procure, get hold.
foraivert *adj* much fatigued.
foraneen *n* the time between breakfast and midday, forenoon.
foranent *same as* **forenent**.
for-as-meikle-as *conj* forasmuch as.
forat *v* to forward.

for a that *conj* notwithstanding.
forbear, forbeir, forbeer *same as* **forebear**.
forbearer *n* **1** an ancestor. **2** progenitor.
Forbes' hour *phr* eleven o'clock, p.m., when public houses, etc, had to close under the Forbes Mackenzie Act.
forbodin *adj* **1** unlawful. **2** unhappy.
forby, forbye, forbyse *prep* **1** besides, in addition to. **2** with the exception of.—*adv* **1** besides, in addition, over and above. **2** on one side, out of the way. **3** near by. **4** apart, aside.—*adj* uncommon, superior.—*n* an addition, appendix.
forcasten *adj* **1** cast off. **2** neglected.
force *n* **1** a great number. **2** the greater part. **3** consequence, importance.
forced fire *n* fire from the friction of two pieces of dry wood together.
forcely *adv* forcibly.
forcing *adj* (*used of the weather*) likely to bring crops to maturity.
forcy *adj* **1** (*used of the weather*) forcing (qv). **2** forward with work. **3** pushing on work.
fordal *n* **1** progress, advancement. **2** (*in pl*) stock not exhausted.—*adj* in advance, ready for future use.—*v* to store up for future use.
fordal rent *n* rent paid in advance on entry.
fordeddus *n* the violence of a blow.
fordel *n* progress.—*v* to store up for future use.
forder *v* **1** to further, promote. **2** to succeed, advance.—*adj* **1** further. **2** progressive.—*adv* moreover, further.
forderance *n* advancement.
forder-'im-hither *n* a piece of showy dress worn by a woman to draw young men to court her.
fordersome *same as* **forthersum**.
fordling *n* stock or provision for the future.
for-done *adj* quite worn out.
for-drunken *adj* **1** quite worn out with drinking. **2** quite drunk.
fordwart *adv* forward.—*v* to forward.
for-dweblit *adj* quite feeble.
fore *adv* before.—*prep* before.—*n* **1** priority. **2** the front. **3** help. **4** advantage. **5** anything cast ashore. **6** a finish.—*phr* **to the fore** remaining.
fore-and-after *n* a hat turned up in front and behind.
fore and back *phr* in front and behind.
fore-bait *n* crushed limpets scattered near the hooks as bait.
fore-bargain *v* to bargain beforehand.
forebear *n* an ancestor.
forebreast *n* **1** the front of a cart. **2** the front seat in a church gallery.
fore-breathing *n* premonitory symptoms.
fore-breed, ~-breadth *n* the front breadth of a dress, petticoat, etc.
fore-brees, ~-broos *n* the forehead.
forebroads *n* the milk that is first drawn from a cow.
foreby *same as* **forby**.
fore-byar *n* a forestaller.
fore-cappy *n* the stone used to sink nets at the bow of a boat.
fore-cast *n* **1** forethought. **2** an omen, forewarning. **3** a premonition of death, etc.
fore-crag, ~-craig *n* the front of the throat.
fore-day *n* the day between breakfast and noon.
fore-days *adv* **1** towards noon. **2** towards evening.
fore-day's dinnertime *n* a late hour for dinner.
fore-done *same as* **for-done**.
fore-door *n* **1** the front door. **2** the front of a common cart.
fore-é-fire *n* **1** the kitchen and living room of an old Caithness house. **2** the part of the kitchen where the family sat.
fore-end *n* **1** the anterior part. **2** the beginning. **3** a first instalment.
forefalted *same as* **forfaulted**.
fore-fowk *n* ancestors.
fore-front *n* the forehead.

foregain, foregainst *prep* opposite to.

fore-gang *n* an apparition of a person about to die, a light foreboding death or disaster.

fore-guard *n* an advanced guard.

fore-go *n* a foreboding, an omen.

fore-hammer *n* a sledgehammer.

forehand *n* 1 the start as to time or advantage. 2 the fore-quarters of a horse, cow, etc. 3 the first player in a curling rink.—*adj* first in order.—*adv* beforehand.

forehandit *adj* 1 rash. 2 foreseeing, far-seeing.

forehand-payment *n* payment in advance.

forehand-rent *n* a year's rent paid on entry or six months after entry.

forehand stone *n* the stone first played in a curling rink.

forehead *n* 1 the bow of a boat. 2 effrontery, boldness.

forehorn *n* a projection at the bow of a boat.

foreign *adv* abroad.

foreigneering *adj* foreign, not local.

forelan *n* boxes in a fish-curing yard in which herrings, etc, are placed preparatory to being cured.

foreland *n* a house facing the street.

forelang *adv* erelong.

foreleet *v* to outstrip, surpass.

foreleit *same as* **forleet**².

fore-loofe *n* a furlough.

foreloppen *adj* fugitive.

foremaist *adj* 1 most excellent, first class. 2 foremost.

fore-mak *n* bustling preparation for an event.

foreman *n* the ninth person in a deep-sea fishing boat, who cleans the boat and does odd jobs in it.

foremither *n* an ancestress.

forenail *v* 1 to spend on credit before the money is gained. 2 to anticipate one's wages extravagantly.

forename *n* the Christian name.

foreneen *n* 1 the time between breakfast and midday. 2 the forenoon.

forenent *prep* 1 opposite, facing, over against, in opposition to. 2 in exchange for. 3 towards.

forenicht *n* 1 the early part of the night. 2 the interval between twilight and bedtime.

forenichter *n* one who spends the evening in a neighbour's house.

fore-nickit *adj* prevented by a trick.

forenoon, forenoon bread *n* a luncheon or spirits taken between breakfast and dinner.

forentres *n* 1 a porch. 2 a front entrance to a house.

fore-paid *adj* paid in advance.

fore-pairt *n* the front of a person.

fore-pocket *n* a front pocket.

fore-rent *n* forehand-rent (qv).

fore-rider *n* a leader, forerunner.

fore-room *n* the compartment of a fishing boat next the bow.

fore-run *v* to outrun, outstrip.

fores *n* perquisites given by bargain to a servant in addition to his wages.

fore-seat *n* a front seat.

foreseen *adj* 1 provided, supplied. 2 acquainted, thoroughly understood or instructed. 3 well-known, famous.

fore-sey *n* 1 that side of the backbone of beeves which is not the sirloin. 2 the short ribs.

foreshot¹ *n* 1 the whisky that first comes off in distillation. 2 (*in pl*) the milk first drawn from a cow.

foreshot² *n* the projection of the front of a house over part of the street on which it is built.

foresichted, foresichtie *adj* foreseeing, provident.

foreside *n* the front.

foresinger *n* a precentor.

foreskip *n* 1 precedence of another in a journey. 2 advantage given in a contest, etc.

fore-spaul *n* a foreleg.

forespeak *v* 1 to injure by immoderate praise, according to popular superstition. 2 to bewitch. 3 to consecrate by

charms. 4 to speak of evil beings so as to make them appear.

forespeaker *n* 1 an advocate. 2 one who bewitches another or injures by immoderate praise.

forespeaking *n* immoderate praise supposed to injure the person spoken of.

forespent *adj* prematurely spent or worn out.

forespoken *adj* bewitched.

forespyke *same as* **forespyke**.

fore-start *n* a start before others.

foret *same as* **forrat**.

fore-thinking *adj* prudent.

forethouchtie *adj* provident.

fore-tram *n* the front part of the shaft of a cart.

fore-wark *n* the frontwork of a fortified castle.

fore-winter nicht *n* the early part of a winter night.

forfairn *adj* 1 worn out. 2 forlorn. 3 abused.

forfaughlit *adj* 1 worn out. 2 jaded.

forfaughten *adj* worn out.

forfaulted *adj* subjected to forfeiture, attainted.

forfaulture *n* forfeiture.

forfecht *v* to overtask oneself, to be overcome with fatigue.

forfeit *n* an offence.—*v* to subject to forfeiture.

forfeitry *n* forfeiture.

forfend *v* 1 to prevent. 2 to forbid. 3 to defend.

forfeuchen *adj* exhausted.

forfight *same as* **forfecht**.

forfleeit *adj* terrified, stupefied with terror. *See* **fley**.

forflitten *adj* severely scolded.—*n* a severe scolding. *See* **flite**.

forfluther, forflutter *v* to discompose, disorder.—*n* confusion, discomposure.

forfochen, forfocht, forfochten, forfoochen *adj* worn out. *See* **forfecht**.

forforn *same as* **forfairn**.

forfouchen, forfouchten, forfought, forfoughten, forfowden, forfuchan *same as* **forfochen**.

forfowden *adj* exhausted.

forgadder, forgader *same as* **forgather**.

forgain, forgainst *prep* 1 against. 2 opposite to.

forgather, forgaither *v* 1 to assemble, to meet for a special purpose. 2 to encounter, meet with, meet by chance. 3 to consort with. 4 to come together in marriage. 5 (*with* **up**) to become attached to.

forgathering *n* 1 an assembly. 2 a social gathering. 3 an accidental meeting.

forge *v* (*used of children*) to copy another's work and pass it off as one's own.

forgedder, forgethar *same as* **forgather**.

forgeit *v* let fly.

forger *n* a child who habitually copies another's work.

forget *n* 1 a neglect. 2 an omission. 3 an oversight.

forgettil, forgettle *adj* forgetful.

forgettilness *n* forgetfulness.

forgie *v* to forgive.

forgrutten *adj* tear-stained.

forgya *v* forgave.

forhow, forhoo, forhooie, forhui *v* to forsake, abandon.

forit *phr* if it be not so.

forjaskit, forjeskit *adj* jaded, fatigued.

forjidged *adj* jaded with fatigue.

fork *n* diligent search.—*v* 1 to pitch-fork into. 2 to pitch hay or corn. 3 to search for. 4 to look after one's own interest.

forker¹ *n* one who forks at a stack.

forker² *n* an earwig.

forking *n* 1 the division of a river into one or more streams. 2 a branch of a river at its parting from the main body. 3 the parting between the thighs. 4 looking out or searching for anything.

forknokit *adj* quite knocked up.

forky-, forkit-tail *n* an earwig.

forlaithie *v* 1 to loathe. 2 to disgust.—*n* 1 disgust. 2 a surfeit.

forlane *adj* quite alone, forlorn.

forlat *v* to deal a blow.
forlatten *adj* (*used of a blow*) dealt.
forlay *v* to lie in ambush.
forle *v* to whirl, turn, twist.—*n* **1** a turning, a twist. **2** a small wheel. **3** a whorle. **4** a stone ring on the end of a spindle, making it revolve.
for-lee *n* the lee bow.
forleet[1] *v* dealt a blow. See **forlat**.
forleet[2], **forleit** *v* **1** to abandon. **2** to forget.
forleith *same as* **forlaithie**.
forlet, forlete *same as* **forleet**.
forlethie *same as* **forlaithie**.
forloff *n* a furlough.
forlore *adj* forlorn.
forlorn *adj* (*used of time*) miserable, wretched.
forlut *v* dealt a blow.—*adj* (*used of a blow*) dealt. See **forlat**.
form *v* to point, direct.
formalist *n* an expert in legal forms, writs, styles, etc.
former *n* a kind of chisel.
fornackit *n* **1** a fillip. **2** a sharp blow.
fornail *same as* **forenail**.
fornens, fornenst *same as* **forenent**.
forniaw, fornyauw *v* to fatigue, tire.
fornyawd *same as* **yawd**.
forpit *n* the fourth part of a peck.
forra[1] *same as* **farrow**.
forra[2] *adv* (*a fishing term*) **1** forward. **2** *in phr* **in the same forra** said of two fishing boats which, when casting lines, lie in the same stretch east and west.
forragate *n* the rowing while fishing nets are being hauled.
forrage *n* wadding for a gun or pistol.
forrage-clout *n* wadding for a gun or pistol.
forrat, forret, forrit *adv* forward.
forretsome *adj* of a forward disposition.
forridden worn out with hard riding.
forrow *n* as much as is carted or carried at one time or turn.
forrow cow *n* a cow not in calf. See **farrow**.
forsay *v* to deny, gainsay.
forscomfisht *adj* **1** overcome by heat. **2** nearly overcome by bad smells.
forsee *v* **1** to overlook. **2** to neglect. **3** to oversee, superintend.
forsel *n* a mat to protect the back of a horse carrying a burden.—*v* to harness.
forsens *n* the refuse of wool.
forset *v* **1** to overpower with work. **2** to surfeit. **3** to overload.—*n* surfeit.
forsey *same as* **foresey**.
forslitting *n* **1** castigation. **2** a satirical reprimand.
forsman *n* a foreman.
forspeak *same as* **forespeak**.
forst *adj* embanked.
forsta' *v* to understand.
forstand *v* **1** to withstand. **2** to understand,
fort *adj* fourth.
fortaivert *same as* **foraivert**.
fortak, fortack *v* to aim or deal a blow.
forten *n* **1** fortune. **2** a fortune.
forth *adv* out of doors, abroad.—*prep* forth from, outside of.—*n* the open air.
forthcoming *n* accounting for money, production of accounts.
forther *adv* formerly.
forthersum *adj* **1** rash. **2** of forward manner. **3** of an active disposition.
forthert *adv* forward.
forthgeng *n* the entertainment given at the departure of a bride from her own or her father's house.
forthiness *n* frankness, affability. See **forthy**.
forthink *v* to repent, regret.
forthright *adv* forthwith.—*adj* straight-forward.
forthsetter *n* **1** a publisher. **2** an author. **3** a setter forth.
forthshaw *v* to show forth.

forthy *adj* **1** early in production. **2** productive. **3** frank, cheerful.
fortifee *v* **1** to pet, indulge. **2** to encourage, abet.
fortifier *n* an aider and abettor.
fortravail *v* to fatigue greatly.
fortune-maker *n* one prosperous in business.
forvoo *same as* **forhow**.
forwakit *adj* worn out with watching.
forwandered *adj* lost, strayed.
forward *adv* (*of a clock, etc*) in advance of the correct time.—*adj* **1** eager, energetic, zealous. **2** present, arrived. **3** intoxicated.
forwardness *n* eagerness.
forweery't *adj* worn out with fatigue.
forworn *adj* exhausted with fatigue.
foryawd *adj* fatigued.
foryet *v* to forget.
foryettil *adj* forgetful.
foryoudent *adj* **1** overcome with weariness. **2** breathless.
forzmin *same as* **forsman**.
fosie, fosy *adj* spongy, soft.
fossa *n* grass growing among stubble.
fossee *n* a fosse.
fosset, fossetin *n* a rush mat for keeping a horse's back unchafed.
foster *n* **1** a foster-child. **2** an adopted child. **3** progeny.—*v* to suckle.
Fostern *same as* **Fastern's Eve**.
fotch[1] *v* **1** to change horses in a plough. **2** to change situations. **3** to exchange.—*n* an exchange of one thing for another.
fotch[2] *v* to flinch.
fotch plough *n* **1** a plough that is worked with two yokings a day. **2** a plough used in killing weeds. **3** a plough in which horses and oxen are yoked together.
fother *n* fodder.—*v* to give fodder.
fothering *n* **1** fodder. **2** provisions.
fothersome *same as* **forthersome**.
fots *n* footless stockings.
fottie *n* **1** one whose stockings, trousers, boots, etc, are too wide. **2** a plump, short-legged person or animal. **3** a female wool-gatherer who went from place to place for the purpose of gathering wool.
fottit-thief *n* a thief of the lowest description.
fou[1] *adv* how.
fou[2] *adv* why.
fou[3] *adj* **1** full. **2** well-fed, filled to repletion. **3** intoxicated, drunk. **4** well-to-do, rich. **5** puffed up, conceited.—*adv* **1** very, much. **2** fully.—*n* **1** a fill. **2** tipple. **3** contents, what fills. **4** a firlot, a bushel of grain.—*v* to make full, to fill.
fou[4] *n* **1** a pitchfork. **2** a kicking, tossing. **3** a heap of corn in the sheaves or bottles of threshed straw.—*v* **1** to kick, toss. **2** to throw up sheaves with a pitchfork.
fouat[1] *n* a cake baked with butter and currants.
fouat[2] *n* the houseleek.
fouchen *adj* wearied in struggling.
foucht, fouchten *v*, *adj* fought.—*adj* troubled.
foud *n* **1** the thatch and sods of a house when taken from the roof. **2** foggage, long coarse grass not eaten down in summer.
fouet *n* the houseleek.
fou-ever *adv* however.
fouge *v* to cheat at marbles by unfairly advancing the hand before playing a marble.—*n* the act of playing thus.
fouger *n* one who fouges at marbles.
fou-handit, ~-han't *adj* **1** well-to-do. **2** losing nothing in a bargain.
fou-hoose *n* **1** open house. **2** a hospitable house.
fouish *adj* slightly drunk.
fouk *same as* **fowk**.
foul *adj* (*used of the weather*) bad, gloomy.—*adv* foully.—*n* **1** a storm, bad weather. **2** devil. **3** evil. —*v* to soil legally or find guilty.

foul a-ane, ~-bit, ~-drap *phr* devil a-one, -bit, -drop.
foul and fair *phr* (*with* **come**) whatever may happen.
foulbeard *n* a blacksmith's mop for his trough.
foul-befa', ~-fa' *phr* devil take! evil befall!
foul-be-lickit *n* absolutely nothing.
foul-farren *adj* of foul appearance.
foulmart *same as* **foumart**.
foul-may-care *n phr* devil may care.
foul-tak-ye *phr* devil take you! evil take you.
foul thief *phr* the devil.
foul water *n* part of a Halloween rite, the choice of which by a person blindfolded portended marriage to a widow or to a widower.
foulzie *v* 1 to foil, defeat. 2 to defile.—*n* filth, street sweepings, dung.
foulzie can *n* a pail for holding house refuse, ordure, etc.
foulzie-man *n* a scavenger.
foumart *n* 1 the polecat. 2 an offensive person. 3 a sharp, quick-witted person.
foumart-faced *adj* having a face like a polecat.
foumartish *adj* having a strong or offensive smell.
fou-moo't *adj* having all one's teeth sound.
foun' *n* a foundation.
found *n* 1 the foundation of a building. 2 the area on which the foundation is laid. 3 foundation, truth, substance.—*v* 1 to warrant. 2 to have good grounds for an action at law.
founder *v* 1 to collapse, break down. 2 (*used of a horse*) to stumble violently. 3 to cause to stumble. 4 to fell. 5 to dismay. 6 to perish or be benumbed with cold. 7 to astonish.
founding *n* having the foundation stone.
founding pint *n* drink etc, given to workmen at the laying of the foundation of a house.
foundit *n* (*with a neg*) nothing at all, not the least particle.
foundit-hait *phr* absolutely nothing.
found-stane *n* 1 a foundation stone. 2 origin, beginning.
foundy *v* to founder.
founer *same as* **founder**.
four-hours *n* a refreshment taken about four o'clock.
four-hours-at-een *n* four o'clock in the afternoon.
fourioghie *same as* **fooriochie**.
four-lozened *adj* having four panes of glass in a window frame.
four-luggit *adj* having four handles.
four-nookit *adj* four-cornered.
four-part dish *n* an old measure holding the fourth of a peck.
fours *n* all fours.
foursome, foursum *n* a company of four.—*adj* performed by four together.
four-stoopit bed *n* a four-post bed.
fourthen *adj* fourth.
fourthnight *n* a fortnight.
fourways *n* four crossroads.
fouscanhaud *n* a Celtic keeper of a low public house.
fouse *n* the houseleek.
fousion *same as* **fushion**
fousome¹ *same as* **fulsome**.
fousome² *adj* 1 nauseous. 2 disgusting. 3 dirty.
fousomeness *n* dirtiness.
fousticat *n* what-d'ye-call it? how is it that you call it?
foustie *n* a roll split up and eaten with butter or jelly
fousty *adj* 1 fussy. 2 mouldy, musty. 3 (*used of corn*) mouldy or damp, having a musty smell.
fousun *same as* **fushion**.
fout¹ *n* a spoiled child.
fout² *n* a fool, a simpleton.
fout³ *n* a sudden movement.
foutch *same as* **fotch¹**.
fouter *same as* **footer**.
fouth *n* abundance, fill.
fouthily *adv* prosperously, plentifully.
fouthless *adj* useless.

fouthlie *adv* plentifully.
fouthy *adj* 1 prosperous, well-to-do. 2 hospitable, liberal. 3 abundant.
fouthy-like *adj* having the appearance of prosperity or abundance.
foutie *adj* 1 mean. 2 obscene, smutty. 3 paltry.
foutilie *adv* 1 meanly, basely. 2 obscenely.
foutiness *n* 1 meanness. 2 obscenity.
foutrack *int* an exclamation of surprise.
foutre *n* successful exertion.
foutsome *adj* 1 forward. 2 officious. 3 meddling.
fouty *same as* **foutie**.
fow¹ *v* 1 to kick, toss. 2 to throw up sheaves with a pitchfork.—*n* 1 a corn-fork, a pitchfork. 2 a kicking, tossing. 3 a heap of sheaves or of bottles of straw.
fow² *n* the houseleek.
fow³ *same as* **fou³**.
fow⁴ *adj* foul.
fower *adj* four.
fowie *adj* 1 well-to-do. 2 a term of disrespect. 3 *phr* **a fowie body** an old hunks (qv).
fowk *n* 1 people, folk. 2 menservants, work people.
fowl *n* a bird of any kind.
fowlie *n* a chicken.
fowlie-bree *n* chicken broth.
fowmart *same as* **foumart**
fowner *same as* **fooner**.
fows *same as* **fouse**.
fowsie *same as* **fossee**.
fowsum *same as* **fousome**.
fowt *same as* **fout²**.
fowth *same as* **fouth**.
fowty *same as* **foutie**.
fox *v* to dissemble.
foxter-leaves *n* the foxglove.
foy *n* a farewell feast to or by one leaving a place, ending an apprenticeship or finishing a job.—*v* to be present at such a feast.
foy *adj* foolish, silly.
foyard *n* a fugitive.
foyll *n* a defeat, foil.
foze¹ *v* 1 to wheeze. 2 to breathe with difficulty. 3 to emit saliva.—*n* difficulty in breathing.
foze² *v* to lose flavour, become fussy.
fozie *same as* **fozy**.
foziness *n* 1 sponginess. 2 obtuseness of mind, stupidity.
fozle¹ *n* a weasel.
fozle², fozzle *v* to wheeze.—*n* a wheeze.
fozlin *n* great exertion with want of strength.—*adj* 1 weak. 2 breathing with difficulty.
fozy¹ *adj* 1 wet. 2 moist with saliva, dribbling.
fozy², fozzy *adj* 1 light, spongy, soft, porous. 2 soft and hairy like wool. 3 fat, bloated. 4 stupid, dull-witted. 5 hazy, foggy. 6 obscured by haze or fog.
fra *prep* from.
fraak *n* 1 a whim. 2 a foolish, superstitious fancy.
fraat *adv* 1 nevertheless. 2 for all that.
fracaw *n* 1 a hubbub. 2 a brawl.
fracht *n* 1 what can be carried or carted at one time. 2 *in phr* **a fracht o' water** two buckets of water. 3 *in phr* **a fracht o' corn** two cartloads of corn.
frachty *adj in phr* **gweed frachty** 1 generous. 2 liberal.
frack *adj* 1 ready, eager. 2 bold, forward. 3 stout, firm, hale, vigorous in old age.
fractious *adj* troublesome or particular about one's food.
frae *prep* from.—*adv* from the time that.
fraeca *n* a disturbance, fracas.
fraesta *adv* 1 pray thee. 2 notwithstanding.
fragalent *adj* 1 advantageous, profitable. 2 undermining.
Fraiday *n* Friday.
fraik¹, fraick *v* 1 to cajole, wheedle. 2 to coax.—*n* 1 flattering, coaxing. 2 a flatterer. 3 a wheedling person.
fraik² 1 sulks. 2 fretting. *See* **freak²**.

fraikas *n* much ado in a flattering sort of way.
fraiky *adj* coaxing, wheedling.
frail *n* a flail.
fraim *same as* **frem**.
frain *same as* **frayn**.
fraise[1] *n* **1** a disturbance, fuss. **2** bustle, excitement. **3** flattery, cajolery, vain talk.—*v* to flatter, wheedle.
fraise[2] *n* a calf's pluck.
fraisen *v* to flatter.
fraiser *n* a flatterer, wheedler.
fraisie *adj* given to flattery or vain talk.
fraisilie *adv* in a flattering, fraising (qv) way.
fraisiness *n* addiction to flattery, etc.
fraising *n* flattery, cajolery.—*adj* flattering.
fraisle *v* to flatter, pay court to.
fraist, fraiz'd *adj* **1** greatly astonished. **2** having a wild, staring look.
frait *n* trouble, fret.
fraith *v* to froth, foam.—*n* froth, foam.
fraize *same as* **fraise**[1].
fraizie *same as* **fraisie**.
frake[1] *same as* **freak**[1].
frake[2] *same as* **fraik**[1].
fraky *adj* coaxing, wheedling.
fram *same as* **frem**.
frame *v* to succeed.—*n* a skeleton.
framed, framet, frammit *adj* **1** strange. **2** cold, distant. *See* **frem**.
frample, frammle *v* **1** to gobble up. **2** to put in disorder.—*n* **1** a confused mass. **2** disordered clothes or yarn.
frampler *n* a disorderly person.
frandie *n* **1** a haycock. **2** a small rick of sheaves.
frane *same as* **frayn**.
frank[1] *n* the heron.
frank[2] *adj* (*used of a horse*) willing, eager, not needing whip or spur.
frank-tenement *n* a freehold.
frap[1] *v* **1** to blight. **2** to destroy.
frap[2] *n* a jugful, a capful.
frappe *adj* insane, sullenly, melancholy.
fra't *same as* **fraat**.
frath *adj* reserved in manner.
fraucht, fraught *n* **1** a freight, load, what carts can bring at a time. **2** two bucketfuls of water. **3** passage money, boat hire.—*v* **1** to freight. **2** to load.
frauchtless *adj* **1** insipid. **2** without weight or importance.
frauchty *adj* **1** liberal. **2** hospitable.
fraud *v* to defraud.
fraudling *n* the act of defrauding, committing of fraud.
frawart *adj* froward.
frawfu' *adj* **1** bold, impertinent. **2** sulky, scornful.
fray *n* terror, panic.—*v* **1** to frighten, daunt. **2** to be afraid.
frayn *v* **1** to ask. **2** to insist. **3** to urge strongly.—*n* inquiry.
freachy *adj* **1** spoiled in the making. **2** faded in colour.
freak[1] *n* **1** a strong man. **2** a fellow. **3** a fool. **4** a foolish fancy.
freak[2] *v* to fret.
freak[3] *same as* **fraik**.
freat *same as* **freet**[2].
freath *v* **1** to froth, foam. **2** to make soap suds. **3** to lather. **4** to wash clothes slightly before smoothing them with the iron.—*n* **1** soap suds, froth. **2** a slight washing-up of clothes before ironing them.
freazock *v* to coax, wheedle, cajole.
frecht *same as* **fricht**.
freck[1] *same as* **frack**.
freck[2] *same as* **fraik**.
freckle *adj* active, hot-spirited.
frecky *same as* **fraiky**.
free *adj* **1** frank, outspoken. **2** genial, familiar. **3** liberal, ready, willing, under no restraint of conscience. **4** unmarried. **5** made free of burghal privileges. **6** divested of. **7** friable, easily crumbled. **8** (*used of cakes*) short, brittle. **9** (*of corn*) so ripe as to be easily shaken.—*n* **1**

soft sandstone, freestone. **2** (*in pl*) Free Church members.
free-coup *n* a place for emptying rubbish.
freedom *n* **1** the right of pasturing on a common. **2** permission, leave.
free-gaun *adj* frank, affable.
freelage *n* an heritable property as distinguished from a farm tenanted.—*adj* heritable.
freely *adv* **1** quite, very. **2** thoroughly. **3** exactly. **4** *in phr* **nae freely** used with reference to anything that had been asserted yet was not true.
freeman *n* a neutral party.
free-martin *n* a female twin calf where the other is a bull, supposed naturally incapable of ever having offspring.
freen, freend *n* **1** a friend. **2** a relation.
freenly *adj* friendly.—*adv* in a friendly way.
freesk *v* **1** to scratch. **2** to curry. **3** to rub roughly or hastily. **4** to walk or work briskly. **5** (*with* **up**) to beat soundly.—*n* **1** a hasty rub. **2** work done hastily.
freet[1] *same as* **fret**[3].
freet[2] *n* **1** a superstitious fancy or saying. **2** an omen, a charm. **3** a superstitious ceremony or rite. **4** a fancy, whim, trick. **5** a trifle.
freet[3] *n* **1** anything fried. **2** oatcake, etc, fried with dripping, butter, etc.
freethe *same as* **freath**.
free-trade *n* smuggling.
free-trader *n* a smuggler.
freevolous *adj* **1** trifling. **2** small, simple.
free-ward *n* freedom.
Free-willers *n* Arminians, believers in free will alone.
freff *adj* **1** shy. **2** intimate.
freicht *same as* **fricht**.
freight *same as* **fraucht**.
freik *same as* **freak**[1].
frein *same as* **frine**.
freisk *same as* **freesk**.
freikit *adj* whimsical, odd.
freit[1] *same as* **freet**[2].
freit[2] *same as* **fret**[1].
freith[1] *n* liberal wages.
freith[2] *same as* **freath**.
freitten *adj* pitted, seamed, as with smallpox.
freity *adj* **1** superstitious. **2** credulous as to omens, etc.
freize *v* to freeze.
frem, fremd, freme, fremit, fremmit *adj* **1** strange, foreign. **2** unrelated by blood. **3** distant, reserved. **4** unfriendly, estranged. **5** far off.—*n* **1** a stranger. **2** one not a blood relation.
fremd-folk *n* strangers in contrast with relations.
fremd-sted *adj* forsaken by friends and cast upon strangers.
fren *adj* **1** strange, foreign. **2** acting like a stranger.
frenauch *n* a crowd.
French-butterfly *n* the common white butterfly.
French-jackie *n* the boys' game of gap (qv).
French-pearie *n* a humming top.
French-puppy *n* the eastern poppy.
French-saugh *n* the Persian willowherb.
French-wallflower *n* the purple-coloured wallflower.
frenchy *n* a boys' marble, of greenish-yellow colour.
frend *same as* **friend**.
frenn *v* to rage, to be in a frenzy.
frennishin, frenisin *n* **1** rage, frenzy. **2** a half-asleep, dazed or mentally confused state.
frenyie, frenzie *n* a fringe.—*v* to fringe.
frenzy *v* (*with* **up**) to madden, inflame.
frequent *adj* numerous, great in concourse.—*v* **1** to acquaint, give information. **2** (*with* **with**) to associate with.
frequently *adv* numerously.
frere *n* a brother.
fresch *int* an exclamation of contempt.
fresh *adj* **1** (*used of land*) free from stock. **2** unsalted. **3** novel, new. **4** sober, not drunk. **5** excited with drink. **6**

(*used of the weather*) thawing, wet, cold, open.—*n* **1** a flood in a river. **2** a thaw.—*v* to thaw.

freshwater muscle *n* the pearl mussel.

fret¹ *v* **1** to eat, devour. **2** to eat into.—*n* a quarrel, revolt.

fret², **frett** *same as* **freet**².

fret³ *n* **1** the product of milk. **2** butter, cheese, etc.

fretch *n* a flaw.

fret-taker *n* a woman supposed to have the power of lessening the profit of her neighbours' cows and of increasing that of her own.

fretty *adj* fretful, peevish.

freuch, freugh *adj* **1** (*used of wood*) brittle. **2** (*of corn*) dry.

frey *n* **1** stir, hurry. **2** cause of anxiety, etc.

frezell *same as* **frizzel**¹.

friars' chicken *n* chicken broth with eggs dropped into it.

friar-skate *n* the sharp-nosed ray.

fribble *v* **1** to curl. **2** to frizzle.—*n* a trifler, a good-for-nothing fellow.

fricht *v* to frighten, scare away.—*n* fright.

frichtedly *adv* in a fright.

frichten *v* to frighten.

frichtfu' *adj* **1** frightful, terrible. **2** bad, annoying.

frichtsome *adj* **1** frightful. **2** causing fear.

frichtsomely *adv* fearfully.

fricht-the-craw *n* a scarecrow.

fricksome *adj* **1** vain. **2** vaunting.

Friday's-bairn *n* a child born on Friday.

Friday's-bawbee, ~-penny *phr* a weekly halfpenny or penny given to a child on Friday as pocket money.

frie *adj* friable.—*n* freestone.

fried chicken *n* friars' chicken (qv).

friend, frien' *n* a relation by blood or marriage.—*v* to befriend.

friended *adj* having friends or relations.

friend-stead *adj* befriended, having friends.

friesk *same as* **freesk**.

friet *same as* **fret**¹.

frig *v* **1** to potter about. **2** to be fastidious about trifles.

frigassee *n* a fricassee.

friggle-fraggles *n* **1** trifles. **2** useless ornaments of dress.

frim-fram *n* **1** a trifle. **2** a whim.

frimple-frample *adv* **1** promiscuously. **2** in a tangled fashion. *See* **frample**.

frine *v* **1** to whine. **2** to fret peevishly.

frisk *n* **1** a dance. **2** a caper. **3** a jig.—*v* to cause to dance.

frisksome *adj* sportive, frisky.

frisky *adj* staggering from drink.

frist *v* **1** to delay. **2** to give a debtor time to pay. **3** to give credit, sell on trust.—*n* **1** delay, respite. **2** credit, trust.

fristing *n* delay, suspension.

frith *n* **1** a wood. **2** a clearing in a wood.

frithat, frithit *adv* nevertheless, for a' that (qv).

fritter *v* **1** to scatter. **2** to reduce to fragments.—*n* a fragment.

frizz *n* a curl.

frizzel *n* **1** the hammer of a gun or pistol. **2** a piece of steel for striking fire from a flint.

frizzel-spring *n* the spring of a gun or pistol.

frizzing *n* the hammer of a gun.

frizzle¹ *n* a hissing, sputtering sound, as of frying.

frizzle² *v* **1** to flatter, coax. **2** to make a great fuss.

froad *v* to froth, foam.—*n* froth, foam.

froath stick *same as* **frothing stick**.

froch *same as* **freuch**.

frock¹ *n* a sailor's or fisherman's knitted woollen jersey.

frock² *n* the term used in distinguishing the different pairs in a team of oxen, as hind-, mid-, fore-frock.

frock-soam *n* a chain fixed to the yoke of the hindmost oxen in a plough and stretched to that of the pair before them.

frocky *same as* **freuch**.

froe *n* froth.

frog¹ *v* to snow or sleet at intervals.—*n* a flying shower of snow or sleet.

frog², **frogue** *n* a young horse between one and two years old. **2** a colt about three years old.

froichfu' *adj* perspiring.

froie *same as* **froe**.

from *prep* (*in reckoning time by the clock*) before a certain hour.

frone *n* a sling.

front¹ *n in phr* **in front of** before in point of time.

front² *v* to swell, distend (*used of meat in boiling*).

front-briest *n* the front pew in a church gallery.

fronter *same as* **frunter**.

frontispiece *n* the front or front view of a house.

fronty *adj* **1** passionate. **2** high-spirited, free in manner. **3** healthy-looking.

frooch¹ *same as* **freuch**.

frooch² *adj* unbending.

froon *v* to frown.—*n* a frown.

frost *n* **1** ice. **2** a poor hand at. **3** an ignoramus.—*v* **1** to become frozen or frostbitten. **2** to spoil through frost. **3** to prepare horses' shoes for frost. **4** (*used of the hair*) to turn grey or white.

frost-rind *n* hoarfrost.

frost-, frosty-win' *n* a freezing wind.

frost-, frosty-wise *adj* tending to frost.

frosty-bearded *adj* having a grey or white beard.

frosty-pow *n* a grey head.

frothe *v* to wash slightly.—*n* a slight washing.

frothing stick *n* a stick or horsehair whisk for whipping cream or milk.

frothy *adj* **1** good at early rising. **2** early at work. **3** energetic.

frou *same as* **froe**.

frough *adj* brittle

frow *n* a big, fat woman.

frowdie¹ *n* a big, lusty woman.—*adj* (*used of a woman*) big, lusty.

frowdie² *n* **1** a woman's cap. **2** a sowback mutch (qv) with a seam at the back, worn by old women.

frowngy *adj* frowning, gloomy, lowering.

frozening *n* **1** a freezing. **2** the act of being frozen.

fruesome *adj* **1** coarse-looking. **2** frowsy.

frugal *adj* frank, kindly, affable.

fruize *v* froze.

frump¹ *n* a badly dressed woman.

frump² *n* an unseemly fold or gathering in any part of one's clothes.

frumple *v* **1** to wrinkle. **2** to crease, to crumple.

frumpses *n* ill-humour, sulks.

frumpy *adj* peevish.

frunce *n* a plait.

frunsh *v* **1** to fret, whine. **2** to frown, gloom. **3** to pucker the face.

frunter *n* a ewe in her fourth year.

frunty *same as* **fronty**.

fruozen *adj* frozen.

frush *n* a collection of fragments.—*adj* **1** brittle, crumbling. **2** frail, fragile. **3** (*used of cloth or wood*) rotten. **4** tender-hearted. **5** frank. **6** forward.

frushness *n* brittleness.

fry¹ *n* **1** a number of children. **2** a clique, set, crew.

fry² *n* **1** a disturbance, tumult. **2** stir, bustle.—*v* **1** to be in a passion. **2** to be pestered or in a state of agitation.

frythe *v* **1** to fry. **2** to feel great indignation.

frything pan *n* a frying pan.

fu *same as* **fou**.

fu' *same as* **foul**.

fucher *same as* **fucher**.

fud¹ *n* **1** the buttocks. **2** the female pudendum. **3** the brush of a hare or rabbit. **4** a queue or the hair tied behind.

fud² *v* **1** to whisk, scud, like a rabbit or hare. **2** to frisk. **3** to walk with short, quick steps.—*n* **1** a quick, nimble walk. **2** a small man who walks with short, quick steps.

fudd *adj* afraid.

fudder *n* **1** a gust of wind. **2** a flurry. **3** the shock occasioned by a gust of wind. **4** a sudden noise. **5** a stroke, a blow. **6** a hurry, hasty motion.—*v* **1** to move hurriedly. **2** to patter with the feet. **3** to run to and fro in an excited and aimless manner.

fudder *n* **1** a large quantity. **2** a cartload. **3** a certain weight of lead. **4** a great number. **5** a confederacy.

fudder *conj* whether.

fudder-flash *n* a flash of lightning.

fuddie *n* **1** the fud of a rabbit or hare. **2** a hare.

fuddie-hen *n* a hen without a tail.

fuddie-skirt *n* a short coat or vest.

fuddik *n* a very short person who walks with a quick, nimble step.

fuddle[1] *v* (*with* **in**) to sow seed in wet weather or when the soil is in a puddle.

fuddle[2] *n* **1** a drinking bout. **2** intoxication.

fuddum *n* snow drifting at intervals.

fuddy[1] *n* a name given to the wind personified.

fuddy[2] *n* the bottom of a corn kiln.

fudgel *same as* **fodgel**.

fudgie[1] *adj* short and fat.

fudgie[2] *same as* **fugie**.

fudie-skirt *n* a short coat or vest.

fuding *adj* **1** gamesome, sportive. **2** frisky.

fudle *v* to fuddle.

fueling *n* the cutting of peats for fuel.

fuff *v* **1** to puff, blow. **2** to breathe heavily. **3** (*used of a cat*) to spit, make a hissing sound. **4** to sniff. **5** (*with* **away**) to go off in a huff or fuming. **6** (*with* **off, out, up**) to blaze up suddenly, to explode.—*n* **1** an explosive sound. **2** a splutter. **3** the hissing sound made by a cat. **4** a puff of wind. **5** a short smoke of tobacco. **6** a whiff of any odour. **7** a sudden outburst of anger.—*int* **1** an exclamation of displeasure or contempt. **2** pooh!

fuffers *n* a pair of bellows.

fuffily *adv* **1** hastily. **2** scornfully.

fuffin *n* puffing.

fuffit *n* the British long-tailed titmouse.

fuffle, fuffel *v* **1** to ruffle, rumple. **2** to dishevel.—*n* **1** fuss. **2** violent exertion.

fuffle-daddie *n* a foster father.

fuffy *adj* **1** light, soft, spongy. **2** short-tempered.

fug *same as* **fog**.

fuggie[1] *same as* **fugie**.

fuggie[2] *same as* **foggie**[2].

fuggie-bell *n* a truant.

fuggie-the-skweel *n* a truant from school.

fuggy *same as* **foggy**.

fugie, fuge, fugee *n* **1** a fugitive from law. **2** a cock that will not fight. **3** a coward. **4** a blow given as a challenge to fight.—*adj* fugitive, running away, retreating.—*v* to run away, play truant from.

fugie-blow *n* a blow challenging to fight.

fugie-cock *n* a cock that will not fight.

fugie-warrant *n* a warrant to arrest a debtor intending to flee.

fugle[1] *v* **1** to signal. **2** to give an example of.

fugle[2] *v* to manage so as to cheat.—*n* a clever, cunning cheat.

fugle[3] *n* anything crumpled up and not neatly folded together.

fuhre *v* to go.

fuilteachs *n* half of January and half of February OS.

fuilyie *same as* **foulzie**.

fuir-days *phr* late in the afternoon.

fuir-nicht *phr* late in the night.

Fuirsday *n* Thursday.

fuish *v* fetched.

fuishen *v* fetched.

fuist *n* **1** a fusty smell. **2** rust. **3** mould.—*v* to acquire a fusty smell.

fuit *n* the houseleek.

fule[1] *n* fool.—*adj* foolish.

fule[2] *n* a fowl.

fule-bodie *n* a foolish person.

fule-thing *n* **1** a foolish creature. **2** a silly, giddy coquette.

fulfil *v* to fill up or to the full.

full *same as* **fou**[3].

full-begotten *adj* lawfully begotten.

fulmar *n* a species of petrel.

fulp *n* a whelp.—*v* **1** to whelp. **2** to give birth to.

fulsie *same as* **foulzie**.

fulsome *adj* **1** copious, giving abundance. **2** (*used of a garment*) somewhat too large. **3** (*of food*) satiating, filling, surfeiting, luscious, rich.

fulsomeness *n* lusciousness.

fultacks *same as* **fuilteachs**.

fulthy *adj* mean, niggardly.

fulye, fulzie *n* **1** a leaf. **2** leaf gold.

fulyie, fulzie *same as* **foulzie**.

fulzie can *n* **1** a slop pail. **2** a vessel for holding night soil.

fum *n* a useless, slovenly woman.

fumart *same as* **foumart**.

fume *n* scent, fragrance.

fummer[*adj*] **1** benumbed. **2** torpid.

fummel *same as* **fummle**.

fummils *n* a whip for a top.

fummle[1], **fummel** *v* to upset.

fummle[2] *v* **1** to fumble. **2** to disturb by handling or poking. **3** with out, to extract slowly and unwillingly.—*n* **1** weakly doing of work. **2** needless, foolish or awkward handling.

fummlin' *adj* **1** unhandy at work. **2** weak.

fumper *v* **1** to whimper. **2** to sob. **3** to hint, mention.—*n* **1** a whimper. **2** a whisper.

fun[1] *v, adj* found.

fun[2] *n* gorse.

fun[3] *v* **1** to joke. **2** to indulge in fun.—*n* **1** a hoax. **2** a practical joke.

funabeis *adv* however.

fund[1] *v, adj* found.

fund[2] *same as* **found**.

fundament, fundment *n* **1** a foundation. **2** a founding.

fundamental *n* **1** the seat of the breeches. **2** (*in pl*) the fundamental doctrines of religion.—*adj* adhering to the fundamentals, orthodox.

funder *same as* **founder**.

fundy *v* **1** to founder. **2** to become stiff with cold.

funeral letter *n* an invitation to attend a funeral.

funeralls *n* funeral expenses, escutcheon, ceremonies, etc.

funeuch *adj* glad, pleased, merry.

fung[1] *v* **1** to strike, beat. **2** to kick. **3** to throw with force. **4** to anger. **5** to annoy, offend. **6** to work briskly. **7** to work in a temper. **8** to lose one's temper. **9** to give forth a sharp, whizzing sound. —*n* **1** a blow, thrust, kick. **2** a pet, a fit of bad temper.—*adv* violently.

fung[2] *n* beer.

fung about *v* to drive hither and thither at high speed.

fungel *n* an uncouth, suspicious-looking person or beast.

funger *n* a whinger, hanger.

fungibles *n* movable goods which may be valued by weight or measure, as grain or money.

fungie *adj* apt to take offence.

funk[1] *v* **1** (*used of a horse*) to shy, kick up the heels. **2** (*with* **off**) to throw the rider. **3** (*with* **up**) to lift up smartly. **4** to die.—*n* **1** a kick, a smart blow. **2** a rage. **3** opposition. **4** (*in pl*) humours.

funk[2] *v* **1** to faint. **2** to become afraid. **3** to shirk, fail. **4** to fight shy of. **5** to wince. **6** to cheat in marbles by playing without keeping the hand on the ground or by jerking or stretching the arm and so obtaining an unfair advantage.—*n* **1** a jerk of the arm unfairly accelerating a marble. **2** a fright. **3** alarm, perturbation. **4** a sulking fit.

funker *n* **1** a horse or cow that kicks. **2** a kicker.

funkie *n* one who is afraid to fight.

fun-mill *n* a mill for bruising furze for food for horses, etc.

funnie, funie *same as* **fundy**.

funniet *adj* easily affected by cold.

funny[1] *adj* **1** strange, curious, unwonted. **2** eccentric. **3** merry, producing mirth or ridicule.

funny[2] *n* a game of marbles, where the marbles are set on a line and the ones that are hit are restored to their owners.

funny bone *n* the elbow joint.

funs *n* furze.

funsar *n* an unshapely bundle of clothes.

funschoch, funschick *n* 1 a sudden grasp. 2 energy and activity at work.

funseless *same as* **fushionless**.

fup[1] *same as* **fulp**.

fup[2] *n* 1 a whip. 2 a cut from a whip. 3 a blow. 4 a moment.—*v* 1 to whip, beat. 2 to whip up. 3 to seize.

fuppertie-geig *n* a base trick.

fur *n* 1 a furrow. 2 a furrowing, ploughing.—*v* 1 to furrow. 2 to rib stockings.

furage *n* wadding for gun or pistol.

fur-ahin *n* the hindmost right-hand horse in a plough.

fur-beast *n* the horse that walks in the furrow in ploughing.

furc *n* the gallows.

furder *adj* more remote.—*adv* further.—*v* 1 to aid. 2 to provoke. 3 to speed. 4 to succeed.—*n* 1 luck, success. 2 progress.

furdersome *adj* 1 active. 2 expeditious. 3 rash, venturesome. 4 forward. 5 favourable, forwarding.

fur-drain *n* a small trench ploughed periodically in the land for drainage.

fure[1] *adj* 1 firm, fresh. 2 sound.

fure[2] *same as* **fur**.

fure[3] *v* to go.—*v* went.

fure-days *same as* **fore-days**.

fur-felles *n* furred skins.

furfluthered *adj* 1 disordered. 2 agitated. *See* **forfluther**.

fur-horse *n* the horse that treads the furrow in ploughing.

furhow *same as* **forhow**.

furich *same as* **foorich**.

furiositie *n* madness, insanity.

furious *adj* 1 insane, mad. 2 extraordinary. 3 excessive.—*adv* 1 uncommonly. 2 excessively.

furl *v* 1 to whirl, wheel, encircle. 2 to spin a teetotum, etc.—*n* 1 a short spell of stormy weather. 2 a sharp attack of illness.

furlad, furlet *n* a firlot.

furlie *n* a turner.

furlie-fa' *n* 1 a trifling excuse. 2 a showy, useless ornament.—*v* to make trifling excuses before doing anything.

furligig, furligiggum *n* 1 a whirligig. 2 a light-headed girl. 3 a child's toy of four cross-arms with paper sails attached, which spin round in the wind on the end of a stick. *See* **whirligig**.

furloff *same as* **fore-loofe**.

furlpool *n* a whirlpool.

furly birs *n* the knave of trumps.

furm *n* a form, a bench.

furmage *n* cheese.

furmer *n* a flat chisel.

furnishings *n* 1 furniture. 2 belongings.

furniture *v* 1 to furnish. 2 to have furniture.

furoch *same as* **foorich**.

furr[1] *same as* **fur**.

furr[2] *v* 1 to choke up, clog with anything. 2 to be encrusted, as a kettle.—*n* the encrustation in a kettle.

furrage *same as* **forrage**.

furret *adv* forward.

furrineerer *n* a foreigner.

furrochie *adj* feeble, infirm from rheumatism or old age.

furrow *v* to forage.

furrow cow *n* a cow not with calf. *See* **farrow**.

fur-scam *n* the second horse from the right hand in a four-abreast team in an old Orkney plough.

Fursday *n* Thursday.

fur-side *n* the iron plate in a plough for turning over the furrow.

fur-sin *n* the cord to which the hook of a plough is attached.

furth *adv* forth.—*prep* out of.—*n* the open air.

furthie *same as* **furthy**.

furthilie *adv* 1 frankly. 2 without reserve.

furthiness *n* frankness, affability.

furthsetter *same as* **forthsetter**.

furth-the-gait *adv in phr* **fair furth-the-gait** honestly.—*adj* holding a straightforward course.

furthy *adj* 1 frank, affable. 2 hospitable. 3 thrifty. 4 unabashed. 5 forward, impudent. 6 early in production.

furtigue *n* fatigue.

fury *n* madness.

fuschach, fushach *same as* **fusschach**.

fush[1] *n* fish.—*v* to fish.

fush[2], **fushen** *v* fetched.

fushen, fushon *same as* **fushion**

fushica'd *same as* **fousticat**.

fushica'im *n* what-do-you-call-him?

fushion *n* 1 pith. 2 substance. 3 vigour, power. 4 mettle, backbone. 5 power of feeling. 6 nourishment.

fushionless *adj* 1 pithless. 2 tasteless, insipid. 3 without nutritional value. 4 dry, withered, not succulent. 5 without body or substance. 6 feeble, weak, useless. 7 without mettle or backbone.

fushloch *n* 1 waste straw about a barnyard. 2 a rough bundle, an untidy mass.

fushon *same as* **fushion**.

fusht *int* whisht! hush!

fusion *same as* **fushion**.

fusionless *same as* **fushionless**.

fusker *n* 1 a whisker. 2 beard and whiskers.

fusky *n* whisky.

fusky-pig *n* a whisky jar.

fusle *same as* **fissle**.

fuslin *adj* trifling.

fu'some *same as* **fousome**[2].

fusschach *v* to work hastily and awkwardly.—*n* 1 a rough, untidy bundle. 2 a fluffy mass.

fusschle, fusschal *n* a small, untidy bundle of hay, straw, rags, etc.

fussle[1] *n* a sharp blow.—*v* to beat sharply.

fussle[2] *n* a whistle.—*v* to whistle.

fussle[3] *n* fusel oil.

fussock *same as* **fusschach**.

fustit *adj* musty. *See* **foosht**.

fustle *v* to whistle.

fustle fair oot *phr* to be straightforward.

fute[1], **fut** *same as* **foot**.

fute[2] *same as* **fout**[2].

futer, futor *same as* **footer**.

futher[1] *pron and conj* whether.

futher[2] *n* the future.

futher[3] *n* 1 a large quantity. 2 a number. 3 a gathering.

futher[4] *n* the whizzing sound of quick motion.

futher[5], **futhir** *same as* **footer**[2].

futherer *n in phr* **peat-futherer** one who supplies peats.

futhil *v* to work or walk clumsily.—*n* 1 hasty, clumsy working or walking. 2 a fussy, clumsy person. 3 a short and stout person.

futith, futoch *same as* **footith**.

futrat *same as* **futteret**.

futter[1] *same as* **footer**[2].

futter[2] *same as* **footer**[1].

futteret, futterad *n* 1 a weasel. 2 a term of contempt.

futtle[1] *n* a knife, a whittle.—*v* to whittle.

futtle[2] *same as* **futhil**.

futtle-the-pin *n* an idler.—*v* 1 to be idle. 2 to be too long in doing anything.

futtlie-bealin *n* a whitlow.

futty[1] *same as* **fittie**[3].

futty[2], **futy** *same as* **foutie**.

fuze *n* strength, pith.

fuzen, fuzhon, fuzzen *same as* **fushion**.

fuzzle *n* 1 beverage. 2 a tipple.

fuzzlet *same as* **fussle**[1].

fuzzy[1] *adj* buzzing. **2** fizzing, hissing.
fuzzy[2] *adj* fluffy, feathery.
fy[1] *int* an exclamation calling to notice, hurry or a summons.
fy[2] *n* whey.
fyaach *v* **1** to fidget, to move around restlessly. **2** to work hard but to little purpose.
fyachle *v* **1** to loaf about. **2** to work at anything softly. **3** to move about in a silly, feckless way. **4** (*with* **down**) to fall softly down.
fyak *n* a woollen plaid.
fyantich *adj* **1** in fair health. **2** hilarious.
fyantish *adj* **1** plausible. **2** fulsome in compliments or welcome. **3** fawning. **4** (*used of lovers*) showing or expressing great fondness.
fyarter *n* an expression of contempt for any bad quality that is not immoral or dishonest.
fy-blots *n* the scum formed on boiling whey.
fy-brose *n* brose (qv) made with whey.
fychel *n* **1** a young foal. **2** a fondling name for a young foal.
fye *same as* **fey**[2].
fye-haste *n* a great hurry.

fyeuch *same as* **feuch**[1].
fyeuch *int* an exclamation of disgust.
fyfteen *adj* fifteen.
fy-gae-by *n* a jocular name for diarrhoea.
fy-gae-to *n* a fuss, disturbance, bustle.
fy-gruns *n* the finely divided sediment formed after whey cools.
fyke *n* the fish, Medusa's head.
fyke *same as* **fike**[1].
fyke-fack *same as* **fike-fack**.
fykesome *adj* fidgety.
fykie *adj* **1** very particular. **2** fidgety.
fyle *same as* **file**[2].
fyooack *n* a very small quantity of anything.
fyoonach *n* (*used of snow*) a sprinkling, as much as just whitens the ground.
fyoord *n* a ford.
fyow *adj* few.
fysigunkus *n* a man devoid of curiosity.
fyte[1] *v* to cut wood with a knife.—*n* a cut.—*phr* **fyte the pin** to be too long in doing anything.
fyte[2] *adj* white.

G

ga[1], **gaw**[1] *n* **1** the gall of an animal. **2** a gallnut. **3** a disease of the gall affecting cattle and sheep. **4** spite. **5** a grudge.
ga[2], **gaw**[2] *n* **1** an abrasion or sore on the skin. **2** a trick or bad habit. **3** a crease in cloth. **4** a layer of soil different from the rest intersecting a field. **5** a furrow. **6** a drain. **7** a hollow with water springing in it.—*v* **1** to rub, excoriate. **2** to irritate. **3** to chafe, fret, become pettish.
ga[3] *v* gave.
ga[4] *v same as* **gae**[3].
gaabril *n* a big, uncomely, ill-natured person.
gaa-bursen *adj* short-winded.
gaad *same as* **gad**[1].
gaadie *adj* **1** showy. **2** tricky.
gaa-grass *n* a plant growing in streams, used for disease of the gall.
gaan[1] *adj* straight, near.—*adv* tolerably.
gaan[2] *v* going.
gaap *same as* **gaup**.
gaar[1] *same as* **garr**.
gaar[2] *same as* **gaur**.
gaa-sickness *n* gall disease in cattle and sheep.
gaat *n* a gelded pig.
gaave *same as* **gaff**.
gab[1] *n* **1** impertinent talk. **2** prating. **3** entertaining conversation. **4** the mouth. **5** the tongue. **6** one who talks incessantly. **7** the palate. **8** the sense of taste. **9** appetite.—*v* **1** to speak impertinently. **2** to reply impertinently. **3** to chatter. **4** to tell tales.
gab[2] *n* the hook on which pots were hung at the end of the crook (qv).
gab[3] *n in phr* **the gab o' May** the last days of April, weather anticipating that of May.
gabbart[1], **gabbard** *n* **1** a lighter. **2** an inland sailing vessel.
gabbart[2] *n* **1** a mouthful, morsel. **2** a fragment, bit of anything.
gabber[1] *n* **1** a talkative person. **2** jargon.—*n* to gabble, jabber.
gabber[2] *n* **1** a fragment, a broken piece. **2** that which has come to grief.
gabber-stroke *n* the garboard-strake of a boat.
gabbet *n* **1** a gobblet. **2** a mouthful. **3** the palate. **4** the sense of taste.
gabbie-labbie *n* confused talking.
gabbing *n* talk, chatter, gabble.
gabbing-chat *n* **1** a chatterer. **2** a telltale. **3** a talkative child who tells of all he or she hears.
gabbit *adj* **1** having a mouth or tongue. **2** gossipy. **3** talkative. **4** (*used of milk*) passed through the mouth.—*n* **1** a mouthful. **2** a bit of anything.
gabble *v* **1** to scold. **2** to wrangle.
gabbock[1], **gabbot** *n* **1** a mouthful. **2** a fragment.
gabbock[2] *n* a talkative person.
gabby[1] *n* **1** the mouth. **2** the palate. **3** the crop of a fowl.
gabby[2] *adj* **1** talkative. **2** fluent.—*n* a pert chatterer.
gaber[1] *n* a lean horse.
gaber[2] *same as* **gabber**[2].
gaberlunzie, gaberlunyie, gaberloonie *n* **1** a wallet that hangs on the loins. **2** a licensed beggar. **3** a mendicant. **4** the calling of a beggar.
gaberlunzie-man *n* a beggar who carries a wallet.
gaberosie *n* a kiss.
gabert *same as* **gabbart**[1].
gaberts *n* **1** a kind of gallows for supporting the wheel of a draw well. **2** three poles of wood forming an angle at the top used for weighing hay.
gab-gash *n* **1** petulant chatter. **2** vituperation.
gabiator *n* a gormandizer.
gable-end *n* the end wall of a building.
gable room *n* a room at the gable of a house.
gab-nash *n* **1** petulant chatter. **2** a prattling, forward girl.
gab-shot *n* having the underjaw projecting beyond the upper.
gab-stick *n* **1** a spoon. **2** a large wooden spoon.
gack *n* a gap.
gad[1] *n* **1** an iron bar. **2** a goad for driving horses or cattle. **3** a fishing rod. **4** the gadfly.
gad[2] *n in phr* **a gad of ice** a large mass of ice.
gad[3] *n* a troop or band.
gad[4] *int* an exclamation of disgust.
gadboy *n* the boy who went with the ploughman and goaded his team of horses.
gadder *v* **1** to gather, to assemble. **2** to amass money.
gadderin *n* **1** an assembly, meeting. **2** a festering lump.
gaddery *n* a collection.
gaddie *adj* **1** gaudy, showy. **2** tricky.
gadding pole *n* a goad or pointed stick for driving horses or cattle.
gade[1] *same as* **gad**[1].
gade[2] *v* went.
gade[3] *v* gave.

gadge[1] *v* **1** to dictate impertinently. **2** to talk idly with stupid gravity.

gadge[2] *n* **1** a standard, a measure. **2** a search, scrutiny. **3** a lookout. **4** a hunt or watch for one's own interests.—*v* to measure.

gadger *n* **1** an exciseman. **2** a gauger. **3** one who is on the watch for gifts, etc.

gadie *adj* **1** showy. **2** tricky.

gadje *n* (*used contemptuously*) a person.

gadman, gadsman *n* **1** the man or boy in charge of a plough team, for driving the team of horses with goad. **2** a ploughman.

gadwand *n* a pointed stick for driving horses or cattle.

gae[1] *n* the jay.

gae[2] *n* a sudden break in a stratum of coal.

gae[3] *v* **1** to go. **2** (*used of animals*) to graze. **3** to die.

gae[4] *v* to give.—*v pret* gave.

gae aboot *v* (*of a disease*) to prevail in a locality.

gae awa *int* an exclamation of contempt, ridicule, surprise, etc.—*v* **1** to swoon. **2** to die.

gae back *v* (*used of cows*) to stop or lessen the milk they give.

gae-between *n* a servant who does part of the housemaid's work and part of the cook's.

gaebie *n* same as **gabby**[1].

gae by *v* to befall.

gae-bye *n* **1** a cheat. **2** an evasion.

gae by oneself *phr* to go off one's head.

gaed[1] *v* went.

gaed[2] *v* gave.

gae doon *v* to be hanged or executed.

gae-doon[2] *n* **1** the act of swallowing. **2** appetite. **3** a guzzling or drinking match.

gae-lattan *n* **1** an accouchement. **2** the verge of bankruptcy.

gaen[1] *v* gone.

gaen[2] *v* given.

gaen[3] *prep* (*of time*) before, within.—*conj* **1** before, until. **2** if.

gae owre *v* **1** to swarm. **2** to excel, transcend. **3** to cross, as a bridge.

gaeppie *n* a large horn spoon, requiring a widely opened mouth.

gaet[1] *same as* **gett**[1].

gaet[2] *n* rags. **2** bits.

gaet[3] *same as* **gate**[1].

gae the country *phr* to tramp as a beggar or itinerant hawker.

gae thegither *v* to be married.

gae through *v* **1** to bungle. **2** to waste. **3** to come to grief.

gae-through *n* **1** a great tumult. **2** much ado about nothing.

gae-to *n* **1** a brawl, squabble. **2** a drubbing.

gae to the bent *phr* to abscond from creditors or other pursuers.

gae wi' *v* **1** to court. **2** to go to wreck. **3** to coincide.

gaff *v* **1** to interchange merry talk, to talk nonsense. **2** to laugh loudly.—*n* **1** a loud laugh. **2** rude, loud talk. **3** impertinence.

gaffa, gaffaw *v* **1** to laugh loudly. **2** to guffaw.—*n* a loud laugh, a guffaw.

gaffaer *n* a loud laugher.

gaffer[1] *n* a loquacious person.

gaffer[2] *n* **1** a grandfather. **2** an elderly man. **3** a term of respect. **4** an overseer.—*v* to act as an overseer, to oversee.

gaflin *adj* **1** light-headed. **2** thoughtless, giddy.

gaffnet *n* a large fishing net, used in rivers.

ga-fur *n* a furrow in a field for letting water run off.

gag[1] *n* a joke, hoax.—*v* **1** to ridicule. **2** to hoax, deceive, play on one's credulity.

gag[2] *n* a filthy mass of any liquid or semiliquid substance.

gag[3] *n* **1** a chap in the hands. **2** a deep cut or wound. **3** a rent or crack in wood, a chink arising from dryness.—*v* **1** (*used of the hands*) to chap, crack. **2** to break into chinks or cracks through dryness.

gage[1] *n* wage, salary.

gage[2] *n* **1** a standard, measure. **2** a search.

gager *n* an exciseman.

gaggee *n* one who is hoaxed.

gagger[1] *n* one who hoaxes or deceives.

gagger[2] *n* **1** a large, ugly mass of any liquid or semiliquid substance. **2** the under-lip. **3** a large, ragged cloud. **4** a deep, ragged cut or wound. **5** a large, festering sore.—*v* to cut or wound so as to cause a ragged edge.

gagger-lip *n* a large, protruding lip.

gaggery *n* a deception, hoax.

gagging *n* **1** a hoax. **2** a hoaxing.

gaggle *v* **1** to laugh affectedly or immoderately. **2** to giggle. **3** to chirp mournfully. **4** (*used of geese*) to sound an alarm.

gaibloch *n* **1** a morsel. **2** a fragment.

gaiby *n* a stupid person.

gaid *v* went.

gaig *same as* **geg**[3].

gail[1] *n* a gable.

gail[2] *v* **1** to tingle, smart with cold or pain. **2** to crack, split open with heat or frost. **3** to break into chinks. **4** (*used of the skin*) to chap.—*n* **1** a crack, fissure. **2** a chink, split in wood.

gail[3] *v* to pierce, as with a loud, shrill noise.

gaile *same as* **gale**[4].

gailies, gailins *adv* tolerably, fairly well.

gaily *adj* in good health and spirits, very well.—*adv* tolerably, moderately.

gain[1] *adj* (*used of a road or direction*) near, straight, direct.—*adv* **1** nearly, almost. **2** tolerably, pretty.

gain[2] *v* **1** to fit. **2** to suffice. **3** to suit, correspond to in shape or size.

gain[3] *v* going.

gain[4] *same as* **gaen**[3].

gainage *n* **1** the implements of husbandry. **2** land held by base tenure by sockmen or *villani*.

gain-coming *n* return.

gainder *v* **1** to look foolish. **2** to stretch the neck like a gander.—*n* a gander.

gainer[1] *n* a gander.

gainer[2] *n* a winner at marbles.

gainful *adj* profitable, lucrative.

gain-gear *n* the moving machinery of a mill, etc, persons going to wreck.

gaingo *n* human ordure.

gaining *adj* ingratiating.

gainly *adj* proper, becoming, decent.

gainn *adj* awkward and reckless.

gainstand *v* to withstand, resist, oppose.

gainter *n* one who puts on conceited airs.

gair[1] *n* **1** a strip or patch of green on a hillside. **2** a triangular strip of cloth, used as a gore or gusset. **3** a strip of cloth. **4** anything like a strip or crease. —*v* **1** to dirty. **2** to become streaked. **3** to crease. **4** to become creased.

gair[2] *adj* **1** greedy, rapacious, intent on gain. **2** thrifty, provident. **3** niggardly, parsimonious. —*adv* **1** niggardly. **2** greedily.—*n* covetousness, greed.

gair-carlin *same as* **gyre-carlin**.

gair'd *adj* (*used of a cow*) brindled, streaked.

gairdy *n* the arm.

gairfish *n* the porpoise.

gair-gathered *adj* ill-got.

gair-gaun *adj* rapacious, greedy.

gairie *n* **1** a striped or streaked cow. **2** the black and yellow striped wild bee. **3** the name of a streaked cow.

gairies *n* vagaries, whims.

gairly *adv* greedily.—*adj* rapacious.

gairn *n* a garden.

gairner *n* a gardener.

gairner's-gertans *n* the ribbon grass.

gairock *n* the black and yellow striped wild bee.

gairsy *same as* **gaucy**.

gairten *n* a garter.

gairun *n* a sea trout.
gairy[1] *adj* variegated, streaked with different colours.
gairy[2] *n* **1** a steep hill or precipice. **2** moorland. **3** a piece of waste land.
gairy-bee *same as* **gairock**.
gairy-face *n* a piece of waste land.
gaishen, gaishon *n* **1** a skeleton. **2** an emaciated person. **3** a hobgoblin. **4** anything regarded as an obstacle in one's way.
gaislin *n* **1** a gosling. **2** a fool. **3** a term of disparagement to a child.
gaist *n* a ghost. **2** a term of contempt.
gaist coal *n* a coal that, when it is burned, becomes white.
gait[1] *n* **1** pace, motion. **2** rate of walking.
gait[2] *n* a goat.
gait[3] *v* to set up sheaves on end or singly to dry.
gait[4], **gaite** *n* **1** a way. **2** a fashion. **3** a distance.—*v* to make one's way.
gait-berry *n* a blackberry.
gaited *adj* paced, walking.
gaiten, gaiten *n* **1** the setting up of sheaves to dry. **2** a single sheaf set up to dry.
gaiter-berry *n* a blackberry.
gaitet *adj* (*used of a horse*) broken in, accustomed to the road.
gaither *v* **1** to gather. **2** to meet together. **3** to grow rich. **4** to save money. **5** (*in buttermaking*) to collect or form during churning. **6** to collect corn enough in the harvest field to make a sheaf. **7** to collect money. **8** to pick up anything. **9** to raise from the ground. **10** (*of a rig*) to plough a ridge so as to throw the soil towards the middle.
gaithered, gaithert *adj* (*said of one who has saved money*) rich, well-to-do.
gaithered gear *n* savings, hoard of money amassed.
gaitherer *n* one who collects corn for binding into sheaves, a gleaner.
gaithering *n* **1** a crowd. **2** a company. **3** saving, frugality. **4** (*in pl*) amassed wealth, money saved.
gaithering-bell *n* **1** a tocsin. **2** a bell summoning citizens to a town meeting.
gaithering coal, ~ peat, ~ turf *n* a large piece of coal, peat or turf put on a fire at night to keep it alive till morning.
gaithering-peat *n* a fiery peat sent by Borderers to alarm a district in time of threatening danger.
gaitlin *n* **1** a little child. **2** a brat. **3** the young of animals. **4** (*in pl*) boys of the first year at Edinburgh High School and Edinburgh Academy.
gaitlins *adv* towards, in the direction of.
gaitsman *n* one employed in making passages in a coal-mine.
gaitwards *adv* in the direction of, towards.
gaivel *v* **1** to stare wildly. **2** (*used of a horse*) to toss the head up and down.
gaivin *adj* **1** awkward. **2** reckless.
gaivle *n* **1** the hind parts, posteriors. **2** a gable.
gaivle-end *n* the posterior.
gaizen *adj* **1** (*used of a wooden tub, barrel, etc*) warped, leaking from drought. **2** thirsty.—*v* **1** to warp, leak from drought. **2** to parch, shrivel. **3** to dry up, fade.
gakie *n* the shell, *Venus mercenaria*.
galant *v* to play the gallant.
galash *v* to mend a shoe by a band round the upper leather.
galashoes *n* overshoes.
galasses *same as* **gallowses**.
galatian *n* **1** (*in pl*) a boys' mumming play performed at Hallow'een. **2** the name of a character in it. **3** a mummer. **4** a ninny.
galavant *same as* **gallivant**.
galavanting *n* lovemaking.
galdragon *n* a sorceress, sibyl.
galdroch *n* a greedy, long-necked, unshapely person.
gale[1] *n* an afflatus, an uplifting of the spirit.

gale[2] *n* a gable.
gale[3] *n* (*used of geese*) a flock.
gale[4] *n* **1** a state of excitement. **2** anger.
gale[5] *same as* **gell**.
gall[1] *n* **1** a disease of the gall among sheep and cattle. **2** spite. **3** a grudge.
gall[2] *n* **1** a crease, a wrinkle in cloth. **2** a layer of a different kind of soil from the rest in a field. **3** a wet, spongy, unfertile spot in a field.
gall[3], **gall-bush** *n* the bog myrtle.
gall[4], **gall-flower** *n* a beautiful growth on roses, briars, etc, resembling crimson moss.
gallacher *same as* **golach**.
galla-glass *n* an armour-bearer.
galland *same as* **callant**.
gallan nail *n* one of the bolts that attach a cart to the axle.
gallant *v* **1** to play the gallant or cavalier by escorting a woman in public. **2** to flirt. **3** to go about idly and lightly in the company of men, to gallivant.—*n* a woman who goes about in the company of men.—*adj* **1** large. **2** improperly familiar. **3** jolly.
gallanter *n* a man or woman who goes much in the company of the other sex.
gallanting *adj* roving with men or women.
gallantish *adj* (*of women*) fond of going about with men.
gallan whale *n* a sort of large whale frequenting the Lewis.
gallasches *n* overshoes.
gallayniel *n* a big, gluttonous, ruthless man.
gallehooing *n* a stupefying, senseless noise.
gallet *n* a term of endearment, darling.
galley *n* a leech.
galliard *adj* **1** gallant. **2** brisk, cheerful, lively.—*n* **1** a lively youth. **2** a dissipated character. **3** a quick, lively dance.
galliardness *n* gaiety.
gallion *n* a lean horse.
gallivant *v* **1** to jaunt, go about idly or for pleasure, show, etc. **2** to philander, act the gallant to. **3** to make love to. **4** to keep company with.
gallivanter *n* **1** an incurable flirt. **2** a gasconader.
gallivaster *n* a tall, gasconading fellow.
galloglach *same as* **gallowglass**.
gallon *n* a Scots gallon, equalling nearly three imperial gallons.
gallon tree *n* a cask holding liquor.
galloper *n* fieldpiece used for rapid motion against an enemy in the field.
gallous *same as* **gallus**.
Galloway dyke *n* a wall built firmly at the bottom, but no thicker at the top than the length of the single stones, loosely piled the one above the other.
Galloway whin *n* the moor or moss whin, *Genista anglica*.
gallowglass *n* an armour-bearer.
gallow ley *n* a field on which the gallows was erected.
gallows *n* **1** an elevated station for a view. **2** three beams erected in triangular form for weighing. **3** braces.—*adj* depraved, rascally.
gallowses *same as* **galluses**.
gallows-face *n* a rascal.
gallows-faced *adj* having the look of a blackguard.
gallows foot *n* the space immediately in front of the gallows.
gallows pin *n* the beam or projection of a gallows upon which the hangman's rope could be fastened.
gallows tree *n* the gallows.
gallus *adj* **1** self-confident. **2** brash, cheeky. **3** bold.
galluses *n* **1** braces for holding up trousers. **2** leather belts formerly used as springs for carriages.
gallwood *n* wormwood.
gallyfish *same as* **gallytrough**.
gally-gander *n* a fight with knives.
gallyie *v* **1** to roar, brawl. **2** to scold.—*n* a roar, a cry of displeasure.
gallytrough *n* the char.
galnes *n* compensation for accident at death, paid by the person who occasioned it.

galope *v* to belch.

galopin *n* an inferior servant in a great house.

galore *n* abundance.—*adv* abundantly.

galpin *n* a lad, a gamin.

galravitch, galravidge, galravich, galravish *v* 1 to raise an uproar. 2 to gad about. 3 to romp. 4 to live or feast riotously. 5 to lead a wild life.—*n* 1 uproar, noise, a romp, riot. 2 a drinking bout.

galravitching *n* 1 riotous feasting. 2 noisy, romping merry-making.

galsh *n* foolish or nonsensical talk.

galshachs, galshichs *n* 1 sweetmeats. 2 any kind of food not in common use.

galshin *v* talking rubbish.

galshochs *n* 1 indigestible articles, unsuitable foods. 2 kickshaws.

galsoch *adj* fond of good eating.

galt *n* a sow when castrated or spayed.

galy *n* a quick dance, a galliard.

galyard, galyeard *same as* **galliard**.

galyie *same as* **gallyie**.

gam *n* 1 a tooth. 2 a gum, lip, mouth.—*adj* (*used of teeth*) irregular, overlapping, twisted.—*v* (*used of teeth*) to grow in crooked and overlapping.

gamaleerie, gamareerie *adj* 1 foolish. 2 big-boned, lean, long-necked and awkward. 3 grisly in appearance.—*n* a foolish, clumsy person.

gamashes, gamashins, gamashons *n* leggings, gaiters.

gamawow *n* a fool.

gamb *same as* **gam**.

gambade *v* to prance, strut, march jauntily.

gambadoes *n* leather leggings for use on horseback.

game[1] *n* 1 a trick, knack, dodge. 2 courage, pluck. —*adj* plucky.

game[2] *adj* lame, deformed.

game-fee *n* a fine formerly imposed by church courts for immorality.

game-hawk *n* the peregrine falcon.

game-leg *n* a deformed leg, a leg with club foot.

gameral *same as* **gomeril**.

gamester *n* one who plays in a game, not necessarily a gambler.

gamf[1] *v* 1 to gape. 2 to gulp, devour, eat greedily. 3 to snatch like a dog.—*n* the act of gamfing.

gamf[2] *same as* **gamp**.

gamfle *v* 1 to trifle, idle, neglect work. 2 to spend time in idle talk or dalliance.

gamfrell, gamfrel *n* 1 a fool. 2 a forward, presumptuous person.

gamie *n* a familiar term for a gamekeeper.

gammawshins *same as* **gamashes**.

gammel *v* to gamble.

gammereerie *same as* **gamaleerie**.

gammerstel *n* a foolish, gawky girl.

gammon, gammond, gammont, gamon *n* 1 the leg or the thigh of a person. 2 (*in pl*) the feet of an animal.

gammul *v* to gobble up.

gamon *same as* **gammon**.

gamp[1] *v* 1 to be foolishly merry. 2 to laugh loudly. 3 to mimic, mock.—*n* 1 an idle, meddling person. 2 a buffoon. 3 an empty-headed noisy fellow.—*adj* sportive, playful.

gamp[2], **gamph** *v* 1 to gape. 2 to devour greedily. 3 to snatch like a dog.

gamphered *adj* (*used of embroidery*) flowery, bespangled.

gamphil *v* 1 to sport. 2 to flirt. 2 to run after girls.

gamphrell *same as* **gamfrell**.

gamrel *same as* **gomeril**.

gam-teetht *adj* having twisted or overlapping teeth.

gam-tooth *n* an overlapping tooth.

gan[1] *n* 1 the mouth, throat. 2 (*in pl*) the gums, toothless jaws.

gan[2] *n* the gannet.

gan[3] *v pret* began.

ganch *v* 1 to snap with the teeth. 2 to snarl, bite. 3 to gnash the teeth. 4 to stammer. 5 to be very ugly.—*n* 1 a wide gape. 2 the snapping of a dog.

gandays *n* the last fortnight of winter and the first fortnight of spring.

gander *n* a stupid person.

gandiegow *n* 1 a stroke, punishment. 2 a nonsensical trick, a prank.

gandier *n* a braggart.

gandy *v* 1 to talk foolishly. 2 to brag. 3 to chatter pertly.—*n* 1 a brag, a vain boast. 2 pert, foolish talk. 3 a pert talker.

gandying *n* 1 foolish, boasting talk. 2 pertness.

gane[1] *v* gone.

gane[2] *same as* **gain**[2].

gane[3] *same as* **gaen**[3].

gane[4] *adj* 1 near. 2 short. 3 convenient. 4 active. 5 expert.

ganelie *adj* 1 proper. 2 seemly. 3 decent.

gang[1] *n* 1 gait, style of walking. 2 pace. 3 a journey. 4 a road, path. 5 a drill, furrow. 6 the channel of a stream. 7 a cattle walk for grazing. 8 the right of pasture. 9 a freight of water from a well. 10 as much as can be carried or carted at a time. 11 a family, band, retinue. 12 a company. 13 a flock. 14 a row of stitches in knitting. 15 a set of horseshoes.

gang[2] *same as* **gae**.

gangable *adj* 1 passable, fit for travelling. 2 tolerable. 3 (*used of money*) current.

gang aboot *n* a travelling hawker.

gang aff *v* to waste.

gang agley *v* to go astray.

gang-atween *n* a go-between, an intercessor.

gang awa' *v* to faint.

gang-by *n* 1 a go-by. 2 escape, evasion.

gange *v* 1 to talk tediously. 2 (*with* up) to chat pertly.

ganger[1] *n* 1 a walker, pedestrian. 2 a shopwalker. 3 a fast-going horse.

ganger[2] *n* an overseer or foreman of a gang of workers.

ganger[3] *v* to become gangrenous.

gangeral, gangerel, gangeril *same as* **gangrel**.

gangery *n* finery.

ganging[1] *n* the furniture of a mill which the tenant must uphold.

ganging[2] *adj* 1 going. 2 active. 3 stirring.

ganging-body *n* a tramp, beggar.

ganging-gate *n* 1 a field path. 2 a footpath in contrast to a roadway for carts, etc.

ganging graith *n* the working machinery of a mill.

ganging-gudes *n* movable goods.

ganging-man *n* a male tramp or beggar.

ganging-plea *n* a hereditary or permanent lawsuit.

gangings-on *n* ongoings, behaviour.

ganging-water *n* something laid past for future needs, a nest egg.

ganglin *adj* 1 straggling. 2 of awkward tallness.

gang on *v* to behave.

gang ower *v* to transcend.

gangrel, gangril *n* 1 a vagrant, tramp. 2 a child beginning to walk, an unsteady walker. 3 (*in pl*) furniture, movables.—*adj* 1 creeping. 2 walking with short steps. 3 vagabond, itinerant, vagrant, strolling. 4 applied to creeping vermin.

gangrill-gype *n* a spoiled child.

gangs *n* spring shears for clipping sheep or grass borders in gardens.

gang-there-out *adj* wandering, vagrant.

gang throw *v* 1 to waste. 2 to bungle.

gang together *v* to be married.

gangway *n* a field path, a footpath in contrast to a roadway.

gang wi' *v* 1 to go to ruin, break down. 2 to waste.

gangyls *n in phr* **to be a guts and gangyls** to be fit for nothing but eating and walking.

ganien *same as* **gandying**.

ganj *same as* **gange**.

ganjin *n* impudently speaking back.

gank *n* an unlooked-for trouble.

ganna *v* going to.

ganne *same as* **gan**[1].

gannyie *same as* **gandy**.

gansald *same as* **gansel**.

gansch *same as* **ganch**.

gansel, gansell *n* **1** a garlic sauce for goose. **2** an insolent retort, something spicy, snappish or disagreeable in speech.—*v* **1** to scold, upbraid. **2** to bandy testy language. **3** to gabble.

gansey, ganzy *n* a seaman's jersey.

gansh *same as* **ganch**.

ganshel *same as* **gansel**.

gant *v* **1** to yawn, gape. **2** to stutter.—*n* **1** a yawn. **2** a stutter.

gant-at-the-door *n* an indolent lout.

gantree *same as* **gantress**.

gantress *n* a wooden stand for barrels.—*v* to set barrels on a gantress.

ganzh *same as* **gange**.

gap *same as* **gaup**.

gape *n* a gap.—*v in phr* **to gape one's gab** to open wide one's mouth.

gape-shot *adj* open-mouthed.

gappock *same as* **gabbock**.

gapus *same as* **gaupus**.

gar *v* **1** to make, cause. **2** to induce, compel.—*adj* compulsory, forced.

garavitch *same as* **galravitch**.

garb[1] *same as* **gorb**[1].

garb[2] *n* any thin, coarse cloth.

garbals *n in phr* **guts and garbals** entrails.

garbel[1] *same as* **gorbal**.

garbe[2], **garboil, garbulle** *n* a broil, uproar, brawl. —*v* to make a brawling, scolding noise.

gardeloo *same as* **gardyloo**.

garden *v* to plant in a garden.

gardener's-gartens, ~-garters *n* the ribbongrass.

garderobe, gardrop *n* a wardrobe.

gardevin *n* **1** a big-bellied bottle. **2** a square bottle. **3** a bottle holding two quarts. **4** a whisky jar. **5** a case or closet for holding wine bottles, decanters, etc. **6** a cellaret.

gardie, gardy *n* the arm.

gardin *n* a large chamber-pot.

gardy-bane *n* the bone of the arm.

gardy chair *n* an armchair.

gardyloo *n* a warning cry about dirty water and household slops thrown from windows on to the streets.

gardy-moggans *n* long sleeves or moggans for covering the arms.

gardy-pick *n* an expression of great disgust.

gare[1] *adj* **1** keen, eager, ready. **2** rapacious. **3** parsimonious. **4** intent on making money. **5** active in managing a household.

gare[2] *same as* **gair**[1].

gare[3] *n* **1** that part of the body close to which is the gusset of a shirt. **2** a strip large enough to make a bandage.

gare[4], **gare-fowl** *n* the great auk.

gare-gaun *adj* rapacious, greedy.

garg *v* to creak.—*n* a creaking sound.

gargle *n* a cant name for liquor.

gargrugous *adj* austere in person and in manners.

garlands *n* straw ropes put round the head of a stack.

gar-ma-true *n* **1** a hypocrite. **2** a make-believe.

garmunshoch *adj* ill-humoured, crabbed.

garnel *same as* **girnel**.

garnet *n* the gurnard.

garr *n* **1** mud. **2** slime, filth. **3** rheum. **4** a thin mixture of oatmeal and water used as a poultice.

garraivery *n* **1** folly, frolicsome rioting, revelling. **2** loud uproar.

garrard *n* **1** a hoop, a gird. **2** *in phr* **ca the garrard** keep the talk going.

garravadge *same as* **galravitch**.

garrer *n* one who makes a boy his fag.

garret *n* **1** the head. **2** the skull.

garrie-bee *n* the black-and-yellow striped bee.

garrin' law *n* the system or law of fagging at a school or at a boys' school.

garrochan *n* a kind of oval shellfish, three inches long, found in the Firth of Clyde.

garron[1], **garran** *n* **1** an inferior kind of horse, small and used for rough work. **2** an old, stiff horse. **3** a thickset animal. **4** a stout, thickset person.

garron[2] *n* a large nail, a spike-nail.

garry-bag *n* the abdomen of unfledged birds.

garse *n* grass.

garsummer *n* gossamer.

gart *v* made, compelled. *See* **gar**.

garten, gartan, gartane, garton *n* a garter.—*v* to bind with a garter.

garten-berries *n* blackberries, brambles.

garten-leem *n* a portable loom for weaving garters.

garten-man *n* one who does the swindling trick of prick-the-garter. *See* **garter**.

garten-pricker *n* a garter-man.

garter *n* the game of **prick-the-garter**, a form of fast-and-loose.

garth *n* **1** a house and the land attached to it. **2** an enclosure for catching salmon. **3** a shallow part or stretch of shingle on a river, which may be used as a ford.

garvie, gaarvock *n* the sprat.

garwhoungle *n* **1** the noise of the bittern in rising from the bog. **2** the clash of tongues.

gascromh *n* a trenching spade of semicircular form, with a crooked handle fixed in the middle.

gash[1] *n* **1** a chin. **2** a projection of the underjaw.—*adj* (*used of the chin*) projecting.—*v* **1** to project the under-jaw. **2** to distort the mouth in contempt.

gash[2] *n* **1** talk, prattle. **2** loquacity. **3** pert language. **4** insolence.—*adj* **1** talkative. **2** affable, lively. **3** wise, sagacious. **4** shrewd. **5** witty, sharp. **6** trim neatly dressed. **7** well-prepared. **8** (*used of the weather*) bright, pleasant.—*v* **1** to talk freely. **2** to converse, chatter. **3** to gesticulate and screw the mouth in an ugly way.

gash[3] *adj* grim, dismal, ghastly.—*adv* dismally.

gash-beard *n* **1** a person with a long, protruding chin. **2** one with a long, peaked beard.

gash-gabbit *adj* **1** having a long, protruding chin. **2** having a distorted mouth. **3** loquacious. **4** shrewd in talk.

gashin[1] *adj* having a projecting chin.

gashin[2] *adj* **1** chattering. **2** insolent in speech. **3** talking. **4** gesticulating and screwing the mouth in an ugly way.

gashle *v* **1** to distort, writhe. **2** to argue fiercely or sharply.

gashlin *n* a noisy, bitter argument.—*adj* wry.

gashly *adv* shrewdly, wittily, smartly.

gash-moo't *adj* having a distorted mouth.

gashy[1] *adj* wide, gaping, deeply gashed.

gashy[2] *adj* **1** talkative, lively. **2** stately, handsome, well-furnished.

gaskin *n* a rough, green gooseberry, originally from Gascony.

gasoliery *n* a chandelier.

gasping *adj* **1** feeble. **2** fainting. **3** expiring.

gast[1] *n* a fright, a scare.—*adj* **1** frightened. **2** terrible.

gast[2] *n* a surprise.

gast[3] *n* a gust of wind.

gaste *n* a term of contempt.

gastly-thoughted *adj* frightened at, or thinking of, ghosts.

gastrel *n* the kestrel.

gastrous *adj* monstrous.

gastrously *adv* monstrously.

gat *v* got.

gate[1] *n* **1** a way. **2** route. **3** distance. **4** a street, thoroughfare. **5** a journey.

gate² *same as* **gait**.
gate³ *same as* **gait**².
gate⁴ *same as* **gait**⁴.
gate-end *n* **1** a road-end. **2** quarters, place of abode. **3** a neighbourhood.
gate-farren *adj* **1** comely. **2** of respectable appearance.
gateless *adj* pathless.
gatelins *adv* directly, in the way towards.
gate-slap *n* an opening in a wall, hedge, etc, for a gateway.
gateward, gatewards *adv* straight, directly.
gather *same as* **gaither**.
gatheraway *n* a travelling rag-and-boneman.
gathering *n* a collection of pus under the skin.
gathering-bodie *n* one who accumulates goods or money through industy and thrift
gatten *v* got.
gatty *adj* **1** enervated. **2** gouty.
gaubertie-shells *n* a hobgoblin supposed to combine loud roaring with barking like little dogs and the sound of shells striking against each other.
gauciness *n* stateliness.
gaucy *adj* **1** plump, jolly. **2** large. **3** portly, stately. **4** well-prepared. **5** comfortable, pleasant.
gaucy-gay *adj* fine, handsome, gay.
gaud¹, **gaude** *n* **1** a prank. **2** a habit, custom. **3** a toy, plaything. **4** an ornament. **5** (*in pl*) pomps.—*v* to make a showy or gaudy appearance.
gaud² *n* **1** a rod. **2** a goad. **3** a rind of board, about nine feet long, used on a calm day to lay the corn slightly before the person who cuts it.
gaude-day *n* a festive day.
gauden *adj* golden.
gaudering, gaudery *n* finery, tawdriness.
gaud-flook *n* the saury pike.
gaudnie *n* a semi-aquatic bird, perhaps the water ouzel.
gaudsman *same as* **gadman**.
gaudy *adj* **1** tricky. **2** mischievous.
gauff *same as* **gaff**.
gauffin *same as* **gaff**.
gaufnook *same as* **gaud-flook**.
gauge *same as* **gadge**².
gauger *n* one who is ever looking after his own interests.
gaugnet *n* the sea needle or needlefish.
gauk¹ *v* (*used of young women*) to behave foolishly or lightly with men.
gauk² *n* a fool, a lout.
gaukie, gauky *n* **1** a foolish, forward, vain woman. **2** a foolish person.—*v* to play the fool, to gauk with men.—*adj* giddy, foolish.
gaukit *adj* **1** foolish, stupid. **2** giddy. **2** awkward.
gaukitness *n* stupidity, lack of sense.
gaul *n* **1** bog myrtle. **2** Dutch myrtle.
gaulf *same as* **gaff**.
gaulp *same as* **gaup**.
gaum *same as* **goam**.
gaumit *n* gamut.
glaumeril, gaumeral *same as* **gomeril**.
gaump¹ *same as* **gamp**¹.
gaump² *same as* **gamf**¹.
gaun¹ *v* to go.—*adj* going.—*n* lapse.
gaun², **gaund** *n* the butterbur.
gaun-a-du *n* a resolution never acted on.
gaunch *same as* **ganch**.
gaun-days *same as* **gan-days**.
gauner *v* **1** to bark. **2** to scold loudly.—*n* **1** a barking. **2** a fit of scolding.
gaunge *same as* **gange**.
gaunna, gauna *v* going to.
gaunt *same as* **gant**.
gaun-to-dee *n* a state near death.
gauntrees *same as* **gantress**.
gaup *v* **1** to gape, yawn. **2** to open the mouth widely. **3** to gaze vacantly or with open mouth. **4** to swallow greed-

ily, gulp.—*n* **1** a vacant, staring person. **2** a stupid, vacant stare. **3** a wide, open mouth. **4** a large mouthful. **5** chatter.
gaup-a-liftie *n* one who carries his or her head high.
gaupish *adj* inclined to yawn.
gaupus *n* **1** a vacant, staring person. **2** a booby, blockhead.
gaupy *n* same as **gaupus**.—*adj* gaping.
gaur¹ *same as* **gar**.
gaur² *v* **1** to scratch. **2** to seam or cut into. **3** to gore. —*n* a seam, scratch, a cut made by a sharp point drawn over a smooth surface.
gausy *same as* **gaucy**.
gaut¹ *n* **1** a boar pig. **2** a gelded boar. **3** a sow.
gaut² *v* galled.
gautseam, gautsame *n* hog's lard.
gavall, gavawll *v* to revel, live riotously.
gavalling *n* **1** revelling, riotousness. **2** a feast, a merry-making.
gavel *n* a gable. **2** the gable end of a building.
gavelag, gavelock *n* **1** an earwig. **2** an insect like an earwig but longer.
gavelock *n* an iron crowbar, a lever.
gavel winnock *n* a gable window.
gavil, gavel² *n* a railing, a hand-rail.
gaw¹ *n* **1** a channel or furrow for drawing off water. **2** a hollow with water springs in it.
gaw² *n in phr* **gaw o' the pot** the first runnings of a still.
gaw³, **gaw**⁴ *same as* **ga**¹, **ga**².
gawan *same as* **gowan**.
gawd¹ *same as* **gad**¹.
gawd² *same as* **gaud**¹.
gawdnie *same as* **gaudnie**.
gawe *v* to go about staring.
gawf *same as* **gaff**.
gaw-fur *n* a furrow for draining off water.
gaw-haw *v* to talk loudly.
gawk¹, **gawkie** *same as* **gauk**¹.
gawk² *same as* **gauk**².
gawk³ *v* to stare idly or vacantly.
gawkie¹ *v* to stroll about.
gawkie² *n* the horse-cockleshell.
gawkit *same as* **gaukit**.
gawkitness *n* stupidity, lack of sense.
gawky, gawkie *same as* **gaukie**.
gawless *adj* **1** without gall or bitterness. **2** harmless. **3** innocent.
gawlin *n* a fowl less than a duck, regarded as a prognosticator of fair weather.
gawmfert *same as* **gamphered**.
gawmp *same as* **gamp**.
gawn *v* going.
gawntress *same as* **gantress**.
gawp *same as* **gaup**.
gawrie *n* the red gurnard.
gawries *same as* **gairies**.
gawsie, gawsy *same as* **gaucy**.
gay *same as* **gey**.
gay-carlin *same as* **gyre-carlin**.
gaye *same as* **gey**.
gaylies, gayly *adj* in fair health.—*adv* pretty well.
gaynoch *same as* **geenyoch**.
gayt *same as* **get**.
gaze *n* a sight, spectacle.
gazen *same as* **gizzen**.
gazzard *n* talk, gossip.
geal *same as* **geel**.
geal-caul *adj* cold as ice.
gean *n* **1** the wild cherry. **2** its fruit.
gear *n* **1** dress, garb. **2** accoutrements. **3** a sword, weapon, etc. **4** harness. **5** apparatus of all kinds. **6** household goods. **7** property. **8** money, wealth. **9** livestock, cattle. **10** stuff, material. **11** fare, food. **12** spirits. **13** trash, rubbish. **14** doggerel. **15** an affair, matter of business. **16** goings on. **17** the smallest quantity, atom. **18** (*in pl*) the

twisted threads through which the warp runs in the loom.—*v* to harness a horse.

gear-carlin *same as* **gyre-carlin**.

gear-gatherer *n* **1** a money-making man. **2** one prosperous in business.

gear-grasping *adj* money-grabbing, avaricious.

gearing *n* **1** dress. **2** fishing tackle.

gearless *adj* **1** moneyless. **2** without property.

gear nor gweed *phr* neither one thing nor another.

gear-pock *n* **1** purse. **2** moneybag.

geat[1] *same as* **gate**.

geat[2] *same as* **get**.

geave *same as* **goave**.

gebbie *same as* **gabby**.

geb-shot *same as* **gab-shot**.

geck *v* **1** to mock, deride, scoff at. **2** to trifle with. **3** to deceive. **4** to toss the head in scorn or pertness. **5** to look derisively. **6** to look shyly. **7** to exult. **8** to look fondly. **9** to be playful or sportive. —*n* **1** scorn, contempt, derision. **2** a passing sarcasm, scoff. **3** a toss of the head. **4** a scornful air. **5** an act of deception, a cheat.—*phr* **to geck one's heels** to dog one's heels, pursue.

geckin'*adj* **1** pert. **2** light-headed. **3** lively, sportive.

geck-neck *n* a wry neck.

geck-neckit *adj* having a wry neck.

ged, gedd *n* **1** the pike. **2** a greedy or avaricious person. **3** anything under water fastening a hook so that it cannot be pulled out.

gedder *same as* **gaither**.

gedderer *same as* **gaitherer**.

geddery *n* a miscellaneous collection, a heterogeneous mass.

geddock *n* a small staff or goad.

ged-staff *n* a pointed staff.

gedwing *n* **1** an ancient-looking person. **2** an antiquary.

gee[1] *int* **1** a call to horses to start or move faster. **2** a call to horses to turn to the left. **3** an exclamation of surprise.—*v* **1** to stir, move, change place. **2** to move aside. **3** to turn, tilt. **4** to swerve from, shirk.—*n* **1** a move, motion to one side. **2** a turn.

gee[2] *n* **1** a fit of ill-temper, sullenness, stubbornness. **2** a sudden pique, offence. **3** a whim, fit of doing anything. **3** a knack, facility for anything.

geeble *n* a small quantity of any liquid (*used contemptuously*).—*v* **1** to shake a liquid, spill, splash over. **2** to lose, destroy. **3** to cook badly. **4** (*with* **on**) to use constantly, as an article of food.

geeblick *n* a very small quantity of liquid.

geebloch *n* a quantity of worthless liquid.

geed *adj* good.

geeg[1] *same as* **gag**.

geeg[2] *v* **1** to laugh in a suppressed way, giggle. **2** to quiz, laugh at.—*n* **1** fun, frolic. **2** a gibe.

geegaw *n* a gewgaw, a trifle.

geegs *n* the sounding boards, pegs and wheels in a mill.

geel *v* **1** to freeze. **2** to congeal.—*n* **1** jelly. **2** ice.

geelim *n* a rabbet plane.

geems *n* the gums.

geen[1] *n* *same as* **gean**.

geen[2] *v* gone.

geen[3] *same as* **gien**.

geenyoch, geenoch *adj* **1** gluttonous, voracious. **2** avaricious.—*n* a covetous, insatiable person.

geenyochly *adv* **1** gluttonously. **2** greedily.

geenyochness *n* gluttony, covetousness.

geer *same as* **gear**.

geese *n* **1** a goose. **2** a large curling stone.

geet *same as* **gett**.

geetle *v* to spill over.—*n* a small quantity.

geetsher *same as* **gutcher**.

geevelor *n* a jailer.

gee-ways *adv* **1** aslant. **2** obliquely.

geezen *same as* **gizzen**.

geg[1] *n* an implement for spearing fish.—*v* to poach fish by a geg.

geg[2] *same as* **gag**.

geg[3] *n* **1** a crack in wood. **2** a chink caused by dryness. **3** a chap in the hands.—*v* **1** to chap. **2** to break into clefts and chinks through dryness.

geg[4] *n* **1** the article used in the game of **smuggle the geg**. **2** the holder of the article.

gegger *n* the under-lip.

geggery *n* a deception.

geggie *n* the shows and stir of a fair.

gehl rope *n* the rope that runs along the end of a herring net.

gehr *same as* **gair**.

geig *n* a net for catching the razorfish.

geik *same as* **geck**.

geill *same as* **geel**.

geing[1] *same as* **gaingo**.

geing[2] *n* any intoxicating liquor.

geir *same as* **gear**.

geisan, geisen *same as* **gizzen**.

geit[1] *same as* **gett**.

geit[2] *same as* **gyte**.

geitter *v* **1** to talk much and foolishly. **2** to work awkwardly and triflingly.—*n* **1** nonsense. **2** foolish chatter. **3** a stupid person. **4** ruin.

geitteral *n* a very stupid person.

geizen *same as* **gizzen**.

geiz'ning *adj* growing parched.

gekgo *n* **1** a jackdaw. **2** a magpie

gelaver *same as* **glaiver**.

gell[1] *same as* **yell**.

gell[2] *same as* **gavel**.

gell[3] *v* **1** to sing loudly. **2** to bawl in singing. **3** to quarrel noisily.—*n* **1** a shout, yell. **2** a brawl, wrangle. **3** sport, a frolic. **4** glee. **5** a spree. **6** a drinking bout. **7** briskness of sale.

gell[4] *adj* **1** (*used of the weather*) sharp, keen. **2** (*of persons*) sharp, keen in business. **3** (*of a market*) brisk in the sale of goods.

gell[5] *v* *same as* **gail**.

gell[6] *n* **1** a leech. **2** a tadpole.

gell[7] *v* to cheat, fleece, gull.

gelleck[1] *same as* **gavelock**.

gelleck[2] *same as* **golach**.

gellie[1] *same as* **gallyie**.

gellie[2] *n* **1** a leech. **2** a tadpole.

gelloch[1] *n* a shrill cry, a yell.

gelloch[2] *same as* **gavelock**.

gelloch[3], **gellock** *same as* **golach**.

gelly *same as* **jelly**.

gellyflower *n* the gillyflower.

gelore *same as* **galore**.

gelt[1] *n* money.

gelt[2] *adj* barren.

gemlick, gemblet *n* a gimlet.

gemm *n* a game.

gemmle *n* a long-legged man.

gen[1] *int* a word used as a cry of pain.

gen[2] *same as* **gin**.

gend *adj* playful.—*adv* playfully.

gener *n* a gender in grammar.

geng *same as* **gang**[2]. *See* **gae**.

genie, geni *n* genius.

genious *adj* **1** ingenious. **2** having genius or intelligence.

genivin *adj* genuine.

gennick *adj* genuine, not spurious.

gent[1] *n* **1** a very tall, thin person. **2** anything very tall.

gent[2] *v* to spend time idly.

gentilities *n* gentlefolk, gentry.

gentiness *n* **1** gentility. **2** genteel manners. **3** daintiness, elegance.

gentle *adj* **1** well-born. **2** gentlemanly.—*n* **1** one of gentle birth. **2** (*in pl*) gentry.—*phr* **gentle and simple** high and low.

gentle-beggars *n* poor relations.
gentle gates *n* delicate habits.
gentlemanie, gentlemanny *adj* **1** belonging to a gentleman. **2** like a gentleman.
gentle-persuasion *n* the Episcopal form of religion.
gentle-woman *n* the name formerly given to the housekeeper in a family of distinction.
gentrice *n* **1** good birth. **2** people of gentle birth. **3** honourable disposition, generosity. **4** gentleness.
genty, gentie *adj* **1** noble. **2** courteous. **3** high-born. **4** having good manners. **5** neat, dainty, trim. **6** tasteful, elegant. **7** (*used of dress*) well-fitting, becoming, genteel.
genyough *same as* **geenyoch**.
geordie *n* **1** a guinea in gold. **2** a name given to a rustic. **3** a coarse, cheap roll or bap.—*phr* **by the Geordie** by St George.
George *n in phr* **1 George's daughter** a musket. **2 yellow George** a guinea in gold.
ger[1] *same as* **gar**.
ger[2] *same as* **gird**.
geravich *same as* **galravitch**.
gerg *same as* **jirg**.
gerletroch *same as* **gallytrough**.
gern *n* a boil, tumour.
gernis *same as* **jarness**.
gerr *adj* awkward, clumsy.
gerrack *n* a coalfish of the first year.
gerran[1] *n* a sea trout.
gerran[2], **gerron** *same as* **garron**.
gerrit, gerrat *n* a little salmon.
gerrock *n* a layer in a pile that is gradually built up.
gerse, geres *n* grass.—*v* **1** to pasture, graze. **2** to eject, cast out of office.
gerse-cauld *n* a slight cold affecting horses.
gersie *adj* **1** grassy. **2** interspersed with grass.
gerslouper *n* a grasshopper.
gersome *same as* **grassum**.
gerss-fouk *n* cottars.
gerss-gawed *adj* cut or galled by grass.
gerss house *n* a house possessed by a tenant, with no land attached to it.
gerss-ill *n* a disease among sheep.
gerss-man *n* the tenant of a house without land attached to it.
gerss-meal *n* the grass that will keep a cow for a season.
gerss-nail *n* a long piece of hooked iron, with one end attached to the scythe blade and the other to its handle.
gerss-park *n* a field in grass.
gerss-puckle *n* a blade of grass.
gerss-strae *n* hay.
gerss-tack *n* the lease which a gerss-man (qv) has of his house.
gert *v* made, compelled. *See* **gar**.
gertan, gertin *same as* **garten**.
geshon *same as* **gaishen**.
gesning *same as* **guestning**.
gess[1] *v* **1** to go away clandestinely. **2** to play truant.
gess[2] *n* a measure by guess.
gest *n* a joist.—*v* to place joists.
gester *v* **1** to walk proudly. **2** to make conceited gestures.
get[1] *v* **1** to beget. **2** to earn. **3** to learn by heart. **4** to take. **5** to find. **6** to marry. **7** to be called. **8** to manage. **9** to manage to reach a place or thing. **10** to cause cream to turn to butter by churning. **11** to receive a blow. **12** to be deceived.—*n* **1** the food brought by birds to their young. **2** a catch of fish. **3** begetting, procreation. **4** offspring. **5** a contemptuous name for a child, a brat. **6** a bastard.
get[2] *same as* **gett**[1].
get a' by *phr* to finish off.
get ahin *v* to fall into arrears.
get awa' *v* to die.
get hands on *phr* to strike, assault.
gether *same as* **gaither**.

get in ahin *phr* to prove the wiser or cleverer, to get the better of.
get it *v* **1** to be scolded, chastised. **2** to suffer. **3** to pay for it.
get one's bed *phr* (*used of a woman*) to be confined.
get owre *v* to get the better in a bargain.
get roon *v* **1** to master. **2** to accomplish.
gett[1], **get** *n* **1** a child. **2** a bastard. **3** (*in pl*) boys attending the lowest class, or junior classes, of an academy.
gett[2], **gett**[3] *same as* **gate**.
gettable *adj* attainable.
gett-farrant *same as* **gate-farren**.
get the cauld *phr* to catch cold.
get the length of *phr* to go as far as.
gettlin *n* **1** a little child. **2** a brat. **3** the young of animals.
gettward *adv* on the way towards.
get upon *v* to be struck on.
get with *v* to be struck with a missile, etc.
geudam *same as* **gudame**.
gevil[1] *same as* **gavel**.
gevil[2] *same as* **gavil**.
gewgaw *n* a Jew's harp.
gewlick[1] *same as* **golach**.
gewlick[2], **gewlock** *same as* **gavelock**.
gey *adj* **1** wild. **2** tolerable. **3** large, great. **4** considerable.—*adv* **1** very, considerably. **2** quite, rather, tolerably. **3** indifferently.
gey an, gey and *adv* **1** somewhat, tolerably. **2** considerably, rather.
gey-geddert, ~gethered *n* used to describe one who has become well-off through industry and thrift.
geyl *same as* **gavel**.
geylies, geyly *adv* rather, much.—*adj* in fair health.
gey loon *n* **1** a rather wild young fellow. **2** a scamp, scoundrel.
geysan, geysen, geyze, geyzen *same as* **gizzen**.
gezling *n* **1** a gosling. **2** a fool.
geyzenin *n* the craving for alcoholic drink.
ghaist *n* **1** a ghost. **2** a piece of coal that burns white, retaining its shape.
ghaist-coal *n* a piece of coal that burns white, retaining its shape.
ghaist-craft *n* a place haunted by ghosts.
ghaist-cramp *n* an injury supposed to be owing to a ghostly visitation.
ghaistlin *n* a ghost (*used contemptuously*).
ghaistrid *adj* ghost-ridden.
ghast *same as* **gast**.
ghoul *n* **1** a ghastly or terrible spectacle or object. **2** an envious, grudging, gloomy person.
ghoulie *adj* haunted by frightening spectres.
giann *n* a giant.
gib[1] *n* **1** a tom cat. **2** a castrated cat.
gib[2] *n* the beak or hooked upper-lip of a male salmon.
gib[3] *n* **1** toffee, candy. **2** a sweetmeat made of treacle and spices.
gibain *n* an oily substance procured from the solan goose, used as a sauce for porridge.
gibb *n in phr* **Rob Gibb's contract** a toast expressive of mere friendship.
gibbag *n* a roll of flax prepared for spinning on the distaff.
gibber *n* nonsense, foolish talk.
gibber-gabber *v* to talk idly and confusedly.
gibberish *n* **1** a confused mixture. **2** idle talk.
gibbery *n* gingerbread.
gibbery-man, ~wife *n* a man or woman who sells gingerbread.
gibbet *n* a chimney crane for suspending a pot over a fire.
gibbet-gab *n* a strong double hook for suspending pots.
gibbet pan *n* the largest pan used in cooking.
gibbie-gabble *n* nonsense.—*adj* foolish.—*v* to babble.
gibble[1] *same as* **geeble**.
gibble[2] *n* **1** a tool of any kind. **2** (*in pl*) particles, wares. **3** odds and ends.

gibble-gabble *n* idle, confused talk, babble.—*v* to talk loudly or rapidly.

gibblet, giblet *n* any small iron tool.

gibby *n* the bent end of a walking stick.

gibby-gabble *same as* **gibble-gabble**.

gibby stick *n* **1** a stick with a turned handle. **2** a walking stick.

gib-gash *n* a fluent talker about nothing.

giblet-check *n* a check in a wall to let a door fold back close to it.

giblich *n* an unfledged crow.

gibloan *n* a muddy lane or miry path, so soft as not to admit of walking on it.

gibrie, gibbrie *same as* **gibbery**.

gid *v* went.

gidd *same as* **ged**.

giddack *n* the sand eel.

gidder *v* **1** to gather. **2** to lift and put on one's hat or cap.

gie¹ *same as* **gey**.

gie² *v* to pry.

gie³ *v* **1** to give. **2** to relax. **3** to give way. **4** to thaw. **5** to give a blow.

giean¹ *adj* given to prying.

giean² *same as* **geyan**.

giean-carlins *n* old women of a prying nature, supposed to be troublesome at Hallowe'en to anyone they found alone.

gied¹ *v* gave.

gied² *v* went.

giein' *v* giving.

gielainger, gielanger *same as* **gileynour**.

gi'en *adj* **1** gratuitous, given as a gift. **2** plighted, pledged. **3** (*with* **to**) inclined to, having a propensity to.

gi'en-horse *n* a gift-horse.

gi'en-rig *n* a piece of land set apart for the devil, the gudeman's croft.

gie's *v* give us.

gies't *v* give us it.

giezie *adj* given to prying into matters which do not concern oneself.

gif *conj* **1** if. **2** whether.

giff-gaffy *n* **1** reciprocity, mutual services, giving and taking. **2** mutual conversation.—*v* **1** to exchange in a friendly way. **2** to bandy words, to converse promiscuously.

giff-gaff *adj* **1** friendly. **2** talkative.

gift *n* a contemptuous term for a person.—*v* to give as a present,

giftie *n* a gift. —*adj* **1** (*used of a crop*) large. **2** abundant.

gig¹ *n* **1** a silly girl. **2** a prostitute. **3** a silly, flighty fellow. **4** a trifler.

gig² *same as* **jeeg**.

gig³ *n* **1** anything that whirls. **2** an ingenious artifice. **3** a curiosity. **4** a charm. **5** a winnowing fan. **6** a jig. **7** a state of flurry.

gig⁴ *v* to laugh in a suppressed manner, giggle.—*n* **1** fun, frolic. **2** a gibe. **3** a prank, trick. **4** a whim.

gig⁵ *same as* **geg**.

gig⁶ *v* to trot, to walk briskly. **2** to jerk.

giggery *n* odds and ends, things of little value.

giggie *adj* brisk, lively, hearty. **2** full of tricks.

giggle *v* to jog, shake about.—*n* a slight jerk, shake.

giggleby *n* a silly, giggling girl.

giggle-trot *n in phr* **tak' the giggle-trot** (*of a woman*) to marry late in life.

giggum *n* a trick.

giglet *n* a girl.

gigmaleeries *n* young people frolicking at a fair.

gimma *v with pron* give it to me.

gigot *n* the hind haunch of a sheep, a leg of mutton.

gig-trot *n* **1** habit. **2** jogtrot.

gihoe *n* a kind of conveyance.

gike *n* **1** the stalk of lovage, hemlock, etc, of which children make squirts. **2** keksy.

gil *same as* **gill**.

gilainger *same as* **gileynour**.

gilaver *v* to chatter, talk foolishly.—*n* idle or gossiping talk.

gilbert *n* an ill-shapen piece of dress.

gilbow *n* a legacy.

gild *adj* **1** clever, capable. **2** full-grown. **3** great. **4** loud. **5** light-hearted.—*n* **1** clamour, uproar. **2** noise. **3** an outburst.—*v* **1** to make a clamour about. **2** to pay court to.

gildee *n* the whiting pout.

gileynour *n* **1** a cheat, swindler. **2** a bad debtor.

gilgal *n* a hubbub, confused noise.

gilkie *n* a lively young girl.

gill¹ *n* **1** the lower jaw, the flesh under the chin or ears. **2** the mouth. **3** throat.

gill² *n* **1** a ravine. **2** a narrow glen with precipitous or rocky sides or wooded and with a stream running at the bottom. **3** a dingle. **4** a mountain stream.

gill³ *n* **1** a leech. **2** a tadpole.

gill⁴ *v* to cheat.

gill⁵ *v* to tipple, drink, tope.

gille-gapous *same as* **gilligachus**.

gillem *same as* **geelim**.

gillet *n* **1** a giddy young woman, a flirt. **2** a young woman approaching puberty.

gill-flirt *n* a thoughtless, giddy girl.

gill-gatherer *n* a leech-gatherer.

gill-ha' *n* **1** a house that cannot protect dwellers from the weather. **2** a house where workers live communally during a job or where each prepares his own food. **3** a lonely house in a glen.

gillhoo *n* a woman who is not counted economical.

gillie¹ *n* a gill of whisky, etc.

gillie² *n* a giddy young woman.

gillie³ *n* **1** a manservant. **2** a male attendant.

gillie-birse *n* an ornament or headdress consisting of a hair cushion or pad worn on a woman's forehead, over which her hair was combed.

gillie-callum the Highland sword dance and its tune.

gillie-casfliuch, ~-casflue *n* the one of a chief's attendants who had to carry him over fords.

gillie-comstrian *n* one who led his chief's horse in difficult places.

gillie-gascon *n* one who talks in an empty, unimportant way.

gillie-more *n* a chief's armour-bearer.

gillie-trusharnish *n* a chief's baggage-man or knapsack-bearer.

gillie-wetfoot *n* **1** a chief's attendant for beating the bushes. **2** a worthless fellow, swindler, a debtor who runs off. **3** a running footman. **4** a bum-bailiff.

gillie-wheesels, ~-wheesh *n* **1** gipsies. **2** robbers.

gillie-whitefoot *n* a beater of the bushes.

gilligachus *n* a fool, a booby.

gilliver *n* the gillyflower.

gill-kickerty *n in phr* **gang to gill-kickerty** to go to Jericho.

gill-maw *n* a glutton, a voracious eater.

gillock *n* **1** a gill. **2** a small measure of drink.

gillore, gillour *same as* **galore**.

gill-ronie *n* a ravine abounding with brushwood.

gill-rung *n* a long stick used by leech-gatherers to rouse leeches from deep holes.

gill-sipper *n* a tippler.

gill stouo *n* **1** a drinking vessel holding a gill, a pitcher. **2** the common periwinkle, from its resemblance to a pitcher.

gill-towal *n* the horse leech.

gill-wheep *n* **1** a cheat. **2** a jilting.

gill-wife *n* an ale-wife, one who sells liquors.

gillycacus *same as* **gilligachus**.

gillyflower *n* **1** the clove pink or carnation. **2** wallflower. **3** the hoary, shrubby stock. **4** a thoughtless, giddy girl.

gilly-gaukie *v* to spend time idly and foolishly.

gilly-gaupus, ~-gaupie *same as* **gilligachus**.

gilly-vine *same as* **keeli-vine**.

gilp[1] *n* **1** a big, fat person or animal. **2** a person of disagreeable temper.

gilp[2] *n* **1** a small quantity of water, etc. **2** a dash or splash of water. **3** thin, insipid liquid.—*v* **1** to jerk, spurt. **2** to spill, splash, dash liquids. **3** to be jerked.

gilpin[1] *n* **1** a very big, fat person. **2** a child or young animal when large and fat.

gilpin[2] *n* **1** a smart young fellow. **2** a gilpy (qv).

gilpy[1] *adj* (*used of eggs*) not fresh, stale.

gilpy[2], **gilpey** *n* **1** a lively young person. **2** a roguish or mischievous boy. **3** a soft, stupid person. **4** a brisk, light-hearted girl. **5** a young, growing girl.

gilravage, gilravachy *same as* **galravitch**.

gilravager *n* **1** a riotous, forward fellow. **2** a depredator. **3** a wanton fellow.

gilravaging *same as* **galravitching**.

gilreverie *n* **1** revelry. **2** riotousness and wastefulness.

gilse *n* a young salmon, a grilse.

gilt[1] *n* a young sow when castrated.

gilt[2] *n* money.

gilt[3] *n* **1** a haystack with rectangular base. **2** a construction made of cleaned straw.

gilter *adj* lively, light-hearted.

giltit *adj* gilded.

gim *same as* **jim**.

gimblet *same as* **gemlick**.

gimcrack *adj* **1** tawdry. **2** fantastic.

gimlet-tool *n* a gimlet.

gimmels *n* tools, implements of various kinds.

gimmer[1] *n* **1** a ewe from one to two years old or that has not yet borne young. **2** a contemptuous name for a woman.

gimmer[2] *v* to court and enjoy.

gimmer-hill, ~-hillock *n* *in phr* **on the gimmer-hill** *or* **gimmer-hillock 1** unmarried. **2** childless.

gimmer-pet *n* a two-year-old ewe.

gimp *same as* **jimp**.

gin[1] *prep* **1** (*used of time*) against. **2** by. **3** in time for. **4** within.—*conj* **1** by the time that, until. **2** if, whether.

gin[2] *n* **1** the bolt or lock of a window or a door. **2** the lever of a latch.

gin[3] *adj* greedy for meat.

ginch[1] *same as* **ginge**.

ginch[2] *n* a small piece.

ginchick *n* a very small piece.

ginchock *n* a rather small piece.

gin-cough *n* the whooping cough.

gindle *same as* **ginnle**.

gineough *same as* **geenyoch**.

ging[1] *same as* **gang**[2]. *See* **gae**.

ging[2] *same as* **gang**[1].

ging[3] *n* filth.

ging-bang *same as* **jingbang**.

ginge *n* ginger.—*adj* made with ginger.

ging-brace,-bras *n* gingerbread, spice cake.

gingebread *n* gingerbread.—*adj* **1** flimsy, soft, delicate. **2** affecting dignity. **3** gaudy. **4** made of gingerbread.

gingebread-man, ~-wife *n* **1** a man or woman who sells gingerbread. **2** the figure of a man or woman in gingerbread. **3** a flighty, delicate, affected man or woman.

ginger *n* a child's posterior.

ging-go *n* **1** nonsense. **2** a confused mass.

gingich *n* the chief climber or leader in rock-climbing for sea fowl in the Western Isles.

gingie *adj* filthy.

gingle *same as* **jingle**.

gingling *adj* noisy, chattering.

gin-goon *adv* ding-dong.

gink *v* **1** to titter. **2** to laugh in a suppressed fashion.—*n* **1** a trick. **2** a tittering.

ginker *n* a dancer.

ginkie *adj* light-headed, giddy, tricky, frolicsome. —*n* **1** a giddy, light-headed girl. **2** a giglet.

ginkum *n* **1** a trick. **2** an inkling. **3** a hint.

ginnaguid *adj* ne'er-do-well, good-for-nothing.

ginnel[1] *n* a street gutter.

ginnel[2] *same as* **ginnle**[1].

ginners *n* the gills of a fish.

ginnle[1] *v* to tickle trout, catch fish by groping under banks and stones with the hands, to guddle.

ginnle[2] *v* **1** to tremble, shake. **2** to cause to tremble. —*n* **1** tremulous motion. **2** the sound caused by vibration.

ginnles *n* the gills of a fish.

ginnling *n* tickling trout.

ginnling *n* the noise caused by vibration.

gin'st *phr* than it has.

gip[1] *n* the point of a fish's jaw.

gip[2] *v* to gut fish for curing.

gipe[1] *n* one who is greedy, voracious or avaricious. — *adj* **1** keen, ardent. **2** very hungry.

gipe[2] *n* **1** a stupid, awkward, foolish person. **2** a foolish stare.—*v* **1** to stare foolishly. **2** to act foolishly.

gipper *n* **1** a woman who guts or cleans fish. **2** a gippie (qv).

gippie *n* a small knife used in gutting fish.

gipping *n* gutting fish in the herring season.

gipsy *n* **1** a term of contempt for a woman or girl and sometimes of endearment. **2** a woman's cap plaited on the back.

gipsy-herring *n* the pilchard.

gird[1] *n* **1** a girth. **2** a hoop for a barrel or tub. **3** a child's hoop.—*v* **1** to put on a hoop. **2** to ring a wheel. **3** to encircle with a belt or girth. **4** to keep fast to a thing.

gird[2] *v* **1** to strike, push. **2** to drive smartly. **3** to erect oneself with energy or violence. **4** to drink hard. **5** to scoff at.—*n* **1** a push, thrust. **2** a blow, knock. **3** a gust of wind. **4** a very short space of time. **5** a reproach, rebuke.

gird and cleek *n* a child's plaything consisting of a hoop and a hook-shaped piece of metal or wire used to guide and control the rolling of the hoop.

girden, girdin *n* **1** a ligament that binds a thing round. **2** a saddle girth.

girder *n* a cooper.

girderings *n* suckers from an ash tree used as hoops.

girding *adj* belonging to the trade of coopers.—*n* girthing.

girdit *adj* hooped with wood or iron.

girdle *n* a circular iron plate with bow handle, for baking oatcake, scones, etc.

girdle-braid *adj* of the breadth of a girdle (qv).

girdle cake *n* a cake baked on a girdle (qv).

girdle farl *n* a quarter of a circular oatcake which is cut into four while baked on the girdle (qv).

girdle scone *n* a flour or barley-meal scone baked on a girdle (qv).

girdlesmith *n* a maker of girdles (qv).

girdless *adj* without hoops.

gird-the-cogie *n* the name of an old Scots tune.

girg *same as* **jirg**.

girkienet *same as* **jirkinet**.

girl[1] *n* a girdle (qv).

girl[2], **girle** *v* **1** to tingle, thrill. **2** to shudder, shiver. **3** to set the teeth on edge.

girl[3] *same as* **grill**.

girn[1] *v* **1** to grin. **2** to snarl. **3** to show or gnash the teeth in rage or scorn. **4** to twist the features, grimace. **5** to gape, like a dress so tightly fastened as to show the undergarment.—*n* **1** a snarl, grin. **2** a whimper. **3** fretful fault-finding. **4** a smile. **5** distortion of the face. **6** a gape in a too tight dress.

girn[2] *n* **1** a snare, trap, gin, noose of wire or cord to catch birds, rabbits, trout and other small animals. **2** a seton to keep up an issue, an issue.—*v* to catch birds, rabbits, etc, by means of a girn.

girn[3] *same as* **kirn**.

girn-again *n* **1** a peevish, cross-grained person. **2** an habitually fretting child.

girnel, girnal *n* **1** a granary. **2** a meal chest.—*v* to store up in granaries.

girnel house *n* **1** a large granary. **2** a miller's granary.

girnel kist *n* a meal chest.

girnel-man *n* a land steward in charge of the grain and meal paid as part of the rent.

girner *n* **1** a garner. **2** a meal chest.

girnie *n* **1** a peevish person. **2** a fretting child.—*adj* peevish, fretful.

girnie-gib, ~-gibbie *n* a peevish person.

girnigo, girnigae *n* a peevish person.—*adj* peevish, fretful.

girnigo-gash, ~-gibbie *n* a peevish person.

girningly *adv* **1** with a grin. **2** fretfully.

girnot *same as* **garnet**.

girr *same as* **gird**.

girran[1], **girron** *n* a small boil.

girran[2] *same as* **garron**.

girrebbage *same as* **gilravage**.

girrel *same as* **girl**.

girs, girse, girss *same as* **gerse**.

girsie *same as* **gersy**.

girskaivie *adj* harebrained.

girsle *n* **1** gristle. **2** a quill pen. **3** the throat.

girslie *same as* **grisly**.

girslin *n* a slight frost, a thin scurf of frost.

girst[1] *adj* pastured on grass.

girst[2] *same as* **grist**.

girst[3] *n* **1** size, measurement, texture, thickness. **2** the form of the surface of linen, wood, etc, as to smoothness.

girster *n* one who brings grain to be ground at a mill.

girt[1] *adj* great, large.

girt[2] *n* **1** the girth. **2** a girth.

girth[1] *n* **1** a neckcloth. **2** a hoop of iron or wood.

girth[2] *n* **1** a sanctuary, place of refuge. **2** a circle of stones environing the ancient places of judgment, popularly supposed to be sanctuaries.

girthgate *n* **1** a safe road. **2** the way to a sanctuary.

girthing *n* a saddle girth, harness.

girtholl *n* a sanctuary.

girtle *n* a small quantity of any fluid.—*v* **1** to pour in small quantities. **2** to work with liquids. **3** (*with* **up**) to throw up, splash. **4** (*with* **out, over**) to spill in small quantities. **5** (*with* **at, with**) to use constantly, as an article of food.

girt o' the leg *phr* the calf of the leg.

girzy, girzie *n* a maidservant.

gisn *same as* **gizzen**.

gite[1] *adj* **1** mad. **2** enraged.—*n* a madman, an idiot.

gite[2] *same as* **gett**.

gitters *same as* **gutters**.

gitty *n* a term of endearment to a child.

give[1] *same as* **gif**.

give[2] *same as* **gie**.

gizen[1] *same as* **gizzen**.

gizen[2] *same as* **gizzen**.

gizy *n* a wig.

gizy-maker *n* a wig-maker.

gizz *n* **1** a wig. **2** the face, countenance.

gizzen[1] *n* childbed.

gizzen[2] *n* **1** the gizzard of a fowl. **2** a person's throat.

gizzen[3] *adj* **1** (*used of wooden vessels*) leaking owing to drought. **2** dry. **3** thirsty. **4** parched.—*v* **1** (*used of wooden vessels*) to warp, twist or crack and become leaky from drought. **2** to dry up from heat. **3** to be parched. **4** to wither, fade, shrivel. **5** to parch from thirst.

gizzen-bed *n* childbed.

gizzen-clout *n* an infant's binder.

gizzy-maker *n* a wig-maker.

glaamer *v* to grope.

glaar *same as* **glaur**.

glabber *v* **1** to chatter, gabble. **2** to speak indistinctly.—*n* foolish, idle talk.

glack[1] *v in phr* **glack one's mitten 1** to bribe. **2** to tip.

glack[2] *same as* **glaik**.

glack[3] *n* **1** a ravine, a defile. **2** the fork of a tree, road, etc. **3** the angle between the thumb and the forefinger. **4** an opening in a wood where the wind blows briskly. **5** a handful or small portion. **6** as much grain as a reaper holds in his left hand. **7** a snack, slight repast.

glad, glade *adj* **1** smooth, easy in motion. **2** slippery. **3** not to be trusted.

glad content *phr* especially content.

glaff[1] *n* a glimpse

glaff[2] *n* a sudden blast or puff of wind.—*v* to waft, blow gently.

glag *v* to make a choking noise in the throat.—*n* a choking sound in the throat.

glagger[1] *same as* **glag**.

glagger[2] *v* to search, pursue or desire eagerly.—*n* **1** a keen pursuit. **2** avaricious greed.

glaggy *adj* soft, sticky.

glaiber *same as* **glabber**.

glaid[1] *same as* **gled**.

glaid[2] *same as* **glid**.

glaid[3] *same as* **gled**.

glaiger *n* a hard, whitish marble made of earthenware.

glaik *n* **1** a trick. **2** a deception. **3** an illusion of the eye. **4** a gleam, reflection of light. **5** a glance of the eye. **6** the bat. **7** (*in pl*) scoffs, gibes. **8** a jilting. **9** an idle, good-for-nothing person. **10** a puzzle game. **11** a child's puzzle.—*v* **1** to trifle. **2** to flirt. **3** to fool. **4** to wanton. **5** to wander idly. **6** to spend time playfully. **7** to jeer, make game of. **8** to shine, dazzle. **9** to deceive, beguile.

glaikery *n* coquetry, trifling, light-headedness.

glaiket *adj* inattentive to duty.

glaikie *same as* **glaiky**.

glaikit, glaigit *adj* **1** senseless, foolish, silly. **2** giddy, thoughtless. **3** affected. **4** petted.

glaikitly *adv* **1** lightly, foolishly. **2** affectedly. **3** pettishly.

glaikitness *n* **1** levity, giddiness. **2** affectation. **3** petteness.

glaiks *n* an instrument for twisting straw ropes.

glaiky *adj* **1** giddy, thoughtless. **2** pleasant, charming.—*n* a giddy girl.

glaim *v* to burn with a bright flame.—*n* a flame.

glaip *v* to gulp food or drink.

glair *same as* **glaur**.

glair-hole *n* a mire.

glairie *n* mud.

glairie-flairies *n* **1** gaudy trappings. **2** glare.

glairy *adj* showy.

glairy-flairy *adj* gaudy, showy.

glaise *same as* **glaize**.

glaister[1] *n* a thin covering of snow or ice.

glaister[2] *v* **1** to babble, talk indistinctly. **2** to howl. **3** to bark. **4** to speak foolishly.

glaisterie *adj* **1** sleety. **2** miry.

glaive *n* a glove.

glaiver *same as* **claver**[2].

glaize[1] *v* **1** to smooth over. **2** to graze in passing. **3** to glaze.

glaize[2] *n* a warming at a fire.

glaizie *adj* **1** glittering. **2** glossy. **3** smooth, sleek. **4** shining like glass.

glak *same as* **glaik**.

glakit *same as* **glaikit**.

glam[1] *n* **1** a loud, prolonged cry. **2** noise, clamour.

glam[2] *same as* **glaum**.

glamack *n* **1** a snatch. **2** an eager grasp. **3** a handful. **4** a mouthful.—*v* **1** to snatch at, clutch. **2** to eat greedily.

glamer[1] *n* glamour.—*v* **1** to bewitch, fascinate. **2** to dazzle.

glamer[2] *n* noise, clamour.

glamer bead *n* an amber bead used in enchantment.

glamerie *same as* **glamourie**.

glamerify *v* to bewitch, cast a spell.

glamer-micht *n* power of enchantment.

glammach *v* **1** to snatch at, clutch. **2** to grope for. **3** search one's pocket. **4** to eat greedily.—*n* **1** a clutch, grasp. **2** a handful. **3** a morsel.

glammer *n* **1** a spell, fascination. **2** witchery.—*v* **1** to bewitch, beguile. **2** to dazzle. **3** to bind with a spell.

glammie *same as* **glaum**.

glamorous *adj* magical, supernatural.

glamour gift *n* the gift of fascinating or enchanting.

glamourie *n* **1** witchcraft. **2** fascination. **3** a spell.

glamshach *adj* **1** greedy, grasping. **2** gluttonous.

glamp *v* **1** to grasp, clutch at. **2** to grope. **3** to gulp, eat greedily. **4** to sprain.—*n* **1** a snatch, gulp, grasp. **2** a groping search in the dark. **3** a sprain.

glance *v* **1** to cause to glance. **2** to brighten the eye.

glancing glass *n* **1** a glass used by children to reflect sunrays on any object. **2** applied to a minister of the gospel who has more show or flashiness than solidity.

glancy *adj* glancing.

glant *v* shone.

glar, glare¹ *same as* **glaur**.

glare² *v* to cause to glare.

glare³ *n* a fine show, a gaudy appearance.

glarry *same as* **glaurie**.

Glasgow-magistrate *n* a red herring.

glash *n* a hollow on the slope of a hill.

glashan *n* the coalfish.

glashtroch *n* continuous rain causing dirty roads.

glasin-wricht *n* a glazier.

glasp *n* a clasp, grasp.

glass *n* (*in pl*) glasses filled with water and having the white of an egg dropped into them, used at Fastern's E'en and Hallowe'en as predictions of the future.—*v* to glaze, furnish windows with glass.

glassack *n* a glassey (qv).

glass-breaker *n* a tippler, a hard drinker.

glass-chack *v* to plane down the outer part of a sash to fit it for receiving the glass.

glassen *adj* made of glass.

glasser¹, **glassier** *n* a glazier.

glasser² *n* a marble made of glass.

glassey *n* **1** a sweetmeat made of treacle. **2** a glass marble.

glassin *n* glasswork, panes of glass.

glassing *n* a planing, smoothing.

glassin wright *n* a glazier.

Glassites *n* followers of the Rev. John Glas (1695–1773), otherwise called Sandemanians.

glassock *n* the coalfish.

glaster *same as* **glaister**.

glasterer *n* a boaster.

glastrious *adj* **1** contentious. **2** boastful.

glatton *n* a handful.

glaum¹ *v* **1** to clutch. **2** to grope.—*n* **1** a clutch. **2** a mouthful.

glaum² *v* to stare, glower.

glaumer, glaumour *same as* **glamer**.

glaump *same as* **glamp**.

glaums *n* a horse-gelder's instruments.

glaund, glaun *n* a clamp of iron or wood.

glaur, glawr *n* **1** mud, dirt, ooze. **2** slippery ice, slipperiness.—*v* **1** to make muddy or dirty. **2** to make slippery. **3** to wade or stick in mud.

glaur-hole *n* a mud-hole.

glaurie *adj* muddy, filthy. **2** smooth and shining like wet mud. **2** (*used of the weather*) wet, causing mud.—*n* mire, soft mud.

glauroch *n* a soft, muddy hole.

glaver *same as* **claver**².

glawnicy *n* an ocular deception caused by witchcraft.

glazen *adj* **1** made of glass. **2** (*used of weak arguments*) easily refuted.

glazie *same as* **glaizie**.

glead¹ *same as* **gleed**.

glead², **gleade** *n* **1** the kite. **2** a kite's feathers used for dressing salmon hooks.

gleait *same as* **glaikit**.

gleam *n in phr* **gang gleam** to take fire.

glebber, glebor *same as* **glabber**.

glebe *n* the piece of land provided for the use of the minister of a parish.

gled¹ *adj* glad.

gled², **glede** *n* **1** the kite. **2** the buzzard. **2** a greedy person.

glede's whissle *n* an expression of triumph.

glede-wylie *n* a children's game.

gledge *v* **1** to glance at, take a side view. **2** to look askance. **3** to leer. **4** to look slyly or archly. **5** to spy.—*n* **1** a glance, glimpse. **2** an oblique look. **3** a sly or arch glance.

gled-like *adj* like a kite.

glee¹ *v* **1** to squint. **2** to look sideways.—*n* **1** a squint. **2** a mark, track, straight course.—*adv* awry.

glee² *adj* merry, gleeful.

glee³ *n* a glove.

gleed¹ *same as* **glead**.

gleed² *adj* **1** squinting. **2** blind in an eye. **3** crooked, awry. **4** oblique.—*adv* **1** crookedly. **2** astray.

gleed-eyed *adj* squinting.

gleed-looking *adj* appearing to have a squint.

gleed-necked *adj* wry-necked, crooked.

gleeitness *n* **1** obliqueness. **2** the state of being squint-eyed.

gleek *same as* **glaik**.

gleemock *n* a faint or deadened gleam, like that of the sun through fog.

glee-mou'd *adj* having the mouth awry.

gleen *v* to shine, glitter, gleam.—*n* a bright light, gleam.

gleesh *v* to burn with a strong, clear fire.—*n* a strong, clear fire.

gleeshach *n* a strong, clear fire.

gleet¹ *v* to shine, glance, glitter.—*n* a glance, a glitter, the act of shining.

gleet² *adj* **1** squinting. **2** blind of an eye. **3** awry, crooked.—*adv* crookedly.

gleeyed *adj* squinting.

gleg *same as* **cleg**.

gleg¹ *n in phr* **be aff the gleg** to be off the track, to miss the mark.

gleg² *adj* **1** clear-sighted, of quick perception. **2** keen, sharp, eager. **3** brisk, nimble. **4** quick in movement. **5** bright, smart. **6** gay. **7** vivid, sparkling. **8** keen of appetite, hungry. **9** sharp-edged. **10** (*of ice*) slippery. **11** clever. **12** pert in manner. **13** attentive. **14** avaricious.—*adv* cleverly.

gleg-e'ed *adj* sharp-eyed.

gleg-gabbit *adj* **1** sharp-tongued. **2** nimble or fluent of speech.

gleg-glancing *adj* quick-sighted.

gleg-hawk *n* the sparrow-hawk.

gleg-lug'd *adj* quick of hearing.

glegly *adv* **1** cleverly. **2** keenly, attentively. **3** briskly, quickly. **4** brightly, flashingly.

glegness *n* **1** keenness. **2** quick perception.

gleg-set *adj* sharp, keen.

gleg-sichted *adj* quick-sighted.

gleg-sure *adj* certain, cocksure.

gleg-tongued *adj* sharp-tongued.

gleg-witted *adj* sharp-witted.

gleib *n* a piece, part of anything.

gleid¹ *same as* **gleed**.

gleid² *same as* **glee**.

gleig *n* clear-sighted.

glen *n* **1** a narrow valley. **2** a daffodil.

glender-gane *adj* in a bad condition, physical, moral or financial.

glender-gear *n* ill-gotten substance.

glendrie-gaits *n* far-away errands.

Glendronach *n* a particular brand of whisky.

glengarry *n* a man's or boy's oblong woollen cap.

glengore *n* venereal disease.

Glenlivat, Glenlivet *n* whisky distilled at Glenlivet.

glent *v* **1** to shine, sparkle. **2** to flash, twinkle. **3** (*of flowers*) to blossom. **4** to glance, peep. **5** to squint. **6** to pass suddenly.—*n* **1** a gleam, sparkle. **2** an instant. **3** a sudden blow. **4** a glance, glimpse. **5** a sly look.

glentin-stanes *n* small white stones, used by children to strike fire.

Glesca *n* Glasgow.

gleshan *same as* **glashan**.

gless *n* a glass.—*v* to drink a glass of spirits, etc.

glesser *same as* **glasser**.

glessy *same as* **glassey**.

glet *same as* **glitt**.

gletty *same as* **glitty**.

gleuve *n* a glove.

gley *same as* **glee**.

gleyd *same as* **glyde**.

gley'd, gleyed, gleyt *adj* squinting.

gley-eyed, ~-e'et *adj* cross-eyed.

gley-mou'd *adj* having a crooked mouth.

gleytness *n* 1 obliqueness. 2 obliqueness of vision.

glib[1] *adj* 1 cunning, sharp or slippery in one's dealings. 2 easily swallowed.

glib[2], **glibbe** *n* a twisted lock of hair.

glibbans *n* a sharp person.

glibber-glabber *v* to talk idly and confusedly.—*n* frivolous and confused talk.

glibby *adj* 1 talkative. 2 glib.

glibe *same as* **gleib**.

glib-gabbit, ~-mou'd, ~-tongued *adj* fluent, voluble, talkative.

glibly *adv* smoothly.—*adj* easily swallowed.

glibe *n* a sharper.

glid *adj* 1 slippery. 2 smooth. 3 polished.

glide *adj* squinting.

glide-aver *n* an old horse.

glie *same as* **glee**.

glieb *n* 1 a field. 2 a glebe.

gliff *n* 1 a glimpse, glance, a brief view. 2 a flash, gleam, anything appearing for a moment. 3 an instant, a moment. 4 a sudden fright or shock. 5 a glow, an uneasy feeling of heat. 6 a short sleep.—*v* 1 to look quickly, glance. 2 to flash, gleam. 3 to frighten, startle. 4 to surprise. 5 to evade quickly or suddenly.

gliffie *n* a moment, a small moment.

gliffin *n* 1 a gleam. 2 a sudden glow or heat. 3 a sudden sensation. 4 an instant. 5 a surprise, fright. 6 something very small.

glifring *n* a feeble attempt to grasp anything.

glim[1] *n* 1 a candle. 2 a lantern. 3 a light. —*v* 1 to light up. 2 to gleam.

glim[2] *adj* blind.—*n* 1 an ineffectual attempt to lay hold of an object. 2 a slip, tumble. 3 a disappointment.

glim[3] *n* venereal disease.

glime *v* 1 to look askance or asquint. 2 to glance slyly. 3 to gaze impertinently with a side look.—*n* a sly glance, a sidelong look.

glim-glam, ~-glanm *n* blind-man's buff.

glimmer *v* 1 to blink, as from defective vision. 2 to wink. 3 (*with* **owre**) to overlook.—*n* mica.

glimmie *n* the person blindfolded in blind man's buff.

glimp *n* 1 a glimpse, glance, cursory look. 2 the least degree.—*v* to blink.

glinder *v* to peep through half-closed eyes.

glink *v* 1 to sparkle, gleam. 2 to cast a side glance, catch a glimpse of. 3 to give a fleeting glance. 4 to jilt.—*n* 1 a gleam, flash. 2 a light affection. 3 a side look.

glinkit *adj* 1 light-headed. 2 giddy.

glint *same as* **glent**.

glintin *n* 1 a gleam. 2 early dawn.

glintle *v* to sparkle, gleam, flash.

glisk *n* 1 a flash, sparkle, gleam of light. 2 a passing glance, a transient view. 3 an instant, a moment. 4 anything transitory or slight. 5 a short, brisk movement. 6 a glance at or over.

gliskie *n* a rapid glance.

gliss *v* 1 to shine, gleam, glisten. 2 to glance.

glist *v* to glisten.

glister *n* a clyster.

glister *same as* **glaister**.

glitt *n* 1 slime, ooze. 2 phlegm.

glittilie *adv* slimily.

glittiness *n* ooziness.

glitty *adj* 1 oozy, slimy. 2 having a smooth surface.

gliv, glive *n* a glove.

gloam *n* the gloaming, dusk, evening.—*v* to become dusk, to grow dark.

gload *n* the twilight at evening.

gloamin *adj* belonging to evening twilight.—*v* to darken, become dusk.—*n* twilight.

gloamin'-fa' *n* 1 dusk. 2 fall of evening.

gloamin'-grey, ~-hour *n* twilight.

gloamin'-hushed *adj* still as in twilight.

gloamin' light *n* twilight.

gloamin'-shot *n* 1 an interval at twilight which workers within doors take before using lights. 2 a twilight interview. 3 nightfall.

gloamin' star, ~ starn *n* the evening star.

gloamin'-tide, ~-time *n* twilight.

gloamin'-tryst *n* an evening tryst or appointment.

gloam't *adj* dusk, in the state of twilight.

gloan *n* substance, strength.

gloan, gloanin *n* feverish excitement.

glock *v* 1 to gulp. 2 to gurgle. 3 to flow through too narrow an opening.—*n* 1 a gulp. 2 a gurgle. 3 the noise of water, etc, flowing through too narrow an opening.

glocken *v* 1 to astound. 2 to start from fright.—*n* 1 a frightened start. 2 a sudden shock. 3 an unlooked-for disaster.

glockenin' *n* a sudden shock from fright, a glocken (qv).

gloff[1] *n* 1 a sudden fright. 2 a sudden change of atmosphere or of temperature. 3 a twinge.—*v* 1 to take fright. 2 to feel a sudden shock. 3 to shiver or shudder from shock, as of plunging into cold water.

gloff[2] *v* to have unsound sleep.—*n* disturbed sleep.

gloffe, gloffin *n* a short, unquiet sleep.

glog[1] *v* 1 to gulp down. 2 to shake a liquid, causing it to gurgle.—*n* 1 a hasty draught. 2 a gurgling sound.

glog[2] *adj* 1 black, dark. 2 appearing deep. 3 slow.

gloggie[1] *adj* 1 insipid. 2 artificial, unnatural.

gloggie[2] *adj* (*used of the atmosphere*) 1 dark. 2 hazy. 3 muggy.

glogger *n* the gurgle of a liquid when poured quickly from a bottle.

glog-rinnin *adj* (*used of a river*) 1 running slowly. 2 dark and deep.

gloidin *adj* awkward.

gloit[1] *v* 1 to work with the hands in any liquid, miry or viscous substance. 2 to do anything dirtily or awkwardly.

gloit[2] *n* 1 a blockhead, a lout. 2 a soft, delicate person.

gloitry *adj* 1 dirty, miry. 2 sloppy, wet and slippery.

gloken *same as* **glocken**.

glomin *n* the gloaming.

glonders *n* the sulks, a bad temper, frowns.

glone *same as* **gloan**.

gloom *n* (*in pl*) the sulks, depression.

gloomer[1] *n* one who frowns.

gloomer[2] *same as* **glaamer**.

glooming *adj* frowning.

gloot *same as* **glout**.

gloove *n* a glove.

glore[1] *n* glory.—*v* to glory.

glore[2] *v* to glow, shine.

glorg *n* to do dirty work.—*n* a nasty compound of any kind.

glorgie *adj* 1 bedaubed, miry, dirty. 2 (*used of the weather*) sultry, warm, suffocating.

glorious *adj* excited or hilarious from drink.

glory *int in phr* **my glory!** an exclamation of surprise.—*n* fun, merriment, hilarity.

glose[1] *same as* **gloze**[1].

glose[2] *n* 1 a blaze. 2 a glow of light. 3 the act of warming oneself at a quick fire.—*v* to blaze.

gloss[1] *n* 1 a low, clear fire, without smoke or flame. 2 the act of warming oneself at such a fire.

gloss[2] *v* **1** to adorn. **2** to give a bright hue to.
gloss[3] *v* to sleep lightly.
glossator *n* **1** a glosser. **2** a commentator.
glossins *n* flushings in the face.
glotten *v* to thaw gently.—*n* a partial thaw.
glottenin *n* **1** a partial thaw. **2** a slight rise in a river, with change of colour and froth on the surface.
glouf *n* **1** a sudden blast. **2** a fright.—*v* to scare.
glouk *n* the sound made by crows or ravens over carrion.
gloum *v* to gloom, frown.—*n* **1** a frown. **2** the gloaming.
glouminly *adv* in a frowning manner.
gloup *same as* **glupe**.
glour *same as* **glower**.
glourer *n* **1** an eye. **2** a starer. **3** a merely curious onlooker at a deathbed.
glourie *n* one who stares.
glouriks *n* the eyes.
glourin'-fow *adj* at the staring stage of tipsiness.
gloushteroich *n* the dregs of soup.
gloushteroich *adj* (*used of the weather*) boisterous, gusty.
glousterie, glousteroich, glousterin *adj* (*used of the weather*) gusty, blustering.—*n* boisterous, changeable weather.
glout *v* to pout, sulk.—*n* a pout, sullenness.
glouten *same as* **glotten**.
glow, glowe *n* a blaze.
glower, glowr, glowre *v* **1** to stare, gaze. **2** to look threateningly. **3** to scowl.—*n* **1** an intent or angry look. **2** a stare. **3** a frown. **4** a leer. **5** vision.
glowert-like *adj* stormy-looking.
glowering *adj* **1** vacant-looking. **2** overcast. **3** scowling. **4** gleaming, clear.
glowm *v* **1** to frown. **2** to gloom.—*n* **1** a frown. **2** the gloaming.
gloy *n* **1** straw. **2** cleaned straw. **3** straw used for thatching, etc. **4** a superficial threshing.—*v* to give grain a hasty threshing.
gloyd *same as* **glyde**.
gloy-stane *n* the stone or floor on which grain is threshed.
gloze[1] *n* a specious show, delusion, mistaken idea.
gloze[2] *same as* **glose**[2].
glozing[1] *adj* blazing.
glozing[2] *adj* flattering, fawning, deceitful.—*n* romancing.
gluck *same as* **glock**.
gludder *n* the sound of a body falling into mud, slush, etc.—*v* **1** to do dirty work or work in a dirty manner. **2** to swallow food in a slovenly or disgusting way.
gluddery *adj* **1** wet. **2** slippery to the touch. **2** unctuous.
glue[1] *n in phr* **candy-glue** candy of a sticky kind, in stalks or lumps.
glue[2] *n* a glove.
gluff[1] *same as* **gloff**.
gluff[2] *adj* sullen, gloomy.
gluff[3] *v* to puff and blow after a plunge into cold water.
gluffin *n* **1** a boisterous brawler. **2** a frightful appearance.
gluffus *n* an ugly person.
glugger *v* to swallow liquids with a noise in the throat.
gluggery *adj* flaccid, like young and soft animal food.
gluive *n* a glove.
glum *adj* sour, sulky, moody.
glumch *same as* **glumsh**.
glumf *v* to look sulky.
glumfie *adj* moody. **2** grumpy.
glumly *adv* sullenly, moodily.
glump *v* to look sulky, gloomy, discontented.—*n* **1** a morose or sulky person. **2** (*in pl*) the blues.
glumph *same as* **glump**.
glumpish *adj* **1** sulky, surly. **2** moping. **3** morose.
glumpy *adj* **1** sour-looking. **2** grumpy. **3** low-spirited.
glumsh[1] *v* **1** to look sulky, frown. **2** to whine, grumble, be querulous. **3** to be dogged.—*n* **1** a frown, pout, sulky look or fit. **2** (*in pl*) the blues. —*adj* gloomy, sour-looking.
glumsh[2] *same as* **glunsh**.
glumshous *adj* sulky.

glunch *v* **1** to frown. **2** to grumble.—*n* **1** a sullen look. **2** a dogged fit.—*adj* sour-looking.
glunchingly *adv* moodily, fretfully.
glunchy *adj* **1** morose, bad-tempered. **2** dogged.
glunder *v* to look sulky.
glundering *adj* gaudy, glaring, calculated to please a vulgar taste.
glundie *n* **1** an inert, awkward lout. **2** a fool. **3** a sullen look. **4** a plough redder, one who clears the plough of earth, etc.—*adj* **1** sullen. **2** inactive.
glune-amie, glunimie *n* **1** a Highlander. **2** a rough, unpolished, boorish man. **3** a term of endearment for a cow.
glunner *same as* **glunter**.
glunny *same as* **glundie**.
glunsch *v* to look sulky.
glunsh[1] *same as* **glunsch**.
glunsh[2] *v* to swallow food hastily and noisily.
glunshoch *n* **1** one who has a morose look. **2** a sulky person.
glunt[1] *same as* **glent**.
glunt[2] *v* **1** to look sullen. **2** to pout, scowl.—*n* **1** a sour look, a suspicious look over the shoulder or sideways. **2** (*in pl*) the sulks.
gluntch *same as* **glunch**.
glunter *n* **1** one who has a morose look, an ignorant, sour-tempered person. **2** (*in pl*) the sulks.
gluntie[1] *n* a sour look.
gluntie[2] *adj* tall, thin and haggard.—*n* an emaciated woman.
gluntoch *n* a surly, sullen, stupid person.
glunyieman *same as* **glune-amie**.
glup *v* **1** to beguile, wheedle. **2** to make a conquest of.
glupe *n* a great chasm or cavern.
glush *n* **1** anything pulpy. **2** sleet, slush. **3** mud.
glushie *adj* **1** slushy. **2** abounding in half-melted snow.
glut[1] *n* a drink, gulp.—*v* to swallow with effort at one gulp.
glut[2] *n* phlegm ejected from the throat.
glut[3] *v* to gush.
gluther *v* **1** to swallow greedily. **2** to splutter. **3** to make a gurgling sound in the throat.—*n* **1** a rising or filling of the throat. **2** a gurgling sound in it caused by emotion and preventing distinct articulation. **3** an ungraceful noise made in swallowing.
gluthery *adj* (*used of roads*) muddy.
gluts *n* **1** two wedges used as leverage in tempering a plough. **2** wedges used in tightening the hooding of a flail.
glutter *v* to swallow quickly.
glutters *n* wet mud, soft earth.
gly *v* to squint.
glyack *same as* **clyack**.
glybe *n* glebe land.
glyde[1] *n* **1** an old horse. **2** an old fellow. **3** a person of disagreeable temper.
glyde[2] *n* **1** an opening. **2** a road. **3** a glade.
glysterie, glysterin *adj* boisterous, gusty, storm.
gly't *adj* squinting.
gnaff *n* **1** any small or stunted creature. **2** a poor-looking creature.
gnap, gnape *v* **1** to gnaw, bite, nibble. **2** to snap at. **3** to attempt to mince ones words affectedly. **4** to taunt, censure snappishly.—*n* **1** a bite, mouthful, morsel of anything eatable. **2** mincing, affected speech.—*adj* hungry.
gnapper *n in phr* **gnipper nor gnapper** not the least particle.
gnapping, gnaping *adj* **1** eager, earnest. **2** given to fault-finding and taunting.
gnap-the-ween *n* **1** very thin oatcake. **2** any kind of very light bread.
gnap-the-win' *n* **1** a disastrous policy. **2** an issue that is unexpectedly bad.
gnarl *n* rough treatment.
gnarlish *adj* (*used of temper*) crusty, crabbed.

gnarly *adj* **1** twisted. **2** cross-grained.

gnarr[1] *n* a hard knot in wood.

gnarr[2] *v* **1** to find fault in a snarling manner. **2** to quarrel.—*n* **1** the growl of an angry dog. **2** peevishness.

gnash *n* **1** pert, insolent talk. **2** bluster.—*v* **1** to be insolent or pert. **2** to bluster.

gnashicks *n* the red bear-berry.

gnat *v* **1** to gnaw. **2** to grind the teeth.—*n* **1** a bite. **2** a snap.

gnatter *v* **1** to grumble, worry. **2** to wrangle.

gnattery *adj* ill-tempered, peevish, querulous.

gnaw *n* a slight, partial thaw.

gneck *n* a notch.—*v* to cut notches.

gneck-in-the-neck *n* a person's manifest peculiarity or weakness.

gneep *n* **1** a booby, ninny. **2** a foolish fellow.

gnegum *n* **1** a tricky disposition. **2** a fiery, pungent flavour in edibles.

gneggum *n* a nasty taste or smell.

gneigie *adj* sharp-witted.

gneip *same as* **gneep**.

gneisle *v* to gnaw.

gneut *n* a stupid person.

gneutick, gneutickie *n* a stupid person.

gneutie *same as* **gneut**.

gnew *v* gnawed.

gnib *adj* **1** ready, quick, clever in action. **2** light-fingered. **3** stingy, mean. **4** sharp-tempered, curt. **5** sharp in demanding one's own. **6** keen of appetite.

gnibbich *n* a little person of thin, sharp features and curt manners.—*adj* **1** mean, stingy. **2** curt in manners.

gnidge *v* **1** to press, squeeze. **2** (*with* **off**) to rub off. **3** to peel off by rubbing.—*n* a squeeze.

gnip *v* **1** to eat, crop. **2** to taunt. **3** to complain constantly about.—*n* a morsel, mouthful.

gnipick, gnipickie *n* a morsel of anything edible.

gnipper *n* the smallest piece of anything edible.

gnipper for gnapper *or* **gnopper** *phr* **1** the sound made by a mill in grinding. **2** the very smallest particle.

gnipper nor gnapper *phr* not the least particle.

gnippin *n* continual petty taunting.

gnissle *same as* **gneisle**.

gnorly *same as* **gnarly**.

gnyauve *v* to gnaw.

go[1] *same as* **gae**.

go[2] *n* **1** distress. **2** excitement, fuss. **3** a drunken frolic, spree.

goab *n* the worked-out part of a mine.

goab-fire *n* the spontaneous ignition of small coal in a worked-out part of a mine, producing white damp.

goad *same as* **gad**.

goadloup *n* the military punishment of running the gauntlet.

goadsman *same as* **gadsman**.

goaf *same as* **gowf**.

goafish *adj* stupid, foolish.

goak *int* an exclamation of surprise and of imprecation.

goal *n* a jail.

goam[1] *v* **1** to pay attention to, heed, take notice of. **2** to acknowledge by curtsy.

goam[2] *v* to gaze about wildly or idly.

goan[1] *v* to lounge.

goan[2] *n* a wooden dish for meat.

goare *n* a hurt, wound.

goarling *same as* **gorlin**.

goarling baird *n* the first downy hairs appearing on the chin.

goarling hair *same as* **gorlin hair**.

go-ashores, go-shores *n* better clothes than working or sea-going clothes.

goat *same as* **gote**.

goat-chaffer *n* the nightjar.

goat's beard *n* vapour in the sky foreboding storm.

goat-whey quarters *n* a place of resort for the drinking of goat's milk.

goave *v* **1** to stare idly or vacantly. **2** to look with a roving

eye. **3** to look steadily with uplifted face. **4** to throw up and toss the head from side to side. **5** to gaze with fear. **6** to flaunt. **7** to play the flirt, to wander aimlessly.—*n* a broad, vacant stare.

goave-i-th'-wind *phr* a vain, foolish, light-headed person.

goavie *same as* **govie**.

goaving *adj* **1** stupid. **2** staring. **3** coquetting. **4** startled. **5** tossing the head.

goaving-wild *adj* **1** staring stupidly. **2** foolishly eager.

gob[1] *n* **1** a lump of meat, etc. **2** a mouthful.

gob[2] *n* **1** the mouth. **2** a beak. **3** a grimace.

gobich *n* the goby.

goblet, gobblet *n* a cast-iron kettle.

goch *int* an exclamation. of pain.

gock[1] *n* a deep wooden dish.

gock[2] *same as* **gowk**.

gock-a-hoy *adj* silly and childish in speech and behaviour.

gockie[1] *same as* **gowky**.

gockie[2], **gockie-cog** *n* a deep wooden dish.

gockit *same as* **gowkit**.

gockmin *n* a sentinel, watchman.

godderlitch *same as* **gotherlisch**.

godin *n* the smallest amount or atom, a trace.

god-left *adj* godforsaken.

godrate *adj* cool, deliberate.

godrately *adv* coolly.

godsend *n* **1** (*used in Orkney and Shetland*) a shipwreck. **2** flotsam and jetsam coming ashore. **3** a drove of whales. **4** a boat fare.

god's-penny *n* earnest money.

god's truth *n* the very truth.

goer-bye *n* a passer-by.

goff *same as* **gowff**.

goffish *adj* foolish.

gog *n* the mark aimed at in playing quoits, etc.

gogar *n* whey boiled with a little oatmeal, used as food.

gogar-worm *n* a worm of serrated form used as bait in fishing.

gogge *v* to blindfold.

goggie *adj* elegantly dressed.

goggle *n* (*in pl*) **1** the eyes, especially when protruding. **2** spectacles. **2** blinds applied to horses that are apt to be scared.

goggle-eyes *n* **1** spectacles. **2** goggles worn by stone-breakers.

goglet, goglet-pot *n* a small pot with a long handle.

gohams *n* bent pieces of wood on each side of a horse to support panniers.

go-harvest, goe-hairst, ~-harst *n* **1** the latter end of summer. **2** the time from the end of harvest till the beginning of winter.

goit *n* a young unfledged bird.

goitling *same as* **goit**.

goke-a-day *int* an exclamation of wonder and satisfaction.

gokit *same as* **gowkit**.

gokman *same as* **gockmin**.

golach *n* **1** a beetle. **2** an earwig. **3** a centipede.

golaichie, golaigh *n* a low, short-legged hen. **2** a low, short-legged woman.

golden-crest, ~-cuttie *n* the gold-crest.

golden grass *n* the seed of the crested dog's-tail grass.

golden-maw *n* the glaucous gull.

golden-wren *n* the goldcrest.

golder *same as* **gollar**.

gold-foolyie *n* leaf gold.

goldie *n* **1** the goldfinch. **2** the ladybird. **3** a cow of a light-yellow colour. **4** the yellow gurnard.

goldie-duck *n* the golden-eye.

gold-spink *same as* **gowdspink**.

goles[1] *n* the corn marigold.

goles[2] *n* disguised form of God, used in petty oaths.

golinger *same as* **gileynour**.

golk *same as* **gowk**.

gollan *same as* **gowan**.
gollar *same as* **goller**.
goller *v* 1 to emit a gurgling sound. 2 to speak indistinctly and loudly. 3 to bark violently. 4 to growl.—*n* 1 a gurgling sound. 2 a shout. 3 a fierce bark.
gollering *n* a gurgling sound, as of an animal being strangled.
gollersome *adj* 1 passionate. 2 boisterous.
gollie *same as* **goller**.
gollie *v* 1 to weep noisily, to bawl. 2 to scold.—*n* 1 noisy weeping, bawling. 2 a scolding.
gollimer *n* one who eats greedily.
golling *n* a method of trenching moss to produce new soil.
gollop *v* 1 to gulp. 2 to swallow hastily.
golly[1] *same as* **goles**[2].
golly[2] *same as* **gollie**.
goloch *same as* **golach**.
golore *same as* **galore**.
goloshin, goloshan *same as* **galatian**.
gomach *n* a fool.
gome, gom *same as* **goam**.
gomer *n* coursing term, used of a greyhound or a hare.
gomeril[1] *n* a gambrel.
gomeril[2], **gomeral, gommeral** *n* a fool, blockhead. —*adj* half-witted, stupid.
gomf *same as* **gumph**.
gommoch *n* a fool, idiot, simpleton.
gomrell *same as* **gomeril**.
gone *adj* 1 (*of a woman*) pregnant. 2 thin, wasted. —*adv* ago, since.—*conj* since.
gone-away land *phr* Hades.
gone a week, month, etc *phr* a week, month, etc, ago.
gone corbie *n* a dead man.
gone man *n* a man who is done for.
goner[1], **gonner** *n* 1 a mouth disease in cattle. 2 a pig's snout.
goner[2] *n* a person in bad health and not likely to recover.
gonial *n* 1 a large, ill-shaped person. 2 a stupid fellow. 3 flesh of a sheep fit for food, though not killed by the knife of a butcher.
gonial-blast *n* a great storm in January 1794, in the south of Scotland, destroying many sheep.
goniel *same as* **gonial**.
gonk *same as* **gunk**.
gonsir *same as* **gunsar**.
gonterniblicks *n* gladness.
gonternichs *int* an exclamation of delight.
gonterns, gontrans, gontring, gontrum *int* an exclamation of joyous admiration.
gontrum-niddles *int* an exclamation of joy, etc.
gonyell *same as* **gonial**.
goo[1] *n* 1 the gull. 2 a fool.—*v* to seduce, allure.
goo[2] *n* 1 taste. 2 relish, liking, gusto. 3 odour, smell.
goo[3] *v* (*used of infants*) to coo.
good *same as* **gude**[2].
good cheap *adj* cheap.—*adv* cheaply, gratis.
good dame *n* a grandmother.
good deed *n* a benefaction, a gift.
goodin *n* 1 manure. 2 manuring.
goodly *adj* godly, religious.—*adv* well, conveniently.
goodly-neighbour *n* a fairy.
goodman *same as* **gudeman**.
good neighbour *n* a fairy, a brownie.
good place *n* a child's name for heaven.
goodsir *n* a grandfather.
goodwife *same as* **gudewife**.
good-willer *n* a well-wisher.
good-willie *adj* wishing well.
goody *n* 1 an old woman. 2 a child's name for a sweet.
goog *n* 1 an unfledged bird. 2 the young of animals. 3 soft young meat. 4 any soft, moist stuff.
googg *n* 1 a large, open, festering sore. 2 a heavy cloud.
google *v* 1 to deceive. 2 to juggle.

googlie *n* a deceptive ball at cricket.
gook *same as* **gowk**.
gool[1] *same as* **gowl**.
gool[2], **goold** *n* the corn marigold.
goold *n* gold.—*adj* golden.
gooldie *n* the goldfinch.
gool-fittit *adj* (*used of fowls*) having yellow legs and feet.
goolie *same as* **gully**.
gool-riding *n* an old custom of riding through a parish to watch against the growth of the gools (qv).
gooms *n* gums.
goon *n* a gown.
goonie *n* a child's nightdress.
goor[1] *n* broken ice and half-melted snow in a thaw.—*v* (*used of streams*) to become choked with masses of ice and snow in a thaw.
goor[2] *n* stagnant water full of animal and vegetable life.
goord *same as* **gourd**.
goorie *n* same as **gouries**.
goose *v* 1 to iron linen clothes. 2 to use a tailor's goose. 3 to smooth.—*n* a large stone used in curling.
goose-cleavers *n* the catchweed or cleavers.
goose-corn *n* wild oat or field brome grass.
goose-dub *n* a goose pond.
goose-ee *n* a blind eye.
goose-girse *n* 1 the soft brome grass. 2 the rough brome grass.
goose pan *n* 1 a pan for stewing a goose. 2 the largest pot or pan used in cooking.
goose-pear *n* a kind of pear.
goose-seam, ~-same *n* goose grease.
goose-wings *n* the peculiar appearance which the foresail and mainsail of a schooner-rigged vessel assume when it is running before the wind, these sails being then spread to opposite sides.
goosey-weasen *n* 1 a goose's neck. 2 a person's long neck.
gooshet *n* a gusset.
goosing iron *n* a flatiron.
goosy *same as* **gussie**.
gootar *same as* **gutter**.
gope *same as* **gowp**.
gopin *same as* **gowpen**.
gor *same as* **gore**.
gorachen *n* hard work.
goravich *same as* **galravitch**.
gorb[1] *n* 1 an unfledged bird. 2 a young child.
gorb[2] *adj* greedy, voracious.
gorbal, gorbel *n* an unfledged bird.
gorbie *n* a raven.
gorbit, gorbet *n* 1 a newly hatched bird. 2 a child.
gorble *v* 1 to eat greedily. 2 to swallow voraciously.
gorblet *n* 1 an unfledged bird. 2 a child.
gorblet hair *n* the down of unfledged birds.
gorblin *n* 1 an unfledged bird. 2 anything very young and bare.
gor-, gore-crow *n* the carrion crow.
gord *same as* **gourd**.
gorded *adj* 1 frosted over. 2 covered with crystallizations. 3 benumbed.
gordlin *same as* **gorblin**.
gore[1] *same as* **gaar**.
gore[2] *int* a disguised form of God, used in exclamations and oaths.
gore[3] *same as* **gair**.
gore-pate *int* an exclamation. See **gore**.
gorfy *adj* coarse in appearance.
gorge *v* 1 to squeak. 2 to make a squelching sound, as when one walks with shoes full of water.
gorgetches *n* 1 a calf's pluck. 2 the heart, liver and lights.
gorglyum *n* a young bird in the nest.
gorie *int* a disguised form of God, used in expletives.
gorkie *adj* nauseous, disgusting.
gorl *v* to surround the thatch of a stack with straw ropes.
gorlin *n* a neckcloth.

gorlin, gorlan *adj* bare, unfledged.—*n* a nestling, unfledged bird.

gorlin hair *n* the down of an unfledged bird.

gorlins *n* a ram's testicles.

gormaw *n* **1** the cormorant. **2** a greedy person, a glutton.

gorr *same as* **gore**.

gorroch, gorrach *v* **1** to mix and spoil porridge. **2** to imbed in mire. **3** to spoil, bungle.—*n* **1** anything dirty and sticky. **2** a sloppy mess, mud. **3** a bungle, 'hash'. **4** a bungler. **5** an untidy, slovenly worker.

gorsh *int* an exclamation or oath.

gorsk *n* strong, rank grass.—*v* (*used of grass*) to grow in luxuriant patches through cattle droppings.

gorsy *adj* furze-clad.

gort *n* a gout of blood, etc.

gos *n* the goshawk, used in expletives.

goshen, goshins *int* gosh!

gosk[1] *n* chickweed.

gosk[2] *same as* **gorsk**.

gosky *adj* **1** rank, coarse. **2** luxuriant. **3** (*used of animals*) large in size, but feeble.

goslin *n* **1** an unfledged bird. **2** a fool.

gospel-greedy *adj* fond of attending church.

gospel-hearer *n* a church-attender.

gospel-hearted *adj* truly pious.

gospel-kail *n* evangelical preaching.

gospel-lad *n* a covenanter.

gospel-minister *n* an evangelical minister.

goss[1] *n* **1** a silly, good-natured man. **2** a mean, griping person.

goss[2] *n* a close friend, a gossip (qv).

goss[3] *n* the goshawk.

gossie *n* **1** a close friend, a gossip (qv). **2** a fellow, person.

gossie-fain *adj* fond of a gossip.

gossip *n* **1** a godparent, sponsor at baptism. **2** an intimate friend invited to a baptism. **3** a boon companion, crony.

gossiprie *n* intimacy.

gossips' wake *n* a gathering of friends and neighbours after the mother's recovery from a birth to congratulate the parents and drink to the child's prosperity.

gossok *n* a term applied in derision to an old type of an inhabitant of Wigtownshire.

go-summer, go o' summer *n* the latter end of summer.

got *n* **1** a drain, a ditch. **2** a narrow inlet of the sea. **3** a slough, etc.

gotch *v* to botch, mar.—*n* a bungle, muddle.

gote *same as* **got**.

goth *int* a disguised form of God used in oaths, etc.

gotherligh *adj* (*used of persons*) confused, in disorder.

gotherlisch, gotherlitch *adj* **1** sanctimonious, of unreal but pretentious piety. **2** foolish, godless. **3** sluttish.—*n* want of delicacy of feeling and manner.

gothill *n* *in phr* **an** *or* **in gothill** if God will.

gott *same as* **gott**.

gou *same as* **goo**.

gouch *same as* **guff**.

goucher *same as* **gutcher**.

gouck[1] *same as* **gouk**.

gouck[2] *same as* **gowk**.

goud[1] *v* began.

goud[2] *same as* **gowd**.

gouden *same as* **gowden**.

gouden-bobbed *adj* with golden blossoms.

gouden-knap *n* a variety of pear.

goudie[1] *n* the keeper of a key of the box of a Glasgow trade incorporation, the boxmaster.

goudie[2] *n* a Gouda cheese.

goudie[3] *n* a blow, stroke.

goudie[4] *same as* **gowdie**[1].

goudie[5] *n* *in phr* **heels o'er-** *or* **heelster goudie** head over heels, topsy-turvy.

goudie[6], **goudie**[7], **goudie**[8] *same as* **gowdie**[2], **gowdie**[3], **gowdie**[4].

goudnie *n* the gowdie duck.

goudriff *adv* reverently, respectfully.

goudspink *same as* **gowdspink**.

goudy-aumous *n* a feast, a merrymaking, a gaudeamus.

gouff[1] *same as* **gowff**.

gouff[2] *n* **1** a blow, stroke. **2** ruin, wreck.—*v* to strike, hit, cuff.

gouff[3] *same as* **guff**[2].

gouff[4] *v* to reel off verses, etc, in recitation.

goufmalogie *n* a woollen petticoat formerly worn by women, having on its border large horizontal stripes of different colours.

goug *n* a young solan goose.

gouk[1] *same as* **gawk**.

gouk[2] *same as* **gowk**.

gouken *n* a handful.

goukmey *n* the grey gurnard.

goul[1] *n* the soul.

goul[2] *same as* **gowl**.

gould *n* gold.—*adj* golden.

gouldie, gouldspink *n* the goldfinch.

goule *n* **1** the throat. **2** the neck. **3** the gullet.

goulie *adj* **1** sulky. **2** scowling.

gouling *adj* (*used of weather*) stormy.

goulkgalister, goulkgaliter *n* **1** a pedantic, conceited fellow. **2** a simpleton. **3** a wanton rustic.

goull-bane *n* the top of the thighbone as it enters the cavity in which it moves.

goulmaw *same as* **gormaw**.

goulock *same as* **golach**.

gounk *same as* **gunk**.

goup[1] *same as* **gowp**.

goup[2] *v* **1** to scoop up (water). **2** to wash with the two hands. **3** to hollow out.

goup[3] *same as* **gaup**.

goupen, goupan, goupin *n* **1** the hollow of the hand in semiglobular shape to receive anything. **2** a handful. **3** a perquisite of a miller's servant in the shape of a handful of meal.

gouph *same as* **gaffa**.

goupin *n* the throbbing of a wound or sore.

gourd[1] *adj* **1** stiff, unwieldy, difficult to open or move, stiffened by exposure to the air. **2** (*used of ice*) not slippery.

gourd[2] *v* **1** (*used of running water*) to be pent up, stop. **2** to stop running water by earth or ice.

gourdness *n* **1** stiffness. **2** want of slipperiness.

gouries *n* the entrails of salmon.

gourlins, gourlock *n* the root of the earth chestnut.

gouster *v* **1** to bully. **2** to storm with wind and rain. —*n* **1** a passionate outburst of scolding. **3** a violent, unmanageable fellow. **4** a swaggerer.

gousterous, goustrous *adj* **1** boisterous. **2** violent. **3** (*of the weather*) dark, wet, blustering, stormy. **4** frightful. **5** rude.

gousterous-looking *adj* stormy-looking.

gousty[1] *adj* tempestuous, stormy, gusty.

gousty[2] *adj* **1** waste, desolate. **2** dreary, gloomy. **3** ghastly, ghostly, unearthly. **4** haggard by age or disease. **5** emaciated. **6** pale, sickly.

gout *n* taste.

goutcher *same as* **gutcher**.

gouthart *adj* frightened, scared.

goutherfow *adj* amazed, terrified.

goutte *n* **1** a drop. **2** a large drop of rain.

govan *adj* flaunting, coquetting.

govance *n* good breeding.—*adj* well-bred.

govanendy *int* an exclamation of surprise.

gove[1] *same as* **goave**.

gove[2], **govy** *n* a name given to the headmaster of a school

govellin *adj* **1** staggering, as if drunk. **2** hanging loosely and ungracefully (*used of the appearance of the eyes in intoxication*).

govie *int* an exclamation. of surprise.

govie-dick *int* exclamation of surprise.

goving *adj* (*used of startled cattle*) staring, tossing the head.

govit *adj* hollowed out.

govus *n* a simple, stupid person.

govy *same as* **gove**.

gow[1] *n* **1** the gull. **2** a fool.—*v* **1** to entice, seduce. **2** to sway. **3** to persuade by argument. **4** to bend, lead.

gow[2] *n* a halo, circle round the sun or moon, a brough (qv) portending bad weather.

gow[3] *n in phr* **tak the gow** to run off without paying one's rent, debts, etc.

gow[4] *adj* (*used of a pampered dog*) petted, spoiled.

gowan[1] *n* the buttercup.

gowan[2] *n* **1** the generic name for the daisy. **2** the common or mountain daisy.—*phrs* **1 not to care a gowan** not to care in the least. **2 to cow the gowan** an expression of surprise, to beat everything.

gowan-gabbit *adj* **1** (*used of the sky*) bright, fine, deceptively clear. **2** (*of the face*) having much red and white, marking a delicate constitution.

gowan head *n* the head or flower of a daisy.

gowan-shank *n* the stalk of a daisy.

gowan-sparkled *adj* sprinkled with daisies.

gowan-speckled *adj* speckled with daisies.

gowan-tap *n* the flower of a daisy.

gowaned *adj* daisied.

gowany *adj* **1** daisied. **2** bright, fair in appearance. **3** deceptively fine.

gowd *n* gold.—*adj* golden.

gowd links *n* golden locks.

gowdanook *same as* **gowdnook**.

gowden *adj* golden.

gowdie[1] *n* **1** a jewel. **2** gold cloth, gold lace. **3** a term of endearment.

gowdie[2] *n* **1** the dragonet. **2** the gurnard.

gowdie[3] *n* **1** the goldfinch. **2** the ladybird.

gowdie[4] *n in phr* **heels o'er gowdie** *same as* **heels o'er goudie**. *See* **goudie**[5].

gowdie[5] *n* a yellow-coloured cow.

gowdie-duck *n* the goldeneye duck.

gowdnie[1] *n* the yellow gurnard.

gowdnie[2] *n* the goldeneye duck.

gowdnook *n* the saury pike.

gowds *n* a term of familiarity used by old women in conversing.

gowdspink, gowdspring *n* the goldfinch.

gower *v* **1** to induce. **2** to tempt. **3** to draw over.

gowet *v* induced, persuaded. *See* **gow**[1].

gowf *n* a bad savour affecting the throat.

gowfer *n* a golfer.

gowff[1] *n* **1** a stroke. **2** golf.—*v* to strike.

gowff[2] *n* a fool, simpleton.

gowff[3] *same as* **gouff**[2].

gowfin *n* **1** a noisy, silly fellow. **2** a fool. **3** a soft, pliable person. **4** a coward.

gowgair *n* a mean, greedy, selfish person.

gow-glentie *n* a sharp, interesting child.

gowkishness *n* folly.

gowk[1] *same as* **gauk**.

gowk[2] *v* to wander up and down.

gowk[3] *n* **1** the cuckoo. **2** a fool, blockhead. **3** a clumsy person, a clown.—*adj* foolish.

gowk and titling *n phr* **1** the cuckoo and any bird of the tit species. **2** the young cuckoo and its foster mother. **3** an incongruous pair. **4** a pair of inseparable friends.

gowk-bear *n* the golden maidenhair.

gowken *n* a handful.

gowkit *adj* **1** foolish, stupid, awkward. **2** (*used of a woman*) light-headed, giddy.

glowkitly *adv* stupidly, foolishly.

gowk-like *adj* like a fool.

gowkoo *n* the cuckoo.

gowkoo-clock *n* a cuckoo clock.

gowk's errand *n* a fool's errand.

gowkship *n* a fool.

gowk's hose *n* the Canterbury bell.

gowk's meat *n* the wood sorrel.

gowk's shillins *n* the yellow rattle.

gowk's spit, ~ spittle *n* the froth on plants discharged by the insect Cicada.

gowk's-thimmles, ~-thummles *n* the harebell.

Gowkston *n in phr* **make John Gowkston of** to make a cuckold of.

gowk-storm *n* **1** a storm of several days at the end of April or the beginning of May. **2** an evil or obstruction of short duration.

gowky *n* a fool.

gowl[1] *n* **1** a hollow between hills, a defile. **2** a gap, opening.

gowl[2] *n* anything large and empty.

gowl[3] *v* **1** to howl, yell, growl. **2** (*used of wind*) to blow fitfully with a hollow sound.—*n* a howl, yell, growl.

gowling *adj* **1** howling, growling. **2** boisterous, stormy. **3** sulky, scolding.—*n* loud and angry scolding.

gowlock, gowlick *same as* **golach**.

gowls *n* the private parts.

gowlsome *adj* large.

gowly *adj* **1** howling, growling. **2** boisterous. **3** scolding.—*n* a fretful, crying child.

gowmeril *same as* **gomeril**.

gown-alane *adj* **1** without a cloak or upper covering for a gown. **2** dowerless.

gownie *same as* **goonie**.

gow'ny *adj* daisy-clad.

gown-men *n togati*.

gowp[1] *same as* **gaup**.

gowp[2], **gowpen** *v* **1** to throb, palpitate. **2** to ache.—*n* a throb of pain.

gowp[3] *n in phr* **a gowp in the lift** a squint.

gowpen[1], **gowpan, gowpin** *same as* **goupen**.

gowpen[2] *same as* **gowp**.

gowpin *n* the throbbing of a wound or sore. *See* **gowp**[2].

gowpinfu' *n* as much as the two hands can hold when in a concave form.

goupinfu' o' a' thing *phr* a contemptuous term to designate one who is a medley of every absurdity.

gowrie *n in phr* **heels o'er gowrie** topsy-turvy.

gowries *same as* **gouries**.

gowst *same as* **gouster**.

gowstly *adj* ghastly.

gowsty *same as* **gousty**.

goy *same as* **gow**[1].

goyit *adj* foolish, silly.

goyler *n* the Arctic gull.

gozen *same as* **gizzen**.

graapus *same as* **grampus**.

grab[1] *v* **1** to seize with violence or unfair means. **2** to cheat. **3** to filch.—*n* **1** a grasp, clutch. **2** the number of things seized. **3** an advantageous bargain. **4** a grasping, miserly person.

grab[2] *n* food, provisions.

grabbin' *adj* inclined to cheat.

grabble *v* to grope with the hands for stones on the ground.

grabbles *n* a disease of cows affecting their limbs and rendering them unable to walk.

grabby *adj* greedy, avaricious, grasping.

grace *n* good qualities, virtue.

grace an' growin' *phr* a good wish for a newborn child, spiritual and temporal prosperity.

grace drink *n* a drink taken after grace at the close of a meal.

gracie[1] *adj* **1** well-behaved. **2** devout, religious.

gracie[2] *n* **1** a pig. **2** a fat, ungraceful woman of loose character.

gracious *adj* **1** pleasant, friendly. **2** agreeable.

graddan *n* **1** a coarse kind of oatmeal, prepared by scorching grain in a pot over the fire and then grinding it in a handmill. **2** coarse snuff in large grains, made from toasted tobacco leaves.—*v* to parch grain by scorching the ear.

grade *same as* **graid**.
graduality *n in phr* **by a graduality** gradually.
graduwa, gradawa *n* **1** a graduate. **2** a doctor with a medical degree.
graen *v* **1** to groan. **2** to clear the throat.
grafel *v* to grovel.
graff[1] *n* **1** a grave. **2** a ditch, trench, hole. **3** the sea bottom.
graff[2] *same as* **groff**.
graff[3] *n* a graft.
graffstanes *n* a gravestone.
graft[1] *v* to grapple, wrestle.
graft[2] *n* a grave.
grafter *n* an engrafter.
graicie *same as* **gracie**[2].
graid *v* to prepare, make ready.
graidly *adj* **1** orderly. **2** proper, fit.—*adv* **1** decently. **2** thoroughly.
graig *v* **1** to belch. **2** to make a noise in the throat. **3** to hesitate in speech. **4** to utter an inarticulate sound of contempt or scorn. **5** to find fault. **6** to grumble about.
graigin *n* hesitation.
grain[1] *n* **1** a branch of a tree. **2** a branch of a river, of a valley or ravine. **3** the prong of a fork.
grain[2] *n* **1** a particle. **2** a little bit. **3** (*in pl*) the refuse of malt, used for feeding cattle.
grain[3] *v* to groan.—*n* a groan.
grainer *n* a tanner's or skinner's knife for taking hair off skins.
graintal-man *same as* **grintal-man**.
grainter *same as* **grinter**.
graip *n* a three- or four-pronged fork used in farming and gardening operations.
graiper *v* **1** to gripe. **2** to grope. **3** to cross-examine.
graiper *n* **1** a blind man. **2** one who gropes.
grait *n* a grating.
graith *v* **1** to make ready for use. **2** to equip. **3** to steep in a ley of stale urine for bleaching.—*n* **1** accoutrements. **2** clothes. **3** furniture. **4** equipment. **5** harness for horses. **6** apparatus. **7** tools. **8** machinery, etc. **9** substance, wealth. **10** stuff, material. **11** company, companions. **12** a lather for washing clothes. **13** stale urine, used for washing.
graithing *n* **1** any kind of equipment, furnishing, provision or preparation. **2** vestments.
graithlie *same as* **graidly**.
gralloch *v* to disembowel the carcass of a deer, etc.
gram *n* anger, passion.
gramacie *int* many thanks.
gramarie *n* magic.
gramashes, gramashons *n* **1** gaiters reaching to the knees. **2** riding hose.
gramloch *adj* avaricious, grasping.
gramlochlie *adv* graspingly.
gramlochness *n* a very worldly disposition.
grammar, grammarian *n* a grammar-school boy.
grammar folk *n* educated people.
grammaticals *n* grammar.
grammaw *n* a voracious eater, a greedy person.
grammle *v* to scramble.
gramoches *same as* **gramashes**.
gramowrie *same as* **gramarie**.
grampus *n* **1** an ignoramus. **2** a greedy fellow.
gramshoch *adj* **1** (*used of grain, etc*) coarse, rank. **2** (*of the sky*) heavy, lowering, portending heavy snow or rain.—*n* an appearance in the sky portending snow, etc.
gramultion *n* common sense.
gran[1] *n* a grandmother.
gran[2] *v* ground.
grand, gran' *adj* **1** capital, first-rate, excellent. **2** eloquent. **3** (*used of the weather*) fine. **4** showily dressed.—*adv* grandly, finely.
grandam *n* a grandmother.
grand-bairn *n* a grandchild.
granddad, ~daddy *n* a grandfather.
grandery *n* grandeur, display.

grandey, grandie *n* **1** a grandfather. **2** an old man.
grandgore *n* venereal disease.
grand-gutcher *n* **1** great-grandfather. **2** ancestor.
grandsher *n* a great-grandfather.
grane[1] *same as* **grane**.
grane[2] *same as* **grain**.
grange *n* **1** a barn or granary. **2** the granary of a religious house.
graniean *n* **1** crying or screaming. **2** a prolonged scream.
grannam, grannum *n* a grandmother.
granniedey *same as* **grandey**.
granny *n* **1** a grandmother. **2** an old woman. **3** an old, tough hen. **4** a grandfather.
granny moil *n* a very old, false, flattering woman.
granny's mutches *n* the columbine.
grant[1] *v* to consent.
grant[2] *v* to grunt, moan.
grap, grape[1] *v* **1** to grope. **2** to examine. **3** to search.
grape[2] *same as* **graip**.
graper *n* a blind man, one who gropes his way.
grapple *v* to drag for dead bodies in water.—*n* a grip in wrestling.
grapple airn *n* a grappling iron.
grappling *n* a method of catching salmon.
grapploch *v* to grasp, seize.
grapus *n* **1** a hobgoblin. **2** the devil.
grashloch, grashlagh *adj* stormy, boisterous, blustering.
grass *same as* **gerse**.
grassum *n* a payment to a landlord by a tenant on entering a farm.
grat[1] *v* wept.
grat[2], **grate**[1] *n* a grating.
grate[2] *adj* **1** grateful. **2** friendly. **3** on terms of intimacy.
grate[3] *v* **1** to annoy, irritate. **2** to hurt, grieve. **3** to grate upon.
grathe *same as* **graith**.
gratification *n* a reward, a tip, a douceur.
gratify *v* **1** to recompense. **2** to tip, give a gratuity. **3** requite. **4** (*in passive*) to receive a gratuity.
gratis, gratus *adj* gratuitous.
graulse *n* a young salmon.
grauvat *n* **1** a cravat. **2** a knitted woollen comforter for the neck.
gravaminous *adj* **1** serious, of grave import. **2** grievous. **3** burdensome. **4** irritating.
gravat *same as* **grauvat**.
grave *n* a pit or hollow.—*v* **1** to dig ground with a spade. **2** to dig for shellfish in the sand. **3** to bury, inter persons.
gravel *v* **1** to embarrass, confuse. **2** to bring to a standstill.
gravestane-gentry *n* the dead and buried.
graveyaird-chorus *n* a cough symptomatic of approaching death.
graveyaird-deserter *n* a sickly person who lingers long.
gravitch *same as* **gilravage**.
grawl[1] *same as* **graulse**.
grawl[2] *v* to grope, search for.
gray[1] *n* **1** a slight breath of wind. **2** a taste or small amount of spirits. **3** a drubbing, thrashing.
gray[2] *n* an arithmetic book in use about the middle of the 19th century, so named from its author.
gray[3] *adj* **1** sombre. **2** sad. **3** disastrous.—*n* **1** morning twilight. **2** evening twilight. **3** a badger. **4** (*in pl*) a dish of kale and cabbage beaten together.—*v* to dawn.
gray-beard *n* a large earthenware jar for holding liquor, etc, a whisky jar.
gray bread *n* coarse bread made of rye or oats.
gray-corn *n* light corn.
gray-crow *n* the hooded crow.
gray-dark *n* dusk.
gray daylight *n* dawn.
gray diver *n* the red-breasted merganser.
gray duck *n* the wild duck.
gray fish *n* **1** the fry of the coalfish. **2** the coalfish.
gray folk *n* the fairies.

gray gate *n* **1** an evil course. **2** a bad end.

gray geese *n* large boulders on the surface of the ground.

gray groat *n* a silver groat.

gray heads *n* heads of grey-coloured oats, growing among others of another colour.

gray heads *n* coalfish of the size and firmness of haddock.

gray hen *n* the female blackcock.

grayjar, ~jug *same as* **gray-beard**.

gray-lennart, ~-linnet, ~-lintie *n* the limpet.

gray ring *n* the coalfish.

gray lord *n* a fully grown coalfish.

gray mare *n* a wife who rules her husband.

gray meal *n* oatmeal.

gray oats *n* a kind of oats yielding a good crop on thin, gravelly soil.

gray paper *n* brown packing paper.

gray-pig *same as* **gray-beard**.

gray-plaidit *adj* wearing a grey plaid.

gray plover *n* the knot.

gray podley *n* the coalfish.

gray school *n* a particular shoal or school of salmon.

gray thrums *n* the purring of a cat.

gray thrush *n* the fieldfare.

gray yogle *n* the short-eared owl.

greaf *same as* **graff**.

grean *n* the muzzle or upper lip of cattle, pigs, etc.

greasehood *n* a long, shallow, iron vessel for melting tallow.

greaser *same as* **greezer**.

greasy *adj* **1** (*used of roads*) slippery from mud or wet. **2** (*of the sky*) dim, misty, portending rain.

great[1] *adj* **1** of large dimension, of large build. **2** pregnant. **3** full. **4** overflowing with emotion, ready to weep. **5** (*used of a river*) flooded, swollen. **6** boastful, vain.—*n* **1** piecework. **2** sum total. **3** gross amount.

great[2] *same as* **grate**.

greatably *adv* greatly, much.

great-bred *adj* high-bred.

great-ewe *n* a ewe big with young.

great-hearted *adj* having a full heart, ready to cry.

great line *n* a line used in catching fish of large size.

greatness *n* width, girth, circumference of a body.

great-printed *adj* having large type.

great whaup *n* the French curlew.

greave *same as* **grieve**.

grecie *n* a little pig.

gredden *same as* **graddan**.

greddon *n* **1** the sweepings of a peat stack or peat box. **2** the remains of fuel.

gree[1] *n* **1** the first place. **2** palm, prize, highest honours. **3** vogue. **4** celebrity. **5** a gradation.

gree [2]*n* **1** tinge, dye. **2** ichor from an animal's sore. **3** the fat exuding from boiling fish.

gree[3] *n* **1** favour. **2** goodwill.

gree[4] *v* **1** to agree, come to an agreement. **2** to reconcile. **3** to arrange.

greeable *adj* **1** harmonious. **2** living in peace and goodwill. **3** kind. **4** obliging.

greeance *n* **1** concord, agreement. **2** the first of the festivities incident to a fisher's bridal, when the betrothal took place formally in presence of parents and friends.

gree'd[1] *adj* boiled so as to exude fat.

gree'd[2] *adj* **1** agreed. **2** reconciled.

greed *v* to covet.—*n* covetousness.

greedy gled *n* **1** the kite. **2** a term of disparagement for a grasping person. **3** a children's game.

Greek[1] *n in phr* **become short of the Greek** to become speechless.

greek[2] *n* daybreak.

greek[3] *n* the grain or peculiar distinguishing texture or quality of a stone.

greement *n* agreement, concord.

green[1] *v* to long for, yearn after.

green[2] *adj* **1** young, vigorous. **2** fresh, not dry. **3** simple, inexperienced. **4** immature. **5** unseasoned. **6** fresh, unsalted. **7** raw. **8** mild. **9** without frost or snow. **10** rainy. **11** (*used of a grave*) recently opened.—*n* **1** a bleaching ground. **2** lawn. **3** grassland. **4** the sods that cover a grave.—*v* to grow green.

green-back *n* the viviparous blenny.

greenbone *n* **1** the garpike or sea needle. **2** the viviparous blenny.

green-brees *n* **1** a cesspool. **2** a stagnant pool beside a dunghill.

green coaties *n* fairies.

green corn *n* corn sown with vetches for green fodder in summer.

green cow *n* a cow recently calved.

green crop *n* a turnip crop.

greeney *n* the greenfinch.

green gaisling *n* a foolish person.

green goose *n* a young goose.

green gown *n* **1** the loss of virginity in the open air. **2** sod. **3** turf on a grave.

green grass *n* a children's singing game.

green horn *n* a horn spoon of greenish colour.

green-horned *adj* simple, silly, foolish.

greenichy *adj* greenish.

greening *adj* becoming green.

green kail *n* plain green colewort.

green-kail-worm *n* **1** a green caterpillar. **2** a person of puny appearance or girlish look.

Greenland dove *n* the black guillemot.

green-lennart, ~-linnet, ~-lintie, ~-lintwhite *n* the greenfinch.

green milk *n* the milk of a newly calved cow.

green-milk-woman *n* a cow recently calved.

green sloke *n* the oyster green or sea lettuce.

Green Tables *n* the Court of Session.

green-wife *n* a female greengrocer.

green yair *n* a species of pear.

greep *same as* **gruip**.

greese *n* a step.

greesh *n* a fireplace of clay built against the gable of a cottage.

greeshoch, greeshough *n* **1** a red, glowing, flameless fire. **2** red-hot embers. **3** a glowing affection.

greesome *adj* gruesome.

greet[1] *v* **1** to cry, weep. **2** to lament.—*n* **1** a fit of weeping. **2** a tear. **3** sob. **4** whine.

greet[2] *same as* **great**.

greet[3] *same as* **greek**.

greetie *n* a child's short cry or whimper.

greetin' *n* crying, tears.

grestin'-cheese *n* a cheese from which oily matter oozes.

greetin'-faced *adj* looking as if ready to cry, puling.

greetin' fu *adj* maudlin drunk, at the tearful stage of drunkenness.

greetin'-meetin' *n* **1** the last meeting of a town council, etc, before new members are elected. **2** a farewell meeting.

greetin-washin *n* the last washing a servant does before leaving her job.

greety *n in phr* **be on the greety** to be always crying.

greezer *n* a thrashing, a beating.

Gregory *n* Gregory's powder.

greice *same as* **grice**.

greik *n* daybreak.

greim, greme *n* soot, grime.—*v* to begrime.

grein *same as* **green**.

greit *same as* **greet**.

greking *n* daybreak.

gress *n* grass.

gressum *same as* **grassum**.

greth *same as* **grain**.

grett *same as* **great**.

grettin *v* wept.

grettlin *same as* **great line**.
grew[1] *n* a greyhound.
grew[2] *adj* grey.
grew[3] *same as* **grue**.
grewan, grewdog, grewhund, grew'n *n* a greyhound.
grewing *n* a shivering. **2** an aguish feeling of cold.
grewse *same as* **growse**.
grewsome *adj* gruesome.
grey, grey dog *n* a greyhound.
grey-grooning *adj* hunting with greyhounds.
gribble *v* **1** to feel with the fingers. **2** to make a manual examination.
grice *n* a young pig.
grice-mites *n* small potatoes for feeding pigs.
grice pan *n* a pan or pot for boiling pigs' meat.
grice-sty *n* a pigsty.
griddled *adj* **1** completely entangled. **2** nonplussed.
grie *same as* **gree**.
grien *same as* **green**.
grieshoch, griershach *same as* **greeshoch**.
grieve *n* a farm overseer or foreman.—*v* to act as an overseer or foreman.
grieveship *n* the situation occupied by a grieve (qv).
grill *same as* **girl**.
grimalder *n* an ugly person.
grime *n* **1** coal dust. **2** soot. **3** smoke.—*v* **1** to sprinkle. **2** to cover thinly.
grimes-dike *n* a ditch made by magic.
grimie *adj* **1** swarthy in complexion. **2** blackened with soot.
griming *n* a sprinkling.
grimly *adj* grim, terrible.
grin *same as* **girn**.
grind[1] *adj* ground.
grind[2] *v* **1** to study hard. **2** to prepare a student for examination. **3** (*used of a cat*) to purr.
grindable *adj* (*used of grain*) fit for grinding.
grinder *n* **1** a difficult student. **2** a student's coach.
grinstane *n* a grindstone.
grinstane-ways *adv* like a grindstone.
grintal-man *n* the keeper of a granary.
grinter, grinter-man *n* one who had charge of a laird's granary.
grinwan *n* a rod or stick with a hair noose for catching trout.
grip[1] *same as* **gruip**.
grip[2] *v* **1** to grasp with the arms, embrace, seize. **2** to apprehend, arrest. **3** to catch after pursuit or in a trap. **4** to search, feel with the hands.—*n* **1** a seizure. **2** an embrace. **3** a struggle. **4** intelligent comprehension. **5** (*in pl*) a sharp pain. **6** colic. **7** a wrestling. **8** blows.
gripe *v* to grip.
gripper *n* **1** a midwife. **2** (*in pl*) antennae. **3** grippers, a shoemaker's tool.
grippie *n* a grasp of the hand.
gripping *n* a disease of sheep disabling them from moving the neck except in one way.—*adj* avaricious, grasping.
grippit *adj* **1** greedy, grasping. **2** sprained.
gripple *adj* griping, grasping, miserly.
grippy *adj* **1** disposed to defraud. **2** greedy. **3** close-fisted. **4** griping.
grisel *same as* **grissel**.
grisk *adj* greedy, avaricious.
griskin *n* a young pig.
grisle *same as* **girsle**.
grissel, grisel *n* a grey horse.
grisy *adj* gristly, full of gristles.
grisset *n* a long, shallow, iron vessel for melting tallow.
grist[1] *same as* **girst**.
grist[2] *n* the multure or fee paid in kind at a mill for grinding.—*v* to grind and dress grain.
grister *n* one who brings grist to a mill.
grit[1], **grite** *same as* **great**.
grit[2] *same as* **great**.

grit[3] *n* **1** a grinding sound. **2** a gnashing of teeth. **3** the grain of stones.
grithe *same as* **girth**.
grit-hearted *adj* ready to cry, having a full heart.
gritness *same as* **greatness**.
grit-yowe *n* a pregnant ewe.
grizzie *n* the name often given to a cow.
grizzle *n* a gooseberry.
groak *v* **1** to look at one watchfully and suspiciously. **2** to whimper, cry for anything.
groaning-malt, ~-maut *n* ale brewed on occasion of a confinement.
groatie[1] *adj* made of groats.
groatie[2], **groatie-buckie** *n* a species of cowrie shell found about John o' Groat's.
grobble *same as* **grouble**.
groff *adj* **1** large. **2** coarse, rough. **3** thick. **4** coarse-featured. **5** (*used of language*) coarse, vulgar, obscene, gross.
grofflin *same as* **grouflins**.
groff-meal *n* coarse, large-grained meal.
groff-write *n* large text in handwriting.
groilach *same as* **gralloch**.
grole *n* porridge, gruel.
gromish *v* to crush severely parts of the body.
groncie *n* anything large or fine of its kind.
grone *n* a pig's snout.
groo *same as* **grue**.
groof *n* the belly.
groofflins *same as* **grouflins**.
groofling *adj* lying close wrapped up.
groogle *same as* **gruggle**.
grool[1] *n* **1** a stone bruised to dust. **2** refuse. **3** a kind of moss beaten into peat.—*v* **1** to bruise. **2** to dust. **3** to crush in battle.
grool[2] *v* to growl.
groop *same as* **gruip**.
grooschin, grooshan *n* any disgusting liquid or viscous stuff.
groose *same as* **growse**.
groosh *adj* excellent.
groosie *adj* (*used of the face*) coarse of skin, greasy. —*n* a big, fat, awkward person.
groot *same as* **grute**.
grootins *n* any dirty, oily thing.
grooze *same as* **growse**.
groozle *v* **1** to breathe with difficulty. **2** to speak huskily.
groozlins *n* intestines.
groozy *adj* shivering.
gropsey *n* a glutton.
gropus *n* a stupid person.
grose *v* **1** to graze, rub off the skin. **2** to rub off the sharp edge of a tool.
groser, grosar, grozer *n* a gooseberry.
grosie *same as* **groosie**.
gross *v* to total, to amount to.
grossart, grossert *n* a gooseberry.
grosset *same as* **grossart**.
grosset buss *n* a gooseberry bush.
grotty *same as* **groatie**.
grou, groue *same as* **grue**.
grouble *v* to swallow hastily.
grouf[1], **grouff**[1] *n* the front of the body, especially of the stomach.—*v* to lie flat on the face or prone.
grouf[2] *same as* **groff**.
grouff[2] *v* **1** to sleep in a restless manner. **2** to breathe heavily. **3** to snore, grunt.—*n* **1** a short, restless sleep. **2** a sleep with a short noisy snore.
groufflins *adv* **1** prone. **2** in a grovelling position.
grougrou *n* the corn-grub.
grouk[1] *n* to become enlivened after sleep.
grouk[2] *same as* **groak**.
grounch *v* **1** to grunt like a pig. **2** to growl, to grumble. **3** to give a droning sound.—*n* **1** a grunt, growl. **2** the droning sound of a bagpipe. **3** a grumble.

ground *n* **1** a grave belonging to a person or family. **2** a ground lair (qv). **3** a farm. **4** the bottom of anything.—*v* **1** to bring to the ground. **2** to strengthen.

ground ebb *n* **1** extreme low water. **2** the lower part of the foreshore.

groundie-swallow *n* groundsel.

ground lair *n* the burial ground pertaining to a family or person.

ground maill *n* the duty or fee paid for the right of interment in a churchyard.

ground master *n* a landlord.

ground-rotten *n* the brown rat.

grounds *n* refuse of flax.

ground-sill, ~-sel *n* **1** the threshold of a house. **2** a door sill of wood or stone.

ground-stane *n* **1** a foundation stone. **2** a basis, foundation.

ground-wa-stane *n* the foundation stone of a wall.

ground-wren *n* the willow warbler.

grounge *same as* **grounch**.

grouse *same as* **growse**.

groushan *same as* **grooschin**.

grousome *adj* **1** gruesome. **2** very uncomely.

grousy[1] *same as* **growse**.

grousy[2] *same as* **groosie**.

grout *same as* **grute**.

grouty *adj* **1** full of sediment, muddy. **2** somewhat rough. **3** rough in manners, rustic, unpolished.

grovel *v* to grope in a stooping posture.

grow[1] *n* **1** growth. **2** a crop.—*adj* favourable to growth.

grow[2], **growe** *same as* **grue**.

growble *same as* **grouble**

grow-grey *adj* becoming grey.—*n* clothes made of wool of the natural colour.

grow-grey wool *n* wool of the natural colour.

growing *n* growth. **2** produce.

growk *same as* **groak**.

growl[1] *n* a grumbler.

growl[2] *same as* **gruel**.

growp *n* a greedy person.

growse *v* to shiver.—*n* a chill.

growshie *adj* favourable for vegetation.

growsin *n* **1** a shivering fit. **2** the feeling of the skin when chilled.

growsome *adj* gruesome.

growth *n* **1** an excrescence on the body. **2** full growth, maturity.

growthilie *adv* luxuriantly.

growthiness *n* luxuriance, fertility.

growthy *adj* **1** well-grown, tall. **2** luxuriant, fertile. **3** growing fast and large. **4** favourable for vegetation.

growthy-tasted *adj* (*of potatoes*) having a taste peculiar to their beginning to sprout in the spring.

grow-weather *n* weather good for vegetation.

growy *adj* promoting growth and vegetation.

growze *v* **1** to shiver, tremble. **2** to have a chill before an ague fit.—*n* a chill, a shivering-fit, a cold, aguish feeling.

grozart, grozert *n* a gooseberry.

grozen *v* to crush, bruise.

grozle *same as* **groozle**.

gru[1] *same as* **grue**.

gru[2] *n* a particle, an atom.

gruan, gruant *same as* **grewan**.

grub[1] *n* food.

grub[2] *v* **1** to toil for. **2** to grasp at parsimoniously. —*n* a greedy or stingy person.

grubbing *adj* grasping, greedy.

grubby *adj* dirty, grimy.

grudge *v* to murmur at, bear a grudge against.

grudge *v* **1** to squeeze, press down. **2** (*with* **up**) to press up. **3** (*used of water checked in its course or ice with water swelling underneath*) to rise, to bulge up.

grudgeful *adj* unforgiving, bearing malice.

grue[1] *v* **1** to shudder with fear or repulsion. **2** (*used of the flesh*) to creep. **3** to feel chilled. **4** to sigh or groan like wind before a storm.—*n* **1** a shiver, tremor. **2** a feeling of horror.—*adj* **1** afraid, suspicious of danger. **2** horrible, frightful.

grue[2] *n* **1** half-frozen water. **2** floating snow or ice. —*v* (*with* **up**) (*used of water*) to be choked up with floating snow or melting ice.

grue[3] *n* a greyhound.

grueing *n* **1** a shuddering repulsion or fear. **2** an aguish sensation of cold.

gruel *n* oatmeal porridge.

gruel tree *n* a porridge stick, a spurtle.

grufe[1] *same as* **grouf**.

grufe[2] *same as* **grouff**.

grufeling *adj* closely wrapped up and comfortable in a lying posture (used in ridicule).

grufelins *same as* **groufflins**.

gruff[1] *same as* **grouff**.

gruff[2] *n* a thick, well-dressed man.

gruff[3] *adj* (*used of the voice*) hoarse, rough.

gruff[4] *same as* **grouf**.

gruffer *n* a grandfather.

grufflins *same as* **groufflins**.

gruggle *v* to put out of order by much handling.

grugous *adj* grim, grizzly.

gruif *same as* **grouf**[1].

gruilch *same as* **grulsh**.

gruilchin, gruilchinie *n* a very thick, squat, fat person or animal.

gruinnich *n* disgust, repulsion.—*v* to disgust.

gruip *n* a cow-house drain.

gruishack *same as* **greeshoch**.

gruive *v* graved.

gruize *same as* **growze**.

grule *n* a mixture of fluid and solid parts in an effusion from an old wound.

grull *same as* **grool**.

grullion *n* **1** a hotchpotch. **2** a mixture of various foods.

grulsh, grulch *n* a thick, squat, fat person or animal.

grulshy *adj* **1** clumsy, awkward. **2** coarsely grown.

grumly[1] *adj* **1** fault-finding, irritable, given to grumbling. **2** surly. **3** grim.

grumly[2] *adj* **1** thick, muddy, full of dregs. **2** gravelly. **3** unpleasant. **4** unsociable. **5** not affable.

grumly-like *adj* forbidding in manner and look.

grummle[1] *v* **1** to grumble. **2** to grudge, have a spite against.—*n* **1** a grudge, spite. **2** a quarrel, misunderstanding. **3** a grumble.

grummle[2], **grummel** *n* **1** crumbs, fragments. **2** dregs, mud.—*v* to make muddy or turbid.

grummlie, grummely *adj* **1** thick. **2** muddy

grumous *n* a bloody effusion from an old wound.

grump *v* to crunch a hard or brittle substance with the teeth.

grumph *v* to grunt, grumble.—*n* **1** a grunt. **2** a pig.

grumphie *n* a pig.

grumple *v* to feel with the fingers.

grumply *adj* surly, out of humour, grumpy.

grun *n* an inclination to evil.

grun[1], **grund**[1] *v* to grind.—*adj* **1** ground. **2** whetted on a stone.

grun[2], **grund**[2] *same as* **ground**.

grunch *same as* **grounch**.

grundable *same as* **grindable**.

grundavie *n* ground ivy.

grunded *adj* **1** ground. **2** whetted on a stone.

grunded-spice *n* ground pepper.

grundie-swallie, grun-i-swallow *n* groundsel.

grund-rotten *n* the brown rat.

grunge *same as* **grounch**.

grungy *n* **1** a grudge. **2** a deep, revengeful feeling.

grunie *n* a small farm.

grunistule, grunnishule *n* groundsel.

grunkle *same as* **gruntle**.

gruns *n* grounds, sediment.

grunsie *n* a sour fellow.

grunstane *n* **1** a foundation stone. **2** a foundation.

grunstane *n* a grindstone.

grun-swall, ~-swallow *n* groundsel.

grunt *v* to grumble, complain.—*n* a grumble, complaint.

grunter *n* a pig.

gruntie, grunty *n* a pig.

gruntle[1] *n* a grain, fragment.

gruntle[2] *v* **1** to grunt in a low key. **2** to groan slightly. **3** (*used of infants*) to make a low cooing sound.—*n* **1** a grunting noise. **2** the moan of a sick cow. **3** an infant's cooing.

gruntle[3], **gruntill** *n* **1** the snout. **2** the face in general.

gruntle-thrawn *adj* wry-faced.

gruntling *n* a groaning noise.

grun-wark *n* **1** the preparatory work in laying the foundation of a building. **2** groundwork.

grunyie[1] *v* **1** (*with* **at**) to grumble, find fault with. **2** (*with* **at** *or* **with**) to disgust.—*n* disgust.

grunyie[2], **grunzie** *n* **1** the snout, mouth. **2** the face, visage. **3** turmoil. **4** dirty work. **5** a mess,

grunzie *adj* having sediment, with dregs.

gruous *adj* **1** grim, grizzly. **2** awe-inspiring.

grup *same as* **grip**.

grupe *same as* **gruip**

gruppit *same as* **grippit**.

gruppy *same as* **grippy**.

gruse[1], **gruss** *v* to crush, press, squeeze.

gruse[2] *same as* **grue**.

grush[1] *v* to crumble.—*n* what has crumbled down.

grush[2], **grushie** *adj* **1** of thriving growth. **2** thick. **3** flabby. **4** frowsy.

grushach, grushaw *same as* **greeshoch**.

grusle *same as* **groozle**.

grut[1], **grute** *n* the refuse of fish livers after oil has been extracted.

grut[2] *same as* **great**.

gruttin, grutten *v* cried. *See* **greet**.

gruze *same as* **growze**.

gruzin *n* **1** a creeping of the flesh. **2** a shivering.

gruzlins *same as* **groozlins**.

gruzzle[1] *v* to bruise, press together.

gruzzle[2], **gruzle** *same as* **groozle**.

gryce, gryse *same as* **grice**.

gryfe *n* a claw, talon.

gryking *n* dawn.

grymie *same as* **grimie**.

gryming *n* a sprinkling.

grype *same as* **grip**.

gryte *adj* great, big.

gu[1] *same as* **gow**.

gu[2] *n* a seagull

guad *v* (*used of a horse*) to be restive or troublesome in harness.

guard *n* **1** the old name for an Edinburgh night-watchman. **2** a guardhouse, prison. **3** a ward. **4** one curling stone preventing another from being dislodged.—*v* to protect a curling stone from being dislodged by putting another in front of it.

guardfish *n* the sea pike.

guardsman *n* **1** a warder. **2** a sentinel, watcher.

gub *n* the mouth.

guck *n* a duck.

guckrie *n* folly.

Gud *n* God.

gudame *n* a grandmother.

gud day *same as* **gude day**.

guddle[1] *v* **1** to catch trout by groping with the hands under the stones or banks of a stream. **2** to dabble as a duck. **3** (*used of children*) to play in the gutters, mud or puddles. **4** to do work of a dirty or greasy nature.—*n* toil, turmoil. **5** dirty work. **6** a mess, muddle.

guddle[2] *v* **1** to mangle. **2** to haggle. **3** to cut awkwardly.

guddler *n* one who catches fish with his hands.

Gude *n* God.

gude[1] good.

gude[2] *adj* **1** large. **2** long. **3** of good birth.—*n* **1** wealth, substance. **2** (*in pl*) cattle, sheep. **3** smuggled articles.— *v* to manure.

gude anes *n* one's best clothes.

gude-billie *n* a brother-in-law.

gude-bit *n* **1** a good berth. **2** a long time. **3** long space.

gude-bluid *n* a brave fellow.

gude-breid *n* bread baked for special domestic events, as marriages, etc.

gude-brither *n* a brother-in-law.

gude-cheap *n* a good bargain.—*adj* costing little or nothing.

gude day *n* a salutation, bidding good day.

gude-deed[1] *n* **1** a bribe. **2** a favour. **3** a benefaction.

gude-deed[2] *int* a mild expletive.

gude-dochter, ~-dother *n* a daughter-in-law.

gude e'en *n* a salutation, bidding good evening.

gude-father, ~-faither, ~-fader *n* a father-in-law.

gude few *phr* a good many.

gude-folk, ~-fowk *n* fairies, elves, brownies.

gude fores *n* good qualities.

gude-for-nocht *n* a good-for-nothing person.—*adj* worthless.

gude-gaun *adj* proceeding steadily.

gudeless *adj* **1** wicked, hurtful. **2** terrible, frightful.—*adv* exceedingly, very.

gudelie[1] *adj* godly.

gudelie[2] *adj* goodly.—*adv* easily, conveniently, well, properly, with a good grace.

gudelie-neighbour *n* a fairy, brownie.

gudeliheid *n* glory, goodliness.

gude-livin' *adj* pious.—*n* good or luxurious food.

gude lock *n* a good quantity.

gudeman *n* **1** the master of a house. **2** a husband. **3** a master, chief. **2** the head of a prison. **2** a farmer who is not a proprietor. **4** a yeoman, a small farmer who farms his own land. **5** the devil. **6** (*with* **the**) a child's designation of God.

gudemanlike *adj* becoming a husband.

gudeman's acre *n* the spot of ground reserved by a farmer for himself when he resigns his farm to his son.

gudeman's-craft, ~-field, ~-taft *n* a portion of land dedicated to the devil and left untilled.

gudeman's milk *n* the milk first skimmed from the pan after the cream has been taken off.

gude-mither *n* a mother-in-law.

gude neighbours *n* fairies, brownies.

gude nicht *n* **1** a salutation, bidding goodnight. **2** a farewell.

gude rest *n* an evening salutation, goodnight.

gude-sister *n* a sister-in-law.

gude-son *n* a son-in-law.

gude troth *int* a mild expletive.

gudewife *n* **1** the mistress of a house, a wife. **2** the landlady of an inn, etc. **3** a woman farmer.

gudewill *n* **1** love, affection. **2** a gratuity, a tip. **3** the perquisite of an under-miller. **4** the parents' consent to a daughter's marriage.

gude-willie, ~-willied, ~-willit *adj* **1** hospitable. **2** hearty. **3** kindly, generous, liberal.

gude words *n* a child's name for its prayers.

gudge[1] *n* **1** anything short and thick. **2** a short, thickset person.

gudge[2] *v* **1** to probe, poke. **2** to press out or make to bulge by wedges or a lever. **3** to poke or probe for trout under the stones or banks of a stream. **4** to stuff, cram with food, play the glutton.

gudgeon *n* a fool, one easily deceived.

gudget[1], **gudgeat** *n* a camp servant.

gudget[2] *n* a glutton.—*v* to be gluttonous.—*adj* short and thick, fat from over-eating.

gudgick *n* a short, thickset person.
gudgie *adj* short and thick, stout.
gudin *same as* **goodin**.
gueed[1] *n* god.
gueed [2]*same as* **gude**.
gueedly[1] *adj* religious, godly.
gueedly[2] *adv* easily, with a good grace.—*adj* goodly.
gueel *n* the corn marigold.
guerdon *n* protection, safeguard.
guergous *adj* **1** martial. **2** warlike in appearance.
guess *n* a riddle, conundrum. **2** an opinion.
guessie *n* a principal actor in the child's game of namie and guessie.
guest[1] *n* anything which the superstitious think portends the arrival of a stranger.
guest[2] *n* a ghost, spectre.
guesten *v* to lodge as a guest.
guesthouse *n* a house of entertainment.
guestning *n* reception as a guest.
guff[1] *n* **1** a puff of wind. **2** a whiff, savour. **3** an inhalation. **4** a bad smell.
guff[2] *v* **1** to laugh boisterously or immoderately. **2** to babble. **3** to let wind from the mouth.—*n* **1** a guffaw. **2** a loud, sudden noise. **3** a suppressed bark or snort.
guff[3] *same as* **gowff**.
guffa *same as* **gaffa**.
guffer *n* the viviparous blenny.
guffie[1] *adj* foolish, stupid.—*n* **1** a fool. **2** a rustic, clown. **3** a noisy person.
guffie[2] *adj* **1** chubby. **2** fat about the cheeks or temples.
guffiness *n* fatness about the cheeks or temples.
guffish *adj* foolish.
guffishlie *adv* foolishly.
guffishness *n* foolishness.
guffle *v* to puzzle, nonplus.
guff nor sty *phr* nothing at all.
guggle *v* to gurgle hysterically.
Guid *n* God.
guid *same as* **gude**[1].
guidal *n* guidance, control, management.
guide *v* **1** to treat. **2** to try. **3** to handle, use. **4** to manage, control, look after. **5** to manage economically. **6** to save. **7** to keep (*in exclamations of surprise*) .—*n* a manager in control of money or property.
guider *n* **1** the leader of a party or faction. **2** a guardian, adviser. **3** (*with* **good**) a managing, economical housewife.
guideship *n* **1** guidance. **2** usage, treatment. **3** management.
guidet *adj* harassed, troubled.
guide ye *int* an exclamation of contempt.
guid-fit *n* a lucky foot.
guid-fitter *n* one who has a lucky foot.
guidsake *int* for god's sake!
guid-the-fire *n* a poker.
guid-the-gate *n* a halter for a horse.
guik *same as* **gowk**.
guild[1] *n* the society of the burgesses of a royal burgh.
guild[2], **guild tree** *n* the barberry.
guild[3] *n* the corn marigold.
guild *same as* **gild**.
guildee *n* the young of the coalfish.
guilder-faugh *n* old lea land, once ploughed and then left to lie fallow.
guild o' glee a merry group of playmates.
guildry *n* the society of the burgesses of a royal burgh.
guile[1] *v* to beguile.
guile[2] *n* the corn marigold.
guilish *adj* **1** guileful. **2** beguiling.
guillie *n* a big knife.
guiltfou *adj* full of guilt.
guind *same as* **gean**.
guinea gowd *n* a fine quality of gold of which guineas were coined.

guinea note *n* a banknote for a guinea.
guisard *n* a mummer.
guise *v* **1** to go mumming, especially on Hallowe'en. **2** to masquerade to decorate.—*n* **1** a merrymaking, frolic. **2** a mumming, masquerade. **3** the parts in a play.
guiser *n* **1** a mummer, especially at Hallowe'en. **2** a masquerader.
guissern *same as* **gusehorn**.
guissie *same as* **gussie**.
guissock *n* a superstitious observance.
quiz *same as* **gizz**.
guizard *n* a mummer.—*v* to act as a mummer.
guize *same as* **guise**.
gukkow *n* **1** the cuckoo. **2** a simpleton.
gulch *v* to eructate.—*n* **1** a glutton. **2** a thick, ill-shaped person. **3** an eructation.
gulchin *n* a big, fat, short person.
gulchy *adj* of gross, thick of body.
gulder *v* **1** to shout, speak boisterously. **2** to bark threateningly. **3** to growl loudly and with menace. **4** to make a gurgling sound. **5** to speak indistinctly.—*n* **1** a loud, sudden shout of surprise or anger. **2** the angry growl of a dog. **3** a gurgling sound. **4** the sound of water escaping through a narrow orifice or channel. **5** the sound of choking or strangulation. **6** half-articulate speech. **7** the sound of a turkey cock.
guldersome *adj* **1** passionate. **2** boisterous. **3** given to snarling.
guldie *n* a tall black-faced, gloomy-looking man.
gule[1] *n* the corn marigold.
gule[2] *adj* yellow.
gulefittit *adj* yellow-footed or yellow-legged.
guleravitch *same as* **galravitch**.
gulf *n* a big hole or rut caused by a rooting sow.
gulghy *n* a beetle, a cockchafer.
gull[1] *v* to flout, sneer at, make fun of.
gull[2] *n* a large trout.
gull[3] *n* **1** a thin, cold mist, accompanied by a slight wind. **2** a chill. **3** a rather low estimate of a person or thing.—*adj* chill, marked by a cold wind.—*v* to be covered with a thin mist, to grow misty.
gull[4] *v* **1** to thrust the finger forcibly under the ear, to catlill. **2** to shout. **3** to growl loudly.—*n* **1** a loud shout. **2** a growl.
guller *same as* **gulder**.
guller's spree *phr* a heavy drinking bout.
gullet, gullot *n* a water channel.
gulliegaup *v* **1** to injure severely. **2** to take by the throat, strangle.
gulliegaupus *n* a big, stupid person.
gulliegaw *v* to wound with a sharp weapon.—*n* **1** a deep cut or gash with sword or knife. **2** a broil.
gulliewillie *n* **1** a blustering, quarrelsome fellow. **2** a swamp covered with grass or herbs. **3** a quagmire.
gullimont *n* a glutton.
gullion[1] *n* a mean wretch.
gullion[2] *n* **1** a quagmire. **2** mud.
gull-maw *n* the greater black-backed gull.
gulloot *n* a big, ugly fellow.
gully[1] *n* **1** a large knife. **2** a butcher's knife. **3** a carving knife. **4** a sword.—*v* to cut, gash.
gully[2] *v* **1** to swallow. **2** to gulp.
gully[3] *n* a sink.
gully[4] *n* human excrement.
gully-gander *n* a fight with knives.
gully-hole *n* **1** the orifice of a sink. **2** a gutter hole, mouth of a drain or sewer.
gully-knife *n* a large knife.
gullymudge *v* to stick or stab with a large knife.
gullyvant *same as* **gallivant**.
guloch *n* an iron lever.
gulp *n* a big, unwieldy child.
gulpin *n* **1** a young child. **2** a simpleton, greenhorn. **3** a raw, unwieldy fellow.
gulsach[1], **gulsoch** *n* **1** a surfeit. **2** a voracious appetite.

gulsach[2], **gulschoch** *n* the jaundice.—*adj* jaundiced.
gulsch, gulsh *same as* **gulch**.
gulschy *same as* **gulchy**.
gulset *n* the jaundice.
gulshock *adj in phr* **gulshock scoot** a boy's popgun made from a hollow-stemmed plant.
gulzie *same as* **gully**[1].
gum[1] *n* **1** the condensed moisture on the windows and walls of a crowded church, hall, etc. **2** a thin film on anything. **3** coal or peat dust.—*v* to become covered with condensed vapour or with a thin film.
gum[2] *n* the palate.
gum[3] *n* **1** disturbance. **2** a misunderstanding. **3** a variance.
gum[4] *n* a disguised form of God, used as an expletive.
gumflate *v* **1** to swell, inflate. **2** to perplex, bamboozle.
gumflerman *n* the bearer of a funeral banner.
gumflower *n* an artificial flower.
gumly *adj* **1** muddy. **2** gloomy.
gummel, gummul *v* to gobble up.
gummeril *same as* **gomeril**.
gummle *v* **1** to make muddy. **2** to confuse, perplex.
gump[1] *v* **1** to grope. **2** to grope for trout.
gump[2] *n* **1** the whole of anything. **2** a large piece or portion.
gump[3], **gumph**[1] *n* **1** a fool, blockhead. **2** a silly woman. **3** a plump child, rather overgrown. **4** (*in pl*) the sulks.—*v* **1** to go about in a stupid way. **2** to sulk.
gumph[2] *v* to beat, defeat, get the better of.
gumph[3] *n* **1** a bad smell. **2** the entrails of a skate.
gumphie *n* a fool, a simpleton.
gumphieleerie *adj* stupid, silly.
gumphion *n* a funeral banner.
gumping *n* **1** a piece cut out of the whole of anything. **2** the part of a rigg (qv) on a harvest field, separated from the rest, that is left uncut.
gumple *v* **1** to become sulky. **2** to show bad humour.—*n* **1** a surfeit. **2** (*in pl*) the sulks.
gumple-face *n* a downcast face.
gumple-faced *adj* chop-fallen, sulky.
gumple-feast *n* a surfeit.
gumple-foisted *adj* sulky, ill-humoured.
gumplin *n* a long, sulky fit.
gumpshion *same as* **gumption**.
gumption *n* **1** common sense. **2** shrewdness. **3** quickness of understanding.
gumptionless *adj* **1** foolish. **2** without gumption.
gumptious *adj* self-gumption.
gumpus *n* a fool.
gumral *adj* **1** foolish. **2** frivolous.
gumsheon, gumshion, gumtion *same as* **gumption**.
gumstick *n* a stick used by teething children.
gun[1] *v* to interchange talk, to gossip.
gun[2] *n* a tobacco pipe.—*v* (*used of blasting charges*) to explode without effect.
gun[3] *n in phr* **great gun** a great friend.
gunch *n* a large piece.
gundie[1] *n* the father-lasher.
gundie[2] *adj* greedy, voracious.
gundie-guts *n* **1** a voracious person. **2** a fat, pursy fellow.
gundy[1] *n* **1** a sweetmeat made of treacle and spices. **2** candy, toffee.
gundy[2] *n* a push, shove.
gundy-balls *n* globular gundies. *See* **gundy**[1].
gundyman[1] *n* a seller of gundies. *See* **gundy**[1].
gundyman[2] *n* a ploughman's assistant, who, with a long pole fastened to the plough beam, had to help the ploughman by pushing the plough off or to him, as occasion required.
gundymonger *n* a seller of sweetmeats or gundy (qv).
gundywife *n* a female gundymonger (qv).
gunk *v* **1** to jilt, disappoint. **2** to take or set aback. —*n* **1** a disappointment. **2** a jilting.
gunkerie *n* the act of duping, jilting, tricking.
gunkie *n* a dupe.

gunnack *n* a species of skate.
gunnald *adj* with great jowls.
gunnals *n* **1** gills. **2** jowls, great hanging cheeks.
gunner[1] *n* a sportsman, one who takes a shooting.
gunner[2] *n* the yellowhammer.
gunner[3] *v* **1** to gossip. **2** to talk loud and long.—*n* **1** gossip. **2** noisy talk. **3** a blustering talker.
gunnerflook *n* the turbot.
gunner room *n* a sort of committee room or meeting room in which matters are discussed
gunning[1] *n* a familiar talk.
gunning[2] *n* the sport of shooting.
gunled *adj* having large jowls.
gunnled *n* **1** gills. **2** jowls.
gun-plucker *n* a kind of fish with a wide mouth.
gunpowder *n* tea.
gunsar, gunsir *n* a big, clumsy, ungainly, stupid person.
gunsh *n* a short, thickset fellow.
gunshy *adj* thickset.
gun-sleeves *n* sleeves wider at the shoulder than at the wrist.
gun-stane *n* a gun flint.
guran *n* a pustule, a small boil.
guranie *adj* full of small boils.
gurbit *same as* **gorbit**.
gurg *v* to make a creaking noise.
gurgrugous *same as* **gargrugous**.
gurgy *adj* **1** fat. **2** short-necked. **3** with protuberant belly.
gurious *same as* **gruous**.
gurk, gurkas *n* **1** a fat, short person. **2** a fine, well-conditioned fellow. **3** the thriving young, large for their age, of any livestock. **4** a term of address.
gurkin *n* a very fat, short person.
gurkie *same as* **gurk**.
gurl[1], **gurle** *v* **1** to growl as a dog. **2** to snarl, mutter. **3** (*of the wind*) to rush, roar, howl as in a storm. **4** (*of water*) to issue or escape with a gurgling noise. **5** (*of an infant*) to crow, coo, gurgle. —*n* **1** a growl. **2** a narrow spot where a confined stream pours with force and gurgling sound.—*adj* **1** surly, quarrelsome. **2** rough, stormy, bitter.
gurl[2] *v* to flatter.—*n* flattery, deceit.
gurliewhirkie *n* **1** unforeseen evil. **2** premeditated revenge.
gurlin' *n* flattery.
gurling *adj* **1** growling, snarling. **2** surly. **3** (*used of rivulets*) gurgling, running noisily.
gurly[1] *adj* **1** (*of a dog*) given to growling, growling loudly. **2** (*of the weather*) boisterous, threatening to be stormy, bitter, bleak. **3** (*of fluids*) gurgling. **4** (*of infants*) crowing, gurgling. **5** (*of persons*) surly, rough, cross. **6** (*of a tree*) gnarled.
gurly[2] *adj* deceitful, fair-spoken.
gurn *same as* **girn**[2].
gurnel, gurnle *n* **1** a strange-shaped, thick man. **2** a fisherman's tool for fixing stakes in the sand to spread nets on.
gurnet *n* the gurnard.
gurr[1] *v* **1** to growl as a dog, snarl. **2** to rumble. **3** to purr as a cat.—*n* the growl or snarl of a dog.
gurr[2] *n* **1** mud. **2** hardened rheum of the eyes.—*v* to soil, defile.
gurr[3] *n* a strong, thickset person. **2** a knotty stick or tree.
gurr[4] *n* courage, bravery.
gurrag *n* a pimple, pustule.
gurran *n* **1** a very strong, thickset person. **2** one with a stubborn temper.
gurr-gurr *v* to growl continuously or for a time.
gurr-gurring *n* **1** a long, low growl or snarl. **2** a rumbling, snarling sound.
gurrie *n* to growl, snarl.
gurring *n* a low growl.
gurron *same as* **garron**.
gurry *n* **1** a dog-fight. **2** a loud, angry wrangle. **3** a brawl. **4** a hurry, bustle, confusion.
gurry-wurry *n* a dogfight, wrangle.—*adj* snarling, growling.

gurth *n* crushed curd.

gurthie *adj* **1** heavy, oppressive. **2** weighty, solid. **3** corpulent, fat. **4** nauseating, burdensome to the stomach.

guschach *n* the fireside.

guschet[1] *n* **1** a gusset. **2** a pocket at or near the armpit. **3** the clock of a stocking. **4** a triangular piece of land, interposed between two other properties.

guschet[2], **gusset house** *n* a house at a corner, forming a division between two streets.

guschetie *n* a small guschet. *See* **guschet**[1].

guse[1] *n* a goose.

guse[2] *n* the long gut or rectum,

gusehorn[1] *n* a coarse, lusty woman.

gusehorn[2] *n in phr* **play gush** to bleed profusely.

gushat, gushet *same as* **guschet**[1].

gushel[1] *n* a small dam made in a gutter or streamlet to intercept water.

gushel[2] *n* **1** an awkward lout. **2** a clumsy, untidy worker.— *v* to work untidily.

gush-hole *n* an outlet in a wall for the escape of water.

gushing *n* the grunting of a pig.

gussie[1] *n* **1** a young sow. **2** a call to a sow.

gussie[2] *n* a coarse, lusty woman.

gussie[3] *n* a division of an orange.

gusslin *n* boasting.

gust[1] *n* a taste, relish, liking, gusto.— *v* **1** to taste, smell. **2** to give relish or appetite. **3** to please the palate. **4** to flavour.

gust[2] *n* a contemptuous term for an officious, flighty, talkative woman who means nothing in her talk.

gustard *n* the great bustard.

gustfu' *adj* **1** full of relish. **2** palatable, savoury. **3** enjoying a relish.

gustily *adv* luxuriously, daintily.

gustless *adj* without taste or appetite, with no power to relish.

gusty *adj* **1** pleasing the palate, savoury, appetizing. **2** fond of good living. **3** with an appetite.

gut[1] *n* the gout.

gut[2], **gutt** *same as* **goutte**.

gut[3] *n* **1** (*in pl*) the belly, stomach. **2** the contents of anything. **2** the inside of anything.

gut an' ga' *phr* the whole contents of the stomach violently ejected.

gutcher *n* **1** a grandfather. **2** grandsire.

gut-haniel *n* a colic.

gut-pock *n* **1** the stomach, belly. **2** the crop of a fowl.

gut-pot *n* a receptacle for the entrails of herrings.

gutrake *n* provisions got with difficulty or improperly.

gut-scraper *n* a fiddler.

gutser[1] *same as* **gutcher**.

gutser[2] *n* **1** a greedy person. **2** a person who eats too much.

gutsie *same as* **gutsy**.

gutsily *adv* gluttonously.

gutsiness *n* **1** gluttony, voracity. **2** greediness.

gutsy *adj* **1** greedy, gluttonous, voracious. **2** (*used of a house*) capacious, roomy, commodious.

guttag *n* a knife for gutting herrings.

guttam *n* a drop.

gutter[1] *n* **1** the mark or trace of tears on the cheeks. **2** mud, mire, puddles. **3** the act of doing work untidily or dirtily. **4** a dirty, untidy worker. — *v* **1** to bemire, bedaub with mud. **2** to work dirtily, slovenly and unskilfully. **3** to eat into the flesh, fester. **4** to lay a gutter.

gutter[2] *n* **1** a person who guts herrings. **2** a person who unpacks herring boxes.

gutter[3] *v* (*used of running water*) to gurgle, make a noise.

gutter-blood, ~-bleed, ~-bluid *n* **1** a homeless child. **2** a low-born person. **3** one born within the same town or city as another. **4** one whose ancestors have been in the same town or city for some generations.—*adj* brought up in the same locality and in the same rank of life.

gutterel *adj* rather gluttonous.—*n* a fat, young pig.

gutterer *n* an unskilful, dirty worker.

gutter-gaw *n* a sore caused by mud, etc, in one who walks with bare feet.

gutter hole *n* **1** a sink or kennel. **2** a receptacle for kitchen refuse or filth.

gutterin' *adj* untidy and unskilful in work.

gutters *n* mud, mire.

gutter-teetan *n* the rock pipit.

guttery *adj* **1** muddy, full of puddles, miry. **2** mud-stained.

guttie[1] *same as* **gutty**.

guttie[2] *n* **1** rubber. **2** a gym shoe.

guttiness *n* **1** capaciousness of belly. **2** thickness. **3** grossness.

guttle *v* **1** to gorge, guzzle. **2** to reach to the guts.

guttrell *same as* **gutterel**.

gutty *adj* **1** pot-bellied, corpulent. **2** thick, gross. **3** greedy, gluttonous.—*n* **1** a fat, corpulent person. **2** a minnow.

gutty bottle *n* a big-bellied bottle.

guy[1] *adv* rather, very.

guy[2] *v* **1** to guide. **2** to have charge of a bill in parliament.

guylte *n* a full-grown pig.

guynoch *same as* **geenyoch**.

guyser *same as* **guiser**.

guzle *v* to guzzle.

guzzhorn *n* the gizzard.

guzzle *v* to take by the throat, throttle, choke.—*n* the throat.

g'wa *int* an exclamation.of surprise, incredulity.

Gweed *same as* **Gude**.

gweed *same as* **gude**[1].

gweed-frauchty and gweed-willie *phr* generous and ready to give to the poor.

gweedin *n* manure.

gweed-wully *same as* **gude-willie**.

gweel *same as* **gule**[1].

gweeshie, gweeshtins *int* a disguised form of God, used in exclamations of great surprise and mild oaths.

gwick *n* the movement of the mouth and the sound made in swallowing.—*v* **1** to move the mouth in swallowing. **2** to make the sound as of swallowing.

gwite *same as* **gett**.

gy[1] *n* **1** a scene, show, performance. **2** a gathering. **3** estimation, respect. **4** a strange, hobgoblin-looking fellow, a guy.

gy[2] *same as* **gey**.

gya *v* gave.

gyaan, gyaen, gyan *v* going.

gyad *same as* **gad**[4].

gyaggers *n* an exclamation of disgust.

gyang *same as* **gang**.

gyangals *same as* **gangyls**.

gyangrel *same as* **gangrel**.

gyang-water *same as* **ganging-water**.

gyaun *v* going.

gy-carlin *same as* **gyrecarlin**.

gye *same as* **gey**.

gyed *same as* **gad**[4].

gyem *n* a game.

gyld *same as* **gild**.

gyle[1] **1** *n* wort. **2** the vat in which wort is fermented. **3** a tun dish.

gyle[2] *n* a jail.

gyle[3] *n* a gable.

gyle-fat *n* the vat used for fermenting wort.

gyle house *n* a brew house.

gylie, gylies *adv* **1** considerably. **2** rather.

gymp *v* **1** to talk freely. **2** to taunt, gibe.—*n* **1** a quirk. **2** a gibe.

gynk *same as* **gink**.

gynkie *adj* giddy, tricky, frolicsome.—*n* **1** a reproachful designation of a woman. **2** a light-hearted girl.

gyp *n* a woman's skirt or short petticoat.

gype *same as* **gipe**.

gypelie *adv* **1** keenly. **2** quickly. **2** nimbly.

gype-like *adj* like a fool or a lout.

gyper *n* **1** nonsense, fun. **2** joking.

gyperie *n* foolishness.
gype-written *adj* written by a fool.
gypical *adj* characteristic of a fool, foolish.
gypit *adj* 1 foolish. 2 made a fool of.
gypitness *n* foolishness.
gyre[1] *n* a powerful, malignant spirit.
gyre[2] *adj* 1 gaudy. 2 glaring.
gyre-carle *n* 1 a water sprite, kelpie. 2 a giant, an ogre.
gyre-carlin *n* 1 a mother witch, a witch. 2 a hobgoblin. 3 a scarecrow.
gyre-fu' *adj* 1 fretful, ill-tempered. 2 discontented.
gyre-leukin *adj* 1 impish-looking. 2 odd-looking.
gyrie *n* 1 a stratagem. 2 circumvention.
gyrin' *adj* gaudy, of a bright or glaring colour.
gyrn *same as* **girn**.
gysan, gysen *same as* **gizzen**.

gysard, gysart *same as* **guizard**.
gyse[1] *same as* **guise**.
gyse[2] *n* 1 mode, fashion. 2 guise.
gyser *n* a mummer.
gyte[1] *adj* mad, out of one's senses.—*n* 1 a madman. 2 a foolish, idiotic person. 3 ruin. 4 pieces.
gyte[2] *same as* **gett**.
gyte[3] *n* a goat.
gyte[4], **gytt** *same as* **gait**.
gytlin[1] *adj* rural, belonging to the fields.
gytlin[2] *same as* **gettlin**.
gytting *same as* **gaiten**.
gyve-airns *n* gyves, fetters for the legs.
gyzen *same as* **gizzen**.
gyzen clout *n* an infant's binder.

H

ha'[1] *n* 1 a hall. 2 a house, home. 3 a farmhouse. 4 a cottage. 5 the chief manor house. 6 a house in a township. 7 a room of a house. 8 the kitchen of a farmhouse.
ha'[2] *same as* **haugh**[2].
haadie *same as* **haddie**.
haaf[1] *n* 1 the deep or open sea. 2 deep-sea fishing ground.
haaf[2] *adv* half.
haaf-boat *n* a boat adapted for deep-sea fishing.
haaf-eel *n* the conger eel.
haaffish *n* the great seal.
haaf-fishing *n* deep-sea fishing.
haafing *n* deep-sea fishing.
haaflin *same as* **haflin**.
haaf lines *n* deep-sea fishing lines.
haaf-man *n* a deep-sea fisherman.
haaf-seat *n* a deep-sea fishing ground.
haal *n* 1 a hold. 2 the support given to a child learning to walk. 3 walk.—*v* to offer sufficient resistance.
haaliget *same as* **hallockit**.
haalyan *same as* **hallion**.
haanyal *same as* **haniel**.
haap[1] *same as* **hap**[3].
haap[2] *v* (*used of horses*) to turn to the right from the driver.—*int* a call to a horse to turn to the right.
haar[1] *n* 1 a raw, foggy, easterly wind. 2 a mist. 3 drizzling rain. 4 hoarfrost.
haar[2] *n* 1 a huskiness in the throat. 2 an impediment of speech.—*v* to speak hoarsely and thickly.
haar-cluds *n* clouds brought by a raw, cold wind from the east.
haary *adj* (*used of wind*) cold, keen, biting.
haas *same as* **halse**.
haave[1] *n* a large pock-net used in fishing.—*v* to fish with a pock net.
haave[2] *adj* pale, wan.
haaver *n* 1 a half-share. 2 a sharer who holds a half. 3 (*in pl*) children's claim to have half of any treasure trove. 4 *in phr* **haavers and shaivers!** a children's exclamation when they find anything of the nature of treasure.—*adj* (*used of cattle, etc*) held in partnership.—*v* 1 to halve. 2 to share in partnership. 3 to divide into two.
hab *n* the hob of a fireplace.
habber *n* 1 a stammerer. 2 one who speaks thickly. 3 a clumsy person. 4 snarling or growling like a dog.—*v* 1 to stutter, stammer. 2 to snarl.
habberdyn fish *n* 1 dried cod. 2 barrelled cod.
habbergaw *n* 1 hesitation. 2 suspense. 3 an objection.
habberjock *n* 1 a turkey cock. 2 a big, stupid person who speaks thickly.
habbernab *v* to touch glasses in drinking.
habbers *n* a copartnership of equal shares between two.
habbie[1] *adj* stiff in motion as a hobbyhorse.

habbie[2] *n* a hobby.
habbie-gabbie *v* to throw money to be scrambled for.
habble[1] *n* 1 the act of snapping. 2 a dog's growling noise. 3 perplexity, a fix. 4 tumult, disorder. 5 a squabble.—*v* 1 to snap like a dog. 2 to confuse. 3 to stammer. 4 to speak confusedly. 5 to gabble, talk fast. 6 to wrangle.
habble[2] *v* 1 to hobble, walk with difficulty. 2 to limp. 3 to shake, jolt. 4 to candle, toss. 5 to move unsteadily with a quivering motion. 6 to swarm with insects or vermin. 7 to embarrass.—*n* a shake, toss.
habble[3] *n* 1 an unsuccesful or botched attempt. 2 a mess.
habble-hobble *n* a rumpus, hubbub.
habblejock *n* a turkey cock.
habbler *n* a squabbler, one who provokes or likes squabbles.
habble-sheuf *n* an uproar, tumult, confusion.
habbleshow *n* 1 a disorderly crowd, rabble. 2 a hubbub.
habblie *adj* 1 (*used of cattle*) having big bones, ill-set. 2 (*used of ground*) soft, quaking.
habbling *n* 1 confusion. 2 wrangling. 3 confused talk.—*adj* given to petty quarrelling.
habbocraws *int* a shout to scare crows from cornfields, etc.
habby *adj* stiff in motion.
habeek-a-ha *int* a cry that marbles, etc, forfeited in school hours are to be scrambled for out of doors.
haberdash *n* small wares, miscellaneous articles.
haberschon *n* an habergeon, a jacket of mail or scale armour.
ha'-bible *n* a large family Bible.
habieshaw *v* to scatter sweets among children to scramble for.
habil, habile *adj* 1 competent. 2 able, qualified. 3 passable. 4 liable.
habiliments *n* outfit.
hability *n* legal competence.
ha'-bink *n* the bank of a haugh (qv) overhanging a stream.
habit and repute *phr* 1 notorious. 2 held and reputed to be.
habit sark, ~ shirt *n* a woman's riding shirt.
hable *same as* **habil**.
hachle *n* 1 a sloven, slut. 2 a dirtily dressed person.
hack[1] *v* (*used of the stomach*) to turn against.
hack[2] *n* 1 a pronged implement for drawing dung from a cart. 2 a mark. 3 a fissure. 4 a crack or graze in the skin. 5 an indentation, or piece of indented sheet iron, for steadying a curler's feet when playing.—*v* 1 to chop. 2 to chap. 3 to be cracked.
hack[3] *v* to hawk, to peddle.
hack[4] *n* a wild, moorish place.
hack and manger *phr* free quarters.
hack and sweep *phr* a clean sweep.

hack-a-thraw *n* a determined fellow.
hackberry *same as* **hagberry**.
hack-door *n* a door between a farm kitchen and the farm-yard.
hacker *v* **1** to hack in cutting. **2** to cut small, hash.
hackery-lookit *adj* **1** rough, gruff. **2** marked by smallpox.
hacking *n* the chapping of hands or feet from cold.
hacking-stock *n* a butcher's block.
hackit[1] *adj* **1** (*used of the tongue*) biting, caustic. **2** (*of hands or feet*) having hacks, chapped.
hackit[2] *same as* **hawkit**.
hackit[3] *adj* ugly, unattractive.
hackit-flesh *n* a charm of carrion for injuring a neighbour's livestock.
hackit-kail *same as* **hackum-kail**.
hackster *n* **1** a butcher. **2** a cutthroat.
hackstock *n* a butcher's block.
hackum-kail *n* chopped colewort, etc.
hackum-plackum *adv* in equal shares of payment.
ha'clay *n* **1** potter's earth. **2** a tough, clammy, blue clay used for colouring the walls of farm cottages.
had[1] *n* **1** a hold, grip. **2** a holding. **3** a house. **4** a den, an animal's hole. **5** a place of retreat or concealment. **6** a support. **7** a leading string. **8** restraint. **9** power of retention.
had[2] *v* **1** to hold. **2** to keep, maintain. **3** to look after, preserve. **4** to uphold. **5** to occupy, to keep busy. **6** to burden, harass. **7** to restrain, hinder, detain. **8** to withhold. **9** to be held as true or generally accepted. **10** to bet, wager. **11** to accept as a bargain. **12** to regard an engagement binding. **13** to preserve for stock. **14** (*of seeds*) to keep to the ground, come up short. **15** to go on one's way. **16** (*of things*) to go on. **17** (*of health*) to progress. **18** (*of the weather*) to continue. **19** to stay, remain. **20** to restrain oneself, refrain from. **21** to cease, stop. **21** (*used of fish*) to lurk for shelter.
had[3] *v* **1** took. **2** taken.
had a care *phr* **1** to take care. **2** to beware.
had aff *v* to keep off.—*int* a ploughman's call to his horses, in some districts to turn to the right, in others to the left.
had affen *v* to defend, protect.
had aff ye *phr* go ahead!
had again *v* **1** to resist. **2** to arrest, stop.—*n* a check, opposition.
had a hough *phr* to assist at a confinement.
had at *v* **1** to persist in. **2** not to spare or let alone.
had awa *v* **1** to hold off, keep away. **2** to wend one's way.
had awa frae *phr* except.
had back *int* a ploughman's call to his horses to turn to the left.
had by *v* **1** to go past. **2** to refrain from.
haddag *n* a haddock.
hadden *adj* held.
hadden and dung *phr* sorely worried and troubled.
hadder[1] *n* **1** a holder. **2** the part of a flail held by the thresher. **3** a needle cushion. **4** a niggard.
hadder[2] *same as* **hether**.
hadder and pelter *n* a flail.
haddie *n* a haddock.
haddies *n* a measure of dry grain.
haddies cog *n* a measure of dry grain, one-third or one-fourth of a peck.
haddin[1] *adj* **1** holding. **2** certain, sure.
haddin[2] *n* **1** the act of embracing. **2** a holding of house or land on lease. **3** property, living. **4** furniture, equipment. **5** farm stock. **6** an entertainment, feast, merrymaking.
haddin-caaf *n* a calf preserved for stock.
haddish *n* one-third of a peck, or, according to some, one-fourth.
haddo-breeks *n* the haddock's roe.
haddock-sand *n* sea ground frequented by haddocks.
had dog *n* a sheepdog.
hadds ye *phr* expressing the acceptance of an offer or bargain.

hade *v* hid.
had fit wi' *phr* to keep pace with, equal.
had forrit *v* to go forward.
had haal *n* a hold, grip.—*v* **1** to keep hold. **2** to offer sufficient resistance.
had in *v* **1** to confine. **2** to contain without leaking. **3** to save or limit expenses. **4** to keep up supply.
had in wi' *phr* **1** to curry favour. **2** to keep in one's good graces.
had o' health *n* a sign of health.
had on *v* **1** to stop. **2** to continue.
had out *v* **1** to pretend. **2** to affirm strenuously. **3** to dwell, lodge. **4** to present a gun. **5** to be of full measure or weight. **6** to suffice to the last. **7** to frequent regularly.
had-poke *n* **1** a beggar. **2** a churl.
had sae *v* to cease, give over.—*n* a sufficiency.
had the crack *phr* to keep conversation going.
had till'd *v* to be in health.
had to *v* **1** to maintain. **2** to go one's way. **3** to shut, keep shut. **4** to keep going or at work.
had up *v* (*used of weather*) to keep fair.
had up to *phr* to make up to, court, woo.
had up with *phr* to keep pace with.
had with *v* **1** to agree with. **2** to consume. **3** to indulge in.
hae *v* **1** to have. **2** to take. **3** to receive. **4** to carry to burial. **5** to understand.—*n* property.
hae and cry *n* **1** a fuss. **2** a hue and cry.
hae-been *n* an ancient rite, custom, institution or person.
haed[1] *v* had.—*ppl* taken for burial. *See* **hae**.
haed[2] *n* an atom, particle.
hael *same as* **heal**[2].
haellens *same as* **haillins**.
haem *n* (*in pl*) the two curved pieces of wood or iron resting on a horse's collar and supporting the traces.
haem-blade *n* the half of a horse's collar.
haem-houghed *adj* having troughs shaped like hames.
haemilt *same as* **hamald**.
ha'en *v* **1** had. **2** had to.
haen *same as* **hain**[2].
haerst *same as* **hairst**.
haet *n* an atom, whit, particle (*used generally with negatives*).
haev *n* a fisherman's hand basket for carrying bait.
haf[1] *same as* **haaf**[1].
haf[2] *same as* **haaf**[2].
hafer, haffer *same as* **haaver**.
haffet, haffat, haffit *n* **1** the side of the face. **2** the temple. **3** (*in pl*) locks of hair, especially on the temples.
haffet-clawing *n* face-scratching.
haffet-close *adv* very close together, cheek to cheek.
haffet-links *n* locks of hair on the temples.
haffins[1] *n* manners.
haffins[2] *same as* **halflins**.
hafflin[1] *n* a trying plane, used by carpenters.
hafflin[2], **haflin** *same as* **halflin**.
haft[1] *n* the right-hand side of a band of reapers.
haft[2] *same as* **heft**[1].
haft and point *n* the outermost party on each side in a field of reapers.
hag[1] *n* **1** an ill-tempered, violent woman. **2** a scold. **3** a dirty, slovenly woman.
hag[2] *v* **1** to hew, chop. **2** to hack. **3** to cut or carve clumsily. **4** to bungle.—*n* **1** a hack. **2** notch. **3** a stroke with an axe, etc. **4** a selection of timber for felling. **5** brushwood.
hag *n* wild, moorish, broken ground.
hag-a-bag *n* refuse of any kind.
hag-airn *n* a blacksmith's chisel.
hag and hash to hack and hew.
hagberry *n* the bird cherry.
hag-block, --clog *n* a chopping block.
hagsa *int* a disguised form of Jesus used in petty oaths and exclamations.
hagg[1] *n* **1** wild, broken ground. **2** a piece of soft bog in a moor. **3** a hole in a moss from which peats have been

cut. **4** a water hollow, wet in winter and dry in summer. **5** an islet of grass in the midst of a bog.

hagg² *n* **1** a stall-fed ox. **2** one who tends fat cattle.

hagg³ *v* **1** to harass. **2** to fatigue.

hagg⁴ *v* (*of cattle*) to butt with the head, to fight.

hagg *same as* **hag²**.

haggart¹ *n* a stack yard.

haggart² *n* an old, useless horse.

hagger¹ *n* **1** one who uses a hatchet. **2** one employed to cut down trees.

hagger² *v* to cut roughly and unevenly, hack, mangle.—*n* a large cut with a jagged edge.

hagger³ *v* to rain gently.—*n* fine, small rain.

haggeral *n* **1** a very large cut. **2** an open, festering sore.

hagger'd *adj* **1** mangled. **2** full of notches.

haggerdash *n* **1** disorder. **2** a broil.—*adv* in confusion.

haggerdecash *adv* topsy-turvy.

haggerin'¹ *n* the act of cutting unevenly.

haggerin'² *adj in phr* **haggerin' and swaggerin** in an indifferent state of health, not prospering in business, etc.

haggersnash *n* **1** offals. **2** a spiteful person. **3** tart language.—*adj* **1** spiteful. **2** tart.

haggerty-tag, ~-tag-like *adv* in an untidy, ragged manner.—*adj* ragged.

haggerty-taggerty *adj* tattered, ragamuffin.

haggies *n* a haggis.

haggils *n* trammels.

haggin *adj* given to butting with the head.

haggis, haggise *n* a sheep's stomach containing the minced lungs, heart and liver of the sheep, mixed and cooked with oatmeal, suet, onions, pepper and salt.

haggis-bag *n* **1** the sheep's stomach containing the ingredients of a haggis. **2** a windbag. **3** a contemptuous term for anything. **4** the paunch. **5** a lumpish, soft-headed person.

haggis-fed *adj* fed on haggis.

haggis-fitted *adj* (*used of a horse*) having the pasterns swelled like a haggis.

haggish *n* a haggis.

haggis-headed *adj* soft-headed, stupid.

haggis-heart *n* a soft, cowardly heart.

haggis kail *n* the water in which a haggis is boiled.

haggis supper *n* a supper mainly of haggis.

haggit *adj* **1** tired. **2** careworn.

haggle *v* **1** to mar a piece of work. **2** to work clumsily or improperly. **3** to struggle. **4** to advance with difficulty.

haggle-bargle *n* **1** one with whom it is difficult to come to terms in bargaining. **2** a stickler.

hagglie *adj* **1** rough, uneven. **2** unevenly cut.

hagglin *adj* rash, incautious.

haggling *adj* (*used of the weather*) vexatious, trying.

haggrie *n* an unseemly mass, a mess.

haggy *adj* **1** rough, broken. **2** boggy.

haghle *same as* **hechle**.

hagil *v* to haggle.

hagil-bargain, ~-bargin *n* **1** a stickler in bargaining. **2** a keen wrangle in cheapening a thing.

hagmahush *n* a sloven.—*adj* slovenly and awkward.

hagman *n* **1** a wood-cutter. **2** one who fells and sells wood.

Hagmana *same as* **Hogmanay**.

hagmark *n* a boundary mark.

hag-rid *adj* suffering from nightmare.

hag-ride *v* **1** to bewitch. **2** to give a nightmare to.

hag-stane *n* a boundary stone.

hag-wife *n* a midwife.

hagwood *n* a copsewood fitted for a regular felling of trees in it.

hag-yard *same as* **haggart**.

ha' hoose *n* the manor house.

hah-yaud *int* a shepherd's call to his dog to make a wide sweep round the flock he is driving.

haiches, haichus *n* **1** force, impetus. **2** a heavy fall and its noise.

haid¹ *same as* **haet**.

haid² *v* hid.

haid nor maid *phr* extreme poverty.

haig¹ *same as* **hag¹**.

haig² *same as* **hagg⁴**.

haig³ *same as* **haik²**.

haigel, haigle *v* to haggle.

haigh *n* a steep bank, a precipice.

haigle *same as* **hauchle**.

haigs *same as* **hegs**.

haik¹ *n* **1** a rack or manger for fodder. **2** a sparred box for holding turnips, etc, for sheep feeding in a field. **3** a triangular wooden frame with small nails for drying fish. **4** a rack on which cheeses are hung to dry. **5** an open cupboard hanging on a wall. **6** the part of a spinning wheel, armed with teeth, which guides the spun thread to the pirn (qv).

haik² *v* **1** to wander aimlessly. **2** to loiter. **3** to lounge. **4** to drag about to little purpose. **5** to tramp, trudge. **6** to beat, batter. **7** to kidnap, abduct.—*n* **1** an idle, lounging fellow. **2** an animal that wanders restlessly in a field or strays from it. **3** a forward, tattling woman, a gossiping gadabout.

haiked, haikit *same as* **hawkit**.

haiker *n* an animal that haiks in a field or from it. *See* **haik²**.

hail¹ *n* small shot, pellets.

hail² *v* to shout, roar.

hail³ *v* to drive a ball to the goal.—*n* **1** the cry raised when the ball is so driven. **2** the act of driving the ball so. **3** the goal at shinty, football, etc. **4** (*in pl*) a game resembling hockey played at the Edinburgh Academy. **5** the place for playing off the ball.

hail⁴ *n* **1** a small quantity of a liquid. **2** a drop.—*v* **1** to flow, run down in large and rapid drops. **2** to pour down.

hail⁵ *v in phr* **hail a hundred** a weaver's term.

hail⁶, haill *v* to haul, pull, drag along.—*n* a haul of fish.

hail⁷, haill *adj* **1** hale. **2** free from injury. **3** safe and sound. **3** healthy, vigorous, robust. **4** whole, complete, entire.— *n* **1** health, vigour. **2** soundness. **3** welfare, well-being. **4** the whole, sum total.—*adv* wholly.

hail an' a-hame *phr* **1** quite at home. **2** in good spirits.

hail an' fere *phr* in perfect health.

hail-an-hadden *phr* complete, entire.

hail-ba' *n* a boys' game at ball, known also as **han-an-hail**.

hail head *adv in phr* **to go hail head** to go on express errand or sole purpose.

hail-headit *adj* **1** unhurt. **2** whole and entire.

hail-heartit *adj* **1** of unbroken spirit. **2** with the whole heart.

hail-hide *adj* **1** unhurt. **2** safe and sound. **3** with a whole skin.

hailick *same as* **hallock**.

hailing-muff *n* a mitten used by fishermen to protect their hands when hauling their lines.

haill¹, haill² *same as* **hail⁶, hail⁷**.

haillick *n* the last blow or kick of the ball that sends it beyond the line and gains the game.

haillins *adv* **1** certainly. **2** completely.

hailly *adv* wholly, utterly.

hail-oot drinks *n* a toast calling to leave no heel taps.

hail-ruck *n* **1** the sum total of a person's property. **2** the whole of a collection of things.

hail-scart *adj* without a scratch, quite safe or unhurt.

hail-skinn't *adj* having a whole, unbroken or healthy skin.

hailsum *adj* **1** wholesome, health-giving. **2** sound.

hailumly *adv* certainly, completely.

hailware *same as* **hailwort**.

hail-water *n* **1** a heavy fall of rain. **2** a rush of rain like a waterspout.

hail-wheel *adv* **1** in wholesale fashion. **2** in quick succession.

hailwort, hailwur *n* the whole number of things or persons.

hailzin *n* **1** a vigorous setting-down. **2** a rude or angry salutation.

haim[1] *same as* **hame**[3].
haim[2] *same as* **haem**.
haimald *same as* **hamald**.
haimart, haimert *adj* **1** belonging to home. **2** home-grown. **3** home-keeping. **4** homely, simple. **5** condescending in manner. **6** not haughty. —*adv* homeward.
haimartness *n* a childish attachment to home.
haimhald *same as* **hamhald**.
haimo'er *same as* **hame-owre**.
hain[1] *n* **1** a haven. **2** a shelter, place of refuge.
hain[2] *v* **1** to enclose, defend by a hedge. **2** to preserve grass for hay. **3** to preserve from harm. **4** to shield. **5** to economize. **6** to hoard, to save for posible future use. **7** to be penurious. **8** to save exertion, spare trouble, etc. **9** (*with* **off** *or* **from**) to abstain from. **10** to cease raining. **12** to keep oneself chaste.
hainberries *n* **1** raspberries. **2** wild raspberries.
hainch[1] *n* the haunch.—*v* **1** to throw under the leg or thigh, by striking the hand against the thigh. **2** to jerk.
hainch[2] *v* to halt, limp.
hainch bane *n* the haunch bone.
hainch-deep *adv* up to the haunches.
hainch hoops *n* hoops over which the skirts were draped.
hainchil *v* to roll from side to side in walking.
hainch knots *n* bunches of ribbons worn on the hips.
hainch vent *n* a triangular bit of linen or gore between the front and back tails of a shirt.
hainer *n* a thrifty, saving person who takes care of his or her property, etc.
haing *v* to hang.
haingle *v* **1** to go about feebly. **2** to loaf about. **3** to dangle.—*n* **1** a lout, booby, a clumsy fellow. **2** (*in pl*) influenza. **3** a state of ennui.
haining *adj* thrifty, penurious.—*n* **1** a field in which a crop or grass is protected. **2** thrift, parsimony. **3** (*in pl*) earnings, savings.
haining broom *n* broom reserved for use.
haining time *n* the time of cropping, when fields or crops were enclosed for protection from cattle.
haip *n* a sloven.
hair[1] *n* **1** a filament of flax or hemp. **2** the sixth of a hank of yarn. **3** a very small portion of anything. —*v* to free from hairs.
hai[2] *n* the last pickle corn to be cut on a farm.
hair-and-wair *n* contention, disagreement.
hair-breed *n* a hairbreadth.
haired *adj* (*used of a cow*) having a mixture of white and red or of white and black on the skin.
hairen *adj* made of hair.
hairey *n* the devil.
hair-frost *n* hoarfrost.
hair-hanged, ~-hung *adj* hanging by the hair, like Absalom.
hairiken *n* a hurricane.
hair-kaimer *n* a hairdresser.
hair-knife *n* a knife used to free butter from hairs.
hair-lug *same as* **hare's lug**.
hairm[1] *n* harm.—*v* to harm.
hairm[2] *v* **1** to grumble, fret. **2** to be ill-tempered. **3** to keep on about a trifling fault, etc, and upbraid the offender.
hairmer *n* one who keeps on about trifles.
hairmin' *n* **1** fretfulness, grumbling. **2** the continuous harping on faults or trifles.
hairmless *adj* **1** unharmed. **2** safe and sound.
hair-mould *n* mouldiness caused by dampness.
hairn *n* (*in pl*) brains.
hairn pan *n* the skull, brainpan.
hairp *v* **1** to harp. **2** to keep on about something. **3** to grumble. **4** to reflect on one with repeated upbraiding.—*n* **1** a harp. **2** a wire instrument for sifting.
hairriel *n* what impoverishes land.
hairry *v* **1** to harry, plunder. **2** to rob nests.
hairse[1] *adj* hoarse.

hairse[2] *n* **1** a lustre. **2** a triangular frame for holding lights in a church.
hairselie *adv* hoarsely.
hairseness *n* hoarseness.
hair-shagh, ~-shard, ~-shaw *n* a harelip, a cleft lip.
hairshill *v* **1** to injure. **2** to waste.
hairship *n* **1** a foray. **2** booty, prey. **3** plundering by force.
hairst *n* **1** harvest. **2** an engagement for harvest. **3** any kind of autumn crop.—*v* to harvest, to work in the harvest field.
hair-stane *n* boundary stone.
hairst-bap *n* a large white roll given at lunch on the harvest field.
hairst-day *n* a day during harvest.
hairst-folks *n* harvesters.
hairst-hog *n* a sheep smeared at the end of harvest, when it ceases to be a lamb.
hairst-home *n* winter.
hairst-maiden *n* a figure formed of a sheaf, surmounting the last load of corn brought home.
hairst-Monday *n* a fair on the Monday occurring four weeks before the anticipated beginning of the local harvest.
hairst mune, ~ meen *n* the harvest moon.
hairst play *n* the school holidays during harvest.
hairst queen *n* the belle of the harvest-home dance.
hairst rig *n* **1** the harvest field or a section of it. **2** the man and woman who reap together on a rig (qv) of the field.
hairst roup *n* a sale by auction at a harvest fair.
hairst-shearer *n* a reaper at harvest with the hook.
hairst vacance *n* school vacation in harvest.
hairt[1] *n* heart.
hairt[2] *adj* (*used of clothes, linen, etc, in the open air*) partly dry.
hair-tether *n* a tether made of hair, supposed to be used in witchcraft.
hairturk *n* a cloth used for women's riding skirts.
hairy[1] *v* to harry.
hairy[2] *n* **1** a prostitute. **2** a slut.
hairy-brotag *n* any large, hairy caterpillar.
hairy-bummler *n* a name given to certain kinds of crabs.
hairy-hutcheon *n* the sea urchin.
hairy-moggans *n* hose without feet.
hairy-oobit, ~-oubit *n* any large, hairy caterpillar.
haiser, haisre *v* to dry clothes in the open air and sun.
haisert *adj* half-dried, surface-dried.
haisk *v* to make a noise like a dog when anything sticks in the throat.
haisle *v* **1** to dry, mellow in the sun. **2** to dry on the surface.—*n* the first process in drying linen.
haiss *adj* hoarse.
haist[1] *n* to make haste.
haist[2] *n* the harvest.
haister *v* **1** to speak or act without consideration. **2** to do anything in a slovenly manner. **3** to toast bread badly. **4** to serve a great dinner confusedly. —*n* **1** a person who does things confusedly. **2** a slovenly woman. **3** a confusion, hodgepodge, mess. **4** a great dinner confusedly set down.
haisters *n* one who speaks or acts confusedly.
haistert *adj* hurried.
haistines *n* early peas.
haistow *n* a call to make haste.
hait *same as* **haet**.
haith *int* an exclamation of surprise, etc, faith!
haitsum *adj* **1** unkind. **2** hateful.
haive *v* to heave.
haiveless *adj* **1** wasteful. **2** slovenly. **3** incompetent.
haiver[1] *a* gelded he-goat.
haiver[2] *same as* **haver**[2].
haiverel *n* a foolish talker.—*v* to talk nonsense.
haives *n* hoofs.
haivins, haivens *n* **1** manners. **2** good behaviour.
haiviour *n* behaviour.

haivrel *same as* **haiverel**.
haivrelly *adj* talking like a fool.
haizart *v* **1** to venture to do or to conjecture. **2** to hazard.
haizer, haizre *same as* **haiser**.
haizert *adj* half-dried.
haizie *adj* **1** dim. **2** not seeing distinctly. **3** muddled. **4** crazy.
hake *same as* **haik**.
hal' *same as* **ha'¹**.
halakit *same as* **hallockit**.
halan-~, halin-shaker *same as* **hallanshaker**.
halbert *n* **1** a halberd. **2** a very tall, thin person.
hald *v* **1** to hold. **2** to cease. **3** held.—*n* **1** a hold. **2** the bank of a stream under which trouts lie. **3** a dwelling.
halden *v* held.
halder *n* a holder.
hale *n* health.
hale an' wale *n* health and wealth, given as a toast.
hale head *adv in phr* **go hale head** to go on an express errand.
halelie *adv* wholly.
halend *same as* **hallan**.
halescart *adj* safe and sound.
halesome *same as* **hailsum**.
haleumlie *same as* **hailumly**.
haleware, halewar, halewur *n* **1** the whole. **2** the whole number of things or persons. **3** the whole caboodle.
hale-water *n* a heavy fall of rain, as if from a waterspout.
hale-wheel *adj* all at once, wholesale.
halewort *same as* **hailwort**.
half *n* (*in pl*) equal shares claimed by children who find anything.—*adj* (*preceding numerals indicating an hour*) half-past the preceding hour.—*v* to halve.
half-acre *n* a small field or allotment.
half-auld *adj* middle-aged.
half-bend *adv* (*used of a gun*) half-cock.
half-cousin *n* a first cousin once removed.
half-dealsman *n* a fisherman who shares in the profits.
halfer *same as* **haaver**.
half-fou *n* two pecks or half a bushel.
half-fou *adj* half-drunk.
half-gable *n* a gable common to two houses.
half-gane *adj* about the middle of pregnancy.
half-gates *adv* halfway.
halfjack *adj* half-witted.
half-lade *n* a large straw basket, two of which when filled and slung on a pony's back form a load.
halflin¹ *n* a carpenter's plane.
halflin² *adj* half-grown, youthful.—*n* **1** a half-grown boy, a stripling. **2** a farm- or stableboy. **3** a hobbledehoy. **4** a half-witted person, a fool.
halflins *adv* **1** half, partially. **2** nearly. **3** halfway, in equal shares.—*adj* **1** half, partial. **2** half-grown, young.
halflinswise *adv* **1** partly, in a slight measure. **2** half-heartedly.
half-loaf *n* half of a loaf which happens to exceed the number allotted to the reapers, which loaf, divided into two, is given, one half to the men and the other to the women, to be scrambled for.
half-mark ~, ~-merk bridal *n* a clandestine marriage.
half-mark kirk *n* a church in which clandestine marriages were formerly celebrated.
half-mark marriage *n* a clandestine marriage.
half-mark-marriage kirk *same as* **half-mark kirk**.
half-marrow *n* **1** a spouse. **2** yoke fellow. **3** mate.
half-moon flask *n* a large flask formerly used in smuggling and almost encircling the body of the smuggler.
half-mutchkin *n* half a pint.
half-net *n* the right to half of the fishing by one net.
half-nothing *n* **1** little or nothing. **2** next to nothing, a very small sum.
half-on *adj* well on the way to become drunk.
half-one *n* (*used in golfing*) the handicap of a stroke deducted every second hole.

half-penny deevil *n* a kind of cheap sweetcake.
half-roads *adv* halfway.
half-sarkit *adj* half-clothed.
half-sea *adj* tipsy.
half-water *adv* halfway between the boat and the sea bottom.
halfways *adv* half, partly.
half-web *n* **1** the red-necked phalarope. **2** the grey phalarope.
half-whaup *n* the bar-tailed godwit.
halicat, halicut *same as* **hallockit**.
halick *same as* **hallock**.
halidome *n* the lands holding of a religious foundation.
halison *n* a comfortable saying.
halk-~, hawk-hen *n* a hen formerly demanded from each house in Orkney to feed the king's hawks when his falconer went there to collect hawks.
halkit *same as* **hawkit**.
hall *same as* **ha'¹**.
hallach, hallach'd *same as* **hallock**.
hallachin *n* noisy, foolish conduct.—*adj* noisy, foolish.
hallack *n* a hillock.
Halla'-day *n* All Hallows Day.
hallan, hallen *n* **1** a partition wall in a cottage between the door and the fireplace. **2** the space within the partition. **3** a porch, lobby. **4** a screen. **5** a dwelling, cottage. **6** a buttress built against a weak wall to keep it from falling. **7** the space above the crossbeams of the couples of a house. **8** a turf seat outside a cottage.
hallan-door *n* an outer door.
hallanshaker *n* **1** a ragged fellow, tramp, beggar. **2** a knave, rascal of shabby appearance.
hallanshaker-looking *adj* unkempt, ragged in appearance.
hallan-stane *n* a doorstep, threshold.
hallarackit *same as* **hallirackit**.
hallens¹, hallins *same as* **halflins**.
hallens² *n in phr* **gae by the hallens** (*of a child*) to go by holds.
hallick, hallik *same as* **hallock**.
hallickit *same as* **hallockit**.
hallie *n* romping.
hallie-balloo *n* a hubbub, uproar.
hallier *n* a half-year.
halligit *adj* wild, giddy.
hallion *n* **1** a clumsy fellow. **2** a clown. **3** an idle, lazy scamp. **4** a servant out of livery. **5** an inferior servant doing odd jobs. **6** a domineering, quarrelsome, vulgar woman.
hallior *n* the last quarter of the moon when much on the wane.
hallirackit, hallyrackit *adj* **1** giddy, romping. **2** harebrained.
hallirakus *n* a giddy, harebrained person.
hallock *v* to behave foolishy and noisily.—*adj* crazy.—*n* a hoyden.
hallockit *adj* **1** wild, giddy, romping. **2** half-witted.—*n* **1** a romp, a hoyden. **2** a noisy, restless person.
halloo-balloo *n* an uproar.
hallop *v* to frisk about precipitately.—*n* a hasty, precipitate person.
halloper *n* a giddy and precipitate person.
hallopin *adj* unsteady, unsettled, foolish.
hallow *adj* hollow, sunken.—*n* a hollow, valley.—*v* to hollow, make hollow.
hallow-baloo *n* an uproar.
Hallow-day *n* All Hallows Day.
Hallowe'en *n* the eve of All Hallows Day.
Hallowe'en-bleeze *n* a bonfire kindled on Hallowe'en.
Hallow-fair *n* a fair held in the beginning of November.
Hallow-fire *n* a Hallowe'en bonfire.
Hallow-market *n* a market held on All Hallows Day.
Hallowmas *n* **1** the season of All Hallows. **2** the first week of November.
Hallowmas-rade *n* the general assembly of warlocks and witches supposed to have been held about Hallowmas (qv).

halls *same as* **hallens**.
hallum *n* the woody part of flax.
hally *adj* holy.
hally-balloo, ~-baloo *n* an uproar.
hally-bally *n* a great noise or uproar.
hallyie *n* romping.
hallyoch *n* a gabbling noise as heard in listening to a strange tongue.
haloc, halok *same as* **hallock**.
haloo-balloo *n* an uproar.
halowhou *n* **1** a child's caul. **2** a membrane.
halse, hals *n* **1** the neck. **2** the throat, gullet. **3** a defile. **4** a shallow in a river. **5** a hug.—*v* to hug, embrace.
halser *n* a hawser.
halshe *n* a noose, loop.
halt *n* **1** a defect. **2** a defect of speech.
halter *v* **1** to bridle. **2** to secure a husband.
haluck *same as* **hallock**.
haluckit *same as* **hallockit**.
halve-net *same as* **haave**.
halver *same as* **haaver**.
haly[1], **halie** *adj* holy.
haly[2] *adj* cautious, in no hurry.
halyear *same as* **hallier**.
ha'-maiden *n* **1** the bridesmaid at a wedding. **2** the maiden kimmer (qv) who lays the infant in the father's arms at a baptism.
hamald[1] *v* to prove anything to be one's own property.
hamald[2] *adj* **1** homely, domestic, household. **2** home-grown. **3** home-made, not foreign. **4** vernacular. **5** tame, not wild.—*v* to domesticate.
hamart *same as* **hameart**.
hame[1] *n* a ham.
hame[2] *same as* **haim**[2].
hame[3] *n* home.—*adj* to the point, direct.
hame-airted *adj* directed homewards.
hameald *same as* **hamald**[2].
hameart, hame-at *same as* **haimart**.
hame-blade[1] *n* a ham bone.
hame-blade[2] *n* the half of a horse collar.
hame-body *n* one not a stranger.
hame-bred *adj* unpolished.
hame-bringing *n* **1** bringing home. **2** importation, importing.
hamecoming *n* **1** arrival home. **2** festivities, etc, on an arrival home.
hame-dealing *n* plain speaking.
hame-drauchtit *adj* selfish, looking after one's own interests.
hame-drawn *same as* **hame-drauchtit**.
hame-fair, ~-fare *n* **1** the removal of a bride from her own or her father's house to that of her husband. **2** the homecoming of a newly married couple.
hame-gain, ~-gaun *n* a return journey.—*adj* going homeward.
hame-girse *n* private pasture in contrast to common.
hame-hatched *n* hatched at home.
hame-houghed *adj* (*used of a horse*) straighter above than below the hough.
hameil *same as* **hamald**[2].
hameit *same as* **haimart**.
hamel *same as* **hamald**[2].
hame-lan' *adj* (*used of farm servants*) living in the farmhouse.
hameld, hamelt *same as* **hamald**[2].
hameliness *n* **1** homeliness. **2** familiarity.
hamely *adj* **1** friendly. **2** familiar, at home.
hamely-spoken *adj* **1** plain-spoken. **2** unaffected.
hame-made *n* a home-made article.
hame-o'er, ~-owre *adj* **1** homely, humble. **2** rude, rustic. **3** coarse, unpolished. **4** home-keeping.—*adv* homewards.
hame-rout *n* the homeward way.
hamert *same as* **haimart**.
hame-sang *n* a song of home, country, etc.

hamesome *adj* homely.
hamespun *adj* **1** spun at home. **2** mean, contemptible, vulgar. **3** rustic, homely, humble.
hamesucken *n* the crime of violently assaulting a person in his or her own house.—*adj* **1** fond of one's home. **2** selfish.
hamet *same as* **haimart**.
hameward, hamewart *same as* **haimart**.
hamewith, ~wuth *adj* homeward.—*adv* homewards.—*n* self-interest.
hamhald *same as* **hamald**[2].
hamie *adj* homely, domestic, suggestive of home.
hamil, hamilt *same as* **hamald**[2].
hamit *same as* **hameart**.
hamlan, hamlin *n* a trick, wile.
hamly *adj* homely.
hammal, hammel *same as* **hamald**.
hammel *n* **1** an open shed for sheltering cattle. **2** a stage on posts to support hay, corn, etc.
hammer[1] *v* **1** to thrash. **2** to work or walk noisily and clumsily. **3** to walk carelessly. **4** to stumble. —*n* **1** a blow with a hammer. **2** clumsy, noisy walking. **3** a noisy, clumsy person. **4** the sledgehammer in athletic games.
hammer[2] *v* **1** to stammer. **2** to hesitate in speaking, hum and haw.
hammer-and-block, ~-study *n* a boys' bumping game.
hammer and tongs *phr* **1** high words. **2** (*in curling*) a stone played with sweeping force.
hammerer *n* **1** a big, clumsy person with unwieldy feet. **2** a noisy, clumsy worker.
hammerflush *n* sparks from an anvil.
hammergaw *v* to argue pertinaciously.
hammerin' *n* a severe thrashing.
hammerman *n* **1** a worker in iron, tin, etc. **2** a member of a blacksmiths' incorporation.
hammer-thrower *n* one who throws a large hammer in athletic games.
hammil, hammle *same as* **hummel**.
hammirt *same as* **haimart**.
hammit, hammot *adj* (*used of corn*) **1** growing close but short in the straw. **2** plentiful, with many grains on one stalk.
hammle *v* to walk in an ungainly, stumbling way.
hamp *v* **1** to halt in walking. **2** to stutter. **3** to read with difficulty and much mispronunciation.—*n* **1** a halt in walking. **2** a stutter.
hamper *n* one who cannot read fluently.
hamphis *v* **1** to surround. **2** to confine.
hamrel *n* **1** a heedless walker. **2** a frequent stumbler.
hamsh *v* to eat noisily and voraciously.
hamshackle *v* to prevent an animal from straying by fastening its head to one of its forelegs.
hamshoch, hamsheugh *n* **1** a sprain or contusion on the leg. **2** a severe bruise accompanied by a wound. **3** a severe laceration of the body. **4** a misfortune, an untoward accident. **5** a disturbance. **6** a harsh and unmannerly intermeddling in any business.—*adj* **1** much bruised and lacerated. **2** (*used of critics*) severe, censorious.
hamstram *n* difficulty.
han *n* hand.—*v* to hand.
han-an-hail *n* a game of handball played at Dumfries.
han'-ban' *n* a wristband.
hanbeast *n* the horse a ploughman guides with the left hand.
hanch *v* to snap like a dog when anything is thrown to it. **2** to devour greedily.—*n* a voracious snatch.
hanchman *n* a personal attendant, henchman.
hand *n* **1** an adept, clever performer. **2** handwriting. **3** a business or job, good or bad. **4** help. **5** the horse that walks on the left-hand side in ploughing. **6** direction. **7** a fuss. **8** (*in pl*) the use of her hands for a servant's own benefit in her spare time.
hand-afore *n* the fore-horse on the left hand in a plough.
hand-ahin *n* the last horse on the left hand in a plough.

hand-bellows *n* a small pair of bellows.

hand-bind *n* a grip in wrestling.

hand-bound *adj* fully occupied.

hand-braid, ~-breed, ~-brode *n* a handbreadth.

hand-canny *adj* handy with tools.

hand-canter *n* a quick canter.

hand-clap *n* a moment, instant.

hand-darg *n* **1** handiwork, toil. **2** wages of manual labour.

handed *adj* hand in hand.

handel *n* a slight refreshment before breakfast, a morning snack.

hander *v* to give assistance to someone in a fight by joining in.

hand-fast *v* **1** to betroth by joining hands for cohabitation before marriage. **2** to contract in order to marriage.

hand-fasting *n* cohabitation for a year with a view to ultimate marriage.

hand-frandie *n* a small stack of corn that can be reached by the hand.

handful *n* a heavy charge, task or responsibility.

handgun *n* **1** a pistol. **2** a popgun.

hand-habble *adv* **1** summarily and quickly. **2** off-hand.

hand-haill *adj* **1** hand-whole. **2** fit for one's work.

hand-hap *n* a chance, hazard.

handiconeive *adv* **1** in company. **2** conjunctly.

handicuff *n* a blow with the hand.

hand-idle *adj* idle, with unoccupied hands.

hand-ladder *n* a light ladder, easily carried by the hand.

handlawwhile *n* a little while.

handle, han'le *n* fishing tackle.—*v* **1** to secure. **2** to get money from. **3** to treat, deal with. **4** to drag up a curling stone by the handle.

hand-lecks *n* mittens.

handler *n* one who handles a cock in a cockfight.

handless *adj* **1** awkward in the use of the hands. **2** clumsy in working. **3** apt to let things fall.

handling *n* **1** business. **2** stewardship, charge. **3** interference. **4** an entertainment. **5** a merrymaking.

hand-making *n* manufacturing by hand and not by machinery.

hand-money *n* ready money.

hand-payment *n* a beating.

hand-plane *n* a smoothing plane.

hand-prap *n* a walking stick.

hand-rackle *adj* **1** rash in striking. **2** careless, inconsiderate. **3** active, ready.

hand reel *n* an old reel used for winding and numbering the hanks of yarn.

hand rick *n* a small stack not too high to be reached by the hand.

handsel *n* **1** an inaugurative gift for luck. **2** an auspicious beginning. **3** a good omen. **4** the first money received for sale of goods. **5** the first purchaser. **6** a morning snack given before breakfast. **7** guerdon, reward. **8** a punishment, a smack of the hand. **9** the earnest given on completing a bargain.—*v* **1** to give money, etc, to celebrate a new undertaking, possession, etc. **2** to inaugurate. **3** to drink success. **4** to pay earnest money on a bargain. **5** to try or use a thing for the first time.

Handsel E'en *n* the eve of the first Monday of the New Year.

handselling *n* the inauguration, first use, payment, purchase, etc.

Handsel Monday *n* the first Monday of the New Year.

handsel-smell *n* a smell instead of a taste in handselling liquor.

Handsel Tuesday *n* the first Tuesday of the New Year.

handsel-wife *n* the woman, usually the bride's mother, who distributes the gifts at a marriage.

handshaking *n* **1** close engagement, grappling. **2** an intermeddling. **3** a correction, punishment.

hand shoes *n* gloves.

hand-skair *n* the lowest part of a fishing rod.

handsome *adj* (*used of the weather*) fine, bright.

hand-spaik, ~-spake *n* a hand spike, used for carrying the dead to the grave.

hand-staff *n* **1** the handle of a flail. **2** a walking stick.

hand-stone *n* a pebble, a stone that can be lifted by the hand.

hand-streik, ~-straik *n* **1** a blow with the hand. **2** (*in pl*) hand-to-hand fighting.

hand's-turn *n* a single act of doing a piece of work.

hand's-while *n* a little while.

hand-thief *n* one who thieves with the hands.

hand-wailed, ~-waled *adj* **1** carefully selected. **2** picked by hand. **3** remarkable.

hand-wailling *n* particular or accurate selection.

hand-wave *v* **1** to strike a measure of grain with the hand. **2** to give good measure.

hand-waving *n* a mode of measuring grain by striking it with the hand.

hand-wealed *adj* picked by hand.

hand-write *n* **1** handwriting. **2** penmanship.

handy[1] *adj* **1** dexterous, clever. **2** useful, good. **3** suitable, seemly. **4** near by, close at band.—*adv* easily, without trouble.—*n* a child's hand, a small hand.

handy[2] *n* **1** a small tub or pail with an upright handle for carrying milk, water, etc. **2** a milk pail. **3** a wooden dish for food.

handy-fu' *n* the fill of a milk pail, etc.

handy-grips *n* close quarters in grappling.

handy-micht *n* main force, strength of hand.

handy-stane *n* a stone that can be thrown with the hand.

hane *same as* **hain**[2].

ha'net *same as* **half-net**.

han'-for-nieve *phr* **1** cheek by jowl. **2** abreast. **3** walking in familiar, friendly fashion.

hangall *v* to entangle.

hangarel *n* a stick, post or peg on which halters, bridles, etc, or anything may be hung.

hang-choice *n* the necessary choice of one of two evils.

hangers *n* braces for trousers.

hangie *n* **1** a hangman. **2** the devil. **3** a drift net.

hanging gate *n* a bar hung across a small stream to prevent anyone passing it.

hanging-lock *n* a padlock.

hanging-side *n* the side of a door to which the hinges are usually attached.

hanging-tow *n* a hangman's rope.

hangit *adj* cursed, damned.

hangit-faced *adj* having a look that seems to point to the gallows.

hangit-like *adj* shamefaced, hangdog-like.

hangle *v* **1** to delay a decision. **2** to hang in suspense.

hang-net *n* a net with a very large mesh.

hangrell *same as* **hangarell**.

haniel *n* **1** a greedy dog. **2** an idle, slovenly person. **3** a term of abuse.—*v* to have a jaded appearance from extreme fatigue or from slovenliness.

haniel slyp *n* an uncouthy-dressed person, an ugly fellow, a vulgar dependant.

haning *same as* **haining**.

hank[1] *n* **1** a rope, coil. **2** a knot, loop. **3** a lock of hair. **4** a skein of cotton, thread, etc. **5** hold, influence.—*v* **1** to make up into coils, etc. **2** to fasten, tie up. **3** to put together. **4** to gall with a rope or cord by tying it too tightly. **5** to catch or hang on a hook. **6** to muzzle.

hank[2] *n* the lee side of a boat.

hank[3] *v* to compress.

hanker *v* **1** to loiter, linger. **2** to loaf about. **3** to hesitate, ponder, hesitate in speaking.—*n* hesitation, doubt, regret.

hankering *n* hesitation.

hankie *n* a bucket narrower at the top than the bottom with an iron handle, used for carrying water.

hankle[1] *v* **1** to fasten by tight tying. **2** to entangle, involve. **3** to wind up into a coil.

hankle[2] *n* the ankle.

hankle[3] *n* **1** a quantity. **2** a considerable number.

hank-oarsman *n* the rower who sits near the helmsman.

hanky *n* a handkerchief.

hannie *same as* **handy**.

hanniel *same as* **haniel**.

hannies *n* oatcakes.

hanniwing *n* a term of contempt.

hanny *adj* light-fingered.

hans *n in phr* **hans in kelder** an unborn child, a toast formerly drunk to the health of an expected infant.

hansel *v* to handsel.

hansh *same as* **hanch**.

hant *v* **1** to practise. **2** to haunt. **3** to frequent, resort to. **4** to provide a haunt for.—*n* a custom, practice, habit.

hanterin, hantrin *n* a moment, a short space of time.—*adj* occasional.

hantle *n* **1** a large quantity or number. **2** much.

hanty *adj* **1** convenient, handy. **2** manageable with ease. **3** handsome.

hanyel, hanziel *same as* **haniel**.

hap[1] *v* **1** to cover, envelop, surround. **2** to cover for warmth, tuck up in bed. **3** to clothe, dress. **4** to cover over, bury. **5** to protect with a covering of earth, straw, litter, etc. **6** to thatch. **7** to conceal, hush up. **8** cover out of sight. **9** to shield, shelter. **10** to make up a fire so as to keep it alive through the night.—*n* **1** a covering, wrap. **2** a coverlet, rug. **3** a thick outer garment. **4** dress. **5** (*with* **up**) a heavy fall or cover of snow.

hap[2] *v* (*used of horses or yoke oxen*) to turn to the right.—*int* a call to a horse to turn to the right.

hap[3] *v* **1** to hop. **2** to dance. **3** to caper. **4** to limp. **5** to revolve. **6** to cause to hop. **7** (*of tears*) to drop fast.—*n* **1** a hop. **2** a rustic dance. **3** a light leap.

hap[4] *n* the fruit of the briar.

hap[5] *v in phr* **hap weel, rap weel** hit or miss.

hap[6] *n* an implement for scraping up sea ooze to make salt with.

hap-border *n* the border of a shawl or wrap.

hape[1] *same as* **hap**[2].

hape[2] *n* a halfpenny.

happen[1] *n* the path trodden by cattle, especially on high grounds.

happen[2] *v* **1** to befall, happen to. **2** (*with* **out**) to light upon, meet in with, come upon by chance.

happening *n* **1** an event. **2** a casual occurrence.—*adj* **1** casual, chance. **2** occasional.

happer[1] *n* the hopper of a mill.

happer[2] *n* a vessel made of straw for carrying grain to the sower.

happer-arsed *adj* shrunken about the hips.

happer bauk *n* the beam on which the hopper rests.

happered *adj* shrunken.

happer-gaw, ~-gall *v* to sow grain unevenly.—*n* a blank in growing corn, caused by unequal sowing.

happer-hippit *adj* **1** shrunken about the hips. **2** lank.

happie *n* **1** a rustic dance. **2** a short hop.—*v* to hop.

happins *n* clothes.

happit[1] *adj* **1** covered, wrapped up. **2** buried.

happit[2] *v* to hop.

happity *n* a man with a club foot.—*adj* lame.

happity-kick *n* (*used of an ill-assorted couple*) inability to walk together in step, incompatibility.

happle *v* (*used of tears*) to trickle, roll down the cheeks.

happorth *n* halfpennyworth.

happy *adj* lucky, fortunate, boding good luck.

happy-go-lucky *adj* at all hazards, by chance.

haps *adv* perhaps, perchance.—*n* **1** happenings. **2** strange occurrences.

hapshackle *v* to bind the feet of cattle together, to keep them from straying.—*n* **1** a shackle, fetter. **2** a ligament for confining a horse or cow.

hap-stap-and-loup *n* hop, skip and jump.

hap-stumble *n* a chance stumble.

hap-the-beds *n* the game of hopscotch or pallall (qv).

hap-warm *n* a warm wrap or covering.—*adj* covering to create or maintain warmth.

har[1], **harr** *same as* **haar**[1].

har[2] *n* the post of a door or gate to which the hinges are fastened.

harberie *n* **1** a port, harbour. **2** harbourage. **3** shelter.

harborous *adj* furnishing shelter.

harbour *n* **1** lodging. **2** hospitable entertainment. —*v* to give house room, hospitality, etc.

hard[1] *v* heard.

hard[2] *adj* **1** close-fisted. **2** (*used of spirits*) strong, undiluted. **3** (*of ale*) sour. **4** having unequal surfaces so as to prevent close contact of parts.—*adv* **1** (*used of the wind*) strongly, boisterously. **2** tightly, quickly.—*n* **1** whisky. **2** difficulty. **3** hardship. **4** the place where two pieces of wood join too closely together.

harden[1] *n* **1** coarse cloth made of the herd (qv) of flax or hemp. **2** sackcloth.—*adj* made of sackcloth or harden.

harden[2] *v* **1** to roast on embers. **2** to toast bread. **3** (*used of prices*) to advance.

harden-gown *n* a coarse linen or sackcloth gown, worn by offenders against the Seventh Commandment when under church discipline.

harden-poke *n* a bag or sack made of sackcloth.

hardens *n* the thin, hard cakes that come off the sides of a pot in which porridge has been boiled.

harden-sark *n* a coarse linen or hempen shirt.

harden-wab *n* a web of coarse linen cloth.

hard-fish *n* dried and salted cod, ling, etc.

hard-food *n* **1** dry food and corn as opposed to grass. **2** dry victuals as opposed to fluid or semifluid.

hard-handed *adj* stingy, niggardly, close-fisted.

hard-head[1] *n* **1** the grey gurnard. **2** the father-lasher. **3** a kind of sea scorpion.

hard-head[2] *n* a small coin of mixed metal formerly current.

hard-head[3] *n* the sneezewort.

hard-headit *adj* unyielding, stubborn.

hard-heartit *adj* heartbreaking, distressing.

hard-horn *adv* tightly.

hardiness *n* bravery.

hardlies *adv* hardly, scarcely.

hardlins *adv* hardly, scarcely.

hard-meat *n* hay and oats as opposed to grass or to boiled bran, etc.

hard-nickle-down *n* a game of marbles.

hard-pushed *adj* **1** hard-pressed. **2** hard put to it.

hards[1] *n* remains of boiled food, as porridge, etc, which adheres to the pot.

hards[2] *n* torches of rags dipped in tar.

hard-set *adj* scarcely able.—*adv* hardly.

hardship *n* a difficulty, a strait, a tight corner.

hard stuff *n* spirits, especially whisky.

hard-tree *n* hardwood, close-grained timber.

hard-words *n* abusive language, vituperation.

hard-wrocht *adj* hard-earned.

hardy *adj* **1** strong, robust. **2** of good constitution. **3** (*used of the weather*) frosty.

hare-bouk *n* the body of a hare.

hare-shard, ~-straw, ~-shie, ~-skart *n* a harelip.

hare's-lug *n* a particular kind of fishing fly.

haricles *same as* **harigalds**.

harie-hurcheon, hutcheon *n* a children's game in which the players hop round in a ring with their bodies resting on their hams and arms akimbo.

ha'-rig *n* **1** the right-hand rig (qv) of a company of reapers. **2** the first ridge in a harvest field, so called because reaped by the farm domestics or members of the farmer's family.

harigald *n in phr* **head and harigald money** a sum payable to colliers and salters in bondage when a female of their number, by bearing a child, added to their owner's property or livestock.

harigalds, harigals, harigells *n* **1** the pluck or entrails of an animal. **2** locks of hair.

hark *v* to whisper.—*n* **1** a whisper. **2** a secret wish or desire.

harken *v* **1** to hearken. **2** to hear one repeat a lesson.

harker *n* a listener.

harkie, harky *n* **1** a pig or sow. **2** a boar pig.

harking *n* a whispering.

harl[1], **harle** *n* **1** the reed or brittle stem of flax separated from the filament. **2** the side fibre of a peacock's tail feather, used for dubbing flies in fishing.

harl[2], **harle** *v* **1** to drag, tug, pull. **2** to trail along the ground. **3** to drag one's way with difficulty. **4** to draw oneself along feebly. **5** to scrape or rake together. **6** to grapple with.—*n* **1** the act of dragging or trailing. **2** a haul, collection, gathering of things. **3** money or property wrongly acquired. **4** a small quantity of anything. **5** that which is obtained with difficulty or rarely. **6** a mud rake or scraper for roads. **7** a slattern. **8** a big, untidy, coarse, cross person.

harl[3], **harle** *v* to roughcast a wall with a mixture of mortar and small gravel.—*n* the mixture used for roughcast.

harle[1] *same as* **harl**[1].

harle[2] *same as* **harl**[2].

harle[3], **harle-duck** *n* the goosander. **2** the redbreasted merganser.

harle[4] *same as* **harl**[3].

harle-a'-hame *adj* **1** selfish. **2** grasping.

harle net *n* a haul net.

harley *n* the swift.

harlin[1] *n* **1** roughcasting. **2** the mixture used for roughcasting.

harlin[2] *adj* slight.

harlin[3], **harlin-favour** *n* **1** some degree of affection. **2** an inclination or liking.

harl in the throat *n* hoarseness.

harmless *adj* unharmed, safe and sound.

harn[1] *n* coarse cloth of flax or hemp.

harn[2] *n* **1** (*in pl*) the brain. **2** brains.

harness cask *n* a receptacle on board ship in which meat, after being taken from the pickle cask, is kept ready for use.

harness lid *n* the lid or covering of a harness cask with a rim coming a small way down the outside of the cask.

harness plaid *n* a plaid of fine manufacture, formerly an indispensable part of a respectably married bride's outfit.

harnless *adj* brainless.

harnpan *n* the skull, brainpan.

harn-wab *same as* **harden-wab**.

haroosh *same as* **huroosh**.

harp *n* **1** a mason's oblong riddle for riddling sand, etc. **2** a kind of search (qv) for cleansing grain. **3** the part of a mill which separates the dust of grain from the shilling (qv).—*v* to riddle or sift with a harp.

harper crab *n* the crab, *Cancer araneus*, the Tammy Harper.

harr[1] *same as* **haar**[1].

harr[2] *same as* **har**[2].

harrage, harriage *n* service due by tenants in men and horses to their landlords.

harragles, harrigals *same as* **harigalds**.

harragraf *n* a designation of men not usually taken out to curling matches by the Kippen Club.

harran, harren *same as* **harden**[1].

harrie *adj* stubborn.

harren *n* (*in pl*) the brain.

harriment *n* spoliation.

harriat *n* harvest.

harro *int* **1** hurrah! an exclamation of surprise. **2** an outcry for help.—*v* to hurrah, halloo.

harrow *v* to arouse, stir.

Harrow Fair *n* an annual fair held in Edinburgh.

harrow plough *n* a plough for killing weeds in turnip fields.

harrow-slaying *n* the destruction of grass seeds by rain before they have struck root, when the mould has been too much pulverized.

harrowster *n* a spawned haddock.

harrow-teeth *n* **1** oppression. **2** exaction, extortion.

harry[1] *n* a harrow.

harry[2] *same as* **harrie**.

harry[3] *n* **1** the devil. **2** an opprobrious epithet applied to a woman.

harry[4] *same as* **herry**.

harry-hurcheon, ~-hurtchon *same as* **harie-hurcheon**.

harry-purcan *n* blind man's buff.

harship *same as* **herschip**.

hart *n* the heart.—*v* to stun by a blow given over the heart.

harvest kemp *n* a keen competition on the harvest field.

hary *same as* **harro**.

hasbeen *n* **1** a custom of long standing. **2** one of the old school. **3** a thing past service.

hase-bane *n* the neck bone.

hash *n* **1** a mess, muddle. **2** a confused mass. **3** a great crash. **4** careless, wasteful use. **5** noisy tumult, riotous strife. **6** nonsense. **7** ribaldry. **8** a heavy fall of rain. **9** a wasteful, slovenly person. **10** a foolish, nonsensical person, a blockhead. **11** a scamp. **12** a vulgar term of endearment for a boy. **13** work done at great speed and under great strain.—*v* **1** to slash. **2** to damage, destroy. **3** to bruise, ill-treat, abuse. **4** to make a mess of. **5** (*in harvesting with the scythe*) to cut so fast that the man behind the scytheman falls to the rear or the man in front is pushed forward by the man behind. **6** to move about or do something in a hurried or flustered way. **7** to overwork a person.

hash-a-pie *n* a lazy, slovenly fellow who is fonder of eating than of working.

hasher *n* a long knife with a handle, fixed on a board and worked with the hand, for slicing turnips, etc.

hashie *adj* coarse, rough.

hashieness *n* slovenliness in dress.

hash-loch *n* waste, refuse.

hashlock *n* the fine wool on a sheep's throat.

hashy *adv* in a slovenly manner.

hash-mash *adv* slapdash.

hash-methram *adv* **1** topsy-turvy. **2** in a state of disorder.

hashrie *n* careless destruction, reckless waste.

hashter *n* ill-planned or slovenly executed work. —*v* to work in a hurried, slovenly, wasteful manner.

hashter't *adj* hurried, flustered, flurried.

hashy *n* **1** a mess, muddle, noise, riot. **2** an old sermon preached over again.—*adj* **1** wet, sleety, slushy. **2** slovenly, careless. **3** wasteful, destructive.

hashy-holey *n* a boys' game.

hask *adj* **1** hard and dry to the touch. **2** harsh and dry to the taste. **3** rigorous, harsh.—*v* **1** to give a short, dry cough. **2** to clear the throat, hawk.

hask *n* the throat, soft palate.

hasky *adj* **1** dry, parched. **2** husky. **3** rank in growth. **4** coarse to the taste. **4** dirty, slovenly. **5** of coarse workmanship.

haslet *n* the liver, lights, etc, of a pig, etc.

haslie *adj* covered with hazels.

haslig *same as* **hashlock**.

hasloch *same as* **hashloch**.

haslock *same as* **hashlock**.

hasp[1] *n* a latch, clasp.—*v* to fasten with a latch.

hasp[2] *n* **1** a hank of yarn, worsted, etc. **2** the fourth part of a spindle. **3** (*with* **ravelled**) a difficulty. **4** confusion, disorder.

haspal, hasple *n* **1** a sloven, with his shirt neck open. **2** a clownish fellow.

haspan, haspin *n* a stripling.

hass *n* **1** the neck, throat. **2** a gap, opening.—*v* **1** to clasp round the neck. **2** to kiss.

hassie *n* a confused mass, a heterogeneous mixture.

hasslin tooth *n* a back tooth.

hassock, hassick *n* **1** a tuft of coarse grass. **2** anything bushy. **3** a shock of hair. **4** a large, round turf used as a seat.

hastard *adj* irascible.

haster, hasther *v* **1** to hurry. **2** to drive to work. **3** to fluster.

hastern, hastered *adj* (*of oats, etc*) early, soon ripe.

hastings *same as* **haistines**.

hastow *v with pron* hast thou?

hastrel *n* **1** a confused person. **2** one who is always in haste.

hasty *n* murrain in cattle.

hasty brose *n* brose (qv) hastily made with oatmeal and boiling water or milk.

hat¹ *v* did hit.

hat² *n* a heap.

hat³ *n* a salutation with the uplifted hat.—*v* to salute by raising the hat.

hat⁴ *v* to hop.—*n* a hop.

hatch *same as* **hotch**.

hatch-door *n* a wicket or half-door.

hatchel *v* to shake in carrying.

hatch-hole *n* a trap door.

hatchway *n* the sliding panel of a box-bed.

hate *same as* **haet**.

hateral *same as* **hatterel**.

haterent *n* hatred.

hatery *same as* **hatry**.

hatesum *adj* **1** unkind. **2** hateful.

hather *n* heather.

hathish *same as* **haddish**.

hatrel *same as* **hatterel**.

hatry *adj* **1** matted. **2** disordered, dishevelled.—*n* a jumble.

hatter *n* **1** an irregular and numerous gathering of any kind. **2** a great number of small insects crawling together. **3** a jumble. **4** an eruption on the face. **5** a collection of sores, a rush of pimples. —*v* **1** to harass. **2** to vex, hurt. **3** to exhaust. **4** to move in confusion and a mixed state. **5** to gather in crowds. **6** to speak thickly and confusedly.

hatterel *n* **1** a large quantity. **2** a jumble. **3** a collection of sores.

hatting owre the bonnets *n* a boys' game.

hattit kit *n* **1** a dish of sour or coagulated cream. **2** a preparation of new milk and fresh buttermilk.

hattock *n* a small hat.

hattrel *n* the core or flint of a horn.

hatty *n* **1** a form of the game of leapfrog, each boy leaving his cap on the back as he leaps over. **2** a game played with pins on the top of a hat.

hauber *n* oats.

hauch¹ *n* low-lying, level ground by the side of a river or stream.

hauch² *v* **1** to hawk, clear the throat of phlegm. **2** to expel anything from the throat by force of the breath. **3** to hesitate, hum and haw. **4** to make a fuss before doing anything.—*n* an effort to clear the throat.

hauchal *n* a deformed or crippled person.

hauchan *n* mucus expelled from the throat.

hauch-grund, ~-land *n* low-lying land by the side of a river or stream.

hauchle *v* **1** to walk lamely or with difficulty. **2** to hobble, drag the feet in walking. **3** to shamble.

hauchlin' *same as* **hachle**.

hauchs *n* the three points into which the upper part of a ploughshare is divided and by which it clasps the wood.

hauchty *adj* haughty.

haud¹ *n* a hold.—*v* **1** to hold. **2** to preserve a calf for stock.

haud² *n* a squall.

hauden held.

haudin *n* a holding.

haudin-calf *n* a calf kept to grow to maturity.

haud-richt *n* a safe, right and wise counsellor.

hauf¹ *adj* half.—*n* a half-measure or small glass of whisky.

hauf² *n* **1** a resort, place of resort. **2** a haunt.

hauf an a hauf *n* a whisky served with a half-pint of beer as a chaser.

hauf-an-snake *v* to divide equally.

hauf-cod *adj* half-tipsy.

hauflin *same as* **halflin²**.

hauf-on *adj* half-drunk.

haugaw *same as* **hawgaw**.

haugh¹ *n* a hough, hock.—*v* to throw a stone under the hough.

haugh² *n* low, level ground beside a stream.

haugh³, haught *v* to clear the throat.

haugh-grun' *same as* **haugh²**.

haugull *n* a cold, damp, easterly wind blowing from the sea in summer.

haugullin *adj* drizzling, damp and cold.

hauk *same as* **hack²**.

hauka *same as* **hawgaw**.

haukie, hawky *same as* **hawkie**.

haukit *same as* **hawkit**.

haukum-plaukum *adj* every way equal.

haul¹ *n* a large quantity or amount, as of money.

haul², hauld *v* **1** to hold. **2** (*used of trout*) to flee under a stone or bank for safety.—*n* a habitation.

hauking *n* fishing with a pock net.

haulket *same as* **hawkit**.

haully *n* a hauling, rough handling in dragging a prisoner, etc.

haumer¹ *n* a hammer.

haumer² *same as* **hammer¹**.

haumshoch *same as* **hamshoch**.

haun *n* a hand.—*v* to hand.

haunch *same as* **hanch**.

haunch buttons *n* the buttons on the back of a coat.

haunch knots *n* bunches of ribbon worn on women's gowns at the haunches.

haunchman *n* a henchman.

haunie *same as* **hannie**.

haunle *v* to handle.—*n* a handle.

haunless *same as* **handless**.

haunlins *n* festive parties.

haunsh *same as* **hanch**.

haunt *same as* **hant**.

hauntskip *n* a place of resort.

haunty *adj* **1** convenient. **2** not troublesome. **3** handsome.

haup¹, haup², haup³ *same as* **hap², hap³, hap⁴**.

haupie-stap-and jump *n* hop, step and jump.

haur *same as* **haar²**.

haur *same as* **haar¹**.

haurk *int* a huntsman's encouraging call to foxhounds.

haurl *same as* **harl²**.

haurn *v* **1** to roast. **2** to toast on the embers. **3** to fire a bannock.

haurrage *n* a blackguard crew of people.

haury *adj* foggy, misty.

hause *same as* **halse**.

hause-bane *n* the neck bone.

hauselet *same as* **haslet**.

hauselock, hausslock *same as* **hashlock**.

haut¹ *v* **1** to limp. **2** to hop.—*n* **1** limping. **2** a hop.

haut² *n* a grove, holt.

haut³ *v* to gather or rake with the fingers.

hauter *n* one who can hop.

haut-stap, ~-stride, ~-and-loup *n* hop, step and jump.

hauve *same as* **haave**.

hauve net *same as* **halve net**.

hauver *same as* **haver¹**.

hauver meal *n* oatmeal.

have *same as* **hae**.

haveless *adj* **1** wasteful, incompetent. **2** slovenly. **3** (*of manners*) unrefined.

havence, havens *same as* **haivins**.

haver¹ *n* oats.

haver² *v* **1** to talk at random. **2** to talk incoherently or nonsensically. **3** to hesitate. **4** to fuss about little or nothing. **4** to work lazily.—*n* **1** nonsense, foolish talk. **2** a piece of folly or nonsense. **3** a silly whim. **4** a stupid chatterer. **5** a lazy, idle fellow. **6** fussy hesitation. **7** one who hesitates.

haver[1] n (used as a legal term) **1** a possessor. **2** one who has information or deeds bearing on a case in court.

haver[2] same as **haaver**.

haver[3] v to toast before the fire.

haveral n **1** a half-witted person. **2** a talkative, garrulous person. **3** a fool.—adj **1** foolish, silly, nonsensical. **2** talking foolishy.—v to talk nonsense.

haveral-hash n a silly nonsensical person.

haver-bannock n an oatmeal bannock.

haverel n a gelded he-goat.

haverelism n a habit of foolish, nonsensical talking.

haveren n a sloven.

haverer n a foolish talker.

haver jannock n an oatmeal cake or bannock.

haver-meal n oatmeal.—adj made of oatmeal.

haveron same as **haverel**.

havers n **1** nonsense. **2** foolish talk.—int nonsense!

haversack n a bag hung at a horse's head, containing his oats, etc.

haver-straw n oat straw.

havres n **1** goods. **2** effects.

havings[1] n possessions.

havings[2] same as **haivins**.

haviour n behaviour.

havoc-burds n the large flocks of small birds that fly about the fields after harvest.

haw[1] adj **1** bluish-grey or pale-green. **2** livid, pale, wan.

haw[2] same as **ha'**[1].

hawberry n the fruit of the hawthorn.

haw-buss n the hawthorn tree.

hawflin same as **halflin**[2].

hawgaw n **1** a rag-gatherer. **2** a midden-raker.

hawgh same as **hauch**[2].

Hawick-gill n a liquid measure of half an English pint.

hawing adj **1** huzzaing. **2** resounding.

hawk[1] n a dung fork.

hawk[2] v to hesitate. **2** to hum and haw.

hawkathraw n a country carpenter.

hawk-hen same as **halkhen**.

hawkie n **1** a white-faced cow. **2** a name for a cow. **3** the bald coot. **4** a stupid, clumsy fellow. **2** a whore.—phr **brown hawkie** a barrel of ale.

hawkin' and swaukin' or **swappin'** phr **1** irresolute, wavering in mind. **2** in indifferent health. **3** struggling with difficulties in worldly circumstances, borrowing from one to pay another.

hawking adj sharp, hawk-like.

hawkit adj **1** (of animals) having a white face. **2** foolish, stupid.

hawk-studyin' n the steady hovering of a hawk over its prey before pouncing upon it.

hawk-teuchin clearing the throat of phlegm.

hawm v **1** to waste time. **2** to loiter. **3** to work in a slovenly way.

hawmer v to hammer.

hawmerer n a big, clumsy person with ungainly feet.

hawmering adj big and clumsy.

hawnet same as **half-net**.

hawnie same as **handy**[2].

hawse same as **halse**.

haw-stones n the seeds contained in the haw.

hawstane adj haughty.

hawthorndean n a species of apple.

hawtree n the hawthorn tree.

hawy adv heavily.

haw-year n a year in which haws abound.

hay[1] v to hie, hasten.

hay[2] n hay harvest.

hay-bird n the willow warbler.

hay-bog n a damp hay meadow.

hay-broo n a decoction of hay.

hay-dash n the turning and tossing of hay in drying.

ha' year olds n cattle eighteen months old.

hay-fog n **1** aftermath. **2** foggage after hay.

hay-folk n haymakers.

hay-fow n a hay fork.

hay-knife n a large knife for cutting hay in the stack.

haymakers n a country dance.

hay-mow n a large haystack.

hay-neuk n the stall where hay is stored for immediate consumption when brought in from the stack.

hays, hayes n the steps of a round country dance.

hay-soo n a large, oblong stack of hay, shaped like a sow.

hay spade n a sharp, heart-shaped spade for cutting the hay in stack.

hayworker n a haymaker.

hazardful adj hazardous.

haze[1] v to half-dry, dry on the surface in the open air.

haze[2] n the glazing of the eyes of the dying.

hazel oil n a drubbing.

hazel-raw n the lungwort.

hazel-shaw n an abrupt flat piece of ground, at the bottom of a hill, covered with hazels.

hazely, hazelly adj (used of soil) poor, light, loose.

hazie, hazzie, hazy adj **1** weak in understanding, crazy. **2** muddled. **3** dim. **4** not seeing distinctly. —n a stupid, thick-headed person, a numskull.

hazley, hazelly adj covered with hazels.

he n **1** the man of the house. **2** a male. **3** a man. **4** anybody.—adj having masculine manners or appearance.

head[1] same as **haet**.

head[2] n **1** the hair of the head. **2** the ears of grain on a single stem of corn. **3** the froth of ale, etc. **4** the hood of raw hide on the upper end of the soople (qv) of a flail. **5** a measure of wool or twine. **6** the higher part of a street. **7** a hill, an eminence. **8** the source of a river. **9** the volume of water in a stream. **10** (in curling) one single contest between two rinks, the majority of twenty-one heads winning the game.—adj **1** chief. **2** best.—v **1** to behead. **2** to have as a head or top. **3** to put in the head of a cask.

head and hide, head and tail adv completely.

headback n the rope that runs along the side of a herring net and carries the corks.

headband n **1** the band or rope fastening a cow to the stall. **2** the band at the top of a pair of trousers. **3** a headback (qv) of a herring net.

headbilke-dawkus n the person in chief charge, the presiding genius.

headbuil n **1** the best family residence on an estate, the manor house. **2** the chief estate.

head bummer n **1** the head of the house. **2** the principal person.

headbusk n a headdress, an ornament for the head.

headcadab n **1** a clever, sharp person. **2** an adept. **2** one quick of understanding.

head court n **1** formerly a court of justice for a county, a sheriffdom and a regality. **2** a special meeting of citizens called by the magistrates of a burgh for counsel and decision on matters affecting the community.

headcut n the cut of a fish which includes the head.

head dyke n a wall dividing the green pasture of a farm from the heather.

header n a stone or brick in a wall having the end outwards.

head hing n a droop of the head.

head hurry n the thick or the midst of any pressing business.

head ice n the ice at the tee of a curling rink.

head-ill n jaundice in sheep.

heading n scorn.

heading n an execution by beheading.

heading-hill n the hill where criminals were beheaded.

heading-man n a headsman, executioner.

heading-sheaf n **1** the sheaf placed on the top of a stack. **2** the crowning act.

headlace n a narrow ribbon for binding the head.

headless adj **1** thoughtless, heedless. **2** fatherless, orphaned.

head-light *adj* giddy, dizzy, light-headed.
head-lightness *n* dizziness.
headlins *adv* headlong, precipitately.
headman, headsman *n* **1** the master or chief. **2** an overseer. **3** a stalk of ribgrass.
head maud *n* a plaid covering head and shoulders.
headmost *adj* topmost.
headocks *n* a children's game of chance, with pins as stakes.
headrig *n* the strip of land in a field on which the plough turns.
headroom *n* **1** a sufficient height of ceilings, etc, room to move the head. **2** freedom. **3** opportunity to take liberty to do one's will. **4** the ground lying between a haugh (qv) and the top of a hill.
headrowm *n* the outer boundaries of a feu or toft (qv).
headset *n* a Highland reel or dance.
headshave, ~-sheaf *n* **1** the last sheaf placed upon the top of a stack. **2** the climax, finishing touch.
headskair *n* the highest part of a fishing rod.
headspeed *n* a state of great excitement
headstall *n* the head of a house.
headstock *n* a leader for the yearly cockfight, formerly common in schools.
headstone *n* (*in pl*) stones resembling various members of the body and lying round healing wells, used to rub the affected parts of the body corresponding to them.
headstoop *adv* in headlong haste.
headsuit *n* a headdress, a covering for the head.
headswell *n* jaundice in sheep.
head-theekit *adj* having the head covered.
head town *n* a county town.
head-washing *n* an entertainment given to his comrades and friends by one who has newly entered a profession, received promotion or made an expedition he never made before.
head-win *n* the leading band of reapers on the harvest field.
heady *adj* clever, giving proof of brains.
heady-craw *n* **1** the hoodie crow. **2** a somersault.—*adv* head-foremost.
heady-maud *same as* **head maud**.
heady-peer, head-y-peer, ~-a-peer *adj* equal in height.— *n* (*in pl*) equals, compeers.
heague *v* (*used of cattle*) to push with the head in trying their strength.
heal¹ *adj* **1** healthy. **2** whole.—*n* **1** health. **2** welfare. **3** nourishment.
heal² *v* to conceal.
heald twine *n* the thread of which the healds are made.
healey *same as* **heally**.
healfull *adj* healthy, healthful.
heal-hadin', ~-makin' *n* salvation.
healing-blade, ~-leaf *n* the leaf of the plantain.
heally *adj* **1** haughty. **2** disdainful. **3** high and mighty. **4** illtempered.—*v* **1** to esteem slightly. **2** to disdain. **3** to take an affront in silence. **4** to abandon, to forsake in contempt.—*n* **1** dudgeon. **2** consciousness of insult.
heally-fu' *adj* full of disdain.
health *v* to drink healths.
healthsome *adj* **1** wholesome. **2** health-giving.
healy *int* softly!—*adv* fairly, gently.—*v* to wait, be patient.
heam-houghed *adj* (*of a horse*) having its hindlegs shaped like the haims (qv) of a horse's collar.
heap *n* **1** one fill of the firlot, heaped till it can hold no more. **2** a great deal. **3** a slovenly woman.—*adv* **1** very much. **2** higgledy-piggledy.
heap-mete *n* liberal measure.
hear *v* **1** to treat. **2** to reprove.—*phr* **be heard for** to be heard of, or on account of, to be known for.
hearing *n* **1** information. **2** news. **3** a scolding. **4** an opportunity of preaching to a congregation as a candidate for the pastorate.
hearken *v* **1** to listen by stealth. **2** to hear a lesson repeated.

3 to listen to. **4** to whisper. **5** (*with* **in**) to prompt secretly. **6** to pay a visit.
hearkenin' *n* encouragement.
hearkenin'-win' *n* a comparative lull in a storm, followed by a destructive blast.
hearse¹ *n* **1** a lustre, a sconce with lights. **2** a frame for holding candles in a church.
hearse² *adj* hoarse.
hearst *n* harvest.
hearsto *v with pron* hearest thou?
heart *n* **1** the stomach. **2** spirits, cheer. **3** the middle of anything. **4** (*used of land*) good, fertile condition.—*v* **1** to strike or fall on the region of the heart. **2** to stun, to deprive of the power of breathing, sensation, etc, by a blow near the region of the heart. **3** to sicken, nauseate. **4** (*with* **up**) to hearten.
heart-anguished *adj* heartsore.
heart-axes *n* the heartburn.
heart-brunt *adj* very fond, greatly enamoured.
heart-eident *adj* with a firm or steadfast heart.
heartening *n* encouragement.
heartful *adj* sad-hearted.
heart-gashed *adj* cut or stricken to the heart.
heart-hale *adj* **1** heart-whole. **2** inwardly sound and healthy.
heart-hankering *n* heart-longing.
heart-hanking *adj* (*used of a maiden*) attractive and entangling the affections.
heart-heezer *n* a comfort, what cheers the heart or raises the spirits.
heart heezing *adj* exhilarating, heart-cheering, encouraging.
hearth money *n* a tax levied on each hearth in a house.
heart hole *n* the centre of a fire.
heart-hoves *adj* heaved from the heart, deep.
heart-hunger *n* a ravenous desire for food.
heart-hunger'd *adj* starved, very hungry.
heartie *n* **1** a little heart. **2** a child's heart.
heart-kittlin' *adj* heart-affecting.
heart-loup *n* a heartbeat.
heart-o'-the-earth' *n* the self-heal.
heart o' the nut *n* the main point.
heart-richt *n* the right or due of the heart or affections.
heart-sabbit *adj* sad, mournful.
heart-sair *adj* **1** heartsore. **2** annoyed.—*n* a great vexation.
heart-scad, ~-scald, ~-scaud *n* **1** heartburn. **2** bitter grief.
heart's-gree *n* delight.
heart-shot *n* a hearty burst of laughter.—*int* an exclamation after sneezing.
heartsome *adj* hearty.
heartsomely *adv* merrily, cheerfully.
heartsomeness *n* cheerfulness.
heart-thirled *adj* bound by the affections.
heart-wear *n* an illness of the heart.
heartworm *n* heartburn.
hearty *adj* **1** cheerful. **2** liberal. **3** exhilarated by drink. **4** having a good appetite. **5** plump, inclining to corpulence. **6** (*used of land*) in good condition.—*n* a term of address, a good fellow.
heary *same as* **herie**.
hease *same as* **heeze**.
heasie *same as* **heezy**.
heastie *n* the murrain.
heasty *adj* hasty.
heat *n* **1** a heating, warming. **2** a thrashing. **3** a round, bout.—*v* **1** (*used of hay or corn*) to become hot in the stack through premature stacking. **2** to thrash so as to heat the skin affected.—*adj* hot.
heathens *same as* **heath-stones**.
heather and dab *n* an obsolete style of roofing houses, etc.
heather-and-dub *adj* rough, poor, tawdry.
heatherbell *n* the flower of the heath.
heatherbill *n* the dragonfly.

heather-birn *n* the stalks and roots of burnt heather.
heather-bleat, ~-bleet *n* the common snipe.
heather-bleater, ~-bluiter, ~-blutter *n* the common snipe.
heather brae *n* a heather-clad slope.
heather-cat *n* **1** a cat becoming wild and roving among the heather. **2** a wild, roving person.
heather-clu *n* the ankle.
heather-cock *n* the ring ouzel.
heather-cowe *n* **1** a tuft of heather. **2** a broom made of heather.
heather-lintie *n* **1** the linnet. **2** the mountain linnet or twite.
heather-pesp, ~-peeper *n* the common sandpiper.
heather-range, ~-reenge *n* the hydrangea.
heather-tap *n* **1** a tuft of heather. **2** a broom made of heather.
heather-theekit *adj* thatched with heather.
heather-wight *n* a Highlander.
heathery *adj* **1** abounding in heather. **2** living among heather. **3** rough, dishevelled, hairy.
heather-heidit *adj* **1** (*used of a mountain*) having the summit clad with heather. **2** (*of the human head*) rough, dishevelled, with untidy hair.
heathshield-fern *n* the shield fern.
heath-stones *n* gneiss.
heauveless *same as* **haveless**.
heave *v* **1** to rise up, come into view. **2** to become swollen. **3** to puff up. **4** (*used of cattle*) to become distended by overeating fresh clover, etc. **5** to exalt, puff up with conceit.—*n* **1** a push, shove. **2** a throb, a heaving motion.
heaven's-hen *n* the lark.
heaviers *n* large-sized cattle, taken in to be kept during winter.
heavy¹ *adj* **1** (*used of the uterus*) pregnant. **2** advanced in pregnancy. **2** large, copious.
heavy² *n* a type of beer roughly eqivalent to English bitter.
heavy charge *n* a heavy trial or burden, such as the care of a number of young children.
heavy end *n* the worst, heaviest part.
heavy-fitted *adj* advanced in pregnancy.
heavy handful *same as* **heavy charge**.
heavy-headit *adj* dull, slow of apprehension.
heavy-heartit *adj* (*used of the atmosphere*) lowering, threatening rain.
heavysome *adj* **1** heavy, weighty. **2** dull, drowsy.
heawe-eel *same as* **haaf-eel**.
heben *n* ebony.—*adj* made of ebony.
hebenwood *n* ebony.
he-broom *n* the laburnum.
hebrun, heburn *n* a goat of three years old that has been castrated.
hech *int* an exclamation of surprise, contempt, sorrow, weariness, pain.—*v* **1** to cry 'hech!' **2** to pant.—*n* the act of panting, hard breathing.
hechen *n* the fireside.
hech-hey *int* heigh-ho!
hech-how *n* the hemlock.
hech-how *int* an exclamation of weariness or sorrow.—*adj* wearisome, causing one to say hech-how!—*n* bad circumstances or health.
hech-how-aye *int* heigh-ho! aye!
hech-how-hum *int* an exclamation of despondency.
hechle *v* **1** to breathe shortly and rapidly after exertion. **2** to exert oneself in climbing a steep incline or surmounting a difficulty. **3** (*with* **on**) to advance with difficulty as to bodily health or temporal circumstances.
hecht¹ *n* **1** height. **2** a hill, elevation. **3** a help, a lift up. **4** the greatest degree of increase.—*v* to lift up, raise.
hecht² *v* **1** to promise. **2** to vow. **3** to offer. **4** to threaten. **5** to call or name. **6** to be called or named.—*n* a promise, offer, engagement.
hecht³ *v* promised.
hech-wow *int* an exclamation of regret, depression.
heck¹ *n* a whore.
heck² *int* a call to horses to come to the left or near side.

heck³ *n* **1** a rack for cattle. **2** a wooden grating placed across a stream.
heckabirnie *n* any lean, feeble creature.
heckam-peckam, heckam-peckam-lass *n* the name of an angler's fly.
heck-door *n* the door between a farm kitchen and the byre or stable.
hecked *adj* (*used of cows*) white-faced.
heckery-peckery *n* a boys' game.
hecket *n* a hay rack in a stable.
heck-hens *n* an additional rent charge paid in fowls and eggs.
heckie-~, heckle-birnie *n* **1** a substitute for the word hell. **2** a children's game, of the nature of running the gauntlet.
heckle¹ *n* **1** a sharp pin. **2** a hackle, a comb with steel teeth for dressing flax and hemp. **3** a thorn in one's side.—*v* **1** to dress flax with a heckle. **2** to cross-question a candidate for parliamentary or municipal honours at a public meeting. **3** to examine searchingly. **4** to scold severely. **5** to tease, provoke.
heckle² *n* the neck feathers of a cock.
heckle-back *n* the fifteen-spined stickleback.
heckle biscuit *n* a kind of biscuit, punctured in baking by a wooden disc full of spikes or heckles.
heckle pins *n* the teeth of a heckle. *See* **heckle¹**.
heckler *n* **1** a flax-dresser. **2** a severe examiner. **3** a chastiser.
heckling *n* **1** flax-dressing. **2** questioning. **3** scolding. **4** a dispute.
hecklin kame *n* a comb with steel teth for dressing flax or hemp.
hector *v* to oppose with vehemence.
hed *v* hid.
hedder *n* heather.
hedder hillock *n* a heather-clad hill.
hedder-reenge *n* the hydrangea.
heddery *same as* **heathery**.
heddle twine *same as* **heald twine**.
hedge *v* **1** to protect. **2** to equivocate. **3** to shuffle in narration.
hedgehog-holly *n* the holly.
hedge-root *n* the foot of a hedge as a shelter.
hedge-spurgy *n* the hedge sparrow.
hedry *same as* **heathery**.
hedy-pere *same as* **heady-peer**.
hee *adj* high.
hee-balou *n* a lullaby.
heed *n* the head.
heed *v* held. *See* **had**.
heedrum-hodrum *n* a derogatory way of referring to traditional Gaelic music or singing.
heef *n* a hoof.
hee-haw *n* nothing at all.
heel¹, heel² *same as* **heal¹, heal²**.
heel³ *n* **1** the part of an adze into which the handle is fixed. **2** the part of a golf club nearest the handle. **3** the stern of a boat. **4** the bottom crust of a loaf. **5** the last remaining part of a cheese. **6** the end, finish, winding-up, close. **7** (*in pl*) increased speed to a curling stone by sweeping before it.—*v* **1** to take to one's heels. **2** to strike with the heel of a golf club. **3** to haul by the heels. **4** to send one heels over head on to one's back.
heelan' *same as* **hielan**.
heel-and-fling board *n* a springboard.
heel-cap *v* to patch stocking-heels with cloth.
heel-cutter *n* **1** a shoemaker's shaping-knife. **2** a shoemaker.
heeld *v* **1** to hold. **2** held.
heeld *v* to bend downwards or to one side.
heel-hole *n* the hole in the handle of a spade.
heelie¹ *same as* **heally**.
heelie² *same as* **healy**.
heeliegoleerie *adv* topsy-turvy.—*n* (*in pl*) frolicsome tricks.

heelifow *same as* **heally-fu'**.
heel-pins *n* two pieces of wood driven into the ground, forming a frame for the treddles of a loom.
heel-ring *n* a shoe heelpiece.
heel-seat *n* **1** a board over the bottom of a boat. **2** a seat at the stern.
heel-shakin' *n* dancing.
heel-shod *adj* having iron heelpieces.—*n* an iron heelpiece.
heele ower-body, ~-craig, ~-gowdie, ~-gowrie *advs* topsy-turvy, in great disorder.
heels-ower-head *adv* **1** topsy-turvy. **2** without particular enumeration or distinction.
heelster-gowdie *adv* head over heels.
heelster-head *adv* heels over head.
heel-strop *n* **1** the parting kick. **2** the finishing touch.
heely[1] *same as* **heally**.
heely[2] *same as* **healy**.
heemlin *adj* humbling, humiliating.
heemlin *adj* used of a continuous rumbling sound.
heep *same as* **heap**.
heepie-creep *adv* in a creeping, sneaking manner.
heepocreet *n* a hypocrite.
heepy *n* **1** a fool. **2** a stupid person. **3** a melancholy person.
heer, heere *n* **1** a filament of flax or hemp. **2** the sixth part of a hank or the twenty-fourth part of a spindle.
heeroad *n* the highway.
heery *same as* **herie**.
heeryestreen *n* the night before last.
heese *same as* **heeze**.
heesh *v* to scare away birds, etc.
heest *n* haste.—*v* to hasten, make haste.
heesty *adj* hasty.
heet *same as* **haet**.
heetie-kneetie *n* (*with a neg*) **1** absolutely nothing. **2** neither one thing nor another.
heevil *same as* **haaf-eel**.
heeze *v* **1** to hoist, heave. **2** to exalt. **3** to dance vigorously. **4** to carry hurriedly. **5** to travel fast.—*n* **1** a hoist. **2** help, furtherance. **3** a toss or lift of the head. **4** a swing. **5** swinging.
heezy *n* **1** a hoist, heave. **2** a lift or help upwards. **3** a tossing. **4** one who tosses another. **5** anything discomposing.
heezy *adj* creaking.
heff *same as* **heft**.
heffing *n* keep, maintenance.
heft[1] *n* **1** an accustomed pasture. **2** a resting place. **3** a domicile.—*v* **1** to accustom sheep or cattle to new pasture. **2** to dwell. **3** to domicile. **4** to become familiarized to a station or work.
heft[2] *v* **1** to confine or restrain nature. **2** to let a cow's udder get hard and large by not withdrawing her milk.
heft[3] *v* **1** to lift up. **2** to carry aloft.
heft[4] *v* **1** to pose. **2** to nonplus.
heft[5] *n* a heft, a handle.—*v* to fix, as a knife in its heft.
heft and blade *n* **1** the whole disposal of a thing. **2** the whole.
hefted *adj* (*used of cattle*) swollen.
hefted-milk *n* milk not drawn off from a cow for some time.
hefter *n* one who watches sheep in new pasture to keep them from straying.
heftet *adj* accustomed to live in a place.
hefty *adj* **1** weighty. **2** not easy to lift.
heg-beg *n* the nettle.
hegh *same as* **hech**.
heghen *same as* **hechen**.
hegh-hey, ~-how *int* heigh-ho!
heghe *same as* **hechle**.
heght[1] *n* a heavy fall.
heght[2] *same as* **hecht**[2].
hegs *int* an exclamation, a petty oath.
heh *int* an exclamation of surprise.

heich[1] *int* **1** a call to attract attention. **2** an exclamation of surprise, sorrow, etc.—*v* to cry 'heich!'
heich[2] *adj* **1** high. **2** tall. **3** (*used of an animal's ears*) pricked, erect. **4** protuberant, big. **5** (*of the wind*) north. **6** proud, haughty. **7** in high spirits, excited.—*n* **1** a height, hill. **2** a slight eminence, a knoll.
heichness *n* **1** height. **2** highness.
heicht *n* height.—*v* to raise.
heid[1] *same as* **head**.
heid[2] *n* state or quality, -hood.
heid an' heels *adv* completely, wholly.
heid-banger *n* **1** a wild person. **2** a crazy person.
heid-deester *n* the chief actor in a function.
heidie[1] *n* an informal name for a head teacher.
heidie[2] *n* an example of using the head to hit the ball when playing football.
heid-speed *n* a landlord, as contrasted with his factor.
heidsteen *n* a headstone.
heid-turning *adj* (*used of liquor*) intoxicating.
heidy *same as* **heady**.
heifer *v* to earmark castrated cows.
heiffle *n* a tussle with a young wench.
heigh[1] *same as* **heich**.
heigh[2] *adj* high.—*n* a height.
heigh-hey,-how *same as* **hech-how**.
heigh-jing-go-ring *n* a girls' game.
heigh-ma-nannie *n* in *phr* **like heigh-ma-nannie** at full speed.
height[1] *same as* **hecht**.
height[2] *v* promised.
heik *int* a call to horses to go to the left.
heild[1] *same as* **heal**[2].
heild[2] *same as* **heeld**[2].
heildit, heilit *v* held.
heilie *same as* **heally**.
hein-shinned *adj* with large, prominent shinbones.
heir-oye *n* a great-grandchild.
heirscap, heirskip *n* heirship, inheritance.
heirship *n* **1** a foray. **2** booty. **3** ruin. **4** mischief.
heirs-portioners *n* co-heirs or co-heiresses.
heis, heise, heize *same as* **heeze**.
heisie *same as* **heezy**.
heiyearald *same as* **high-year-old**.
held *v* **1** ran off. **2** took to heels. *See* **heel**[2].
helden *v* held.
heldigoleerie *same as* **heeliegoleerie**.
hele *same as* **heal**[2].
helie *same as* **haly**[1].
helie *same as* **heally**.
heliefu' *same as* **heally-fu'**.
helie-how *n* a caul or membrane.
helimly *same as* **hailumly**.
helit *adj* concealed. *See* **heal**[2].
helkite *n* a dishonest or shady person.
hell *same as* **hail**[7].
helldom *n* misery, utter wretchedness.
hellenshaker *same as* **hallanshaker**.
hell-, hell's-holes *n* dark nooks supposed to be haunted by ghosts.
hell-hot *adj* as hot as can be.
hellicat, hellicate *adj* **1** wild, unmanageable. **2** giddy, lightheaded. **3** extravagant.—*n* **1** a wicked creature. **2** a villain.
hellie-lamb *n* a ludicrous designation of a hump on the back.
hellie-man *n* the devil.
hellie-man's rig *n* a piece of land dedicated to the devil.
hellier, hellzier *same as* **hallier**.
hellim *n* a helm.
hell-jay *n* the razorbill.
hellocat *same as* **hellicat**.
hellock *n* a romp.
hellweed *n* the lesser dodder.
hellwords *n* words or spells of evil omen.

helly *same as* **haly**[1].
helm[1] *n in phr* **helm of weet** a great fall of rain.
helm[2] *v* **1** to turn. **2** to guide, govern.
helm[3] *n* a noisy crowd.
helmy *adj* rainy.
help *v* **1** to mend, repair. **2** to lift, to relieve of a burden. **3** (*with* **to**) to refrain from.
helpener, helpender *n* an assistant.
helper *n* **1** an assistant teacher. **2** an assistant to a minister.
helply *adj* helpful.
helter *n* a halter.—*v* to put on a halter.
helter-cheeks *n* **1** a halter or bridle encompassing the head of a horse or cow. **2** a cow wearing such a halter.
helter-shank *n* a rope attached to a horse's headstall.
helter-skelter *adj* **1** confused. **2** careless.
helter-skeltering *n and adj* hurrying.
hely *same as* **haly**[1].
hem[1] *n* the edge of a stone.
hem[2] *same as* **haem**.
hemlock *n* any hollow-stemmed umbelliferous plant.
hemlock-skite *n* a squirt made of the stem of a hemlock.
hemmel *same as* **hammel**.
hemmil *n* **1** a heap. **2** a crowd, multitude.—*v* **1** to surround a beast in order to capture it. **2** to surround with a multitude.
hemp *n* **1** a rope. **2** a halter. **3** a hangman's halter. **4** *in phr* **haud the hemp on the hair** to push on with arrears of work.
hempie *n* the hedge sparrow.
hemp-looking *adj* fit for the gallows.
hemp-riggs *n* fertile land on which hemp was formerly grown.
hempshire-gentleman *n* one who is qualifying for the gallows.
hemp-string *n* a hangman's halter.—*v* to hang by the neck.
hempy *adj* **1** wild, riotous. **2** giddy, reckless, romping.—*n* **1** a rogue, one who deserves to be hanged. **2** a giddy, wild, romping, mischievous girl.
hen *n* **1** a term of address applied to a woman or girl. **2** a term of endearment for a wife, etc.—*v* to break a bargain, withdraw from an engagement.
hen-a-haddie *n* a a fuss, an outcry.
hen-bauk *n* a rafter on which hens roost.
hen-bird *n* **1** a chicken following its mother. **2** a hen.
hen broth *n* chicken broth.
hench[1] *same as* **hainch**[1].
hench[2] *same as* **hainch**[2].
hench-hoop *n* the hoop worn by ladies in the 18th century.
henchil *same as* **hainchil**.
hench-vent *n* a gore, a piece of linen put into the lower part of a shirt to widen it so as to give vent for the haunch.
hend, hende *adj* **1** (*used in ballad poetry*) clever. **2** courteous.—*n* a young fellow.
hender *v* to hinder.—*n* hindrance.
hendersun *adj* causing hindrance.
hen-hearted *adj* timid, cowardly, chicken-hearted.
hen-laft *n* the joists of a country cottage on which the poultry roosted.
henmaist *adj* last, hindmost.
hen-man *n* a poultry-tender.
hen-mou'd *adj* toothless.
henners *n* a boys' swing-game.
hennie *n* a term of endearment for a woman.
henny[1] *n* honey.
henny[2] *adj* apt to draw back from a bargain.
henny byke, ~ beik *n* a honey hive.
henou *int* an order to a number of persons to pull or lift all at once.
hen-party *n* a tea party of wives exclusively.
hen-pen *n* **1** a hen coop. **2** the dung of hens.
hen's care *n* care exercised without judgment.
henscarts *n* fleecy clouds thought to betoken wind or rain.

hen's cavey *n* a henhouse.
hen's croft *n* a portion of a cornfield frequented and damaged by fowls.
hen's flesh *n* the state of the skin when the pores stand up through cold, making it rough like a plucked fowl, gooseflesh.
hen's gerse, ~-girss *n* a hen's keep.
hen's taes *n* **1** bad writing. **2** pothooks.
hen-toed *adj* pigeon-toed.
hensure *n* a giddy young fellow.
hen's ware *n* the edible fucus.
hent[1] *v* caught, laid hold of.
hent[2] *n* a moment of time.
hent[3] *adj* posterior, hind.
hen-wife *n* **1** a woman in charge of poultry or who sells poultry. **2** a man who meddles with his wife's department of domestic affairs.
hen-wifely *adj* like a hen-wife (qv).
hen-wile *n* a stratagem.
herald *n* **1** the diving goose. **2** the heron.
herald-duck *n* **1** the diving goose. **2** the dundiver.
herb *n* any wild plant used medicinally.
herbery *n* **1** a haven or harbour. **2** a shelter. **3** a small loch, a stream.
herbour *n* a shelter.—*v* to give shelter.
herd[1] *n* **1** a shepherd. **2** a farm servant or boy who tends cattle. **3** a pastor. **4** a guard placed on the ice in curling to prevent the winning stone being displaced.—*v* **1** to tend cattle, etc. **2** to drive away, scare. **3** to gather in a crop. **4** to keep in trust or charge.
herd[2] *n* the coarse refuse of flax.
herd club *n* the stick, partly notched in a peculiar way and generally made of ash, formerly used by herd boys in the northeast of Scotland.
herding *n* the place and work of a herd.
herding tree *n* a herd boy's stick.
herdship *n* the driving away of cattle wrongfully.
herd's-man *n* the common skua, thought to protect young lambs from the eagle.
herd-widdiefows *n* cattle-stealers.
hereabout *adj* belonging to the immediate neighbourhood.
here and were *n* contention, disagreement.
hereanent *adv* concerning this.
hereawa' *adv* in or to this quarter.—*adj* belonging to this quarter.
herefore *adv* on this account, hence.
hereschip *n* the plundering of cattle.
hereward *adv* hither, hitherward.
hereyesterday *n* the day before yesterday.
hereyestreen *n* the night before yesternight.
herezeld *n* the best beast on the land, given to the landlord on the death of the tenant.
herie *n* **1** a conjugal term of endearment. **2** a term addressed to a female inferior.
heritor *n* a landed proprietor in a parish, liable to pay public burdens.
heritrix *n* a female heritor (qv).
herle *n* **1** a heron. **2** a mischievous dwarf. **2** an ill-conditioned child or little animal.
herling *n* the salmon trout.
herling house *n* a net in which herlings are caught.
hern[1] *n* the heron.
hern[2] *same as* **harn**.
hern-bluter, ~-bliter *n* the snipe.
hern-fern *n* a plant taken from ditches for protection against witches, etc.
heron-bluter *n* the snipe.
heronious *adj* **1** careless. **2** bold, daring.
heronsew, heronshew *n* the heron.
herral *same as* **herle**.
herral-necked *adj* long-necked.
herrial, herrieal *n* **1** what causes loss, ruin. **2** a great, costly expenditure.
herrier *same as* **herryer**.

herrinband *n* a string warped through the different skeins of yarn to keep them separate when boiled.

herring drave *n* a drove or shoal of herring.

herring drewe *n* a herring drave (qv) as an attraction to idle fellows and bankrupts, so that a bankrupt who fled from his creditors was said to have gone to the herring drewe.

herring-soam *n* the fat of herrings.

herring-tack *n* a shoal of herrings.

herrin head *n* **1** a retreating forehead. **2** a person with a retreating forehead (*used contemptuously*).

herry *v* **1** to plunder. **2** to rob nests, etc.

herryer *n* **1** a robber. **2** a plunderer of birds' nests.

herrying the per man *n* a boy's game like smuggle-the-gig (qv).

herryment *n* **1** plunder. **2** the cause of plunder.

herry-water *n* **1** a net that catches small fish. **2** a person who takes all he or she can get.

hersche, herse *same as* **hairse**[1].

hersel' *pron* **1** used by a Highlander as the same as himsel' (qv). **2** a nickname of a Highlander.

hersel *same as* **hirsel**[1].

herseness *n* hoarseness.

hership, herschip *same as* **hereschip**.

herskit *n* heartburn.

hersum *adj* **1** strong, rank. **2** harsh.

hert *n* heart.

hert-sair *adj* heartsore.

hert-stawed *adj* thoroughly surfeited.

hervy *adj* **1** mean. **2** having the appearance of great poverty.

heshie-ba *n* a lullaby.—*int* a call to a baby to sleep.

he-slip *n* a lad, young boy.

hesp *same as* **hasp**.

hespy *same as* **hie-spy**.

hess *same as* **haiss**.

hester *v* **1** to hesitate. **2** to pester, trouble.

het[1] *v* to strike, hit.

het[2] *adj* hot, warm, comfortable.—*n* heat.

het[3] *n* the person who does the choosing in a game such as tig, it, etc.

het a hame *adj* comfortable at home.

het beans and butter *n* a children's game, like hunt the thimble.

het bitch *n* a bitch in the rutting season.

het drinks *n* warm, cordial drinks.

het-fit *adv* at full speed, immediately.

heth *int* an expletive meaning 'faith!'

het hands *n* a children's game of piling hands one on another and withdrawing them in rotation.

hether *n* **1** heath. **2** ling.

hetherig *n* the end of a field on which the horses and plough turn.

hethery *same as* **heathery**.

hetly *adv* hotly.

het pint *n* a drink composed of ale, spirits, etc, drunk on New Year's Eve, on the night preceding a marriage and at childbearing.

het rows and butter-bakes *n* a boys' game.

het seed *n* **1** early grain. **2** early peas.

het skin *n* a drubbing, thrashing.

het-skinned *adj* irascible, hot-tempered.

het-spurred *adv* at full speed, at once.

het stoup *n* a het pint (qv).

hettle[1] *adj* **1** fiery. **2** irritable. **3** hasty, eager.

hettle[2] *n* the name given by fishermen on the Firth of Forth to a range of rocky bottom lying between the roadstead and the shore.

hettle codling *n* a species of coaling caught on the hettle.

het tuik *n* a bad taste, as of meal made from corn heated in the stack.

het waters *n* ardent spirits.

het weeds *n* annual weeds, like field mustard, etc.

heuch[1], **heugh**[1] *n* **1** a crag, cliff, rugged steep. **2** a hollow,

a deep glen. **3** a deep cleft in rocks. **4** a coal pit. **5** the shaft of a coal mine. **5** a hollow made in a quarry.

heuch[2] *same as* **hooch**.

heuch[3], **heugh**[2] *n* a disease of cows supposed to arise from lack of water or from bad water attacking the stomach and eventually inflaming the eyes.

heuch[4] *v* hewed.

heuch bone, heuk bone *n* a kind of steak for grilling or frying.

heuch head *n* the top of a cliff or precipice.

heuchle-bane *n* the hipbone or joint, the huckle bone.

heuch-~, heugh-man *n* a pitman.

heuchster, heughster *n* a pitman.

heuch-stone *n* sulphate of copper applied to the inflamed eyes of cattle.

heuck[1] *n* **1** a reaping hook. **2** a reaper in harvest.—*v* to hook.

heuck[2] *same as* **heuch**[3].

heuck-bane *n* the hipbone, huckle bone.

heuck-stane *n* blue vitriol, used for removing the heuch disease among cattle. *See* **heuch**[3].

heuk[1] *v* to itch.

heuk[2] *v* to hook.—*n* **1** a hook. **2** a reaping hook.

heul *n* **1** a mischievous boy. **2** one who acts in a headstrong, regardless or extreme fashion. **3** a cross-grained person.

hevicairies *int* an exclamation of surprise, a contraction of 'have a care of us!'

hew[1] *same as* **heuch**[1].

hew[2] *n* **1** look, appearance. **2** a slight quantity, a 'dash'.—*v* to colour.

hew[3] *v* hoed.

hewl *same as* **heul**.

hewmist *adj* last, hindmost.

hexe *n* a witch.

hey[1] *int* a call to attract attention.—*v* to cry 'hey!'

hey[2] *n* hay.

hey-ma-ninnie *n* full speed.

heynd *same as* **hend**.

heypal *v* to limp, go lame.—*n* **1** sciatica. **2** rheumatic pains in the upper part of the thigh. **3** a cripple. **4** a good-for-nothing fellow. **5** a term of contempt.

heypalt *n* **1** a cripple. **2** an animal whose legs are tied. **3** a sorry-looking fellow or horse. **4** a sheep that casts its fleece as the result of some disease.

heyrd, heyrt *adj* furious, raging.

heytie *n* the game of shinty or hockey.

hey wullie wine and how wullie wine *n* an old fireside play of country people, the aim of which was, by rhyming question and answer, to find out the sweethearts of the players.

hezard *v* to dry clothes by bleaching.

hezekiah *n in phr* **proud as hezekiah** excessively proud.

hibble *v* to confine.

hic *v* to hesitate.

hiccory *adj* cross-grained, ill-tempered.

hich[1] *v* **1** to hoist. **2** to hitch. **3** to lift with an upward heave.—*adj* high.

hich[2] *int* an exclamation of surprise, sorrow, contempt, etc.

hichen *v* **1** to heighten. **2** to raise the price of an article.

hicht *same as* **hecht**.

hichtit *adj* in great anger, raised.

hick[1] *v* to hesitate in bargaining or speaking.—*n* **1** an expression of hesitation. **2** a stammer.—*int* a call to horses to turn to the right.

hick[2] *v* **1** to make a clicking sound in the throat like a sob. **2** to hiccup. **3** to cry at short intervals. **4** to whimper.—*n* **1** a clicking sound in the throat. **2** the hiccup.

hickertie-pickertie *adv* higgledy-piggledy, one upon another.

hickery-pickery *n* hiera picra, a drug compounded of Barbadoes aloes and canella bark.

hickety-bickety *n* a boys' outdoor game.

hid[1] *pron* it.

hid[2] *v* had.
hidance *n* shelter. **2** a hiding place.
hidder *adv* hither.
hidder and tidder *adv* hither and thither.
hiddie *same as* **hoodie**.
hiddie-giddie[1] *n* a disorderly noise, a disturbance. —*adv* **1** topsy-turvy, in confusion. **2** hither and thither.—*adj* confused, giddy, wanton.
hiddie-giddie[2] *n* a short piece of wood with a sharp point at each end, fixed on the trace for keeping horses or oxen apart in ploughing.
hiddie-pyke *n* **1** a miser. **2** niggard.
hiddils, hiddles *n* **1** shelters, hiding places. **2** concealment.
hiddle *v* to hide.—*adv* secretly, mysteriously.
hiddlin *adj* hidden, secret.
hiddlins *adj* secret, clandestine.—*adv* secretly, stealthily.— *n* a place or state of concealment.
hiddlinsly *adv* secretly.
hiddlinways, hiddlinwise *adv* secretly, by stealth.
hiddly *adj* **1** hidden. **2** sheltered from view. **3** concealing.
hiddrick *n* the head ridge on which a plough turns.
hide[1] *n* **1** the skin of a human being. **2** a term of contempt applied to the females of domestic animals, also to human beings, especially women. **3** the nap of a hat.—*v* **1** to beat, thrash. **2** to curry. **3** to skin an animal.
hide[2] *v* **1** to put carefully by. **2** to treasure.—*n* a hiding place.—*int* the cry given by the concealed player in hide-and-seek.
hide-o-seek *n* the game of hide-and-seek.
hide and hair *n* the whole of a thing.
hide-and-seek *n* blind man's buff.
hide-bind *n* a disease of horses and cattle causing the hide to stick closely to the bones.
hidee *n* the player who hides himself in hide-and-seek.
hide-i'-the-heather *n* a tramp, vagrant.
hidet *v pret* **1** hid. **2** hidden.
hide-the-mare *n* a child's game of searching for a hidden article.
hiding *n* a severe thrashing.
hidlance *n* **1** secrecy. **2** concealment.
hidle *v* to hide.
hidlin *same as* **hiddlin**.
hidlins *same as* **hiddlins**.
hidmaist *adj* hindmost.
hidy *adj* **1** hidden. **2** secret. **3** hiding.
hidy-corner *n* a secret corner in which to hide things.
hidy-hole *n* **1** a place in which a person or thing is hidden. **2** a subterfuge.
hie[1] *adj* high.
hie[2]**, hie-here** *int* a call to horses to turn to the left.
hielan', hieland, hielant *adj* **1** Highland. **2** silly. **3** clumsy.
hielan *adj in phr* **nae sae hielan** not so bad.
hielan' blue *n* Highland whisky.
hielan' Donald *n* a pony or sheltie (qv) formerly reared in the Highlands by the crofters and brought to the Lowlands.
hielan' fling *n* a Highland step-dance.—*v* to dance the hielan' fling.
hielan'-man's funeral *n* a funeral lasting more than a day and occasioning much whisky-drinking.
hielan'-man's ling *n* walking quickly with a jerk.
hielan' passion *n* a violent but temporary outburst of anger.
hield *v* to shield, protect.
hier *same as* **hair**[1].
hiersome *adj* coarse-looking.
hiertieing *n* a mocking or jeering salutation.
hiese *same as* **heeze**.
hie-spy *n* a form of the game of hide-and-seek.—*int* the call given by the players when ready in their hiding places.
hie-wo *int* **1** a call to horses to turn to the left. **2** also to turn to the right.

higgle *v* to argue.
high *same as* **heich**[2].
high-bendit *adj* **1** dignified in appearance. **2** aspiring, ambitious.
high-cocked hat *n* a hat with the brim thrice cocked.
High Court *n* the supreme criminal court in Scotland,
Highers *n* a Scottish school leaving certificate.
high-fies *n* swings at fairs.
high gate *n* the high-road, highway.
high-henched *adj* having high or projecting thighbones.
high heid yin *n* **1** a person in a position of authority. **2** an important person.
high jinks *n* an obsolete drinking game.
high-jumper *n* a parasite found in wool.
high-kilted *adj* **1** with short or tucked-up petticoats. **2** verging on indecency.
highland gill *n* two gills.
highle *v* to carry with difficulty.
high sniffingness *n* airs of importance.
high street *n* the highway.
high-style *adj* bombastic, grandiose.
hight[1] *same as* **hecht**[2].
hight[2] *v* to trust, resort to.
hight[3] *v* to raise, heighten, enhance.
high-twal' *n* midday.
high-year-old *adj* (*used of cattle*) a year and a half old.
hig-rig-ma-reel *adv* higgledy-piggledy.
high tea *n* a meal usually taken in the late afternoon or early evening consisting of one savoury course plus an assortment of scones cakes, etc, of the kind usually eaten at afternoon tea.
hig-tig-bizz *n* a form of words used by boys to startle cattle.
hike[1] *n* **1** to move the body suddenly by the back joint. **2** (*of a boat*) to toss up and down, swing.
hike[2] *same as* **heck**[2].
hilch[1] *v* to halt, hobble.—*n* a halt, a limp.
hilch[2] *n* a shelter from wind or rain.
hilch[3] *n in phr* **the hilch of a hill** the brow or higher part of the face of a hill from which one can get a full view on both hands of that side of the hill.
hildegaleerie, hildegulair, hiligulier *adv* topsy-turvy.
hildie-gildie *n* an uproar.
hill[1] *n* **1** a heap of rubbish or things in disorder. **2** a common moor.
hill[2] *n* a hull, a husk.
hillan *n* **1** a hillock. **2** a small artificial hill. **3** a heap.
hill-ane *n* a fairy.
hillan-piet *n* the mistle thrush.
hill-bird *n* the fieldfare.
hill-burn *n* a mountain stream.
hill-chack *n* the ring ouzel.
hill dyke *n* a wall dividing pasture from arable land.
hiller[1] *n* a small heap, a mound of rubbish.
hiller[2] *n* a stout, untidy person.
hill folk *n* **1** dwellers in hilly regions. **2** Covenanters, Cameronians or Reformed Presbyterians. **3** fairies.
hill-gait *n* **1** a hilly road. **2** a hill road.
hill head *n* the top of a hill or of an acclivity.
hilliebalow, ~baloo, ~belew, ~bullow, ~buloo *n* a hullabaloo, an uproar.
hilliegeleerie *n* a frolic.—*adv* topsy-turvy.
hilling *n* grazing on hill pasture.
hill-linty *n* the twite.
hillman *n* **1** a dweller among hills. **2** a Covenanter, a Cameronian.
hilloa *n* a call to attract attention.—*int* 'hullo!'
hillocket *same as* **hallockit**.
hill-plover *n* the golden plover.
hill-slack *n* a pass between two hills.
hill-sparrow *n* the meadow pipit.
hill-worn *adj* wearied with hill-walking.
hilly *adj* (*used of the sea*) rough, heaving, having huge waves.

hilly-baloo *n* an uproar.
hilly-ho *int* a hunting cry, 'tally-ho!'
hilsh *same as* **hilch**.
hilt *n in phr* **hilt and hair 1** every particle. **2** (*with* **nor**) nothing at all.
hilted-rung, ~-staff *n* a crutch.
hilter-skilter *adv* in rapid succession, helter-skelter.
hiltie *n* a crutch.
hiltie-skiltie, hilty-skilty *adv* helterskelter.
him lane *phr* himself alone.
himpie *n* a half-angry word called by a mother to a child.
himsel', himsell *pron* **1** the head of the house. **2** the husband as spoken of to or by his wife. **3** the master as spoken of to or by his servant. **4** one in full possession of his faculties.
hin *same as* **hind**[3].
hinch *same as* **hainch**.
hincher *n* a lame person.
hincum *same as* **hinkum**.
hind[1] *n* a farm servant, hired yearly and occupying a farm cottage.
hind[2] *n* a thin layer.
hind[3] *adj* **1** rearward. **2** belonging to the back. **3** spare, extra.—*n* **1** the rear, back. **2** the very last.—*adv* behind.—*prep* behind.
hindberry *n* the wild raspberry.
hind-chiel *n* **1** a youth. **2** a young fellow.
hind-door *n* the movable backboard of a box cart.
hinderin *n* the close, latter end, hind end.
hinderlets *n* the back parts, posterior.
hinder-line *n* the posterior.
hinder nicht *n* last night.
hinding work *n* a farm servant's work.
hindish *adj* **1** rustic. **2** clownish. **3** clumsy.
hindling *n* one who falls behind, a loser in a game.
hindmaist *adj* hindmost.
hind-squire *n* **1** a young fellow. **2** a young squire.
hine *adv* away, afar, to a distance.—*v* to take oneself off.—*n* a departure.
hine-awa *adj* faraway.—*adv* to a distance.
hin'-en' *n* **1** the last part, the latter end. **2** the backside, the buttocks.
hiner *same as* **hinner**.
hine-till *adv* **1** as far as. **2** to the distance of.
hing *v* **1** to hang, be suspended. **2** to hang, suspend. **3** to be in suspense.—*n* **1** the trick, fashion of a thing. **2** the knack of putting a thing.
hing an' hangie *v* to delay, dawdle.
hingar, hinger *n* **1** a curtain, hanging. **2** a pendant. **3** a necklace.
hingar-at-lug *n* an earring.
hing-dringing *adj* lingering, dwelling tediously on a topic.
hinged-brig *n* a drawbridge.
hinging[1] *n* a courting, wooing.
hinging[2] *adj* (*of a market or sale*) dull, not brisk.
hinging-chafted *adj* having pendulous cheeks.
hinging-lug *n* **1** a grudge or enmity towards one. **2** (*in pl*) despondency.
hinging-luggit *adj* **1** having drooping ears. **2** disappointed. **3** dull, despondent. **4** sulky, out of temper. **5** having a grudge at one.
hinging-mou'd *adj* in low spirits.
hingings *n* bed-curtains.
hinging-shouthered *adj* having sloping shoulders.
hingle *same as* **haingle**.
hing-thegither *adj* clannish.
hingum-tringum *adj* **1** in weak health. **2** in low spirits. **3** disreputable, worthless.
hin-hairst *n* **1** the end of harvest. **2** the time between harvest and winter.
hin-han' *adj* last.—*n* **1** the last of a series. **2** the last player in a curling rink.
hin-heid *n* the back of the head.
hink *v* to hesitate.—*n* hesitation, a misgiving.

hinklin *n* an inkling.
hink-skink *n* very small beer.
hinkum *n* **1** what is tied up into balls. **2** a young and mischievous boy or girl.
hinkum-booby *n* a children's singing game.
hinkum-sneevie, ~-snivie *n* a silly, stupid person. —*adj* stupid, lounging, slothful.
hinmaist *adj* the last, latest, final.—*n* the end, the last remains.
hin-man *n* **1** the man behind. **2** the man who is last.
hinner[1] *v* **1** to hinder. **2** to withhold or keep back from.—*n* hindrance.
hinner[2] *adj* **1** hind, hinder, back, posterior. **2** last, latter, as regards time.—*n* (*in pl*) **1** the posterior. **2** the hindquarters of an animal.
hinner en *n* **1** the back of anything. **2** the end. **3** the end of life. **4** the last remnant of anything. **5** refuse, the worst of anything.
hinner lans, ~ lats, ~ lets, ~ lins, ~ liths *n* **1** back parts, buttocks. **2** hindquarters.
hinnerly *adv* **1** at the last. **2** finally.
hinnermaist *adj* last.—*n* the latest.
hinner nicht *n* the last or latest night.
hinnersum *adj* **1** tedious. **2** wearisome. **3** causing hindrance or delay.
hinny *n* **1** honey. **2** a term of endearment.
hinny crock *n* a honey jar.
hinny mark, honey mark *n* a mole on the body.
hinny pig *n* a honey jar.
hinny-pigs, ~-pots *n* a children's game.
hin-shelving *n* an extra board put on the backboard of a box cart.
hin-side *n* the back, the rear.
hint[1] *v* **1** (*with* **about** *or* **after**) to watch quietly. **2** to go about quietly or slyly. **3** to teach quietly. **4** to indicate slightly.—*n* **1** an opportunity, occasion. **2** a moment of time.
hint[2] *v* **1** to disappear quickly, vanish. **2** (*with* **back**) to start back.
hint[3] *v* to throw a stone by striking the hand sharply against the thigh
hint[4] *v* to hurt.
hint[5] *v* to lay hold of.
hint[6] *v* to plough up the bottom furrow between rigs. *See* **rig**.
hint[7] *adv and prep* behind.
hint-a-gowk *n* the derisive name given to an April fool.
hin-the-han'*n* anything stored for future use.
hintins *n* the furrows with which ploughmen finish their rigs. *See* **rig**.
hint o' hairst *n* **1** the end of harvest. **2** the time between harvest and winter.
hip[1] *v* **1** to skip over, omit, miss. **2** to hop.—*n* an omission, the passing over.
hip[2] *n* **1** the border or edge of a district. **2** the shoulder of a hill. **3** a round eminence towards the extremity or on the lower part of a hill. **4** a protection, shelter.
hip[3] *same as* **hup**.
hip and hollion *adv* entirely.
hip-hop *adv* with repeated hops.
hiplocks *n* the coarse wool about the hips of sheep.
hippal *n* **1** sciatica. **2** rheumatic pains in the upper part of the thigh.
hippen, hippin *n* a baby's hip-napkin.
hippertie-skippertie *same as* **hippity-skippertie**.
hippertie-tipperty *same as* **hippity-tippertie**.
hippet, hippit *adj* **1** hurt in the thigh. **2** having the muscles of the back, loins and thighs overstrained by stooping at work. **3** wearied.
hip-piece *n* a piece of beef from the thigh of an ox.
hippie-dippie *n* **1** a castigation. **2** a slapping on the hips or buttocks.
hippit *adj* **1** passed over. **2** exempted. **3** excused.
hippity-haincher, ~-hincher *n* a lame person.

hippiter-skippertie *adv* in a frisking, skipping fashion.

hippity-tippertie *adj* **1** unstable. **2** flighty, frivolous. **3** childishly exact. **4** affectedly neat.

hip-shot, ~-shotten *adj* lamed in the hip, with a sprained or dislocated thigh.

hip-the-beds *n* the game of hopscotch.

hirch *v* **1** to shiver. **2** to thrill with cold. **3** to shrug the shoulders.—*n* a shrug.

hirch and kick *n* a kicking game in which the player had no other impetus than a shrug of the shoulders when toeing the line.

hird *v* to tend cattle.—*n* **1** a flock, a herd. **2** a cattle-tender, shepherd.

hirdie-club *n* a herd's stick or club.

hirdie-girdie *same as* **hiddie-giddie**.

hirdsale, hirdsel *same as* **hirsel**.

hirdum-dirdum *n* **1** confusion. **2** noisy mirth, uproar.—*adj* uproarious, confused.—*adv* topsy-turvy.

hire[1] *v* **1** to enrich land with various manures. **2** to make food palatable or appetizing.

hire[2] *v* **1** to let on hire. **2** to engage as a servant. **3** to accept, welcome.—*n* a dealing, trading transaction.

hired *adj* (*used of food*) seasoned with various condiments.

hire house *n* **1** service. **2** the place or house to which a servant is engaged to go.

hire-man *n* a hired servant, farm labourer.

hire-quean *n* a servant girl.

hirer *n* **1** a person engaged for farm work by the day or for a short time. **2** one who lets on hire. **3** a horse jobber.

hireship *n* **1** service. **2** the place of a servant.

hirewoman *n* a maidservant.

hirie-harie *same as* **hirrie-harrie**.

hiring pint *n* drink consumed at the hiring of a horse, etc.

hirling *same as* **herling**.

hirm *same as* **hairm**[2].

hirne *n* a corner, recess.

hirp *same as* **harp**.

hirple, hirpil *v* **1** to limp, walk as a cripple. **2** to move unevenly, hobble.—*n* **1** a limp, halt. **2** a cripple.

hirpledird *v* to walk lamely with a rebounding motion.

hirploch, hirplock *n* a cripple, a lame creature.

hirr *v* to hound on a dog.— *int* **1** an expression used in hounding on a dog. **2** a herd's call to his dog to drive up cattle.

hirrie *same as* **herry**.

hirrie-harrie *n* **1** the hue and cry after a thief. **2** a broil, tumult.—*adv* tumultuously.

hirro *int* hurrah! an outcry for help.—*v* to hurrah, halloo.

hirsel[1]**, hirsle**[1] *n* **1** a flock of sheep. **2** the stock of sheep on a farm. **3** a spiritual flock. **4** the feeding place of a flock of sheep. **5** a gathering, company. **6** a large collection of people or of things.—*v* **1** to arrange different kinds of sheep in separate flocks. **2** to arrange or dispose persons in order.

hirsel[2]**, hirsle**[2]**, hirschle** *v* **1** to move or glide resting on the hams. **2** to slide with grazing or friction. **3** to move in a creeping or trailing manner with a slight grating noise. **4** to move a body with much friction or effort. **5** to cause to slide. **6** to work in a hurried, careless or slovenly fashion. **7** to be slovenly in dress.—*n* **1** a sliding, grazing movement. **2** the noise made by a heavy body being drawn over another. **3** an auger used for boring when red-hot.

hirsel aff *v* to die easily or gently.

hirsel yont *v* to move farther off.

hirsil-rinning *adj* gathering sheep at a distance.

hirsp *v* **1** to jar. **2** to rasp.

hirst[1] *n* **1** a resting place. **2** a small eminence on rising ground. **3** a small wood. **4** a ridge. **5** a bank. **6** the bare, hard summit of a hill. **7** a sandbank on the brink of a river. **8** a shallow in a river. **9** a sloping bank or wall of stonework, formerly used in mills as a substitute for a stair.

hirst[2] *n* **1** a great number. **2** a large quantity of anything.

hirst[3] *v* to slide with grazing or friction.

hirstin *n* a dwelling place.

hirstle *same as* **hurstle**.

hirstlin *n* the sound of rough breathing.—*adj* wheezing.

hirsty *adj* dry, bare, barren.

hirtch *v* **1** to move gradually or with jerks. **2** to approach slyly or in wheedling fashion.—*n* a slight motion or jerk, a slight push.

hirtchin-harie *n* a children's game.

His *poss pron* God's.

hise *same as* **heeze**.

hish[1] *same as* **hiss**.

hish[2] *n* hush!

hishie[1] *v* to lull to sleep, to sing a lullaby.

hishie[2] *n in phr* **neither hishie nor wishie** not the slightest sound.

hishie-ba, ~-baw *int* an expression used in lulling a child to sleep.—*n* a lullaby.—*v* to lull to sleep.

hisht *int* hush!

hisk, hiskie *int* a call to a dog.—*n* **1** a dog. **2** a hissing sound.

his lane *phr* himself alone.

hiss *v* to drive off an animal or hound on a dog by making a hissing sound.—*n* a sound used in so doing.

hissel *same as* **hirsel**.

hissel', his sel' *pron* himself (*used emphatically*).

hissie *n* **1** a housewife. **2** a hussy (*used contemptuously*). **3** a young girl, a lass, wench. **4** a mare, a jade. **5** a needle case, a case for needles, thread, etc.

hissieskip *n* housewifery.

hist[1] *same as* **hirst**[2].

hist[2] *v* **1** to haste. **2** to hasten.

hist away by *int* a shepherd's call to his dog to be off.

hist-hast *n* a confusion, disorder.

histie *same as* **hirsty**.

historicals *n* historical statements, history.

hit[1] *v* **1** to throw forcibly. **2** (*with* **if**) to manage, succeed. **3** to agree.

hit[2] *pron* **1** it (*used emphatically*). **2** the 'he' or 'she' in certain games.

hitch *v* **1** to move about with jerks. **2** to hop on one leg. **3** to creep. **4** to linger.—*n* **1** a sudden movement. **2** a push, a slight temporary assistance. **3** a difficulty. **4** an obstruction in mining when the coal seam is interrupted by a different stratum or sudden rise or inequality. **5** a row of knitting.

hite *adj* **1** furious, mad. **2** excessively keen.

hither-and-yont *adv* **1** hither and thither. **2** backwards and forwards. **3** topsy-turvy, in confusion.

hitherwa *adv* hither.

hither-come *n* advent, descent, pedigree.

hither-thither *adv* hither and thither.

hithin *n* the eye of the souple (qv) of a flail, the hooding (qv).

hithom-tithom *n* a dish of sweet and sour sowens (qv).

hitten *v* hit, struck.

hiv[1] *n* a hoof.

hiv[2] *v* to have.

hive[1] *n* a crowd, a swarm of people.—*v* to go in crowds.

hive[2] *v* **1** to swell. **2** to cause to swell.

hive[3] *n* a haven.

hives *n* **1** any eruption on the skin from an internal cause. **2** the red and the yellow gum. **3** a feverish complaint among children.

hivie *adj* **1** in easy circumstances. **2** well-to-do. **3** affluent.

hiving-sough *n* the peculiar buzzing sound made by bees before they hive.

hiz[1] *pron* us.

hiz[2] *v* has.

hizard *same as* **hezard**.

hize *v* **1** to ramble. **2** to romp about.

hizzie *same as* **hissie**.

hizzie-fallow, ~-fellow *n* a man who does what is considered to be the work of a housewife.

hniusle *v* to nuzzle.

ho[1] *n* a stop, delay, cessation.

ho[2] *n* a stocking.

ho[3] *n* **1** a cover. **2** a coif, headdress. **3** a nightcap. **4** a child's caul.

hoak *same as* **howk**[2].

hoakie[1] *n* a fire that has been covered up with cinders, when all the fuel has become red.

hoakie[2] *int* used as a petty oath.

hoam[1] *n* **1** level, low ground beside a stream, a holm. **2** an islet, an island in a lake. **3** a depression, hollow.

hoam[2] *n* the dried grease of a cod.

hoam[3] *v* **1** to give a disagreeable taste to food by confining the steam in the pot when boiling. **2** to spoil provisions by keeping them in a confined place.

hoam'd *adj* (*used of animal food*) having a stale taste from being kept too long.

hoars *n* white hairs. **2** old age.

hoarse *n* a hoarse note of a fowl.

hoars-gowk *n* **1** the common snipe. **2** the green sandpiper.

hoast *n* **1** a cough. **2** a hem, a vulgar mode of calling on one to stop. **3** a matter attended with no difficulty.—*v* **1** to cough. **2** to belch up, bring forth. **3** to hem, to call on one to stop.

hoatching *adj* very busy or crowded. —*in phr* **hoatching with 1** full of. **2** infested with

hoatie, hoats *n* a term used in the game of pearie (qv) or peg-top, of a pearie that bounces out of the ring without spinning.

hob-and-nob *v* to hobnob.

hobble, hoble *same as* **habble**[2].

hobble *n* **1** a fool. **2** a blockhead.

hobble-bog *n* **1** a quagmire. **2** soft, wet, quaking ground.

hobbled *adj* **1** perplexed. **2** put about. **3** confined.

hobble-quo *n* **1** a quagmire. **2** a scrape, dilemma.

hobbler *n* a stout ferry-boat.

hobbleshow, hobbleshaw, hobbleshew, hobbleshue *n* **1** a hubbub, tumult. **2** commotion. **3** a rabble. **4** a tumultuous gathering.

hobblie *adj* (*used of ground*) soft, quaking under foot.

hobby *n* the merlin.

hobby-horse *n* a hobby, favourite avocation.

hobby-tobby *n* the appearance, dress, etc, of an awkward, tawdry woman.

hob collinwood *n* the four of hearts in the game of whist.

hobois *int* a hunting cry to the dogs.

hoboy *n* **1** a hautboy or oboe. **2** a player on the hautboy.

hobshanks *n* knees.

hoburn saugh *n* the laburnum.

hoch[1] *n* **1** the leg of an animal. **2** the leg or lower part of a person's thigh. **3** the ham, thigh, hip.—*v* **1** to hamstring. **2** to throw a missile under the thigh. **3** to throw the leg over a person in contempt of his small stature. **4** to tramp, trudge along.

hoch[2] *int* an exclamation of grief, weariness, joy, etc.

hoch-anee *int* an exclamation of grief.

hoch-ban *n* a band passing round the neck and one of the legs of a restless animal.—*v* to tie a hoch-ban to a cow, etc.

hoch-bane *n* the thighbone.

hoch-deep *adv* **1** up to the thighs. **2** as deep as the thighs.

hochen *same as* **hechen**.

hocher *n* one who houghs cattle.

hoch-hey *int* an exclamation of weariness.

hoch-hicht *v* to stand on one leg and put the other over any object.

hoch-hiech *adj* as tall as a full-grown person's leg.

hoch-hone *int* an exclamation of grief.

hochie *n* a keg, cask, small barrel.

hochimes *same as* **houghams**.

hochle *v* **1** to walk with short steps. **2** to sprawl, shamble, shuffle in walking. **3** to walk clumsily. **4** to do anything clumsily or awkwardly. **5** to make love to women in open day.—*n* **1** a sloven. **2** a person regardless of dress or appearance.

hochmagandy *n* fornication.

hoch-on *n* help given to mount on horseback, a leg-up.

hoch-wow *int* an exclamation of grief, weariness, etc.

hock *same as* **howk**.

hocker s*ame as* **hoker**.

hockerie-topner *n* the houseleek.

hockerty-pockerty *adv* riding on a person's shoulders with a leg over each.

hockery-packery, ~-pokery *n* **1** sharp practice. **2** anything mysterious or underhand, hocus-pocus.

hocking *n* scraping out a hole with the hands or with a hoe.

hocus[1] *n* a stupid fellow, fool, simpleton.

hocus[2] *n* juggling, artful management, hocus-pocus.

hod[1] *v* **1** to jog along. **2** to ride badly.

hod[2] *v* **1** to hide. **2** to put carefully by. **3** to treasure.

hod[3] *v* hid, hidden.

hod[4] *n* **1** a hood. **2** the hob of a fireplace. **3** the back of a fireplace. **4** a small enclosure or shelf built at the side of a fireplace. **5** a portion of a wall built with single stones or with stones that go from side to side at short intervals.

hodded *v* did hide.

hodden[1] *v* hid, hidden.

hodden[2], **hoddin** *n* **1** homespun cloth of wool of the natural colour, a coarse, thick cloth worn by the peasantry and smaller farmers. **2** a covering made of hodden.—*adj* **1** clad in homespun. **2** made of hodden. **3** homely, coarse.

hodden-breeks *n* homespun breeches.

hodden-clad *adj* clad in homespun.

hodden-grey *n* grey homespun.—*adj* clad in hodden-grey.

hoddie *same as* **hoodie**.

hoddin *v* riding heavily.

hoddins *n* small stockings, such as are worn by children.

hoddit *v* hid.

hoddle[1] *v* **1** to waddle. **2** to walk awkwardly. **3** to dance clumsily.—*n* a waddle, jog trot. **2** a step, a pace.

hoddle[2] *n* a clumsy rick of hay or corn.

hoddler *n* one who waddles.

hoddle-tronsie *n* bread twice steeped in hot water and pressed twice.

hoddy[1] *adj* in good condition.

hoddy[2] *adj* **1** hidden, concealed. **2** suitable for concealment.

hoddy-corner *n* a cunning place for hiding things.

hoddy-table *n* a small table that goes under a larger one when not in use.

hode *v* **1** to hide. **2** hid.

hoden *same as* **hodden**[2].

hodge *v* **1** to move with an awkward, heaving motion. **2** to stagger. **3** to shake with laughter. **4** to hitch up. **5** to push roughly.—*n* **1** a shove. **2** a jolt. **3** a big, awkward person, a fool.

hodgil *n* a dumpling.

hodgil *v* **1** to move by jerks and with difficulty. **2** (*with about*) to carry about constantly. **3** to hobble. **4** to move slowly and clumsily.—*n* **1** a push. **2** a stout, clumsy person.

hodin *n* same as **hodden**.

hodlack *n* a rick of hay.

hodle[1] *n* a small roadside inn.

hodle[2] *same as* **hoddle**[1].

hodle-makenster *adj* rustling.

hodler *n* one who waddles.

hodlins *adv* secretly.

hoe *same as* **ho**.

hoeshin *same as* **hoshen**.

hog[1] *n* a cant name for a shilling.

hog[2], **hogg**[1] *n* **1** a young sheep before it has lost its first fleece. **2** a curling stone that does not pass over the distance score. **3** the distance score or line in curling.—*v* to clip or make pollards of trees.

hog[3], **hogg**[2] *v* to jog, shog.

hog and score *n* one sheep added to every twenty.

hog and tatie *n* mutton stewed with potatoes, onions, pepper and salt.

hog-backed *adj* round-backed.

hoger *same as* **hogger**.

hog-fence *n* **1** a feeding ground for sheep. **2** a fence for enclosing sheep.

hoggart *adj* (*of stockings*) footless. *See* **hogger**.

hogged *adj* fallen behind in means or business.

hogger *n* **1** a footless stocking worn as a gaiter. **2** an old stocking used as a purse.

hogget *n* a hogshead, a large cask or barrel.

hoggie *n* a young sheep.

hogging *n* a place where sheep, after becoming hogs, are pastured.

hogging-score *same as* **hog-score**.

hoggling *adj in phr* **hoggling and boggling** unsteady, moving backwards and forwards.

hogg-reek *n* a blizzard of snow.

hog-ham *n* hung mutton of a sheep that has died of disease or been smothered in the snow.

hoghle *v* to hobble, to limp.

Hoghmanay *same as* **Hogmanay**.

hog-house *n* a pigsty, a piggery.

hog in hairst *n* a young sheep sheared at the end of harvest and ceasing then to be a lamb.

hog-lamb *n* a sheep of about a year old.

hogling *n* a pig.

Hogmanay, ~-ae, ~-ee *n* **1** the last day of the year. **2** a gift given to children who ask for it on New Year's Eve. **3** an entertainment given to visitors on Hogmanay.

Hogmena, ~-ay *n* Hogmanay.

Hogmina, ~-ay *n* Hogmanay.

Hogmonay, Hogmynae *n* Hogmanay.

hogrel, hoggrel *n* a sheep of about a year old.

hogry *same as* **huggerie**.

hogry-mogry *same as* **huggry-muggry**.

hog score *n* the distance line in curling.

hog shouther *n* a game in which the players push each other with the shoulders.—*v* to jostle or push with the shoulders.

Hoguemennay *n* Hogmanay.

hogyet *same as* **hogget**.

hoichle, hoighle *same as* **hochle**.

hoighlin *adj* doing anything clumsily.

hoilie *same as* **haly**[2].

hoise *v* **1** to hoist, elevate, raise. **2** to brag, vaunt. **3** to bluster, rant. **4** to talk, gossip.—*n* a hoist, a lift upward.

hoispehoy *same as* **hie-spy**.

hoist *same as* **hoast**.

hoisting *same as* **hosting**.

hoit *n* **1** a foolish, awkward, clumsy person. **2** a hobbling or awkward motion. **3** a shrug, a motion of the shoulders.—*v* **1** to move awkwardly. **2** to run or walk clumsily.

hoited *adj* **1** clumsy, awkward. **2** clumsily shaped or made.

hoitering *adj* moving in a stiff, clumsy manner.

hoity-toity *n* an awkward, tawdry appearance.

hoke *same as* **howk**.

hoker *v* **1** to crouch over the fire. **2** to bend over.

hokery-packery,-pokery *n* **1** sharp practice. **2** anything underhand or mysterious, cantrips.

hoky *int* an expletive.

holden *ppl* held.

holder *n* a needle-cushion.

holding *adj* sure, certain.

hole[1] *n* **1** cover, shelter. **2** a sheep mark. **3** (*in pl*) a game of marbles, the kypes (qv).—*v* **1** to bore a hole, perforate. **2** to wear into holes. **3** to have holes. **4** to dig, dig out. **5** to hide. **6** to disappear. **7** to take to earth.

hole[2] *v* to stay in a place longer than seems necessary.

hole-ahin *n* a term of reproach for one who falls behind.

holen *n* the holly.

holie *n* a game of marbles, the kypes (qv).

hollie-pie-thingies *n* **1** patterns of sewing and knitting. **2** small holes cut out of linen and stitched round.

holing *n* the depth of coal displaced at a blasting.

holk *same as* **howk**.

holl[1] *v* **1** to excavate, to hollow out. **2** to pierce, penetrate.

holl[2] *v* **1** to stay in a place without occupation, to haunt a place in a lazy, idle fashion. **2** to loaf. **3** to be content with mean work. **4** to work hard and accomplish little. **5** to work sluggishly and dirtily.—*n* a lazy, idle meeting or gossiping.

hollan *same as* **hallan**.

hollan, holland *n* the holly.

Holland, Hollan *adj* Dutch.

Holland-bools *n* Dutch marbles, striped and variegated.

holland-bush *n* a holly bush.

holland-duck *n* the scaup.

holland-hawk *n* the great northern diver.

hollen *n* the holly.

holleu, holo *n* a halloo, loud shout.

hollie *adj* having holes, holed.

hollin *same as* **hallan**.

hollin *n* the holly.

hollin, hollin-aboot *adj* **1** lazy. **2** unskillful, awkward.

hollion *n in phr* **o'er hip and hollion 1** completely. **2** entirely.

hollis-bollis, hollos-bollos *same as* **holus-bolus**.

hollow *n* **1** a carpenter's tool, plane. **2** *in phr* **hollows and rounds** casements used in making any kind of moulding in wood, whether large or small.

hollow *adj* **1** moaning, having a dismal sound. **2** speaking in hollow tones.

hollow meat *n* poultry.

holsie-jolsie *n* **1** a confused mass of food. **2** swine's meat.

holt[1] *v* **1** to halt. **2** to stop.

holt[2] *n* **1** a wooded hill. **2** a small haycock. **3** a small quantity of manure before it is spread.

holus-bolus *adv* completely, all at once.

holy band *n* the kirk session.

holy-dabbies *n* cakes of shortbread, formerly used as communion bread.

holy-doupies *same as* **holy-dabbies**.

holy-fair *n* a name formerly given to the days set apart in connection with the Lord's Supper in a district.

holy-how *n* a membrane on the head, with which some children are born, the loss of which was regarded as a bad omen.

home *n* a holm.

home-bringer *n* an importer from abroad.

home-dealing *n* close dealing with a man's conscience.

homester *n* a stay-at-home.

homie-omrie *n* a hotchpotch, a miscellany.

homing *n* level and fertile ground, properly on the bank of a stream or river.

hommel *same as* **hummel**[2].

hommel-corn *n* beardless grain.

hommelin *n* the fish, rough ray.

hone *v* **1** to whine, complain. **2** to murmur.

honest *adj* **1** honourable. **2** respectable. **3** chaste.—*adv* honestly.

honest-come *adj* **1** honestly obtained. **2** well-earned.

honest hour *n* the hour of death.

honest-like *adj* **1** good-looking. **2** of respectable appearance. **3** goodly, substantial. **4** liberal. **5** (*of a child*) plump, lusty.

honestly *adv* decently, respectably, honourably.

honest man *n* a kindly designation of an inferior.

honesty *n* **1** honour. **2** respectability. **3** what becomes one's station in life, kindness, liberality. **4** a handsome, valuable gift. **5** a thoroughly good article worthy of the giver.

honey *n* **1** a pet. **2** a sweetheart. **3** a term of endearment for a woman or child.—*adj* honeyed, sweet as honey.

honeybee *n* a working bee.

honey-blab, ~-blob *n* **1** the contents of a bee's honey bag. **2** a term of endearment. **3** a variety of gooseberry.

honey-byke *n* a hive of honey.
honey-cherrie *n* a sweet variety of cherry.
honey-doo *n* a pet, sweetheart.
honey-drap *n* a mole on the skin.
honeyflower *n* any flower yielding honey.
honey month *n* the honeymoon.
honey mug *n* a vessel containing honey.
honey-oil *v* to flatter, make up to.
honey-pear *n* a variety of pear.
honey-spot *n* a mole on the skin.
honey-ware *n* a species of edible seaweed.
honner *v* to honour.
honneril *n* a foolish, talkative person.
honnie *n* a term of endearment.
hoo[1] *int* **1** a cry intended to scare. **2** a call to draw attention.—*v* **1** to frighten away birds. **2** to drive away. **3** to holloa, shout. **4** (*used of an owl*) to hoot. **5** (*of the wind*) to sigh, moan, howl drearily.
hoo[2] *adv* **1** how. **2** why.
hoo[3] *same as* **ho**[3].
hoo[4] *same as* **how**[2].
hooch[1] *int* an exclamation of disgust.
hooch[2] *int* **1** an exclamation of joy, etc. **2** a shout during the dancing of a reel.—*v* to cry hooch!—*n* **1** a shout. **2** the hooch used in reels. **3** the sound made by forcing the breath through the narrowed lips. **4** a smell, savour.
hood[1] *n* **1** a sheaf of corn placed on the top of a stook (qv) to protect it from rain. **2** the hob at the side of a fireplace for pots, etc. **3** the back of a fireplace, built like a seat. **4** a small enclosure or shelf built at the side of a fireplace. **5** a space of a stone wall built at short intervals and marked by stones which go from side to side.—*v* to cover a corn stook (qv) by putting on a hood sheaf (qv).
hood[2] *n* the joining of the two parts of a flail, generally of leather, sometimes of eel's skin.
hooded *adj* (*of a hen*) tufted, having a tuft on the head.
hooded crow *n* **1** the pewit gull or black-headed gull. **2** the carrion crow.
hooded mew *n* the pewit gull.
hoodie *n* 1 the hooded crow or the carrion crow. **2** a hired mourner.
hoodie-craw *same as* **hoodie**.
hooding *n* the leather strap or thong connecting the hand staff and the souple (qv) of a flail.
hoodling-how *n* a kind of cap.
hood neuk *n* the corner beside the fireplace.
hoodock *adj* foul and greedy, like a hoodie (qv) or carrion crow, miserly.
hood sheaf *n* a sheaf of corn laid on the top of a stook (qv) to protect it from rain.
hoodstane *n* **1** a flagstone set on edge as a back to a fire on a cottage hearth. **2** a stone used in building as a hood (qv) or portion of a wall.
hooferie *n* folly.
hooger *same as* **hogger**.
hooh *int* a cry.
hoo-hooing *v* crying out, calling out.
hooick *n* a small stack in a field, built in a wet harvest.
hooie *v* to barter, exchange.—*n* **1** an exchange. **2** barter. **3** a boys' word in exchanging knives under cover.
hooing *n* loud shouting.
hook[1] *n* **1** the bend of a river. **2** the land enclosed by such a bend. **3** a reaping hook. **4** a reaper, a shearer.
hook[2] *v* to run off.
hook[3] *same as* **howk**.
hook-bane *same as* **heuck-bane**.
hook-busser *n* one who dresses fly hooks.
hooker *n* a reaper, one who wields a sickle.
hooker *n* **1** whisky. **2** a drink of whisky.
hookers *n* the bended knees.
hookie *n* a meaningless exclamation or mild expletive.
hook-penny *n* a penny given weekly to reapers in addition to their wages.
hool[1] *v* **1** to remove the outer husk of any vegetable or fruit.

2 to geld.—*n* **1** a husk, pod, outer skin of fruit. **2** a case. **3** a shell. **4** a cheese rind.
hool[2] *v* **1** to conceal. **2** to cover, wrap up.—*n* **1** an outer covering. **2** the pericardium. **3** the body.
hool[3] *adj* **1** beneficial. **2** friendly, kind.
hoolachan *n* a Highland reel.
hoolat *v* **1** to henpeck. **2** to look miserable.
hoolet *n* **1** an owl. **2** an owlet.
hooley *n* a wild party.
hoolie *adv* softly.
hoolie-gool-oo-oo *n* the hoot of an owl.
hooliness *n* slowness, tardiness.
hooloch *n* **1** a falling or rolling mass. **2** an avalanche of stones, etc.
hooly, hoolyie *same as* **haly**[2].
hooly and fairly *adv* fair and softly, slowly and gently.
hoom[1] *n* a herd, a flock.
hoom[2] *same as* **hoam**[3].
hoomet *n* **1** a large flannel nightcap. **2** a child's under-cap. **3** a man's Kilmarnock bonnet.
hoometet *adj* covered with a hoomet (qv).
hoon[1] *v* (*with* **off**) to delay, postpone.
hoon[2] *same as* **hone**.
hoop[1] *n* the circular wooden frame surrounding the millstones and keeping the meal from being lost.—*v* to speed, hurry.
hoop[2] *v* to hope.
hoor *n* **1** a whore, a prostitute. **2** a term of abuse for a woman.
hoord *v* to hoard.
hoose *n* a house.
hoosht *int* hush!—*v* to order silence.
hoosie *n* a small house.
hoot, hoots *int* an exclamation of doubt, contempt, irritation, dissatisfaction.—*v* to pooh-pooh, discredit, cast doubt on.
hoot awa *int* tuts! nonsense!
hoot ay *int* to be sure!
hoot fie *int* o fie!
hoot-toot, ~-toots *int* an exclamation of strong dissatisfaction or jocular contradiction.
hoot-toot-toot *int* an exclamation of annoyance.
hooze *v* to stay, tarry.
hoozle[1] *n* the housel, sacrament of the Lord's Supper.
hoozle[2] *n* **1** a socket for a handle in tools. **2** the head of a hatchet, etc. **3** a paper band round a bundle of papers, keeping them together.
hoozle[3] *v* **1** to wheeze. **2** to breathe with a wheezing sound, as if out of breath.—*n* **1** heavy breathing. **2** an inhalation. **3** a big pinch of snuff.
hoozle[4] *v* **1** to perplex, puzzle. **2** to pose. **3** to drub smartly.
hoozling[1] *adj* breathing hard.—*n* a wheezing.
hoozling[2] *n* a severe drubbing.
hop *same as* **hap**[3].
hop-clover *n* yellow clover.
hope, hop *n* **1** a hollow among the hills. **2** a hill.
hope *n* **1** a small bay. **2** a haven.
hoped *v in phr* **better hoped** more hopeful.
hope-fit *n* the lowest part of a hope (qv) or valley among hills.
hope head *n* the highest part of a hope (qv) or valley among hills.
hop-my-fool *n* a game of chance.
hopple *v* to fasten two legs of an animal to prevent it from straying.—*n* the rope or strap so used.
hoprick *n* a wooden pin driven into the heels of shoes.
horal *same as* **horl**.
hork *v* to grub like a pig.
horl, horal *n* **1** a small iron or wooden ring used as a pulley. **2** a castor. **3** a small wheel.
horn *n* **1** a drinking vessel. **2** a draught of liquor. **3** a comb. **4** a spoon made of horn. **5** a snuffbox made from the sharp end of a horn. **6** a horn formerly used as a cupping glass. **7** a hard excrescence on the foot. **8** a hair comb. **9**

the continuation of the stern of a boat. **10** the nose. **11** the spout of a teapot. **12** part of a large bell. **13** a cloud resembling a boat in shape.—*v* **1** to make hard and horny. **2** to bleed by cupping. **3** to cuckold. **4** to draw up a curling stone by the handle and so put it out of play.

horn bouet, ~ bowet *n* a hand lantern in which thin horn was used for glass.

horn cutty *n* a short spoon made of horn.

horn-daft *adj* **1** quite mad. **2** outrageous. **3** very foolish.

horn-dry *adj* **1** very dry. **2** thirsty. **3** craving for drink.

horneck *n* the root of the earthnut.

horned *adj* cuckolded.

hornel *n* the sand lance when of large size.

horn-end *n* the parlour or better end of a house.

horner *n* **1** a maker of horn spoons. **2** one who is sent to Coventry. **3** one who was 'put to the horn'.

horn-golach *same as* **hornie-golach**.

horn-haft *n* a heft made of horn.

horn-hard *adj* very hard.—*adv* soundly, profoundly.

horn-head *adv* **1** with full force. **2** without pause.

horn-idle *adj* quite idle, thoroughly at leisure.

hornie[1] *n* the horneck (qv).

hornie[2] *n* the devil.

hornie *n* a children's game, played with clasped hands and thumbs extended.

hornie[3] *n* **1** a horned cow. **2** the name of such a cow.

hornie[4] *n in phr* **fair hornie** fair play.

hornie-golach *n* an earwig.

hornies *n* horned cattle.

horning *n* **1** a supply of drink. **2** a cuckolding. **3** *in phrs* **letters of horning, horning and caption 1** an order requiring a debtor to pay a debt on pain of being declared a rebel. **2** a letter of amercement.

horn-mad *adj* **1** raving mad. **2** outrageously irritated.

horn mark *n* a mark branded on the horn of a sheep, ox, etc.

hornock *n* the devil.

horns *n* in the game **a' horns to the lift** where the horn represents the forefinger.

hornshottle *adj* **1** (*used of the limbs*) dislocated. **2** (*of the teeth*) loose. **3** shaken to pieces.

horn spune, ~ speen *n* a spoon made of horn.

horn-tammie *n* a laughing stock, a butt.

horny *adj* **1** having horns. **2** strong, fortified. **3** noisy as a horn. **4** amorous, lecherous. **5** having corns on the feet.

horny-goloch *n* an earwig.

horny-holes *n* a game of four persons, played with a bat like a walking stick and frequently a sheep's horn for a cat (qv).

horny-hoolet *n* the long-eared owl.

horny-luck *n* a variety of the game of tig.

horny-rebels *n* a children's game.

horny-worm *n* a short, thick worm with a tough skin, enclosing a sort of chrysalis, which becomes the long-legged fly called by children 'spin-Mary'.

horrals *same as* **horl**.

horrid *adj* great, extraordinary.—*adv* exceedingly, extraordinarily.

horse *n* **1** horses. **2** a mason's large trestle. **3** a mason's hod. **4** a frame or rack for drying wood. **5** a screen or frame for airing linen, a clotheshorse. **6** a wooden implement for drawing off liquors, a faucet.—*v* **1** to mount. **2** to ride on horseback. **3** to punish or hurt by striking or bumping the buttocks of a person on a stone, etc.

horse and hattock *int* **1** a call to get ready to ride off. **2** the witches' and fairies' call to be off.

horse-beast *n* a horse.

horse-buckie *n* the white whelk.

horse-cock *n* a small kind of snipe.

horse-corn *n* the small corn separated by riddling.

horse-couper, ~-cowper *n* a horse-dealer.

horse-coupin *adj* horse-dealing.—*n* the trade of a horse-couper (qv).

horse-feast *n* food without liquid of any kind.

horse-foal *n* a colt.

horse-gang *n* a fourth of land that is ploughed by four horses, belonging to as many tenants.

horse-gear *n* harness, saddlery.

horse-gell *n* the horse-leech.

horse-gowan *n* the ox-eye daisy.

horse-gowk *n* **1** the green sandpiper. **2** the snipe.

horse-grace *n* a rhyme describing how a horse should be treated by its driver on a journey.

horse-hirer *n* one who lets out horses for riding, etc.

horse-hoe *n* a hoe, or hoeing implement, drawn by a horse.—*v* to use a horse-hoe.

horse-kirn *n* a churn driven by a horse.

horse-knot *n* the black knapweed.

horse-load *n* the load which a horse can carry.

horse-mackerel *n* the scad.

horse-magog *n* a boisterous, frolicsome clown.

horse-malison *n* one who is very cruel to horses.

horseman *n* a farm servant in charge of a pair of horses.

horseman's word *n* the secret password which a farm servant got from his fellows in order to become a member of the Horseman's Society and receive help in the training of a refractory horse.

horse-meal *same as* **horse-feast**.

horse muscle, ~ mussel *n* **1** a large mussel. **2** the pearl mussel.

horse-nail *n in phr* **make a horse-nail of a thing** to do something clumsily and imperfectly.

horse-orts *n* horse dung.

horse-setter *n* one who lets out horses for riding, etc.

horse sheet *n* a horse cloth.

horse-stang *n* the dragonfly.

horse-supperin' *n* the horse's evening meal.

horse-tailor *n* a saddler.

horse-thristle *n* the bur.

horsetree *n* the swingletree, to which the horse was harnessed when drawing a pair of harrows.

horse troch *n* a drinking trough for horses, etc.

horse-well-grass *n* the brooklime.

horsing wadge *n* a large wedge used in quarrying.

hort *v* **1** to maim. **2** to hurt.—*n* a hurt.

hose, hosen *n* **1** a single stocking. **2** a footless stocking. **3** the sheath of corn. **4** the seed leaves of grain. **5** a socket for the handle of a tool.

hose-doup *n* the medlar.

hosefish *n* the cuttlefish.

hose-gerse *n* meadow soft grass.

hose net *n* **1** a small net, resembling a stocking, affixed to a pole. **2** an entanglement, a difficulty.

hoshen *n* **1** a footless stocking. **2** a wide, loose house slipper. **3** a term of abuse. **4** a bad, pithless worker.

hosie *n* the cuttlefish.

ho-spy *same as* **hie-spy**.

host *same as* **hoast**.

hosta *same as* **husta**.

host-bell *n* **1** the bell rung at the celebration of mass. **2** used in one place in Perthshire formerly to call children into school.

hostee *n* the host.

hostilar *same as* **hostler**.

hostillar, hostellar *n* a hostelry.

hostilogies *n* retainers, henchmen.

hosting *n* the raising or gathering of an army or host.

hostler, hostlier *n* an innkeeper.

hostler house *n* **1** a hostel. **2** a house of public entertainment.

hostler-wife *n* **1** a landlady. **2** an innkeeper's wife.

hot[1]**, hott** *n* **1** a small heap of anything carelessly put up. **2** a pannier used for carrying dung. **3** a small heap of manure or lime drawn from a cart in a field for spreading.

hot[2] *same as* **het**[3].

hotch, hotchen *v* **1** to jerk, lurch. **2** to move clumsily. **3** to fidget. **4** to hitch. **5** to shake with laughter. **6** to shrug the shoulders. **7** to move along in a sitting posture. **8** to sit closer. **9** to limp. **10** to swarm. **11** to cause to jerk. **12** to heave.—*n* **1** a jerk, jolt, shove, shrug. **2** a big, unwieldy person.

hotchie *n* a general name for puddings.

hotching *same as* **hoatching**.

hotchin-hippit *adj* having hips that cause clumsy walking.

hotchle *v* **1** to walk clumsily. **2** to hobble, to limp. —*n* a jerk, a hitch.

hotch-potch *n* **1** a vegetable soup with pieces of mutton boiled in it. **2** a medley. **3** a confused jumble.

hot-load *n* a heap of manure or lime in a field for spreading.

hots *n* a term used in the game of pearie (qv) or peg-top.

hott *v* **1** to move by sudden jerks. **2** to shake with laughter.

hotten *v* hit.

hotter *v* **1** to move unsteadily or awkwardly. **2** to hesitate. **3** to shake with laughter. **4** to totter, hobble. **5** to shudder, shiver. **6** to shake, jolt, vibrate. **7** (*used of the heart*) to palpitate. **8** to shake with fear. **9** to boil slowly, simmer. **10** to make a bubbling noise in boiling. **11** to crowd together. **12** to move like a toad. **13** to rattle, clatter, make a loud noise.—*n* **1** a swarm. **2** a crowd of small animals in motion. **3** the motion made by such a crowd. **4** the agitation of boiling water. **5** a jolting, shaking-up. **6** a shaking, heaving mass.

hotter-bonnet *n* a person overrun with vermin, lice, etc.

hottie *n* a name given to one who has something pinned to his or her back of which he or she is unconscious.

hottish *adj* rather hot.

hottle, hottel *n* an hotel.

hottle[1] *n* the bubbling sound of boiling.

hottle[2] *n* anything tottering or not firmly based.

hot-trod, ~-bed *n* the pursuit of Border rievers (qv) with bloodhounds and bugle horn.

hou *same as* **hoo**.

houan *adj* howling.

houch *v* to hoot as an owl.—*n* the moaning of the wind.

houchty-pouchty *adj* high and mighty.

houck *n* **1** a haunt. **2** a continued stay in one place in idleness.—*v* **1** to haunt, frequent. **2** to loaf, lounge.

houd *same as* **howd**[1].

houdee *same as* **howdoye**.

houdin-tow *n* a swing rope.

houdle *same as* **howdle**.

houdy *same as* **howdie**[2].

houe *v* **1** to hoot. **2** to howl. **3** to scare away.

houff *same as* **howff**.

houffie *adj* (*used of a place*) snug, comfortable.

houg *n* **1** a grip, grasp. **2** a hug.

hough[1] *v* to cry hooch! *See* **hooch**.

hough[2] *same as* **hoch**[1].

hough[3] *adj* **1** giving a hollow sound. **2** empty, hollow. **3** low, mean. **4** in poor health. **5** in low spirits.

hougham *n* bent pieces of wood slung on each side of a horse to support dung panniers.

hougheneugh *adj* but so-so or middling.

houghle *v* to limp, to hobble.

houghlin *n* sexual intercourse.

houghmagandie *same as* **hochmagandie**.

hought *adj* undone, overthrown.

hough up *adv* as high as the thigh.

houh *same as* **howe**[1].

houin *n* **1** the dreary whistling of the wind. **2** the cry of the owl in warm weather.

houk[1] *v* to heap.

houk[2] *same as* **howk**.

houlat *v* **1** to reduce to a henpecked state. **2** to go about downcast and peevish. **3** to look miserable.

houlat, houlet, houlit *same as* **hoolet**.

houlat-like *adj* **1** having a meagre, feeble appearance. **2** puny.

hound *n* **1** a large, ill-favoured dog. **2** a low, mean fellow.

3 a greedy, avaricious, grasping person. —*v* **1** to hunt with dogs. **2** (*with* **out**) to instigate, incite to mischief.

hounder-out *n* **1** an inciter to mischief. **2** an instigator.

hound-hunger *n* the ravenous appetite of a dog.

hound-thirsty *adj* thirsty as a hound.

houp[1] *n* hope.

houp[2] *n* hops.

houp[3] *n* **1** a mouthful of any drink. **2** a mouthful of food. **3** a taste of any liquid.—*v* to drink by mouthfuls.

houpin *n* the drinking by mouthfuls.

hour *n* (*in pl*) o'clock, time of day.

housal *adj* domestic, household.

house *n* **1** the workhouse, poorhouse. **2** a portion of a house occupied by one tenant. **3** (*in curling*) the circle round the tee within which stones must lie to count.—*v* **1** to shelter. **2** (*used of hay or corn*) to get under cover in rick or in barn.

hous an' ha' *phr* house and hall, completely, a clean sweep.

house-ba' *n* a girls' game of ball.

house-carle *n* a household servant.

house-devil *n* from the saying **a devil at home, a saint abroad**.

house-dirt *n* the dust of a house.

house-end *n* the gable of a house.

house-fast *adj* confined to the house by illness, duty, etc.

house gear *n* household goods.

house-haddin' *n* housekeeping.

house head, ~-heid *n* **1** the head of the house. **2** the ridge of the house roof.

house-heat, ~-heating *n* a house-warming on entering a new house.

house-hicht *n* a person of small stature.—*adj* in an excited or angry state.

householdry *n* **1** charge of a household. **2** household utensils.

housel *adj* belonging to the house, household.

housel *n* the socket of the handle of a dung fork.

house-maill *n* house rent.

housen *n* houses.

house-riggin' *n* the ridge at the top of a house.

house-side *n* a big, clumsy person.

house-things *n* **1** articles of furniture. **2** household goods.

housewifeskep *n* housekeeping.

housie *n* a small house.

houster *v* to gather together confusedly.—*n* one whose clothes are ill put on.

houstrie *n* **1** soft, bad, nasty food. **2** trash, trumpery.

houstring *adj* bustling but confused.

hout *int* tuts!—*v* **1** to pooh-pooh. **2** to flout.

hout fy *n* for shame!

houther *v* **1** to push. **2** to blow fitfully.—*n* **1** a push. **2** a rocking motion. **3** the act of fornication. **4** a violent tossing. **5** confusion, havoc. **6** a blast of wind.

houthering *n* rough, clumsy romping.

houtie croutie *n* the haunches, hams.

houttie *adj* testy, irritable.

houxie *int* a call to a cow.

houzle *same as* **hoozle**[3].

hove[1] *v* **1** to rise up, come into view. **2** to heave. **3** to swell. **4** to puff up. **5** (*used of cattle*) to become distended by overeating fresh clover, etc. **6** to exalt, puff up with conceit.

hove[2], **hove lady** *int* a call to a cow to come and be milked.

hoved *adj* (*used of light, loose soil*) puffed up.

hoven, hoving *n* (*used of cattle*) flatulence, distention from overeating. **2** (*of cheese*) swelling or undue rising. **3** swollen.

hover *v* **1** to stay, pause. **2** to take time, wait.—*n* **1** suspense, hesitation, uncertainty. **2** (*of the weather*) a state of uncertainty.

how[1] *same as* **ho**[3].

how[2] *n* a piece of wood which joins the couple wings together at the top on which rests the rooftree of a thatched house.

how³ *v* **1** to reduce. **2** to drain. **3** to thin.—*n* reduction, diminution.

how⁴, **howe** *int* **1** an exclamation to draw attention. **2** one of joy or grief.—*v* to cry 'how!' with grief.

howanabee, howanawbee *adv* however.

howanever *adv* however.

how-backit *same as* **howe-backit**.

howch *adj* hollow.

howd¹ *v* **1** to sway, rock. **2** to wriggle. **3** to bump up and down, move by jerks.—*n* **1** a motion from side to side. **2** swaying, jerking. **3** wriggling. **4** a sudden gust of wind.

howd² *v* to hide.

howd³ *v* **1** to act as a midwife. **2** to deliver a woman in labour.

howd⁴*n* a great quantity.

howder¹ *v* **1** to heap together confusedly. **2** to crowd, swarm, huddle. **3** (*with* **on**) to put on one's clothes hurriedly and carelessly.

howder² *v* to push.—*n* **1** a pushing. **2** a strong blast of wind.

howder³ *v* to hide.

howdie¹ *n* **1** a young hen. **2** a young unmarried woman.

howdie² *n* a midwife.

howdie-fee *n* a midwife's fee.

howdiefication *n* a confinement, accouchement.

howdieing, houdying *n* a confinement, childbed.

howdieing-fee *same as* **howdie-fee**.

howdie-trade *n* the practice of midwifery.

howdle *v* **1** to move up and down. **2** to sway. **3** to rock to sleep. **4** to crowd together, swarm, move hither and thither. **5** to limp. **6** to walk in a heaving, clumsy way. **7** (*with* **about**) to carry clumsily. —*n* **1** a swarm, a wriggling mass. **2** the motion of such a mass of small creatures. **3** a crowd in motion.

howdler *n* one who walks in a limping, heaving manner.

howdlins *adv* secretly, clandestinely.

howdoye *n* a sycophant.

howdy-towdy *same as* **how-towdie**.

howe¹ *adj* **1** hollow, concave. **2** empty. **3** hungry, famished. **4** (*used of sounds*) hollow, deep, low, guttural. **5** poor, humble, mean. **6** in low spirits. **7** in bad health.—*n* **1** a hollow. **2** a hollow space. **3** a valley, glen. **4** a flat tract of land. **5** the track of a curling stone towards the tee. **6** the depth or middle of a period of time. **7** reduction, diminution.—*v* **1** to reduce. **2** to thin. **3** to drain, diminish in quantity or number.

howe² *n* a hoe.—*v* to hoe.

howe-backit *adj* hollow-backed, sunk in the back.

howe-doup *n* the medlar.

howe-dumb-dead *n* (*used of night*) the middle, when silence reigns.

howe-hole *n* **1** a hollow. **2** a valley. **3** a depression. **4** a hole.

howe-hoose *n* **1** an area-dwelling. **2** a house below the street level.

howe-howm *n* a vale, a low-lying plain.

howen¹ *adj* hewn.

howen² *adj* hoed.

howe o' the year *n* the winter solstice.

hower *n* a hoer.

howe-speaking *n* **1** speaking in a low deep voice. **2** speaking like a ventriloquist.

howe-wecht *n* a circular implement of sheepskin stretched on a broad hoop for lifting grain, chaff, etc, in barns.

howf¹ *n* a severe blow on the ear, given with a circular motion of the arm.

howf² *n* liking, desire for.

howff, howf³ *n* **1** a place of resort or concourse. **2** haunt. **3** a much frequented tavern. **4** an abode, residence. **5** a stay at a place. **6** a shelter. **7** a cemetery, burial place, mausoleum.—*v* **1** to haunt, frequent. **2** to lodge, abide, reside, take shelter. **3** to lodge, house, cause to live, shelter. **4** (*with* **up**) to bury.

howffie *adj* comfortable, cosy.

howffin, howfin *n* a clumsy, foolish person.

how-hum *int* alas.

howick *same as* **hooick**.

howie *n* a small plain.

howk¹ *n* an internal disease of common occurrence among cattle, of the nature of acute indigestion.

howk² *v* **1** to dig out, to excavate. **2** to burrow. **3** to grub. **4** to pull out, draw out. **5** to rummage, to search out, hunt out. **6** to sound out or quiz a person.—*n* the act of digging, excavation.

howk-back *n* a sunk back.

howk-backit *n* having a sunk back.

howk-chowk *v* to make a noise as if poking in deep mud.

howker *n* a digger.

howking *n* **1** an excavation. **2** the act of sounding out or quizzing anyone.

howl *n* a hollow, a depression.

howlet *n* **1** an owl. **2** an owlet. **3** a term of reproach.

howlet-blind *adj* blind as an owl.

howlet-een *n* eyes like an owl's, large and staring.

howlet-faced *adj* having a face like an owl's.

howlet-haunted *adj* frequented by owls.

howlety *adj* like an owl.

howlety-hoo *n* the cry of an owl.

howm *same as* **hoam**¹.

howmet *n* a little cap.

hownabe *same as* **howanabee**.

hownicht *n* midnight.

howp¹ *n* hope.—*v* to hope.

howp² *same as* **houp**³.

how-sheep *int* a shepherd's call to his dog to pursue sheep.

howsoever *adv* indeed, in fact.

howsomever *adv* **1** however. **2** nevertheless. **3** in any case.

how soon *adv* as soon as.

howster *same as* **houster**.

howstrie *same as* **houstrie**.

howther *same as* **houther**.

howthering *same as* **houthering**.

howthir *v* **1** to hobble in walking. **2** to work hastily and untidily.—*n* **1** an awkward, hasty walker. **2** a sloven, slattern. **3** unseemly haste.

howtie *same as* **houttie**.

howtilie *adv* in an angry and sulky manner.

howtiness *n* anger and sulkiness.

how-towdy *n* **1** a hen that has never laid. **2** a fat young chicken to be cooked. **3** a chicken dish. **4** a young unmarried woman.

howts *int* tuts!

hoxter-poxter *adv* in great confusion.

hoy *int* an exclamation to draw attention.—*n* a shout, cry.—*v* **1** to call to, hail, summon. **2** to incite, provoke. **3** to set on dogs.

hoyden *adj* **1** inelegant. **2** homely, commonplace.

hoyse *v* to hoist.—*n* a lift by a rope or by an upward thrust.

hoys net *same as* **hose net**.

hoyster *v* to hoist.

hoyte *v* to hoist, raise on the shoulders.

hoyte *same as* **hoit**.

hu *int* an exclamation of anger, rage, etc.

huam *n* the moan of an owl in the warm days of summer.

hubbie *n* a dull, stupid, slovenly fellow.

hubble¹ *n* **1** an uproar, tumult. **2** a stir, bustle.

hubble² *v* **1** to shake, dandle, quiver. **2** to limp.—*n* a shake.

hubblebub *n* the riffraff, the rabble.

hubbleshow, ~shew, ~shoo *same as* **hobbleshow**.

huch *v* to warm the hands by breathing on them.

huck *v* to haggle, play the huckster.

huckerspoke *adj* showing dignity.

huckie *n* the pit in which ashes are held under the fire.

huckle-buckie *n* a game in which children slide down a hill sitting on their hunkers. *See* **hunker**.

hud¹ *same as* **hod**².

hud² *same as* **had**¹.

hud³ *n* a mason's hod.

hud[4], **hudd** *n* **1** the back of a fireplace in the houses of the peasantry, built of stone and clay, not unlike a seat. **2** a small enclosure or shelf at the side of the fire, formed of two stones set erect, with one laid across the top as a cover. **3** the flat plate that covers the side of a grate. **4** the seat opposite the fire on a blacksmith's hearth. **5** a portion of a wall built with single stones going through from side to side.

hudden[1], **huddem** *same as* **hodden**[2].

hudden[2] *adj* held.

hudder *v* **1** to heap together in disorder. **2** to crowd, swarm. **3** to huddle. **4** to work confusedly.

hudderin *n* meat condemned as unwholesome.

hudderon, hudderen *same as* **huddroun**.

hudderone *n* a young heifer.

huddery *adj* **1** rough, shaggy. **2** dishevelled. **3** tawdry. **4** slovenly.

huddin[1] *same as* **hodden**[2].

huddin[2] *n* a child's cap or hood.

huddle *v* **1** to gather together greedily. **2** to crowd together in a little room or space. **3** to lie down in the grave.

huddle-muddle *adv* secretly.

huddroun *adj* **1** hideous, ugly. **2** flabby and slovenly in person. **3** empty, ill-filled.—*n* **1** a dirty, ragged person. **2** a big, fat, flabby woman.

huddry *same as* **huddery**.

hudds *n* hardened clay, used as a back to a grate.

huddy, huddy-craw *same as* **hoodie**.

huddy-droch *n* a squat, waddling person.

hude *same as* **hud**[4].

huderon *same as* **huddroun**.

hudge[1] *v* to amass.—*n* a great quantity.

hudge[2] *v* **1** to speak in a suppressed manner. **2** to spread evil reports.—*n* suppressed talking.

hudge-mudge *n* **1** secrecy, hugger-mugger. **2** a suppressed talking. **3** a talk aside in a low voice. —*adv* secretly, underhand.—*v* to whisper, talk in a suppressed voice.

hudgie-drudgie *n* **1** a drudge. **2** an incessant talker.—*v* to toil, drudge.—*adj* toiling, slaving.

hudibrass *v* to hold up to ridicule.

hud-nook *n* the corner beside the fireplace.

hudron, hudroun *n* veal fed on pasture and not on milk.

hudroun veal *n* veal of the worst quality.

hud-stane *n* **1** a flagstone set on edge as a back to a fire on a cottage hearth. **2** a stone used in building a hud. *See* **hud**[4].

hue *n* **1** look, appearance. **2** a slight quantity, a soupçon.—*v* to colour.

hue and hair *n* **1** main force. **2** every effort or inducement.

huerunt *n* the heron.

hueta *int* an exclamation of surprise and hesitancy: 'see here!'

huferie *same as* **hooferie**.

huff[1] *v* **1** (*used of a bruise*) to swell. **2** (*in baking*) to rise. **3** to become angry, take offence. **4** to offend. **5** to scorn. **6** to bully. **7** to get rid of by bullying. **8** to get on smartly with work.—*n* **1** a fit of temper. **2** offence. **3** haste, hurry.

huff[2] *v* **1** to humbug. **2** to disappoint. **3** to illude.—*n* **1** a humbug. **2** a disappointment.

huff[3] *int* an exclamation of surprise or suddenness.

huff[4] *v* (*in draughts*) to remove a piece from the board, which an opponent should have played to take another piece.

huffle-buffs *n* old clothes.

hufflit *n* a blow with the hand on the side of the head.

huffy *adj* **1** proud. **2** choleric.

hufud *n* a stroke on the head.

hug *v* to cling close to.

hugeous *adj* huge, large.

hugert *adj* wearing footless stockings.

hugger[1] *same as* **hogger**.

hugger[2] *v* **1** to shudder, shiver. **2** to crouch with cold or disease. **3** to crowd together from cold.—*n* a state of shivering or crouching from cold or disease.

huggerfu' *n* a stockingful.

huggerie *adj* awkward and confused in dress or manner.

huggerin *adj* bent down from cold or disease.—*n* the shaky, creepy feeling caused by intense cold.

huggermagrillian *n* a coarse, slovenly woman.

hugger-mugger *n* secrecy.—*adv* secretly.—*v* **1** to act or speak secretly. **2** to conceal.

huggert[1] *adj* **1** wearing footless stockings. **2** (*used of stockings*) footless.

huggert[2] *adj* **1** bent with cold or disease. **2** shrunken.

hugget *same as* **hogget**.

huggrie *same as* **huggerie**.

huggry-muggry *adj* **1** secret. **2** slovenly, untidy, disorderly.—*n* clandestine conduct.—*adv* secretly.

hughyal *v* to hobble.

hugrie *same as* **huggerie**.

hugy *adj* huge.

hui *int* begone!

huick, huickie *same as* **hooick**.

huie *v* to frighten away birds.—*int* a cry to scare birds.

hui-hoi *int* a cry used by fishermen when heaving all together in launching their boats.

huik *n* a hook.

huil[1] *same as* **haly**[2].

huil[2] *same as* **hool**[1].

huild *v* did hold.

huird *n* a hoard.

huish *n* a lumpish, slovenly woman.

huisht *int* hush!

huisk *n* an untidy, dirty, unwieldy woman.

huist *n* **1** a heap. **2** an overgrown, clumsy person.

huister *n* an uncomplimentary term for a woman, implying lasciviousness.

huister *same as* **houster**.

huistrie *n* **1** bad food. **2** trash. **3** the contents of a beggar's wallet.

huit *n* a heap.

huive *v* **1** did heave. **2** did swell. *See* **hove**[1].

huke *same as* **heuck**[1].

huke-bane *n* the haunch bone.

hulbie *n* any object that is large and unwieldy.

huldie *n* a nightcap.

hule[1] *same as* **heul**.

hule[2] *n* **1** a pod. **2** a husk. **3** a child's caul. **4** a covering.

hule[3] *n* a hovel.

hulgy *adj* having a hump.

hulgy-back *n* a hunchbacked person.

hulgy-backed *adj* hunchbacked.

hulie *same as* **haly**[2].

huliness *n* tardiness.

hulk *v* **1** to skulk lazily about. **2** to hang about a place.—*n* **1** a lazy, clumsy person. **2** an idle, good-for-nothing lout.

hulking *adj* **1** skulking. **2** idle.

hull[1] *n* **1** a hill. **2** the elevated site of a peat stack.

hull[2] *v* to hurry.

hullachan *same as* **hoolachan**.

hull-cock *n* the fish smooth hound.

huller *same as* **hiller**[2].

hullerie[1] *adj* **1** erect, bristling. **2** (*used of a hen*) with feathers standing up. **3** (*of the head*) confused after hard drinking. **4** slovenly. **5** (*of walls*) ill-built, crumbling, friable.

hullerie[2] *adj* (*of the weather*) raw, damp and cold.

hullie-bullie, ~-bulloo *n* a noisy tumult, outcry, hurly-burly.

hullion *n* **1** wealth. **2** goods. **3** property. **4** a burden, heap.

hullion *same as* **hallion**.

hullockit *same as* **hallockit**.

hully *adj* **1** having a husk or shell or rind. **2** husky, hoarse.

hully-belloo *n* a noisy tumult.

hulster[1] *n* a holster.

hulster[2] *v* **1** to carry a burden with difficulty and awkwardly. **2** to burden oneself needlessly. **3** to throw upon back or shoulder. **4** to walk with heavy, ungraceful step.—*n* **1** a load of any kind. **2** the pushing up of a burden. **3** a big, awkward person.

hulter-corn *n* **1** hulled grain. **2** husked corn.

huly *same as* **haly**².

hum¹ *n* the milt of a cod fish.

hum² *v* **1** to stammer. **2** to speak hesitatingly. **3** to whip a top. **4** to strike.—*n* **1** hesitation, indecision. **2** an evasive answer. **3** an expression of scorn.

hum³ *v* to cheat, impose upon, humbug.—*n* a cheat, trick, sham.

hum⁴ *v* **1** to feed, as birds do their young by billing. **2** to transfer food from one's mouth to an infant's. **3** to chew food for infants.—*n* **1** a morsel of chewed food given to infants. **2** (*in pl*) mouthfuls of chewed food.

hum⁵ *adj* **1** out of humour. **2** sullen.

humanity *n* **1** the classics, especially Latin. **2** a classical education.—*phr* **the humanities** the study of the classics.

humble *same as* **hummel**.

humble-bummel *n* a deep ravine with a stream flowing through it over numerous cataracts.

humch *v* to be in a sulky mood.—*n* a fit of sulking.

humdrum *n* **1** a dull, stupid person, without interest in anything. **2** (*in pl*) dejection.—*v* to talk in a humdrum, prosy way.

humdrumming *n* hesitation, insincerity.

humdudgeon, ~durgon *n* **1** needless complaint, fuss or noise. **2** a big, stupid person of an evil disposition.

humet *same as* **hoomet**.

humil *same as* **hummel**².

humist *adj* hindmost.

humlag *n* a hornless cow.

humle *adj* hornless.

humlie *n* a hornless ox, cow, etc.

humlock, humloch *n* **1** hemlock, the cow parsley. **2** any hollow-stemmed, umbelliferous plant.

humlock *n* **1** a hornless cow. **2** a person with a shaved head or whose hair has been cut off.

humlock-skite *n* a squirt made from the hollow stalk of hemlock.

humma *same as* **hummie**².

hummel¹, **hummle** *v* **1** to humble. **2** to cast down, overthrow.—*adj* **1** downcast. **2** at a loss. **3** low-lying.

hummel², **hummil, hummle** *adj* **1** hornless. **2** wanting. **3** lacking. **4** (*of handwriting*) plain, without flourishes.—*v* **1** to remove the beards of barley after threshing. **2** to chew carelessly.

hummelcorn *n* **1** beardless grain. **2** the lighter kind of grain.—*adj* poor, mean, shabby.

hummel-doddy *adj* hornless.—*n* **1** a woman's flat and mean headdress. **2** a hornless ox, polled Angus, Aberdeen or Galloway. *See* **doddy**.

hummel-drummel *adj* morose and taciturn.

hummel-mittens *n* woollen gloves with only the thumb separated.

hummer¹ *v* to murmur, grumble.

hummer² *n* a small top.

hummie¹ *n* a hump.

hummie² *n* **1** a grasp taken with the thumb and four fingers pressed together. **2** the space thus included, excluding the palm. **3** a pinch of anything, as much as can be taken up between the thumb and the four fingers.—*v* to lift up the thumb and fingers.

hummie³ *n* **1** the game of shinty or hockey. **2** the hooked stick used in the game.—*int* a cry used in the game to a player to keep on his own side.

hummie-fou *n* a pinch of anything.

hummilt *adj* having no horns.

humming *adj* (*used of ale or liquor*) strong, heady, foaming.

humming-buming *n* a humming sound.

hummlie *n* a hornless ox, cow, etc.

hummock *same as* **hummie**².

humorous *adj* **1** whimsical, capricious. **2** inconstant. **3** pettish.

humour *n* **1** pus or matter from a sore. **2** bad temper. **3** advice, opinion.

humourousness *n* **1** caprice. **2** pettishness, bad temper.

humoursome *adj* **1** capricious. **2** fanciful. **3** droll, witty, humorous.

hump *n* **1** an arched back. **2** a hillock, knob. **3** ill-humour. **4** the sulks.—*v* **1** to be dissatisfied, sulk. **2** to carry on the back or shoulders.

hump-glutteral *n* the flesh of a sheep that has died a natural death and not of disease.

humph¹ *n* coal when it approaches the surface of the ground and becomes useless.

humph² *n* a hum or hesitation in speech.

humph³ *n* a bad smell or taste as indicating some degree of putridity.—*v* **1** to sniff as if detecting a bad smell. **2** to smell or taste of putridity. **3** to begin to putrefy.

humph⁴ *n* a hump.—*v* **1** to carry on one's back. **2** to carry. **3** to carry with difficulty, to lug.

humph-backit *adj* hunchbacked.

humphed *adj* having a tainted smell.

humpher *n* a hurried movement in rising.

humphy¹ *adj* tainted, having a bad taste or smell.

humphy² *n* a hunchback.—*adj* hunchbacked.

humphy-back *n* a hunched back.

humple¹ *n* a hillock.—*v* **1** to exhibit a hump. **2** to walk with a stoop. **3** to hump the shoulders. **4** to assume a semicircular form.

humple² *v* **1** to walk lame, limp. **2** to stumble. **3** to walk feebly and awkwardly.

humple³ *v* to ride at the crupper behind another.

humpling¹ *adj* shambling.

humpling² *adj* exhibiting a hump.

humplock *n* **1** a small heap. **2** a knoll. **3** a lump. **4** a protuberance.

hump-shouldered, ~-shouthered *adj* hunchbacked, high-shouldered.

humpy-back *n* a hunched back.

humpy-backit *adj* hunchbacked.

hums *n* expressions of love, endearing names.

humsh *same as* **hamsh**.

humstrum¹ *n* a slight peevish fit, the pet.

humstrum² *n* inferior music.

hun' *v* to run about from place to place like a hound.

hunch *v* **1** to hoist up, shove. **2** to push. **3** to shrug the shoulders up.—*n* an awkward bending movement of the body.

hund *n* **1** a hound. **2** an avaricious person.—*v* to incite.

hunder *n* **1** a hundred. **2** a measure of garden ground, 15 feet by 18 feet in extent.—*phr* **a lang hunder** six score.

hune¹ *v* **1** to loiter. **2** to stop.—*n* **1** delay. **2** a loiterer. **3** a lazy, silly person.

hune² *v* to stammer from shyness or from conscious guilt.—*n* one who stammers.

hune³ *same as* **hone**.

hung *adj* (*used of milk*) coagulated by the heat of the weather, placed in a linen bag and hung up until the whey, etc, has dripped from it and only a thick, creamy substance is left.

hunger *v* **1** to starve, withhold necessary food. **2** (*used of land*) to manure insufficiently.—*n* a period of privation.

hunger-rot *n* rot in sheep arising from a deficiency of every kind of food.

hungersome *adj* **1** hungry. **2** causing hunger. **3** with a rather keen appetite.

hungrisum *adj* voracious, eager.

hungrisumlike *adv* somewhat voraciously.

hungrisumness *n* a state of hunger.

hungry ground *n* ground credited to be so much enchanted that a person passing over it would faint if he did not use something to support nature.

hungry-haunch *adj* starved, poorly fed.

hungry hillock *same as* **hungry ground**.

hungry hour *n* the dinner hour from noon to one o'clock.

hungry welcome *n* a cold reception.

hungry-worm *n* a worm supposed to cause hunger, especially in children.

hunker *v* **1** to squat on the haunches with the hams near the heels. **2** to make one squat down so. **3** to watch in a crouching position. **4** to stoop, yield, submit.—*n* (*in pl*) the hams resting on the legs near the heels.

hunkerings *n* genuflections, prostrations.

hunker-slide *v* **1** to slide sitting on one's hunkers. **2** to act in a mean, unmanly underhand way.

hunkerticur *v* to slide sitting on one's hunkers.

hunker-tottie *adv* in a squatting position.

hunkert-wise, hunkertys *adv* in a squatting position.

hunks *n* a lazy slut. **2** a drab.

hunner *n* a hundred.

hunt *v* **1** to drive by force. **2** to search for. **3** to frequent, haunt.—*n in phr* **neither hunt nor hare** absolutely nothing.

hunter *n* (*used of a cat*) a good mouser, one which preys on birds, rats, young rabbits, etc.

hunter's beer *n* a weaver's treat.

huntiegouke *same as* **hunt-the-gowk**.

hunting hawk *n* the peregrine falcon.

huntsman's moon *n* the October moon.

hunt-the-glaiks *v* to go on a fool's errand.

hunt-the-gowk *v* to go on a fool's errand.—*n* **1** a fool's errand, an April errand. **2** an April fool, a person sent on a fool's errand.—*adj* of the character of a fool's errand.

hunt-the-hare *n* the game of hare and hounds.

hunt-the-slipper *n* a young people's sport.

hunt-the-staigie *n* a boys' game in which one player tries to catch the others with his hands clasped; if he catches one, the two join hands and try to catch another, and so on.

hunt-the-unity-staigie *n* the game of hunt-the-staigie (qv).

hunty *n* the game of hare and hounds.

huoven *adj* **1** heaved. **2** swelled.

hup *int* **1** a call to a horse to go to the right. **2** a call to a horse, cow, etc, to go on.—*v* **1** to cry hup to a horse, etc. **2** to go forward.

hupe *n* the wooden circular frame surrounding millstones.

hur *same as* **hurr**[2].

hurb *n* **1** a term of endearment applied to a mischievous child. **2** a term of contempt for a short, thickset person. **3** an awkward fellow. **4** a puny, dwarfish person.

hurble *n* a lean, meagre object.

hurcheon, hurchent, hurchin *n* a hedgehog.

hurd *same as* **huird**.

hurdie-rickle *n* rheumatism.

hurdies *n* the buttocks and hips.

hurdle *v* **1** to crouch, squat like a hare. **2** to contract the body like a hedgehog, cat, etc. **3** to curtsy, bow.

hurdon *n* a woman with large hips.

hurdy-bane *n* the thighbone.

hurdy-caikle *n* pain in the loins of reapers from stooping.

hurdy-gurdy *n* a contemptuous name for a harp.

hure *n* a whore.

huredom *n* whoredom.

hure-quean, ~quine *n* a whore.

huril *same as* **herle**.

hurk *v* **1** to stay idly in a place. **2** to do little. **3** (*with* **about**) to go about in a lazy, underhand fashion.

hurkel *same as* **hurkle**[3].

hurker *n* a semicircular piece of iron put on an axletree, inside the wheel, to prevent friction on the cart body.

hurkie *n* the fish, bib.

hurkle[1] *n* a horse-hoe for cleaning turnips.

hurkle[2] *adj* **1** lazy, careless, slovenly. **2** troublesome, unmanageable. **3** unpleasant.

hurkle[3] *v* **1** to crouch, cower, squat down. **2** to draw oneself together. **3** to submit. **4** to shrug the shoulders. **5** to walk with difficulty owing to rickety legs. **6** to advance in a crouching position or on hands and feet.

hurkle-backit *adj* **1** hunchbacked. **2** having stooping shoulders.

hurkle-bane *n* the hipbone.

hurkle-beens *n* the projecting points of the thighbones.

hurkled *adj* wrinkled.

hurkle-durkle *n* laziness, sluggishness.—*v* **1** to lie long in bed. **2** to lounge.

hurkles *n* the hams.

hurklin *adj* misshapen, drawn together.

hurl[1] *n* a kind of Dutch tobacco.

hurl[2] *n* **1** a drive. **2** a lift or journey in a vehicle. **3** a train journey. **4** an airing in a carriage, etc. **5** a confused mass of material thrown or falling down with violence. **6** the noise caused by the violent fall of material or of carts on a hard road. **7** a scolding.—*v* **1** to wheel, trundle. **2** to whirl. **3** to rush. **4** to roll. **5** to drive in a conveyance.

hurl[3] *v* **1** to toy. **2** to dally amorously.

hurl[4] *n* the snoring sound in the chest during a bronchial attack.

hurl-barrow *n* **1** a wheelbarrow. **2** a handcart.

hurl-come-gush *n* a great and sudden rush or onset.

hurler *n* **1** one who wheels a barrow. **2** a peat-wheeler.

hurley[1] *n* **1** a wheel. **2** a two-wheeled barrow used by hawkers, porters, etc. **3** a handcart for light goods. **4** a truckle bed.

hurley[2] *same as* **hurly**[2].

hurley barrow *n* a two-wheeled barrow or handcart.

hurley bed *n* a truckle bed.

hurley cart *n* **1** a handcart. **2** a toy cart.

hurley-hacket *n* **1** a small trough or sledge for sliding down an inclined plane or a hillside, a toboggan. **2** an ill-hung carriage. **3** a sliding game down a smooth bank.

hurley house *n* a large house fallen into disrepair or nearly in ruins.

hurley-load *n* **1** the load of a handcart. **2** a heavy burden.

hurlie *n* a tumult.

hurling[1] *adj* quickly passing. **2** rushing.

hurling[2] *n* rough dalliance, as on the harvest field.

hurlmaadie *n* an ancient style of headgear.

hurloch[1] *n* **1** a falling or rolling mass. **2** an avalanche of sand, stones, etc.

hurloch *adj* cloudy.

hurly[1] *n* a noise, tumult.

hurly[2] *adv and adj* last.

hurly[3] *n* **1** a wheel. **2** a handcart.

hurly[4] *int in phr* **hurry hawkie!** a milkmaid's call to her cows.

hurly-buck-out *n* the last, the hindmost person.

hurly-burey *n* the last, the hindmost person.

hurly-burly *n* a storm of wind.—*adj* tempestuous, tumultuous.

hurly-go-thorow *n* a racket, disturbance.

hurly-gush *n* the gushing forth of water.

hurly-hacket *n* a racket, disturbance.

hurly-hindmost *n* the last, the hindmost person.

huron *n* the heron.

huroosh *n* a disturbance.

hurr[1] *v* to whir round.

hurr[2] *v* to snarl like a dog.—*n* **1** rough breathing. **2** hoarseness.

hurried *adj in phr* **hurried enough 1** having enough to do, having one's work cut out before one, an expression of difficulty. **2** busy. **3** having much to do in little time. **4** in a hurry.—*adv* quickly.

hurrok *n* the brent goose.

hurroo, hurroe, hurro *int* hello! hurrah!—*n* **1** a hello. **2** a murmuring noise as of the sea on a pebbly shore. **3** a hurly-burly. **4** a noisy commotion.

hurry *n* **1** a press of work. **2** a riot, commotion. **3** a quarrel, scolding.—*v* to raise a disturbance.

hurry-burry *n* **1** confusion. **2** noise.—*adv* **1** with extra hurry. **2** in confusion.

hurry-scurry *n* an uproar, tumult.

hurschle, hurstle *v* to move or slide with grazing or friction.

hurstle *v* to breathe roughy from phlegm in the windpipe.—*n* a rattling sound in the windpipe.

hurstling *n* **1** the sound of rough breathing. **2** wheezing.

hurst-rigg *n* the harvest field.
hurtit *adj* hurt.
hurtsome *adj* hurtful.
husband-land *n* a division of land such as might be ploughed or mown with a scythe.
husband-toon *n* a farmstead.
husband work *n* household work.
husch[1] *same as* **hush**[3].
husch[2] *same as* **hush**[1].
huschle *v* to move with friction.
huschle-muschle *n* great confusion.—*v* to put into great confusion.
huschoue *v* to frighten birds.—*int* a cry to scare birds away.
hush[1] *v* **1** to lull asleep, sing a lullaby. **2** to go to sleep.—*n* a whisper, the slightest noise.—*adj* hushed, quiet.
hush[2] *n* **1** a sudden gush or rush. **2** a swell or rolling motion of the sea. **3** abundance.—*v* **1** to rush, gush forth. **2** to force forward, cause to rush.
hush[3] *int* a cry in order to scare birds.—*v* to scare birds by a slight noise.
hush[4] *n* the lumpfish.
hush-a-baa *n* a lullaby.—*v* to lull a child to sleep.
hushel[1] *v* to move or slide with friction.
hushel[2] *n* **1** a worn-out implement. **2** a person out of order or useless for work. **2** a sloven. **3** a confused mass of things.
hushel-bushel *n* an uproar.
hushel-mushel *n* a state of great confusion.—*v* to put into great confusion.
hushie[1] *v* to lull a child.
hushie[2] *n in phr* **hushie or whishie** the slightest intimation given most cautiously.
hushie-ba *n* a lullaby.—*v* to lull asleep.—*int* an expression used to lull a child to sleep.
hushion *same as* **hoshen**.
hushle *same as* **hushel**.
hushloch *same as* **hushoch**.
hushlochy *adv* all of a heap.—*adj* **1** hurried. **2** careless. **3** slovenly.
hushly *adj* disordered, untidy.
hush-mush, ~-musch *n* **1** secret talking, rumour. **2** bustling disorder.—*v* to speak much secretly. —*adv* in bustling disorder.
hush nor mush *phr* not a single whisper.
hushoch *v* **1** to work carelessly or hurriedly. **2** to dress in a slovenly style. **3** to heap up loosely.—*n* **1** a confused heap. **2** a loose quantity of anything. **3** slovenly work.
hushochy *adj* **1** hurried. **2** careless. **3** slovenly.
husht *int* hush!—*v* to order silence.
hushter *same as* **hashter**.
hushy-baa, ~-baw *n* a lullaby.—*v* to lull to sleep.
huskit *adj* husky, hoarse.
hussey-skep *n* housewifery.
hussil, hussle *v* to move the clothes about the shoulders.
hussle-bussle *n* a confusion.
hussock *n* **1** tuft of coarse grass. **2** a shock of hair. **3** the earth adhering to the root of a cabbage stalk when pulled.
hussyfe *n* **1** a housewife. **2** a wench, hussy.
hussyfe-skep *n* housewifery.
husta, husto *int* an exclamation of surprise and hesitance.
huster *n* a contemptuous designation of a woman.
hustle[1] *v* **1** to work hard. **2** to shrug the shoulders.
hustle[2] *v* **1** (*used of a child*) to coo. **2** (*of a cat*) to purr.
hustle-farrant *n* one who wears tattered clothes.
hut[1] *n* **1** an overgrown, indolent person. **2** a slattern.
hut[2] *n* **1** a small heap. **2** a heap of dung laid down in a field. **3** a small stack built in the field.—*v* to put up grain in the field in a small stack.
hut[3] *int* a call to a careless horse.
hut[4] *n* a square basket formerly used for carrying out dung to the fields, the bottom of which opened.
hutch[1] *n* **1** a cottage. **2** an embankment to hinder water from washing away the soil. **3** a deep pool in a river underneath an overhanging bank.

hutch[2] *n* **1** a small heap of dung. **2** a small rick or temporary stack of corn.
huther[1] *n* **1** a slight shower. **2** a wetting mist.—*v* **1** to fall in slight showers. **2** to rain intermittently.
huther[2] *v* to work confusedly.
hutherin *n* **1** a young heifer. **2** a stupid fellow. **3** a mongrel sort of greens, raised from the seed of common greens and cabbages grown too near each other.
huthering, hutheron *adj* **1** confused. **2** awkward. **3** hurried in walking or working. **4** (*of a stout woman*) slovenly.—*n* a lazy, slovenly girl or woman, a slattern.
huther-my-duds *n* **1** a tatterdemalion. **2** a ragged person.
huthery *adj* untidy.
huthir *v* **1** to walk clumsily, hobble. **2** to work hurriedly and slovenly.—*n* **1** a slattern. **2** a slovenly worker. **3** a hasty walker. **4** unbecoming haste.
huthran *adj* huthering, acting with confused haste.
hutie-cuittie *n* a copious draught of intoxicating liquor.
hutock *n* a small stack.
huts *int* tuts!
hutten *v* hit.
huuy *int* begone!
huz *pron* us.
huzle, huzzle *same as* **hoozle**[3].
huzzh *v* to lull a child to sleep.
huzzh-baw *n* a lullaby.
huzzie, huzzy *n* **1** a hussy. **2** a lass, a wench. **3** a jade.
huzzie *n* a case for needles, thread, etc.
huzzie-baw *n* a lullaby.
hwill *n* a small skiff.
hwrinket *n* improper language.—*adj* perverse, stubborn.
hy *int* a call to horses to turn towards the left.
hyaave *adj* **1** grey. **2** black and white. **3** sallow. **4** livid.
hyank *v* to cut in lumps.—*n* **1** a lump. **2** a big slice.
hyauve *same as* **hyaave**.
hyauve-leukin' *adj* of sallow complexion.
hychle *v* to walk with difficulty while carrying a burden.
hyde *n* **1** a hide. **2** a disagreeable fellow.
hyeave *same as* **hyaave**.
hy jinks *n* drinking by lot.
hyke *v* **1** to hoist. **2** to toss up and down.
hykerie-pykerie *same as* **hickery-pickery**.
hymnler *n* a hymn-singer.
hynail *same as* **haniel**.
hynd, hynde *same as* **hind**[1].
hynd-wynd *adv* **1** straight. **2** by the nearest road.
hyne[1] *same as* **hind**[1].
hyne[2] *adv* far away.—*n* a departure.
hyne[3] *v* to hoist.
hyne-awa *adj* distant.—*adv* to a great distance.
hynt *v* **1** caught up. **2** laid hold of.—*v* gathered up.
hyow *v* to hoe.—*n* a hoe.
hypal[1] *v* to limp.—*n* sciatica.
hypal[2] *n* **1** a good-for-nothing person. **2** a person with loose, tattered clothes. **3** one who is hungry or voracious.
hypalt, hypald *adj* crippled.—*n* **1** a cripple. **2** a strange-looking fellow. **3** a sheep that casts its fleece from disease. **4** a lean, old, starved horse. **5** an animal whose legs are tied.
hype[1], **hyp** *n* the fruit of the dog rose.
hype[2] *n* **1** a big, unruly person. **2** a term sometimes of respect, sometimes of disrespect.
hyple[1] *same as* **hypal**[1].
hyple[2] *n* a dishonest old woman.
hypocreeties *n* shams, hypocrisies.
hypocrip *n* a hypocrite.
hypothec *n* **1** a legal security for rent or money due. **2** the former right of a landlord to claim rent of his tenant, in preference to other creditors. **3** *in phr* **the whole hypothec** the whole concern or collection.
hyppal *same as* **hypal**.
hyppel *n* an opprobrious name given to anyone.
hysch *v* to lull a child to sleep.
hyse *v* **1** to hoist. **2** to romp. **3** to banter. **4** to brag. **5** to

bluster, rant.—*n* **1** an uproar, rant. **2** a wild frolic. **3** a brag. **4** banter. **5** a practical joke. **6** a cock-and-bull story.

hy-spy *same as* **hie-spy**.

hyste *v* to hoist.

hyster *v* to hoist.

hyte¹ *int* a call to horses to go on.—*v* to urge a horse.

hyte², **hyt** *adj* mad, raging.

hyter *v* **1** to walk with tottering gait. **2** to work weakly and clumsily.—*n* **1** weak and clumsy working. **2** walking with tottering steps. **3** confusion. **4** ruin. **5** nonsense. **6** a weak, stupid person.—*adv* **1** with weak, tottering steps. **2** in a state of ruin.

hytering *adj* **1** weak. **2** stupid. **3** unskilful.

hyter-skyter *n* **1** walking with tottering steps. **2** a lot of arrant nonsense.—*v* to walk with tottering steps.—*adv* **1** with weak steps. **2** in ruin.

hyter-styte *n* **1** stupidity. **2** nonsense. **3** utter ruin. —*adj* stupid, silly, mad-like.—*adv* **1** madly, stupidly. **2** in ruin.—*v* to walk with tottering steps.

hyte-styte *adj* **1** mad-like. **2** in a state of madness. —*n* **1** nonsense. **2** utter ruin.

hyuck, hyuk *n* a hook.

hyule *n* an out-of-the-way person. **2** a mischievous person. **2** a rake.

hyve *v* to heave.

hyven *n* heaven.

hyves *same as* **hives**.

hyvie, hyvy *adj* in easy circumstances.

hyze *same as* **hyse**.

hyzzie *same as* **hissie**.

I

i *prep* in.

ice ground *n* a curling rink.

ice hill *n* an iceberg.

icelet *n* an icicle.

iceshoggle, iceshockle *n* an icicle.

ice skid *n* a skate.

ice stane *n* a curling stone.

ice tangle *n* an icicle.

ichie nor ochie *adj* irresolute, wavering.—*n* not a sound, nothing.

icker *n* an ear of corn.

icksy-picksy *adj* alike.

id *v* would.

idder¹*conj and adv* either.

idder², **ider** *adj* **1** other. **2** each other.

idderwise *adv* otherwise.

ident *adj* diligent, industrious.

idiot *n* an uneducated person.

idioticals *n* **1** foolish things, nonsense. **2** things of no importance.

idiotry *n* **1** idiocy. **2** folly.

idiwut *n* an idiot, a simpleton.

idledom *n* idleness.

idleset, idleseat *n* **1** idleness. **2** a useless or frivolous amusement.—*adj* disposed to idleness.

idleteth, idelty *n* **1** idleness. **2** (*in pl*) idle frolics.

I dree, I dree, I dropped it *n* a girls' singing game.

ie *n* an island.

ield *adj* (*used of a cow*) not giving milk.

ieroe *n* a great-grandchild.

ieskdruimin *n* a species of salmon at the isle of Harris.

ignorant *n* an ignorant person.

ile¹ *n* the fishing ground inside the main tidal current, in the space between two points where there is a counter-current.

ile² *n* **1** a wing of a church. **2** a half-transept. **3** an aisle.

ile³ *n* oil.

ilk¹ *n* the same name, place, nature or family.—*phr* **of that ilk** indicating that the person so designated has the same surname as his or her property or title.

ilk² *adj* **1** each. **2** every.—*n* each one.

ilka *adj* **1** each. **2** every. **3** common, ordinary.

ilka body's body *n* **1** a universal favourite. **2** a toady.

ilka day *n* **1** a lawful day. **2** a weekday.—*adv* daily. —*adj* pertaining to the weekdays. **2** ordinary.

ilka-day's claise *n* weekday garments in contrast to Sunday's.

ilka-deal *adv* **1** every whit. **2** altogether.

ilk ane *n* each one.

ilka-where *adv* everywhere.

ilky *same as* **ilka**.

ill *adj* **1** vicious, immoral. **2** (*used of money*) forged. **3** noxious. **4** grieved, sorrowful. **5** stormy. **6** hard, difficult. **7** unkind, cruel, harsh. **8** severe. **9** angry. **10** (*with* **about**) eager after, very fond of. **11** (*with* **for**) having a vicious propensity to. **12** (*with* **to**) hard to bargain with or to deal with in settling an account.—*adv* badly.—*n* **1** misfortune, harm. **2** illness. **3** pain. **4** disease. **5** difficulty.

ill able *adj* **1** hardly able. **2** unable.

ill-aff *adj* **1** poor. **2** miserable, ill-used. **3** perplexed.

ill-ane *n* **1** a bad character. **2** the devil.

ill-best *n* **1** the best of a bad job. **2** the best of the bad.

ill-bind *n* a bad shape or form of an article of dress.

ill-bit *n* hell.

ill-boden *adj* poorly furnished or stocked.

ill-brew, ~-broo *n* **1** an unfavourable opinion. **2** no great liking.

ill-brocht-up *adj* badly trained.

ill-canker't *adj* not well-disposed.

ill-chance *n* bad luck.

ill-cleckit *adj* misbegotten, baseborn.

ill-coloured *adj* discoloured.

ill-contrickit *adj* knavish, mischievous.

ill-contrived *adj* **1** crafty, mischievous. **2** badly behaved, ill-tempered. **3** awkward. **4** badly constructed.

ill-convenient *adj* inconvenient.

ill-cuisten *adj* badly sown with the hand.

ill-curponed *adj* **1** ill-conditioned. **2** surly, churlish. **3** cross.

ill-deedy, ~-deedly *adj* mischievous, evilly disposed.

ill-dereyt *adj* untidy, disorderly.

ill-designed *adj* evilly disposed.

ill-doer *n* an evildoer.

ill-doin', ~-deein' *adj* **1** badly behaved. **2** leading an evil life.

ill-done, ~-deen, ~-dune *adj* **1** wrong, mischievous. **2** cruel. **3** ill-advised.

ill-dread *n* an apprehension of evil, of something bad.

ill-dreaded *adj* fearing or expecting evil.

ill-dreader *n* one anticipating or suspicious of evil.

ill-eased *adj* **1** reduced to a state of inconvenience. **2** inconvenient.

ill-e'e *n* **1** the evil eye. **2** dislike.

ill-eed *adj* having an evil or an unfriendly eye.

illegal *n* an illegality.

ill-end *n* a bad end, a miserable death.

illest *adj* worst.

ill-farrant *adj* **1** ugly. **2** unpleasant in behaviour or appearance.

ill-fashed *adj* **1** greatly troubled. **2** much worried.

ill-fashioned *adj* **1** vulgar in habits, ill-mannered. **2** quarrelsome.

ill-faur'd, ~-far'd *adj* **1** unbecoming. **2** unmannerly. **3** out of place. **4** unpleasant, unsavoury. **5** not looking well or healthy. **6** ill-tempered. **7** mean. **8** scurvy. **9** clumsy. **10** ugly, not good-looking.

ill-fauredly *adv* **1** clumsily. **2** meanly, shabbily.

ill-fit *n* a person supposed to bring bad luck.

ill-fitter *same as* **ill-fit**.

ill-gab *n* **1** bad language, abusive talk. **2** insolence of speech.—*v* to use such language.

ill-gabbit *adj* **1** foul-tongued. **2** vituperative.

ill-gainshoned, ~-gaishoned *adj* **1** mischievous. **2** mischievously disposed.

ill-gait, ~-gate *n* **1** an evil way. **2** a bad habit.

ill-gaited, ~-gaetit, ~-gettit *adj* having bad habits.

ill gi'en *adj* **1** evilly disposed, given to evil. **2** niggardly.

ill-gotten *adj* **1** baseborn. **2** illegitimate.

ill-greein' *adj* quarrelsome.

ill-grun, ~-grunyie *n* a bad, knavish disposition.

ill-gruntet *adj* grumpy, ill-natured.

ill-grunyiet *adj* evilly disposed.

ill-guide *v* **1** to mismanage. **2** to ill-treat. **3** to train or bring up badly. **4** to advise wrongly.

ill-hadden *adj* unmannerly, ill-mannered.

ill-hain't *adj* saved with no good result.

ill-hair't *adj* **1** ill-conditioned. **2** surly, churlish.

ill-hairtit, ~-heartit *adj* **1** malevolent. **2** illiberal. **3** easily daunted.

ill-hairtitness *n* malevolence.

ill-happit *adj* **1** ill-clad. **2** with poor or scanty clothes.

ill-hauden-in *adj* saved to no good purpose.

ill-hear *v* to chide, scold.

ill-hearing *n* a scolding.

ill-hertit *same as* **ill-hairtit**.

ill-hivard *same as* **ill-hyvered**.

ill-hued *adj* ill-favoured.

ill-hung *adj* (*used of the tongue*) **1** impudent, insolent. **2** vituperative.

ill-hyver *n* **1** awkward behaviour. **2** ill-humour.

ill-hyvered *adj* **1** awkward. **2** abusive. **3** ill-looking. **4** ill-tempered.

illighten *v* to enlighten.

illiquid *adj* not legally ascertained.

ill-jaw *n* **1** bad language. **2** an abusive tongue.—*v* to use abusive language.

ill-jaw't *adj* foul-tongued, abusive.

ill-kennin' *adj* hardly knowing.

ill-kessen *adj* badly sown with the hand.

ill-learned *adj* **1** badly taught. **2** inexperienced.

ill-leggit *adj* having unshapely legs.

ill-less *adj* **1** harmless, innocent. **2** with no evil disposition.

ill-less guidless *adj* having neither good nor bad habits, character, etc.

ill-like *adj* **1** not looking well. **2** ugly.

ill-likit *adj* unpopular.

ill-liver *n* an immoral person.

ill-living *adj* immoral.—*n* immoral conduct.

ill-luckit *adj* **1** unlucky. **2** bringing bad luck.

ill-making *adj* mischief-making.

ill-man *n* a child's name for the devil.

ill-minded, ~-min't *adj* evil-minded.

ill-min'in *n* forgetfulness, unmindfulness.

ill-minted *adj* **1** ill-meant. **2** with evil intentions.

ill-mou *n* abusive, insolent language.—*v* to use such language.

ill-mou'd *adj* **1** insolent. **2** vituperative.

ill-muggent *adj* **1** abusive, insolent. **2** evilly disposed.

ill-name *n* **1** a bad name. **2** a bad reputation.

ill-nature *n* bad temper.

ill-natured *adj* **1** bad-tempered. **2** irritable.

ill-off *same as* **ill-aff**.

ill-one *same as* **ill-ane**.

ill-paid, ~-pay't *adj* very sorry.

ill-paired *adj* badly matched, ill-assorted.

ill-part *n* hell.

ill-payment *n* a bad debt.

ill-place *n* hell.

ill-prat, ~-prot *n* a mischievous trick.

ill-prattie, ~-pretit, ~-prottit *adj* mischievous, roguish.

ill-put-on *adj* badly or carelessly dressed.

ill-red-up *adj* **1** untidy. **2** in a state of disorder.

ill-saired, ~-ser'd *adj* **1** badly served. **2** not having enough to eat at a meal.

ill-santafied *adj* not spiritually edifying.

ill-sar'd *adj* unsavoury.

ill-scrapit *adj* (*used of the tongue*) abusive, rude.

ill-set *v* to become badly.—*adj* **1** evilly disposed. **2** spiteful. **3** selfish.

ill-setness *n* **1** opposition. **2** spite. **3** churlishness. **4** selfishness.

ill-shaken-up, ~-shakken-up *adj* **1** (*used of dress*) disordered, untidy, uncomely. **2** (*used of a person*) careless as to personal appearance.

ill-shapit *adj* badly behaved.

ill-side *n* a defect, blemish.

ill-sitten *adj* ungainly in gait from long sitting at work.

ill-sorted *adj* **1** displeased, dissatisfied. **2** ill-assorted.

ill-speaker *n* an evil speaker, a slanderer.

ill-spent *adj* misspent.

ill-ta'en *adj* taken amiss.

ill-tasted *adj* unpleasant.

ill-teen *n* a bad humour.

ill-teth'd *adj* **1** malevolent. **2** ill-conditioned.

ill-thief, ~-thing *n* the devil.

ill-thochted *adj* **1** suspicious. **2** evilly disposed.

ill-thriven *adj* lean, not thriving.

ill-tochered *adj.* having a poor dowry.

ill-tongue *n* **1** evil speaking. **2** bad language.

ill-tongued *adj* **1** foul-tongued. **2** difficult to pronounce.

ill-trick *n* a mischievous trick.

ill-trickit, ~-tricky *adj* mischievous, roguish.

ill-turn *n* a turn for the worse.

ill-upon't *adj* **1** in bad health. **2** much fatigued. **3** spiritless, woebegone.

ill-used *adj* put to a wrong use.

ill-waled *adj* badly chosen.

ill-wared *adj* **1** ill laid out. **2** misspent.

ill-washen *adj* **1** badly washed. **2** expressive of contempt.

ill-ween *n* **1** bad language. **2** bad news.—*v* to use abusive language.

ill-weirdit *adj* ill-fated.

ill-will *v* to wish evil.

ill-willed, ~-willied *adj* **1** sulky. **2** ill-tempered. **2** grudging. **2** unwilling.

ill-willer *n* an adversary. **2** one who wishes evil to another.

ill-willie, ~-willy *adj* **1** ill-tempered, spiteful. **2** disobliging. **3** grudging, niggardly. **4** reluctant.—*adv* reluctantly.

ill-win¹ *adj* ill-won.

ill-win² *n* an evil report, slander.

ill-wish *n* **1** an imprecation. **2** a malicious wish.

ill-words *n* swear words.

ill-wull *n* ill-will.

i-lore *int* woe is me!

image *n* **1** a wooden figure carved by the fairies in the likeness of a person intended to be stolen. **2** a figure of clay or wax used in witchcraft. **3** a pitiful object. **4** an oddity. **5** a sight.

imaky-amaky *n* the ant.

imbase *v* to debase coin.

imbecill *v* to damage.

imber *n* the great northern diver.

imbezilling *v* exposing to loss or damage.

imbog *v* to engulf, as in a bog.

ime *n* **1** soot. **2** a thin coat or scum deposited on a surface.

imey *adj* sooty.

imhim *int* an exclamation of assent.

immedant *adj* immediate.

immedantly *adv* immediately.

immer *same as* **imber**.

immick, imok *n* the ant.

immis *adj* **1** variable. **2** (*of the weather*) changeable, variable. **3** foggy.

imp *n* **1** a shoot, a sucker. **2** a length of hair twisted, forming part of a fishing line.

impasch, impeach *v* to hinder.

imper *v* to be overbold, to presume.

imperence *n* impudence.

impertinence *n* **1** petulance. **2** an insolent person.

impertinent *adj* uncivil, petulant.

imphim, imph, imphm *int* an exclamation of assent.

impident, impiddent *adj* impudent.

implement *n* fufilment.

importance *n* **1** means of support. **2** source of gain.

imposition *n* the right or permission to levy a tax.

imprestable *adj* impracticable.

imprieve[1] *v* **1** to disprove. **2** to impeach.

imprieve[2] *v* to improve.

improbation *n* (*used as a legal term*) the act of improving. See **improve**.

improve *v* (*used as a legal term*) to prove a statement untrue or that a thing has not taken place.

improver *n* (*used as a legal term*) one who proves a writ to have been forged or that an allegation is false.

impune *n* impunity.

impunge *v* to impugn.

imrie *n* the smell of roasted meat.

imrigh *n* a kind of strong soup made from the best parts of beef.

in[1] *prep* **1** in the midst of, occupied with. **2** near, close. **3** into. **4** on, upon. **5** with.—*adv* **1** inside, within the house. **2** at home. **3** (*used of a gathering*) met, going on. **4** (*used of the harvest*) gathered, stacked. **5** shrunken. **6** fallen in. **7** (*of the sea*) at high tide. **8** (*of a railway train, etc*) arrived at a station. **9** on good terms. **10** friendly. **11** approving of, agreeing to.—*v* **1** to go or come in. **2** to put, push or get in.—*n* an entrance.

in[2] *conj* if.

in about *adv* in or to the immediate neighbourhood, near.

inairt *adj* **1** inward. **2** quite genuine, sincere.

in and in *adj* (*used of cattle, sheep, horses, etc*) bred wholly from the same stock.

in at *prep* to, at.

in atween *prep* between.

inawe, inawn *v* to owe.

inbearing *adj* **1** officious, meddlesome. **2** eager to ingratiate oneself. **3** persuasive, impressive in speech.

inbiggit *adj* **1** selfish. **2** morose. **3** reserved.

inbreak *n* **1** a portion of infield (qv) pasture land broken up or tilled. **2** a breach in or into.

inbred fever *n* a disease similar to influenza.

inbring *v* **1** to import. **2** to bring in. **3** to pay in. **4** to collect forces or taxes.

inbringer *n* **1** an importer. **2** an introducer, one who brings in.

inbrocht *adj* **1** imported. **2** introduced. **3** paid in.

in-by, ~-bye *adj* low-lying.—*adv* **1** nearer towards the speaker. **2** in the inner part of a room, house, etc.—*v* to come near.—*prep* beside.

incall *v* **1** to invoke. **2** to pray. **3** to call in or on.

incaller *n* a petitioner.

incalling *n* invocation, prayer.

incast *n* what is given over and above the legal measure or exact sum.

incastred *adj* imprisoned.

inch[1] *n* **1** an island. **2** low-lying land near a river or stream.

inch[2] *n in phr* **an inch of time** the least moment of time.—*v* to live sparingly, to grudge spending.

inch-muckle *n* a piece as small as an inch.

incident *adj* **1** incidental. **2** occurring as a possible consequence.

incidently *adv* not of set purpose.

income *n* **1** advent. **2** entrance. **3** a newcomer, an arrival. **4** an internal disease not caused by an accident or contagion, an ailment without apparent external cause. **5** an

abscess, running sore. **6** deficiency from a stated or expected quantity of things weighed or measured. **7** what is thrown ashore by the sea.—*adj* **1** introduced. **2** come in.

income ware *n* weeds or wrack cast ashore by the sea.

incoming *n* conversion and accession to the church.—*adj* ensuing, succeeding.

incontinent *adv* forthwith, immediately, at once.

inconvene, inconveen *adj* inconvenient.—*n* inconvenience.

inconveniency *n* **1** hardship. **2** inconvenience.

inconvenient *n* inconvenience.

incormant *n* a share, portion.

in-country *n* **1** the interior of a country. **2** an inland district.

ind *v* **1** to bring in. **2** to house or stack grain.

indecent *adj* disreputable.

indecent-like *adj* **1** disreputable-looking. **2** apparently unseemly.

indeed no *phr* no, indeed.

indemnify *v* **1** to compound a felony by relieving the criminal from penalties. **2** to free from the consequences of rebellion, etc.

indent *v* **1** to carve, engrave. **2** to engage. **3** to warrant. **4** to make a compact.—*n* an indenture.

indew *adj* indebted.

India *n* India rubber.

Indian fuel *n* tobacco.

Indian rubber *n* India rubber.

indict *v* **1** to appoint a meeting authoritatively. **2** to summon.

indicted *adj* **1** addicted. **2** inclined.

indignance *n* indignation.

indignify *v* to disgrace.

inding *adj* **1** unworthy. **2** shameful.

indiscreet *adj* rude, uncivil.

indiscreetly *adv* rudely, uncivilly.

indiscretion *n* incivility, rudeness, discourtesy.

indite *v* **1** to indict. **2** to summon a meeting.

indoor-face *n* a face not affected by exposure to the weather.

indorsate *adj* endorsed.

indraught *n* **1** suction of air. **2** a strong current, vortex. **3** toll or duty collected at a port.

indrink *n* shrinkage, diminution of quantity or number.—*v* to shrink in, turn out less.

indumious *adj* **1** very bad. **2** (*of the weather*) extraordinarily stormy.

induring *prep* during.

indwall *v* to inhabit.

indwelling *n* a habitation, residence.

indy *n* a peculiar way of pitching a marble by placing the thumb of the left hand on the ground with the hand held up, placing also the marble in front of the middle finger of that hand and with the right hand propelling it forward.

inease *v* to allay, set at rest.

infall *n* **1** an invasion. **2** a hostile attack. **3** an onslaught.

infamous *adj* branding with infamy.

infang *v* **1** to cheat, gull. **2** to get into one's clutches.

infang thief *n* **1** a thief caught by a baron within his own territory. **2** the privilege conferred on a landlord of trying such a thief.

infar, infare *n* **1** the homecoming of a bride. **2** the feast given at her reception in her new home.

infar cake *n* a cake broken over the bride's head as she crossed the threshold of her new home.

infatuate *adj* **1** infatuated. **2** mad, foolish.

infauld *v* to enfold.

infeft *v* to invest formally with property, enfeoff. —*adj* invested with, possessed of.

infeffment *n* investiture, legal possession.

linfestuous *adj* extraordinary.

infield *n* arable land continually cropped and manured.—*adj* pertaining to infield.

infit *n* **1** an introduction. **2** influence. **3** footing.
infittin *n* **1** influence. **2** footing.
inflame *n* inflammation.
infleenzy *n* influenza.
inforce *v* **1** to aid, to second, to abet. **2** to compel by inward impulse.
infore *same as* **infar.**
ingaan, ingain *n* an entrance.—*adj* entering, assembling, ingoing.
ingaan mouth *n* the mouth of a coal pit with a horizontal direction.
ingadder, ingaither *v* to collect, to gather
ingae *v* to enter.
ingain' tenant *n* a tenant who succeeds another on a farm, etc, which has been let.
ingan *n* an onion.
ingang *n* **1** lack, deficiency. **2** shrinkage. **3** entrance. **4** beginning.
ingangs *n* intestines.
ingate *n* an entrance.
ingate and outgate *adv* within and without, completely.
ingeniously *adv* **1** ingenuously. **2** frankly.
ingenuity *n* ingenuousness.
inger *n* a gleaner.
inger's pot *n* a quantity of all kinds of grain dried in a pot and ground into meal.
ingetting *n* **1** a gathering in. **2** a receiving. **3** collection.
ingine[1] *n* **1** an engine. **2** a weapon used with gunpowder.
ingine[2] *n* **1** ingenuity. **2** quickness of intellect. **3** ability. **4** knowledge. **5** invention. **6** disposition. **7** a person of ability. **8** a genius. **9** an ingenious person.
ingiver *n* one who delivers a thing, either for himself or herself or for another.
ingle *n* **1** fire, flame. **2** a fire in a room. **3** the furnace of a kiln. **4** a hearth, fireplace, fireside. **5** a chimney corner. **6** a faggot or bundle of fuel. **7** a burning peat, coal or log.
ingleberry *n* a fleshy growth on the bodies of oxen.
ingle-biel *n* fireside shelter.
ingle-bole *n* a chimney recess for holding small articles.
ingle-blink *n* the flickering light from the ingle (qv).
ingle-bred *adj* home-bred.
ingle-cheek *n* the fireside.
ingle-end *n* the end of a room where the fire is.
ingle-gleed *n* **1** the blaze of a fire. **2** a blazing fireside. **3** hearth coal.
ingle-lichtit *adj* lighted by the fire.
ingle-lowe *n* the flame or blaze of a fire, firelight.
ingle-lug *n* the fireside, the hearth.
ingle-mids *n* the centre of a fire.
ingle-neuk, ~-nook *n* a chimney corner, a corner by the fireside.
ingle-ring *n* the fireside circle.
ingle-save *n* a device for saving fuel.
ingle-side *n* the fireside.
ingle-stane *n* the hearthstone.
inglin *n* fuel.
Inglisher *n* an Englishman.
ingo *v* to enter.
ingothill *phr* if God will, God willing.
ingrat *n* an ungrateful person.—*adj* ungrateful.
ingrate *adj* ungrateful.
ingrowth *n* increase.
ingrowth *n* **1** a abscess. **2** a tumour.
ingy *v* to bring forth lambs.
ingyang *same as* **ingang.**
ingyre *v* **1** to push oneself forward artfully. **2** to worm one's way into.
inhabile *adj* **1** incompetent. **2** disqualified. **2** inadmissible as a witness.
inhabilitie *n* **1** disability. **2** unfitness. **3** inability.
inhable *v* **1** to disable. **2** to disqualify. **3** to prevent.
inhadden, inhaudin *adj* **1** continuously supplied. **2** selfish. **3** fawning, cringing, ingratiating. **4** frugal, penurious.—*n* frugality, parsimoniousness.

inhaddin eldin *n* fuel that needs constant renewal.
inhaudin *same as* **inhadden.**
iniquious *same as* **iniquous.**
iniquity *n* inequity.
iniquous *adj* **1** iniquitous. **2** unfair.
injury *n* contumely, reproach, abuse.
injustified*adj* not put to death.
inker *n* an ink bottle.
inker-pinker *n* small beer.
ink-holder *n* a vessel containing ink.
inkle-weaver *n* a weaver of coarse tape.
inkling *n* **1** a faint or half-concealed desire or inclination. **2** a small measure or degree.
in-kneed *adj* knock-kneed.
ink-pud *n* a vessel for holding ink.
inks *n* **1** low-lying lands on the banks of a river, overflowed by the sea at high tide and covered by short, coarse grass. **2** shore pasture.
ink-standish *n* an inkstand.
inlaik, inlack, inleak *n* a deficiency, lack.—*v* **1** to be deficient, to lack. **2** to die.
inlair *n* a mill lade.
inlat *n* an inlet.
inler *n* **1** one who is in office. **2** one of the government party.
in-life *adj* alive.
in-liftin' *adj* (*used of animals*) too weak to rise without help.
inlucky *adj* dirty.
inlying *n* **1** child-bearing. **2** a confinement.
in-meat *n* **1** the edible viscera of any animal. **2** food given to animals within doors.
in-nix *v* to interfere.
inn *v* to bring in grain from the field.
inn *n* **1** a house. **2** (*in pl*) an inn. **3** (*in games*) the goal.
inner *adj in phr* **inner water** water entering a house through the foundation.—*n* (*in pl*) undergarments.
innerly *adj* **1** situated in the interior of a country. **2** low-lying. **3** snug, not exposed. **4** (*used of land*) fertile. **5** towards the shore, keeping near the land. **6** in a state of near neighbourhood. **7** neighbourly, sociable. **8** affectionate, compassionate.
innerly-hearted *adj* of a feeling or sympathetic disposition.
innes *n* an inn.
inning *n* the bringing of corn from the field.
inno *prep* **1** in. **2** into. **3** within. **4** close beside.
innocent *n* **1** an imbecile, idiot. **2** a half-witted person.
inorderlie *adv* irregularly.
in-ower, ~-o'er, ~-owre *adv* **1** near, close to the speaker. **2** over. **3** beside, close to. **4** close at hand. **5** within, to within, on the premises. **6** in and over.
in-owre and out-owre *phr* **1** backwards and forwards. **2** thoroughly. **3** violently. **4** with complete mastery.
inpervenient *adj* **1** unforeseen. **2** unprovided for.
inpit[1] *n* the gaining for someone a footing in favour or in a company.
inpit[2] *same as* **input.**
input, inpit *v* to put in.—*n* **1** a contribution to a collection. **2** help, assistance. **3** entrance. **4** beginning. **5** the feeding of children. **6** balance in change of money. **7** what one is instructed or inspired by another to do in a bad cause. **8** a setting up or settlement in business with financial help.
inputtin, inpitten *n* the feeding of children.
inputter *n* **1** one who instructs, or suggests to, another. **2** one who places another in a certain situation.
inquest *adj* inquired at.
inquietation *n* disturbance.
inring *n* **1** a movement of a curling stone, either to displace the winner or to lie within the ring around the tee. **2** the segment of the surface of a curling stone which is nearest the tee. *See* **outring.**
inscales *n* the racks at the lower end of a cruive (qv) in a river.

inseam *n* the seam attaching the welt to the insole and upper of a shoe or boot.

inseam-elshin *n* a shoemaker's awl for making the inseam (qv).

inseat, inset *n* **1** the kitchen of a farmhouse. **2** the mid-room between the kitchen and the parlour.

insense *v* **1** to make to understand. **2** to explain. **3** to instil. **4** to enlighten as to, to put sense into regarding.

insett *adj* substituted temporarily for another.

insh *same as* **inch**.

inside *n* the inner parts of the body.—*adv* in a room, house, etc, within.

insight, insicht *n* **1** the furniture of a house, household goods. **2** implements of agriculture kept within doors.—*adj* relating to insight.

insightit *adj* having insight into.

insight-kennage *n* knowledge, information.

insignificate *v* **1** to make void. **2** to reduce to nothing. **3** to deprive of authority.

insist *v* **1** to prolong a discourse. **2** to persevere. **3** (*with* **for**) to insist upon having.

in sma' *adv* briefly.

insnorl *v* **1** to entangle. **2** to inveigle.

insook[1] *n* **1** (*used of frost*) a touch, a slight amount. **2** (*of the tide*) an inrush.

insook[2] *n* **1** a bad bargain. **2** a fraud.

inspraich, inspraith, inspreght *n* furniture, household goods.

inspreight *adj* **1** domestic. **2** pertaining to what is within a house.

instance *n* **1** insistence. **2** effort.

instancy *n* **1** eagerness. **2** urgency.

insteid, instede *adv* instead.

instore *v* to store up.

instriking *n* the throwing back into the body of an eruption through cold, etc.

instruct *v* **1** to prove or show clearly. **2** to equip, furnish.

instrument *n* a formal document in proof of any deed of a civil or an ecclesiastical court or of a member of that court.

insucken-multure *n* the duty payable at a mill by tenants whose land is astricted to it.

in't *conj* with.—*pron* if it.

intack *adj* intact.

intae *prep* **1** into. **2** in.

in-taed *adj* having the toes turned inward.

intak[1] *n* **1** an inhalation. **2** the bringing home of the crop. **3** a contraction. **4** the narrowing of a stocking in knitting. **5** the place in a seam where the dimensions are narrowed. **6** a piece of land enclosed from moor, common, etc, for cultivation. **7** the part of the body of flowing water taken from the main stream. **8** the place where this water is taken off. **9** a dam across a stream to turn off water. **10** a cheat, swindle, fraud. **11** a swindler.—*v* to take a fortified place.

intak[2] *v* **1** to cheat. **2** to lift stitches in knitting.

intaker *n* a receiver of stolen goods.

intakin' *n* the part of a farm newly reclaimed from moor.—*adj* **1** deceptive. **2** fraudulent, swindling.

intear *adj* entirely intimate or dear.

inteer *adj* entire, unbroken.

intellects *n* wits, senses.

intellectuals *n* intellect, mental capacity.

intelligence *n* a friendly understanding, agreement.

intend *v* (*used as a legal term*) **1** to prosecute. **2** to raise an action.

intenet *adj* intended.

intent *v* **1** to intend. **2** to raise an action.—*n* **1** a litigation, lawsuit. **2** superintendence. **3** onlooking.

intention *v* to intend.

intercommon, ~-commune *v* **1** to hold intercourse with proscribed persons. **2** to forbid such intercourse.

intercommuner *n* **1** one who holds intercourse with proscribed persons. **2** one who treats between persons at variance.

intercommuning *n* holding intercourse with proscribed persons.

interdict *n* a court order placing a ban on something until a court can decide whether or not it is legal or lawful and injunction.—*v* to place under interdict.

interdick *v* to interdict.

interesse *v* **1** to interest. **2** to have an interest.

interlocutor *n* (*used as a legal term*) a judgment exhausting the points immediately under discussion in a cause, which becomes final if not appealed against in due time.

intermell *v* **1** to intermingle. **2** to intermeddle.

interpell *v* **1** to importune. **2** to interdict. **3** to warn against.

interpone *v* to interpose.

interrogator *n* a judicial examination.

interteen, intertenie *v* **1** to entertain. **2** to support. **3** to maintain. **4** to pay for the support of.

interteniement *n* support, maintenance.

interval *n* **1** the time between the hours of public worship. **2** a school break.

intervald *v* to interrupt, cause an interval.

intervert *v* **1** to intercept. **2** to appropriate to another than the original purpose.

in-through, ~-throw *adv* towards the fireplace, or the speaker, in a room.—*prep* by means of, through from the outside to the centre.

inthrow and outthrow *phr* in every direction.

intill *prep* **1** into. **2** in, within.

intimmers *n* the intestines.

intire *adj* intimate, very familiar.

into *prep* in, within.

intown, intoon *n* land or pasture adjacent to the farmhouse.—*adj* adjacent to the farmhouse.

in-town, ~-toon weed *n* an annual weed.

intrals *n* the entrails, the interior of the body.

intromission *n* **1** interference with another's money or effects. **2** (*in pl*) goings on with a person.

intromit *v* **1** to meddle with another's effects, etc. **2** to interfere. **3** to associate with.

invade *v* to assail, assault a person.

invaird *v* to put within, place inside.

invasion *n* an assault on a person.

inveet *v* to invite.—*n* an invitation.

inveetors *n* articles taken over by inventory at a valuation in taking a farm.

inventor *n* an inventory.

invert *v* **1** (*used of money*) to pervert to wrong ends. **2** to practise malversation.

invest *v* to take possession of one's own property.

invigor *v* to invigorate.

invitor *n* an inventory.

invitors *n* the crops, fencing, etc, paid by the incoming tenant of a farm.

invock *v* to invoke.

invyfull *adj* envious.

inward, inwaird *adj* living within.—*v* to put within, place inside.

inwick *v* (*used as a curling term*) to send a stone through a port (qv) or wick (qv), to strike the inring (qv) of a stone seen through that wick.—*n* (*in curling*) a station in which a stone is placed very near the tee after passing through a narrow port (qv).

inwith *adv* **1** to within. **2** towards the low country. **3** secretly. **4** inclining downwards. **5** inclining inwards.—*prep* within.

inwork *n* indoor or domestic work.

ion *n* **1** a horse. **2** a cow a year old.

ire *n* a passion.—*in phr* **an ire o' wraeth** a fit of wrath.

irie, irey *adj* **1** melancholy, gloomy. **2** causing fear.

Irish *n* an Irishman.

Irish blackgauds *n* a variety of potato.

Irish blackguard *n* a variety of snuff.

Irisher *n* an irishman.

irk *n* **1** weariness. **2** pain.—*v* to grow weary.

irm *v* **1** to whine. **2** to question fretfully and persistently.

iron, irne *n* **1** a sword. **2** a horseshoe. **3** a girdle (qv) for baking. **4** (*in pl*) the coulter, sock, etc, of a plough. **5** thin plates on the edges of the soles of clogs.

iron eer, ~ ever, ~ near *n* iron ore, chalybeate matter.

iron-eer spot *n* a spot on linen caused by oxide of iron.

iron-eer well *n* a mineral well.

iron-eery *adj* **1** chalybeate. **2** impregnated with iron.

iron-heater *n* a toaster made of strong iron wire or slender rods.

iron house *n* a room in a prison where prisoners were put or kept in irons.

iron-soupled *adj* having links or hinges of iron.

iron tings *n* fire tongs.

irony *adj* hard or strong as iron.

irr *int* a shepherd's call to a dog to pursue cattle.

irremediless *adj* irremediable.

irrepairable *adj* irreparable.

irresponsal *adj* insolvent.

irresponsality *n* **1** irresponsibility. **2** insufficiency.

irritancy *n* (*used as a legal term*) the rendering void of a contract, lease or deed, the terms of which are no longer observed.

irritate *v* to render a deed, etc, null and void, the terms of which are no longer observed by the party in whose favour it was granted.

irrnowt *same as* **irr**.

irrogat *adj* (*of a sentence or doom*) judicially pronounced.

is *conj* as.

i's, i'se *pron with v* **1** I shall. **2** I am.

isca *same as* **isk**.

isdel, isel *n* a hot cinder.

ish *n* **1** issue, exodus. **2** the act of passing out. **3** termination.

isher *n* an usher.

isherie *n* an usher's office.

ish-wish *int* a call to a cat to come for its food.

ising *n* the silvering of a looking glass.

isk, iskie, iskey, iskiss *int* a call to a dog.

iskie-bae *same as* **usqueba**.

isle¹*n* anger.—*v* to be angry.

isle² *same as* **isel**.

isle³ *same as* **aisle**.

is na, is nae *neg v* is not.

I-spy *n* the game of hie-spy (qv).

iss *int* a call to a dog to attack.

it *pron* that.—*adv* there.—*n* **1** (*in games*) the chief player. **2** (*used possessively*) its.

item *n* **1** a small creature. **2** a puny creature. **3** an object

ither *n* the udder of a cow, mare or goat.

ither *adj* **1** other. **2** each other.

itherwhere *adv* elsewhere.

ithin *prep and adv* within.

itinerarly *adv* in an itinerant way, in one not stationary.

its *poss pron in phr* **its lane** by itself, alone.

itsel' *pron* itself.

iver *adv* ever.

ivry *int* the call of a boy in playing marbles for liberty to play in any position he chose.

ivver-yestreen *n* the day before yesterday.

ivy-tod *n* an ivy bush.

iwis *adv* certainly.

iwyte *adv* assuredly.

ixey-pixey *same as* **icksy-picksy**.

izel, izle *n* **1** a smut or flake of soot from a chimney. **2** a hot cinder.

izzat, izzit, izzard *n* the letter Z.—*adj* zigzag.

J

jaabard *same as* **jabart**.

jaager *same as* **jagger**.

jaap *same as* **jaup**.

jab *v* to prick sharply.—*n* a prick.

jabart *n* **1** an animal in poor condition. **2** a fish out of season.

jabb¹ *n* a large, open creel lined with a net for catching the fry of coalfish.

jabb² *v* to fatigue, exhaust.—*n* **1** a big, lean, uncomely person. **2** a big-boned, lean, weakly animal.

jabber *n* chatter, idle talk.

jabbit *adj* fatigued, exhausted, worn-out.

jabbit-leukin' *adj* looking as if tired.

jabble¹ *v* **1** (*used of water*) to ripple, break in irregular wavelets. **2** to shake the liquid in a vessel. **3** to spill. **4** to cook badly. **5** to use constantly an article of food.—*n* **1** a ripple on the surface of water, small broken waves of the sea. **2** a confusion of a liquid and its sediment. **3** weak soup, tea, etc. **4** a quantity of any liquid or of wishy-washy drink. **5** turmoil, confusion.

jabble² *n* **1** a large, blunt needle. **2** a knife. **3** a curved sword.

jabbled *adj* **1** agitated. **2** stormy.

jabblick *n* a quantity of worthless liquid or half-liquid food.

jabblin *adj* weak, washy, insipid.

jabbloch *n* **1** a mess of liquid or half-liquid food. **2** weak, watery liquor.

jacey *n* **1** a jersey made of coarse wool. **2** any coarse woollen fabric.

jachlet *adj* blown or bent to one side.

jack¹ *n* **1** a half-contemptuous name for a single person. **2** a fellow. **3** a leather drinking vessel. **3** a jackdaw. **4** a roller for a towel. **5** a lavatory. **6** (*in pl*) small bones, pebbles, etc, used in children's games.

jack² *n* a jacket.

jack and the lantern *n* will-o'-the-wisp.

jacket *n* the skin of a potato.

jack in the bush *n* the navelwort.

jacko *n* **1** the jackdaw. **2** the magpie.

jack's alive *n* a game played with a lighted piece of paper or match.

jacksnipe *n* **1** the snipe. **2** the dunlin.

jacky-forty-feet *n* a centipede.

jacky-tar *n* **1** a sailor. **2** the sailor's hornpipe.

Jacob's ladder *n* the belladonna.

jacobus *n* a kind of gold coin.

jacolet *n* chocolate.

jad *n* **1** a worthless woman. **2** a lass, girl. **3** a mare, a horse. **4** an old, worn-out horse.—*v* to jade.

jadden *n* the stomach of an animal such as a sow.

jadstane *n* the common white pebble, found on the sand or beds of rivers

jae *same as* **jaw**².

jaffled *adj* tired, worn-out.

jag¹ *n* **1** calf leather. **2** jackboot.

jag² *n* **1** a leather bag or wallet. **2** a pocket. **3** a saddlebag.

jag³ *n* fatigue.

jag⁴ *v* to jolt or jerk roughly.—*n* **1** a sharp jerk, a jolt. **2** a rut.

jag⁵ *v* **1** to pierce, prick with a sharp instrument, thorn, etc. **2** to vex, irritate. **3** to rankle. **4** to pain. —*n* **1** a prick or tear made by nail, thorn, etc. **2** a thorn, prickle.

jag-armed *adj* armed with a sharp point or sting.

jager *n* *same as* **jagger**.

jagg *same as* **jougs**.

jagger¹ *n* a prickle.

jagger² *n* **1** a pedlar, a hawker, a fish-hawker. **2** a boat that is used to land the first-caught herrings in deep-sea fishing.

jagger steamer *n* a steamer for the transport of herrings.

jagget¹ *n* a full sack or pocket dangling at every motion from an awkward position.

jagget[2] *adj* prickly.
jaggie[1] *adj* **1** prickly, sharp-pointed, piercing. **2** stinging.
jaggie[2] *adj* **1** full of ruts. **2** having a jerking or jolting motion.
jag the flea *n* a contemptuous name for a tailor.
jaiket *n* a jacket.
jaip *v* to jape, jest.—*n* a jest.
jaiper *n* a jester, a buffoon.
jairble *same as* **jirble**.
jaisy *n* a wig.
jake, jak *v same as* **jauk**.
jake-easy *adj* quite willing.
jaker *n* an idler, trifler.
jackman *n* a retainer.
jallup *n* **1** a brisk purgative. **2** something to stir one up.
jalouse, jaloose *v* **1** to suspect, be suspicious. **2** to guess, imagine.
jalousings *n* suspicions.
jalp *same as* **jaup**.
jam[1] *v* **1** to put to inconvenience. **2** to press or corner in an argument.
jam[2]**, jamb** *n* **1** a projection, buttress or wing of a building. **2** the projecting side of a fireplace, **3** the upright support of a fireplace. **4** a corner made by a projection. **5** anything large and clumsy. **6** a big, ugly animal.
jamb-~, jam-stane *n* the side stone of a fireplace.
jamb-friends *n* intimate or fireside friends.
jamb o' a hoose *n* a badly built house, cheerless, cold, with the wind whistling through crevices in walls, doors and windows.
jamf *same as* **jamph**.
jamfle *same as* **jamphle**.
jamie *n* a rustic, clown.
jammer *same as* **yammer**.
jammerer *same as* **yammerer**.
jammie *n* a hovel.
jamp *v* jumped.
jamper *n* a tool for boring rocks, stones, etc, a jumper.
jamph[1] *v* **1** to make game of, to mock, jeer, sneer. **2** to shuffle, make false pretences. **3** to act the part of a male jilt. **4** to trifle, spend time idly. **5** to walk slowly and idly, lounge.—*n* **1** a mock, jeer, sneer. **2** an habitual trifler. **3** trifling over work.
jamph[2] *v* **1** to tire, fatigue. **2** to destroy by jogging or friction. **3** to chafe. **3** to drive to difficulties, straits or extremities. **4** to travel with extreme difficulty, as through mire, to trudge, plod.
jampher *n* **1** a male jilt. **2** an idler. **3** a scoffer.
jamphit *adj* reduced to extremities.
jamphle *v* to shuffle in walking owing to wearing too wide shoes.
jander *same as* **jaunder**.
jandies *n* jaundice.
Janet-Jo *n* a children's singing. game
jangle *v* to chatter.
jangler *n* a chatterer.
janitor *n* a school caretaker.
Janiveer *n* January.
jank *v* **1** to evade. **2** to trifle.—*n* a trick to give someone the slip.
janker *n* a long pole attached to two wheels, for carrying logs fastened to it by chains.
jankit *adj* fatigued.
jank off *v* to run off.
jank the labour *v* to waste time at work.—*n* an idler at work.
janner *same as* **jaunder**.
jannock *n* a thick oatmeal bannock.
jant *v* **1** to go on a journey for pleasure. **2** to go along in a merry, jaunty way.—*n* a journey for pleasure.
janting bottle *n* a pocket flask.
janty *adj* jaunty, cheerful.
Januar, Janwar *n* January.
jap *same as* **jaup**.

japandet *adj* japanned.
japin *same as* **jaupin**.
japper *n* a hollow, broken wave.
japple *v* **1** to stamp on clothes when washing them. **2** to get the feet wet. **3** to splash.
jarble *n* an old, tattered garment.
jarg[1] *v* to make a harsh, grating or creaking sound, to creak.—*n* a harsh, grating or shrill sound as of a rusty or creaking hinge.
jarg[2] *n* a trick played on one.
jargative *adj*. argumentative.
jargle *v* to produce a shrill sound repeatedly.
jargon *n* chatter, banter.
jargoning *n* idle talk, chattering.
jar-hole *same as* **jaw-hole**.
jarie *same as* **jaurie**.
jarness *n* a marshy place.
jarr *v* **1** to wrangle, quarrel. **2** to disturb, ruffle.
jasey *same as* **jeezy**.
jaskit *adj* jaded, worn-out.
jasp *n* **1** a spot, blemish. **2** a particle.
jass *n* **1** a violent throw. **2** a heavy blow. **3** the noise of a heavy blow.—*v* to dash, throw with violence.
jassich *n* a dull, heavy blow or fall.—*v* to shake violently.
jatter *v* (*of the teeth*) to chatter.
jaub *same as* **jab**.
jaubber *same as* **gabber**.
jauchle *v* **1** to walk as with feeble joints. **2** to make shift, do with difficulty.
jaud *same as* **jad**.
jaudie[1] *n* **1** the stomach of a pig or sheep. **2** an oatmeal pudding. **3** a haggis.
jaudie[2] *n* a little girl running wild on the streets, ragged, dirty and unkempt.
jaug *same as* **jag**.
jauk *v* (*used of shoes*) to be too large and loose upon the feet in walking.
jauk[1] *v* **1** to spend time idly. **2** to walk slowly.—*n* **1** an idler, a time-waster, **2** slacking over work.
jauk[2] *v same as* **jouk**.
jauker *n* a trifler, idler.
jaukery *n* trifling, slacking.
jaukin *n* **1** delay, idling, slacking, trifling. **3** dawdling. **4** flirting.—*adj* habitually slacking or idling at work.
jaumle *v* **1** to jumble. **2** to shake.
jaumph[1]**, jaumph**[2] *same as* **jamph**[1]**, jamph**[2].
jaumpt *v pt* jumped.
jaunder *v* to talk idly and foolishly, to maunder.—*n* **1** idle talk, maundering. **2** an idle talker, a chatterer, a maunderer.
jaunder aboot *v* to go idly about from place to place with no proper object.
jauner *same as* **jaunder**.
jauner aboot *same as* **jaunder aboot**.
jaunt[1] *same as* **jant**.
jaunt[2] *v* to taunt, gibe, jeer.—*n* a taunt, a gibe.
jauntingly *adv* jauntily.
jaup[1] *v* **1** (*used of water*) to dash and rebound in waves. **2** (*of the liquid contents of a vessel*) to dash against its side. **3** to splash. **4** to bespatter with mud or water, to throw water, etc, over anything or any person. **5** to spill. **6** to exhaust, to tire out. —*n* **1** a dash of water. **2** a broken wave. **3** a short, cross sea. **4** a spot or splash of mud, dirty water, etc. **5** a quantity of liquid. **6** dregs. **7** the sound made by shoes full of water. **8** a slap, a slight blow. **9** ruin, destruction.
jaup[2] *v* to fatigue, weary.
jaupie, jauppie *v* to spill, scatter, separate into small portions of liquid.
jaupin *n* a jerk, a smart stroke.—*adj* breaking in waves.
jaupit *adj* **1** exhausted, tired out. **2** empty-looking. **3** thin.
jaur[1] *same as* **jarr**.
jaur[2] *n* a jar.
jaur-hole *n* a sink, jawhole.

jaurie *n* an earthenware marble.
jaurnoch *n* **1** filth. **2** washings of dishes, etc.
jave[1] *v* to push hither and thither.
jave[2] *n* the upper crust of a loaf of bread.
javel *n* a blow, an injury.
javell *n* **1** a jail. **2** *same as* **jevel**[1].
jaw[1] *n* **1** talk, chatter. **2** abusive or insolent talk. **3** coarse banter.—*v* **1** to talk, chatter. **2** to vituperate, give insolence or abusive language.
jaw[2] *v* **1** (*used of water*) to dash, splash, surge. **2** to dash or pour a quantity of water.—*n* **1** a dash or spurt of water. **2** a quantity of water thrown out with a jerk or dash. **3** a wave, billow, breaker. **4** a large quantity of any liquid.
jaw-blade *n* the jaw.
jawbox *n* a sink under a tap, an indoor sink for dirty water.
jawcked *adj* baffled in an attempt.
jawd *same as* **jad**.
jawdie *same as* **jaudie**.
jawhole *n* **1** a place into which dirty water, etc, is thrown, a cesspool, midden. **2** a sink leading to a sewer.
jawlock *n* lockjaw.
jawner *same as* **jaunder**.
jawp[1] *same as* **jaup**.
jawp[2] *n* a jape, a nasty, mean trick.
jawther *v* to engage in idle or frivolous talk.—*n* (*in pl*) idle, frivolous talk.
jay-piet, ~-pyet *n* the jay.
jay-teal *n* the common teal.
jeal *v* **1** to freeze. **2** to be benumbed with cold. **2** to congeal as jelly.—*n* **1** extreme cold. **2** jelly.
jealous *adj* suspicious, apprehensive.
jealouse *same as* **jalouse**.
jealousy *n* suspicion.
Jeanie *n* a generic name for a country girl.
jeast *n* a joist.
jebber *same as* **gebber**.
jeck[1] *v* **1** to neglect (a piece of work). **2** to dislocate.
jeck[2] *v* to go rightly or smoothly.
jeck up *v* to abandon, to discard.
jecko *n* **1** the jackdaw. **2** the magpie.
Jeddart *adj* connected with Jedburgh.
Jeddart cast *n* a legal trial after the infliction of punishment.
Jeddart jug *n* a brass jug containing about two pints, used as a standard of dry and liquid measure.
Jeddart jury *n* a jury that tries a case after the infliction of punishment.
Jeddart justice *n* **1** punishment before trial. **2** a general condemnation or acquittal.
Jeddart law *n* punishment before trial.
Jeddart staff *n* a kind of battle-axe, a halbert.
jedge[1] *n* the order or warrant of a Dean of Guild.
jedge[2] *n* a gauge or standard measure.
jedgry *n* the act of gauging.
jee *v* **1** to stir, to move. **2** to cause to move. **3** to move aside, to swerve.—*n* **1** a move. **2** a turn, a swerve, a side motion.—*int* a call to horses.
jee *same as* **gee**[2].
jeeack, jeeak *v* to squeak, to creak.—*n* a creaking noise.
jeeble-jabble *n* any weak fluid, any mixture spoilt by being tossed about
jeed *adj* awry, squint.
jeedge *v* to judge, to adjudge.
jeeg[1] *v* to creak.—*n* a creaking noise.—*adv* with a creaking noise.
jeeg[2] *n* **1** a silly fellow. **2** a giddy girl. **3** a prostitute.
jeeg[3] *v* **1** to dance briskly as in a jig. **2** to trot, walk briskly
jeeg[4] *v* to taunt, to scoff.—*n* **1** a taunt, gibe. **2** an oddity.
jeeg[5] *v* **1** to laugh in a suppressed fashion. **2** to quiz.—*n* fun, frolic.
jeegets *n* little sounding boards, pegs and wheels in a piece of machinery.
jeeggit *v* **1** to move from side to side. **2** to jog, to ride or walk at a jog trot.

jeegin *n* a creaking sound.
jeegle[1] *same as* **giggle**.
jeegle[2] *v* to make a jingling or creaking noise.—*n* the creaking of a door on its hinges.
jeegler *n* an unfledged bird.
jeel *v* **1** to freeze. **2** to congeal as jelly.—*n* **1** extreme cold. **2** jelly.
jeelie *n* jelly.
jeelie piece *n* a piece of bread spread with jelly or jam.
jeelie pig *n* a jamjar.
jeel o' caul *n* a chill, a cold.
jeelt *adj* **1** chilled, frozen. **2** jellied.
jeel wi' caul *v* to catch cold, get a chill.
jeer *n* the seat of the trousers.
jeery *adj* jesting.
jeest[1] *n* a joist.
jeest[2] *n* a jest, a joke.
jeestie *n* **1** a joke. **2** a jesting matter or manner.—*adj* jesting.
jeet *n* **1** a worthless person. **2** a general term of contempt.
jeetle[1] *same as* **juitle**.
jeetle[2] *n* a small quantity.—*v* to spill, shake over.
jeety *adj* **1** bright. **2** neat. **3** fastidious.—*adv* neatly.
jeezy *n* a wig.
jeggin *adj* creaking.
jeggle-jaggle *v* to waver to and fro in order to save oneself from a fall.
jeho, jehoy *v* to cease, give over.
jeissle *n* a multitude of things thrown together without order.
jeist *n* *same as* **jeest**[2].
jeistiecor *same as* **justiecoat**.
jellily *adv* merrily, gaily.
jelly *adj* **1** upright, worthy. **2** excellent of its kind. **3** pleasant, agreeable. **4** jolly.
jellyflower *n* **1** the clove pink. **2** the wallflower.
jellyteen *n* gelatine.
jelouse *same as* **jalouse**.
jemmies *n* a species of woollen cloth.
Jen *same as* **Jeanie**.
jenk *same as* **jink**.
jenk amang the whins *n* the linnet.
Jenkin's hen *n* an old maid.
jennock *same as* **jonick**.
Jenny *same as* **Jeanie**.
jenny[1] *n* a spinning wheel.
jenny[3] *n* a centipede.
Jenny a' thing shop *n* a general dealer's shop.
Jenny cut-throat *n* the whitethroat.
jenny guld-spinner *n* the daddy-longlegs.
jenny heron *n* the heron.
jenny langlegs *n* the daddy-longlegs.
Jenny Mac *n* a girls' game.
jenny mony-feet *n* a species of centipede.
jenny nettle *n* the daddy-longlegs.
jenny spinner *n* **1** the daddy-longlegs. **2** a toy.
jenny wren *n* the wren.
jentie *same as* **genty**.
jeoparty-trot *n* **1** a quick motion between walking and running. **2** a contemptuous designation for one who walks in this fashion. **3** a coward.
jeopardie, jeoperd *n* a risky undertaking, a bold venture.
jerg *same as* **jirg**.
jerk *v* **1** to eject a person. **2** to walk smartly. **3** to make a splashing sound as of water in one's shoes. **4** to move, to rise briskly or suddenly.—*n* **1** a smart blow. **2** a stroke of good fortune. **3** a trick. **4** an instant.
jerkin[1] *n* a beating, thrashing.
jerkin[2] *n* **1** a gathering. **2** a kind of picnic.
jerkined *adj* wearing a jerkin.
jerniss *same as* **jarness**.
jesmie *n* jasmine.
jesp *n* **1** a gap or flaw in the weave of a fabric. **2** a seam in one's clothes. **3** a gap or small opening. **4** a stain, a blemish.

Jessie *n* a contemptuous name for an effeminate man.
jessie *same as* **jeezy**.
jet, jett *n* to strut.
Jethart *same as* **Jeddart**.
jether *same as* **jawther**.
jeuk¹ *same as* **jouk**.
jeuk² *n* a duck.
jeve *same as* **jave**.
jevel¹ *n* **1** a rascal, ne'er do weel. **2** a jailbird.
jevel², **jevvel** *v* **1** to joggle, to shake. **2** to spill a large quantity of any liquid at once. **3** to move obliquely.—*n* the dashing of water.
jevelor *n* a jailer.
Jew's ear *n* a species of lichen.
Jew's roll *n* a penny loaf, round on the top and with a reddish-brown glaze.
jib, jibb *v* **1** to milk a cow to the last drop. **2** to fleece.
jibber *v* to chatter, talk nonsense.—*n* (*in pl*) silly talk.
jibberage *n* gibberish.
jibber-jabber *v* to talk foolishly.—*n* noisy, foolish talk.
jibbings *n* the last milk taken from a cow.
jibble *v* **1** to spill. **2** to lose, to destroy. **3** to cook badly.—*n* a quantity of any liquid.
jick *v* **1** to avoid by a sudden jerk of the body. **2** to elude. **3** (**jick school**) to play truant.—*n* **1** a sudden jerk. **2** the act of eluding.
jicker *v* **1** to ride smartly, to trot. **2** to go quickly about anything.
jickering *adj* gaudy but tawdry in dress.
jicky *adj* (*used of a horse*) apt to shy and swerve suddenly.
jie¹ *v* to turn aside quickly.
jie² *same as* **gee**.
jiff *n* a giddy girl.
jiffer *n* a contemptuous name applied to an odd person, a jigger (qv).
jiffing *n* an instant.
jiff-jaffs *n* a fit of dependency.
jiffle *v* to shuffle restlessly, to fidget.—*n* **1** a shuffling movement. **2** a fidget.
jiffy, jiffey *n* **1** an instant. **2** a hurry.—*v* to hurry. —*adv* with haste.
jig¹ *n* **1** a jerk, shake, swing. **2** a sudden pull. **3** an illegal fishing instrument.—*v* **1** to dance vigorously or boisterously. **2** to play the fiddle. **3** to walk briskly. **4** to jerk, tilt. **5** to rock or sway, as a ladder under a person's movement. **6** to give a sudden pull. **7** to catch fish illegally with a jig.
jig² *n* **1** a certain measure of yarn. **2** a method of measuring yarn.
jig³ *n* **1** a spinning top. **2** anything that whirls. **3** a winnowing fan.
jig⁴ *same as* **jeeg**.
jiggate *n* a sail shaped like a leg of mutton.
jigger *n* one who jigs for herrings. *See* **jig¹**.
jigger *n* **1** a general term of contempt applied to a person. **2** an oddity.
jigger *n* a vehicle for carrying trees from a wood.
jigget, jiggot *n* a leg of mutton, a gigot (qv).
jigget *v* **1** to jog. **2** to move from side to side.
jiggle *v* **1** to make a jingling noise. **2** to creak.—*n* a creaking noise.
jiggle-jaggle *adj* irregular, uneven, zigzag.
jile *n* jail.—*v* to put in jail.
jiling *n* imprisonment.
jill-bow *same as* **gilbow**.
jillet, jilly *n* **1** a giddy girl. **2** a flirt, a jilt. **3** a young woman entering puberty.
jill-flirt *n* a flirting girl.
jilp¹ *v* to dash water upon one.—*n* **1** a spurt of water. **2** a small quantity of liquid. **3** an insipid, weak drink.
jilp² *same as* **gilp**.
jilpert *n* **1** anything too thin, as soup. **2** milk deficient in fat. **2** any liquid having little more than water in it.

jilt *v* to throw water upon one.—*n* a dash of water.
jim *adj* neat, spruce.
jimmer *v* to make a disagreeable noise on a violin. —*n* the sound made by a badly played violin.
jimmy *adj* **1** neat, spruce, smart. **2** handy, dexterous. **3** neatly made.
jimp¹ *n* a thin piece of leather, put between the outer and inner soles of a shoe.
jimp² *adj* **1** slender, small. **2** graceful. **3** neat, dainty. **4** scanty, meagre. **5** tight, close-fitting. **6** narrow.—*adv* scarcely, narrowly.—*v* **1** to curtail, contract. **2** to make too narrow. **3** to give too little measure, weight, room, etc.
jimp³ *n* **1** a coat, a loose jacket. **2** (*in pl*) easy stays, open in front.
jimp⁴ *v* to leap.
jimper *n* a fisherman's jersey.
jimpey *n* **1** a short gown without skirts, reaching only to the middle. **2** a kind of easy stays.
jimply *adv* scarcely, narrowly.
jimp-middled, --waisted *adj* slender-waisted.
jimpy *adj* slender.—*adv* tightly.
jimrie-cosie *n* a comfortable supply of drink.
jimy *n* a white pudding.
jin *n* the bolt or lock of a door.
jinch *adj* neat, spruce, smart.
jine *v* to join.
jing *n* a mild oath.
jing-bang *n in phr* **the hale jing-bang** the whole lot.
jingle¹ *n* gravel, shingle.
jingle² *n* the smooth water at the back of a stone in a river.
jingle³ *n* **1** noisy mirth. **2** an instant.
jingle the bonnet *n* a game in which the players put a coin each into a cap and, after shaking them together, throw them on the ground. The player who has most heads when it is his or her turn to jingle, gains the coins put into the cap.
jingle the key *n* the cry of the yellowhammer.
jingling *adj* **1** noisy, chattering. **2** wordy and unmeaning.
jingo-ring, -ringle *n* a girls' game in which, hand in hand, they dance in a circle singing.
jinipperous *adj* **1** spruce, trim. **2** stiff.
jink¹ *n* a chink, a long, narrow aperture, as when a window is slightly open.
jink² *v* **1** to elude. **2** to escape, to avoid. **3** to dodge, swerve quickly aside. **4** to slouch behind a wall. **5** to play tricks, to fool around. **6** to cheat, trick. **7** to move nimbly. **8** to turn quickly. **9** to spend time idly. **10** to move the arm, as in fiddling. **11** (*with* **in**) to enter a place suddenly and secretly. **12** to dance briskly.—*n* **1** a sudden turn. **2** a slip. **3** a trick, a lark. **4** a game. **5** an escape. **6** a particular point or turn in a dispute.
jinking's hen *same as* **jenkin's hen**.
jinker *n* **1** a fast horse. **2** a lively, giddy girl. **3** an immoral woman. **4** a wag.
jinket *v* **1** to make merry. **2** to gad about.
jinkie¹ *n* a small chink.
jinkie² *n* a children's game of sudden turns to avoid being caught.
jinking *n* **1** a trick, a lark. **2** a quick movement.—*adj* **1** wriggling. **2** dexterous. **3** evasive. **4** crafty. **5** merry, sportive.
jinniprous *same as* **jinipperous**.
jinny *same as* **jeanie**.
jipper *v* to imperil, to jeopardize.
jipperty, jippordy *n* jeopardy.
jirble *v* **1** to shake the liquid contents of a vessel so as to spill them. **2** to pour out unsteadily. **3** to empty a small quantity of liquid backwards and forwards from one vessel to another.—*n* (*in pl*) the dregs left by one often drinking from the same glass, cup, etc.
jirbling *n* **1** the spilling of liquids. **2** the changing of liquids from vessel to vessel. **3** (*in pl*) dregs of tea, etc. **4** (*in pl*) spots of liquid spilt here and there.

jird *same as* **gird**.

jirg *v* **1** to creak, grate, jar. **2** to grate, to grind. **3** to hesitate.—*n* a creaking sound.

jirge *v* **1** to churn. **2** to move violently.

jirger *n* anything that causes a creaking sound.

jirgle *v* to empty a small quantity of liquor from one vessel to another.—*n* **1** a small quantity of liquor. **2** (*n pl*) dregs left in a glass.

jirgum *v* to jerk, as if using a fiddle bow.

jirk¹ *v* to gnash one's teeth.

jirk² *v* **1** to unload, disburden. **2** to unload a vessel so as to defraud the revenue.

jirk³ *v* **1** to jerk. **2** to fidget.

jirkin *n* a sort of bodice worn by women.

jirkinet *n* a woman's outer jacket or jirkin.

jirt *v* to squirt.

jirt *n* **1** a jerk. **2** a sudden or sharp blow

jisk *v* to caper.

jisp *same as* **jesp**.

jist *adv* just.

jit *n* sour or dead liquor.

jivvle *n* **1** a jail. **2** a house sparsely furnished like a jail.

jizzen, jizzen-bed *n* childbed.

jizzy *dame as* **gizz**, **gizzy**.

jo *n* **1** a sweetheart. **2** a term of endearment.

Joan Thomson's man *n* a man who yields to the influence of his wife.

joater *v* to wade in mire.

joatrel *n* one who wades in mire.

job¹ *same as* **jab**.

job² *n* **1** a difficult or unfortunate affair. **2** an affair, illicit sexual intercourse

jobber *n* one who does odd jobs of work.

jobbernowl *n* the head.

jobbet *same as* **jabbet**.

jobbie¹ *adj* prickly.

jobbie² *n* a little job, a small piece of business.

job-troot *n* a jogtrot.

jock *n* **1** a country fellow. **2** a bull.

jockey *n* **1** a gipsy. **2** a strolling minstrel.

jockey coat *n* a greatcoat.

jockey's-grun, -ground *n* a boys' game.

jock-hack *n* **1** a farm servant in working clothes. **2** a horse-breaker.

Jock Hector *n* an exclamation equivalent to Jack Robinson.

jockie, jocky *n* **1** a country fellow, rustic. **2** a pig.

jockie-blindman *n* blind man's buff.

jock-landy *n* a foolish, destructive person.

jock-leg *n* a large clasp knife.

jock-neb *n* a turkey cock's nose.

jock-needle-jock-preen *n in phr* **to play jock-needle-jock-preen** to play tricks on one, to play fast and loose.

jock-startle-a-stobie *n* exhalations from the ground on a warm summer day.

jock-strike-the-knock *n* the striking hammer of a clock.

Jock Tamson *n* whisky.

Jock Tamson's bairns the human race, humankind.

jock-te-leear *n* a small almanac, the weather predictions of which seldom came true.

jockteleg, jock-tae-leg, jocktaleg *n* **1** a clasp knife. **2** a large pocketknife. **3** a large knife for kitchen use.

jocktie *same as* **joctibeet**.

jocky-haggis *n* part of the intestines, the stomach.

Jocky Ketch *n* a hangman, Jack Ketch.

joco *adj* pleased with oneself, happy, jocose.

joctibeet *n* **1** the wheatear. **2** the whinchat. **3** the stonechat.

joe *same as* **jo**.

jog *same as* **jag**⁵.

jogg *v* to confine in the jougs or pillory.—*n* (*in pl*) the jougs. *See* **jougs**².

jogger *n* a state of tremulousness.

joggle *v* **1** to lurch. **2** to jog on. **3** to cause oscillation. —*n* **1** a push. **2** a lurch. **3** the reeling of a carriage.

jogglie *adj* shaky, tottering.

john¹ *n* a country fellow, a rustic.

john² *n* a demijohn.

John Barley *n* John Barleycorn (qv).

John Barley-bree *n* **1** malt liquor. **2** whisky.

John Barleycorn *n* **1** malt liquor. **2** whisky.

johndal *n* a contemptuous name for a young ploughman or bothy lad.

John Dominie *n* a schoolmaster.

John Heezlum Peezlum *n* the man in the moon.

Johnie Barley *n* John Barleycorn (qv).

john jillets *n* a term of contempt for a man.

johnny *n* **1** a countryman. **2** a greenhorn, a simpleton. **3** a half-glass of whisky. **4** whisky.

johnny-cheats *n* a cheating pedlar.

johnny ged's hole *n* a grave-digger.

Johnny Lindsay *n* a young people's game.

Johnny Maut *n* John Barleycorn (qv).

Johnny Pyot's term-day *n* the day after the Day of Judgment, never and for ever.

johnny-raw *n* a greenhorn.

johnny rover *n* a boys' game.

johnny-stand-still *n* a scarecrow.

John o' Groat's buckie *n* the *Cyproea europoea*.

Johnsmas *n* St John's Day, Midsummer Day.

John's nut, St *n* two nuts growing together in one husk, supposed to secure one against witchcraft.

Johnstone's ribband, ~-tippet, St *n* a halter for hanging a criminal.

John Thomson's man *n* a husband who yields to his wife's influence.

joice *n* juice.

joined *adj in phr* **a joined member** a church member.

joinering *n* carpentry, joinery.

joiner-word *n* the password of a carpenters' guild.

joiner work *n* carpentry.

joint *n in phr* **a word out of joint**, a word improper in any respect, as approaching profanity or indecency.

joint-harl *v* to point a wall or fill its joints with mortar.

jointure *n* a juncture.

joise *same as* **joyse**.

joiter *n* an idler, loiterer, ne'er-do-weel.

joke-, jack-, jock-fellow *n* an intimate, one treated as an equal.

joke-fellow-like *adj* apparently intimate or friendly.

jokelar *adj* jocular.

jokie *adj* jocular, fond of a joke.

jolliment *n* mirth, jollity.

jollock *adj* **1** jolly, hearty. **2** fat. **3** healthy.

jolly-cheekit *adj* **1** bright, jolly. **2** comely.

jolster *n* **1** a mixture, a hodgepodge. **2** a quantity of ill-prepared victuals.

jonick *a* **1** genuine. **2** honest. **3** fair, just.

joog-jooging *adj* going pit-a-pat.

jook *same as* **jouk**.

jookerie *same as* **joukerie**.

jookery-cookery *n* artful management.

jookery-pawkrie, ~-paikerie *n* **1** artful management. **2** juggling. **3** roguery.

jookie *n* a slight swerve.

joop, joopan *same as* **jupe**.

joot *n* **1** sour or dead liquor. **2** used contemptuously of tea. **3** a tippler.—*v* to tipple.

jordan *n* **1** a chamber pot. **2** a urinal. **3** an open cesspool.

jordeloo *n* **1** a warning cry formerly given by servants in the higher stories of Edinburgh houses when about to throw dirty water, etc, into the streets. **2** the contents of the vessel used. *See* **gardyloo**.

jore *n* **1** a mixture of semiliquid substances. **2** a mire, slough.

jorg *n* the noise of shoes when full of water.

jorgle *n* the noise of broken bones grating.

jorinker *n* a bird of the titmouse species.

jork *v* to make a grating noise.

jorram *n* a slow and melancholy rowing song.

jorum[1] *n* a loud thunder crash.

jorum[2] *n in phr* **push about the jorum** the name of an old Scottish reel or the tune adapted to it.

jorum-jingler *n* a fiddler.

joskin *n* **1** a raw country youth. **2** a country bumpkin, a yokel. **3** a farm servant.—*adj* of the nature of a joskin.

joss *v* to jostle.—*n* a jostle.

jossich *n* **1** a dull, heavy blow or fall. **2** the dull sound of such.—*v* **1** to shake or dash violently. **2** to shake to pieces. **3** to jerk heavily backwards and forwards.

jossle *v* **1** to push through a crowd. **2** to hustle. **3** to shake.—*n* **1** a push, shake. **2** a big, clumsy cart or gig.—*adv* roughly, by pushing.

jossler *n* **1** a big person of rude manners. **2** an ugly, clumsy conveyance.

jossling *adj* wobbling, having an unsteady motion.

jot *n* **1** a light job. **2** an occasional piece of work. **3** (*in pl*) petty domestic work.—*v* (*with* **about**) to engage in light kinds of work.

jotter[1] *v* to engage idly in light and petty kinds of work, to do odd jobs.

jotter[2] *n* a notebook, an exercise book.

jotteral *n* **1** odd jobs. **2** mean or dirty work. **3** anything about to fall in pieces.

jotterie *n* **1** odd jobs. **2** mean or dirty work.

jotterie-horse *n* a horse of all work.

jotterie-man *n* a man of all work.

jotterie-wark *n* work of all kinds, such as does not belong to a regular worker, odd jobs.

jottle *v* to busy oneself with trifles, to accomplish little.

jottler *n* a man of all work, an odd-job man.

jottling-man *na* jottler.

jottrell *same as* **jotteral**.

joucat *n* a liquid measure, a quarter of a pint

jouf *n* a sort of nightgown.

joug *v* to shake, jog, jolt.

jougging *n* shaking, jolting,

jougs[1] *n* bad liquors.

jougs[2] *n* an instrument of public punishment which consisted of a hinged iron collar placed round the offender's neck, attached to a wall or post by a chain and locked

jouk, jouck *v* **1** to duck so as to avoid a blow. **2** to evade, dodge. **3** to swerve suddenly. **4** (*used of a stream*) to wind, meander. **5** (*of a light*) to flicker, to appear and disappear. **5** to bow, make obeisance, curtsy. **6** to cheat, swindle. **7** to jilt. **8** to play truant.—*n* **1** a swerve, stoop or duck to avoid a blow. **2** a bow, curtsy. **3** a shelter from a storm or a blow. **4** a dodge, trick.

jouker *n* a truant.

joukerie *n* **1** trickery, double-dealing. **2** jugglery.

jouking *adj* cunning, deceitful.—*n* cunning conduct.

joukit *adj* cunning.

joukrie-pawkrie *n* deceit.

jouk-the-squeel *n* a truant from school

jouky-daidles *n* a term of affection given to a child.

joundie *same as* **jundy**.

joup *same as* **jupe**.

jourdan *same as* **jordan**.

journey-wark *n* journeyman's work.

jouse *adj* proud, joyous.

joust *n* a joist.

joustle *same as* **jossle**.

jow[1] *v* **1** to ring or toll a bell. **2** to knell, ring, toll. **3** to ring a bell by moving its tongue. **4** to move, to attract attention. **5** to rock, roll. **6** to surge, come in waves or floods. **7** to spill the liquid contents of a vessel by moving it from side to side. **8** (*used of a river*) to roll forcibly in flood. **9** (*with* **in**) to ring a bell quickly, so as to indicate that the ringing will soon stop. **10** (*with* **on**) to jog on. — *n* **1** a knock, push. **2** a single pull or toll of a bell. **3** the ringing of a bell. **4** the sound of a bell. **5** the dashing of water in waves, wavelets or ripples. **6** water thus dashed.

jow[2], **jowie** *n* a fir cone.

jowgs *same as* **jougs**[2].

jowing-in bell *n* the curfew bell.

jowel *n* a jewel.

jowl[1] *n in phrs* **1 jowl to jowl** close together, cheek to cheek. **2 cheek for jowl** side by side.

jowl[2] *v* to jolt or shake rudely.—*n* the knell or clang of a bell.

jowler *n* **1** a heavy-jawed dog. **2** a foxhound.

jowp *n* **1** a skull, head. **2** a term of contempt denoting stupidity.

joy *n* a term of endearment or friendly address.

joyeusity *n* jollity, joyousness.

joy-glad *adj* glad and joyous.

joyse *v* **1** to have the use of, to possess. **2** to take pleasure in, to rejoice in.

jubilee *n* any merrymaking, as at the New Year.

jubious *adj* dubious, suspicious.

jubish *v* to suspect.—*adj* dubious.

jucat *same as* **joucat**.

juck[1] *n* a duck.

juck[2], **juckie** *n* a large, white, earthenware marble.

judaism *n* **1** treachery. **2** the being two-faced, like a Judas (qv).

Judas *n* one who is one thing to your face and another behind your back.

Judas-limmer, ~-scoundrel *n* a Judas (qv).

judge *v* to curse.

judgeable *adj* that may be judged.

judgment *n* one's senses, wits.

judgment-like *adj* **1** threatening some token of divine judgment. **2** mysterious, awful.

judgment-timed *adj* indicative of judgment by coincidence of time.

judicate *v* to think, imagine.

judicious *adj* intelligent.

juffle *v* **1** to shuffle. **2** to fumble.—*n* (*in pl*) old shoes down at the heels.

juffler *n* a shuffler in walking.

jug *n* an old measure of capacity kept at Stirling.

juge *v* to judge.—*n* a judge.

juggie *n* a jug or small vessel for drinking punch.

juggins, juggons *n* rags.

juggle[1] *v* to cheat, swindle.

juggle[2] *v* to shake.

juggs *same as* **jougs**.

jugle *same as* **juggle**.

juice *n* **1** gravy, sauce. **2** a soft drink. **3** the moisture of the body coming out in perspiration.

juik *same as* **jouk**.

juip *same as* **jupe**.

juist *adv* **1** very. **2** quite. **3** only.

juit *same as* **joot**.

juitle *v* **1** to delay. **2** to be idle or dilatory.

juitlin' *adj* **1** dilatory. **2** tricky.

juke *same as* **jouk**.

juliflower *n* the gillyflower.

jum[1] *n* a clumsily built, awkward-looking house.

jum[2] *adj* reserved, not affable.

jumle *v* jummel.

jumly *same as* **jummlie**.

jumm *n* the hollow moaning of the sea in a storm.

jummel, jummle *v* **1** to jolt. **2** to jumble. **3** to suffer from shock. **4** to be insane.—*n* **1** a splash, dash. **2** a shock.

jummlie *adj* muddy, turbid.—*n* the sediment of ale.

jump[1] *n* **1** a coat, a loose jacket. **2** (*in pl*) easy stays, open in front.

jump[2] *v* **1** (*of a garment*) to make too tight. **2** to burst asunder. **3** to tally, coincide. **4** (*of a gun*) to recoil at one's shoulder. **5** (*of crops*) to start growing.

jump[3] *adj* jimp.

jumpables *n* **1** a bodice. **2** corsets.

jumper *n* a maggot found in cheese, cooked meat, ham, etc.

jumpie *n* a short-tailed spencer worn by women.

jumping cattle *n* fleas.

jumping jack *n* **1** a child's toy made from the wishbone of a fowl, thread and shoemaker's wax. **2** a figure of a man made of pasteboard or thin wood, the limbs of which are pulled by a string. **3** a fickle, unstable person.

jumping-on-lid *n* the lid of a ship's cask in which pickled meat is kept ready for use.

jumping rope, ~ tow *n* a skipping rope.

jump-strap *n* a strap for a pair of corsets.

jump-the-cuddy *n* a boys' game.

jumze *n* anything larger than needful.

juncturer *n* an old name for a greatcoat.

jund *same as* **junt**.

jundie[1] *n* anything larger than strictly needful.

jundie[2]**, jundy** *v* **1** to jog with the elbow, **2** to jostle. **3** to move or rock from side to side. **4** to gush.—*n* **1** a shake, push. **2** a wrench causing pain. **3** a blow, a blow from being knocked about. **4** a dash. **5** a sudden impulse to one side.

jundy[1] *same as* **jundie**[2].

jundy[2] *n* **1** the trot. **2** the ordinary course.

Juniper *n in phr* **Janet Juniper's stinking butter** a nickname for a wife's daughter whom no man will marry because of her laziness, conceit and pride, and who, if married, would lie like stinking butter on her husband's stomach while she lived.

juniper-nebbed *adj* self-conceited.

junkit *adj* stout, sturdy.

junky *adj* stout, sturdy.

junnice *n* **1** a jostle. **2** a blow. **3** a jog.

junnie, junny *v* **1** to jog. **2** to shake a vessel containing liquor so as to produce the sound of dashing. **3** to irritate one by doing what he or she forbids. **4** to provoke to anger. —*n* **1** a severe blow. **2** a painful sprain or wrench.

junrell *n* a large, irregular mass of stone or other hard matter.

junt[1] *n* **1** a large piece of anything. **2** a large quantity of any liquid. **3** a squat, clumsy person.

junt[2] *n* **1** a jolt. **2** a heavy fall or blow.

jupe, jup *n* **1** a woman's skirt. **2** a woman's short gown, upper garment or nightgown. **2** a man's loose coat, a greatcoat. **3** a flannel shirt or jacket. **4** (*in pl*) loose stays. **5** a piece of flannel used instead of stays. **6** a kind of pelisse for children.

jurble *same as* **jirble**.

jurg, jurge *v* to make a creaking noise.

jurmummle *v* **1** to crush, **2** to disfigure. **3** to bamboozle.—*n* the act of crushing or disfiguring.

jurnal *v* to coagulate.

jurr[1] *n* the noise of a small waterfall descending among stones and gravel.

jurr[2] *n* a servant girl.

jurram *same as* **jorram**.

jurrie-worrieing *n* a growling noise like that of a dog about to worry.

juskal *n* a tale, traditional tale.

just[1] *v* to adjust.—*adj* accurate, exact.

just[2] *adv* **1** very, extremely. **2** quite. **3** only. **4** none other than.

justiciary power *n* the power of judging in matters of life and death.

justicoat, justiecor *n* a sleeved waistcoat.

justify *v* **1** to inflict capital punishment or other penalty. **2** to punish arbitrarily. **3** to judge. **4** to acquit legally.

just na *int* just so!

just now *adv* immediately, by-and-by.

jute[1] *n* a a term of reproach applied to a woman.

jute[2] *same as* **joot**.

jute[3] *n* whisky.

jutter *n* a tippler.

juttie *n* a tippler.

juttle *v* **1** to shake liquids. **2** to tipple.

juttler *n* a tippler.

juttling *adj* weak, wishy-washy.

juxter *n* a juggler.

jybe *v* to taunt.—*n* a taunt, a gibe.

jyple *n* a person with badly made clothes.

K

ka *same as* **kae**.

kabbelow[1] *n* salted codfish hung for a few days.

kabbelow[2] *n* potatoes and cabbage mashed together.

kabbie-labbie, ~-llaby, ~-lyabbie *n* a wrangle, gabble.— *v* to wrangle, dispute.

kabbie-llabiein *adj* fretful.

kach *same as* **keech**.

keech *n* excrement.—*v* to void excrement.—*int* an exclamation warning children not to touch anything dirty.

kacky *v* **1** to void excrement. **2** to befoul with excrement.

kade *same as* **ked**.

kadgie *adj* in high spirits.

kae[1] *n* **1** the jackdaw. **2** a thievish or mischievous person. **3** the jay. **4** a neat, little person. **5** the jackdaw's cry. **6** a caw.—*v* to caw.

kae[2] *v* to invite; *in phr* **kae me and I'll kae you** invite me and I'll invite you.

kae[3] *int* an exclamation of disbelief, contempt, disgust.

kaebie *n* the crop of a fowl.

kae-hole *n* a jackdaw's hole or nest in a tower.

kaery *same as* **kairy**.

kae-wattie *n* the jackdaw.

kae-witted *adj* scatterbrained.

kahute *n* **1** a little house. **2** a ship's cabin.

kaiber *n* **1** a pole. **2** rafter.

kaible *n* the crop of a fowl.

kaid[1] *same as* **ked**.

kaid[2] *v* (*used of cats*) to desire the male.

kaiding *n* the state of a cat desiring the male.

kaiding time *n* the time when a cat desires the male.

kaif *adj* familiar.

kaigh *int* an exclamation of contempt, disgust.

kail[1] *n* a race at a wedding, the prize being a kiss from the bride.

kail[2] *n* **1** colewort. **2** broth made of colewort and other greens. **3** food, dinner.

kail bell *n* the dinner bell.

kail blade *n* a leaf of colewort.

kail broo *n* water in which colewort has been boiled.

kail brose *n* the scum of kail broth (qv) mixed with oatmeal.

kail broth *n* vegetable soup boiled with meat.

kail castock, ~ custock *n* the stem of the colewort.

kail cog *n* a wooden bicker (qv) for holding broth, mashed colewort, etc.

kail-gully *n* a large knife for cutting down and slicing colewort.

kailie *adj* of colewort.

kail-kennin *n* cabbages and potatoes mashed together.

kail-kirk *n* a Glassite church, where the members dined together after service.

kailly *adj* **1** (*used of colewort, cabbage, etc*) producing leaves fit for the pot. **2** smeared with broth, greasy.

kailly brose *same as* **kale brose**.

kailly worm *n* the cabbage caterpillar.

kail-pat *n* **1** a large broth pot. **2** the extreme division at either end of the space divided into eight parts in the game of hopscotch.

kail-pat-whig *n* one who stays at home from church on Sundays.

kail root, ~ reef *n* the stump of a colewort stem that has been cut.

kail runt *n* **1** a colewort stem stripped of its leaves. **2** a full-grown plant of colewort. **3** a term of contempt.

kail runtle *n* a kail runt (qv) (*used contemptuously*).

kail seed *n* **1** colewort seed. **2** wild oats.

kail-seller *n* a greengrocer.

kail stick *n* a rod for stirring boiling broth.

kail stock *n* a plant of colewort.

kail-straik *n* straw laid on beams, anciently used instead of iron for drying corn.

kail-supper *n* one who is fond of broth, a name given to people from Fife.

kailtime *n* dinnertime.

kailwife *n* **1** a woman who sells colewort. **2** a scold.

kailworm *n* **1** a caterpillar that feeds on kail and cabbage. **2** a tall, slender person dressed in green.

kailyard *n* **1** a kitchen garden. **2** a small cottage garden. **3** the name given to a genre of sentimental fiction dealing principally with domestic life, making use of dialect speech and popular in the late 19th and early 20th centuries.

kaim[1] *n* **1** a comb. **2** a honeycomb.—*v* to comb.

kaim[2] *v* (*with* **down**) (*used of a horse*) **1** to strike with the forefeet. **2** to rear.

kaim[3] *n* **1** a low ridge. **2** the crest of a hill. **3** a pinnacle resembling a cock's comb. **4** a camp or fortress. **5** a mound.

kaim-cleaner *n* horsehair used for cleaning combs.

kaiming stock *n* the stock on which the combs were fixed for dressing wool, rippling lint and breaking flax.

kain *n* rent in kind.

kainer *n* a water bailiff.

kaip *same as* **keep**.

kair[1] *n* **1** mire. **2** a puddle.

kair[2] *v* to take the broken straws and grass out of corn after threshing.

kair[3] *v* **1** to toss to and fro. **2** to mix up. **3** to handle too much.—*n* much handling.

kaird *n* a gipsy, tinker.

kaird-turners *n* small bad money forged by tinkers.

kairins *n* pieces of straw, grass, etc, removed from newly threshed grain by turning it over with outspread fingers.

kairn *n* a cairn.

kairney *n* a small heap of stones.

kairs *n* rocks through which there is an opening.

kairy *adj* having different coloured stripes.—*n* **1** wool of different colours. **2** a small breed of sheep.

kaisart *n* **1** a cheese press. **2** a frame on which cheeses are placed to ripen.

kaivan *n* **1** the act of rearing. **2** the act of climbing.

kaive *v* **1** to topple over. **2** (*used of a horse*) to toss the head, to paw the ground, rear, plunge. **3** to climb. **4** to push backwards and forwards. **5** to walk awkwardly.—*n* the act of climbing.

kaiver *v* to waver in mind.

kaiving *adj* rearing and plunging, as a habit.

kaivy *n* a great number of living creatures, especially human beings.

kale *same as* **kail**.

kalwart *adj* (*used of the weather*) keen, very cold.

kamb, kame *same as* **kaim**[1].

kame *n* **1** a low ridge. **2** the crest of a hill.

kamshacle *adj* difficult to repeat.

kamster *n* a wool-comber.

kane *n* rent in kind.

kaner *same as* **kainer**.

kannie, kanny *adj* **1** careful. **2** prudent.

kaper *n* a piece of buttered oatcake bearing a piece of cheese.

kaping *n* a coping.

kar *adj* left-handed.

karrach *n* the game of shinty.

karriewhitchet *n* term of endearment for a child.

karshab *int* a cry used in the game of shinty.

kartie *n* a kind of louse resembling a crab, a crab-louse.

katabella *n* the hen harrier.

kate *same as* **kaid**.

katherane *n* a cateran (qv) riefer (qv).

kathil *v* **1** to beat very severely. **2** to pulp.—*n* **1** pulp. **2** an egg beaten up.

katie-~, katty-clean-doors *n* a child's name for the snow.

katie-hunkers *n* sliding on the ice in a crouching position. *See* **hunker**.

katie-wren *n* the common wren.

katty *n* the jack in the game of bowls.

katy-handed *adj* left-handed.

kauch *n* a bustle, fluster, uneasiness of mind, anxiety.—*v* to bustle, fluster.

kaur *n* calves.

kaur-~, kaury-handit *adj* left-handed.

kave[1] *n* **1** a bottle. **2** a spirit flask.

kave[2] *n* a hen coop.

kave[3] *v* to clean grain from broken straws, chaff, etc.

kavel[1] *n* a lot.—*v* to divide by lot.

kavel[2] *n* a low, mean fellow.

kavel-mell *n* **1** a sledgehammer. **2** a large hammer for breaking stones.

kaver *n* a gentle breeze.

kay *same as* **kae1**.

kay *same as* **kae**[3].

kazzie *n* a sack or net of plaited straw.

keach, keagh *same as* **kauch**.

keady *adj* wanton.

keal *same as* **kail**.

keallach *same as* **kellach**.

keam *n* **1** a honeycomb. **2** a young girl's bosom.

keam-drappit *adj* (*used of honey*) dropped from the comb.

keaming stock *same as* **kaiming stock**.

keapstone *n* a copestone.

keasen *same as* **kizen**.

keave[1] *v* (*used of horned cattle*) to toss the horns threateningly. **2** to threaten.

keave[2] *same as* **keeve**.

keavie *n* a species of crab.

keavie-cleek *n* a hooked iron implement for catching crabs.

keavle *n* that part of a field that falls to one when divided by lot.

keaw *same as* **kae**[1].

keb[1] *n* **1** the sheep louse. **2** any small creature. **3** an infant.

keb[2] *v* to beat severely.—*n* **1** a blow. **2** a thrust.

keb[3] *v* (*used of ewes*) **1** to bring forth a stillborn lamb. **2** to abandon a lamb. **3** (*with* **at**) to refuse to suckle.—*n* **1** a ewe that has brought forth immaturely or been accidentally prevented from suckling. **2** a sow pig that has been littered dead.

kebar, kebbre *n* **1** a rafter. **2** a strong person of stubborn disposition. **3** a companion, neighbour.

kebback *same as* **kebbuck**.

kebbie[1] *v* **1** to chide. **2** to quarrel.

kebbie[2]**, kebbie stick** *n* **1** a walking stick with a curved handle. **2** a shepherd's crook.

kebbie-lebbie *n* an altercation when a number of people talk at once.—*v* to carry on an altercation.

kebbuck, kebbock *n* a whole cheese.

kebbuck creel *n* a cheese basket.

kebbuck end *n* the remains of a cheese.

kebbuck heel, ~ stump *n* the end of a cheese.

kebec *same as* **kebbuck**.

keb ewe *n* a ewe that has lost her lambs.

keb house *n* a shelter for young lambs in the lambing time.

kebrach, kebritch *n* very lean meat.

kebrock *n* anything big and clumsy.

kebruch *n* meat unfit for use.—*adj* **1** lean. **2** rapacious.

kebs *n* the game of knuckle-bones (qv).

kebuck *same as* **kebbuck**.

kech *n* a girl's shoe.

kecher *v* to cough continuously.

kecht *n* a consumptive cough.

keck¹ *v* **1** to draw back from a bargain. **2** to flinch.

keck² *v* to faint or swoon suddenly.

keck³ *n* a linen covering for the head and neck.

keckle *v* **1** to cackle. **2** to laugh heartily. **3** to chuckle. **4** to giggle. **5** to show signs of eager ness, joy, temper.—*n* **1** a chuckle. **2** noisy laughter. **3** giddy behaviour. **4** loud chatter. **5** foolish, idle talk.

keckle ~, keckling pins *n* knitting pins, knitting wires.

keckler *n* a hen.

ked *n* a sheep tick.

kedge¹ *v* **1** to stuff. **2** to fill with food.

kedge² *adj* active, brisk.

kedge³ *v* **1** to toss about. **2** to move a thing quickly from one place to another.

kedge-kyte *n* **1** a large, protuberant belly. **2** a glutton.

kedgie *adj* brisk, lively.

kee *n* humour.

keechan *n* a small rivulet.

keechie *adj* dirty.

keechin *n* in distillation, the liquor after it has been drawn from the grains and fermented, before going through the still.

keechle *same as* **keuchle.**

keed *n* the cud.

kee-how *n* the game of hie-spy (qv).—*int* a cry made in the game.

kee-hoy *n* a variety of hie-spy (qv).

keek¹ *same as* **keck³.**

keek² *v* **1** to look, peep, glance. **2** to pry.—*n* a peep, a stolen glance.

keek-a-bo, keek-bo *n* the game of peepboo.—*int* a cry during the game.

keek-bogle *n* the game of hide-and-seek.

keeker *n* **1** a gazer, spectator. **2** a black eye. **2** (*in pl*) the eyes.

keek-hole *n* a peephole.

keeking-glass *n* **1** a looking glass. **2** a telescope.

keek-keek *int* a cry in the game of hide-and-seek.

keek-roon-corners *n* a spy.

keeky-bo *same as* **keek-a-bo.**

keel¹ *n* **1** a small vessel, a lighter. **2** the spine. **3** the lower part of the body, the breech.—*v* **1** (*of a ship*) to plough the seas. **2** to overturn, knock down.

keel² *adj* cool.—*v* to cool.

keel³ *n* **1** ruddle. **2** any marking substance, black or red.—*v* **1** to mark with ruddle. **2** to mark a person or thing as an expression of dissatisfaction, contempt, jealousy, etc.

keel⁴ *n* a large, clumsy person, animal or thing.

keel⁵ *v* **1** to cease. **2** (*with* **in**) to give over, come to an end.

keel⁶ *n* a mark on the warp showing the weaver where to cut his cloth.

keelack *same as* **kellach.**

keelan *n* a big, awkward person.

keelavine, keelavine pen *n* a pencil of black lead.

keel-draught *n* **1** the part of the keel below the garboard strake. **2** a false keel.

keel-hauled *v* intoxicated.

keel-hauling *n* **1** a severe questioning. **2** a scolding, berating.

keelick *n* **1** anger. **2** trouble. **3** vexation. **4** a stroke, a blow.

keelie¹ *adj* **1** reddish. **2** coloured by ruddle.

keelie² *n* **1** a street Arab. **2** a pickpocket. **3** a young working-class male from an urban area. **4** a rough, tough person.

keelie³ *n* **1** a long plank or beam for amusing children. **2** the game played, a kind of seesaw.—*v* to play the game on a keelie.

keelie⁴ *n* the kestrel.

keelie-craig *n* a crag on which the kestrel nests.

keelie-hawk *n* the kestrel.

keeling *n* a large cod.

keel-row *n* **1** a Galloway country dance. **2** a popular bridal tune.

keelup *same as* **keelick.**

keelyvine, keelivine *same as* **keelavine.**

keen¹ *v* to wail over a corpse.

keen² *adj* **1** (*used of a horse, dog, etc*) eager. **2** (*of the weather*) severe, cold. **3** avaricious. **4** devoted to self-interest. **5** (*with* **for**) desirous of. **6** (*with* **to**) eager, anxious to.

keen-bitten *adj* **1** eager, sharp. **2** hungry.

keenk *v* **1** to cough. **2** to labour for breath.

keen killer *n* an eager shooter of game.

keep¹ *v* **1** to watch over. **2** to fare in health. **3** to attend regularly.—*n* **1** possession. **2** charge, keeping. **3** (*in pl*) marbles kept by a winner. **4** food kept up from previous meals.

keep² *v* to catch what is thrown to one.

keeper *n* **1** the catch of a clasp. **2** the guard ring of a wedding ring. **3** (*in pl*) store cattle.

keepet, keeped, keepit *v, adj* kept.

keeping *n* **1** board and lodging. **2** guard.

keeping off *prep* except.

keep's *int* an exclamation of surprise.

keer *n* a cure.—*v* to cure.

keerie *n* a call to a lamb or sheep.

keerie-oam *n* a game similar to hie-spy (qv).

keerikin *n* **1** a sharp and sudden blow that knocks one down. **2** a fall.

keeriosity *n* **1** curiosity. **2** (*in pl*) curious habits.

keerious *adj* curious.

keeroch *n* **1** a contemptuous name for any strange mixture, particularly a medicinal compound. **2** a soss (qv).—*v* to mess about.

keers *n* a thin gruel given in the spring to feeble sheep.

keesich *int* a word used by one entering a room where a person is already seated and requesting a seat.

keeslip *n* **1** the dried stomach of a calf used for curdling milk. **2** rennet. **3** a plant resembling southernwood, used as a substitute for rennet.

keessar, keeser *n* a big, strongly built, ugly person or animal, particularly a woman.

keest¹ *n* **1** sap. **2** substance.

keest² *v* **1** cast. **2** vomited.

keestless *adj* **1** tasteless, insipid. **2** giving no nourishment. **3** without substance. **4** spiritless.

keet *n* the ankle.

keeth *same as* **kythe.**

keething-sight *n* the view of the motion of a salmon, by marks in the water.

keetikiins *n* gaiters.

keeve *n* **1** a tub. **2** a mashing vat.

keezlie *adj* (*used of soil*) unproductive, barren.

keff *n* *in phr* **be in a gay keff** to have one's spirits elevated.

keffel *n* an old or inferior horse.

keh *same as* **kae³.**

keig, keik *n* a wooden trumpet, formerly blown in the country districts of Aberdeenshire at 5 p.m.

keik *same as* **keek².**

keil¹ *n* a haycock.—*v* to put hay into cocks.

keil² *same as* **keel³.**

keill *n* a small vessel, a lighter

keilling *same as* **keeling.**

keiltch *v* **1** to heave a burden farther up on one's back. **2** to jog with the elbow.—*n* **1** an upward heave. **2** one who heaves upwards.

keilup, keilop *same as* **kellup.**

keis *n* a large straw basket for carrying on the back.

keisen, keizen *same as* **kizen.**

keist *same as* **keest².**

keisty *adj* lecherous.

keisyl stane *n* a flintstone.

keith *n* a bar laid across a river to prevent salmon going farther up.

keit you *int* **1** an exclamation of impatience. **2** get away!

keize, keizie *n* a sort of basket made of straw.

kekle *same as* **keckle**.

kelch *n* a thump. **2** a push.—*v* to push.

kelder *n* the womb.—*phr* **Hans in kelder** a child in the womb.

kelk *n* the roe of cod, ling, etc.

kell *n* **1** a child's caul. **2** an incrustation of grime, etc. **3** the scurf, etc, on a child's head. **4** dandruff. **5** a scabbed head. **6** a network cap for a woman's hair. **6** the hinder part or crown piece of a woman's cap.

kellach, kellachy *n* **1** a small cart of wicker fixed to a square frame and tumbling shafts. **2** a conical basket of coarse wicker for carrying manure to the fields. **3** anything built high or narrow or in a slovenly way.

kellop *n* a stroke, blow.

kelp *n* a raw-boned youth.

kelpie *n* **1** a water sprite, a river horse. **2** a raw-boned youth.

kelshie *adj* crabbed, rude.

Kelso boots *n* heavy shackles put on prisoners' legs.

Kelso convoy *n* escorting a friend a short distance.

Kelso-rung *n* a Kelso cudgel, classed along with Jeddart staves (qv).

kelt[1] *n* a salmon spent after spawning, a foul fish.

kelt[2] *n* frieze cloth, generally of native black wool.

kelt-coat *n* a coat of coarse homespun made of black and white wool.

kelter[1] *n* money.

kelter[2] *v* **1** to move at full speed. **2** to move in an undulating manner. **3** to move uneasily. **4** (*used of the stomach and of the conscience*) to be uneasy with qualms. **5** to tilt. **6** to upset. **7** to fall headlong. **8** to struggle violently, as a hooked fish.—*n* a somersault, a fall heels over head.

kelt-hooks *n* hooks for catching a kelt (qv).

keltie *n* the kittiwake.

keltie's mends *n* a bumper to be drunk by a reluctant or unfair drinker in a company.

kelty *n* a child.

kelty, keltie *n* **1** plenty. **2** a bumper to be drunk by those who do not drink fair. **3** a reluctant or unfair drinker.

kem[1], **keme, kembe** *same as* **kaim**[1].

kem[2] *v in phr* **kem one's croon 1** to tear one's hair. **2** to strike one's head.

kembit *n* the pith of hemp.

kembo *adv* akimbo.

kemester *n* a wool-comber.

keming stock *same as* **kaiming stock**.

kemmin *n* an active and agile child or small animal.

kemp[1] *n* **1** a stalk and seed head of ribgrass or lancet-leaved plantain. **2** a game played with these. **3** crested dog's-tail grass.

kemp[2] *v* **1** to fight, struggle. **2** to contend for mastery. **3** to compete, especially in the harvest field. **4** to take food hurriedly so as to finish first.—*n* **1** a competition. **2** strife. **3** a champion. **4** an impetuous person.

kempel *v* **1** to cut in separate parts for a purpose. **2** to cut wood into billets.—*n* **1** a piece, fragment. **2** a piece cut off.

kemper *n* **1** a reaper who kemps in harvest (*see* **kemp**[1]). **2** one who strives. **3** a competitor.

kempin *n* **1** striving on the harvest field. **2** a struggle for superiority in any form.

kemple *n* a measure of straw or hay, containing forty bottles.

kemps *n* a variety of potatoes.

kemp seed *n* **1** a name given to the seed of the ribgrass. **2** (*in pl*) the 'seeds' or husks of oats, when meal is made. **3** the reeings or riddlings of the sieve.

kempstane *n* a stone placed to mark where the first player reaches with the putting stone, the player who throws farthest beyond being the winner.

kempy *n* a bold, impetuous person. *See* **kemp**[2].

kemster *n* a wool-comber.

kemetock *n* a capstan.

ken[1] *same as* **kenn**.

ken[2] *v* **1** to know. **2** to be acquainted with to recognize. **3** to destroy.—*n* **1** knowledge. **2** one's own mind. **3** recognition. **4** sight, view.

ken[3] *n* **1** 300-stone weight of cheese. **2** the quantity of cheese made by a farmer in one season.

kenable *adj* easily known or recognizable.

kendal-ben *n* very thick shoe leather for soles.

kendle[1] *v* to kindle, to bring forth.

kendle[2] *v* to kindle a fire, etc.

kendlin' *n* what is used to kindle a fire.

kendlin brand *n* a brand or live coal for kindling a fire.

kendlin peat *n* a live peat for kindling a fire.

kendlin stuff *n* materials for lighting fires.

kendlin wood *n* matchwood, splinters or chips of wood for lighting fires.

ken-gude *n* **1** a caveat. **2** a lesson or example to teach, warn or profit by.

kenilt *v, adj* kindled.

kenk *same as* **kink**[2].

kenkind *same as* **kinkind**.

kenle *v* to kindle a fire.

kenless *adj* unknown.

kenlin *n* what is used to light a fire.

ken-mark *n* a distinguishing mark.

kenn *n* a headland, point.

Kenns *n* the district along the banks of the Ken in Galloway, the Glenkens.

kennan *same as* **kenning**.

kenna-what *n* a nondescript.

kenned *v* known.

kennelling *n* firewood.

kenner *n* **1** a water bailiff. **2** the overseer of the crew of a salmon coble.

kennet, kenet *n* a small hound, a beagle.

kenning, kening *n* **1** knowledge, experience. **2** recognition, acquaintance. **3** a small portion of anything. **4** a very little. **5** the distance a person can see.

ken-no *n* a cheese made to be eaten at a birth by the gossips. *See* **gossip**.

kens *n* rent paid in kind.

kensie *same as* **kenyie**.

kenspeck, kenspeckle *adj* **1** easily recognized from some peculiarity. **2** conspicuous, notable.—*n* a distinguishing mark or feature.

kent[1] *n* **1** a long pole used by shepherds for leaping ditches, etc. **2** a long, lank person.— *v* to pole a boat or punt.

kent[2] *v* knew.—*adj* known, familiar.

kent-face *n* an intimate, an acquaintance.

kent-fit *n* a familiar footstep.

kent-fowk *n* people familiarly known.

kent-grun' *n* a familiar district.

kenyie, kenzie *n* **1** a rustic. **2** (*in pl*) fighting fellows.

keoch *n* a wooded glen.

kep[1] *n* a cap.—*phr* **to hing up one's kep to** to pay one's addresses to, to court.

kep[2], **kepp** *v* **1** to catch anything thrown or falling. **2** to catch with the hand. **3** to fasten up the hair. **4** to intercept. **5** to hinder progress, turn or head back an animal. **6** to encounter, meet accidentally. **7** to prepare for. **8** to gather up on the way. —*n* **1** reach, range. **2** a catch.

kep[3] *v* to keep.

kep o' steill *n* a steel headpiece.

keppie *adj* quick at turning back an animal.

kepping kaim *n* a large comb for keeping up a woman's hair on the back of her head.

keppit *adj, v* kept.

kepstone *n* the copestone.

ker[1] *n* the soft kernel of suet.

ker[2] *adj* **1** left-handed. **2** awkward. **3** morally wrong.

kerbit *adj* peevish, cross.

ker cake *n* a cake baked specially for Fastern's E'en.

kerd *v* to card wool.

ker-handit *adj* left-handed.

kerk v **1** to scold. **2** to nag.

kerl n a tall candlestick.

kerlin n an old woman.

kern, kerne n a foot soldier armed with a dart or a skean. **2** a vagabond, a sturdy beggar.

kernel n a hard gathering or gland in the neck.

kerrag n a contemptuous term applied to a woman.

kerse[1] n **1** a watercress. **2** a cress.

kerse[2] n an alluvial plain near a river.

kerse[3] n a cherry.

kersen v to baptise, to christen.

kertch n a woman's headdress.

kertie same as **kartie**.

kerve v to carve.—n a cut, an incision.

kerwallop adv pit-a-pat.

kest[1] same as **kist**[1].

kest[2] same as **keest**[2].

ket[1], **kett** n **1** carrion. **2** the flesh of animals that have died of disease, braxy. **3** a worthless fellow. **4** a term of contempt.

ket[2], **kett** n **1** couch grass. **2** a spongy peat composed of tough fibres of moss, etc. **3** exhausted land. **4** a fleece.

ket[3] adj irascible.

ketch v to catch hold of and throw down.

ketle v to kitten.

ketlin n a kitten.

ketrail n a term of great contempt and abhorrence.

kett[1] v to shield, protect.

kett[2] same as **ket**[2].

kettach n the fishing frog or sea devil.

kettie-neetie n the dipper.

kettle n **1** a church bell (used in contempt). **2** a Tweedside feast or social party in which salmon is the main dish.

kettle of fish n a salmon feast.

kettle pan n a cooking utensil.

kettlin n a kitten.

kettrin n a cateran (qv).

ketty adj **1** (used of grass) matted with couch grass. **2** (of peats) spongy, fibrous.

keuchle v to cough.—n **1** a cough. **2** the act of coughing.

keude adj harebrained, wild.

keuill v to have intercourse.

keuk v to cook.—n a cook.—phr **keuk one** to get what one wants of a person.

keul same as **kevel**[5]

keulins n young people in general.

keuter v to coax, wheedle.

keuve v **1** kneaded. **2** chewed much. See **kiauve**.

keve same as **kaive**.

kevee n in phr **on the kevee** with a flow of spirits bordering on derangement, with a bee in the bonnet.

kevel[1] n a staff, cudgel.

kevel[2], **kevil** v **1** to walk or climb clumsily. **2** to hold or wield awkwardly.

kevel[3] n a low, mean fellow.

kevel[4] v **1** to quarrel, wrangle. **2** to scold.—n a quarrel.

kevel[5] n a lot.—v to cast lots.

kever n a gentle breeze, causing a slight motion of the water.

kevie same as **kave**[2].

kevins n the refuse separated from grain.

kew[1] v struggled. **2** wrought hard.—n an overset from great fatigue. See **kiauve**.

kew[2] v to clew up.—n **1** a clew. **2** a queue.

kewl n a halter put under the jaws and through the mouth of a horse not easily managed.

kex n human excrement.

key n **1** the seed of the ash. **2** a spanner, screw-wrench. **3** mood, frame of mind.—v to fasten with a key, lock.

key-cold adj **1** cold as a key, quite cold. **2** thoroughly indifferent or unconcerned.

keysart same as **kaisart**.

keyse same as **keis**.

keystane n a masonic symbolical decoration.

keytch v **1** to toss. **2** to drive backwards and forwards.—n a toss.

kiaugh same as **kauch**.

kiauve v **1** to knead. **2** to chew hard. **3** to struggle, sprawl. **4** to pull to and fro. **5** to work hard.—n **1** a kneading. **2** hard chewing. **3** a struggle, tumbling. **4** hard toil.

kibble adj **1** strong, active. **2** compactly framed. **3** smart at walking.

kibbling n **1** a cudgel. **2** a roughly cut stick.

kibbock same as **kebbuck**.

kich same as **keech**.

kichen, kichin adj **1** disgusting. **2** disagreeble. **3** (used of children especially) having a disagreeable temper.

kick[1] n a novelty.

kick[2] v **1** to walk with a silly, haughty air. **2** to show off. **3** to beg successfully for money. **4** to play tricks. **5** to tease. **6** (with up) to make or raise disturbance, etc, to die.—n **1** a trick, practical joke. **2** a puzzle. **3** the knack, trick. **4** contemptuous and summary dismissal. **5** (in pl) fine airs.

kick-at-the-benweed adj headstrong, unruly.

kickba n **1** a football. **2** the game of football.

kick-bonnety n a boys' game in which one boy's cap is used as a football until the owner can seize another's cap, which then becomes the football.

kicken-hearted adj faint-hearted.

kicker v **1** to titter. **2** to laugh in a suppressed manner.—n a titter. **2** a suppressed laugh.

kickers n in phr **stand one's kickers** to withstand one.

kickshaw n **1** a novelty. **2** a curio.

kick-up n **1** a tumult, uproar. **2** a great stir or row.

kicky adj **1** smartly dressed, showy. **2** aspiring beyond one's station. **3** pert, clever, lively. **4** saucy. **5** repulsive.

kid[1] v **1** to toy. **2** to render pregnant.

kid[2] same as **ked**.

kiddie n a candle.

kiddet adj pregnant, with child.

kiddy same as **keady**.

kidgie adj **1** friendly. **2** familiar. **3** lovingly attached.

kie v **1** to detect. **2** to show.

kiel same as **keel**[3].

kies n keys.

kiest v cast.

kiff n a fool.

kiffle v to cough from a tickling sensation in the throat.—n a tickling or troublesome cough.

kiffling cough n a slight cough, caused by a tickling.

kift n a talk, a chat, a gossip over liquor.

kigger v to mess about with soft or semiliquid foods.—n a wet mass.

kiggle-kaggle v (in curling) to make a succession of inwicks (qv) up a port to a certain object.

kigh v to cough from a tickling in the throat.—n a short, tickling cough.

kighen-hearted same as **kicken-hearted**.

kigher[1] same as **kecher**.

kigher[2] same as **kicker**.

kighle v to have a short, tickling cough.—n a short, tickling cough.

Kilbaigie n whisky formerly distilled at Kilbaigie in Clackmannan county.

kilch[1] v **1** (used of horses) to throw up the hind legs, especially when tickled on the croup. **2** (with up) to raise one end of a plank by sitting on the other.

kilch[2] same as **kelch**.

kilches n wide-mouthed trousers worn by male children.

kildoch n the herring.

kile same as **kyle**[3].

kiles n ninepins.

kilfud-yoking n a fireside disputation.

kilk same as **kelk**.

kill[1] v **1** to overcome. **2** to exhaust. **3** to hurt severely.

kill[2] n the opening in a stack for ventilation.

kill[3] n a kiln.—v to dry in a kiln.

killach same as **kellach**.

kill-barn *n* a barn attached to a kiln.
kill-beddin *n* the straw in a kiln on which grain was spread to dry.
kill-briest *n* the part of a kiln built above the arch of the open space in front of the fireplace.
kill-cow *n* a matter of consequence, a serious affair.
kill-door *n* the raised steps at the entrance to a kiln.
kill-dry *v* to dry in a kiln.
kill-ee *n* the fireplace of a drying kiln.
killer *n* a finishing blow.
kill-fuddie *n* the aperture by which fuel is put into the kiln, the inner part of the killogie (qv).
kill-fudyoch *n* a fireside disputation.
kill-head *n* (*in curling*) a large number of stones all lying near the tee.
kill-huggie, ~-hogie *same as* **killogie**.
killick *n* 1 the fluke of an anchor. 2 the 'mouth' of a pickaxe.
killicoup *n* a somersault, a tumble head over heels.
killie *same as* **keelie**³.
killieleepsie, killileepie *n* the common sandpiper.
killiemahou *n* 1 an uproar. 2 a confusion.
killimanky *n* 1 a petticoat made of calamanco. 2 a petticoat.
killin *same as* **keeling**.
killing clothes *n* clothes worn by a butcher in the slaughter house.
killing times *n* the times immediately preceding the Revolution of 1688, during which the Covenanters suffered.
killin-kites *n* a designation of the inhabitants of Colvend in Galloway, from codfish being their chief sustenance.
kill-kebber *n* 1 a kiln rafter. 2 a support for a kiln.
kill-man *n* the man in charge of a kiln.
kill-meat *n* a perquisite of the shillings (qv) of a mill, falling to the under-miller.
kill-moulis *n* a hobgoblin, represented as having no mouth.
killogie *n* the open space in front of the fireplace in a kiln.
killogue *v* 1 to confer secretly. 2 to plot, conspire.
kill-pot *n* the pot in which grain was dried in a kiln at a farmstead.
kill-ravage *n* a disorderly mob, engaged or engaging in some outrage.
kill-rib *n* 1 a support for a kiln. 2 a kiln rafter.
kill-ring *n* the open space in front of the fireplace in a kiln.
kill-spendin *n* an old name for the kiln fire.
kill-stickles *n* pieces of drawn straw on which grain was laid to dry in strae kilns (qv).
kill-strae *n* straw used in kilns, on which grain was laid.
kill-trees *n* thin laths on which straw was laid, to bear the corn spread on it for kiln drying.
Killum-callum *n* the Highland sword dance, Gillie-callum.
killyvie *n* a state of alertness.
killy-wimple *n* 1 a gewgaw. 2 an ornament. 2 a grace note in singing.
Kilmarnock *n* 1 a Kilmarnock cowl (qv). 2 a man's woven cap in the shape of a Tam o' Shanter.
Kilmarnock whittle *n* a betrothed person of either sex.
kiln *n* a frame of wood on a corn staddle for ventilating a stack.
kilpin *n* a stout, muscular person.
kilsh *same as* **kelch**.
kilshes *n* wide trousers worn by children.
kilt¹ *n* the proper way or knack of doing a thing. —*v* to do a thing neatly and skilfully.
kilt² *n* 1 the slope of a stone, especially in a staircase. 2 an unnatural or ungraceful elevation of the voice.
kilt³ *v* 1 to tuck up the skirts, etc. 2 to roll up the sleeves. 3 to elevate. 4 to lift up quickly. 5 to run quickly. 6 to pack off with.—*n* 1 a tuck.
kilt⁴ *v* to overturn.—*n* an upset.
kilt⁵ *n* 1 a Hebridean name for home-made cloth of any or no colour. 2 a knee-length skirt now made from tartan material, pleated at the sides, worn by men and women.

kilter *n* cheer, entertainment.
kiltie *n* 1 one who wears a kilt or a very short dress. 2 a soldier in a Highland regiment.— *adj* wearing a kilt.
kiltie *same as* **kelt**¹.
kiltimmer *n* an opprobrious epithet applied to a woman of doubtful character.
kilting *n* 1 the portion of a dress, etc, that is tucked up. 2 the lap of a woman's petticoat that is tucked up.
kiltit *adj* tucked up.—*phr* **high-kiltit** (*used of language*) verging on indecency or coarseness.
kilt-rack *n* the machinery for raising the rack of a mill.
kilty *n* fornication.
kim *n* 1 a cistern, a tub. 2 a large baling ladle.
kim *adj* 1 keen. 2 spirited. 3 spruce.
kimmen, kimmin *n* 1 a milk pail. 2 a small tub. 2 a large, shallow tub used in brewhouses.
kimmer *n* 1 a gossip (qv). 2 a godmother. 3 a midwife. 4 a young woman. 5 a contemptuous name for a woman. 6 a reputed witch. 7 a male companion.—*v* to bring forth a child.
kimmerin *n* an entertainment at the birth of a child.
kimpal *n* a truss of drawn straw for thatch.
kimplack *n* a very large piece.
kimple *n* a piece of any solid substance.
kimplet *n* a piece of moderate size.
kin *v* to kindle, light.
kin'¹ *adj* kind.
kin'² *n* 1 kind. 2 nature. 3 custom, wont. 4 sort.—*adv* somewhat, in some degree.
kin-awa *n* kindred abroad.
kin-a-wise *adv* in a way, in a sort.
kin-bot, ~-boot *n* a fine paid to the kindred of a slaughtered person as compensation.
kinch *n* the armpit.
kinch *n* 1 a loop. 2 a twist or doubling given to a rope, etc. 3 a sudden twist in wrestling. 4 an unfair or unexpected advantage. 5 a favour. 6 a hold. —*v* 1 to twist, loop. 2 to tighten by twisting.
kinch pin *n* a pin or stick used in twisting ropes, etc, to tighten them.
kin cogish *n* the law by which a chief was answerable for every member of his clan.
kind gallows *n* a name given to the gallows of Crieff.
kindle *v* (*used of small animals*) to litter.
kindlie *n* the tenure of a kindlie tenant (qv).
kindlie-possession *n* the land held by a kindlie tenant (qv).
kindlie rowm, ~ room *n* a kindlie possession (qv).
kindlie tenant *n* a tenant whose ancestors have long resided on a farm and who claims a right to retain a farm through long possession by his family.
kindlike *adv* in a kindly manner.
kindling *n* fire or light applied to combustibles.—*adj* blushing, ruddy.
kindly *adj* 1 natural, according to nature. 2 thriving, in good condition. 3 favourable for growth, etc.—*adv* heartily, cordially.
kindness *n* 1 friendship, affection, liking. 2 the right on which a man claimed to retain a farm in consequence of long possession by his ancestors.
kine *adj* kind.
king *n* 1 an adept. 2 the ladybird.
King and Queen of Cantelon *n* a boys' game in which the boy who is king tries to catch the other players when running between two goals.
king-coll-awa', ~-gollowa *n* the ladybird.
king-collie *n* the ladybird.
king-come-a-long *n* a boys' game in which the two sides strive which can secure most captives for the king.
king cup *n* the marsh-marigold.
King Dr Ellison *n* the ladybird.
kingame *n* a species of wrasse.
King Henry *n* a boys' game.
kingle-kangle *n* loud, confused and ill-natured talk.

King of Bane, King of the Bean n a character in Christmas revels.

King of Cantland n a children's game. *See* **King and Queen of Cantelon**.

king of the herringe n the fish *Chimaera monstrosa*.

king's chair n **1** the hands crossed to form a seat. **2** a game played with the hands so crossed.

king's claver n melilot, a species of trefoil.

King's Covenanter n a children's game. *See* **King and Queen of Cantelon**.

king's cushion n **1** a seat formed by crossing the arms. **2** the game played with such a seat.

king's ellwand n Orion's belt.

king's hat n the second stomach of a ruminant.

king's head n the king's hat (qv).

king's hood n **1** the king's hat (qv). **2** the great gut, part of a sheep's tripe.

king's horn n the hue and cry.

king's keys n *in phr* **to mak king's keys** to force open the door of a house, room, chest, etc, by virtue of a legal warrant in the king's name.

king's land n land formerly in possession of the crown.

king's man n an exciseman.

king's weather n the exhalations rising from the earth on a warm day.

king's will n the king's good pleasure as to a sentence.

kink[1] n **1** a bend. **2** a crease. **3** a fold.—v to curl.

kink[2] v **1** to laugh restrainedly. **2** to choke with laughter. **3** to choke, catch the breath convulsively, cough, as in whooping cough. **4** to vomit. —n **1** a convulsive fit of laughter, a catch of the breath. **2** the sound of whooping cough. **3** a faint. **4** a whiff. **5** (*in pl*) the whooping cough.

kinken n a small barrel, a keg.

kinkens n an evasive answer to an inquisitive child.

kink-host, ~-hoast n **1** the whooping cough. **2** a severe loss. **3** an utter disgust.

kinkin adj (*used of a cough*) choking, convulsive.

kinkind, kinkine, kinkin n kind, variety, sort.

kinkin-pin *same as* **kinchpin**.

kinkit adj (*used of twisted ropes when untwisted*) knotted, curled.

kinkoch n the whooping cough.

kinnen, kinning n a rabbit, a coney.

kinrent, kinred n **1** a kindred. **2** a clan.

kinrick n a kingdom.

kinsh[1] n a lever used in quarrying, etc, a 'pinch'.

kinsh[2], **kinsch** *same as* **kinch**[2].

kinshens *same as* **kinkens**.

kintra n a country, region, district.—adj **1** belonging to the country. **2** rustic. **3** rural.

kintra clash n country or district gossip or news.

kintra clatter n talk or reports current in a district.

kintra cleadun n rustic apparel, homespun.

kintra crack n country talk.

kintra-cuisser, ~-cousser n an itinerating stallion serving mares.

kintra dance n a country dance.

kintra fowks n country people, rustics.

kintramen n rustics.

kintra-side n a country district.

kintye n the rooftree.

kinvaig n **1** a tippet. **2** a small plaid.

kiow-ow n (*in pl*) **1** tittle-tattle, foolish talk. **2** trifles, things of a trivial nature.—v to trifle in discourse or conduct.

kiowowy adj **1** particular. **2** fastidious.

kip[1] v to take another's property by fraud or force.

kip[2] v to play truant.—n a truant.

kip[3] n a house of ill-fame.

kip[4] n haste, hurry.

kip[5], **kipp** n **1** a hook. **2** a tilt or upward turn of the nose. **3** anything that is beaked. **4** a sharp-pointed hill. **5** a jutting point or knob on a hill. —v **1** to turn up at the point of a horn, nose, etc. **2** to turn up at the side of a hat or bonnet.

kipe *same as* **kype**.

kiple v to couple.

kip-nebbit, ~-nosed adj **1** (*used of the nose*) tip-tilted, turned up at the tip. **2** having a pug nose.

kipp *same as* **kip**[5].

kippage[1] n a ship's crew or company.

kippage[2] n **1** disorder, confusion. **2** a dilemma, fix. **3** a paroxysm of rage, a passion.

kippen n a rabbit.

kipper[1] n **1** a salmon after spawning. **2** a salmon or herring salted and cured.—v to cure fish by salting and hanging them up or drying them in smoke.

kipper[2] n **1** a large bowl. **2** a large quantity of food. —v to eat heartily.

kipper[3] v to trifle.

kipperdy smash n a children's game.

kipper-kaper adj easy-going, as of a tired or lazy horse.

kipper-nose n a hooked or beaked nose.

kippie n a small hill.—adj having the points of the horns turned up.

kipping n truancy.

kipple n **1** a couple, pair. **2** a rafter beam.—v **1** to couple, fasten together. **2** to marry, match.

kipple-bawk n a roof beam, rafter.

kipple-fit n the foot of a rafter.

kipple-hoe n a straight piece of wood laid across the top of the couple or rafter.

kippling n **1** a rafter. **2** a coupling.

kippling kaim n a comb for fastening up the hair.

kir adj **1** cheerful. **2** fond, amorous, wanton. **3** consequential.

kire n a choir.

kirk n **1** a church. **2** the church. **3** a congregation. **4** the building set apart for public worship. **5** ecclesiastical courts.—v **1** to attend church. **2** to church a woman after childbirth. **3** to escort a newly married couple to the church on the first Sunday after marriage. **4** to lodge the ball into the hole in the game of kirk-the-gussie (qv).

kirk-attender n a churchgoer.

kirk beadle n the church officer.

kirk bell n the churchgoing bell, summoning to church.

kirk book n the kirk session's record or minute book.

kirk box n the name formerly given to the fund for the church poor, derived from fines, gifts, collections, legacies, etc.

kirk brae n the hill on which a church stands.

kirk brod n the plate at the church door, or the ladle (qv), for receiving collections.

kirk clachan n a village or hamlet containing a church.

kirk claes n Sunday clothes.

kirk court n a church court or judicature.

kirk door n a church door.—phr **do anything at the kirk door** to do it openly and unblushingly.

kirk-door plate n the offertory plate at the main entrance of a church.

kirk dyke n a churchyard wall.

kirk dues n **1** fines formerly exacted for breaches of the seventh commandment, etc. **2** church dues, contributions regularly paid for church purposes.

kirker n a member or adherent of a church.

kirk fever n excitement over church affairs.

kirk fouk n **1** the members of a congregation. **2** churchgoers. **3** those going to or returning from church. **4** church officials. **5** ecclesiastical office bearers.

kirkfu' n a churchful, a congregation.

kirk gate n **1** the churchyard gate. **2** the way leading to a church.

kirk-gaun' adj **1** churchgoing. **2** frequenting church. —n attendance at church.

kirk-gaun claes n Sunday clothes.

kirk-greedy adj eager and regular in church attendance.

kirk green n **1** a church green. **2** a churchyard.

kirk hammer n the tongue of a church bell.

kirk herd n **1** a minister, a pastor. **2** a ruling elder.

kirk hill *n* a hill on which a church stands.

kirk hole *n* a grave in a churchyard.

kirking *n* 1 churchgoing. 2 the first attendance of a newly married couple at church, generally on the first Sunday after marriage.

kirking party *n* the newly married couple and their friends met to attend church for the first time after the marriage.

kirk-keeper *n* a regular church attender.

kirk knock *n* the church clock.

kirk knowe *n* the knoll on which a church stands.

kirk ladle *n* a box with a long wooden handle for taking collections inside a church.

kirklands *n* lands formerly belonging to a church, glebe lands.

kirkle *same as* kirtle.

kirkless *adj* 1 (*used of a minister or preacher*) without a church or charge. 2 (*of people*) not attending church.

kirk liggate *n* a churchyard gate.

kirk loaning *n* a lane leading to a church.

kirk loom *n* a pulpit.

kirk-lover *n* a lover of church.

kirkman *n* an ecclesiastic.

kirk master *n* 1 a deacon of an incorporated trade. 2 a member of a town council, whose office is to take charge of the fabric, etc, of the churches that are under the care of the council.

kirk member *n* a communicant of a church.

kirk mouse *n* a church mouse.

kirk occasion *n* 1 church service. 2 the dispensation of the communion. *See* occasion.

kirk officer *n* the kirk beadle (qv).

kirk park *n* a park adjoining a church.

kirk pad, ~ path *n* a path leading to a church.

kirk plate *n* the plate at the church door for the offertory.

kirk-reekit *adj* bigoted.

kirk road *n* 1 a church road. 2 a right of way leading to a church.

kirk-scandalisin' *n* a causing of scandal to a church.

kirk seat *n* a church pew.

kirk session *n* the lowest Presbyterian church court, having spiritual oversight of the congregation.

kirk shoon *n* Sunday shoes reserved for churchgoing.

kirk shot *n* fishings on a river, near or belonging to a church.

kirk skailing *n* dismissal of a congregation after service.

kirk steeple *n* a church steeple, formerly used often as a prison.

kirk stool *n* a stool taken to church before the introduction of pews.

kirk style, ~ stile *n* 1 the gate of a churchyard or of a wall round the church. 2 steps in a churchyard wall by which persons pass over. 3 the houses adjoining a churchyard.

kirk supper *n* the festivity after the kirking (qv) of a newly married pair.

kirk tables *n* communion tables at which communicants sit.

kirk-the-gussie *n* a game with a large ball which one set of players strive to beat with clubs into a hole, while the other set strive to drive it away.

kirktime *n* 1 the hour for beginning public worship. 2 the time during which it lasts.

kirktown *n* a village or hamlet where there is a parish church.

kirk wa' *n* a church wall.

kirk waddin *n* a marriage in church.

kirkward *adv* towards church.

kirk wark *n* the church fabric and what concerns it.—*phr* maister of the kirk wark a kirk master (qv).

kirk weather *n* weather admitting of churchgoing.

kirk-wipe *n* a club foot.

kirk-wiped *adj* having a club foot.

kirk wynd *n* a church lane.

kirkyard *n* a churchyard.

kirkyard-deserter *n* a very aged or infirm person.

kirkyard gate *n* the way to the churchyard.

kirkyard-like *adj* apparently likely to die soon.

kirk yett *n* the churchyard gate, church gate.

kirn *n* 1 a churn. 2 the act of handling or nursing too much. 3 the act of working in a lazy, slovenly manner. 4 a disgusting mixture, mire. 5 the last handful of grain cut on the harvest field. 6 the harvest home.—*v* 1 to churn. 2 to mix, stir up. 3 to handle constantly and messily. 4 to overnurse or take too much care of a child. 5 to work in a disgusting way. 6 to be improperly familiar.

kirn *n* 1 a kernel. 2 a grain of corn.

kirnan rung *same as* kirn rung.

kirn bannock *n* a bannock specially baked for the harvest home.

kirn-cut *n* the last cut handful of corn on the harvest field.

kirn-dancing *n* dancing at the kirn supper (qv).

kirn dollie *n* a female figure or image made of the last cut of grain.

kirnel *n* a kidney.

kirnen *n* 1 familiarity. 2 improper familiarity.

kirn feast *n* the harvest-home festival.

kirnie *n* a pert, impudent boy who apes a man and would be thought one.

kirning *n* 1 a churning. 2 what has been churned at a time.

kirning stone *n* a stone heated red-hot to heat the churn before use.

kirning water *n* hot water to mix with buttermilk in a churn.

kirn milk *n* 1 buttermilk. 2 the precipitate of curd which occurs when hot water is poured into a churn containing buttermilk.

kirn rung *n* the rod used for stirring milk in a churn.

kirn staff *n* the kirn rung (qv).

kirn-staff *n* the sun spurge.

kirn stick *n* a stupid person.

kirn supper *n* the harvest-home feast.

kirn-swee *n* an implement for lightening the manual labour of churning.

kirny *adj* (*used of corn*) full of grains.

kirr *same as* kir.

kirry-wirry *n* a burlesque serenade given to old people marrying again or marrying young people.

kirsen *v* to baptise, christen.—*adj* 1 Christian. 2 proper, suitable, decent.

Kirsenmas, Kirsmas *n* Christmas.

kirsnin *n* baptism.

kirssan crab *n* a blackish variety of crab.

kirstal *n and adj* crystal.

kirsty *n* a whisky jar.

kirtle *n* 1 a woman's outer petticoat or short skirt. 2 a gown. 3 dress.—*v* to clothe, dress.

kiryauw *v* to caterwaul.—*n* 1 a noise, great outcry. 2 an ado.

kish *n* shining powdery matter that separates from pig iron too long kept molten.

kisle stane *n* a flintstone.

kislop *n* the fourth stomach of a calf.

kissie *n* a kiss.

kissing-kind *adj* seemingly, but not really, kind.

kissing signal *n* at rustic balls, the signal given by the fiddler making a squeaking sound like a kiss, at which the men kiss their partners and then begin dancing.

kissing strings *n* strings tied under the chin.

kissing time *n* the time for kissing at a rustic ball.

kiss-my-loof *n* 1 a fawner. 2 a useless person.

kiss-the-caup *v* to drink, take refreshment.—*n* a tippler.

kist[1] *n* 1 a chest, box. 2 a chest of drawers. 3 a coffin. 4 a cruive. 5 a shop counter. 6 the chest of the body.—*v* 1 to lay up in a chest. 2 to place in a coffin.

kist[2] *n* 1 sap, substance. 2 spirit. 3 taste.

kistfu' *n* a boxful.

kistfu' o' whistles *n* an organ.

kisting *n* 1 the act of placing a dead body in a coffin. 2 the religious service often accompanying that act.

kistit[1] *adj* 1 dried up, sapless. 2 without substance.

kistit[2] *adj* 1 put in a chest. 2 put in a coffin.

kistless *same as* **keestless**.
kist lid *n* the lid of a chest.
kist locker *n* a box-like locker in a chest for holding valuables, etc.
kist neuk *n* the corner of a chest, where money was often concealed.
kist o' whistles *same as* **kistfu' o' whistles**.
kist-shaped *adj* shaped like a chest.
kist weed *n* the woodruff.
kit[1] *n* **1** any wooden vessel used for milk, salted butter , sugar, etc, or for washing dishes. **2** a small fiddle. **3** a set of tools.—*v* to pack in a kit.
kit[2] *n* the whole collection of persons or things.
kit[3] *same as* **keet**[1].
kit[4] *v* **1** to pack off. **2** *in phr* **kit ye** get out of the way!
kitchen *n* **1** a relish or condiment with food. **2** something to make plain fare more palatable. **3** an allowance for milk, butter, beer, to servants. **4** a tea urn.—*v* **1** to season. **2** to give a relish to food. **3** to save. **4** to be sparing of.
kitchener *n* a cook.
kitchen fee *n* dripping.
kitchen fowk *n* servants.
kitchen lass *n* a maidservant, kitchen maid.
kitchenless *adj* without relish, seasoning or condiment.
kitchen lum *n* the kitchen chimney.
kitchie *n* **1** a kitchen. **2** an addition or relish to plain fare.—*v* to season, give a relish to.
kitchie-boy *n* a boy who serves in a kitchen.
kitchie-umman *n* a kitchen maid.
kitching *n* a kitchen.
kite *n* the stomach.
kite-clung *adj* **1** having the belly shrunk from hunger. **2** herring-gutted.
kited *adj* intestinal.
kitefu' *n* a bellyful.
kith[1] *n* acquaintance, friends not related by blood or not kin.
kith[2] *same as* **kythe**.
kithag *n* an unmanageable woman.
kithan *n* an unmanageable rogue.
kithless *adj* friendless.
kit-kae *adv* pit-a-pat.
kitlin *n* a kitten.
kitly *same as* **kittly**.
kitt[1] *n* a brothel. **2** a privy. **2** a urinal.
kitt[2] *v* to lose all one's money at the gaming table or otherwise.
kitt[3] *n* the whole number or quantity.
kitter *v* to fester.
kittle[1] *int* get out of the way!
kittle[2] *n* a name given to any kind of cow.
kittie[3] *n* **1** a loose woman,. **2** a term of disrespect for a woman who may not, however, be light-headed. **2** a romping, merry girl.
kittie-cat *n* a bit of wood, or any substitute for it, hit in the game of shinty or other games.
kitting *n* the act of packing in a kit.
kittit *adj* stripped of all one's possessions, by misfortune or otherwise. *See* **kitt**[2].
kittle[1] *v* **1** to tickle. **2** to please, flatter. **3** to caress, fondle, cuddle. **4** to itch. **5** to stir up, enliven, stimulate what is jaded. **6** to rouse, interest. **7** to prick, stab. **8** to puzzle, perplex. **9** to get or put into a bad humour. **10** to sweep before a curling stone in motion. **11** to strike up a tune on an instrument. **12** to warm up and show life in speaking. **13** (*used of a horse*) to become restive or excited. **14** (*of the wind*) to rise. **15** to compose, work at, make up.—*n* **1** a tickling sensation. **2** cunning, cleverness, skill.
kittle[2] *adj* **1** easily tickled, sickly, ticklish. **2** itching. **3** difficult, not easily managed or done, ticklish. **4** unsteady, nicely balanced. **5** uncertain, fickle. **6** variable. **7** dangerous, critical. **8** obscure, intricate, not easy to understand or to pronounce. **9** excitable, nervous, fidgety. **10**

skittish. **11** touchy, easily angry, keen-tempered. **12** clever, apt. **13** cunning, smart. **14** humorous, entertaining. **15** (*used of an angle*) sharp. **16** scrupulous, squeamish.
kittle[3] *v* **1** (*of cats, etc*) to bring forth young. **2** to be generated in the imagination or affections.
kittle-breeks *n* a nickname for a person of irascible temper.
kittle-leggit *adj* nimble, quick at dancing.
kittlesome *adj* **1** sensitive to tickling. **2** itchy.
kittle-strips *n* a rope with a noose at each end into which a person's feet are put, he being placed across a joist or beam in which position he has to balance himself so nicely as to be able to lift something laid before him with his teeth without being overturned.
kittlet *adj* **1** interested. **2** aroused. **3** excited.
kittle thairm *v* to play the fiddle.
kittley *same as* **kittly**.
kittlie-cowt, ~-kow *n* a children's game of searching for a hidden handkerchief or other article.
kittling[1] *n* **1** a tickling sensation. **2** the act of being tickled. **3** anything that tickles the fancy.—*adj* stirring, affecting.
kittling[2] *n* **1** a kitten. **2** the bringing forth of kittens.
kittly *adj* **1** itchy. **2** ticklish. **3** difficult. **4** intricate.
kitt-neddy *n* the sandpiper.
kittock *n* **1** a romping girl. **2** a loose woman.
kitty[1] *same as* **kittie**[3].
kitty[2] *n* a small bowl.
kitty[3] *same as* **kittie**[2].
kitty[4] **1** the kittiwake. **2** any of the smaller gulls.
kitty[5] *n* the jack in a game of bowls.
kitty-langlegs *n* the daddy-longlegs.
kitty-needy, ~-neddy *n* the sandpiper.
kitty stick *n* a small stick on which the pirns (qv) are put in order that the thread may be wound off them.
kitty-wren *n* the common wren.
kiutle *v* **1** to fondle. **2** to embrace.
kivan *same as* **kivin**.
kive *same as* **keeve**.
kiver *v* to cover.—*n* a cover.
kivering *n* **1** a covering. **2** woollen cloth for bedcoverings and saddle cloths.
kivilaivie *n* a crowd of low persons.
kivin, kivvan *n* **1** a gathering of people. **2** a promiscuous crowd. **3** a bevy. **4** a covey.
kivvy, kivy *n* **1** a covey. **2** a bevy.
kizen, kizzen[1] *v* **1** to dry up. **2** to parch. **3** to shrink. **4** to wither.
kizzen[2] *n* a cousin.
klamoos, klamoz *n* an outcry, a loud noise.
kleckit oot *adj* knocked out.
kleg *n* a gadfly.
klem *adj* **1** imperfectly done, badly done, of little value. **2** unprincipled.
klint *n* **1** a rough stone. **2** an outlying stone.
klippert *n* a shorn sheep.
klipsheers *n* the earwig.
kllauch *v* to work in a filthy, disgusting manner. —*n* the act of working so.
klot *v* to scrape up mud, dung, ashes, etc.—*n* a hoe for scraping.
klyak *v* to gossip.—*n* a gossip.
klyock *n* the last sheaf in harvest.
klyte *n* a heavy fall.—*v* to fall heavily.
knab[1] *v* to strike, to beat.—*n* a blow.
knab[2] *n* **1** the apex of a rock or hill. **2** a rocky headland.
knab[3] *n* **1** a sturdy boy. **2** a stout, thickset animal.
knabb, knab[4] *n* **1** a person of consequence, rank, wealth, etc. **2** a pretentious, conceited person. **3** a chief, leader.
knabberie *same as* **knabbry**.
knabbish *adj* **1** well off pecuniarily or socially. **2** pretentious, dressing above one's means or station. **3** genteel.
knabbry *n* the lower class of gentry.

knabby *adj* **1** well-to-do. **2** pretentious. **3** wealthy.
knablich *n* a strong, thickset person or animal.—*adj* sour, cantankerous.
knablick *adj* irregularly shaped.—*n* a stone or pebble with several angles that moves under the foot when trod on.
knabrie *same as* **knabry**.
knabsie *n* a short, stout, strong person or animal.
knack[1] *v* **1** to crack, snap with a clicking sound, as with finger and thumb. **2** to strike together. **3** to make a harsh sound with the throat. **4** to talk amusingly, chatter. **5** to tell, narrate. **6** to indulge in repartee. **7** to poke fun at.— *n* **1** a snap, crack. **2** a click, a clicking noise in the throat. **3** a habit. **4** a scheme, a tricky pretence, trick. **5** a knick-knack. **6** a joke, a witty saying, a smart answer.
knack[2] *v* to knock.—*n* a knock.
knackers *n* **1** two flat pieces of wood or bone used as castanets. **2** the testicles.
knacket *n* one smart in reply or retort.
knackety *adj* **1** handy, expert at nice work. **2** finical. **3** self-conceited.
knacks *n* a disease in the throat of fowls fed on too hot food.
knacksy *adj* **1** quick at repartee. **2** pleasant, amusing. **3** clever.
knackum *n* a sharp blow.
knack up *v* to compliment, flatter.
knackuz *n* **1** a chatterer. **2** a quick, snappish speaker.
knacky *adj* **1** handy, ingenious, expert. **2** acute and facetious. **3** entertaining, vivacious, cunning, crazy.
knag[1] *n* **1** a knob or peg on which to hang articles. **2** the projection of a knot in a tree.
knag[2] *same as* **knog**.
knag[3] *n* the green woodpecker.
knag[4] *n in phr* **at the knag and widdie thegither** at loggerheads.
knaggie *n* a small barrel.
knaggie *adj* **1** having protuberances like rock, etc. **2** bony. **3** tart, ill-humoured. **4** (*of wood*) full of knots.
knaggim *n* a disagreeable aftertaste.
knaglie *adj* having many protuberances.
knaist, knaisht *n* a lump of anything.
knaivatick *adj* mean, knavish.
knak *same as* **knack**[1].
knap[1] *n* **1** a knob, protuberance, bump. **2** a knot in wood. **3** a hillock, knoll. **4** a bunch of heather. **5** the ascent of a rising ground. **6** the kneecap. **6** the point of the elbow. **8** a stout, thickset person. **9** a wooden vessel, a milkvat.
knap[2] *n* an eccentric person.
knap[3] *v* **1** to knock. **2** to strike sharply. **3** to pat. **4** to break stones, chip, hammer. **5** to snap in two. **6** to cleave. **7** to snap with the teeth. **8** to eat greedily. **9** (*of a clock*) to tick. **10** to speak affectedly, to try to speak fine English, to clip one's words.—*n* **1** a blow. **2** a tap, slight stroke. **3** a bump. **4** a knock on the head. **5** a snap, bite. **6** a morsel.
knap-darlichs *n* lumps of dung hanging from the hindlegs of cattle.
knap-dodgil, ~-dogik *n* any person, animal or thing that is short and stout.
knap-dorlak, ~-dorle *n* a large piece of anything solid.
knaper *n in phr* **ilka knipper and knaper** every particle.
knap-for-naught *n* any morsel that just serves for a mouthful.
knapgrass *n* knotgrass.
knap-knap *v* **1** to tap. **2** to knock against.
knap-knapping *n* **1** a tapping. **2** the sound of tapping.
knaplich *n* a bit broken off.
knap of the knee *n* the kneepan.
knappal *n* a boy between ten and sixteen years of age.
knapparts, knapperts *n* the bitter vetch.
knappel, knappild *n* a thick stick or staff
knapper *n* a hammer for stone-breaking.
knappery *adj* (*used of roads*) having loose road metal, causing jolting.
knappik *n* a stout, thickset person or animal.

knappin' *n* the noise of tapping or smart strokes.
knappin' hammer *n* a hammer used in stone-breaking.
knappin' hole *n* the hole out of which two shinty players try to drive the ball in opposite directions.
knappish *adj* tart, snappish.
knappit *adj* affected, spoken mincingly.
knapplach, knapplack *n* **1** a large lump or protuberance. **2** a stout, thickset person or animal.
knapply *adj* short and stout, dumpy, thickset.
knappy[1] *adj* abounding in lumps, in small, roundish lumps.
knappy[2] *adj* brittle. *See* nappie.
knappy[3] *adj* (*of ale, etc*) strong.—*n* strong liquor.
knapsack[1] *n* a boys' game.
knapscap[2] *n* a steel bonnet, a headpiece.
knapseck drill *n* a severe scolding.
knapskull *n* a knapscap (qv).
knark *v* **1** to crunch with the teeth. **2** to crack, creak.—*n* a snap with the teeth, a bite.
knarlich *same as* **knorlack**.
knarly *adj* gnarly, knotty.
knarrie *n* **1** a bruise. **2** a hurt. **3** an abrasion.
knash *v* **1** to strike. **2** to gnaw.
knat *n* **1** a solid body. **2** *in phr* **knat o' a littlin** a child who is solid fat.
knauperts *same as* **krauperts**.
knaur *same as* **knirr**.
knave *n* **1** a manservant, a lad. **2** an under-miller.
knave-bairn *n* a man-child.
knave-servant *n* a dishonest servant.
knaveship *n* a customary due of meal paid to the under-miller.
knaw *v* to know.
knawlege *n* **1** knowledge. **2** trial, examination. **3** an inquest.
kned *v* **1** (*generally used of animals*) to pant, breathe heavily. **2** to exhaust.—*n* short, laboured breathing.—*adj* **1** exhausted. **2** hard pushed or driven.
knedeuch *n* a musty taste or smell.
knee *v* **1** to bend in the middle. **2** to be broken down. **3** to mend or patch clothes at the knees. **4** to press down with the knees.—*n* **1** a bow, curtsy. **2** a crank. **3** a small hill.
knee-bairn *n* a child too young to walk.
knee-breekit *adj* wearing knee breeches.
knee breeks *n* knee breeches.
knee breekums *n* knee breeches.
kneef *adj* **1** alert, active. **2** fairly healthy, in good spirits after illness. **3** vigorous for one's age. **4** intimate. **5** in thorough intimacy and sympathy. **6** quick-tempered. **7** difficult.
kneef-like *adj* **1** healthy-looking. **2** of strong appearance.
kneefly *adv* briskly.
kneefy *adj* **1** stout and active. **2** agile.
knee-heigh *adj* as high as one's knee.
knee-height *n* the height of one's knee.
knee-ill *n* a cattle disease affecting the knees.
kneep *n* **1** a lump. **2** a promontory. **3** a big, stupid person.
kneeplach *n* **1** a big lump. **2** a large clot.—*v* to strike and cause a lump.
kneeple *n* a big lump.—*v* to cause a big lump.
knee-pock *n* a baggy trouser knee.
knee-shell, ~-shall *n* the kneepan.
kneetle *v* **1** to strike with the knuckles. **2** to hit, knock, tap.
kneetling *n* a thrashing.
kneeve *n* the fist.
kneevick *adj* grasping, covetous.
kneevle[1] *n* **1** a lump. **2** a clot. **3** a knot.
kneevle[2] *same as* **knevell**.
kneevlick, kneevlack *v* **1** to press down with force. **2** to strike so as to cause a lump.—*n* **1** a stroke producing a lump. **2** a severe beating. **3** a large lump. **4** a large protuberance.
kneggum[1] *same as* **knaggim**.
kneggum[2] *n* **1** a trick, prank. **2** a bad practice.
kneif *adj* **1** alert. **2** intimate. **3** quick-tempered.

kneip *same as* **knap**[3].

kneister *v* **1** to creak. **2** to smother a laugh.

knell *v* to talk loudly.

knelling *adj* **1** sounding an alarm. **2** uneasy, alarmed, troublesome.

knell-kneed *adj* knock-kneed.

knet *v* **1** knitted. **2** knotted.

knevell *v* **1** to beat severely. **2** to thump with fists. **3** to knock about.—*n* a severe thrashing.

knewel *n* **1** a wooden pin in the end of a halter for holding by. **2** the crossbar of an Albert watch chain.

knib *n* a small piece of wood fixed in the end of a rope, fixed also in the loop in the end of another rope, so as to act like a swivel.

knibblach, knibbloch *n* **1** a lump, a knob, a small piece. **2** a small, round stone or clod. **2** the swelling caused by a fall or blow. **4** the barb of a harpoon.

knibblochis, knibblockie *adj* **1** rough, uneven. **2** used of a road in which many small stones rise up and make walking hurtful.

knible *adj* nimble, clever.

knicht *n* a knight.

knick *same as* **knack**[1].

knickity-knock *adv in phr* **fa' knickity-knock** to fall so as to strike the head first on one side and then on the other.

knick-knack, knick-nack *n* **1** a whim, caprice. **2** a precise person. **3** one who is neat and skilful in delicate work.

knick-knacket *n* **1** a knick-knack, a trifle. **2** (*in pl*) odds and ends, curios.

knickle *n* a knuckle.

knickum *n* a tricky boy.

knidder *v* to keep under.

knidge *n* **1** a strong squeeze, heavy pressure. **2** a nudge. **3** a short, strong person or animal.—*v* **1** to press down forcibly, squeeze. **2** to nudge.

knidgel *n* a short, strong person.

knidget *n* a mischievous, saucy boy or girl.

knidgie *adj* short, strong and thick.

knief *same as* **kneef**.

kniefly *adv* vivaciously.

kniel *same as* **knewel**.

knievel *same as* **kneevle**[1].

knife *n in phr* **a black knife** a small dirk.

kniff *same as* **kneef**.

kniffy *same as* **kneefy**.

kniggum *same as* **knaggim**.

knight *n* a close stool.

knip[1] *v* to bite, nibble.

knip[2] *same as* **knyp**.

knip[3] *n* a small bundle of things strung together at one end of a string.

kniper *n in phr* **ilka kniper and knaper** every particle.

knippach *n* two or three small fish tied together.

knipper-knatlich *adj* **1** stingy. **2** particular and slightly eccentric.

knipperty-knaps *n* odds and ends, knick-knacks.

knipsie *n* a malapert, mischievous boy or girl.

knirls *n* **1** a kind of measles. **2** chickenpox.

knirr *n* **1** a knot of wood. **2** a wooden ball or knot of wool used in the game of shinty. **3** anything small or stunted in growth (*used contemptuously of a decrepit old woman who outlives the usual span of life*).

knit *v* **1** to tie. **2** to overfill, burst.

knitch *n* a bundle tied round.—*v* to truss, tie, bundle, tie round.

knitchell *n* a bundle, a number of things tied together.

knite *same as* **knoit**[2].

knittal *n* **1** braces. **2** a trouser belt.

knittan *n* a surfeit.

knitten[1] *adj* knitted.

knitting, knitten[2] *n* tape.

knitting pins *n* knitting needles.

knitting sheath *n* a small sheath, generally of a hen's quills, into which knitters thrust their needles.

knivel *n* **1** the short horn of a young beast. **2** a snuffbox made from such a horn.

knivel, knivvle *same as* **knevell**.

knivelach *n* a blow that causes a swelling.

knivvelin *n* a thumping.

knob *n* **1** a lump. **2** the head.

knobbet *adj* having knobs.

knobby *adj* **1** having knobs. **2** short and plump.—*n* a walking stick with a hooked head.

knock[1] *n* a little sheaf of cleaned straw of four or five inches in diameter.

knock[2] *n* a hill, a knoll.

knock[3] *n* **1** a clock. **2** *in phr* **Jock-strike-the knock** the hammer of a clock, which jerks back before striking.

knock[4] *v* **1** to strike with a sharp blow. **2** to pound. **3** to hull barley.—*n* **1** a sharp blow. **2** a door-knocker. **3** a sort of beetle for beating yarn webs, etc, in bleaching.

knock-beetle *n* one who is severely beaten.

knock-dodgel *adj* short and thick.

knock-him-doon *adj* **1** downright. **2** turbulent.

knock house *n* a clock house.

knockie *adj* clever, smart.

knockin'-knees *n* knock-knees.

knockin' mell *n* a mallet for beating the hulls off barley or linen after bleaching.

knockin' stane *n* **1** a stone mortar in which barley was hulled by the knockin' mell (qv). **2** a large, flat stone on which linen was beaten after bleaching.

knockit *n* **1** a lunch between breakfast or dinner. **2** a midday meal. **3** a small cake or loaf baked for children.

knockit-barley,-bear *n* barley hulled in the knockin' stane (qv) with the knockin' mell (qv).

knockles *n* the knuckles.

knock-maker *n* a clockmaker.

knock-me-down *adj* knock-down.

knock-strings *n* the cords supporting the weights of a clock.

knog, knogie *n* **1** anything short, thick and stout. **2** a small cask, a firkin.

knoist *same as* **knoost**.

knoit[1] *n* **1** a large piece of anything. **2** a knob. **3** a stout person.

knoit[2] *v* **1** to strike, knock, beat. **2** (*used of the knees*) to knock together, tremble. **3** to plod on. **4** to gnaw.—*n* **1** a sharp blow. **2** the sound of a heavy stroke.

knoiter *v* **1** to knock, strike sharply. **2** (*used of the knees*) to tremble.

knoity *adj* knobbed, knobby.

knoll[1] *n* a large piece of anything, a lump.—*v* to knead.

knoll[2] *n* **1** a knell. **2** the sound of a bell tolling.

knooff *same as* **knuff**.

knool[1] *v* **1** to beat with the knuckles or clenched fist. **2** to beat on the knuckles in a game of marbles. **3** to knuckle down.

knool[2] *same as* **knewel**.

knoop *n* **1** a knob. **2** a lump. **3** a peg to hang anything on. **4** that part of a hill which towers or projects above the rest.

knoose *same as* **knuse**.

knoost *n* a large lump, a piece.

knoozing *n* a beating.

knop[1] *same as* **knoop**.

knop[2] *same as* **knap**[3].

knorel, knorle *same as* **knurl**.

knorelick *same as* **knorlack**.

knorlack, knorlag *n* **1** a large lump, a protuberance. **2** a large clot. **3** a swelling.

knorlie *same as* **knurly**.

knorrie *same as* **knorlack**.

knot *n* **1** a lump. **2** a pretty large piece of anything round or square. **3** a lump of sugar. **4** used of a little dry oatmeal in porridge. **5** a clod of earth. **6** a short, strong, thickset person or animal. **7** the mark, where a branch has budded in the wood, at the bottom of a boat, supposed in Shetland and Orkney to betoken the fortune of the boat. **8** a lot to be cast. **9** a joint in straw, grass, etc. **10** a cluster, group. **11** *in phr* **aff at the knot** crazy, insane.—*v* **1** to gather together, to form groups. **2** to knot thread in a particular way. **3** to do tatting. **4** to knit.—*adj* knotted.

knot² *v* (*used of turnips*) to suffer from finger and toe (qv).

knotgrass *n* the oatgrass.

knotless *adj* (*used of thread*) without knots.—*phr* **like a knotless thread** quietly, easily, without check.

knottik *n* a small, strong, thickset person.

knotty *n* **1** a game like shinty. **2** the ball used in the game.

knotty-porridge *n* porridge with lumps of dry or uncooked oatmeal in it.

knotty-sowans *n* sowans (qv) badly boiled so as to have lumps.

knotty tams, ~ tammies, ~ tommies *n* lumps of meal in porridge.

knoul¹ *same as* **knule**.

knoul² *same as* **knewel**.

knout¹ *n* the ball or piece of wood used in shinty.

knout², **knowt** *n* cattle.

knoutberry *n* the cloudberry.

know¹ *v* to press down with the fists or knees.

knowe, know² *n* **1** a knoll. **2** a protuberance. **3** the head.

knowel *same as* **knewel**.

knowie *adj* full of knolls.

knowing *adj* intelligent, well-instructed.—*n* a very small quantity.

knowledge *n* a trial or inquest by a jury.

knowledgeable *adj* intelligent, well-informed.

knowledge box *n* **1** the head. **2** anyone full of information.

knowpert *same as* **krauperts**.

knowsh *n* a lump, a large protuberance.

knowt *v* to plod on.

knub *n* **1** a smart blow. **2** a short club.—*v* to thump.

knublack, knublock *n* **1** a lump, knob. **2** a small, round object. **3** a swelling caused by a blow or fall.

knuckle *n* the length of the second finger from the tip to the knuckle.—*v* **1** to measure a knuckle. **2** (*with* **in**) a term in playing marbles. **3** (*with* **down**) to shoot a marble with the knuckles on the ground, to expose the knuckles to the 'nags' as a punishment. **4** to bend, submit. **5** to knead.

knuckled cake *n* oatcake or bannocks kneaded with the knuckles instead of being rolled out with a rolling pin.

knuckler *n* a marble.

knuckles *n* a punishment at the game of marbles.

knudge *n* a short, thickset, strong person or animal.

knudgie *adj* short, thickset and strong.

knuff, knuiff *v* to converse familiarly.

knuist *same as* **knoost**.

knule¹ *same as* **knewel**.

knule² *same as* **knool**¹.

knule³ *n* **1** a knob, knot. **2** a swelling, excrescence.

knuled *adj* henpecked.

knule-kneed *adj* **1** having swelled or enlarged knee joints. **2** knock-kneed.

knule-knees *n* swollen knee joints.

knule-taed *adj* having toes with swollen joints.

knule-taes *n* toes swollen at the joints.

knurl, knurle *n* **1** a lump, protuberance, knob. **2** a clot. **3** a game resembling cricket in which a wooden ball or 'knurl' is struck with a bat. **4** a knot in twine, thread, etc. **5** a dwarf, hunchback. **6** a term of contempt.—*v* to strike so as to raise a lump.

knurley *adj* having small lumps or knobs.

knurlin *n* a dwarf.—*adj* dwarfish.

knurly *adj* **1** (*used of wood*) knotty, hard. **2** ill-shapen, rough. **3** stunted in growth.

knurr *same as* **knirr**.

knuse *v* **1** to press down with the hands or knees, to bruise. **2** to beat with the fists. **3** to knead.

knushy *adj* thick, gross.—*n* a strong, firm boy.

knusly *adv* snugly, comfortably.

knut *v* **1** to halt slightly. **2** (*used of a horse*) to jerk on its pasterns when setting a foot on a round stone.—*n* a slight halt.

knutle *v* **1** to strike with the knuckles. **2** to repeat feeble blows frequently.

knuve *same as* **knuff**.

knuzle *same as* **knuse**.

knyaff *n* a dwarf, a very small person or animal.

knyockles, knyockels *n* the knuckles.

knyockles of the queets *n* the anklebones.

knyp, knype *n* a sharp blow, the sound of a blow. —*v* **1** to inflict a smart blow. **2** to knock with violence.

knyte *same as* **knoit**.

kob *n* a gold coin, a jacobus (qv).

kok *v* to faint.

koks *n* a child's name for excrement.

koky *v* to evacuate excrement.

kook *v* to appear and disappear by fits.

kool *n* a sailor's souwester.

koom *n* **1** coal or peat dust. **2** crumbs.

koopie *v* to chide.

koost *v* did cast.

koot *n* the ankle.

korkalit, korkie-lit *n* a red dye.

korkir *n* the lichen which furnishes korkalit (qv).

korter *n* a quarter of oatcake.

kouk *v* to retch.

koum *n* soot, dust.

kounger *v* to snub.

kow *n* a goblin.

kowe *n* what cows one.

koyt *v* to beat, flog.

kracht *n* craft, wickedness.

krang *n* the body of a whale divested of blubber.

krauperts *n* the crowberry.

krechle *v* to make a hoarse, croaking sound.

kreish *n* grease.

krocket *n* the oystercatcher.

krunkled *adj* wrinkled, crinkled.

kued *adj* harebrained.

kuit, kute *n* an ankle.

kurchie *n* **1** a kerchief for neck or head. **2** a curtsy.

kurt *adj* sparing.

kustril *n* a foolish fellow.

kuter *v* **1** to coax, wheedle. **2** to nurse delicately. **3** to talk secretly. **4** to converse clandestinely and intimately.

kuttikins *n* gaiters.

kweed *n* the cud.

kweeger *n* a mess, an untidy mixture.

kweel *v* to cool.

kweetin *n* a coverlet.

kwile, kwyle *n* a piece of burning peat or coal.

kwintra *n* the country.

kwyte *n* a coat.

kyaak, kyak *n* **1** a cake. **2** (*in pl*) oatcakes.

kyaard *n* a tinker.

kyan *n* cayenne pepper.

kyard *n* a tinker.

kyardin *n* a scolding.

kyarlin *n* an old man.

kyarn *n* a heap, cairn.

kyauve *same as* **kiauve**.

kye, ky *n* cows, kine.

kye-herd *n* a cowherd.

kye time *n* the time of milking cows.

kyeuk *v* to cook.

kyle¹ *n* a sound, a strait.

kyle² *n* **1** a ninepin. **2** (*in pl*) the game.

kyle³ *n* a chance, opportunity.

kyle⁴ *n* a haycock.—*v* to put hay into cocks.

kyle-alley *n* a ninepin alley.

kylenne *same as* **keelavine**.

kyloe, kylie, kylock *n* a breed of small Highland cattle.
kymond *same as* **kimmen**.
kyob, kyobie *n* a bird's crop.
kyow-ow *same as* **kiow-ow**.
kyowowy *same as* **kiowowy**.
kype *n* **1** a cup-shaped hole in the ground used in playing marbles. **2** (*in pl*) the game played with such holes.
kypie[1] *n* a game played with a bat and a soft ball.
kypie[2] *adj* left-handed.
kypie-hole *n* a hole in the game of kypes (qv).
kyrtle *same as* **kirtle**.
kysle-stane *n* a flintstone.
kyst *same as* **keest**[1]
kystless *same as* **keestless**.
kytch *same as* **keytch**.

kyte *same as* **kite**.
kyte-clung *same as* **kite-clung**.
kyted *adj* intestinal.
kyte-fu' *n* a bellyful.
kyth *n* kith.
kythe *v* **1** to show. **2** to make known. **3** to become known. **4** to appear, show oneself. **5** to look, seem. **6** to become friendly.—*n* an appearance, show.
kythesome *adj* of prepossessing appearance.
kything *n* an appearance, manifestation.— *adj* **1** revealing itself. **2** (*used of the sky*) brightening.
kything-sight *n* a salmon fisher's sight of a fish by marks in the water.
kytie *adj* corpulent from good living.
kytock *n* the belly.

L

laaboard *same as* **labord**.
laager *same as* **lagger**.
laan *n* land, ground.
lab[1] *n* **1** a blow. **2** a throw with a swing.—*v* **1** to beat severely. **2** to pitch or toss with a swing. **3** to walk with a swinging gait. **4** to fall flatly.
lab[2], **labb**[1] *n* **1** a piece, lump. **2** a portion.—*v* to devour in lumps.
lab[3] *adj* drunk.
labach *same as* **llabach**.
labb[1] *same as* **lab**[2].
labb[2] *n* the sound of lapping waves.
labber *v* **1** to slobber in eating or drinking. **2** to let fall food in eating. **3** to soil, bespatter.—*n* the act of slobbering and the noise it causes.
labbich *same as* **llabach**.
labe *v* to lay on a burden.
labey, labie, labbie *n* the flap or skirt of a coat or shirt.
labich *same as* **llabach**.
labichrie *n* a long story about nothing.
labie *n* a large, irregular piece.
labile *adj* liable or apt to err.
labord, labroad *n* a tailor's lapboard.
labour *v* **1** to till land. **2** to plough.—*n* tillage. **3** labouring.—*n* a farm.
labourous *adj* labouring.
labster *n* a lobster.
labster-tae *n* a lobster's claw.
lace *v* to mix spirits with tea, etc.
lacer[1] *n* a shoe tied with a lace.
lacer[2] *n* spirits for mixing with tea, etc.
lacerate *v* to destroy a deed by tearing it up.
lacht *n* **1** a loft. **2** an upper floor or room.
lachter *n* **1** a sitting of eggs. **2** all the eggs laid by a hen before clocking (*see* **clock**). **3** a brood of young chickens, etc. **4** as much cut grain as a reaper carries in one hand. **5** a lock of hair or wool. **6** a flake or layer of hay, etc. **7** the site of a house.—*v* to gather up cut grain.
lachter-stead *n* the site of a house.
lack *v* **1** to slight, deprecate. **2** to vilify.—*n* **1** vilification. **2** scandal, disgrace, slight.
lackanee *int* alas!
lacken *n* coarse German cloth.
lad *n* **1** a kindly term of address to a man. **2** a bachelor. **3** a male sweetheart. **4** a young manservant. **5** a term of commendation or the reverse.
lad-bairn *n* a male child.
ladder *n* **1** the framework of a cart for carrying straw, etc. **2** a gallows.—*v* to apply a ladder for ascending.
ladder-to-heaven *n* the Jacob's ladder plant.
laddie *n* **1** a boy. **2** a term of affection for a boy or youth. **3** a male sweetheart.
laddie-bairn *n* a male child.

laddie band *n* a band of boys.
laddie-days *n* boyhood.
laddie-herd *n* a herd boy.
laddie-hood *n* boyhood.
laddie-in-jacket *n* a novice.
laddie-wean *n* a male child.
laddikie *n* **1** a little lad. **2** a term of endearment for a lad or boy.
laddock *same as* **laddikie**.
lade[1] *n* a watercourse leading to a mill.
lade[2] *v* to lead.
lade[3] *v* to load.—*n* a load.
lade[4] *v* laden.
lade-man *n* a miller's carter.
laden *v* to load, to burden.—*n* a load, a burden.
ladenin time *n* the time of laying in winter provisions.
lading *n* a burden.
ladle *n* **1** a small wooden box with a long handle, formerly in general use in collecting offerings in churches. **2** a tadpole.
lad o' pairts a clever, talented young man, especially one from a poor or humble background.
lad's love *n* southernwood.
lad-wean *n* a male child.
lady *n* a laird's wife.—*adj* fit for a lady.—*v* **1** to be the mistress. **2** to be the wife of a laird.
lady-bracken *n* the female fern.
lady-hen *n* a lark.
lady landers *n* the ladybird.
ladyness *n* ladylikeness.
lady of the meadows *n* meadowsweet.
lady-preen *n* a small kind of pin.
lady's-, ladies'-bedstraw *n* the yellow bedstraw.
lady's-, ladies'-fingers *n* **1** the kidney vetch. **2** the honeysuckle.
lady's-, ladies'-garten-berries *n* brambleberries.
lady's-o'-heaven's-hen *n* the wren.
lady's-, ladies'-smock *n* the cuckooflower.
lady-toed *adj* (*used of a horse*) turning out the hoofs of the forefeet in running.
lae *v* to leave.—*n* the rest, remainder.
laenarly *adj* **1** lonely. **2** exceptional.
laep *v* to lap as a dog.
laesion *n* **1** lesion. **2** injury.
laesir *n* leisure.
laethran *same as* **latheron**.
lafe *same as* **lave**.
laffin *same as* **lafting**.
laffy *adj* **1** soft, flaccid. **2** not pressed together.
laft[1] *n* **1** an upper floor. **2** a church gallery. **3** a loft.
laft[2] *n* fitness of soil for seed.
lafting *n* **1** a boarded ceiling. **2** a ceiling, flooring. **3** a storey.

laftit *adj* (*used of grain*) kept on the floor of a loft or granary.

lag[1] *n in phr* **lag at the boors** a challenge to play at marbles.

lag[2] *adj* **1** slow, sluggish. **2** laggard. **3** late, last of all.

lagabag *n* **1** the hindmost. **2** a loiterer.

lagen, laggan *same as* **laggen**.

laggan *adj* fatiguing.

laggen *n* **1** the projection of the staves of a barrel, etc, beyond its bottom. **2** the angle formed by the side and bottom of a barrel, etc.—*v* to repair the laggen of a hooped vessel.—*phr* **to ungirth the laggen** to give birth to a child.

laggen ~, lagen gird *n* the bottom hoop of a tub, barrel, etc.—*phr* **to cast a laggen gird** to give birth to an illegitimate child.

lagger *v* **1** to bemire. **2** to sink in a mire. **3** to overburden. **4** to stagger under a load. **5** to walk with difficulty. **6** to walk loiteringly.—*n* **1** a miry place, mud. **2** (*in pl*) spots of mud.

laggert *dj* **1** miry. **2** overburdened.

laggery *adj* miry, dirty.

laggie[1] *n* a goose.—*int* a call to geese.

laggie[2] *adj* slow, inactive.

laggie bag *same as* **lagabag**.

lagging *adj* **1** toilsome. **2** exhausting. **3** slow-moving.

laggit-oot *adj* worn-out.

laggin *n* the junction of the bottom of a pot or pan with its sides.

lags *n* small tufts of corn left uncut.

laich *adj* **1** low. **2** short of stature. **3** below the level of a street, etc, underground. **4** prostrate. **5** sick. **6** in low spirits. **7** lowly, of low birth, humble. **8** (*used of the wind*) southerly.—*n* **1** a hollow, low-lying land. **2** a plain. **3** the lower part or side of anything, years of age, etc.—*v* **1** to lower. **2** to cease, stand still. **3** to higgle about a price.

laich browed *adj* (*used of a close*) with a low entry.

laich country *n* **1** the low country. **2** the Lowlands.

laich croft *n* a low-lying croft.

laichen[1] *v* to lower.

laichen[2] *same as* **laigan**.

laich kirk *n* t1 he area of a church, in contrast to the galleries. **2** the low church of a town, in contrast to the high or principal church.

laich-lifet *adj* pertaining to low life, mean, despicable.

laichness *n* lowness.

laich shop *n* a shop below the level of a street.

laich-sprung *adj* of lowly birth.

laid[1] *n* the pollack.

laid[2] *adj* **1** (*used of crops*) flattened by a storm. **2** lain. **3** compelled.—*v* lay.

laid[3] *n* a load.

laid-drain *n* a drain in which stones were so laid as to give free passage to the water.

laidle *n* **1** a ladle. **2** a box with a long handle for collecting the offertory.

laidlick *n* a tadpole.

laidly *adj* **1** loathly. **2** lascivious. **3** clumsy.

laidner *n* **1** a larder. **2** provisions for winter.

laidron *same as* **latheron**.

laif *n* a loaf.

laig[1] *n* **1** silly talk, gossip. **2** a gossiper.—*v* **1** to talk idly. **2** to talk loudly. **3** to talk foolishly. **4** to gossip.

laig[2] *v* to wade.

laigan *n* a large quantity of anything.

laigen, laiggen *n* the angle between the staves of a barrel and the bottom.

laiger, laigger *same as* **lagger**.

laigh *same as* **laich**.

laighen *same as* **laichen**.

laighie-braid *n* a thickset person or animal.

laighland *adj* lowland.

laiglen *n* a milk pail.

laik[1] *n* **1** a toy. **2** (*in pl*) marbles staked in playing.

laik[2] *v* to leak.—*n* a leak.

laikinadj (*used of rain*) intermittent.

laik-wake *n* a watch by the dead.

laiky *adj* **1** moist. **2** (*used of showers*) intermittent.

lailly *adj* loathly.

laim *n* earthenware.

laimiter *n* a lame person.

lain *same as* **lane**[3].

lainch, lainsh *v* **1** to throw. **2** to launch. **3** to pay out. **4** to set about vigorously. **5** to spring.—*n* a launch.

laing *v* to take long strides.

laip *v* to lap like a dog.

lair[1] *n* **1** a bed. **2** a resting place. **3** a family grave. —*v* **1** to lie, rest. **2** to sink to rest. **3** to bury.

lair[2] *n* **1** a quagmire, bog. **2** quicksand. **3** mud.—*v* **1** to sink in mud, snow, etc. **2** to stick fast in mud, snow, etc. **3** to struggle in a lair.

lair[3] *n* **1** lore. **2** learning. **3** education. **4** schooling.—*v* **1** to learn. **2** to teach.

lair[4] *n* **1** a layer. **2** a slice of beef, etc. **3** a patch of moss for drying peats.—*adj* thick in layers.

lairach *n* **1** the site of a building. **2** the traces of a foundation or ruin. **3** the foundation on which a stack rests. **4** a peat moss. **5** a heap of materials. **6** a cairn of stones.

lairach cairn *n* a heap of stones.

lairag *n* the lark.

laird *n* **1** a lord. **2** a landlord of a house. **3** a landed proprietor.

lair'd *adj* stuck in mud, snow, etc.

lairdie *n* a small laird.

lairdlin *n* **1** a lordling. **2** a petty laird.

lairdlineas *n* lordliness.

lairdly *adj* lordly.

lairdship *n* **1** lordship. **2** landed or house property. **3** ownership of land or houses. **4** the rank or dignity of a laird.

lairer *n* a herd boy's staff for driving cattle, etc, to their resting place.

lairge *adj* **1** large. **2** plentiful.

lairick *same as* **larick**[1].

lair-igigh *n* the green woodpecker.

lairing staff *n* a herd boy's lairer (*qv*).

lairoch *same as* **larach**.

lairock *n* the lark.

lair-stane *n* a tombstone.

lairt *same as* **lyart**.

lairy *adj* **1** wet, slushy. **2** boggy, swampy.

laish *n* a heavy fall of rain.

laist *v* to last.

lait[1] *same as* **lythe**.

lait[2] *n* **1** manner, bearing. **2** a habit, custom. **3** a trick, prank. **4** a bad habit.

lait[3] *v* **1** to search for. **2** to induce. **3** to entice.

lait[4] *v* **1** to reduce the temper of iron when too hard. **2** to plate with tin, etc.

laiteran *same as* **lateran**.

laith[1] *same as* **lythe**.

laith[2] *adj* loath.—*n* a loathing.—*v* to loathe.

laithfu' *adj* **1** bashful. **2** shy of invitations. **3** loathsome. **4** wilful.

laithfu-like *adj* seemingly shy or reluctant.

laithless *adj* **1** unregretful. **2** quite willing. **3** not shy.

laith-lounkie *adj* in low spirits.

laithly *adj* **1** foul. **2** repulsive. **3** loathly. **4** lascivious.

laithron *same as* **latheron**.

laitin *n* **1** thin sheet metal. **2** tin plate.

laive[1] *same as* **lave**.

laive[2] *v* **1** to bale water. **2** to throw water with the hand or with a vessel.—*n* **1** a quantity of water thrown. **2** the drawing or throwing of water.

lake[1] *v* to undervalue.—*n* **1** a disgrace. **2** want.

lake[2] *n* a small, stagnant pool.

lake[3] *n* **1** play. **2** a plaything. **3** (*in pl*) marbles staked in various games.—*v* to play, sport.

laldie *n* **1** punishment. **2** a beating.—*in phr* **gie it laldie** to do something with great vigour.

lall *same as* **loll**.

Lallan *adj* belonging to the Lowlands of Scotland. —*n* **1** the Lowland dialect. **2** (*in pl*) the Lowlands of Scotland.

lamar, lamer *same as* **lammer**.

lamb *n* a term of endearment.

lamb-gimmer *n* a ewe lamb of a year old.

lambie *n* **1** a young lamb. **2** a term of endearment.

lamb's lettuce *n* corn salad.

lamb's tongue *n* corn mint.

lamb-tiend *n* the tithe of wool.

lamb-time killing *n* the time when lambs are killed for food.

lame¹ *adj* **1** slow-footed. **2** clumsy.

lame² *n* **1** crockery, earthenware. **2** a broken piece of earthenware.—*adj* made of earthenware or porcelain.

lamely *adj* **1** slow. **2** halting.

lament *n* a slow piece of music composed for the bagpipes in mourning for a death or deaths.

lame pig *n* an earthenware jar or other vessel.

lamer *n* **1** a thong. **2** the lash of a whip.

lamgammachy *n* **1** a long, rambling speech. **2** much foolish talk. **3** rhymes repeated in girls' games.

lamiter, lameter *adj* lame.—*n* **1** one who is lame. **2** a cripple. **3** one who is deformed.

Lammas *n* **1** the beginning of August. **2** a Scottish term.

Lammas-fair *n* a fair held at Lammas.

Lammas-flood, ~-rain, ~-spate *n* heavy rain and floods about Lammas.

Lammas-nicht *n* the night of 1 August.

Lammas-stream *n* a strong and high spring tide in August.

Lammas-tide *n* the Lammas season.

lammas-whiting *n* the young of the salmon trout.

lammer *n* amber.—*adj* made of amber.

lammer-bead *n* an amber bead.

Lammermoor lion *n* a sheep.

lammer wine *n* amber wine, an imaginary liquor esteemed a sort of elixir of immortality.

lammie, lammikie, lammikin *n* **1** a young lamb. **2** a term of endearment. **3** a kid.

lammie-loo *n* a darling child.

lammie-sourocks *n* the sorrel dock.

lamoo *n in phr* **gang down like lamoo** to be easily swallowed.

lamp¹ *n in phr* **lamp o' the watter** phosphorescence on the sea.—*v* to shine as a lamp.

lamp² *v* **1** to stride. **2** to walk quickly and with long steps. **3** to beat, thrash. **4** to hammer on a sole, heel, etc. **5** to vanquish, conquer.—*n* a long, heavy step, a great stride.

lamp³ *v* (*used of the ground*) to be covered with gossamer from dew or slight frost.

lamper¹ *n* one who takes long, heavy strides.

lamper², lamper-eel *n* a lamprey.

lamper *v* (*used of milk*) to coagulate, to lapper (qv) without artficial means.

lampin' *n* **1** a beating. **2** a defeat.

lampit *n* a limpet.

lampy *adj* having a striding gait.

lamy *n* the common guillemot.

lan *same as* **laan**.

lance¹ *n* a lancet.—*adj* lancet-shaped.

lance² *v* to leap, bound forward.

lancers *n* teeth.

land¹ *n* **1** that portion of a field or rig (qv) that a band of reapers could cut together at one bout. **2** arable land. **3** a house of different storeys, let out in tenements. **4** a storey, a tenement in such a house.—*v* to end, to finish a business.

land² *n* a hook like the letter S.

landart *adj* rustic.

land-biding *adj* stay-at-home.

land-burst *n* a series of a few breakers at a tidal change or occasionally during a storm.

land-fall *n* the flood tide.

land-folk *n* country people, rustics.

landgates *adv* towards inland.

land-horse *n* the horse that treads on the unploughed land.

landimere, landemeer *n* **1** the march of a property. **2** the ceremony of beating the bounds.

Landimere's Day *n* the day on which the bounds are beaten or the marches are examined.

landin, landen *n* **1** the end of a furrow in a ploughed field. **2** the name given by a band of reapers to the rig (qv) on which they worked. **3** the reaping of their rig.

landlash *n* a great fall of rain with high wind.

landlord *n* the head of the family.

land-louper *n* **1** a vagabond. **2** an adventurer. **3** an unsettled person. **4** one who flees the country to escape his creditors or arrest.

land-loupin' *adj* rambling from place to place as a vagrant.

land lubbing *adj* pertaining to a landlubber or rustic.

landmail *n* rent of land in money or kind.

landman *n* **1** a landowner. **2** a landsman. **3** an inhabitant of the country.

land-march, ~-merch *n* a boundary.

land-~, land's-mark day *n* the day on which a burgh's boundaries are beaten or marches ridden.

land master *n* landowner.

land-metster *n* a measurer of land, a land surveyor.

landrien *adv* in a straight course and quickly.

land-sea *n* heavy breakers on a beach.

land-setting *n* land-letting.

land-setting cop *n* a fee paid by the tenant at the letting of a farm.

land-side *n* the side of a plough next the unturned soil.

land's lord *n* a landowner.

landstail *n* **1** the parapet of a bridge. **2** the part of a dam head which connects it witn the adjoining land.

landstane *n* a stone found in the soil of field.

land-tide *n* the undulating motion of the air, seen on a hot day.

land-tow *n* a cable for fastening a boat to the shore.

land-tripper, -tuppit *n* the common sandpiper.

landwart *n* **1** the country. **2** inland districts.—*adj* **1** rural, rustic. **2** boorish.—*adv* towards the country.

landwart-bred *adj* brought up in the country.

landwart-men *n* rustics in contrast with citizens.

landwart-town *n* **1** a country farmhouse. **2** a country house.

land-waster *n* a spendthrift.

landways *adv* by land.

land-whaup *n* the curlew.

lane¹ *n* **1** a brook, the motion of which is scarcely perceptible. **2** the hollow course of a large rivulet in meadow land. **3** the smooth, imperceptible flow in a river.

lane² *v* to hide, keep secret.

lane³ *adv* alone.—*adj* **1** lonely. **2** solitary. **3** dreary. —*n with pers pron and poss adj* self, selves.—*phrs* **1 him lane, his lane** by himself. **2 her lane** by herself. **3 them lane, their lane** by themselves.

laneful *adj* forlorn.

lanely *adj* **1** lonely. **2** alone. **3** single.

lan'en *n* the end of a furrow.

lanerly *adj* **1** alone. **2** single. **3** exceptional, singular.

lanesome *adj* lonely.

lang¹ *v* to long for.—*n* **1** homesickness. **2** desire.

lang² *prep* along.—*adv* for a long time.

lang³ *adj* **1** long. **2** tall. **3** great. **4** slow. **5** tedious, wearisome. **6** lasting.—*n* **1** length. **2** extent. **3** a long time. **4** tedium.

langainsyne *adv* long ago.

langal *same as* **langel**.

lang-back-seen *adv* long ago.

lang board *n* a long table in a farmhouse, at which master and servants sat at meals.

lang bowls *n* a game in which heavy leaden bullets were thrown from the hand and in which he who threw the farthest or reached a fixed point with fewest throws was victor.

lang bullet *n* an iron bullet or a round stone round which a broad garter was wound, the end of which was held in the hand while the bullet was forcibly thrown forward on the highway and acquired a rotary motion, making it move forward with extreme rapidity.

lang-chafted *adj* having long jaws.

lang-craig *n* **1** a long neck. **2** a purse. **3** an onion that goes to stalk.

lang-craigit *adj* long-necked.

lang-craigit heron *n* the heron.

Lang Day *n* the Day of Judgment.

lang-draughtit *adj* very foreseeing or politic.

langel *n* **1** a tether fastening an animal's fore- and hindlegs together on one side. **2** a hindrance.—*v* **1** to hobble an animal. **2** to fetter. **3** to hinder.

langelt *n* a shackle.—*v* to shackle an animal.

langemark-day *same as* **landmark-day**.

lang-endwise *adv* lengthwise.

langer *n* **1** weariness. **2** tedium. **3** ennui. **4** longing. **5** homesickness.

langersome *adj* **1** tedious. **2** slow. **3** causing ennui.

langet *n* a shackle for an animal.—*v* to shackle an animal.

lang-eyed, ~-e'ed *adj* **1** long-sighted. **2** sharp-sighted.

lang-fingert *adj* thievish.

lang fras syne *adv* long ago.

lang-gabbit *adj* talkative.

lang gae *n* a long time.

lang-gaithered *adj* (*used of money, etc*) taking long to accumulate.

lang-gammachy *n* a long, rambling speech or story.

Lang-Gate *n* the path skirting the old Nor' Loch, now Princes Street, Edinburgh.

lang halter time *n* the season of the year when, the fields being cleared, travellers and others claimed a common right of occasional passage.

lang hame *n* **1** the grave. **2** heaven.

lang-heidit *adj* **1** shrewd. **2** far-seeing. **3** intelligent.

langie-spangie *n* a game of marbles, played with large marbles out along a road.

langije *n* abusive language.

lang kail *n* a colewort or cabbage unmeshed or unchopped.

lang-kail-gullie, ~-knife *n* a knife for cutting lang kail (qv).

langle *same as* **langel**.

lang-least-buik *n* a ledger.

lang-leggit-tailor *n* the daddy-longlegs.

lang length *n* **1** full length. **2** full extent. **3** a long time.

lang-lenth *n in phr* **at lang-lenth** at last.

langletit *adj* having a fore- and a hindleg shackled, to prevent straying or running. *See* **langel**.

langlins *prep* along.—*adv* **1** slowly. **2** long-drawn-out.

lang-lip *n* **1** a fit of sulking. **2** a sulky, morose person.

lang-lippit *adj* **1** sulky. **2** morose. **3** melancholy.

langlit, langlet *n* a shackle for an animal.

lang-lonen *n* long-continued loneliness.

lang-lowrie *n* a large bell tolled at 10 p.m. in many towns.

lang-lug *n* **1** a large portion. **2** (*in pl*) a donkey. **3** an eavesdropper.

lang-luggit *adj* **1** long-eared. **2** quick of hearing. **3** given to eavesdropping.

lang megs *n* a kind of apple.

lang-neb *n* **1** a long beak or nose. **2** a forward intrusion.

lang-nebbit *adj* **1** long-nosed. **2** quick of understanding. **3** prying, intrusive. **4** having a long point or prong. **5** preternatural. **6** (*used of words*) difficult to pronounce or to understand, polysyllabic. **7** pedantic.

langour *same as* **langer**.

langrin *n* the long run.

langs *prep* along.

lang saddle *n* **1** a long wooden seat with a high back and ends. **2** a folding bed.

lang sands *n in phr* **leave one to the lang sands** to

throw one out of a share of property to which he has a just claim.

lang sang *n* a noise made by the waves on the bar of a harbour.

lang seat *n* a lang saddle (qv).

lang seen *adv* long ago.

lang settle *n* a lang saddle (qv).

lang-shankit *adj* **1** long-legged. **2** having a long handle.

lang-shanks *n* death.

lang sheep *n* sheep of the Cheviot breed.

lang sicht *n* a great deal.

langside *adv* alongside.

lang siller *n* a large price.

lang since syne, lang sin syne *n and adv* long ago.

langsome, langsum *adj* **1** slow. **2** tedious, weary. **3** rather long. **4** rather tall. **5** lengthy. **6** late, behind time.

langsomelie *adv* tediously.

langsomeness *n* **1** tediousness. **2** delay.

langspiel *n* a small harp.

lang-spool *adj* long-limbed.

langsyne *adv* long ago.—*adj* **1** ancient. **2** old-time. —*n* **1** ancient days. **2** days of old.

lang-taed *adj* (*used of a schoolteacher's punishment belt*) having long strips at its end.

lang-tailed *adj* **1** tedious. **2** prolix. **3** longing, covetous.

lang-taw *n* a game of marbles.

lang tholance *n* long-suffering.

lang-tochered *adj* having a substantial dowry.

lang-tongued *adj* **1** voluble, garrulous. **2** tale-bearing. **3** unable to keep secrets. **4** given to exaggeration.

languish *adj* **1** longish. **2** (*used of a forehead*) high.

langure *n* longing.

lang-war-day *n* the month of March.

langways, ~wise *adv* lengthways.

Lang Whang *n* the bleakest part of Carnwath Moor.

langwidge *n* languor, languishing.

lang-wund *adj* **1** tedious. **2** long-winded, involved.

Lanimer Day, Lanimers *same as* **Landimere's Day**.

lanland *n* all the stories of a house.

lannimor *n* an adjuster of marches between conterminous landowners.

lanstell *same as* **landstail**.

lant[1] *n* **1** three-card loo. **2** a cheat. **3** a dilemma.—*v* **1** to play the game of lant. **2** to cheat. **3** to bring to a stand. **4** to reduce to a dilemma. **5** to jeer at.

lant[2] *n* **1** confusion. **2** commotion.

lant[3] *n* land, ground.

lante *v* lent.

lanter-loo *n* five-card loo.

lantern chafts *n* lantern jaws.

lantron[1] *n* a lantern.

lantron[2] *same as* **lentrin**.

lap[1], **lapp**[1] *n* **1** a drink. **2** what can be licked by the tongue. **3** the noise of water among stones. **4** a splash. **5** a pool.

lap[2], **lapp**[2] *v* **1** to mend, patch. **2** to wrap round.—*n* **1** a wrap. **2** a patch. **3** a flap. **4** the lobe of the ear. **5** the lapel of a coat, etc. **6** a saddle flap.

lap[3] *v* leapt.

lap[4] *n* a small quantity.

lap-love *n* **1** the climbing buckweed. **2** the corn convolvulus.

lapp *same as* **lap**[1], **lap**[2].

lapper[1] *same as* **lipper**.

lapper[2] *v* **1** to clot, curdle, coagulate. **2** to besmear. **3** to cover so as to clot. **4** to cover or become covered with blood. **5** (*used of damp soil*) to harden by drought. **6** to become lumpy, craggy. **7** to make soil muddy by working it in wet weather. —*n* **1** a clot of blood. **2** a coagulated mass. **3** curdled or sour milk. **4** snow in a slushy state.

lappert milk *n* milk coagulated without artificial means.

lapperty *n* milk that has stood until it is curdled.

lappie *n* **1** a plash (qv). **2** a pool.

lappings *n* slaver from an animal's mouth.

lapron *n* a leveret.
lapster *n* a lobster.
lapster-clap *n* a stick with an iron hook for catching lobsters on the shore at extreme low tide.
lapstone *n* the stone on which a shoemaker hammers his leather.
larach *same as* **lairach**.
larbal *adj* 1 lazy. 2 sluggish.
larboard *adv* beneath board.
larcenry *n* larceny.
lard *int* an exclamation of disgust.
lare *same as* **lair**[1], **lair**[3], **lair**[4].
lare-maister *n* a schoolmaster, teacher.
large *adj* 1 liberal. 2 self-important. 3 plentiful.
larick[1] *n* the larch.
larick[2] *n* the lark.
larick's lint *n* the great golden maidenhair.
larie[1] *same as* **lorie**.
larie[2] *n* laurel.
lark *v* 1 to play, frolic. 2 to make mischievous fun. —*n* 1 a frolic. 2 a spree. 3 mischievous fun.
larrie *n* 1 jesting, gibing. 2 a practical joke, hoax.
larrup *v* to thrash, beat soundly.—*n* a blow.
larry, lary *n* a servant.
larum *n* 1 an alarm. 2 noise. 3 stir, bustle.
las-a-day *int* an exclamation of fear, surprise, etc.
lash[1] *n* 1 a heavy fall of rain. 2 a dash of water. 3 a quantity. 4 a great abundance.—*v* 1 (*with* **out**) to kick from behind. 2 to lavish money, live extravagantly. 3 to dash water, etc. 4 to throw forcibly. 5 to act violently. 6 (*used of water*) to fall with violence, dash, splash, rush. 7 (*used of rain*) to fall in torrents. 8 to work vigorously.
lash[2] *adj* 1 relaxed from weakness or fatigue. 2 feeble. 3 lazy.
lashings *n* 1 abundance. 2 great quantities.
lashness *n* 1 relaxation through great exertion. 2 looseness of conduct.
lask *n* diarrhoea or scour (*qv*) in cattle.
laskar *n* a large armful of hay or straw.
laskit *n* elastic.
lass *n* 1 a girl. 2 a young woman. 3 a female sweetheart. 4 a daughter. 5 a maidservant. 6 a woman. 7 a term of address.
lass-bairn *n* a female child.
lass-fond *adj* fond of a lass or of the lasses.
lassie *n* 1 a young lass, a girl. 2 a term of endearment. *See* **lass**.
lassie-bairn *n* a female child.
lassie-boy *n* a tomboy.
lassie-days, lassiehood *n* girlhood.
lassie-lad *n* an effeminate boy.
lassie-like *adj* 1 girlish. 2 (*used of a boy*) effeminate.
lassie-wean *n* a female child, a daughter.
lassikie, lassockie *n* a young or little lassie (qv).
lassock *n* a young lass (qv).
lassock-love *n* a girl sweetheart.
lass-quean *n* a female servant.
lass-wife *n* a girl wife.
last[1] *n* 1 a measure of herrings. 2 a measure of arable land. 3 a measure of tonnage. 4 a dry measure of varying amount.
last[2] *n* 1 durability, continuance. 2 staying power, power of lasting.—*v* 1 to hold out. 2 to live on, survive.
last-day *n* 1 yesterday. 2 the other day, a day or two ago.
lasten *adj* last.
laster *adj* later.—*adv* later.
lastest *adj* latest.—*adv* last, lastly.
lasty *adj* 1 lasting, durable. 2 serviceable.
lat[1] *v* to let, hinder.—*n* a hindrance.
lat[2] *v* to let, allow.
lat[3] *v in phr* **lat a raught** to aim a blow.
lata *same as* **lawtie**.
lat a be *phr* 1 not to mention. 2 to omit.
latace *n* lettuce.

lat be *v* to let alone.—*adv* much less.
latch[1] *n* a mire, swamp. 2 a rut, the track of a cartwheel.
latch[2] *n* 1 a loop of thread on the edge of a garment for fastening on a hook or button. 2 the cord connecting the footboard and the wheel of a spinning wheel.
latch[3] *v* to catch.
latch[4] *n* part of a moss where peats are spread to dry.
latch[5] *v* to idle, to loiter.—*adj* indolent.—*n* an idler or indolent person.
latchard *n* 1 a loop of thread on the edge of a dress for fixing on a button or hook. 2 a loop of thread fixing a footless stocking by passing over the second toe.
latchet *n* a smart blow.
latchy *adj* full of ruts.
late[1] *same as* **lait**[4].
late[2] *n* 1 a late hour. 2 a recent time.
lateran, latern *n* 1 the preceptor's desk below the pulpit. 2 the raised pew round the foot of the pulpit, where the elders sat and parents brought their children for baptism.
lateth *same as* **lawtie**.
late-wake *same as* **lyke-wake**.
lat-gae *v* 1 to let off, fire. 2 to break wind. 3 to raise a psalm tune.
lather[1] *v* to work vigorously.
lather[2] *n* a ladder.
lather[3] *n* leather.
latheron, latherin, lathron *n* 1 a lazy, idle person. 2 a sloven, slut. 3 a loose woman. 4 a term of contempt.— *adj* 1 lazy, vulgar. 2 slovenly, sluttish.
lathie *same as* **laddie**.
Latiner *n* one who is learning Latin.
latna *v* let not.
lat o'er *v* to swallow.
lat oot *v* to pay out straw gradually in twisting straw ropes.
latron *n* a latrine.
latt *n* a shelf formed of laths.
latten *v* let, allowed.
latter-meat *n* meat sent from the master's to the servant's table.
latteron *same as* **lateran**.
latter-oot *n* the person who pays out straw in twisting straw ropes.
lat wi' *v* to yield to, indulge.
lauch[1] *n* 1 law. 2 custom. 3 condition. 4 fitness of soil. 5 a tavern bill.
lauch[2] *v* 1 to laugh. 2 (*used of the eye*) to light upon with pleasure.—*n* a laugh.
lauchablest *adj* most laughable.
lauchen *v* laughed.
laucher *n* a laughter.
lauchfull *adj* lawful.
lauchter *same as* **lachter**.
lauchterins *n* what remains after a mass of anything has been removed.
lauchty *adj* (*used of teeth*) projecting, long, tusk-like.
laudron *same as* **latheron**.
laudry *n* a heated discussion or questioning.
laugen *v, adj* gossiping. *See* **laig**.
laugh *n* a loch, lake.
laughen *v* laughed.
laughify *v* to laugh at.
laughing rain *n* rain from the southwest, with a clear skyline.
laumer *same as* **lammer**.
laun *same as* **laan**.
launder *n* a laundrymaid.—*v* to wash and dress clothes.
laup *v* leaped.
lave[1] *n* the remainder.
lave[2] *v* to lavish.
lave[3] *v* 1 to draw water. 2 to bale. 3 to throw water. —*n* a quantity of water thrown.
lave[4] *n* the guillemot.
lavellan *n* 1 a kind of weasel. 2 a mythical creature, living in lakes, etc, and squirting poison to a great distance.

lave-luggit *adj* having long, drooping ears.

laverock, laveruck *n* the lark.

laverock-heich *adv* as high as the lark soars.

laverock-heicht *n* the height to which a lark soars.

laverock's-lint *n* 1 the golden maidenhair. 2 the dwarf flax.

lavrick, lavrock *same as* **laverock**.

lavrie *adj* (*used of broth*) 1 well-cooked. 2 having good and plentiful ingredients.

lavy[1] *adj* lavish, profuse, liberal.

lavy[2] *same as* **lave**[4].

law[1] *n* 1 litigation, lawsuits. 2 disputatious talk. 3 so much time or space granted in a race and pursuit of game.—*v* 1 to go to law. 2 to take every advantage of law against the defender. 3 to lay down the law. 4 to determine.

law[2] *n* a roundish or conical hill.

lawage *n* acting lawfully.

law-biding *adj* 1 able to answer a charge. 2 waiting the regular course of law instead of fleeing. 3 observing the laws.

lawbor *n* labour.—*v* 1 to labour. 2 to cultivate the soil.

lawborable *adj* that may be ploughed.

law-brod, ~-buird *n* a tailor's lapboard.

law burrows *n* legal security given by a person that he will not injure another in person or property.

lawe *same as* **lowe**.

law-folk *n* lawyers.

law-free *adj* not legally convicted or condemned.

lawful-day *n* an ordinary weekday.

lawin *n* 1 a tavern bill. 2 a reckoning.

lawin-clink, ~-coin *n* money for payment of the lawin (qv).

lawin-free *adj* scot-free, exempt from paying a share of the lawin (qv).

Lawland *same as* **Lallan**.

lawly *adv* in legal form.

lawman *n* a lawyer, solicitor.

lawn, lawning *n* grass land.

law-paper *n* a will, a testamentary deed.

law-plea *n* a lawsuit.

law-pleaing *n* litigation.

Lawrence-fair *n* a fair held on St Lawrence's Day.

Lawrencemas *n* 23 August.

lawrie *same as* **lowrie**.

law-sovertie *n* legal security.

Law Sunday *n* the name given to a particular Sunday between the end of March and Whitsuntide.

lawtie, lawtith *n* loyalty, fidelity, honesty.

lawtifull *adj* most loyal, full of loyalty.

law-work *n* the experience of conviction of sin or repentance under the law.

lax[1] *n* relief, release.—*v* 1 to relax. 2 to grow feeble.

lax[2] *n* a salmon.

laxat *adj* laxative, aperient.

lax-fisher *n* a salmon fisher.

lay[1] *n* a slip of wood coated with sand or emery for sharpening a scythe.

lay[2] *n* 1 the slay of a loom. 2 that part to which the thread is fixed and which, as it moves, lays the threads of the web parallel, shot by shot, in weaving.

lay[3] *n* grassland, pasture, lea.

lay[4] *n* a turning lathe.

lay[5] *v* 1 (*used of crops*) to flatten by wind or rain. 2 to wager. 3 to alleviate. 4 to allay. 5 to repair the worn edge of a plough coulter by adding fresh iron. 6 to smear sheep with ointment. 7 to thresh. 8 to lie, rest.—*n* 1 the parting of the wool when the sheep is smeared. 2 the lie of the land, the direction in which a thing lies or moves. 3 a foundation. 4 a temporary lull of waves. 5 a chance.

lay[6] *v in phr* **lay up one's mittens** to beat out one's brains.—*n* a footing.

lay about *v* 1 to turn, put about. 2 to fight vigorously.

lay aff *v* 1 to talk volubly. 2 to hurt, injure.

layan *n* the curing of a rickety child in a smithy by bathing it in a tub of water heated by plunging hot irons into it.

lay at *v* to beat severely. 2 to work vigorously.

lay away *v* (*used of hens, etc*) to lay eggs in out-of-the-way places.

lay-buird *n* a lapboard.

lay by *v* 1 to stop, cease. 2 to injure oneself by overwork. 3 to be laid aside from illness.

lay down *v* 1 to knock or trample down. 2 to sow out in grass. 3 to bury. 4 to seduce a woman.

laydron *same as* **latheron**.

layer[1] *same as* **lair**[1].

layer[2] *n* the Manx shearwater.

lay-fitted *adj* (*used of the foot*) flat-soled, springless and much turned out.

lay from *v* (*used of a horse*) to kick violently.

lay in *v* 1 (*used of a woman*) to be confined. 2 to work vigorously.

laying money *n* money in hand.

laying time *n* the season, about November, for smearing sheep.

lay into *v* 1 to beat severely. 2 to work vigorously. 3 to eat greedily.

lay money *n* false coin.

layne *same as* **lane**[2].

lay on *v* 1 to beat severely. 2 to work hard. 3 (*used of rain, etc*) to fall heavily. 4 to fall on food, to eat much.—*n* a good meal.

lay on to *v* to thrash, beat severely.

lay out *v* to explain clearly.

lay out for *v* 1 to get ready for. 2 to abuse, scold.

lay past *v* to put by.

lay pock *n* the ovary of a fowl.

layt *same as* **lait**[3].

lay-to, -tae *n* 1 a contest, fight. 2 a holdfast at the head of a cow's stall to which the cow is tied.

lay to, ~ till *v* 1 to shut a door, etc. 2 to lay hold of. 3 to apply, put on. 4 to lay to the charge of. 5 to work vigorously. 6 to set to work. 7 to eat greedily.

lay up *v* 1 to serve a meal. 2 to cast on stitches in knitting.

lay upon *v* to strike, beat severely.

lazy *v* to render lazy.

lazy bed *n* a method of planting potatoes, which secures the trenching of the plot in two or three years.

lea[1] *adj* unploughed.—*adv* in grass.

lea[2] *v* to leave.

lead[1] *v* 1 to play first in a curling rink. 2 to carry, cart, hay, straw, peats, etc.—*n* 1 a millrace, an artificial watercourse. 2 as much hay, etc, as a horse and cart can take in one journey. 3 the course over which curling stones are driven. 4 the first player in a curling rink. 5 (*in pl*) a game of curling.

lead[2] *n* 1 a dialect. 2 a rhyme, song. 3 a screed.

lead[3] *n* 1 the weight at the end of the pendulum of a clock. 2 a weaving term.

lead-brash *n* a disease affecting animals at leadhills.

lead-bullaxe *n* a roughly pointed piece of lead used as a pencil or as a ruler.

lead-draps *n* small shot.

leaden-heart *n* a charm hung round the neck to promote recovery from unaccountable ailments.

leader[1] *n* 1 the person who plays the first stone in a curling rink. 2 a carrier, carter. 3 a tendon, sinew. 4 a pipe for conveying water.

leader[2] *n* a leaden bullet, sometimes used as a boy's marble.

leading *n* 1 carting hay, straw, peats, etc. 2 provisions.

lead master *n* 1 a leader. 2 a general.

lead-pike *n* a lead-bullaxe (qv).

lead-stane *n* the weight that sinks a fishing line.

lead-stone *n* the first stone played on a curling rink.

leaf *same as* **laif**.

leaf-alane *adj* quite alone.

leaful[1] *same as* **leiful**.

leaful[2] *adj* 1 sad, lonely. 2 wistful.

leafu'-lane *adj* quite alone.

leag *same as* **laig**[1].

leager *v* to encamp.

leager-lady *n* **1** a soldier's wife. **2** (*used contemptuously*) a female camp follower.

league *v* to hurry off.

leaky *n* an irregularity in the tides in the Firth of Forth.

leaky-tide *n* the leaky (qv) in the Firth of Forth.

leal *adj* **1** loyal, faithful. **2** sincere, true. **3** genuine. **4** true to the mark. **5** (*of a blow*) severe, smart, well-directed.— *n* truth.—*adv* truly.

lea-laik[1] *n* natural shelter for cattle, such as is furnished by glens or overhanging rocks.

lea-laik[2], **-gair** *n* **1** well-sheltered grazing ground. **2** the place where two hills join together and form a kind of bosom.

lea-lane *adj* quite alone.

lea-lang *adj* livelong.

leal-come *adj* honestly gained.

leal-gede *adj* truly good.

leal-heartit *adj* true-hearted, faithful, loyal.

leal-loved *adj* dearly and truly loved.

leally *adv* loyally, honestly.

lealty *n* loyalty, fidelity.

leam[1] *n a* **1** gleam, flash. **2** flame, blaze.—*v* **1** to gleam, shine. **2** to flash.

leam[2] *v* to take nuts out of the husk.

leam[3] *n* a dog-leash.

leam[4] *same as* **lame**[2].

leamer *n* a ripe nut ready to fall from the husk.

leaming *adj* (*used of nuts*) ripe and separating easily from the husk.

lean[1] *v* (*with* **down**) to be seated, to lie down, recline.—*n* **1** means of leaning. **2** a resting place.

lean[2] *same as* **lane**[2].

lean[3] *adv* scantily.

leanet *adj* **1** well-inclined. **2** affable. **3** frank.

leaning stock *n* a post or block of wood for resting on.

leap[1] *same as* **lap**[4].

leap[2] *same as* **loup**[1].

leaping ague *n* St Vitus's dance.

leaping-block *n* a horse block.

leaping-ill *same as* **louping-ill**.

leaping-on-stone *n* a stone horse block.

lear[1] *same as* **lair**[3].

lear[2] *v* **1** (*with* **up**) to brighten up. **2** to lighten.

lear[3] *adv* rather.

lea-rig *n* a grass field, an unploughed rig (qv).

learless *adj* unlearned.

learn *v* **1** to teach. **2** to threaten punishment. **3** to accustom.

learning *n* education, schooling.

learock *n* the lark.

leary *n* **1** the light of a candle, lamp, etc. **2** a lamplighter.

leary-licht-the-lamps *n* **1** a lamplighter. **2** a teasing name given to a lamplighter by children.

lease[1] *v* to hold, possess.

lease[2] *v* to injure.

lease-haud *n* possession, holding by a lease.

lease-me-on *same as* **leese-me-on**.

leash[1] *n* **1** a long piece of rope, cord, etc. **2** rope enough, freedom, liberty. **3** anything very long. —*v* **1** to tie together. **2** to marry. **3** to tie up with twine. **4** to walk or move quickly. **5** (*with* **off**) to unroll. **6** (*with* **off**) to speak from memory. **7** (*with* **off**) to speak much. **8** (*with* **at**) to work vigorously and with speed. **9** (*with* **away**) to go cleverly off.

leash[2] *same as* **lish**.

leashing-maker *n* **1** a liar. **2** a spreader of lies.

leasing *n* lying. **2** slandering.

leasing-making *n* **1** lying. **2** the uttering of falsehood against the king or his counsellors to the people or to the king or government against the people.

leasome *same as* **leesome**.

least[1] *adv* at least.

least[2] *conj* lest.

leastways' -wise *adv* at least, at any rate.

leasum *same as* **leesome**[3].

leasumlie *adv* lawfully.

leath[1] *n* the lay (qv) of a weaver's loom.

leath[2] *v* to loiter. **2** to delay.

leath[3] *same as* **laith**[2]

leather[1] *n* **1** the skin. **2** untanned hide. **3** a cow's udder. **4** a heavy blow.—*v* **1** to beat, thrash. **2** to do anything vigorously and speedily. **3** to hurry. **4** to plod on or pound away at anything. **5** to scold. **6** to tie tightly. **7** to cover with leather.

leather[2] *n* a ladder.

leathering *n* **1** a thrashing. **2** a scolding.

leatherjacket *n* a name given to the corn grub.

leather-shod *adj* supplied with boots and shoes.

leatherty-patch *n* a country dance.

leathfow *same as* **laithfu'**.

leaugh *same as* **laich**.

leauw, leaw *n* a place for drawing nets on at a riverside.

leave[1] *v* **1** to allow, permit, let. **2** to have leave.

leave[2] *same as* **lave**.

leave[3] *same as* **lief**.

leave aside *v* **1** to put aside. **2** not to count, to except.

leave be *v* to let alone, let be.

leaven *n* dough set for fermentation.

leave out *n* permission to leave school for a few minutes.

leaves *n* leavings, scraps.

lebb, leb *n* as much liquid, meat, etc, as can be taken into the mouth or thrown by the hand at one time.—*v* **1** to lick up food. **2** to swallow hastily. **3** to throw small quantities of liquid or of meal by hand or a small vessel into the mouth. **4** to get through work quickly.

lebber, leber *same as* **lebber**.

lebber-beards *n* broth made of greens, thickened with oatmeal.

lebbie *same as* **labey**.

leck[1] *n* **1** a flagstone. **2** any stone that stands a strong fire. **3** a hard subsoil of clay and gravel.

leck[2] *v* **1** to moisten. **2** to sprinkle. **3** to pour water over a substance to get a decoction. **4** to drip, ooze. **5** to leak. **6** to drain off.—*n* **1** a leak, a drip. **2** a pit for soaking bark in tanning.

leck-ee *n* the pit that holds the tan liquor and supplies the tan pits.

lectern *same as* **lateran**.

ledder[1] *n* a ladder.

ledder[2] *n* leather.

leddy *n* a lady.

leddy-lannners *n* the ladybird.

led-farm *n* a farm on which the tenant does not reside.

ledge[1] *v* **1** to allege. **2** (*with* **upon**) to accuse.

ledge[2] *v* **1** to jut out. **2** to overhang.

ledge[3] *v* **1** (*with* **on**) to travel at a good pace. **2** to work quickly. **3** (*with* **out**) to go fast at the start. **4** to begin work with a dash.

ledgin' *n* a parapet, especially of a bridge.

ledgit *n* the top of the inner half of a window.

ledington *n* a kind of apple.

lee[1] *n* shelter from wind or rain.—*adj* sheltered.

lee[2] *n* the ashes of green weeds.

lee[3] *adj* (*used as an intensive*) lonely.

lee[4] *n in phr* **little fee** slender means of escape.

lee[5] *n* lea, grassland.—*adj* untilled.

lee[6] *v* to leave.

lee[7] *v* to tell lies.—*n* a lie.

lee[8] *v* to love.

lee-a-lawly *n* a children's game.

leear, leearie *n* a liar.

leeberal *adj* liberal.

leebrary *n* a library.

leech[1] *n* a doctor, surgeon.—*v* **1** to bleed. **2** to doctor.

leech[2] *v* to pin or splice two pieces of wood together.—*n* a piece of wood used to splice a broken shaft, etc.

leechence *n* license.

leed[1] *n* the metal lead.
leed[2] *n* **1** a dialect, language. **2** a song, rhyme. **3** a long, rambling speech. **4** a yarn. **5** a particular line of argument or talk.—*v* to speak much with little meaning.
leef[1] *adj* unwilling.
leef[2] *same as* **loof**.
leefer *same as* **liefer**.
leefow[1], **leefu'** *adj* kindly, compassionate.
leefow[2] *adj* wilful, obstinate.
leefow, leeful[3] *adj* **1** lonely. **2** sad, wistful.
leefow-heartit *adj* kindly, sympathizing.
leeft *v* left.
leefu-lane, ~-leen *adj* all alone, quite by oneself.
leein'-like *adj* unlike the truth.
leek *n in phr* **as clean as a leek** completely, perfectly.
leekrife kail *n* broth with an abundance of leeks.
leek-strae *n* straw placed under a dead body in a bed.
leeky *adj* (*used of the hair*) lank, much in need of the curling tongs.
leel *same as* **leal**.
lee-lane, ~-lone *phr with a poss pron* **1** quite alone. **2** single.
lee-lang *adj* **1** livelong. **2** whole.
lee-like *adj* having the appearance of falsehood.
leem[1] *n* a tool, an implement.
leem[2] *n* a loom.
leem[3] *same as* **leam**[1].
leem[4] *same as* **lame**[2].
leem[5] *same as* **leam**[2].
leemer *same as* **leamer**.
leemit *n* limit.
leen[1] *n* **1** a wet, grassy place in a moor. **2** a low-lying piece of grass in a farm.
leen[2] *int* cease!—*v* to cease.
leen[3] *same as* **lane**[3].
leenge *v* **1** to slouch. **2** to lounge.
leenger *n* **1** a slouching. **2** a lazy fellow.
leengyie *adj* (*used of a weaver's web*) of a raw or thin texture.
leeno, leenon *n* thread gauze.
leenzie *n* the loin.
leep[1] *v* **1** to parboil, scorch, scald. **2** to warm hastily. **3** to boil for a short time. **4** to perspire freely. **5** to sit over a fire.—*n* **1** a great heat. **2** a hasty warming. **3** a lounge over a fire.
leep[2] *v* to cheat, cozen, deceive.
leepan day *n* a hot, moist day.
lee-penny *n* a charm, consisting of a stone set in gold, in the possession of the Lockharts of Lee.
leeper *adv* very, superlatively.
leeping *adj* (*used of the weather*) hot and moist.
leepit *adj* **1** chilly, loving a fire. **2** meagre, thin.
leepit thing *n* a dog or cat that presses near to a fire.
leer[1] *n* a look, glimpse.—*v* to scowl, frown.
leer[2] *adv* rather.
leeret-gray *same as* **lyart**.
leerie[1] *adj* **1** blinking. **2** casting sidelong glances.
leerie[2] *same as* **leary**.
leerie[3] *n* a cock, chanticleer.
leerie-la, ~-law *n* **1** the crow of a cock. **2** cockcrow.
leerielarach *n* a wrangle, a brisk quarrel.
leerip *same as* **larrup**.
leeroch, leerrach *same as* **lairach**.
leerrach *v* **1** to talk much foolishly. **2** to deliver a long, uninteresting speech, etc. **3** (*with* **aboot** *and* **at**) to repeat from memory. **4** to speak in an unknown tongue.—*n* **1** rambling talk. **2** a foolish book or writing.
leerup *same as* **larrup**.
leese[1], **lees** *v* **1** to unravel, disentangle. **2** to arrange ravelled bits of packthread by collecting them into one hand. **3** to gather anything into the hand. **4** to pass a coil of rope through the hand. **5** to arrange, sort. **6** to trim. **7** to loosen the fibres of a rope. **8** (*with* **out**) to spin out, to prolong. **9** to be prolix.—*n* the thread in winding yarn—

phr **get the lees of a thing** to get a right understanding of something.
leese[2] *v* to be pleased to.
leese[3] *v* **1** to lose. **2** to cause to lose.
leese-me-on *phr* an expression of extreme pleasure in, or affection for, a person or thing.
leesh[1] *same as* **lash**[1].
leesh[2] *same as* **leash**[1].
leesh[3] *n* a large slice.
leeshach *n* a long piece of rope, twine, etc.—*v* **1** (*with* **off**) to unroll. **2** to speak from memory. **3** to tell news at length.
leeshince, leeshins *n* **1** licence. **2** leisure.
leesing *n* **1** falsehood. **2** a lie.
leesk *same as* **lisk**.
leesome[1], **leesim** *adj* **1** pleasant. **2** lovable.
leesome[2] *adj* lonely.
leesome[3] *adj* **1** lawful. **2** permissible.
leesome[4] *adj* easily moved to pity.
leesome-lane *adj* quite alone.
leesome-like *adj* eerie, ghostly.
leester *n* a salmon spear.
leesum *adj* speaking in a lying or hyperbolical manner.
leesumlie *adv* lawfully.
leesum-like *adj* like lying.
leet[1] *n* **1** a lot, portion. **2** a separate division. **3** a selected list of candidates or nominees. **4** a nomination to office by election.—*v* **1** to nominate, to make a select list of candidates. **2** to enrol. **3** to establish.
leet[2] *n* **1** an unseemly mass of liquid or semiliquid stuff. **2** ichor distilling through the pores of the body. **3** a watery sore.—*v* to ooze slowly.
leet[3] *v* **1** to pretend, feign. **2** to make a thing appear so or so. **3** to notice, mention. **4** to attend to, listen to.
leet[4] *same as* **leed**[2].
leet[5] *same as* **lait**[4].
leet[6] *v* **1** to let, allow. **2** allowed.
leetach[1] *n* **1** an unseemly mass of any liquid or semiliquid substance. **2** a watery sore.
leetach[2] *v* **1** to talk a great deal foolishly. **2** to deliver a speech or sermon. **3** to repeat from memory.—*n* incoherent talk, rambling speech. **4** a poor, lengthy piece of literature.
leetch *same as* **leech**[2].
leeth *same as* **laith**[2].
leethfu' *same as* **laithfu'**.
leethfu', leethfow *same as* **leefow**.
leet-lyte *v* to fall flat violently.—*n* a heavy fall.—*adj* flat.
leeve *v* to live.
leeve *same as* **lief**[2].
leevin *n* a living being.
leevin-lane *same as* **leefu'-lane**.
leeze *same as* **leese**[1].
leeze-me-on *phr* an expression of great pleasure.
left *adj* **1** destitute, abandoned. **2** godforsaken. **3** widowed.
left-about *n* an abrupt dismissal.
left ane *n* the largest bannock of a batch.
lefter *n* a shallow wooden vessel, larger than a cog (qv).
left-hand *adj* wrong.
left-handed *adj* **1** sinister. **2** malicious. **3** dubious, doubtful. **4** (*used of a child*) illegitimate.
left-loof *adj* **1** sinister. **2** malicious.
leg[1] *v* **1** to lie. **2** to sleep with.
leg[2] *n* **1** a flat, wooden, leg-shaped board for stretching stockings after washing. **2** an upright post resting on the ground, giving support to a house. **3** a leg-dollar (qv). **4** (*in pl*) increased speed to a curling stone.—*v* **1** to walk. **2** to run away, to take to one's heels.
legacie *n* the state or office of a papal legate.
legacy *v* to bequeath.
legal *n* time allowed before the foreclosure of a mortgage.
legality *n* **1** legal proof. **2** legal knowledge. **3** legal action. **4** a lawsuit.
legate *v* to bequeath.

legation *n* a legal formality.
legator *n* a legatee.
leg bail *n* **1** a kick on the legs. **2** escape. **3** flight from justice instead of seeking bail.
leg bane *n* the shin.
leg-brod *n* a leg-shaped frame for stretching stockings.
leg-dollar, legged-dollar *n* **1** a Manx dollar. **2** a dollar worth £2 16s. Scots, bearing the impression of a man in arms with one leg visible and a shield covering the other.
lege *v* to allege.
legen-girth *same as* **laggen-gird**.
leg-foot *n* the foot or bottom of a thing.
leggat *n* a stroke at golf or ball which for some reason or other is not counted.
leggate *same as* **liggate**.
leggen, leggin *same as* **laggen**.
leggen-gird *same as* **laggen-gird**.
leggie *v* to run, to use one's legs.—*n* a child's leg.
leggin *n* loose bits of wool from near the sheep's feet.
leggums *n* leggings, gaiters.
legible *adj* fair, equitable.
leg-ill *n* a disease in sheep causing lameness.
legitun *n* the lawful share of movables falling to a child on the father's death.
legitime *adj* legitimate.
leg-length *n* the length of a stocking.
leglin *n* a milk pail with an upright handle.
leglin-girth *n* the lowest hoop of a milk pail.—*phr* **to cast a leglin-girth** to bear an illegitimate child.
leg-o'er-im *adv* with one leg over the other.
leg-o'-mutton *adj* huge, brawny.
leg-on *n* brisk walking or working.
leg-out *n* a quick walk.
legs *n* legends.
legs and arms *n* currency given to a story.
leid[1] *n* the metal, lead.
leid[2] *n* a load.
leid[3] *same as* **lade**[1].
leid[4] *same as* **leed**[2].
leid[5] *n* an inkling, a partial idea.
leif *same as* **leef**.
leifer *adv* rather.
leifsum[1] *same as* **leesome**[1].
leifsum[2] *same as* **leesome**[4].
leifu'[1] *adj* lawful.
leifu'[2] *adj* discreet, modest.
leifu'[3] *same as* **leefow**.
leifu'-lane *adj* quite alone.
leil *adj* **1** loyal, honest, upright. **2** (*used of a blow*) smart.— *adv* smartly, severely.
leill *n* a single stitch in marking on a sampler.
leillie *n* in the lullaby, 'leillie-baw loo-loo'.
lein[1] *same as* **lane**[2].
lein[2] *same as* **leen**[2].
leinfou, leinfu-heartit *adj* **1** kindly. **2** feeling. **3** sympathetic.
leingie *n* the loin.
leingie-shot *adj* (*used of a horse*) having the loins dislocated.
leip *same as* **leep**[1].
leippie *same as* **lippie**.
leir *v* to teach.
leirichie-larachie *v* to whisper together.—*n* mutual whispering.
leis *v* to arrange.
leisch *same as* **leash**[1].
leish[1] *same as* **lish**.
leish[2], **leisch** *same as* **lash**[1].
leish[3] *same as* **leash**[1].
leisher *n* **1** a tall, active fellow. **2** an extensive tract. **3** a long journey.
leishin'*adj* **1** tall and active. **2** (*used of a field farm, parish, etc*) extensive. **3** (*of a journey*) long.
leisin *same as* **leasing**.

leis-me-o' *phr* an expression of great pleasure.
leisome[1] *same as* **leesome**[3].
leisome[2], **leisum** *same as*. **leesome**.
leisome[3] *adj* warm, sultry.
leissure *n* **1** pasture between two cornfields. **2** any grazing ground.
leister *n* a barbed fish spear with prongs.—*v* to spear fish.
leit[1] *n* a piece of horsehair used as a fishing line.
leit[2] *same as* **leet**[2].
leit[3] *same as* **leet**[3].
leit[4] *same as* **leet**[1].
leitch *v* to loiter.
leiugh *same as* **laich**.
leive[1] *same as* **lief**[2].
lieve[2] *same as* **loof**[1].
lek *same as* **leck**[2].
le-lane *int* be quiet! let alone!.
lele *same as* **leal**.
lell *v* to mark, take aim.
leloc *adj* lilac-coloured.
lema *n* broken pieces of crockery.
lemanry *n* **1** an illicit amour. **2** harlotry.
leme[1] *same as* **leam**[1].
leme[2] *same as* **lame**[2].
lemp *same as* **lamp**[2].
lempit *n* a limpet.
lempit-cuddie *n* a small creel for gathering limpets.
lempit-ebb *n* the shore between high and low tide, where limpets are gathered.
lempit-pick *n* an iron chisel for detaching limpets from rocks.
len[1] *same as* **lane**[2].
len[2] *same as* **lean**[1].
len' *v* to lend.—*n* a loan.—*in phr* **tak' a/the len' o'** to make a fool of, to deceive.
lench[1] *same as* **lainch**.
lench[2] *v* to pay out money unwillingly.
lend[1] *v* to give a blow—*n* a loan.
lend[2] *n* the loin.
lendit *adj* (*used of black cows*) having a white stripe over the loins.
length *n* **1** stature, tallness. **2** a point of distance or time. **3** (*with poss adj*) one's house.
lenk *n* a link of horsehair connecting hooks and fishing line.
lenner *n* a lender.
lenno *n* a child.
lennochmore *n* a big child.
lent[1] *adj* slow.
lent[2] *same as* **lant**[1].
lented *adj* beaten in the game of lent (qv).
lenten[1] *n* the spring.
lenten[2] *v* allowed, let.
lent fever *n* a slow fever.
lent-fire *n* a slow fire.
lenth *n* length.
lenthie *adj* prolix, long.
lently *adv* slowly.
lentrin, lentren, lentron *n* **1** Lent. **2** the spring.
lentrin kail *n* **1** broth made without beef. **2** poor fare.
lentrins *n* lambs that die in spring soon after birth.
leomen *n* **1** a leg. **2** the bough of a tree.
lep *v* **1** to sup or lick with the tongue. **2** to lap.
lepe *same as* **leep**[1].
leper-dew *n* a cold, frosty dew,.
lepit peats *n* peats dug out of the solid moss, without being baked.
leppie *same as* **lippie**.
lerb *n* a sip of liquid lapped like a dog.
lerk *v* **1** to contract. **2** to shrivel.
lerrick, lerrock *same as* **larick**[1].
lerroch *same as* **lairach**.
lese *v* **1** to injure, wrong. **2** to offend.
lesed *adj* (*used as legal term*) injured, wronged.

lesion *n* (*used as a legal term*) injury, wrong.
lesk *same as* **lisk**.
less[1] *conj* unless.—*prep* except, with the exception of.
less[2] *conj* lest.
lesser *n* a smaller quantity or amount.
lesum *same as* **leesome**[3].
let *v* **1** to let go. **2** to emit, give out. **3** to lance.
let at *v* to assail.
let bug *v* **1** to give a hint. **2** to divulge, tell.
let gae *v* to raise a tune.
leth *n* disgust.
lethargy *n* **1** coma. **2** a trance.
lether[1] *v* to leather, beat.
lether[2] *n* a ladder.
letherin *n* **1** a beating. **2** a scolding.
lethfu' *same as* **laithfu'**.
lethie *n* **1** a surfeit. **2** a disgust.
let intil *v* to strike.
let licht *v* to admit, allow.
let off *v* **1** to fire a gun. **2** to break wind. **3** to make a great display.
let on *v* **1** to make known, mention, divulge. **2** to indicate by signs. **3** to take notice of. **4** to pretend, feign. **5** to give oneself concern about. **6** to explain.
let on the mill *v* to scold.
let out *v* **1** to go on. **2** (*used of a school, church, etc*) to be dismissed.
let out on *v* to break out into scolding.
lett *n* **1** a lesson. **2** a piece of instruction. **3** a ticket on a house showing it is to be let.
letten *v* permitted, suffered.
lettengo-wort *n* a laxative.
letter *n* **1** a spark on the wick of a candle, supposed to indicate the arrival of a letter. **2** (*in pl*) legal writs.—*v* **1** to write, paint or carve letters on signboards, gravestones, etc. **2** to teach letters, instruct.
letteran, letterin *same as* **lateran**.
lettered *adj* **1** bearing an inscription. **2** (*used of invitations*) sent by letter.
lettered cakes *n* cakes with words inscribed on them, generally with sugar.
lettered sweeties *n* large, flat lozenges with mottoes, etc, printed on them, also known as **conversation lozenges**.
letterene *same as* **lateran**.
letter-gae *n* the preceptor in a church.
lettering *n* letter-cutting on a tombstone.
lettern, letteron, lettrin *same as* **lateran**.
lettrin *n* **1** a latrine. **2** the channel in a stable for carrying off urine.
let wit, let to wit *v* to inform, give to know.
let with it *v* **1** to admit. **2** to mention, inform.
leuch[1], **leugh** *v* laughed.
leuch[2], **leugh** *adj* **1** low in situation. **2** squat, not tall.—*n* **1** the low part. **2** a dale.
leuchen, leughen *v* laughed.
leuchly *adv* in a low situation.
leuchness *n* **1** lowness of stature. **2** lowness of situation.
leug *n* a tall, ill-looking man.
leuk *v* to look.—*n* a look.
leur *adv* rather.
leure *n* a gleam, a faint ray.
leusking *v, adj* absconding.
leut *n* a sluggard.
levellers *n* a name given to the Galloway peasantry who objected to landlords fencing in fields, on the ground that herding cattle by their children would no longer be necessary.
leven[1] *n* lightning.
leven[2] *n* **1** a lawn. **2** an open space between woods.
lever[1] *v* to unload from a ship.
lever[2] *adv* rather.
levin-bolt *n* a thunderbolt.
levrick *n* the lark.
lew *v* to warm, make tepid.—*n* a heat.—*adj* lukewarm.

lewands *n* buttermilk and meal boiled together.
lewder *v* to move heavily.—*n* **1** a blow with a cudgel. **2** a handspike for lifting a millstone.
lewer, leivre *n* **1** a handspike. **2** a long pole. **3** a lever.
lewgh *adj* low.
lew-warm *adj* lukewarm.
ley *n* grassland.
ley-cow *n* a cow not giving milk and not in calf.
ley-crap *n* a lea crop.
ley-metal *n* an alloy of tin and lead.
leytch *v* to loiter.
lezzure *n* pasture.
liam *n* a hair rope.
liart *same as* **lyart**.
lib, libb *v* to geld.
libbag *n* a short-handled horn spoon.
libber[1] *n* **1** a castrator. **2** a sow-gelder.
libber[2] *n* a lubberly fellow.
libberlay *n* a long, rambling story.
libby *same as* **lippie**.
libel *n* a legal indictment, the formal statement of a charge.—*v* **1** to indict. **2** to draw up a libel.
libelt *n* **1** a long discourse. **2** a long treatise.
liberality *n* a gift, present.
libet *n* **1** a eunuch. **2** a gelded animal.
lice *n* the seeds of the wild rose.
licent *adj* licensed.
lich bird *n* the nightjar.
liche-fowl *n* the nightjar.
licht[1] *v* to light, kindle.—*n* **1** a light. **2** light. **3** a will-o'-the-wisp. **4** a corpse candle. **5** (*in pl*) (*with* **auld**) conservatives in theology and ritual. **6** (*with* **new**) progressives in theology and ritual.
licht[2] *adj* **1** not heavy. **2** dizzy. **3** giddy. **4** thoughtless, foolish.—*v* **1** to lighten. **2** to make light of. **3** to under-value.
licht[3] *v* **1** to alight. **2** to reach one's destination. **3** to happen.
licht-avised *adj* of light, fair complexion.
licht-coal *n* a piece of splint coal put on a fire to give a light.
lichten[1] *v* to give light, enlighten.—*n* a flash of lightning.
lichten[2] *v* to lighten, alleviate.
lichtening *n* **1** dawn, daybreak. **2** lightning.
lichtenly *adv* disparagingly, scornfully.
lichter *adj* (*used of a woman*) delivered of a child. —*v* **1** to unload. **2** to deliver a woman of a child.
lichters *n* a horse's blinkers.
licht-farran *adj* light in conduct, giddy.
licht-fit *adj* **1** nimble. **2** giddy, flighty. **3** of loose character.
licht-heeled *adj* active, nimble.
lichtie *adj* light-headed, foolish.—*n* a giddy woman.
lichtin'-in-eldin *n* small brushy fuel, as furze, thorns, etc.
lichtless *adj* despondent.
lichtlie[1] *adj* light of foot.—*adv* expeditiously.
lichtlie[2] *v* **1** to make light of, disparage. **2** to undervalue, think little of. **3** (*of a bird*) to forsake its nest.—*n* **1** scorn. **2** a slight. **3** jilting.
lichtliefow *adj* scornful, haughty.
lichtlifie *v* **1** to make light of, slight. **2** to undervalue.
lichtlifiean *n* **1** disparagement. **2** the act of disparaging.
lichtly shod *adj* bare-footed.
licht-o'-day *n* the white phlox.
licht-o'-spald *adj* light of foot.
lichts *n* the lungs.
lichtsome[1] *adj* **1** well-lighted. **2** light in colour.
lichtsome[2] *adj* **1** light in weight. **2** nimble. **3** cheerful, lively. **4** pleasant, delightful. **5** (*used of a sick person*) easier, better, brighter. **6** light, trifling, fickle.
lichtsomely *adv* **1** pleasantly. **2** joyously. **3** brightly.
lichtsomeness *n* **1** cheerfulness, gaiety. **2** pleasant variety.
lichty *adj* near daylight.
lick *v* **1** to strike. **2** to fight. **3** to carry on a prosecution.—*n*

1 a taste, a small quantity. **2** a pinch of snuff. **3** a daub of paint, etc. **4** a blow. **5** speed. **6** a wag, a fellow. **7** a cheat. **8** (*in pl*) a thrashing, punishment, deserts.

licken *v* to lay to one's charge.

licker *n* liquor.

lickie *n* a small hooked wire for drawing the thread through the hack of a spinning wheel.

licklie *v* to lay to one's charge.

lick-lip *adj* fawning.

lick-ma-dowp *n* a servile flatterer.

lick-my-loof *adj* fawning, cringing.

lick-penny *n* a scamp, rascal.

lick-apit *n* a servile flatterer.

lick-up *n* **1** a lock of hair that will not lie flat. **2** a horse's martingale. **3** a lock-up, prison. **4** a bar of iron hindering the chains from slipping off the swingletree of a plough. **5** a scrape. **6** a plight, difficulty.

licquory stick *n* a stick of liquorice or liquorice root.

lid *v* to shut, close.

lidded *adj* furnished with flaps.

lidder *adj* **1** idle, lazy. **2** loathsome.—*n* laziness.

lidderie *adj* feeble and lazy.

lidderlie *adv* lazily.

lidderon, lidrone *same as* **latheron**.

Liddisdale-drow *n* a shower that wets an Englishman to the skin.

lide¹ *v* to glide through.

lide² *same as* **lithe**³.

lie¹ *n* **1** a sheltered, warm place. **2** a calm.—*adj* warm, sheltered.

lie² *n* a black speck on a tooth.—*v* to make an erroneous statement without intending to lie.

lie³ *v* **1** to be ill in bed. **2** to lie idle. **3** to sleep. **4** (*used of a ewe*) to bring forth lambs. **5** to lay.—*n* **1** (*used of a place*) exposure. **2** a natural situation. **3** the direction in which a thing moves or is placed. **4** the situation of a golf ball. **5** rest.

lie-a-bed *n* a late riser, a sluggard.

lie-by *v* **1** to lie idle. **2** to lie unused. **3** to keep off. —*n* **1** a mistress. **2** a neutral.

lied *same as* **leed**².

lie-day *n* an idle day.

lief¹ *same as* **loof**¹.

lief² *adj* dear, beloved.—*adv* gladly, willingly.

lief-alane, -on-lone *adj* quite alone.

liefer *adv* rather.

liefhebber *n* a lover.

liefaum *adj* pleasant.

liefu' lane *adj* quite alone.

lie in *v* to be in childbed.

lien by *v* refrained from.

lie out *v* **1** (*used of cattle*) to lie in the fields at night. **2** to be delayed in receiving money due or in entrance on inherited property.

lierachie *n* a hubbub.

liesh *same as* **lish**.

lies-making *n* treasonable falsehood.

liesome¹ *adj* warm, sultry.

liesome² *same as* **leesome**³.

liesome³ *same as* **leesome**¹.

liesome-like, ~-looking *adj* having the appearance of lies.

lie throut *n* to lie out of doors.

liethry *n* a crowd.

lie time *n* days on which harvesters are not engaged on harvest work proper.

lie to *v* to incline to love.

lieugh *adj* low.

lieutenantry *n* the lieutenancy of a county or district.

lieve *same as* **lief**².

liever *same as* **liefer**.

lievetenant *n* lieutenant.

life *n* a living person or animal.

life-knife *n* a pocket-knife.

life-like *adj in phrs* **1** life-like and deathlike used of the

uncertainty of life. **2** living and life-like in vigorous health.

life-safe *n* a warrant to spare an offender's life.

life-sick *adj* sick of life.

life-stoup *n* a mainstay, chief support of life.

life-thinking *adj in phr* living and lifethinking in vigorous health.

life-tie *n* **1** a hold on life. **2** one for whose sake alone another lives.

liffy *same as* **loofie**.

lifie, lifey *adj* **1** lively, spirited. **2** merry. **3** active. **4** life-giving, exhilarating.—*adv* quickly, alertly.

lilieness *n* vigour, vitality.

lifily *adv* **1** vigorously, briskly. **2** heartily. **3** merrily.

lift¹ *n* the firmament, sky.

lift² *v* **1** to gather root crops. **2** to cut corn, hay, etc. **3** to collect money, rates, taxes, subscriptions, etc. **4** to steal, pilfer. **5** to steal cattle, etc. **6** to exhume a dead body. **7** to move house. **8** to remove, transport, shift cattle. **9** to break up ground. **10** to take out of pawn. **11** to strike up a tune, raise the psalm, etc. **12** to rise and depart. **13** to disperse. **14** to ascend. **15** to carry out the dead to burial. **16** (*of the chest*) to heave.—*n* **1** a burden. **2** a weight to be lifted. **3** the lifting of a burden. **4** a large quantity. **5** a theft. **6** a drove of cattle. **7** a trick in a game of cards. **8** the first break or ploughing. **9** help, encouragement. **10** promotion. **11** a helpful drive given on a road to one on foot. **12** a heave of the chest in difficult breathing or oppressive sickness. **13** the rise of a wave, the swell of the sea. **14** an ill-turn. **15** a large sum of money. **16** the matter.—*int* a call to a horse to lift its foot.

lift and lay *n* a number of men wielding the scythe.—*adv* **1** stroke for stroke. **2** on an equality.

lifted *adj* **1** elated. **2** conceited. **3** joyously grateful.

liften *v* lifted.

lifter *n* **1** one who gathers corn in harvest fields or gathers root crops. **2** a cattle-stealer. **3** a shallow wooden bowl in which milk is set for cream. **4** a flat, rectangular, perforated door key that lifted the latch. **5** the valve of a pair of bellows. **6** (*in pl*) the name formerly given to those who held that the minister, at the Communion, should lift the bread before the thanksgiving.

lift-fire *n* lightning.

lift hanse *n* the left hand.

liftie *n* dirt on the streets adhering to the feet.

lifting *n* **1** removal. **2** the carrying forth of a coffin from the house to burial. **3** (*used of the mouth*) something to eat.

liftward *adj* and *adv* heavenward.

lig¹ *v* **1** to talk much. **2** to gossip.—*n* **1** much talk. **2** gossip. **3** the noise of talking.

lig² *v* to lag, fall behind.

lig³ *v* (*used of ewes*) to bring forth.

lig⁴, **ligg** *v* **1** to lie, recline. **2** to lodge. **3** to know carnally, to have had sexual intercourse with. **4** to lay, let lie.

liggate, ligget *n* a self-closing gate.

ligger, liggar *n* a foul salmon.

ligger-lady *same as* **leager-lady**.

light *same as* **licht**².

lighter *n* (*in pl*) the blinkers of a horse.

lighter *same as* **lichter**.

lightfeet *n* a greyhound.

liglag *n* **1** a confused noise of tongues. **2** a great deal of idle talk. **3** a strange language. **4** an unintelligible discourse.—*v* to prate.

lignate *n* an ingot or mass of metal that has been melted.

likamy-docks *n* the pillory, jougs (qv), etc.

like¹ *adj* **1** (*in golf*) equal, even. **2** likely, probable. —*adv* **1** probably. **2** about, nearly.—*conj* **1** as, just as. **2** as if.—*n* **1** a match, equal. **2** the even stroke in golf.—*v* to be on the point of, to be likely.

like² *v* (*used impersonally*) to please, be agreeable to.

like³ *same as* **lyke**.

like as *conj* **1** as if. **2** as also.

likeliness *n* comeliness, good looks.

likely *adj* **1** promising. **2** likely to do well. **3** good-looking.—*adv* probably.—*n* likelihood, probability.

likelys *adv* likely.

liken, liking *adj* on the point of, likely to do, bear, etc.

liker *adj* **1** better fitted for. **2** more suitable to.—*adv* more likely.

likery stick *n* a stick of liquorice or liquorice root.

likesome *adj* like.

likewake *same as* **lykewake**.

liking[1], **likein** *n* **1** appearance. **2** condition.

liking[2] *n* **1** favour. **2** good graces. **3** a darling.

likmy-docks *same as* **likamydocks**.

lill *n* the hole of a wind instrument.

lillilu, lillyloo *n* **1** a lullaby. **2** a refrain.

lilly *adj* charming, lovely.

lilly-lowe *n* a bright flame, blaze.

lilt *v* **1** to sing softly. **2** to hum. **3** to sing briskly. **4** (*with* **out** *or* **off**) to finish off one's drink merrily or quickly. **5** (*with* **up**) to begin a song or music. **6** to dance to music. **7** to leap lightly over a fence.—*n* **1** a song. **2** a cheerful tune. **3** a mournful tune. **4** the hole of a wind instrument. **5** a long and frequent pull in drinking.

lilti-cock *n* one who walks limping or jerking himself or herself.—*adj* walking in a limping or jerking way.

lilting *adj* limping.

liltit *adj* paired for a dance.

lily[1] *adj* charming, lovely.

lily[2] *n* aphthae or thrush in children.

lily[3] *n* **1** the white lily or poet's narcissus. **2** the daffodil.

lily-can *n* the yellow water lily.

lily-oak *n* the lilac.

limb, lim *n* **1** the butt of a fishing rod. **2** (*used contemptuously*) a creature, a tool, agent. **3** a mischievous child or person.

limb-free *adj* with relaxed limbs, as in sleep.

lime *n* glue.

lime-man *n* **1** a lime-burner. **2** a dealer in lime.

lime-quarrel *n* a lime quarry.

lime-red *n* the rubbish of lime walls.

lime-shells *n* burnt lime unslaked.

limestone beads *n* St Cuthbert's beads, fossil *entrochi*.

lime-wark *n* a place where limestone is dug and burnt.

limm *n* a mischievous child or woman.

limmer[1] *n* **1** a rascal, rogue. **2** a prostitute. **3** a loose woman or girl. **4** a playful or contemptuous term applied to a woman, without any charge of immorality. **5** a familiar term of address to a man or a woman.

limmer[2] *n* a wagon or cart shaft.

limp *v* to cause to limp.

limpus *n* a worthless woman.

lin[1] *same as* **lint**[2].

lin[2] *n* a waterfall.—*v* to hollow out the ground by force of water.

lin[3] *n* a shrubby ravine.

lin[4] *same as* **lint**[1].

linarich *n* a green sea plant, used as an astringent.

linch *v* **1** to halt. **2** to limp. **3** to hop.—*n* a hop.

Lincum green *n* a green-coloured cloth manufactured at Lincoln.

Lincum twyne *n* **1** packthread. **2** a very fine thread. **3** a Lincoln texture.

lind *same as* **lend**[2].

linder *n* a woollen or flannel undershirt.

lindsay *n* linsey-woolsey.

line[1] *n* **1** the boundary of the Highlands. **2** any written or printed authority. **3** a doctor's prescription. **4** a certificate of proclamation of banns or of marriage or of Church membership or of character. **5** a short letter of introduction. —*v* **1** to measure with a line. **2** to thrash.

line[2] *v* (*used of dogs*) to impregnate.

line[3] *n* flax.

line[4] *v* **1** to bestow gifts. **2** (*with* **one's roof**) to bribe one.

lineboard *n* the starboard.

line-grip *n* strength and skill to handle a fishing line.

line-him-out *n* a boys' game in which the players beat one of their number with their caps.

line-man *n* a line- or white-fisher.

linen, linnen *n* **1** the white sheet worn by immoral offenders in doing public penance. **2** (*in pl*) underclothing, shirts. **3** a shroud, winding sheet.

linen-winsey *n* linsey-woolsey.

liner *n* one who measures by line.

liner-out *n* one who prefers the reading of a psalm line by line before singing.

line-scoll *n* a box to hold fishing lines.

ling[1] *n* a long, thin grass or species of rush.

ling[2] *n* **1** a line. **2** a quick career in a straight line. —*v* **1** to walk quickly with long steps. **2** to gallop.

lingal, lingel *same as* **lingle**.

lingan, lingin *n* **1** shoemakers' thread. **2** the taw or lash to a whip.

lingcan *n* the body.

linge *v* to flog, beat.

lingen-ends *n* shoemakers' thread ends.

linget[1] *n* a rope binding a forefoot of a horse to a hind one.

linget[2] *n* **1** the seed of flax, linseed. **2** flax thread.

linget oil *n* linseed oil.

linget seed *n* the seed of flax, linseed.

lingit[1] *adj* **1** narrow. **2** thin. **3** small. **4** (*used of an animal*) very lank in the belly.

lingit[2] *adj* **1** flexible, supple. **2** pliant. **3** agile.

lingit-claith *n* cloth of a soft texture.

lingity *adj* slender.

lingle *n* **1** shoemakers' thread. **2** a leather thong. **3** a fetter. **4** anything to tie with. **5** anything of considerable length. **6** a tall, lanky person.—*v* **1** to fasten with shoemakers' thread. **2** to fasten, fetter. **3** to hobble an animal. **4** (*with* **off**) to unwind, unroll. **5** to reel off a speech, etc.

lingle-back *n* a person with a long, weak back.

lingle-end *n* the point of a shoemaker's waxed thread.

lingle-tailed *adj* draggle-tailed.

lingle-threeder *n* one who uses lingles or shoemakers' threads.

lingo *n* a long story.

ling tow *n* a rope used by smugglers.

ling-tow man *n* **1** a smuggler. **2** one who carried inland smuggled goods.

lingy *adj* **1** trashy. **2** limp. **3** helpless.

lining[1] *n* **1** a measurement. **2** permission to build from the Dean of Guild's Court of a burgh according to plans given in to, and passed by, the Court.

lining[2] *n* food and drink.

lining-out *n* the old practice of reading the psalms to be sung line by line.

linjet *same as* **linget**[2].

link[1] *n* **1** a length of hair or fine gut, attaching a hook to a line. **2** a joint. **3** the division of a peat stack. **4** a straw rope fastening the thatch of a stack, etc. **5** a lock of hair. **6** (*in pl*) the chain by which a pot, etc, hangs over a fire from the crook (qv). **7** a string of sausages resembling links in a chain.—*v* **1** to walk arm in arm. **2** to join. **3** to twine arms. **4** to marry. **5** to cease moving about. **6** to lift a pot from the links of a crook (qv). **7** (*with* **down**) to lower on the links of a chain, to unhook. **8** (*with* **on**) to hang upon a chain or crook (qv). **9** (*with* **away**) to carry off by the arm.—*phr* **the links of misery** the extreme of starvation.

link[2] *v* **1** to walk briskly. **2** to trip along. **3** (*used of money*) to flow in rapidly and in plenty.

link[3] *n* (*in pl*) **1** the windings of a river. **2** the rich ground lying among these windings. **3** sandy knolls, a stretch of sandy, grass-covered ground near the seashore. **2** a golf course.

lin-~, linn-keeper *n* a large freshwater trout, supposed to keep possession of a particular pool or linn.

linket *adj* swift.

linkie *adj* sly, roguish, waggish.—*n* **1** a wag, rogue. **2** a person on whom no reliance can be placed.

linkingly *adv* 1 swiftly. 2 lightly.
Linkome green *same as* Lincum green.
Linkome twyne *same as* Lincum twyne.
links[1] *n* sausages that are sold linked together like a chain. *See* link[1].
links[2] *same as* link[3].
links goose *n* the common sheldrake.
link-stane *n* a stone attached to a rope to keep a link (*see* link[1]) of a peat stack upright.
linky *adj* flat and grassy.
linn[1] *n* 1 the precipice over which water falls. 2 the cascade of water. 3 the pool at the base of the fall. —*v* to hollow out the ground by the force of water.
linn[2] *n* a piece of wood placed under a boat's keel to facilitate drawing it up on the beach.
linnen *n* a lining.
linn-lier *same as* lin-keeper.
lin pin *n* a linchpin.
lins *n* rollers by which a boat is drawn over the beach and by which it is propped up.
linset *n* linseed.
linset-bows *n* the pods containing the flaxseed.
linsey *n* linsey-woolsey.
linsh *same as* linch.
lint[1] *v* 1 to relax. 2 to unbend. 3 to cease from work.—*phr* lint one's trough to sit down for a little.
lint[2] *n* flax.
lint bells *n* the flowers of the flax.
lint-bennels *n* the seed of the flax.
lint-bow *n* the pod containing flax seed.
lint brake *n* an implement for breaking and softening flax.
lint coble *n* a pond or pit for steeping flax.
lintel ale *n* ale given at the completion of building work.
lint-haired *adj* having flaxen locks.
lint-hole *same as* lint-coble.
lintie *n* the linnet.
lintie-whytie, lintiwhite *n* the linnet.
lint-locks *n* flaxen hair.
lint pot *same as* lint coble.
lint-ripple *n* a toothed implement for separating the seeds of flax from the stalk.
lintseed *n* linseed.
lint-straik *n* a handful of newly dressed flax.
lint-tap *n* as much flax as is put on the distaff at a time.
lint wheel *n* a spinning wheel.
lintwhite *adj* flaxen-coloured.
lint-white *n* the linnet.
linty *adj* flaxen.
lion *n* an old coin of the value of £2 8s. Scots.
lip *n* 1 edge. 2 boundary.—*v* 1 to taste. 2 to be full to the brim. 3 to rise to the edge of a bank. 4 to break pieces from the face of edge tools.
lip-deep *adj* 1 superficial, only from the lips. 2 very deep, up to the brim. 3 up to the lips.
lip-fou *adj* 1 quite full. 2 tipsy.
lip-licker *n* one who licks his lips at the sight of some dainty.
lipp *n* the broad brim of a soft hat.
lippen[1] *v* 1 to trust. 2 to depend upon. 3 to have confidence in. 4 to entrust to. 5 to expect.
lippen[2] *same as* luppen.
lippen[3] *v* 1 to taste. 2 to sip, put one's lips to.
lippening *adj* 1 occasional. 2 thoughtless. 3 accidental.
lipper[1] *n* 1 a slight swell or ruffle on the surface of the sea. 2 a ripple, wavelet.—*v* 1 to ripple, break in small waves. 2 to rise and fall gently on the waves.
lipper[2] *n* a large festering surface on the skin.—*adj* covered with smallpox or any cutaneous eruption.
lipper[3] *n* 1 a leper. 2 a contemptuous term applied to a dog.
lipper[4] *v* to lap up.
lipper[5] *adv* very, exceedingly, superlatively.
lippering *adj* full, overflowing.
lipperjay *n* a jay or jackdaw.
lipper owre *v* to be so full as to run over.
lippet *ppl adj* edged, having a border.

lippie[1] *n* 1 the fourth part of a peck. 2 a liquid measure. 3 a bumper.
lippie[2] *n* a child's lip.
lipping, lipping-fou *adj* full to the brim.
lip-rapping *adj* 1 lip-knocking. 2 (*used of a kiss*) resounding.
liquefy *v* to spend money in drink.
liquidly *adv* clearly beyond dispute.
liquor-, liquorry stick *n* a stick of liquorice.
liquory *adj* sweet-toothed, fond of sweets.
liquory-knots *n* the bitter vetch.
lirb *v* to sip.
lire[1] *n* 1 the flesh or muscles of any animal, as distinguished from the bones. 2 lean beef.
lire[2] *n* 1 the complexion. 2 that part of the skin which is colourless. 3 the air.
lire[3] *same as* lure.
lirk *n* 1 a crease, wrinkle. 2 a fold in the skin or flesh. 3 a double. 4 a subterfuge. 5 a crevice or hollow in a hill.—*v* 1 to fold. 2 to crease, rumple. 3 to contract, shrivel.
lirky *adj* full of creases, wrinkled.
lirt *v* 1 to deceive. 2 to jilt. 3 to beguile.—*n* 1 deception. 2 fooling. 3 cheating.
liry *same as* lyrie.
lish *adj* 1 lithe. 2 supple. 3 agile.
lisk *n* the groin, flank.
liss *v* to cease, stop.—*n* 1 cessation. 2 release. 3 respite from pain.
lissens *n* 1 release. 2 an interval free from pain, etc.
lissim *adj* lawful.
list[1] *adj* 1 agile. 2 lively. 3 eager.—*n* appetite.—*v* to choose.
list[2] *v* 1 to write down on a list. 2 to enlist as a soldier.
list[3] *v* to listen to.
listen *v* to listen to.
listener *n* the ear.
lister[1] *same as* litster.
lister[2] *same as* leister.
listing *n* list for stockings.
lit *same as* litt[1].
litt *same as* litt[2].
litany *n* a long, unmeaning effusion.
litch[1] *n* a smart blow.—*v* to strike over.
litch[2] *same as* latch[5].
lite *same as* loit[1].
lit-fat *n* a dyer's vat.
lith[1] *n* 1 a gate. 2 a gap in a fence.
lith[2] *same as* lithe[4].
lith[3] *n* 1 a joint of the body. 2 a division of an orange or onion, etc. 3 a ring round the base of a cow's horn.—*v* to disjoint, dislocate.
lithe[1] *v* to listen, hearken.
lithe[2] *n* a shelter.—*adj* sheltered.—*v* to shelter.
lithe[3] *v* 1 to thicken broth, etc, by adding oatmeal. 2 to thicken water with mud, etc.
lithe[4] *adj* 1 soft, gentle. 2 mild. 3 pleasant. 4 agile, active.—*n* encouragement, favour.
litheless *adj* 1 comfortless. 2 cold.
lithely *adv* warmly, genially.
litheness *n* genial warmth.
lither[1] *adj* idle, lazy.—*n* sloth, laziness.—*v* to idle, loaf.
lither[2] *adj* 1 yielding. 2 undulating.
litherlie *adv* lazily.
litheside *n* a liking, kindly regard.
lithesome[1] *adj* 1 active. 2 brisk. 3 agile.
lithesome[2], lithsome *adj* 1 sheltered, shady. 2 warm, cosy.
lithet *adj* 1 thickened. 2 spiced.
lithics *same as* lythocks.
lithie *adj* 1 warm. 2 comfortable.
lithie *v* to break the neck.
lithing *n* a paste of flour or oatmeal for thickening broth, gravy, etc.
lithry *n* a crowd.
lithy *adj* 1 thickened. 2 thick and smooth, as porridge.
litigious *adj* prolix, lengthy. 2 tedious. 3 vindictive.

litster *n* a dyer.

litt[1] *n* **1** a dye. **2** a tinge, hue, stain, any colouring liquid.— *v* **1** to dye. **2** to colour. **3** to stain. **4** to blush.

litt[2] *v* to edge.

litterstane *n* a brick-shaped stone, about two feet long and one foot in breadth and depth, formerly borne to builders in litters.

litt-fat, --vat *n* a vat for dyestuff.

litt house *n* a dye house.

littin' *adj* blushing.

litt-kettle *n* a dyer's kettle.

little ane *n* **1** a baby. **2** a small child.

little boukit *adj* **1** of small size. **2** of small authority or influence.

little-coatie *n* a petticoat.

little-dinner *n* a morsel taken in the morning before going to work.

little-doucker *n* the little grebe.

little-ease *n* a lockup.

little-felty-fare *n* the redwing.

little-good, -goodie *n* the sun spurge.

little-gude *n* the devil.

littleman *n* **1** a young ploughman. **2** a learner at the plough.

littlenie *n* a very small or young child.

little-pickie *n* the little tern.

littler *adj* less.

little room *n* a room smaller than the best room in a farmhouse and used by the farmer's family for common meals, talk, etc.

littlest *adj* least.

little-whaup *n* the whimbrel.

little-wit *adj* of little intelligence.

littleworth *adj* worthless.—*n* a worthless person.

littlie *adj* rather little.

littlin *n* a baby, young child.

litt-pat *n* a pot used in dyers' work.

liung *n* an atom, whit.

liv *n* the palm of the hand.

live-day-long *n* the livelong day.

livefu-, livin-lane *adj* quite alone.

livellan *same as* **lavellan**.

liven *v* **1** to enliven. **2** to brighten.

liver[1] *v* to unload a vessel.

liver[2] *adj* **1** active. **2** sprightly, lively.

liver-bannocks *n* bannocks baked with fish livers between them.

liver-crook, --croke *n* intestinal inflammation in calves.

liver cup *n* a cup-shaped dumpling filled with fish livers.

liver grass *n* the liverwort.

liver-head *n* the head of a fish stuffed with livers.

liverock *same as* **laverock**.

livery-downie *n* a haddock stuffed with livers, meal, etc.

liveryman *n* a livery servant.

livery meal *n* meal given to servants as part of their wages.

livfu' *n* as much liquid as will lie on the palm of the hand.

living *adj* **1** alive, in life. **2** (*used of fire*) blazing, glowing.—*n* **1** a living being, a person. **2** food, fare. **3** a farm.

living body *n* a live person too weak to do anything.

living-like *adj* **1** likely to live long. **2** healthy, healthy-looking.

livrie *adj* **1** well-cooked. **2** (*used of liquid food*) well-thickened.

lixie *n* a woman who collected knives, forks and spoons on loan for a penny bridal (qv) and got her dinner for her trouble.

lizures *n* selvages of cloth or of a weaver's web.

lizzure *same as* **leissure**.

llabbach *v* **1** to speak in an unknown tongue. **2** to speak much with little meaning. **3** to talk incoherently. **4** to repeat from memory. **5** to unroll. —*n* **1** incoherent talk or writing. **2** a long piece of worthless cloth. **3** an uncomely article of dress. **4** a long piece of twine, etc. **5** a quantity of strong drink.

llarg *v* to lodge in wet masses, as grass, corn.—*n* a wet mass in the midst of a dry sheaf.

llauve-cairn *n* a beacon cairn.

lloostrie *n* idleness.

lloostre *n* **1** sloth. **2** a slothful person.—*v* to remain slothful.

lo[1] *v* to allow, grant, let.

lo[2] *n* a corpulent person.

load *n* **1** a large number or quantity. **2** (*used of illness*) a very severe cold.—*v* to lay to one's charge.

loaden[1] *adj* laden, loaded.

loaden[2] *v* **1** to load, burden. **2** to load a gun.

loadning *n* lading.

load-stone *n* a curling stone.

loadstone-watch *n* a compass.

loaf bread *n* a wheaten loaf.

loags *n* footless stockings.

loake *n* one of the multures of a mill.

loal *v* to mew, to caterwaul.

loamy *adj* slothful.

loan[1] *n* **1** provisions. **2** rations. **3** pay, wages.—*v* to lend.

loan[2] *n* **1** a lane. **2** a narrow street. **3** the space between the middle of a street and the houses on either side. **4** an opening between fields of corn for driving cattle home. **5** a small piece of ground near a farm or village where cows are milked, a milking park. **6** a paddock. **7** a small common.

loan end *n* the end of a lane or narrow street.

loan head *n* the upper end of a lane or narrow street.

loaning *n* **1** a lane, a bypath. **2** a milking park. **3** a paddock.

loaning-dyke *n* a wall dividing arable from pasture land.

loaning-green *n* a milking green.

loan money, ~ silver *n* **1** pay, wages. **2** bounty.

loan soup *n* **1** milk given to passengers through the milking park at milking time. **2** milk fresh from the cow.

loatch *same as* **lotch**[2].

loave *v* **1** to offer for sale. **2** to offer at lower price for anything in purchasing.

loavenenty *same as* **lovanenty**.

lob *n* a lump.

lobbach *n* a lump.

lobster-clap *n* a hooked staff for picking out lobsters from crevices in the rocks.

lobster kist *n* a floating box in which lobsters are kept alive until sold.

lobster-toad *n* the deep-sea crab, *Cancer araneus*.

local *v* to assign among different landholders their respective portions of an increase of the parish minister's stipend.

locality *n* **1** the apportioning of the increase of a parish minister's stipend. **2** the lands held by a widow in life rent, in terms of her marriage contract.

lochaber-axe *n* a halberd hooked at the back.

lochaber-trump *n* a jew's-harp.

lochan, lochen *n* a small loch or lake.

locherin' *same as* **loggerin'**.

loch head *n* the head of a loch.—*phr* (*used in curling*) **loch head of desolation** driving a stone with extreme vigour so as to scatter all before it.

loch-learoch *n* a small, grey water bird, seen on Loch Leven.

loch-leech *n* the medicinal leech.

loch-liver *n* a jellyfish.

loch-lubbertie *n* the jelly tremella, a gelatinous plant found in pastures after rain.

loch-reed *n* the common reed grass.

lochter *same as* **lachter**.

lochy *adj* **1** having a loch. **2** abounding in lochs.

lock[1] *n* **1** a difficulty. **2** deadlock. **3** a dilemma, a knotty point.—*v* **1** to enclose. **2** to clutch. **3** to embrace.

lock[2] *n* **1** a small quantity of anything. **2** one of the multures of a mill.

lockanties *int* an exclamation of surprise.

locken-gowlan, lockin-gowlan *n* the globeflower.
locker[1] *n* the globeflower.
locker[2] *v* to curl.
lockerby-lick *n* a wound in the face.
locker-gowlan *same as* **locken-gowlan**.
lockerie *adj* (*used of a stream*) rippling.
locker-strae *n* a school pointer.
lockfast *n* a locked cupboard, etc.—*adj* shut and locked.
lockhole *n* a keyhole.
lockhole execution *n* serving a writ by leaving it in the defendant's keyhole.
lockintee *same as* **lockanties**.
lockin' tree *n* the rung (qv) that served to bar the door.
lockman, locksman *n* the public executioner.
locus *n* ashes so light as to be easily blown about.
Lod *int* Lord!
lodamy *n* laudanum.
loddan, lodden *n* a small pool.
lodden[1], **loden** *same as* **loaden**[2].
lodden[2] *same as* **loddan**.
lodge *n* a fishing hut.—*v* (*used of grain*) to lie flat through wind or rain.
lodge-fish *n* fish caught by lodgemen.
lodgeman *n* the occupant of a fishing hut.
lodging *n* a dwelling house.
lodging maill *n* the rent of lodgings, house rent.
lodomy *same as* **lodamy**.
loe *v* to love.—*n* love.
loesome *adj* **1** lovable. **2** lovely. **3** winsome beloved. **4** affectionate.
loft *v* to lift the feet high in walking.
lofted house *n* a house of two or more storeys.
loft house *n* **1** the upper part of a house used as a warehouse. **2** the whole building of which the loft is so used.
lofting *same as* **lafting**.
loftit *same as* **laftit**.
log[1] *n* the substance that bees gather to make their wax.
log[2] *same as* **loags**.
logamochy *n* a long, rambling dull story or speech.
logan *n* **1** a handful of money, marbles, etc, thrown to be scrambled for by a crowd of boys. **2** a scramble for such things.—*v* to throw any articles to be scrambled for.
logerhead *n* a blockhead.
logg *adj* lukewarm.
loggar, logger *v* to hang loosely and largely.—*n* **1** a stocking without a foot. **2** a gaiter.—*adj* loose-hanging, drooping.
loggerin' *adj* drenched with moisture.
loggie[1] *same as* **luggie**.
logie, loggie[2] *n* **1** the open space before a kiln fire. **2** a fire in a snug place. **3** a snug place for a fire. **4** a ventilating hole at the foundation of a stack.
logies *int* an exclamation of surprise.
logive *adj* **1** extravagant. **2** careless.
log-water *n* lukewarm water.
loichen *n* a quantity of anything soft, like porridge.
loin *n* an allowance.
loit[1] *n* **1** a turd. **2** a horse's dropping.—*v* to excrete.
loit[2] *n* **1** a spirt of boiling water ejected from a pot. **2** any liquid suddenly ejected from the mouth. —*v* **1** to spirt. **2** to bubble forth. **3** to eject from the stomach.
loit[3] *same as* **loyt**.
lokadaisy *int* an exclamation of surprise.
loke, loks *int* an exclamation of surprise and mirth.
lokker *same as* **locker**[2].
lolaby *n* a screaming child.
loll[1] *v* to embrace, fondle.—*n* a lazy fellow.
loll[2] *v* to excrete.—*n* human excrement.
loll[3] *same as* **loal**.
lolling *adj* lazy, indolent.
loltidoll *n* the largest species of potato.
lome *same as* **loom**[1].
lomon, lomin' *n* a leg.
lon *v* to lend.

lonachies *n* **1** couch grass. **2** couch grass gathered in heaps for burning.
londer *v* to tramp heavily and wearily.
London pride *n* the common rose campion.
lone[1] *same as* **loan**[2].
lone[2] *same as* **lane**[3].
lone[3] *n* a place of shelter.
lone[4] *same as* **loan**[1].
loneful *adj* forlorn.—*adv* forlornly.
lonely *adj* **1** alone, single. **2** exceptional.—*adv* singly, only.
lonesum-like *adj* lonely.
long[1] *v* to become weary.
long[2] *same as* **lang**[3].
long[3] *adv and prep* along.
longavil, longueville *n* a species of pear.
longe *v* **1** to tell a fair story. **2** to flatter.
longie *n* the guillemot.
longish *adj* (*used of the forehead*) high.
long lie *n* an occasion of staying in bed later than usual in the morning.
longsome *same as* **langsome**.
loning *same as* **loaning**.
lonkor *n* a hole in a dyke through which sheep may pass.
lonnach *n* **1** a long piece of twine or thread. **2** a ragged article of dress. **3** a long rigmarole.—*v* **1** to talk a great deal. **2** to unroll. **3** to deliver a speech, etc.
lonnachs *same as* **lonachies**.
lonnie *n* a small milking park.
loo[1] *v* to love.
loo[2] *same as* **lew**.
lood *adj* **1** loud. **2** famous.—*adv* aloud.
lood-spoken *adj* outspoken.
loof *n* **1** the palm of the hand. **2** help. **3** a hoof.
loof bane *n* the centre of the palm of the hand.
loof bread *n* a hand's-breadth.
looffin, loof-fu' *n* a handful.
loofie *n* **1** a stroke on the palm of the hand. **2** a fingerless mitten for the hand. **3** a flat stone resembling the palm and formerly used in curling.
loofie channel stane *n* a loofie (qv), formerly used in curling.
loofie-lair *n* proficiency in fisticuffs, etc.
loof-licker *n* a fawning, cringing person.
loogan *n* a rogue.
loogard *same as* **lugard**.
look *v* **1** (*with* **in on**) to call on. **2** (*with* **on**) to watch beside a dying person. **3** to inspect, examine.—*n* the face, the appearance.
looker *n* the eye.
lookin' to *n* a prospect, a future.
lool *v* to sing in a dull and heavy manner.
loom[1] *n* **1** an implement. **2** utensil. **3** a vessel of any kind.—*v* to weave.
loom[2] *n* **1** mist, fog. **2** the hazy appearance of land as seen from the sea or on the horizon.
loombagus *n* lumbago.
loom-bred *adj* bred to weaving.
loom-post *n* a post forming part of a loom.
loom shop *n* a weaving shop.
loom-sprung *adj* said of those who have risen in the world by the toil of the weavers in their employment.
loomstance, ~stead *n* the place where a loom stands.
loomy[1] *adj* misty, hazy.
loomy[2] *n* a small loom.
loon[1] *same as* **lunyie**.
loon[2] *n* **1** a rascal. **2** a ragamuffin. **3** an idle, stupid fellow. **4** a fellow. **5** the native of a place. **6** the follower of a trade. **7** a servant. **8** a person of low rank. **9** a peasant, rustic. **10** a boy, a lad. **11** a loose woman. **12** a paramour.
loonder *same as* **lounder**.
loonfow *adj* rascally.
loonie[1] *n* a boy, a little lad.
loonie[2] *adj* **1** imbecile. **2** crazy. **3** lunatic.—*n* **1** a person who is mentally retarded. **2** an idiot. **3** a lunatic.

loonikie *n* a very small boy.

loon-ill *n* malingering to shirk work.

loon-like *adj* **1** rascally. **2** shabby, tattered. **3** like a lad or boy.

loon-looking *adj* rascally.

loon-quean *n* a loose woman.

loon's-piece *n* the uppermost slice of a loaf.

loop¹ *n* **1** a stitch in knitting. **2** a piece of knitting. **3** the winding of a river, lake or glen. **4** the channel of a stream left dry by the water changing its course.—*v* **1** to join in marriage. **2** to hang in a noose.

loop² *n* **1** a trick, a tricky scheme. **2** a wile.

loop o' the shank *n* the knitting of stockings.

loopy *adj* crafty. **2** deceitful.

loor¹ *adv* rather.—*v* to prefer.

loor² *v* **1** to lurk. **2** to crouch. **3** to skulk.—*n* a lurking place.

loorach *n* rags.

loordy *same as* **lourdy**.

loosable *adj* that may be loosed.

loose¹ *same as* **lowse**.

loose² *n* a louse.

loose³ *v* to lose.

loose-behind *adj* not costive.

loose-footed *adj* **1** disengaged. **2** free from entanglements.

loose-tongued *adj* voluble, gossiping.

loosey *adj* having lice.

loosht *n* a lazy lounger.

looshtre *n* a heavy, soft blow.—*v* to strike with a heavy, soft blow.

looshtrin *n* a heavy beating.

loosie *same as* **loossie**.

loosing *adj* laxative, purgative.

loosome *adj* lovable.

loossie *adj* (*used of the skin*) covered with dandruff.

looster *v* to lounge, idle.—*n* **1** indolence. **2** a lazy, slothful person.

loostrie *adj* lazy, idle.

loot¹ *same as* **lout**.

loot² *v* permitted, let.

looten *v* allowed, let.

looten o' *adj* esteemed.

loothrick *n* a wooden lever.

lootin o' *adj* esteemed, held in estimation.

loot on *v* (*with neg*) did not give any sign.

loove *n* **1** love. **2** a lover.

looves *n* the palms of the hands. *See* **loof**.

loozy *same as* **loosy**.

lope¹ *v* to lop off.

lope² *v* leapt.

lopper¹ *same as* **lapper²**.

lopper² *same as* **lipper¹**.

lopper-gowan *n* the yellow ranunculus.

lord *n* **1** a judge of the Court of Session. **2** a laird. —*int* an exclamation of surprise.

Lord Harry *int* an expletive.

lordlifu' *adj* **1** rich, sumptuous. **2** extravagantly liberal.

lordly *adj* **1** proud. **2** difficult to please. **3** very liberal.

Lord Lyon the chief herald of Scotland.

lordsake *int* an exclamation of surprise.

lord's fool *n* **1** a born fool. **2** a person who is mentally retarded.

lore *n* talk, conversation.

lorie, lorie-me *int* an exclamation of surprise.

lorimer *n* a clockmaker.

lorrach *n* **1** a disgusting mess. **2** ill-cooked food. **3** a long piece of wet, dirty cloth, twine, etc.

lorum *n* lore, learning.

lose *adj* loose.

losel, lossel *n* a lazy rascal.

lose-leather *n* loose skin from the falling away of flesh.

losh *n* a corrupt form of 'Lord'.—*int* an exclamation of surprise or wonder, used alone and in various combinations.

loshie, loshie-goshie *int* an exclamation of surprise.

loshins, loshtie *int* an exclamation of surprise.

losin *same as* **lozen**.

losing one's sel *phr* losing care for one's personal appearance.

loss *v* to lose.

lossie *adj* (*used of a crop*) causing loss, waste by vacancies.

lossiness *n* the state of being unprofitable.

lost *adj* at a loss.

lot *n* **1** a building feu (qv). **2** a quantity of grain, generally the twenty-fifth part, given to the thresher as wages. **3** a great number, the whole of several articles.

lotch¹ *n* a handful or considerable quantity of something semiliquid.

lotch² *n* a corpulent, lazy person.—*adj* lazy.

lotch³ *v* **1** to limp. **2** to jog.

loth *same as* **laith²**.

lotman *n* a thresher, at so much per boll.

lotten *v* allowed, let.

lottie *n* a small collection or number.

louable *adj* praiseworthy.

louch *same as* **loutch**.

louchter *same as* **lachter**.

loud *same as* **lood**.

lougs *same as* **loags**.

loun¹ *same as* **loon²**.

loun², lound *adj* **1** quiet, calm. **2** sheltered.

lounder, louner *v* **1** to beat severely. **2** to do anything with vehemence. **3** to scold.—*n* **1** a heavy blow. **2** energy at work.

loundering *n* a severe beating.—*adj* (*used of a blow*) resounding.

lounfow *same as* **loonfow**.

lounge *v* to thrust forward violently.—*n* a lunge.

lounlie *same as* **lownly**.

loun's-piece *n* the uppermost slice of a loaf.

loup¹ *v* **1** to leap, jump, spring. **2** to jump over. **3** to throb, pulsate. **4** to dance, frisk. **5** to run, run off, escape. **6** to move quickly. **7** to run like a hare or rabbit. **8** (*used of horses and bulls*) to engender. **9** (*of frost*) to give way at sunrise. **10** to burst, break out of an enclosure. **11** to swell with anger, heat, etc. **12** to pass from one owner to another. **13** (*with* **aff**) to ramble in a speech or story. **14** (*with* **back**) to refuse suddenly to keep a bargain. **15** (*with* **down**) to lower one's first offer in bargaining. **16** to dismount. **17** (*with* **on**) to mount on horseback, to equip a company of horse. **18** (*with* **up**) to raise one's price in bargaining.—*n* **1** a leap, spring, bound. **2** the distance jumped. **3** a place where a river becomes so contracted by rocks that it can be easily leapt. **4** a small cataract. **5** a disease of sheep affecting their limbs.

loup² *n* a loop.

loup³ *v* (*used of a boot or shoe*) to open between the upper and the sole.

loup-counter lad *n* **1** a shopkeeper. **2** a salesman.

loupen *v* leapt.

loupen-steek *n* **1** a broken stitch in a stocking. **2** anything amiss.

louper *n* a vagabond, a fugitive from the law.

louper-dog *n* the porpoise.

loup-garthe *n* a gauntlet to be run.

loup-hunt *n* **1** an idle errand. **2** the search for adventure.—*v* **1** to go abroad early in the morning. **2** to go in search of adventures.

loupie *same as* **loopy**.

loupin' ague *n* St Vitus's dance.

loupin and leevin *adj* **1** (*used of fish*) freshly caught. **2** (*of persons*) in health and spirits.

loupin'-ill *n* the disease of sheep affecting their movements.

loupin'-on-stane *n* a horse block.

loup-the-bullocks *n* the game of leapfrog.

loup-the-cat *n* a term of contempt.

loup-the-dyke *adj* **1** unsettled. **2** runaway, not keeping in bounds.

loup-the-tether *v* **1** to break bounds. **2** to throw off restraint.—*adj* wild, that cannot be restrained.
loupy *n* a short leap.
loupy for loup *adv* with short leaps.
loupy for spang *phr* with short leaps.
lour[1] *v* **1** to lurk, crouch. **2** to skulk.—*n* a lurking place.
lour[2] *v* to prefer.
lourd[1] *v* rather; *in phr* **I had lourd** I had much rather.
lourd[2] *adj* **1** dull. **2** lumpish. **3** stupid. **4** sottish, gross.
lourdand *same as* **lurdane**.
lourdly *adv* stupidly.
lourdy *adj* lazy, sluggish.
lourie *n* the name of a bell rung at 10 o'clock p.m. in some towns.
lour-shouthered *adj* round-shouldered.
loury *adj* (*used of the weather*) gloomy, threatening.
lousance *n* freedom from bondage.
louse[1] *same as* **lowse**[1].
louse[2] *v* **1** to look for lice. **2** to take lice from the person or clothes.
lousen *same as* **lowsen**.
louss *same as* **lowse**[3].
louster *same as* **looster**.
lousy *adj* **1** dirty. **2** having lice. **3** shabby. **4** mean.
lousy-arnut *n* the earthnut.
lout *v* **1** to stoop. **2** to bend low. **3** to bow. **4** to curtsy.
loutch *v* **1** to slouch. **2** to bow down the head and raise the shoulders. **3** to have the appearance of a blackguard. **4** to loiter.
louthe *n* abundance.
louther[1] *v* **1** to loiter, idle. **2** to walk or move with difficulty. **3** to carry anything with difficulty. **4** to be entangled in mire, snow, etc. **5** to beat severely.—*n* **1** an idler, trifler, a good-for-nothing person. **2** a tall, uncomely person. **3** a sharp blow.
louther[2] *same as* **lowder**.
louthering *adj* **1** lazy. **2** awkward, lumbering.
louthertree *n* a lever for lifting millstones.
louthrick *same as* **lowder**.
lout-shouthered *adj* **1** round-shouldered. **2** off the perpendicular.
louty *adj* slow, lazy.
louze *same as* **lowse**[3].
lovanenty, loveanendie, lovenanty *int* an exclamation of surprise, alarm, etc.
love-bairn *n* an illegitimate child.
love-begot *n* an illegitimate child.—*adj* illegitimate.
love-begotten *adj* illegitimate.
love-blink *n* a glance of love.
love-clap *v* to embrace fondly.
love-daft *adj* madly in love.
love-darg *n* a friendly day's ploughing given to a neighbour.
love-dotterel *n* the doting love felt by old unmarried people.
love-fraucht *adj* full of love.
love-glint *n* a glance of love.
love-in-idleness *n* the *Viola tricolor*.
loveit, lovite *n* a term expressing the royal regard for a person mentioned or addressed, as in a Royal Commission.
love-lichtit *adj* (*used of the eyes*) lighted by love.
love-links *n* the creeping Jenny.
love-lowe *n* the flame of love.
lovenenty *same as* **lovanenty**.
lovens, loving *int* an exclamation of surprise.
loverin-iddles *int* an exclamation of surprise.
lovers' links *n* stonecrop.
lovers' loaning *n* a lane frequented by lovers.
lover's loup *n* **1** the leap of a despairing lover over a precipice. **2** the place where such a leap has occurred.
love-stoond, ~stound *n* the pang of love.
lovetenant *n* lieutenant.
love-tryste *n* a lovers' meeting by appointment.

lonch, lontch *adj* lavish.
lovy-ding *int* an exclamation of surprise.
low[1] *v* **1** to degrade. **2** to lower. **3** to abate, cease. **4** to haggle as to a price.
low[2] *same as* **lo**[1].
low[3] *adj* **1** weak, extremely weak. **2** of small stature. **3** lower, downstairs. **4** (*used of the wind*) blowing from the south.
low[4] *same as* **lowe**.
lowan *same as* **lown**[2].
lowance *n* **1** allowance. **2** share. **3** permission.
lowdamer, lowdamy *same as* **lodamy**.
lowden *v* **1** to lull, abate. **2** to reduce to calmness, to quiet. **3** to silence. **4** to bring down. **5** to speak a little. **6** to stand in awe of another.
lowder *n* **1** a wooden lever. **2** a handspoke for lifting a millstone. **3** any long, stout, rough stick. **4** a stroke or blow.—*v* **1** to beat. **2** to move heavily.
lowdomary *same as* **lodamy**.
lowe *n* **1** a flame, blaze, light. **2** a glow. **3** a rage.—*v* **1** to flame, blaze. **2** to glow. **3** to parch with thirst from great heat.
lowed *v* lowered.
lowen *same as* **lown**[2].
lowering *adj* stooping.
lowie *n* a big, lazy person.
lowie-lebbie *n* a hanger-on about kitchens.
lowins *n* liquor after it has once passed through the still.
lowins *same as* **lowance**.
lowland *adj* low-lying.
low-lifed *adj* **1** mean, despicable. **2** of low habits.
lowly-legged *adj* short-legged.
lowmin *same as* **loymin**.
lowmost *adj* lowest.
lown[1] *same as* **loon**[2].
lown[2] *adj* **1** calm, serene. **2** tranquil, unagitated. **3** sheltered. **4** silent. **5** quiet. **6** soft, gentle, low. **7** secret.—*adv* softly, in a low voice.—*n* **1** stillness. **2** shelter. **3** a sheltered place.—*v* **1** (*used of the wind*) to abate. **2** to fall.
lownder *same as* **lounder**.
lowness *n* **1** shortness of stature. **2** extreme weakness.
lown-hill *n* the sheltered side of a hill.
lownly *adv* **1** in shelter. **2** quietly. **3** softly. **4** in a low tone. **5** in stillness. **6** languidly.
lownness *n* stillness, quietness.
lown-side *n* the sheltered side of a wall, hill, etc.
lown-warm *adj* soft and warm.
lowp[1] *same as* **loup**[1].
lowp[2] *v* to lop.
Lowren-fair *n* an Aberdeenshire fair held on St Lawrence Day, 23 August.
lowrie *n* the fox.
lowrie-like *adj* having the crafty look of a fox.
lowrie-tod *n* the fox.
lowsance *n* **1** liberty. **2** deliverance.
lowse[1] *adj* **1** loose, free, unrestrained. **2** lax in morals. **3** thoughtless. **4** (*used of the weather*) mild, genial.
lowse[2] *v* to lose.
lowse[3] *v* **1** to loosen. **2** to set free. **3** to stop working for the day. **4** to unharness, unyoke. **5** to unload, discharge a cargo. **6** (*used of perspiration*) to break out. **7** to set to work energetically, to begin. **8** to say grace before a meal. **9** to redeem an article pawned. **10** (*used of a cow*) to show signs of milk in the udder. **11** to thaw.—*n* a rush, a race.—*phr* **lowse us** say grace for us.
lowse leather *n* pendulous skin on one that has lost flesh.
lowsely *adv* loosely.
lowsen *v* **1** to loosen. **2** to unyoke horses or cows.
lowseness *n* **1** diarrhoea. **2** dysentery.
lowse siller *n* small change.
lowsing *n* the end of working.
lowsing time *n* **1** the end of a day's work. **2** the time for unyoking horses and stopping farm work.
lowsy naturae *n* a *lusus naturae*.
lowt *same as* **lout**.

lowter *same as* **lowder**.
lowttie *adj* **1** loutish. **2** heavy and inactive.
lowying *adj* **1** idling. **2** lounging.
loy *adj* sluggish, inactive.
loyester *n* a stroke, a blow.
loymin, loym *n* a limb.
loyness *n* inactivity.
loyt *n* a lazy person.
lozen, lozin, lozzen *n* a pane of glass.
lozenge-lion *n* an ancient coin.
lozenger *n* a lozenge.
Luac ~, Luag Friday *n* a fair held in Tarland, in Aberdeenshire, on a Friday in July.
lub *n* anything heavy and unwieldy.
lubbard, lubbert *n* **1** a lout. **2** a coward. **3** a lubber.
lubber-fiend *n* a benevolent sprite.
lubbertie *adj* **1** lazy. **2** sluggish, lubberly.
lubin *n* a children's singing game.
lubrick *adj* **1** vacillating. **2** slippery.
luce¹ *n* brightness.
luce² *n* **1** scurf, dandruff. **2** the slimy matter scraped off in shaving.
lucht *n* a lock of hair.
luchter *same as* **lachter**.
luck¹ *v* **1** to prosper. **2** to have good luck. **3** to happen by good fortune.
luck² *n* a lock.—*v* **1** to shut up, fasten. **2** to enclose.
luck-daddy *same as* **lucky-dad**.
lucked*adj* **1** fated. **2** having good or ill luck or fate.
lucken¹ *n* a bog.
lucken² *v* **1** to prosper. **2** to cause to thrive.
lucken³ *n* the globeflower.
lucken⁴ *v* **1** to knit the brows. **2** (*used of cloth, etc*) to pucker, gather into folds. **3** (*of a cabbage*) to grow firm in the heart.
lucken⁵ *adj* **1** close. **2** shut up. **3** contracted. **4** locked, bolted. **5** webbed.
lucken⁶ *n* an unsplit haddock, half-dried.
lucken-booth *n* **1** the old Tolbooth in Edinburgh. **2** (*in pl*) booths made to be locked up by day or night.
lucken-browed *adj* **1** heavy-browed. **2** having the eyebrows close to each other.
lucken-footed *adj* **1** web-footed. **2** having the toes joined by a film.
lucken-gowan, ~-gowlan *same as* **locken-gowlan**.
lucken-haddock *n* an unsplit haddock, half-dried.
lucken-handed *adj* **1** having the fist contracted, with the fingers drawn down to the palm. **2** close-fisted.
lucken-toed *adj* web-footed.
lucken-toes *n* toes joined by a film or web.
lucker *n* an eye.
luck-minnie *same as* **lucky-minnie**.
luck-penny *n* money given back by the seller to the buyer for luck.
luckrass *n* a cross-grained, cantankerous old woman.
lucky¹, **luckie** *n* **1** a familiar term of address to an elderly woman. **2** a midwife. **3** a grandmother. **4** a grandfather. **5** a wife, mistress. **6** a helpmate. **7** a landlady, mistress of an alehouse. **8** a witch.
lucky² *adj* **1** of good omen. **2** over and above the standard measure or stipulated quantity. **3** abundant, full. **4** larger. **5** bulky. **6** more than enough.—*adv* perhaps.
lucky-dad, ~-daddy, ~-deddy *n* a grandfather.
lucky-foot *n* a person whom it is lucky to meet on a road.
lucky-like *adj* looking like good fortune.
lucky-measure *n* **1** that which exceeds what can legally be claimed. **2** overflowing measure.
lucky-minnie *n* **1** a grandmother. **2** a term of reproach to a woman.
lucky-minnie's 'oo' *n* a fleecy substance growing on a plant in wet ground.
lucky-plack *n* the fee for the proclamation of marriage banns.
lucky-pock *n* a lucky bag.

lucky-roach *n* the hardhead (qv).
lucky's lines *n* a plant growing in deep water near the shore.
lucky's-mutch *n* the monkshood.
lucky's 'oo' *same as* **lucky-minnie's 'oo'**.
lucky words *n* words that Shetland fishermen use only at the deep-sea fishing.
lucre *n in phr* **lucre of gain** profit, gain.
lucriss *same as* **luckrass**.
lucy-arnut *same as* **lousyarnut**.
ludging *n* a lodging, a house.
ludibris *n* **1** derision. **2** an object of derision.
lue¹ *same as* **lew**.
lue² *same as* **loe**
luely *adv* softly.
luesome *adj* **1** lovely. **2** lovable.
lue-warm *adj* lukewarm.
lufe, luff *same as* **loof**.
luffie *same as* **loofie**.
lug¹ *adj* (*used of crops*) growing too little to ear or root and too much to stem.
lug², **lugg** *n* **1** the ear. **2** the handle of a jar, cup, jug, etc. **3** the projection on a bucket, etc, to which the handle is attached. **4** a tuft or tassel at the side of a bonnet or cap. **5** a knot. **6** one of the two tufts at the top of a full sack by which it is lifted and carried on the back. **7** a corner, recess. **8** the side of a chimney. **9** a corner of a herring net, the loop on the end of a fishing line. **10** the tongue of a boot or shoe.—*v* to cut off the ears.
lug³ *n* the sandworm, the lugworm.—*v* to dig for lugworms.
lugard *n* a blow on the ear.
lug-bab *n* **1** an earring. **2** a tuft or knot of ribbons or tassel on the side of the cap over the ear.
lug-bane, ~-been *n* part of the head of a fish.
lug-drum *n* the eardrum.
lug-fin *n* the fin of a fish nearest the ear.
luggerheids *n* loggerheads.
luggie¹ *n* **1** the horned owl. **2** a crop-eared person.
luggie² *adj* heavy, sluggish.
luggie³ *n* **1** a wooden pail or dish with a handle formed by the projection of one of the staves above the others. **2** a boys' game.
luggie⁴ *n* **1** a hut or lodge in a park. **2** a very small cottage.
luggie⁵ *n* a window-like aperture in a room of an old baronial castle from which the baron could hear and survey unseen what went on in the room underneath.
luggit *adj* **1** having ears. **2** having handles.—*n* a blow on the ear.
luggy *adj* (*used of crops*) growing more to stem than to grain or root.
lug-haul *v* to pull by the ears.
lug-horn *n* **1** a stethoscope. **2** an ear trumpet.
lught *same as* **lucht**.
lughter *same as* **lachter**.
lug-knot *n* a knot of ribbons at the side of the bonnet over the ear.
lug-lachet *n* a box on the ear.
lug-length *n* the distance at which one can hear another speak.
lug-locks *n* curls hanging behind the ear.
lug-mark *n* a distinguishing mark cut on the ear of a sheep.—*v* **1** to cut such marks, to earmark. **2** to punish by cropping the ears.
lug of *adv phr* near to.
lug-stanes *n* stones attached as sinkers to the lower side of a herring net.
lug-storming *adj* assailing or deafening the ears.
lug-yerkit *adj* **1** struck on the ear. **2** pulled by the ears.
luiffie *n* a morning roll.
luig *same as* **luggie**⁴.
luik *v* to look.
luin *n* the red-throated diver.
luive, luif *same as* **loof**.
luke¹ *adj* lukewarm, tepid.
luke² *v* to look.

Luke's-mass *n* the festival of St Luke, 18 October.
lull *v* to sleep gently.
lulls *n* bagpipes.
lum[1], **lumb** *n* **1** a chimney. **2** a chimney corner. **3** a chimney stalk. **4** the chimney top. **5** a dress hat shaped like a chimney.
lum[2] *v* to rain heavily.—*n in phr* **a lum of a day** a very wet day.
lumberload *n* **1** a heavy, useless load. **2** a corpulent, overfed body.
lumbersome *adj* cumbrous.
lumbery *adj* useless, rubbishy.
lum-cheek *n* the fireside, the side of the chimney.
lum-cleek *n* the hook on which a pot is hung in cooking.
lume *same* as **loom**[1].
lum hat *n* a dress hat, shaped like a chimney.
lum-heid *n* the chimney top.
lummle *n* the filings of metal.
lump *n* **1** a fat pig. **2** a dull, heavy person. **3** a mass, quantity. **4** a great wave, a large mass of water. —*v* **1** to beat, thump. **2** to raise a lump by a fall or blow.
lumper *n* one who furnishes ballast for ships.
lum-pig *n* a chimney can or cowl.
lumping pennyworth *n* good measure or weight.
lumpit *adj* collective.
lump o' butter *n* a soft, easy-going, useless person.
lum-reek *n* smoke from a chimney.
lum-root *n* the base of a chimney where it rises from the roof.
lum-sooper *n* a chimney sweep.
lum-tap *n* the top of a chimney or of the funnel of a steamer.
lum-tile *n* a chimney can made of clay.
luncart *n* a temporary fireplace out of doors for the use of washerwomen.
lunch, luncheon *n* a large piece of anything, of food.
lunchick *n* a bulky package carried on the haunch under the coat.
lunchock *n* the angle made by the thighs and belly.
lunder, lundre *same as* **lounder**.
lunets *n* spectacles.
lungie *same as* **longie**.
lunie, luny *same as* **loonie**[2].
lunie *same as* **lunyie**.
lunie-bane *n* the hipbone.
lunie-joint *n* the hip joint.
lunie-shot *adj* having the hip joint dislocated or sprung.
lunk *adj* lukewarm.
lunkie[1], **lunky** *n* **1** a small hole left for the admission of animals. **2** a hole for sheep in a stone dyke.
lunkie[2] *adj* (*used of the weather*) close and sultry.
lunkie-hole *n* a hole in a stone dyke (qv) for sheep.
lunkieness *n* oppressiveness of atmosphere, sultriness.
lunkit *adj* **1** lukewarm. **2** half-boiled.
lunner *same as* **lounder**.
Lunnon *n* London.
lunnie *same as* **loonie**[2].
lunsh *v* to loll.
lunshach *n* a large supply of food.
lunshing *adj* idle, lounging.
lunt[1] *n* **1** a light. **2** a match. **3** a lighted match. **4** smoke. **5** the smoke of a pipe. **6** smoke with flame. **7** anything used to light a fire. **8** a column of flame. **9** hot vapour of any kind.—*v* **1** to emit smoke in puffs or columns. **2** to blaze. **3** to smoke a pipe.
lunt[2] *v* **1** to walk quickly. **2** to walk with a great spring.—*n* a great rise and fall in walking.
lunt[3] *v* to sulk.—*n* a fit of sulking.
luntus *n* a contemptuous name for an old woman.
lunyie, lunzie *n* the loin.
luppen[1] *v* leapt.
luppen[2] *adj* **1** (*used of a boot or shoe*) opened between the upper and the sole through stitches giving way. **2** *in phr* **luppen a gutter** escaped some danger.
luppen-steek *n* a dropped stitch.

luppin *n* looping for a hat.
lurch *n* a tricky way.
lurd *n* a blow with the fist.
lurdane, lurden, lurdoun *n* **1** a lazy, stupid person. **2** an idle fellow. **3** a worthless man or woman.—*adj* **1** lazy, stupid, worthless. **2** heavy. **3** severe.
lurdenly *adv* **1** stupidly. **2** lazily. **3** clownishly.
lurder *n* a lazy, worthless person.
lurdy *adj* lazy.
lure[1] *adv* rather.
lure[2] *n* the udder of a cow, as used for food.
lure[3] *same as* **lire**[1].
lurk[1] *v* **1** to live quietly in seclusion. **2** to idle, loaf about. **3** to lower so as to hide.
lurk[2] *same as* **lirk**.
lusbirdan *n* **1** a low-statured people once living in the Hebrides. **2** pigmies.
luscan *n* a sturdy, thieving beggar.
lush *n* strong drink.
lusking *adj* absconding.
lusome *adj* **1** not smooth. **2** rough, unpolished.
lusome *adj* lovable.
luss *same as* **luce**[2].
lust *n* an appetite for food.
lustheid *n* amiableness.
lusty *adj* **1** pleasant. **2** sturdy. **3** healthy-looking. **4** fat. **5** powerful.
lute *n* **1** a sluggard. **2** a lout.
lute *v* allowed, let.
luthir *same as* **lither**[1].
luther, luthir *n* a heavy blow.
lutten *v* let, allowed.
luve *v* to love.
luves *n* hands.
ly *n* the pollack.
lyaach *adj* low.
lyach-fire *n* a fire on a hearthstone and not in a grate.
lyaag *same as* **laig**[1].
lyaagen *same as* **laggen**.
lyaagens o' the air *n* the extreme edge of the visible sky, the horizon.
lyaager *same as* **lagger**.
lyaat *n* a very small quantity, especially of liquid.
lyabach *same as* **llabach**.
lyabber *same as* **labber**.
lyam *same as* **liam**.
lyardly *adv* sparingly.
lyart *adj* **1** (*used of hair*) streaked with grey, hoary. **2** streaked with red and white. **3** (*of fallen leaves*) variegated, changed in colour.
lyaug *same as* **laig**[1].
lyawger *n* gossiping.
lybbich *same as* **llabach**.
ly-by *adj* standing aside, neutral.
lychtle, lychtlie *same as* **lichtlie**[2].
lydder *same as* **lither**[1].
lye *n* pasture-land.
lying-in-wife *n* a midwife.
lying-money *n* money not used.
lying-side *n* the side of a carcass of beef that has all the spinous processes of the vertebræ left on it.
lying-storm *n* a prolonged storm.
lying time *n* the time worked by a miner between the date of making up the paybill and the date of the payday.
lyke *n* **1** an unburied corpse. **2** the watch kept over a dead body until the funeral.
lyke-wake *n* the watch kept over a body between death and burial.
lyke-waker *n* a watcher by the dead.
lymphad, lymfad *n* a galley.
lyowder[1] *same as* **lowder**.
lyowder[2] *v* to amble, or sway from side to side, in walking.
lyre[1], **lyrie** *n* the Manx shearwater.
lyre[2] *same as* **lire**.

lyred *adj* having locks of hair of iron-grey. *See* **lyart**.
lyrie *n* **1** the pogge. **2** the whiting pollack.
lyse-hay *n* hay from pasture land, not from meadow.
lyst *v* to listen.
lyt *n* **1** a few. **2** a small quantity or number.
lytach *n* **1** a large mass of wet substance. **2** speech in an unknown tongue. **3** a long, rambling piece of news. **4** a long, disconnected piece of literature.—*v* **1** to work with liquid or semiliquid substances to perform domestic work. **2** to work unskilfully and awkwardly. **3** to speak in an unknown tongue. **4** to speak much in a rambling, confused manner.
lyte *n* **1** an untidy mass of any wet substance. **2** a heavy fall. **3** the sound of a heavy fall.—*v* **1** to throw any wet substance in a mass to the ground. **2** to fall flat. **3** to work unskilfully.—*adv* flat and heavily.
lyter *n* a large mass of any wet substance.
lythe *n* the immature pollack.

lythe[1] *same as* **lithe**[3].
lythe[2], **lyth** *same as* **lithe**[4].
lythe, lyth *same as* **lithe**[2].
lythesome[1] *adj* **1** sheltered, shaded. **2** warm, genial.
lythesome[2] *adj* engaging, of genial disposition.
lythet *adj* **1** thickened. **2** spiced.
lythie *same as* **lithie**.
lything *n* **1** softening. **2** soothing. **3** a smooth paste of flour or oatmeal and water or milk for thickening soup, gravy, etc.
lythocks *n* a mixture of oatmeal and cold water stirred over a fire until it boils and thickens, used as a poultice.
lythy *adj* **1** thickened. **2** thick and smooth like porridge.
lytrie *n* **1** a mass of anything in disorder. **2** a crowd of small creatures in disorder.—*adj* (*used of a mass of semiliquid substance*) dirty and disordered.
lytt *same as* **leet**.

M

ma[1] *same as* **mae**[1].
ma[2] *same as* **maw**[3].
ma[3] *adj* my.
maa[1] *same as* **maw**[4].
maa[2] *same as* **maw**[3].
maa[3] *n* **1** a whit. **2** a jot.
maa[4] *n* the bleat of a lamb.
maa-craig *n* a rock frequented by gulls.
maad *same as* **maud**[1].
maader *int* a call to a horse to come to the near side.
maain *adj* mowing.—*n* what a man can mow in a day.
maak[1] *n* the milt of a fish.
maak[2] *same as* **maik**[3].
maan *adj* mown.
maavie *n* **1** the maw of a fish. **2** any small animal's stomach. **3** a rennet bag.
mabbie *n* a woman's cap.
macabaa, macabaw *n* a kind of snuff.
macalive-cattle *n* cattle appropriated, in the Hebrides, to a child sent out to be fostered.
macaroni, maccaroni *n* a fop, dandy.
Macdonald's disease *n* an affection of the lungs.
macer *n* a macebearer, an officer who keeps order in law courts.
Macfarlane's bouat *n* the moon.
mach[1] *n* might.
mach[2] *same as* **mawk**.
machair *n* a stretch of low-lying sandy ground that lies close to the seashore and is covered with coarse grasses.
Machars *n* the part of Wigtownshire washed by the Solway Firth and the Bay of Luce.
machers *n* bent-grown, sandy tracts by the sea.
machie *n* a conveyance, a gig, a cart.
machine *n* a vehicle, carriage, cart.
machle *v* to busy oneself in vain.
machless *adj* **1** feeble. **2** powerless.
macht *same as* **maught**.
mack[1] *v* to make.
mack[2] *n* **1** fashion. **2** shape.—*adj* neat, tidy.
mackaingie *n in phr* **fair mackaingie** full scope.
mackdom *same as* **makedom**.
mackerel-sture *n* the tunny.
macker-like *adj* **1** more becoming. **2** more suitable.
mack-like *adj* **1** tidy, neat. **2** seemly. **3** suitable. **4** well-proportioned.
mackly *adj* mack-like (qv).
Macmillan-folk, Macmillanites *n* the followers of Macmillan, one of the founders of the Reformed Presbyterian Church.
macon *n* a hare.

macrel *n* a mackerel.
mad[1] *adj* **1** keen, eager. **2** angry, vexed.—*v* to madden.
mad[2] *n* a sort of net, fixed on four stakes, for catching salmon and trout.
mad[3] *n* **1** a maggot. **2** the larva of a maggot.
mad[4] *same as* **maud**[1].
madam *n* **1** a fine lady. **2** a mistress. **3** a hussy.
madded *adj* mad, foolish.
madden *v* to anger, vex.
madden drim *same as* **madder drim**.
madder *n* a vessel used in mills for holding meal.
madder drim *n* **1** madness. **2** folly. **3** mad pranks.
maddie[1] *n* a large species of mussel.
maddie[2] *n* a lunatic.
made[1] *adj* fatigued.
made[2] *same as* **mad**[3].
made with *adj* affected by.
madge *n* a playul or contemptuous term for a woman.
mad-leed *n* a mad strain.
madlins *adv* madly.
madlocks *n* milk brose.
mae[1] *adj* more.
mae[2] *n* **1** the bleat of a sheep or lamb. **2** a child's name for a sheep. **3** a sheep call.—*v* to bleat softly.
maeg *n* **1** a hand. **2** a big, clumsy hand. **3** (*in pl*) the flippers of a seal.—*v* **1** to handle. **2** to handle injuriously.
maegsie *n* the possessor of big, clumsy hands.
mael *n* **1** a spot or stain on cloth. **2** an iron stain.—*v* to spot, stain.
maelyer *n* the quantity of corn ground at a time.
maen *n* **1** a moan. **2** lamentation. **3** complaint.—*v* **1** to moan. **2** to pity. **3** to show signs of pain. **4** to mourn. **5** to condole with.
maese *v* **1** to allay. **2** to soothe. **3** to settle. **4** to mellow fruit.
maeslie *adj* **1** speckled, spotted. **2** poor, inferior.
maeslie-shankit *adj* having the legs spotted from being too near a fire.
maet *same as* **meat**.
maet-haill *same as* **meat-hale**.
maether *int* a carter's call to his horse to come to the near side.
maffling *n* blundering, bungling.
mag[1] *same as* **maeg**.
mag[2] *same as* **magg**[1].
magerful *adj* masterful, exercising undue influence.
magg[1], **mag**[2] *n* **1** a halfpenny. **2** a small gratuity, tip.
magg[2] *v* to carry off clandestinely.
maggateevish *same as* **maggative**.

maggative, maggativous *adj* **1** full of whims. **2** crotchety. **3** changeable in moods.

magger *prep* in spite of.

maggie[1] *n* **1** a young woman or girl. **2** a jade. **3** a collier's term for a kind of till or clay.

maggie[2] *n* **1** the common guillemot. **2** a magpie.

Maggie Findy *n* a woman capable of shifting for herself.

maggie-mony-feet *n* a centipede.

Maggie-Rab, ~-Robb *n* **1** a bad halfpenny. **2** a bad wife.

maggit *same as* **magot**.

maggle *v* **1** to mangle. **2** to bungle.

maggoty-heidit *adj* whimsical, capricious.

maggoty-pow *n* a whimsical, crotchety person.

magin *adj* **1** wondering. **2** speculating. **3** talking as if at a loss.

magistrand *n* a student about to become MA at Aberdeen University.

magistrate *n* a red herring.

magot *n* **1** a maggot. **2** a whim, fancy. **3** a fad.

magowk *v* to make an April fool of one.

magpie *n* a chatterer.

magre *same as* **magger**.

mags *same as* **magg**[2].

magyers *v* to spite.

mahers *n* a tract of low land of a marshy and moory nature.

mahoun *n* a name given to the devil.

maich *n* **1** marrow. **2** might. **3** strength. **4** an effort.

maicherand *adj* **1** weak, feeble. **2** incapable of exertion.

maichless *adj* wanting bodily strength.

maick *same as* **magg**[2].

maid *n* **1** a maggot. **2** the larva of a maggot.

maid[1] *same as* **made**[1].

maid[2] *n* the last handful of corn cut in harvest.

maiden *v* **1** to lay a child in the arms of its parent when it is presented for baptism.—*n* an old maid. **2** a designation formerly given to the eldest daughter of a farmer. **3** the bridesmaid at a wedding. **4** she who laid the child in the arms of its parent when it was presented for baptism. **5** the last handful of corn cut in harvest, dressed with ribbons to resemble a young woman. **6** the feast of harvest home. **7** a wisp of straw put into a hoop of iron, used by a smith for watering his fire. **8** an ancient instrument for holding the broaches of pirns until the pirns are wound off. **9** an instrument for beheading, like the guillotine. **10** the skate, thornback.

maiden chance *n* a first chance.

maiden day *n* the day when the last sheaf of the harvest is cut.

maiden feast *n* the feast given on the last day of harvest.

maiden-hair *n* the muscles of oxen when boiled.

maiden-kimmer *n* **1** the maid who attends the kimmer (qv) or matron who has the charge of the infant at a kimmerin (qv) and baptisms. **2** the maid who lays the infant in the father's arms at a baptism.

maiden night *n* the night of the harvest feast.

maiden-play *n* the harvest-home amusement.

maiden-skate *n* the skate, thornback.

Maiden Trace *n* the name of an old popular tune, often played when a bride and her maidens walked thrice round the church before the celebration of the marriage.

maid-in-the-mist *n* navelwort.

maidship *n* **1** a maiden condition. **2** an unmarried state.

maie *same as* **mae**[2].

maig *same as* **maeg**.

maigers *same as* **magger**.

maighrie *n* **1** money. **2** valuable effects.

maigintie, maiginties *int* an exclamation of surprise.

maik[1] *n* **1** a halfpenny. **2** a small gratuity.

maik[2] *n* **1** fashion. **2** design. **3** figure, shape. **4** kind, species. **5** variety. **5** quantity of what is made.

maik[3] *n* **1** an equal, match. **2** an image, model. **3** resemblance.

maikint *same as* **makint**.

maikless *adj* matchless.

mail[1], **maill** *same as* **meal**[4].

mail[2] *same as* **mael**.

mail[3] *same as* **meal**[3].

mail[4] *n* a travelling bag.

mail-duty *n* rent.

mailen *same as* **mailin**.

mailer *same as* **maelyer**.

mail-free *same as* **meal-free**.

mail garden *n* a garden, the produce of which is grown for sale.

mailie, maillie *n* **1** a pet ewe. **2** the name for a pet cow or ewe.

mailin[1] *n* a purse.

mailin[2], **mailen** *n* **1** a farm, holding. **2** its rent.

mailinder *n* the holder of a farm.

maille *n* a gold coin.

mailler, mailer *n* **1** a cottager who gets waste land rent-free for a number of years to improve it. **2** a rent-paying farmer.

maillyer, mailyer *same as* **maelyer**.

mail-man *n* a farmer.

mail-payer *n* a rent-paying farmer.

mailrooms *n* hired lodgings.

mails[1] *n* various species of goosefoot.

mails[2] *n* small perforated scales of metal attached to the heddle through which the warp passes, used in weaving.

mailt house *n* a house for which rent is paid.

main[1] *n* patience.—*adj* **1** thorough. **2** staunch.—*adv* **1** very much. **2** quite.

main[2] *same as* **maen**.

main-braces *n* part of the equipment of a carriage of the old fashion for supporting its body.

main-comb *n* a comb for a horse's mane, etc.

maine bread *n* fine white bread.

maingie *n* **1** a family household. **2** a retinue. **3** a crowd.

mainly *adv* very, exceedingly.

mainners *n* manners.

main-rig *n* land of which the ridges were possessed alternately by different persons.

mains *n* the home farm on an estate.

mainsmore *n* goodwill or free grace.

mains o' *n* **1** the upper hand of, the advantage over. **2** the best of a bargain or argument.

mainswear *same as* **manswear**.

main-sweat *n* the death sweat.

mainto *n* **1** obligation to one. **2** debt.

mair *adj* more.

mairattour *adv* moreover.

mairch *n* a march, a boundary

mairdil *v* to be overcome with fatigue.—*adj* moving heavily from fatigue, size or bodily weakness.

mairdle *same as* **meirdel**.

mairower *adv* moreover.

mairritch lickness *n* a likelihood of marriage.

mairt *n* winter provision of beef, made at Martinmas.

Mairtimas *n* Martinmas.

maischloch *same as* **mashloch**.

mais *same as* **maise**.

maise[1], **mais** *n* a measure of herrings.

maise[2] *same as* **mease**.

maise[3] *v* **1** to mix. **2** to blend or incorporate in one mass.

maised *adj* (*used of fruit*) mellow, spoiled from too long keeping. *See* **mease**.

maiser[1] *n* a macer.

maiser[2] *n* a drinking cup of maple, a mazer.

maishie *same as* **maizie**[1].

maison dieu, ~ dew *n* a hospital.

maissery *n* macership.

maist, maista *adj* most.—*adv* almost.—*n* the greatest number, degree, etc.

maister[1] *n* **1** master. **2** an overmatch. **3** a schoolmaster.—*v* to master.

maister[2] *n* **1** stale urine. **2** chamber lye.

maister can *n* an earthen vessel for preserving stale urine.
maisterfu' *adj* masterful.
maister laiglen, ~ tub *n* a wooden vessel for holding stale urine.
maister wud *n* the timber of agricultural buildings originally paid for by the landlord.
maistlins *adv* **1** mostly. **2** almost.
maistly *adv* **1** mostly. **2** almost.
maistry *n* **1** mastery. **2** skill, power.
mait *n* meat, food.
maith *n* a maggot.—*v* to become infested with maggots.
maitter *n* **1** matter. **1** pus.
maivie *same as* **mavis**.
maize *v* to wonder.
maizick *n* music.
maizie[1] *n* a basket made of straw rope for holding odds and ends.
maizie[2] *n* **1** a binder (qv). **2** a flannel undershirt.
majirk *n* an odd old-fashioned article or machine.
major *v* to walk to and fro with a military air, swagger.
major-mindit *adj* haughty in demeanour.
mak[1] *v* **1** to make. **2** to compose poetry. **3** to make up accounts. **4** (*of dung*) to become fit for use. **5** to do, to have business. **6** to meddle. **7** to pretend. **8** to matter, be of consequence. **9** to reach. **10** (*of the tide*) to rise, flow.
mak[2], **mak**[3] *same as* **maik**[2], **maik**[3].
mak aff *v* to run away, scamper off.
make[1], **make**[2] *same as* **maik**[1], **maik**[2].
make-bate *n* a mischief-maker.
makedom *n* figure, shape.
make-down *v* **1** (*used of spirits*) to dilute. **2** (*of a bed*) to make it ready.
maker *n* a poet.
mak for *v* to prepare for.
mak fore *v* to be of advantage.
making *n* **1** (*used of tea, etc*) the quantity made at a time. **2** (*in pl*) the materials of which a thing is made. **3** germs.
makint *adj* **1** assured. **2** confident.
makintly *adv* **1** assuredly. **2** confidently.
mak into *v* to make one's way into, sail into.
mak in wi' *v* to get into one's good graces.
makly[1] *adv* equally.
makly[2] *adj* mack-like (qv).
mak of *v* **1** to make much of. **2** to profit by. **3** to do with. **4** to pat.
mak-on *n* a pretence.
mak oneself away *v* to commit suicide.
mak oot *v* **1** to extricate oneself. **2** to prove. **3** to find out truth or fact.
mak sleepy *adj* soporific.
maksna *v neg* matters not.
mak stead *v* to be of use.
mak throw *v* to struggle through.
mak to *v* **1** to make towards. **2** to approximate so far towards.
mak up *v* **1** to intend, decide. **2** to get out of bed. **3** to arrange, prepare. **4** to raise, collect. **5** to invent. **6** to make a fortune. **7** to break.—*n* a **1** fabrication. **2** anything made up of odds and ends.
mak up for *v* (*used of rain*) to threaten.
mak upon *v* to prepare.
mak up oneself *v* to recoup oneself for expenditure, labour, etc.
mak up to, ~ till *v* **1** to overtake. **2** to accost. **3** to make matrimonial overtures.
mak up with *v* to be pleased with, satisfied with, profited by.
mal-accord *n* **1** disagreement. **2** disapproval.
malagruized *adj* disordered, rumpled.
malagruze *v* **1** to bruise. **2** to rumple.
malapavis *n* **1** a mischance. **2** a misfortune.
malavogue *v* to beat, chastise.
malchance *n* mischance.
male[1] *same as* **meal**[4].

male[2] *n* a meal.
male[3] *n* five hundred herrings.
male[4] *same as* **mael**.
male-a-forren *n* **1** a meal over and above what is consumed. **2** a meal beforehand.
malefice *n* **1** a bad action. **2** injury by witches.
maleficiat *adj* injured by witchcraft.
male-free *same as* **meal-free**.
malegrugrous *adj* **1** grim, ghastly. **2** looking discontented.
maliceful *adj* **1** sickly. **2** in bad health.
malicin, mallasin *n* a curse.
maligrumph *n* the spleen.
malishy *n* the militia.
Malison *n* the Evil One.
malkin *n* **1** a half-grown girl. **2** a girl engaged to do light housework. **3** a hare.
mall *n in phr* **mall in shaft** all right, fit for work.
mallachie *adj* of a milk-and-water colour.
mallagrugous *adj* **1** grim. **2** ghastly. **3** looking discontented.
mallat *v* to feed.
malleables *n* iron work.
mallow *n* the sea wrack *Zosrera marina*.
malm *v* **1** to soften and swell by means of water. **2** to steep. **3** to become mellow.
malmieness *n* mellowness.
malmy *adj* **1** (*used of fruit*) mellow. **2** juiceless. **3** (*of food*) vapid, tasteless. **4** soft, yielding, gentle.
malorous *adj* **1** evil, unfortunate. **2** malicious.
malt *n* any liquor made from malt.
malt and meal *n* food and drink.
malvader *v* **1** to stun by a blow. **2** to injure.
malvadering *n* **1** a beating. **2** a defeat.
malverish *adj* **1** ill-behaved. **2** good for nothing.
malverse *n* **1** a crime. **2** a misdemeanour.—*adj* criminal—*v* **1** to do wrong. **2** to give an erroneous judgment. **3** to misemploy or pervert an office, trust, etc.
malvesy *n* malmsey wine.
mam *n* a child's name for mother.
mament *n* a moment.
mamie *n* **1** a wet nurse. **2** a foster mother.
mamikeekie *n* a smart, sound blow.
mammock *n* **1** a fragment. **2** a bit.
mammy *n* **1** a child's name for mother. **2** a midwife. **3** a nurse. **4** a foster mother.
mamore *n* a big field.
mamp *same as* **mump**[2].
mam's-fout, -pet *n* a spoiled child.
man[1] *n* **1** a husband. **2** a familiar term of address.
man[2], **man**[3] *same as* **maun**[1], **maun**[2].
manadge, manawdge *n* a kind of club or benefit society of near neighbours.
manadge circle *n* the whole number of contributors to the manadge (qv).
manadge wife *n* the woman treasurer of the manadge (qv).
manage *v* **1** to get through with. **2** to reach with some difficulty.
man-body *n* a full-grown man.
man-bote *n* compensation fixed by law for manslaughter.
man-browed *adj* having hair growing between the eyebrows.
manco *n* calamanco, a kind of cloth.
mand *n* a bread basket shaped like a corn sieve and made of plaited willows and straw, a hamper.
mandate *v* to commit a sermon to memory before preaching it.
mandel-buttons *n* mantle buttons, buttons for a loose upper garment.
mander *v* **1** to handle. **2** to deal.
mane[1] *same as* **maen**.
mane[2] *n* **1** the wool on a sheep's neck. **2** the top of a sheaf of oats.
manelet *n* the corn-marigold.
man-faced *adj* having masculine features.

manfu'-like *adj* manly, man-like.
mang[1], **mangs** *prep* among.
mang[2] *v* **1** to maim, bruise. **2** to overpower.
mang[3] *same as* **meing**. *See* **ming a mang**.
mang[4] *v* **1** to become frantic. **2** to render frantic. **3** to feel great but suppressed anxiety. **4** to long for eagerly. **5** to gall. **6** (*with* **at**) to be angry with. —*n* strong, suppressed feeling or anger.
manglumtew *n* a heterogeneous mixture.
manheid *n* **1** bravery. **2** fortitude.
man-hive *n* a populous town.
manish *v* **1** to manage. **2** to pull through.
manitoodlie *n* a term of endearment for a male child.
mank *v* **1** to fail. **2** to be deficient. **3** to impair, spoil.—*n* **1** a want. **2** a deficiency, short-coming. **3** an objection. **4** a complaint. **5** a disturbance. **6** the shying of an animal, causing it to stop.—*adj* **1** defective. **2** at a loss.
mankeeper *n* **1** the water newt or esk. **2** a small lizard.
mankey *same as* **manco**.
mankie[1] *v* **1** to miss. **2** to fail.—*n* a pear that misses its aim and remains in the ring in the game of pegtop.
mankie[2] *same as* **manco**.
man-life *n* **1** human life. **2** life as a man.
manling *n* a mannikin.
man-muckle *adj* come to the height of a full-grown man.
mann *same as* **maun**[2].
mannagie *n* a mannikin.
manner *v* **1** to mock. **2** to mimic. **3** to sound indistinctly or mockingly as an echo.
mannerin' *n* **1** mockery. **2** mimicry.
mannie, manikie, mannikie *n* **1** a little man. **2** a term of endearment for a small boy.
mannin' *adj* imperious. *See* **maun**[1].
manno *n* a big man.
mannor, manor *v and n* manure.
man o' mean *n* a beggar.
man o' sin *n* the Pope.
mauritch *adj* (*used of a woman*) masculine.
manse *n* a Scottish minister's official residence.
Maneemas Day *n* **1** 31 December NS. **2** 20 December OS.
mansie *n* a mannikin.
manswear *v* to commit perjury.
mansworn *adj* perjured.
mant *v* to stammer, stutter.—*n* a stutter.
mantay *same as* **manty**.
manteel *n* a mantle.
manter *n* a stammerer.
manting *n* **1** stuttering. **2** stumbling.—*adj* stammering.
manto *n* a mantle, gown.
manty *n* **1** a gown. **2** the stuff of which the gown is made.
manty-coat *n* a woman's loose coat.
manty-maker *n* a dressmaker.
manumission *n* graduation, as making free of a university.
manumit *v* **1** to confer an academic degree. **2** to laureate.
many *adj* much.—*n* **1** (*with* **a**) a great number. **2** (*with* **the**) the majority. **3** (*with* **the**) the departed.
manzy *same as* **menyie**.
maoil *n* a promontory.
map[1] *n* a portrait, likeness.
map[2] *v* to nibble as a sheep, rabbit, etc.—*n* a rabbit.—*int* a call to a rabbit.
map and mell *v* to live at board and bed as a wife with a husband.
mappy *n* a rabbit.—*int* a call to a rabbit.
mappy *n* a boys' marble marked with lines like a map.
mapsie *n* **1** a pet sheep. **2** a young hare.
mar *n* **1** an impediment in speech. **2** a defect.—*v* to irritate, annoy.
marb *n* the marrow.
marbel *adj* **1** feeble, inactive, slow, lazy. **2** reluctant.
marble *n* an alley made of fine white clay and streaked with red and blue lines.
marble-bools *n* marbles used in playing.

marbled *adj* (*used of meat*) composed of fat and lean in layers.
Marce Billion *n* the feast of the translation of St Martin, 4 July.
marchandye *n* merchandise.
marchant *n* a merchant.
march-balk *n* a narrow ridge, serving as a march between the contiguous lands of different proprietors.
march-dyke *n* a boundary wall or fence.
marches *n* part of a weaver's loom.
march-man *n* a Borderer.
march stane *n* a boundary stone.
mardel *n* a fat, clumsy woman.—*adj* **1** big, fat. **2** clumsy.
mardle[1] *same as* **meirdel**.
mardle[2], **mardel** *n* **1** a gossiper. **2** an idle, lounging woman.
mare *n* **1** the wooden figure of a horse, used as a military punishment. **2** a trestle supporting scaffolding. **3** a mason's or bricklayer's hod or trough.
marefu' *n* a hodful.
mareillen *n* the frogfish.
mare's-tails *n* long, streaky clouds portending rain.
marestane *n* a rough, hatchet-shaped stone, hung up in a stable to protect the horses from being hag-ridden.
margent *n* **1** a margin, bank. **2** a beach.
margullie, margulie *v* **1** to disfigure, mangle. **2** to bungle. **3** to abuse.
marican *n* a kind of pear.
mariken *n* a dressed goatskin, morocco.
mariken shoon *n* morocco-leather shoes.
marinel *n* a mariner.
marish *adj* marshy.
maritage *n* money paid to the superior by the heir of his dead vassal, if unmarried before the death or at puberty, as the value of his tocher (qv).
mark[1] *n* **1** a silver coin worth 13s. 4d. Scots or 13$^{1}/_{3}$d. sterling. **2** a division of land. **3** a nominal weight.
mark[2] *same as* **mirk**.
mark[3] *n* **1** a conspicuous figure, a spectacle. **2** the supposed mark of the devil on a witch's body. **3** the aim in shooting.—*v* to aim in shooting.
market *n* **1** sale. **2** traffic. **3** a matrimonial engagement or match.
market-fare *n* a fairing (qv) bought for a sweetheart at a market.
market-ripe *adj* (*used of a woman*) marriageable.
marketstance *n* the field, etc, on which a market is held.
marketstead *n* the site of a market.
markland *n* a division of land, varying in extent.
mark nor burn, mark nor horn *n* not the least vestige or trace of anything lost.
mark o' mouth *n* indication of age by the teeth.
markstane *n* **1** a boundary stone. **2** (*in pl*) stones defining the extent of a mark (qv) of land.
marl[1], **marle** *v* **1** to become mottled, variegated. **2** to streak, spot.—*n* **1** a mottle, an indistinct mark on the skin caused by cold. **2** (*in pl*) the measles.
marl[2], **marle** *v* to marvel.
marle[1] *same as* **marl**[1].
marle *same as* **marl**[2].
marled *adj* **1** mottled. **2** chequered.
marled salmon *n* the grey trout, a species of salmon.
marley *n* a red clay marble.
marlion, marlin *n* **1** the merlin. **2** the sparrowhawk. **3** the kestrel.
marl-midden *n* a compost of marl and earth.
marmaid *n* **1** a mermaid. **2** the frogfish. **3** a species of limpet.
marmite *n* a large cooking pot.
maroonjus, marounjous *adj* **1** harsh. **2** outrageous. **3** obstreperous. **4** in bad humour.
marr[1] *v* **1** (*used of a cat*) to purr. **2** (*of an infant*) to coo. **3** (*with* **up**) to make a noise like two cats provoking each other to fight. **4** to urge or keep one to work.
marr[2] *same as* **mar**.

marra *same as* **marrow**.

marriage *n* the duty payable on the marriage of a ward whose lands were held of a superior.

marriage bone *n* a fowl's merrythought.

marriage check *n* a sound like the ticking of a watch, portending marriage.

marriage lines *n* a marriage certificate given to the bride.

marriage sark *n* a shirt made by the bride to be worn by the bridegroom on their marriage day.

marrott *n* **1** the common guillemot. **2** the razorbill.

Marrow *n* a name given to *The Marrow of Modern Divinity*, a work published in 1718 by Edward Fisher, the doctrines of which influenced the Evangelicals of the Scottish Kirk in the 18th century.

marrow *n* **1** a match, equal. **2** a facsimile. **3** one of a pair. **4** a partner, mate, companion. **5** a spouse, lover. **6** an atom.—*v* **1** to match. **2** to wed, mate. **3** to pair. **4** to unite. **5** to keep company with.

Marrow kirk *n* a Church that favoured the Marrow (qv) doctrine.

marrowless *adj* **1** without a peer or equal. **2** odd, not of a pair, not matching. **3** companionless. **4** without a husband or wife. **5** widowed, unmarried.

Marrowmen *n* ministers who preached the Marrow (qv) doctrine.

marry *v* (*with* **on** *or* **upon**) to be married to.

marsh-bent, marsh-bent grass *n* the fine-top grass.

marshlick, marshlach *n* a collection of things, no two of which are alike.—*adj* untidy.

marsh woundwort *n* the marsh betony.

Mar's year *n* the year 1715.

mart *n* **1** a cow or ox fattened, killed and salted about Martinmas for winter use. **2** meat pickled and stored for winter. **3** one who lives in ease and prosperity.

marter *same as* **martyr**.

marth *n* marrow, pith.

Martin-a-bullimus, --of-bullion's Day *n* 4 July, the feast of the translation of St Martin.

Martinmas *n* **1** St Martin's Day. **2** 11 November. **3** the November term day.

Martinmas-foy *n* a ploughman's farewell feast at Martinmas.

martin-swallow *n* the martin.

martlet *n* the marten.

martyr *n* **1** a dirty or spoilt condition. **2** a mess. **3** anything causing a mess.—*v* **1** to mutilate. **2** to bruise severely. **3** to torture. **4** to subject to great pain. **5** to bungle, confuse. **6** to work in a dirty, clumsy fashion. **7** to bedaub, bespatter with dirt.

martyreese *v* to victimize, martyr (qv).

martyring *n* ill-treatment.

marval *n* marble.

marvel *v* to marvel at.

mary, marie *n* **1** a maid of honour. **2** a female attendant.

Mary-knot, St *n* a triple knot.

Marymas *n* 8 September, the festival of St Mary.

Mary's knot, St *n in phr* **tie with St Mary's knot** to hamstring.

Mary-sole *n* the smear or dab.

maschle, mashle *n* **1** a mixture. **2** a mess. **3** a state of confusion.—*v* **1** to reduce to a confused mass. **2** (*with* **up**) to be closely related by marriage and blood.

mash[1] *n* **1** a mess. **2** a soft, pulpy mass.

mash[2] *n* a mason's large hammer.—*v* to crush stones.

mash-fat *n* a large tub for mashing malt in brewing.

mash hammer *n* a mason's large hammer.

mashie *n* a particular kind of golf club.

mashlach, mashlich *same as* **mashloch**.

mashlam *same as* **mashlum**.

mashlie *n* **1** mixed grain, peas and oats. **2** the broken parts of a moss.

mashlie-moss *n* a moss that is much broken up.

mashlin *adj* **1** mixed. **2** blended carelessly or coarsely.—*n* mixed grain.

mashloch, mashlock *n* **1** a coarse kind of bread. **2** mixed peas and oats.—*adj* **1** mingled, blended. **2** promiscuous.

mashlum *n* **1** mixed grain. **2** the flour or meal of different kinds of grain. **3** a mixture of edibles. —*adj* **1** mixed. **2** made from different kinds of grain.

mashman *n* one who has charge of the mashing of malt at a brewery.

mashpot *n* a teapot.

mash-rubber *n* a mashpot (qv).

mask[1] *n* **1** a mesh of a net. **2** a crib for catching fish.—*v* to catch fish in a net.

mask[2] *n* **1** a quantity. **2** a mass.

mask[3] *v* **1** to infuse tea, malt, etc. **2** (*used of a storm*) to be brewing. **3** to be in a state of infusion or preparation.—*n* a mash for a horse.

maskert *n* the marsh betony.

masking *n* a sufficient quantity of tea, etc, for an infusion.

masking fat *n* a large tub for mashing malt in brewing.

masking loom *n* a brewing utensil.

masking pat *n* a teapot.

masking rung *n* a rod for stirring mash in the mash tub.

maskis *n* a mastiff.

mask rudder *n* an instrument for stirring the mash in the vat.

masle *n* mixed grain.

maslin *same as* **mashlum**.

mason due *n* a hospital. *See* **maison dieu**.

mason word *n* a masonic password.

mass[1] *n* a title prefixed to the Christian name of a minister of religion.—*int* used in exclamations and in oaths.

mass[2] *n* **1** pride, haughtiness. **2** self-conceit.

mass and meat *n* prayers and food.

masser *same as* **macer**.

mass-John *n* a minister of religion.

massy *adj* **1** self-important. **2** conceited. **3** boastful.

master[1] *n* **1** a landlord, laird. **2** a schoolmaster. **3** a baron's or viscount's eldest son.

master[2] *same as* **maister**[2].

masterdom *n* mastery.

masterful *adj* **1** great in size. **2** powerful. **3** violent, forcible.

master-graith *n* the chain fastening the harrow to the swingletree.

masterman *n* **1** an employer. **2** an overlooker.

master of mortifications *n* the member of a town council who has charge of funds mortified or bequeathed to the town.

master pen *n* a bird's chief feather.

mastertree *n* the swingletree nearest the plough, etc.

master wood *n* the principal beams in the roof of a house.

masterwork *n* work on the home farm exacted from the neighbouring tenants of small holdings.

masthead *n* the extreme, the utmost limit, the very end.

mastin *n* a mastiff.

mat[1] *n* a woollen bedcoverlet.

mat[2] *v* may.

ma't *n* malt.

matash *n* a moustache.

match *v* to marry, mate.

match paper *n* brown paper soaked in a solution of saltpetre and used with flint and steel for lighting pipes, etc.

matchstick *n* a splint of wood tipped with sulphur for kindling.

mated-out *adj* exhausted with fatigue.

mat grass *n* the wire-bent.

mather *same as* **madder**.

mathy *adj* warm and misty

matie, mattie *n* **1** an immature herring. **2** a fat herring.

matrimonial *n* an affair of marriage.

matter *n* a quantity or variety of food.

mattle *v* to nibble.

matty *adj* matted.

mauch[1] *same as* **mawk**.

mauch[2] *same as* **maught**.

mauch³ *same as* moch³.
mauchless *same as* maughtless.
maucht *adj* 1 tired, worn-out. 2 puzzled, baffled. 3 out of heart.
maucht *same as* maught.
mauchy *same as* mochie².
maud¹ *n* a shepherd's plaid.
maud² *same as* mad².
maudin-plaid *n* a shepherd's plaid.
maudlin-hood *n* a woollen hood.
maughsome *adj* loathsome.
maught *n* 1 strength, ability. 2 an effort. 3 marrow.
maughtless *adj* feeble, impotent.
maughtlessly *adv* feebly.
maughtly *adv* mightily, strongly.
maughty *adj* 1 mighty. 2 powerful.
maugre¹ *n* 1 ill-will. 2 spite. 3 vexation. 4 blame. 5 injury.
maugre² *n* to overpower in spite of.
maugres o' *adv* in spite of.
mauk *same as* mawk.
maukie *adj* full of maggots.
maukin *same as* mawkin.
maukiness *n* the state of being maukie (qv).
maukin-mad *adj* mad as a hare.
maukrel *n* a mackerel.
maul *n* a female paramour.
maulifuff *n* 1 a young woman without energy. 2 one who fusses to little effect.
mauly *n* a maulifuff (qv).
maum *same as* malm.
maument *n* a moment.
maumie *same as* malmy.
maumieness *n* mellowness.
maun¹ *v* 1 must. 2 to order imperiously.
maun² *v* 1 to manage. 2 to accomplish by energy or by any means.
maun³ *adv* (*used as a superlative*) very.
maun⁴ *same as* maund².
mauna *v neg* must not.
maun-be *n* a necessary act or result.
maund¹ *v* to beg.
maund² *same as* mand.
maunder¹ *n* a beggar.
maunder² *n* 1 a gossip. 2 a babbler.—*v* 1 to talk idly, incoherently, foolishly. 2 to sound indistinctly as an echo.
maundrel *n* 1 a gossip, a babbler. 2 (*in pl*) idle tales. 3 foolish, fevered fancies.—*v* to babble.
maund-wecht *n* a winnowing sieve of untanned sheep or calfskin stretched on a wooden hoop.
mauner *v* to maunder (qv).
mauning *adj* imperious.
maunna *v neg* must not.
maunnering *n* incoherent talk.
maunt *same as* mant.
mausie *same as* mawsie.
maussie *same as* mawse².
mauzie *same as* mawse.
maut *n* malt.
maut bree *n* malt liquor.
mauten¹ *v* 1 (*used of bread*) to become tough and heavy. 2 (*of grain*) to sprout when being steeped.
mauten², mautent *adj* 1 (*used of grain*) having a peculiar taste because not properly dried. 2 (*of bread*) not properly baked, moist. 3 dull, sluggish.
mauten'd-loll, ~-lump *n* a heavy, sluggish person.
mautit *adj* malted.
maut-kiln *n* a malt kiln.
mautman *n* a maltster.
maut-ailler *n* money for malt.
mauvering *n* threatening language or demeanour.
mauvie *n* 1 the maw of a fish. 2 the stomach of any small animal. 3 a rennet bag.
maverish *same as* malverish.
mavie *n* the slightest noise. *See* meevie.

mavis, mavie, mavish *n* the song thrush.
mavis-skate *n* the sharp-nosed ray.
maw¹ *v* (*used of a cat*) to mew.
maw² *n* the human mouth.
maw³ *v* to mow.—*n* a single sweep of the scythe.
maw⁴ *n* the common gull.
maw⁵ *n* an atom, whit.
maw⁶ *n* a word fo mother.
maw bag *n* an animal's stomach.
mawch¹ *same as* mawk.
mawch² *same as* maught.
mawd *same as* maud¹.
mawer *n* a mower.
mawin *n* the quantity mowed in a day.
mawk *n* 1 a maggot. 2 the larva of the bluebottle fly.—*v* to be infested with maggots.
mawkin *n* 1 a half-grown girl. 2 a girl engaged to do light housework. 3 a hare.
mawkiness *n* the state of being infested with maggots.
mawkin-fly *n* the bluebottle fly.
mawkin-hippit *adj* having thin hips like a hare.
mawkin-mad *adj* mad as a March hare.
mawkit *adj* 1 infested with maggots. 2 very dirty, filthy.
mawkworm *n* a maggot.
mawky *adj* full of maggots.
mawm *same as* malm.
mawment *n* an image, effigy.
mawn *same as* maund².
mawner *same as* manner.
mawp *v* 1 to mope. 2 to wander about thoughtfully or listlessly.
maws *n* the mallow.
mawse¹ *same as* mows.
mawse² *adj* 1 quiet. 2 wary.
mawsie *adj* 1 stout, strapping, sonsie (qv). 2 thick, strong.—*n* 1 a stout woman. 2 a stupid, slovenly woman. 3 a drab, a trollop. 4 a poor-sounding fiddle. 5 a piece of thick, strong, warm dress material. 6 a knitted semmit (qv) worn over the shirt by old men.
mawster *n* a mower.
mawten *same as* mauten¹.
maxie *n* a maximus, or the gravest, error in a Latin version.
may *n* a maid, maiden.
may *same as* mae².
maybe, maybes *adv* perhaps, possibly.—*n* a possibility.
Maybird *n* 1 the whimbrel. 2 a person born in May.
May-gobs *n* cold weather about the second week of May.
May-gosling *n* a fool made on May Day, as on 1 April.
mayock-fluke *n* the flounder.
may-puddock *n* a young frog.
may-shell *n* the bone of a cuttlefish.
may- skate *same as* mavis-skate.
may-spink *n* the primrose.
maze¹ *same as* maise¹.
maze² *v* 1 to wonder. 2 to be amazed.
mazerment *n* 1 bewilderment. 2 confusion.
mazie *same as* maizie¹.
mazing *adv* amazingly.
meace *n* 1 a meal, dinner. 2 mess.
mead *same as* meid¹.
meadow *n* boggy land producing coarse grass.
meadow-hay *n* the hay produced on boggy land.
meadow-kerses *n* the cuckooflower.
meadow-queen *n* the meadowsweet, spiraea.
meadow-rocket *n* the marsh orchis.
meagries *n* 1 miseries. 2 ills.
meagrim *n* 1 a whim, fancy. 2 an absurd notion. 3 a caprice.
meal¹ *same as* meel².
meal² *n* oatmeal.—*v* (*used of grain*) to produce meal.
meal³ *n* 1 food. 2 the quantity of milk given by a cow or herd at one milking.—*v* 1 to feed. 2 to have meals.

meal[4] *n* **1** rent. **2** payment of dues on land let. **3** a contribution levied.

meal-a-forren *n* a meal of meat over and above what is consumed.

meal-and-ale *n* a mixture of oatmeal, ale, sugar and whisky, prepared when all the grain crop is cut.

meal-and-bree *n* brose (qv).

meal-and-bree-nicht *n* Hallowe'en.

meal-and-kail *n* oatmeal and mashed kail (qv).

meal-and-thrammel *n* a little meal in the mouth of a sack at a mill, having some water or ale poured in and stirred about.

meal ark *n* a large meal chest.

meal bowie *n* a meal barrel.

meal cog *n* a small wooden vessel for holding meal.

mealer *same as* **maelyer**.

meal-free *adj* rent-free.

meal-girnel *n* a meal ark (qv).

meal-hogyett *n* a barrel for holding oatmeal.

mealie *n* a mob. **2** a melee.

mealin *n* **1** a meal ark (qv). **2** oatcake or barley scones soaked in milk. **3** (*in pl*) meal for dusting over bannocks before baking them.—*v* to dust or sprinkle with meal.

mealing *n* **1** a farm. **2** a holding. **3** rent of a farm.

meal in wi' *v* **1** to share with. **2** to make friends with. **3** to mingle with.

me-alive *int* **1** an exclamation of surprise. **2** a mild oath.

meal-kail *same as* **meal-and-kail**.

meal kist *n* a meal chest.

meal kit *n* a kit for holding meal.

mealler *n* **1** a cottager who, rent-free for so many years, improves waste land. **2** a farmer paymg rent.

meal-maker *n* a miller.

mealmonger *n* a meal-seller.

meal-mou'd *adj* **1** soft-spoken. **2** plausible. **3** afraid to speak out.

mealock, meallock *n* a crumb of oatcake, etc.

mealom *n* a very mealy potato.

meal o' meat *n* **1** a meal. **2** victuals.

meal pock *n* **1** a meal bag. **2** a beggar's wallet for holding meal.

meal's corn *n* **1** any species of grain. **2** any food made of corn.

meal seeds, ~-sids *n* the husks of oats sifted out of the meal.

meal-shells, ~-shillings *n* mill seeds (qv).

meal's meat *n* food for one meal.

mealstand *n* a ploughman's barrel for holding his oatmeal.

mealstane *n* a rough stone weighing generally about 17 lb, formerly used in weighing oatmeal.

mealtith *n* **1** a meal. **2** the quantity of milk given by a cow or herd at one milking.

meal-wind *v* to rub a cake or bannock over with meal before putting it on the girdle (qv) and again after it is first turned.

mealy *adj* **1** dusty with meal. **2** stained with meal.

mealy bag *n* a beggar's wallet for holding meal.

mealy-mou'd *adj* **1** afraid to speak out. **2** plausible. **3** soft-spoken.

mean[1] *n* **1** a means, instrumentality. **2** means, property.

mean[2] *adj* **1** held in common or equal shares. **2** in bad health or condition.

mean[3] *same as* **maen**.

mean-born *adj* of lowly birth.

meaner *n* **1** an arbiter who adjusts in equal portions land held in common by various tenants. **2** (*in pl*) common lands.

meantime *n in phr* **in the middle of meantime** meanwhile.

mear *n* a mare.

mearen *n* a strip of uncultivated ground of various breadth between two corn ridges.

mease *v* **1** to soothe, assuage, calm. **2** to settle. **3** to soften, mellow fruit,.

measie *same as* **maizie**[1].

measle *v* **1** to have the legs spotted by sitting too near a fire. **2** to speckle, blotch, mottle.

measly *same as* **maeslie**.

measly-shankit *same as* **maeslie-shankit**.

measure *n* moderation.

measurely *adv* in moderation, moderately.

meat *n* **1** victuals. **2** board. **3** food. **4** food for animals. **5** flesh.—*v* **1** to feed. **2** to board. **3** to fill out the corn for a horse.

meat-hale, ~-haill *adj* having a good, healthy appetite.

meathie *same as* **meethe**.

meaths *n* maggots. *See* **maith**.

meaties *n* food for infants.

meat-like *adj* like one well-fed.

meat loom *n* a vessel in which food is cooked or served.

meat-mither *n* **1** the mistress of a house. **2** one who serves out food.

meat-rife *adj* abounding in meat.

meat-wedder *n* a wedder ready for the butcher.

meat-year *n* the season for crops, etc.

meazie *same as* **maizie**[1].

meazle *same as* **measle**.

meble *adj* movable.

meckant *adj* romping, frolicsome.

med *v* must.

meddem *n* a tickling in the nose, portending the arrival of a visitor.

medding *n* a dung heap.

meddle *v* **1** to meddle with. **2** to hurt. **3** to assault. **4** to annoy. **5** to have to do with.

medicamenting *n* medical attendance.

medicine *n* anything nauseous, bitter or disagreeable.

mediciner *n* a doctor, physician.

meduart *n* meadowsweet.

meed[1] *same as* **meid**[1].

meed[2], **meedge** *same as* **meethe**.

meef *same as* **meeth**[1].

meek-tasted *adj* sweet or mild of taste.

meel[1] *n* oatmeal.

meel[2] *same as* **mool**[3].

meelack *same as* **mealock**.

meelick *n* the same spot where the pitcher spins in striking a marble.

meen[1] *n* the moon.

meen[2] *same as* **maen**.

meen[3] *same as* **mean**[2].

meener *same as* **meaner**.

meenint, meenont *n* a minute.

meenit *same as* **meenint**.

meenlicht *n* moonlight.

meenlichty flitting *n* a moonlight flitting (qv) by a tenant unable to pay his rent.

meer *n* a mare.

meeran *same as* **mirran**.

meer-browed *adj* having the eyebrows meeting so as to cover the bridge of the nose.

meerie *n* a young or little mare.

meer-swine *same as* **mere-swine**.

mees *same as* **mease**.

meeschle *same as* **maschle**.

meeschle-maschle *n* **1** great confusion. **2** a confused mass.—*adj* **1** confused. **2** much intermarried.

meese *n* locating a spot at sea by observing certain landmarks.

meesery *n* misery.

meesh-mash *same as* **mish-mash**.

meet[1] *adj* **1** exact, exactly corresponding to. **2** close-fitting.

meet[2] *v* (*with* **in with**) to meet with.

meet-bodied coat *n* a meet-coat (qv).

meet-coat *n* a coat exactly fitting the body, as distinguished from a greatcoat.

meeten *v, adj* measured, meted.

meeth[1] *adj* **1** hot, sultry, close. **2** exhausted with heat.
meeth[2] *adj* **1** modest. **2** mild. **3** gentle.
meeth[3] *same as* **meethe**.
meethe, meeth *n* **1** a measure. **2** a mark. **3** a landmark for vessels at sea. **4** a mark by which observations are made or an object is detected. **5** a hint, innuendo.—*v* to mark a place at sea by the bearings of landmarks.
meethness *n* **1** sultriness. **2** extreme heat.
meeths *n* bodily activity, alertness.
meet-marrow *n* **1** a facsimile. **2** a fellow, companion.
meeve *v* to move.
meevie *n* the slightest noise.—*phr* **neither meevie nor mavie** not the slightest sound. *See* **mavie**.
meexter-maxter *same as* **mixie-maxie**.
meezle *same as* **measle**.
meg *n* **1** a woman. **2** a country girl.
Meg-cut-throat *n* the whitethroat.
Meg Dorts *n* a sulky, pettish woman or girl.
meggification *n* **1** an exaggeration. **2** an untruth.
meggy-mony-feet *n* the centipede.
megh *n* the big toe.
megirkie *n* the woollen cloth worn by old men in winter to protect head and throat.
megirtie *n* a kind of cravat, held by two clasps.
megisty *same as* **megsty**.
meg-mony-feet, meg-o'-mony-feet *n* the centipede.
megrim, megram *n* **1** a whim. **2** a foolish fancy.
megsty, megsty me *int* an exclamation of surprise.
meg-wi'-the-mony-feet *n* **1** the centipede. **2** the crab. **3** the lobster.
meid[1] *n* **1** appearance. **2** bearing, courage. **3** mood, disposition.
meid[2] *same as* **meethe**.
meid[3] *n* a reward, recompense.
meigh *same as* **meeth**[1].
meikle *same as* **mickle**.
meikledom *n* size.
mein[1] *same as* **mean**[2].
mein[2] *n* an attempt.
mein[3] *same as* **maen**.
meing *v* **1** to mingle, blend, mix. **2** (*of corn*) to become mixed in colour.
meinging *n* the act of mixing.
meingyie[1] *v* (*of grain*) to begin to change colour.
meingyie[2] *v* **1** to hurt. **2** to lame.
meingyie[3], **meinzie** *same as* **menyie**.
meir *n* a mare.
meirdel *n* **1** a confused crowd of persons or animals. **2** a large family of little children. **3** a huddled mass of small insects.
meirie *n* a young mare.
meise[1], **meis** *same as* **mease**.
meise[2] *same as* **maise**[3].
meishachan *n* a subscription dance.
meisle, meissle *v* **1** to waste imperceptibly. **2** to crumble down in eating. **3** to expend on trifles. **4** to eat little and slowly.—*n* a small piece.
meislen, meisslen *v* **1** to waste away by degrees. **2** to eat little and slowly.—*n* a very small piece.
meit *n* meat.
meith[1] *same as* **meeth**[1].
meith[2] *same as* **meethe**.
meith[3] *v* might.
mekil, mekle *same as* **mickle**.
mekildom *n* largeness of size.
mekilwort *n* the deadly nightshade.
mel *n* meal, ground grain.
melancholious *adj* **1** melancholy. **2** sombre. **3** bilious.
melancholy *n* **1** lovesickness. **2** mischief.
melder *n* **1** the quantity of oats ground at one time. **2** (*with dusty*) the last milling of the crop of oats. **3** the last child born in a family.
meldren *n* a melder (qv).
meldrop *n* **1** the foam that falls from a horse's mouth or

the drop at the bit. **2** the drop at the end of an icicle. **3** any drop in a pendent state, as a drop at the nose.
meldweed *n* the white goosefoot.
melg *n* the milt of fish.
melgraf, mellgrave *n* **1** a quagmire, quicksand. **2** a break in a highway.
meliorat *v* to improve.
mell[1] *n* **1** a mallet. **2** a beetle. **3** a large wooden hammer. **4** a big, heavy fist. **5** the prize given to the last in a race or contest. **6** a blow with a mallet. **7** a heavy blow with any weapon. **8** a big, strong, stupid person.—*phr* **mell for mell** blow for blow.—*v* **1** to hammer. **2** to beat with a mell.
mell[2] *v* **1** to feed. **2** to have meals.
mell[3] *v* **1** to mix. **2** to be intimate. **3** to meddle, interfere. **4** to join battle. **5** to match, equal.—*n* a company.
mell[4] *adj* mellow.
mell[5] *v* (*used of corn in the straw*) to become damp.
meller *same as* **melder**.
mellering *n* **1** waste meal. **2** the refuse meal gathered after grinding the sweepings of a meal mill.
mellin *same as* **mealin**.
melling *n* a mixture.
mellison *n* a curse, malison.
mellow *adj* **1** genial by drink. **2** ripe, ready.
mellowish *adj* slightly intoxicated.
mells *n* *in phr* **gree like butter and mells** not to agree well.
mellsman *n* **1** a stonemason. **2** one who can wield a mell. *See* **mell**[1].
melly *adj* **1** mellow. **2** pleasant, tender.
melmont-berry *n* the juniper berry.
melodious *adj* used as an intensive adj.
melt[1] *v* **1** to be almost overcome with heat. **2** (*used of money*) to spend in drink.
melt[2] *n* the milt of a fish.
melt[3] *v* **1** to knock down by a stroke on the side. **2** to bruise, knock.
melt[4] *n* the male fish.
melt[5] *n* the spleen.
melt-hole *n* the space between the ribs and the pelvis in human beings and in animals.
meltie-bow *n* a mystic figure on a herd-boy's club that was supposed to protect the cows from hurt if the club chanced to strike them on the side.
meltin-blow *n* the finishing stroke.
meltith, melteth, meltaith, meltit *same as* **mealtith**.
meltith-buird *n* a table on which meals are served.
meltith-hale *adj* having a good appetite.
melvie *v* to cover or soil with meal.—*adj* soiled with meal.
melvyin *n* a dusting with meal.
melwand *same as* **meal-wind**.
melyie *n* a coin of small value.
mem *n* madam, ma'am.—*v* to call one madam or ma'am.
Memmel *n* timber from Memel.
memorandun *n* a memorial inscription.
memt *adj* connected by, or attached from, blood, alliance or friendship.
men *n* laymen who occupied a prominent place in the religious life of the Highlands.
men' *v* to mend.
menage *same as* **manadge**.
mend *v* **1** to make better. **2** to mend for one. **3** to become convalescent. **4** to reform, improve in character.—*n* **1** a patch, repair. **2** improvement or recovery of health.
mendable *adj* **1** reparable. **2** capable of amendment.
mendiment *n* amendment.
mends *n* **1** amends, compensation. **2** revenge. **3** amendment. **4** improvement.—*phr* **to the mends** over and above.
mene[1] *same as* **maen**.
mene[2] *n* an attempt.
mene[3] *same as* **mean**[2].
menfolk, ~fowk *n* males, men.

meng *same as* **meing**.
menge *v* to soothe.
mengie, mengyie, menji *same as* **menyie**.
meniment *same as* **mendiment**.
mennent, mennon, menon *n* a minnow.
mens, mense *n* amends.
mensal kirk *n* a church appropriated by the patron to the bishop and made thenceforth a part of his own benefice.
mense *n* **1** honour, respect, reverence. **2** a great deal. **3** recompense. **4** thanks. **5** decency, propriety. **6** discretion. **7** good manners. **8** a credit. **9** an ornament.—*v* **1** to adorn. **2** to do credit or honour to. **3** to make up for. **4** to become.—*phr* **mense a board** to preside at table.
menseful *adj* **1** becoming. **2** seemly. **3** discreet. **4** creditable, respectable. **5** courteous, respectful, mannerly. **6** hospitable, liberal. **7** clean, neat.
mensefullie *adv* **1** with propriety. **2** becomingly.
menseless *adj* **1** unmannerly, ill-bred. **2** uncultured. **3** greedy. **4** selfish. **5** immoderate in price. **6** incalculable.
men's house *n* a farm bothie (qv) where menservants cook their own food.
menstril *n* a minstrel.
mensworn *same as* mansworn.
ment[1] *v* **1** to pretend or threaten to strike. **2** to attempt ineffectually. **3** to attempt. **4** to aim at. **5** to venture, dare. **6** to intend, purpose. **7** to hint, insinuate. **8** to feign. *n* —**1** an aim. **2** an attempt. **3** a threat. **4** a blow. **5** a stroke. **6** an insinuation, hint. **7** a feint.
ment[2] *v, adj* mended.
ment[3] *n* mental capacity.
mentals *n* wits.
mention *n* **1** a trifle. **2** a little bit of anything.
mentith *same as* **mealtith**.
mento *same as* **mainto**.
meny *same as* **maenn**.
menyie, menze, menzie *n* **1** a household, family. **2** a train of followers, a company of retainers. **3** a crowd of persons. **4** a multitude of things.—*v* **1** to crowd. **2** to mix confusedly.
menzie *same as* **menyie**.
meow *v* to mew.—*n* a cat's mew.
mercat *n* a market.
mercatable *adj* marketable.
mercatorian *adj* commercial.
merch[1] *n* **1** a march. **2** a boundary.
merch[2] *n* **1** marrow. **2** pith, strength.
merchandise *v* to trade as a merchant.
merchandising *n* **1** shopping. **2** retailing, shopkeeping.
merchant, merchan' *n* **1** a shopkeeper, a retailer. **2** a buyer, customer. **3** shopping.
merchiness *n* the state of being marrowy.
merchless *adj* **1** without marrow. **2** pithless.
merchy *adj* **1** marrowy. **2** full of marrow.
merciful *adj* **1** (*used of the weather*) favourable, seasonable, mild. **2** lucky, fortunate.
merciment *n* **1** mercy. **2** discretion. **3** disposal.
mercury-docken *n* the smear-docker (qv), the good King Henry.
mercury-leaf *n* the plant, dog's mercury.
mercy *int* used in exclamation of surprise.—*n* (*in pl*) whisky, etc.
merdal *same as* **mardel**.
merdle *same as* **meirdel**.
mere *n* **1** a small pool caused by moisture of the soil. **2** a pool easily dried by the heat.
mere-swine *n* **1** the dolphin. **2** the porpoise.
mergh *same as* **merch**[2].
merghless *adj* without marrow, pithless.
mergie me *int* an exclamation of surprise.
mergin *adj* **1** largest. **2** most numerous.
mergle *v* **1** to wonder. **2** to express surprise.
meridian *n* a midday drink of liquor.
merk[1] *same as* **mark**[1].
merk[2] *same as* **mirk**.

merkerin *n* the spinal marrow.
merl *v* **1** to candy. **2** to become sweet and gritty.
merlady *n* a mermaid.
merle *n* the blackbird.
merled *adj* **1** variegated. **2** mottled. *See* **marl**[1].
merlie *adj* candied.
merligo *same as* **mirligo**.
merlin *n* a mermaid.
merlins *int* an exclamation of surprise.
mermaid *n* the frogfish.
mermaid's-glove *n* a kind of sponge.
mermaid's purse *n* the egg case of fishes whose skeleton is cartilaginous.
merridge *n* a marriage.
merrigle *n* **1** a miracle. **2** a ridiculous spectacle. **3** a mischievous boy.—*adj* mischievous.
merrily-go *same as* **mirligo**.
merriment *n* a source of merriment.
merry *v* to marry.
merry-begotten *adj* illegitimate.—*n* an illegitimate child.
merry-dance *n* the aurora borealis.
merry-dancers *n* **1** the aurora borealis. **2** vapours rising from the earth on a warm day and seen flickering in the atmosphere.
merry-hyne *n* **1** a disgraceful dismissal. **2** a good riddance.
merry-man *n* **1** a merry-andrew, a clown. **2** a chieftain's retainer.
merry-matanzie *n* **1** an expression in the girls' singing game of jingo-ring. **2** a children's singing game.
merry-meat *n* a feast at the birth of the first child.
merry-meetings *n* New-Year's Day merrymaking.
merry-night *n* a festive entertainment.
merry-pin *n* an excited or merry mood.
merse *n* **1** a fertile spot of ground between hills. **2** alluvial land beside a river. **3** ground gained from the sea, converted into moss.
mert *same as* **mart**.
merter *same as* **martyr**.
Mertimes *n* Martinmas.
mert-maill *n* rent due at Martinmas.
mertyreese *same as* **martyreese**.
mervadie *adj* (*used of cake*) sweet and brittle.
merve *same as* **mervy**.
mervel *v* to marvel.
mervil *adj* **1** nervous, trembling. **2** inactive in mind or body.
mervy *adj* **1** (*used of fruit*) rich, mellow. **2** savoury.
mes, mess *same as* **mass**[1].
meschant *adj* **1** wicked. **2** mischievous. **3** worthless.—*n* a worthless person.
mese *same as* **mease**.
mesh *n* a net for carrying fish.
meshie *n* a basket made of straw rope.
meslin *same as* **mashlum**.
mess[1] *n* a meal.—*v in phr* **mess and mell 1** to have familiar intercourse. **2** to mingle at one mess.
mess[2] *n* **1** a muddle. **2** a scrape, plight.
messages *n* **1** shopping, groceries. **2** *in phr* **go the messages** to shop for ordinary household goods.
messan, messin, messen, messon *n* **1** a small dog. **2** a small, insignificant person.
mesan dew *n* a hospital. *See* **maison dieu**.
messanter *same as* **mishanter**.
messenger, meseenger-at-arms *n* a sheriff's officer.
mess-John *n* a minister.
mess-priest *n* a Roman Catholic priest.
mester *same as* **maister**[2].
met[1] *v* may.
met[2] *same as* **mett**.
metal *v* to make or repair a road with broken stones.
meter *n* a person legally authorized to measure.
meth *same as* **meethe**.
methe *same as* **maith**.
methody *n* a methodist.
metster *n* a person legally authorized to measure.

met stick *n* a piece of wood for measuring the foot.
mett *n* **1** a measure of herring, of coals, etc. **2** a boundary, a boundary stone.—*v* to measure.
mettage *n* measurement.
mettle *adj* **1** capable of enduring great fatigue. **2** spirited.
met-wand *n* a measuring-rod.
meugle *v* to dabble in mud.
meul *same as* **mewl**.
mevies *same as* **mavis**.
mew[1] *n* a son-in-law.
mew[2] *n* an enclosure.
mewl *v* **1** to cry, whine. **2** to mew like a cat.
mewt *v* to mew as a cat.
mewtle *v* (*used of cows and ewes*) to cry.
mey *same as* **mae**[2].
meycock *n* the maycock, the grey plover.
meyse *same as* **mease**.
meysel, meyzle *same as* **meisle**.
meyseln *same as* **meislen**.
miauve *v* to mew as a cat.—*n* a cat's mew.
micel *same as* **meisle**.
michael *n* a term applied to a girl.
Michaelmas-moon *n* **1** the harvest moon. **2** the produce of a raid at this season, as constituting the portion of a daughter.
michen *n* the common spignel.
micht *n* might.—*v* might.
micht-be-better *adj* showing some signs of improvement.
michty *adj* **1** mighty. **2** stately. **3** haughty. **4** strange, surprising. **5** (*used of liquor*) strong.—*adv* very, exceedingly.
michty me *int* an exclamation of surprise.
mickle *adj* **1** great, big. **2** much. **3** abundant. **4** grown-up. **5** eminent, important. **6** proud, haughty.—*adv* **1** much, greatly. **2** very.—*n* a large amount, a great deal.
mickle bag *n* the stomach.
mickle-bookit *adj* **1** full-bodied. **2** great with child. **3** bulky.
mickle chair *n* a large armchair.
mickle-cheild *n* the devil.
mickle-coat *n* a greatcoat.
mickle-deil *n* the devil.
mickledom *n* size, bulk.
mickle-Friday *n* the Friday on which a large fair is held.
mickle-hell *n* hell itself.
mickle-horned *adj* having large horns.
mickle-man *n* **1** a head farm servant. **2** a man of means.
mickle-maun *adj* very big, very fine.
mickle-mou'd *adj* having a large mouth.
mickle-neived *adj* large-fisted.
mickleness *n* size, bulk.
mickle-preen *n* a large pin for fastening shawls.
mickle-rin wheel *n* the large wheel of a spinning wheel.
mickle-Sunday *n* a communion Sunday.
mickle-tochered *adj* largely dowered.
mickle-toe, ~-tee *n* the big toe.
mickle wame *n* **1** a big belly. **2** the stomach of a cow.
mickle wheel *n* the large wheel of a spinning wheel.
mickle-worth *n* **1** great value. **2** great reputation.
mickly *adv* greatly, much.
mid-aged *adj* middle-aged.
mid-couple *n* the swipple of a flail.
midden *n* **1** a dunghill. **2** a refuse heap, a tip. **3** a dirty, slovenly women. **4** a dirty, untidy place.
midden cock *n* **1** a dunghill cock. **2** the principal cock in the poultry yard.
midden creel *n* a basket for manure, etc.
midden-croon *n* the top of a dunghill.
midden dub *n* a dunghill pool.
midden-dung *n* dung from a dunghill.
midden-dyke *n* the wall of a dunghill.
midden-feil *n* turf mixed with manure to form a dung heap.
midden head *n* the top of a dunghill.—*phr* **to be heard on the midden head** to quarrel openly.
midden-heap *n* a dunghill.
midden-hen *n* a common barn-door hen.

midden-hole *n* **1** a dunghill. **2** a dunghill puddle.
midden-lairach *n* the site of a dunghill.
midden-makin' *n* the making of a dunghill.
midden-mavis *n* a raker of dustbins, dung heaps, etc.
midden monarch *n* a cock.
midden-mount *n* a rampart or mound made of dung, rubbish, etc.
midden-mylies *n* **1** the goosefoot. **2** the wild spinach.
midden-peel *n* a dunghill pool.
midden-scarter *n* a hen.
midden-stead *n* the site of a dunghill.
midden-tap *n* the top of a dunghill.
midder *n* a mother.
middle[1] *n* the waist.
middle[2] *v* to meddle.
middled, midled *adj* (*used of sheep*) earmarked by a bit cut out of the middle of the ear.—*n* a sheep-mark so made.
middle-erd *n* **1** the earth, the world. **2** the nether regions.
middlemaist *adj* nearest the middle.
middlin *adj* **1** tolerable. **2** mediocre, fair, indifferent, not very well.—*adv* moderately, tolerably.
middlinly *adv* **1** not perfectly. **2** moderately.
middlins *adv* moderately.
middrit *n* **1** the midriff. **2** (*in pl*) the heart and skirts of a bullock.
midge *n* **1** a mosquito. **2** a very diminutive person. —*v* to move slightly.
midge-merchant *n* a petty trader or shopkeeper.
mid-grund *n* a fishing ground in a middle position.
midgy *n* a midge.
mid-house *adv* halfway.
midlen *same as* **middlin**.
midlert *same as* **middle-erd**.
mid-man *n* a mediator.
mid-noon *n* noon.
midperson *n* a middleman between two others.
midplace *n* **1** a middle room between a but (qv) and a ben (qv) in a three-roomed house. **2** a bedcloset.
midroom *n* **1** a midplace (qv). **2** the middle compartment in a boat.
mids, midse *n* **1** the midst, middle. **2** a medium. **3** a middle course. **4** the open furrow between two ridges. **5** (*in pl*) means, ways, methods.—*v* **1** to strike a medium. **2** to come to an agreement.
mids-day *n* midday.
mid-seas *adj* half-tipsy.
mids-man *same as* **midman**.
midstick *n* the middle stick of a kite, etc.
midtime o' day *n* midday.
midwart *adv* towards the middle.
mid-water *n* the middle of a stream, lake or sea.
midwife-gallop *n* **1** full gallop. **2** a great speed.
mields *n* the dust of the grave.
miff *n* a slight quarrel.—*v* to offend.
mights *n* means, help.
mighty *same as* **michty**.
milcie *same as* **milk-sye**.
milcie wall *same as* **milsie wall**.
mildrop *same as* **meldrop**.
milds *n* the goosefoot.
mile[1] *n* the wild celery.
mile[2] *n* millet.
milens *n* crumbs.
miles[1] *n* **1** wild spinach. **2** the goosefoot.
miles[2] *n* small insects in the diseased entrails of sheep.
militate *v* **1** to take effect. **2** to operate without opposition.
milk *n* **1** an annual school holiday on which the scholars presented their teacher with a small offering, of which milk originally formed the chief part. **2** the semiliquid of the ear of corn before it hardens.—*v* **1** (*used of a cow*) to yield milk. **2** to steal, pilfer. **3** to rook.—*adj* milch.
milk and meal *n* **1** milk porridge. **2** milk brose (qv).
milk-ass *n* an ass giving milk.
milk-bowie *n* a milk pail.

milk-boyne *n* a milk tub.
milk-brose *n* a dish of milk and raw oatmeal.
milk broth *n* broth made of milk and barley.
milk cattle *n* milch cows.
milk cow *n* a milch cow.
milk cum, --kim *n* a milk tub.
milker *n* a cow that gives milk.
milk-gowan *n* a yellow flower, the dandelion.
milk-herrie *n* the loss of milk, or of profit of milk, through witchcraft.
milk house *n* **1** the dairy. **2** the house or room where milk is stored.
milking-kye *n* milch cows.
milking-loan *n* the milking park.
milking shiel *n* a milking shed.
milking-slap *n* the entrance to the milkingfield.
milk keg *n* a milk tub.
milk kye *n* milch cows.
milk-lue *adj* lukewarm, of the temperature of milk warm from the cow.
milk-madlocks *n* milk porridge.
milkmaid's path *n* the Milky Way.
milk-may *n* a milkmaid.
milk-meat *n* **1** milk porridge. **2** any food of which milk is an ingredient.
milkness *n* **1** dairy produce. **2** milk. **3** a dairy. **4** dairy work.
milk-ort, --wort *n* the root of the harebell.
milk-potage *n* milk porridge.
milk-saps *n* bread steeped in boiled milk and sweetened.
milk-sieve *n* a milk strainer.
milk-sile *n* a milk strainer.
milk-span *n* a milk pail.
milk-stoup *n* a milk pail.
milk-sye, -syth *n* a milk strainer.
milk-woman *n* a wet nurse.
milky *adj* used of grain when the ear is soft and fills but does not grow white.
mill[1] *n* a snuffbox.—*v* **1** to manufacture. **2** to steal.
mill[2] *n* **1** a boys' fight. **2** a scrimmage.—*v* to beat, drub.
mill bannock *n* a large circular cake of oatmeal, a foot in diameter and one inch thick.
mill-bitch *n* a small bag clandestinely hung up by the miller to receive meal for his own profit.
mill-burn *n* a stream driving a mill.
mill-capon *n* a person begging of those who had corn grinding at a mill.
mill-claise *n* a miller's working clothes.
mill-clap *n* a piece of wood, or clapper, that strikes and shakes the hopper of a mill.
mill-cloose *n* **1** the boxed woodwork that conducts the water into the millwheels. **2** the sluice of a millrace.
milldew *n* **1** cold, raw weather. **2** wet, foggy weather.
mill-dozen *n* every thirteenth peck of grain milled, payable to the owner or laird of the mill.
milled *adj* intoxicated.
mill-e'e *n* the 'eye' or opening in the cases of a mill, through which the meal falls into the bin.
miller[1] *same as* **melder**.
miller[2] *v* to crumble.—*n* (*in pl*) small crumbs.
millering *same as* **mellering**.
miller's-thumb *n* **1** the young of the bib. **2** the river bullhead. **3** the goldcrest.
millert *n* a miller.
millert's lift *n* an upward thrust with a lever.
millfish *n* the turbot.
mill-fud *n* a girl who works in a mill or factory.
mill gruel *n* milk porridge.
mill knave *n* a vessel for measuring mill shillings.
millie *n* a small mill.
millin *n* **1** a crumb of bread. **2** the least bit of solid food. **3** a particle.
mill knave *n* the miller's man who received the knaveship (qv) as his perquisite.
mill lade *n* a millrace or its channel.

mill lichens *n* the entry into the place where the inner millwheel goes.
mill reek *n* the lead distemper to which workers in lead are subject.
mill-ring *n* **1** the open space in a mill between the runner and the wooden frame surrounding it. **2** the meal remaining in the ring or on the millstones, which becomes the miller's perquisite. **4** the dust of a mill.
mill shilling *n* husked grain running from the mill-e'e (qv).
mill-steep *n* a lever fixed to the machinery of corn mills by which the millstones can be adjusted closer or otherwise.
mill-stew *n* the dust of a mill.
mill-swine *n* a miller's swine.
millthromie *n* the fish, hardhead.
mill timmer *n* a thick, round piece of timber, used as a prop in a mill.
mill-trows *n* the sluice of a millrace.
millvader *v* to confuse, bamboozle.
mill-wand *n* a beam or pole used for transporting a millstone from a quarry to the mill.
milne-clap *n* the clapper of a mill.
milne-knave *n* the miller's man who received the knaveship (qv) as his perquisite.
milnhirst *n* the place on which lie the crubs, within which the millstone rubs.
miln't *v, adj* milled.
milord *n* a haggis, as 'chieftain of the pudding race'.
milryn *n* a coin worth £2, 17s. Scots.
milsie *same as* **milk-sye**.
milsie wall *n* **1** a wall with crenated battlements. **2** the wall of a dairy with a sort of window of perforated tin.
milt *v* to melt.
milt-hole *n* the space between the ribs and the pelvis.
milt-token *n* prognosticating weather from cuts in the spleen of an ox killed about Martinmas.
mim *adj* **1** prudish, prim. **2** demure. **3** affecting great moderation in eating or drinking. **4** affecting squeamishness in admitting what cannot be denied. **5** quiet. **6** silent, mute.—*v* **1** to act in a prim, affected manner. **2** to protest affectedly.
mimicate *v* **1** to mimic. **2** to pretend, sham.
mimin *n* affected protesting.
mimlie *adv* primly, affectedly.
mim-mou'd *adj* **1** affectedly proper in speech or action. **2** shy at speaking out, reticent. **3** soft-spoken.
mim-mou'dnees *n* affected modesty in speech.
mimness *n* prudishness.
mimp *v* to speak or act affectedly.—*adj* prim, demure.—*n* **1** affected speech. **2** an affected gait.
mim-spoken *adj* shy at speaking out.
min[1] *n* **1** man. **2** a familiar term of address.
min[2] *v* must.
min' *v* to mind.—*n* mind.
minace *v* to threaten, menace.
minawa *n* a minuet.
mince[1] *v* **1** to dance with short steps. **2** to tone down, lessen, extenuate. **3** to derogate from. **4** to disown.
mince[2] *n* nonsense, rubbish.
minch *v* **1** to cut into very small pieces. **2** to mince. —*n* a crumb.
minch house *n* a small alehouse or inn.
minchick *n* a very small piece.—*v* to cut or break into small pieces.
minchickie *n* a very small piece indeed.
minchmeat *n* mincemeat.
mincing *adj* **1** trivial, trifling. **2** disparaging.
mind[1] *v* **1** to mine. **2** to dig in a mine.—*n* a mine.
mind[2] *n* **1** memory. **2** a reminder. **3** affection.—*v* **1** to remember. **2** to remember in a will. **3** to remind. **4** to notice. **5** to take care of. **6** to have a mind to. **7** to wish.
minding *n* **1** recollection. **2** a very small quantity.
mindless *adj* **1** heedless. **2** forgetful.
mine *n* **1** mien. **2** figure. **3** carriage.

mineerum *n* **1** a stir, fuss, a great ado. **2** an awkward plight, a scrape. *See* **minneer**.

minent *n* a minute.

mines *pron* mine.

ming *same as* **meing**.

ming a mang *v* to mix up together. *See* **mang**.

mingle-mangle *adj* confused, irregular.

ming-mang *n* confusion. *See* **ming a mang**.

mingee, minkee *v* to mingle.

mingin *adj* having an unpleasant smell, stinking

minikin *n* anything very small.—*adj* of the smallest size.

minikin preen *n* the smallest size of pin.

minister[1] *n* a member of the clergy in the Church of Scotland.

minister[2] *n* (*in pl*) small spiral shells found on the seashore.

ministerial *adj* becoming a minister.

minister's-mark *n* **1** a mark on sheep, having both ears cut off.

mink *n* **1** a noose. **2** a ring of straw or rushes, used in adjusting the yoke on an ox.—*v* **1** to tie fast. **2** to halter. **3** with up, to coil a rope in the hand.

minkie *n* a noose. *See* **mink**.

minkster, minxter *n* a mixture.

minna *v neg* **1** may not. **2** must not.

minneer *n* a great noise.—*v* to make a great noise.

minnie[1] *adj* many.

minnie[2] *n* **1** a mother. **2** a pet name for mother. **3** a dam.—*v* **1** to join a lamb to its own mother in a flock. **2** (*used of a lamb*) to run to its own mother.

minnie[3] *n* the cup of remembrance, a toast on Yule Eve formerly in the north.

minnie's bairn *n* mother's pet.

minnie's daut, ~ dawtie *n* mother's pet.

minnie's man *n* a henpecked husband.

minnie's-mouthes *n* those who must be wheedled into any measure by kindness, coaxing, etc.

minnin, minnon *n* the minnow.

minnock *n* the minnow.

minnoyt *adj* (*perhaps*) annoyed.

minowaye *same as* **minawa**.

minsh *same as* **minch**.

minshach *adj* **1** mean, niggardly. **2** inhospitable.

minshoch *n* a two-year-old she-goat.

minstrell *n* a minster.

minswear *same as* **manswear**.

mint[1] *n* peppermint.

mint[2] *n* a very large quantity or sum of money.

mint[3] *v* **1** to insinuate, hint, use innuendo. **2** to feign. **3** to aim at. **4** to attempt. **5** to intend, purpose. **6** to venture, dare.—*n* **1** an aim. **2** an attempt, effort. **3** a threat. **4** a blow, stroke. **5** an insinuation, hint. **6** a feint.

minteen *v* to maintain.

minua *same as* **minawa**.

minum *n* **1** a minim. **2** a musical note, a song.

minute *n* **1** a first draft of a written agreement. **2** (*in pl*) a short interval for play during school hours.—*v* to make short notes or a first draft of a written agreement.

minute time *n* the short interval for play during school-hours.

minxter *same as* **minkster**.

minyar *n* anything untoward.

miogs *n* clumsy hands. *See* **maeg**.

miol *v* to cry or mew like a cat.

miracle, miraikle *n* **1** an object of amazement. **2** a spectacle. **3** a mockery. **4** a mischievous boy. **5** a very large quantity, an amazing amount.—*v* **1** to wonder. **2** to tease.

mirac'lous *adj* **1** very drunk. **2** clumsy, helpless.—*adv* excessively.

mird *v* **1** to meddle. **2** to venture, attempt. **3** to make amorous advances. **4** to toy amorously. **5** to fawn upon, coax.—*n* flattery, coaxing.

mire *n* a bog, swamp.—*v* **1** to bog (qv). **2** to lair (qv). **3** to entangle in a dispute.

mire-bumper *n* the bittern.

mire-duck *n* the wild duck.

mireena *n* merino.

mire-side *n* the edge of a bog.

mire-snipe *n* **1** the snipe. **2** an accident, misfortune. **3** a plight. **4** a person with hard features.

mirk *adj* **1** dark, murky. **2** dusky. **3** obscure.—*n* **1** darkness, gloom. **2** night. **3** obscurity.—*v* to darken, overcast.

mirk dim *adj* dark, gloomy.

mirk-eyed *adj* dark-eyed.

mirkin *n* darkness, nightfall.

mirkins *adv* in the dark.

mirklins *adv* in the dark.

Mirk Monanday *n* Monday 24 March 1652 when the sun was totally eclipsed.

mirkness *n* darkness.

mirk-night *n* **1** midnight. **2** the darkest hour of night.

mirknin *v, adj* darkening, growing dark.—*n* the dusk, twilight.

mirksome *adj* **1** rather dark. **2** somewhat gloomy. **3** dusky.

mirky[1] *adj* dark, gloomy, murky.

mirky[2] *adj* **1** merry, smiling. **2** light-hearted.

mirl[1] *same as* **murle**.

mirl[2], **mirle** *same as* **marl**[1].

mirligo, mirlego, mirlygo *n* **1** a small, upright, fast-revolving spinning wheel. **2** dizziness, vertigo, causing disordered vision. **3** (*in pl*) ridiculous fancies. **4** mad frolicsomeness, the effect of drinking.

mirly *adj* speckled, spotted, variegated.

mirly-breasted *adj* having a speckled breast.

mirran *n* a carrot.

mirrot *n* a carrot.

miregim *n* the angler fish.

mirthsome *adj* mirthful, merry.

misacker *same as* **missaucher**.

misanter *same as* **mishanter**.

misbeet *v* **1** to disarrange. **2** to mismatch.

misbegot, misbegotten *adj* illegitimate.—*n* an illegitimate child.

misbegowk *n* **1** a deception. **2** a disappointment.

misbehadden *adj* **1** (*used of language*) unbecoming. **2** ill-natured. **3** ill-trained. **4** indiscreet. **5** incautious.

misbelief *n* unbelief.

misbeseem *v* **1** to misbecome. **2** not to suit.

miscall, misca' *v* **1** to speak evil of. **2** to scold, vituperate. **3** to call names.

miscaller, misca'er *n* one who mispronounces in reading.

miscarriage *n* **1** a misfortune. **2** misconduct.

miscarry *v* **1** to misbehave. **2** to behave indecently.

mischancy *adj* **1** unlucky. **2** risky, dangerous.

mischant *adj* **1** wicked. **2** mischievous. **3** worthless.

mischanter *n* **1** a misfortune. **2** *in phr* **auld mischanter** the devil. *See* **mishanter**.

mischant-fow *adj* cruel.

mischantlie *adv* wickedly.

mischantness *n* wickedness.

mischant--, mischan-pratt *n* a mischievous trick.

mischief *n* **1** a severe hurt. **2** injury, harm. **3** a mischievous, vexatious person. **4** the devil.

mischieve *v* **1** to injure, hurt. **2** to damage.

mischievin *n* **1** a severe injury. **2** a cruel beating.

mischievous, mischeevous *adj* **1** hurtful. **2** painful. **3** cheating, tricky.

miscomfit *v* to displease.

miscomfist *adj* nearly stifled by a bad smell.

misconstruct *v* to misconstrue.

miscontent *adj* discontented.

miscontented *adj* discontented.

miscontentment *n* **1** discontent. **2** a grievance.

misconvenient *adj* inconvenient.

miscook *v* **1** to cook badly. **2** to bungle, mismanage.

miscounselled *adj* ill-advised.

misdeedy *adj* mischievous.

misdiet *v* to have food irregularly.
misdoot *v* **1** to doubt, disbelieve. **2** to suspect. **3** to mistake.—*n* a doubt, mistrust.
misdootins *n* doubts, suspicions.
misemployment *n* malversation of money, etc.
miser *n* **1** a wretch. **2** a miserable being.
misert *adj* **1** miserly. **2** parsimonious. **3** avaricious. —*n* a miser.
misertish *adj* miserly, very parsimonious.
misert pig *n* a child's moneybox made of earthenware.
misfarin *adj* ill-grown.
misfet *v* to offend one.
misfit *v* to displease.
misfortunate, misfortinit *adj* unfortunate.
misfortune *n* the giving birth to an illegitimate child.
misfuir *v* to fare badly.
misgae *v* **1** to go wrong. **2** to miscarry. **3** (*of a cow*) to abort.
misgate *n* a going astray, transgression, misdeed.
misgie, misgive *v* **1** to fall through, miscarry. **2** (*used of a pistol etc*) to misfire.
misgieins *n* misgivings.
misgien *adj* (*used of a crop*) failed.
misgoggle, migoogle *same as* **misguggle**.
misgrow *v* to grow stunted, crooked, ill-shaped.
misgrugle *v* **1** to rumple, handle roughly. **2** to disfigure. **3** to deform.
misguggle *v* **1** to disfigure, mar. **2** to handle roughly. **3** to misgrugle (qv).
misguide *v* **1** to mismanage. **2** to waste, misspend. **3** to ill-use, injure.
misguided *adj* (*used of a woman*) seduced.
misgully *v* **1** to handle a gully (qv) clumsily. **2** to mangle in cutting or carving.
mishandle *v* **1** to mismanage, bungle. **2** to handle awkwardly.
mishanter *n* **1** a misfortune, accident. **2** ill-luck. **3** a name for the devil.—*v* to meet with an accident, hurt or bruise.
mishappens *n* unfortunateness.
mishent *adj* wicked.
mishently *adv* wickedly.
mishguggle *same as* **misguggle**.
mish-mash *n* **1** a hodge-podge. **2** a muddle.—*v* to mingle. **3** to throw into confusion.—*adv* in confusion.—*adj* put in confusion.
mish-masherie *n* things in a confused state.
misimproven *adj* not improved, wrongly improved.
misinclined *adj* disinclined.
misinformer *n* a false informer.
misk *n* **1** a piece of land, partly earth, partly moss. **2** land covered with coarse, rough, moorish grasses.
misken *v* **1** not to recognize. **2** to ignore. **3** to disown. **4** not to know of. **5** to misunderstand. **6** to leave unnoticed. **7** not to meddle with. **8** to assume airs of superiority. **9** (*with* **oneself**) to forget one's proper station.
misk grass *n* the grass growing on a misk (qv).
misknow *same as* **misken**.
mislair *same as* **mislear**.
misle[1] *n* the mistletoe.
misle[2] *same as* **mizzle**[2].
mislear *v* **1** to misinform. **2** to lead astray, seduce.
misleard, misleart, misleer'd *adj* **1** unmannerly, ill-bred. **2** mischievous. **3** greedy.
mislearin *n* an error, mistake.
misle-shinned *adj* having speckled legs. *See* **mizzle**[2].
mislike *v* to displease.
misliken *v* **1** to disparage, depreciate. **2** to do discredit to.
mislippen *v* **1** to disappoint. **2** to deceive. **3** to distrust. **4** to suspect. **5** to mismanage. **6** to neglect.
mislooin *n* derision.
misluck *n* **1** misfortune. **2** ill-luck.—*v* **1** to miscarry. **2** not to prosper.
mislushious *adj* **1** rough. **2** malicious. **3** ill-natured.
mismacht, mismaight *adj* **1** mismatched. **2** disordered.

mismae *v* to disturb.
mismaggle *v* **1** to disarrange, rumple. **2** to mar, spoil.
mismake, mismack *v* **1** to shape clothes improperly. **2** to trouble, disturb, unsettle. **3** to blush.
mismannered *adj* **1** unmannerly, uncivil. **2** unbecoming.
mismanners *n* **1** ill-breeding. **2** incivility.
mismar *v* to disarrange, mar.
mismarrow, mismorrow *v* to mismatch.—*n* anything that is wrongly matched.
mismaucher *v* to render useless.
misminnie *v* **1** (*used of a lamb*) to lose its mother, to be put to suck a strange ewe. **2** (*of a child*) to miss its mother.
mismove, mismove, mismuive *v* **1** to disturb. **2** to disconcert, fluster.
misnurtured *adj* ill-bred.
misorder *n* **1** irregularity. **2** disorderly proceeding.
misportion *v* (*with* **oneself**) to eat to excess.
misprood *adj* unduly proud.
misreckon *v* to miscalculate.
misred, ~rid *adj* **1** entangled, ravelled. **2** complicated.
misremember *v* to forget.
misrestit *adj* having broken sleep or disturbed rest.
misrid *same as* **misred**.
miss[1] *n* a paramour, mistress.
miss[2] *v* **1** to avoid. **2** to fail to happen. **3** to fail to germinate or grow. **4** to dispense with, do without. **5** (*with* **oneself**) to be deprived of pleasure or enjoyment by not being present at an enjoyable occasion.—*n* **1** absence. **2** loss. **3** one whose death or removal is regretted. **4** a fault.
missaucher, missaucre *v* **1** to destroy, ruin. **2** to hurt severely. **3** to bruise. **4** to mangle.—*n* **1** ruin. **2** severe injury. **3** pain caused by bruises, etc.
miss but *v* **1** to fail to. **2** to avoid.
mis-seem *v* to ill-become.
mis-set *v* **1** to put out of temper. **2** to displease. **3** to disorder.
misshieff *same as* **mischief**.
missing *adj* (*used of the tide*) not full.
mission *v* to send on a mission.
missionar *n* an itinerant preacher.
missive *n* **1** a provisional lease. **2** an informal contract preceding the formal one.
miss-John *same as* **mass-John**.
missle *same as* **mizzle**[1].
misslie *adj* **1** lonely or unhappy because of missing someone or somewhere. **2** dull, dreary. **3** much missed, regretted.
misslieness *n* **1** loneliness. **2** regret for one absent.
missour *n* measure.
misspeak *v* to speak favourably of one whose conduct does not justify such praise.
mis-swear *v* to swear falsely.
mis-sworn *adj* perjured.
mistaen, misteen *v*, *adj* mistaken.
mistak *v* **1** to mistake. **2** to do wrong.—*n in phr* **nae mistak but** without doubt.
mistell *v* to misinform.
mistemper *v* to put out of gear.
mistent *v* **1** to neglect. **2** not to take heed to.—*n* a slip, mistake.
mister[1] *n* **1** a master. **2** a term of address, sir.
mister[2] *same as* **maister**[2].
mister[3] *v* **1** to lack. **2** to be necessary. **3** to need.—*n* want, need, necessity.
misterfu' *adj* needy, in straits.
misteuk *v* mistook.
mist fawn *n* mist like a white spot of ground.
mis-thrift *n* thriftlessness, wastefulness.
misthrive *v* to thrive badly.
mistime *v* **1** to play out of tune or time. **2** to put out of one s usual routine.
mistimeous *adj* **1** unpunctual. **2** not to be trusted for punctuality. **3** untidy, clumsy. **4** not to be depended on.
mistiming *n* irregularity or unpunctuality as to times.

mistlie *same as* **misslie**.
mistraucht *adj* distraught.
mistress *n* **1** a title formerly given to the wife of a principal tenant and to a minister's wife. **2** a familiar term for a wife.
mistryst *v* **1** to miss an appointed meeting. **2** to fail to keep a promise. **3** to visit with trouble, etc. **4** to frighten, perplex without cause or against expectation.
misuser *n* one who injures another.
mitch *n* the support near the stern of a large boat, on which the lowered mast rests.
mite *v* to pick out mites.—*n* anything small and inferior.
mitel *v* **1** (*used of mites*) to eat away. **2** (*of money when changed*) to be spent gradually. **3** to waste slowly
mith[1] *v* might.
mith[2] *same as* **meethe**.
mither *n* **1** mother. **2** the origin, source. **3** an old potato.
mither-in-law *n* a stepmother.
mitherland *n* native land.
mither-nakit *adj* quite naked.
mither-o'-the-mawkins *n* **1** the little grebe. **2** a witch. **3** an uncanny person.
mither-o'-thousands *n* the ivy-leaved toadflax.
mither's heart *n* the shepherd's purse.
mither-wife *n* a wife and mother.
mithrate, mithret *n* the diaphragm.
mitle *same as* **mitel**.
mitten *n* **1** a glove, especially a worsted glove. **2** a gauntlet.
mittilat *v* to mutilate, to maim.—*n* a person with disabled limbs.
mittle *v* to mutilate, to hurt.
mix *v* **1** (*used of grain*) to change colour. **2** to grow pale from illness. **3** to disorder the body. **4** to join with a company.
mixed *adj* muddled with drink.
mixen-varlet *n* a contemptuous designation.
mixie-maxy *n* **1** a miscellaneous mixture. **2** a state of confusion.—*adj* confused, jumbled.
mixter-maxter *same as* **mixie-maxie**.
mixty-maxty, ~-maxtie *same as* **mixie-maxie**.
mizzle[1] *v* to decamp.
mizzle[2], **mizle** *v* to speckle.—*n* (*in pl*) measles.
mizzle-shinned *adj* with the shins speckled by the heat of a fire.
mizzlie, mizly *adj* **1** speckled. **2** variegated.
mo *same as* **mae**[1].
moach *same as* **moch**[3].
moagre *same as* **mogre**.
moakie *n* a pet name for a calf.
moals *n* earth.
moan *same as* **maen**.
moary *same as* **moory**.
moat[1] *n* **1** a mote. **2** an atom. **3** a minute creature.
moat[2] *n* an earthen mound.
moat-hill *n* an earthen mound of considerable size.
moatie *adj* **1** tiny. **2** full of motes.
mob *n* a school of whales.
mobile *n* the mob, rabble.
moch[1] *n* a moth.
moch[2] *same as* **mawk**.
moch[3] *adj* **1** moist, damp. **2** close. **3** foggy. **4** mouldy, putrescent.—*v* **1** to grow mouldy. **2** to approach putrescence. **3** to be putrid.
moch[4] *n* a heap.
moch-eaten *adj* moth-eaten.
mocher, mochre *v* **1** to coddle. **2** (*used of cows*) to soothe before milking. **3** to busy oneself with trifles or paltry work. **4** to work in the dark.
moch-flee *n* a moth.
mochie[1] *adj* full of moths.
mochie[2]**, mochy** *adj* **1** moist. **2** misty. **3** muggy. **4** dirty. **5** becoming mouldy or putrid.
mochness *n* moistness causing mouldiness or putrescence.

Mochrum-elder, ~-laird *n* the cormorant.
mocht *adj* becoming putrid.
mock *n* **1** fun. **2** a jest. **3** a flout. **4** a sham. **5** a swindle.
mockage *n* mockery.
mockrife, mockriff *adj* scornful.
Mod *n* an annual festival devoted to Gaelic culture in which prizes are given for singing, etc.
modder *v* to mutter.
model *n* the very image.—*v* to organize.
moderate[1] *v* **1** to preside in a Presbyterian Church court. **2** to preside at the election, calling or ordination of a pastor.
moderate[2] *adj* **1** composed, calm, cool. **2** (*used of the weather*) calm.—*n* a name given to a party in the Church of Scotland in the 18th and 19th centuries, in contrast to the Evangelical party.
moderation *n* **1** presiding in a Church court at the election, calling or ordination of a pastor. **2** calmness. **3** settled weather.
moderator *n* the minister who presides in a Presbyterian Church court.
modgel *n* **1** a noggin. **2** the usual quantity of drink.
modie-brod *same as* **mowdie-brod**.
modification *n* **1** arrangement. **2** adjustment.
modify *v* **1** to arrange proportionally. **2** to arrange the contributions of heritors to a parish minister's stipend.
modish *adj* polite, courteous.
modywart *same as* **moudiewarp**.
moe *same as* **mae**.
moem *n* a scrap.
moen *n* *same as* **moyen**.
mogan *n* a hidden or secret purse.
mogen *adj* **1** (*perhaps*) common, public. **2** watched.
moggan, moggen, moggin *n* **1** a stocking. **2** a footless stocking. **3** a stocking used as a purse. **4** a long stocking-like sleeve for a woman's arm. **5** (*in pl*) the legs. **6** *in phr* **wet the sma' end o' a moggan** to find great difficulty.
mogh *same as* **moch**.
moghie *same as* **mochie**[1].
mogran *adj* clumsy.
mogre *n* **1** a bungle. **2** a clumsy mess.—*v* **1** to work in a dirty way. **2** to handle clumsily.
moich *same as* **moch**[3].
moichness *n* **1** mouldiness. **2** damp causing putrescence.
moider *v* **1** to stupefy. **2** to dull the brain by drinking.
moiken *same as* **michen**.
moil *n* **1** drudgery, hard labour. **2** bustle. **3** turmoil. **4** din.
moilie, moiley *n* **1** a hornless bullock or cow. **2** a mild, good-natured person, who is tame even to silliness.
moist *v* to moisten.
moisterless *adj* lacking moisture.
moistify *v* to moisten.
moisty *adj* moist.
mokie *n* a stupid, silly fellow.
mokre *same as* **mocher**.
mokriff *same as* **mockrife**.
molashed *adj* drunk.
molass, molash *n* whisky made from molasses.
moldewort *n* the mole.
mole-blind *adj* blind as a mole.
moleery-tea *n* **1** the common milfoil. **2** the goose-tongue.
moley, molie *n* a familiar name for a mole-catcher.
mollachon *n* a small cheese.
mollan *n* a long, straight pole, such as is used in fish yards.
mollat *n* the bit of a bridle.
mollets *n* **1** sly winks. **2** fantastic tricks.
mollify *v* to tone down a charge, statement, etc.
molligrant, molliegrunt, moligrant, mollygrant *n* whining, complaining.—*v* to whine.
molligrubs, molligrumphs *n* **1** a stomach ache. **2** a fit of temper.
mollion *n* the mass of the people.
moll-on-the-coals *n* a gloomy-minded, melancholy woman.

mollop, mollup *v* to toss the head haughtily.
molloping *adj* haughty, disdainful.
molluka *n* the molucca bean or nut, once used as a charm in the Western Islands.
moloss *adj* 1 loose. 2 dissolute in conduct.
molten *v* 1 to melt. 2 to melt into laughter, tears, etc.
moment-hand *n* the second hand of a clock or watch.
mon *same as* **maun**[1].
mon *n* man, a term of address.
Monanday, Mononday *n* Monday.
Monday's haddie *n* a stale fish.
mone *same as* **maen**.
money-nifferer *n* a moneychanger.
monger *n* a trader, dealer.
mongs *prep* among.
monie, mony *adj* many.
monie lang *adv* for a long time past.
moniest, monniest *adj* most in number.
moniment *n* 1 a monument. 2 a spectacle. 3 a ridiculous or insignificant person. 4 a fool.
moniplies, monieplies, monnyplies, monyplies *n* 1 the third stomach of a ruminant, with its many parallel folds. 2 the human intestines.
monk *same as* **munks**.
monkfish *n* the angler fish.
monk's-rhubarb *n* the patient dock.
monshie, monzie *n* a Frenchman.
Month *n* the Grampian range towards its eastern extremity.
monthly bird *n* the fieldfare.
mony *same as* **many**.
monyest *adj* most.
monyfaulds *same as* **moniplies**.
moo[1] *n* the mouth.
moo[2] *v* to low as a cow.—*n* the low of a cow.
moo[3] *same as* **mow**[1].
moo band *same as* **mow band**.
moo-bit *n* 1 a morsel. 2 food.
mooch *v* 1 to sneak about. 2 to play the spy.
moocher *n* 1 a loafer on the lookout for what he can pick up on the sly. 2 a sharper.
mooching *n* a kind of sly begging.
moo-cue *n* a twisted halter for curbing a young horse.
moodle[1] *n* a mole.
moodle[2] *adj* down-hearted.
moodle[3] *adj* gallant.
moodle-hill *n* a molehill.
moodge *same as* **mudge**.
moody-warp *n* the mole.
moo-frachty *adj* palatable, pleasant to the taste.
moofu' *n* 1 a mouthful. 2 a meal. 3 a scanty livelihood.
moofu' o' a prayer *n* a short prayer.
moogan *same as* **moggan**.
moogard[1] *n* the mugwort.
moogard[2] *n* 1 a worthless person or thing. 2 a mess, a muddle.
moo-hause *n* a trap-door opening.
moo-heich *adv* as high as one's mouth.
mool[1] *n* a bluff headland.
mool[2] *n* a slipper. See **mulls**.
mool[3] *n* 1 (*in pl*) broken chilblains. 2 a disease of the heels.
mool[4] *n* 1 a mould. 2 the small piece of bone etc, round which cloth is wrapped to form a button.
mool[5] *n* 1 mould. 2 soil good for working. 3 pulverized dry earth. 4 the soil for a grave, the grave. 5 (*in pl*) a grave, the earth of a grave, dust. —*v* 1 to bury. 2 to crumble. 3 to have carnal intercourse with.
moolating *adj* whimpering, whining.
moolboard *n* the mouldboard of a plough.
mool button *n* a button of cloth wrapped round a piece of bone.
moold *same as* **mould**[1].
mooler *v* to crumble, moulder.
moolet, moolat *v* 1 to whine. 2 to murmur. 3 to sob.

moolicks *n* crumbs.
moolie *n* a soft, ill-baked marble.—*adj* 1 full of crumbs or small pieces of soil, friable, crumbling. 2 soft, flabby.
moolie-pudding *n* a boys' game, in which one boy with clasped hands tries to touch the others.
mooligh *v* to whimper.
mooligrubs *same as* **molligrubs**.
moolin *n* a crumb.
mooliness *n* the state of being full of crumbs.
mooly[1] *adj* mouldy.
mooly[2] *adj* 1 earthy. 2 earth-stained. 3 savouring of the grave.
mooly-heel *n* 1 a heel affected by chilblains. 2 (*in pl*) chilblains.
moo-maein *n* the lowing of cattle.
moo-mawin *ppl* 1 hinting. 2 mooting.
moon, moonie *n* the goldcrest.
moon broch *n* a halo round the moon.
moonge *same as* **munge**[1].
moonlicht-flittin' *n* a decamping by night with one's goods to escape from one's creditors or landlord.
moonog *n* the cranberry or crawberry.
moony *same as* **moon**.
moop[1] *v* 1 to nibble. 2 to mump. 3 to keep company with. 4 (*used of nose and chin*) to approach each other through loss of teeth in old age.
moop[2] *v* 1 to impair by degrees. 2 to fall off, fail. 3 to decline in health.
moop[3] *v* 1 to have sexual intercourse. 2 to consort with.
mooping *n* fantastic conduct. 2 grimacing.
moo-pock *n* a horse's nosebag.
moor *n* 1 peaty land. 2 peat mud.
moor band *n* a surface of peat moss wasted to a kind of light black earth, often mixed with sand.
moorbird *n* any bird nesting on a moor.
moor-burn *n* 1 the annual burning of part of a moor. 2 an outbreak of temper. 3 a dispute, conflict.
moor duck *n* the wild duck.
moor-fail *n* turf cut from the surface of a moor.
moor-~, muir-fowl-egg *n* a species of pear.
moorgrass *n* the silverweed.
moor hags *n* holes made in moor or moss by peat-cutting.
moor-ill *n* the red water in cattle.
moor-poot,-pout *n* 1 the young of a moorbird. 2 a young grouse.
moor-sickness *n* a wasting sickness affecting sheep in autumn.
moor-spade *n* a spade for cutting the turf of moor or peat.
moory *adj* 1 heathy. 2 of a brown or heather colour.
moose[1], **moosie** *n* a mouse.
moose[2] *same as* **mouse**.
moose-web *n* 1 a cobweb. 2 gossamer. 3 phlegm in the throat.
moosie *adj* downy, covered with soft hair.
moost[1] *n* a nasty smell.—*v* to grow mouldy.
moost[2] *n* hair powder.—*v* to powder the hair.
moosty *adj* covered with hair-powder.
moot[1] *v* to hint, suggest.
moot[2] *same as* **mout**.
mooten'd *adj* moulted.
mooter[1] *n* a multure.—*v* to take multure for grinding corn.
mooter[2] *v* to mutter.
mooter[3] *v* 1 to fret. 2 to fall off through faction. 3 to take away piecemeal.
mooter-the melder *n* a miller.
mooth[1] *adj* 1 foggy, misty. 2 damp and warm. 3 soft. 4 calm. 5 comfortable. 6 cheerful, jolly.
mooth[2] *n* the mouth.
moothfu' *n* a mouthful.
moothlie *adj* softly.
mooth-ruif *n* the palate.
moothu *n* a mouthful.
mootie[1] *same as* **moatie**.
mootie[2] *adj* parsimonious, niggardly.

mootit-like *adj* **1** puny. **2** looking like shrinking in size.
mootle *same as* **moutle**.
mootre *n* the miller's payment in meal.
moozlie *v* (*used of hay, etc*) to become mouldy or rot through damp.—*n* dry-rot.
mop *n* a grimace.
moral *n* the exact likeness.
moral-legger *n* a boys' marble, hard, ring-streaked or pie-bald.
Moray coach *n* a cart.
morbid *adj* morbific, causing disease.
morbleu, morblue *n* a murder cry.—*adv* with vigour.
mord-de-chien *n* a disease of horses, glanders.
more *same as* **mair**.
morgoz'd *adj* confused.
morie-morning *n* tomorrow morning.
morken, morkin *n* **1** a dead sheep. **2** the skin of a dead sheep.
morn *n* (*with* **the**) tomorrow.
morn-come-never *adv* never.
mornie-~, morn-i-'e-morning *n* the early morning.
morning *n* **1** a glass of liquor taken before breakfast. **2** a slight repast taken some hours before breakfast.
morning-blink *n* early morning light.
morning bout *n* a morning walk.
morning drink *n* alcoholic refreshment before breakfast.
morning gift *n* a husband's gift to his wife on the morning after marriage.
morning mun *n* **1** the dawn. **2** increasing daylight.
morn wind *n* morning wind.
morrice dance *n* a morris dance.
morroch *v* **1** to trample in mud. **2** to soil.
morrot *same as* **marrott**.
morrough *n* a merman.
morrow *same as* **marrow**[2].
morsel *n* **1** a slight meal. **2** food spoilt in cooking.
morsing horn *n* a powder flask.
mort *n* the skin of a sheep that dies.—*adj in phr* a **mort cauld** a very severe cold.
mortal *adj* **1** great, extreme. **2** single, individual. **3** complete, whole. **4** dead-drunk.—*adv* very, exceedingly.—*n* the mortal remains.
mortal drunk, -fou *adj* dead-drunk.
mortally *adv* excessively, very.
mortar *n* coarse reddish clay.
mortar stone *n* a hollow stone formerly used as a mortar for husking grain.
mort cloth, ~-claith *n* a funeral pall.
mortersheen *n* the most fatal species of glanders.
mortfundit *adj* **1** chilled to death, cold as death. **2** foundered with cold.
morth *same as* **murth**.
morth *n in phr* a **morth o' cauld** a very severe cold.
mort-heid *n* **1** a death's-head. **2** a turnip hollowed out and cut in the form of a face and lighted with a candle. **3** the death's-head moth.
morthling *same as* **murling**.
mortichien *same as* **mortersheen**. *See* **mord-de-chien**.
mortification *n* **1** giving in mortmain. **2** lands or funds so given.
mortifier *n* one who bequeaths lands or funds in mortmain.
mortify *v* to give in mortmain for religious, etc, purposes.
mort-safe *n* a cast-iron frame, formerly used to prevent a grave being violated by resurrectionists.
mort woo' *n* the wool from the skin of a sheep that has died a natural death.
morungeous *same as* **maroonjus**.
moses' table *n* a kind of granite.
moshin-hole *same as* **motion-hole**.
mosker *v* to decay, crumble away.
moss *n* **1** a place where peats may be dug. **2** peat. **3** various kinds of cotton grass.—*v* to cut and prepare peats.
moss bailie *n* one who has charge of a peat moss.
moss bluter *n* **1** the common snipe. **2** the bittern.

moss boil *n* a fountain that boils up in a moss.
moss-bummer *n* the bittern.
moss-cheeper *n* the meadow pipit, titlark.
moss-corn *n* the silverweed.
moss-crop *n* **1** various species of cotton grass. **2** the silverweed.
moss-duck *n* the wild duck.
moss-earth *n* peaty soil.
mosser *n* one who cuts and prepares peats.
moss-fa' *n* a ruinous building.
moss-fa'en *adj* (*used of trees*) fallen into a bog and gradually covered with moss.
moss farmer *n* a moorland farmer.
moss-flow *n* a watery moss.
moss fog *n* mosses growing in a bog or swamp.
moss grieve *n* a moss bailie (qv), one in charge of a peat moss.
moss hag *n* a place out of which peats have been cut.
mossin' *n* peat-cutting.
mossin' time *n* the peat-cutting season.
moss laird *n* the owner of a moorland farm.
moss-leerie *n* a will-of-the-wisp.
moss maill *n* rent for right of cutting peats.
moss-mingin *n* the cranberry.
moss oak *n* **1** bog oak. **2** a seat made of bog oak.
moss-owl *n* the short-eared owl.
moss seat *n* a mossy seat.
moss stock *n* trunks and stumps of bog oak.
moss thief *n* a Border riever.
moss-thristle *n* the marsh thistle.
moss-trooper *n* a Border freebooter.
moss-willow *n* the *Salix fusca*.
most *adj* chief, principal.—*adv* **1** almost. **2** mostly. —*n* the majority.
most *n* a mast.
mosted *adj* crop-eared.
mot, mote *v* **1** may. **2** might.
mot[1] *same as* **mote**[3].
mot[2] *n* **1** a speck of dust. **2** a mote. **3** a dot. **4** a mark aimed at.
motch *v* **1** to eat little slowly and secretly. **2** to waste imperceptibly.—*n* **1** slow, quiet eating. **2** fondness for dainties. **3** imperceptible use. **4** thriftlessness.
mote[1] *n* **1** a very small particle. **2** a crumb. **3** a tiny creature. **4** a single stalk of straw or hay. **5** a flaw, drawback from.—*v* **1** to pick motes out of anything. **2** to search for and catch lice.—*phr* **mote the blankets** to pick at the bedclothes, a sign of the approaching death of a patient.
mote[2] *adj* (*used of money*) gradually spent.
mote[3] *n* a rising ground, a knoll.
mote-hill *n* a little hill on which conventions were held.
motey *adj* **1** full of motes or minute creatures. **2** tiny.
moth *same as* **mooth**[1].
motheat *v* to injure one's reputation secretly and slowly.
mother *n in phr* **the mother on beer** the lees working up and forming a thick mould on the top.
moth-hawk *n* the nightjar.
motie *adj* (*used of the cheeks*) ornamented with black patches.
motion-hole *n* the touchhole of a cannon.
mott *n* an earthen mound.
mottie[1] *adj* profane.
mottie[2] *n* **1** a mark to be aimed at. **2** a dot.
motty *adj* **1** spotted. **2** full of minute creatures. **3** full of motes. **4** tiny.
mottyoched *same as* **muttyoched**.
motty-sun *n* the appearance when a sunbeam shines through an aperture and shows floating atoms of dust.
mou[1] *same as* **moo**[1].
mou[2] *same as* **mow**[1].
mou-ban *same as* **mow-band**.
moubit *n* **1** a mouthful. **2** food.
mouch[1] *same as* **moch**[1].
mouch[2] *v* **1** to idle or lounge about. **2** to sneak about.

moucher *v* to sneak about, to spy.
moud[1] *n* a moth.
moud[2] *n* **1** mould, earth. **2** the grave.
mouden *same as* **mouten**.
moudie *n* **1** a mole. **2** a mole-catcher.
moudie-hillan, -hill *n* a molehill.
moudie-hoop *n* a molehill.
moudie-man *n* a mole-catcher.
moudie-poke *n* a bag to put moles in.
moudie-skin *n* a moleskin.
moudiewarp, moudiewart, moudiewort *n* **1** a mole. **2** a short, dark person with a profusion of hair. **3** a term applied to children.
moudiewarp burd *n* the mouldboard of a plough.
moudiewarp-hill *n* a molehill.
moudiwort *n* a very slow worker.
moug *n* a mug.
mougart *n* mugwort.
mought *same as* **maught**.
mougre *v* to creep, crawl over.
moul[1] *v* to become mouldy.
moul[2] *same as* **mool**[3].
moul[3] *same as* **mool**[5].
mould[1] *n* **1** the grave. **2** soil.
mould[2] *adj* mouldy.
mould[3] *n* a candle made in a mould.
moulder away *v* (*used of laws, customs, etc*) to become obsolete.
mouldie *adj* savouring of the grave.
mouldywarp burd *n* the mouldboard of a plough.
moulie-draps *n* drops left in the bottom of a glass.
mouligh *v* to whine, whimper.
mouligrant *same as* **molligrant**.
mouligrubs *same as* **molligrubs**.
moull *n* refuse of meal at a mill, generally used to feed swine.
moulter[1] *n* **1** a multure. **2** payment for grinding corn.
moulter[2] *v* **1** to crumble. **2** to take away piecemeal.
mouly, moully *adj* mouldy.
mouly-heels *n* chilblains on the heels.
mouly-penny *n* a miser.
mounge[1] *same as* **munge**[1].
mounge[2] *same as* **munge**[2].
mount *v* **1** to make ready. **2** to equip. **3** to get ready for setting off.—*n* a weaving term.
mountain-blackbird *n* the ring ouzel.
mountain dew *n* whisky.
mountain-dulse *n* the mountain laver.
mountain folks, ~ men *n* **1** the Covenanters. **2** the sect of the Cameronians.
mountain-spate *n* a mountain torrent.
mountain-thrush *n* the ring ouzel.
mount-caper *n* the marsh orchis.
mounting *n* **1** furnishing. **2** a trousseau. **3** a mount in weaving, a weaver's apparatus.
moup[1] *same as* **moop**[1].
moup[2] *same as* **moop**[2].
mouper *v* to nibble continuously.
moupit-like *adj* in apparent ill-health, drooping.
mourie *n* **1** a gravelly sea beach. **2** a stratum of mixed sand and gravel.
mourn *v* (*used of cattle*) to moan.—*n* a murmuring sound.
mournings *n* mourning garb.
mourning-string *n* a streamer worn on the hat in token of mourning.
moury *adj* mellow.
mous *same as* **mows**.
mouse *n* the bulb of flesh at the end of a shank of mutton.
mouse-ear *n* the mouse-ear chickweed.
mouse-end *n* the end of a leg of mutton where the mouse (qv) is situated.
mouse-fa' *n* a mousetrap.
mouse-web, ~-web, ~-wob *n* **1** a cobweb. **2** phlegm in the throat.

mouse-webbed *adj* covered with cobwebs.
moust[1] *same as* **moost**[1].
moust[2] *same as* **moost**[2].
mou'-strings *n* the strings that tie the open end of a pillowslip, etc.
mout *v* **1** to moult. **2** (*with* **away**) to lessen gradually, take away piecemeal.
moutch *same as* **mouch**[2].
moutchit *n* **1** a contemptuous term applied to children. **2** a smatchet (qv).
mouten *v* **1** to melt. **2** to clarify.
mouter[1] *same as* **mooter**[3].
mouter[2] *same as* **mooter**[1].
mouth *n* **1** a mouthful. **2** a trap-door opening. **3** the bowl of a spoon.—*v* **1** to speak. **2** to proclaim. **3** to feel hungry. **4** to crow.
moutin' *adj* moulting.
moutle *v* **1** to nibble. **2** to fritter away, to take away piecemeal.
mouze[1] *same as* **mows**.
mouze[2] *v* to plunder clandestinely.
mow[1] *n* **1** a large rectangular stack of hay, etc. **2** a heap, pile.—*v* to pile up hay, etc.
mow[2] *n* a grimace.
mow[3] *same as* **mow**[1].
mow band *n* **1** a halter. **2** speech.—*v* **1** to articulate. **2** to mention. **3** to understand.
mowbit *n* **1** a morsel. **2** food.
mowoh *same as* **mouch**[2].
mowdie *same as* **moudie**.
mowdie-brod *n* the mouldboard of a plough.
mowdie-hoop *n* a molehill.
mowdiewark, ~-wart, ~-wort *same as* **moudiewarp**.
mowe[1] *n* dust.
mowe[2] *v* to copulate.
mowes *same as* **mows**.
mowr *n* a mock, jeer, flout.
mows, mowse, mowze *n* a joke, jest.
moy *adj* **1** affecting great moderation in eating or drinking. **2** modest. **3** demure.
moyen, moyan *n* **1** means. **2** ability. **3** influence. **4** management.—*v* **1** to accomplish by means. **2** to manage. **3** to succeed through influence.
moyener *n* one who uses his influence for another.
moyenless *adj* **1** powerless, inactive. **2** without influence.
moylie *same as* **moilie**.
mozie[1] *adj* **1** swarthy, dark in complexion. **2** acrimonious. **3** ill-natured. **4** sour-looking.
mozie[2] *n* a person of weak intellect, an idiot.—*adj* **1** rotten, mouldy, decayed. **2** over-ripe.
mucht *same as* **maught**.
muchty *adj* **1** close. **2** musty. **3** stale.
muck *n* **1** dung in a wet state. **2** mud, mire. **3** any kind of filth. **4** a worthless person.—*v* **1** to clean a byre (qv) or stable. **2** to manure with dung. **3** to soil oneself. **4** to use dirty practices in any way.
muckafy *v* to defile, soil.
muck creel *n* a large creel or hamper, formerly used for carrying dung to the fields.
muck-fail *n* a mixture of sward and dung used as a manure.
muck-hawk *n* a dung fork.
muck-heap *n* a dunghill.
muck-hole *n* an opening in a cow-house wall for throwing out dung.
muck-kishie *n* a muck creel (qv).
muckle *adj same as* **muckle**.
muckle chair *n* an armchair.
muckle-coat *n* a greatcoat.
muckle Friday *n* the Friday on which a large fair is held.
muckle man *n* **1** a full-grown and qualified farm servant. **2** a man of means.
muckle-mou'd *adj* having a large or wide mouth.
muckleness *n* largeness of size.

mucklest *adj* biggest.

muckle-worth *adj* of great value.

muckly *n* the fair on muckle Friday (qv).

muck-man *n* a scavenger.

muck-midden *n* a dung heap.

muck-rotten *adj* quite rotten.

mucky *adj* **1** dirty. **2** slatternly. **3** messy, untidy.—*n* a privy.

mucky-fit *n* **1** a ploughman. **2** a farm labourer.

mucky-heap *n* a dirty, slatternly woman or girl.

mucky house *n* a privy.

mud *n* a small nail used in the heels of shoes, having a small head.

mud *v* must.

mud-bedraiglet *adj* mud-bedraggled.

muddle *v* **1** to work fussily and do little. **2** to be busy clandestinely. **3** to lie upon and tickle a person. **4** to have carnal knowledge of a woman.

muddock *n* a child's name for mother.

muddy *adj* **1** (*used of style*) not lucid, obscure. **2** confused. **3** muddled with drink.—*v* to make muddy.

mud fever *n* an affliction of the legs of horses that are clipped in winter, occasioned by muddy roads.

mudfish *n* fish salted in barrels.

mudge *v* **1** to move, stir. **2** to budge. **3** to talk of secretly. **4** to hint at.—*n* **1** a movement. **2** a stir. **3** a rumour.

mudgeon, mudyeon *n* a movement of the face, indicating displeasure, contempt, mockery, etc.

mudwart *same as* **moudiewart**.

mue *same as* **moo**[2].

muff *v* **1** to mow. **2** to trim the beard, etc.

muffatees, muffitees *n* wristlets of knitted wool, etc, worn in cold weather.

muffed *adj* (*used of a hen*) tufted.

muffle-wren *n* the willow warbler.

muffit *n* the whitethroat.

muffe *n* a mitten with only two divisions.

mufty *n* a tufted fowl. *See* **muffed**.

mug[1] *v* to drizzle.—*n* a drizzling rain.

mug[2] *n* **1** the mouth. **2** the face.

mug[3] *v* **1** to soil, defile. **2** to use dirty practices.—*n* dung.

mug[4] *n* the hole into which a ball or marble is thrown or rolled.—*v* to play a marble as in kypes or throw a ball into a hole. **2** to strike a ball out from a wall.

mug[5], **mugg** *n* a kind of sheep with a good coat of wool.

muggan *same as* **moggan**.

muggart, mugger *same as* **moogard**[1].

muggart kail *n* **1** a dish composed of mugwort. **2** mugwort broth.

mugger *n* a hawker of crockery.

mugg-ewe *n* a sheep with a good coat of wool.

muggie *n* **1** a small mug. **2** a game of marbles, the kypes. **3** the hole into which a marble or ball is played.—*v* **1** to put the marble or ball into the hole. **2** to strike a ball out from a wall.

muggin *same as* **moggan**.

muggle *v* to drizzle.—*n* a drizzle.

muggly *adj* **1** drizzling. **2** damp, foggy.

muggons, muggins *n* mugwort.

muggy *adj* **1** drizzling. **2** foggy. **3** tipsy.

mugg-yarn *n* wool from a mug sheep. *See* **mug**[5].

muil *same as* **mool**[5].

muilcioun *n* the spignel.

muilen *n* a crumb of bread.

muilie *same as* **moolie**.

muils *n* slippers, cloth or list shoes. *See* **mool**.

muin *same as* **moon**.

muir *same as* **moor**.

muir-burn *same as* **moorburn**.

muis *n* **1** heaps. **2** parcels.

muist[1] *same as* **moost**[1].

muist[2] *same as* **moost**[2].

muist[3] *n* musk.

muist box *n* **1** a musk box. **2** a box for smelling at.

muisty[1] *adj* **1** mouldy. **2** musty.

muisty[2] *same as* **moosty**.

muith *same as* **mooth**[1].

muithly *same as* **moothlie**.

mulberry *n* the whitebeam tree.

mulde *n* **1** earth, mould. **2** (*in pl*) the grave.

mulde-meat *n* *in phr* **give one his mulde-meat** to kill him.

mulder *v* **1** to crumble. **2** to moulder.—*n* (*in pl*) small crumbs.

mule[1], **mule**[2] *same as* **mool**[4], **mool**[5].

mule[3] *same as* **mull**[1].

mule[4] *same as* **mool**[3].

mule in *v* *in phr* **mule in with one** to be familiar, on intimate terms, with one.

mules *same as* **muils**.

mulie *same as* **moolie**.

mulin, mullen *same as* **moolin**.

muliness *n* the state of being full of crumbs.

mulk *n* milk.

mull[1] *n* a promontory.

mull[2] *n* a mill.

mull[3] *n* a mule.

mull[4] *n* a snuffbox.

mull[5] *n* the mouth.

mullach *n* a term of endearment among women.

muller *v* to crumble.—*n* **1** (*in pl*) small crumbs. **2** mould, soil.

muller, mullert *n* a miller.

mulligrumphs *same as* **molligrubs**.

mullion *n* a shoe made of untanned leather.

mulliwark *same as* **moudiewarp**.

mulloch *n* the crumbled dust of a peat stack.

mullock *n* a hornless cow.

mully *n* a small tin snuffbox.

mullygrubs *same as* **molligrubs**.

mulock *same as* **mealock**.

mulrein *n* the frogfish.

multer *n* multure.

multiples *n* the folds of a dress.

multure *n* **1** the toll of meal taken by a miller for grinding corn. **2** a miller.—*v* **1** to take toll of meal for grinding corn. **2** to defraud.

multure-free *adj* exempt from multure dues.

multure-man *n* a miller's man.

multurer *n* the tacksman of a mill, a miller.

mum *v* **1** to talk or sing in a low, inarticulate voice. **2** to mutter.—*n* **1** a mutter. **2** a low, inarticulate sound.—*adj* silent.—*int* hush!

mumbudjit *n* silence.

mumge *same as* **munge**.

mummed *adj* **1** benumbed. **2** tingling from heat after cold.

mummer *n* one who speaks or sings in a low, inarticulate voice.

mummle *v* **1** to mumble. **2** to chew without teeth.

mummy *n* bits, fragments.

mumness *n* numbness.

mump[1] *v* **1** to hint. **2** to aim at. **3** to whisper.—*n* **1** a whisper. **2** surmise.

mump[2] *v* **1** to nibble. **2** to chew without teeth. **3** to gnaw. **4** to grimace, screw up the mouth. **5** to mimic. **6** to speak affectedly or mincingly. **7** to complain, murmur. **8** to mope.—*n* used contemptuously of a toothless old woman.

mump[3] *v* **1** to hitch. **2** to move by jerks.

mumpit-like *adj* dull, stupid-like.

mumple *v* **1** to seem as if going to vomit. **2** to chuckle.

mump-the-cuddie *n* a children's game in which they sit on their hams with a hand on each hough and thus hitch forward to reach the goal.

mumt-like *same as* **mummed**.

mun[1] *same as* **maun**[1].

mun[2] *n* **1** a small, trifling article. **2** a short-handled spoon.

mun[3] *n* man.

mun[4] *n* **1** an old person with a very little face. **2** (*in pl*) the mouth, the face, the hollow behind the jawbone. **3** the jaws.

Munanday, Munnonday, Munonday, Mununday *n* Monday.

munch *v* **1** to chew without teeth. **2** to eat voraciously. **3** to mumble. **4** to grumble.

mund *same as* **mun**⁴.

munder *same as* **maunder**².

mune *n* the moon.

munelichty *adj* moonlight.

munge¹ *v* **1** to mumble. **2** to grumble. **3** to moan. **4** to bellow. **5** to betray a secret. **6** to mention.

munge² *v* **1** to munch, chew. **2** to chew with difficulty.

munk *v* **1** to diminish. **2** to bring below the proper size. **3** to cut the hair of the head very close.

munkie *n* a short rope with a loop at one end for receiving a knool (qv) or peg at the other, used for fastening up cattle in a byre (qv).

munks *n* a halter for a horse.

munn¹ *same as* **mun**².

munn² *same as* **mun**⁴.

munshock *n* the red bilberry.

munsie *n* a short-handled spoon. *See* **mun**².

munsie *n* **1** a designation of contempt or ridicule. **2** a contemptible figure. **3** a spectacle through ill-treatment. **4** the knave in a pack of cards.

munt¹ *v* to go off, take oneself off.

munt² *v* to mount.

munt³ *same as* **mint**³.

muntin *n* **1** a bride's trousseau. **2** mounting. **3** the whole of a weaver's apparatus.

mupetigage *n* a term of endearment addressed to a child.

mur *same as* **murr**.

murbled *same as* **murmled**.

murchen *n* (*perhaps*) a hare.

murder *v* **1** to kill by accident. **2** to harass, trouble.

murdiegrups *same as* **molligrubs**.

mure *same as* **moor**.

mure *v* to immure.

mure-burn *same as* **moor-burn**.

mureland *adj* pertaining to a moor.—*n* an upper and less cultivated region.

murelander *n* a dweller in a mureland (qv).

mureman *n* a murelander (qv).

murgeon *v* **1** to mock. **2** to grumble. **3** to make faces. **4** to mimic.—*n* **1** a murmur. **2** muttering, mumbling. **3** (*in pl*) grimaces. **4** violent gesture. **5** taunts. **6** grumblings.

murgeon-maker *n* one who makes murgeons. *See* **murgeon**.

murgully *same as* **margullie**.

murjin *n* **1** *same as* **murgeon**. **2** *in phr* **no murjins at a place** no movement or sign of life about a place.

murk *same as* **mirk**.

murkie *same as* **mirky**².

murkle *n* a term of reproach or contempt.

murlain *n* **1** a round, narrow-mouthed basket. **2** a wooden half-peck measure.

murle¹ *v* **1** to crumble, pulverize. **2** to moulder away. **3** to eat slowly and in small portions.—*n* **1** a fragment, crumb. **2** the act of eating in a slow, quiet manner.

murle² *v* **1** (*used of an infant*) to coo, murmur, croodle (qv). **2** to talk to oneself in a low voice. **3** to reduce to a murmur. **4** to hum a tune.

murlick *same as* **murlock**.

murlin *same as* **murlain**.

murling¹ *n* a crumb, fragment.—*v, adj* **1** crumbling. **2** eating slowly and quietly. **3** dainty in eating.

murling² *n* **1** a gentle noise, a soft murmur. **2** a very froward, whining, ill-natured child.

murling³ *n* the skin of a young lamb or sheep after it has been shorn.

murloch *n* **1** the young dogfish. **2** the smooth hound.

murlock *n* a crumb, fragment.

murly *adj* friable, crumbly.—*n* **1** any small object. **2** a

crumb. **3** a fondling term for an infant.

murly-fikes *n* an infant.

murmell *v* **1** to murmur. **2** to croodle like an infant. *See* **croodle**².

murmled *adj* halting, lamed.

murmur *v* to murmur at, complain or grumble against.

murmuration *n* **1** murmuring. **2** mumbling.

murn *same as* **mourn**.

murneful *adj* mournful.

murphy¹ *n* a potato.

murphy² *n* morphia.

murr *v* **1** to purr as a cat. **2** (*used of infants*) to make a low, murmuring sound.

murrain *n* **1** a nuisance. **2** used as an execration.

murre *n* the razorbill.

murreungeous *same as* **maroonjus**.

murrie *adj* merry.

murtlin *n* **1** a froward child. **2** a gentle noise, whining.

murroch *n* shellfish.

murrs *n* the edible roots of *Potentilla anserina*.

murt *n* the skin of a young lamb or of a sheep soon after it has been shorn or before castration.

murth *n* murder.

murther¹ *v* to murmur softly as a child.

murther² *v* **1** to kill by accident. **2** to harass, trouble.

murther³ *same as* **muther**.

musch *n* a small person with a shock of dark hair.

muschin *adj* **1** bad. **2** mischievous.

muschin-pratt *n* **1** a mischievous trick. **2** (*used ironically*) a great deed.

muschle *same as* **mushle**.

muscle *n* a mussel.

museock *n* a familiar or contemptuous name for the muse.

mush¹ *n* **1** a mash. **2** a pulp. **3** a mass of things tossed together in confusion. **4** the slow, constant consumption of anything.—*v* to consume or use slowly and wastefully.

mush² *n* **1** a muttering. **2** whisper, hint.

mush *v* **1** to cut out with a stamp. **2** to nick, notch, scallop. **3** to make into flounces. **4** to plait.—*n* a nick, notch, as is made by scissors.

mush³ *n* one who goes between a lover and his sweetheart.

mushed-out *adj* **1** scalloped. **2** flounced.

mushie *n* a mushroom.

mushik *same as* **musch**.

mushin¹ *n* **1** scalloped or crimped work. **2** plaiting. **3** cloth so ornamented.

mushin² *adj* bad, mischievous.

mushinfow *adj* cruel.

mushle *v* **1** to throw into confusion. **2** to mix clumsily. **3** to be connected by blood and affinity. **4** to consume slowly. **5** to eat slowly.—*n* **1** confusion. **2** slow and constant consumption of anything. **3** the act of eating slowly.

mushlin *n* one who is fond of dainty food eaten secretly.

mushoch *n* a heap of grain laid aside in a corner for seed.

mushoch rapes *n* ropes for surrounding a mushoch (qv).

music *n* instrumental music in churches, in contrast to vocal music alone.

musicianer, musitioner *n* a musician.

musicker *n* **1** a musician. **2** a player on any musical instrument.

music tunes *n* **1** church music. **2** psalm tunes.

musk *same as* **mush**¹.

musk almond *n* **1** a sweetmeat. **2** an almond coated with sugar.

musken *n* a measure equal to an English pint.

muslin-kail *n* broth made simply of water, barley and greens.

muslin-mouth *n* a prim mouth.

mussel ~, mussle brose *n* brose (qv) made from mussels boiled in their own sap, which is mingled with oatmeal.

mussel draig *n* an implement for gathering mussels.

mussel ebb *n* the mussel ground as exposed at low tide.

mussel-mou' *n* a mouth shaped like a mussel and closing tightly.

mussel-mou'd *adj* having a mussel-mou (qv).
musselpecker, ~picker *n* the oystercatcher.
mussel scaup *n* a bed of mussels.
mussle *same as* **mushle**.
mussy *adj* **1** messy. **2** slippery.
must[1], **must**[2] *same as* **moost**[1], **moost**[2].
must[3] *same as* **muist**[3].
mustard bullet *n* a bullet used for bruising mustard seed.
mustard stone *n* a stone used for bruising mustard seed in a stone or wooden vessel.
musted[1] *adj* mouldy, musty.
musted[2] *adj* **1** powdered. **2** covered with hair powder.
muster *v* to talk with great volubility.—*n* extreme loquacity.
musterer *n* an incessant talker.
musty *same as* **moosty**.
mutch *n* **1** a woman's cap. **2** an infant's cap. **3** a man's nightcap.
mutch-bord *n* the border of a woman's cap.
mutch-cap *n* a nightcap.
mutched *adj* wearing a mutch (qv).
mutchit *n* a contemptuous name for a child.
mutchkin *n* a liquid measure equal to an English pint.
mutchkin bottle, ~ bowl, ~ cup, ~ stoup *n* vessel large enough to hold a mutchkin (qv).
mutch string *n* the string of a woman's cap.
mute[1] *v* **1** to complain. **2** to reveal a secret.—*n* **1** a quarrel. **2** a whisper. **3** a grievance.
mute[2] *n* a small utensil fixed on the bridge of a violin to deaden or soften the tone.
muter, mutter *n* multure.
muth *same as* **mooth**[1].
muther *n* a great number.
mutineer *v* to mutiny.
muttie, mutty, muttie-measure *n* a measure like a bushel, though smaller, with a division or bottom at a particular point within the circular walls, one end of the measure holding half a peck of oatmeal, and the other holding the same, used in taking multure.
mutton ham *n* a leg of mutton cured like ham.
mutton kail *n* mutton broth.

mutton tee *n* a mutton ham (qv).
muttyoched *adj* matted together.
mutur, muture *n* multure.
muxter-maxter *n* **1** a confused heap. **2** a miscellaneous collection.
muzzel-thrush *n* the mistle thrush.
muzzle *n* **1** the face. **2** the lower part of the face.
muzzy *adj* **1** muddled with drink. **2** dazed from injury to the head.
my *int* an exclamation of astonishment or surprise.
myaakin *same as* **mawkin**.
myaat *n* **1** the short, faint mew of a cat. **2** the slightest sound.
myach *same as* **maught**.
myak *same as* **maik**[3].
myarl *same as* **marl**[1].
myarter *same as* **martyr**.
myaut *same as* **myaat**.
myauve *same as* **miauve**.
myckie *adj* dirty.
myginich *n* **1** a coward. **2** a beaten one.
myid, myed *n* a measure.
myles *n* various species of goosefoot.
mylies *n* the small rings on a fishing rod through which the line runs.
mylk *n* milk.
mynd *n* a mine in which metals or minerals are dug.—*v* to dig in a mine.
myogre *same as* **mogre**.
myowt *n* **1** a mustering. **2** a complaint, a peevish utterance.
mype *v* **1** to speak a great deal. **2** to be very diligent.
mysel *n* a leper.—*adj* leprous.
mysel, myeell *pron* **1** myself. **2** by myself.
myster *same as* **mister**[3].
mystification *n* mystery.
myth[1] *v* **1** to measure. **2** to mark.
myth[2] *n* marrow.
mythie *adj* marrowy, full of marrow.
myting *n* a fondling name for a child.

N

na[1] *int* an exclamation of surprise.
na[2] *adv* not.
na[3] *conj* than.
na[4] *adj* no, none.
naag *v* **1** to tease. **2** to nag.
naak *n* the great northern diver.
naar *adv, prep and adj* near.
nab[1] *n* **1** a smart stroke. **2** a blow on the head.—*v* **1** to strike. **2** to peck.
nab[2] *n* **1** an important person. **2** a conceited person. **3** *in phr* **his nabs** his lordship.
nab[3] *n* the head.
nab[4] *v* **1** to catch, seize suddenly. **2** to steal. **3** to take into custody.—*n* **1** a snatch. **2** a theft.
nab[5] *v* **1** to speak affectedly. **2** to attempt to speak fine English.
nab[6] *n* **1** the summit of a rock or hill. **2** a rocky headland.
nabal *n* **1** a narrow-minded, greedy person. **2** a churlish person.—*adj* **1** churlish. **2** crusty. **3** stingy. **4** narrow-minded.
nabaler *n* a covetous person.
nabalish *adj* covetous, griping, grasping.
nabb *n* a peg or nail on which anything is hung.
nabber *n* a pilferer, thief.
nabbery[1] *n* theft, pilfering.
nabbery[2] *n* the lesser gentry.
nabble[1] *same as* **nabal**.

nabble[2] *v* to work fast, to hurry through with one's work
nabbler *n* a nabaler.
nabby *adj* **1** well-to-do. **2** of rank. **3** trim, well-dressed. **4** pretentious, dressed above one's station.
na be here *int* an exclamation of surprise or pleasure.
nabity *n* a well-dressed person.—*adj* neat, trim.
nable *same as* **nabal**.
nabrie *same as* **nabbery**.
nace *adj* destitute.
nack *n* a trick, knack.
nacket[1] *n* **1** an impertinent, mischievous child. **2** a precocious child. **3** a smart young fellow. **4** a person of small size.
nacket[2] *n* **1** the bit of wood, stone or bone used in the game of shinty. **2** a small roll of tobacco. **3** a quantity of snuff made up.
nacket[3] *n* **1** a small cake or loaf. **2** a piece of bread eaten at noon.
nacketie *adj* **1** expert in doing any piece of nice work. **2** self-conceited.—*n* one neat in person and work.
nackie[1] *n* **1** a loaf of bread. **2** a small cake.
nackie[2] *adj* clever, ingenious, expert
nackit[1] *same as* **nacket**[3].
nackit[2] *same as* **nacket**[1].
nacks *n* **1** a disease in the throat of fowls fed on too hot food. **2** pip.
nackuz *n* one who tells a tale pretty sharply.

nadder *n* an adder.
nadkin *n* **1** the taint of meat too long kept. **2** any disagreeable taste or odour.
nae *adj* no, none.—*adv* not.
naegait *adv* **1** in no wise. **2** nowhere.
nae ho *adv* nohow.—*n* no other way or resource.
nae idder *adj* and *n* no other.
nael *n* the navel.
naelins *adv* used as a negative interrogative.
nael-string *n* the umbilical cord.
nae mows *phr* **1** no joke. **2** dangerous.
nae rizzon *n* an insufficient reason.
nae-say *n* **1** a refusal. **2** the option of refusing. **3** what is undeniable.—*v* **1** to refuse. **2** to contradict.
naeslin *adj* (*used of horses*) **1** nuzzling. **2** pulling well in double harness. **3** well-matched.
naet[1] *same as* **nate**[2].
naet[2] *n* nought.
naether *pron, adj and conj* neither.
naething *n* nothing.
naetie *same as* **naitie**[2].
nastly *adv* **1** neatly. **2** completely. **3** exactly.
naff *same as* **nyaff**[2].
naffin *n* idle talk, chatter.
naffle[1] *same as* **nyaffle**.
naffle[2] *v* to rumple.
naffy *adj* **1** affable. **2** on good terms. **3** gossipy. **4** newsy.
nag[1] *v* **1** to strike smartly. **2** to snap, bite. **3** to nick, notch. **4** to find fault with continually and peevishly. **5** to jeer. **6** to labour persistently and painfully.—*n* **1** a snap, bite. **2** a nick, notch, a hack. **3** an indentation with a sharp instrument. **4** a snappish retort. **5** a stroke in the game of nags. **6** (*in pl*) a game at marbles in which the loser is struck on the knuckles by other players with their marbles.
nag[2] *n* the ball used in shinty, etc.
nag[3], **nagg** *n* **1** a peg or nail on which to hang hats, clothes, etc. **2** the short stump of a broken-off branch.
nag[4] *n* a saddle horse.
naggie *same as* **noggie**.
naggle *v* to fret continuously.
naggly *adj* **1** touchy, fretful. **2** peevish, ill-natured. **3** sarcastic.
naggy *adj* snappish, cross.
nag-nail *n* **1** an ingrowing nail. **2** a bunion.
nagy *n* a pony.
naig *n* **1** a riding horse. **2** a nag. **3** a stallion. **4** a pony.—*v* (*with* **awa'**) to move like a horse that has a long, quick and steady pace.
naig-graith *n* harness.
naigie *n* a horse, a pony.
nail[1] *n* **1** a trigger. **2** (*in pl*) loose tufts of wool. **3** refuse of wool.—*v* **1** to catch unawares. **2** to arrest. **3** to steal. **4** to settle a bargain. **5** to clench an argument. **6** to aim at successfully. **7** to kill. **8** to strike. **9** (*with* **off**) to say or repeat rapidly.
nail[2] *n* a particular pain in the forehead.
nailer *n* a clincher.
nailerel *adj* insignificant-looking.
nail horn *n* a nail.
nailing *n* a beating.
nail-pinn *n* a nail or pin used in boatbuilding.
nain *adj* own.—*phr* **by one's nain** by oneself.
nain folk *n* **1** one's particular friends or supporters. **2** one's kinsfolk.
nainsel' *pron* **1** one's own self. **2** a nickname for a Highlander.
naip *n* the ridge of a roof.
naipkin *n* **1** a napkin. **2** a handkerchief.
naipry *n* napery.
nairrow *adj* **1** narrow. **2** stingy.
naise *same as* **neeze**.
naish *same as* **nesch**.
naisty *adj* nasty.

nait *adj* neat.
naither *conj, pron and adj* neither.
naitherans *adv and conj* neither.
naithers *adv and conj* neither.
naithing *n* nothing.
naithless *adv* nevertheless.
naitie[1] *same as* **nittie**[2].
naitie[2] *adj* **1** natty. **2** neat, tidy. **3** handy. **4** clever in mechanical operations.
naitir *n* nature.—*adj* **1** natural. **2** growing naturally.
naitir-woo' *same as* **nature-wool**.
naitral *adj* natural, native.—*n* **1** one's nature. **2** an imbecile.
naivel *same as* **nevell**.
nake *v* **1** to bare. **2** to make naked.
naked, nakit *adj* **1** scanty, insufficient. **2** unarmed, defenceless. **3** destitute. **4** sole. **5** simple.
naked-corn *n* thin-eared corn.
naked-truth *n* spirits neat.
nale *n* an alehouse.
nam *v* to seize quickly and rather violently.
name *n* **1** a clan. **2** a group of persons bearing the same name. **3** a reputation for. **4** a report.—*v* **1** to report that two persons are courting or engaged to each other. **2** to baptise.
name-daughter *n* a girl who bears one's name.
name-father *n* a person whose Christian name one bears.
nameliheid *n* fame, glory.
namely *adj* famous, celebrated.
namers-and-guessers *same as* **namie-and-guessie**.
name-son *n* a boy who bears one's name.
namie-and-guessie *n* a children's guessing game.
nam-nam *adj* **1** pleasant to the taste. **2** sweet.
namshach *v* to hurt severely.—*n* an accident, misfortune.
nancy-pretty *n* London pride, none-so-pretty.
nane[1] *adj* none.
nane[2] *same as* **nain**.
nanse *n* the nonce.
nanny *n* a she-goat.
nap[1] *n* a soporific, a soothing.
nap[2] *n* **1** a wooden vessel or dish made with staves. **2** a milk vat.
nap[3] *n* **1** ale, strong beer. **2** the head on ale. **3** the head.
nap[4] *n* **1** a bit. **2** a morsel. **3** a snack.—*v* to bite.
nap[5] *n* **1** a joke, jest, fun. **2** a trick.
nap[6] *n* a shin of beef.
nap[7] *v* (*used of a fishing line*) to be released when a hook is caught on the bottom by means of the recoil of a strong pull suddenly stopped.
nap[8] *adj* **1** expert, clever. **2** ready, eager.
nap[9] *n* an eccentric person.
nap[10] *v* **1** to knock. **2** to hammer.—*n* a blow, tap.
naper *n* the head.
napery *n* **1** bed and table linen, sometimes including blankets. **2** a closet for household linen.
napkin *n* **1** a pocket handkerchief. **2** a kerchief for the head or neck.
napper *n* a mallet, beetle.
nappie *n* a short sleep.
nappit *adj* **1** crabbed. **2** ill-humoured.
napple, napple-root *n* the heath pea.
nappy[1] *n* **1** strong ale. **2** any alcoholic drink.—*adj* **1** (*used of ale or beer*) foaming. **2** (*of any liquor*) strong, heady. **3** excited by liquor, tipsy. **4** strong, vigorous.
nappy[2], **nappie** *adj* **1** brittle. **2** (*used of the tongue*) snappish, tart.
nappy *n* a wooden dish.
nappy-boin *n* a small tub.
napron, naperon *n* an apron.
napsie *n* a little, fat animal, such as a sheep.
napskap *n* a headpiece, a steel bonnet.
nar[1] *conj* **1** nor. **2** than, if, that.
nar[2] *adv, prep and adj* near.
narder *adv and adj* nearer.

nardest *adv and adj* nearest.
narg *v* 1 to nag. 2 to fret. 3 to jeer.—*n* continual quarrelling.
nargle *adj* jeering.
nar-hand *adv* 1 near at hand. 2 hard-by. 3 nearly. —*prep* near to.—*adj* 1 neighbouring. 2 niggardly.
narly *adv* narrowly.
narr *v* to snarl, as dogs.
narration *n* a great noise or clamour.
narrow *adj* 1 stingy. 2 close. 3 searching.
narrow-nebbit *adj* narrow-minded, bigoted.
nar-side *n* the left side of a horse, etc.
na-say *same as* **nae-say**.
nase *n* the nose.
nash[1] *v* 1 to prate. 2 to talk pertly.—*n* pert, insolent talk.
nash[2] *same as* **nesch**.
nashag *n* the bearberry.
nash-gab *n* 1 a forward, prattling girl. 2 insolent talk.
nash-gabbit *adj* pert, talkative, gossiping.
nashie *adj* talkative, chattering.
na, sirs *int* an exclamation of surprise.
nask *n* a withe for binding cattle.
nastified *adj* nasty, disgusting.
nasty *adj* ill-tempered.—*v* to commit an annoying act, to act like a nuisance.
nat *n* a person of short stature and short temper.
natch *v* 1 to lay hold of violently. 2 to notch. 3 to loop or sling.—*n* a notch, an incision made in cutting cloth.
nate[1] *v* 1 to need. 2 to use.—*n* use, employment.
nate[2] *adj* 1 neat. 2 pretty. 3 exact. 4 precise. 5 identical. 6 mere.—*adv* exactly.
nateral *adj* natural.
natheless, nathless *adv* nevertheless.
nather *conj, pron and adj* neither.
nathing *n* nothing.
nation *n* a division of students according to birthplace in the universities of Glasgow, St Andrews and Aberdeen.
native *n* one's birthplace.
natkin *same as* **nadkin**.
natrie, nattrie *adj* 1 ill-tempered. 2 grumbling. 3 querulous.
natter *v* 1 to grumble, fret. 2 to tease, worry, nag. 3 to talk in an unfriendly way. 4 to debate, to wrangle.—*n* peevish chattering, grumbling.
natterin *adj* chattering fretfully.
nattle *v* 1 to nibble. 2 to gnaw.
natty *same as* **naitie**[2].
natural *adj* 1 due to birth alone. 2 affable. 3 simple, kind. 4 (*of the weather*) genial.—*n* 1 an idiot, imbecile, half-witted person. 2 one's nature or constitution.
naturality, naturalty *n* 1 natural affection. 2 natural disposition.
nature *adj* 1 spontaneously producing rich herbage, etc. 2 rich, nourishing.
nature-clover *n* rich natural clover.
nature grass *n* rich natural grass.
nature-ground *n* land producing rich natural grass.
nature hay *n* hay produced by the ground spontaneonsly.
natureness *n* 1 spontaneous fertility in rich herbage. 2 richness and exuberance of natural grass.
nature-wid *n* natural wood.
nature-wool *n* 1 fine wool. 2 wool pulled off from the sheep's back instead of being shorn.
naubal *same as* **nabal**.
nauborly *adj* close-fisted.
nauchle *n* a dwarf.
nauchlie *adj* dwarfish.
naucht *n* naught, nought.
naughtafee *v* 1 to make naught of. 2 to disparage.
naukie *adj* 1 asthmatic. 2 short-winded.
nauks *same as* **nacks**.
naum *n* a heavy blow with a bludgeon.
naup *n* a nap, short sleep.
naur *adj, prep and adv* near.

naval *same as* **nevell**.
nave *same as* **neive**.
navel *n* 1 the very centre. 2 the very front.
navus-bore *n* a hole in wood where a knot has dropped out.
nawn *same as* **nain**.
nawus-~, nawvus-bore *same as* **navus-bore**.
nax *n* a schoolboy's humiliating birching, etc.
naxie *same as* **nackuz**.
nay-say *same as* **nae-say**.
nay-sayer *n* one who denies.
nay-saying *n* a refusal.
naze *n* a promontory.
neal *v* to soften.
neap[1] *n* a turnip.
neap[2] *n* the nape.
neaphle *n* a thing of no value.
neapit *adj* (*used of tides*) low.
near[1] *n* a kidney.
near[2] *adv* 1 nearly. 2 exactly. 3 narrowly. 4 sparingly.—*adj* 1 close. 2 short. 3 left. 4 narrow. 5 stingy, niggardly.
near-about *adv* almost.
near-begaun *adj* stingy, parsimonious.
near-behadden *adj* stingy, miserly.
near-bludit *adj* closely connected by blood.
near-by *adv* 1 close to, near at hand. 2 almost.
near-cut *n* a short cut, the nearest way.
nearer-hand *adv* nearer.
near-friend *adj* closely related.
near-gaun *adj* stingy, miserly.
near-geddert *adj* (*used of money*) gathered by parsimony.
near-hand *same as* **nar-hand**.
near-hand gate *n* the nearest way.
near-handness *n* 1 nearness. 2 a short distance. 3 niggardliness.
near-hand road *n* a short cut.
nearlins *adv* nearly, almost.
nearmaist *adj* nearest.—*adv* almost.
near miss *n* 1 almost a miss. 2 almost a hit.
nearness *n* niggardliness.
near-o' ane *n* not one.
near oneself *adj* 1 niggardly. 2 tenacious of one's own property. 3 very careful as to one's self-interest.
near-strings *n* the strings connected with the kidneys.
near the bane *adj* niggardly.
nease *n* the nose.
neast *same as* **neist**.
neat *adj* 1 pretty, pleasing to the eye, exact. 2 mere. 3 identical.—*adv* 1 exactly. 2 nett.
neath- *prep* beneath.—*adv* under, lower than.
neath-maist, -mest *adj* lowest, undermost.
neat land *n* land for grazing neat cattle.
neat's-fire *same as* **need-fire**.
neaty *adj* 1 mere. 2 identical.
neave *same as* **neive**.
neavil *same as* **nevell**.
neb, nebb *n* 1 the tip or point of anything. 2 the snout. 3 the nib of a pen. 4 oatmeal and water mixed up together in a wooden dish, rolled like cucumbers and boiled. 5 the time between dawn and sunrise. 6 pungency. 7 pungency in liquor. —*v* 1 to peck, to scold. 2 to bill and coo, kiss, caress. 3 to make a pen of a goose quill.
neb and feather *phr* completely.
nebbily *adv* sharply, smartly.
nebbit *adj* 1 having a beak or nose. 2 pointed, edged. 3 having a hooked head on a staff.
nebbock *n* the nose.
nebby *adj* sharp, ill-natured, smart.
neb-cap *n* an iron toe plate on shoe or clog.
nebed *same as* **nebbit**.
nebfu' *n* 1 a beakful. 2 a very small quantity of whisky, etc.
neb-o'-the-mire-snipe *n* the utmost extremity.
neb-o'-the-morning *n* the time between dawn and sunrise.

nebsy *n* an impudent old woman.

necessar *adj* necessary.—*n* (*in pl*) necessary things.

necessitat *adj* necessitated, compelled.

necessitous *adj* necessary.

nechram *n* horse leather.

neck *n* **1** the neck piece or cape of a coat, covering the neck and shoulders. **2** a weaving term.—*v* **1** to kill, behead. **2** to put the arm round the neck. **3** to court.

neck-break *n* **1** ruin, destruction. **2** what brings to an unlooked-for end.

neck-cutter *n* a headsman, executioner.

neck-deep *adv* up to the neck.

neck-herring *n* a smart stroke.

necking *n* courting.

neckit *n* a tippet for a child.

neckle *v* to entangle.

neckless *adj* (*of a button*) without a shank.

neck-napkin *n* a neckerchief.

neck-verse *n* Psalm 51, 1, sung at executions.

ned, neddy *n* **1** a donkey. **2** a simpleton.

neddar, neddir *n* an adder.

nedder *conj, pron and adj* neither.

neddercap *n* a cross-grained person.

nedderin *conj and adv* neither.

nedeun *n* a gnawing pain.—*v* **1** (*of pain*) to gnaw. **2** to mutter curses to oneself.

neebour *n* a neighbour.

need *v* **1** to do of necessity. **2** to use.

need-be *n* **1** a necessity. **2** expediency.

needcessitate *v* to necessitate.

needcessity *n* **1** necessity, a state of need. **2** (*in pl*) things needful for life.

need-fire *n* **1** fire caused by friction of two pieces of wood, used as a charm for murrain, etc. **2** a beacon fire. **3** spontaneous ignition.

needfu' *adj* needy, necessitous.—*n* (*in pl*) necessaries.

needlach *n* a small, young eel.

needle *n* **1** a fallen leaf of the larch or Scotch fir. **2** a spark of fire or boiling matter that pricks the spot of skin on which it falls. **3** a cheat, swindle. **4** anything of the smallest.—*v* **1** to sew with a needle. **2** to work backwards and forwards. **3** to thread one's way through.

needle-cases *n* a children's singing game.

needle-dumper *n* a seamstress.

needle-e'e *n in phr* **through the needle-e'e 1** the children's game of thread-the-needle. **2** the game of oranges and lemons.

needlefish *n* **1** the shorter pipefish. **2** the sea needle.

needles-e'e *n* a nutshell.

needle-speed *n* the utmost speed.

needle-steik *n* a needle stitch.

need-made-up *adj* hastily prepared as immediately necessary.—*n* anything so prepared.

needment *n* a requirement, anything necessary.

neednail *v* to clinch a nail.

neef *n* need, difficulty.

neeger[1], **neegre** *n* **1** a Negro. **2** a hard worker. **3** an adept.

neeger[2], **neigre** *same as* **niggar**.

neek-nack *adv* rapidly moving in and out, or to and fro, as in play.

neemit *n* dinner.

neen[1] *adj* none.

neen[2] *n* noon.

neep[1] *n* **1** a turnip. **2** a bulky, old-fashioned watch in a hinged case. **3** a disagreeable person. **4** anything ugly of its kind. **5** (*in pl*) the time between the final hoeing of turnips and the harvest.—*v* to serve cattle with turnips.

neep[2] *n* a promontory.

neep-brose *n* a dish of oatmeal mixed with mashed turnips.

neep-cutter *n* a turnip-cutter.

neep-grun' *n* ground in which turnips are sown.

neep-hack, ~-hawk *n* **1** a pronged mattock for raising tur-

nips from the frozen ground. **2** a turnip rack for feeding cattle or sheep out of doors with turnips in winter.

neep-heid *n* **1** a turnip head. **2** a stupid person.

neep-heidit *adj* dull, stupid.

neepkin *n* **1** a napkin. **2** a pocket-handkerchief.

neep-like *adj* **1** like a turnip. **2** stupid.

neepour *n* a neighbour.

neep-reet *n* growing turnips.

neep seed *n* **1** turnip seed. **2** the time for sowing turnip seed.

neep-shaw *n* a turnip top.

neepyun *n* a napkin.

neer *same as* **near**[1].

ne'er-be-licket *phr* not a whit.

Ne'er-Day *n* **1** New Year's Day. **2** a New-Year's Day present.

neerder *adj* nearer.

ne'er-do-gude *adj* **1** past mending. **2** irreclaimable.

ne'er-do-weel *n* an incorrigible in wickedness, folly or indolence.

ne'erless *adv* nevertheless.

ne'er may care *adv* nevertheless.

neese *same as* **neeze**.

nesshin *v* (*used of an animal*) to desire the male.

neeshin *n* **1** sneezing. **2** snuff.

neeshin-mill *n* a snuffbox.

neest *adj* nearest, next.

neet[1] *n* a parsimonious person, a niggard.

neet[2] *n* **1** a nit, the egg of a louse. **2** a louse.

neetie *adj* miserly, stingy.

neety-cud *n* a low fellow who does mean things.

neeve *same as* **neive**.

Neever-day *n* New Year's Day.

Neever-e'en *n* New Year's Eve.

neevie-neevie-nick-nack *n* a guessing game played with a small article hidden in one closed hand moved over the other.

neeze[1] *v* to sneeze.—*n* a sneeze.

neeze[2], **neez** *n* the nose.

neffit *n* **1** a pigmy. **2** a chit.

neffle *same as* **nevell**.

neffow, neffu' *n* a handful.—*v* **1** to take in handfuls. **2** to handle an animal.

neg[1] *v* **1** to bite, snap. **2** to nag.

neg[2] *same as* **naig**.

negleck *v* to neglect.—*n* neglect.

negleckfu' *adj* negligent, apt to neglect.

neibour *n* a neighbour.

neicher, neigher *same as* **nicker**[2].

neidfire *same as* **need-fire**.

neidnail *same as* **need-nail**.

neif[1], **neif**[2] *same as* **neive**.

neiffer *same as* **niffer**.

neighbour *n* **1** a companion, comrade, good friend. **2** a partner. **3** a fellow servant. **4** a bedfellow. **5** a husband or wife. **6** a friend. **7** a match, one of a similar pair.—*adj* neighbouring, fellow. —*v* **1** to consort with. **2** to work along with or in partnership. **3** (*with* **ill**) to disagree.

neighbourhood *n* friendly, social relations.

neighbourless *adj* not matching, not of a pair.

neighbourlike *adj* **1** like one's neighbours. **2** friendly, sociable.

neighbourliness *n* friendship, companionship.

neigher *same as* **nicker**[2].

neigre *same as* **niggar**.

Neil *n in phr* **Auld Neil** the devil.

neilship *n in phr* **his neilship** the devil.

neip *same as* **neep**[1].

neiper *n* a neighbour.

neiperheed *n* friendship, social relations.

neiperty *n* **1** partnership. **2** the embrace of copulation. **3** companionship.

neir *same as* **near**[1].

neis *n* **1** the nose. **2** a ness.

neisht *adj* next.

neist *adj* nearest.—*adv* next.—*prep* next to, on this side of.

neistmost *adj* next.

neistways *adv* in a short time after.

neis-wise *adj* **1** having an acute sense of smell. **2** quick of perception or pretending to be so.

neith *same as* **neath**.

neithers *adv* notwithstanding, either.

neive *n* **1** the fist. **2** the hand. **3** the closed hand. **4** a handful. **5** cheating at marbles by stretching the hand over the score. **6** a measure of length. **7** (*in pl*) fisticuffs, boxing.—*v* **1** to catch with the hands, guddle (qv). **2** to turf the ridge of a house so as to hold and cover the ends of the thatch. **3** to cheat at marbles by extending the hand unduly.

nievefu' *same as* **nievefu'**.

neive-shaking *n* **1** a women's quarrel, scolding match. **2** a windfall.

neivie-nick-nack *n* a guessing game played with the neives or closed hands. *See* **neive**.

nek *same as* **neck**.

nell *v* to talk loudly or fluently.

nellin *adj* **1** loquacious. **2** frivolous.

nell-kneed *adj* knock-kneed.

nens, nenst, nent *prep* **1** opposite to. **2** regarding.

nepos, nepus-gable *n* a gable in the middle of the front of a house.

neppit *same as* **nippit**.

ner *conj* than.

nerby *prep* near to.—*adv* **1** nearly. **2** almost.

nerlins *adv* nearly, almost.

nerr *v* **1** to snarl or growl as a dog. **2** to purr as a cat, to fret.—*n* **1** a growl. **2** a purr.

nerve *n* **1** capacity, ability. **2** (*in pl*) an attack of nervousness. **3** strong excitement.

nervish *adj* nervous.

nervously *adj* forcibly.

nesch *adj* of delicate health.

ness *same as* **nace**.

nesscock, nesscockle *n* a small boil, a hot pimple.

nesslin *n* the smallest and weakest bird in the nest.

net[1] *adv* neatly.

net[2] *n* the omentum or caul covering the intestines.—*v* to enclose sheep by nets.

neth *prep* beneath.—*adv* under.

nether[1] *adj* **1** lower. **2** nearer, next.

nether[2] *n* an adder.

nether[3] *pron and conj* neither.

netherans *same as* **naitherans**.

nether-end *n* the posteriors.

nethermaist *adj* lowest.—*n* the lowest part.

nether-stane *n* an adder-bead (qv), used as a charm against elf-shots (qv).

nethmist *adj* undermost.

net-silk *n* knitted silk, used for stockings.

nett *adv* exactly.

nettercap *n* a spider.

netterie *adj* **1** ill-natured. **2** sarcastic.

nettery *n* a spider.

nettle *v* to puzzle.

nettle broth *n* broth made of young nettles, as a substitute for greens.

nettle-earnest *adj* in deadly earnest.

nettle kail *same as* **nettle broth**.

nettlesome *adj* **1** peevish. **2** quarrelsome. **3** irritating.

nettlie *adj* **1** ill-humoured, fretful. **2** exasperating.

nettly *adv* exactly.

netty[1] *adj* mere, sheer.

netty[2] *n* a woman who traverses the country in search of wool.

neucheld *adj* (*of a cow*) newly calved, with calf.

neuck, neuk *n* **1** a nook, recess, interior angle. **2** a niche, crevice. **3** a corner seat by the fire. **4** an out-of-the-way place. **5** childbed. **6** a corner, the corner of a garment or any piece of cloth. **7** a fair share of work, of a treat, etc.—*v* **1** to curb, humble. **2** to outwit, take in, trick.

neukatyke *n* a shepherd's collie.

neukie *adj* having corners.

neukit *adj* **1** having corners. **2** crooked. **3** short-tempered, sharp.

neuk-stane *n* a cornerstone.

neuktime *n* twilight, as the season for pastime or gossiping among workpeople.

neull *same as* **nool**[1].

neulled *adj* having very short horns.

nev, neve *same as* **neive**.

neval *adv in phr* **to fa' a-neval** (*used of an animal*) lying helpless on its back.

nevell, nevel *v* **1** to strike with the fist, pommel. **2** to grasp, pluck out. **3** to knead. **4** to pinch with the fingers.—*n* a blow with the fist or elbow.

nevermas *n* a time that never comes.

nevilling *n* a pommelling.

nevil-stone *n* the keystone of an arch.

nevo, nevoy, nevey *n* nephew.

new[1] *v* **1** to curb, master, humble. **2** to beat severely.

new[2] *adj* recently happened.—*adv* newly.—*n in phr* **in the new** anew.

newan *n* a drubbing, a beating.

newance *n* **1** something new or unusual. **2** the first kiss given to a person by a child on getting a new garment.

new bread *n* a novelty.

new-brent *adj* quite new.

new-cal', -ca'd *adj* (*used of a cow*) **1** lately calved. **2** with calf, pregnant.

new-cheese *n* a cheese made of the milk of a newly calved cow.

newcome *adj* newly come, fresh.

newfangle *n* a novelty.—*adj* **1** fond of novelty. **2** pleasant to strangers. **3** new-fashioned.

newfangled *adj* **1** vain of a new thing. **2** in a new and strange position. **3** innovating.

newfangledness *n* **1** love of novelty. **2** an innovation, novelty.

Newhaven gill *n* a measure of two gills.

newing *n* **1** barm. **2** yeast.

newings *same as* **newance**.

newis *adj* **1** earnestly desirous. **2** parsimonious, greedy, keeping in.

new light *adj* liberal and progressive in doctrine.

newline, newlans *adv* **1** very lately. **2** newly, recently.

newmost *adj* nethermost, lowest.—*n* the nethermost.

newous[1] *same as* **newis**.

newous[2] *adj* fond or full of what is new, newfangled.

newouslie *adv* in a novel or new-fashioned way.

newousness *n* **1** newfangledness. **2** an innovation. **3** love of novelty.

new-pan *n* a widow's second husband.

newrgift *n* a New Year's Day gift.

news, newse *n* **1** gossip. **2** talk. **3** the subject of talk. **4** a newspaper.—*v* **1** to tell as news. **2** to talk over the news. **3** to gossip, talk.

New's Day *n* New Year's Day.

newser *n* **1** a retailer of news. **2** a gossip.

newsfu' *adj* full of gossip.

news-gizzened *adj* empty of, or hungering for, news.

newsie *adj* talkative. **2** gossiping.

newsing *n* gossip.—*adj* gossiping.

news-lassie *n* a newspaper-girl.

newspaper billy *n* a press reporter.

newspaper-woman, ~-man *n* a great reader of newspapers.

New-Year-Day *n* **1** New Year's Day. **2** a present given on New Year's Day.

next *adj* next but one.

nextan, nexten *adj* next.

neypsie *adj* **1** prim. **2** precise in manners.

niaff *same as* **nyaff**².
nib *n* **1** the human nose. **2** a narrow strip of land. **3** a long, projecting headland. **4** a point, tip. **5** a nibble, a snapping bite.
nibbawa, nibawa *adj* **1** snappish, crusty. **2** thin, emaciated-looking.
nibbie *n* **1** a walking stick with a crooked head. **2** a shepherd's crook.
nibbits *n* two pieces of oatcake buttered and placed face to face.
nibble¹ *n* the stump of a pen.
nibble² *v* **1** to fidget with the fingers. **2** to snatch stealthily.
nibbock *n* a beak, bill.
niber *n* a neighbour.
nibwise *adj* ready to take offence or take up a wrong meaning.
niccar *same as* **nicker**³.
nice *adj* **1** difficult, critical. **2** fine.
nice-gabbit *adj* **1** difficult to please with food. **2** prim, particular of speech.
nicelies *adv* nicely.
niceness *n* **1** a difficulty. **2** a ticklish business.
nicety *n* a dainty, a luxury. **2** a nice thing.
nicher *same as* **nicker**³.
nicherin *same as* **nickerin**.
nichil *n* nothing.
nicht *n* **1** night. **2** the evening. **3** a curtain lecture. —*v* **1** to darken. **2** to benight. **3** to spend the night, lodge for the night. **4** to spend the evening with. **5** to visit after dark. **6** to stop work for the day. **7** to cease working at the close of daylight.
nicht-at-eenie *n* the time of night when children play, etc, before bedtime.
nicht-bour *n* a bedchamber.
nicht-bussing *n* a woman's nightcap.
nicht-cap *n* some liquor taken before going to bed.
nicht-come *n* nightfall.
nicht-cowl *n* a nightcap.
nicht-cowled *adj* wearing a nightcap.
nicht-hawk *n* **1** a large white moth that flies about hedges on summer evenings. **2** a person who ranges about at night.
nicht-hawking *adj* given to roaming at night.
nichting time *n* the time when daylight closes and outdoor labour ceases.
nichtit *adj* **1** benighted. **2** darkened by night.
nicht-kep *n* a nightcap.
nichtless *adj* with no night.
nicht-mirk *n* the darkness of night.
nicht-mutch *n* a woman's nightcap.
nicht-rail *n* **1** a covering for the head worn at night. **2** a nightdress.
nichtside *n* the course of the evening.
nicht-things *n* coal, peats, water, etc, brought in at night for use next morning.
Nick *n* a name for the devil.
nick¹ *n* **1** a score, mark. **2** a cleft, crevice, grove. **3** the angle between the beam and handle of a plough. **4** a hollow or pass through hills. **5** (*in pl*) the knuckles.—*v* **1** to cut. **2** to reap. **3** to stab. **4** to wrinkle. **5** to bite. **6** to snap off. **7** to thwart. **8** to cut one short. **9** to refuse curtly. **10** to deprive.
nick² *n* **1** a wink. **2** a gibe, jeer. **3** a retort.—*v* to answer in a mocking or insulting way.
nick³ *v* **1** to click. **2** to play a marble smartly with thumb and first finger. **3** to aim at marbles.—*n* **1** a creaking sound. **2** a click. **3** a smart blow.—*phr* **to play nick** to sound like something suddenly giving way.
nick⁴ *v* **1** to steal. **2** to cheat. **3** to seize. **4** to catch away.—*n* **1** an act of trickery or deceit. **2** a policeman.
nick⁵ *v* to drink heartily.
nickelty *n* the letter N on a teetotum, signifying nothing.
nickem, nickim *n* **1** a mischievous, tricky boy. **2** a wag.
nicker¹ *n* a water sprite.

nicker² *n* the marble with which a boy aims, a pitcher.
nicker³ *v* **1** to neigh, whinny. **2** to give a suppressed laugh, snigger.—*n* **1** the neighing of a horse. **2** light laughter. **3** a snigger.
nickerers *n* creaking shoes, new shoes that creak.
nickerie *n* a term of endearment for a child.
nickerin' *n* a neighing, whinnying.
nickery *adj* knavish.
nickey, nickie, nickie-ben *n* the devil.
nickie frog *n* a contemptuous name for a Frenchman.
nick-in-the neck *n* a person's manifest weak point or peculiarity
nickit, nicket *n* a small notch.
nickle¹ *v* **1** to aim with a marble briskly. **2** to handle. **3** to set up type.—*n* **1** a sharp stroke such as impels a pitcher at marbles. **2** a player at marbles.
nickle² *n* a knuckle.
nickle³ *n* **1** *in phr* **N-nichil, nickle-naething** said when the teetotum displays N uppermost. **2** nothing at all.
nickle doon *v* to propel a marble with the knuckles touching the ground.
nickle in *v* to propel a marble with the hand inverted in a strained position, so as to reduce the chance of hitting a marble in the ring.
nickler *n* a boys' marble used as a pitcher.
nickling *n* the act of propelling a marble.
nick-nack *adv* with steady motion or clicking sound.
nick-nack *n* **1** a gimcrack. **2** (*in pl*) small wares.
nick-nacket *n* a trinket.
nick-nackity *adj* precise, punctilious.
nick-nacky *adj* dexterous in doing nice work.
nick on the horn *n* another year of life.
nicks *v* to aim at anything near.
nickstick *n* a tally.
nickstick bodie *n* **1** one who proceeds exactly by rule. **2** one who does nothing without a return in kind.
nickum *same as* **nickem**.
nicky-nacky *adj* **1** gimcrack. **2** useless, trifling. **3** speaking mincingly.
nid *v* to nod slightly.
nidder¹ *conj* neither.
nidder² *adj* lower.
nidder³ *n* the second shoot made by growing grain.
nidder⁴ *v* **1** to depress. **2** to straighten. **3** to undervalue, depreciate. **4** to put out of shape by frequent handling.
nidder⁵ *v* **1** to shiver. **2** to shiver with cold. **3** to subject to hunger. **4** to pinch with cold. **5** to shrivel. **6** to pine, fret, wither. **7** to blast and bite with frost or wind. **8** to plague.
niddle¹ *v* **1** to work quickly with the fingers without doing much. **2** to trifle with the fingers.
niddle² *v* to overcome and rob.
niddle³ *v* (*used of birds*) to bill and coo, to frisk about each other at pairing time.
niddling, nidling *adj* trifling.
niddy-noddy *n* **1** a palsied movement of the head. **2** (*in pl*) assumed airs, showy manners, as shown by the movement of the head.
nidge *n* **1** a heavy squeeze, pressure. **2** a nudge.—*v* **1** to squeeze, press down. **2** to nudge.
nidgell *n* **1** a fat, forward young man. **2** a lover no one can displace.
nidity-nod *adv* bobbing up and down.
nid-noddy *adj* falling asleep.
nidy-noy *adv* **1** with affected gait. **2** with mincing or bobbing step.
nief *n* a female bondservant.
niegre *same as* **niggar**
niest *adj* next.
nieve, niev *same as* **neive**.
nievefu' *n* **1** a handful. **2** a small quantity of anything dry. **3** any person or thing very small and puny. **4** anything comparatively of little or no value. **5** a death's hold of what is viewed as worthy of grasping.

nieveshaking *n* **1** something dropped from the hand of another. **2** a windfall.

nievle *same as* **nevell**.

nievling *n* milking a cow by grasping the teat with the whole hand.

niffer *v* **1** to exchange, barter. **2** to haggle in bargaining.— *n* an exchange, barter.

nifferer *n* a barterer.

niffle *v* **1** to trifle. **2** to be in any respect insignificant.

niffle-naffle *v* to trifle away time.

niff-naff *n* **1** a trifle. **2** anything very small. **3** a small person. **4** a silly peculiarity of temper. **5** fussiness.—*v* **1** to trifle. **2** to talk in a silly way. **3** to toy. **4** to take finicking trouble.

niff-naffy *adj* **1** fussy. **2** over-particular about trifles.

nif-niff, niffy-naff *v* to trifle.

nig *n in phr* **nigs and news** knick-knacks, oddments.

nigg *v* **1** to complain, fret. **2** to nag.

niggar *n* **1** a niggard. **2** a mean fellow. **3** a lout. **4** an iron cheek to a grate, used for economy of fuel.

nigger *same as* **neeger**[1].

niggerality *n* meanness, niggardliness.

nigger'd *adj* in reduced circumstances.

niggerhead *n* a white cowrie.

niggerhead *n* negrohead tobacco.

niggle *v* **1** to hack. **2** to cut with a blunt implement.

nigher *same as* **nicker**[3].

nigh-hand *adv* nearly.

night *same as* **nicht**.

night-gown *n* a dressing gown.

nightingale *n* a moth.

nig-ma-nies *n* **1** sundry trifles. **2** needless ornaments. **3** gewgaws. **4** a bride's things.

nig-nag, ~-nac *n* **1** a knick-knack. **2** a worthless trifle.

nig-nay, -nae, -new, -eye *n* **1** a trifle. **2** a knick-knack. **3** a plaything. **4** a gewgaw.—*v* **1** to do what is useless or is without good result. **2** to show reluctance. **3** to work in a trifling way.

nig-nayin *adj* **1** whimsical. **2** full of crotchets.

nigre *same as* **niggar**.

nikkienow *n* a term of reproach.

nil *same as* **nill**.

nile *n* a plug for the water hole in the bottom of a boat.

nile-hole *n* the hole for the nile (qv).

nill, nil *v* **1** to be unwilling. **2** *in phr* **nill ye, will ye** whether you will or no.

nim[1] *n* steam, vapour, warm air.

nim[2] *v* **1** to catch up quickly. **2** to walk with brisk, short steps or mincingly.

nimble *adj* clever, astute.

nimble-gawn *adj* **1** nimble. **2** loquacious.

nimious *adj* oppressive, exceeding due bounds, excessive.

nimle *adj* nimble.

nimmit *n* dinner.

nimp *n* a very small piece.

nine-eyed-eel *n* the lamprey.

nineholes *n* **1** the game of nine-men's morris. **2** the piece of beef that is cut out immediately below the breast.

nine O's *n* a game in which nine O's in three parallel columns are to be joined by lines that must not cross each other.

ninepence *n in phr* **to a ninepence** to a T.

ninesome *adj* consisting of nine.

nineteen *n* a nineteen years' lease of a farm.

ninny-niawing *n* whinnying.

ninyoumpook *n* a nincompoop.

nip *v* **1** to graze. **2** to eat daintily. **3** to taste sharp. **4** to smart. **5** to tingle with cold. **6** to be niggardly, to stint. **7** to cheat. **8** to snatch. **9** to steal. **10** to run off quickly.—*n* **1** a squeeze. **2** a bite, a bite in fishing. **3** the pain of a pinch or bite. **4** a sharp, pungent flavour. **5** a burning, biting taste. **6** a keen feeling in the air. **7** a small bit of anything. **8** a share of a burden, etc. **9** an advantage in bargaining. **10** speed, rate.—

in phr **take a nip of one** to take undue advantage of one.

nip-caik *n* an eater of delicacies in secret.

nipick *same as* **nippock**.

nipkin *n* **1** a napkin. **2** a pocket handkerchief.

nip-lug *n* **1** a schoolmaster. **2** quarrelling to the point of blows.

nip-necks *v* (*of horses*) to bite each other's neck.

nipour *same as* **neiper**.

nipper[1] *n* a small quantity of strong liquor.

nipper[2] *n* **1** a sharp retort. **2** a settler (qv).

nipper[3] *n* **1** a niggard. **2** a tooth. **3** (*in pl*) tongs. **4** forceps.

nipperkin *n* a small measure of liquor.

nipper-nebbit *adj* having a sharp beak.

nipperren *n* a small quantity.

nipperty *adj* mincing, affected.

nipperty-tipperty *adj* **1** childishly exact, affectedly neat. **2** quick, rattling in rhythm.

nippily *adv* smartly, sharply.

nipping *n* **1** a smarting pain. **2** a tingling.—*adj* **1** sharp. **2** pungent. **3** tingling, aching. **4** cold, freezing. **5** short in size or weight. **6** niggardly. **7** tricky.

nippit *adj* **1** niggardly. **2** short in size or weight. **3** scanty. **4** (*used of clothes*) tight-fitting, pinched-in. **5** starved-looking. **6** apt to give short weight or measure. **7** narrow-minded, bigoted. **8** snappish, short-tempered.

nippitness *n* stinginess.

nippock *n* a very small piece.

nippy *adj* **1** sharp. **2** pungent, biting, causing to tingle. **3** bitter of speech. **4** scanty. **5** tight in fit. **6** too little. **7** stingy. **8** keen to take advantage. **9** tricky.—*n* a very small bit.

nippy sweetie *n* a bitter person, especially a woman.

niprikin *same as* **nipperkin**.

nipecart *n* **1** a niggard. **2** a cross, ill-tempered person.

nipshot *adv* aslant, backwards.

nipsicker *adj* **1** cross, captious. **2** severely exact.

nir *n* **1** anything small or stunted. **2** a term of contempt.

nirb *n* **1** a dwarf. **2** anything of stunted growth.

nirl *n* **1** a knot. **2** an induration on the skin. **3** a fragment. **4** a small piece. **5** a dwarfish person.—*v* **1** to pinch with cold. **2** to cause to shrink or shrivel. **3** to break into small pieces.

nirled *adj* **1** shrunken, shrivelled. **2** stunted.

nirlie *adj* **1** stunted in growth. **2** puny. **3** niggardly.

nirlie-headed *adj* (*used of wheat*) having a small head.

nirling *adj* keen, nipping, frosty, drying.

nirlock *n* a small, hard lump or swelling on the feet or hands.

niris, nirles *n* an eruption on the skin, like measles or chickenpox.

nirr *same as* **nurr**[1].

nirrange *n* an orange.

nirt *n* a very small piece.

nirty *adj* small.

nis, nise *same as* **neeze**.

nis-bit *n* the iron or bit that passes across the nose part of a horse's bridle or branks (qv).

nisser *same as* **nizzer**.

nissle *v* **1** to beat with the fists. **2** to thrash.

nissling *n* a thrashing.

nistie-cock *same as* **nesscock**.

nis-wise *same as* **neis-wise**.

nit[1], **nite** *n* **1** the egg of a louse. **2** a louse.

nit[2] *v* **1** to knit. **2** to fasten.

nit[3] *n* **1** a nut. **2** a hazelnut.

nit[4] *n* a female wanton.

nit-brown *adj* nut-brown.

nitch[1] *n* a bundle or truss.

nitch[2] *n* a notch, incision.

nite *same as* **nyte**.

nitfu' *n* (*used of whisky*) a 'thimbleful', a nip.

nit-grit *adj* as large as a nut.

nither[1] *same as* **nidder**[4].

nither[2] *v* **1** to shiver. **2** to shrivel. **3** to pine away. **4** to pinch with cold.

nither[3] *adj* lower, nether.

nither[4] *conj, adj and pron* neither.

nithered *adj* **1** trembling with cold. **2** withered, wasted.

nitherie *adj* withered, blasted, feeble.

nitmyug *n* a nutmeg.

nit-saw *n* a salve for clearing the head from lice.

nitter[1] *v* to grumble constantly.

nitter[2] *same as* **nither**[5].

nitteret *adj* **1** sulky. **2** ill-natured.—*n* a sulky looking face.

nitterie *adj* ill-natured.

nitters *n* a greedy, grubbing, impudent, withered woman.

nittie *n* a female wanton.

nittie *same as* **neetie**.

nitting *n* tape.

nittle *v* to irritate.

nittled *adj* having small, stunted horns.

nittles[1] *n* **1** horns peeping through the skin. **2** the small, stunted horns of sheep.

nittles[2] *n* pieces of string used for tying full sacks.

nitty[1] *adj* lousy.

nitty[2] *n* **1** a knave, a rascal. **2** a term of abuse.

nitty[3] *same as* **naitie**[2].

nitwud *n* a wood of hazelnut trees.

niv, nivv *same as* **neive**.

nivel *same as* **nevell**.

nivie-nick-nack *same as* **nievie-nick-nack**.

nivlock *n* a handle of wood, round which the end of a hair tether is fastened.

nivvi-nivvi-nak-kak *same as* **nivie-nick-nack**.

nivvil *n* a handful.

nix *same as* **nicks**.

nixie *n* a water nymph.

nixin *n* a game resembling rowly-powly (qv).

niz, nizz *n* the nose.

niz-bit *same as* **nis-bit**.

nizzart *n* a lean person with a hard, sharp face.—*adj* contracted.

nizzelin' *adj* **1** niggardly. **2** from greed, spending time on trifles.

nizzer *v* **1** to contract. **2** to become dried up or stunted in growth.

nizzertit *adj* stunted in growth.

nizzey *n* the nose.

nizzin, nizin *n* **1** a drubbing. **2** exposure to the weather.

nizzle *same as* **nissle**.

nizzlin *n* direct exposure to a severe storm.

no *adv* **1** not. **2** used as an interrogative after a positive statement.

Noah's ark *n* clouds assuming the shape of a boat, regarded as a sign of the weather.

nob[1] *n* **1** a knob. **2** a rounded hill. **3** the nose. **4** the toe of a boot.

nob[2] *n* **1** an interloper in a trade. **2** a blackleg.—*v* to act as a blackleg.

nob[3] *n* a swell.

nobberry, nobe-berry *n* the cloudberry.

nobbut, nobut *adv* **1** only. **2** nothing but.

nobby *n* **1** a rich man. **2** a swell.

nobilitat *v* to confer a peerage, ennoble.

noble *n* the armed bullhead.

nocent *adj* guilty.

nocht *n* nought.

nochtie *adj* **1** puny in size. **2** contemptible in appearance. **3** bad. **4** unfit for any purpose. **5** valueless. **6** trifling.

nock[1] *n* **1** a notch. **2** the notch on a spindle or arrow.

nock[2] *n* a clock.

nock[3] *n* a hill.

nock[4] *n* the corner of a sailyard.

nock[5] *v* to tire out, exhaust.

nocket *n* **1** a luncheon. **2** a slight repast between breakfast and dinner. **3** a small cake.

nocket time *n* the time for taking a nocket (qv).

nod *v* **1** to fall asleep in one's chair. **2** to go on one's way briskly and carelessly.—*n* a nap.—*phr* **the land of nod** sleep.

nodder *same as* **nowther**.

noddis *n* a slight nod.

noddle *n* **1** the temper. **2** the head, used contemptuously.

noddle-araid *adv* head-foremost.

noddy[1] *n* a sleepy person.

noddy[2] *n* a kind of teacake baked with currants.

noddy[3] *n* a simpleton.

noddy[4] *n* **1** a one-horse coach, moving on two wheels and opening behind. **2** a one-horse coach of the ordinary kind, with four wheels.—*phr* **on Shanks' noddy** on foot.

nodge[1] *v* to strike with the knuckles.—*n* a stroke with the knuckles.

nodge[2] *v* **1** to sit or go about in a dull, stupid state. **2** (*with* **along**) to travel leisurely.

nodie *n* the head.

nog[1] *n* **1** a small wooden vessel. **2** a mug.

nog[2] *n* **1** a wooden peg used in thatching with sods. **2** a knob. **3** a hooked stake driven into the wall. **4** a projecting small handle of a scythe.

nogg *v* to stroll leisurely nodding the head.

noggan *n* a noggin.

noggie *n* a small wooden vessel, a mug.

noggit *same as* **nocket**.

noint *v* to anoint.

nointment *n* ointment.

noisome *adj* noisy.

noit[1] *n* **1** a small rocky height. **2** a projecting knob on the foot.

noit[2] *v* to strike smartly.—*n* a smart stroke.

noiting *n* a beating.

noitled *adj* drunk with spirits.

noityon *n* a noit (qv) on the foot.

nokkit *same as* **nocket**.

noll[1] *v* to press, beat or strike with the knuckles.—*n* a strong push or blow with the knuckles.

noll[2] *n* **1** a knoll. **2** a large piece of anything.

noll[3] *n* a noodle.

nolt *n* **1** cattle. **2** black cattle. **3** a stupid fellow.

noltish *adj* stupid.

nolt-tath *n* luxuriant grass manured by cattle.

nombles *n* the entrails of a deer, sheep, etc.

no mere man *n* a supernatural being, a goblin.

non *n* a name given towards the middle of the 19th century to the non-intrusion section of the Church of Scotland.

non-compear *v* not to appear in answer to a citation.

non-conform *adj* not conforming.

none *adv* **1** not. **2** in no wise.

nonentity *n* **1** a sinecure. **2** a nonplus. **3** a deadlock.

none-so-pretty *n* London pride.

none-such, nonsuch *adj* unparalleled.—*n* a quite exceptional person or thing.

non-fiance *n* want of confidence.

non-plush *v* to nonplus.

non-residentin *adj* nonresident.

noo-a days *adv* now, in these days.

noof[1] *adj* **1** sheltered from the weather. **2** snug. **3** neat, trim.—*v* **1** to enjoy oneself leisurely. **2** to be snug and comfortable. **3** to be neat.

noof[2] *v* to chat familiarly.

noofly *adv* **1** neatly. **2** handsomely.

noofy *adj* **1** silly. **2** feckless.

nooh *same as* **nough**.

nook *same as* **neuck**.

nookit *adj* **1** crooked. **2** sharp. **3** short-tempered.

nool[1] *n* **1** a small horn. **2** one not part of the skull, but attached to the skin.

nool[2] *v* to beat with the knuckles.

nooled *adj* having mere stumps of horns.

nool-kneed *adj* knock-kneed.

noonin *n* noon.

nooning piece *n* a piece of bread as luncheon.

noonog *n* the cranberry. **2** the heath.
noony *n* a luncheon.
noop[1] *same as* **nup**.
noop[2] *n* **1** a round projection. **2** a pin.
noop[3] *v* to walk with downcast eyes and nodding head.
noor *adv* not.
noorish *n* a nurse.
noos *n* **1** news. **2** gossip.
noosle *v* **1** to nuzzle. **2** to nestle close for warmth. **3** to root with the snout like a pig. **4** to seize by the nose.
noost[1] *v* to cudgel, belabour.
noost[2] *n* the action of the grinders of a horse in chewing.
noost[3] *n* a sheltered landing place for a boat.
noot *n* the ball struck in playing at shinty.
noosle *v* to nuzzle.
noosly *adv* snugly.
noozle *v* **1** to squeeze. **2** to press down with the knees—*n* a squeeze.
nor *conj* **1** than. **2** although. **3** if. **4** that. **5** *in phr* **deil nor** little would one care although.
Norawa' *n* Norway.
Norawa'-wifie *n* the little auk.
Nordereys *n* the northern Hebrides.
norie[1] *n* a whim, fancy.
norie[2] *n* the puffin.
norish *same as* **noorish**.
norit *adv* northward.
norl *n* **1** a lump. **2** a protuberance.—*v* to rise in lumps.
norland *n* **1** the north country. **2** a north country man.—*adj* northern.
norland-blue *n* Highland whisky.
norlander *n* one who lives in the north.
norland nettie *n* a Highland woman who bartered small articles of dress for wool.
norlick *n* a tumour caused by a blow.
norlin *adj* northern.
norlins *adj* northwards.
norloc *n* a large cyst or growth on a person's head.
nor'loch trout *n* a jocular term formerly applied to a joint or leg of mutton.
normost *adj* northmost.
norrat, norrart *same as* **norward**.
norrie[1] *n* a name for a sow.
norrie[2] *same as* **norie**[1].
north *v* (*used of the wind*) to blow from the north. —*n in phr* **cock o' the north** a name for the dukes of Gordon.
northart *same as* **norward**.
north-bye *adv* towards the north.
north-cock *n* the snow bunting.
north-dancers *n* the aurora borealis.
northern hareld *n* the long-tailed duck.
northlins *same as* **norlins**.
norward *adv* northward.—*adj* northern.—*n* the north, the direction of the north.
nor-wastert *n* **1** a bitter blast. **2** anything of a cold, rude nature.
Norwegian teal *n* the scaup.
nose *n* **1** the projecting part of anything. **2** a promontory. **3** an immediate approach.—*v* **1** to rub with the nose. **2** to suck.
noseband *n* a loop of stout cord to which one end of a lead stone or sinker is attached, the other being fastened to the fishing line.
nose feast *n* a storm.
nosel *n* a small socket or aperture.
nose-nippin, *adj* (*of the weather*) cold, freezing.
nose-o'-wax, nosy-wax *n* **1** a pliable fellow. **2** an easily imposed on simpleton.
noseskip *adj* nasal.
nose-specks *n* spectacles.
nosetirl, nostirle *n* a nostril.
nose-wise *same as* **neis-wise**.
noshin *n* a notion.
nosie-nappie *n* a nursery term for the nose.

nosie way *n* one with little knowledge.
nossock *n* a good drink of liquor, a dram.
nost *n* **1** noise. **2** talking. **3** speculation about any subject.
not[1] *n* **1** a knob. **2** a ball. **3** a point, conclusion. **4** a head.
not[2] *v* needed.
notable *adj* (*used of a woman*) clever, industrious, capable.
notandums *n* notes, memoranda.
notar, nottar *n* a notary.
not-a-will *adv* not voluntarily.
notch up *v* to reckon, count.
note[1] *n* **1** a spoken remark. **2** a saying. **3** notice. **4** a banknote for £1.
note[2] *same as* **not**[1].
note[3] *n* **1** necessity, need. **2** occasion for.—*v* **1** to use, have occasion for. **2** to enjoy. **3** to need.
noteless *adj* **1** unknown. **2** unnoted.
noth *n* **1** nothing. **2** the cipher 0.
notice *v* to attend to, to take care of.
notion *n* **1** a fancy that may lead to lovemaking. **2** a liking for. **3** a whim. **4** a pretence of being, doing, etc.
notionate *adj* **1** self-opinionated. **2** fanciful.
notour *adj* **1** notorious. **2** determinedly persistent.
notourly *adv* notoriously.
not-payment *n* non-payment.
not proven *phr* a verdict returned by a jury in a Scottish criminal trial as an alternative to guilty or not guilty where the jury has felt that the prosecution has produced insufficient evidence to prove the accused guilty but where there is enough evidence to prevent a verdict of innocent being given.
not-swearer *n* a nonjuror.
nott[1] *v* needed.
nott[2] *same as* **not**[1].
nott-and-loopwark *n* a process in weaving.
notten *adj* needed.
noture *same as* **notour**.
nouchtie *same as* **nochtie**.
noud *n* the grey gurnard.
nough *v* (*used of the wind*) to blow gently.
nought[1] *adj* worthless.—*adv* in no wise.
nought[2] *same as* **nowt**[1].
noup *n* a nob.
nourice *n* a nurse.
nourice-fee *n* a wet nurse's wages.
nouricerie *n* a nursery.
nourice-skap, ~-ship *n* **1** the place of a nurse. **2** a nurse's wages.
nouse[1] *n* sense, intelligence.
nouse[2] *n* nothing.
nout *same as* **nowt**[1].
novation *n* an innovation.
novelles *n* **1** novels, works of fiction. **2** news.
novels *n* tidings, news.
novity *n* a novelty.
now[1] *int* an exclamation of discontent.—*n* the present time.
now[2] *v* **1** (*used of the wind*) to blow gently. **2** to talk foolishly.
nowan *adj* silly, loquacious.
now and talk *v* to talk loudly and in a silly manner.
nowd *n* the grey gurnard.
no weel *adj* unwell.
nown *same as* **nain**.
nowt[1] *n* **1** cattle. **2** black cattle. **3** a stupid fellow, a lout.
nowt[2] *v* **1** to injure. **2** to beat.
nowt-beast *n* an animal of the ox family.
nowt-doctor *n* a veterinary surgeon.
nowt-feet *n* **1** calves' feet. **2** cow heel.
nowt-feet-jeel *n* calf's-foot jelly.
nowt-head *n* **1** a blockhead. **2** a coward.
nowther *conj* neither.
nowt-herd *n* **1** a cattle herd. **2** a keeper of black cattle.
nowt-hide *n* ox leather.
nowt-horn *n* an ox horn, used as a trumpet.

nowtit *adj* (*used of a potato*) hollow in the heart.
nowt-leather *n* ox leather.
nowt-market *n* a cattle market.
nowt-tath *same as* **nolt-tath**.
no-wyss *adj* **1** foolish. **2** thoughtless. **3** deranged.
noy *n* **1** annoyance. **2** harm. **3** mischief.
noyit *adj* **1** vexed. **2** wrathful.
nozle *same as* **nosel**.
nozzle *same as* **noosle**.
nub *n* a club foot.
nubberry *same as* **nobberry**.
nubbie *n* a staff with a hook or knob.—*adj* **1** short and plump. **2** dumpy. **3** having knobs.
nubbie *n* an unsocial person, worldly yet lazy.
nubblock *n* **1** a knob. **2** an induration. **3** the swelling made by a blow or fall.
nuce *same as* **nace**.
nuck¹ *same as* **neuck**.
nuck² *v* **1** to notch. **2** to make nooks or angles. **3** to make verses the lines of which are not of equal length.
nuckle, nuckelt *adj* (*of a cow*) newly calved.
nucky *n* **1** a small corner. **2** the tassel of a cap, the knob of a nightcap. **3** a fish hook.
nud *n* the pull of a fish on a fishing line.
nudge¹ *n* **1** a stroke or push with the knuckles. **2** a slight movement. **3** exertion. **4** grief, annoyance, pain.—*v* **1** to stir oneself. **2** to molest.
nudge² *n* a short, thick-set person.
nudie *same as* **noddy**³.
nufe *same as* **noof**¹.
nug, nugg *v* **1** to nudge, jog with the elbow. **2** to nod.—*n* the pull of a fish on a fishing line.
nuget, nugget *n* **1** a lump of anything. **2** a short, thickset person.
nuif¹ *adj* intimate.
nuif² *same as* **noof**¹.
nuik *same as* **neuck**.
nuikey *adj* having corners.
nuil *same as* **nael**.
nuisant *adj* hurtful.
nuist¹ *n* a large piece of anything.
nuist² *v* **1** to eat continually, to be ever munching. **2** to beat, bruise.—*n* **1** a greedy, ill-disposed, ignorant person. **2** a blow.
nule¹ *v* to beat with the knuckles.
nule² *n* a knob.
nule-kneed *adj* knock-kneed.
null¹ *v* **1** to finish off. **2** to reduce to nothing.
null² *same as* **nool**¹.
null³ *v* to beat with the knuckles.
nully *v* to nullify.
numb *adj* (*of a boat*) slow in sailing, almost motionless.
number, nummer *n* a statement of quantity.
number-sorrow *adj* **1** hardy. **2** rough, weakly
numeration *n* the counting of money in paying it over.
numerosity *n* numbers.
nump *v* to nibble.
numpty *n* a fool, an idiot
nun *n* the blue titmouse.
nunce *n* a nuncio.
nup, nupe *n* the fruit of the cloudberry.
nupe *same as* **noop**².
Nurday *n* New Year's Day.—*adj* appropriate to New Year's Day.
nure-gift *n* a New Year's gift or treat.
nurg, nurgle *n* a short, squat, savage man.
nurgling *n* a person of cat-like disposition.
nurice, nurish *n* a nurse.
nurl, nurle *n* **1** a knot. **2** a lump. **3** a tumour.—*v* **1** to strike so as to raise lumps. **2** to become knotty. **3** to rise in lumps.
nurling *n* a person of an ill-tempered disposition.
nurlock *n* a small, hard swelling, an induration on the skin.
nurly *adj* lumpy, knotty, hard.

nurr¹ *v* **1** to snarl or growl like a dog. **2** to purr as a cat. **3** to fret, be discontented.—*n* the sound made by a cat.
nurr² *n* **1** a hard knot of wood. **2** the ball used in the game of **knur and spell**.
nurr³ *n* a decrepit person.
nurrilled *same as* **nirled**.
nurring *adj* feline, cat-like.
nurris-braid *adv* working too eagerly to last long.
nurrish *n* a nurse.
nurrit *n* an insignificant or dwarfish person.
nurse *n* a hardy tree planted to shelter a more tender one.
nuse *v* to knead.
nut *n* the head.
nutbrae *n* a brae or hill abounding in hazelnut trees.
nutting tyne *n* a nut hook.
nutyon *same as* **noit**¹.
nuzzle *same as* **noosle**.
nyaakit *adj* naked.
nyaakit-like *adj* scantily clad.
nyabok *n* a small, talkative person.
nyaff¹ *n* **1** a trifle, a thing of no value. **2** anything small of its kind. **3** a dwarf. **4** a worthless annoying person. **5** a term of abuse.
nyaff² *v* **1** to bark, yelp. **2** to talk forwardly and frivolously. **3** to argue snappishly. **4** to trifle and be weakly in working. **5** to take short steps.—*n* **1** a little dog's yelp. **2** frivolous chatter. **3** a wrangle over a trifle. **4** a pert chatterer.
nyaffet *n* a conceited little creature.
nyffing *adj* **1** chattering. **2** peevish. **3** haggling. **4** idle, insignificant. **5** contemptible.—*n* idle talk, prattle.
nyaffle *v* **1** to trifle away time. **2** to potter about. **3** to loiter. **4** to take short steps.—*n* **1** a trifle. **2** a thing of no value. **3** anything very small.
nyam *v* to chew.—*int* a child's exclamation over anything good to eat.
nyamff *adj* hungry.
nyap *v* to snap or bite at.
nyaph *n* the female nymphae, etc.
nyarb *v* **1** to fret. **2** to be discontented.—*n* a peevish complaint, a fretful quarrel.
nyarbit *adj* of a peevish disposition.
nyarg *same as* **narg**.
nyargie *adj* jeering.
nyargle *v* to wrangle.—*n* one who loves to wrangle or dispute.
nyarr *v* **1** to snarl as a dog. **2** to cry, as an angry cat. **3** to find fault peevishly.—*n* **1** a dog's growl. **2** peevishness. **3** peevish fault-finding.
nyat *v* to strike sharply with the knuckles.—*n* a smart stroke with the knuckles.
nyatrie *same as* **natrie**.
nyatt *same as* **nat**.
nyatter¹ *v* **1** to chatter. **2** to speak fretfully. **3** to scold. **4** to tease. **5** to gossip in an unfriendly fashion. **6** to gnash the teeth like a trapped rat. **7** to quarrel, wrangle.—*n* peevish chatter.
nyatter² *v* to rain slightly with a high wind.
nyatterie *adj* cross-tempered.
nyauchle *same as* **nauchle**.
nyaukit *adj* naked.
nyauve *v* to gnaw.
nyawn *same as* **nain**.
nyber *n* a neighbour.
nyim, nyimmie *n* a very small piece.
nyirb *same as* **nyarb**.
nyirr *same as* **nyarr**.
nyit *v* to strike sharply with the knuckles.
nyle *n* the navel.
nyod *int* a modified form of 'God', used as an exclamation or oath.
nyow¹ *v* **1** to curb. **2** to maul.
nyow² *adj* new.
nyowan *n* a beating.
nyowmost *adj* nethermost, lowest.

nyse *v* to pommel.
nyte *v* **1** to strike smartly. **2** to rap.
nyuckfit *n* the snipe.
nyuk *same as* **neuck**.

nyum *same as* **nyam**.
nyum-nyam *int* a child's exclamation of pleasure in anything good to eat.
nyurr *same as* **nyarr**.

O

o¹ *same as* **oe²**.
o² *prep* of.
o³ *prep* on.
o⁴ *int* oh!
oachening *n* **1** early dawn. **2** the night just before daybreak.
oaf *n* **1** an elf. **2** an animal whose face is so covered with hair that it can scarcely see.—*v* to walk stupidly.
oaff *adj* decrepit. **2** worn down with disease.
oak *n* an oaken cudgel.
oak-eggar *n* a moth.
oakie *n* the common guillemot.
oak nut *n* an acorn.
oam *n* **1** steam, vapour. **2** a blast of warm air. **3** a close, warm air.—*v* to blow with a warm, close air.
oar *v* **1** to row. **2** to ferry.
oast *n* a dug-out place above high water into which a boat is drawn when it is to be some time on shore.
oat-fowl *n* the snow bunting.
oath *n in phr* **to gi'e one's oath** to take an oath.—*v* to swear to anything.
oat-land *n* land for growing oats.
oat-leave *n* (*in old husbandry*) the crop after bear or barley.
oats and beans and barley *n* a singing game.
oatseed *n* **1** oats for seed. **2** the time of sowing oats.
oat-skiter *n* the wild angelica, through the hollow stems of which children shoot oats.
o ay *int* o yes!
obedience *n* **1** obeisance. **2** a bow. **3** a curtsy.
obeisance *n* subjection.
obering *n* **1** a hint. **2** an inkling of something important.
obfusque *v* to darken.
obit *n* a particular length of slate.
objeck *n* **1** a miserable creature. **2** one diseased or deformed. **3** an objection.—*v* to object.
obleegement *n* a favour, service.
obleish *v* to oblige.
obleisment, obleistment *n* an obligation, bond.
obleist, oblist *ppl* come under obligation.
oblish *v* to oblige.
oblishment *n* an obligation.
obscure *adj* **1** secret. **2** concealed. **3** clandestine.—*v* to conceal, hide.
observe *n* an observation, remark.—*v* to guard.
obstic *n* **1** an obstacle. **2** an objection.
obstrapulosity *n* obstreperousness, restiveness.
obstrapulous, obstropalous *adj* **1** obstreperous. **2** unmanageable, refractory.
obtemper *v* **1** to obey. **2** to fulfil an injunction, etc.
occasion *n* **1** cause, reason. **2** necessity. **3** the dispensation of the sacrament of the Lord's Supper.
occupier *n* one engaged in business, work, etc.
occupy *v* to labour, work.
occur *same as* **ocker**.
och *int* an exclamation of sorrow, etc.
ochaine, ochanee, och-hey, och-hey-hum, och-hone, och-hon-a-rie, och-hon-o- chrie, och-how *ints* exclamations of sorrow, etc.
ochening *same as* **oachening**.
ochie *n in phr* **neither eechie nor ochie** absolutely nothing.
ocht¹ *n* **1** aught. **2** anything. **3** a whit. **4** a person of consequence.—*adj* any.

ocht² *v* ought.
ocht³ *v* possessed of.
ochtlins *same as* **oughtlins**.
ocker, ockar *n* interest, usury.—*v* to increase, add to.
ockerer *n* a usurer, a moneychanger.
ock-name *n* a distinguishing name or to-name (qv).
od *n* a disguised form of God, a minced oath, an expletive, used in various combinations.
odd *adj* **1** occasional. **2** sequestered, solitary.—*adv* singularly, out of the usual course, fashion, etc.—*n* **1** a point of land. **2** a handicap to a weaker player.
odd-come-shortlies *n* an occasion close at hand.
odd-like *adj* strange-looking.
odd or even *n* a guessing game played with small articles in a closed hand.
odds *n* **1** consequence. **2** change.
oddses *n* differences.
odd time *n* **1** leisure. **2** a chance time.
odious *adj* exceeding.—*adv* exceedingly, used as an intensive.
odiously *adv* exceedingly, terribly.
od-zookers *int* an exclamation of surprise, etc.
oe¹ *n* a small island.
oe² *n* a grandchild.
oen *n* an oven.
o'er *prep* **1** over. **2** upon. **3** on account of. **4** concerning. **5** across, on the other side of. **6** past, beyond.—*adv* **1** across. **2** off. **3** asleep. **4** too, too much. **5** very.—*adj* upper, higher. **6** superior in power, etc.—*v* **1** to cross. **2** to go, jump, run, swim, etc, across. **3** to endure, surmount, survive. **4** to recover from. **5** (*with refl pron*) to manage for oneself, control oneself.
o'er-abürd *adv* overboard.
o'er-anent *prep* over against.
o'erback *n* a cow that has failed to have a calf when three years old.
o'er-bladed *adj* hard-driven in pursuit.
o'erblaw *v* **1** (*used of a storm*) to blow over. **2** to cover with driven snow.
o'er-bogie, ~-boggle *n* a marriage not celebrated by a minister.—*v* to contract such a marriage.
o'er-brim *v* to overflow.
o'er-by *adj* **1** neighbouring. **2** past and gone.—*adv* at no great distance.—*n* a place not far off.
o'ercast *v* **1** to overturn. **2** to cloud over. **3** to overlay. **4** to recover from, as an illness or wound.—*n* an outcast, castaway.
o'erclad *adj* overspread, thickly covered.
o'ercome *v* **1** to come or cross over. **2** to surpass. **3** to prove too much for, baffle. **4** to revive from a swoon. **5** to recover from.—*n* **1** surplus. **2** the refrain of a song, the burden of a discourse or speech. **3** a hackneyed phrase or one frequently used by a person. **4** a voyage, a journey, passage across the sea. **5** outcome, issue.
o'er-coup *v* **1** to upset, capsize. **2** to retch.
o'er-crow *v* **1** to overcome. **2** to exult over. **4** to overlook a view, house, etc.
o'er-crown *n* a particular kind of woman's cap or mulch (qv), so cut as not to require a crown and rendering a bonnet unnecessary.
o'er-driven *adj* (*used of persons*) overworked, oppressed with work.
o'er-end *v* **1** to set on end. **2** to turn over endwise. **3** to be turned topsy-turvy.—*adj* erect, upright, on end.

o'er-fa'in *n* the time of childbirth, a woman's confinement.

o'er-foughten, ~-fochen *adj* 1 over-exhausted. 2 quite prostrate.

o'er-fret *adj* decorated all over.

o'er-gae *v* 1 to go over. 2 (*used of time*) to elapse. 3 to become overdue. 4 to overrun. 5 to overburden, exhaust. 6 to domineer over, oppress. 7 to superintend.

o'er-gaff *v* 1 to cloud over. 2 to overcast.

o'er-gane *adj* past and gone.

o'er-gang *v* 1 to overrun, overspread. 2 to outrun. 3 to elapse. 4 to exceed. 5 to surpass. 6 to master, overpower. 7 to superintend.—*n* 1 a right of way. 2 oppression. 3 superintendence. 4 an overseer. 5 the director of a gang of workmen. 6 a coat of paint, plaster, etc. 7 a scraping, raking, harrowing.

o'er-ganger *n* an overseer, superintendent, etc.

o'er-gangin *adj* 1 unmanageable. 2 domineering.

o'er-gaun *n* 1 a passage, crossing. 2 a going or falling over. 3 a falling asleep. 4 a coat of paint, etc. 5 a washing, scouring, etc. 6 a raking, harrowing, etc.—*adj* unmanageable.

o'ergaun rapes *n* the vertical ropes keeping down the thatch of a stack.

o'er-get *v* 1 to overtake, come up with. 2 to overreach.

o'er-gilt *adj* gilded over.

o'er-grip *v* to strain, overstrain.

o'er-gyaun *n* a fault-finding.

o'er-hand *n* the upper hand, mastery.

o'er-harl *v* 1 to oppress. 2 to treat with severity, to 'haul over the coals'. 3 to turn over. 4 to examine roughly.

o'er-heeze *v* to elate unduly.

o'er-heid *adv* 1 overhead. 2 wholly. 3 on an average. 4 taken in the gross.

o'erhie, o'erhigh, o'er-hye *v* to overtake.

o'erhing *v* to overhang.

o'er-hip *n* a way of fetching a blow with the sledgehammer over the arm.

o'erlay *n* 1 a cravat, neckcloth. 2 a kind of hem, in which one part of the cloth is laid over the other.—*v* 1 to belabour, drub. 2 to hem in such a way that one part of the cloth is laid over the other.

o'erleat, o'erleet *n* something that is folded over another.

o'erling *adj* covering over.

o'erloup, o'erlop *n* 1 a trespass. 2 excess, occasional self-indulgence. 3 the stream tide at the change of the moon. 4 an occasional trespass of cattle. 5 the act of leaping over a fence.—*v* to overleap.

o'erlyin *n in phr* **at the o'erlyin** ready to lie or fall down from fatigue.

o'ermills *n* 1 remnants. 2 the remains of anything.

o'ermist *adj* 1 uppermost. 2 farthest off.

o'er mony *phr* 1 too many. 2 too strong. 3 more than a match.

o'er nice *adj* too fastidious.

o'er ocht *phr* beyond comparison.

o'erpeer *n* 1 one who excels. 2 a superior.

o'erplush *n* surplus, overplus.

o'erput *v* 1 to recover from. 2 to survive.

o'er-qualled *adj* overrun, overspread.

o'er-rack, ~-rax *v* 1 to overreach. 2 to overstrain.

o'errin *v* 1 to run over. 2 (*used of animals*) to multiply too greatly.

o'ers *n* excess.

o'ersea *adj* foreign.

o'ersee *v* 1 to manage, superintend. 2 to overlook, pass over, forget.

o'erseen *adj* watched over when dying.

o'erset *v* 1 to upset, overturn, disorder. 2 to upset mentally.— *adj* deranged.

o'ershot *n* the surplus, remainder.

o'erside *adv* overboard, over the side.

o'erslide *v* to slide or glide past.

o'erspade *v* to cut land into narrow trenches.—*n* heaping the earth upon an equal quantity of land not raised.

o'erspang *v* 1 to pursue. 2 to overleap. 3 to bound over.

o'erstent, o'erstented *adj* exorbitant, overcharged.

o'erswak *n* the rush or noise of a wave breaking on the beach.

o'ersyle *v* 1 to cover, conceal. 2 to beguile.

o'ertack *v* to overtake.

o'ertake *v* 1 to take aback, put to confusion. 2 to overcome. 3 to succeed in a task though pressed for time. 4 to fetch one a blow. 5 (*in passive*) to become drunk.

o'ertap *v* to overtop.

o'ertirvie *v* 1 to overcome. 2 to upset.

o'ertramp *v* 1 to oppress. 2 to trample on.

o'ertree *n* the single handle or stilt of an Orcadian plough.

o'erturn *n* 1 the refrain or chorus of a song. 2 an upheaval, revolution, change of circumstances, etc. 3 (*used of money*) turning over for profit in business.

o'erwales *n* the refuse of anything from which the best is taken.

o'erway *n* the upper or higher way.

o'erweek *v* to overstay one's welcome by not departing in the week of arrival.

o'erweekit *adj* (*used of meat*) kept too long.

o'erweill *v* to exceed.

o'er wi' *adj* done with, finished with.

o'er-woman *n* a woman chosen to give a casting vote in a cause in which the arbiters are equally divided.

o'erword *n* 1 a word or phrase frequently repeated. 2 the chorus or burden of a song.

o'eryeed *v* overwent, overpassed.

oey *same as* **oye**.

of *prep* 1 from, out of. 2 on. 3 during. 4 on account of. 5 as regards. 6 at. 7 (*used of time*) to, before.

off *prep* 1 beyond, past. 2 without. 3 from.—*adv* out of.— *adj* committed to memory.—*v* 1 to go off. 2 (*with* **with**) to doff.

off-cap *n* a salutation by lifting the cap.

off-casten *adj* 1 cast off. 2 rejected.

off-come *n* 1 an apology. 2 a subterfuge, pretext.

offend *v* to injure.

offer *v* 1 to attempt. 2 to show promise or intention.—*n* 1 choice, disposal. 2 an attempt. 3 a projecting or overhanging bank that has been undermined by the action of a stream.

offering *n* 1 a small quantity. 2 an imperfect performance.

off-faller *n* 1 an apostate. 2 one who falls away.

off-falling *n* 1 defection. 2 a declension in health or appearance. 3 moral declension.

offgang *n* the firing of a cannon, etc.

offgoing *n* 1 death. 2 departure from life. 3 the firing of a cannon.

offhand *adv and adj* extempore.

officiar *n* 1 an officer. 2 an official.

offish *n* an office.

offishness *n* reserve.

offnin *adv* often.

offput *n* 1 an excuse. 2 postponement.

offset *n* a recommendation.

offskep *n* the utmost boundary of a landscape.

ofi *n* 1 an outhouse. 2 a privy.

o-fish *n* the cuttlefish.

oft *adj* frequent.

ogertful *adj* 1 nice, fastidious. 2 squeamish. 3 affecting delicacy of taste.

oggie *same as* **ogie**.

oggit *adj* surfeited.

oghie *same as* **ochie**.

ogie, oggie *n* 1 the open space before the fireplace of a kiln. 2 a killogie (qv).

oglet *n* a theodolite, as something to spy with.

ogress *n* a giantess with large, fiery eyes, supposed to feed on children.

ogrie *n* a giant with the same character and propensities as the ogress.

ohn- *neg prefix* equivalent to un-.

ohon *int* alas!

ohoy *int* ahoy!

oie, oi *same as* **oye**.

oil *v* 1 to soothe, comfort. 2 (*with* **lug**) to flatter in speech.

oilan-auk *n* the great northern diver.

oilcoat *n* an oilskin coat.

oil muggie *n* a vessel for holding oil.

oil of aik *n* a beating with an oaken cudgel.

oil of hazel *n* a beating.

oil of malt *n* 1 whisky. 2 malt liquor.

oily-gaun *adj* plausible, flattering.

oily pig *n* an oil jar.

oindroch *same as* **undoch**.

oisie *int* an exclamation of wonder or as a call to attention.

oist *n* a host, an army.

old *adj* eldest.

old-mouthed *adj* toothless from age.

oleit, olied, olicht, olit, ollath *adj* 1 prompt, willing. 2 active, nimble. 3 sprightly. 4 handsome.

ome *same as* **oam**.

omne-gatherum, ~-gaddrum *n* 1 a miscellaneous collection. 2 a medley. 3 the unincorporated craftsmen of a burgh.

on[1] *neg pref* generally used with *ppls*.

on[2] *prep* 1 on to, upon. 2 in. 3 about. 4 regarding. 5 of. 6 for. 7 to. 8 at. 9 against. 10 by means of.—*adv* 1 continually. 2 agoing. 3 on the fire, cooking, boiling. 4 with speed, force of forward movement. 5 in drink, tipsy. 6 (*with* **with**) courting, keeping company.—*v* (*with* **with**) to put on.

onbeast *n* 1 a monster. 2 a ravenous beast. 3 a noxious member of human society. 4 a raging toothache.

onbethankit *adj* unthanked.

onbraw *adj* 1 ugly. 2 unbecoming. 3 unhandsome.

onbrawness *n* ugliness.

oncarry, oncairy *n* 1 a stir, bustle. 2 frolic, merriment. 3 flighty conduct.

oncarryings *n* behaviour, ongoings, carryings-on

oncast *n* 1 a misfortune, burden. 2 the first row of loops in knitting. 3 the casting of a row of loops. —*v* to begin knitting with an oncast.

once-, one's-errand *n* a special errand.—*adv* purposely, expressly.

oncome *n* 1 a fall of rain or snow. 2 the beginning of any business or movement, as an assault. 3 an attack of disease the cause of which is unknown. 4 how an affair goes on and issues.

oncost *n* 1 expense before profit. 2 extra expense. —*adj* causing extra expense.

ondeemas *adj* 1 incalculable. 2 extraordinary. 3 incredible. 4 what cannot be reckoned.

ondeemously *adv* excessively.

onding *n* 1 a heavy fall of rain or snow. 2 an attack. 3 oppression. 4 turmoil.—*v* to rain heavily.

ondingin' *n* 1 an onding (qv) of rain or snow. 2 a torrent of words.

ondo *v* to undo.

ondocht *n* a weak, puny creature.

ondraw *n* a wrapper or garment for occasional use.

one *adj* only.—*n* 1 a degree, step. 2 a blow, rebuff. 3 someone.

one-erie *n* a child's word in counting out rhymes for regulating games.

oner *prep* under.

onerosity *n* the payment of an onerous (qv) price.

onerous *adj* 1 not gratuitous. 2 sufficiently advantageous. 3 implying the payment of a sufficient price.

onfa', onfall *n* 1 a heavy fall of snow or rain. 2 a misfortune. 3 an onslaught, attack. 4 a mysterious disease.

onfa'en *adj* unfallen.

onfarrant *adj* 1 senseless. 2 rude.

onfeel, onfeelin *adj* 1 unpleasant. 2 disagreeable. 3 uncomfortable. 4 rough, not smooth.

onfeirie *adj* 1 infirm. 2 unwieldy.

onfrack *adj* inactive, not alert.

ongae *n* 1 stir. 2 fuss. 3 'to-do'.

ongäines, ongauns, ongyauns *n* 1 procedure. 2 conduct, behaviour. 3 fuss.

ongang *n* 1 the starting of machinery. 2 proceedings. 3 conduct.

ongangings *n* conduct, behaviour.

ongetting *n* welfare, manner of getting on.

ongoings *n* proceedings, conduct, behaviour.

ongraithe *v* to unharness.

onhing *n* 1 patient waiting. 2 a mean and lazy staying in a place.

onie, ony *adj* any.

onie-gate *adv* 1 any way. 2 in any place or direction.

onie-gates *n* (*used in the game of marbles*) the claim of a player to play at any part of the ring.

oniehow *adv* 1 anyhow. 2 at any rate.

oniewhaur *adv* anywhere.

onken *v* not to know or recognize.

onkennable *adj* 1 unknowable. 2 immemorial.

onkent *adj* unknown.

onker *n* a small portion of land.

onlat *n* 1 the setting of machinery in motion. 2 the allowing of water to flow to move machinery.

onlauchful *adj* unlawful.

onlay *n* 1 a fall of snow or rain. 2 a surfeit.

onlayin' *n* castigation, the act of beating severely.

onless *prep* except.

onlife *adj* alive.

onlouping *n* the act of mounting a horse.

onmarrow *n* a partner in business, a sharer in a concern.

onnawars *adv* unawares, unexpectedly.

onnerstan' *v* to understand.

onnersteed *v* understood.

on o', on on *prep* on upon.

onpricket *adj* (*used of cattle*) without pricking (*see* **prick**) or startling (*see* **startle**) in hot weather.

onputting *n* dress, clothes.

onricht *adj* 1 dishonest. 2 unjust.

onset[1] *n* 1 an outhouse. 2 a farmstead.

onset[2] *v* to attack.

onsettin' *adj* not handsome, ugly.

onsleepit *adj* not having slept.

onstanding *adj* determined.

onstead *n* 1 a farmstead. 2 a homestead.

ontack, ontak *n* 1 a bustle, fuss. 2 airs. 3 assumption.

ontakin' *n* 1 approach. 2 beginning.—*adj* 1 taking on airs. 2 taking or buying on credit. 3 reckless in expenditure, dishonest.

onter[1] *v* (*used of horses*) to rear.

onter[2] *v* to venture.

ontill *prep* 1 on to, upon. 2 unto.

onto *prep* same as **ontill**.

ontron *same as* **orntren**.

on-uptaken *adj* not taken up.

onwaiter *n* a patient waiter for a future good.

onwaiting *adj* patiently waiting.—*n* patient waiting.

onwal *n* interest on money, profit on capital.

onweetin *adj* 1 unknowing. 2 involuntary. 3 unknown.

onwittins *adv* 1 without being privy to. 2 without the knowledge of.

onwyns *n* the left hand.

onwyner *n* the foremost ox on the left hand in ploughing.

onwyte *n* 1 an expectant wait. 2 waiting on a sick person or on one dying.

onwytin *same as* **onwaiting**.

oo[1] *n* wool.

oo[2] *pron* we.

oo[3] *int* o! oh!

oo[4] *n* a grandson.

oo ay *int* o yes!.

oobit *n* 1 a woolly worm or long-haired caterpillar. 2 a hairy, unkempt person.

ooder *same as* **ouder**.

oof, ooff[1] *n* **1** an elf. **2** a lout. **3** a weak, harmless person.—*v* to walk stupidly.

ooff[2] *v* **1** (*used of peaty soil*) to cause oats to die out before ripening.—*adj* decrepit. **2** worn down by disease.

oof-looking *adj* wearing a stupid look.

ooin'[1] *n and adj* wooing.

ooin'[2] *n* woollen material.—*adj* woollen.

ook *n* a week.

ookday *n* a weekday.

ook-oyn *n* a weekend.

ookly *adj* weekly.

ool *v* **1** to treat harshly. **2** to treat as an oddity.

oolat, oolert *n* **1** an owl. **2** an owlet.

oolt-leukin *adj* **1** cowed. **2** terrified

ooly *n* oil.

oom *same as* **oam**.

ooman *n* a woman.

oon[1] *n* a wound.

oon[2] *same as* **oen**.

oon[3] *adj* **1** addled. **2** applied to an egg without a shell.—*n* an egg without a shell.

oon- *neg prefix* un-.

oondisjeested *adj* undigested.

oondomious, oondeemis *adj* incalculable.

oon egg *n* a wind egg, a soft egg without a shell.

oonermine *v* to undermine.

oonerstan' *v* to understand.

oonfashed *adj* untroubled.

oonfersell *adj* **1** inactive, inert. **2** not lively.

oonleedful *adj* lacking in diligence or industry.

oonless *conj* unless.

oonlicklie *adj* unlikely.

oonpatientfu' *adj* impatient.

oonsizzonable *adj* unseasonable.

oonslocken, oonslockened *adj* unslaked, unquenched.

oontimeous *adj* untimely, unseasonable.

oonweelness *n* an illness.

oonwutty *adj* wanting wits.

oop *v* **1** to splice, to bind with thread or cord. **2** to unite.

oor[1] *poss adj* our.

oor[2] *pron and v* we are.

oor[3] *n* hour.

oor[4], **ool** *v* **1** to creep, cower, crouch. **2** to move slowly and feebly.

oora *same as* **orra**.

oorat[1], **oorit** *adj* **1** cold, miserable, shivering. **2** weak, drooping.

oorat[2] *n* a wart.

oore *adv, prep and conj* before.

oorie *adj* **1** eerie. **2** apprehensive. **3** superstitious, afraid, melancholy, depressing dismal. **4** languid, sickly-looking, drooping,.

oorie-like *adj* looking much fatigued.

oorieness *n* chilliness.

ooriesum *adj* timorous.

oorit *adj* with the hair standing on end

oorlich *adj* **1** cold, chilly. **2** raw, damp.

oose[1] *n* a house.

oose[2] *same as* **ooze**.

oosie *adj* having a fine woollen nap

oot *same as* **out**[1].

ootaltie *n* anything that sets off the person.

ootbrack *n* **1** an eruption. **2** a quarrel.

ootbract *n* a quarrel.

ooten *prep* out of.

ooterin, ootrin *adj* outward, from without.

ooth *n* value, worth.

ootlie *n* outlay.

ootlin *n* **1** a stranger. **2** an outcast. **3** the despised or neglected member of a family.

ootmaist *adj* outermost.

oot-turn *n* the yield of grain in threshing.

ootwyle *n* refuse.—*v* to select.

oowen *adj* woollen.

ooy *adj* woolly.

ooze *n* **1** the nap or caddie (qv) that falls from yarn, cloth, etc. **2** cotton or silk. **3** fluff. **4** fibrous stuff put into an inkstand to prevent the ink from spilling.

oozlie *adj* **1** slovenly, unkempt. **2** broken-down. **3** miserable. **4** dark-featured.—*adv* in a slovenly way.

oozlie-looking *adj* slovenly in appearance.

oozlieness *n* slovenliness.

ope *v* to open.—*adj* open.

open *adj* **1** (*used of the weather*) mild, without frost or snow. **2** (*of a sow or heifer*) unspayed.—*n* an opening, a hole. **3** the front suture of the skull.

open-steek *n* a peculiar kind of stitch in sewing.—*adj* having like ornaments in architecture.

open the mouth *v* to begin to preach as a licentiate of the Church.

opentie *n* an opening.

operate *v* **1** a legal term. **2** *in phr* **to operate payment** to procure or enforce payment.

opery *n* belongings, tackle, miscellaneous property.

opignorate *v* **1** a legal term. **2** to pledge.

opine *n* opinion.

opingyon *n* opinion.

oppone *v* **1** to oppose. **2** to bring forward evidence against a prisoner at the bar.

opprobry *n* **1** reproach. **2** opprobrious language. **3** scornings.

optics *n* eyes.

or *prep* **1** before. **2** until.—*conj* **1** than. **2** before. **3** till.

ora *same as* **orra**.

orange-fin *n* sea-trout fry in the River Tweed.

oranger *n* an orange.

orchin *n* a hedgehog.

orchle *n* a porch.

ord *n* a steep hill or mountain.

ordeen *v* **1** to ordain. **2** to design for a special purpose.

order *v* to put in order.—*n in phr* **to take order** to adopt measures for bringing under proper regulations or to secure a certain result.

orderly *adv* regularly.

ordinances *n* the administration of the Lord's Supper and the services connected with it.

ordinar, ordnar *adj* **1** ordinary. **2** usual.—*adv* ordinarily, fairly, rather.—*n* **1** custom, habit. **2** usual condition or health.

ordinarie *n* one's usual course, health, etc.

ordinary[1] *n* what happens in the ordinary course of things

ordinary[2] *n* a Lord Ordinary in the Court of Session.

ore *conj* before.

orf *n* a puny, contemptible creature.

orhie *same as* **o'erhie**.

orie *same as* **oorie**.

origin *n* an orange.

original sin *n* **1** debt on an estate to which one succeeds. **2** the living proofs of youthful incontinence. **3** a cant term.

orishen *n* a reproachful term for a savagely behaved person.

orlache, orlage, orloge *n* **1** a clock. **2** the dial plate of a clock.

orlang *n* a complete year.

Orlie *adj* relating to Orleans.

orling *n* a dwarfish person or child.

or'nar *same as* **ordinar**.

orntren *n* **1** evening. **2** the repast between dinner and supper.

orow *same as* **orra**.

orp *v* **1** to weep convulsively. **2** to fret, repine. **3** to chide habitually.

orphant *n* an orphan.

orphelin *n* an orphan.

orpie-leaf *n* orpine.

orpiet, orpit *adj* fretful, querulous.

orpy, orpey, orpie *n* orpine, a species of houseleek.

orra, orrie, orro, orrow *adj* **1** unmatched, odd, without a fellow. **2** occasional, doing odd jobs. **3** having no settled occupation. **4** spare, superfluous. **5** unoccupied, not engaged. **6** sundry. **7** idle, low, worthless, vagabond, disreputable. **8** out of the common, strange.—*adv* **1** oddly. **2** unusually.—*n* what is left over. **3** a fragment, scrap. **4** (*in pl*) odds and ends. **5** (*in pl*) superfluous things.

orra-beast *n* an odd horse used in doing odd jobs.

orraest *adj* most orra (qv).

orra fowk *n* beggars, tramps.

orra lad, ~ loun *n* a boy employed on odd jobs.

orrals, orrels *n* **1** anything left over. **2** refuse, odds and ends.

orra man *n* a farm labourer who does odd jobs and not stated work.

orraster *n* **1** a low, vagabond fellow. **2** a term of contempt.

ort *v* **1** to pick out the best part of food and leave the rest. **2** to throw away provender. **3** to crumble or waste food. **4** to reject anything. **5** to give away a daughter in marriage without regarding the order of seniority of the others.— *n* (*in pl*) refuse.

orte *n* horse dung.

orzelon *n* a kind of apple.

oshen *n* a person of mean disposition.

osler *n* an ostler.

oslin *n* a species of apple.

Osnaburgh, Osenbrug *n* coarse linen cloth or ticking.

ostensible *adj* (*used of persons*) prominent, conspicuous in public life.

ostentation *n* too much of any article.

ostler *n* an innkeeper.

osy *n* an easy-going, good-tempered person.

o' them *phr* some of them.

o'-them-upo'-them *n* **1** cold flummery, used instead of milk, with boiled flummery. **2** the same substance used at once both as meat and drink or in a solid and fluid state.

other *adj* **1** additional, successive, another. **2** next, succeeding.—*pron* each other, one another.—*adv* otherwise, else.—*n* other way or thing.

other gaits *adv* in another direction.

othersome *pron* some others.

otherwheres *adv* elsewhere.

otherwhiles *adv* at other times.

otter *n* **1** the barb of a fish hook. **2** an illegal fishing implement used by poachers.

otter-grains *n* the dung of the otter.

otterline *n* a cow in calf in her second year.

ou¹ *same as* **oo¹**.

ou² *int* oh!—*v* **1** to ejaculate. **2** to say 'ou!'

ou ay *int* oh yes!

oubit *same as* **oobit**.

ouch *same as* **ough¹**.

ouchin' *adj* (*used of the wind*) sighing, blowing gently.

oucht *same as* **ocht¹**.

ouchtlans *same as* **oughtlins¹**.

ouder *n* **1** a haze, light mist. **2** flickering exhalations from the ground on a warm day.

ouer *prep* over.

ouf *n* **1** an elf. **2** a lout.

ouf-dog *n* a wolf-dog.

ouff *v* to bark.—*n* the sound of a dog barking.

oufish *adj* elvish.

oufish-like *adj* elf-like.

oug *v* **1** to surfeit. **2** to loathe. **3** to disgust.

ough¹ *int* ugh! an exclamation of pain or disgust. —*n* the sound of forcible expulsion of breath.

ough² *v* (*used of the wind*) to blow gently.

ought *v* to own.

oughtlins¹ *adv* **1** at all. **2** in any degree.—*n* anything at all.

oughtlins² *n* anything that ought to be done, duty.

ougsum *adj* horrible.

ouk *n* a week.

oukly *adj* weekly.

oulie *n* oil.

ouncle-weights *n* weights formerly used about farmhouses, generally of sea stones of various sizes, regulated to some standard.

oup *same as* **oop**.

ouph, ouphe *same as* **oof**.

ouphish *adj* **1** elfin. **2** loutish.

ouphish-like *adj* elf-like.

our, oure *v* to overawe.—*prep* over, beyond.

ourback *same as* **o'erback**.

ourheld *adj* untidy.

ourie, oury *same as* **oorie**.

ourinesa *n* sadness, melancholy.

ourlay *n* a cravat.

ourman *n* an arbiter, overman.

oursel's *refl pron* ourselves.

ourthort *prep* athwart.

ourword *same as* **o'erword**.

ouse *n* an ox.

ouse ~, oussen bow *n* a wooden collar used for draught oxen.

ouse-John *n* a cowherd.

ousel¹ *n* the blackbird.

ousel² *n* the sacrament of the Lord's Supper.

ousen milk *n* flummery unboiled, used as milk.

ousen staw *n* an ox stall.

ouster *same as* **oxter**.

out¹ *adv* **1** (*used of a meeting, etc*) dispersed. **2** over. **3** projecting, curving outwards. **4** current, published, circulating. **5** aloud. **6** fully. **7** throughout. **8** finished.—*adj* **1** gone, empty. **2** worn-out, torn. **3** mistaken, in error. **4** extintinguished, gone out. **5** not in friendship.—*prep* **1** beyond. **2** along. **3** without, free from.—*n* (*in pl*) those out of office, etc.—*phr* **outs and ins** the whole details, particulars.

out² *v* **1** to eject, oust. **2** (*with* **with**) to pull or draw out, to tell out, divulge. **3** to betray speak aloud. **4** to vent, expend.

out³ *int* an exclamation of surprise, reproach, etc.

out-about *adj and adv* out of doors.

out alas *int* alas!

out-amo' *adv* away from.

outance *n* **1** an outing. **2** a going out.—*adv* out of doors.

out-an'-out *adv* wholly, entirely.

out ay *int* a strong affirmative.

outback *adv* back foremost.

outbaits *n* common for pasture.

outbearing *n* endurance to the end.—*adj* blustering, bullying.

outbock *v* **1** to vomit forth. **2** to pour out.

outbrade *v* **1** to draw out. **2** to start out.

outbreak *n* **1** an eruption on the skin. **2** a quarrel, a strife. **3** a fit of drinking. **4** transgression. **5** an outcrop. **6** land recently improved.

outbreaker *n* an open transgressor of the law.

outbreaking *n* transgression, sin.

outburst *v* to burst out, break forth.

outburthen *v* to overburden.

outby *adv* **1** outside, out of doors. **2** near by. **3** at a distance. **4** in the direction of.—*adj* **1** out of doors, openair. **2** out-of-the-way, more remote.

outca' *n* **1** a pasture to which cattle are ca'd or driven. **2** a wedding feast given by a master to a favourite servant.

outcast *n* a quarrel, disagreement.—*v* to quarrel, fall out.

outcasten *n* a dispute, contention.

outcome *n* **1** appearance. **2** increase, product. **3** termination. **4** upshot. **5** surplus, excess beyond a measured quantity.

outcoming *n* development of youthful promise.

out-dichtins *n* the refuse of grain.

outdo *v* to overcome.

outdoor *n* work out of doors on a farm.

out-dyke, out-o'-dykes *adv* in unfenced pasture.

out-edge *n* the cutting edge of a knife, sword, etc.

outen *adv* out of doors.—*prep* out of.

outen-under *prep* out from under.

outer *n* one who frequents balls and entertainments.

outerlin' *n* **1** an alien. **2** an outcast. **3** the member of a family who is treated as an outsider. **4** the weakling of a brood, etc.

outerly *adv* outwards.—*adj* (*used of the wind*) blowing from the shore.

outfall *n* **1** the water that escapes from or runs over a weir or dam. **2** a fall of rain, etc. **3** an incident, accident. **4** a quarrel, contention. **5** the ebb tide.

outfalling *n* a quarrel.

outfang-thief *n* **1** the right of a feudal lord to try a thief who was his own vassal, although taken with the fang or booty within the jurisdiction of another. **2** the thief so taken.

outfarm *n* an outlying farm on which the tenant does not reside.

outfeedle *n* **1** an outlying field. **2** the land farthest from the farmstead.

outfield *n* arable land, not manured but constantly cropped, lying some distance from the farmstead.—*adj* (*used of land*) outlying and of inferior quality.

outfight *v* **1** to confront. **2** to fight to the last.

outfit *n* the expense of fitting out.

outflow *n* the ebb tide.

outfoul *n* wildfowl.

outfy *int* an exclamation of reproach.

outgae *n* outlay, expenditure.—*v* to expend.

outgaein *n* **1** a going out of doors. **2** a removal, departure. **3** the feast given to a bride before she leaves her father's or master's house for that of her husband.— *adj* **1** expiring. **2** removing, moving.

outgane *adj* **1** past, beyond, older than. **2** exceeding a limit.

outgang *n* **1** a departure. **2** the giving up of a tenancy. **3** exit, egress. **4** excess over a certain weight or measure.

outganging *n* **1** an outgoing. **2** a going out of doors.

outgate, outgaet *n* **1** a way out, exit, outlet, an issue. **2** gadding about, visiting. **3** ostentatious display. **4** a market, a demand, sale.

outget *n* **1** a way out, deliverance. **2** an opening, opportunity, demand.

outgie *n* expenditure, outgiving, outlay.

outgoer *n* a removing tenant.

outgoing *same as* **outgaein**.

outheidie *adj* rash, hot-headed.

outher *adv and conj* either.

outherans *adv* either.

outhery *adj* (*used of cattle*) not in a thriving state, as shown by their leanness, rough skin and long hair.

outhounder *n* an instigator, an inciter to mischief.

out-hoy *n* an outcry.

outing *n* **1** a vent for commodities. **2** the act of going out or abroad. **3** a gathering of men and women for amusement. **4** the open sea.

outish *adj* **1** roguish. **2** showy. **3** fond of public amusements.

outheek *n* an outlook, a peep out.—*v* to peep out.

outlabour *v* to exhaust by too much labour.

outlack, outlaik *n* **1** overweight. **2** overmeasure.

outlaid, outlayed *adj* expended.

outlair *n* an egg laid by a hen out of her proper nest.

outlan *n* **1** an alien, stranger. **2** an incomer from the country to the town or from one parish to another.—*adj* **1** outlying, distant. **2** far from neighbours. **3** strange, alien. **4** wandering.

outlander *n* a stranger, foreigner.

outlandish *adj* out-of-the-way, remote.

outlans *n* **1** freedom to go in and out. **2** holidaying.

outlayer *n* **1** a hen that lays out of the regular nest. **2** an egg laid by such a hen. **3** a stone lying detached in a field.

outlay gear *n* a stock of furniture, implements, plenishin (qv).

outlaying *adj* (*used of a hen*) laying eggs away from the regular nest.

outleap *n* an outbreak, outburst.

outlens *same as* **outlans**.

outler *adj* not housed.—*n* **1** a beast that lies outside in winter. **2** one who is out of office.

outletting *n* **1** an emanation. **2** the operation of divine grace.

outlie *n* outlay, expenditure.

outlier *n* **1** an outler (qv). **2** a stone lying out detached in a field.

outlin *same as* **ootlin**.

outlins *same as* **outlans**.

outloup *v* to leap out.

outly[1] *n* money that lies out of the hands of the owner, either in trade or at interest.

outly[2] *adv* fully, completely.

outlyer *n* a person who sleeps in the open air at night.

outlying *adj* **1** (*used of cattle*) lying out at night in winter. **2** distantly related. **3** (*used of money*) spent on, laid out, put out.

outmarrow *v* **1** to outmatch. **2** to outmanoeuvre.

out of *prep* **1** in excess of, going beyond. **2** destitute of.

out on *adv* hereafter, by-and-by.—*prep* out of.

out oner *prep* from under.

outouth *adv* outwards.

outowre *adv* **1** out from any place. **2** quite over. **3** across, beyond. **4** outside.

out-owre-by *adv* at a good distance.

outplay *v* to beat at play.

outpittin *n* **1** the excrement of infants. **2** attending to this.

outpour *n* a downpour of rain or snow.

output *n* appearance, style of dress, get-up.—*v* **1** to dismiss, eject. **2** to furnish, equip soldiers. **3** to issue coin. **4** to publish.

outputter *n* **1** one who furnishes and equips soldiers. **2** an employer, instigator. **3** one who passes counterfeit coin. **4** one who circulates false or calumnious reports.

outputting *n* **1** passing coin. **2** equipment. **3** the publishing of libels, etc.

outrake *n* **1** an extensive walk for sheep or cattle. **2** an expedition.

outrate *v* **1** to outnumber. **2** to outdo, outrun.

outred *v* **1** to extricate. **2** to finish out a business. **3** to clear off debt. **4** to fit out. **5** to clear out, put in complete order.—*n* **1** rubbish, what is cleared off or swept out. **2** clearance, finishing.

out-red *n* a military expedition.

outreike *n* outfit, rigging out.—*v* to fit out, equip levies.

outreiker *n* one who equips others for service.

outrigg *n* **1** equipment. **2** appearance, preparation. —*v* to equip.

outring *n* (*a curling term*) the outward bias given to a stone by touching the outside of another.

outrook, outrug *n* the backward wash of a wave after breaking.

outrun *v* to run out, come to an end.—*n* pasture land attached to a farm.

outrunning *n* expiration, termination.

outs *int* an exclamation of impatience.

outscold *v* to scold excessively or loudly.

outseam awl *n* a peculiar kind of shoemaker's awl.

outset *v* **1** to set out, start, set about. **2** to set off ostentatiously, to make a tawdry display of finery. —*n* **1** an outfit. **2** a start in life. **3** the provision for a child leaving home or a daughter at her marriage. **4** the publication of a book. **5** an ornament, offset, what sets off the appearance. **6** an ostentatious display of finery, etc. **7** an outhouse, an addition enlarging a room or building. **8** waste land brought under cultivation. **9** patches of newly cultivated land.

outshinned *adj* having the shins turned outwards.

outshoot *v* **1** to outwit. **2** to overreach. **3** to overshoot.

outshot *n* **1** the projection of a building or wall. **2** an outbuilding or lean-to of a house. **3** pasture, untilled ground on a farm. **4** ebb tide. **5** a visible attack of illness.—*adj* projecting outside.

outshot window *n* a bay window.

outside *n* **1** the farther side of anything. **2** the heart of the matter. **3** the utmost extent.—*prep* beyond the usual course of.

outsider *n* one who is not a relative.

outside worker *n* a fieldworker.

outsiftins *n* the refuse of grain.

outsight *n* goods or implements for use out of doors.

outsight *n* prospect of egress.

outsight-plenishing *n* implements for use out of doors.

outsole *n* the outer sole of a boot.

outspeckle *n* a laughing stock.

outspew *v* to pour forth.

outspout *v* **1** to spout forth. **2** to dart out.

outstaffs *n* the poles of a poke or pout net.

outstand *v* to stand out against, withstand.

outstander *n* **1** an opponent. **2** a firm opposer.

outstanding *n* resistance, opposition.—*adj* great, enormous.

outsteek *n* a kind of shoe.

outstrapolous, outstropolous *adj* obstreperous.

outstriking *n* an eruption on the skin.

outstrucken *adj* having an eruption on the skin.

outsucken *n* **1** the freedom of a tenant from thirlage (qv) to a mill. **2** duties payable by those who have such freedom.—*adj* free from thirlage to a mill.

outsuckener *n* one not thirled to a mill—*see* **thirl**.

outsucken-multure *n* the duties payable by those who come voluntarily to a mill.

out-tak *n* **1** goods bought on credit. **2** outlay. **3** yield, return.

out-taken *ppl as prep* except, excepting.

outter *same as* **outer**.

out-the-gait *adj* honest.

out-things *n* objects outside.

out-through, ~-throw *prep* **1** through to the opposite. **2** completely through.—*adv* thoroughly.

outtie *adj* **1** addicted to company. **2** much disposed to go out.

out-tope *v* to overtop.

out-town *n* an outlying field on a farm.

out-town multures *n* duties payable by those who come voluntarily to a mill.

out-trick *v* to outdo by trickery.

out-turn *n* **1** a finish, result in the end. **2** increase, productiveness.

out upon *prep* advanced in.

out upon *int* an exclamation of reproach or anger.

outwag *v* **1** to wave. **2** to hold out and wave.

outwair *v* to expend.

outwairin *adj* wearisome.

outwale *n* **1** refuse. **2** the pick or choice.—*v* to choose out, select.

outwalins *n* **1** refuse. **2** leavings.

outward *adj* **1** cold, distant, reserved. **2** not kind.

outwardness *n* **1** distance. **2** coldness. **3** unkindness.

outwards *n* externals.

outwatch *n* an outpost, picket, watch.

outweel *adv* assuredly

outwick *n* (*a curling term*) the bias given to a stone by touching the outside of another.

outwinterers *n* cattle not housed in winter.

outwith, outwuth *prep* outside of, beyond.—*adv* **1** separate from. **2** beyond.—*adj* **1** abroad. **2** more distant, not near.—*n* the outlying parts.

out with *phr* **1** at variance with. **2** fallen out with.

outwittins *adv* **1** unwittingly. **2** without the knowledge of.

outwoman *n* a woman who does outdoor work.

outwork *n* **1** outdoor work. **2** fieldwork.

outworker *n* a fieldworker.

outworthy *v* to excel.

outwuth *same as* **outwith**.

outwyle *v* to select.

ouze *same as* **ooze**.

ouzel *same as* **ousel**.

ouzily *same as* **oozlie**.

oven *n* **1** a shallow pan or metal pot with a lid in which loaves are baked, burning peats being piled on the top of the lid. **2** the closeness felt on opening a room long shut up.—*v* to bake in an oven.

oven-builder *n* the willow warbler.

oven cake *n* a cake made of oatmeal and yeast and baked in an oven.

over *same as* **o'er**.

overbalance *v* **1** to outnumber. **2** to get the better of.

overbid *v* to outbid.

overcap *v* to overhang, project over.

overcoming *n* crossing over.

overdraw *v* to over-induce.

overenyie *n* southernwood.

overgive *v* to give up, surrender.

overing *n* **1** superiority. **2** control. **3** a by-job. **4** (*in pl*) odds and ends.

overish *adj in phr* **all overish** feeling creepy.

overitious *adj* **1** excessive, intolerable. **2** boisterous, violent, headstrong.

overlap *v* **1** to be folded over. **2** to lay one slate or stone so as partially to cover another.—*n* the place where one thin object partially covers another. **3** a surplus. **4** the hatches of a ship.

overlarded *adj* covered with fat or lard.

overleather *n* the upper leather of a shoe.

overlook *v* **1** to bewitch. **2** to look on one with the evil eye.—*n* an omission, oversight.

overlouping *adj* exultant.

overly *adj* **1** excessive. **2** superficial. **3** careless. **4** remiss. **5** incidental.—*adv* **1** excessively, very. **2** too, too much. **3** superficially, briefly, hastily. **4** accidentally, by chance.

overreach *v* **1** to overtake. **2** to overrate, assess too highly. **3** to extend over.

oversailyie *v* **1** to build over a close, leaving a passage below. **2** to arch over.

oversman *n* **1** a foreman, overseer. **2** an umpire when two arbiters disagree.

overspaded *adj* half-trenched.

over-the-matter *adj* excessive.

overthink *v* to think over.

overthwart *prep* across.

overture *n* (*in Presbyterian churches*) the opening up or introduction of a subject to the notice of a superior court.—*v* to bring up an overture.

overward *n* the upper ward or district of a county.

ow *int* an exclamation of surprise.

ow ay *int* oh yes!

owder *same as* **ouder**.

owdiscence *n* a hearing, audience.

owe[1] *v* to own, possess.

owe[2] *adj* owing, indebted to.

ower *same as* **o'er**.

owerling *adj* covering over.

owerlippin *adj* overflowing.

owerthrang *adj* **1** too busy. **2** too crowded.

owff *same as* **ouff**.

owg *v* to shudder.

owght *n* a cipher, nought.

owing *n in phr* **eghin and owing** humming and hawing.

owk, owke *same as* **ouk**.

owme *same as* **oam**.

own *v* **1** to claim as owner. **2** to recognize. **3** to identify. **4** to acknowledge relationship. **5** to support, favour. **6** not to let a curling stone alone but help it up by sweeping before it.

owrance *n* **1** ability. **2** superiority. **3** mastery.

owre *same as* **o'er**.

owrhye *same as* **o'erhie**.

owrie *same as* **oorie**.

owrun and owrim *n* the shearing by a band of reapers of grain not portioned out to them by rigs.

owrter *adv* farther over.

owsal *n* the blackbird.

owse *same as* **ouse**.

owssen-staw *n* an ox stall.

owther *same as* **outher**.

owtherins *same as* **outherans**.

owthor *n* an author.

ox *n* a steer of the third year.

ox-e'e *n* **1** the blue tit. **2** the. **3** ox-eye daisy.

oxengate, oxgang, oxgate *n* a measure of land varying according to the nature of the soil.

ox-money, ~-penny *n* a tax on oxen paid to a landlord by tenants.

oxter *n* **1** the armpit. **2** the armhole of a coat, etc. **3** the breast, bosom.—*v* **1** to go arm in arm. **2** to lead by the arm. **3** to embrace. **4** to take by the arms. **5** to carry under the arm. **6** to elbow.

oxter-deep *adv* up to the armpits.

oxterfu' *n* an armful.

oxterfu'-ket *n* a worthless fellow.

oxter-lift *n* as much as can be carried between the arm and the side or in a semicircle formed by the arms and the breast.

oxter pocket, ~ pouch *n* a breast pocket.

oxter staff *n* a crutch.

oy *same as* **oye**.

oye *n* **1** a grandchild. **2** a grandson. **3** a nephew.

oyess *n* oyez, as used by heralds and public criers three times in succession, to give legal effect.

oyess *n* a niece.

oyse[1] *n* oysters.

oyse[2] *n* oyez.

ozelly *same as* **oozlie**.

ozle *n* the line attaching cork buoys to a herring net.

P

pa'[1] *same as* **pall**[2].

pa'[2] *same as* **paw**[1].

pa'[3] *same as* **paw**[3].

paak *same as* **paik**[2].

paal *same as* **pall**[1].

paalie-maalie *adj* in bad health, sickly.

paamie *same as* **palmy**.

paat *same as* **paut**.

pab *same as* **pob**.

pabble *v* to bubble like boiling water.

pace *same as* **paise**[1].

Pace *n* Easter.

Pace-day *n* Easter Day.

Pace-egg *n* an Easter egg, hard-boiled and coloured, given as a toy to a child.

Pace-even *n* Easter Saturday.

Pace-market *n* a market held at Easter.

Pace-ree *n* a time about Easter when storms were expected.

Pace Saturday *n* Easter Saturday.

Pace-Sunday *n* Easter Day.

pachty *same as* **paughty**.

pack[1] *n* a pact, compact.

pack[2] *n* the shepherd's part of a flock, which is allowed free grazing in return for his services in looking after the whole herd.

pack[3] *n* **1** property, belongings. **2** a measure of wool, 18 stones Scots or 240 pounds. **3** a heavy mass of clouds, a thundercloud.—*v* **1** to play as partner at cards. **2** (*with* **upon**, *used of a retort*) to come home.—*adj* intimate, familiar, friendly.

packad *n* a shallow wooden box or backet (qv) for carrying ashes.

packald *n* a pack load.

pack and peil *v* **1** to load and unload. **2** to trade unfairly.

packet *n* a pannier.

pack-ewes *n* the ewes allowed to a shepherd instead of wages.

packhouse *n* a warehouse for goods imported or to be exported.

packie *n* a packman, pedlar.

packies *n* heavy masses of clouds.

packlie *adv* familiarly.

packman-rich *n* a species of bear (qv), having six rows of grains to the ear.

packmantie *n* a portmanteau.

pack-merchant *n* **1** a packman. **2** (*in pl*) *same as* **packies**.

packness *n* familiarity, intimacy.

paction *v* **1** to bargain. **2** to make an agreemeet.

pad[1] *n* a nag.

pad[2] *n* **1** a path. **2** a beaten track.—*v* **1** to make a path on a new track. **2** to go on foot. **3** to send away on foot.

padda, paddan *n* a frog.

padder *same as* **patter**[1].

paddie stule *n* a toadstool.

paddit *adj* (*of a track*) beaten hard by treading.

paddle[1] *n* **1** a long-handled spud for cutting thistles, weeds, etc. **2** a stake net.—*v* **1** to cut off with a spud. **2** to hoe.

paddle[2] *n* the lumpfish.

paddle[3] *v* **1** to walk slowly or with short steps. **2** to toddle. **3** to tramp about in wet and mud.—*n* the act of walking with short, quick steps or tramping in mud or water.

paddle[4] *v* to finger, handle, feel lovingly.

paddle-doo *n* a frog formerly kept in a cream jar for luck.

paddled-rounall *n* a circular space in a field worn bare by oxen following one another round and round.

paddler *n* **1** a child just beginning to walk. **2** a small person walking with short, uncertain steps.

paddling *adj* **1** walking, wandering aimlessly. **2** trifling, petty. **3** useless.

paddock[1] *n* **1** a frog. **2** a toad. **3** a term of reproach or contempt. **4** a low, frog-shaped sledge for carrying large stones.

paddock[2] *n* a small farm.

paddock-cheeks *n* yellow, inflated cheeks, like those of a frog.

paddock-cruds *same as* **paddock-rud**.

paddock-dabber *n* one that dabs at or kills frogs.

paddock flower *n* the marsh-marigold.

paddock-hair *n* the down on unfledged birds and on the heads of babies born without hair.

paddock-loup *n* **1** as far as a frog can leap. **2** the game of leapfrog.

paddock pipe *n* various species of the horsetail.

paddock-rud, -rude, -reed *n* the spawn of frogs or toads.

paddock-spit, -spittles *n* the cuckoo spit, the white froth secreted on plants by cicadas.

paddock-spue *n* frogs' spawn.

paddock stone *n* the toadstone.

paddock stool *n* **1** a toadstool. **2** a term of contempt.

paddock-stool bonnet *n* a cap shaped like a toadstool.

paddow *n* **1** a frog. **2** a toad.

paddy[1] *n* a frog.

paddy[2] *n* a packman, pedlar.—*phr* **to come paddy** to befool.

paddy-fair *same as* **paldy-fair**.

paddy-ladle *n* a tadpole.

padell *same as* **paddle**[1].

padjell *n* **1** an old pedestrian. **2** one who has often won foot races.

padle[1], **padle**[2] *same as* **paddle**[1], **paddle**[2].

padroll *v* to patrol.
pady *n* a frog.
Paece *same as* **Pace**.
paedaneous judge *n* a petty judge who tried only trifling cases and sat only on a low seat.
paedle[1], paedle[2] *same as* **paddle**[2], **paddle**[3].
paelag *same as* **pellock**.
paet *n* a peat.
pae-wae *adj* **1** woebegone. **2** out of sorts.
paffle *n* **1** a small portion of land. **2** a pendicle (qv).
paffler *n* one who occupies a small farm.
paght *n* the custom on goods.
paick *same as* **paik**[2].
paid[1] *same as* **pad**[2].
paid[2] *adj in phr* **ill-paid** very sorry.
paidle[1] *v* to hoe.—*n* **1** a hoe. **2** a short spud.
paidle[2] *same as* **paddle**[3].
paidle[3] *n* a nail bag.
paiferal *n* a stupid fellow.
paighled *adj* **1** overcome with fatigue. **2** panting with exertion. *See* **peghle**.
paigle *n* the dirty work of a house.—*v* to do such work.
paik[1] *n* **1** a low character. **2** a term of reproach for a woman.
paik[2], paike *v* **1** to beat, strike. **2** to chastise. **3** to walk steadily and continually.—*n* **1** a stroke, blow. **2** (*in pl*) a deserved punishment.
paiker *n* a street-walker.
paiket *adj in phr* **paiket wi' poverty** pinched by poverty.
paikie[1] *n* a female streetwalker, a prostitute.
paikie[2] *n* a piece of skin doubled, for defending the thighs from the peat spade in cutting peats.
paikie[3] *n* an occasional day labourer.
paikie-dog *n* a dogfish.
paiking *n* a beating, chastisement.
paikit-like *adj* **1** like a prostitute. **2** looking shabby and worn-out.
paikment *n* a beating, paiking (qv).
pail[1] *n* a hearse.
pail[2] *same as* **pale**[1].
pailie[1] *same as* **paulie**.
pailie[2] *n* a small pail.
pailin *n* a stake fence.—*v* to surround with a paling.
paill *n in phr* **to haud paill wi'** to match a thing with another.
pain *n* **1** pains, trouble. **2** a penalty. **3** (*in pl*) rheumatism.
painch *n* **1** a paunch. **2** (*in pl*) tripe.
painch-lippit *adj* (*used of a horse*) having lips like a painch (qv).
painful *adj* **1** painstaking. **2** laborious.
pain-piss *n* a disease of horses, the bats (qv).
painsfu' *adj* painful.
paint *n* the painted woodwork in a room or house.
Paip *n* the Pope.
paip[1] *same as* **pop**[2].
paip[2] *n* **1** a cherry stone used in a children's game. **2** the game played with cherry stones.
paipie *n* the game played with cherry stones.
paipoch *n* the store of cherry stones from which the castles or caddies are supplied. *See* **castle; caddle**.
pair[1] *n* **1** a set or number of anything. **2** a single article. **3** (*in pl*) a card game.—*v* **1** to marry. **2** (*with* **with**) to match with, agree with.—*phr* **a pair o' carritches** a catechism.
pair[2] *v* **1** to grow worse. **2** to diminish.
pairing *adj* matrimonial.
pairis' *n* a parish.
pairk *n* **1** a park. **2** a field.
pairle *n* two rounds of a stocking in knitting.
pairless *adj* companionless, without a fellow or match.
pairnmeal, pairns *n* the coarsest kind of meal, made of bran and wheat siftings.
pairt *same as* **part**.
pairtisay *n* anything done by or belonging to more persons than one.
pairtisay wa' *n* a party wall.

pairtisay wark *n* work done by a number of persons.
pairtisay web *n* a web worked for several owners, each of whom contributes a share of the materials.
pairtrick *n* a partridge.
pairt tak' *v* **1** to side with. **2** to defend.
paise, pais *v* **1** to weigh in the hand. **2** to poise.—*n* **1** the weight of a clock. **2** a weight used by a weaver to keep his web extended.
Paise, Paiss *same as* **Pace**.
pait *n* **1** a pet. **2** an advocate related to a judge and favoured by him.
paiter[1] *same as* **patter**[1].
paiter[2], paitter *same as* **patter**[2].
paith *same as* **path**.
paitlich *adj* favourite, favoured.
paitlich-gown *n* (*perhaps*) a kind of neckerchief.
paitric, paitrick *n* a partridge.
pake[1], pake[2] *same as* **paik**[1], **paik**[2].
pakey *same as* **pawky**.
pakkald *same as* **packald**.
palach *same as* **pellock**.
palall *same as* **pall-all**.
palaulays *same as* **pall-all**.
palaver, palaiver *n* **1** idle talk, nonsense. **2** a wearisome talker. **3** a silly, ostentatious person. **4** fussy show.—*v* **1** to talk over. **2** to gossip. **3** to behave ostentatiously. **4** to jest.
Paldy fair *n* a fair held at Brechin in memory of St Palladius.
pale[1] *v* **1** to test a cheese by an incision. **2** to tap for the dropsy.—*n* an instrument for testing cheese.
pale[2] *n* (*in pl*) a paling.
pale[3] *n* a faucet.
pale[4] *same as* **pall**[1].
pale[5] *v* **1** to call, summon. **2** *in phr* **to pale a candle** on seeing a dead candle, to demand a view of the person's face whose death it portends.
palerine *n* a woman's cloak or tippet, a pelerine.
paley[1] *same as* **paulie**.
paley[2] *adj* pale, pale-faced.
paley-footed *adj* flat-footed, splay-footed, having the feet turned in.
paley-lamb *n* a very small or feeble lamb.
palie *adj* delicious, palatable.
paling *v* to surround with a paling.
paling wall *n* a paling.
palinode *n* **1** a legal term. **2** a recantation demanded of a libel in addition to damages.
palissade *n* a row of trees planted close.
pall[1] *n* **1** a large pole. **2** a mooring post. **3** a stay for the feet in pulling horizontally.—*v* to get a purchase for the feet against a post in pulling. **4** (*of a horse*) to strike with the forefeet.
pall[2], palls *n* any rich or fine cloth.
pall[3] *v* **1** to puzzle, baffle. **2** to beat, surpass.—*n* a puzzle.
pallach, pallack *same as* **pellock**.
pallach *same as* **pall**[3].
pallaldies *same as* **pall-all**.
pall-all, pallalls, pallally *n* **1** hopscotch. **2** the piece of slate, stone, etc, with which the game is played.
pallawa *n* **1** a species of sea crab, a keavie or pillar. **2** a dastardly fellow.
pallet[1] *n* **1** the head. **2** a ball.
pallet[2] *n* **1** a pelt. **2** an undressed sheepskin.
pallie *same as* **paulie**.
pallo *n* a porpoise.
pally *adj* palsied.—*n* a palsied hand.
pally-wat *n* a term of contempt. *See* **pallawa**.
palm[1] *n* **1** the common willow. **2** (*in pl*) its catkins.
palm[2] *n* the palm of the hand.—*v* **1** to lay hands on, finger. **2** to squeeze the hand.
palmer *v* **1** to wander about. **2** to saunter. **2** to walk clumsily, feebly or with a shuffling gait. **3** to move about noisily.—*n* **1** clumsy walking. **2** one who goes about in shabby clothes, either from poverty or from slovenliness.

palmerer *n* a clumsy, noisy walker.
palmering *adj* **1** rude, clumsy. **2** walking feebly. **3** wandering.
Palm-fair *n* a fair beginning on the fifth Monday in Lent and lasting two days.
palmy[1] *adj* abounding in catkins.
palmy[2] *n* a blow on the palm of the hand from a schoolteacher's tawse (qv) or cane.—*v* to inflict palmies.
palsified *adj* palsied.
paly *adj* pale, whitish.
pamisaple *n* the shell *Bulla lignaria*.
pammy *same as* **palmy**[2].
pamphie *n* **1** the knave of clubs. **2** the knave of any suit of cards. **3** the pam.
pamphil *same as* **pumphel**.
pamphlete, pamphelet *n* a plump young woman.
pan[1] *n* **1** the skull, head. **2** a piece of timber laid lengthwise on the top or posts of a house to which the roof is attached.
pan[2] *v* **1** to correspond. **2** to tally. **3** to unite.
pan[3] *same as* **pawn**[1].
pan[4] *n* a hard, impenetrable crust below the soil.
pan[5] *v* to tie a pan or kettle to a dog's tail.
pan and kaiber *n* a peculiarly constructed roof. *See* **pan**[1].
panash *n* a plume worn in the hat.
pancake *n* a kind of round flat cake, thicker and smaller than an English pancake, cooked on a griddle, a drop scone.
pance *same as* **panse**.
pand *n* the valance of a bed.
pander *v* **1** to wander about in a silly, aimless way from place to place. **2** to trifle at work.
pandomie *n* pandemonium.
pandore, pandoor *n* a large oyster.
pan drop *n* a kind of hard, round, mint-flavoured sweet.
pandy *n* a stroke on the palm of the hand with a tawse (qv) or cane.—*v* to inflict pandies. *See* **palmy**.
panel, pannel *n* **1** the bar or dock in a court of justice. **2** a prisoner at the bar.—*v* to bring to the bar for trial.—*phr* **to enter upon panel** to appear at the bar.
pang[1] *v* **1** to pain. **2** to ache.
pang[2] *v* **1** to pack to the utmost. **2** to cram, stuff full.—*adj* close-packed, choke-full, crammed.
pang[3] *n* strength, force.
pang fu' *adj* crammed to the full.
panicat *adj* panic-stricken.
pan-jotrals *n* **1** a dish made of various kinds of meat. **2** a sort of fricassee. **3** a gallimaufrie (qv). **4** the slabbery (qv) offals of the shambles.
pan kail *n* broth made of coleworts cut small, seasoned with kitchen fee (qv), butter or lard and thickened with oatmeal.
pan-loaf *n* a baker's loaf baked in a pan and hard and smooth on the sides and bottom as well as the top.
pannel *n* **1** a sack filled with straw. **2** same as **panel**.
pannelling *n* part of a saddle.
pans *n* a description of Church lands.
panse *v* **1** to think. **2** to dress a wound.
pan-soled *adj* (*used of a bap* (qv)) flat and hard on the underside, from being fired there.
pant[1] *n* the mouth of a town well or fountain.
pant[2] *n* a backstroke.
pantin, pantoun *n* a slipper.
pantouffles *n* slippers.
pantry *n* **1** a larder. **2** a press (qv).—*v* to lay up in store.
pant well *n* a covered well.
pan velvet *n* **1** rough velvet. **2** plush.
pan wood *n* **1** fuel used at salt pans for purposes of evaporation. **2** small coals, coal dust.
pany *adj* (*used of a field*) difficult to plough, owing to stones, etc, on it.
pap[1] *n* **1** the projection of the mouth. **2** a teat.
pap[2] *n* weavers' paste for dressing their webs.
pap[3], **pap**[4] *same as* **pop**[1], **pop**[2].

paparap *n* a pronged implement.
pap-bairn *n* a sucking child.
pape[1] *same as* **pap**[3].
pape[2] *same as* **paip**[2].
Pape *n* the Pope.
papejay *same as* **papingoe**.
paper *n* **1** the manuscript of a sermon not preached extempore. **2** accommodation bills. **3** bills instead of cash. **4** banknotes. **5** a begging petition written for a person begging.—*v* **1** to advertise in the newspapers. **2** to report to the newspapers.
paper-dragon *n* a boy's paper kite.
paper-glory *n* glory or fame by writings.
paperie *n* **1** a small paper. **2** a short paper.
paper-lead *n* **1** sheet lead. **2** tinfoil paper.
paper-lord *n* a lord by courtesy alone.
paper-minister *n* a minister who reads his sermons.
paper-news *n* newspapers.
paper-note *n* a banknote.
paper-pound *n* a banknote of £1.
paper-sermon *n* a sermon read and not preached extempore.
papery *n* popery, Catholicism.
papin *n* a beverage of whisky, small beer and oatmeal.
papingoe, papinjay *n* **1** a parrot. **2** a wooden bird formerly shot at in a yearly trial of skill, a popinjay.
papingoe ball *n* the yearly ball held at the shooting of the papingoe (qv).
papish *n* a papist, a Roman Catholic.
papism *n* popery.
papist-stroke *n* **1** a cross. **2** a ludicrous term used by young people.
papistry *n* Romanism, popery.
paple *same as* **papple**[2].
pap milk *n* breast milk.
pap-o'-the-hass *n* the uvula.
pappan *v* **1** to pamper, spoil. **2** to bring up young people or animals too indulgently or delicately.
pappant *adj* **1** rich. **2** rising in the world. **3** rendered pettish by over-indulgence. **4** very careful of one's health.
pappin[1] *n* weavers' paste.
pappin[2] *n* **1** a thrashing. **2** the sound made by hail, etc, beating against anything.
papple[1] *n* the corncockle and its seed.
papple[2] *v* **1** to bubble, boil up like water. **2** to tumble about or swirl with a quick, bubbling motion. **3** to purl. **4** to boil with indignation. **5** to perspire violently.
papple roots *n* the roots of the corncockle.
pappy *adj* **1** conceited, puffed up with pride. **2** presumptuous.
par *same as* **parr**.
parade *n* a procession.—*v* to cut a dash, strut about.
para-dog *same as* **pirrie-dog**.
parafle, paraffle *n* **1** ostentatious display. **2** embroidery.
parafling *n* a trifling evasion.
paragon *n* a rich cloth imported from Turkey.
paraleeses *n* paralysis.
paralytic *n* a stroke of paralysis.
paramuddle *n* the red tripe of cattle.
paraphernally *n* **1** a matter, an affair, occurrence. **2** a story. **3** a rigmarole.
paraphernala, parapharnauls *n* a wife's personal dress and ornaments.
paraphrases *n* the Scottish metrical version of other portions of Scripture than the psalms.
paratitle *n* an explanatory subtitle.
paraud, parawd *same as* **parade**.
pardi *int* an oath derived from French: by God!
pardoos *n* **1** violence. **2** a bang.—*adj* violently.
pare *v* **1** to cut off the surface of a moss or moor. **2** to run a plough lightly among thinned turnips to check weeds.
paregally *adv* particularly.
parfait *v* to perfect.
parich *same as* **parrich**.

parish *n* the ring with the tee in the centre at the end of a curling rink.

parishen *n* a parish.

paritch *same as* **parritch**.

park *n* **1** a grass field. **2** a paddock.

park-breed *n* the breadth of a park (qv).

park dyke *n* a wall of stone or turf enclosing a field or paddock.

parl *same as* **pall**[3].

parlamentar *n* a member of parliament.

parle *n* **1** speech. **2** a talk, conversation. **3** an argument, a war of words.—*v* to talk, converse.

parled *adj* paralysed.

parley, parlie *n* **1** a small, thin gingerbread cake sprinkled with small sweeties (qv). **2** a parliament (qv).

parley, parlie, parly *v* to converse.—*n* **1** a long conversation. **2** a truce, especially in certain games.

parleyvoo *v* to speak French or in a foreign tongue. —*n* **1** speech, talk, used in ridicule of the French. **2** a lover's talk.—*adj* **1** foreign. **2** French.

parliament[1], **parliament cake** *n* a cake, supposed to have been used by members of the Scottish parliament during their sittings. *See* **parley**.

parliament[2] *n in phr* **free parliament** freedom of speech.

parliamenter, parlimenter *n* a member of parliament.

parliamentin chield *n* a member of parliament.

parliament man *n* a parliamenter (qv).

parlicue *n* **1** a résumé of various speeches, sermons or addresses, given at their close. **2** a flourish at the end of a word in writing. **3** the space between the thumb and the forefinger when they are extended. **2** (*in pl*) peculiarities of conduct, whims, oddities.—*v* to give a résumé of speeches and especially of sermons preached at a communion season.

parlously *adv* in an extraordinary manner.

parochial *n in phr* **to gang on the parochial** to accept parish relief.

parochine *same as* **parishen**.

parochiner *n* a parishioner.

parpane *n* **1** the parapet of a bridge. **2** a partition wall. **3** a wall.

parpane wall *n* a partition wall.

parpell wall *n* a partition wall.

parpin *adj* perpendicular.

parqueer, parquier *adj* **1** accurate. **2** skilful. **3** thoroughly instructed.—*adv* by heart.

parr *n* a young salmon.

parrach *n* oatmeal porridge.

parrach, parrich, parrick *n* **1** a small field, a paddock. **2** a small enclosure in which a ewe is confined to suckle a strange lamb. **3** a crowd, a collection of things huddled together. **4** a group.—*v* **1** to shut up a ewe with a strange lamb to induce her to suckle it. **2** to crowd together confusedly.

parrich *n* **1** a person of small stature, very neatly and finely dressed. **2** a term of endearment to an infant or young child.

parritch, parridge *n* (*used as a pl*) oatmeal porridge.

parritch bicker *n* a porringer.

parritch broo *n* water for boiling porridge.

parritch cap, ~ coggie *n* a porringer.

parritch-hale *adj* quite able to take one's ordinary food.

parritch-hertit *adj* soft-hearted.

parritch hours *n* mealtimes, breakfast.

parritch kettle *n* a porridge pot.

parritch luggie *n* a porringer.

parritch meal *n* oatmeal for porridge.

parritch pan *n* a porridge pot.

parritch pat, ~ pingle *n* a porridge pot.

parritch spurkle, ~ spurtle *n* a rod for stirring porridge.

parritch time *n* mealtime.

parritch tree *n* a rod for stirring porridge.

parrlie *n* a small barrel.

parrock, parrok *same as* **parrach**.

parrot, parrot coal *n* a species of coal that burns very clearly, a cannel coal, giving a loud, cracking noise on being placed on the fire.

parry[1] *v* to put off, delay, tarry, loiter.

parry[2] *n in phr* **when ane says parry a' says parry** when anything is said by a person of consequence it is echoed by everyone.

parry *v* to fight in play.

parrymyak *n* a match, equal.

parsel *n* parsley.

parsley-breakstone *n* the lady's mantle.

parson-gray *adj* dark grey.

part *n* **1** a place, a district. **2** that which is incumbent on, or becomes, one. **3** interest. **4** share. **5** concern.—*v* **1** to part with, abandon. **2** to divide. **3** to share. **4** to distribute. **5** to side with, favour. **6** to depart.—*phrs* **to part with bairn** *or* **with Patrick** to abort, to give birth prematurely.

partail *n* bait taken from the tail of a young salmon or parr.

partal door *n* the door leading from the dwelling house to the byre (qv).

partal wall *n* the wall separating the dwelling house from the byre (qv).

partan, parten, partin, parton *n* **1** the common crab. **2** a term of contempt.

partan bree *n* crab soup.

partan cage *n* a crab trap, a sparred cage for keeping crabs alive when caught.

partan cartie *n* an empty crab shell used as a toy cart.

partan crab *n* a crab.

partan-face *n* a term of contempt.

partanfu' *adj* as full as a crab.

partan-haar *n* a seasonable time for catching crabs.

partan-handit *adj* **1** close-fisted. **2** gripping like a crab. **3** greedy.

partan-, partan's-tae *n* a crab's claw.

partawta *n* a potato.

parteeclar *adj* particular.

partic *adj* particular.

particate *n* a rood of land.

particle *n* a small piece of land.

particular *adj* **1** precise. **2** careful. **3** very attentive.

particularities, partickilarities *n* **1** the particulars, details. **2** whims, particular fancies.

particularness *n* **1** caution. **2** precision.

partiere wall *n* a boundary wall common to two proprietors.

partisie *same as* **pairtisay**.

partle *v* to trifle at work.—*n* **1** a trifle. **2** a small part.

partlet *n* a woman's ruff.

partner *n* a spouse.—*v* to be a partner of or to.

partrick *n* a partridge.

part-take *v* to side with.

party *v* to side with.

party match *n* a party contest.

party pot *n* a pot with several owners.

pas *v* to pace, measure.

Paach *n* Easter.

paseyad *n* a woman who has nothing new to wear at Easter.

Pase *same as* **Pace**.

pash[1] *v* to bruise to powder.

pash[2] *n* the head.

pashy *adj* having a good head, clever.

pasment *n* livery.

pasper, paspie *n* samphire.

paspey *n* a kind of dance.

pass *v* **1** (*with* **off**) to spend. **2** to let a thing go or slip. **3** to remit. **4** to have or finish a meal. **5** to pass by, avoid. **6** to surprise, puzzle.—*n* an aisle, a passage in a church or between rows of seats.—*phr* **to draw one's pass** to withdraw oneself or one's offer.

passage *v* to progress.

passe *n* a hint to resign an office.

passeneip *n* parsnip.

passers *n* a pair of compasses.

pass-gilt *n* current money.
passingly *adv* occasionally.
passivere *v* to exceed.
pastorauling *v, adj* **1** playing at shepherds and shepherd-esses. **2** used of lovers walking in the fields together.
pastoraulity *n* the act of pastorauling (qv).
past-ordinar *adj* extraordinary.
pasty[1] *adj* pale, sallow.
pasty[2] *n* a nickname for a billsticker.
pat[1] *n* a pot.
pat[2] *v* put.
pat[3] *n* **1** the head, pate. **2** the top of the head.
pat[4] *v* (*used of the heart*) to beat fast.
pat[5] *adj* **1** appropriate. **2** ready, fluent. **3** pleasant.
pat[6], **pate** *n* a judge's favourite advocate through whom interest was made for clients.
patawtie *n* a potato.
patelet *same as* **partlet**.
patent *adj* **1** ready, willing. **2** disposed to listen. **3** open. **4** available.
pater *same as* **patter**[2].
pates *n* steps at the corners of the roofs of houses to facilitate reaching the top.
path *n* **1** a steep, narrow way. **2** the world, the way through life.
pathed *adj* (*used of a subject*) often treated of or discussed.
pathlins *adv* by a steep and narrow way.
patience *n* used as an expletive.
patient *n in phr* **patient of death 1** a death agony. **2** one who waits. **3** one who delays a decision.
patientfu' *adj* very patient.
patlet *same as* **partlet**.
pat-luck *n* potluck.
paton *n* a patter.
patrick, patridge *n* a partridge.
patron *n* a pattern.
patronate *n* the right of presenting to a benefice.
patron-call *n* the patronage of a church.
patship *n* the being a judge's pat. *See* **pat**[6].
patter[1] *v* **1** to move with quick, sounding steps. **2** to tread down, trample underfoot.—*n* the act of walking with quick, short steps.—*adv* **1** with a quick succession of sharp strokes. **2** with quick, sharp-sounding steps.
patter[2] *v* **1** to be loquacious. **2** to mutter, mumble. **3** to engage in a low or whispering conversation.
patterar *n* one who repeats prayers.
patter-patter *v* **1** to fidget about. **2** to move restlessly in and out.
pattie[1], **patty** *n* a small pot.
pattie[2] *adv* pit-a-pat.
pattle[1] *n* a plough staff, a small, long-handled spade used for cleaning a plough.
pattle[2] *v* to move the hands backwards and forwards in any yielding substance.
pauce *v* **1** to prance with rage. **2** to stride in irritation.
pauchle, pauchel[1] *v* **1** to tout for tips by slight services. **2** to take something without permission, to steal, to swindle. **3** to rig something dishonestly. —*n* **1** a package. **2** an instance of cheating or swindling.
pauchle[2] *v* to struggle, make way with difficulty.
pauchler *n* a small farmer who works on his own land.
pauchty *same as* **paughty**.
paucky *same as* **pauky**.
pauge *v* **1** to prance or to pauce (qv). **2** to pace about artfully till an opportunity occurs for fulfilling any plan. **3** to tamper with. **4** to venture on what is hazardous in a foolhardy manner.
paughtily *adv* haughtily.
paughty *adj* **1** haughty, proud. **2** ambitious. **3** consequential, impertinent, forward. **4** saucy, insolent. **5** discreet.
pauk *n* **1** a trick, wile. **2** a sly, clever way.
paukerie, paukery *n* slyness, craftiness.
paukily *adv* shrewdly, craftily, cleverly.
paukiness *n* **1** shrewdness. **2** cunning. **3** craftiness.

pauky *adj* **1** shrewd. **2** cunning. **3** knowing, artful. **4** insinuating. **5** (*of the eye*) wanton, arch. **6** lively.
paul[1] *same as* **pall**[1].
paul[2] *same as* **pall**[3].
paule *n* the half of one's allowance of bread.
paulie *adj* **1** (*of a bodily member*) impotent, feeble. **2** (*of lambs*) small in size. **3** (*of the mind*) insipid, inanimate. **4** lame, dislocated. **5** distorted.—*n* **1** an inferior or sickly lamb. **2** the smallest lamb in a flock. **3** a feeble, inanimate being.
paulie-footed *same as* **paley-footed**.
paulie-merchant *n* one who traverses the country buying inferior lambs.
paum[1], **paum**[2] *same as* **palm**[1], **palm**[2].
paumer *same as* **palmer,**
paumy *same as* **palmy**[2].
paunch *same as* **painch**.
paunchings *n* tripe.
paut *v* **1** to paw. **2** to push out the feet alternately when one is lying down. **3** to stamp with the foot in anger. **4** to strike with the foot, kick. **5** to move the hand, as if groping in the dark. **6** to search with a rod or stick in water or in the dark. **7** to make a noise when so searching. **8** to make short, convulsive movements with the hands. **9** to pat. **10** to set to work slowly or aimlessly. **11** to move about gently or leisurely.—*n* **1** a kick, a stamp on the ground. **2** a pat. **3** a heavy, weary walk. **4** a poker.
pauw *same as* **paw**[3].
pavean, paveen *adj* pretentious.
pavee *same as* **pavie**.
pavement *v* **1** to pave. **2** to furnish with a flooring.
paver *n* a paving stone.
pavie *n* **1** a trick. **2** a part in a play or business. **3** exertion. **4** a bustle. **5** quick muscular movement.—*v* to make fantastic gestures, to act as a clown.
paw[1] *n* a hand.
paw[2] *n* **1** a step. **2** gait.
paw[3] *n* **1** a trick. **2** the slightest motion. **3** one who cannot make the slightest exertion. **4** a quick, ridiculous or fantastic movement. **5** a ceremonious fluster. **6** a stir, bustle. **7** a conceited, dressed-up person.—*v* to make fantastic movements.
pawchle, pawchlie *n* **1** a frail, old body. **2** one low in stature and weak in intellect.
pawk *same as* **pauk**.
pawkery, pawkrie *same as* **paukerie**.
pawkie *n* a woollen mitten having a thumb and without fingers.
pawky *same as* **pauky**.
pawl *v* to claw the air, to make an ineffectual effort to clutch.
pawlie[1] *n* the stone, etc, used in hopscotch.
pawlie[2] *same as* **paulie**.
pawm[1] *n* the uppermost grain in a stalk of corn.
pawm[2], **pawm**[3] *same as* **palm**[1], **palm**[2].
pawmer *same as* **palmer**.
pawmie *n* **1** the knave of clubs. **2** the knave of any suit of cards.
pawmie *same as* **palmy**[2].
pawn[1] *n* a narrow curtain fixed to the top or the bottom of a bed.
pawn[2] *n* a pawnshop.—*v* to palm off a worthless thing as one of great value.
pawn[3] *n* the timbers in a thatched roof placed under the cabers and stretching from gable to gable.
pawnd *n* a pledge, security.—*v* to pledge, pawn.
pawrlie *same as* **parley**.
pawt *same as* **paut**.
pawns *v* to dally with a girl.
pay *v* **1** to beat, drub. **2** to punish. **3** to defeat, conquer. **4** to smart. **5** to pay the penalty, suffer. **6** to run, walk smartly. **7** (*with* **up**) to work energetically.—*n* **1** a drunken bout following the payment of wages. **2** (*in pl*) punishment.
payment *n* a thrashing.
Pays *n* Easter.

paysyad *same as* **paseyad**.
payway *adj* valedictory.—*n* a farewell.
pay wedding *n* a wedding at which guests contribute to the cost of the feast.
pea *adj* **1** tiny. **2** as small as a pea.—*n* (*in pl*) peasemeal.
pea-and-thummils *n* a thimble-rigging game.
Peace *same as* **Pace**.
peace warn *v* to serve a notice of ejectment.
peae-warning *n* a notice of ejectment.
peaceyaud *same as* **paseyad**.
pea-claw *n* a name for pea soup.
peagun *n* a peashooter.
peak[1] *n* **1** the sharp point of a sea cliff or rock. **2** a triangular piece of linen, binding the hair below a cap. **3** a very small quantity. **4** a ray.—*v* **1** (*used of a spire, mast, etc*) to end in a sharp point. **2** to show a peak or sharp point.
peak[2] *v* **1** to chirp. **2** to squeak. **3** to cry, weep. **4** to speak in a whisper or thin, weak voice. **5** to complain of poverty.—*n* **1** the chirp of a bird. **2** the squeak of a mouse. **3** an insignificant voice. **4** a small person with a thin, weak voice.
peakie *same as* **pickie**[2].
peaky *adj* sharply pointed.—*n* **1** a steel knitting pin. **2** a knitter. **3** (*in pl*) knitting.
peaky worker *n* a knitter.
peal[1] *same as* **pale**[5].
peal[2] *same as* **peel**[1].
peal[3] *same as* **peil**[2].
pealings *n* strippings, the last milk drawn from a cow.
peaner *n* a small, cold-looking, ill-clad person.
peanerflee *n* one with the appearance of lightness and activity.
peanie[1] *n* a turkey hen.
peanie[2] *n* a pinafore.
pea-pluffer *n* a tin peashooter.
pear[1] *n* a peg-top.
pear[2] *v* to appear.
pearl[1] *v* to stud with pearls.—*n* a cataract in the eye.
pearl[2] *n* a kind of ornamental lace used for edging. —*v* **1** to edge with lace. **2** to border. **3** to ornament with a knitted border.
pearl[3] *n* **1** *in phr* **to cast up a pearl** to purl a stitch instead of making it plain. **2** the seam stitch in a knitted stocking.
pearled *adj* bordered with lace.
pearlin *n* **1** lace. **2** a kind of thread lace.
pearling *n* **1** a string of pearls. **2** (*in pl*) tears.
pearlin-keek *n* a cap with a lace border.
pearl-lace *n* an ornamental lace, used as an edging.
pearl-shell *n* the pearl mussel.
peart *adv* **1** scarcely, hardly. **2** smartly.
peary[1], **peary**[2] *same as* **peerie**[1], **peerie**[2].
peas *n* glassy marbles used as pitchers.
pease *same as* **pees**.
pease bannock *n* a bannock made of peasemeal.
pease-bogle *n* a scarecrow set up in a field of peas.
pease-bread year *n* a year towards the close of the 18th century when peasemeal was used as a substitute for oatmeal and barley meal.
pease brose *n* brose (qv) made of peasemeal.
pease-bruizle *n* field peas boiled in their pods.
pease-clod *n* a coarse roll or bap (qv) made of peasemeal.
pease-cod tree *n* the laburnum.
pease-kill *n* **1** pease-bruizle (qv). **2** a confused scramble.
pease-lilts *n* pease brose (qv).
peasemeal *n* meal made from peas.—*adj* **1** soft, flabby. **2** doughy.
pease-mum *n* *in phr* **to play pease-mum** to mutter.
pease-pudding-faced *adj* mealy-faced.
peaser *n* a strong bumper of liquor.
peaseweep *same as* **peesweep**.
peasie *int* a call given to calves, pigeons, etc. *See* **pease**.
peasie-whin *same as* **peysie-whin**.
pea-splitting *adj* **1** hair-splitting. **2** driving hard bargains.

peas-scone *n* a scone made of peasemeal.
peat[1] *n* **1** a pet. **2** a term of endearment. **3** used also contemptuously. **4** a name formerly given to advocates who were related to judges and favoured by them.
peat[2] *same as* **pyat**[2].
peat bank *n* the place whence peats are cut.
peat bree, ~ brew *n* peaty water.
peat breest *n* the peat bank (qv).
peat broo[1] *n* peat bree (qv).
peat broo[2] *n* the peat bank (qv).
peat cashie *n* a large basket or creel for holding or carrying peats.
peat-caster *n* one who cuts peats.
peat-castin' *n* peat-cutting.
peat claig *n* a place built for holding peats.
peat clod *n* **1** a single peat. **2** a piece of peat.
peat coom *n* peat dust.
peat corn *n* peat dust, peat dross.
peat creel *n* a peat basket.
peat crue *n* the place where peat is stored.
peat days *n* days on which peats are cut or are taken home.
peat-digger *n* a peat-cutter.
peat-fitter *n* one who sets peats on end to dry.
peat-futherer *n* a retailer or carter of peats.
peat-grieshoch *n* red-hot peat.
peat hagg *n* **1** a hole from which peat has been cut. **2** a peat hole containing water. **3** the rough, projecting margin of a peat hole when the hole has grown up again. **4** a hump of peat on the surface of a moss.
peat hole *n* a hole from which peats have been dug.
peat house *n* a house where peats are stored.
peat lair *n* the place where peats are spread and 'fitted' to dry.
peat lowe *n* the blaze of a peat fire.
peatman *n* a retailer of peats.
peat meal *n* peat dust.
peat mould *n* **1** peat dust. **2** peaty soil.
peat mow *n* **1** a large stack of peats. **2** a heap of peat dust.
peat neuk *n* **1** the corner at the kitchen fireside, where peats were stored for immediate use. **2** a place facing the entrance door, between two doors, one of which opened into the kitchen and the other led to the other rooms of the house.
peat o' sape *n* a bar of soap, so called from its resemblance to a peat.
peat pot, ~ pat *n* a hole from which peat has been dug.
pea tree *n* the laburnum.
peat reek *n* **1** peat smoke. **2** the flavour imparted to whisky distilled by means of peat. **3** Highland whisky.
peat-reekit *adj* filled, discoloured or flavoured by peat smoke.
peat-reek-whisky *n* Highland whisky, distilled over peat fires.
peat shieling *n* a hut built of peat.
peat spade *n* a flaughter spade (qv), used for cutting peats.
peat stane *n* the cornerstone at the top of a house wall.
peaty *n* a judge's peat. *See* **peat**[1].
peavor *same as* **peever**[1].
pech[1] *same as* **pecht**.
pech[2] *v* **1** to pant, puff. **2** to breathe hard. **3** to sigh heavily. **4** to cough shortly and faintly.—*n* **1** a heavy sigh, deep breath. **2** laboured breathing. **3** an exclamatory, forcible expiration after exertion.
pechan *n* **1** the gullet, the crop. **2** the stomach.
pechie *adj* short of breath, given to panting.
pechin *n* a fit of short, faint coughing.
pechle[1] *n* a parcel or packet carried secretly.
pechle[2] *v* to pant.
pech-pech *n* the sound of forcible expiration during violent exertion.
pecht *n* **1** a Pict. **2** a term of contempt.
pecht--, pech-stane *n* a prehistoric monumental stone.
peck[1] *n* a large quantity or number.
peck[2] *same as* **paik**[2].

peck-bit *n* that part of a muttie measure which holds a peck. *See* **muttie**.

peckin *n* a small quantity.

peckish *adj* hungry.

peckle *v* to peck.

peckman *n* one who carried smuggled spirits through the country in a vessel like a peck measure.

peculiar *n* **1** a particular line of business, work. **2** a peculiarity.

ped *n* **1** a professional runner. **2** the tramp, walking.

pedaneous *adj* used of inferior judges who had not a bench but sat on a low seat.

pedder *n* a pedlar.

pedee *n* a kind of footboy.

pedlar's drouth *n* hunger.

pedrall *adj* toddling.—*n* a child beginning to walk.

pee *v* **1** (*of children*) to urinate. **2** to wet with urine.

peeack, peeak *v* to chirp.—*n* one with a thin, insignificant voice. *See* **peak**[2].

peeackin *adj* speaking or singing in a thin or querulous voice.

peeak *v* to look sickly.

peeble *n* **1** a pebble. **2** an agate.—*v* to throw pebbles at.

peabruch *n* a pibroch.

peece *n* a piece.

peechack *n* a small-sized marble.

peefer *same as* **piffer**.

peefering *adj* **1** insignificant. **2** useless. **3** trifling.

peeggirin-blast *n* **1** a heavy shower. **2** a stormy blast.

peek[1] *v* **1** to look sickly. **2** to peak.

peek[2], **peek**[3] *same as* **peak**[1], **peak**[2].

peekie[1] *n* a small ray or point of light.

peekie[2] *same as* **pickie**[2].

peeking *adj* **1** ill-tempered. **2** complaining.

peeky *same as* **peaky**.

peel[1] *v* **1** to rub or take off the skin. **2** to take off one's clothes.—*n* **1** a particle. **2** a blade of grass.

peel[2] *n* a pool.

peel[3] *n* **1** a pill. **2** anything disagreeable, unpleasant, nauseous.—*v* to prescribe or administer pills.

peel[4] *same as* **pell**[1].

peel[5] *v* to shear corn with a sickle.

peel-a-bane *n* very freezing weather.

peel-a-flee *n* **1** a person insufficiently clad. **2** a creature out of its element.

peel-an'-eat[1] *adj* sickly-looking, delicate.

peel-an'-eat[2] *n* **1** potatoes presented at table unpeeled. **2** the eating of such potatoes.

peeled egg *n* a windfall.

peelemel *adv* pell-mell.

peeler *n* a crab that has cast its shell.

peeler *n* a policeman.

peel-garlick *n* **1** a simpleton. **2** a weak, wasted, miserable-looking person.

peelie *adj* thin, meagre.—*n* a scarecrow.

peelie-wally *n* **1** a tall, slender, sickly-looking young person. **2** a tall, slender plant or shoot. **3** very weak stuff.—*adj* pale, ill-looking.

peeling[1] *adj* travelling lightly clad on a windy day. —*n* **1** a paring. **2** peel. **3** skin.

peeling[2] *n* a thrashing.

peelock *n* a potato boiled in its skin. **2** peel-an'-eat (qv).

peel-reestle *n* a stirring, mischievous child or youth.

peel-ringe, ~-range *adj* **1** thin. **2** not able to endure the cold.—*n* **1** a skinflint. **2** a tall, thin person. **3** a cold person.

peelrushich *n* **1** anything that comes with a rush or in a torrent. **2** a rush, a torrent.

peel-shot *n* the dysentery of cattle.

peel-wersh *adj* wan, sickly-looking.

peem-pom *n* a pompom, the ball of coloured worsted once worn by infantry in front of the shako.

peen[1] *n* a pin.

peen[2] *n* a pane of glass.

peen[3] *n* the sharp point of a mason's hammer.—*v* to strike with a hammer.

peenge *v* **1** to whine, fret. **2** to complain of cold or hunger. **3** to pretend poverty.

peenged *adj* **1** delicate. **2** shrunken.

peenging *adj* **1** starved-looking. **2** sickly. **3** fretful.

peengy *adj* **1** fretful, ill-tempered. **2** pinched with cold. **3** unable to bear cold.

peenie[1] *same as* **pinny**.

peenie[2], **peenie rose** *n* a peony.

peenish *v* to stint, limit.

peenjure *v* **1** to hamper. **2** to confine.

peeoye, peeoe *n* a small cone of moistened gunpowder, made by boys as a firework.

peep[1] *n* **1** the dawn. **2** a peephole.

peep[2] *v* **1** to whine, complain. **2** to pure.—*n* **1** the meadow pipit. **2** a feeble sound. **3** a whisper.

peepag *n* a reed or pipe made of green straw, used by boys to make a sound.

peeper[1] *n* **1** a looking glass. **2** (*in pl*) spectacles. **3** the eyes.

peeper[2] *n* a complaining person.

peep-glass *n* a telescope.

peepie *adj* fretful, whining.—*n* a fretful and tearful child.

peepie-weepie *adj* used of a whining disposition.

peep-sma' *n* **1** one who is weak in body and mind. **2** one who keeps in the background.—*v* **1** to keep in the background. **2** to take a humble place. **3** to sing small.

peer[1] *n* a match, equal.—*v* **1** to equal. **2** to match.

peer[2] *adj* poor.

peer[3] *n* **1** a pear. **2** a peg-top.

peerer *n* one who stares.

peerie[1] *n* **1** a peg-top. **2** the game of top-spinning.

peerie[2] *adj* small.

peerie[3] *adj* timid, fearful.

peerie[4] *adj* **1** peeping, peering. **2** sharp-looking. **3** disposed to examine narrowly.

peerie[5] *v* **1** to flow in a small stream, as through a quill. **2** to purl.—*n* a small quantity of fluid.

peerie-breeks *n* **1** short trousers. **2** a person with short legs.

peerie-foal *n* a small bannock.

peerie-man *same as* **poor-man**.

peerie-pinkie *n* the little finger.

peerie-wee *adj* very small.

peerie-weerie[1] *n* a slow-running stream.

peerie-weerie[2] *adj* **1** blinking. **2** small-eyed. **3** sore-eyed.— *n* a mysterious, hidden person.

peerie-weerie[3], **~-wirrie** *adj* very small.—*n* **1** anything very small. **2** the little finger or toe.

peerie-weerie-winkle *adj* excessively small.

peerie-winkie *n* **1** anything very small. **2** the small finger or toe.

peerie-write *n* small-text handwriting.

peer-man *same as* **poor-man**.

peer-mate *adj* of equal rank.

peer-page *same as* **poor-page**.

peer's house *same as* **poor's house**.

pees *int* a call to pigeons, calves, etc.

peeser *n* an unfledged pigeon.

peesie the peesweep (qv).

peeskie *n* **1** short wool. **2** stunted grass.—*adj* **1** dry, withered, shrivelled. **2** short, stunted.

peesweep, peesweep *n* the lapwing.

peesweep-like *adj* sharp-featured, with a feeble appearance and a shrill voice.

peesweepy *adj* **1** poor, pitiful. **2** silly. **3** whining.

peesweet *n* **1** the lapwing. **2** the cry of the lapwing.

peetly-pailwur *n* an endearing term for a child.

peety *n* pity.

peeuk *v* **1** to chirp. **2** to peep.

peevee *n* **1** a trick. **2** a fantastic bodily movement. **3** bustle. **4** a conceited, dressed-up person.—*v* to make fantastic gestures.

peever[1], **peevor** *n* **1** the game of hopscotch. **2** the stone or slate used in the game.

peever[2] *v* (*used of children*) to urinate.

peever[3] *v* to shake, tremble, quiver.

peeveralls, peeveral-al *n* the game of hopscotch.

peevor *same as* **peever**[1].

peewit, peeweep *n* **1** the cry of the lapwing. **2** the lapwing.

peff *n* **1** a dull, heavy blow or fall. **2** the sound made by such. **3** a dull, heavy step in walking. **4** the sound of such. **5** a big, stupid person.—*v* **1** to beat with dull, heavy blows. **2** to beat severely. **3** to walk with heavy step. **4** (*with* **in** *or* **down**) to drive.—*adv* **1** with heavy step. **2** with a dull, heavy fall.

peffin *n* a very big, stout person.

peg[1], **pegg** *n* **1** a leg, foot. **2** a step. **3** the ball used in shinty. **4** a blow with the fist.—*v* **1** to hammer, beat. **2** to hurry on. **3** to work hard. **4** to eat greedily. **5** (*with* **out**) to pay or give out.

peg[2] *n* a policeman.

pegg *same as* **peg**.

peggin'-awl *n* a shoemaker's awl for entering pegs driven into the heels of shoes.

pegh *same as* **pech**[2].

peghin *same as* **pechan**.

peghle *same as* **pechle**[2].

peght *same as* **pecht**.

pegil *n* the rough or dirty work of a house.—*v* to do such work.

peg-pie *n* a magpie.

peg-puff *n* an 'old' young woman, a young woman with the manners of an old one.

pegral *adj* paltry.

pehoy *n* a sneeze.

pehts *n in phr* **to make pehts and kail of 1** to beat very severely. **2** to destroy.

peifer[1] *same as* **peever**[3].

peifer[2] *same as* **piffer**.

peik *n* a long piece of lead used for ruling paper.

peikthank *adj* ungrateful.

peil[1] *v* to equal, match.—*n* a peer, an equal.

peil[2] *v in phr* **to pack and peil** to conduct business in an unfair way.

peild *adj* bald, made bald.

peinge *same as* **peenge**.

peinor-pig *n* an earthenware moneybox.

peir *same as* **peer**[1].

peise *same as* **paise**.

peisled *adj* **1** in easy circumstances. **2** smug.

peist *v* to work feebly.—*n* a little, weak person.

pejorate *v* **1** (*a legal term*) to prejudice. **2** to make worse.

pele *v* to puncture.

peley-wersh *same as* **peel-wersh**.

pell[1] *n* **1** a useless, worn-out thing. **2** a thick, dirty piece of cloth. **3** a term of abuse. **4** a lazy, dirty, worthless person. **5** a tuft of clotted wool. **6** dried dirt adhering to an animal's hindquarters. **7** (*in pl*) rags, tatters.

pell[2] *n* very sour buttermilk.

pell[3] *n* **1** a heavy dash, blow or fall. **2** the sound of such a blow or fall.—*v* **1** to dash, drive, strike violently. **2** to walk with a heavy, dashing step. —*adv* with great force or violence.

pell[4] *same as* **pale**[5].

pell[5] *n* a salted hide.

pellack-whale *same as* **pellock**.

pellad *n* a tadpole.

pell and mell *v* to rush pell-mell.

pell-clay *n* pure, tough clay, ball clay.

pellet, pellot *n* a skin.

pellets *n* two leaden compresses applied to prevent undue bleeding.

pellile *n* the redshank.

pell-mell *n* **1** a scrimmage. **2** a headlong rush. **3** confusion.—*adj* confused, haphazard.

pellock, pelloch, pelluck *n* the porpoise.

pelonie *n* a dress for young boys: an old-fashioned, long, tight-fitting overcoat.

pelt[1] *n* **1** rags, rubbish. **2** a piece of thick, dirty dress.

pelt[2] *v* **1** to beat, strike, thrash. **2** to work with energy. **3** to hurry.—*n* **1** a stroke or blow. **2** a downpour. **3** a heavy fall. **4** the noise made by a falling body.—*adv* violently.

pelt[3] *n* **1** a sheepskin without the wool. **2** used as a term of reproach in *phr* **foul pelt**.

peltag *n* a coalfish in its second year.

pelter *n* **1** a passion, temper. **2** a state of excitement.

peltin-pock *n* **1** a bag for guarding the thighs from the flaughter spade (qv) in peat-cutting. **2** a worthless dress or bag.

peltry[1] *n* a skin.

peltry[2] *n* **1** trash, rubbish. **2** ill-cooked food. **3** wet and stormy weather.—*adj* **1** worthless. **2** wet and stormy.

pemmint *n* **1** a thrashing. **2** payment.

pen[1] *n* **1** a feather, quill. **2** part of a kail stem or castock (qv). **3** a snuff spoon, a piece of quill used for taking snuff. **4** a spoon.—*v* to take snuff with a pen.

pen[2] *n* **1** a hill. **2** a high, pointed, pyramidal hill.

pen[3] *n* the dung of fowls.

pen[4] *n* an old, saucy man with a sharp nose.

pen[5] *n* **1** condition. **2** humour.

pen[6] *same as* **pend**.

pence *n* **1** money. **2** a fortune.

pencefu' *same as* **pensefu'**.

penceless *adj* penniless.

pence-pig *same as* **penny-pig**.

pencey *same as* **pensy**.

pench *same as* **painch**.

pend *n* **1** an archway. **2** a covered way. **3** a covered sewer, a conduit.—*v* to arch.

pendenter-knock *n* a clock hanging on a wall, a wag-at-the-wa (qv).

pendice of a buckle *n* that which receives the one latchet before the shoe is straightened by means of the other.

pendicle *n* **1** an appendage. **2** a pendant. **3** a small piece of land attached to a larger. **4** a small farm, a croft. **5** a church or parish depending on another.

pendicler *n* **1** one who farms a pendicle (qv). **2** an inferior tenant.

pending *n* **1** an archway, a pend (qv). **2** making a pend (qv).

pendit *adj* arched.

pendle, pendule *n* **1** a pendant. **2** an earring.

pen-driver *n* **1** a clerk. **2** an author.

pend-stane *n* a stone for building an arch.

pen fauld *n* the close in a farmstead for holding cattle.

penfu' *n* **1** a spoonful. **2** a mouthful. **3** a good meal.

pen gun *n* **1** a child's popgun made of a quill. **2** a loquacious person of small stature.

pen head *n* the upper part of a mill lead, where the water is carried off from the pond to the mill.

penkle *n* a rag, a fragment.

pen-mouth *n* the entrance to a pend (qv) or covered gateway.

penn *same as* **pend**.

pennander *n* a standard-bearer, one who carries a pennant.

pennar, pennart *n* **1** a pen case. **2** a tin cylinder for holding pens, etc. **3** a penman. **4** a composer. **5** a scribbler.

pennarts *same as* **pennyworth**.

penned *adj* arched.

penneth *n* a pen case.

pennirth *same as* **pennar**.

penny[1], **pennie** *n* **1** money. **2** cash. **3** earnings. **4** a fortune. **5** a sum of money.

penny[2] *n* **1** the act of eating. **2** daintier fare than ordinary.—*v* **1** to eat much with gusto. **2** to feed, fare.

penny-bake *n* a penny biscuit or roll.

penny-boo *n* a large top.

penny-brag *n* a game.

penny-breid n 1 a penny loaf. 2 penny loaves.
penny bridal n a wedding at which the guests contribute to the cost of the feast.
penny cookie n a penny bun.
penny-cress n the wild cress.
penny-dog n 1 a person who dogs another's footsteps, as a dog follows his master. 2 a mean, sneaking fellow.
penny-fee n wages in money.
penny-friend n a deceitful, interested friend.
penny-Herioters n balls formerly made by the boys of George Heriot's Hospital.
penny-maill n rent paid in money.
penny-maister n 1 an old term for the treasurer of a town guild or incorporated trade, etc. 2 a box- master (qv).
penny-note n a forged £1 note.
penny-pap n a penny roll.
penny-pig n an earthenware moneybox used by children.
penny reels n dances at which admission was paid for.
penny-rent n rent paid in money.
penny-sillor n 1 money. 2 hard cash. 3 a dowry.
penny-stane n 1 a flat, circular stone, used as a quoit. 2 a quoit. 3 (in pl) the game played with these stones.
penny-stane-cast n the distance to which a person can throw a quoit.
penny stipend n a minister's salary in money.
penny-wabble n very weak beer sold at a penny a bottle.
penny wedding, ~ waddin n a penny bridal (qv).
penny-whaup, ~-wheep, ~-whip n very weak beer sold at a penny a bottle.
penny-widdie same as **pin-the-widdie**.
penny-winner n a scanty wage-earner.
pennyworth n 1 a purchase. 2 a bargain. 3 revenge, retribution. 4 value for money paid. 5 also a term of contempt.
pen-point n a pen nib.
pense v to walk conceitedly, with measured step.
pensefu' adj 1 thoughtful, meditative. 2 proud, conceited.
pensefu'ness n conceit, affectation.
pensel n a banneret, a small pennon.
penshens same as **painch**.
pensieness n self-conceit, affectation.
pensilie adv in a self-important manner.
pension n 1 pay. 2 salary.
pensioner n a boarder en pension.
penstraker n 1 the whin-lintie. 2 the yellowhammer.
pensy adj 1 quiet, thoughtful. 2 pensive. 3 sedate. 4 proud, affected. 5 smart, foppish. 6 tidy in dress and appearance.
pent n paint.
penty v to fillip.—n a fillip.
penure adj penurious.
penure-pig n a miser, niggard.
penury n 1 scarcity. 2 lack, deficiency.
penwork n 1 copying. 2 writing.
pep same as **paip**².
peppen, peppin, pepin same as **pappan**.
pepper v 1 to dust or sprinkle with powder, etc. 2 to tickle.—n irritation, passion.
pepper-curn, -curns n a handmill for grinding pepper.
pepper-dulee, ~-dilse n the edible jagged fucus.
pepper-quern n a handmill for grinding pepper.
peppin n a baby.
peppoch n the store of cherry stones from which the castles, or caddles, of paips are supplied. See **caddle**; **paip**².
perambulation n the itinerating of a judge gomg on circuit.
perconnon, percunnance n condition, term, understanding.
perdé same as **pardi**.
perdews n the forlorn hope.
perdue adj driven to extremities, so as to use violent means.
pere v 1 to pour. 2 to stream.
perelt adj paralytic. See **perils**.
perempt adj peremptory.

peremptor, peremper adj 1 peremptory. 2 exact. 3 precise.—n 1 a peremptory demand. 2 an allegation for the purpose of defence.—phrs 1 **at one's peremptors** at one's wits' end. 2 **upon one's perempers** being so very exact and precise.
peremptourly adv 1 precisely. 2 unalterably.
perfeck adj 1 perfect. 2 thorough, utter.—adv thoroughly, utterly.
perfeckshous adj perfect.
perfite, perfit, perfyt adj 1 perfect. 2 exact. 3 neat. 4 finished, complete, utter.—v to finish, bring to completion or perfection.
perfite age n 1 the age of twenty-one. 2 majority.
perfitely adv thoroughly, in finished style.
perfiteness n 1 exactness. 2 neatness. 3 perfection.
perfumed adj thorough, out-and-out, used intensively.
perfurnish v to furnish thoroughly.
pergaddus n a heavy fall or blow.
perie same as **peerie**¹.
perils, perls n a shaking of head or limbs, resulting from a paralytic affection.
perish v 1 to kill or starve with cold or hunger. 2 to be numb with cold. 3 to destroy, injure, murder. 4 to devour, eat up. 5 to squander, waste.
perishment n 1 severe cold. 2 a severe chill.
perjim adj neat.
perjink, perjinct adj 1 precise, particular, finicky, nice. 2 neat.—n 1 a precise, particular, finical person. 2 (in pl) p's and q's.
perjinkety adj extreme as to neatness, etc, finical. —n (in pl) 1 preciseness, niceties, particulars, details. 2 peculiarities. 3 odd ways. 4 naughty tricks.
perk n 1 a bird's perch. 2 a clothesline. 3 a peg. 4 a small wooden skewer for plugging a hole. 5 an affected little girl. 6 a pole, a perch.—v 1 to perch. 2 to brighten up.
perkin n a thin, round gingerbread biscuit, with a piece of almond in the centre.
perk tree n a pole to support a clothesline.
perky adj saucy, pert.
perlie¹ n a moneybox.
perlie² n 1 anything small. 2 the little finger.—adj difficult to please.
perlin same as **pearlin**.
perlyaag n 1 rubbish, bits of all kinds. 2 a mixture of odds and ends. 3 something nauseous or unpalatable.
permusted adj scented.
pernickety, pernackety, pernicketty, perneekity, pernickity, pernicked, pernicky adj 1 particular, fastidious, finical, difficult to please. 2 dainty, nice.—adv particularly, fastidiously, daintily.—n (in pl) niceties, p's and q's.
perpen same as **parpane**.
perple n a wooden partition.
perplin n a cat and clay (qv) wall between the kitchen and the spence (qv) of a cottage.
perqueer, perquire, perqueir, perquer same as **parqueer**.
perqueerly adv accurately, by heart.
perr same as **pirr**¹.
perrackit n 1 a little, smart child. 2 a sagacious, talkative child.
perrie same as **peerie**².
perris, perrishin n a parish.
pershittie adj 1 precise. 2 prim.
persil same as **parsel**.
personality n 1 personal peculiarity. 2 personal appearance.
persowdy n a medley, an incongruous mixture.
perteen v to pertain, belong to.
pertrick n a partridge.
pertrubill v to perturb, trouble greatly.
pery same as **peerie**¹.
pesky adj tiresome, annoying
pesse-pie n a pie baked for Easter.

pessments *same as* **pasment**.
Pess Sunday *n* Easter Sunday.
pest *v* to pester, plague.
pestillette *n* a small pistol, a pistolet.
pestration *n* annoyance, worry, plague.
pesty *adj* troublesome, annoying.
pet *n* a very fine day in the midst of bad weather. —*v* **1** to feed delicately, pamper. **2** to sulk, take offence.
petal *same as* **pattle**¹.
pet day *n* a fine day in bad weather.
Peter *n in phrs* **1 to make a Peter of** to befool, ill-use. **2 to put the Peter on** to snub, annoy.
Peter-Dick *n* a dancing step in which the movements of the feet correspond to these words when said at the same time.
Peter's pleugh *n* the constellation Ursa major.
Peter's staff *n* the constellation Orion's sword or belt.
peth *same as* **path**.
pether, pethir, pethirt *n* a pedlar.
pethlins *adv* by a steep declivity.
petitour *n* one entitled to raise an action by which something is sought to be decreed by the judge in consequence of a right of property in the pursuer.
pet-loll *n* a favourite, darling.
petrie ball *n* a black ball used by shoemakers.
pett, pettit *n* the skin of a sheep without wool.
petticoat-tails *n* **1** a kind of teabread baked with butter. **2** small cakes. **3** small triangular pieces of shortbread cut from a round.
pettie¹ *n* a sea bird.
pettie² *adj* small.—*n* a man's short woollen undervest.
pettie-pan *n* a white-iron pastry mould.
pettie-point *n* a particular kind of sewing stitch.
pettle¹ *n* a foot.
pettle² *v* **1** to pet, spoil, indulge. **2** to make much of. **3** to take care of oneself.
pettle³ *same as* **pattle**¹.
petts *n* projections on the slanting part of a gable resembling steps.
petty-whin *n* the needle furze.
peuchling *n* a slight fall of snow. *See* **peughle**.
peugh¹ *int* an exclamation of disgust, contempt, etc.
peugh² *v* to breathe shortly and spasmodically.
peughle *v* **1** to attempt anything feebly. **2** to do anything inefficiently. **3** to cough in a stifled manner. **4** (*used of rain or snow*) to drizzle continuously. **5** (*of snow*) to fall in fine particles. **6** to eat little and slowly, nibble without appetite. **7** to sneak off. **8** to whine.—*n* **1** a stifled cough. **2** a nibble, a small bit such as a sick ox takes at a time.
peught *adj* asthmatic.
peuk *v* to whine, whimper, wail.
peul *same as* **peughle**.
peust *same as* **puist**.
peuter¹ *v* to whine, whimper.
peuter², **peuther** *v* **1** to canvass. **2** to bustle about seeking votes. **3** to go about aimlessly. **4** to potter. **5** to appear to be working yet accomplishing nothing.
peuter-fac't *adj* having a complexion of the colour of pewter.
peuther *same as* **peuter**².
peutherer *n* a worker in pewter.
peutring *n* the act of canvassing.
peveral *same as* **peeveralls**.
pew *n* **1** the least breath of wind or smoke. **2** the least ripple on the sea. **3** a small quantity.—*v* (*used of smoke*) to rise, be wafted.
peweep *same as* **peewit**.
pewel *same as* **peughle**.
pewil, pewl *same as* **peughle**.
pewit *same as* **peewit**.
pewter¹ *same as* **pewter**¹.
pewter² *same as* **peuter**².
pewtung *adj* bungling.
pey *v* **1** to pay. **2** to punish.

peyay *int* a milkmaid's call to calves to come to their mothers.
peychle *n* a fat person.
peysie-whin *n* the greenstone.
peysle, peyzle *n* any small tool used by rustics.
peyster *n* a miser who feeds voraciously.
peyvee *same as* **pavie**.
peyzart, peysert *n* a miser.—*adj* miserly.
peyzle *same as* **peysle**.
phairg *v* **1** to work vigorously. **2** to rub or beat severely.—*n* the act of rubbing.
phaple *n* **1** the under-lip. **2** the countenance.
pheare *n* a companion.
pheer *v* (*in ploughing*) to mark off the ridges by one or two furrows.
pheerin *n* **1** the act of turning a plough. **2** the furrow or furrows that mark off the breadth of the ridges.
pheerin pole *n* a pole used by ploughmen in opening up the furrows.
pheugh, pheuch *int* an exclamation of contempt, disgust, etc.
phieton *n* a phaeton.
philabeg *n* **1** the leather pouch worn in front of a Highlander's kilt. **2** a kilt. **3** a fillibeg.
philander *v* to prance, caper, as a horse.
phingrim *n* a coarse woollen cloth.
phink *n* a species of the finch.
phinnick, phinoc *n* a species of grey trout.
phizz *n* a beard.
phleme *n* a farrier's lances.
phraise, phrase *v* **1** to talk insincerely. **2** to use coaxing, flattering, fussy speech glibly. **3** to brag. —*n* **1** smooth, insincere, glib speech. **2** voluble, unmeaning talk. **3** fuss, ado.
phraiser *n* **1** a braggart. **2** a wheedling person.
phraising *adj* given to flattery, etc.—*n* **1** fair speech, flattery. **2** the act of cajoling.
phrenesie *n* frenzy.
phring *n* a wife, a consort.
physical *adj* **1** relating to physic, drugs, etc. **2** medical. **3** medicinal, healing.
pibrach, pibrugh *n* **1** Highland bagpipe music. **2** a pibroch.
pibroch-reed *n* a bagpipe.
picher *n* **1** a flurry, bustle. **2** work done with bustle and uselessly. **3** a bother, perplexity. **4** a weak, bustling person. **5** one who works in a flurry without plan or method.—*v* **1** to work in a hurry and bustle. **2** to be bothered or perplexed in one's work.
picherty *same as* **pickelty**.
picht *v* to work weakly.—*n* a very diminutive and deformed person.
pick¹ *n* **1** a pickaxe. **2** a soldier's pike. **3** an instrument for detaching limpets from a rock.—*v* **1** to indent. **2** to hew stone. **3** to detach limpets.
pick² *n* pitch.—*v* to bedaub with pitch.
pick³ *v* **1** to throw stones at. **2** (*of animals*) to abort.
pick⁴ *v* **1** to pilfer. **2** to peck, eat in small quantities or with poor appetite. **3** to choose. **4** to find fault with.—*n* **1** choice. **2** a selected article. **3** a peck. **4** a very small quantity. **5** a little food. **6** a meal. **7** pique. **8** a grudge. **9** a quarrel.
pick⁵ *n* **1** a spade in playing cards. **2** (*in pl*) the suit of spades.
pick⁶ *v* to dress, beautify.—*n* **1** a thread of gold, silk, etc. **2** an implement used in embroidering.
pick⁷ *n* a marble used as a mark to aim at.
pickal *n* a miller.
pick and dab *n* potatoes and salt.
pick and wale *n* **1** the best choice. **2** a selection to choose from.
pickaternie *n* **1** the common tern. **2** the Arctic tern.
pick-black *adj* black as pitch.
pick-dark *adj* pitch-dark.
pickelty *n* **1** a difficulty. **2** a plight. **3** embarrassment. **4** suspense, eagerness.

picken[1] *n* a picking, a scrap of food.
picken[2], **pickenie** *adj* (*used of cheese*) pungent from the action of mites.
picker[1] *n* a young fish, a coaling.
picker[2] *same as* **picher**.
picker[3] *n* a petty thief.
picker[4] *n* the implement for pushing the shuttle across the loom.
picker[5] *n* an implement of embroidery.
pickerel *n* the dunlin.
pickery *n* petty theft.
picket *v* to dash a marble against the knuckles of losers in a game.—*n* **1** such a blow on the knuckles. **2** (*in pl*) the penalty of losing at tennis, paid by holding up the hand against the wall while others strike it with the tennis ball.
picketarnie *same as* **pickaternie**.
pickie[1] *n* hopscotch.
pickie[2] *adj* **1** insignificant. **2** petty.
pickie[3] *n* a wooden pole with an iron hook used for striking fish into a boat.
pickie-burnet *n* a young black-headed gull.
pickie-fingered *adj* given to pilfering.
pickie-laird *n* a small proprietor.
pickie-man *same as* **pikeman**.
pickietar, pickietarnie *same as* **pickaternie**.
pickin *same as* **picken**[2].
pickindail *n* a ruff or collar with star-shaped points, a piccadill.
pickit *adj* **1** meagre. **2** bare. **3** niggardly.
pickle[1] *n* **1** a grain of corn. **2** any small seed. **3** a small particle. **4** a small quantity. **5** a few.
pickle[2] *v* **1** to pilfer. **2** to pick up, as a bird. **3** to pick up a tune note by note. **4** to dawdle.
pickle[3] *n* the brain.
pickled primineary *n* a quandary.
pickman *same as* **pikeman**
pickmaw, pickmire *n* the black-headed gull.
pick-mirk *adj* pitch-dark.—*n* total darkness.
picktelie *same as* **pickelty**.
pickthank *adj* ungrateful.—*n* **1** a mischief-maker. **2** a faultfinder.
picktooth *n* a toothpick.
pi-cow *n* hide-and-seek, a game of assaulting and defending a castle or fort.
pictarnie, pictarn *same as* **pickaternie**.
pictarnitie *n* the black-headed gull.
Picts' houses *n* underground erections.
pictur', pickter *n* a sight, spectacle (*used contemptuously*).
piddie *v* to urinate (*a child's term*).
piddle[1] *v* to urinate (*a child's term*).
piddle[2] *v* **1** to trifle with one's foot. **2** to take short steps.
pidge *v* to confine in small space.
pie[1] *n* **1** a mess, scrape. **2** a conical potato pit.
pie[2] *n* a magpie.—*v* **1** to peer like a magpie. **2** to squint.
pie[3] *n* **1** an eyelet for a lace. **2** a hole made in patterns of knitting, embroidery, etc.
piece[1] *conj* although.
piece[2] *n* **1** (*with of omitted*) a part of anything. **2** an abusive term for a woman. **3** a recitation. **4** an indefinite space or distance. **5** a slice of bread, etc, given to children, workers, etc, as lunch. **6** a place, room. **7** a hogshead of wine. **8** (*with the*) apiece.
piecetime *n* lunchtime.
piefer *same as* **piffer**.
piege *n* a snare, trap for rats or mice.
pie-hole *n* **1** an eyelet for a lace. **2** a hole in patterns of knitting or embroidery. *See* **pie**[3].
piel *n* an iron wedge for boring stones.
piepher *same as* **piffer**.
pier *n* a quay or wharf.
piercel *n* a gimlet.
pierie[1], **pierie**[2] *same as* **peerie**[1], **peerie**[2].
piet *same as* **piot**.
piew *same as* **pew**.

piffer *v* **1** to whimper. **2** to complain peevishly. **3** to do anything feebly in a trifling way.—*n* an utterly useless person, a cypher.
pifferin' *adj* **1** trifling, insignificant. **2** complaining.
pig, pigg *n* **1** an earthenware jar or pitcher. **2** a stone bottle. **3** a hot-water bottle. **4** a chamber-pot. **5** an ornamental or common flowerpot. **6** a chimney can. **7** any article of crockery. **8** a potsherd.
pig and ragger *n* a pedlar who exchanges crockery for rags and bones.
pig ass *n* an ass for drawing a cart with crockery for sale.
pigful *n* what fills an earthenware pig (qv).
pigger *n* an earthenware marble.
piggery *n* a collective name for pigs.
piggery *n* **1** a pottery. **2** a crockery shop. **3** earthenware.
piggie *n* a small earthenware jar or bottle.
piggin *n* an earthenware swine trough.
pigman *n* a male seller of crockery.
pigs and whistles *n* **1** wreck and ruin. **2** useless knickknacks.
pigshop *n* a crockery shop.
pigwife *n* a female seller of crockery.
pik[1] *v* to strike lightly with anything sharp-pointed.
pik[2] *same as* **pick**[2].
pike[1] *n* **1** a tall, thin, sharp-featured person. **2** the rib of an umbrella. **3** a cairn of stones on the highest point of a hill.
pike[2] *v* **1** to pick. **2** to gather. **3** to pick bare. **4** to scratch with the finger-nail. **5** to pilfer, practise petty thieving. **6** to trim and clean flowerbeds. **7** to nibble, to eat sparingly or with little appetite. **8** to eat pasture bare. **9** to emaciate.—*n* **1** a small quantity of food. **2** anything to pick up and eat.
pike[3] *same as* **pick**[5].
pike[4] *n* a pique.
pike[5] *same as* **pick**[6].
pike-a-plea-body *n* a litigious person.
pikeman *n* **1** a miller. **2** a miller's servant.
pike out *v* **1** to delineate. **2** to prick out.
piker *n* a wire for cleaning the vent of a gun.
pikes[1] *n* short, withered heath.
pikes[2] *n* a drubbing.
pikethank *same as* **pickthank**—*phr* **for pikethank** for mere thanks.
pikie *adj* given to pilfering.
piking *n* **1** nourishment, food. **2** livelihood,.
pikit[1] *adj* emaciated, lean, pinched.
pikit[2] *adj* spiked, pointed.
pikle *n* a pitchfork.
pik-mirk *adj* pitch-dark.
pi-ku *same as* **pi-cow**.
pilch[1] *n* anything hung before the thighs to preserve them from injury in the casting of peats with a flaughter spade (qv).
pilch[2] *n* **1** a tough, skinny piece of meat. **2** anything short and gross. **3** a short, fat person.—*adj* thick, gross.
pilcheck *same as* **pilshach**.
pilcher *n* the marble that a player uses in his hand to pitch with, a pitcher.
pile[1] *n* a small quantity.
pile[2] *n* **1** fat or grease as a scum on soup, etc. **2** grease skimmed off the liquor in which fat meat has been boiled.
pile[3] *n* **1** a blade or stalk of straw, grass, etc. **2** a single grain.
pile[4] *n* the motion of the water made by a fish rising to the surface.
pile[5] *n* **1** the reverse of a coin. **2** money. **3** *in phr* **with neither cross nor pile** without a single coin.
pilget *n* **1** a quarrel, broil. **2** a conflict. **3** a difficulty, plight.—*v* **1** to quarrel. **2** to get into difficulty.
pilgeting, pilgatting *n* the act of quarrelling.
pilgie *n* a quarrel.—*v* **1** to quarrel. **2** to toil, struggle.
pilgrim *v* to go on pilgrimage.
pilgrimer *n* a pilgrim.

pilk *v* **1** to pick, pluck. **2** to take out of a husk or shell. **3** to pilfer.

pilkings *n* the last-drawn milk.

pill *n* **1** anything unpleasant. **2** anything very small.

pillan *n* a small, greenish sea crab, used for bait, the shear crab.

pillarachie *n* hubbub, confusion.

pillenrichie *same as* **pillarachie**.

pillgarlic *same as* **peelgarlick**.

pillie *n* a pulley.

pilliewinkes *same as* **pilniewinks**.

pillie-winkie *same as* **pinkiewinkie**.

pillions *n* rags, tatters.

pillonian *n* a kind of coarse blue cloth. *See* **pollonian**.

pillow *n* a tumultuous noise.

pillowbere *n* a pillowslip.

pilly *n* a boys' game, the cry used in the game.

pillyshee *same as* **pullisee**.

pilniewinks *n* an instrument of torture formerly used, of the nature of thumbscrews.

pilshach, pilshock *n* **1** a piece of thick, dirty cloth. **2** a dirty, ugly piece of dress. **3** a low coarse, dirty fellow.

piltack, piltock, piltick *n* a coalfish in its second year.

piltin-pyock *n* a bag for guarding the thighs from the flaughter spade (qv) in peat-cutting.

pimginet *n* **1** a small red pimple. **2** one resulting from over-indulgence in spirits.

pimpin *adj* mean, scurvy.

pimrose *n* the primrose.

pin[1] *n* **1** a small, neat person or animal. **2** a person of small stature. **3** the latch of a door. **4** a fiddle peg. **5** humour, temper. **6** a point, peak, summit. **7** the hip-bone. **8** a leg. **9** anything used for closing or filling up, a small stone for filling up a crevice in a wall.—*v* **1** to attach. **2** to fasten. **3** to stop a hole or crevice in masonry by driving something in. **4** to fill. **5** to seize, grasp. **6** to steal, pilfer.

pin[2] *v* **1** to strike by throwing or shooting. **2** to make a small hole by throwing a stone, etc. **3** to drub.—*n* **1** a sharp stroke or blow, a blow from an object thrown. **2** a severe beating. **3** speed, haste in running.

pinch[1] *v* **1** to economize. **2** to stint. **3** to puzzle.—*n* **1** hunger. **2** the smallest possible portion. **3** a difficulty.

pinch[2] *n* an iron crowbar.

pincher *n* (*in pl*) pincers, tweezers.

pincie *same as* **pensy**.

pincing *adj* **1** pinching. **2** chilling.

pind *same as* **poind**.

pinding *n* costiveness in lambs.

pine[1] *v* **1** to suffer pain. **2** to inflict pain. **3** to take pains, toil. **4** to fret, complain. **5** to dry or cure fish by exposure to the weather.—*n* **1** grief, pain, misery. **2** pains, trouble. **3** (*used of sheep*) a wasting disease.

pine[2] *v* (*used of wind*) to blow strongly.

pine-, piner-pig *n* an earthenware moneybox.

piner[1] *n* a strong breeze from the north or northeast.

piner[2] *n* an animal that does not thrive.

piner[3] *n* **1** one who prepares mortar for the mason. **2** a labourer. **3** a carter. **4** a scavenger. **5** a porter.

ping *v* to strike, dash against.—*n* the noise of a hard substance striking against metal, etc.

pinge *same as* **peenge**.

pingil *same as* **pingle**[2].

pinging[1] *adj* thumping, resounding.

pinging[2] *adj* **1** sordid. **2** miserly, mean, penny-pinching.

pingle[1], **pingle-pan** *n* **1** a small saucepan. **2** a small tin pan with a long handle.

pingle[2] *v* **1** to strive, compete. **2** to quarrel. **3** to struggle, toil, contend with difficulties.—*n* **1** a struggle for a livelihood. **2** a combat. **3** a turmoil. **4** a difficulty. **5** labour, toil without much result.

pingles *n* a pedlar's varied stock-in-trade made up in bundles.

pingling *n* **1** striving for subsistence with not much success. **2** constant, irksome application. **3** difficult or tiresome work.

ping-pong *n* a jewel fixed to a wire with a long pin at the end and worn in front of the cap.

pinie *n* a game.

pining, pining and vanquishing *n* **1** a wasting disease of young sheep. **2** tubercular consumption.

pinion *n* a pivot.

pinit *adj* starved, hungry-looking.

pink[1] *v* to deck, to dress up.—*n* **1** an example or type of utmost perfection. **2** a term of endearment used by a young man to his sweetheart. **3** the prettiest, the best.

pink[2] *v* **1** to contract the eye. **2** to glimmer.—*n* a small gleam of light.

pink[3] *v* **1** to trickle, drop, drip. **2** to bespot.—*n* **1** a drop. **2** the sound of a drop. **3** a very small hole. **4** a very small spot.—*adv* drop by drop, in drops.

pink[4] *v* **1** to strike smartly with any small object, as a marble. **2** to poke, push. **3** to beat, punish.

pinkerton *n* a person of little intelligence.

pinkie[1] *n* the clove pink.

pinkie[2] *adj* **1** small. **2** glimmering. **3** (*used of the eyes*) narrow, drooping.—*n* **1** a blindfolded person. **2** a person of small intelligence. **3** anything very small. **4** the little finger. **5** the smallest size of candle. **6** the weakest small beer.

pinkie finger *n* the little finger.

pinkie nail *n* the nail of the little finger.

pinkie-amall *n* anything very small.

pinkie-winkie *n* a barbarous pastime against birds among young children.

pinkle-pankle *n* the tinkling sound of a little liquid in a bottle, jar, etc.—*v* to make a tinkling sound, as of a little liquid in a jar, etc.

pinking *n* a thrilling, tinkling motion.

pink-pank *v* to make a tinkling sound, as by twitching the strings of a musical instrument.

pin-leg *n* a wooden leg.

pinler *n* **1** a forester. **2** a field-watcher.

pin mittens *n* woollen gloves knitted on wooden pins.

pinn[1] *same as* **pine**[1].

pinn[2], **pinn**[3] *same as* **pin**[1], **pin**[2].

pinnace *n* a pinnace.

pinner[1] *v* **1** to dash, roll. **2** to move quickly and noisily.

pinner[2] *n* a woman's headdress, with lappets pinned to the temples, reaching down to the breast and fastened there.

pinner[3] *n* a heavy drinking bout.

pinner-pig *same as* **pine-pig**. *See* **penny-pig**.

pinnet *n* **1** a streamer. **2** a pennant.

pinning[1] *n* diarrhoea in sheep.

pinning[2] *n* a surfeit.

pinning[3] *n* a small stone for fitting into a crevice in a wall.

pinning[4] *n* running quickly.

pinning awl *n* a shoemaker's awl for pegging shoes.

pinnit *adj* (*used of lambs*) seized with diarrhoea.

pinny *n* a pinafore.

pinnywinkler, *same as* **pilniewinks**.

pinsel *n* **1** a streamer. **2** a banneret.

pint[1] *n* a measure equal to two English quarts.

pint[2] *v* to point.

pint[3] *n* **1** a point. **2** a shoe tie.

pintacks *n* a children's game in which the stakes are pins.

pin-the-widdie *n* **1** a small dried haddock, unsplit. **2** a very thin person.

pintill fish *n* the pipefish.

pinto, pintoe *n* a wooden lever for turning a weaver's beam.

pin-tooth *n* a pincushion.

pin-pig *same as* **pine-pig**.

pint-stoup *n* **1** a pint measure. **2** a drinking vessel. **3** a spiral shell of the genus Turba, resembling a pint stoup.

piona *n* the peony.

piot *n* the magpie.

pioted *adj* **1** variegated. **2** piebald.

pi-ox *same as* **pi-cow**.

pioy, pioye *same as* **peeoye**.

pipe *n* **1** the throat. **2** (*in pl*) the bagpipe.—*v* **1** (*used of the wind*) to whistle loud, howl. **2** to cry, weep. **3** to frill with an Italian iron.

pipe-bent *n* a stalk of the dog's-tail grass.

pipe gun *n* a popgun.

piper[1] *n* **1** a singer, vocalist. **2** a half-dried haddock. **3** the sea urchin. **4** the daddy-longlegs or cranefly.

piper[2] *n* a marble made of pipeclay.

pipe-reek *n* tobacco smoke.

piper-faced *adj* pale, delicate-looking.

piper-fu' *adj* very drunk.

piper's invite *n* the last asked to a convivial meeting or party.

piper's news *n* stale news.

pipe-shank *n* a pipe stem.

pipe-shankit *adj* (*used of the legs*) long and thin.

pipe-skill *n* skill in playing the bagpipe.

pipe-small *same as* **peep-sma'**.

pipe-stapple *n* **1** the stem of a clay pipe. **2** anything very brittle. **3** a blade of dog's-tail grass. **4** (*in pl*) broken pieces of a pipe stem. **5** a children's plaything, consisting of a green pea pierced by two pins at right angles and placed at the upper end of a pipe stem, which is held vertically and blown gently through.

pipin'-fou *adj* very drunk.

piping *n* a frill.

piping-hot *adj* (*used of lessons*) said by a pupil fresh from learning them and not likely to remember them long.

piping-iron *n* an Italian iron.

pipple *v* **1** to cry. **2** to whimper.

pipple-papple *v* **1** to patter. **2** to pop, do anything with a sudden noise or motion.—*adv* with a popping sound or motion.

pir *same as* **pirr**[1].

pirie *same as* **peerie**[1].

pirie's chair *n* a punishment in a boys' game, when a wrong answer to a question was given.

pirjinct, pirjink *same as* **perjink**.

pirk *same as* **perk**.

pirkas, pirkuz *n* **1** a perquisite. **2** a thing not worth having.

pirkle *v* to prick.—*n* a thorn.

pirl *v* **1** to spin round as a top. **2** to push or roll gently along. **3** (*used of a brook*) to purl. **4** to whirl. **5** to twist, twine, curl. **6** to twist horsehair into a fishing line. **7** to poke. **8** to stir. **9** to fumble, grope. **10** to handle overmuch. **11** to work needlessly, in a trifling way, or easily. **12** to move slowly and lazily. **13** to shoot.—*n* **1** a whirl, a twist, curl. **2** a ripple on the surface of water. **3** a gentle stirring. **4** undue handling. **5** work done easily, with little accomplished.

pirlag *n* a small, round lump of dung.

pirlet *n* a puny, contemptible figure.

pirlewoot *n* marmalade.

pirley pease-weep *n* a boys' game.

pirl grass *n* creeping wheatgrass.

pirlicue, pirliecue *same as* **parlicue**.

pirlie[1] *n* a moneybox.

pirlie[2] *n* **1** anything small. **2** the little finger.—*adj* difficult to please.

pirlie[3] *adj* **1** crisp. **2** tending to curl up.

pirlie-pig *n* an earthenware moneybox.

pirlie-skinned *adj* having a crisp, curly coat.

pirlie-wee *adj* small.

pirlie-weeack *n* anything small of its kind.

pirlie wheel *n* the small spinning wheel.

pirlie-winkie *n* the little finger.

pirlie-wirlie *n* a term of contempt.

pirlin[1] *adj* **1** crisp. **2** curly.

pirlin[2] *n* the selecting of potatoes by feeling for them with the hand.

pirlin stick, ~ wand *n* a rod for stirring shilling seeds (qv) to make them burn when they are used as fuel.

pirlit *same as* **pirlet**.

pirn *n* **1** a reel or bobbin on which yarn or thread is wound. **2** the bobbin of a shuttle. **3** yarn wound on pirns. **4** a reel of cotton. **5** the reel of a fishing rod. **6** a wheel. **7** an illturn.—in *phr* **wun in a pirn** entangled without easy extrication.—*v* **1** to reel. **2** to run to and fro.

pirn cap *n* a wooden dish used by weavers for holding their quills or reeds round which the yarn was wound.

pirned *adj* **1** having unequal threads or colours. **2** striped.

pirn-girnel *n* a box for holding pirns while being filled. *See* **pirn**.

pirn house *n* a weaver's shed.

pirnickerie *same as* **pernickety**.

pirnie *adj* (*used of cloth or a web*) **1** of unequal threads or unlike colours. **2** striped, variegated. —*n* a nightcap.

pirnie-cap *n* a striped woollen nightcap.

pirnie-castle *n* a contemptuous designation for the harvester on the rig (qv) who is generally behind the rest.

pirn of ale *n* three gallons of ale.

pirn stick *n* **1** the wooden broach (qv) on which the quill or pirn (qv) is placed while the yarn is reeled off. **2** (*in pl*) thin legs, spindle-shanks.

pirn wheel *n* a wheel for winding bobbins.

pirnwife *n* a woman who fills the pirns with yarn. *See* **pirn**.

pirn-winding *n* the act of winding pirns.—*adj* engaged in winding pirns. *See* **pirn**.

pirr[1] *n* **1** a gentle breath of wind. **2** a breeze. **3** a stirring up. **4** vigour, energy. **5** a flurry. **6** a pettish fit.—*v* **1** to blow gently, to freshen. **2** to spring up or forth, as blood from a lancet wound.

pirr[2] *adj* **1** neat, trim. **2** gaily dressed. **3** precise in manner. **4** having a tripping mode of walking. **5** walking with a spring.

pirr[3] *n* **1** the common tern. **2** the tern's cry.

pirr-egg *n* the tern's egg.

pirrie[1] *adj* **1** neat. **2** precise. *See* **pirr**.

pirrie[2] *v* to follow a person from place to place like a dependent.

pirrie-dog *same as* **para-dog**.

pirrihouden *adj* fond, doting.

pirwee *n* a flighty or excited mood.

pirweeans *n* a conceited, flighty person.

pirsie *adj* conceited.

pish *v* to urinate.—*n* a jot.

pishminnie *n* an ant.

pishminnie-hillan, ~-tammock *n* an ant hill.

pishmother *n* an ant.

pisk *n* a dry, scornful-looking girl.

pisket *adj* **1** dried, shrivelled. **2** dry, reserved in manner.

piskie[1] *adj* **1** dry, withered, shrivelled. **2** short, stunted.

piskie[2] *adj* marshy.

pisminnie *n* an ant.

piss *int* **1** a call to a cat. **2** an exclamation to drive away a cat.—*v* **1** to hiss in order to drive off. **2** to incite a dog to attack.

pise-a-bed *n* the dandelion.

pistolet, pistolette *n* a small pistol.

pisweip *same as* **peesweep**.

pit[1] *v* to put.—*phrs* **1 to pit one down** to execute one. **2 to pit oneself down** to commit suicide.

pit[2] *n* **1** a colliery. **2** a dungeon. **3** a pit for drowning women. **4** a conical heap of potatoes, turnips, etc, partially sunk in the ground and covered with straw and earth.—*v* **1** to cover a heap of potatoes, etc, with straw and earth. **2** to mark, as with smallpox.

pitata, pitawta, pitatay, pitattie *n* a potato.

pit-bank *n* the mound around a coal mine.

pitcake *n* the plover.

pitch *v* **1** to affix. **2** to start a tune. **3** (*with* **into**) to attack, assail vigorously.

pitcher *n* **1** the marble with which a boy aims. **2** the piece of slate or stone used in hopscotch.

pitchie *n* the game of hopscotch.

pitching-ring *n* the ring in playing marbles.

pitch pea *n* the wild vetch.
pit-dark *adj* dark as a pit.
pit-for pat *adv* pit-a-pat.
pith *n* **1** substance. **2** marrow.—*phrs* **1 pith of hemp** the hangman's rope. **2 pith of malt** whisky.
pithfu' *adj* (*used of words*) powerful, pithy.
pithy *adj* (*used of ale*) strong.
pitiful *adj* to be regretted.
pitifu' market *n* the marriage market for widows.
pitleurachie *n* hubbub, confusion.
pit-life *n* a collier's life.
pit-mirk *adj* dark as a pit.—*n* intense darkness.
pit-mirkness *n* intense darkness.
pit stones *n* boundary stones that mark different parts of a peat moss.
pitt *n* a peat.
pitten *v* put, placed.
pitter-patter *v* **1** to beat continuously with light, rapid strokes. **2** to fall in hasty, repeated drops, like hail. **3** to walk to and fro, in and out of doors. **4** to move up and down with a clattering noise with the feet. **5** to repeat prayers hastily and mechanically.—*n* **1** the act of making light, rapid strokes. **2** the sound of such strokes. **3** the act of walking with a quick, short step. **4** the sound of such steps.—*adv* all in a flutter.
pitterty-pat *adv* pit-a-pat.
pittivout *n* a small arch or vault.
pitty *adj* **1** small. **2** petty.
pitty-patty, ~-pat *adv* pit-a-pat.—*adj* unsteady, tottering, pattering.—*n* the fluttering movement of a perturbed heart.
pity *n in phrs* **1 it's a pity of one** expressive of compassion for one. **2 to think pity of one** to feel sorry for one.—*int* **pity me! 1** an exclamation of surprise or self-commiseration.—*v* to be sorry. **2** (*used impersonally*) it fills one with pity.
piver *v* to shake, tremble, quiver.
piwipe *same as* **peesweep**.
piz¹, **pizz** *n* **1** peas. **2** a single pea.
piz² *same as* **pizie**.
pizan *n in phr* **to play the pizan with one** to get the better of one.
pize *n* a mild form of execration.
pizen *n* poison.
pizie, pizzie *n* **1** a very small marble. **2** a dwarf. **3** a mischievous child.
pizzant-like *adj* **1** poisoned-like. **2** shrivelled, wasted, withered.
placad *n* a placard.
place *n* **1** a passage of Scripture, the text of a sermon. **2** a landed proprietor's mansion house. **3** a small holding.—*v* to ordain or settle a minister in a charge.
placing *n* a minister's settlement in a charge.
plack¹ *n* **1** a copper coin, worth one-third of a penny sterling or four pennies Scots. **2** the smallest coin. **3** the least amount of money.
plack² *same as* **playock**.
plack and farden *n* every penny, the uttermost farthing.
placket *n* **1** a placard. **2** a public proclamation.
plackless *adj* penniless, poor.
plack-pie *n* a pie costing a plack. *See* **plack**¹.
plack's-worth *n* what is of very little value.
pladd *n* a plaid.
plaff *adv* **1** suddenly. **2** with the sound of a slight explosion.
plagiary *n* **1** an abductor. **2** a legal term.
plague *n* (*used in various expletives*) trouble.
plagued, plagit *adj* used as a term of abuse or as an intensive.
plaguely *adv* **1** very, greatly. **2** excessively.
plaguesome *adj* annoying, troublesome.
plaguey *adv* very, excessively.
plaick *same as* **playock**.
plaid *n* a plaid used as a blanket.—*v* to clothe.

plaiden *n* coarse woollen twilled cloth.—*adj* made of plaiden.
plaiden-ell *n* an ell of 38.416 inches, used in measuring plaiden (qv).
plaiden-merchant *n* a dealer in plaiden (qv).
plaid-neuk *n* the sewed-up corner of a plaid, used for carrying a lamb, etc.
plaig, plaik *same as* **playock**.
plaik *n* **1** a plaid. **2** a loose covering for the body.
plain¹ *adj* (*used of a court, meeting, etc*) full.
plain² *v* to complain.
plain³ *v* to play plaintive music.
plainen *n* coarse linen.
plain-soled *adj* flat-footed.
plain-~, plane-stanes *n* **1** the pavement. **2** a flagged roadway. **3** the exchange of a town, as paved with flat stones.
plaint *v* to complain.
plaintless *adj* uncomplaining.
plainyie *v* to complain.—*n* **1** a complaint. **2** a dissent.
plait *v* **1** to cross the legs. **2** to throw one leg over the other in walking or running. **3** to mark with folds or wrinkles.—*n* a fold, a pleat.
plait-backie *n* a nightgown reaching to the knees, with three plaits on the back.
plaithie *n* a plaid.
plaitings *n* the two pieces of iron below the sock of a plough.
plane *n* the sycamore.
plane-footed *adj* flat-footed.
plane-soled *adj* flat-footed.
plane tree *n* the maple.
plank *n* **1** a regular division of land, in contrast to the irregular divisions of run-rig (qv). **2** a piece of land in cultivation, longer than broad. **3** a strip of land between two open furrows.—*v* **1** to place, settle. **2** to divide or exchange pieces of land possessed by different people and lying intermingled with one another so that each person's property may be thrown into one field.
planker *n* a land-measurer.
planky¹ *n* **1** candy. **2** a sweetmeat.
planky² *n* a large marble.
plant *v* to supply a district with a minister.
plant-cot *n* a small enclosure for rearing cabbage plants.
planting *n* a plantation.
plantry *n* **1** garden grounds. **2** plantations.
plant-toft *n* a bed for rearing young cabbages, etc.
plap *adv* **1** plop. **2** with a sudden splash.
plapper *v* to make a noise with the lips or by striking a flat-surfaced body in water.—*n* **1** the act of doing so. **2** the noise so made.—*adv* with a splashing noise.
plapperdosh *n* a tremendous fall. *See* **plapper**.
plash *v* **1** to dash through water. **2** to rain heavily. **3** to wash or scour perfunctorily. **4** to work with the hands in a liquid. **5** to work ineffectually.—*n* **1** a splash of rain, mud. **2** a heavy downfall of rain, snow, etc. **3** a quantity of liquid or semiliquid dashed violently. **3** a mess of ill-cooked liquid food.—*adv* with a splash.
plash-fluke *n* the plaice.
plashie¹ *n* the plaice.
plashie² *adj* **1** wet. **2** wetting. **3** miry. **4** apt to daub. **5** full of dirty water.
plashing-wet *adj* (*used of clothes*) soaked with water so as to make a splashing sound.
plash-mill *n* a fulling mill.
plash-miller *n* a fuller.
plasket *n* an evil trick.
plat¹ *n* a plot of ground.
plat² *adj* **1** flat. **2** clear, plain, distinct.—*adv* **1** very, quite. **2** due, direct.—*n* a cake of cow's dung.
plat³ *v* **1** did intertwine. **2** (*with* **up**) erected.—*n* a plait of hair.
plat⁴, **platt** *n* **1** a plot. **2** a plan. **3** those who form a plan.
platch¹ *n* a flat foot.—*v* to make a heavy noise in walking with short, quick steps.

platch[2] *v* **1** to splash. **2** to bespatter, besmear.—*n* **1** a splash. **2** a clot. **3** a large piece of anything. **4** a big spot.

platch[3] *v* **1** to patch. **2** to mend clumsily.—*n* **1** a patch. **2** a piece of cloth used as a patch.

platchack *n* a large patch.

platchen[1], **platchin** *v* **1** to cover with spots. **2** to besmear.— *n* a very big spot or clot.

platchen[2] *v* to patch, mend clumsily.—*n* a big or clumsy patch.

platchie *adj* splashy, bespattering, besmearing.

plate *v* to clinch a nail.

platejack *n* ancient coat-armour, platemail.

plate-man *n* the man in charge of the offertory plate at a church door.

platoon *n* **1** a volley. **2** the report of a shot. **3** a sudden scare or shock.

platten *v* **1** to rivet. **2** to clinch a nail.

platten stone *n* a large flat stone used by blacksmiths in riveting horseshoe nails to prevent their coming out.

platter *v* **1** to dabble among a liquid or semiliquid. **2** to walk smartly in water or mud.—*n* **1** dabbling in water, mud, etc. **2** the noise so caused.—*adv* with such a sharp, continuous noise.

play[1] *v* to boil with force.

play[2] *n* **1** any game. **2** a holiday. **3** a school vacation.

play-act, ~ack *v* **1** to act plays. **2** to recite.

play-acting *n* acting.— *adj* theatrical.

play-actoring *adj* **1** dramatic. **2** theatrical.

play at *v* **1** to nibble at. **2** to begin to enjoy.

play brown *v* (*used of strong broths*) to take on a brown colour in boiling.

play by *v* **1** to play against. **2** to play false.

play-carl-again *v* to give as good as one gets.

playday *n* **1** the day when school holidays are given out. **2** a day that is a half-holiday at school.

playding *same as* **plaiden**.

playfair *n* a toy, plaything.

playing-at-the-pitcher *n* the game of hopscotch.

playing-bairn *n* a playmate.

play-marrow *n* a playmate.

playock, playick, playke *n* **1** a plaything, toy. **2** a trifle.

playrife *adj* playful.

playrifety *n* **1** playfulness. **2** fondness of sport. **3** abundance of play, sport, fun.

playsome *adj* playful, sportive.

plea *n* **1** a lawsuit. **2** the subject of a lawsuit. **3** a quarrel, debate. **4** wrangling, strife.—*v* **1** to go to law. **2** to plead, sue. **3** to quarrel, wrangle.

plead *v* **1** to argue, debate. **2** to quarrel.—*n* a quarrel, strife.

plea house *n* a law court, courthouse.

plean *same as* **plain**[2].

pleasance *n* pleasure, delight.

please *v* to relish, like.—*n* **1** pleasure. **2** a pleasant word. **3** a choice, a say.

pleat *v* to plait.—*n* a plait.

pleck-pleck *n* the cry of the oystercatcher.

pledge *v* **1** to be sure. **2** to provide, furnish.

pledge house *n* a house in which debtors were confined.

plee *same as* **plea**.

pleen *same as* **plain**[2].

pleengie *n* the young of the herring-gull.

pleep *v* **1** to chirp. **2** to speak in a fretful tone of voice.—*n* the plaintive chirping of seafowl.

pleepin *n* the chirping of a bird.—*adj* complaining, pleading poverty or sickness.

pleesh-plash *same as* **plish-plash**.

pleesk *v* to dash and wade through water.

pleesure *v* to please, gratify.—*n* pleasure.

pleet *v* to complain in a low, peevish tone.

pleeter *n* **1** a complaint. **2** a peevish tone.

plencher-nails *n* large nails used in planking.

plene *same as* **plain**[1].

plenish *v* **1** to furnish a house. **2** to stock a farm.—*n* furniture.

plenisher *n* one who plenishes. *See* **plenish**.

plenishing *n* **1** furniture, furnishing. **2** goods. **3** stock.

plenishment *n* furnishing.

plenishing-nail *n* a flooring nail.

plenshir *n* a large nail for floors.

plenstanes *same as* **plainstanes**.

plent, plente *same as* **plaint**.

plenty *adv* sufficiently.

plenyie, plenzie *same as* **plainyie**.

pleoch, pleochan *n* a plough.

plep *n* anything weak or feeble.

pleppit *adj* **1** feeble. **2** creased. **3** not stiff. **4** flaccid.

plesk *v* to dash through water.

plet[1], **plett** *v* to plait.—*v* plaited.

plet[2] *v* **1** to rivet. **2** to clinch.

plet[3] *adv* due, direct.

plettin *same as* **platten**.

plettin-stone *same as* **platten-stone**.

pleuat *n* a green turf or sod, used for covering houses.

pleuch, pleugh *n* **1** a plough. **2** as much land as a plough can till. **3** a plane for making a groove and feather (qv). **4** a match plane.—*v* **1** to plough. **2** to groove and feather. **3** to use a match plane.

pleuch-airns, ~-irnes *n* the coulter and ploughshare of a plough.

pleuch-bred *adj* bred to the plough.

pleuch-bridle *n* what is attached to the head of a plough beam, to regulate the breadth or depth of the furrow.

pleuch-fittit *adj* having heavy, dragging feet.

pleuch-gang, ~-gate *n* as much land as can be properly tilled by a plough, about forty Scotch acres.

pleuch-gear, ~-graith *n* the harness and equipment of a plough.

pleuch-godes, ~-goods *n* plough oxen.

pleuchlad *n* **1** a ploughboy. **2** a ploughman.

pleuchland *n* arable land.

pleuchman *n* a ploughman.

pleuch pettle *n* a small paddle for clearing earth from the plough.

pleuch shears *n* a bolt with a crooked head for regulating the bridle and keeping it steady, when the plough requires to be raised or depressed on the furrow.

pleuch sheath *n* the head of a plough on which the sock or ploughshare is put.

pleuch staff *n* the pleuch pettle (qv).

pleuch stilts *n* the handles of a plough.

pleuchtail *n* **1** the pleuch stilts (qv). **2** the rear of a plough.

pleugh *same as* **pleuch**.

pleuk *same as* **plook**.

pleuter *same as* **plouter**.

pleutery *same as* **ploutery**.

plew *same as* **pleuch**.

plewman *n* a ploughman.

pley *same as* **plea**.

plichen[1] *n* a plight, condition.

plichen[2] *n* a peasant.

plicht[1] *v* plighted.

plicht[2] *n* a plight.

plie *v* **1** to ply. **2** to fold, plait.—*n* a fold, plait.

plies *n* thin strata of freestone.

plingie *same as* **pleengie**.

plime *n* the young of the herring gull.

plish *v* to splash.

plish-plash *v* to splash.—*adv* in a splashing manner.—*n* **1** a splashing in a liquid. **2** the noise so made.

plisky *n* **1** a trick, prank. **2** a mischievous trick. **3** a practical joke. **4** a plight. **5** a fray, scrimmage.—*adj* **1** tricky, mischievous. **2** frolicsome.

plit *n* **1** the slice of earth turned over by a plough. **2** a furrow.

plitch-platch *same as* **plish-plash**.

pliver *n* the plover.

plleuter *same as* **plouter**.

plloud, pllout *same as* **ploud**.

ploat *same as* **plot**[1].
plock *same as* **plack**[1].
plodder *v* to toil continuously.
ploiter *same as* **plouter**.
ploiterie *same as* **ploutery**.
plonk *n* a tree buried in a moss.
ploo *same as* **pleuch**.
plood *n* a green sod.
ploog *same as* **plook**.
plook *n* **1** a pimple. **2** a spot on the skin. **3** a small knob near the top of a metal measure for liquid. —*v* to set the plook on a vessel for measuring liquids.
plook-besprent *adj* pimply, covered with pimples.
plook-faced *adj* having pimples on the face.
plookie *adj* **1** full of little knobs. **2** pimply.
plookie-faced *same as* **plook-faced**.
plookiness *n* the being covered with pimples.
plook-measure *n* measure up to the plook (qv) of a vessel.
plooky *n* a slight stroke or blow.
ploom *n* a plum.
plooman *n* a ploughman.
plooster *v* **1** to toil in mud or filth. **2** to splash among water.—*n* a mess, muddle bungle.
plop, plope *v* **1** to plunge, plump, flop. **2** to fall or drop suddenly and noisily into water.—*n* the sound made by a small object falling into water from a height.—*adv* suddenly, with a plop.
plopper *v* to bubble like boiling water.
plopperin' *n* the noise made by anything boiling in a pot.
plore *v* to work among mire, as children amusing themselves.
plorie *adj* a piece of ground converted into mud by treading, etc.
plot[1]**, plote** *v* **1** to plunge into boiling water. **2** to scald. **3** to make boiling hot. **4** to burn, scorch, make hot.—*n* **1** a scald or burn with boiling water. **2** to be very hot. **3** a hot, stewing or perspiring condition.
plot[2]**, plott** *v* **1** to pluck off feathers. **2** to make bare, fleece, rob.
plotch *v* **1** to dabble. **2** to work slowly.
plotcock *n* the devil.
plot-het *adj* so hot as to scald.
plotter *v* to wade through water or mud.
plotter plate *n* a wooden platter with a place in the middle for salt.
plottin *n* a plan, scheme.
plottin' *v, adj in phr* **plottin' wi' rage** very angry, boiling with indignation.
plotting *adj* sweating profusely.
plottin-het *adj* scalding hot.
plottit[1] *adj* fleeced, plucked.
plottit[2] *adj* **1** fond of heat. **2** unable to bear cold.
plotty *n* **1** a rich and pleasant hot drink made with spices, wine and sugar, mulled. **2** any hot drink, as tea.
plouckie *adj* pimpled.
ploud[1] *same as* **plood**.
ploud[2] *v* **1** to waddle in walking. **2** to fall with a short, heavy fall. **3** to endeavour.—*n* **1** a waddling pace. **2** a short, heavy fall. **3** a thickset, fat person or animal. **4** a plump child.
plouder *v* to wade or walk with difficulty through water, mud, etc.
ploudie *n* a fat or plump child.
plouk *same as* **plook**.
ploumdamia *n* a damson.
plounge *v* to plunge.—*n* a plunge.
ploup *same as* **plop**.
ploussie *adj* plump, well-grown.
plout *v* **1** to splash. **2** to fall with a splash suddenly. **3** to put down suddenly and heavily. **4** to wade through water or mud.—*n* **1** a fall into liquid. **2** a splash. **3** the noise of a fall or splash. **4** a heavy shower of rain. **5** the act of walking in water, mud or wet soil.—*adv* suddenly, plump.

plout[1] *same as* **plot**[1].
plout[2] *v* to poke.—*n* a poker.
plouter *v* **1** to wade through water or mud. **2** to flounder, splash. **3** to dabble in liquid. **4** to do wet or dirty work. **5** to work awkwardly or slovenly. **6** to dawdle. **7** to potter about at trifling tasks.—*n* **1** a splash, plunge. **2** a splashing sound. **3** walking through water or mud. **4** wet, disagreeable work. **5** ill-cooked food.—*adv* with a noisy splash.
plouterin' *adj* weak, unskilful at work, laborious with little result.
ploutery *n* **1** anything wet, dirty or disagreeable. **2** wet weather. **3** refuse. **4** ill-cooked food.—*adj* wet and dirty, disagreeable.
ploutie *n* a sudden fall.
ploutin' *adj* weak and clumsy at work.
plout-kirn *n* the common churn, worked by an upright staff.
plout net *n* a small, stocking-shaped net, affixed to two poles.
ploutter *n* **1** a clumsy, untidy person. **2** a great and noisy talker.
plover *n* the golden plover.
plover's page *n* **1** the dunlin. **2** the jacksnipe.
plow *same as* **pleuch**.
plowable *adj* arable.
plowp *same as* **plop**.
plowster *v* to toil in mud or filth.—*n* a bungle, muddle.
plowt *same as* **plot**[1].
plowter *same as* **plouter**.
ploy *n* **1** amusement, sport. **2** a frolic, escapade. **3** a practical joke. **4** employment, business. **5** a serious matter. **6** a procession. **7** a quarrel.
pluchie *n* a ploughman.
pluck[1] *n* **1** courage, spirit. **2** what can be plucked. **3** a small quantity of grass, etc. **4** a two-pronged implement, with teeth at right angles to the shaft, for taking dung out of a cart or for uprooting turnips in hard frost. **5** the armed bullhead. **6** a reverse of fortune, a loss, a calamity. **7** (*in pl*) herrings damaged by the net.
pluck[2] *same as* **plook**.
plucked *adj* **1** high-spirited. **2** brave.
plucker *n* **1** the great fishing frog. **2** the father lasher.
plucking pin *n* a weaving implement used in hand looms for pushing or pulling the shuttle across the loom.
pluckless *adj* spiritless.
pluck-msasure *n* measure up to the plook (qv) of a drinking vessel.
pluck-up *n* **1** an eager struggle or demand for an article on sale or for gift. **2** a rise in price of an article because of its scarcity.
plucky-face't *adj* having a pimpled face.
pluff *v* **1** to emit a short, sharp breath. **2** to puff, pant, blow. **3** to blow peas, pellets, etc, through a tube. **4** to set fire to suddenly. **5** to explode gunpowder. **6** to throw out hair powder in dressing the hair. **7** to throw out smoke in quick, successive whiffs.—*n* **1** a puff, blast. **2** a shot. **3** a slight explosion. **4** a pinch, a small quantity of snuff, powder, etc. **5** a powder puff. **6** a piece of bored bourtree (qv), used as a bellows. **7** a rotten and dried mushroom (the devil's snuff mill), which falls to dust when touched. **8** a pear with a fair outside but rotten inside. **9** the act of throwing on hair powder.
pluffer *n* **1** a peashooter. **2** a shooter, marksman.
pluff grass *n* the creeping, and the meadow, soft-grass.
pluff gun *n* a popgun, a peashooter.
pluffins *n* anything easily blown away, as the refuse of a corn mill.
pluffy *adj* fat, swollen, chubby.
plug *v* to strike with the fist.
pluke, pluik *same as* **plook**.
plum *n* **1** a deep pool in a river or stream. **2** the noise made by a stone when plunged into a deep pool. **3** the straight, the right direction.
plumache, plumashe *n* a plume of feathers.

plumb[1] *n* a plum.
plumb[2] *n* a plunge.
plum-dames, ~-dames, ~damis, ~-damy *n* **1** a damson. **2** a Damascene plum.
plum duff *n* a suet dumpling, usually originally eaten with beef.
plume[1] *n* a plummet, plumb weight.
plume[2] *n* a plum.
plummet *n* the pommel of a sword.
plump[1] *n* **1** a plunge. **2** a heavy shower falling straight down. **3** a ducking.—*v* to rain heavily, like a thunder shower.—*adv* falling heavily and perpendicularly.
plump[2] *n* a clump of trees.
plumpit *adj* **1** plump. **2** protuberant.
plump-kirn *n* a common upright churn.
plump-shower *n* a sudden, heavy shower.
plumpy *adj* **1** plump. **2** chubby.
plumrock *n* the primrose.
plumy *adj* (*used of birds*) feathered.
plunge churn *n* a churn driven with an upright staff.
plunk[1], **plung** *n* **1** the sound made by a heavy body falling from a height into water. **2** the sound of a cork being drawn. **3** the sound of emitting tobacco smoke. **4** a sound imitating the cry of the raven. **5** a sudden blow or stab. **6** the pitching of a marble by thumb and forefinger. **7** a short, stout, thickset person, animal or thing.—*v* **1** to drop or throw anything so as to produce a hollow sound ot a crackling noise. **2** to plump, plunge. **3** to draw a cork. **4** to croak like a raven. **5** (*used in the game of marbles*) to give a fair and full hit, to pitch a marble.—*adv* **1** suddenly, smartly. **2** at once.
plunk[2] *v* **1** to desert, shirk. **2** to play truant. **3** to stand still, balk, like a vicious horse.
plunkart *n* a person or thing, short, stout and thickset.
plunker[1] *n* a large marble.
plunker[2] *n* **1** a truant. **2** a horse given to balking.
plunkie[1] *n* **1** a trick. **2** a practical joke.—*adj* tricky, not to be trusted.
plunkie[2] *n* a sweetmeat made of molasses.
plunkin *n* a game at marbles.
plunky *n* a game of marbles in which large marbles are used.
pluskie *same as* **plisky**.
plut *same as* **plout**.
ply[1] *v* **1** (*with* **on**) to push on. **2** to fold, plait.—*n* a plight, condition.
ply[2] *same as* **plea**.
ply[3] *same as* **ploy**.
plyaak, plyaack *same as* **playock**.
plyde *n* a plaid.
plype *v* **1** to walk or dabble in water, mud, etc. **2** to fall plunge into water. **3** to work in slovenly fashion among any liquid.—*n* **1** dabbling or walking in water, mud, heavy ground, etc. **2** working in a slovenly way in liquids. **3** a fall into water. **4** the noise made by a fall into water or mud. **5** a heavy fall of rain.—*adv* with a plype.
plypper *same as* **plapper**.
plyvens *n* the flowers of the red clover.
po[1] *n* a chamber pot.
po[2] *int* pooh!
poach *v* **1** to poke. **2** (*used of cattle*) to trample soft ground into mud and holes. **3** to poke in a wet substance. **4** to work in a wet or semiliquid substance in a dirty, slovenly way. **5** to drive backwards and forwards. **6** to play about with food, mess.—*n* **1** a puddle. **2** wet soil trampled by cattle. **3** a muddle, mess, confusion.
poacher court *n* a nickname for a kirk session.
poachie[1] *n* a child's game.
poachie[2] *n* a nursery name for porridge.
poaching *n* the trampling of sward into holes.—*adj* clumsy and dirty at work.
poachy *adj* (*used of land*) soft, wet, full of puddles, trampled into holes.
poan *same as* **powan**.

poatch *same as* **poach**.
pob *n* **1** the refuse of flax, often used for popguns. **2** a rope or twine shredded into its original material.
pobbob *n* a hubbub.
pobtow *n* pob (qv).
pochle *same as* **pauchle**.
pock[1] *n* **1** a bag, poke, sack. **2** a wallet. **3** a bag-shaped fishing net. **4** the stomach of a fish. **5** a bag growing under the jaws of a sheep, an indication of the rot. **5** the rot.—*v* **1** to catch fish in a net. **2** to be seized with the rot.
pock[2] *n* **1** the pustule caused by vaccination. **2** (*in pl*) smallpox.
pock and string *n* **1** a state of beggary. **2** begging for a livelihood.
pock-arr *n* a mark left by smallpox.
pock-arred, pockard *adj* marked with smallpox.
pock-arrie *adj* full of the marks of smallpox.
pock-broken *adj* marked with smallpox.
pocked *adj* **1** marked with smallpox. **2** (*used of sheep*) having a disease resembling scrofula.
pocket-hankie *n* a pocket handkerchief.
pocket-napkin, ~-naipkin *n* a pocket handkerchief.
pocket-pick *v* to pick one's pocket.
pockey-ort, pockiawrd *adj* marked with smallpox.
pock-faced *adj* having the face marked with smallpox.
pock-freitten *adj* pitted by smallpox. *See* **freitten**.
pockmanteau, pockmanky, pockmanty *n* a portmanteau.
pock-markit *adj* marked with smallpox.
pock net *n* a bag-shaped fishing net, a ringnet.
pock-neuk *n* **1** the bottom corner of a sack. **2** one's own resources or means.
pockpit *n* a scar left by smallpox.—*v* to mark with smallpox.
pock-pud, ~-pudding *n* **1** a bag pudding. **2** a term of contempt for an Englishman. **3** a glutton.
pock-shakings *n* **1** the youngest and last child of a family. **2** the small, weak pigs of a litter.
pock staff *n* the pole to the end of which a pock or ring net is suspended.
pocky *adj* subject to smallpox.
pockyawr'd *same as* **pock-arred**.
pod[1] *n* **1** a little person. **2** a small and neat animal.
pod[2] *v* to walk with short steps.
pod[3] *n* a louse.
pod[4] *int* a call to pigeons.
podder *v* **1** to potter. **2** to dawdle. **3** to walk slowly to and fro. **4** to produce slowly and with difficulty.
poddle *v* to walk with short, unsteady steps.
poddlie *n* an immature coalfish.
poddlit *adj* (*of poultry*) plump, in good condition.
poddock, podduck *same as* **paddock**.
poddock-cruds *same as* **paddock-rud**.
podge[1] *n* a short, fat person.
podge[2] *n* **1** hurry, bustle, confusion. **2** a jumble, mixture.
podgel, podgal *n* a strong, thickset person.
podls *n* a tadpole.
podle *n* a fondling name for a thriving child.
podle *same as* **poddle**.
podley, podlie, podle *n* **1** an immature coalfish. **2** the pollack.
podsy *adj* pudgy.
poem book *n* a book of poems.
poeteeze *v* to write poetry.
poeter *n* **1** a poet. **2** a poetaster.
poffle *same as* **paffle**.
poik *n* a poke, bag.
poind[1] *n* **1** a silly, inactive person. **2** a person easily imposed on.
poind[2], **poin** *v* **1** to distrain. **2** to impound.—*n* a distraint.
poindable *adj* capable of being distrained.
poinder *n* a distrainer.
poind fauld *n* **1** a pound. **2** an enclosure for strays.
poinding *n* **1** a distraint. **2** a warrant for distraint.

poinding plea *n* an action or suit to distrain.
poiner *same as* **piner**[3].
point *n* **1** a bodkin. **2** a boot or shoelace. **3** a stay lace. **4** the left-hand side of a bandwin (qv). **5** the portion of a harvest field reaped by the left half of a bandwin. **6** the leader of a bandwin. **7** state of body.—*phr* **to be first in the point** to lead as scythesman in harvest.
point-bitch *n* a bitch pointer.
pointed *adj* (*used of a person*) **1** particular, precise, exact. **2** punctual. **3** tidy.
point-game *n* (*in curling*) a game played by each player for himself or herself, at the various shots, to win the single-handed medal.
poinyel *n* a burden carried by a traveller.
poison *n* **1** anything offensive. **2** a term of contempt.—*v* **1** to spoil food. **2** to mar.—*adj* (*used of persons*) bad, disgusting.
poisonable *adj* poisonous.
poist[1] *same as* **poost**.
poist[2] *n* a post.
poister *v* to pamper, pet, spoil.
pok *same as* **pock**[1].
poke[1] *n* the smallpox.
poke[2] *v* **1** to do digging work lazily. **2** to dawdle. **3** to grope about in the dark. **4** to walk with a dull, heavy footfall. **5** to carry the head and shoulders thrust forward. **6** (*with* **at**) to meddle with. **7** to make fun of.—*n* **1** a blow. **2** the hollow sound of a blow. **3** the act of groping in the dark or in a hole.—*adv* **1** suddenly and with a hollow sound. **2** awkwardly and with heavy footfall.
pokeful *n* **1** a sufficiency. **2** surplus.
pokemantie *same as* **pockmanteau**.
poke-up *adj* turned up.
pokey *same as* **pawky**.
pokey hat *n* an ice-cream cone.
pol, pole *same as* **pow**[4].
poldach *n* marshy ground beside a body of water.
pole *n* a walking stick.
pole tree *n* the pole of a carriage.
police *n* a policeman.
police dung *n* town manure applied to fields.
policy *n* (*in pl*) the pleasure grounds of a country mansion.
polis *n* the police.
polisher *n* a policeman.
polist, polisht *adj* **1** polished. **2** accomplished educationally. **3** finished, complete (*in an opprobrious sense*). **4** fawning, designing.
polist lair *n* a finishing education.
politique, politick *n* **1** policy. **2** a plan.
polka *n* a woman's jacket.
poll *same as* **pow**[4].
pollac *n* the guiniad powan.
pollachie *n* the crabfish.
pollan *same as* **powan**.
pollicate *n* a kind of web or cloth.
pollie, polly *same as* **poullie**[1].
pollie-cock *n* a turkey cock.
pollock *n* the young of the coalfish.
pollonian, polonian *same as* **polonaise**.
polly-shee *n* a pulley attached to a pole from which a rope runs to a window for hanging clothes to dry, peculiar to Dundee.
polly-wag, ~-woug *n* a tadpole.
polonaise, polonie *n* **1** a dress for young boys, including a sort of waistcoat with loose, sloping skirts. **2** a greatcoat for boys, a dress formerly worn by men in the Hebrides. **3** a surtout. **4** a person clad in old-fashioned garments.
polsterer *n* an upholsterer.
pomate, pomet *n* pomade.—*v* to grease with pomade.
pome *n* a poem.
pompidoo *n* **1** an article of feminine apparel. **2** a kind of chemise. **3** a dress cut low and square in the neck.
ponage *n* **1** portage. **2** the place of a ferry.

pones *n* **1** long meadow grass. **2** the duffel grass.
poney-cock *n* **1** a turkey. **2** a peacock.
pong *n* a kind of embroidery.
pong-pong *n* a trinket.
poo[1] *same as* **pow**[1].
poo[2] *v* to pull.—*n* a pull.
pooch *v* to pouch.—*n* a pocket.
poochle *adj* **1** shy, reserved. **2** proud. **2** prim. **3** tidy, neatly dressed.
poodle *na* plough staff.
poodge, pooge *same as* **pudge**.
pooer *same as* **power**.
poof *same as* **puff**.
poom *n* a pulling.
pook *v* **1** to pull with nimbleness or force. **2** to pull gently. **3** to pluck a fowl. **4** to pull the hair. **5** to moult. **6** to take or eat in small quantities, peck. —*n* **1** the disease to which moulting fowls are subject. **2** declining health. **3** a very small quantity. **4** (*in pl*) the feathers on a fowl when they begin to grow after moulting. **5** down, or any like stuff, adhering to one's clothes. **6** the ends of threads. **7** unconsidered trifles.
pook and rook *v* to pillage.
pookie, pookit *adj* **1** starved-looking, thin and bony. **2** shabby in appearance.
pookit-like *adj* **1** looking like a plucked chicken. **2** puny, meagre, diminutive.
poolie *n* a louse.
poollie *n* a turkey.
poolly-woolly *n* the cry of the curlew.
poon[1] *same as* **poind**.
poon[2] *n* a pound.
poop *v* to break wind backwards.—*n* the act of doing so.
poopit *n* a pulpit.
poopit fit *n* a pulpit foot.
poopit man *n* a minister, preacher.
poor[1] *adj* **1** out of condition. **2** used endearingly.—*n* a poor or unfortunate or contemptible creature.—*v* to impoverish.
poor[2] *v* to pour.
poorail *n* the poorer people.
poor-bodie *n* **1** a poor creature. **2** a delicate person. **3** a beggar.
poorie[1] *n* a small, meagre person.
poorie[2] *same as* **pourie**.
poorin' *same as* **pourin'**.
poorish *adj* not very well.
poorit *adj* **1** impoverished. **2** meagre.
poor John *n* a cod in poor condition.
poorly *adv* **1** in poverty. **2** softly, gently.
poor-man *n* **1** a beggar. **2** a frame of iron or wood on a rod three or four feet long, set in a stone socket and holding fir candles for lighting a room. **3** a heap of four upright sheaves of corn with one laid on the top in wet weather. **4** the blade bone or broiled remains of a shoulder of mutton.
poor-man of mutton *n* the remains of a shoulder of mutton broiled for supper or for next day.
poor man's weather-glass *n* **1** the common pimpernel. **2** the knotted figwort.
poor-page *n* an iron or wooden frame for holding fir candles.
poor's house *n* the workhouse.
poortith, poortha, poortoth *n* **1** poverty. **2** leanness, weakness from lack of food.
poortith-struck *adj* poverty-stricken.
poor widow *n* a children's game.
poor Willis *n* the bar-tailed godwit.
poos *n* a sort of sour cake, the dough of which was moistened with water poured off sowens (qv).
poosion, pooshan *same as* **pousion**.
poosioning *same as* **pousioning**.
poossie *n* **1** a kitten. **2** a cat. **3** a hare.
poost *v* **1** to push. **2** to overload the stomach.

poot *same as* **pout**⁶.
pootch¹ *n* a pocket.
pootch² *v* to eat with relish.
pootchin *adj* **1** fond of good things. **2** big-bellied, corpulent.
poother *same as* **powder**.
poother-deelie *same as* **podwer-deil**.
pootie *adj* niggardly, mean, stingy.
poot-poot-poot *int* a call to young pigs at feeding time.
pop¹ *v* **1** to fire a gun. **2** to shoot. **3** to put, place. **4** (*with* **up**) to startle, rouse up suddenly. **5** (*with* **about**) to go about. **6** to drop. **7** to fall quickly or lightly.—*n* a spot, speck.
pop² *v* **1** to strike, knock. **2** to shoot at. **3** to pelt, throw.—*n* **1** a knock, blow. **2** a pat, tap.
pope *n* a name given by seamen to the puffin.
poper *n* the boy who swept out a schoolroom instead of paying fees.
popeseye steak *n* a cut of beef for frying or grilling, like rump steak.
popingoe *same as* **papingoe**.
popist *n* a papist.—*adj* popish.
pople, popple *same as* **papple**².
poppin, popin *same as* **pappin**.
poppin' job *n* **1** an odd job. **2** a small piece of work.
popple *same as* **papple**¹.
poppy-show *same as* **puppie-show**.
pop-the-bonnet *n* a game played with two pins on the crown of a hat.
popular *adj* populous.
pore *v* to purge or soften leather, so that the stool or bottom of the hair may come easily off.
poring iron *same as* **purring iron**.
pork *v* **1** to grub, poke about, rout about. **2** to poke, thrust.
pork bree *n* soup made of fresh pork.
pork-ham *n* a ham in contrast to a mutton ham.
porkling *n* a young pig.
porkmanky, porkmanty *same as* **pockmanteau**.
porky *n* a pig.
porpus *n* **1** a porpoise. **2** a stupid or self-important person.
porpy *n* a porpoise.
porr *same as* **purr**¹.
porrage, porritch *same as* **parritch**.
porridge tree *n* a rod for stirring porridge.
porring iron *same as* **purring iron**.
port¹ *n* the carriage of an article.
port² *n* **1** a gate, gateway. **2** (*in curling or bowling*) a passage left between two stones or bowls.
port³, **porte** *n* **1** a lively tune on the bagpipe. **2** a catch, glee.
port⁴ *v in phr* **port the helm** a boys' game, suggested by contact with seafarers.
portage *n* the goods allowed to be put on board a vessel as a passenger's private store or luggage.
Port-day *n* the day (in old times) for hiring harvesters near the West Port of Edinburgh.
Porteous-roll *n* **1** a list of persons indicted to appear before the Justice-aire, given by the Justice Clerk to the Coroner, that he might attach them in order to their appearance. **2** the list of criminal cases to be tried at the circuit courts.
porter *n* **1** in weaving, a certain number of threads forming a section of a warp. **2** a ferryman.
porterage, porterer, porteretch, portridge *n* a portrait.
portie *n* air, mien, bearing.
portioner *n* **1** the occupier of part of a property originally divided among co-heirs. **2** the possessor of a small portion of land.
portmantle, portmankle, portmanty *n* a portmanteau.
portridge *same as* **porterage**.
portule *same as* **port-youl**—*phr* **to sing portule** to cry out.
portus *n* a skeleton.
port-vent *n* part of the bagpipe.

port-youl, ~-yeul *n* a cry, howl.
pory *adj* (*used of bread*) light, spongy, porous.
pose¹ *n* **1** a hoard. **2** a secret store. **3** savings.—*v* to hoard up, amass.
pose² *v* to examine, question.
posel *n* a small heap.
posellie *n* a very small heap.
posh, poshie *n* a nursery name for porridge.
positeevest *adj* most positive.
posnett *n* **1** a bag for holding money. **2** a net purse.
poss¹ *v* **1** to push. **2** to pound. **3** to dash violently backwards and forwards in water for the purpose of cleaning or rinsing clothes, etc.
poss² *same as* **pose**¹.
posee, possey *n* a large muster of men.
possess *v* to give legal possession or investiture.
posset-masking *n* the making and drinking of possets.
possibles *n* means, wherewithal.
possile *same as* **posel**.
possing tub *n* a tub for washing clothes or tramping blankets.
possit *adj* possible.
possody *same as* **powsowdy**.
post¹ *n* a stratum in a quarry.
post² *n* **1** a postman. **2** postage.—*v* to convey, accompany.
post³ *same as* **poss**¹.
post and pan *n* a method of building walls with upright posts tied with pans or crosspieces of timber, making a framework to be filled up with stones and clay or mud.
postie *n* a familiar name for a postman/woman.
postit *adj in phr* **postit wi' sickness** overpowered by sickness.
post-letter *n* a letter posted.
post-sick *adj* bedridden, confined to bed with illness.
posture *n* site, local position.
posy *n* **1** a cluster. **2** a small collection. **3** an unsavoury smell.
pot¹ *n* **1** a small still. **2** the last division in the game of hopscotch. **3** ruin.—*v* **1** to stew. **2** to boil in water to reduce to a jelly when cold. **3** to boil in order to preserve.
pot², **pott** *n* **1** a pit. **2** a deep hole or cavity. **3** a deep pool or hole in water. **4** a hole from which peats have been dug.—*v* **1** to plant or set in a pit. **2** to dig peats out of a hole.
pot³ *v* to trample soft or wet soil, as cattle do.
pot⁴ *n* a name for porridge.
potards *n* dotards.
potato beetle *n* a potato masher.
potato bing *n* a covered potato heap.
potato bogle *n* a scarecrow.
potato box *n* the mouth.
potato bread *n* bread made of flour and mashed potatoes.
potato doolie *n* a scarecrow.
potatoes and point *n* only potatoes to eat.
potato mould *n* a field on which potatoes have been grown and which is considered rich enough to give a crop of oats without further manure.
potato scones *n* scones made of flour and potatoes.
pot brod *n* a pot lid (qv).
pot brose *n* oatmeal stirred quickly into hot milk.
potch¹ *same as* **poach**.
potch² *n* a jumble, a hodge-podge.
potching *adj* clumsy and dirty at work.
potchy *n* a name for a poacher.
pot-cleps *n* pot-hooks.
pot-dyed *adj* dyed in a pot.
pote *same as* **pout**⁴.
potecarg *n* an apothecary.
potent *n* a crutch.
pot-head *n* the caain' whale.
potie¹ *same as* **pottie**¹.
potie² *same as* **pottie**².
potingarie, potinger *n* **1** an apothecary. **2** a cook.
potle bell *n in phr* **to ring the potle bell** a children's way of confirming a bargain by hooking together the little

fingers of the right hand and shaking the hands up and down and repeating, 'Ring the potle bell, gin ye brack the bargain ye'll gang to hell'.

pot-lid *n* a curling stone played so as to rest on the tee.

pot-metal *n* cast-iron.

pot-piece *n* an old name for the piece of ordnance called a mortar.

potridge *same as* **porterage**.

pot-shkirt *n* **1** a piece of a broken kettle for holding oil. **2** a potsherd.

pot stick *n* stirring rod.

pot still *n* a small whisky still.

pot-stuff *n* **1** vegetables for cooking. **2** plants grown in pots.

pottage, pottish *n* porridge.

pottage-meal *n* oatmeal.

pottage pan *n* porridge pot.

potterlow *n* **1** fragments, small pieces. **2** utter ruin.

potter-skink *n* **1** wreck and ruin. **2** bits.

potterton-hen *n* the black-headed gull.

pottie[1] *n* a little pot.

pottie[2] *n* a red clay marble.

pottie[3], **potty** *adj* stewed or preserved in a pot.—*v* to stew in a pot.

pottie head *n* a dish made from the flesh of an ox head or pig's head boiled to a jelly.

pottingar *n* **1** a cook. **2** a druggist.

pottinger *n* **1** a jar, a small earthen vessel. **2** a porringer.

pottit-heid *same as* **pottie-heid**.

potty *n* putty.—*v* **1** to putty. **2** to suit, work, do.

pou[1] *n* **1** a pool. **2** a slow-running stream.

pou[2] *v* to pull, pluck.—*n* a pull.

pouce *n* a flea.

pouch *n* **1** a pocket. **2** a purse.—*v* **1** to pocket. **2** to steal. **3** to pocket food, etc. **4** to swallow. **5** to eat greedily.

pouch clout *n* a pocket handkerchief.

pouch companion *n* a pocket companion.

poucher *n* one who pockets food, etc, on the sly.

pouch-flap *n* a pocket flap.

pouchie *n* **1** a child's pocket. **2** a small pocket.

pouchfu' *n* a pocketful.

pouching *adj* **1** greedy. **2** fond of good living.

pouchless *adj* **1** pocketless. **2** poor. **3** impecunious.

pouch lid *n* a pocket flap.

pouch pistol *n* a pocket pistol.

pouch room *n* pocket space.

pouch strings *n* purse strings.

pouder *n* **1** dust. **2** gunpowder. **3** hair powder.—*v* **1** to powder. **2** to wear hair powder. **3** to corn beef, salt it slightly.

pouff *n* **1** a dull, heavy blow or fall. **2** the sound of such. **3** the act of walking heavily or wearily. **4** a big, stupid person.—*v* **1** to give dull, heavy blows. **2** to dash down violently. **3** to drive, hammer. **4** to fall heavily. **5** to walk with dull, heavy step.—*adv* **1** with a dull, heavy blow. **2** with heavy or weary steps.

pouffin *n* a big, stupid person.

pouk[1] *same as* **poke**[2].

pouk[2] *n* a mischievous sprite, puck.

pouk[3] *n* **1** a small pit or hole containing water or mud. **2** a deep hole.

pouk[4] *n* a poke, bag.

pouk[5] *same as* **pook**.

pouken-pin *n* (*weaving term*) a plucking pin, used in hand-loom weaving.

poukery *same as* **pawkery**.

poukit *as* **pookie**.

poulie *n* a louse.

poullie[1] *n* a turkey.

poullie[2] *v* to look plucked-like.

poullie-hen *n* a turkey hen.

poullie hens *n* plucked-looking hens.

pounce *v* to spring or pounce upon.

pound[1], **poun** *n* a weight varying in locality and as to articles weighed.

pound[2] *n* **1** a small enclosure. **2** a sheepfold.

poundlaw *n* money paid for delivery of goods poinded or impounded. *See* **poind**.

pound-piece *n* a sovereign.

pound Scots *n* the twelfth of a pound sterling.

pounie[1] *n* a pony.

pounie[2] *same as* **pownie**.

pount *n* a point.

pouny *adj* puny, little.

poupit *same as* **poopit**.

pour[1] *adj* poor.

pour[2] *same as* **power**.

pour[3] *v* **1** to drain off water in which potatoes have been boiled. **2** to dish a meal by emptying the vessel in which it has been cooked. **3** to rain heavily and fast.—*n* **1** a steady flow. **2** a heavy shower. **3** a small portion of liquid.

pourie *n* **1** a vessel with a spout. **2** a decanter. **3** a cream jug. **4** a very small quantity of any liquid or dry substance.—*adj* (*of a stream*) rushing, rapid.

pourin' *n* **1** a small quantity of liquid or spirits. **2** (*in pl*) the thin liquid poured off from sowens (qv) after fermentation. **3** the dregs or leavings of a liquid.

pourit *same as* **poorit**.

pour taties *v* to kill by blood-letting.

pourtith *same as* **poortith**.

pous *same as* **poos**.

pouse *v* **1** to push. **2** to thrust.—*n* **1** a push. **2** a blow.

pousion, pousin, poushon, pushion *n* **1** poison. **2** used as a term of contempt for a disagreeable person. **3** an eyesore. **4** anything offensive.—*v* **1** to spoil. **2** to spoil food in cooking.—*adj* (*used of persons*) bad, contemptible, disgusting.

pousioning *adj* poisonous, noisome.

pousle *v* **1** to puzzle. **2** to search uncertainly for anything. **3** to trifle.—*n* **1** an airy and finical person. **2** one who boasts of wealth with little reason for doing so.

pousowdy *n* **1** sheep's-head broth. **2** a mixture of meal and milk. **3** any mixture of incongruous foods.

pouss[1], **pousse** *same as* **poss**[1].

pouss[2], **poust** *v* to snuff a candle.

poussie *n* **1** a cat. **2** a hare.

poust[1] *n* **1** strength, vigour. **2** bodily power.

poust[2] *n* the person who plays second of three players in the game of marbles or buttons.—*v* to put a person in such a position.

pouster, pousture *n* bodily ability, the power of using a limb, arm.

poustie *n* **1** power. **2** ability, bodily strength. **3** *in phr* **lege poustie** full strength. **4** legitimate power.

pout[1] *n* *in phr* **to play pout** to make the least noise or exertion.

pout[2], **poutworm** *n* a grub destructive of springing grain, the tory, the larva of the daddy-longlegs.

pout[3] *v* to cause to pout, render sullen.

pout[4] *n* a poker.—*v* **1** to poke. **2** to push with the foot.

pout[5] *v* **1** to start up suddenly, as from under water. **2** to make a noise when doing so.

pout[6] *n* **1** a pullet. **2** a young turkey. **3** a young partridge or moorfowl. **4** an unfledged bird. **5** the sound made by a chicken. **6** a term of endearment for a young child, young girl, a sweetheart. **7** anything small. **8** a small haddock. **9** a small trout.—*n* to shoot at young partridges.

pout[7] *v* to stumble or stagger from drink.

pouter[1] *n* a sportsman who shoots young partridges or moorfowl.

pouter[2] *v* **1** to poke. **2** to stir with finger or instrument. **3** to rake as among ashes. **4** to work carelessly and unskilfully. **5** to go about aimlessly or to the annoyance of others. **6** to walk backwards and forwards. **7** to trifle. **8** to make a noise or splash in liquid.—*n* **1** a careless worker. **2** an aimless walker. **3** a poking, stirring.

pouther[1] *n* pewter.

pouther[2] *same as* **peuter**[1].

pouther³ *same as* **powder**.
poutie *same as* **pootie**.
pouting *n* spearing salmon.
pouting-season *n* the shooting season.
pout net *n* a round net fastened to two poles, thrust under the banks of a river to force out fish.
poutry *n* poultry.
pouzle *same as* **pousle**.
povereeze *v* **1** to exhaust. **2** to impoverish.
poverty-pink *n* the clover *Trifolium*.
povie *adj* **1** snug, comfortable, well-off. **2** spruce. **3** self-conceited.
pow¹ *n* a crab.
pow² *n* **1** a slow-running stream in flat lands. **2** a marshy place. **3** a small creek with a landing place for boats. **4** the wharf itself.
pow³ *v* to strike.
pow⁴ *n* **1** the head, the poll. **2** a head of hair. **3** the head of a hammer.—*v* **1** to cut the hair. **2** (*with* **up**) to raise up the head. **3** to win, secure.
powan¹ *n* **1** the freshwater herring, the guiniad. **2** the vendace.
powan², **powin** *n* a pound.
powart¹ *n* a seal.
powart² *n* a tadpole.
powder *n* **1** dust. **2** powder. **3** gunpowder. **4** (*used in curling*) strength in driving a stone.—*v* **1** to sprinkle butter or beef slightly with salt. **2** (*with* **up**) to powder the hair.
powder-brand *n* a disease in grain.
powder-deil *n* a small cone of moistened gunpowder, used as a firework.
powder pan *n* the priming pan of a firelock.
powder pouch *n* a powder flask.
powder room *n* a powder magazine.
pow-ee *n* a small fresh haddock.
poweed *same as* **pow-head**.
power *n* **1** a large number or quantity, a great deal. **2** a military force. **3** power to dispose of. **4** possession.
powerful *adj* **1** (*of liquor*) strong, potent. **2** plentiful.
powet *same as* **pow-head**.
pow-head *n* **1** a tadpole. **2** a vesuvian match. **3** the minute hand of a clock.
pow-high *adv* as high as the head.
powie¹ *same as* **poullie**¹.
powie², **powit** *n* a tadpole.
powin *same as* **pownie**².
powit *same as* **powie**².
powk¹ *same as* **pock**¹.
powk² *same as* **pook**.
powk³ *same as* **poke**².
powk-powking *n* **1** repeated poking. **2** digging. **3** groping. **4** walking heavily.
powl¹ *v* to walk or move rapidly.
powl² *n* a pole.
powlick *n* a tadpole.
powlie *same as* **poulie**.
pownie¹ *n* **1** a pony. **2** a trestle for support of temporary tables, etc.
pownie², **powney** *n* **1** a peacock. **2** a turkey hen.
pownie-cock *n* a peacock.
powowit, **powrit** *n* a tadpole.
powsowdy, **pow's-sowdy**, **pow-sodie** *n* **1** sheep's-head broth. **2** milk and meal boiled together. **3** a mixture of incongruous foods.
powster *n* **1** posture. **2** local position.
powstit *adj* exhausted, overcome. *See* **postit**.
powt¹ *same as* **paut**.
powt² *same as* **pout**⁶.
pow-tae *n* a crab's claw.
powter *same as* **pouter**.
powtle *v* to creep out like a mole.
pow-wow *n* a child's head.
pox *n* **1** a plague. **2** an imprecation.—*v* **1** to plague. **2** to break so as to render useless.

poy *v* **1** to work diligently and anxiously. **2** (*with* **upon**) to use persuasion so as to exercise undue influence.
poyn, **poynd** *same as* **poind**.
practicate *adj* practised.
practician *n* one who treats of legal procedure.
practick, **practique** *same as* **pratick**.
practise *v* **1** to suborn, bribe a witness. **2** to tamper with.
practiser *n* one who practises.
practitioner *n* a writer on practicks. *See* **pratick**.
prad *n* a steed.
praise *n* a name for God.
praise-be-thankit *int* an exclamation of thanks to God.
praiss *same as* **priest**⁶.
pran, **prann** *v* **1** to wound, bruise. **2** to squeeze. **3** to scold, reprimand.—*n* **1** a bruise, squeeze. **2** anything crushed to fragments. **3** coarsely ground oatmeal. **4** the bran of oatmeal.
prance *v* **1** to dance, caper. **2** to dance vigorously.
prancer *n* a vigorous dancer.
prang *n* **1** a prong. **2** a prop, support.
prank *v* **1** to play tricks on. **2** to play fast and loose with. **3** to prance.
pranket *n* a childish prank.
pranksome *adj* full of pranks, lively.
pranning *same as* **pran**.
prap *n* **1** a prop. **2** a molehill. **3** a tall chimney stalk. **4** a mark.—*v* **1** to prop. **2** to set up as a mark. **3** to aim at, throw at a mark. **4** to assist. **5** to pelt.
prapper *n* a prop, support.
prappin *n* a game in which stones are thrown at a mark.
prap-prap *v* (*used of tears*) to trickle, to roll quickly down in drops.
prat, **prate**, **pratt** *n* **1** a trick. **2** a roguish or wicked act.—*v* to become restive, as a horse, etc.
pratfu' *adj* **1** tricky. **2** (*of children*) mischievous.
pratick, **prattick**, **prattik** *n* **1** practice. **2** legal procedure. **3** a precedent. **4** a piece of policy. **5** an experiment. **6** a project. **7** a mischievous trick. **8** a trick of legerdemain. **9** a warlike exploit. **10** an achievement of stratagem or policy. **11** any wicked act.
prattle *v* (*used of a stream*) to flow noisily.
pratty *adj* tricky, mischievous.
prawn *same as* **pran**.
prawta *n* a potato.
preace, **preas** *v* **1** to press. **2** to importune. **3** to endeavour, make an effort.—*n* **1** pressure, trouble. **2** a difficulty.
preaching *n* **1** a sermon. **2** a religious service, especially at a Communion season.
preaching-tent *n* a covered erection for an open-air pulpit at a Communion season.
preceese *adj* precise, particular.—*adv* precisely, exactly.
precent *v* to lead the singing as a preceptor.
precentor *n* an official in the Presbyterian church who was appointed to lead the singing of the congregation.
precept *n* **1** a legal injunction. **2** a written order from a superior. **3** an order to pay money.
precognition *n* **1** a preliminary judicial examination of witnesses. **2** a legal term.
precognosce *v* **1** to make preliminary judicial investigation of a case by examination of witnesses. **2** a legal term.
precunnance *n* an understanding, condition.
predick *v* to predict.
predominant *n* a dominant passion or sin.
pree *v* **1** to prove, experience, venture upon. **2** to attain. **3** to taste, partake of. **4** to give relish to. **5** to kiss. **6** to stop at a place to try for fish.—*n* a taste, a small portion.
preeay *int* a call to calves.
preef, **prief** *n* proof.
preeint *n* **1** proof, experience. **2** a testing, tasting. **3** a taste, bite, sup. **4** a tippling.
preek *same as* **prick**.
preekin *same as* **prickin**.
preen¹ *n* **1** a pin. **2** a fish hook. **3** (*in pl*) a game played

with pins lifted from the ground by wetted thumbs.—*v* to pin.

preen[2] *v* **1** to deck oneself out. **2** to dress the hair.

preen-cod, ~-cushion *n* a pincushion.

preen-heid *n* a pinhead.

preen-heidit *adj* small-brained.

preen-holed *adj* pricked by a pin.

preen-hook *n* a fish hook.

preening *adj* (*used of water*) just at the boiling point, when small bubbles like pinpoints shoot to the surface.

preen-point *n* a pinpoint.

preen's-worth *n* a pin's worth.

prees *n* a crowd, a press—*v* to press.

preest *n* a minister.

preest-cat *same as* **priest-cat**.

preeve *v* **1** to prove. **2** to try, test. **3** to taste. **4** to experience, enjoy. **5** to meddle with.—*n* a taste.

preface *n* **1** profession, pretence. **2** a short explanation of the verses of a psalm given by the minister before they were sung at the beginning of the service.—*v* to give such a preface.

preferment *n* preference.

pregnancy *n* fullness, ripeness, richness of promise.

pregnant *adj* **1** full, complete. **2** rich in promise. **3** clever. **4** solid, weighty.

prein *same as* **preen**.

preise *same as* **prees**.

prejinctly *adv* with minute nicety.

prejink, prejinct *same as* **perjink**.

prejinkitie *n* minute nicety or accuracy.

prejinkness, prejinctness *n* **1** niceness. **2** insistence on trifles.

prejudge *v* **1** to prejudice. **2** to be to the prejudice of.

prejudice *n* injury, damage.

premit *v* to premise.

premunitories *n* premonitory symptoms of illness.

prent *n* **1** print. **2** a pat of butter marked with a die. **3** (*in pl*) newspapers.—*adj* printed.

prent-buik *n* a printed book.

prentice-foy *n* a feast at the end of an apprenticeship.

prentice-haun' *n* **1** a novice. **2** a novice's effort.

prequeer *same as* **parqueer**.

presairve *v* to preserve.

presbytery *n* a kind of church court or council in the Presbyterian church to which several churches in an area each send a minister and one elder.

prescript *n* a doctor's prescription.

prescrive, prescryre *v* to prescribe.

present *n* a white speck on a fingernail, as an augury of a gift.—*v* to bring before a judge.—*phr* **present to** (*used of a pistol*) to present at.

presently *adv* just now.

preserve *v* used in exclamation of surprise.—*n* (*in pl*) spectacles used to preserve the sight but magnifying little or nothing.

preses *n* a president or chairman.

press *v* **1** to crowd a room, etc. **2** to urge a guest to eat or drink.—*n* **1** a squeeze, pressure. **2** a wall cupboard with shelves, etc.

press-bed *n* a box bed with doors.

press-door *n* the door of a wall cupboard.

pressfu' *n* what fills a press (qv).

press-gang *n* a group of romping children.

prestable *adj* payable.

Prestoune-ale *n* Prestonpans beer.

pret *same as* **prat**.

pretfu' *adj* full of tricks.

prethy *int* prithee!

prettick, prettikin *same as* **pratick**.

pretty *adj* **1** small. **2** small and neat. **3** handsome, well-made. **4** bold, stalwart. **5** warlike. **6** polite, cultured. **7** fine, excellent. **8** considerable. **9** insignificant, petty.—*adv* **1** prettily. **2** tolerably.—*phr* **pretty little girl of mine** a children's singing game.

pretty dancers *n* the aurora borealis.

Pretty Nancy *n* the London pride.

prevade *v* to neglect.

preveen *v* **1** to prevent, hinder. **2** to anticipate. **3** to interpose in another judge's jurisdiction.

prevention *n* (*a legal term*) the interposition of one judge in another's jurisdiction.

preventive-man *n* a coastguard.

prestry *n* a presbytery.

price *v* to ask in marriage.—*n in phr* **to speer a woman's price** to ask her in marriage.

pricle *n* a small or low price.

prick *n* **1** a wooden bodkin or pin for fastening one's clothes. **2** a pike. **3** an iron spike.—*v* **1** to pin. **2** to fasten. **3** to discover a witch by searching for and pricking the supposed devil's marks on her person. **4** (*used of cattle*) to run fast, startle (qv) in hot weather, from the torment of flies, etc. **5** to dress gaudily, adorn. **6** to stimulate. **7** to copy music in manuscript. **8** to stick. **9** to set forward prominently.

pricker *n* **1** the basking shark. **2** a contemptuous name for a tailor. **3** one who discovered witches by pricking. *See* **prick**.

prick-haste *n* hot haste.

prickie-and-jockie *n* a child's game played with pins, like odds or evens.

prickie-sockey *n* the game of prickie-and-jockie (qv).

prickin *n* a method of killing oxen, etc, with a sharp chisel driven home on the neck behind the animal's head.—*adj* **1** sharp-pointed, piercing. **2** fond of dress. **3** conceited. **4** forward.

prickle *v* **1** (*used of the hair*) to stand up. **2** to have a pricking sensation.—*n* **1** a pricking sensation. **2** a muzzle set with projecting nails. **3** a tool used by bakers for pricking holes in bread. **4** the crampit or perforated sheet iron on which a curler stands to play.

prickly-tang *n* the *Fucus serratus*.

prickmaleerie *adj* stiff, precise.

prickmedainty, prickmadenty, prickmy-dainty *adj* finical in language and manners, conceited. —*n* one who is finical in dress and carriage.

prick's-worth *n* anything of the lowest imaginable value.

prick-the-clout-loon *n* a nickname for a tailor.

prick-the-garter *n* a cheating game played at fairs.

prick-the-loops *n* the same cheating game played at fairs.

prick-the-louse *n* a contemptuous designation of a tailor.

pride *v* to be proud of, take pride in.

prided *adj* proud.

priding *n* the pride of something or somewhere, one of whom others are proud.

prie *same as* **pree**.

prief *same as* **preeve**.

priest[1] *n* **1** used of a presbyterian minister. **2** *in phr* **to be one's priest** to kill one.

priest[2] *n* a strong but ineffectual inclination to go to stool.

priest-cat *n* a children's or fireside game, played with a stick made red in the fire and handed round.

priest-dridder *n* the dread of priests.

priest's pintle *n* the rose root.

prieve *same as* **preeve**.

prig, prigg *v* **1** to importune, plead. **2** to haggle. **3** to beat down the price.—*n* entreaty, pleading.

prigger *n* **1** one who beats down the price of an article. **2** an importunate person.

prigging *n* **1** haggling. **2** entreaty.

prigmedainty *same as* **prick-medainty**.

prignickitie *same as* **pernickety**.

priler *n* a marble that, on striking another, spins round in the place of contact.

prim *v* **1** to close firmly. **2** to press closely or primly.

primadainty *same as* **prickmedainty**.

primanaire *n* trouble, confusion.

primar *n* the *primerius*, or principal, of a college or university.

primariat *n* the principalship of a college or university.

prime[1] *adj* **1** ready, eager. **2** primed with liquor.—*adv* capitally.—*n* the best.

prime[2] *v* **1** to fill, load. **2** to intoxicate, excite with drink. **3** to excite to the point of an outburst of temper.

primely *adv* capitally, very well.

primp *v* **1** to dress smartly or affectedly. **2** to deck. **3** to behave prudishly or affectedly.—*n* a person of stiff, affected manner.

primpie *adj* affected in dress or manner.—*n* an affected person.

primpit *adj* **1** primpie (qv). **2** pursed-up, primly set. **3** ridiculously stiff in demeanour.

primpsie, primsie *adj* **1** demure, precise. **2** affected.

prin, prine *same as* **preen**[1].

principal *adj* (*used of the weather*) excellent, prime.

pringle *n* a small silver coin about the value of a penny.

prinkin' *n* the act of twinkling or shining brightly.

prinkle *v* **1** to tingle, prickle. **2** to touch. **3** to cause to tingle. **4** (*used of a boiling pot*) to send up small bubbles.

prinkle *n* a young coalfish.

prinkling *n* a tingling sensation arising from stoppage of the circulation of the blood.

print *n* **1** a pat of butter impressed with a die. **2** (*in pl*) newspapers.—*adj* printed.

priperty miss *n* a children's singing and dancing game.

prise *v* to wrench, force open.—*n* **1** a lever. **2** a push with a lever.

prison *v* to imprison.

prisoners, prisoners'-relief *n* the game of prisoners' base.

prisoning, prisonment *n* imprisonment.

privado *n* a confidential private supporter.

privates, privities *n* the privy parts.

priving *n* a tasting. *See* **preeve**.

privy, privy-saugh *n* the privet.

prization *n* valuation.

prize[1] *v* to set a value on, appraise.

prize[2] *v* to capture, to seize as a prize.

prizer *n* an appraiser.

proadge *v* to push with a stick.

prob *v* **1** to probe. **2** pierce, stab. **3** to lance. **4** to prod.—*n* **1** a prod. **2** a jog.

probable *adj* provable.

probationer *n* a licensed preacher eligible for a settled charge and ordination.

process *v* **1** to bring to trial. **2** to raise an action in a court. **3** to try judicially.

prochy *same as* **proochy**.

prockie *int* a call to horses.

proctrie *n* procuration.

procurator fiscal *n* an official who institutes and carries on criminal proceedings in the inferior courts in Scotland.

procutor *n* **1** a procurator. **2** a solicitor.

prod[1] *n* a prodigal.

prod[2] *v* **1** to stir about, shuffle. **2** to jog.—*n* **1** a wooden skewer. **2** a prick with a pointed instrument. **3** a stake. **4** a thorn, prickle. **5** a sting. **6** a craw-prod (qv) or pin fixed on the top of a gable to which the ropes fastening the thatch of a cottage were attached. **7** a house-thatcher. **8** a poke, a stir.

prod[3] *v* to move with short steps like a child.

proddle *v* to prick, goad, stab.

prodie *n* **1** a toy. **2** a trinket.

prodigious *adj* prodigal, very wasteful.

prodin *n* **1** a child's foot. **2** a small foot.

proditor *n* (*a legal term*) a traitor, a betrayer.

prodle *v* to move quickly with short steps.—*n* a small horse that takes short steps.

prodler *n* a small horse, one that prodles. *See* **prodle**.

profane *v* to swear.

profession *n* **1** a religious denomination. **2** a yearly examination formerly held in some of the universities as to the progress of the students during the preceding year.

professionist *n* a professing Christian whose profession is an empty one.

professor *n* **1** a professing Christian. **2** one who claims an unusual amount of religious faith and fervour.

proffer *n* **1** an offer of marriage. **2** a tender of services.

profit *n* the expected yield of milk or butter, etc.

profite *adj* **1** exact. **2** clever.

prog, progg *v* **1** to probe. **2** to prod, prick. **3** to stir up, poke.—*n* **1** a goad. **2** a prick. **3** a probe. **4** a spike. **5** a thorn, prickle. **6** an arrow. **7** a sting. **8** a poke, thrust. **9** a pointed sarcasm, a retort. **10** food.

proggles *n* the spines of a hedgehog.

progne *n* the swallow.

prognostic, prognostication *n* an almanac.

prog-staff *n* an iron-pointed staff.

progue *same as* **prog**.

proitle *v* **1** to stir. **2** to poke out trout from under banks.

projeck *n* **1** a project. **2** resource.

proke *v* **1** to poke. **2** to poke the fire.

proker *n* a poker.

prokitor *n* a procurator, solicitor.

proll *v in phr* **to proll thumbs** to lick and strike thumbs in confirmation of a bargain.

promiscuously *adv* by chance, casually.

promish *v* to promise.

promoval *n* promotion, furtherance.

promove, promuve *v* **1** to promote, further. **2** to prompt.

pron *same as* **pran**.

pronack *n* **1** a fragment, splinter. **2** a crumb. **3** a crumb of dough in kneading oatmeal.

prone *same as* **pran**.

pronn *n* provisions.

pronning *n* a bruise, a squeeze.

prontag *same as* **pronack**.

proo *int* **1** a call to oxen to come near. **2** a gentle call to a horse.

proochy *int* a call to a cow or oxen.

proochy-lady, ~-madame *int* a call to a cow.

prood *adj* proud.

proof *n* **1** a scripture text proving a doctrine, especially in the Shorter Catechism. **2** a proof text. **3** a mode of ascertaining the amount of grain in a corn stack when it is to be sold.

proof a-shot *adj* shot-proof.

proof-barley, ~-corn *n* barley or corn from selected sheaves.

proof-man *n* a person appointed to determine the amount of grain in a stack.

proof of lead *or* **shot** *n* a fancied protection from leaden bullets by witchcraft.

proonach *same as* **pronack**.

proop *same as* **poop**.

prop *same as* **prap**.

propale *v* to publish, proclaim abroad.

proper *adj* **1** thorough, complete. **2** excellent, fine. **3** well-made or grown.

property *n* a good quality, as opposed to a failing.

prophet's chamber *n* a room occupied by a probationer or minister going from home on duty.

propine, propyne *v* **1** to present, give. **2** to propitiate. **3** to pledge in drinking. **4** to touch glasses.—*n* **1** a gift, a gift in recognition of services. **2** drink money. **3** the power of giving. **4** disposal.

propone *v* **1** to bring forward a legal defence. **2** to propose. **3** to lay down.

proportion *n* the district in a parish under the care of an elder for visitation.

proppit *adj* marked out, appointed.

proqueer *same as* **parqueer**.

prorogat *adj* used of a jurisdiction to which a defendant submits willingly, though it be not altogether otherwise competent.

prose *v* to put into prose.

prose-folk *n* people who talk in prose.

prose-hash *n* a prosy fool or blockhead.
proselyte *v* to proselytize, bring over to one's views or ways.
prospect, prospect-glass *n* a telescope.
pross *v* 1 to give oneself airs. 2 to behave overbearingly.
prossie *adj* annoyingly nice and particular in dress or work.
prostrate *v* to prostitute.
prot *same as* **prat**.
protick, prottik *same as* **pratick**.
protty¹ *same as* **pratty**.
protty² *same as* **pretty**.
prou *same as* **proo**.
proud¹ *adj* 1 glad, pleased. 2 protuberant. 3 (*used of the projection in a haystack during building whence it needs dressing; of a roof*) highly pitched.
proud² *v* to prod.
proudful *adj* 1 full of pride. 2 (*used of skins*) swollen by the operation of lime.
proudish *adj* rather proud.
proudness *n* (*used of skins*) the state of being swollen out.
prove *same as* **preeve**.
proven *v, adj* 1 proved. 2 (*a legal term*) attested.
provend, provand *n* 1 provender. 2 provisions.
proverb *v* to quote proverbs.
proves' *same as* **provost**.
provide *v* 1 to furnish a bride's outfit of dress, household linen, etc, and also the bridegroom's contribution. 2 to promote.
providing *n* a bride's outfit, trousseau.
provo' *same as* **provost**.
provokesome *adj* provoking.
provoking *adj* tempting the appetite.
provokshon *n* provocation.
provost *n* the chief magistrate of a burgh.
provostry *n* a provost's tenure of office.
prow *same as* **proo**.
prowan *n* provender.
prowie *n* a cow.
prowse *same as* **pross**.
prowsie *same as* **prossie**.
pru, prui, prroo *int* a call to cattle.
prutchee *same as* **proochy**.
prute no *int* an exclamation of contempt.
prove *same as* **preeve**.
pry¹ *n* the carex grass.
pry² *n* 1 refuse, small trash. 2 inferior vegetables.
prym *same as* **prime**².
pryze *same as* **prize**¹.
psalm *n in phr* **to take up the psalm** to act as preceptor.
ptru, ptroo, ptrui *same as* **proo**.
ptruch, ptruchie *same as* **proochy**.
ptrueai, ptrua, ptrumai, ptruita *int* a call to cattle.
pu' *v* to pull.—*n* a pull.
puady *same as* **puddy**.
public *n* a public house, inn.—*adj* adapted to the times.
public room *n* a reception room.
public school *n* a school under the auspices of the local authority as opposed to a private, fee-paying school.
publisht *adj* plump.
puchal, puchil *adj* 1 well-off, thriving. 2 of small stature. 3 neat. 4 conceited. 5 consequential.
pucker *n* 1 a state of perplexity, agitation, etc. 2 a difficulty, confusion.
puck-hary *n* a certain sprite or hobgoblin.
puckle *n* a small quantity.
pud¹ *n* a pudding.
pud² *n* 1 the belly. 2 a plump, healthy child. 3 an endearing name for a child.
pud³ *n* an ink-holder.
pud⁴ *n* an innkeeper.
pudden band *n* catgut.
pudder *n* 1 bustle. 2 to-do. 3 pother.
puddie *n* a fondling term for a child. *See* **pud**¹.

puddill *n* 1 a pedlar's pack. 2 a pedlar's wallet.
pudding, puddin *n* 1 (*in pl*) the intestines. 2 the intestines of a pig, etc, filled with various ingredients.
pudding bree, ~ broo *n* the water or broth in which puddings have been boiled.
pudding-heidit *adj* stupid, thick-headed.
pudding-leather *n* the stomach.
pudding-leggie *n* a fat, chubby leg.
pudding pin *n* a skewer or pin for pricking puddings when boiling.
pudding prick *n* a pudding pin (qv).
puddle *n* 1 a state of disorder or perplexity. 2 the act of working in such a state. 3 a slow, dirty, untidy worker.—*v* 1 to walk through puddles or on muddy roads or on marshy ground. 2 to play with hands and feet in water. 3 to work dirtily and untidily. 4 to engage laboriously and frivolously in the popish ceremonies. 5 to tipple.
puddling *adj* 1 weak, trifling. 2 untidy, dirty.
puddock *same as* **paddock**.
puddock-pony *n* a tadpole.
pud-dow *n* a pigeon.
puddy *same as* **padda**.
puddy *n* 1 a kind of cloth, paduasoy.
pudge *n* 1 a small house, a hut. 2 anything small and confined. 3 a short, thickset, fat person or animal. 4 anything short and fat.
pudgel *adj* fond of good living.
pudget *n* a short, fat person.—*adj* 1 short, fat, corpulent. 2 inclined to feed well.
pudgettie *adj* 1 short and fat. 2 having a large belly.
pudgick *n* a short, fat person or animal.—*adj* short and fat, corpulent.
pudgy *adj* podgy, short and fat.
pudill *same as* **puddle**.
pudjel *n* a fat, round person.
pue *same as* **pew**.
pueshen *n* poison.
puff *n* 1 breath, one's wind. 2 panting. 3 flattery.—*v* 1 to pant. 2 to boast, brag.—*adv* in a breath, all at once.
puffer *n* one who bids at a sale, not to purchase but only to raise the price, one who 'sweetens'.
puffery *n* puffing advertisements.
puffing *n* pastry puffs.
puffle *v* to puff up, swell.
puff-the-wind *n* bellows.
puft *n* a puff of wind.
pug¹ *n* 1 a monkey. 2 a small locomotive engine.
pug² *v* to pull.
puggled *adj* exhausted, worn-out
puggy *n* 1 a monkey. 2 a drunken man.—*v* to play tricks, befool.
puggy *v* (*with* **up**) to show temper.
puggy-like, pug-like *adj* like a monkey.
pugh *int* pooh!
puh *same as* **pew**.
pui *int in phr* **pui ho, pui hup!** calls to calves.
puik *same as* **pook**.
puin *same as* **poind**.
puint *n* a point.
puir *adj* poor.—*v* to impoverish.
puirtith *same as* **poortith**.
puist¹ *adj* 1 in comfortable circumstances. 2 snug and self-satisfied.—*n* one who is thick and heavy.
puist² *same as* **poost**.
puist-body *n* a person in easy circumstances.
puistie *adj* in easy circumstances.
puk *same as* **pook**.
puke *same as* **pouk**².
pulchrie *adj* beautiful.
pule¹ *n* a puff of smoke.—*v* to puff out smoke.
pule² *v* 1 to eat without appetite. 2 to sneak off.
pulicate *same as* **pollicate**.
pull *v* to trim the sides of a rick by pulling out the projecting straw.

pulley *n* a wooden frame, used to dry clothes inside and consisting of long parallel horizontal bars, the frame being suspended from a ceiling and raised and lowered by a rope.

pullion *n* a saddle.

pullisee, pullishee *same as* **polly-shee**.

pull-ling *n* the mosscrop, cotton grass.

pulloch *n* a young crab.

pully *same as* **poullie**[1].

puloch *n* a patch, a clout.

pult *n* a dirty, lazy woman.—*v* to go about in a lazy, dirty manner.

pultie *n* **1** a short-bladed knife. **2** one that has been broken and has had a new point ground on it.

pultring *adj* **1** rutting. **2** lascivious,.

pultron *n* a poltroon.

pultrous *adj* lustful, lascivious.

pumfil, pumfle *same as* **pumphel**.

pump[1] *n* a beer shop.

pump[2] *v* to break wind backwards.—*n* wind broken backwards.

pumphel pumppil *n* **1** a railed-in enclosure for cattle. **2** a square church pew.—*v* to enclose cattle in a pumphel.—*adj* enclosed, boxed-in.

pumpit *adj* **1** hollow. **2** (*of trees*) rotten at the core.

pumrose *same as* **pimrose**.

pun[1] *n* a sham.

pun[2] *n* a pound in weight or money.

punce[1] *v* **1** to beat. **2** to push by striking. **3** to push with the head or a stick.—*n* **1** a blow with the fist. **2** a thrust.

punce[2] *v* to pierce or punch with a bradawl.

punch[1] *v* **1** to strike with the foot. **2** to jog with the elbow.—*n* a slight push, a jog.

punch[2] *same as* **pinch**[2].

punch[3] *adj* thick and short.

Punch and Polly *n* a Punch and Judy show.

punchbowl *n* *in phr* **the bottom of the punchbowl 1** a figure in an old dance. **2** a girls' dancing and singing game.

punchik *n* any person, animal or thing that is short, stout and strong.

punckin *n* the footsteps of horses or cattle in soft ground.

punctual *adv* **1** precisely. **2** especially.

punctuality *n* **1** a detail, point. **2** nicety, technicality.

pund[1] *same as* **pound**[2].

pund[2] *n* a pound in money or weight.

pundar *n* a person who has charge of hedges, woods, etc, and who impounds straying cattle.

pundie *n* **1** a small tin mug for heating liquids. **2** a drinking jug. **3** drink, liquor.

pundler, punler *n* **1** a stalk of peas bearing two pods. **2** one who watches fields or woods to prevent thefts and impound straying cattle.

punger *n* the large edible crab.

punish *v* **1** to reduce much in cutting or dressing, a workman's term. **2** to devour. **3** to eat or drink heavily of.

punk-hole *n* a peat pot (qv) or hole in a moss.

punkin *same as* **punckin**.

punky *n* the game of kypes at marbles.

puns *n* the duffel grass.

punse *v* to emboss.

punsh *v* to punch.

punyie, punzie *v* to prick, spur.—*n* a prick.

puock *same as* **pock**[1].

pup-gallanter *n* a coxcomb who plays the gallant.

puppie show *n* a puppet show.

puppish *adj* puppyish.

pur *same as* **purr**.

purchase *n* **1** an amour. **2** an intrigue. **3** one's wits. —*v* to obtain, procure, secure.

purcill, pursill *n* the edible fucus, *Fucus esculentus*.

pure *same as* **puir**.

pure pride *n* ostentatious grandeur without means of supporting it.

purfeit, purfittie *adj* short-necked, corpulent, of asthmatical make.

purfile, purfloe *n* **1** an edging. **2** the border of a woman's dress.—*v* to purfle.

purfillit, purfied *adj* short-winded.

purfling *adj* causing shortness of breath.

purge *v* **1** to acquit. **2** to clear a court of those who are not members.

purie *same as* **pourie**.

purify *v* to fulfil the conditions of a bond.

purl[1] *n* **1** a portion of the dung of sheep or horses. **2** dried cow dung used for fuel.

purl[2] *v* **1** to spin round. **2** to twine, curl. **3** to grope for potatoes. **4** to fumble. **5** to form the stitch that produces the fur (qv) in a stocking.—*n* the seam stitch in a knitted stocking.

purled-steek, purlin-steek *n* the stitch that produces the fur (qv) in a stocking.

purled stocking *n* a ribbed or furred (qv) stocking. *See* **fur**.

purlicue *same as* **parlicue**.

purlie, purlie-pig *same as* **pirlie**[1].

purlusion *n* anything noxious or disgusting.—*v* to render noxious.

purn *n* a quill or pirn of yarn. *See* **pirn**.

purpie[1] *n* purslane.

purpie[2] *adj* of purple colour.—*n* the colour purple.

purpie fever *n* typhus.

purple *n* blood.—*v* to appear as purple.

purply *adj* purple.

purpose *n* **1** neatness, tidiness. **2** exactness. **3** taste. —*adj* **1** exact, methodical. **2** neat, neatly dressed. **3** well-adjusted.

purposedly *adv* purposely.

purpose-like *adj* **1** suitable to its purpose. **2** (*used of a woman*) capable, managing.—*adv* suitably to an end.

purposeness *n* **1** neatness, exactness. **2** method. **3** capacity.

purr[1] *v* **1** to prick, stab. **2** to poke. **3** to kick.—*n* **1** a kick. **2** a stab. **3** the sound of a sharp instrument piercing the flesh.

purr[2] *n* a buzzing sound.

purring-iron *n* a poker.

purry *n* a kind of porridge or pudding made of kail and oatmeal.

purse-browed *adj* having a pursed-up forehead.

purse-hingers *n* **1** purse strings. **2** purse strings attaching a purse to the person.

purselin *n* purslane.

purselled *adj* (*used of the mouth*) pursed.

purse-moo *n* **1** the purse mouth. **2** a boat-shaped cloud.

purse-penny *n* any coin kept in the purse and neither exchanged nor given away.

purse-pest *n* **1** a highwayman. **2** a pickpocket.

purser *n* a town treasurer.

pursikie *n* **1** a small purse. **2** a small fortune.

pursill[1] *n* as much money as fills a purse.

pursill[2] *same as* **purcill**.

pursuable *adj* that may be prosecuted at law.

pursual *n* **1** most earnest urging. **2** a prosecution. **3** a trial, attempt.

pursue *v* **1** to walk or run with great energy. **2** to assault. **3** to urge earnestly. **4** to prosecute at law.

pursuer *n* a plaintiff, prosecutor in an action in a civil court.

pursuit *n* **1** an assault. **2** a prosecution.

pursy *adj* purse-proud.

purvey *n* refreshments provided after a funeral, at a wedding reception, etc.

push *n* pressure of work, etc.

pushen, pushion, pushon, pusion *same as* **pousion**.

pushlock, puslick *n* **1** cows' dung left in the fields. **2** dung of cattle, horses and sheep.

push-pin *n* a child's game, played with three pins.

pussickie *n* **1** a kitten. **2** a fondling term for a child.

pussy-bawdrons *n* a cat.
pussy-nickle *n* the method of propelling a marble by placing it in the hollow made by the bent forefinger and the thumb.
put[1] *v* 1 to send. 2 to compel.
put[2] *n* a dimple. 2 a hollow in the cheek or chin.
put about *v* 1 to put on clothes. 2 to annoy, inconvenience. 3 to vex, harass. 4 to disconcert. 5 to report, circulate. 6 to publish.
put afore *v* to put in front of.
put against *v* to oppose.
put at *v* 1 to set to, apply oneself. 2 to dun. 3 to appeal for help. 4 to push against.
put away *v* to lay by, save.
put-back *n* a disadvantage, drawback.
put-by *n* 1 a makeshift, a substitute. 2 a hoard, a nest egg.— *v* 1 to lay carefully aside. 2 to hoard, save. 3 to bury. 4 to support, satisfy, entertain. 5 to defray cost. 6 to delay, postpone. 7 to divert from a purpose, etc. 8 to hold out beyond. 9 to serve one's turn, do for an occasion or as a makeshift.
put by on *v* 1 to serve one's turn. 2 to be satisfied with.
put by oneself *adj* greatly excited.
put down *v* 1 to kill, execute, hang. 2 to bury. 3 *in phr* **to put oneself down** to commit suicide.
put-hand-~, ~-hands-~, ~-in, ~-to, ~-on *v* 1 to lay violent hands on, assault. 2 to kill, to kill oneself.
puther[1] *same as* **peuter**.
puther[2] *n* pewter.
put in *v* 1 to unharness, put in the stable. 2 to advance, deposit or invest money. 3 to pass. 4 to fulfil. 5 to endure. 6 to suffer as punishment. 7 to cart corn, etc, from the field to the farmyard.
put in a foot *v* to hurry.
put in for *v* to tender, give in an offer.
put in the cries *v* to give in for publication the banns of marriage.
put in the pin *v* to give up drinking.
put-off *n* 1 an excuse, evasion, pretext. 2 unnecessary delay.—*v* to squander, waste.
put on *n* a style of dress, clothes.—*v* 1 to clothe, dress. 2 to put or keep on one's hat, cap, etc. 3 to dun. 4 to press, embarrass. 5 to push forward, to hasten with increasing speed. 6 to pretend. 7 to acquire a language. 8 to impute to.
put out *v* 1 to discover. 2 to publish. 3 to make a person known who wishes to be concealed. 4 to exert, put forth. 5 to expend, lay out money. 6 to bake.
put owre *v* 1 to survive, last until. 2 to tide over, suffice for. 3 to swallow.
put past *v* 1 to lay aside, save. 2 to dissuade. 3 to give a distaste to. 4 to exempt one from an imputation or charge.
putt *v* 1 to push, thrust. 2 to butt. 3 to pat. 4 to push gently as a hint. 5 to throw a heavy stone from the shoulder in athletic games. 6 to throb.—*n* 1 a push. 2 a thrust. 3 the recoil of a gun. 4 the act of putting the stone in athletic games. 5 (*used in golf*) a slight push of the ball into a hole. 6 position, ground. 7 attempt, effort. 8 a buttress of a wall. 9 a jetty, a mass of stones placed in a river to divert the current. 10 one's ground or point.
putt and row *n* great exertion.
putten *v, adj* put.
putter[1] *n* 1 one who putts the stone in athletic games. 2 an animal that butts.
putter[2] *n* a small petard or piece of ordnance.
putterling *n* a small petard.
put through *v* to publish, spread abroad.
put til *same as* **put to**.
putting *v, adj* pouting.
putting stane *n* a heavy stone used in putting the stone in athletic games. *See* **putt**.
put to *or* **til** *v* 1 to interrogate straitly. 2 to straiten. 3 to be put out of countenance. 4 to shut, close. 5 to harness, yoke. 6 to put together in order to propagate. 7 to ap-

prentice to a trade or profession. 8 to set to work, begin. 9 to subject to, make to endure or suffer.
puttock *n* the buzzard.
put up *v* 1 to be lodged. 2 to raise, erect. 3 to settle, have a home of one's own. 4 to endure. 5 to vomit. 6 to incite.
put upon *v* 1 to put on one's clothes. 2 to oppress. 3 to impose upon. 4 to put pressure on.—*adj* oppressed, hardly treated.
put up to *v* 1 to incite. 2 to teach, instruct.
puzhun *n* poison.
puzzle *v* 1 to cause intricacy. 2 to get bewildered on a strange road or in a fog.
py[1] *n* a loose riding coat or frock.
py[2] *same as* **pie**[2].
pyaavan *adj* peevish, sickly.
pyaavie *n* a short turn of illness.
pyardie *n* the magpie.
pyat[1] *n* the boy or man who, when a stack begins to taper, is perched on its eaves to catch the sheaves from the fork and toss them to the builder.
pyat[2] *n* 1 a magpie. 2 a forward child. 3 a chatterer.—*adj* 1 piebald. 2 having large white spots. 3 (*of words*) meaningless, chattering. 4 ornate.
pyated *adj* 1 freckled. 2 piebald.
pyat-horse *n* a piebald horse.
pyatie *adj* 1 parti-coloured. 2 freckled. 3 cloudy in appearance.
pyck *n* a pike.
pydile *n* a cone made of rushes, for catching fish.
pye *n* a magpie.—*v* 1 to pry. 2 to peer. 3 to squint.
pyet *same as* **pyat**[2].
pyetty *same as* **pyettie**.
pyfer *same as* **piffer**.
pygral *same as* **pegral**.
pyke[1] *same as* **pick**[6].
pyke[2] *same as* **pike**[2].
pyke[3] *v* to pick.
pyke[4] *same as* **pike**[4].
pyker, pycker *n* one charged with petty theft.
pykering *n* petty theft, pilfering.
pyket, pykeit *adj* (*used of wire*) barbed.
pykie *adj* given to stealing.
pykie-pock *n* chickenpox.
pykin-awl *n* a shoemaker's awl for picking out pegs, etc.
pykis *n* short, withered heath.
pykit, pykeit *adj* meagre-looking. 2 shrunken.
pykle *n* a hayfork.
pyle[1] *n* a Border peel or fortress.
pyle[2] *same as* **pile**[2].
pyle[3] *n* a small quantity.
pyle[4] *n* 1 a blade or stalk of grass. 2 a single grain of corn.
pyne *same as* **pine**.
pyne doublet *n* a hidden coat of mail.
pyne-~, pynt-pig *n* a child's earthenware moneybox.
pyocher *n* a troublesome cough.
pyochter *v* to cough vigorously to get rid of phlegm.
pyock *same as* **pock**[1].
pyotie *same as* **pyatie**.
pyoul *v* 1 to fret, whine. 2 to eat without appetite, little and slowly. 3 to sneak off. 4 (*used of snow*) to fall in a continuous drizzle.—*n* 1 a small bite. 2 a stifled cough.
pyowe *same as* **peeoye**.
pyowter *same as* **pouter**[2].
pyrl *same as* **pirl**.
pyrn *same as* **pirn**.
pyrr *n* 1 the par or samlet. 2 the salmon.
pysent *adj* of light behaviour.
pysert *same as* **peyzart**.
pyslit *same as* **peisled**.
pyssle *n* 1 a thing of no value. 2 a trifle.
pyster *v* to hoard up.
pystery *n* a hoard, anything hoarded up.
pytane *n* 1 a term of endearment. 2 a young child.

Q

qua[1] v (*used in the imperative*) to come away.
qua[2], quaa *same as* quaw.
quaaakin *adj* quaking.
quack *n* an instant.
quacking *adj* quaking.
quad *adj* base, bad, vile.—*n* a bad state.
quadre *v* to square, quadrate.
quadruply *n* 1 a fourth reply. 2 (*used as a legal term*) a defender's rejoinder to a pursuer's triply (qv).—*v* to make such reply or rejoinder.
quaff *n* a draught.—*v* to drink one's health.
quag *n* 1 a quagmire. 2 the soft part of a bog.
quaich[1] *v* to scream wildly.—*n* a wild scream.
quaich[2] *n* a two-eared drinking cup.
quaick *n* a heifer.
quaigh *n* a small, shallow drinking cup with two 'ears' for handles.
quaik *same as* quaick.
quaikin-ash *n* the aspen.
quail *v* 1 to quell. 2 (*used of the wind*) to lull. 3 to quiet down.
quaintance *n* acquaintance.
quair, quaire *n* a quire of paper.
quairn[1] *n* a small stone handmill for grinding corn, a quern.
quairn[2] *n* 1 a grain. 2 a seed. 3 a a small particle.
quairny *adj* 1 granulated. 2 in small particles.
quaist *n* 1 a rogue. 2 a wag.
quaisten *n* a question.—*v* to question.
quaisten-buik *n* the Shorter Catechism.
quait *adj* 1 quiet. 2 secret, private.—*v* to silence.
quaiten *v* 1 to quiet. 2 to assuage pain.
quait-tongued *adj* 1 not talkative. 2 of sober and gentle speech.
quake *same as* quaick.
Quakers' meeting *n* a silent gathering or assembly.
quaking, quakkin *adj* (*used of a bog*) moving, trembling.
quaking ash *n* the aspen.
quaking bog *n* a moving quagmire.
quaking qua *n* a moving quagmire.
qualify *v* 1 to prove. 2 to authenticate. 3 to make good. 4 to testify to.
quality *n* 1 the gentry. 2 the upper classes. 3 reservation, condition.
quality binding *n* a sort of worsted tape used for binding the borders of carpets.
quall *v* 1 to quell. 2 to be subdued. 3 to quail.
quantance *n* acquaintance.
quar *same as* quair.
quarnelt *adj* having angles.
quarrant *n* a kind of shoe made of untanned leather.
quarrel *n* 1 a stone quarry. 2 materials from a quarry.—*v* 1 to quarry. 2 to raise stones from a quarry.
quarrel *v* 1 to challenge. 2 to reprove, check. 3 to object to, question.
quarrel-head *n* the head of a dart for a crossbow.
quarrellable *adj* open to challenge, challengeable.
quarrelsome *adj* 1 fault-finding. 2 litigious. 3 fond of contradicting.
quarry-hole *n* a disused quarry.
quartan *n* 1 a quart. 2 a quarter.
quarter *n* 1 the quarter of a circular oatcake. 2 a quarter of a pound.
quarter cake *n* a farl (qv) or fourth part of a circular oatcake.
quarterer *n* 1 a respectable beggar who was furnished with lodgings in parish. 2 a lodger.
quarter-ill *n* a disease affecting one of the quarters of sheep or young cattle.

quartering house *n* a lodging, quarters.
quarterly *adv* through each quarter of a town.
quarter-wife *n* a poor woman quartered in a house by the parish.
quartril *same as* quarter-ill.
quat[1] *v* 1 to quit, give over. 2 to abandon. 3 to resign. 4 to exonerate. 5 to stop working.
quat[2] *v* omitted.—*adj* rid, free.
quate *adj* quiet.
quaten *v* to quiet.
quattit *v* quit, quitted.
quauk *v* to quake.
quaukin-aish *n* the aspen.
quave *v* (*used of a hill or incline*) to go up or down zigzag.
quaver *n* a tremulous cry or voice.
quaw *n* 1 a quagmire. 2 a hole out of which peats have been cut. 3 an old pit overgrown with grass, etc.
quay[1] *same as* qua[1].
quay[2] *same as* quey.
quay-neb *n* the point of a pier, the projecting part of a quay.
quazie *adj* queasy.
que *same as* quey.
queach *same as* quaich.
queak *v* to squeak or cry like the young of rats, mice, etc.—*n* 1 a gentle squeak. 2 the cry of the young of small animals.
quean-bairn, --lassie *n* 1 a female child. 2 a young girl.
quease *v* to wheeze.
quech *same as* quaich.
qued *same as* quad.
quee-beck *n* the cry of a startled grouse.
queecher *v* to work lazily and unsatisfactorily.
queed[1] *n* 1 a tub. 2 a vessel formerly used for holding fish. 3 a wooden chamber pot.
queed[2] *n* the cud.
queedie *n* 1 a small tub. 2 a small wooden chamber pot, used in a nursery.
queedie *n* the cud.
queek *same as* queak.
queel *v* to cool.—*n* 1 a cooling. 2 what cools one.
queem *adj* 1 pleasant. 2 calm, smooth. 3 neat. 4 filled up to the general level. 5 close and tight, fitting exactly. 6 deep.—*v* to fit exactly.
queemer *n* 1 one skilled in fitting joints. 2 a wheedler.
queemly *adj* exactly adapted.—*adv* calmly, smoothly.
queemness *n* exact adaptation.
queen[1] *n* 1 a queen. 2 a girl, a young woman. 3 a loose woman. 4 a term of endearment or of contempt.
queen[2] *n* a quern.
Queen Anne *n* 1 a girls' rhyming game in which a ball is used. 2 a gun such as was used in Queen Anne's reign.
Queen Anne's thrissel *n* the musk thistle.
queen cake *n* a small sweet cake made without pastry.
queen's chair *n* a method of carrying a person.
queen's cushion *n* a queen's chair (qv).
queen's cushion *n* the cropstone.
queen's head *n* a postage stamp.
queentra *same as* quintry.
queeple *v* to quack like a duckling.—*n* a duckling's quack.
queer[1] *n* 1 the choir or chancel of a church. 2 a vault in a church. 3 the persons composing a choir.
queer[2] *adj* entertaining, amusing, humorous.—*adv* queerly.—*n* (*in pl*) news, any things odd or strange.—*v* 1 to puzzle. 2 to treat curiously.
queerach *v* 1 to work weakly and triflingly. 2 to nurse too daintily.—*n* 1 working in a weak and trifling way. 2 overnursing daintily.

queer-gotten *adj* used of uncertain parentage.
queerikens *n* the hips.
queerish *adj* **1** feeling rather unwell. **2** rather queer.
queerishness *n* an uneasy sensation.
queersome *adj* rather queer.
queerways *adj* strange, nervous, squeamish.
queery[1] *n* **1** a queer thing. **2** a curious circumstance.
queery[2] *n* a query.
queese *v* to wheeze.
queesitive *adj* inquisitive.
queesitiveness *n* inquisitiveness, curiosity.
queest[1] *v* did cast.
queest[2] *n* the wood pigeon.
queet *n* **1** the ankle. **2** a gaiter.
queeter *v* to work in a weak, trifling manner.—*n* working in a weak, trifling manner.
queeth *n* the coalfish in the second year.
queetie *adj* low, mean.
queetilrins *n* **1** gaiters. **2** short leggings.
queezie *adj* queasy.
queez-maddam *n* the French jargonelle pear.
queff, quegh, queich *same as* **quaich**.
queine *same as* **queen**[1].
queir *same as* **queer**.
queit *adj* quiet.
quell *v* **1** to quench, extinguish. **2** to quail. **3** to cease. **4** to grow quiet.
quelt *n* a kilt.
queme *same as* **queem**
quene *same as* **queen**[1].
quentry *same as* **quintry**.
quenyie *n* a corner.
querd *same as* **queed**[1].
quenous *adj* curious.
quern[1] *n* the gizzard of a fowl.
quern[2] *same as* **quairn**[2].
querney *n* a species of rot in sheep.
quernie[1] *same as* **quairny**.
quernie[2] *n* **1** a grain of corn. **2** an indefinite number or quantity.
quernie[3], **quernock** *n* a small quern or stone handmill for grinding corn.
querty *adj* **1** lively, possessing a flow of animal spirits. **2** active.
query *same as* **queery**[2].
quest *v* **1** to search for game. **2** (*used of a dog*) to give tongue on a scent, to hunt.—*n* a request, petition.
question *n* (*in pl*) the Shorter Catechism.
questionary *adj* (*of examinations*) oral, viva voce.
question book *n* the Shorter Catechism.
quet *n* the guillemot.
quey, queyag *n* a heifer until she has had a calf.
queyit *adj* quiet.—*n* rest, quietude.
queyl *n* a haycock.
queyn, queynie *same as* **queen**[1].
quoyoch *n* a heifer.
queyt *same as* **quite**[2].
quhaip, quhawp *n* an evil spirit, a goblin, supposed to haunt the eaves of houses at night on the lookout for evil-doers.
quhey *same as* **quey**.
quhult *n* anything big of its kind.
qui *n* a heifer.
quib *n* **1** a quip. **2** a gibe.
quibow *n* the branch of a tree.
quich *n* a small round-eared cap, worn by women under another and showing only the border.
quicher *n* any needless work in household duties.
quick *adj* piercing, sharp.
quick-and-quidder *adv* quickly, swiftly.
quicken *n* **1** the mountain ash, rowan. **2** the couch grass.
quickenin *n* fermenting ale or beer thrown into ale, porter, etc, that has become dead or stale.
quick-horn *n* a horn taken from a living animal.

quid *n* the cud.
quiddie[1], **quiddie**[2] *same as* **queedie**[1], **queedie**[2].
quide *same as* **queedie**[1].
quie *same as* **quey**.
quierty *same as* **querty**.
quiet *adj* (*used of persons*) concealed, skulking.
quieten *same as* **quaten**.
quietlin-wise *adv* quietly.
quiff *n* a whiff of a pipe, a short smoke.
quile[1] *n* **1** a coal. **2** a burning coal.
quile[2] *n* a haycock.—*v* to pile haycocks.
quill[1] *v* to write.—*n* the throat.
quill[2] *n* **1** a weaver's reed. **2** a bobbin.
quill[3] *n* a bung.
quill-fatt *n* a vat having a bung.
quilt *v* to thrash.
quim *adj* familiar.
quim and cosh *adj* familiarly intimate.
quin *v in phr* **to quin thanks** to give thanks.
quine *same as* **queen**[1].
quinie *n* a young girl.
quinkins *n* **1** the scum or refuse of any liquor. **2** nothing at all.
quinter *n* a ewe in her third year.
quintry, quintra *n* country.
quinzie *same as* **queynie**.
quirk *n* an advantage, not positively illegal but inconsistent with honour and strict honesty.—*v* **1** to cheat. **2** to elude by stratagem.
quirkle *n* a puzzle, the answer to which depends on a catch or quibble.
quirklum *n* a little arithmetical puzzle, the answer to which depends on a quibble.
quirksome *adj* subtle.
quirky *adj* **1** intricate. **2** playful.
quirn *n* a small stone handmill.
quirty *same as* **querty**.
quisquous *adj* **1** nice, perplexing, subtle. **2** difficult to discuss.
quistical *adj* whimsical, fantastic, queer, odd-looking.
quit *same as* **queet**.
quitchie *adj* very or scalding hot.
quit-claim *v* to renounce a claim.
quite[1] *adj* quiet.
quite[2] *n* **1** a coat. **2** a petticoat.
quite[3] *v* **1** to play quoits. **2** to skate. **3** to play at curling.—*n* **1** a quoit. **2** the act of skating.
quiting *n* the game of curling.
quiting stone *n* a curling stone.
quittance *n* riddance.
quiyte *same as* **queet**.
quiz *v* to question closely.
quizzing-glass *n* an eyeglass.
quo' *v* pret quoth.
quoif *n* a cap, mulch (qv), coif.
quoit *same as* **quite**[3].
quoiting stane *n* a curling stone.
quoits *n in phr* **a' oot o' the quoits** quite astray, all wrong.
quorum *n* a company, assemblage
quote *v in phr* **to quote a paper** (*used as a legal term*) to endorse the title of a paper.
quott, quote *n* the portion of goods of one deceased, appointed by law to be paid for the confirmation of his or her testament or for the right of intromitting with his or her property.
quoy, quoyach *same as* **quey**.
qurd *n* **1** a clot of excrement. **2** a term of reproach for a person.
quy, quyach *same as* **quey**.
quyle[1], **quyle**[2] *same as* **quile**[1], **quile**[2].
quyne *same as* **queen**[1].
quynie, quynyie *same as* **queynie**.
quyte[1] *same as* **quite**[2].
quyte[2], **qwyte** *same as* **quite**[3].

R

ra[1] *n* a roe deer.
ra[2] *adj* raw.
raakin *v* to reckon.
raal *adj* real.—*adv* very.
ra'an *adj* riven, torn.
raan *same as* **rowan**[3].
raand *same as* **rand**[1].
raan-fleuk *n* the turbot.
raaze *same as* **raise**[1].
rabate *v* to abate.
rabbie-rinnie-hedge *n* the goosegrass.
rabbit's kiss *n* a penalty in the game of forfeits in which a man and a woman have each to nibble an end of the same piece of straw until their lips meet.
rabblach *n* 1 nonsense. 2 incoherent speech or nonsense. 3 a confused mass. 4 an ill-built wall, etc. 5 a stunted tree.—*v* 1 to rattle off nonsense. 2 to repeat a lesson, etc, carelessly or hastily. 3 (*with* **up**) to build carelessly and in a hurry.
rabble, rable *v* 1 to speak indistinctly and quickly. 2 to gabble. 3 to work hastily or carelessly. 4 to mob riotously.—*n* 1 confused, careless speech. 2 incoherent reading or talking. 3 a gabble. 4 hasty, careless work. 5 a ruinous mass, a building falling to decay. 6 a careless, hurried worker. 7 a foolish story.
rabblement *n* 1 confused talk. 2 chatter.
rabbler, rabler *n* 1 a quick reader. 2 one who speaks or reads indistinctly. 3 a careless, hasty worker. 4 a rioter, mobber.
rabbling *n* 1 the act of mobbing. 2 a violent ejectment.
rabiator, rabiawtor *n* 1 a violent bully. 2 a robber, plunderer.
rabscallion *n* 1 a low, worthless fellow. 2 a tatterdemalion.
race *n* 1 a freight of water from a well. 2 a quick errand. 3 the train of historical narration.
racer *n* 1 a common bull. 2 an attendant at races.
racer-horse *n* a racehorse.
rach *same as* **ratch**[3].
rachan *n* 1 a plaid worn by men. 2 rough cloth from which sailors' dreadnoughts were made. 3 a scarf, cravat.
rachle[1], **rachlie**[1] *same as* **ruckle**[1], **ruckle**[2].
rachled *adj* (*used of faces*) wrinkled, worn.
rachlie *adj* dirty and disorderly.
rachlin *adj* 1 unsettled. 2 hare-brained. 3 noisy, clamorous.
rack[1] *n* 1 a blow. 2 a shock. 3 ruin.
rack[2] *n* (*used of mutton*) the neck or scrag.
rack[3] *n* 1 a racking pain. 2 a wooden shelved frame attached to a wall, for holding plates, etc. (*in pl*) an apparatus for roasting meat. 4 a piece of wood used in feeding a mill. 5 reach, extent. 6 a shallow ford of considerable breadth.—*v* 1 to suspend. 2 to strain. 3 to wrench.
rack[4] *n* the course in curling over which the stones are driven.
rack[5] *v* (*used of the clouds*) to clear.—*n* 1 the foam of the sea. 2 driving clouds, mist, smoke, etc.
rack[6] *same as* **reck**[2].
rack[7] *n* couch grass.
rackabimus *n* a sudden or unexpected stroke or fall.
rackad, rackart *n* 1 a racket, noise. 2 uproar. 3 hurly-burly. 4 reproof. 5 a crashing blow.
rackbone *n* that part of the harness of a twelve-ox plough by which the first pair was connected with the bridle.
rackel *same as* **rackle**[2].
racket *n* 1 a spasm of pain. 2 a smart and violent blow.
racket *n* a dress frock.
racking pin *n* a piece of wood used to tighten ropes.
racking wage *n* a too liberal wage.

rackle[1], *same as* **ruckle**[1].
rackle[2] *same as* **raucle**.
rackle[3] *n* 1 a chain. 2 the chain of a tin pipe lid. 3 the clank of a chain.—*v* 1 to clank rattle. 2 to shake forcibly. 3 to chain. 4 to take the kinks out of a rope for one winding it into a ball.
rackle-handit *adj* 1 careless. 2 headstrong. 3 ready to strike.
rackleness *n* vigorous health and briskness in old age.
rackler *n* a land surveyor.
rackless *adj* reckless.
rackless-handit *adj* reckless, headstrong.
racklessly *adv* recklessly.
rackle-tongued *adj* rough-tongued, harsh of speech.
rackligence *n* accident, chance.
rackmereesle *adv* higgledy-piggledy.
rackon *v* 1 to reckon, suppose. 2 to fancy.
rack-pin *same as* **racking pin**
racks *same as* **rax**[3].
rack-staff, ~-stick *n* a racking pin (qv).
rack-stock *n* 1 a rack. 2 the rack for torture.—*phrs* 1 **tak rack-stock** to claim everything that belongs to one. 2 **tak' one owre the rack stock** to call one to account severely for some mistake.
racky *adj* (*used of the weather*) gusty, stormy.
rad[1], **rade** *adj* afraid, timorous.—*v* to fear.
rad[2] *adj* quick.
raddle *v* to beat soundly with a stick.
rade[1] *same as* **raid**[1].
rade[2] *v* rode.
rade[3] *same as* **rad**[1].
rade goose *n* the barnacle goose.
radgie *same as* **rajie**.
radicle *n* a reticule.
radly *adv* quickly.
rae[1] *same as* **ree**[1].
rae[2] *n* a roe deer.
rael[1] *same as* **rail**[2].
rael[2] *same as* **real**[1].
rael[3] *same as* **ravel**[2].
raeling *same as* **ravelling**.
raem *same as* **ream**[1].
raen[1] *n* a raven.
raen[2] *same as* **rane**[1].
raep *v* to reap.
raeper *n* a reaper.
raff[1] *n* a flying shower.
raff[2] *n* 1 a rank, rapid growth. 2 worthless stuff, refuse. 3 the riffraff. 4 plenty, abundance.—*v* 1 to abound, overflow. 2 to rant, roar. 3 to carouse.—*adj* cheerful. 4 contented.
raffan, raffing *adj* 1 ranting, roaring. 2 merry. 3 carousing. 4 roving. 5 hearty.
raffel *n* doeskin.
raffish *adj* 1 sportive. 2 rough.
raffy *adj* 1 (*of corn*) rank, coarse, rapidly growing. 2 (*of a crop*) thick and thriving. 3 drunken, dissipated. 4 liberal, generous. 5 plentiful.—*n* a large quantity of forced growth, exhausting the soil.
raft *n* 1 a large number or quantity. 2 a crowd.
rag[1], **ragg** *n* 1 a low, worthless person. 2 a contemptuous designation of anything very lean and thin. 3 (*used of corn*) a partial winnowing.—*v* 1 to pierce a fish with the hook in fishing. 2 (*used of corn*) for the ear to show out of the shot blade. 3 to put corn for the first time through a winnowing machine.
rag[2] *v* 1 to tease. 2 to reproach, scold violently, abuse.—*n* 1 rough chaffing. 2 a debate, quarrel. 3 the act of severe reproaching.

ragabanes *n* the skeleton of a fish, etc.

rag-a-bash, rag-a-brash, rag-a-buss, ~-bush *n* **1** a tatterdemalion. **2** a low rascal. **3** a vagabond.—*adj* **1** very poor. **2** mean, paltry, contemptible. **3** good-for- nothing.

rag-a-tag *n* an old horse.

rag-fallow, ~-fauch *n* grassland broken up in the summer after the hay is cut, ploughed three times and then dunged.

ragg *same as* **rag**[1].

ragger *n* a ragman, one who exchanges crockery, etc, for rags.

raggety *adj* ragged, untidy.

raggle[1] *v* **1** to ruffle the skin. **2** (*used in architecture*) to jag, to groove one stone to receive another. **3** to winnow corn partially.—*n* **1** a reglet in architecture. **2** a partial winnowing of corn.

raggle[2] *v* to wrangle, dispute.—*n* a wrangle, a bicker.

raggling, ragling *n* the vacant space between the top of the walls and the slates of a house.

ragglish, raglish *adj* **1** (*used of the weather*) rough, boisterous. **2** harsh, severe. **3** coarse. **4** worthless.

raggy *n* a ragman.—*adj* ragged.

raggy-folks *n* rag-gatherers.

raglat-plane *n* a plane used by carpenters in making a groove for shelves of drawers, etc.

ragnails *n* broken bits of skin round the fingernails.

rag-pock *n* a bag for holding rags, etc.

rag-tag *adj* reduced to rags by drink.

ragweed *n* ragwort, *Senecio*.

raible *same as* **rabble**.

raichie *v* to scold.—*n* the act of scolding.

raid[1] *n* **1** a rapid journey. **2** a ridiculous enterprise or expedition.

raid[2] *n* a road for ships.

raid[3] *same as* **rade**[2].

raid goose *same as* **rade goose**.

raik[1] *same as* **rake**[1].

raik[2] *same as* **reck**[2].

raik[3], **raik**[4] *same as* **rake**[2], **rake**[3].

raik[5] *same as* **reak**[2].

raik[6] *n* a weed that grows around a water spring or in a well.

raiker *same as* **raker**.

raikin *adv* readily.

rail[1] *n* **1** a woman's jacket. **2** an upper garment worn by women. **3** the upper portion of an infant's nightdress.

rail[2] *n* a line or row.—*adj* railed.—*v* **1** to fit with a band, bar or border. **2** to enclose. **3** to set in a row.

rail[3] *v* to rail at, abuse.

rail[4] *same as* **ravel**[2].

railed entangled, ravelled.

rail-ee'd *adj* wall-eyed.

railie, railly *n* a woman's jacket.

raillich *n* a thin, worthless piece of cloth.

rail stick, ~ tree *n* a large beam in a byre (qv), fixed about two feet above the heads of the cows, into which the upper ends of stakes are fixed.

rail-train *n* a railway train.

rail-tree *same as* **rail stick**.

rail-wand *n* the railing of a stair.

raim *same as* **ream**[1].

rain *same as* **rane**[1].

rainbird *n* the green woodpecker.

raing[1] *n* **1** a circle. **2** a circular streak.—*v* to encircle, to streak in a circular manner.

raing[2] *n* a row, a rank.—*v* **1** to rank up. **2** to follow in a line.

rain goose *n* the red-throated diver.

rainie *n* idle, unmeaning talk. *See* **rane**[1].

rainiebus *n* a boys' game, to recover caps scattered at a distance from a line drawn across the playground.

rain-tree[1] *n* an umbrella.

rain-tree[2] *same as* **ran-tree**[1].

rainy day *n* a day of adversity.

raip *same as* **rape**.

raipie, raipy *adj* **1** viscous, ropy. **2** (*used of thread, etc*) coarse, rough.

rair *same as* **roar**.

raird *v* **1** to brag. **2** to bandy ill-language. **3** to roar. **4** to break wind backwards. **5** to make a noise by eructation. **6** to make a loud noise. **7** to scold. **8** to make a crackling sound. **9** (*used of sheep and cattle*) to bleat, to low.—*n* **1** a loud noise, clamour. **2** a riot. **3** confusion. **4** a sudden report. **5** the noise of eructation. **6** the backward breaking of wind. **7** lowing. **8** bleating. **9** a scold.

rairdie *n* **1** a wild frolic. **2** a riot. **3** a quarrel.

rairuck *n* a small rick of corn.

raise[1] *v* **1** to cause bread to rise. **2** to leaven. **3** to cause to ferment. **4** to start a tune. **5** to sing. **6** to excite, infuriate, madden. **7** (*used in curling*) to move a stone out of the way.—*n* a jest, wild fun.

raise[2] *v* arose, rose.

raise-an'-wand, raise-an'-dwang *n* an apparatus for bringing a millstone home from the quarry.

raised-like *adj* **1** apparently under great excitement. **2** madlike.

raise net *n* a net that rises and falls with the tide.

raise-net fishing *n* allowing the lower part of the net to rise and float with the flowing tide and to fall with the ebbing.

raiser *n* one who helps another to rise in life.

raising *n* an alarm, rousing.

raising-dwang *same as* **raise-an'-wand**.

raisin-wine *n* a name given to French brandy.

rait *same as* **ratt**.

raith[1] *n* a quarter of a year.

raith[2] *n* a circular earthwork or mound.

raither *adv* rather.

raitherly *adv* rather.

raivel[1], **raivel**[2] *same as* **ravel**[1], **ravel**[2].

raivelin, raivlin *same as* **ravelling**.

raivel stick *same as* **rail stick, ~ tree**.

raivery *same as* **ravery**.

raize *same as* **raise**[1].

rajie *adj* (*used of an animal*) becoming excited and plunging about wildly.

rak[1] *same as* **rack**[5].

rak[2] *same as* **reck**[2].

rak[3] *same as* **rawk**[3].

rake[1] *v* **1** to clear a grate or fire of ashes. **2** to turn and stnooth burning seaweed in kelpmaking. **3** to accumulate, gather. **4** to search thoroughly. **5** to recall old scandals, etc. **6** to bank up a fire. **7** to bury. **8** to clear the eyes. **9** to rub any part of the body with the hands. **10** (*of food*) to disagree with.—*n* an implement like a rough golf iron with a handle like a spade's used in kelp-making.

rake[2] *n* **1** a track, path. **2** a walk for cattle, etc. **3** the extent of pasturage for sheep or cattle. **4** the extent of a fishing ground. **5** the direction of clouds driven by the wind. **6** a journey. **7** a journey to and fro to fetch anything, the thing so fetched, a load. **8** a large quantity. **9** a swift pace. **10** a rapid growth of crops, etc. **11** great energy. **12** work done speedily. **13** work to be done within a given time. **14** one who works with fuss, but carelessly. **15** (*in pl*) the duty exacted at a mill of three gowpens (qv).—*v* **1** to do anything with speed or energy. **2** to run. **3** to fly. **4** (*used of cattle, etc, ploughing*) to turn to the left.

rake[3] *v* **1** to range, stray. **2** to roam, wander. **3** to stroll idly. **4** to walk about late at night.—*n* **1** a lounger. **2** one who roams at night. **3** an aimless wanderer.

rake[4] *same as* **reek**[3].

rake[5] *same as* **reak**[2].

rakel *adj* **1** rash, fearless. **2** strong, stout.

raker[1] *n* a hard worker.

raker[2] *n* a vagabond.

raking *n* a flight, clearance.—*adj* **1** energetic. **2** quick. **3** (*used of clouds*) gathering, scouring.—*adv* readily.

raking coal, ~ piece *n* a large lump of coal used to keep a fire alight through the night.
rakless *adj* **1** rash. **2** careless.
rale *adj* **1** real. **2** true.
ralliach *adj* slightly stormy.
rallion *n* a ragged fellow.
rallion *n* clattering noise.
rallion shout *n* a loud, noisy shout.
rally[1] *v* **1** to crowd. **2** to sport in a disorderly fashion. **3** to go to and fro in disorder.—*n* **1** a rush, quick pace. **2** a crowd.
rally[2] *v* to scold.
rally[3] *adj* mean, not handsome or genteel.
rally[4] *same as* **railie**.
ralyie *same as* **rally**[1].
ram[1] *n* a headstrong fellow.
ram[2] *v* **1** to push violently. **2** to stuff with food. **3** to use a person as a battering ram by way of punishing him. **3** (*with* **about**) to knock about. **4** (*with* **in**) to crush or burst in.
ramack[1] *n* **1** a stick. **2** a large, rugged piece of stick. **3** a scrap. **4** a worthless article.
ramack[2] *n* **1** a large, raw-boned person who speaks and acts heedlessly. **2** a backbiter. **3** a double-dealer. **4** a false-hearted fellow.
ramack-a-dodgil *n* anything large.
ramagiechan *same as* **ramack**[2].
ramasht *adj* summed-up, totalled.
rambaleugh *adj* **1** tempestuous, stormy. **2** (*used of the temper*) stormy.
rambarre *v* **1** to repulse. **2** to stop, restrain.
rambask *same as* **rambusk**.
rambaskious, rambaskish *adj* rough, rude, unpolished.
ramble[1] *v* **1** to dance. **2** to wander or talk in sleep or delirium.—*n* **1** a digression in writing or speaking. **2** a drinking bout. **3** a spree.
ramble[2] *same as* **rammel**[2].
ramblegarie *same as* **rumblegarie**.
ramblin' *adj* **1** loose. **2** talkative. **3** untrustworthy.
ramblin-~, ramlin-lad *n* a tall, fast-growing boy. *See* **rumbling**.
ramblin-syver *n* a drain filled up to the surface with loose stones. *See* **ramle**[2].
rambooze *adv* suddenly and with headlong speed.
rambounge *n* a severe bout of labour.
rambusk, rambust *adj* robust.
rambusteous *adj* rude, of boisterous manners.
rame *v* **1** to shout, roar. **2** to talk nonsense. **3** to ask for anything repeatedly and fretfully. **4** to whimper. **5** to ply with questions. **6** to keep reiterating the same words.—*n* **1** a cry. **2** a reiterated cry. **3** repetition of the same sound.
ramfeezled *adj* **1** fatigued, exhausted. **2** overworked. **3** worn-out. **4** confused.
ramfeezlement *n* **1** disorder, caused by fatigue or otherwise. **2** confused discourse. **3** a violent quarrel.
ramfoozle *v* **1** to disorder. **2** to turn topsy-turvy.
ramgeed, ramjeed *adj* **1** furious, crazy. **2** confused with drink.
ramgunshoch *adj* **1** rugged. **2** morose. **3** rough, rude.
ramiegeister *n* **1** a sharp stroke. **2** an injury.
ramished, rammist *adj* **1** furious, crazy. **2** confused with drink. **3** ill-rested. **4** sleepy from broken sleep. *See* **rammage**.
ram-lamb *n* a male lamb.
ramle[1] *same as* **rammel**[3].
ramle[2] *n* **1** rubbish. **2** fragments of stones. **3** a wall, etc, unsubstantially built. **4** a heap of ruins. **5** brushwood.—*adj* (*used of drains*) filled with broken stones.
ramlin *same as* **ramblin**.
rammack[1], **rammack**[2] *same as* **ramack**[1], **ramack**[2].
rammage[1] *adj* (*used of a road*) rough-set.
rammage[2] *n* the sound emitted by hawks.
rammage[3] *adj* **1** rash, thoughtless. **2** furious. **3** of strong sexual instinct. **4** violent. **5** strong.—*v* **1** to be driven

about under the impulse of any powerful passion. **2** to go about in an almost frenzied state.
rammaged *adj* delirious from drink.
rammekins *n* a dish of eggs, cheese and breadcrumbs mixed like a pudding.
rammel[1] *same as* **ramle**[2].
rammel[2] *n* mixed grain.
rammel[3] *n* a big-boned, scraggy animal.—*adj* (*used of straw*) rank and strong.
rammelin *same as* **ramlin**.
rammelsome *adj* rough, troublesome.
rammely *adj* (*used of persons and animals*) tall, loosely made.
rammer *n* a knock, rap.
rammish, rammis *same as* **rammage**.
rammle *same as* **ramble**[1].
rammleguishon *n* a sturdy, rattling fellow.
rammy *n* a horn poon.
ramp[1] *v* **1** to romp. **2** to prance. **3** to stamp about in fury. **4** to use violent language. **5** to boil vigorously. **6** to trample.—*n* **1** a romp. **2** a tomboy. **3** passion.—*adj* **1** riotous. **2** vehement, violent, disorderly. **3** headstrong.
ramp[2] *v* (*used of milk*) to become ropy.
ramp[3] *adj* **1** rank. **2** rancid. **3** strong-smelling.
ramp[4] *n* a shirt.
rampage, rampauge *v* **1** to prance about with fury. **2** to rage, storm. **3** to romp about noisily.—*n* **1** disorderly conduct. **2** a rage, fury.
rampageous, rampaginous *adj* **1** boisterous, noisy. **2** furiously angry.
rampager, rampauger *n* one who rampages, a restless, romping person.
rampan *adj* (*used of bread, of bannocks*) kept too long and showing small white filaments like gossamer.
rampar, ramper *n* the lamprey.
rampar-eel *n* the lamprey.
ramper *n* a noisy, stamping fellow.
rampier, rampire *n* a rampart.
ramping-mad, ~-wud *adj* raving mad.
rample *v* **1** to romp. **2** to scramble.
ramplon *n* the lamprey.
ramplor, rampler *n* a merry roving fellow.—*adj* roving, unsettled.
ramplosity *n* **1** a roving disposition. **2** boisterousness.
rampron-eel *n* the lamprey.
ramps *n* a kind of garlic, the wild garlic.
rampse *adj* **1** harsh to the taste. **2** rank. **3** (*used of spirits*) fiery, strong.
ram-race, ~-rats *n* **1** the race taken by two rams before each shock in fighting. **2** a short race to give impetus in leaping. **3** running with the head down, as if to butt with it. **4** a headlong rush. **5** a boys' rough game, sometimes given as a punishment.—*adj* headstrong, impetuous, precipitate.
ram-reel *n* a reel danced by men alone.
ramscooter *v* to send flying in a panic.
ramscullion, ramscallion *n* **1** an offensively dirty person. **2** a low vagrant.
ramse *same as* **ramsh**[2].
ramsh[1], **ramsch** *same as* **ransh**.
ramsh[2] *adj* **1** strong, robust. **2** harsh to the taste. **3** rash, arrogant. **4** acting too soon or too forcibly. **5** lascivious, lustful. **6** rank, foul. **7** (*used of spirits*) strong, fiery.
ramsh[3] *n* wild garlic.
ramshackle[1] *adj* **1** rickety. **2** unmethodical. **3** disorderly, wild. **4** dissipated, unsteady.—*n* **1** a wild, idle fellow. **2** a thoughtless fellow.
ramshackle[2] *v* **1** to ransack. **2** to search for closely.
ramshackled, ramshachled *adj* **1** loose, disjointed. **2** rickety. **3** in a crazy state.
ramskeerie *n* **1** a wild restless romp. **2** a madcap, tomboy.
ramskerie *adj* restive and lustful as a ram.
ram-skulled *adj* sheepish.

ramstacker, ramstalker *n* a clumsy awkward, blundering fellow.—*v* to act in a blundering, awkward manner.

ramstageous *same as* **ramstougar**.

ramstam, ram-stram *adj* **1** headlong, precipitate. **2** headstrong, heedless, impetuous. **3** forward. **4** thoughtless.— *adv* **1** precipitately. **2** at random. **3** rudely. **4** regardlessly of obstacles, at headlong speed.—*n* **1** a giddy, forward person. **2** an impetuous, reckless person. **3** the strongest home-brewed beer.—*v* to walk push or run forward in a headlong, rude, reckless manner.

ramstam-like *adv* as with headlong speed.

ramstamphish *adj* **1** rough, blunt, unceremonious. **2** forward and noisy.

ramstamran *adj* rushing headlong.

ramstougar, ramstougerous *adj* **1** rough and strong. **2** (*used of cloth*) rough. **3** (*of a woman*) big, vulgar, masculine. **4** boisterous in manner. **5** disposed to be riotous. **6** quarrelsome. **7** austere. **8** heedless. **9** harebrained.

ramstugious *same as* **ramstougar**.

ram-tam *adv* precipitately.

ramtanglement *n* confusion, disorder.

ran[1], **ran**[2] *same as* **rowan**[1], **rowan**[3].

ran[3] *same as* **rand**[1].

rance *v* **1** to prop with stakes. **2** to barricade. **3** to fill completely. **4** to choke up.—*n* **1** a wooden prop. **2** the crossbar that joins the lower part of the frame of a chair together. **3** the cornice of a wooden bed.

rancers *n* the bars running across the bottom of an open kitchen dresser on which bowls, pots, could be placed.

rancie *adj* (*used of the complexion*) red, sanguine.

rancil, ransel *v* **1** to search for missing goods. **2** to rummage, ransack. **3** to grope for.

rancor *v* to cause or enhance rancour.

rancountor *v* to encounter.—*n* a rencontre.

rand[1] *n* **1** a border. **2** a strip or selvage of cloth, list. **3** a stripe. **4** a strip of leather securing the heel of a shoe to the sole.

rand[2] *n* what can be melted at a time.

rand[3] *v* **1** to thicken, strengthen by thickening or doubling. **2** to strengthen a stocking heel by darning or doubling.

ran-dan *n* **1** a carouse. **2** a boys' holiday without leave. **3** violence.

rander[1] *v* **1** to ramble in talk. **2** to talk idly.—*n* **1** a great talker. **2** (*in pl*) idle talk. **3** idle rumours.

rander[2] *n* order.

rander[3] *v* **1** to render. **2** to surrender. **3** to melt down fat, etc.

rander[4] *same as* **ranter**[2].

randified *adj* scolding.

randit *adj* streaked.

randivoo *n* rendezvous.

random-splore *n* a chance frolic.

randon *n* **1** a drunken carouse. **2** force, violence.

randy *n* **1** a frolic. **2** a wild practice. **3** a wild, reckless person. **4** a beggar. **5** a ruffian. **6** a scolding virago. **7** a loose, disorderly woman. **8** an indelicate, romping hoyden, a tomboy. **9** a thief. **10** occasionally a term of affection for a young, lively female child.—*adj* **1** wild, unmanageable. **2** disorderly. **3** disreputable. **4** vagrant. **5** quarrelsome. **6** scolding. **7** abusive.—*v* **1** to scold, vituperate. **2** to frolic.

randy-beggar *n* **1** a beggar who extorts alms by menaces. **2** a tinker.

randy-like, ~-looking *adj* looking like a randy (qv).

rane[1] *n* **1** idle talk frequently repeated. **2** a frequent repetition of one sound. **3** a metrical rigmarole. **4** a fable.—*v* **1** to repeat the same thing over and over. **2** to murmur monotonously. **3** to rhyme. **4** (*with* **down**) to speak evil of, to disparage.

rane[2] *same as* **rand**[1].

ranegill *n* a masterful, turbulent person or criminal.

rang[1] *same as* **raing**[2].

rang[2] *v* reigned.

range[1] *v* **1** to search for thoroughly. **2** to rush about noisily

and rougllly. **3** to give a clattering, ringing motion, as when crockery or a piece of iron falls. **4** to crash. **5** to poke a fire. **6** to clear out the bars of a grate. **7** to agitate water by plunging, for the purpose of driving fish from their holds.—*n* **1** a thorough search. **2** a clearing out. **3** a stroll. **4** a clattering or clanging noise. **5** a strip of land. **6** a shelf. **7** a settle. **8** the seat round the pulpit that was reserved for the elders or for parents bringing their children for baptism. **9** a row, a rank.

range[2] *v* **1** to clear out. **2** to rinse.—*n* a handful of heather tied together to clean out pots and pans, etc, a heather ranger. *See* **ranger**[2].

rangel, rangle *n* **1** a crowd. **2** (*used of stones*) a heap.

ranger[1] *n* one who goes about noisily.

ranger[2] *n* a scrubber made of heather for pots, pans, etc, a heather ranger.

rangiebus, range-the-bus *same as* **rainiebus**.

rangle tree *same as* **rantle tree**.

rangunshock *v* to roar incessantly.

rank[1] *adj* **1** strong, sturdy, formidable. **2** thorough. **3** wild, rugged. **4** (*used of a boat*) top-heavy.

rank[2] *v* **1** to arrange one's costume. **2** to get oneself ready in regard to clothes. **3** (*with* **out**) to bring forward and arrange. **4** to rummage. **5** to bung out, prepare.

rankreenging, rankringing *adj* **1** wild, coarse. **2** lawless.

rannel ~, rannle, ~ bauk, ~ tree *same as* **rantle tree**.

rannie *n* the wren.

rannoch *n* bracken.

rannock *n* **1** lake weed. **2** ooze.

rannygill *same as* **ranegill**.

ranse *same as* **rance**.

ransh *v* **1** to take large mouthfuls, eat voraciously. **2** to crunch with the teeth.

ranshackle, ransheckle *same as* **ramshackle**[2].

ransie *same as* **rancie**.

ransivall *n* a garden pea, a large, pasty pea.

ransom *n* an extravagant price or rent.

rant *v* **1** to frolic, romp. **2** to revel. **3** to live a fast life. **4** to roister. **5** (*used of a fire*) to roar, blaze.—*n* **1** a merrymaking. **2** a rough, noisy frolic. **3** a jollification. **4** a lively story or song.

ranter[1] *n* **1** a roving, jovial fellow. **2** a reveller. **3** a scold.— *v* to roam, to rove about, as an animal broken loose.

ranter[2] *v* **1** to sew a seam across roughly. **2** to darn coarsely. **3** to join. **4** to attempt to reconcile statements that do not tally. **5** to work hurriedly and carelessly.—*n* **1** one who does anything carelessly. **2** anything badly done.

ranting *adj* **1** roistering. **2** blazing. **3** in high spirits. **4** exhilarating.—*n* noisy mirth in drinking.

rantingly *adv* **1** with great glee. **2** in a jovial, riotous fashion.

ranting place *n* a place for revelling.

rantle tree[1] *n* **1** the crossbeam in a chimney. **2** the end of a rafter or beam. **3** a tall, raw-boned person.

rantle tree[2] *same as* **rowan tree**.

ran-tree[1] *same as* **rantle tree**[1].

ran-tree[2] *same as* **rowan tree**.

rantry, rantry-tree *same as* **rowan tree**.

rant up *v* to mend, repair clothes. *See* **ranter**[2].

ranty *adj* **1** lively, cheerful, gay. **2** tipsy, riotous.

ranty-tanty *n* **1** a weed with reddish leaf, growing among corn. **2** the broad-leaved dock. **3** a kind of beverage distilled from heath and other vegetable substances, formerly used by the peasantry.

ranverse *v* **1** to reverse. **2** to overturn a decision on appeal. **3** to refute.

rap[1] *n* **1** a counterfeit copper coin of the nominal value of a halfpenny, used in Ireland in the reign of George I. **2** a counterfeit coin of any kind. **3** a cheat. **4** an impostor.

rap[2] *n* **1** a rope. **2** *in phr* **rap and stow** root and branch.

rap[3] *v* **1** to rap at. **2** to knock heavily. **3** to tap. **4** to arouse by knocking. **5** (*used of tears*) to fall in quick succession, in pattering drops. **6** to sound as if knocked on. **7** (*with* **off**) to go off hastily and with a noise. **8** to act expeditiously. **9** (*with* **to**) to fasten a door, etc. **10** (*with* **up**) to knock up, awaken by knocking. **11** (*with* **upon**) to come upon, knock up against.—*n* **1** a moment. **2** a knock at a door. **3** a stroke.

rap⁴ *v* **1** to seize, snatch. **2** to carry off.

rap⁵ *n* the vegetable, rape.

rape *n* **1** a rope. **2** a line of rope carried across a room or the front of the fireplace. **3** a band for a sheaf or stack. **4** any worthless piece of dress or cloth of considerable length. **5** a measure, a rood. —*v* **1** to wind up in a ball. **2** to coil. **3** to bind sheaves or stacks. **4** to tie clumsily. **5** to unroll, wind out. **6** to fray out.

raperie *n* a ropery, a ropewalk.

rape-thackit, ~-theekit *adj* with thatch secured by ropes.

raping band *n* a rope band for carrying a basket on the shoulder or for tying it so as to keep in its contents.

raploch, raplock, raplach, raplack *n* **1** coarse woollen cloth, homespun and undyed. **2** a plaid of such cloth. **3** the skin of a hare littered in March and killed at the end of the year.—*adj* **1** coarse. **2** homely. **3** rough. **4** homespun.

rapper¹ *n* wrapper leather.

rapper² *n* **1** the tongue of a bell. **2** the hammer of a clock.

rapperdandy *n* the bear-bilberry.

rapple¹ *n* the beat of a drum.

rapple² *v* **1** to grow quickly and rankly (*used of vegetation and of young people*). **2** to do work hurriedly and imperfectly. **3** to intertwist threads in sewing.

rapple³ *v* **1** to put on clothes in haste. **2** to wrap clothes around.

rapple-rat-tat *n* the beat of a drum.

rapt *n* **1** robbery. **2** rapine. **3** abduction.

rapture *n* **1** a fit of temper. **2** a state of violent anger or strong excitement.

rapturous *adj* outrageous.

rare¹ *same as* **raird**.

rare² *adj* grand, fine.—*adv* very.

raree *n* a raree show, a spectacle.

rarely *adv* excellently, capitally.

rarish *adj* rather rare.

rasch¹, rasch², rasch³ *same as* **rash¹, rash², rash³**.

rase¹ *same as* **raze**.

rase² *v* rose.

rash¹, rasch¹ *adj* **1** brisk, agile. **2** hale, hearty in old age.—*v* (*with* **out**) to blab, to publish imprudently.

rash², rasch² *v* **1** to pour down. **2** to descend heavily. **3** to dash down. **4** to dash, rush about. **5** to thrust. **6** to make any forcible exertion. **7** to twinge with pain.—*n* **1** a sudden fall. **2** a sudden twinge or twitch. **3** a rush of rain, etc.

rash³, rasch³ *n* **1** a crowd, a number of anything. **2** a row of any article, as needles used in weaving.

rash⁴ *n* the rush.

rash-bonnet *n* a cap made of rushes.

rash-buss *n* a clump of rushes.

rashen *adj* made of rushes.

rash hat *n* a hat made of rushes.

rashie *adj* covered with rushes.

rashie wick *n* a rush wick.

rash-~, rashie-mill *n* a toy mill made of rushes.

rash-pyddle *n* a bagnet of rushes, for catching fish.

rash-rape, ~-tow *n* a rope made of rushes.

rash-whish *n* a whizzing sound.

raskill *n* a young deer.

rasp¹ *v* **1** to rub a ring up or down over a twisted rod attached to a door, the sound serving as a bell or knocker. **2** to tirl at the pin (*see* **tirling-pin**) **3** (*used of the heart*) to make it sore, to cut it to the quick.

rasp² *n* **1** a raspberry. **2** a raspberry plant.

rasper *n* one who speaks in an exasperating manner.

rasp house *n* a house of correction.

rat¹ *n* rote. See **rat-rhyme**.

rat² *n* **1** a scratch. **2** a rut, a wheel track on a road. —*v* **1** to scratch, score. **2** to make deep ruts.

rat³ *n* a wart.

ratch¹ *n* the little auk.

ratch² *n* a white mark or streak, generally on the face of a horse.—*v* to mark with lines, stripes, etc.

ratch³ *n* **1** a hound. **2** a poacher. **3** a night wanderer.—*adj* unsteady, loose in morals.

ratch⁴ *n* the lock of a musket.

ratch⁵ *v* to tear away so roughly or clumsily as to cause a fracture.

ratchal, ratchell *n* **1** a hard, rocky crust below the soil. **2** the stone called wacken porphyry.

ratch't *adj* **1** ragged. **2** in a ruinous condition.

rate¹ *v* to be priced.

rate² *same as* **ratt**.

rate³ *v* to beat, flog.

rath, rathe *adj* early, quick.—*adv* soon.

rathely *adv* quickly.

ratherest, ratherly *same as* **raitherly**.

rathest *adv* sooner, much rather.

rathy, rathie *n* a good, quick-growing crop of hay, weeds, etc.

ratify *v* to clear up, settle.

ratihabit *v* to confirm, approve.

ratihabition *n* (*a legal term*) confirmation, approval.

ration *n* reason.

rationality *n* reason, sense.

ratling *n* the death rattle.

rat-rhyme, rat-rythm *n* **1** anything repeated by rote. **2** a long rigmarole. **3** nonsense.—*v* to repeat from memory without attaching any meaning to the words.

rat's-tail *n* the greater plantain.

ratt *n* a file of soldiers.

rattan, ratten, ratton *n* **1** a rat. **2** a small person or animal. **3** a sly person. **4** a term of endearment.

rattan fa' *n* a rat trap.

rattan-flitting *n* the removal of rats in a body from one haunt to another.

rattan-houkit *adj* dug or holed by rats.

rattan's-rest *n* a state of perpetual turmoil or bustle.

rattan-stamp *n* a rat trap.

rattle *v* **1** to pronounce the letter 'r' with a burr. **2** to do anything with energy and speed. **3** to talk much loosely and foolishly. **4** (*with* **down**) to undo work carelessly. **5** to strike, beat.—*n* **1** a sudden smash. **2** impetus. **3** a chatterer. **4** a stupid fellow. **5** a smart, quick blow.

rattle bag *n* **1** anything that makes a rattling noise. **2** a loud clatter. **3** a noisy, fussy person who excites alarm.

rattler *n* **1** a loud, noisy, talkative fellow. **2** a child's rattle.

rattle-shot *n* a shot fired as a salute.

rattle skull *n* **1** one who talks much without thinking. **2** a stupid, silly fellow.

rattle-trap *adj* rickety, worn-out.—*n* (*in pl*) odds and ends.

rattley, rattlie *n* a child's rattle.

rattling *adj* **1** rollicking. **2** lively. **3** wild, noisy.

rattling fou *adj* boisterously drunk.

rattrum *same as* **rat-rhyme**.

rauch *same as* **rauk¹**.

rauchan *same as* **rachan**.

rauchel *same as* **raucle**.

rauchl *same as* **ruckle¹**.

rauchly *adj* rough, boisterous.

raucht¹ *adj* frosted.

raucht² *same as* **raught**.

raucie *adj* coarse.

rauck *v* **1** to scratch with anything pointed. **2** to mark with a nail. **3** to rummage.—*n* a mark, scratch.

raucking *n* the noise of a nail scratching a slate.

raucle, rauckle *adj* **1** fearless. **2** boisterous. **3** headstrong. **4** strong and sturdy in old age.—*n* **1** any rough person or thing. **2** a term of contempt.

rauckle *same as* **raucle**.

raucle-haundit *adj* ready to strike.

raucleness *n* vigour in old age.

raucle-tongue *n* a rough, vigorous, plain-speaking tongue.

raucle-tongued *adj* plain-speaking, outspoken.
raugh *v* **1** to reach. **2** to hand, fetch. **3** to stretch, hold out. **4** to give a blow.
raughan, raughen *same as* **rachan**.
raughel *same as* **raucle**.
raught *v* **1** reached. **2** reached for.—*n* **1** the act of reaching. **2** a blow, dash.
rauhhel *n* a small three-pronged fork, used to break potatoes boiling in a pot.
rauk[1] *adj* **1** hoarse. **2** misty.—*n* a mist, fog.
rauk[2] *v* **1** to stretch. **2** to reach.
rauk[3] *same as* **rauck**.
rauky *adj* misty, foggy.
raul *same as* **rail**[2].
raullion *same as* **rullion**.
raul tree *same as* **rail stick**.
raun[1], **raun**[2] *same as* **rowan**[1], **rowan**[3].
raun'd *adj* having roe.
raunel ~, raunle tree *same as* **rantle tree**.
rauner *n* the female salmon, having roe.
raun-fleuk *n* the turbot.
rauns *n* the awns of barley.
raun tree *same as* **rowan tree**.
raup *n* a three-pronged instrument for bruising potatoes for supper.—*v* to prepare potatoes thus.
raut[1], **raut**[2] *same as* **rat**[2], **rat**[3].
raux *same as* **rax**[3].
rave[1] *v* **1** to bawl. **2** to make a loud noise. **3** (*used of the wind*) to make a wild, roaring sound.—*n* **1** a vague report. **2** an almost incredible story.
rave[2] *v* **1** to roam, stray. **2** to rove.
rave[3] *v* tore, did tear.
rave[4] *v* to take by violence.
ravel[1] *n* **1** a rail, railing. **2** the crossbeam in a byre (qv) to which the tops of the cow stakes are fastened. **3** an instrument with pins in it for spreading out yarn on the beam before it is wrought. **3** the rowel of a spur. **4** (*in pl*) the tops of a cart. —*v* to fit or enclose with a railing.
ravel[2] *v* **1** to wander in speech. **2** to unravel the loops in knitting. **3** to tangle or curl up like a hard-twisted thread.—*n* **1** a ramble. **2** a tangle. **3** confusion. **4** incoherent speech. **5** (*in pl*) ravelled thread.
ravelled-hesp *n* an intricate business.
ravelling, ravelin' *n* **1** a tangled thread. **2** a loose, unravelled thread. **3** frayed textile fabric. **4** odds and ends of rhyme.
ravel lock *n* a kind of river lock.
ravel stick, ~ tree *same as* **rail stick**.
ravery *n* **1** delirium. **2** a violent fit of temper and loud vociferation.
ravin *adv* exceedingly.
raving *adj* riving.
ravlin' *same as* **ravelling**.
raw[1] *n* undiluted whisky.—*v* (*used of corn*) to grow soft.—*adj* (*of the weather*) cold and damp.
raw[2] *same as* **row**[2].
rawchan *same as* **rachan**.
rawel *same as* **ravel**[1].
raw-footed *adj* barefooted.
raw-gabbit *adj* speaking confidently on a subject of which one is ignorant.
rawk[1] *same as* **rauk**[1].
rawk[2] *same as* **rauck**.
rawk[3] *n* **1** the rheum that gathers about the eyes in sleep. **2** the scum on stagnant water.
rawky *same as* **rauky**.
rawlie, rawly *adj* **1** unripe. **2** not fully grown. **3** moist, damp, raw.
rawn[1] *n* the fragment of a rainbow.
rawn[2] *n* **1** a scratch. **2** a furrow. **3** a discoloured stripe.
rawn[3] *adj* afraid.
rawn[4] *same as* **rowan**[3].
rawned *adj* **1** furrowed. **2** striped so as to be disfigured. **3** streaked.

rawn-fleuk *n* the turbot.
rawn-tree *same as* **rowan tree**.
rawsie *same as* **raucie**.
rawt[1], **rawt**[2] *same as* **rat**[2], **rat**[3].
rax[1] *n* **1** an andiron. **2** (*in pl*) an iron instrument consisting of links or hooks on which the spit was turned at the fire.
rax[2] *n* a boys' game, also called cock. *See* **cock**[1].
rax[3] *v* **1** to extend, stretch. **2** to hand, pass, reach. **3** to stretch out the body or limbs on waking. **4** to strain, overstrain. **5** to wrench. **6** to rack. **7** to grow.—*n* **1** a stretch, reach. **2** the act of stretching or reaching. **3** a strain. **4** a sprain. **5** a wrench of limb or muscle.
raxed craig, ~ neck *n* the neck of a person who has been hanged.
raxing *adj* **1** elastic, easily stretched. **2** (*used of pain*) racking. **3** increasing, growing.—*n* a hanging.
rax-king-of-Scotland, raxis-boxie *n* a boys' game in which one player tries to catch others as they rush across a line.
rax-me-doon *n* a better kind of coat that can readily be put on in place of one's working coat.
raxter *n* a long walk.
ray[1] *v* **1** to array. **2** to make ready.
ray[2] *n* rye.
ray[3] *adj* mad, wild.
ray[4] *n* a song, poem.
raze *v* **1** to abrade the skin. **2** to shave.—*n* an erasure.
razer *n* a measure of grain.
razonberry *n* the redcurrant.
razor-ride *v* to shave.
re *int* a call to a horse to turn to the right.
rea *n* an evil spirit.
reable *same as* **rehable**.
reach[1] *same as* **reak**[1].
reach[2] *v* to retch.
read[1], **read**[2] *same as* **red**[4], **red**[1].
read[3] *same as* **redd**[3].
read[4] *same as* **reed**[2].
reade *n* a kind of sceptre.
reader *n* **1** a preacher who reads his sermons. **2** one who read the lessons and prayers when ministers of the Scottish Church were few. **3** (*used of cups*) a fortune-teller examining grounds of tea in a cup.
readily, readilys, read'ly *adv* **1** probably. **2** naturally. **3** easily.
reading *n* family worship.
reading priest *n* a minister who reads his sermon.
ready *adj* on the point of.—*v* **1** to prepare food. **2** to put on one's things.—*n* ready money.
ready-handit *adj* **1** clever with the hands. **2** quick and handy.
reak[1] *n* **1** a trick. **2** an artifice.
reak[2] *v* **1** to reach. **2** to hand. **3** to fetch. **4** to extend. **5** to thrust. **6** to arrive. **7** to fetch a blow.—*n* **1** ability, capacity. **2** attainment.
reak[3] *same as* **reek**[3].
real[1] *adj* **1** eminently good. **2** true, staunch. **3** (*used of money, rent, etc*) paid in cash.—*adv* **1** very. **2** thoroughly.—*n* reality.
real[2] *same as* **rail**[2].
real[3] *n* a gold coin.
real tree *same as* **rail stick**.
ream[1] *n* **1** cream, thick cream. **2** froth, foam. **3** water lying near the surface of a well, etc.—*v* **1** to skim off cream. **2** to rise as cream. **3** to froth, foam, mantle. **4** to overflow. **5** to buzz. **6** (*of thoughts*) to keep hold of the mind.—*adj* **1** smooth as cream. **2** used as cream. **3** made of cream.
ream[2] *v* **1** to talk or write at length. **2** to cry fretfully and repeatedly. **3** to repeat the same sound.
ream bowie *n* a small barrel in which cream is kept.
ream breid *n* oatcake or bannocks baked with cream.
ream-cheese *n* a cheese made from cream.
ream-crowdy *n* oatmeal mixed with cream.
ream dish *n* a dish for holding cream.

reamed milk *n* skim milk.
reamer *n* a milk-skimmer.
ream-fu' *adj* full to overflowing.
reaming-calm *n* a calm with the sea smooth as cream.
reaming cap, ~ dish *n* a milk-skimmer.
reaming fu' *adj* full to overflowing.
reamish *same as* **reemish**.
reamishing *adj* noisy, disturbing.
ream jug *n* a cream jug.
ream kirn *n* a churn.
ream milk *n* unskimmed milk.
ream pig *n* a jar for holding cream.
reamy *adj* creamy.
reard *same as* **raird**.
reardie *same as* **rairdie**.
rearie, rearum *same as* **rairdie**.
reason *n* **1** a reasonable price. **2** justice, right.
reasonable *adj* (*used of distance*) fairly near, not very far.
reast[1] *n* a hen roost.
reast[2] *same as* **reest**[2].
reath *same as* **raith**[1].
reathy *adj* ready.
reave[1] *same as* **rave**[2].
reave[2] *See* **rive**[1].
reave[3] *same as* **reeve**[6].
reavel[1], **reavel**[2] *same as* **ravel**[1], **ravel**[2].
reaver *same as* **reever**[2].
reaverie *n* robbery, spoliation.
reaving *same as* **reeving**.
reaving wind *same as* **reeving wind**.
rebaghle *n* reproach.
rebat[1] *n* the cape of a mantle.
rebat[2] *v* **1** to retort. **2** to draw back. **3** to prove recalcitrant.
rebbit *n* a polished stone for a window, door or corner.
rebig *v* to rebuild.
rebleat *v* (*of a ewe*) to bleat in response to her lamb.
rebook *v* to rebuke.
reboon, rebound *v* **1** to vomit. **2** to be squeamish. **3** to be like to vomit. **4** to repent.—*n* the sound of a shot fired.
rebunctious *adj* refractory.
rebute *n* a rebuff.
recant[1] *v* to revive from debility or sickness.
recant *n* to recite or tell over again.
receipt, receit *n* **1** accommodation, capacity. **2** shelter. **3** the harbouring of criminals. **4** the receiving of stolen goods. **5** a receiver of stolen goods.—*v* **1** to receive, welcome. **2** to entertain. **3** to shelter a criminal or outlaw. **4** to receive stolen goods.
receipter *n* **1** one who entertains. **2** one who shelters criminals. **3** a receiver of stolen goods.
receive *n* **1** a power of receiving. **2** an appetite, a good stomach.
recently *adv* early.
recept *same as* **receipt**.
reck[1] *same as* **rack**[4].
reck[2] *v* **1** to take heed of. **2** to care. **3** to matter.
reck[3] *v* to reckon, deem, think.
reck[4] *same as* **reak**[2].
reckle *same as* **rackle**[3].
reckon *v* **1** to conjecture. **2** to pretend.
reclaim *v* **1** (*a legal term*) to object, oppose. **2** to appeal against a decision.
reclaiming note *n* a formal notice of appeal.
reclamation *n* an appeal to a higher court.
recognosce *v* **1** (*a legal term, used of a superior*) to reclaim heritable property from a vassal who has failed to observe the terms of his tenure. **2** to rejudge.
recognose *v* to reconnoitre.
recollection *n* the memory of the dead.
reconvalesce *v* to recover health after a relapse.
reconvene *v* to cite again a person for the same crime of which he was proved innocent.
reconvention *n* **1** a countercharge. **2** a renewed citation. **3** a legal process raised by a person prosecuted for a crime

in which he calls for the defence all such witnesses as he thinks might be brought to testify against him.
recounter *v* **1** (*a tradesman's technical term*) to invert. **2** to reverse.
recour *v* **1** to recover. **2** to regain health. **3** to obtain.
recrue *v* to recruit.—*n* a party of recruits.
recule *v* to recoil, retreat, revert.
recuperate *v* (*a legal term*) to recover, regain.
recur *v* to have legal recourse for recovering damages or the relief of expenses.
recusance *n* refusal.
red[1] *adj* bloody.—*v* to redden, to become red.
red[2] *n* the green ooze found in the bottom of pools.
red[3] *same as* **rad**[1].
red[4] *v* **1** to advise, counsel. **2** to warn. **3** to explain, solve. **4** to foretell, predict. **5** to guess. **6** to imagine, suppose. **7** to beware, be cautious.—*n* advice, counsel, warning.
red[5] *v* rode.
red[6] *n* **1** the rood, the cross. **2** Rood-day (qv).
red[7], **red**[8] *same as* **redd**[1], **redd**[2].
redact *v* to reduce.
red-aitin *same as* **red-etin**.
redargue *v* **1** (*a legal term*) to contradict. **2** to accuse, blame.
redbelly *n* the char.
redcap, red-capie-dossie *n* a spectre or elf with very long teeth, supposed to haunt old castles.
red-close *n* the throat, the gullet.
redcoat *n* **1** a name specially given during the rebellion to those who served under King George. **2** a ladybird.
redcock *n* an incendiary fire.
redcock crawing *n* fire-raising.
red cole, ~ coal *n* red cabbage.
red-comb *n* a large-toothed comb.
red-cowl *n* a redcap (qv).
red cross *n* the fiery cross.
redd[1] *v* **1** to set in order. **2** to prepare. **3** to tidy, clean up. **4** to dress or comb the hair. **5** to disentangle, unravel. **6** to clear up, sort. **7** to clear, clean out, open up. **8** to adjust. **9** mark out. **10** to arbitrate, judge. **11** to quell a fray. **12** to compose a quarrel. **13** to separate combatants. **14** to correct, set right. **15** to criticize, sum up faults. **16** to scold, rebuke.—*n* **1** tidying, cleaning. **2** a clearance. **3** the removal of an obstruction. **4** litter, rubbish, remains. **5** a cleaner, an instrument for cleaning or clearing out anything. **6** energy, speed, ability to work. **7** progress, despatch. **8** a will, a testamentary settlement of affairs.
redd[2] *adj* **1** ready, willing, prepared. **2** active, able. **3** clear, not closed up, free from crowd, obstacles, encumbrances. **4** clear, fluent, distinct. **5** done with one's work or business.—*adv* readily.
redd[3] *n* **1** spawn. **2** a spawning ground.—*v* to spawn.—*adj* (*used of fish*) in the spawning state.
redd[4] *v* to rid, to free.—*adj* rid, free.
redd[5] *same as* **red**[5].
redd[6] *same as* **rad**[1].
reddance *n* riddance, clearance.
reddand *n* the bend of the beam of a plough at the insertion of the coulter.
reddans *n* **1** combings. **2** odds and ends left over.
Red-day *same as* **Rood-day**.
redden *v* to cause to blush.
reddendo *n* the clause in a feu charter defining the duty that the vassal had to pay to the superior.
redder[1] *adv* rather.
redder[2] *n* **1** a large-toothed comb. **2** one who tries to settle a dispute or part combatants.
redder's blow, ~ lick *n* the blow that falls on one who tries to part combatants.
redder's-part *n* the redder's blow (qv).
redd-hand *n* a clearance.
redd-handit *adj* **1** active. **2** capable. **3** neat, tidy. **4** having little in possession.

reddin n a clearance, a riddance.
reddin' blow, ~ straik n the redder's blow (qv).
reddins n spawn.
red-doup n a kind of bumblebee.
redd thrums v to quarrel about trifles.
redd-up adj 1 neat, tidy. 2 put in order.—n the making of things neat, clean and orderly.
reddy same as **ready**.
rede¹ n a fairy of some kind.
rede² n 1 a wraith. 2 the apparition of a person, seen when he or she is alive.
rede³ same as **reed²**.
rede⁴ same as **red⁴**.
rede⁵ adj 1 fierce, impetuous, wild. 2 excited. 3 drunk.
rede⁶ n 1 a reed. 2 part of a weaver's loom.
rede⁷ same as **rad¹**.
rede⁸ n adj aware.
rede⁹ same as **redd³**.
red-early n grain that begins to sprout in the stack.
rede goose same as **rade goose**.
red-etin, ~-eitin n 1 the name of a giant or monster. 2 a savage, barbarous person.
Red Even, ~E'en same as **Rood Eve**.
red fish n fish in a spawning state.
red-fisher n a salmon fisher.
red-glove grozer n a kind of red gooseberry.
red-gown n an arts student of the universities of St Andrews, Glasgow and Aberdeen.
red-hand n a bloody hand.—adv in the very act.
red hawk n the kestrel.
red-headit adj hot-tempered.
red heckle n a kind of fishing fly.
red-hunger, reid-hunger n the rage of hunger.
red-hungered adj ravenous from hunger.
redie n a red clay marble.
red-kail same as **red-cole**.
red-kaim same as **red-comb**.
red-land n ploughed land.
red-lane n the throat, gullet.
redlins adv 1 readily. 2 perhaps, probably.
red-mad adj 1 raging mad. 2 furious. 3 intensely eager.
redment n 1 a putting in order. 2 a settlement of affairs, etc.
red-nakit adj quite naked.
red-neb n the kidney-bean potato.
redound v (of money) to fall to be paid.
red rab n the robin.
red-rot n the sundew.
red-sauch n a species of red willow.
red-shank n 1 the dock, after it has begun to open. 2 a contemptuous name for a Highlander, from his bare legs.
red-sheuch, ~-seuch n the stomach.
redsman n 1 one who clears away rubbish. 2 one who tries to settle a dispute or part combatants.
redtail n the redstart.
red the rook v to detect a fraud.
red-wame n the char.
redware n sea girdles, seaweeds growing in shallow waters.
redware-cod, ~-codlin n a species of cod.
redware fishick n the whistlefish.
red-wat adj 1 wet with blood. 2 bloodstained.
red-water n a disease of cattle and sheep.
redwing mavis n the redwing.
red-wode, ~-wood, ~-wud adj 1 raging mad. 2 insane. 3 furious. 4 eager.
redwood n the reddish wood found in the heart of trees.
red-waur n a name given by Newhaven fishermen to a species of fucus used by children for painting their faces.
ree¹ n 1 an enclosure from a river or the sea, open towards the water, to receive small vessels. 2 a harbour. 3 the hinder part of a mill dam. 4 a sheepfold, an enclosure for cattle. 5 an enclosure for coal on sale. 6 a wreath (qv) of snow.—v 1 to enclose with a wall of stone or turf. 2 (used of snow) to drift into wreaths.
ree² n a period of stormy weather occurring about Whitsuntide.—adj 1 (used of weather) windy, clear and frosty. 2 bleak.
ree³ v to riddle corn, beans, etc, by an eddying movement.—n a riddle smaller than a sieve.
ree⁴ adj 1 crazy, delirious. 2 rude, wild. 3 unmanageable. 4 (used of a horse) high-spirited, restive. 5 excited with drink, tipsy.—n 1 a state of temporary delirium. 2 excitement.—v to become excited.
reeans n the coarser damaged beans that do not pass through the sieve.
reeble¹ same as **rabble**.
reeble² n a greedy person or animal.
reebler n a careless worker or speaker.
reeble-rabble n 1 a rabble. 2 great confusion.—adv in great confusion.—v to crowd in great confusion.—adj confused, disorderly.
reechnie adj rough in appearance or manner.—n a person of ungainly, rough appearance or manners.
reed¹ n part of a weaver's loom.
reed² n the fourth stomach of a ruminant.
reed³ same as **ree¹**.
reed⁴ conj lest, for fear that.—v to fear, apprehend.
reed⁵ same as **red⁴**.
reed⁶ n a cross, the rood.
reed⁷ same as **redd³**.
reed⁸ same as **red¹**.
reed⁹ same as **rede⁵**.
reediemadeasy, reedy-ma-deezy n 1 a child's first reading book. 2 reading made easy.
reeding plane n 1 a carpenter's plane that forms three rows at once. 2 a centre-bead plane, making two or more beads.
reed-mad same as **red-mad**.
reeds n a method of catching young coalfish with a handline from a boat anchored near the shore.
reef¹ same as **reeve³**.
reef² n 1 a skin eruption. 2 mange. 3 the itch.
reef³ n a roof.
reefart, reefort n the radish.
reefart nosed adj having a nose coloured or shaped like a radish.
reef'd adj rumoured.
reef-saw n an ointment for the itch.
reefu' same as **rierful**.
reefy adj 1 scabby. 2 having the itch.
reegh same as **ree¹**.
reeing riddle n the sieve for reeing beans. See **ree³**.
reek¹ n 1 smoke. 2 a smoke, a whiff of a pipe. 3 mist, fog. 4 scent, smell. 5 a house with a chimney. 6 a quarrel among people in the same house. 7 a family misunderstanding.—v 1 to smoke. 2 to soil with smoke. 3 to perspire.
reek² n a blow.
reek³ v 1 to equip. 2 to rig out. 3 to dress, accoutre. 4 to make ready.
reek⁴, reek⁵ same as **reak¹, reak⁴**.
reeker n anything out of the common.
reek fowl, ~ hen n 1 a hen paid as a tax. 2 the tax itself.
Reekie, Auld Reekie n Edinburgh.
reekim, reekum n 1 a smart blow. 2 a riot, quarrel. —v 1 to strike a smart blow. 2 to box.
reekin' n 1 an outfit. 2 plenishing (qv).
reekiness n smokiness.
reekin' house n 1 an inhabited house. 2 a household.
reekit adj 1 rigged out. 2 well-dressed. 3 furnished with an outfit.
reek money, ~ penny n a tax on every chimney.
reek-ridden adj smoke-ridden.
reek-shot adj (used of the eyes) sore and watery without apparent cause.
reek-stained adj smoke-begrimed.
reeky adj smoky, smoking.

Reeky Peter *n* a candlestick for fir candles.
reel[1] *n* a lively dance peculiar to Scotland.—*v* to dance a reel.
reel[2] *n* **1** the spool of a spinning wheel. **2** the spinning wheel. **3** a bobbin.—*v* **1** to wind or unwind a bobbin. **2** (*with* **on**) to rattle on. **3** to push on rapidly.
reel[3] *v* **1** to romp. **2** to travel. **3** to roam. **4** to roll. **5** to knock violently. **6** (*used of thunder*) to peal. **7** to wrestle, contend.—*n* **1** a confused or whirling motion. **2** turmoil. **3** mental confusion. **4** a loud, rattling noise. **5** a peal, a thunderclap.
reel[4] *n in phr* **oot o' reel** not in a healthy condition.
reel[5] *same as* **rail**[2].
reel-about *v* **1** to go to and fro in a rambling and noisy way. **2** to romp. **3** to whirl round in a dance.—*n* a lively, romping person.
reel-fittit *adj* **1** club-footed. **2** having the feet turned inwards so that the legs are crossed in walking and the feet make a curve.
reeling *adj* **1** in confusion. **2** intoxicated. **3** disordered in thought and speech.—*n* **1** a whirling motion made by bees. **2** confusion of ideas. **3** intoxication. **4** bustle. **5** a loud, clattering noise.
reel-rall, ~-rawl *n* a state of confusion turmoil.—*v* **1** to move or work confusedly. **2** to walk in an aimless, disorderly fashion.—*adv* **1** in confusion. **2** topsy-turvy, helter-skelter.
reel-rally *adj* staggering under the influence of liquor.
reel-tree *same as* **rail-stick**.
reel-yeukin *adj* itching to dance a reel. *See* **reel**[1].
reem[1] *n* **1** a rumour. **2** a false report.
reem[2] *same as* **ream**[1].
reemage *v* to rummage noisily.
reemish, reemis *n* **1** a loud, rumbling noise. **2** the sound of a heavy fall or blow. **3** a disturbance, row. **4** stir, bustle. **5** a thorough and noisy search. **6** a weighty blow.—*v* **1** to make a loud, rumbling noise. **2** to search thoroughly and noisily.
reemle *v* **1** to emit or cause a sharp, tremulous noise. **2** to roll or push forward.—*n* **1** a continuous sharp, tremulous sound or motion. **2** a confused, falling sound, a rumble.—*adv* with a sharp, tremulous sound.
reemle-rammle *v* **1** to make a great deal of noise. **2** to behave noisily and rompingly.—*n* **1** a great noise. **2** noisy, rollicking behaviour. **3** rambling speech or talk.—*adv* **1** in a rude, noisy manner. **2** with a low, heavy sound. **3** with a jingling and confused sound.
reemmage *same as* **reemage**.
reemous *same as* **reem**.
reenge[1], **reenge**[2] *same as* **range**[1], **range**[2].
reenger *same as* **ranger**[1].
reep *same as* **rip**[1].
reepal *n* a person, irrespective of character.
reepan, reepin *n* **1** a lean person or animal. **2** a low character. **3** a telltale.
reerd *same as* **raird**.
reerie *same as* **rairdie**.
ree-ruck *n* a small rick of corn put up to be easily dried.
reese[1] *v* to blow briskly.—*n* a puff, blast.
reese[2] *same as* **roose**[1].
reeshle, reeshil *v* **1** to rustle. **2** to clatter, crackle. **3** to beat soundly. **4** to hustle. **5** to drive with blows. **6** to shake up. **7** to knock up against.—*n* **1** a rustle. **2** a loud clattering or rattling sound. **3** the ringing of a bell. **4** a sounding blow. **5** a sharp shaking. **6** a tottering ruin. **7** a loose heap. —*adv* with a crackling sound.
reeshler *n* a noisy or flurried worker.
reeshlin' *adj* forward bustling, prompt.
reeshlin-bland *n* a scourge.
reeshlin-dry *adj* so dry as to make a rustling sound.
reeshly *adj* **1** rude, rowdy. **2** troublesome. **3** given to rows. **4** stirring. **5** rattling. **6** noisy.
reesie *adj* **1** blowing briskly. **2** (*of a horse*) frisky.
reesil *same as* **reeshle**.

reesin *adj* vehement, forcible, strong.
reesk *n* **1** coarse grass growing on downs. **2** wasteland yielding only benty grasses. **3** a marshy place.
reeskie *adj* abounding in reesk (qv), coarse grass, etc.
reesle *same as* **reeshle**.
reest[1] *v* **1** to be restive. **2** to refuse to proceed. **3** (*of a horse*) to baulk, to turn.—*n* **1** a fit of stubbornness or refusal to move on. **2** one who becomes stubborn.
reest[2] *v* **1** to smoke. **2** to dry in the sun or by fire. **3** (*used of a well*) to dry up.—*n* the place where fish, hams, etc, are smoked.
reest[3] *same as* **rest**[2].
reest[4] *n* a roost.—*v* to roost.
reested[1] *adj* **1** restive. **2** stiff, tired. **3** unwilling.
reested[2] *adj* **1** smoke-dried. **2** shrivelled up.
reester[1] *n* **1** a restive, baulking horse. **2** a resister. **3** an obstinate, wayward person.
reester[2] *n* **1** a salted and dried salmon. **2** a kipper.
reestle[1] *same as* **reeshle**.
reestle[2] *same as* **rizzle**.
reestlin,-rustlin *adj* (*used of corn*) so dry as to rustle. *See* **reeshle**.
reesty *adj* **1** restive, unwilling to move. **2** obstinate, mulish.
reet[1] *n* root.—*v* to uproot.
reet[2] *same as* **root**[2].
reeve[1] *n* **1** a cattle pen. **2** a sheepfold.—*v* to shut up in a reeve.
reeve[2] *v* to burn with a strong, bright flame.
reeve[3] *v* **1** to talk vivaciously and incoherently. **2** to rumour.—*n* a rumour.
reeve[4] *same as* **roove**.
reeve[5] *same as* **rive**[1].
reeve[6] *v* to rob, plunder.—*n* robbery, plundering.
reeve[7] *same as* **rove**[3].
reever[1] *n* **1** anything large or quickly moving. **2** a roaring fire. **3** a high wind. **4** a swift boat. **5** a stout, active person.
reever[2] *n* a robber, freebooter.
reeving *adj* **1** high, strong. **2** burning brightly.
reeving-wind *n* a high wind.
reeze[1] *v* (*with* **behind**) to break wind.
reeze[2] *same as* **roose**[1].
reeze[3] *v* to pull one about roughly.
reeze[4] *same as* **reese**[1].
reezie *same as* **reesie**.
reezing-horse *n* a healthy horse.
reezlie *adj* (*used of ground*) having a cold bottom, producing coarse grass.
refe *same as* **reef**[2].
refeese *v* to refuse.
refeir *n in phr* **to the refeir** in proportion.
refell *v* to refute, repel.
refer *n* **1** a reference. **2** a thing referred.—*v* to delay, defer.
reff *v* to rob, spoil.
refind *v* to refund.
refleck *v* to reflect.
reform *v* to repair.—*n* repair.
refound *v* **1** to charge to the account of. **2** to refund.
refresher *n* liquid refreshment.
reft[1] *v* **1** stole. **2** stolen.—*adj* stolen. *See* **reave**[6].
reft[2] *same as* **rive**[1].
refted *v, adj* stolen. *See* **reave**[6].
refuse *n* a refusal, rejection.
refusion *n* the act of refunding.
refusticat *v* to recover consciousness, revive.
regalia *n* privileges pertaining to the Crown.
regalis, regalles *n* districts having the privileges of a regality.
regality *n* a territorial jurisdiction granted by the king, with lands given in free regality and conferring on the person receiving it the title of 'lord of regality'.
regard, regaird *v* **1** to fall to the lot of. **2** to concern.

regardless, regairdlese *adj* **1** reckless, careless. **2** regardless of God and man.

regent *n* the old title of a university professor.—*v* to discharge the office of a university professor.

regentry, regency *n* a university professor's office.

regibus *same as* **rainiebus**.

regiment *v* to form into a regiment.—*n* government.

registrate *v* **1** to register. **2** registered.—*adj* registered.

reglar *adj* **1** regular. **2** thorough, complete.—*adv* regularly, always.

regorge *v* to regurgitate.

regret *n* **1** a complaint. **2** a grievance.

rehable *v* **1** to rehabilitate. **2** to reinstate. **3** to render an illegitimate child legitimate.

reib *n* **1** colewort growing tall with little or no leaf. **2** a cabbage that does not stock properly. **3** a lean, thin person or animal. **4** an animal that does not thrive.

reibie *adj* **1** tall and thin. **2** lean, lank, slender.

reick *same as* **reek**[3].

reid[1] *same as* **reed**[2].

reid[2] *same as* **red**[1].

reid[3] *same as* **redd**[1].

reid[4] *same as* **rede**[5].

reid[5] *same as* **rood**[6].

reid-hunger *n* a ravenous appetite.

reif, reife *same as* **reave**[6].

reif *same as* **reef**[2].

reifart *same as* **reefart**.

reiffar *n* a robber.

reif randy *n* a sturdy beggar.

reif-saw *n* itch ointment.

reify *adj* having the itch.

reigh *same as* **ree**[1].

reik[1], **reik**[2], **reik**[3] *same as* **reek**[1], **reek**[2], **reek**[3].

reik[4], **reik**[5] *same as* **reak**[1], **reak**[2].

reikim, reikum *same as* **reekim**.

reiking *n* an outfit, personal garments.

reikit *adj* furnished with all needful clothes.

reil *same as* **reel**[3].

reilibogie *n* **1** confusion. **2** tumult, disorder.

reiling *n* a loud, clattering noise.

reimis *same as* **reemish**.

reinge[1], **reinge**[2] *same as* **range**[1], **range**[2].

reingin' *n* a hard rapping.

reinzies *n* reins.

reip *same as* **ripe**[2].

reird *same as* **raird**.

reise[1] *same as* **roose**.

reise[2] *same as* **rice**.

reishle, reishil *same as* **reeshle**.

reishlin, reishillin' *adj* **1** noisy. **2** forward. **3** prompt. —*n* a sound beating.

reisk[1] *same as* **risk**[1].

reisk[2], **reisque** *same as* **reesk**.

reiskie *n* a big, boorish person, especially such a woman.

reisle, reissil, reissle *same as* **reeshle**.

reist[1] *n* the instep of the foot.

reist[2] *v* to sprain or strain the wrist.

reist[3], **reist**[4], **reist**[5] *same as* **reest**[1], **reest**[2], **reest**[3].

reister *same as* **reester**[2].

reisum *n* **1** a stalk or ear of corn. **2** an atom, particle. **3** the smallest possible quantity.

reit *n* a root.

reithe *adj* keen, ardent.

reive[1] *n* a name given to circular mounds with regular fosses, which are considered to be ancient Caledonian forts.

reive[2] *same as* **reeve**[6].

reive[3] *same as* **rive**[1].

reiver *same as* **reever**[2].

rejag *v* to give a smart answer or one reflecting on the person to whom it is addressed.—*n* a repartee, retort.

rejeck *v* to reject.

relapser *n* one who relapses into scandalous sin.

release *v* **1** to relax. **2** to remove a duty on goods.

releich *v* to enlarge, release.

relevancy *n* the legal sufficiency of facts stated, in a libel (qv) or in a defence, to infer punishment or exculpation.

relevant *adj* **1** (*a legal term*) valid. **2** sufficient to warrant the conclusion in a libel (qv) or in a defence.

relict *n* **1** a relic. **2** ruins.

relief *adj* an ecclesiastical term, applied to congregations that withdrew from the Church of Scotland in order to be free from the evils of patronage in presentation to livings and free to choose their own ministers.

relish *v* to give relish to.

relisher *n* one who relishes.

remain *n* **1** a posthumous publication. **2** literary remains.

remaining *adj* future.

remaining state *n* a future state.

remanent *adj* remaining, other.—*n* a remainder.

remark *n in phr* **in remark** notable, remarkable, exceptional.

remarkable *n* any thing or event remarkable or noteworthy.

remarking *n* **1** a remark. **2** criticism.

remb *same as* **rame**.

rember *n* one who tells improbable stories.

reme *same as* **ream**[1].

remede, remeed *same as* **remeid**.

remedie *n* a certain latitude of degrees of fineness in silver on either side of the standard in coining formerly, to save the labour of precision.

remeeve *v* to remove.

remeid, remead, remied *n* **1** a remedy, cure. **2** redress, relief.—*v* to remedy, redress.

remeid of law *n* a legal term, applicable to the obtaining of justice by appeal to a superior court.

remember *v* to remind.

rememberful *adj* full of old memories.

remembering prayer *n* the intercessory prayer in public worship.

remigester *same as* **ramiegeister**.

remind *v* to keep in mind, remember.

remish *same as* **reemish**.

remit *v* (*used of a person*) to pardon him.

remm *same as* **rame**.

remnant *n* **1** a small piece. **2** a feeble old creature, a physical wreck.

remove *v* to die.—*n* **1** an intervening degree of relationship. **2** an old horseshoe removed and replaced. **3** the act of reshoeing a horse with the old shoes.

removedly *adv* remotely.

ren *same as* **rin**[1].

renaige *v* to revoke at cards.—*n* a revoke.

renchel[1] *v* to beat with a stick.

renchel[2] *n* a tall, thin person.

rendal *n* **1** land held by a tenant in discontiguous plots. **2** land held by several tenants in one field.

render[1] *v* **1** to melt fat, butter. **2** to discharge pus. —*n* melted fat, dripping.

render[2] *n* **1** a rate. **2** a degree.

rendered fat *n* melted fat.

renderment *n* melted fat, dripping.

renk *n* a curling rink.

rennal *same as* **rendal**.

rennet *n in phr* **rig and rennet** land held by tenants in places here and there or land held by several tenants in one field.

rensh *v* to rinse.

renshel *same as* **renchel**.

rent *v* to rend, tear, crack.

rental *n* **1** a favourable lease. **2** the annual rent.

rentaller *n* one who possesses a farm or land by rental (qv).

rent-dues *n* arrears of rent.

rent-racker *n* **1** a rack-renter. **2** a harsh collector of rents.

rep, repp *v* **1** to rip. **2** (*with* **on**) to unwind anything knitted.

repair *n* a gathering of people, concourse.

reparty *v* to reply, retort.

repeal *v* **1** to recall a sentence. **2** to set aside a verdict on appeal.

repeat *v* **1** to demand money back. **2** to recover. **3** to call back.—*n* the repetition of lines in psalm singing.

repeater *n* a repeating psalm tune.

repentance *n in phr* **stool of repentance** the stool or seat in church formerly occupied by offenders against the Seventh Commandment for public rebuke.

repentance gown *n* a white sheet of coarse linen worn by those who occupied the stool of repentance or had otherwise to undergo public penance.

repentance ~, repenting stool *n* the stool of repentance. *See* **repentance.**

repetition *n* **1** repayment. **2** recovery or restoration of money.

replegiation *n* the handing of a prisoner over to the jurisdiction to which he was subject.

replenish *v* to refurbish, clean up anew.

reploch *same as* **raploch.**

repone *v* **1** to replace. **2** to restore to office or status, etc. **3** to reply.—*n* a legal reply.

report *v* **1** to obtain. **2** to carry off.

repose *v* to replace, reinstate.

reposition *n* **1** reinstatement. **2** restoration to ecclesiastical status.

repouss *v* to repulse, repel.

reppet *same as* **rippet.**

reppoch *n* **1** a ragged garment. **2** (*in pl*) tatters.

repree *v* to reprove.

reprivell *n* a reprieve.

reproach *v* to bring or be a cause of reproach.

reprobate *v* **1** to contradict the evidence of a witness. **2** to challenge a verdict as against evidence (a legal term).

reprobation *n* contradictory evidence of one witness against another.

reprobator *n* one who reprobates evidence or a verdict. *See* **reprobate.**

reprobature *n* the act of reprobating.

repute *adj* **1** reputed. **2** habitually reported.

requeesht *v* to request.

requittance *n* requital.

resaitt *same as* **reset¹.**

reschell, reshill *same as* **reeshle.**

reseeduary *same as* **residuary.**

resent *v* **1** to appreciate. **2** to applaud.

resentments *n* feelings of gratitude, appreciation.

reserve *n* **1** a reservation. **2** a tree reserved in a hag (qv) or cutting of an allotted portion of wood.

reset¹ *v* to receive stolen goods.

reset² *same as* **roset.**

resetter *n* a receiver of stolen goods.

reshill *same as* **reeshle.**

resident *v* to reside.

residenter *n* a resident.

residenting *adj* residing, resident.

residuary *n* a name formerly given to ministers who remained in the Established Church of Scotland at the Disruption in 1843.

resile *v* **1** to flinch, recoil. **2** to withdraw. **3** to beguile, deceive. **4** to resist in argument. **5** to respite.

reskal *n* a rascal.

resolve *v* **1** to terminate. **2** to clear up or settle doubts. **3** to convince.

resp¹, resp² *same as* **risp¹, risp².**

respect¹ *v* **1** to respect. **2** to be solicitous for. **3** to drink one's health.—*n* **1** respect. **2** (*in pl*) interest, emolument, advantage.

respect² *n* a respite.

respective *adj* respectful, full of regard to.

respond *n* the return made by a precept from Chancery on an application for sasine.

responsal *adj* **1** responsible. **2** substantial as to means, etc.

responsible *adj* **1** of good standing. **2** respectable. **3** substantial.

resputt *n* respite.

ress *same as* **race.**

ressum *same as* **rissom.**

rest¹ *n* **1** the place where a curling stone should stop. **2** the part of a spade on which the foot rests.

rest² *v* **1** to make up a fire for the night,. **2** to be indebted to one, owe. **3** to arrest, distrain for debt. —*n* **1** a remnant. **2** a relic. **3** (*in pl*) arrears of money due, rent, etc.

rest³ *v* **1** to twist, sprain. **2** to wrest.—*n* a sprain.

restaur *v* to make restitution.

restauration *n* restitution, reparation for injury, etc.

resting chair *n* a long chair, shaped like a settle.

reating clod, ~ peat *n* a peat sod for resting a fire. *See* **rest².**

resting-owing *adj* remaining indebted to one.

restrick *v* to restrict.

restringent *n* an astringent.

resume *v* **1** to repeat. **2** to recapitulate, summarize.

resurrectioner, resurrector *n* a resurrectionist, bodysnatcher.

ret¹ *v* to steep flax in order to separate the woody core from the fibre.

ret² *same as* **rit¹.**

retard *v* **1** to be late. **2** to fall behind.

reteir *v* to retreat, retire.

reth *same as* **raith¹.**

retical *n* a reticule.

retour *v* **1** to return. **2** to make a return in writing as to the service of an heir or the value of lands. —*n* **1** the legal return made to a brief issued from Chancery or as to the value of lands. **2** a great amount.

retreat *v* to retract.

retrench *v* to reduce the amount of a fine.

retrinch *v* to compel the return of anything unjustly obtained.

retroact *v* to make an Act retrospective.

retrocess *v* to give a back place.

rett *same as* **raith¹.**

retting *n* the steeping of flax or hemp in order to separate the woody core from the fibre.

reunde *same as* **roond.**

reuth¹ *n* wild mustard seed.

reuth² *n* rush, pity.

revally *n* the signal given about daybreak to awaken soldiers.

reve *same as* **reave⁶.**

revel¹ *n* **1** a severe blow. **2** a back-stroke.

revel², revel³ *same as* **ravel¹, ravel².**

rever *same as* **reever².**

reverence *n* **1** a respectful greeting. **2** power. **3** one's mercy. **4** a title of respect given to a minister or priest. **5** *in phr* **to be in one's reverence** to be under obligation to one.

reverie *n* **1** a rumour. **2** a vague report.—*v* to report.

revers *n in phr* **at the revere** at random.

reverser *n* a proprietor who has the right of redemption over lands he has mortgaged by paying the mortgage.

revemion *n* the right of redemption of a mortgaged property.

reverie *same as* **ravery.**

revert *v* to recover from a swoon or from sickness.

revestrie *n* the vestry of a church.

revil *n* the point of a spur, a rowel.

revisie *v* **1** to inspect again. **2** to revise.

revure, revoore *adj* **1** dark and gloomy. **2** thoughtful. **3** having a look of calm scorn or contempt.

rew¹ *v* to roll.

rew², rewe *same as* **rue.**

rewayle, rewayl'd *adj* **1** untidy, slovenly. **2** ravelled, disordered.

rewe *same as* **rew².**

rewl *same as* **ravel**².
rewth *n* a cause for **repentance**.
rex *same as* **rax**².
rexa-boxa-king *same as* **rax-king-of-Scotland**.
rex-dollar *n* a coin worth £2, 18s. Scots.
reyk *same as* **reek**².
reyle *same as* **ravel**².
reyl tree *same as* **rail stick**.
reyve *same as* **rive**¹.
rhaem, rhaim *same as* **rame**.
rhane *same as* **rane**¹.
rheemous *same as* **reem**.
rheum *n* (*in pl*) rheumatism.
rheumateese, rheumatiz *n* rheumatism.
rhematics *n* rheumatism.
rheumatis't *adj* afflicted with rheumatism.
rhind¹ *same as* **rind**².
rhind² *n* a footpath, roadway.
rhind-mart *n* **1** a whole carcass of cow or ox. **2** a mart (qv).
rhone *n* **1** a spout for carrying off rainwater. **2** a small patch of ice formed on a road.
rhume, rhyme *same as* **rame**.
rhymeless *adj* **1** unreasonable. **2** regardless.
rhyming ware *n* **1** compositions in rhyme. **2** minor poetry.
rhynd, rhyne *same as* **rind**³.
rhynde *same as* **rind**¹.
rhyne *same as* **rane**¹.
riach *adj* **1** dun. **2** ill-coloured.
rial *n* **1** a gold coin. **2** a silver coin bearing the name of the reigning sovereign.
riauve *n* a row, a file.
rib *n* **1** a wife. **2** the bar of a grate. **3** a strip of anything. **4** the slight ridge in stockings.—*v* to half-plough land by leaving an alternate furrow unploughed.
ribbing *n* a half-ploughing.
ribbit *same as* **rebbit**.
ribble *same as* **rabble**.
ribble-rabble *n* **1** a rabble. **2** great confusion.—*v* to crowd in great confusion.—*adv* in great confusion.
ribblie *n* a disorderly gathering.
ribblie-rabblie *adj* disorderly.
ribbon *n in phr* **St Johnston's ribbon** a halter.
ribe *n* **1** a colewort tall and with little or no leaf. **2** a cabbage that does not stock properly. **3** a lean person or animal.
ribgrass *n* the ribwort plantain.
ribie *adj* **1** tall, with little foliage. **2** lank, tall and thin.
rib-ploughing *n* ribbing (qv), a particular kind of ploughing. *See* **rib**.
rice *n* **1** a twig, branch. **2** brushwood. **3** branches used for hedging.—*v* to throw branches into a river to frighten the salmon.
rich *adj* full.—*v* to become rich.
richnie *n* a name given in anger to a woman.
richt *same as* **right**.
richteous *adj* righteous.
richtfu' *adj* rightful.
richt-like *adj* **1** according to justice. **2** in good health.
richtly *adv* certainly, positively.
rick¹ *same as* **reek**.
rick² *v* to pierce with a hook by a sudden pull or jerk.—*n* **1** a tug or pull. **2** a sharp movement.
rickam *same as* **reekim**.
ricket¹ *n* **1** a racket, disturbance. **2** a policeman's rattle.
ricket² *adj* unsteady, rickety.
rickety-dickety *n* a wooden toy made for children.
rickle *n* **1** a loose heap, pile or stack. **2** a low stone fence built before a drain. **3** a very lean person or animal. **4** a living skeleton.—*v* **1** to put into a heap. **2** to stack. **3** to pile up loosely.
rickle-dyke *n* a wall firmly built at the bottom but having the top only the thickness of the single stones loosely piled the one above the other.

rickler *n* **1** one who builds up loosely. **2** a bad stone-builder.
rickling¹ *n* a method of preserving corn in small stacks.
rickling² *n* **1** the youngest or smallest of a brood, litter or family. **2** a weakling.
rickly *adj* **1** loosely built. **2** rickety, unsteady. **3** dilapidated.
rickmaster *same as* **rittmaster**.
rickmatick *n* **1** concern, affair. **2** collection, hypothec (qv).
rick-thacking *n* the thatching of ricks.
rick-yard *n* a stackyard.
rictum-tictum *adj* conjuring.
rid¹, rid² *same as* **redd**¹, **redd**².
rid³ *same as* **red**³.
rid⁴ *same as* **redd**³.
rid⁵ *v* rode.
ridable *adj* fordable on horseback.
rid-comb *n* a comb for the hair.
ridden-meal *n* money paid by an incoming tenant for getting the liberty of the farm before the term expires.
ridder *same as* **redder**².
ridding-comb *n* a rid-comb (qv).
riddins *n* spawn.
riddle¹ *v* **1** to pierce. **2** to mangle.
riddle² *v* **1** to puzzle. **2** to solve.
riddle-turning *n* a method of divination by means of a riddle fixed on the extended points of a pair of scissors.
riddlin-heids *n* **1** what has been sifted out. **2** refuse.
riddlin' in the reek *n* a rough and ready method of getting rid of a fairy changeling.
riddlum, riddleum *n* a riddle, conundrum.
ride¹ *same as* **redd**³.
ride² *v* **1** to ford on horseback. **2** to be fordable on horseback. **3** to ride in procession to the Parliament House. **4** to ride on a plundering raid. **5** to drive a curling stone with such force as to knock a rival one out of the way. **6** to bowl strongly.—*n* **1** a hard throw in bowls. **2** a passage by water. **3** the current or swell of the sea.
ride³ *same as* **royd**.
rider¹ *n* a Scottish gold coin worth £8, 2s. Scots.
rider² *n* **1** a curling stone that forcibly dislodges one blocking its way. **2** (*used in bowling*) a forcibly thrown bowl.
ride-tail-tint *v* to back one horse against another in a race so that the losing horse is lost by the owner.
rid-handit *same as* **redd-handit**.
ridicule *n* a practical joke.
ridiculous *adj* (*used of the weather*) unseasonable.
ridie-roosie *n* a ride pick-a-back.
riding *n* **1** marauding, freebooting. **2** a Border raid.
riding graith *n* riding equipment.
riding money *n* a tax paid in connection with the quartering of dragoons on the Covenanters.
riding pie, ~ py *n* a loose riding coat or frock.
riding time *n* the breeding season of sheep.
rief, rieft *same as* **reeve**⁶.
riefer *same as* **reever**².
rien *v*, *adj* riven.
riep *same as* **rip**¹.
rier *same as* **roar**.
rierful *adj* roaring.
riesle *same as* **reeshle**.
riest *same as* **rest**².
rifart *same as* **reefart**.
rife, riff *same as* **reef**².
rife *adj* **1** ready. **2** quick.
riffraff, riraff *n* a low, mean person.—*adj* **1** disreputable. **2** shabby. **3** scurvy.
rifle *v in phr* **rifle the ladies' pouches** the shepherd's purse.
rift¹ *v* **1** to belch, eructate. **2** to come back unpleasantly to the memory. **3** to boast, exaggerate.—*n* **1** an eructation. **2** unbridled talk. **3** exaggeration. **4** frank conversation.
rift² *n* **1** a look. **2** appearance. **3** a slit made in a sheep's ear.—*v* to mark sheep with a rift.
rifted *adj* riven, split.
rifting-full *adj* full to repletion.

rifty *adj* belching forth abuse.

rig[1] *n* **1** a half-castrated animal. **2** a male animal with imperfectly developed organs.

rig[2] *v* to cheat, trick.—*n* **1** a frolic. **2** a trick. **3** a spree.—*phr* **on the rig** wandering about at night.

rig[3] *v* **1** to deck out. **2** to set up. **3** to prepare, trim. —*n* **1** equipment. **2** good condition. **3** working order.

rig[4] *n* **1** a ridge. **2** a long, narrow hill. **3** the spine of a person or animal. **4** the space between the furrows of a field. **5** a section of a ploughed field. **6** a section of a field. **7** a field. **8** the first furrow turned in ploughing. **9** a drill for potatoes, etc.—*v* **1** to plough. **2** to make ridges in a field by ploughing.

rigadoon, rigadown-daisy *n* a lively dance on the grass at a wedding.

rig and bauk *n* a field with alternate strips of corn and pasture.

rig and fur *n* **1** the ridge and furrow of a ploughed field. **2** the whole field. **3** the ribbing of stockings, etc.

rig-and-rendal *n* the old land system of runrig (qv), where the small farms are parcelled out in discontinuous plots. *See* **rendal**.

rig-back, ~-bane *n* the spine, backbone.

rig-end *n* **1** the buttocks. **2** the lower end of the spine. **3** the end of a rig in ploughing or of a section of a field in reaping. *See* **rig**[4].

rig-fidge *n* a gentle blow on the back.

rig-fish *n* the backbone of a fish.

rigg *same as* **rig**[1], **rig**[2], **rig**[3].

rigget-cow *n* a cow with white stripe along the backbone.

riggin *n* **1** a term of reproach to a woman. **2** a tall, ungainly woman.

rigging[1] *n* **1** clothing. **2** outfit.

rigging[2] *n* **1** the backbone. **2** the head, skull. **3** the ridge of a roof. **4** the rafters forming the roof. **5** the roof itself. **6** shelter under a roof.—*v* to roof in, cover with a roof.

rigging stone *n* a stone forming part of the ridge of the roof.

rigging tree *n* **1** the ridge beam of the house. **2** the rooftree (qv).

riggit *adj* (*used of cattle*) having a white streak or white and brown streaks along the back.

rigglin *n* an animal with one testicle.

riggly *adj* unsteady, rickety, wriggling.

riggs and shaws *n* the entire estate.

riggy, rigga *n* a name given to a cow having a stripe along the back.

rig-head *n* the strip of land at the sides of a field where the plough turns.

right *adj* **1** large. **2** good. **3** thorough. **4** sane. **5** canny. **6** in good health. **7** sober.—*adv* thoroughly.—*v* to put in order, repair.

rightlins *adv* **1** by rights. **2** of a certainty. **3** rightly.

right now *adv* just now, immediately.

right-recht *v* to judge justly, aright.

rights *n* title deeds.

right-side *n* the side of a cake that was uppermost when first placed on the girdle (qv).

right-so, ~-sua *adv* in like manner, just so.

right way *n* the true story, the real facts of a case.

rigibus *same as* **rainiebus**.

riglan, riglen *same as* **rigglin**.

rigmalorum *n* a rigmarole.

rigmarie, rig-ma-ree *n* **1** a base coin. **2** a mischievous frolic. **3** a tumult, uproar. **4** any frail, thin membrane.

rigmarole *adj* long-winded and incoherent.

rigs *same as* **rainiebus**.

rigwiddie, rigwoodie, rigwuddie *adj* **1** stubborn in disposition. **2** deserving the widdie (qv) or halter. **3** ill-shaped. **4** lean, bony.—*n* **1** the rope or chain crossing the back of a yoked horse. **2** one who can bear much fatigue or hard usage. **3** a wild trick or prank.

rigwiddie-nag *n* a half-castrated horse.

rike *same as* **reack**[2].

rik-ma-tik *same as* **rickmatick**.

rile[1] *v* to entangle, ravel.

rile[2] *v* to irritate, annoy.

rilling *n* a shoe made of rough, untanned leather.

rim[1] *n* **1** a circular haze, a halo. **2** *in phr* **rim of the belly** the peritoneum.

rim[2] *n* a ream of paper.

rim-bursin *n* a rupture of the abdominal muscles to which horses and cows are subject.

rim-burst *n* hernia.

rim-burstenness *n* the condition of having hernia.

rime *n* **1** a fog, mist. **2** the death sweat.

rim-fou *adj* brimful.

rimil *v* to rumble.

rimless *same as* **rhymeless**.

rimmed *adj* brimmed.

rimmer *n* the iron hoop round the upper millstone, to keep it unbroken.

rimpin *n* **1** a lean cow. **2** an old, ugly woman.

rim-ram *adv* in disorder.

rim-raxin *n* **1** a good feed. **2** a surfeit. **3** what food one can retain, having eaten until the stomach is distended.

rin[1] *same as* **run**[2].

rin[2] *same as* **rand**[3].

rin[3] *same as* **rind**[1].

rin aboot *v* to go about, wander from place to place.

rin-aboot *n* **1** a gadabout. **2** a vagabond. **3** one who tramps the country.—*adj* running about, scampering to and fro.

rin ahin *v* **1** to run at one's heels or behind. **2** to follow closely. **3** to fall into arrears, run into debt.

rin at *v* **1** to assault. **2** to fall upon a person.

rin-awa' *n* **1** a runaway. **2** the bolting of horses. **3** the ring finger.—*adj* runaway.

rind[1] *v* **1** to liquefy fat by heat. **2** to melt. **3** to distil whisky.

rind[2] *n* **1** a piece cut off a board. **2** list, selvage. **3** the wrapping of list on the handle of a golf club, under the leather.

rind[3] *n* hoarfrost.

rindle *v* to trickle, flow gently.—*n* a brook, rivulet.

rin coon wi' *v* to pour down the throat of a hand-fed animal.

rind-shoon *n* shoes with the uppers of cloth woven or plaited out of list.

rine *n* **1** list or selvage. **2** a piece cut off a board.

rine *n* hoarfrost.

rinegate, rinagate *n* a runagate, vagabond.—*adj* worthless.

rin-'em-owre *n* a children's game, played in the open street, in the middle of which one tries to catch those who try to cross within bounds.

ring[1] *n* **1** a prehistoric circular fort or entrenchment. **2** a game of marbles placed in a circle. **3** a mark on a cow's horn by which her age may be known. **4** the meal which falls round the millstone, between it and the surrounding case.—*v* **1** to form a ring. **2** to encircle or surround with a wall. **3** to put a ring in a bull's nose or in a pig's snout. **4** to put a ring round a wheel. **5** (*of a mill*) to fill the crevices round the millstone with the first grain ground after the stones are picked.

ring[2] *v* to tingle, vibrate.—*n* **1** the striking of a public clock. **2** a solitary coin to ring or jingle on a counter. **3** a slap, blow.

ring[3] *v* **1** to reign. **2** to behave noisily or imperiously. **3** to urge on. **4** to overpower.

ring[4] *same as* **rink**[1].

ring[5] *v* to wring.

ring aboot at *v* to make a great noise, to behave imperiously.

ringan *adj in phr* **a ringan deevil** a very devil, used intensively.

ring corn *n* the meal that in grinding falls round the millstone, between it and its case.

ring-cutter *n* an implement used by curlers for marking the rings at the ends of the rinks.

ring down *v* **1** to overpower. **2** to overbear.

ringe[1], **ringe**[2] *same as* **range**[1], **range**[2].

ringe-heather *n* the cross-leaved heather.

ringer[1] *n* a scrubber or whisk for cleaning pots, etc.

ringer[2] *n* one who ranges about noisily.

ringer[3] *n* a stone that lies within the ring immediately surrounding the tee in curling a pot lid (qv).

ring-fowl *n* the reed bunting.

ringie red belt *n* a children's game, played with a burning splint of wood rapidly turned in a circle while doggerel lines are repeated.

ring in[1] *v* **1** (*used of a church bell*) to ring with increased speed, indicating that service is about to begin. **2** to be near death.

ring in[2] *v* **1** to yield. **2** to cease. **3** to acknowledge defeat.

ringing *adj* **1** very energetic. **2** domineering.—*adv* intensely.

ringit *adj* **1** (*used of a sow*) having a ring through the snout. **2** having a great quantity of white visible round the iris of the eye.

ringle[1] *n* a ringing sound, as of a loose horseshoe.

ringle[2] *n* a cluster, group.

ringled *adj* **1** ringed. **2** marked in rings.

ringle-e'e *n* **1** a walleye. **2** a walleyed animal.

ringle-e'ed *adj* **1** wall eyed. **2** having too much white in the eye.

ring-malt *n* ring corn (qv).

ring-necked loon *n* the great northern diver.

ring owre *v* to hold in subjection.

ring-straik *n* an instrument used for stroking down grain in a bushel measure.

ring-tail *n* the hen harrier (female).

ring-tails *n* **1** small remnants. **2** miscellaneous odds and ends. **3** arrears of rent. **4** 'heel-taps'.

ringum-craggum *adv* right through and through.

ringy *n* a game with marbles placed in a ring.

rink[1] *n* **1** a race. **2** a course. **3** the course over which curling stones are driven. **4** a set of players in a rink at curling or quoits. **5** a number of articles set in order. **6** the act of setting in order. **7** a line of division.—*v* **1** to range up and down. **2** to roam hither and thither. **3** to climb about. **4** to clamber on to an elevated position. **5** to mount some forbidden place. **6** to arrange, set in order.

rink[2] *v* to surround, encircle.

rink[3] *v* **1** to rattle. **2** to move with a sharp sound. **3** to search or rummage noisily and thoroughly. —*n* **1** a rattling sound. **2** noisy movement or conduct.

rink[4] *n* a strong man.

rinker *n* **1** a tall, thin, long-legged horse. **2** a tall, raw-boned woman. **3** a harridan.

rinketer *same as* **rinker**.

rink-fair *n* a yearly public market held a few miles south of Jedburgh.

rink medal *n* (*in curling*) the medal played for by rinks and held by the winning rink (qv).

rink room *n* the arena for jousting.

rink's end *n* the goal.

rinlet *n* a small stream.

rinn[1] *same as* **rind**[1].

rinn[2] *same as* **run**[2].

rinnagate *n* **1** a runagate. **2** a worthless person.—*adj* vagabond.

rinnal *same as* **rindle**.

rinner[1] *n* the upper millstone.

rinner[2] *n* **1** a clue of yarn. **2** a stream, brooklet.

rinner[3] *n* butter melted with tar for sheep smearing.

rinnin' *n* **1** a running sore, an ulcer, abscess. **2** the flowing of matter from a sore. **3** (*in pl*) scrofula. **4** (*in pl*) the drift of a remark. **5** the main lines of anything. **6** the run of an argument.

rinning bill *n* a furious or mad bull.

rinning-darn *n* a disease in cows causing a severe flux.

rinning knot, ~ noose *n* a slipknot.

rinning mink *n* a slipknot.

rino *n* ready money.

rin on *v* **1** to push. **2** to butt as a furious bull, etc.

rin out *v* **1** to leak. **2** not to contain.

rin owre *v* **1** to continue without pause. **2** to boil over. **3** to overflow. **4** to overrun.

rinrig *n* **1** a wile. **2** a prank, trick. **3** a deep-laid scheme.

rinse, rinze *v* (*with* **down**) to wash down.—*n* a scrubber of heather stems.

rinse, rinze-heather *same as* **ringe-heather**.

rin-shackel *n* a shackle that runs on a chain, with which a cow is bound in the byre (qv).

rin-the-country *n* **1** a fugitive. **2** one who flees the country for his misdeeds.

rintherout, rin-there-out *n* **1** a gadabout. **2** a needy, homeless vagrant. **3** a tramp.—*adj* given to roaming or gadding about.

rin up *v* to pour into, fill up.

rin wa' *n* **1** a partition. **2** a wall dividing a house from one side to the other.

rin-watter *n* **1** just enough money, laid past or in hand, to pay one's way. **2** a struggle to make ends meet.

riot *n in phr* **in full riot** in full swing.

rip[1] *v* **1** to cleave. **2** to saw wood with the grain. **3** to undo insufficient or badly done work. **4** (*used of cloth*) to shrink so as to tear. **5** (*with* **up**) to disclose, open up. **6** to recall old stories, grievances, etc. **7** to scold. **8** to speak impetuously. **9** to curse. —*n* **1** a rush, great speed. **2** anything worthless. **3** a reckless person. **4** a rascal. **5** a slovenly dressed girl. **6** a cheat.

rip[2] *same as* **ripe**[2].

rip[3], **ripp** *n* **1** a handful of unthreshed corn or hay. **2** an unbound sheaf or part of one.

rip[4] *n* an osier basket for holding eggs, spoons, etc.

ripe[1] *adj* prevalent, abundant, rife.—*v* to ripen.

ripe[2] *v* **1** to search thoroughly. **2** to investigate narrowly. **3** to rob or pick one's pocket. **4** to clear from an obstruction. **5** to clean or clear out a pipe. **6** to break up pasture. **7** *in phr* **to ripe the ribs** to clear the bars of a grate of ashes, cinders, etc.—*n* a clearing out.

ripe-pouch *n* a pickpocket.

riper *n* anything used for clearing a small hole or a tobacco pipe.

ripet *adj* ripened.

riphet *same as* **reefart**.

riple *same as* **ripple**.

riposte *n* **1** a reply, retort. **2** a short, sharp answer. —*v* to retort, reply.

rippadeeity *n* the loud noise caused by romping children.

rippet, rippart, rippit *n* **1** a noisy disturbance. **2** a romp. **3** an uproar. **4** a brisk, short quarrel. **5** mental disturbance or care. **6** a bitter-tempered, chattering creature.—*v* **1** to make a disturbance. **2** to quarrel. **3** to scold. **4** to wrangle.

rippie *n* **1** a poke net fixed to a hoop for catching crabs.

ripping *adj* given to cleaning out. *See* **ripe**[2].

rippish *adj* cleanly, fastidious. *See* **ripe**[2].

ripple[1], **rippill** *v* **1** to separate the seed of flax from the stalk. **2** (*with* **out**) to undo badly done work. **3** to separate. **4** to tear in pieces. **5** (*of birds*) to eat grains of standing corn. **6** to drizzle. **7** (*of clouds*) to open up, disperse, clear off.—*n* an instrument with teeth like a comb for rippling flax.

ripple[2] *n* **1** a painful illness. **2** a fatal disease. **3** (*in pl*) kidney trouble. **4** backache.

ripple-, rippling-grass *n* the ribwort plantain.

rippler *n* one who ripples flax. *See* **ripple**[1].

rippling *n* the operation of separating the seed of flax from the stalks.

rippling kaim *n* a toothed instrument for rippling flax. *See* **ripple**[1].

rippon *n* an old, broken-down horse.

rip-rap *v* (*used in curling*) to drive on with great force, knocking the stones out of the way.—*adv* with great violence.

ris *v* rose.

risart *same as* **rizzard**.

rise[1] *v* **1** (*of soap*) to lather well in washing clothes. **2** to ascend, climb. **3** (*used of food*) to be vomited, to have the taste repeated in the mouth. **4** to raise.—*n* **1** a steep ascent. **2** a practical joke.

rise[2] *same as* **rice**.

rise-up-Jack *n* magic, conjuring.

rishle *same as* **rissle**.

rising *adj* approaching, nearing a certain age.

risk[1] *v* **1** to make a harsh, grating sound, like the tearing of roots. **2** to cut grass with a reaping-hook. **3** to rasp. **4** to thrust, plunge.—*n* **1** a tug, pull. **2** a rasping, grating sound.

risk[2] *same as* **reesk**.

riskish *adj* wet, boggy.

risle *same as* **rissle**.

risp[1] *v* **1** to grate. **2** to rub with a file. **3** to rub hard bodies together. **4** to grind the teeth. **5** to rasp. **6** to whet a knife. **7** to make a harsh, grating sound. **8** to use the tirling pin (qv). **9** to knock, rattle.—*n* **1** a harsh, grating sound. **2** the friction of two rough bodies. **3** a whetting. **4** a carpenter's file. **5** a tirling pin (qv), used as a knocker or a doorbell.

risp[2], **rispie** *n* **1** long, coarse grass. **2** a stalk of hay or straw. **3** a bulrush.

risp grass *n* long, coarse grass.

rispings *n* **1** filings. **2** grated bread.

rissar *same as* **rizzar**.

rissle[1] *n* a rod, wand.

rissle[2] *same as* **rizzle**[1].

rissom *n* **1** a stalk or ear of corn. **2** an atom, particle. **3** the smallest possible quantity.

rist *v* to make up a fire for the night.—*n* rest.

ristle *n* a kind of small plough used to draw a deep line in the ground in order that a big plough might more easily follow.

rit[1], **ritt** *v* **1** to incise, furrow. **2** to score, scratch, mark. **3** to cut open, slit. **4** to plunge. **5** to cut a slit in a sheep's ear.—*n* **1** a scratch, a slight incision. **2** a sheep's earmark. **3** a rent, opening. **4** a chasm. **5** a groove.

rit[2] *n* root.

rit-fure *n* **1** the first furrow opened in ploughing. **2** a furrow to run off surface water in a ploughed field.

ritt-master *n* a captain or master of horse.

rittocks *n* the refuse of tallow, when it is first melted and strained.

riv[1] *v* to sew roughly or slightly.

riv[2] *same as* **roove**.

riv[3] *same as* **reeve**[1].

riv[4] *same as* **rive**[1].

riva chair *n* a cleft in a rock, forming a seat.

rive[1] *v* **1** to tear one's food. **2** to eat ravenously. **3** to pull with force. **4** to burst asunder. **5** to burst from overeating. **6** to plough fallow to break in new land. **7** (*of clouds*) to break. **8** (*of a storm*) to rage. **9** to fight, struggle together, romp roughly. **10** to work energetically. **11** to struggle on. **12** to toil on. **13** to plunge forward.—*n* **1** a rent, a tear. **2** a tug, wrench. **3** a piece torn off. **4** (*used of food*) a piece torn off and hastily eaten. **5** the break of day. **6** a worthless lot. **7** energy in work, much work accomplished. **8** a meal to repletion, a surfeit. **9** a large quantity of anything.

rive[2] *same as* **reeve**[6].

rivel-ravel *n* **1** a rigmarole, rhapsody. **2** nonsense.

riven *adj* stolen, plundered. *See* **reeve**.

riven'd *adj* riven, torn.

river[1] *same as* **reever**[2].

river[2] *n* an energetic worker.

rivin' fu' *adj* full to bursting.

riving *adj* **1** energetic. **2** (*used of a storm*) raging.

riv't haet *n* absolutely nothing.

riz *v* rose.

rizar, rizer, rizar *same as* **rizzar**.

rizer *same as* **rizzard**.

risle *v* to beat violently.

rizzar, rizzer, rizzor *v* **1** to dry in the sun. **2** to cool by drying in the sun. **3** to bleach or dry clothes in the open air.—*n* **1** drying by heat, by sun-heat. **2** a haddock dried in the sun.

rizzard, rizzart, rizzer *n* a redcurrant.

rizzard-haddie *n* a dried haddock.

rizzen *n* reason.

rizzer-berry *n* a redcurrant.

rizzim *same as* **rissom**.

rizzle[1] *n* a redcurrant.

rizzle[2] *v* to dry by the heat of the sun or fire.

rizzle-buse *n* a redcurrant bush.

road *n* a direction.—*v* **1** to make a beaten track by repeated walking. **2** (*used of small birds*) to run along the ground before the sportsman instead of flying. **3** (*of a sporting dog*) to follow game closely, to track by scent.

road-collup *n* a portion of the booty paid by the robber to the laird or chief through whose lands he drove his prey.

roadman *n* **1** a carter, one who drives stones for repair of public roads. **2** a man in charge of the roads in a district. **3** one in charge of the ways of a mine.

road money *n* a tax for the maintenance of the public roads.

road-reddens, ~-ribbing *n* mud raked to the side in cleaning roads.

road-scrapings *n* road-reddens (qv).

road-side room *n* room to pass.

road-stamper *n* a wooden leg.

road-stoor *n* dust on the roads.

roak *same as* **rauk**.

roaky *same as* **rauky**.

roan[1] *n* a roan-coloured cow.

roan[2] *same as* **rowan**[3].

roan[3] *same as* **rhone**.

roan[4] *same as* **rone**[1].

roan[5], **roan tree** *same as* **rowan**[1].

roap *same as* **roup**[4].

roar *v* **1** to cry, weep. **2** (*used of a bird*) to emit a loud cry. **3** to emit a loud continuous report, as the cracking of a field of ice. **4** (*used in curling*) to rush with great speed. **5** (*with* in) to salute loudly.—*n* a loud report, as a noisy eructation.

roarer[1] *n* **1** a broken-winded horse. **2** the barn owl. **3** a curling stone driven too forcibly.

roarer[2] *n* anything large of its kind.

roaring-buckie *n* a kind of seashell.

roaring fou *adj* noisily drunk.

roaring game, ~ play *n* the game of curling.

roary *adj* **1** drunk. **2** noisily drunk. **3** gaudy, glaring, flashy.

roasen *adj* roasted.

roasen-like *adj* looking as if roasted.

roast *v* **1** to scald. **2** to burn severely. **3** to tease, joke, jest.—*n* a rough jest.

roasted cheese *n* toasted cheese.

rob[1] *n* blackcurrant jam or jelly.

rob[2] *n* the robin.

robbie boy, rob-boy *n* a hoyden, a tomboy.

robin a ree *n* a game played with a lighted stick.

robin breestie *n* the robin.

robin redbreast *n* the wren.

robin-rin-the-hedge, ~-roun'-the-hedge *n* the goosegrass.

roborate *v* **1** to corroborate. **2** to confirm legally.

robrie *n* robbery.

robustious *adj* robust, healthy, vigorous.

roch *same as* **rouch**[1].

rock[1] *v* to reel under the influence of drink.

rock[2] *n* a distaff.

rockat, rocket *n* **1** a rochet. **2** a loose upper cloak.

rock banes *n* fossil bones.

rock-blackbird *n* the ring ouzel.

rock-cod *n* the cod fish.

rock-doo *n* the wild pigeon.

rocket *n* a porch, vestibule.

rocker *n* one who frequents a rocking (qv).

rockety-row *n* a game in which two persons stand back to back and, with arms intertwined, lift each other alternately.

rock-heartit *adj* stony-hearted.

rocking *n* **1** a visit to a neighbour's house for the evening with rock (*see* **rock**²) and spindle. **2** a friendly gathering of neighbours with their rocks and spindles. **3** a spinning bee or group. **4** a lovers' assignation.

rocklay, rockley *n* a short cloak.

rockle *n* a pebble.

rocklie *adj* abounding in pebbles.

rock-lintie *n* the rock-pipit.

rockly *n* a distaff. *See* **rock**².

rockman *n* a cragsman who catches seafowl.

rock-starling *n* the ring ouzel.

rocky *n* the twite.

rodd *same as* **redd**³.

rodden, roddin *n* **1** the mountain ash. **2** the fruit of the mountain ash. **3** the red berry of the hawthorn, wild rose and sweet briar. *See* **rowan**.

rodden-fleuk *n* the turbot.

roddie *n* **1** a narrow road. **2** a short footpath. *See* **roddin**¹.

roddikin *n* the fourth stomach of a ruminant animal.

roddin¹ *n* **1** a sheep track. **2** making tracks or narrow paths.

roddin² *same as* **rodden**.

rodding time *n* spawning time.

rode¹ *n* a raid, foray.

rode² *v* ridden.

roden, rodin, roden tree *same as* **rodden**.

rodger *n* **1** anything large and ugly. **2** a big ugly animal. **3** a big person of rude manners.—*v* to beat with violence.

rodikin *same as* **roddikin**.

roebuck-berry *n* the stone-brambleberry.

roen *n* **1** a border, selvage, list. **2** a shred.

rogerowse *adj* free of speech, outspoken.

rogie *n* **1** a little rogue. **2** a term of endearment for a child.

rogue *v* to swindle, cheat.

rogue money *n* a tax for the apprehension and punishment of offenders.

roid *same as* **royd**.

roik *same as* **rauk**.

roil *n* a disturbance, storm.

roil-fittit *adj* having the feet turned outwards.

roin *same as* **royne**¹.

roister *n* **1** a bully. **2** a noisy, blustering fellow. **3** a romp.—*adj* noisy, dissolute, riotous.

roisting *adj* noisy.

roit *v* **1** to go about aimlessly and idly. **2** to be troublesome. **3** to cause confusion and noise. **4** to stir up strife.—*n* **1** a forward, disorderly person. **2** an unruly animal. **3** a babbler. **4** a term of contempt for a woman.

roke *same as* **rauk**.

roke *same as* **rock**².

rokelay *n* a short cloak.

roll *same as* **row**¹.

roller *n* **1** a rolling pin. **2** a roll of carded wool ready for spinning. **3** a strickle for a bushel measure.

rolloching, rollying *adj* frank, free, speaking one's mind freely.

rolment *n* a register, record.

roly-poly, rolli-poly *n* a name given to various games of chance played at fairs.

romage *same as* **rummage**.

Roman Catholic *n* the red admiral butterfly.

romantics *n* **1** romancings. **2** exaggerations.

romble *same as* **rummle**².

Rome-believer *n* a Roman Catholic.

rome-blinkit *adj* become somewhat sour.

romie *n* a small brown marble.

rommle *same as* **rummle**².

rond¹ *same as* **rand**¹.

rond² *same as* **rand**³.

rone¹, **ron** *n* **1** a tangle of brushwood, thorns, etc. **2** a thick growth of weeds. **3** a coarse substance adhering to flax,

which has to be scraped off in heckling (qv).

rone² *same as* **rhone**.

rone³ *n* **1** sheepskin dressed to imitate goatskin. **2** roan leather.

roneless *adj* lacking rain spouts.

rong¹ *v* (*used of a bell*) to toll like a funeral or passing bell.

rong² *same as* **rung**.

ronie *adj* covered with rime or sheets of ice.

ronkly *same as* **runkly**.

ronn *same as* **rhone**.

ronnachs *n* couch grass.

ronnal, ronnel *n* the female of salmon trout or any other fish.

ronnet *n* rennet.

ronnet bags *n* the rennets for coagulating.

roo¹ *n* a pile of peats set on end to dry.—*v* to pile up.

roo² *n* an enclosure in a grass field in which cattle are penned up during the night.

Rood-day *n* the day of the Invention of the Cross, 3 May in the Roman calendar, or the Elevation of the Cross, 25 September (14 September OS).

Rood-day in barlan *n* 3 May.

Rood-day in hairst *n* 25 September.

rooden *same as* **rodden**.

Rood-eve *n* **1** the eve of 3 May. **2** the eve of 25 September. **3** the eve of Beltane, 21 June.

Rood-fair *n* a fair held on Rood-day (qv).

rood goose *same as* **rade goose**.

roodoch, roodyoch *same as* **ruddoch**.

Rood's-mass *n* 25 September.

roof *n* the ceiling of a room.

roof-rotten *n* the black rat.

roof timbers *n* the rafters.

rooftree *n* **1** the beam forming the angle of a roof. **2** one's house, home. **3** a toast to the prosperity of one's family.

roog *v* **1** to pull hastily or roughly. **2** to tear. **3** to pull to pieces.—*n* **1** a rough or hasty pull. **2** an article got much under its value.

rook¹ *n* **1** a disturbance, uproar. **2** a noisy company. **3** a set of boisterous companions. **4** a house swarming with inmates.—*v* to cry like a raven or crow.

rook² *n* a heap, pile.—*v* to pile up in heaps.

rook³ *n in phr* **one's hindmost rook** one's last farthing.

rook⁴ *v* to moult.—*n* **1** moulting. **2** a thin, lean animal. **3** a term of contempt.

rook⁵ *v* **1** to clear, bare. **2** to plunder. **3** to cheat and despoil. **4** to devour. **5** to cut close.

rook⁶ *same as* **rauk**.

rook⁷ *n* **1** to win all one's stock of marbles in playing for stakes. **2** a marble.—*int* a boy's shout when he is to take possession of the marbles of the other players.

rookery¹ *n* **1** a disturbance. **2** a noisy quarrel.

rookery² *n* robbery, pillage.

rooketty-coo, rookitty-coo *v* **1** to bill and coo. **2** to fondle.

rooketty-doo *n* a tame pigeon.

rookit¹ *adj* hoarse.

rookit² *adj* **1** (*used of a bird*) moulting. **2** (*of an article of dress*) bare and scrimpy.

rookit³ *n* a rissole.

rookly *same as* **rokelay**.

rooky¹ *adj* misty.

rooky² *adj* hoarse.

roolye, roolyie *v* **1** to rumble. **2** to stir about things noisily.

roolying tree, ~ stick *n* a stick for stirring potatoes in washing them.

room *n* **1** the best sitting room in a small house. **2** a compartment in a boat. **3** a farm. **4** a portion of land. **5** a possession. **6** an official situation. **7** place in logical sequence. **8** place in a literary work.—*adj* **1** roomy. **2** unoccupied.

room-and-kitchen *adj* two-roomed.

roomatica *n* rheumatism.

room end *n* the end of a cottage in which the best room is situated.

roomily *adj* with abundance of room.

roon[1] *same as* **rowan**[3]

roon[2] *same as* **roun**[2].

roon[3], **roond** *adj* round.

roon[4], **roond** *same as* **rand**[1].

roond[1] *same as* **roon**[3].

roond[2] *same as* **roon**[4]

roond[3] *v* **1** to make a loud, hoarse noise in coughing. **2** to grind. **3** to make a disagreeable noise, as by grinding.

roondshoon *same as* **rundshoon**.

roonses *n* (*used in marbles*) the claim of a player to shift to a better position at the same distance from the ring.

roop[1], **roop**[2], **roop**[3] *same as* **roup**[2], **roup**[4], **roup**[6].

roopit *adj* hoarse.

roos *n* fine rain accompanied by high wind.

roose[1], **roos** *v* **1** to praise, extol. **2** to boast. **3** to exaggerate or flatter in praising. **4** to rouse.—*n* **1** praise, commendation. **2** a laudatory toast. **3** a boast.

roose[2] *v* **1** to water. **2** to sprinkle with water. **3** to use a watering pot.

roose[3] *v* to salt a large quantity of fish together, preparatory to curing them.

rooser[1] *n* **1** a boaster. **2** one given to self-commendation.

rooser[2] *n* a watering pot.—*v* to water with a rooser.

rooser[3] *n* **1** anything very large. **2** a big lie.

roosh *same as* **rush**[1].

rooshie-doucie *n* **1** a tumultuous rush. **2** a scrimmage.

rooshoch *adj* **1** coarse. **2** robust. **3** half-mad.

rooshter *n* a severe blow.

roosil *same as* **reeshle**.

roosing[1] *adj* **1** flattering. **2** praising.—*n* boasting.

roosing[2] *same as* **rousing**.

roost[1] *n* **1** the inner roof of a cottage, composed of spars reaching from the one wall to the other. **2** a garret.—*v* to rest, sleep.

roost[2] *n* **1** rust. **2** a brownish blight on wheat.

roost[3] *same as* **reest**[1].

rooster *n* a cock.

roostit *adj* **1** rusted. **2** parched, dry. **3** grizzled.

roosty[1] *adj* (*used of the throat*) rough, hoarse.

roosty[2] *adj* stubborn, restive, irritable.

root[1] *n* **1** the base of a hedge. **2** *in phr* **root and crap** wholly, root and branch.—*v* to uproot.

root[2] *v* **1** to burrow. **2** to rummage. **3** to turn things over in search of anything. **4** to make shift.

root[3] *same as* **rout**[4].

rooter *v* to work in a rough, hurried manner.—*n* **1** rude, unskilful work. **2** a boorish person.

rootering *adj* **1** unskilful. **2** boorish.

rooth *n* a rowlock.

root-hewn *adj* perverse, froward.

roove *v* **1** to rivet, clinch. **2** to settle a point beyond possible alteration.—*n* **1** an iron rivet. **2** a washer of iron on which a nail is clinched.

rooze *same as* **roose**[1].

roozer *same as* **rooser**[2].

rope *same as* **rape**.

roped e'en *n* sore eyes, with rheumy matter hardened on the eyelashes.

rope-ravel *n* a handrail made of rope.

roper's-ree *n* a ropewalk.

roplaw *n* a young fox.

roploch *same as* **raploch**.

roppin *v* **1** to wrap. **2** to rope, tie.

ropple *v* **1** to draw the edges of a hole coarsely together. **2** to work in a hurry and imperfectly.

ropple *same as* **rapple**[2].

ropy *adj* (*of twine or thread*) very coarse and rough.

ropy-e'en *adj* having rheumy matter hardened on the eyelashes.

rorie[1] *n* a cabbage plant run to stalk without having formed a heart.

rorie[2], **rorie boulder** *n* **1** anything large of its kind. **2** a great lie.

rory *adj* **1** drunk, roaring drunk. **2** gaudy, glaring,.

rosa solis *n* the sundew.

rose *n* **1** erysipelas. **2** (*of potatoes*) the crown end of the tubers. **3** the part of a watering pan that scatters the water.—*v* (*of a wound*) to inflame.

rose fever *n* erysipelas.

roseir *n* **1** a rose bush. **2** an arbour of roses.

rose-kaim *n* a fowl with a red or rose-coloured comb.

rose-kaimed *adj* (*used of fowls*) having a tightly curled comb.

rose-lenart, -lintie *n* the red-breasted linnet.

rose-noble *n* the knotted figwort.

rosert *n* resin.

roset, rosit *n* **1** resin. **2** cobblers' wax.—*v* to rub with resin or with cobblers' wax.—*adj* (*used of wood*) resinous.

roset end, roset-end thread *n* the end of a shoemaker's waxed thread.

rosetty *adj* covered with resin or cobblers' wax.

rosetty-end *n* a shoemaker's waxed threadend.

rosie *n* a red clay marble.

rosieways *adv* like roses.

rosin[1] *same as* **rossen**.

rosin[2] *n* boasting. *See* **roose**.

rosit *n* **1** a quarrel. **2** a disturbance.

rossen *n* **1** a bramble thicket. **2** a clump of thorns or briars.

rosseny *adj* abounding in brushwood.

rosy *adj* red.

rot[1], **rott** *v* **1** used in oaths and imprecations. **2** to steep flax.

rot[2] *n* six soldiers of a company.

rot[3] *same as* **rote**.

rotch, rotchie *same as* **ratch**[1].

rotcoll *n* the horseradish.

rote *n* **1** a line cut or drawn along a surface. **2** a scratch or mark made by a point. **3** a row.—*v* **1** to draw lines along a surface. **2** to scratch with a sharp point. **3** to make rows for cabbage, etc.

rot grass *n* the midge grass.

rothos *n* an uproar, tumult.

rot-master *n* a non-commissioned officer, inferior to a corporal.

rot-~, rott-rime *same as* **rat-rhyme**.

rot-stone *n* a soft stone used for scrubbing.

rott *same as* **rot**[1].

rottack, rottick, rottich *n* **1** old, musty corn. **2** anything stored up until it becomes musty. **3** (*in pl*) grubs in a beehive. **4** old rubbishy odds and ends stored up for possible use but never used. **5** lumber.

rottan *same as* **rotten**[2].

rotten[1] *adj* **1** rainy. **2** damp.

rotten[2], **rottan, rotton, rottin** *same as* **ratten**.

rotten-fa' *n* a rat trap.

rotten-whin *n* whin or trap rock of a brittle or non-adhesive variety.

rotten yow *n* an unwholesome person given to much expectoration.

rottich, rottick *same as* **rottack**.

rouch[1] *adj* **1** rough. **2** (*used of the face*) long bearded and moustached. **3** hoarse. **4** plentiful. **5** well-off. **6** luxuriant, sappy. **7** (*used of a bone*) having plenty of meat left on it. **8** (*of the weather*) stormy.—*adv* roughly.—*n* **1** the coarser part of anything. **2** the greater part of anything.—*v* to roughen the shoes of a horse.

rouch[2] *n* **1** a rowlock. **2** the part of the gunwale between the thowls.

rouch and ready *adj* (*used of a meal*) plentiful, but roughly served.

rouch and richt *adv* entirely.—*adj* **1** indifferently well. **2** rough in manners.

rouch and round *n* rude plenty.—*adj* (*used of a meal*) plentiful, but roughly served.

rouch airs *n* **1** rough benty grass. **2** the rough cock's-foot grass.

rouch-handit *adj* violent, daring.

rouchle *v* to toss about.

rouchness *n* **1** roughness. **2** rude plenty. **3** abundance.

rouch-red *n* a variety of potato.

rouch-rider *n* a circus equestrian.

rouch-rullion *n* a rude, rough fellow.

rouchsome *adj* **1** somewhat rough. **2** rather rude in manners. **3** rustic, unpolished.

rouchsome-like *adj* rough-looking.

rouch-spun *adj* **1** rude, blunt. **2** rough in manner or speech.

rouchton *n* a strong, rough fellow.

roudas, roudes *adj* **1** rude, unmannerly. **2** rough. **3** old, haggard, grim.—*n* **1** a virago. **2** an ill-natured, ugly old woman. **3** a strong, masculine woman.

roudoch *same as* **ruddoch**.

rouen *adj* torn, riven (used especially of old pieces of dress and wooden dishes split).

roufu' *adj* rueful, sorrowful-looking.

roug-a-rug *int* a fishwife's cry.

rough[1] *n* a rush.

rough[2] *adj* raw.

rough[3] *same as* **rouch**[1].

rough bear *n* a coarse kind of barley.

roughie *n* **1** a withered bough, brushwood. **2** dried heather. **3** a torch. **4** the torch used in leistering salmon. **5** a wick clogged with tallow instead of being dipped.

roughish meadow grass *n* the birdgrass.

rough tea *n* a high tea (qv).

roughy *n in phr* **auld roughy** a name given to the devil.

rouk[1] *same as* **rook**[5].

rouk[2], **rouke** *same as* **rauk**.

rouk[3] *same as* **rook**[1].

roukery *same as* **rookery**[2].

rouky *same as* **rauky**.

roul *n* a colt. **2** a pony a year old.

roulie-poulie *same as* **roly-poly**.

roun[1] *same as* **room**.—*v in phr* **to soum and roum** to pasture in summer and fodder in winter.

roun[2] *same as* **rowan**[3].

roun[3], **round** *v* **1** to whisper. **2** to speak much and often about one thing.

roun[4] *same as* **round**[3].

rounall *n* anything circular, as the moon.

round[1] *same as* **roun**[3].

round[2], **roun** *adj* **1** (*used of coals*) consisting of lumps or large pieces free from dross. **2** full, abundant.—*n* **1** the immediate neighbourhood. **2** a round of beef. **3** an accustomed way. **4** the way a thing should go round. **5** a semicircular wall of stone and feal (qv) for sheltering sheep. —*v* to turn round.

round[3], **roun** *adv in phr* **round by** nearer, closer in.—*v in phr* **to get round** to recover health.

round[4] *same as* **roond**[3].

round-aboot-fire *n* the circle of persons sitting round the fire.

roundabout *n* **1** a circular fort or encampment. **2** a fireplace with the grate so detached from the wall that persons may sit round it. **3** an oatcake or gingerbread cake of circular form, pinched all round with the finger and thumb. **4** circumlocution.

round-about fireside *n* a fireplace with a detached grate round which all may sit on every side.

round-eared *adj* (*used of a woman's cap*) shaped like a beehive and surrounding the ears.

rounder *n* a whisperer.

rounders *n* the game of prisoners' base.

round-sound *n* the seed vessels of the honesty.

roung *same as* **rung**[1].

rounge *v* to devour greedily.

rounstow *v* to cut off the ears of sheep and so obliterate distinctive marks of ownership.

roun tree *same as* **rowan tree**.

roup[1] *n* the ore weed.

roup[2] *v* **1** to plunder. **2** to devour. **3** to explore.

roup[3] *v* to vomit.

roup[4] *v* **1** to shout, to cry hoarsely. **2** to croak. **3** to sell by auction. **4** to sell up.—*n* **1** hoarseness. **2** the croup. **3** a disease affecting the throat or mouth of fowls. **4** a sale by auction.

roup[5] *n* a close mist.

roup[6] *n in phr* **stoup and roup** entirely.

roup bill *n* a bill announcing an auction.

roup day *n* the day of sale by auction.

rouped price *n* the price realized at an auction.

rouper *n* **1** one who sells his or her goods by auction. **2** an auctioneer.

roup folk *n* people attending an auction.

roup green *n* the grass plot on which an auction is held.

roupie *adj* overgrown with ore weed.

roupie *adj* hoarse.

rouping *n* an auction.

rouping wife *n* a woman who buys at auctions to sell again.

roupit *adj* **1** hoarse. **2** spent with shouting.

roup roll *n* the list of articles to be sold at auction.

roup wife *n* a female auctioneer.

roupy *adj* viscous, ropy.

roupy weather *n* foggy weather that makes one hoarse.

rouse[1] *v* to stir up a fire.—*n* **1** a reveille. **2** a state of excitement, a hurry.

rouse[2], **rouse**[3], **rouse**[4] *same as* **roose**[1], **roose**[2], **roose**[3].

rouse away *int* haul away! the call of a freshwater boatswain.

rouser[1], **rouser**[2] *same as* **roose**[2], **roose**[3].

rousing *adj* **1** resounding. **2** (*used of a fire*) brisk, blazing, roaring. **3** strong, large. **4** (*used of a lie*) big, massive.— *n* noisy, unruly mirth.

rousing bell *n* a bell rung at 8 a.m. to arouse the upland (qv) people to get ready for church.

rousling *adj* **1** rousing. **2** bustling.

roussil *v* to rouse.

roussillin *same as* **rousling**.

roust[1] *same as* **roost**[2].

roust[2] *v* **1** to rouse. **2** to rout out.

roust[3] *v* **1** to roar. **2** to bellow. **3** to make a loud noise as on a trumpet.—*n* **1** a roar, a bellow. **2** the act of roaring or bellowing.

rouster *n* a stroke, a blow.

roustit *same as* **roostit**.

roustree *n* the crossbar on which a crook is hung.

rousty *same as* **roosty**.

rout[1] *v* to go to parties.—*n* **1** a party. **2** a rabble.

rout[2] *n* the brent goose.

rout[3] *v in phr* **1** **rout about** to poke about, to go from place to place rummaging. **2** **rout out** to clear out.—*n in phr* **1** **rin the rout** to gad or run about. **2** **tak' the rout** to take to flight.

rout[4] *v* **1** to low loudly, as cattle. **2** to bellow, roar. **3** to bray. **4** to make any loud noise. **5** to snore. **6** to break wind backwards.—*n* **1** the prolonged or angry low of a cow. **2** a donkey's bray. **3** a loud noise. **4** a bustle, commotion, disturbance.

rout[5] *v* to strike, beat.—*n* a heavy blow.

router[1] *n* a cow.

router[2] *same as* **rooter**.

routh[1] *n* plenty, abundance.—*adj* abundant, well-supplied.

routh[2] *n* **1** a rowlock. **2** the act of rowing.

routhily, routhlie *adv* abundantly, plentifully.

routhless *adj* **1** profane. **2** regardless of God and man.

routhrie *n* plenty, abundance.

routhy *adj* **1** abundant. **2** well-furnished.

routing *adj* **1** noisy, blustering. **2** loud-sounding.

routing well *n* a well that makes a rumbling noise, predicting a storm.

rove[1] *v, adj* riven.

rove[2] *v* **1** to be delirious. **2** to rave. **3** to talk in one's sleep.

4 to have high animal spirits.—*n* **1** a stroll, ramble. **2** a wandering.

rove³ *v* **1** to twist yarn into rolls preparatory to spinning. **2** to twist. **3** to fasten.—*n* **1** a twist of rope. **2** a roll of cotton or yarn, to be drawn into thread by the spindle.

rovers *n in phr* **at rovers** at random.

roving *adj* **1** of unsettled character. **2** merry, excitable. **3** full of animal spirits. **4** (*of the weather*) unsettled.—*adv* quite, excessively.—*n* delirium, raving.

roving-fu' *adj* full to overflowing.

row¹, **rowe** *v* **1** to roll. **2** to wrap up. **3** to wind, turn, move round. **4** (*with* **up**) to wind up a clock. **5** to tie a sheaf of corn. **6** to make carded wool into a roll for spinning. **7** to nod through drowsiness. **8** (*with* **about**) to be advanced in pregnancy. **9** (*used of tears*) to flow.—*n* **1** a roll of wool. **2** a roll for a woman's hair. **3** a roll of tobacco. **4** a roller. **5** a fat, plump person.

row² *n* **1** a street in a coal-mining village. **2** a ridge of ground. **3** genus, class, set.—*v* **1** to set out, sow, plant, place or stand in rows. **2** to come up in rows.

rowan¹ *n* **1** the mountain ash. **2** its fruit.

rowan² *n* **1** a flake of wool. **2** *in phr* **to cast a rowan** to bear an illegitimate child.

rowan³ *n* **1** the roe of a fish. **2** a turbot.

rowans, rowins *n* wool made up in long rolls ready for spinning.

rowan tree *n* the mountain ash.

rowar *n* a row of carded wool ready to be spun.

row-chow-tobacco, rowity-chow-o'-tobacco *n* a game of boys in a line, holding each other's hands and gradually coiling themselves round one at the extremity (who is called the pin) in imitation of a tobacconist winding up his roll round a pin.

row-de-dow, rowdy-dow *n* **1** a disturbance, uproar. **2** a bitter quarrel.

rowdy-dowdy *adv* **1** with great confusion and noise. **2** in noisy disorder.

rowe *same as* **row**¹.

rower *n* **1** a roller. **2** one who wheels peats for drying.

row-footed *adj* rough-footed, rough-shod.

rowin-pin *n* a roller for flattening dough.

rowk *same as* **rauk**.

rowl¹ *v* to roll.

rowl² *same as* **roul**.

rowle *v* to rule.

rowley-powley *same as* **roly-poly**.

rowm *n* **1** a situation. **2** a possession in land. **3** a place in a literary work or in logical sequence.

rowme *adj* clear, empty.

rowmmil *same as* **rummle**.

rown¹, **rownd** *same as* **rowan**³.

rown² *same as* **roun**³.

rowns *n* the berries of the mountain ash.

rown tree *n* the mountain ash.

rowp *same as* **roup**⁴.

rowsan *same as* **rousing**.

rowt¹, **rowt**², **rowt**³, **rowt**⁴ *same as* **rout**¹, **rout**², **rout**⁴, **rout**⁵.

rowth *same as* **routh**¹.

roxle *v* **1** to grunt. **2** to speak hoarsely.

roy *n* a king.

royal¹ *n* **1** royalty. **2** a gold coin. **3** applied to certain silver coins in conjunction with the name of the reigning sovereign.

royal² *adj* at an advanced stage of drunkenness.

royal blue *n* whisky.

royal bracken *n* the flowering or royal fern.

royaleese *v* to play the king.

royalty, royality *n* territory under the immediate jurisdiction of the king.

royd, royet, rogat, royit *adj* **1** frolicsome, romping, tomboyish. **2** riotous, mischievous. **3** wild. **4** stormy. **5** unruly. **6** dissipated.—*v* **1** to romp. **2** to feast well.

royetnese *n* romping, wildness.

royetous *adj* wild, unruly.

royl-fittit *same as* **roil-fittit**.

royne¹ *n* a selvage.

royne² *same as* **rane**¹.

royst *adj* **1** wild. **2** dissolute.

royster *n* a bully.—*adj* noisy, riotous.

roystering *adj* swaggering, blustering.

roysting *adj* noisy.

royston-crow *n* the hooded crow.

roy't *same as* **royd**.

royt, royte *v* **1** to go aimlessly or idly from place to place. **2** to be troublesome. **3** to cause confusion and noise. **4** to stir up strife.—*n* **1** a forward, disorderly person. **2** an unruly animal.

royter *v* to work unskilfully. **2** to talk foolishly.

rozered *adj* **1** rosy. **2** resembling a rose.

rozet *same as* **roset**.

rub¹ *v* **1** to rob. **2** to practise robbery.

rub² *n* **1** an indirect reproof. **2** an insinuation. **3** a hard, grasping person.—*v* (*with* **on** *or* **upon**) to impute, impose.

rubbage *n* rubbish.

rubber¹ *n* a robber.

rubber² *n* a scrubber.

rubbers and reengers *n* a children's game, through the needle-e'e.

rubbery *n* robbery.

rubbidge *n* rubbish.

rubbing bottle *n* a liniment.

rubbings *n* a liniment.

rubbing stick *n* a stick used by shoemakers to rub leather into smoothness.

rubbing stock *n* a post set up for cattle to rub themselves against.

ruber *n* **1** a cask. **2** a wine cask.

rubiator *same as* **rabiator**.

ruch *same as* **rouch**.

ruck¹ *n* **1** the majority, the bulk. **2** a mass.

ruck² *n* a rick, stack.—*v* to build in a stack.

rucker *n* one who builds in a stack.

ruckle¹ *same as* **rickle**.

ruckle² *n* **1** a crease. **2** a wrinkle.—*v* to rumple, wrinkle.—*adj* rough, uneven.

ruckle³ *v* **1** to breathe with difficulty. **2** to make a harsh, rattling sound in the throat.—*n* **1** a hoarse, gurgling sound made in hard breathing. **2** the death rattle.

ruckly *adj* **1** rickety. **2** unsteady, dilapidated.

ruction, ruckshun *n* **1** a quarrel. **2** a disturbance.

rudas *adj* **1** bold, masculine. **2** stubborn, rude. **3** rough, unmannerly. **4** haggard, old.—*n* **1** a virago. **2** an ill-natured, ugly old woman.

rudd *same as* **redd**³.

rudder¹ *n* wreck, ruin, smash.

rudder² *n* an implement for stirring the mash in brewing.

ruddikin *same as* **roddikin**.

ruddin *same as* **rodden**.

rudding time *n* spawning time.

ruddoch *n* **1** a beldame, hag. **2** a deluded wretch. **3** a monster, villain.—*adj* sour-looking, sulky.

ruddoch, ruddock *n* the robin.

ruddy¹ *n* ruddiness, ruddy complexion.

ruddy² *v* **1** to make a loud, reiterated noise. **2** to rumble.—*n* **1** a thud. **2** a loud, reiterated noise.

ruddying *n* a loud knocking.

rude¹ *n* **1** the complexion. **2** the red colour of the complexion.

rude² *same as* **redd**³.

rude³ *n* the cross, the rood.

rude⁴ *n* a rood of ground.

rude goose *n* the barnacle goose.

rudes *same as* **rudas**.

rud-hand *adj* red-handed.

rudjen *v* to beat.

rudous *same as* **rudas**.

rue *n* **1** regret, repentance. **2** *in phr* **to take the rue** to change one's mind, draw back from a promise or engagement.

rue-bargain *n* smart money for breaking a bargain.

ruech *n* a hill pasture, cattle run, summer shieling.

rueless *adj* unregretful.

ruend *same as* **rand**[1].

ruff[1] *v* **1** to beat a drum. **2** to applaud by stamping with the feet.—*n* **1** the noise made by the beating of a drum. **2** applause made by stamping with the feet.

ruff[2] *n* an eruption on the skin.

ruff[3] *v* **1** to ruffle. **2** to put in disorder.

ruffe *n* fame, celebrity.

ruffle *v* **1** to insult. **2** to threaten.—*n* **1** an insurrection. **2** a skirmish.

rufflet sark *n* a frilled shirt.

ruffy *adj* **1** unkempt. **2** (*used of cabbages*) not properly hearted.

ruffy *same as* **roughie**.

ruffy-headed *adj* having rough, unkempt hair.

ruft *same as* **rift**[1].

rug[1], **rugg** *n* a kind of cloth for clothes.

rug[2], **rugg** *v* to pull forcibly, tug, tear.—*n* **1** a pull, tug, bite. **2** dragging power. **3** a severe throb of pain. **4** an unfair advantage. **5** a good bargain or investment.

rug aud rive *v* **1** to drag forcibly, to contend violently for possession. **2** to pull or haul in a quarrel.

rugg[1], **rugg**[2] *same as* **rug**[1], **rug**[2].

ruggin' *n* a tough fowl, not easy to carve or eat.

ruggly *adj* **1** unsteady, rickety. **2** causing unsteady pulling or tugging. *See* **rug**[1].

ruggy-duggy *n* a rough, boisterous person.

rugh *adj* rough.

rugl *v* to shake, tug backwards and forwards.—*n* a shake, tug, a pull backwards and forwards.

rug-saw *n* a wide-toothed saw.

ruh-heds *n* **1** turfs for fuel, cut with grass adhering. **2** rough heads.

ruik *same as* **ruck**[2].

ruil *n* **1** an unruly person or animal. **2** an awkward female romp.—*v* to romp.

ruin *v* **1** to soil. **2** to spoil.

ruind *same as* **rand**[1].

ruint *same as* **roond**.

ruise, ruiss *same as* **roose**[1].

ruit *n* a root.

ruith *same as* **rueth**.

rule *same as* **ruil**.

rule o' contrary *n* a girls' game.

rule-o'er-thoum *adv* **1** slapdash. **2** off-hand. **3** without consideration or accuracy.

rulie *adj* unruly, talkative. *See* **ruil**.

rullion *n* **1** a shoe made of untanned leather. **2** a piece of thick, rough cloth. **3** a rough dress. **4** a big, coarse-looking person or animal. **5** a term of contempt or pity. **6** a noise, clatter.—*adj* **1** coarse. **2** loud, noisy.

rullion-hand *n* a rude, coarse hand.

rullion-shout *n* a loud, noisy shout.

rullye *same as* **rally**[1].

rum[1] *n in phr* **christened rum** rum and water.

rum[2] *adj* **1** ingenious, especially in mischief or wickedness. **2** excellent of its kind.

rumatics *n* rheumatism.

rumballiach *adj* **1** (*used of the weather*) stormy. **2** (*of a person*) quarrelsome.

rumble *same as* **rummle**[2].

rumblegarie *adj* **1** disorderly. **2** confused in manner. **3** forward.—*n* **1** a forward person. **2** a romp. **3** a rambling, roving person.

rumble-gumption *n* common sense.

rumble-tumble *n* the rumbling sound of rushing water.—*adj* **1** hurried. **2** confused. **3** noisy.

rumbling *adj* hungry, having a growing appetite.

rumel-~, rumle-gumption, ~-gumshion, ~ gumtion *n* **1** common sense. **2** smartness of mind.

rumgumption *n* **1** common sense. **2** shrewdness.

rumgunshoch, rumgunshach *adj* **1** (*used of soil*) rocky, stony. **2** (*of persons*) coarse, rude, unkind. —*n* a coarse, rude person.

ruminage *v* to rummage.

rumish *same as* **reemish**.

rumlieguff *n* a rattling, foolish fellow.

rummage *v* **1** to search untidily. **2** to rampage, storm, rage.—*n* a great noise or disturbance.

rummer *n* the mat on which the toddy tumbler was placed.

rummiss *same as* **reemish**.

rummle[1], **rummell** *same as* **ramle**[2].

rummle[2], **rummil** *v* **1** to rumble. **2** to stir violently. **3** to push or poke about. **4** to beat, knock about. **5** to rummage. **6** to clear a tube or pipe with rod or wire.—*n* **1** a rumble. **2** a thunder peal. **3** anything causing a rumbling sound. **4** a large, inconvenient house or room. **5** a cumbrous piece of furniture.

rummle-de-thump *n* **1** mashed potatoes. **2** a mess of potatoes and cabbage.

rummled tatties *n* mashed potatoes.

rummle-, rummil-gairie *same as* **rumblegarie**.

rummle-~, rummel-~, rummil-gumption, ~-gumshon *n* **1** common sense. **2** shrewdness.

rummle-hobble *n* confusion, disorder.

rummle-kirn *n* a gully on a wild, rocky shore.

rummle-~, rummel shackin *adj* **1** raw-boned. **2** loose-jointed.

rummle-skeerie, ~-skerie *n* **1** a madcap. **2** a wild, reckless romp.

rummle-thump *n* potatoes and cabbage.

rummlety-thump *n* **1** mashed potatoes. **2** rummle-thump (qv).

rummlin kirn *n* a gully on a wild, rocky shore.

rummlin sive, ~ syvrer *n* a drain filled up to the surface with loose stones for percolation.

rump[1] *n* **1** an ugly, raw-boned animal, especially a cow. **2** a contemptuous name for a person.

rump[2] *v* **1** to break. **2** to cut off close. **3** to smash, beat. **4** to deprive a person of all his or her property or money, as by gambling.

rump and dozen *n* the wager of a rump of beef and a dozen of wine as a dinner.

rump and stump *adv* wholly, root and branch.

rumping *adj* **1** reduced in size. **2** growing less and less.

rumping shaft *n* a rod used by the weaver when he went to the warehouse for money for payment in advance.

rumple *n* **1** the rump. **2** the rump bone. **3** the tail.

rumple bane *n* the rump bone.

rumpled *adj* (*used of the brain*) confused.

rumple-fyke *n* the itch when it has got a firm hold.

rumple knot *n* a bunch of ribbons worn at the back of the waist.

rumple-routie *n* the haunch.

rumple-tumple *v* to roll in play down a declivity.

rumption *n* a noisy bustle within doors, driving everything into confusion.

rumpus *v* **1** to quarrel. **2** to behave boisterously.

rumpy bum coat *n* a short, tailless coat.

run[1] *same as* **rand**[1].

run[2] *v* **1** to compete with in running. **2** to land smuggled goods. **3** to fix with melted lead. **4** to leak, let in water. **5** to flow. **6** to suppurate. **7** (*of the eyes*) to water. **8** to curdle.—*n* **1** a smuggling voyage. **2** the track of an animal. **3** a stretch of pasturage. **4** a small water channel. **5** a pipe for carrying water from a roof, a rone. **6** a squall, blast. **7** heavy surge on a shore caused by a past or approaching gale. **8** business, line of goods, etc.

run[3] *same as* **rand**[3].

runagate *adj* **1** vagabond. **2** roving, unsettled.—*n* a worthless person.

runch[1] *n* **1** wild mustard. **2** the wild radish.

runch[2] *same as* **runsheoch**.

runch[3] *n* **1** an iron instrument for twisting nuts on screw bolts. **2** a wrench or screw key.

runch[4] *adj (used of whisky punch)* strong.

runch[5] *v* **1** to crunch. **2** to grind the teeth. **3** to wrench, rive.—*n* **1** the act of crunching any harsh edible substance or of grinding the teeth. **2** a bite, a piece of anything taken out with the teeth. **3** the noise of a sharp instrument piercing the flesh.

runchie-week *n* the first week in May.

runchy, runchie *adj* large, raw-boned.

runckle, runcle *same as* **runkle**.

runcy *n* a woman of coarse manners and doubtful character.

rund[1], **rund**[2] *same as* **rand**[1], **rand**[3].

rund *same as* **roond**.

rundale *same as* **rendal**.

run-deil *n* **1** a thorough devil. **2** an incorrigible villain.

rundge *v* to gnaw.

rund shoon *n* shoes made of list or selvages of cloth.

rune *same as* **rand**[1].

rung[1] *n* **1** a cudgel, staff. **2** a stout piece of wood. **3** a bough. **4** a rail on the side of a cart. **5** a bar in a chair. **6** the spoke of a wheel. **7** an ugly, big-boned person or animal. **8** a contemptuous term for an old person, particularly an old woman. **9** the stroke of poverty.—*v* to cudgel.

rung[2] *v* reigned.

rung[3] *adj* exhausted by running.

rung[4] *n* an edge, selvage, list.

rung cart *n* a cart, the sides of which are made of round pieces of wood.

runge *v* to rummage, to search eagerly.

runged stool *n* a stool or chair with the seat and back formed of rungs.

rung gin *n* a gin worked by a rung wheel (qv).

rung-in *adj* worn-out by fatigue. *See* **ring in**.

rungle, rungil tree *same as* **rantle tree**.

rung wheel *n* a wheel with spokes that are driven by the cogs of a wheel geared into it. *See* **rung gin**.

runigate *same as* **runagate**.

run in *v* to pour in.

runjoist *n* a strong spar laid alongside a roof that is to be thatched.

runk[1] *n* **1** a fold, plait, crease. **2** a term of anger or contempt applied to a woman. **3** a harsh, cruel woman. **4** an old woman, a hag. **5** a scandalmonger, gossip. **6** an old, outworn, lean animal. **7** a broken or twisted and useless branch of a tree.—*adj* wrinkled.

runk[2] *v* **1** to deprive one of one's possessions by any means. **2** to attack or undermine one's character. **3** to ruin. **4** to satirize.

runkar *n* the lumpfish.

runkle *v* to wrinkle, crease, crumple.—*n* a wrinkle, crease, crumple.

runkly *adj* wrinkled, creased, crumpled.

run-knot *n* a slipknot, a knot that cannot be untied.

run-metal *n* cast iron.

run milk *n* curdled milk.

runnagate *adj* **1** vagabond. **2** worthless.

runner *n* **1** a small channel for water. **2** a kennel, gutter. **3** the slice that extends across the forepart of a carcass of beef under the breast.

running-dog *n* a dog given to roaming.

running-trade *n* smuggling.

run off *v* to pour out.

run out *v* **1** to leak. **2** to pour into, fill up.

run-rig, run-ridge *n* land where the alternate ridges of a field belong to different owners or are worked by different tenants.

runse[1] *n* the noise of a sharp instrument piercing the flesh.

runse[2] *same as* **runch**[1].

runsh *same as* **runch**[5].

runshag, runshick *n* **1** the wild mustard. **2** the wild radish.

runsheoch *n* a large, raw-boned person.

runt[1] *n* **1** an ox or cow of small breed. **2** an old ox or cow. **3** a short, thickset person. **4** an old person. **5** a withered old man or woman, a hag. **6** a cabbage or kail stem. **7** the dry, hard stalk of a plant. **8** a short, thick stick, a cudgel. **9** the tail or rump of an animal. **10** a shaft or handle.—*v* to grow old.

runt[2] *v* **1** to rush out. **2** to bounce, prance.

runt[3] *v* **1** to rend, tear. **2** *(used of cloth)* to make a loud ripping sound when cut or torn.

runt[4] *v* to take all a person's money.

runted[1] *adj* stunted in growth.

runted[2] *adj (used in the game of marbles)* having lost all one's marbles.

run-the-road, ~-the-rout *adj* vagrant, gadabout. —*n* **1** one who has no fixed residence. **2** a tramp, a gadabout.

run to *v* to have recourse to, resort to.

run upon *v* to shame, disgust, grieve.

run-wull *adj* **1** run wild. **2** out of reach of the law.

ruppit *same as* **rippet**.

ruralach *n* a rustic, native of a rural district.

ruse[1], **ruse**[2] *same as* **roose**[1], **roose**[2].

ruse[3] *v* did rise.

ruser[1] *n* **1** a boaster. **2** a flatterer.

ruser[2] *n* a watering pan.

rush[1] *n* **1** diarrhoea in sheep, when first put on new or rank pasture. **2** a broil.—*v* to throw down with violence.

rush[2] *n* a rash, skin eruption.

rush-fever *n* scarlet fever.

rushie *n* **1** a broil, quarrel. **2** a tumult.

rushie-doucie *n* **1** a tumultuous rush. **2** a scrimmage.

rushy *adj* thatched with rushes.

rushy wick *n* a rush wick.

rusie *same as* **roose**[1].

rusk[1] *v* **1** to claw, scratch vigorously. **2** to pluck roughly.

rusk[2] *v* to risk.—*n* risk.

ruskie[1], **rusky** *adj* **1** healthy, vigorous, stout. **2** strong, of force.—*n* **1** a strong person of rough manners. **2** a very stout woman.

ruskie[2], **ruskey, rusky** *n* **1** a seed basket used in sowing. **2** a basket of straw for holding oatmeal. **3** a straw beehive. **4** a coarse straw hat worn by peasant girls and others.

russel, russle, rustle *n* a redcurrant.

russel buss *n* a redcurrant bush.

rust *same as* **reest**[1].

rusty[1], **rusty**[2] *same as* **roosty**[1], **roosty**[2].

rute *same as* **rout**[5].

ruth[1] *same as* **routh**[1].

ruth[2] *adj* kind.

ruth[3] *same as* **routh**[2].

ruthag *n* a young edible sea crab.

ruthe *n* the seeds of the spurrey.

ruther[1] *n* a rudder.

ruther[2] *n* **1** an uproar. **2** a noise. **3** outcry.—*v* **1** to storm, bluster. **2** to roar.

rutherair *n* an uproar.

ruthie *n* the noise in the throat or chest caused by oppressed breathing.

rutle *v* **1** to rattle. **2** to breathe with a rattling sound, as in dying persons.—*n* a rattling sound in the throat, the death rattle.

ruve *same as* **roove**.

ruz, ruzie *same as* **roose**[1].

ryal *same as* **royal**.

rybat *same as* **rebbit**.

rybe *same as* **reib**.

ryce *same as* **rice**.

rye-craik *n* the landrail.

rye kail *n* rye broth.

ryefart *same as* **reefart**.

ryfe out *v* **1** to break up land. **2** to reclaim waste land. *See* **rive**[1].

ryke *v* to reach.

ryle *same as* **ravel**[2].

rymeless *same as* **rhymeless**.

rynd[1] *v* to get one's affairs in order.

rynd² *same as* **rind**².
rynes *n* reins.
rynk *same as* **rink**¹.
rynmart *same as* **rhind-mart**.
ryot *n* **1** an assault. **2** an illegal interference. **3** a breach of

the peace.
rype¹ *adj* **1** ripe. **2** ready.—*v* to ripen.
rype² *same as* **ripe**².
ryss *same as* **rice**.
ryve *same as* **rive**¹.

S

s *n* an iron hook shaped like the letter S.
's *v* is.
saal *same as* **saul**.
saan *n* sand.
saan-blin' *adj* purblind.
saat *same as* **saut**.
sab¹ *n* **1** a sob. **2** a gust, a gale of wind. **3** a land storm. **4** the noise of the sea.—*v* **1** to sob. **2** to make a hissing noise, as green wood, etc, in a fire. **3** (*used of flowers*) to fade.
sab² *v* to soak, saturate.
sab³ *v* **1** (*of flooring, etc*) to subside, settle down. **2** (*of a wooden floor*) to make an elastic movement on the fall of a heavy body or the starting of a joist.—*n* such an elastic motion of a floor.
Sabbathly *adv* on every Sabbath.
sabelline *n* sable.
sacban, sackbaun *n* an apparition, preceding a person and portending sudden death in the house at which it stops.
sachet *n* a small sack.
sachless *same as* **sackless**.
sack *n* **1** a sackcloth or coarse linen garment worn by offenders in public penitence. **2** a bottle. **3** a term of contempt for a man.—*v* **1** to put into a sack or pocket.
sacken *n* sacking.
sacken goun, ~ sark, ~ weed *n* a sack goun (qv).
sacket *n* **1** a bag, a small sack. **2** a short, dumpy person. **3** a determined little fellow.
sackety *adj* short and thick.
sack goun *n* the garb of an offender doing public penance.
sackie *adj* short and thick.—*n* a short, dumpy person.
sackit *same as* **sacket**.
sackless *adj* **1** blameless, guiltless, innocent. **2** simple, inoffensive, harmless. **3** useless, silly, feeble.
sackleasly *adv* innocently.
sacrament time *n* a communion season.
sacrify *v* to consecrate.
sacrist *n* a university macebearer, who has also charge of the cleaning of classrooms, etc.
sad *adj* **1** solid, firm, compact. **2** beaten hard. **3** (*used of bread, etc*) heavy. **4** singular, remarkable, uncommon. **5** great. **6** flat. **7** close to the ground.—*v* **1** to consolidate by tramping or otherwise. **2** to sink, settle down. **3** to grow solid. **4** to sadden.—*n* a heavy, downward, consolidating movement.
sadden *v* to consolidate, beat down.
saddle, sadle *n* **1** the part of a stall between the manger and the grip or drain. **2** a settle, a wooden seat.
saddle-gear *n* saddlery.
saddle-irons *n* stirrups.
saddle-my-nag *n* a boys' game.
saddle-seat *n* a saddle horse.
saddle-sick *adj* sore from long riding.
saddle-tae-side, ~-tae-sidlins *adv* side-saddle, not astride.
saddle-tore *n* a saddlebow.
saddle-turside *n* a settle.
sade *n* **1** a thick sod or turf for burning. **2** sward.
sadjell *n* a lazy, unwieldy animal.
sadlies *adv* **1** sadly. **2** to a great degree, greatly.
sae¹ *adv* **1** so. **2** as.
sae² *same as* **sey**⁴.
sae-be, saebeins, saebins *conjs* **1** if so be, provided that. **2** since.
saed *n* a full-grown coalfish.

saeg¹ *v* to set the teeth on edge by eating anything sour.
saeg², **saege** *same as* **segg**².
sael *same as* **seal**¹.
sae-like *adj* similar.
saelkie *n* **1** a seal, sea calf. **2** a big, stout person.
saem *same as* **saim**.
saer *as* **sair**¹.
saet *same as* **saed**.
sae tree *n* a pole for carrying pails.
saewyse *adv* in such wise.
saf, salf, safs *v* to save.
safer *n* a safe.
saft *adj* **1** muddy. **2** (*of the weather*) damp, drizzling, rainy. **3** (*of a horse*) out of condition, tender. **4** pleasant, easy. **5** gentle. **6** weak, simple, effeminate. **7** easily imposed on. **8** half-witted, foolish. **9** amorous, sentimental.—*adv* **1** gently, lightly. **2** easily.—*n* **1** cut tobacco in contrast to cake or twist. **2** ale in contrast to whisky.
saft cake *n* an oatcake before it is dried.
saft e'ened *adj* disposed to weep, softhearted.
saften *v* **1** to soften. **2** to thaw.
saft-fisted *adj* effeminate.
saft-fittit *adv* quietly.
saft-hand *n* a foolish, inexpert person.
saft-heid *n* a simpleton, a fool.
saft-heidit *adj* silly, foolish.
saftick *n* the shore crab after it has cast its shell.
saftness *n* weakness of character.
saft-side *n* in phr **one's saft-side** one's weakness, one's good graces.
saft-skinned *adj* **1** sensitive. **2** thin-skinned.
saft-soles *n* a simpleton, fool.
saft-tobacco *n* cut tobacco.
saft-veal *n* a simpleton.
saft-win' *n* flattery.
safty *n* **1** a crab that has cast its shell. **2** a simpleton. **3** one easily duped. **4** a weak, effeminate person.
sag *same as* **segg**¹.
sagan *n* **1** a devil. **2** Satan.
sag-backit *adj* (*used of a horse*) having a sunk back.
saggon *n* **1** the water flag. **2** various species of rushes, reeds and sedges.
saght *v* sought.
sagor *n* a wild fellow.
saick *same as* **sack**.
saickless *same as* **sackless**.
saicretfu' *adj* secretive.
said¹ *same as* **saed**.
said² *n* a mature coalfish.
saidle *n* a saddle.
saidle-turside *n* a settle.
said-sae *n* a report.
saig¹ *v* **1** to sag. **2** to press down. **3** to cause to bend.
saig² *same as* **segg**¹.
saig³ *same as* **segg**².
saigh *v* to sigh.
saikless *same as* **sackless**.
sail *v* to ride in a vehicle.—*n* **1** a ride in a vehicle. **2** *in phr* **to keep a low sail** to live quietly.
sailfish *n* the basking shark.
sailing-Jack *n* the Blue Peter, the flag used as a signal for sailing.
saille *n* happiness.

sailor-lad *n* a girls' dancing and singing game.
sailzie, sailyie *n* an assault.—*v* to assail.
saim *n* **1** lard. **2** goose grease. **3** fat. **4** fish oil.
sain *v* **1** to make the sign of the cross. **2** to bless. **3** to consecrate. **4** to shield from evil influence of-fairies, witches,
etc. **5** to absolve of.—*n* a blessing.
sainins *n* **1** a scolding. **2** what one thinks of another's bad
conduct.
sainlese *adj* **1** unblessed, graceless. **2** profane.
saint *v* **1** to bless. **2** to turn saint, become devout.
Saint Causlan's flaw *n* a shower of snow in March.
Saint John's nut *n* a double nut.
Saint Mary knot *n* a triple knot.
Saint Mary's knot *n in phr* **to tie with St Mary's knot** to
hamstring.
Saint Monday *n* the day on which workmen spend Saturday's wages on drink.
Saint Peter's wort *n* the hypericum or hard hay.
Saint Sair *n* St Serf.
Saint Sair's fair *n* a fair held on St Serf's Day.
saint's bell *n* the small church bell rung just before service begins.
saip *n* soap.—*v* to soap.
saip-blotts *n* soapsuds.
saipman *n* a soap boiler.
saip-sapples *n* soapsuds.
saipy *adj* soapy.
sair[1] *adj* **1** sore. **2** aching. **3** sad, sorrowful. **4** costly. **5** heavy,
great. **6** sorry, puny, scanty. **7** niggardly. **8** (*of the weather*)
tempestuous.—*adv* **1** sorely, grievously. **2** very, greatly. **3** very
well.—*n* **1** a wound, bruise. **2** a crack, fracture. **3** sorrow.
sair[2] *v* **1** to serve, serve out. **2** to treat. **3** to serve along with
an article of food. **4** to supply with alms. **5** (*used of
clothes*) to fit, be large enough for. **6** to satisfy. **7** to suffice for. **8** (*with* **of**) to satisfy with, to tire of. **9** (*with* **out**)
to deal out, divide.—*n* a small quantity of food, a mor-
sel, a grain.
sair[3] *v* **1** to taste, smell, savour. **2** to be appetizing. **3** (*with*
out) to scent out, smell out.—*n* **1** a taste, smell. **2** a stench.
3 wit, spirit, courage. **4** a gentle breeze. **5** unction.
sair aff *adj* **1** straitened in means. **2** greatly to be pitied.
sairch *v* to search.—*n* a search.
sair-dowed *adj* sorely worn by grief.
sair-dung *adj* hard put to.
sair-fit *n* a time of need.
sair-han' *n* a mess, muddle.
sair-heel *n* **1** a time of need. **2** a tender spot.
sair-heid *n* a headache.
sair-hertit *adj* sad of heart.
sairie *adj* **1** poor. **2** silly. **3** feeble. **4** sorry. **5** sorrowful. **6**
contemptible. **7** innocent. **8** needy. **9** empty.
sairie-man *n* an expression of affection, often used to a
dog.
sairing[1] *n* **1** a serving, a helping. **2** a sufficiency of food. **3**
a sufficient punishment. **4** an alms.
sairing[2] *n* **1** a taste. **2** the smallest quantity or portion of
anything.
sairious *adj* serious.
sairless *adj* savourless, tasteless, insipid.
sair-lump *n* a boil.
sairly *adv* **1** severely. **2** greatly, sorely (*used intensively*).
sairmiss't *adj* **1** greatly missed. **2** deeply regretted.
sairness *n* soreness.
sair pechin' *adj* sorely panting.
sair-six *n* a rotation of crops, two each of grass and cereals, one of turnips and one of cereals.
sair-sought, --socht *adj* **1** much exhausted. **2** nearly
worn-out by age or weakness. **3** eagerly desired, anxiously sought.
sair-sunk *adj* deeply sunk.
sair-wroucht, --wroucht, --wrocht *adj* hard- worked.
sair wame *n* colic.
sair-won *adj* hardly earned.
sairy[1] *adj* sufficiently large.

sairy[2] *same as* **sairie**.
sairy man *same as* **sairie-man**.
sait *n* a seat, chair.
saithe *n* the mature coalfish.
saitisfee *n* **1** what satisfies one, enough. **2** satisfaction.
sakeless *same as* **sackless**.
sakes *int* an exclamation of anger or surprise.
sal[1], **sall** *v* shall.
sal[2], **sall** *int* a strong expletive.
salamander *n* a large poker with a flat heated end for lighting fires.
salariat *adj* salaried, receiving pay.
sald *adj* sold.
salder *v* to solder.
sale *n* (*used of a doctor*) practice.
salebrosity *n* a rough or uneven place.
salerife *adj* saleable.
sal-fat *same as* **salt-fat**.
salie, sallie *same as* **saulie**.
sallet *n* salad.
Sally Walker *n* a children's singing game.
salmon e'en *n* eyes like a salmon's.
salmon-fishers *n* a children's singing game.
salmon-flounder *n* the flounder.
salt *n* **1** a salt cellar. **2** the sea. **3** cost, penalty. **4** sarcasm. **5**
(*in pl*) Epsom salts.—*adj* costly, expensive.—*v* **1** to
pickle. **2** to snub. **3** to have revenge upon. **4** to check. **5**
to heighten in price.
salt-bed *n* the place where ooze fit for making salt is found.
salter *n* **1** one who salts fish. **2** a shrewd, sharp-tongued
person.
salt-fat *n* a salt cellar.
saltie *n* the dab.
saltless *adj* **1** senseless. **2** disappointing.
saltly *adv* **1** smartly. **2** at a heavy price.
salt master *n* an owner of salt pans.
salt pan *n* a shallow pond for making salt by evaporation.
salt-upon-salt *n* refined salt.
salty *adj* salt, tasting of salt.
salvage *n* a savage, barbarian.—*adj* savage.
salve *v* **1** to save. **2** to prevent. **3** to obviate.
saly *same as* **saulie**.
same *same as* **sam**.
same-like *adj* similar.
samen, samine *adj* same.—*n* (*with* **the**) the same.
sammer *v* **1** to adjust. **2** to assort. **3** to match. **4** to agree.
sample-swatch *n* a sample as pattern.
samson *n* an adept, proficient.
san', sand *n* a sandy-bottomed fishing ground.—*v* **1** to
run ashore on sand. **2** to nonplus.
san'-blin' *adj* purblind.
sanchich *same as* **sanshach**.
sand[1] *same as* **san'**.
sand[2] *same as* **sant**[1].
sand-back *n* the sand martin.
sand-bed *n* an inveterate drunkard.
sand-bunker *n* a small well-fenced sandpit.
sand-chappin' *n* the pounding of sandstone finely for
sprinkling on floors.
sandel, sandle, sandile *n* **1** the sand eel. **2** the smelt or
sperling.
sand-fleuk *n* the smear dab.
sandjumper *n* a sand hopper, beach flea.
sand-kep *n* a wall of sand built on the beach by children
to withstand the rising tide.
sand-lairag *n* the common sandpiper.
sand-lark *n* **1** the common sandpiper. **2** the ringed plover.
sandling *same as* **sandel**.
sand-loo *n* the ringed plover.
sand-louper *n* **1** a sand hopper. **2** a small species of crab.
sandrach *n* beebread, the food provided for young bees.
sand-tripper *n* **1** the common sandpiper. **2** the ringed
plover.
sandy *n* **1** the common sandpiper. **2** the sand eel.

Sandy n 1 a nickname for a Scotsman. 2 in phr **Auld Aandy** the devil.
Sandy Campbell n a pig.
Sandy Fry n the devil.
sandy-giddack n the sand eel.
sandy-laverock n the ringed plover.
sandy-loo same as **sand-loo**.
sandy-mill n in phr **to big a sandy-mill** to be in a state of intimacy.
sandy-swallow n the sand martin.
sane¹ same as **sain**².
sane² n 1 a message. 2 a prayer.
sang¹ v singed.
sang² int 1 an oath, expletive. 2 'blood!'
sang³ n 1 song. 2 a note, strain. 3 a fuss, outcry. 4 a saying.
sang-buke n a book of songs.
sang-note n 1 a voice for singing. 2 a singing note.
sangschaw n a competitive exhibition of vocal and instrumental music.
sang-schule n 1 a music school. 2 a class for learning to sing.
sangster v to sing.—n a songster.
sanguine adj bloody, bloodstained.
sanna v neg shall not.
sannal same as **sandel**.
sanneg n (perhaps) a kind of pear, the swan egg.
sannie adj sandy.
Sannie same as **Sandy**.
sannock-garner n the devil.
sanshach, sanshagh, sanshauch, sanaheuch, sanshuch adj 1 wily, crafty. 2 sarcastically clever. 3 proud, distant. 4 disdainful. 5 petulant, saucy. 6 nice, precise. 7 peevish.
sansie same as **sonsy**.
sant¹ v 1 to disappear, be lost. 2 to vanish noiselessly downward.
sant² n a saint.
santliness n saintliness.
sap¹ n 1 liquid of any kind. 2 milk, beer, etc, taken with solid food. 3 juice, gravy. 4 sorrow. 5 tears provoked by vexation or affliction.—v 1 to saturate. 2 to moisten. 3 to flow forth.
sap² n a simpleton, ninny, fool.
sap³ n 1 a sup. 2 a gulp. 3 a mess of food.
sape same as **saip**.
sapless adj (used of the weather) rainless, dry.
sap-money n an allowance to servants for milk, liquor, etc.
sapp n 1 a bunch. 2 a cluster of worms strung on worsted, for eel fishing.—v to catch or bob for eels.
sapple¹ same as **soople**¹.
sapple² n 1 to soak. 2 to rinse or wash out.—n soapy water
sappy adj 1 saturated with moisture. 2 sodden. 3 wet, rainy, muddy. 4 savoury. 5 given to drink. 6 lively in liquor. 7 (used of kisses) sweet, pleasing. 8 fat, plump. 9 (of a sermon) given with unction. 10 (of a bargain) very profitable.
sappy-headed adj 1 silly. 2 stupid.
saps n sops.
sap-spale n sapwood, the soft layer of wood next the bark of a tree.
saps-skull n 1 a simpleton. 2 a blockhead.
sapsy adj 1 soft, weak. 2 overly sentimental
sar same as **sair**¹.
sarbit int an exclamation of sorrow.
sare¹, **sare**² same as **sair**¹, **sair**³.
sareless same as **sairless**.
sargeat n 1 a kind of cloth. 2 (perhaps) serge.
sark n 1 a shirt. 2 a chemise. 3 a nightdress.
sark-alane adj wearing only a sark (qv).
sarken adj belonging to a shirt or to cloth for shirts.
sarkfu' n 1 a shirtful. 2 in phr **a sarkfu' o' sair banes** the result of great fatigue, of violent exertion or of a sound beating.

sarking n 1 coarse linen shirting. 2 the wood above the rafters and immediately under the slates.—adj belonging to a shirt or to cloth for shirts.
sarkit n a short shirt or blouse.—adj 1 dressed in or possessing a shirt. 2 (used of a roof) covered with sarking (qv).
sarkless adj 1 without a shirt. 2 poverty-stricken.
sark-neck n the collar or neckband of a shirt.
sark o' God n a surplice.
sark-tail n 1 the bottom of a shirt. 2 the skirt or lower part of a dress.
sarless adj used of a soft, limp, useless person or of one who does not care to do too much work.
sarrie same as **sairie**.
sasine n investiture.
sasser-meat n sausages.
saster n a pudding of meal and minced meat or of minced hearts and kidneys salted, put into a bag or tripe.
sat same as **saut**.
satchell baggie n a wallet.
satericals n satire.
satire v to satirize.
satisfee n enough.
satisfice v to satisfy.
satteral adj 1 tart. 2 quick-tempered.
Satterday n Saturday.
Satterday's slop n the time from Saturday afternoon till sunrise on Monday, during which it is unlawful to catch salmon.
sattle¹ v 1 to determine a quarrel. 2 to reduce to silence. 3 to settle, decide. 4 to induct a minister into a charge.
sattle² v 1 to settle. 2 to settle down.—n a wooden seat like a sofa. 3 a passageway behind cows in a byre (qv) and between the urine channels.
sattle chair n a long, sofa-shaped chair, frequently found in farm kitchens and farm cottages and used as a bed for children.
sattler n what determines a quarrel or reduces a person to silence.
sattle-stane n a stone at the fireside, used as a seat.
sattril adj sarcastic.
Saturday kebbuck n a cheese made of the overnight and morning's milk, poured cream and all into the yearning tub (qv).
Saturday's-bairn n a child born on Saturday, who is supposed to have to work for a living.
Saturday's bawbee n a halfpenny given every Saturday to a child as pocket money.
sauce n 1 impertinence. 2 vanity, pride, display.
saucer-meat n sausages.
sauch¹ n a willow.
sauch² n a hollow, murmuring sound.
sauch buss n a willow, a willow bush.
sauch creel n a basket made of willow.
sauchen, sauchin, saughen adj 1 belonging to or made of willow. 2 soft, weak, not energetic. 3 of a sour, stubborn disposition. 4 unsociable.—n a willow.—v to make supple or pliant.
sauchen-toup n a simpleton, one easily duped.
sauchen tree n a willow tree.
sauchen-wand n a willow wand, osier.
sauchie adj 1 full of willows. 2 made of willow.
saucht¹ v sought.
saucht² n 1 rest. 2 quiet, peace.
sauch tree n a willow tree.
sauch-wand n a willow wand.
saucy adj scornful. 2 proud, vain, conceited.
saud n a sod.
sauf, sauff v to save.—prep except.—adj safe.
saugh same as **sauch**¹.
saughe n the sum given in name of salvage.
saugher v to walk or act in a lifeless, inactive manner.
saughran, saughrin adj 1 listless, inactive. 2 sauntering. 3 taking good care of oneself.
saugh-shaded adj shaded by willows.

saught *same as* **saucht**.
saul[1] *n* **1** soul. **2** spirit, mettle.—*int* used as an expletive.
saul[2], **sauld** *v, adj* sold.
saulfu' *n* enough to daunt the soul.
saulie, saullie *n* **1** a funeral mute, a hired mourner. **2** a black plume.
saulless *adj* spiritless, dastardly.
saully *v* **1** to move or run from side to side. **2** to rock or swing like a small boat at anchor.—*n* a run from side to side. **3** a continuous rising and falling. **4** a swaying, swinging motion.
saul-sleper, ~-sleeper *n* a minister who neglects the care of souls.
sault *n* **1** a start. **2** a leap. **3** the start of a plough when it meets a stone.
saum *n* a psalm.—*v* to tell a long story.
saumont, saumon *n* a salmon.
saumont-loup *n* a boys' game.
saumont-raun *n* the roe of salmon.
saun *n* sand.
saun-blin' *adj* purblind, near-sighted.
saunt[1], **saunt**[2] *same as* **sant**[1], **sant**[2].
saunter away *v* to waste time.
saup *same as* **sap**[3].
saur[1] *same as* **sair**[3].
saur[2], **saurin** *same as* **sairing**.
saurless[1] *same as* **sairless**.
saurless *same as* **sarless**.
saut *n* **1** salt. **2** the sea. **3** cost, penalty, smart.—*v* **1** to salt, pickle. **2** to snub. **3** to have revenge upon. **4** to check. **5** to heighten in price.—*adj* **1** costly. **2** severe, painful.
saut backet *n* a salt box of wood.
saut bree *n* salt water.
saut-cadger *n* an itinerant seller of salt.
saut cuddie *n* a salt box.
sauter *n* **1** a cadger of salt. **2** a salt-maker.
saut-fat, ~-fit *same as* **salt-fat**.
saut-girnel *n* a salt box.
sautie[1] *n* the dab, a species of flounder.
sautie[2], **sauty** *adj* tasting of salt.
sautie ~, sauty bannock *n* an oatmeal pancake baked for Fastern's Eve.
saut kist *n* a salt box.
sautless *same as* **saltless**.
sautly *same as* **saltly**.
sautman *n* an itinerant seller of salt.
saut-water *n* **1** the sea. **2** the seaside.
saut-water fleuk *n* the dab.
saut-water fowk *n* visitors to the seaside.
savage *n* a young animal difficult to rear.
savendie, sauvendie *n* sagacity, knowledge.
savendle *same as* **sevendle**.
savie *n* common sense, perception.—*adj* wise, sagacious, experienced.
saving *n* the savings bank.—*prep* except.
savour *n* **1** a bad smell. **2** a disgust. **3** unction in preaching.—*v* **1** to taste. **2** to scent out.
savoury *adj* possessing unction.
saw[1] *n* a salve, an ointment.
saw[2] *v* to sow.
sawbill *n* **1** the goosander. **2** the red-breasted merganser.
sawcer *n* a maker or seller of sauces.
sawer *n* a sower.
sawf *n* a prognostication.
sawins *n* sawdust.
sawin' sheet *n* a sheet used in sowing grain.
sawlie *same as* **saulie**.
sawmer *same as* **sammer**.
samnon *n* a salmon.
Sawney, Sawnie *n* a Scotsman.
sawnie *adj* sandy.
sawr *n* **1** a gentle breeze. **2** a disgust.
sawstick, sawstock *n* a log of rough-hewn timber.
sawt *same as* **saut**.

sax[1] *adj* six.
sax[2] *v* to scarify with a sharp instrument.
Saxon shilling *n* a shilling of English money.
saxpence *n* sixpence.
saxt *adj* sixth.
say[1] *n* **1** a speech. **2** a thing to say. **3** a saying. **4** a proverb. **5** an opinion and the right to express it. **6** authority, influence, voice.
say[2], **say**[3], **say**[4] *same as* **sey**[3], **sey**[4], **sey**[5].
say again *v* to disapprove of, find fault with.
say awa' *v* **1** to go on with what one is saying. **2** to say grace. **3** to begin to eat. **4** to fall to.—*n* **1** loquacity. **2** a discourse, narrative. **3** confused talking.
saye *same as* **sey**[4].
sayer *n* a poet.
say for *v* to vouch for.
say-hand *n* an assay, trial.
saylch *same as* **sealch**.
say-piece *same as* **sey-piece**.
say-shot *n* **1** a trial shot. **2** an opportunity in a game to regain by one stroke all that one had previously lost. **3** an attempt.
scaad, scaal *v* to scold.
scaal-pyock *n* a double chin.
scaam *same as* **scaum**.
scaap *same as* **scalp**.
scab *n* the itch, as it appears in the human body.
scabbit *adj* **1** (*used of land*) thin, bare, gravelly, rocky. **2** (*of vegetation*) thin, patchy. **3** mean, paltry. **4** worthless. **5** shabby, ill-looking.
scabble *v* **1** to scold. **2** to squabble.
scabely *adj* **1** untidy. **2** naked.
scabert *n* a scabbard, sheath.
scab-full *adj* chock-full.
scad[1], **scadd** *n* **1** a colour obliquely or slightly seen as by reflection. **2** the reflection itself. **3** a faint gleam. **4** the variegated scum of mineral water.
scad[2] *n* the ray.
scad[3] *v* **1** to soil by frequent use. **2** (*used of dress*) to fade, soil.
scad[4] *v* **1** to scald. **2** to heat a liquid to the boiling point or slightly under. **3** to burn scorch. **4** to be inflamed. **5** to trouble, vex. **6** to disgust.—*n* **1** anything that scalds. **2** any hot drink, as tea. **3** a scorch, burn. **4** an inflamed part of the body. **5** trouble, pain, injury. **6** disgust.
sca'd *adj* **1** scalded. **2** scabbed, scurfy. **3** affected with skin disease, as eczema or ringworm.
scaddaw, scaddow *n* a shadow.
scaddem *n* an incompetent smith.
scadden *adj* thin, not obese.—*n* a person of spare figure.
scadderized *adj* (*used of persons*) dry, withered.
scaddin *n* the quantity scalded or to be scalded.
scaddit ale, ~ beer *n* a drink made of hot ale or beer and a little meal, of the consistency of gruel.
scaddit whey *n* whey boiled on a slow fire so as to become curdy.
scaddit wine *n* mulled wine.
scade *same as* **scad**[1].
scad head *n* a scrofulous disease of the head, causing the hair to fall off.
scadie *adj* burning, causing a tingling sensation.
scadlips *n* thin broth apt to scald the lips.
sca'd-man's head *same as* **scaud-man's head**.
scaff[1] *n* **1** food. **2** provisions. **3** anything got by dishonourable or importunate begging. **4** an idle wanderer. **5** a sponger. **6** the act of going about in an idle or frolicsome manner. **7** merriment, diversion, fun.—*v* **1** to provide food. **2** to devise means for obtaining food. **3** to sponge, sorn (qv). **4** to collect by dishonourable means. **5** to eat greedily. **6** to wander about idly.
scaff[2] *n* a heavy, but brief, shower of rain.
scaff-and-raff *n* **1** abundant provisions. **2** the dregs of the populace.
scafferie *n* the contents of a larder.

scaffie *n* **1** a scavenger. **2** a road-sweeper. **3** a refuse collector.

scaffing *n* **1** food of any kind. **2** abundance of provisions. **3** aimless wandering.

scaff-raff *n* the dregs of the populace, the riff-raff.

scaffy *adj* (*of a shower of rain*) heavy but soon over.

scag *n* putrid fish.—*v* **1** to render putrid by exposure to sun and air. **2** to spoil a dress by carelessness or untidiness in wearing it. **3** to spoil the appearance of a thing.

scaich *same as* **skaigh**.

scaicher *same as* **skaigher**.

scail *same as* **skail**.

scailie *same as* **skelly**⁴.

scaill *same as* **skail**.

scair *same as* **skair**².

scairt¹ *same as* **scart**¹.

scairt² *v* to run quickly.

scairt³ *adj* scared, frightened.

scairy *n* **1** a shadow, reflection. **2** a metaphor.

scaith *same as* **skaith**.

scaithless *adj* **1** unharmed. **2** harmless.

scalbert *same as* **scawbert**.

scalch *n* a morning dram or drink.

scald¹ *v* **1** to heat. **2** to scorch. **3** to vex.—*n* **1** a hot drink. **2** vexation.

scald² *v* to scold.—*n* **1** a scolding. **2** one who scolds.

scal'd *adj* scabbed.

scaldachan *n* an unfeathered nestling.

scald-berry *n* the fruit of the blackberry.

scalder¹ *n* a jellyfish.

scalder² *n* a sore or inflamed place.

scaldricks *same as* **skeldick**.

scale *same as* **skail**.

scale-stairs *n* a straight staircase in contrast to a spiral one.

scalie *v* to squint.

scall¹ *same as* **scald**¹.

scall² *same as* **scad**².

scallag *n* a bondservant who worked five days for his master and one for himself.

scallion *n* the leek.

scallyart *n* a blow, stroke.

scalp *n* **1** the head, skull, as a term of contempt. **2** a small bare knoll. **3** thin soil barely covering rock beneath. **4** a bank of sand or mud exposed at low tide. **5** an oyster or mussel bed.—*adj* (*of soil*) thin, bare, unfertile.—*v* **1** to pare off the surface of soil. **2** to cut turf. **3** to scrape.

scalpy *adj* **1** bare, barren. **2** thinly covered with soil.

scalve *n* a shelf.

scam, scame *same as* **scaum**.

scamble *v* to **1** shamble. **2** to dodge about.

scambler *n* a sponger for food, a mealtime visitor.

scamells *n* shambles.

scamp *v* **1** to roam about idly. **2** (*with* **off**) to hurry off. **3** to play mischievous tricks.—*n* **1** idle wandering. **2** work badly or lazily done. **3** a swindler.

scan *n* **1** what one can see or know. **2** a view.

scance¹ *v* **1** to reflect on, ponder. **2** to glance at, scan. **3** to look with contempt. **4** to give a slight account of. **5** to put to the proof, test. **6** to reproach. **7** to reflect censoriously. **8** to form a hasty judgment.—*n* **1** a glance. **2** a quick look. **3** a hasty survey in the mind. **4** a cursory inspection. **5** a brief calculation. **6** blame, reproach, scandal.

scance² *v* **1** to glitter. **2** to shine. **3** to make a great display. **4** to exaggerate in conversation.—*n* **1** a glance. **2** a gleam.

scancer *n* **1** a showy person. **2** an exaggerator. **3** a gleam. **4** a light.

scancing *adj* **1** good-looking. **2** bouncing.

scanclashin *same as* **scantlishin**.

scandal *v* to scandalize ecclesiastically.

scandal-crack *n* talk involving scandal.

scandaleese *v* to talk or spread scandal

scandal-jobber *n* a scandalmonger.

scandal-potion *n* a sarcastic name for tea.

scannach *v* to gleam, shine.

scanse¹ *v* to climb.

scanse², **scanse**³ *same as* **scance**¹, **scance**².

scansed *adj* seeming, having the appearance of.

scant *adj* **1** scarce, rare. **2** few. **3** deficient, needy. **4** poor, badly off. **5** parsimonious, sparing.—*adv* scarcely.—*n* **1** scarcity, lack. **2** poverty.

scantack *n* a fishing line with hooks for night-fishing in rivers, etc.

scantily *adv* scarcely.

scantling¹ *n* the juncture of a wall with the roof of a house.

scantling² *n* **1** a rude sketch. **2** a rough draft of a deed. **3** a scanty measure or portion.—*adj* small, very scanty.

scantling line *n* a fishing line fixed on the bank of a stream for night fishing.

scantlins *adv* scarcely, hardly.

scantlishin *n* **1** scanty increase. **2** a small remainder.

scantly *adv* scarcely.

scant o' grace *n* a graceless fellow.

scap¹ *same as* **scalp**.

scap², **scape** *same as* **skep**¹.

scaps *n* a landscape.

scape-the-gallows *n* a thoroughly bad fellow.

scapethrift *n* **1** a spendthrift. **2** a worthless fellow.

scar¹ *n* **1** a bare place on the side of a steep hill from which the sward has been washed down by rains. **2** a cliff, precipice. **3** a spit of sand or gravel running into a lake or loch. **4** (*in pl*) rocks through which there is an opening.

scar² *same as* **scare**¹.

scarce *adj* (*with* **of**) short of.

scarcement *n* **1** the row of stones that separates the slates of two adjoining roofs. **2** the edge of a ditch where thorns are to be planted. **3** a projection among rocks. **4** a shelf among rocks. **5** the part that projects when a dyke (qv) is suddenly contracted.

Scarce Thursday *n* a fair held at Melrose on Maunday Thursday.

scarcht *n* a hermaphrodite.

scarcraw *n* a scarecrow.

scare¹ *v* to take fright.—*n* an ugly person.—*adj* **1** easily frightened, shy. **2** wild. **3** affectedly modest. **4** given to shying.

scare², **scare**³ *same as* **skair**², **skair**³.

scarey *adj* terrifying.

scarf *v* to wrap, envelop.

scarf *n* the cormorant.

scar-gait *adj* (*used of a horse*) easily frightened.

scargivenet *n* **1** a girl from twelve to fourteen years of age. **2** a half-grown woman.

scarnoch *n* **1** a number, multitude. **2** a noisy tumult.

scarnoghin *n* a great noise.

scarred *adj* **1** bare. **2** precipitous.

scarrie *adj* **1** bare, rocky. **2** full of precipices.

scarrow *n* **1** faint light. **2** reflected light. **3** a shadow.—*v* **1** to emit a faint light. **2** to shine through clouds.

scarsement *same as* **scarcement**.

scart¹ *v* **1** to scratch. **2** to strike a match. **3** to scrape. **4** to clean any vessel with a spoon. **5** to scrape together money, etc. **6** to oppress by extortion. **7** to make a scraping, rasping sound. **8** to write. **9** to write indistinctly. **10** to draw. **11** to sculpture. **12** to scatter.—*n* **1** a scratch. **2** a scratching. **3** a stroke of the pen. **4** a scrap of writing. **5** the smallest quantity of anything. **6** a puny or meagre-looking person. **7** a saving, industrious person. **8** a niggard. **9** a rasping sound.

scart² *n* the cormorant.

scart³ *adj* scared.

scartel *same as* **scartle**.

scart-free *adj* **1** safe and sound. **2** unharmed. **3** free of expense.

scartins *n* what is scraped out of any vessel.

scartle *v* **1** to scrape together by many little strokes. **2** to collect money by long and continuous small savings. **3**

to scatter.—*n* an iron tool for raking out a stable or byre (qv).

scart-the-bowl *n* a niggard, skinflint.

scash *v* 1 to beat, batter. 2 to crush or press roughly or carelessly. 3 to squabble. 4 to twist turn awry. 5 to tread on the side of one's foot. 6 to turn the toes inward. 7 to walk affectedly. 8 to be careless as to dress.—*n* 1 a blow. 2 a thump. 3 a twist, wrench. 4 a turning to one side.—*adj* twisted, turned to one side.—*adv* 1 in a twisted manner. 2 with a waddling shuffling gait.

scash-foot *n* a foot with the toes turned inward.

scash-footed *adj* having the toes turned inward.

scashie *v* to squabble. *n* a wrangle, squabble. S*ee* **scash**.

scashle *v* 1 to squabble, wrangle. 2 to twist, turn away. 3 to tread on one side of the foot. 4 to turn the toes inward. 5 to waddle or shuffle in walking. 6 to be careless about one's dress.—*n* 1 a squabble, wrangle. 2 a scuffle. 3 a twist, wrench. 4 a turning to one side. 5 a waddling, shuffling walk. 6 the noise of shuffling feet along the ground.—*adv* in a waddling, shuffling manner.

scash-mouthed *adj* having the mouth awry.

scass *v* 1 to beat. 2 to twist.

scat *n* the sharp sound of a bullet striking a hard substance.

scate *n* a skate.

scath *same as* **skaith**.

scatted *adj* (*with* **up**) littered-up.

scatter *v* to stud, dot over.—*n* a dispersion.

scatter-cash, **~good** *n* a spendthrift.

scatterment *n* a scattering, as of shot.

scattermouch *n* an ill-conditioned rascal.

scatter-witted *adj* senseless, harebrained.

scatyun *n* a small potato.

scau *same as* **scaw**².

scaubert *n* a scabbard.

scaud¹, **scaud**² *same as* **scad**¹, **scad**⁴.

scaud³ *adj* 1 scabbed. 2 scurfy.

scaudie *same as* **scadie**.

scauding *same as* **scaddin**.

scaudit *adj* scalded.

scaud-man's head *n* the sea urchin's shell.

scaud o' day *n* the daybreak.

scauff *same as* **scaff**¹.

scaul, scauld *same as* **scald**².

scaul' *same as* **scad**⁴.

scaum *v* 1 to burn, scorch, singe. 2 to envelop in a mist or haze, to shade.—*n* 1 a burn, scorch. 2 the mark of a burn or singeing. 3 a thin haze, a light vapour.

scaumer *n* 1 a pirate. 2 a plunderer. 3 a cattle-stealer.

scaum o' the sky *n* the thin vapour of the atmosphere.

scaumy *adj* misty, hazy.

scaup, scaulp *same as* **scalp**.—*in phr* **a peer scaup** poor soil.

scaur¹ *same as* **scar**¹.

scaur² *same as* **scare**¹.

scaurabee *n* a term of contempt.

scaured *adj* 1 bared. 2 precipitous.

scaurie *same as* **scarrie**.

scaurt *same as* **scart**².

scaut *adj* scabbed.

scavie *n* a trick, prank.

scaw¹ *n* a barnacle.

scaw² *v* 1 to become faded. 2 to change or fade in colour, as a dress. 3 to spoil, destroy. 4 to destroy a colour.—*n* a faded or spoilt mark.

scaw³ *v* to scab.—*n* 1 a scab. 2 a scall. 3 the itch.

scawbert *n* 1 a pretentious person, one who wishes to appear above his or her rank. 2 a strongly made person of a stubborn, disagreeable temper.

scawd¹ *same as* **scad**¹.

scawd², **scaw't** *adj* 1 (*of a dress*) faded in colour. 2 (*of land*) having bare brown patches. 3 worthless.

scaw'd, scaw't *adj* 1 scalled, scabbed. 2 (*used of the face*) having many carbuncles.

scaw'd like *adj* faded in colour.

scawip, scawp *same as* **scalp**.

scelet, scellet *same as* **skelet**.

scent *n* 1 a bad smell. 2 a sniff. 3 the least particle.

scentage *n* aroma, flavour.

scent-bean *n* a fragrant bean carried in snuffboxes to perfume the snuff.

scent-dog *n* a pointer.

sch *for many sch words see sh words*.

schachel *same as* **shachle**¹.

schafe *same as* **shave**¹.

schafts *same as* **shafts**.

schald *same as* **shald**.

schamlich *v* to shamble.—*adj* shambling, weak in the legs, puny.—*n* a weak, puny person or animal.

scharge *n* a puny child.

schavel *n* a rogue.

schaw *n* 1 a wood of small size. 2 a glade. 3 a grove.

schech *v* 1 to search. 2 to obtain by craft. 3 to filch.

schell-fowl *n* the sheldrake.

schelm, schellum *same as* **skellum**.

scheme *n* a housing estate, particularly one built by a local authority, *also called* **housing estate**.

schenachy *same as* **seannachie**.

scheu *same as* **shew**².

schiff *n* a sieve.

schlaffert *n* a blow, buffet.

schluchten *n* a hollow between two hills.

scholard *n* 1 a scholar. 2 one who can read and write.

school¹ *v* to train an animal.

school² *n* 1 a swarm, a great number. 2 a shoal.

schooling-frock *n* a dress worn at school.

school-penny *n* a school tax.

schowd *same as* **showd**.

schowdin-rope *n* a swing.

schowy *adj* containing fragments of broken flax, etc. *See* **shows**.

schroynock *n* noise.

schugh *n* a drain, a furrow.—*v* 1 to furrow. 2 to plant temporarily.

schuip *v* shaped.

schule¹ *same as* **shool**¹.

schule² *n* a school.—*v* 1 to educate. 2 to correct, rebuke. 3 to train an animal.

schule brod *n* a school board.

schule-callant *n* a schoolboy.

schule-craft *n* a school education.

schule-gaen *adj* attending school.

schule-lear, **~lare** *n* education.

schule-wean *n* a schoolchild.

schurling *n* the skin of a newly shorn sheep.

schute-stock *n* a bevel.

sciatics *n* sciatica.

scibe *same as* **skibe**.

scig *n* 1 a shelter. 2 a ruse.—*v* 1 to shade. 2 to hide.

sciver *same as* **skiver**.

sclaff *v* 1 to strike with the open hand or with anything having a flat surface. 2 in golf, to hit the ground a glancing blow with a club before hitting the ball. 3 to throw down flat. 4 to walk clumsily without lifting the feet properly. 5 to shuffle along.—*n* 1 a blow with the open hand. 2 a slight blow. 3 the noise made by a slight blow or a flat, soft fall or in shuffling the feet. 3 a thin, light shoe. 4 an old, worn shoe used as a slipper. 5 anything thin and solid.—*adv* 1 flat, plump. 2 with light, flat step.

sclaffard *n* a slight blow.

sclaffer *v* to sclaff (qv).—*n* 1 a sclaff (qv). 2 (*in pl*) worn-out shoes.—*adv* with a sclaff.

sclaffert¹, **sclafferd** *n* 1 a sclaff (qv). 2 a rock lying horizontally in thin beds.—*v* to sclaff (qv).

sclaffert² *n* the mumps.

sclaff-fitted *adj* flat-footed.

sclaip *same as* **sclaup**.

sclait *n* slate.

sclaitey *n* a marble made of slate.

sclamb *v* climbed. *See* **sclimb**.

sclander *n* slander, scandal.—*v* to slander.

sclanderer *n* **1** a slanderer. **2** one who creates scandal.

sclarried *adj* bedaubed, besmeared.

sclasp *v* to clasp.—*n* **1** a clasp. **2** the act of clasping.

sclatch *n* **1** an unseemly, semiliquid mess. **2** a large clot of mud or filth. **3** a large spot or mark on the skin. **4** an uncomely patch. **5** a big, lubberly fellow. **6** a heavy fall into water or mud, a splash. **7** the noise of a splash. **8** a stroke or slap with the palm of the hand. **9** a bespattering with mud.—*v* **1** to bespatter, bedaub. **2** to perform work inefficiently and clumsily. **3** to dash violently. **4** to fall heavily. **5** to walk with a heavy, lumbering step. —*adv* **1** heavily, violently. **2** with clumsy, lumbering gait.

sclate, sclat *n* a slate.—*v* to cover with slate.—*adj* of slate.

sclate band *n* a stratum of slate among bands of rock.

sclate pen *n* a slate pencil.

sclater[1] *n* a slater.

sclater[2] *n* the woodlouse.

sclater's eggs *n* little white eggs like beads found in ploughed land.

sclate stane *n* **1** a small bit of slate. **2** a stone resembling slate.

sclattie *n* a slate.

sclaty *adj* **1** slaty, like slates. **2** abounding in slates.

sclaup *v* **1** to shuffle in walking. **2** to walk in loose slippers.

sclaurie *v* **1** to splash with mud. **2** to soil one's clothes. **3** to calumniate, vilify. **4** to scold. **5** to call names. **6** to pour forth abusive language.—*n* **1** soft mud. **2** any semiviscous substance, as jelly.

sclave, sclaive *v* to slander, calumniate.

scleeberie, sclibbus *n* a large piece of land of little value.

scleet, scleit *v* **1** to slide or slip smoothly or rapidly. **2** to walk so as to wear down shoes at one side or as if splay-footed.—*adj* smooth, sleek.

scleetin-fittit, scleetan-feeted *adj* **1** having plain soles. **2** splay-footed. **3** given to treading one's shoes on one side.

sclender[1] *adj* slender.

sclender[2], **sclenter** *n* **1** a loose, thin stone lying on the face of a scaur (qv). **2** the face of a hill covered with small, loose stones.

sclenderie *adj* covered with small, loose stones.

sclent *v* **1** to slope. **2** to look obliquely. **3** to look askance. **4** to hit or throw obliquely. **5** to be guilty of immoral conduct. **6** to diverge from truth, fib. **7** to give a slanting direction. **8** to dart askance. **9** (*in relation to the eyes*) to squint. **10** to pass obliquely. **11** to cut so as to produce a slanting side.—*n* **1** obliquity. **2** acclivity, ascent. **3** a glance. **4** a squint.

sclentin-ways *adv* obliquely.

scleurach *n* a person untidy in dress and gait.

sclibbene *same as* **scleeberie**.

sclidder *same as* **slidder**.

scliff *v* **1** to drag the feet in walking. **2** to walk with a dull, heavy step. **3** to stride sideways in passing with anything having a flat surface. **4** to rub against.—*n* **1** dragging of the feet, a dull, heavy step. **2** a side stroke or rub in passing. **3** the noise made by scliffing. **4** an old broken shoe or slipper. **5** an untidy slattern.—*adv* with a trailing, shuffling motion.

scliffan *n* a thin, useless shoe.

scliff-sclaff *adv* with a dragging, shuffling step, as with loose shoes or slippers.

sclimb, sclim *v* to climb.

sclimpet *n* a small, thin piece of rock or anything else.

scliner *adj* slender.

sclither *same as* **slither**.

sclithene *adj* slippery.

sclithers *n* **1** loose stones lying on a hillside. **2** places where numerous small stones lie.

sclitter *adj* uncouth.—*n* a lazy person.

scloit *same as* **sclyte**.

sclon, sclone *n* a large piece of anything flat like a pancake.

sclowff *v* to walk with a heavy tread like a flat-footed person.

scloy *same as* **scly**.

scluchten *same as* **schluchten**.

sclute *v* **1** to throw down or pour out in a mass. **2** to fall flat. **3** to fall flat in mud or loose soil. **4** to walk clumsily and with dragging feet. **5** to walk with the toes much turned out.—*n* **1** a thin, semiliquid mass. **2** the fall of such a mass and its sound. **3** a large, clumsy foot. **4** a lout, an awkward, clumsy fellow. **5** a person of untidy habits. —*adv* **1** flat, plump. **2** with heavy, awkward step.

sclutt *n* soft and coarse till.

sclutter *v* to dawdle.—*n* a sloven.

scly *v* to slide.—*n* **1** a slide. **2** a sliding motion. **3** the place on which one slides.

sclypach *v* to sklype (qv).—*n* a sklype.—*adv* with force.

sclype *same as* **sklype**.

sclyre *same as* **sklyre**.

sclytach *v* (*used intensively*) to sclyte (qv).

sclyte *v* **1** to throw down or pour out so as to cause a sharp sound. **2** to fall heavily.—*n* **1** a thin, semiliquid mass. **2** a heavy fall. **3** the sharp sound made by such a fall. **4** a worn-out shoe. **5** a large, clumsy foot. **6** a clumsy, untidy fellow.—*adv* **1** flatly. **2** suddenly, as with a fall.

sclyter *v* (*used intensively*) to sclyte (qv).—*n* a quantity, mass.

sclyterach *v* (*used intensively*) to sclyter (qv).

scoan *n* a round, flat cake.

scob[1], **scobb** *n* **1** a splint. **2** a wooden gag. **2** a limber rod of willow, hazel, etc, used for fastening down thatch. **3** the rib of a basket.—*v* **1** to put in splints. **2** to gag. **3** to keep the mouth open by crosspieces of wood. **4** to peg down thatch. **5** to take long stitches in sewing. **6** to sew clumsily. **7**to dip the shuttle in weaving, so that the woof appears above the warp.

scob[2], **scobe** *v* **1** to scoop out roughly. **2** to test a cheese by a scoop.—*n* an instrument for scooping.

scob[3], **scobe** *n* an onion planted after vegetation has begun.

scobb *same as* **scob**[1].

scobe[1], **scobe**[2] *same as* **scob**[2], **scob**[3].

scoberie, scobrie *n* the act of careless sewing or sewing with long stitches.

scobie *n* a birchen trout rod.

scob-seibow *n* **1** an onion allowed to remain in the ground during winter. **2** the young shoot from an onion of the second year's growth.

scodge *v* **1** to look sly. **2** to pilfer. **3** to sneak about idly. **4** to do housework. **5** to drudge.

scodger *n* a lazy lounger.

scodgie *n* **1** one who does the dirty work of a kitchen. **2** a drudge. **3** a mean, underhand fellow. **4** a suspicious-looking person.—*v* **1** to act as a drudge. **2** to clean, scrub.

scodgie-lass *n* a female drudge.

scog *same as* **scug**.

scogger *adj* shady.

scogie *same as* **scodgie**.

scoil *v* to squeal.—*n* a squeal.

scok *v* **1** to shelter. **2** to shade.

scokky *adj* shady.

scold[1] *n* a scolding.

scold[2] *v* to drink healths.

scolder *n* a drinker of healths.

scold's bridle *n* the branks (qv), an instrument for punishing scolding women.

scoll, scol *v* **1** to drink to one's health, to toast. **2** to drink hard.—*n* the drinking of healths, a toast.

scolle, scole *n* **1** the skull, head. **2** the brain. **3** brains, ability.

scolp *v* to scallop.

scomfish *v* **1** to suffocate, stifle, choke, from heat, smoke or bad smells. **2** to spoil by heat, etc. **3** to disgust.—*n* **1** a state of suffocation. **2** a dislike.

scon[1] *v* **1** to crush flat. **2** to beat with the open hand or a flat surface. **3** to inflict corporal punishment, generally on the buttocks.—*n* a stroke with the palm of the hand, etc.

scon[2] *v* **1** to make flat stones skip along the surface of water. **2** (*used of flat bodies*) to skip along, as in ducks and drakes.

scon[3] *n* **1** a flat, round cake of flour, etc, baked on a girdle (qv). **2** anything flat or round like a scon. **3** a piece of dried dung used as fuel. **4** a sample or specimen of anything. **5** the old broad Lowland bonnet

scon ~, scone cap *n* a man's flat, broad bonnet.

sconce *n* **1** a slight erection as a shelter from the wind. **2** a stone-hewer's shed. **3** a screen. **4** a seat fixed in the wall or near the fireplace.—*v* **1** to guard, protect. **2** to take up a position of security. **3** to keep off, turn aside. **4** to extort, cheat. **5** to trick out of. **6** to jilt or slight a woman.

scone[1], **scone**[2] *same as* **scon**[1], **scon**[3].

sconfice, sconfis *same as* **scomfish**.

sconner *same as* **scunner**.

scoo[1] *n* a flat basket into which herrings are put when gutted.

scoo[2] *adj* awry.—*n* anything badly made.

scooder *same as* **scowder**.

scooed *adj* **1** twisted. **2** badly made.

scoof *same as* **scuff**[1].

scoog *same as* **scog**.

scouk *same as* **scouk**.

scool[1] *n* a swelling in the roof of a horse's mouth.

scool[2] *same as* **school**[2].

scool[3] *v* to scowl.

scooneral *n* a scoundrel.—*adj* scoundrelly.

scoonge *same as* **scounge**.

scoop[1] *n* **1** an offertory ladle, generally a small box with a long handle. **2** a baler. **3** a spoonful. **4** a wooden drinking cup, a caup (qv). **5** a draught of liquor. **6** the peak of a cap. **7** a poke bonnet.—*v* **1** to core an apple, etc. **2** to dig out the contents and leave the shell, crust or rind of anything. **3** to sup. **4** to drink off, quaff. **5** to bale a boat.

scoop[2] *same as* **scoup**[3].

scoopie *n* an old-style poke bonnet.

scoor[1] *n* **1** the rattle of a hail shower. **2** a shower, a squall with rain.

scoor[2] *v* **1** to scour. **2** to scrub. **3** to clear out a ditch, drain, etc. **4** to clear, rid, free. **5** to purge. **6** (*with* **out**) to drink off. **7** to flog. **8** to whip a top. **9** to scoop.—*n* **1** a cleansing. **2** a laxative, a purgative. **3** diarrhoea. **4** a big draught or dose of liquor. **5** a severe rebuke.

scoor[3] *v* **1** to scamper. **2** to plunge, drive. **3** to discover, lay hands on, find.—*n* **1** pace. **2** a quick walk. **3** a run of water. **4** a channel.

scoorie[1] *n* **1** a squall with rain. **2** a severe scolding. —*adj* squally.

scoorie[2] *adj* **1** shabby, threadbare, ragged. **2** mean in conduct. **3** idle. **4** disreputable. **5** dried, parched in appearance. **6** wasted.—*n* a blackguard, a mean, disreputable person.

scoorin *n* **1** a severe scolding. **2** a drubbing. **3** diarrhoea.

scooriness *n* shabbiness of dress.

scoorins *n* **1** a kind of coarse flannel. **2** serge.

scoorin' things *n* gaudy ornaments.

scoor-the-buggie *n* the youngest child of a family.

scoor-the-gate *n* a kind of ale causing diarrhoea.

scoor-the-huddie *n* a chimney sweep.

scoor-the-kintry *adj* vagrant.—*n* a vagabond.

scoosh *v* **1** to run for shelter. **2** to plunge. **3** to squirt or spurt.—*n* a squirt or spurt.

scoot[1] *n* **1** the common guillemot. **2** the razor.

scoot[2] *n* **1** a term of contempt applied to a man or woman. **2** a camp trull. **3** a braggadocio.

scoot[3] *n* a wooden drinking vessel.

scoot[4] *v* **1** to squirt. **2** to spout. **3** to eject water forcibly. **4** to throw off liquid excrement. **5** to hurry off. **6** to dart away.—*n* **1** a squirt, syringe. **2** a popgun. **3** a gush or

flow of water from a roof and the pipe from which it flows. **4** liquid excrement. **5** diarrhoea.

scoot[5] *v* to loaf about.

scoot-bog *n* a term of reproach.

scooter[1] *n* **1** a squirt. **2** a syringe.

scooter *n* the scattering of money among children at a marriage.—*v* to scatter money in this way.

scoot gun *n* a squirt, syringe.

scooth *same as* **scouth**.

scooti-allan *n* the Arctic gull.

scootie[1] *adj* low, mean, beggar-like.

scootie[2] *n* a wooden drinking vessel.

scootiefu' *n* the fill of a drinking cup.

scootiekin *n* a dram of whisky.

scoot-laniels *n* diarrhoea.

scootle *same as* **scutle**.

scoove *same as* **scove**.

scop *same as* **scoup**[3].

scope *n* a gag.

score *v* to mark a supposed witch with a cross cut on the brow, as a protection from her cantrips.—*n* **1** a line drawn in games. **2** a circle drawn to keep off ghosts, witches, etc. **3** the line in marble-playing. **4** a deep, narrow, ragged indentation on a hillside. **5** a narrow street on a slope. **6** absolution from scandal. **7** matter, affair.

scorie *n* a game of marbles.

scorlins *n* slimy, cord-like seaweed.

scorn *n* **1** jest, ridicule. **2** a slight in love. **3** the rejection of an offer of marriage. **4** insult, reproach, blame.—*v* **1** to mock. **2** to rally a woman about her lover. **3** to allege an existing courtship between a young man and a maiden. **4** to jilt.

scornsum *adj* **1** scornful. **2** troublesome, bothering, slippery.

scory *adj* (*of a hedgehog's cheeks*) wrinkled, lined.

scoscie *n* a starfish.

scot *v* to pay taxes.

Scot *n* **1** a Scotsman as distinguished from a Shetlander. **2** *in phr* **Scots and English** a boys' game.

Scotch *n in phr* **Scotch and English** a boys' game.

scotch *n* an ant.

Scotch-collops *n* **1** beef scotched or sliced and stewed with onions, pepper and salt. **2** beef minced and stewed.

Scotch-~, Scots-convoy *n* the accompanying of a visitor the whole way home.

Scotch cuddy *n* **1** a pedlar. **2** a travelling draper.

Scotch ell *n* 37.0958 inches.

Scotch European *n* a Scotsman living on the Continent.

Scotch fiddle *n* the itch.

Scotch gale *n* the bog myrtle.

Scotch mark *n* a moral or physical defect distinguishing a particular individual.

Scotch mile *n* 1984 yards.

Scotch mist *n* a small but wetting rain.

Scotch nightingale *n* the sedge warbler.

Scotian *adj* Scottish.

scotify *v* to translate into Scotch.

Scots *adj* Scottish.—*n* the Scotch language.

Scots rider *n* a gold coin worth £8, 2s. Scots.

Scots room *n* room to swing the arms.

Scots Willie *n* a small codlin.

scouder *same as* **scowder**.

scouderin' *adj* **1** threatening. **2** chastising, rebuking.

scoudrum *n* chastisement.

scouff[1] *v* **1** to sweep. **2** to swoop.

scouff[2] *n* **1** a low blackguard. **2** a male jilt. **3** a blusterer.—*adj* **1** empty. **2** blustering.

scoug *same as* **scog**.

scougie *same as* **scodgie**.

scouk *v* **1** to skulk. **2** to scowl. **3** to look angry, sulky or furtive. **4** to go about stealthily, as if guilty. **5** to conceal, hide. **6** to seek shelter or hiding. **7** to dash or flow under.—*n* **1** a frown, scowl. **2** a sour, forbidding look. **3** an evil look. **4** a skulking, cowardly fellow. **5** one with a downcast or dogged look. **6** shade, shelter, protection.— *adv* **1** sulkily, sullenly. **2** secretly, clandestinely.

scouking *adj* **1** ill-looking. **2** ashamed to look up. **3** furtive.

scoul *v* to scold.

scoulie-horned *adj* having the horns pointing downwards.

scoulin *n* a scolding.

scoult *same as* **scult**.

scounge *v* **1** to go to and fro like a dog. **2** to fish for invitations. **3** to pilfer.

scoup[1] *v* **1** to run, scamper, move briskly. **2** to skip, leap. **3** to spring from a place. **4** to go off.—*n* **1** a blow. **2** a sudden fall.

scoup[2] *n* a ladle, a scoop.—*v* **1** to hollow out. **2** to quaff. *See* **scoop**.

scoup[3] *n* **1** scope. **2** range. **3** liberty, licence. **4** length of rope. **5** plenty of room.

scouper *n* **1** a dancer. **2** a light, unsettled person.

scoup-hole *n* a subterfuge.

scour[1], **scour**[2], **scour**[3] *same as* **scoor**[1], **scoor**[2], **scoor**[3].

scour[4] *v* to whip off with an article.

scourge *v* **1** to act very severely. **2** to be a hard taskmaster. **3** (*used of land*) to exhaust the strength of the soil.

scourger *n* one whose duty it was to rid a parish of sturdy beggars.

scourging-hyre *n* an executioner.

scourie *v* to upbraid.

scourin' *same as* **scoorin**.

scouriness *n* shabbiness of dress.

scourins *same as* **scoorins**.

scourse *n* a subject of conversation.

scoury[1], **scoury**[2] *same as* **scoorie**[1], **scoorie**[2].

scoury-looking *adj* disreputable in appearance.

scout[1] *n* **1** a small boat. **2** a handy, open sailing boat used by smugglers.

scout[2] *n* a cobbler.

scout[3], **scout**[4], **scout**[5] *same as* **scoot**[1], **scoot**[2], **scoot**[3].

scouth *n* **1** room, freedom, scope, liberty to range. **2** abundance. **3** (*in playing marbles*) ample space or room sufficient for a player to take his shot.

scouth and routh *n* freedom to range and plenty to eat.

scouther[1] *n* **1** a slight, flying shower. **2** a storm of wind and rain. **3** a slight fall of snow.—*v* **1** to rain or snow slightly. **2** to drizzle.

scouther[2] *same as* **scowder**.

scouther[3] *v* to make a stone skim the surface of the water.

scouther[4] *n* sea blubber.

scouthered *adj* spoiled by rain.

scoutherie *adj* **1** abounding in flying showers. **2** threatening rain.

scoutherie-like *adj* like flying showers, threatening such.

scoutherin *n* a slight quantity of fallen snow.

scouthein' *same as* **scouder**.

scootherum *n* a very slight shower.

scouthie *adj* roomy, capacious, of large size.

scouthry *same as* **scoutherie**.

scouti-aulin *same as* **scooti-allan,**

scoutie *same as* **scootie**[1].

scout-mouth *n* a pursed-up mouth.

scout-mouthed *adj* having a scout-mouth (qv).

scove *v* **1** to fly equably and smoothly. **2** (*used of a bird*) to poise on the wing.

scove *n* a fop.—*adj* foppish.

scove-like *adj* having a foppish look.

scow[1] *n* a small boat made of willows, etc, covered with skins.

scow[2] *n* **1** a barrel stave. **2** a thin plank from which barrel staves are made. **3** the outside board of a tree. **4** a stick. **5** a twig. **6** (*in pl*) brushwood, firewood. **7** a bit, fragment. **8** the fragments cut from planks. **9** anything broken in small and useless pieces. **10** anything tall, thin and bony.—*v* **1** to knock in staves. **2** to smash in pieces. **3** to trim. **4** to cut off rags or tatters.

scowb *same as* **scob**[1].

scowb and screw *n* a wattle used in thatching with straw or thin pieces of turf.—*adj* all snug.

scowder *v* **1** to scorch, singe, burn. **2** to brown in toasting.—*n* **1** a burn, scorch, singe. **3** a hasty toasting. **4** sea blubber, for its power of scorching the skin. **5** severity. **6** painful experience.

scowder-doup *n* a ludicrous designation for a smith.

scowff[1] *same as* **scouff**[2].

scowff[2] *v* to swallow at one draught.

scowk *same as* **scouk**.

scowman *n* the man in charge of a scow or a lighter. *See* **scow**[1].

scowner *same as* **scunner**.

scowp[1], **scowp**[2] *same as* **scoup**[1], **scoup**[3].

scowr *same as* **scoor**[1].

scowrie[1] *n* a scurry, bustle.

scowrie[2] *same as* **scoorie**[2].

scowry[1] *same as* **scoorie**[1].

scowry[2] *adj* scouring.

scowth *same as* **scouth**.

scowther[1] *same as* **scouther**[1].

scowther[2] *same as* **scowder**.

scoy *adj* askew, awry.—*n* anything badly made.

scoy'd *adj* **1** twisted. **2** badly made or done.

scoyloch *n* an animal that plaits its legs in walking.

scra' *same as* **scraw**.

scrab[1] *n* **1** a stunted or withered tree or shrub a root. **2** a stump of heather. **3** a puny shrivelled person. **4** a thin, shrivelled limb. **5** an undergrown, scraggy animal.

scrab[2] *v* to scratch, scrape, claw.

scrabbie *adj* **1** stunted. **2** shrivelled.

scrabble[1] *n* **1** a stunted tree or shrub. **2** a thin, shrivelled limb. **3** a puny, shrivelled person. **4** a small, scraggy animal.

scrabble[2] *v* to tease wool.

scrabblich *n* **1** a stunted tree or shrub. **2** a scrabble (qv).

scrabe *n* the Manx shearwater.

scraber, scrabber *n* the black guillemot.

scra'-built *same as* **scraw-built**.

scrach *same as* **scraich**.

scrachle *v* **1** to scramble, crawl, creep. **2** to move with difficulty.—*n* a crawl, clamber.

scrae *n* **1** a shoe. **2** an old, shrivelled shoe. **3** a thin, skinny person or animal. **4** anything thin or shrivelled. **5** a skeleton. **6** fish dried in the sun, unsalted. **7** an ill-natured, fault-finding person. **8** an excitable person.—*adj* spare, meagre, lean.

scrae fish *n* unsalted fish dried in the sun.

scrae-shankit *adj* **1** having long, thin legs. **2** spindle-legged.

scraffle *v* to scramble for loose coins.—*n* a scramble, struggle.

scraggy *adj* **1** small. **2** spare.

scraich, scraigh *v* **1** to shriek, scream. **2** to cry like an alarmed hen. **3** to neigh. **4** to make a harsh, grating sound.—*n* **1** a shriek. **2** a bird's scream or shrill cry. **3** an urgent cry. **4** a harsh, discordant sound. **5** a lean, short person with a shrill voice. **6** (*used of day*) the dawn.

scraicher *n* one who scraichs. *See* **scraich**.

scraighton *n* a person fond of screaming.

scraik *same as* **scraich**.

scraip *v* to scrape.

scrall *v* to crawl.

scrammie *v* to scramble.

scramp *v* **1** to cramp, pinch. **2** to stint of anything.

scran *n* **1** food. **2** a collection of miscellaneous provisions. **3** victuals. **4** ability. **5** means for effecting a purpose.—*v* **1** to gather together. **2** to scrape a livelihood. **3** to save by frugality. **4** to collect. **5** to gain, catch. **6** to spend money on sweets, etc.

scranch *v* to grind between the teeth, crunch.

scranel *n* a morsel.

scrank *adj* **1** lank, lean, ill-shaped, slender. **2** (*of writing*) thin, sprawling, ill-formed.—*n* a lean, slender person. **3** ill-formed, sprawling writing. —*v* **1** to make ill-formed letters. **2** to write in a sprawling hand.

scrankit *adj* shrunken, puny.

scranky *adj* **1** lean, meagre. **2** lank, scraggy. **3** wrinkled. **4** empty, shrunken. **5** (*used of letters*) ill-formed.—*n* a coarse-featured person.

scranky-looking *adj* thin, scraggy in appearance.

scranky-shankit *adj* thin-legged.

scranny *adj* **1** thin, meagre, scraggy. **2** of inferior quality, scanty.—*n* an ill-natured old woman.

scran-pock *n* **1** a beggar's wallet for scraps. **2** a bag carried by camp followers to hold the spoil taken from the dead or wounded in battle.

scran-wallet *n* a beggar's wallet for scraps.

scrap[1] *n* scrap iron.

scrap[2] *n* **1** a wallet. **2** scrip.

scrap[3] *v* **1** to fight. **2** to box. **3** to gather up. **4** to bow, make obeisance.

scrape *v* **1** to make a scraping noise. **2** to grub in the earth. **3** to bow moving the foot. **4** to shave. **5** to gather or save money with difficulty, toil and pinching. **6** (*with* **along**) to manage to live. **7** to express scorn or derision.—*n* **1** a mark or scratch made by a pen. **2** a short letter, writing. **3** a shave. **4** an obeisance. **5** a pinch, difficulty in earning or saving money. **6** a miser.

scrape hard *n* **1** a miser. **2** one who has difficulty in making ends meet.

scraper *n* **1** a barber. **2** a fiddler. **3** an instrument for cleaning a byre (qv). **4** a hat.

scrapie *n* a miser.

scrapit *adj in phrs* **1** **ill-scrapit** ill-speaking, foul-mouthed. **2** **weel-scrapit** well-speaking, civil of speech.

scrapit-face *n* a person of thin, haggard face.

scraple *n* **1** an instrument for cleaning a baking board. **2** one for cleaning a byre (qv) or stable.

scrapon *same as* **scrupon**.

scrapper *same as* **scraper**.

scrat *same as* **scart**[1].

scratch[1] *n in phr* **up to the scratch** thoroughly competent.

scratch[2] *n* a hermaphrodite.

scrath *same as* **scart**[2].

scratter *n* a coarse heather scrubber for cleaning pots, etc.

scratty *adj* small, insignificant, puny, thin.

scrauch, scraugh *same as* **scraich**.

scrauchle *v* **1** to crawl. **2** to scramble.—*n* a clamber.

scraunky *same as* **scranky**.

scraut *same as* **scart**.

scraw *n* **1** a thin strip of turf. **2** a sod for thatching a roof, used also for hens confined to peck at. **3** *in phr* **scob and scraw** giving the idea of snugness, like the roof of a house when the turfs are well secured. *See* **scob**[1].

scraw-built *adj* built of sods.

scrawdyin *n* a sickly, puny child.

scray *same as* **scrae**.

screa *same as* **scrae**.

screak *same as* **scraich**.

scree *n* debris collected on a steep mountainside.

screeby *n* **1** the scurvy. **2** the scurvy grass.

screech *same as* **scraich**.

screech bird, ~ thrush *n* the fieldfare.

screed *n* **1** a long, thin strip of paper, cloth, land, etc. **2** a piece, bit. **3** a rent, tear. **4** a gap. **5** the sound of tearing. **6** the sound of scraping, used of a fiddle bow on the strings. **7** (*used of a pistol*) shot. **8** a large portion. **9** a long discourse or statement. **10** a piece of poetry. **11** a long list. **12** a drinking bout, a revel. **13** a quick movement. **14** a snatch. **15** anything torn off. **16** a lie.—*v* **1** to tear, rend. **2** to scream, to produce a sharp, shrill sound. **3** to play on the fiddle. **4** to talk tediously. **5** to recite rapidly. **6** to reel off. **7** to repeat a lie, to lie. **8** to write down at length. **9** to do anything smartly and with spirit.

screedge *v* **1** to tear. **2** to screed (qv).

screef *n* **1** scurf, dandruff. **2** a thin film or crust. **3** a slight covering. **4** lichen. **5** the hard skin or surface of arable land.—*v* **1** to become covered with scurf, a thin film or hard crust. **2** to pare a surface. **3** to come off in flakes of scurf.

screege *v* to scourge.

screegh *same as* **scraich**.

screek *v* to shriek.—*n* **1** a shriek. **2** (*used of day*) daybreak. **3** cockcrow.

screel *v* to scream.

screemage *same as* **scrimmage**.

screen *v* **1** to hide. **2** to protect. **3** to cover with a plaid or cloak.—*n* **1** a large scarf worn over the head. **2** a plaid, cloak.

screenge *same as* **scringe**[1].

screeny *adj* shady, screening.

screeve[1] *v* **1** to glide along swiftly. **2** to career. **3** to reel off a story. **4** to talk, read or sing fast and continuously.—*n* **1** a lengthy, familiar talk or chat. **2** a learned dissertation.

screeve[2] *same as* **scrive**[1].

screever[1] *n* **1** a clever fellow. **2** an expeditious worker.

screever[2] *n* **1** an inferior writer. **2** a mean scribe.

screg *n* a shoe.

scregh *same as* **scraich**.

screigh[1], **screich** *same as* **scraich**.

screigh[2] *n* whisky.

screigh o' day *n* daybreak.

screik *same as* **scraich**.

screive[1] *same as* **screeve**[1].

screive[2] *same as* **scrive**[2].

scremerston crow *n* the hooded crow.

scremit *adj* stingy.

screnoch *same as* **scroinoch**.

screw[1] *v* **1** to bore or move like a screw. **2** (*used in golf*) to drive widely to the left hand.—*n in phr* **a screw higher** a higher level.

screw[2] *n* the shrewmouse.

screw[3] *same as* **scrow**[3].

screw-driver *n* a carpenter's turnscrew.

screwtore *same as* **scritor**.

screyb *same as* **scribe**[1].

scribble *same as* **scrabble**[2].

scribe *n* a crab apple.

scribe *v* **1** to write. **2** to inscribe.—*n* **1** a mark with a pen. **2** a letter. **3** a scrap of writing.

scriddan, scridan *n* a mountain torrent.

scrie[1] *same as* **scrow**[3].

scrie[2] *same as* **scry**[2].

scriech, scriegh *same as* **scraich**.

scried *same as* **screed**.

scrieve[1] *same as* **screeve**[1].

scrieve[2], **scrieve**[3] *same as* **scrive**[1], **scrive**[2].

scrieving *n* the sound of a player putting very much wind into his bagpipe.

scriff[1] *n* the scruff of the neck.

scriff[2] *same as* **screef**.

scriffin, scriffan *n* **1** a small quantity. **2** a membrane. **3** a film.

scrift *n* **1** a recitation from memory. **2** a long-winded story. **3** a written composition. **4** a fabrication. **5** a falsehood.—*v* **1** to rehearse from memory fluently. **2** to magnify in narration. **3** to fib.

scrim[1] *v* **1** to strike. **2** to beat vigorously. **3** to bustle about. **4** to work with energy and success. **5** to search vigorously. **6** to move swiftly. **7** to rinse. **8** to rub vigorously.

scrim[2] *n* **1** thin, coarse cloth, used for window blinds. **2** buckram.

scrimge *same as* **scringe**[1].

scrimger *n* **1** a greedy, covetous person. **2** a person of disagreeable disposition and manners.

scrimmage *n* **1** a hard rubbing. **2** a severe beating. **3** a thorough, noisy, fussy search.—*v* **1** to skirmish. **2** to scramble. **3** to rub violently. **4** to beat severely. **5** to search thoroughly and noisily.

scrimmish *n* a skirmish.

scrimp[1] *v* **1** to straiten. **2** to straiten as to food or money. **3** to stint, pinch. **4** to oppress by extortion. **5** to give short weight or measure. **6** to dole out scantily.—*adj* **1** narrow. **2** parsimonious, niggardly. **3** short in weight or measure. **4** deficient mentally.—*adv* barely.

scrimp[2] *v* **1** to kick violently. **2** to act energetically.

scrimpiness *n* **1** cutting. **2** measuring or weighing out articles on sale with very great exactness.

scrimpit *adj* niggardly.

scrimpitly *adv* scarcely, barely, hardly.

scrimpitness *n* scrimpness, scantiness.

scrimply *adv* **1** scantily. **2** scarcely, barely. **3** sparingly.

scrimps *n* **1** narrow means. **2** a short allowance.

scrimpy *adj* **1** niggardly, mean. **2** scarlty.

scringe[1] *v* **1** to scrub or rub vigorously. **2** to purge. **3** to scourge, flog. **4** to search carefully, pry about. **5** to run forcibly. **6** to wander about, turning over everything. **7** to glean.—*n* **1** a thorough cleansing. **2** a rub, a rubbing. **3** the sound of rubbing. **4** energetic working. **5** a lash, stroke. **6** a severe beating. **7** a prying, eager search. **8** a thorough rummage. **9** a gleaning. **10** a mean, miserly person. **11** a searcher. **12** a loose woman.—*adv* with a sharp blow.

scringe[2] *v* **1** to shrink. **2** to wince. **3** to shrivel.

scringer *n* **1** a person of energetic character, ill-disposed. **2** a gleaner. **3** one who pries about looking out for trifles. **4** anything large of its kind.

scringing *n* **1** fishing at night with small nets and no torches. **2** (*in pl*) gleanings.

scrip *n* a bill, reckoning.

scripturalist *n* a firm believer in Holy scripture.

scritor *n* an escritoire.

scrive[1] *v* **1** to write. **2** to scrape, peel. **3** to make a harsh sound by scratching metal.—*n* **1** a piece of writing, a letter. **2** a written statement. **3** handwriting. **4** a large scratch.

scrive[2] *v* to tear, drag asunder.

scrive[3] *same as* **screeve**[1].

scrivening paper *n* writing paper.

scriver *n* **1** a writer. **2** a paymaster. **3** a secretary.

scrobe *v* to scratch.

scrobie *same as* **scrooby**.

scroch *v* to scorch (used of a sultry, oppressive day or of a withering wind).

scrocchen't *adj* **1** (*used of peats*) sufficiently dried on the surface to allow them to be footed. **2** twisted or gnarled by excessive heat. *See* **foot**.

scrog[1] *n* the tilt given to a cap or bonnet on the head.

scrog[2], **scrogg** *n* **1** a stunted shrub, tree or branch. **2** a thorn bush. **3** rough land covered with stunted bushes and underwood. **4** the crab apple. **5** a long, crooked, scraggy limb.—*adj* stunted.

scrog apple *n* the crab apple.

scrogg buss *n* a stunted bush.

scrogged *adj* **1** (*of vegetation*) thorny. **2** stunted. **3** twisted.

scroggy, scrogie *adj* **1** stunted. **2** thorny. **3** abounding in stunted bushes or underwood.

scroinoch, scroinach *n* **1** a shrill cry. **2** a yell. **3** a tumult. **4** a noisy fuss. **5** a noisy person.—*v* **1** to shout, yell. **2** to make a noisy disturbance.

scroit *n* (*used of children or grown persons*) a worthless, contemptible number.

scroll, scrol *v* to write.

scronach, scronnoch *same as* **scroinoch**.

scrooby *n* the scurvy.

scrooby grass *n* the scurvy grass.

scrooch, scrouch *same as* **scroch**.

scroof[1] *same as* **scruff**[1].

scroof[2], **scroofe, scrooff** *same as* **scruff**[2].

scroofin *same as* **scruffin**.

scrout *same as* **scroit**.

scrow[1] *n* **1** a scrap. **2** a damaged skin, fit only for making glue. **3** an odd bit or scrap taken from a skin. **4** (*in pl*) various kinds of small insects found in pools and springs.—*v* to cut off scraps, ears and torn pieces from skins.

scrow[2] *n* a slight shower of rain.

scrow[3] *n* **1** a number. **2** a crowd. **3** a swarm. **4** riot. **5** hurly-burly.—*v* **1** to swarm. **2** to gather in numbers.

scrub *n* **1** a joiner's foreplane or jack plane. **2** a niggard, a mean, grasping person. **3** (*in pl*) the husks of oats, etc.—*v* **1** to scrape, scratch. **2** to scrape together money, to live parsimoniously.

scrubber *n* a small bundle of heather for cleaning pots, etc.

scrubbieness *n* sordid parsimony.

scrubble *v* **1** to struggle. **2** to raise an uproar.—*n* **1** a struggle. **3** a difficulty to be overcome in accomplishing any work. **4** a squabble, uproar.

scrubby *adj* lean.

scrubie *same as* **scrooby**.

scrubie grass *same as* **scrooby grass**.

scrubily *adv* scurvily.

scrudge *v* to scourge.—*n* a scourge.

scrufan, scrufin *same as* **scruffin**.

scruff[1] *n* **1** the back of the neck, the nape. **2** the back of a coat collar.

scruff[2], **scruf, scrufe** *n* **1** scurf, dandruff. **2** a thin crust or covering. **3** a film. **4** the surface of land or water.—*v* **1** to take off the surface of anything. **2** to graze, touch slightly. **3** to handle any subject superficially. **4** to plough carelessly and slightly. **5** to be covered with a film.

scruffin *n* **1** a thin covering or scurf. **2** the surface of earth.

scruffin time *n* the time for preparing land for one crop in succession to another and covering the seed.

scrug[1] *v in phr* **to scrug one's bonnet** to cock one's cap in order to look smart or bold. *See* **scrog**[1].

scrug[2] *same as* **scrog**[2].

scruinnich *same as* **scroinoch**.

scruity *n* the scurvy.

scrummage *same as* **scrimmage**.

scrump *v* **1** to make a crackling noise in eating crisp bread. **2** to make crisp. **3** to bake hard. **4** to crunch hard bread. **5** (*used of bread*) to become crisp.—*n* crisp and hard bread.

scrumpie *adj* crisp.

scrumpit *adj* crisp, baked hard.

scrumple[1], **scrumpill** *same as* **scrump**.

scrumple[2] *v* to crease, wrinkle, ruffle.

scrumplie *adj* crisp.

scrunch *v* to eat noisily.—*n* a crunching, grating sound.

scrunge *same as* **scringe**[1].

scrunt[1] *n* **1** anything stunted or worn down. **2** the stump of a quill pen. **3** a cabbage stalk. **4** a stunted, insignificant person. **5** a mean, miserly person. **6** a walking skeleton.

scrunt[2] *v* **1** to grate. **2** to produce a harsh sound by grating or scraping. **3** to scratch, scrape, scrub. **4** to oppress or grind down.—*n* a harsh, grating sound.

scruntin' *adj* stunted, dwarfed.

scruntiness *n* **1** stuntedness. **2** scrubbiness. **3** stubbiness.

scruntit *adj* **1** stunted, dwarfed. **2** meagre, thin, undergrown. **3** raw-boned.

scruntit-like *adj* scruntit (qv) in appearance.

scrunty *adj* **1** stunted in growth. **2** thin, meagre. **3** raw-boned, scraggy. **4** stubbed, short and thick. **5** mean, niggardly, stingy.

scrupon *v* to hamper.—*n* one who hampers.

scrupulous *adj* **1** doubtful, suspicious. **2** curious, inquisitive.

scrutoire *same as* **scritor**.

scry[1] *same as* **scrow**[3].

scry[2] *v* **1** to cry, proclaim. **2** to announce publicly. —*n* **1** noise, clamour. **2** a public proclamation of sales, fairs, banns of marriage, etc. **3** an advertisement in a newspaper.

scrymge *same as* **scringe**[1].

scrymger *same as* **scringer**.
scrynge *same as* **scringe**[1].
scrynoch *same as* **scroinoch**.
scubble *v* to soil, as a schoolboy does his book.
scud[1] *v* **1** to cause a thin stone to skim along the surface of still water. **2** to rain slightly or in drifting showers. **3** to quaff. **4** to raise froth or foam upon. **5** to slap with the open hand, with a tawse (qv) or with a ferule. **6** to dust with a rod. **7** to beat or whip.—*n* **1** a sudden movement. **2** the rush of a stream. **3** a sudden shower with wind, a squall. **4** foam, froth. **5** a blow, a slap. **6** (*in pl*) a whipping. **7** foaming beer or ale.
scud[2] *n* **1** the skin. **2** nudity, nakedness.
scudder[1] *same as* **scowder**.
scudder[2] *v* to shudder.
scudderin *n* shuddering.
scuddie *n* **1** a game like shinty. **2** the club used in it.
scuddievaig *same as* **scurryvaig**.
scudding seat *n* the seat in a school on which punishment was inflicted.
scudding stane *n* a thin stone used in the game of ducks and drakes.
scuddle[1] *v* to cleanse, wash. **2** to act as a kitchen drudge. **3** to do housework in a slatternly way. **4** to soil, sully. **5** to put an article of dress out of shape or colour by careless usage. **6** to walk in a slovenly way.—*n* **1** a cleansing, scrubbing. **2** kitchen drudgery. **3** a kitchen drudge, scullion. **4** a dress much worn or soiled. **5** a slovenly, untidy style of working or walking.—*adv* in a slatternly way.
scuddle[2] *v* **1** to scurry, hurry. **2** to wander from home in order to shirk work or duty.
scuddler[1] *n* a youngster.
scuddler[2] *n* a child who wanders from home to shirk work.
scuddlin boy *n* a young scullion or kitchen boy.
scuddrie *adj* showery.
scuddy *adj* **1** naked. **2** unfledged. **3** scant. **4** too small. **5** penurious.—*n* **1** an undressed infant. **2** an unfledged bird.
scuddy-naked *adj* stark naked.
scudgie *same as* **scodgie**.
scudle *same as* **scuddle**[1].
scue *adj* askew.
scuff[1], **scufe** *v* **1** to shuffle the feet, scrape with the shoes in walking. **2** to graze. **3** to touch lightly in passing. **4** to brush aside. **5** to injure slightly. **6** to cuff, slap. **7** to treat a subject superficially. **8** to tarnish dress by wearing or doing rough work. **9** to work in a light, careless manner.—*n* **1** a shove with the foot in walking. **2** a slight touch or graze in passing. **3** a puff of wind. **4** the slight performance of work. **5** a hasty brushing. **6** a bat for playing at handball, a battledore.—*adv* with a whizzing sound.
scuff[2] *n* the nape or scruff of the neck.
scuff[3] *n* a sudden and passing shower of rain.—*v* to rain slightly.
scuff[4] *n* a mean, sordid fellow.—*v* to pilfer from the poor or in any mean way.
scuff[5] *v* to drink off, quaff.
scuffet *n* a smith's fire-shovel.
scuffle[1] *v* **1** to work roughly and superficially. **2** to shuffle with the feet. **3** to whiz, to grate slightly. **4** to graze. **5** to rub lightly. **6** to tarnish.—*n* **1** a shuffle. **2** a graze. **3** a slight rub. **4** a slight grating sound. **5** doing work superficially.—*adv* with a whizzing sound.
scuffle[2] *n* a Dutch hoe.—*v* to use a Dutch hoe.
scuffle[3] *n* a mop for cleaning out ovens.
scuffy *adj* **1** shabby, flimsy. **2** worthless.
scufter *n* a policeman.
scug[1] *n* **1** a twig. **2** a small branch.
scug[2] *n* **1** a shade. **2** a sheltered place. **3** the declivity of a hill. **4** shelter, protection. **5** a pretext, ruse. **6** a frown, a gloomy countenance.—*v* **1** to shade. **2** to shelter, protect. **3** to hide. **4** to take shelter, refuge. **5** to go in a stooping posture. **6** to flow under. **7** to frown, have a gloomy

countenance. **8** to crouch in order to avoid a blow. **9** to move stealthily.
scuggers *n* footless stockings worn over the shoes as gaiters or over the arms.
scugging-faced, **~-looking** *adj* of a gloomy countenance.
scugways, **scugwise** *adv* stealthily.
scuit[1] *same as* **scoot**[3].
scuit[2] *same as* **skute**[2].
sculder[1] *n* ruin.
sculder[2] *n* an under-cook.
sculduddery, **sculdudry**, **sculduldry** *n* **1** fornication. **2** grossness. **3** obscenity. **4** filthy talk. **5** vulgar, low people. **6** rubbish, tatters.—*adj* **1** adulterous. **2** immoral. **3** obscene, indecent, foul-mouthed.
scule[1] *same as* **schule**[2].
scule[2] *same as* **school**[2].
scule-time *n* the time one is at school.
scule-wean *same as* **schule-wean**.
scull[1] *n* **1** a fisherman's shallow wicker basket. **2** a wicker-work cradle.
scull[2] *v* **1** to walk in zigzag fashion. **2** to wander.
scull[3] *same as* **skull**[1].
scull bonnet *n* a tightly fitting cap formerly worn by judges and lawyers.
scull gab *n* a cloud shaped like a boat.
scull hat *n* a skullcap.
scullion, **scullian** *n* a rogue, knave.
scull row *n* the notch in the stern of a boat for the oar when only one is used to propel the boat.
scult *n* **1** a stroke with the open hand. **2** a blow on the palm of the hand.—*v* **1** to beat with the open hand, thrash. **2** to punish by striking the palm.
scum[1] *n* **1** anything skimmed. **2** skimmed milk. **3** a thin coating of ice. **4** a greedy fellow, a hunks. **5** a scamp, rascal. **6** a worthless person.—*v* **1** to shave. **2** to scrape clean. **3** to catch the herrings that fall from the nets as they are hauled. **4** to glance. **5** to look at hurriedly.
scum[2] *v* to strike on the mouth.
scumfish *v* **1** to suffocate, stifle, choke with heat, smoke or bad smell. **2** to spoil by heat or bad smell. **3** to disgust. **4** to overpower.—*n* **1** a state of suffocation. **2** a dislike, disgust.
scummer *n* **1** the boy who in a herring boat catches the fish that drop from the nets when being hauled. **2** the poke net on the end of a pole by which he catches the falling fish.
scummerins *n* the scrapings of a pot.
scum milk *n* skimmed milk.
scumming *v in phr* **scumming the text** preaching from a text superficially, ignoring its doctrines or only touching lightly on them without pressing them home.
scummings *n* **1** anything skimmed. **2** skimmed milk.
scun *n* **1** plan. **2** craft. **3** intention.
scuncheon *n* **1** the cornerstone of a building. **2** a stone forming a projecting angle. **3** a square dole or piece of bread, cheese, etc.
scunder *same as* **scunner**.
scunfis, **scunfish** *same as* **scumfish**.
scunge *v* **1** to slink about. **2** to fawn like a dog for food. **3** to drive out like a dog. **4** to gallop, run quickly.—*n* **1** a sly fellow. **2** a vicious man.
scunner *v* **1** to loathe. **2** to feel disgust. **3** to shudder with repugnance. **4** to scare. **5** to flinch from. **6** to cause to surfeit. **7** to be sick. **8** to disgust, sicken, cause loathing. **9** to hesitate.—*n* **1** dislike, disgust. **2** a surfeit. **3** the object of loathing. **4** what excites disgust.
scunnerashen *n* anything disgusting, an abomination.
scunnerfu' *adj* disgusting, loathsome, abominable.
scunnersome *adj* loathsome, scunnerfu' (qv).
scuntion *same as* **scuncheon**.
scuppit-beaver *n* a shovel-shaped hat.
scur[1] *n* **1** a small freshwater shrimp. **2** the mayfly, fresh from the larva.
scur[2] *same as* **scurr**.

scurdy n **1** moorstone. **2** a resting place. **3** a favourite seat.

scurfuffle v to tarnish.—n **1** the act of tarnishing. **2** a tarnished article of dress.

scurl n the scab formed over a wound or sore.

scurly adj covered with a scab.

scurly adj **1** scurrile. **2** opprobrious.

scurr n **1** the scab formed over a wound or sore. **2** the rough surface of a stone. **3** a small horn of ox or cow, not fastened to the skull but hanging by the skin alone. **4** a low rascal. **5** a sheriff officer's assistant. **6** anything low.—v (used of a sore) to become covered with a scab.

scurrie[1] n the shag.

scurrie[2] adj **1** low, dwarfish. **2** not thriving.

scurrie[3] n a cow with scurrs or short horns.

scurrie-man n a wandering fellow.

scurrie-whurrie n a hurly-burly, tumult.

scurroch, scurrock n the least particle.

scurry v **1** to scour. **2** to go about from place to place. **3** to wander about aimlessly.

scurryvaig, scurrivaig v **1** to run about in an unsettled manner. **2** to live idly and in dissipation.—n **1** a scamp. **2** a vagabond. **3** a clumsy person. **4** an idle, unsettled person. **5** a course of dissipation. **6** a spree.

scurvy n a mean, contemptible person.

scushel, scushle v **1** to slide. **2** to shuffle in walking. **3** to make a noise in walking in shoes too big or down at the heels. **4** to work carelessly and in slovenly fashion. **5** to spoil an article of dress by bad usage.—n **1** a shuffle. **2** a shuffling noise from walking in old or ill-fitting shoes. **3** an old, wornout shoe. **4** slovenly unmethodical working. **5** work so done. **6** a clumsy person in gait or work. **7** a clumsy, ill-made thing.—adj clumsy, ill-made.

scushy n money, cash.

scutch v **1** to beat. **2** to switch, cane. **3** to shear or trim with a hook. **4** to walk pushing the feet lightly forward. **5** to move quickly. **6** to touch lightly with a duster, etc. **7** to push or carry forward.—n **1** a cut at the top of a twig or thistle. **2** the trimming of a hedge. **3** the cutting down of thistles. **4** a shuffle or scraping movement of the feet. **5** a slight whizzing or grating sound. **6** a light, quick manner of working. **7** a beating, dusting. **8** a billhook.—adv with a grating sound.

scutcher n **1** a dirty, slovenly, clumsy worker. **2** a scutch used in flax-dressing.

scutching n (in pl) **1** waste tow, refuse flax. **2** twigs, thistles, etc, lopped off.

scutching knife n a billhook.

scutching spurkle n a stick for beating flax.

scutching tow n the refuse of flax after scutching.

scute same as **scoot**[3].

scuter-hole same as **scutter-hole**.

scutle v **1** to pour from vessel to vessel, to spill liquid in doing so. **2** to cook.—n (in pl) liquid tossed from vessel to vessel.

scutsh v to dress oneself up.

scuttal n a pool of filthy water.

scutter v **1** to run off hastily, as if in panic, to scuttle. **2** to bungle, make a mess. **3** to work slapdash and in a messy manner.—n **1** a mess. **2** dirty, confused work. **3** dirty, messy working. **4** a slovenly, untidy worker.

scutter-hole n a filthy puddle.

scutterie job n work of an indefinite character.

scuttle dish n a large, flat dish set below the spigot of an ale barrel to catch the drops.

scuttlin-flour n flour made of refuse wheat.

scuttlins n light or refuse wheat, ground apart into inferior flour.

scybel same as **skybal**.

scypal same as **skypal**.

scyre adj sheer, utter, complete.—adv utterly.

scythe v **1** to eject quickly. **2** to squirt from the mouth through the teeth.

scytheman n a mower.

scythe-shank n the long handle of a scythe.

scythe-sned n the handle of a scythe.

scythe-straik n a piece of hardwood covered with sand for sharpening scythes.

se v shall.

sea box n a box for holding fishermen's provisions at the deep-sea fishing.

sea breach, -break n a breaker.

sea bree n the waves of the sea.

sea breed n the food of fishes.

sea breeks n breeches worn by fishermen at sea.

sea-broken adj shipwrecked.

sea candle n the phosphorescence of the sea.

sea-carr v to embank.—n a sea wall, an embankment.

sea cashie n a wicker fish basket.

seacock n **1** the puffin. **2** the foolish guillemot.

sea coulter n the puffin.

sea crow n the razorbill.

sea daisy n the thrift.

seadog n a meteor seen on the horizon before sunrise or after sunset, viewed by sailors as a sure portent of bad weather.

sea dovie n the black guillemot.

sea edge n the margin of the sea.

seafarin' n sea-voyaging.

sea fike n a marine plant that, when rubbed on the skin, causes irritation.

sea fire n the phosphorescence of the sea.

seag same as **segg**[1].

sea goo n a seagull.

sea growth n the names given by fishermen to various species of sertulariae, flustrae, etc, adhering to small stones, shells, etc.

sea haar n a sea fog.

sea hack n **1** a temporary thaw occasioned by the salt vapour during the rising tide. **2** a short thaw between frosts.

sea hen n **1** the common guillemot. **2** the piper or *Trigla lyra*.

seal[1] n a rope or chain for binding cattle in the stall.—v to bind or fasten cattle in the stalls.

seal[2] same as **seel**.

sea lark n the dunlin.

sealch[1] n **1** a pustule, a large blackhead. **2** a bunion.

sealch[2], **sealgh** n a seal, sea calf.

sealch's bubble n a jellyfish.

sealch-skin n a sealskin.

sea-light n the phosphorescence of the sea.

seal of cause n a writing granted to a body of craftsmen or a guild by a royal burgh and sealed with the burgh seal, conveying or confirming privileges.

seam[1] n **1** a crack in crockery. **2** a piece of sewing or weaving. **3** (used of teeth) a row.

seam[2] same as **saim**.

sea maiden n a mermaid.

seaman body n a sailor.

sea maw n **1** the common gull. **2** the blackheaded gull.

sea meath, ~-meeth n a landmark to those out at sea.

sea milkwort n the black saltwort.

sea mouse n the dunlin.

seannachie n **1** a Highland bard. **2** a storyteller. **3** a chronicler of heroic achievements.

seantack n a baited fishing line, one end of which is fastened to the bank of the river and the other kept across the stream by a weight.

seap same as **seip**.

sea peek n the dunlin.

sea pellock n the porpoise.

sea pheasant n the turbot.

sea pie, ~ pyet n the oystercatcher.

sea poacher n the armed bullhead.

sea quhaup,-whaup n a species of gull of a dark colour.

search n **1** a fine sieve. **2** a strainer.—v to sift or strain through a fine sieve.

searcher n a civil officer formerly employed in Glasgow

to apprehend idlers on the streets on Sunday during public worship.

sear-claith *n* a cerecloth.

sea snipe *n* the dunlin.

season-side *n* the duration of the season.

sea spire *n* sea spray.

sea swine *n* the ballan wrasse.

seat *n* **1** one of the boards over the bottom of a boat. **2** a fishing ground. **3** a sitting in a church.

seat-board *n* the seat of a hand loom.

seat-breast, ~-breist *n* the book board of a pew.

seath¹ *same as* **saithe.**

seath² *n* part of a plough.

seat house *n* the manor house on an estate.

seatie *n* a small or low seat.

seat-maill *n* pew-rent.

sea tod *n* the ballan wrasse.

sea tow *n* a rope for fastening or anchoring a fishing boat.

sea tree *same as* **sae tree.**

seat tree *n* a weaver's seat while at the loom.

seawa *same as* **say-awa'.**

sea waur *n* algae thrown up by the sea used as manure.

sea woman *n* a mermaid.

sea worm *n* a crab.

sea wynd *n* an alley leading to the sea.

sebow *same as* **sybo.**

seceder *n* **1** a seceder from the Established Church of Scotland. **2** one who differs from another.

seceder-body *n* a seceder (qv), a member of the Secession Church.

seceder-face *n* a sanctimonious face.

seceder-plan *n* the plan of supporting a Church by voluntary contributions without state aid.

secession *n* the Church of seceders. *See* **seceder.**

sech *same as* **sich.**

seck¹ *n* a sack.

seck² *n* the wine, sack.

seckcloth *n* sackcloth.

seck-gown *n* the garment worn by an offender while doing public penance.

seckless *same as* **sackless.**

secky-ban *same as* **sacban.**

second-handed *adj* second-hand.

second-sichtit *adj* having the power of foreseeing the future.

secret *n* a coat of mail worn under the outer dress.

secretar, secreter *n* **1** a secretary. **2** a keeper of secrets.

secret council *n* the privy council.

secretful *adv* secretly.

sect *n* **1** set, class. **2** sex.

secured *adj* provided for, secured from want.

sedan-bread *n* a soda scone.

sedge band *n* an apparition.

sedge-singer *n* the sedge warbler.

sedging *n* a disease in the roots of oaks caused by insects.

sedimateese *v* to choke or stop up with sediment.

see *v* to give, hand, lend, let one have.

see-about *v* to acquire an accurate knowledge of one's surroundings.

see-after *v* **1** to look after, attend to. **2** to try to find, inquire about.

see and *v* to see if.

see-awa' *v* to outlive, survive.

see'd *v* saw.

seed *n* **1** the husk of oats. **2** the inner covering of grain, recovered in grinding. **3** a very small quantity. **4** a fragment. **5** seed time. **6** spring. **7** a hot-tempered person.— *v* **1** to sow. **2** (*used of mares and cows*) to have the udder begin to swell before giving birth.

seed bird *n* **1** the grey wagtail. **2** the common gull.

seed-fire *n* a fire made with seeds or husks of oats. *See* **seed.**

seed-foullie *n* the pied wagtail.

seed-fur *n* the furrow into which the seed is to be cast.

seedge *n* rate, speed.

seed-lady,-laverock *n* the pied wagtail.

seed-like *adj* (*of land*) apparently fit to receive seed.

seedlins *n* **1** youngsters. **2** learners.

seedsman *n* a sower.

seedy *adj* **1** full of seeds or husks. **2** made of, or containing, the husks of oats. *See* **seed.**

seedy-broo *n* **1** sowens (qv) in the first stage of steeping, before the seeds have fallen to the bottom of the tub. **2** the second brewing of ale or home-made beer. **3** weak ale. *See* **seed.**

seefer *same as* **sieffer.**

seeing glass *n* a looking glass.

seek¹ *v* **1** to fetch, bring. **2** to court, ask in marriage. **3** to invite. **4** to ask as a price. **5** to make a bid, offer a price. **6** to overtask. **7** to attack. **8** to beg. **9** to live by begging. **10** to ask for.

seek² *v* to soak.

seek³ *v* **1** to ooze. **2** to leak.

seek-and-hod *n* the game of hide and seek.

seek awe' *v* to seek to go away.

seek in *v* to seek to enter in.

seek out *v* **1** to fetch out. **2** to ask leave to go out of school.

seel *n* **1** a favourable occasion. **2** happiness.

seelfu' *adj* pleasant, happy, blessed, foreboding good.

seelfu'ness *n* **1** complacency. **2** sweetness of disposition. **3** happiness of temper.

seelible *adj* pleasant, happy, delightful.

seelie-hoo, ~-how *n* **1** a child's caul, thought to bring luck to its possessor. **2** any quaint headdress.

seely *adj* happy, blessed.

seely-court *n* the fairy court.

seely-wight *n* a fairy.

seem¹ *n* resemblance, appearance.

seem² *same as* **saim.**

seemilar *adj* similar.

seemless *adj* unseen.

seemly *adj* comely, winsome.

seen¹ *v* saw.

seen² *adj* **1** looking, showing. **2** familiar, versed, practised, expert.

seen³ *same as* **syne**³.

seen⁴ *adv* soon.

seenil *adv* seldom, rarely.—*adj* **1** rare, infrequent. **2** single. **2** singular.

seenillie *adv* remarkably, singularly.

seenil-times *adv* rarely, seldom.

seenlins *adv* rarely, seldom.

se'ennicht *n* **1** a week. **2** the seventh night.

seep *same as* **seip.**

seep-sabbin' *n* the sound of dripping, trickling water or of a brook.

seer¹ *n* one who has the second sight.

seer² *adj* sure.

seerie *same as* **sairie.**

seerly *adv* surely.

seerup *n* syrup.

seestou, seestow, seestoo *int* an exclamation used as emphasis, to attract attention.

seet¹ *n* soot.

seet² *n* **1** a seat. **2** the cover of the narrow place over the keel of a boat.

seeth, seethe *same as* **saithe.**

seeth *v* **1** to boil. **2** to be nearly boiling.

seethe *same as* **scythe.**

seg¹ *v* **1** to bend down from superincumbent weight. **2** to sink, subside. **3** to press or shake down. **4** (*used of liquids*) to sink down. **5** (*of drink*) to influence the drinker.

seg² *v* to set the teeth on edge by eating anything sour.

seg³ *n* a grip.

seg⁴ *same as* **segg**¹.

seg-backit *adj* (*used of a horse*) having the back hollow or sunk.

segg[1], **seg** *n* **1** a name given to various plants with sword-shaped leaves. **2** the yellow iris.

segg[2] *n* a bull castrated when of full age.

seggan *n* **1** a name given to various plants with sword-shaped leaves. **2** the yellow iris.

seggit *adj* walking heavily and stumbling from weariness.

seggit cow *n* a cow with calf.

seggit-teeth *n* teeth set on edge.

segg-root *n* the root of a segg. *See* **segg**[1].

seggy *adj* sedgy, overgrown with reeds, etc.

seggy boat *n* a toy boat made of sedges, rushes, etc.

seibow *same as* **sybo**.

seich *same as* **sich**.

seiger *n* a besieger.

seik *v* to seek.

seil[1] *v* **1** to strain. **2** to filter. **3** to rinse clothes.—*n* a sieve, strainer for milk, etc.

seil[2], **seile** *same as* **seel**.

seiler *n* a strainer.

seilfu' *same as* **seelfu'**.

seill *same as* **seal**[1].

seily *same as* **seely**.

seim[1] *same as* **saim**.

seim[2] *same as* **seem**[1].

seimly *same as* **seemly**.

seindle, seinle *same as* **seenil**.

seip *v* **1** to ooze. **2** to leak. **3** to percolate slowly. **4** to cause to drop or trickle. **5** to drain to the dregs in drinking. **6** to drain of moisture. **7** to soak through. **8** to sink slowly and disappear.—*n* **1** a leakage. **2** a puddle. **3** a state of wetness. **4** a mouthful of liquid. **5** a sip, drop. **6** what remains in a bottle. **7** a small spring or stream of water. **8** the dregs of a liquid.

seipage *n* leakage.

seiped *adj* dried up, drained of moisture.

seipin' *adj* very wet, dripping.

seirie *adj* **1** distant, reserved, haughty. **2** cynical in manner.

seise *v* to give formal possession.

seissle *v* **1** to confuse, disorder. **2** to trifle. **3** to spend time needlessly. **4** to be inactive or unhandy.

seissler *n* a trifler.

seizer *n* an officer whose duty was to apprehend persons idling in the streets during public worship on Sunday.

sejoin *v* to disjoin, separate.

sek *same as* **seck**[1].

seker *same as* **sicker**.

sekerly *same as* **sickerly**.

sel', sell *pron and adj* self.

selch, selchie, selcht *same as* **sealch**[2].

selcouth *adj* strange, rare, uncommon.

sele[1] *n* **1** a favourable occasion. **2** happiness.

sele[2] *same as* **seal**[1].

self *adj* **1** original, pristine. **2** natural. **3** undyed.

self and same *adj* the very same.

self-tenderness *n* care for one's own health.

selkhorn *same as* **shillcorn**.

selkie *same as* **sealch**[2].

Selkirk bannock *n* a sweet cake of flour baked with currants.

selkit, selkith *adv* seldom.

sell[1], **selle** *n* **1** a seat, stool. **2** a saddle, pillion.

sell[2] *v* to throw away an advantage.

sell[3] *same as* **seel**.

sell[4] *same as* **seal**[2].

sellag *n* the fry of the coalfish.

sellat, sellat-pan *n* a small pan or pot with a lid.

sellet *n* a salad.

sellible *same as* **seel**.

sellie *n* self.—*adj* selfish.

sell't, selt *v* sold.

sel'-sappit *adj* **1** self-satisfied. **2** self-conceited.

selvage *n* **1** a border, edge. **2** the bank of a stream. —*v* to form a border, line or margin.

selver *n* a salver.

sely *same as* **seely**.

sely-how *same as* **seelie-hoo**.

sem *same as* **saim**.

semble *n* the parapet of a bridge.

semi, semie *n* a second year's student at a Scottish university, especially Aberdeen University.

semibachelor *n* an old designation of a second year's student at Edinburgh University.

semibajan *n* a semibachelor (qv).

semiclass *n* second-year students at Aberdeen University.

semiyear *n* the second year of a student's curriculum.

semmit *n* a flannel or knitted woollen undershirt.

semmle *v* to arrange, put in order.

sempeternum *n* a species of woollen cloth.

semple *adj* **1** of lowly birth. **2** in common life.—*n* the commonalty.

sempleness *n* a low condition of life.

sempster *n* a sempstress.

sen[1] *same as* **sain**.

sen[2] *same as* **syne**[3].

sen' *v* to send.

senachie, sennachie *same as* **seannachie**.

send *n* **1** a message. **2** a prayer. **3** a messenger. **4** one sent in advance of the bridegroom to summon the bride.—*v* to require by message something to be done.

send-down *n* a message sent down.

send-up *n* a message sent up.

sengreen *n in phr* **small marsh sengreen** the hairy stonecrop.

senil, sennil *same as* **seenil**.

senlins *adv* seldom.

sen's *int* save us! *See* **sain**.

sense *n* essence, pith.—*v* **1** to put a sense upon. **2** to put meaning into. **3** to scent out.

senselessest *adj* most senseless.

sense-thrawin *adj* (*of drink*) confusing the senses.

senshach *adj* **1** (*of children*) wise, sensible. **2** well-behaved.

sensible *adj* **1** conscious in an illness. **2** evident, beyond doubt.

sensible drunk *adj* drunk but conscious.

sensuals *n* passions.

sen syne *same as* **sin syne**.

sent *same as* **sint**.

sen't *v with pron* send it.

sentence silver *n* money paid by the person losing his case towards the salary of the judges and by the prosecutor also.

sequels *n* **1** small parcels of corn or meal given as a fee to the mill servants in addition to what is paid to the multurer. **2** the young of animals.

sequestrate *v* to set apart a day for a special purpose (a legal term).

ser', sere *same as* **sair**[2].

sere *v* **1** to sear. **2** to wither up, blast.

sereachan-~, (*perhaps*) **screachan-aittin** *n* a bird with a larger body than a large mall, of bluish colour, with a bill of carnation colour and given to shrieking hideously.

serf *n* sowens (qv) before fermentation has fully begun.

serin' *same as* **sairing**.

serk *same as* **sark**.

serplath *n* eighty stones of wool.

serplins *n* the soapy water in which clothes have been boiled.

serse *int* an exclamation of surprise.

ser't *v*, adjsaid of one who has had quite enough.

servad, servat *n* **1** a serviette, table napkin. **2** a towel. **3** a small tray.

servant *same as* **servitor**.

servant-lass *n* a maidservant.

serve[1] *same as* **sair**[2].

serve[2] *v* to deserve.

serve[3] *v* to preserve.

servet *same as* **servad**.

service *n* **1** an assurance of respect. **2** a place of service. **3** assistance given by unskilled labourers to masons and carpenters while building or repairing a house. **4** a round of wine, spirits, etc, formerly given to the persons attending a funeral. **5** any serving of whisky, etc.

servin' *same as* **sairing**.

servin'-chiel *n* a manservant.

servin' lass, ~ woman *n* a maidservant.

servitor *n* **1** an apprentice or clerk of a judge, advocate, etc. **2** a secretary, man of business. **3** a servant, attendant.

servitrix *n* **1** a female servant. **2** a lady's maid.

servitude *n* service, employment.

sesquaster *v* **1** to sequester. **2** to sequestrate.

sess *v* to assess.—*n* an assessment.

session *n* the elders of a Presbyterian congregation in session, the kirk session.—*v* **1** to give in names to the clerk of the kirk session for proclamation of banns. **2** to summon before the session.

session book *n* the kirk-session record of its proceedings.

session clerk *n* th secretary of a kirk session.

sessioner *n* a member of the kirk session.

session saints *n* elders of the kirk.

session siller *n* a parish dole distributed by the kirk session.

sestuna *int* an exclamation of admiration.

set¹, sett *n* **1** a potato or part of one, used for planting. **2** a shape, figure. **3** a pattern, the pattern of a tartan. **4** kind, manner. **5** the knack of doing a thing. **6** the nature or requirement of the material worked. **7** the fixed quantity of an article regularly supplied. **8** a check in growth. **9** an attack, onset. **10** impulse, force. **11** a shock. **12** a difficult task, problem. **13** a disgust. **14** a lease. **15** a billet on a house showing that it is to be let. **16** the chartered constitution of a burgh. **17** a stationary net, the place in a river where it is fixed. **18** a warp, twist. **19** a paving stone. **20** a whetstone for a razor. **21** the pointing of a sporting dog. **22** a band of reapers and the number of ridges they cut at one time. **23** the socket in which a precious stone is set. **24** (*in pl*) corn put up in small stacks.

set² *v* **1** to seat. **2** to place a hen on eggs in order to hatch them. **3** to assign work. **4** to settle, get in order. **5** to put milk into a pan for the cream to rise. **6** to set a fishing line or net. **7** to work according to a pattern. **8** to plant potatoes, kail, etc. **9** to make, impel, induce. **10** to beset. **11** to bring to a halt. **12** to puzzle. **13** to nauseate, disgust. **14** (*of a dog*) to mark game. **15** to let, lease. **16** to escort for part or the whole of a short journey. **17** to send, despatch. **18** to become, suit, beseem. **19** to sit. **20** to cease to grow, become mature. **21** to stiffen, congeal, become hard or solid. **22** to start, begin. **23** to set off.

set³ *adj* **1** stunted in growth, squat. **2** no longer growing. **3** bent, warped. **4** firm, resolute. **5** obstinate, self-willed, settled in opinion or purpose. **6** disposed, affected or inclined, either ill or well. **7** distressed, afflicted, cast down.

set aff *v* **1** to dismiss, turn off. **2** to fob off, shift off. **3** to put away. **4** to take oneself off. **5** to slip off. **6** to loiter, linger. **7** to delay, waste time. **8** to set in motion. **9** to fire off, explode. **10** to deliver a speech glibly, tell a fluent story. **11** to make a great display. **12** to plant. **13** to quit. **14** to keep off.

set-aff *n* **1** a dismissal. **2** a shift, evasion. **3** an offset. **4** anything that counterbalances another. **5** delay. **6** a dilatory person. **7** a pretence. **8** a start. **9** anything that becomes a person.

set after *v* to hurry after, pursue, set out after.

set at *v* **1** to attack. **2** to incite.

set-at *n* a battle, contest.

set awe' *v* to go, set off.

set-back *n* **1** a rebuff. **2** a check. **3** the rejection of an offer of marriage.

set by *v* **1** to lay or put by. **2** to save. **3** not to take into account. **4** to substitute for something better. **5** to make

to suffice. **6** to satisfy. **7** to esteem greatly. **8** to value highly.

set-by *n* **1** a substitute. **2** a makeshift.

set caution *v* to give security.

set down, set doon *v* **1** to place food on the table. **2** to write down. **3** to rebuff, snub. **4** to settle in marriage.

set-down, ~-doon *n* **1** a snub, rebuff. **2** a settlement in marriage.—*adj* (*of a meal*) sit-down, formal, regularly prepared or provided.

set fire *v* (*with* **in** *or* **till**, *of a pipe or cigar*) to light it.

set-gear *same as* **settle-gear**.

seth *same as* **saithe**.

set hame *v* **1** to start for home. **2** to escort homeward.

seth-ill *same as* **side-ill**.

set house *v* to begin housekeeping, set up house.

set in *v* **1** to bring in a meal, to arrange or spread it on a table. **2** (*used of the weather*) to last.

set-in *adj* likely to continue long, permanent.

set on *v* **1** to fall upon, attack. **2** to set to a task. **3** to accommodate. **4** to be well off. **5** to make a start. **6** (*of a fire*) to prepare and light it. **7** (*in curling*) to aim or direct a stone. **8** to do well by.—*n* a violent scolding. **9** a strong effort to persuade.

set-on *adj* **1** provided. **2** treated. **3** resolved upon, bent upon. **4** engrossed with, devoted. **5** (*used of food*) burned in cooking. **6** ill-thriven, short.

set out *v* **1** to eject, put out forcibly. **2** to publish. **3** to array oneself in order to conquest in courting. **4** to embellish. **5** to set off by ornament or contrast.

set-out *n* **1** a feast. **2** a display. **3** an important event. **4** a joke, fun.

set owre *v* to overset, capsize.

set-owre *n* a capsize, overturn.

set-rent *n* a certain portion allotted to a servant or cottager when working for his master.

set-stane *n* a whetstone for a razor, etc.

sett *n* a decree.

setten, settin *adj* set.

setter *n* **1** one who lets anything out for hire. **2** a baker's tool.

setterel *adj* **1** thickset. **2** dwarfish.—*n* a squat person.

setter-out *n* **1** a publisher. **2** one who circulates anything.

setting, settin' *n* **1** the number of eggs a hen sits on to hatch. **2** the letting or leasing of a house, farm, etc. **3** a portion of land. **4** a measure of bulk. **5** a sufficiency of anything.—*adj* **1** growing mature. **2** becoming, suitable. **3** comely, graceful.

setting dog *n* a spaniel, a setter.

setting-down *n* **1** a settlement in marriage. **2** a provision made with a view to marriage.

setting of the sculls *n* the carrying of bride and bridegroom in baskets or sculls. *See* **scull¹**.

setting step *n* a step in the sword dance.

settle *v* **1** to compose a quarrel. **2** to silence. **3** to kill.

settle *v* **1** (*with* **up**) to attend to, make comfortable. **2** to induct or place a minister to a particular charge.—*n* **1** shape, build, form of body. **2** a settling down. **3** the fall of night. **4** calmness, ease.

settle-bed *n* a settle that forms a bed by night.

settle-gear *n* money yielding interest.

settler *n* **1** what reduces one to silence. **2** a conclusive argument or blow.

settlin *n* what reduces one to silence or submission.

settlins *n* **1** the dregs of beer. **2** sediment.

set to *v* **1** to begin. **2** to fight. **3** to turn to. **4** to settle down to. **5** *in phr* **set to the gate** to set off, go off.

set-to *n* **1** a fight. **2** a quarrel. **3** a scolding match. **4** a state of things, pass, crisis.

set together *v* to marry.

settral *adj* unconvinced by argument.

settrel, settril *same as* **setterel**.

settrell *n* young sprouts that shoot forth in spring from coleworts planted in the beginning of winter.

settrin *same as* **set rent**.

set tryst *v* to make an appointment to meet.
set up *v* **1** to cause, occasion. **2** to restore to health or prosperity. **3** to cure, make good. **4** to elate. **5** to ornament, set off. **6** to disgust, nauseate. **7** (*used of razors*) to sharpen.
set-up *adj* **1** conceited, proud, vain, affected. **2** elated.
seuch, seugh *same as* **sheuch**³.
seugh¹ *same as* **sough**¹.
seugh² *same as* **sheuch**²
sevendle, sevennil *adj* **1** strong, secure, sufficient. **2** trustworthy. **3** to be relied on.
seven senses *n* all one's wits.
seven-shift *n* a seven years' course of cropping.
seventeen-hunner linen *n* a very fine linen, produced by a reed with 1700 divisions.
several *n* a piece of land lying apart from the main portion.
severals *n* several persons or things.
severely *adv* thoroughly.
sewawra *n* a kind of cravat.
sewster *n* a sempstress.
sey¹ *n* **1** the opening of a gown or shift through which the sleeve passes. **2** the part of a dress between the armpit and the breast. **3** a part of the back of an ox cut up for beef.
sey² *same as* **saithe**.
sey³ *v* **1** to try, test. **2** to assay, prove. **3** to essay. **4** to taste.—*n* **1** an assay. **2** an attempt. **3** a trial piece of work.
sey⁴ *n* **1** a bucket. **2** a milk pail.
sey⁵ *n* **1** a woollen cloth formerly made by families for their own use. **2** a kind of serge.
sey⁶ *n* a stuff that contained silk.
sey⁷ *v* **1** to strain through a sieve. **2** to strain milk. —*n* **1** a sieve. **2** a strainer for milk, etc.
sey⁸ *v* to see.
seyal *n* a trial.
seybie, seybo, seybow *same as* **sybo**.
sey clout *n* a cloth through which liquid is strained.
seyd *n* a sewer, a passage for water.
sey dish *n* a milk-strainer.
seyer *n* a fine sieve for straining milk.
seyg *same as* **seg**¹.
seyl *same as* **seil**¹.
seyle *same as* **seel**.
segmar *n* **1** a loose upper garment. **2** a scarf.
sey milk *n* a milk-strainer.
seyndle *same as* **seenil**.
sey-piece *n* a trial piece.
sey-sones, ~-sowens *n* a sieve for straining sowens (qv).
seyster *v* to mix incongruously.—*n* an incongruous mixture or medley of edibles.
sgian-dhu *same as* **skeandhu**.
sha *int* an inciting call to a dog to chase another animal.
shaak *n* chalk.
shaal¹, **shaal**² *same as* **shall**¹, **shall**².
shaard *same as* **shaird**.
shaave¹ *same as* **shauve**.
shaave² *same as* **shave**².
shaavin basket *n* a basket for sowing seed.
sha-awa' *int* a call to a dog to chase another animal.
shab, shabb *v* **1** to smuggle. **2** to send anything away privately. **3** (*of the sun*) to sink slowly, set.
shabble, shable *n* **1** a crooked sword or hanger. **2** an old, rusty sword. **3** a small, insignificant person or thing.
shach *v* to distort. **2** to shape anything obliquely. **2** to jilt or desert a woman.
shach-end *n* the fag end of a web where the cloth becomes inferior in quality.
shachle¹, **schachel** *v* **1** to distort. **2** to wear out of shape. **3** to cripple. **4** to walk in a shambling or knock-kneed fashion. **5** to waddle. **6** to wriggle. —*n* **1** a feeble, puny, misshapen person or animal. **2** anything worn-out or badly put together. **3** a shanty. **4** a contemptuous term for a leg.
shachle² *same as* **shackle**¹.

shachled shoes, ~ shoon *n* **1** a person of no further use. **2** a woman discarded by her lover.
shachlieness *n* knock-kneedness.
shachlin' *adj* **1** mean, paltry, unsatisfactory. **2** unsteady, infirm.—*n* a puny weakling.
shachl't *adj* shuffling.
shachly *adj* **1** shambling, shuffling. **2** jolting. **3** shaking.
shack *v* to shake.—*int* a word of incitement to a dog to worry another animal.
shack-a-fa', shackiefa *v* to wrestle.
shackelt *v, adj* hindered, kept down.
shackle¹ *n* **1** a hobble for a horse. **2** the wrist. **3** the ankle.—*v* to hobble horses, to tie their forelegs together.
shackle² *v* **1** to shamble. **2** to distort.
shackle³ *same as* **shockel**.
shackle bane *n* **1** the wrist bone. **2** the knucklebone.
shacky *adj* shaky.
shade¹ *n* a cultivated field.
shade² *n* **1** a sheath. **2** a sheath for knitting pins.
shade³ *same as* **shed**².
shade-knife *n* a knife carried in a sheath.
shadow-half *n* **1** the northern exposure of land. **2** the shady side.
shae *n* a shoe.
shaep *v* to shape.
shaetery *n* cheating.
shaffie *n* a frivolous excuse. *See* **sheeffie-shaffie**.
shaft *v* to put a handle to any implement.
shaftmon, schaftmon *n* the measure of the fist with the thumb extended, taken as six inches.
shafts¹ *n* the cheeks, jaws.
shafts² *n* a kind of woollen cloth.
shag¹ *n* the cormorant.
shag² *same as* **segg**².
shag³, **shagg** *n* **1** tail corn. **2** the refuse of barley or oats.
shag-coat *n* a coat of rough cloth.
shagged *adj* shaggy.
shaghle *same as* **shachle**¹.
shaglie *adj* **1** loose-jointed. **2** bandy-legged.
shagmahoch *n* a small, misshapen person.
shags *n in phr* **to go shags** to go shares.
shamit-reel *same as* **shamed-reel**.
shair¹ *v* **1** to rub one substance against another. **2** to grate, grind.
shair² *adj* sure.
shaird *n* **1** a shard, sherd. **2** a fragment, shred. **3** a small portion. **4** an old, unseaworthy boat. **5** a piece of furniture badly put together. **6** a little, despicable creature. **7** an unhealthy dwarf. **8** a puny or deformed child. **9** a petulant, mischievous child.
shairn, shamn *same as* **sharn**.
shairny *adj* bedaubed with sharn (qv).—*n* the person who cleans out the cow house.
shaivle *same as* **shevel**.
shak, shake *v* to wrestle.—*n* **1** a shock. **2** a wrestling bout. **3** emaciation by disease or long confinement. **4** refuse corn. **5** corn shorn when green.
shak a fa' *v* **1** to wrestle. **2** to exert oneself to the utmost.—*n* a wrestling match.
shak a fit or leg *v* to dance.
shak-and-tremble *n* the quaking grass.
shak-im-troose *same as* **shantrews**.
shaking *n* **1** the smallest quantity. **2** the last remains.
shakin's o' the pock *or* **pot** *n* the youngest child of a family.
shakit *v* shook.
shakker, shaker *n* **1** part of a threshing mill. **2** a fit of ague. **3** nervous tremor.
shakky trimmles *n* nervous tremors.
shaklock *n* **1** a lazy ne'er-do-weel. **2** an idle loafer.
shak o' a fit *n* a dance.
shak o' a hand *n* a very short time.
shak one'a crop *v* **1** to vent one's ill-humour. **2** to speak loudly and vehemently.

shake, shake-rag *n* **1** a beggar. **2** a tatterdemalion.

shak-rag-like *adj* like a tatterdemalion.

shak the feet *v* **1** to shake dust, mud, etc, off one's feet. **2** to dance.

shak-wind *n* **1** a wind that shakes the ripened grain. **2** a blustering wind.

shaky *adj* (*used of a road*) causing jolting.

shaky-mill *n* the deathwatch.

shald *same as* **shall²**.

shale¹ *n* alum ore.

shale² *same as* **shall²**.

shalk *n* **1** a servant. **2** a workman. **3** a farm servant.

shall¹ *n* **1** a shell. **2** part of the old crusie lamp, for holding the oil and wick and for catching the drip. **3** a portion, fragment. **4** the scale suspended from a balance for weighing. **5** (*in pl*) burnt limestone before it is slaked.

shall² *adj* shallow.—*n* a shallow place.—*v* to spear or leister salmon in shallow water.

shall³ *n* a shawl.

shallmillens *n* fragments.

shalloch¹ *adj* **1** plentiful, abundant. **2** (*used of corn*) short in the stalk but growing very close with many grains on one stalk.

shalloch² *n* shallow tin vessel.

shallochy *adj* shallow.

shalt, shaltie *same as* **sheltie**.

sham¹ *v* **1** to cheat, trick, deceive. **2** to shirk. **3** to treat lightly.

sham² *v* to strike.

sham³ *v* to make faces.

sham⁴ *same as* **shaum¹**.

sham⁵ *n* shame.

shamble *v* **1** to rack the limbs by striding too far. **2** to distort, writhe. **3** to make a wry face or mouth.

shamble-chafts *n* a wry, distorted mouth.

shamble-shankit *adj* having crooked legs.

shamble-shanks *n* **1** crooked legs. **2** a person with crooked legs.

shambling *adj* unevenly set.

shambo, shambo-leather *n* chamois leather, shammy.

shame *n* (*in imprecations*) the devil.—*v* **1** to be ashamed. **2** *in phr* **to think shame** to be ashamed.

shamed ~, shame reel *n* the first dance after a marriage ceremony, danced by the bride and best man and the bridegroom and bridesmaid.

shame-fa' *int* an imprecation.

shameful *adj* modest, shy, bashful.

shameful reel *n* the shamed reel (qv).

shame spring *n* the dance music for the shamed reel (qv).

sham-gabbit *adj* having the upper jaw protruding or an underhung mouth.

shamlichin *same as* **schamlich**.

shamloch *n* a cow that has not calved for two years.

shammel, shammil *same as* **shamble**.

shammy *n* hockey, shinty.

shamp *v* to take oneself off.

shan¹ *adj* **1** backward, averse. **2** reluctant.

shan² *adj* **1** pitiful, silly. **2** poor, shabby. **3** paltry.

shanachy *same as* **seannachie**.

shand *adj* worthless.—*n* base coin.

shan-dre-dan *n* **1** any old, rickety, quaint-looking conveyance. **2** a jocular name for a vehicle.

shandy *adj* shy, reluctant.

shane *v* **1** to heal, cure. **2** to break the spell of witchcraft, to wish good luck by superstitious practices.—*n* that which breaks the spell of witchcraft.

shang *n* **1** a sort of luncheon, a snack between meals. **2** a piece (qv).

shan-gabbit *same as* **sham-gabbit**.

shangan, shangin, shanjan *n* a stick cleft at one end for putting on a dog's tail.

shangie¹ *adj* thin, meagre, lean.

shangie², shanjie, shangy *v* to enclose in a cleft piece of wood.—*n* **1** a shangan (qv). **2** an ornament for a

horse's tail. **3** a shackle running on the stake to which a cow is bound in the byre (qv). **4** a chain. **5** a leash or chain for coupling dogs, a loop of gut or hide round the mast of a boat into which the lower end of the sprit is slipped. **6** a trouble, pest. **7** a quarrel, a disturbance.

shanginess *n* leanness, meagreness.

shangy-mou'd *adj* **1** hare-lipped. **2** having a cleft mouth. **3** having the mouth much to one side.

shank¹ *n* **1** the leg of a stocking. **2** a stocking in process of being knitted. **3** a handle, shaft. **4** a stem. **5** the stem of a tobacco pipe. **6** the stalk of a plant. **7** the trunk of a tree. **8** the projecting point of a hill joining it to the plain. **9** the shaft or pit of a coal or lead mine.—*v* **1** to travel on foot, to walk. **2** to run. **3** to hurry off. **4** to send off without ceremony. **5** to depart. **6** to knit stockings. **7** to fit with a handle. **8** to sink a shaft. **9** to shrivel up, shrink, wither.

shank² *n* **1** a salmon after spawning. **2** the smallest of the kelt tribe.

shank³ *v* (*used of a stream*) to join another.

shank-bane *n* **1** a leg. **2** the shinbone.

shanker *n* **1** a knitter of stockings. **2** a sinker of shafts. **3** one present at the throwing of the bride's stocking.

shankie *n* the leg.

shankit *v*, *adj* set or started on the way.

shankless *adj* without a handle or shaft.

Shanks *n* (*with* **Auld**) a name for death.

shank's mare *n* one's own legs.—*adv* afoot.

shank's naig, naigie *or* **naggis** *n* shank's mare (qv).

shank's noddy *or* **pair** *n* shank's mare (qv).

shank-steels *n* the legs.

shankum *n* a man or beast with long, slender legs.

shanky *n in phr* **Auld Shanky** death.

shanna *v neg* shall not.

shannach¹ *same as* **shinich**.

shannach² *same as* **shannagh**.

shannag *n* an ant.

shannagh, shannach *n in phr* **it is ill shannagh in you to do so and so** it is ill on your part or unwise of you or ungrateful of you to do so and so.

shannel *n* **1** subsoil. **2** hard, unyielding subsoil as the foundation of a building.

shanny *same as* **shandy**.

shantrews *n* a Highland tune and dance

shantrum *n* a Highland dance.

shanty *n* a chamber pot.

shap¹ *n* a shop.

shap² *n* the soil at the foot of a wall, hedge, etc.

shap³ *v* to mash.

shap⁴ *same as* **shaup**.

shap⁵ *same as* **shape**.

shape, shap *v* **1** to devise. **2** to cut out. **3** to succeed. **4** to show promise. **5** to go, depart. **6** to drive off. **7** to intend, contrive, manage. **8** to set about.—*n* **1** an attitude. **2** an article. **3** conduct, manner, mood.

shapings *n* the shreds or clippings of cloth.

shapper *n* a beetle for mashing potatoes.

shappin stick, ~ tree *n* a shapper (qv).

shard¹ *same as* **shaird**.

shard² *n* cow dung.

share¹ *adj* sure.

share² *v in phr* **to share a staff** to distribute blows.

share³ *v* **1** to pour off the lighter parts of a liquid. **2** to separate a liquid from the dregs. **3** (*of liquids*) to separate in a vessel into two or more parts.

sharg *adj* **1** tiny, lean, shrivelled. **2** mean.—*n* **1** a starveling. **2** a tiny, mischievous creature.

shargan *n* **1** a lean, scraggy person. **2** a weakly child.

shargar, sharger *n* **1** a thin, stunted person. **2** a weakly child. **3** a starveling. **4** an ill-thriven person or animal.— *v* **1** to stunt in growth. **2** to become stunted.

shargar-like *adj* lean and stunted or ill-thriven in appearance.

shargar stone n a stone that was supposed to stop the growth of anyone who crept underneath it.

sharge v to sharpen, grind.

shargie adj thin, shrivelled.

sharginess n thinness.

sharings n the useless or less valuable part of a liquid, whether poured off or remaining in the vessel.

shark same as **sark**.

sharle-pin n a pin of wood or an iron bolt used instead of hinges.

sharlins n the whole arrangement of pivots for hinges.

sharn n cow dung.—v to soil with sharn.

sharn-hole n the hole that receives the sharn (qv) from a byre (qv).

sharny adj bedaubed with sharn (qv).—n one who cleans out a byre (qv).—v to bedaub with sharn (qv).

sharny-faced adj having a very dirty face.

sharny-peat n sharn (qv) mixed with coal dust, dried in the sun and used for fuel.

sharon same as **sharn**.

sharp adj **1** (used of land) sandy, gravelly. **2** (of weather) cold, frosty, keen, brisk.—adv quickly. —v **1** to sharpen. **2** to rouch (qv) a horse in frosty weather.—n a sharpening.

sharpen v to rouch (qv) a horse in frosty weather.

sharping stone n **1** a whetstone. **2** a severe lesson learned by experience.

sharplyer adv more sharply.

sharps n **1** coarse flour containing much bran. **2** turnip tops. **3** pods of beans.

sharp-set adj **1** keen. **2** sharp-witted.

sharrachie adj (of the weather) cold, chill, piercing.

sharrow adj **1** sharp, sour, bitter in taste. **2** keen.

sharrow-craver n one who acts the part of a dun.

sharry n **1** a quarrel. **2** a dispute.—v to quarrel. See **Sherra-moor**.

shathmont same as **shaftmon**.

shatter[1] v **1** (used of the teeth) to chatter. **2** to rattle, as the windows of a carriage.

shatter[2] v **1** to chirp. **2** to chatter.

shauchle, schaughle same as **shachle**[1].

shaughle-bane same as **shackle-bane**.

shauk v to shake.

shaul, shauld same as **shall**[2].

shault, shaultie same as **sheltie**.

shaum[1] n **1** a leg. **2** a limb.

shaum[2] v to warm oneself by thrusting the lower part of the body close to the fire.—n a warming, a sitting very near the fire to get warm.

shaup n **1** the shell or pod of peas or beans. **2** an empty pod. **3** anything empty, worthless or shrivelled. **4** a fragment, a broken piece.—v to shell peas or beans.

shaupie adj **1** lank, thin. **2** not well filled up.

shaupit adj furnished with pods.

shauve v to saw.—n a saw.

shauvens n sawdust.

shav same as **shauve**.

shave[1] n **1** a slice. **2** the wheel of a pulley.—v to gall.

shave[2] v to sow.

shave[3] same as **shavie**.

shave[4] n a sheaf.

shavel same as **shevel**.

shavelin n a tool for smoothing hollow or circular wood or plaster.

shaver n **1** a wag, a queer fellow. **2** a youngster.

shavie n **1** a trick. **2** a practical joke. **3** an uproar. **4** a disappointment.

shaving n **1** the candle grease that gutters down the side of a candle. **2** a nicety.

shaving whittle n a weaver's tool.

shaviter n **1** a term of contempt. **2** a blackguard.

shaviter-like adj having the appearance of a blackguard.

shavling n **1** a shaveling. **2** a contemptuous name for a priest.

shaw[1] n **1** a grove, a flat piece of ground at the foot of a hill or steep bank. **2** (in pl) the leaves or stalks of turnips, potatoes and other esculent roots.—v to cut off the tops of turnips, potatoes, etc.

shaw[2] same as **shave**[2].

shaw[3] n (in pl) refuse flax or hemp.

shaw[4] v to show.—n **1** a show. **2** a sight, view.

shaw[5] same as **sha**.

shawd adj shallow.

shawintrewse same as **shantrews**.

shawl same as **shall**[2].

shawlie n a small shawl for the shoulders or head.

shawlness n shallowness.

shawlt, shawltie same as **sheltie**.

shawn v shown.

shawp same as **shaup**.

shawpy same as **shaupie**.

shay n a chaise.

she n **1** the mistress of a house. **2** a woman.

sheaf same as **sheave**.

sheal[1], **sheal**[2] same as **sheel**[2], **sheel**[3].

shealin[1], **shealin**[2] same as **sheelin**[1], **sheelin**[2].

shealocks same as **shillacks**.

shear v **1** to cut through. **2** to reap with a sickle. **3** to part.—n **1** a knife. **2** the blade of the maiden (qv) or guillotine. **3** a shorn sheep. **4** a reaping. **5** a cut, slice. **6** a particular sheep mark. **7** the ridge of a hill. **8** the fork of the legs.

shear bane n the pubic bone.

shear blade n **1** a blade of a pair of scissors. **2** a knife for cutting kail.

shear feather n the part of a plough that cuts out the furrow.

shear grass n **1** long, coarse grass. **2** couch grass.

shear keavie n a kind of crab.

shearman n a cloth-worker.

shearn same as **sharn**.

shears n scissors.

shear-smith n a maker of shears.

shear-tail n the tern.

sheath n **1** a metal plough head. **2** a holder of needles during knitting, often made of a tied bunch of hens' quills.

sheath-whittle n a sheath knife.

sheave n a slice.—v to slice.

sheavick n a paring, a small slice.

sheavle same as **shevel**.

shed[1] n **1** a shade, shady place. **2** a shelter.—v to shade.

shed[2], **shede** v **1** to part, separate, divide. **2** to part lambs and calves from their mothers. **3** to rake out a fire. **4** to make a parting in the hair of the head or the wool of a sheep. **5** to cut into slices. **6** to cut off a part. **7** to cease, leave off.—n **1** a parting in the hair or in a sheep's wool. **2** a slice. **3** a piece cut off. **4** (used of land) a particular piece set apart. **5** an interstice. **6** the space between the different parts of the warp in a loom.

shed[3] n an abode.—v to place in sheds.

sheded v shed.

shedder salmon n a female salmon just after spawning.

shedding n **1** a parting of the hair. **2** the intersection of crossroads. **3** the separation of lambs from sheep. **4** the sheep drafted out from the flock.

sheddo n a shadow.

shed of corn n a field set apart for corn.

shed of land n a portion of land.

shed of teeth n the interstices between the teeth.

shee[1] n **1** a slice. **2** a pulley wheel.

shee[2] n a shoe.—v to shoe.

shee-bree n water in the shoes.

sheed same as **shed**[2].

sheeffie v **1** to hesitate. **2** to make frivolous excuses.

sheeffie-shaffle v to shilly-shally.—n a frivolous excuse.

sheeg same as **shieg**.

sheegle same as **shiegle**.

sheel[1] same as **shool**[1].

sheel², **sheeld** *n* **1** a temporary residence for shepherds, etc, in summer. **2** a shelter.—*v* to put sheep under cover.
sheel³ *v* **1** to shell. **2** to husk.
sheeld-peat *n* peat cut horizontally.
sheelfa *same as* **shilfa**.
sheelin¹ *n* **1** a hut. **2** a cottage. **3** a temporary summer residence.
sheelin² *n* the husk of seeds, chaff.—*adj* pertaining to husking.
sheelin coug *n* a dish for holding mussel bait, etc, when shelled.
sheeling hill *n* an eminence where grain can be winnowed.
sheeling seeds *n* the husks of grain.
sheelock *same as* **shillacks**.
sheemach, sheemich *n* **1** a mass of matted hair or fibre. **2** thick matted cloth. **3** a pad of a straw rope used as a packsaddle. **4** a thing of no value. **5** anything much damaged.
sheen¹ *n* shoes.
sheen² *adj* shining.—*n* **1** a gleam, sparkle. **2** the pupil of the eye.—*v* **1** to shine. **2** to glitter.
sheenies *n* children's shoes.
sheep bucht, ~ bught *n* a small sheepfold.
sheep-dead *n* a disease of sheep from flukes in the liver.
sheep drains *n* surface drains on moorland.
sheep faws *n* retreats beneath the moors for sheep in winter.
sheep gang *n* pasturage for sheep.
sheep-head, sheep's-head *n* a dish of boiled sheep's head.
sheep-head broth, ~ kail *n* broth made from a sheep's head.
sheep-head sword *n* a basket-hilted sword.
sheep-herd *n* a shepherd.
sheep-hog *n* a sheep before its first shearing.
sheep-lifter *n* a sheep-stealer.
sheep- ifting *n* **1** sheep-stealing. **2** the removal of sheep by their buyer.
sheep-muckle *adj* as big as a sheep, full-grown.
sheep net *n* a net hung on stakes for enclosing sheep when feeding in a turnip field.
sheep-race *n* **1** a boys' game. **2** a ram-race (qv).
sheep-ree *n* an enclosure for sheep built with stone or turf.
sheep-rent *n* the rent of a sheep farm.
sheep-rive *n* pasturage for sheep.
sheep-rodding *n* a sheep track.
sheep-rot, ~-root *n* **1** the butterwort. **2** the pennywort.
sheep's-cheese *n* the root of the couchgrass.
sheepshank *n* a person or thing of no value or consequence.
sheepshank-bane *n* a nobody.
sheep silver, ~ siller *n* **1** mica. **2** an allowance to ploughmen instead of permission to keep a sheep or two.
sheep-smearing *n* an application of tar and melted butter to sheep in winter for warmth.
sheep's-soorag, ~-sorrel, ~-sourock *n* a kind of sorrel.
sheep-stell *n* an enclosure for sheep.
sheep's tothins *n* sheep's droppings.
sheep-taid, -fade *n* a tick or sheep louse.
sheep-tathing *n* the confinement of sheep to a particular portion of ground until their droppings manure it.
sheep-tiend *n* a tithe on lambs or sheep.
sheep-troddles *n* the droppings of sheep.
sheepwalk *n* a sheep track.
sheer¹ *same as* **shear**.
sheer² *n* a lurch, swerve.
sheer³ *n* the sweeping stroke of a sword.
sheer⁴ *adj* odd, singular.
sheer⁵ *adj* sure.
sheer-blade *n* **1** a blade of a pair of scissors. **2** a lang-kail (qv) knife.
sheer-cloth *n* a cerecloth.
sheerless *adj* without scissors.
sheerly *adv* thoroughly, entirely.

sheerly *adv* surely.
sheerman *same as* **shearman**.
sheermouse *n* the shrew, fieldmouse.
sheers *n* scissors.
sheet¹ *v* **1** to shoot. **2** (*used of rain*) to fall at brief intervals of sunshine.—*adj* shot.
sheet² *n* a winding sheet.
sheets *n* the sweetbread.
sheet-styth *adj* shot dead.
sheeve *same as* **sheave**.
sheenck *n* a small slice, a paring, shaving.
sheevil *same as* **shevel**.
shee-wisp *n* a little straw in the shoes to keep the feet warm.
sheggan *n* a reed.
sheil¹ *same as* **sheel³**.
sheil², **sheild** *same as* **sheel²**.
sheilin¹, **sheilin²** *same as* **sheelin¹**, **sheelin²**.
sheiling hill *n* a winnowing hill.
sheilin mill *n* a mill for husking grain.
sheimach *same as* **sheemach**.
sheive *same as* **sheave**.
sheld-fowl *n* the common sheldrake.
shelf¹ *v* **1** to lay on a shelf. **2** to put past.
shelf² *n* **1** a rock or reef under water. **2** a shoal, shallow.
shelf³ *same as* **skelf**.
shelfa, shelfy *same as* **shilfa**.
shelf press *n* a walled cupboard with shelves.
shelister *n* the water flag.
shelky *same as* **sealch²**.
shell¹ *n* **1** the husk of oats, peas, etc. **2** (*in pl*) burnt limestone before it is slaked.—*v* **1** to husk grain. **2** to pay out or down. **3** (*used of sheep*) to have snow frozen in their wool.
shell² *n* a cell.
shellach *n* a young boy.
shellachie *adj* (*used of the weather*) cold, piercing.
shellaggy *n* the tussilago or coltsfoot.
shell-gold *n* gold leaf.
shelling *n* grain freed from husks.
shelling ~, shellen seeds *n* **1** the fine husks of grain enclosing the meal. **2** the husks of grain, chaff, generally.
shell-lime *n* unslaked lime.
shellocks *same as* **shillacks**.
shell-sickness *n* a disease of sheep, affecting the omentum and larger intestines.
shell-wherry *n* a small boat used along the coast for bringing up cockles and mussels.
shellwife *n* a woman who deals in shellfish.
shell-wing *n* the shelving (qv) of a cart.
shelly-coat, shellicoat *n* **1** a water sprite. **2** a coat made of shells worn by the water sprite. **3** a bum-bailiff, sheriff's messenger. **4** the tortoise-shell moth.
shelm¹ *same as* **skellum**.
shelm² *n* the pieces of wood forming the upper frame of a cart, into which the starts or posts in the sides are mortised.
shelments *n* **1** the frame or rail, extending over the wheels, that is laid on a corn cart for carrying a load of corn or hay. **2** the longitudinal bars of the sides of a close cart.
shelpit *same as* **shilpit**.
shelter-stell *n* an enclosure or shelter for sheep, of stone or a clump of trees.
sheltie, shelt *n* **1** a pony. **2** a Shetland pony.
shelve *same as* **shelf²**.
shelving *n* additional boards fixed to the sides of a cart to increase its capacity.
shelvy *adj* shelving, shoaling.
shend *v* **1** to abash, confound. **2** to disgrace. **3** to chide. **4** to mar, destroy, ruin.
shendship *n* ruin, confusion.
shent *v, adj* destroyed. *See* **shend**.
shenty *n* **1** hockey. **2** shinty.

shepherd check *n* shepherd tartan, a small black-and-white check pattern in cloth.
shepherd land *n* pastoral districts.
shepherd's club, ~ gowd *n* the great mullein.
shepherd's needle *n* the wild chervil.
shephroas *n* kid gloves.
sherarim *n* a squabble. *See* **sharry**.
shere *v* to shear.
sheriff *n* a legal officer who acts as judge in a sheriff court.
sheriff court *n* a court in Scotland that deals with the majority of civil actions and all but the most serious criminal actions.
sheriff gloves *n* an old perquisite of the sheriff of Edinburgh after each of the two great local fairs.
shern *same as* **sharn**.
sheroo *n* the shrewmouse.
sherp *adj* sharp.—*v* to sharpen.
sherra, sherry *n* a sheriff.
sherrakin *same as* **shirrakin**.
Sherramoor *n* 1 the battle of Sheriffmuir in 1715. 2 a row, confusion. 3 a scrimmage. 4 a loud scolding.
sherra ~, sherry officer *n* a sheriff officer.
she-slip *n* a young girl.
sheth, shethe *n* 1 the stick with which a mower whets his scythe. 2 any object coarse and ugly. 3 an ugly person.
sheth *n* the sheath (qv) of a plough.
sheuch[1] *same as* **shach**.
sheuch[2]**, sheugh** *same as* **shoo**[1].
sheuch[3]**, sheugh** *n* 1 a ditch, drain. 2 a furrow, trench. 3 a small stream. 4 a ravine. 5 the hollow of the neck. 6 *in phr* **to be in a sheuch** to be in a difficulty.—*v* 1 to make ditches, furrows, etc. 2 to dig for peats or coals. 3 to plant temporarily in a furrow with a view to transplanting. 4 to cover over.
sheughly *adj* rickety, shaky, unsteady.
sheuk *v* shook.
sheuken *v, adj* shaken.
sheul *same as* **shool**[1].
shevel *v* 1 to distort. 2 to become distorted. 3 to walk unsteadily and obliquely.—*n* a distortion.
shevel-~, sheveling-gabbit *adj* having a distorted mouth.
sheveling-heeled *adj* (*used of a shoe*) twisted or down at the heel.
shevel-mouthed *adj* having a distorted mouth.
shevel-shot *adj* 1 twisted, deformed. 2 having the joints distorted.
shew[1] *v* 1 to swing. 2 to move up and down. 3 to shove.—*n* 1 a swing. 2 a seesaw. 3 a shove.
shew[2] *same as* **shoo**[1].
shew[3] *v* showed.
shew[4] *same as* **shoo**[4].
shewe *v* sowed. *See* **shaw**.
sheyld, sheylt *adj* distorted in any way.
sheyle *v* 1 to distort the face. 2 to make faces. 3 to look askance.—*n* a wry face, a distortion of the features.
shiacks *n* light black oats, variegated with grey stripes and bearded like barley.
shiauve, shiave *same as* **shave**[2].
shick *n* the cheek.—*v* to set the head, as a bull intending to toss.
shick-blade *n* the cheekbone.
shicked *adj* wry-necked.
shie *n* a shoe.
shieg *v* 1 to joggle. 2 to be rickety.
shiegle *v* 1 to joggle. 2 to be loose and rickety.
shiek *n* 1 the cheek. 2 the side of anything. 3 insincere or boastful talk.
shiel[1]**, shield** *same as* **sheel**[2].
shiel[2] *same as* **sheal**[3].
shielin[1]**, shielin**[2] *same as* **sheelin**[1]**, sheelin**[2].
shiemach *adj* 1 malignant. 2 reproachful.
shiffel *n* a shovel.
shiffle-shaffle *v* to shuffle in walking.
shift *v* 1 to escape. 2 to evade, elude. 3 to hesitate. 4 to try

shifts. 5 to swallow.—*n* 1 a rotation of crops. 2 management.
shiftin' claes *n* a change of clothes after working hours.
shifty *adj* 1 ingenious. 2 resourceful.
shig *v* to make temporary small stacks in the harvest field.—*n* a small, temporary stack in the harvest field.
shilbins, shilbands *n* a frame or boards for adding to the carrying capacity of an ordinary cart.
shile *same as* **sheyle**.
shilfa, shilfaw, shilfey, shilfy *n* the chaffinch.
shilfa-cock *n* a male chaffinch.
shilf-corn *same as* **shillcorn**.
shill[1] *n* a 1 shovel. 2 an arrangement on the front of the plough beam to regulate the width and depth of the furrow.
shill[2] *same as* **sheel**[3].
shill[3]**, schill** *adj* 1 shrill. 2 loud, noisy.
shill[4] *adj* chill.
shillacks, shillicks, shillocks *n* 1 the lighter part of grain. 2 light grain blown aside in winnowing.
shillcorn, shilcorn *n* a blackhead.
shilling[1] *n in phr* **to spit shillings** to have the mouth so dry from hard drinking that the saliva spit on the ground lies like a shilling.
shilling[2]**, shillen** *n* grain freed from the husk.
shilling hill *same as* **sheilin hill**.
shilling ~, shillen seeds *n* the husks of oats.
shilly[1] *adj* (*used of the wind*) shrill, howling, loud.
shilly[2] *v* to distort.
shilly-shally *adj* 1 weak, delicate. 2 poor, inferior. 3 undecided.
shilmine *n* a shelmont (qv).
shilmonts *same as* **shelments**.
shilp *n* a pale, sickly girl.—*adj* acid to the taste.
shilpit *adj* 1 pale, sickly. 2 weak. 3 pinched, shrunken and starved-looking. 4 puny, small, insignificant, timid. 5 insipid, tasteless, wersh (qv). 6 thin, inferior, worthless. 7 (*of corn ears*) ill-filled.
shilpitness *n* 1 weakness, feebleness. 2 tremor.
shilpy, shilpie *adj* 1 shilpit (qv). 2 cold and wet.—*n* 1 a weak, sickly, timid person. 2 a sycophant.
shil-shal *n* a dainty, delicacy.
shilt, shilty *same as* **sheltie**.
shilvin *same as* **shelving**.
shim *v* to weed with a hoe.—*n* 1 a hoe. 2 a drill harrow.
shimee *n* a chemise.
shimmer *n* one of the crossbars in a kiln for supporting the ribs on which the grain is laid to dry.
shin[1] *same as* **sheen**[1]
shin[2] *n* 1 the slope of a hill. 2 the ridgy part of a declivity, with a hollow on each side.—*v* to climb with hands and legs, to swarm up.
shincough *n* the whooping cough.
shine *v* 1 to fling. 2 to throw violently.—*n* 1 a display. 2 a treat. 3 a merrymaking.
shiner *n* a candlestick. 2 a light on a branched candlestick.
shinicle *n* a bonfire lighted on Hallowe'en.
shinnen, shinan, shinnon *n* a sinew.
shinners *n* 1 cinders. 2 the refuse of a blacksmith's stithy.
shinnock *n* the game of shinty.
shinny *n* the game resembling hockey, shinty.
shinny ball *n* the ball used in shinty.
shinny club *n* the curved stick used in shinty.
shin-side *n* the front part of the leg, the shin.
shinty *n* 1 the game shinny (qv). 2 the ball and the club used in the game.
shiolag *n* the wild mustard.
shipper *n* a shipmaster, skipper.
Shire *n* Wigtownshire, as distinguished from Kirkcudbright or the Stewartry, in Galloway.
shire *adj* 1 (*used of liquids*) clear, not muddy, thin, watery. 2 (*used of cloth*) thin. 3 scrimp, strait, exact in measure. 4 mere, utter, complete.—*v* to pour off liquor from dregs.
shire-lick *n* a smart fellow.

shirie *adj* 1 (*used of liquids*) thin, watery. 2 (*used of cloth*) thin, loosely woven. 3 proud, conceited.

shirins, schirins *n* liquid poured off.

shirl *adj* shrill.

shirle *same as* **shirrel**.

shirp *v* 1 to shrink, shrivel. 2 to waste or pine away.

shirpit *adj* thin and tapering to a point.

shirpit-looking *adj* of thin, shrunken appearance.

shirra *same as* **sherra**.

shirragh, shirroch *adj* sour, acrid.

shirraghie, shirrochy *adj* looking sour, haughty or passionate.

shirragle, shirraglie *n* a contention, squabble.

shirrakin *n* a severe scolding, especially a public one.

Shirramuir, Shirrameer *same as* **Sherramoor**.

shirrang *v* a wrangle, squabble.—*v* to wrangle noisily.

shirrel *n* a piece of turf for fuel.

shirret, shirrot *n* a turf, a divot

shirrow *n* the shrewmouse.

shirt[1] *n* a woman's shift.

shirt[2] *n* 1 the winter rape. 2 wild mustard.

shirt-gown *n* a bodice.

shirt-washings *n* the water in which clothes have been washed.

shit[1] *n* 1 a chit. 2 a child. 3 a puny, insignificant person or animal. 4 a term of contempt.

shit[2] *v* to shoot.

shite *v* to void excrement.—*n* excrement.

shite house *n* a privy.

shit-faced *adj* having a small face.

shither[1] *v* to shiver.

shither[2] *n* people, folk, a fellow.

shitten *adj* 1 dirty. 2 mean, despicable. 3 insignificant in appearance.

shitten-like *adj* 1 dirty-looking. 2 mean, despicable. 3 insignificant in appearance.

shittle[1] *n* anything good for nothing.

shittle[2] *n* a shuttle.

shiv, shive *v* 1 to push, shove. 2 (*with* **by**) to succeed.—*n* a shove.

shive[1] *n* *same as* **sheave**.—*v* (*with* **aff**) to live upon another, to save or help oneself at another's cost.

shive[2] *n* a chive.

shivel *n* a shovel.—*v* to shovel.

shivelavat's hen *n* 1 a hen that has ceased to lay. 2 a woman past childbearing.

shivereens *n* fragments, atoms, shivers.

shivering bite *n* a piece of bread eaten immediately after bathing.

shiverons, shivrons *n* chevrons.

shivers *n* torn clothes, rags, tatters.

shluist *n* 1 a large, heavy person. 2 an ungainly or ungraceful person. 3 a sluggard.

shluster *v* to swallow ungracefully.

sho[1] *n* a shoe.

sho[2] *same as* **shoo**[1].

shoad *n* a portion of land.

shoak *n* 1 a shock. 2 a moment.

shoar *same as* **shore**[4].

shoas *same as* **shows**.

shochad *n* the lapwing.

shochle[1] *same as* **shachle**[2].

shochle[2] *same as* **shoggle**[1].

shochles *n* legs, a term of contempt.

shochling *adj* 1 waddling. 2 wriggling. 3 mean. 4 paltry.—*n* irregularity of gait.

shock[1] *n* 1 a paralytic stroke. 2 a moment.

shock[2] *v* to choke.

shock[3] *v, adj* shaken.

shockel *same as* **shoggle**[1].

shocking *adv* exceedingly.

shocks *n* the jaws.

shod *v* 1 to furnish with shoes. 2 to shoe a horse. 3 to fit with a metal tip, band or ring. 4 to put a tire on a wheel.

5 to fit iron toe and heel pieces on shoes. 6 to cover the soles with hobnails.—*n* 1 a shoe. 2 an iron tip or point. 3 the tire of a wheel. 4 an iron toe or heel piece on a shoe.

shoddie *n* 1 a child's shoe. 2 the iron point of a pikestaff or pivot of a top.

shodless *adj* shoeless.

shod-shool, ~-shule *n* a wooden shovel fitted with iron.

shoe *v* to put a tyre on a wheel.—*n* the hopper of a mill.

shoe-bree *n* water in the shoes.

shoe-clouter *n* a cobbler, a mender of shoes.

shoel *same as* **showl**.

shoelin *adj* distorted.

shoe-mou' *n* the open part of a shoe.

shoes *same as* **shows**.

shoe-the-auld-mare *v* to play a dangerous game of balancing on a wooden beam slung between two ropes and going through a number of antics.

shoe-the-naig *n* a blacksmith.

shoe-whang *n* a shoe tie.

shoe-wisp *n* a little straw in the shoes or boots in order to keep the feet warm.

shog, shogg *v* 1 to shake. 2 to jog, jolt. 3 to jog along. 4 to swing to and fro, rock a cradle. 5 (*with* **about**) to keep about, remain alive.—*n* 1 a push, nudge. 2 a blow. 3 a swing-rope.

shog-bog *n* 1 a quaking bog. 2 one on which a light person can walk without sinking.

shoggie *v* 1 to swing to and fro as a pendant. 2 to swing.—*n* 1 a push. 2 a slight blow. 3 a swing.—*adj* unstable.

shoggie-shew, ~-shoo, ~-shue *n* 1 a swing. 2 a seesaw. 3 the gallows.—*adv* with a swaying, swinging motion.

shoggie-shooin' *adj* (*used of a long ladder*) unsteady under a person moving on it.

shogging, shogging-tow *n* a swing rope.

shoggle[1] *n* 1 an icicle. 2 a large piece of ice floating down a river when a thaw comes.

shoggle[2] *n* a clot of blood.

shoggle[3], **shogle** *v* 1 to shake, jolt, rock. 2 to totter. 3 to trot slowly, jog along. 4 to shake or settle down.—*n* 1 a jolt, jog. 2 a shake.

shoggly *adj* shaky, insecure, tottering.

shog-shog *v* to jolt or shake frequently or continuously.

shogue *same as* **shog**.

shol *same as* **shool**.

shol-markit *adj* marked with a shool (qv) or born with one. *See* **shool**[1].

shon *n* a bog, quagmire.

shone *n* shoes.

shony *n* a sea god to whom sacrifice was formerly offered in the island of Lewis at Hallowe'en.

shoo[1] *int* 1 an exclamation to scare away poultry and other intrusive birds and animals. 2 an exclamation of surprise, disdain, etc.—*v* 1 to cry shoo! to scare away. 2 to hasten away.

shoo[2] *v* 1 to swing. 2 to rock to and fro. 3 to seesaw. 4 to back water in rowing. 5 to back a cart.—*n* 1 a swing. 2 a rocking motion. 3 a rope on which to swing. 4 a seesaw. *See* **shoggie-shoo**.

shoo[3] *pron* she.

shoo[4] *v* to sew.

shoo[5] *v* to sue.

shooch *same as* **sheuch**[3].

shood *n* the distant noise of animals passing.

shooder *n* the shoulder.

shooder-heid *n* the shoulder blade.

shooer *n* a shower.

shoog *same as* **shog**.

shoogie *same as* **shoggie**.

shoogle *same as* **shoggle**[3].

shooglie *same as* **shoggly**.

shoo-gled's-wylie *n* a children's or boys' game.

shook, shooken *v, adj* shaken.

shooken *n* 1 dues of thirlage (qv) paid at a mill. 2 the tenants of an estate bound to send their grain to the mill belonging to the landlord.

shookie *int* a word used in calling horses.

shool[1] *n* **1** a shovel. **2** a spade. **3** a shovel-shaped distinguishing mark in a sheep's ear.—*v* **1** to shovel. **2** to clean with a shovel. **3** to drag the feet. **4** to shuffle. **5** to mark a sheep's ear with a shovel-shaped mark.

shool[2] *same as* **sheel**[3].

shool[3] *same as* **showl**.

shool bane *n* the shoulder blade.

shoolfu' *n* a shovelful.—*adv* in shovelfuls.

shool staff *n* **1** a shovel handle. **2** a crutch.

shool-the-board *n* the game of shovelboard.

shoomach, shoomich *same as* **sheemach**.

shoon[1] *n* shoes.

shoon[2] *adv* soon.

shoonies *n* a child's shoes.

shoonless *adj* shoeless.

shoop *v* shaped.

shoor *v* shore. *See* **shore**[6].

shoory *adj* showery.

shoost *v* **1** to drive off. **2** (*with* **on**) to urge on. *See* **shoo**[1]

shooster, shooster-body *n* a sempstress.

shoot[1] *n* **1** a throw of a fishing net or lines. **2** a push. **3** a puny or imperfect young animal.—*v* **1** to empty a cart by tipping. **2** to cast fishing lines or nets into the sea. **3** to push, thrust. **4** to push off from the shore in a boat and cast a net in a river. **5** to bulge out and give way. **6** to run to seed. **7** to avoid, escape. **8** to separate the worst animals from a drove or flock. **9** to select in purchasing cattle or sheep. **10** *in phr* **shoot a shower** to avoid a shower.

shoot[2] *v* **1** to suit. **2** to please.

shoot about *v* **1** to get through a time of special difficulty. **2** to be in ordinary health. **3** to satisfy with food.

shoot aff *v* to run off, hurry off.

shoot by *v* **1** to put off, delay. **2** to palm off, substitute. **3** to get through a crisis. **4** to satisfy with a slight or homely meal.

shoot-by *n* a makeshift.

shooter *n* **1** a sportsman. **2** a member of a shooting party.

shoother *same as* **shouther**.

shooting blade *n* the upper leaf of a corn plant.

shooting brod *n* a target.

shoot o'er *v* **1** to overpass, get through a period of time. **2** to satisfy. **3** to palm off upon.

shoot-stick *n* an arrow.

shoot-stock *n* **1** a mason's or joiner's tool. **2** a bevel.

shoow *same as* **shoo**[4].

shop[1] *v* **1** to rap, knock. **2** to hammer.

shop[2] *adj* (*used of certain plants, as comfrey, eyebright, lungwort, speedwell and valerian*) common, officinal.

shop-hauder *n* a shopman, shopkeeper.

shopkeeper *n* an article in a shop remaining long unsold.

shoppie[1] *n* a small shop.

shoppie[2] *n* a teetotum.

shore[1] *n* **1** a steep rock. **2** a rocky coast. **3** a quay, wharf. **4** a game of marbles.

shore[2] *n* a sewer, drain.

shore[3], **schore** *n* a chieftain.

shore[4] *v* **1** to threaten. **2** to scold. **3** to threaten rain. **4** to be cloudy. **5** to call off. **6** to urge. **7** to hound. **8** to offer. **9** to promise. **10** to favour. **11** to bestow upon.

shore[5] *v* to count, reckon.

shore[6] *v* to cut.—*v, adj* shorn.

shoreside *n* the shore.—*adj* pertaining to the shore.

shore-snipe *n* the common snipe.

shore-teetan *n* the rock pipit.

shorling *n* the skin of a newly shorn sheep.

short *adj* **1** laconic. **2** tart. **3** quick, urgent. **4** early.—*adv* **1** soon. **2** recently.—*v* **1** to amuse, divert, make time seem short. **2** to become angry or short-tempered.—*n* a short time.

shortcome *n* a shortcoming.

short coupled *adj* **1** thickset. **2** compact in body.

short-cuts *n* a method of drawing cuts or lots.

shorten *v* to put a baby into short clothes for the first time.

short-ended, ~-ainded *adj* short-winded.

shortener *n* what shortens or lessens.

shortgown *n* a gown without skirts, reaching only to the middle, worn by female cottagers and servants.

short-heeled fieldlark *n* the tree pipit.

short-heeled lark *n* the skylark.

short hours *n* **1** the early morning. **2** the small hours.

shortie *n* shortbread, shortcake.

short kail *n* vegetable broth.

shortlies, shortlins *adv* shortly, quickly, soon.

shortly *adv* tartly.

shorts *n* **1** the refuse of flax. **2** the refuse of hay, straw, etc.

short-set *adj* short and stout, thickset.

short shed *n in phr* **salving from short shed to short shed** smearing sheep slightly on the back, neck and upper parts of the sides. *See* **smear**[1].

short sheep *n* a black-faced forest breed of sheep.

short-shift *n* **1** a day's work of fewer hours than usual. **2** short time.

short side *n in phr* **the short side of day** dawn, early morn.

short sinsyne *adv* lately, not long ago.

shortsome *adj* **1** amusing, diverting, not tedious or dreich. **2** pleasantly situated.—*v* **1** to divert. **3** to while away time. **4** to keep from ennui.

shortsyne *adv* recently, not long ago.

short-trot *n* **1** a fit of temper. **2** snappishness.

short while *adv* recently.

short-writing *n* shorthand.

shot[1] *n* a division of land.

shot[2], **shott** *n* **1** speed, progress. **2** a blasting in quarrying. **3** a blasting charge of gunpowder, dynamite, etc. **4** (*in curling*) a stone lying nearest the tee. **5** a thread shot home when the shuttle passes across the web. **6** a sudden attack of illness. **7** a shooting pain. **8** the spout that carries water to a millwheel. **9** one of the boxes of a millwheel receiving the water carried to it. **10** a compartment in the stern of a fishing boat. **11** a fishing station on a salmon river. **12** a projecting window. **13** a hinged window opening outwards. **14** an ill-grown ewe. **15** a refuse animal left after the best of a flock or herd have been chosen. **16** a young weaned pig. **17** a gelded pig. **18** a set of heavy breakers followed by the lull caused by the backwash. **19** the end or aim of action. **20** an outburst. **21** one's turn to play in any game. **22** a turn at doing something. **23** the temporary use of someone's property. **24** the stroke or move made. **25** very strong whisky.

shot[3] *adj* **1** cast at by fairies. **2** (*used of herring*) recently spawned.—*n* a danger signal of street children on the appearance of a policeman.

shot[4], **shote** *v* to shoot.

shot[5] *v, adj* having been shut, shut.

shot[6] *n* a fabric made of warp and woof threads of different colours.

shot[7] *v* shoved, thrust.

shot-about *n* an alternate move or play in a game. —*adj* striped, of various colours.

shot-about weaver *n* a weaver who produces a fabric of different colours.

shot-a-dead *n* death from a fairy dart.

shot blade *n* the upper leaf of a corn plant, the part of a corn stalk enclosing the ear.

shot brae *n* an avalanche causing a scar on a hillside or bank.

shote *int* a warning cry indicating the approach of someone in authority.

shot heuch *n* a steep bank from which the surface has fallen through the action of rain or flood undermining.

shot-hole *n* a loophole in a wall of an old castle or keep.

shot-pig *n* **1** a young pig taken out of the litter. **2** a gelded pig.

shot star *n* **1** a meteor. **2** the jelly tremella, a gelatinous substance found in pastures, etc, after rain.

shot stern *n* the jelly tremella.

shotten *adj* shot.

shottle[1] *adj* short and thick, squat.

shottle[2], **shottel** *same as* **shuttle**.

shot-whaup *n* a species of curlew.

shot-window *n* a projecting window.

shou *same as* **shoo**[2].

shoud *same as* **showd**.

shoudder bane *n* the shoulder blade.

shough *same as* **sheuch**[2].

shoughie *adj* short and bandy-legged.

shoulfall *same as* **shilfa**.

shoultie *same as* **sheltie**.

shouskie *n* **1** a designation of the devil. **2** a fondling term for a child.—*int* a call to cattle.

shout *v* **1** to shout at, assail with shouts. **2** (*used of a woman*) to be in labour.

shouther *n* the shoulder.—*v* **1** to lift and carry on the shoulder. **2** to push with the shoulder.

shouther bane *n* the shoulder blade.

shouther cup *n* the socket of the shoulder blade.

shouther-heich *adj* as high as the shoulder.

shouther-heicht *n* the height of the shoulder.

shouther-lyar *n* a joint of beef, coarse and fit only for broth or beef tea.

shouther-pick *n* a pickaxe.

shouther-shawl *n* a small shawl thrown over the shoulders or head.

shouting *n* parturition, childbed labour.

shovel-groat *same as* **shool-the-board**.

show[1] *same as* **shoo**[2].

show[2] *n* **1** indication, sign. **2** a sight.

show[3] *n* **1** a coppice. **2** a glade.

showd, showdie *v* **1** to waddle. **2** to swing on a rope or on a seesaw. **3** to rock like a ship tossed by waves. **4** to dandle a child. **5** to rock to sleep. —*n* **1** a swing, a seesaw. **2** the act of swinging. **3** a swing rope. **4** a rocking motion. **5** a jaunt, a short journey. **6** a lift in a vehicle on a road.— *adv* with a rocking motion or a swaying, waddling gait.

showdin-tow *n* a swing rope.

showdy towdy *n* a seesaw.

shower, showre *n* **1** a sharp attack of pain. **2** a throe, a paroxysm. **3** (*in pl*) the pangs of childbirth. **4** a strong push, a sudden turn.—*v* **1** to give a helping hand. **2** to push or turn forcibly.

showerickie, showerockie *n* a slight or gentle shower.

show-fair *n* anything more showy than likely to be useful.

showing-horne *n* any article of food that makes people drink more liquor.

showl *v* **1** to twist, distort the face. **2** to grimace.—*n* a grimace, a distortion of the face.

showlie *adj* deformed by being slender and crooked.

shows[1] *n* the refuse of flax, hemp, hay, straw, etc.

shows *n* a funfair

show-shop *n* a place of great display or show.

show-wife *n* a show-woman.

shrauky *adj* scraggy, shrunken.

shreud *v* to shroud.

shrew *v* to curse.

shriegh *v* to shriek.

shriek o' day *n* daybreak.

shrift *n* one who shrives a penitent.

shrive-days *n* days for shriving penitents.

shroud *n* a piece of charred wick or melted wax or tallow down the side of a candle, regarded as an omen of death or disaster.—*v* to clothe, cover.

shrugg *n* a quiver, a convulsion.

shu *same as* **shoo**.

shuch, shugh *same as* **sheuch**[2].

shuck[1] *v* shook.

shuck[2] *v* to throw out of the hand, to chuck.

shucken *same as* **sucken**.

shuckenwort *n* chickweed.

shud[1], **shude** *n* **1** the coagulation of any liquid body. **2** a large piece of floating ice.

shud[2] *v* should.

shue[1], **shue**[2], **shue**[3] *same as* **shoo**[2], **shoo**[4], **shoo**[1].

shuest *same as* **shoost**.

shuffle *v* (*with* **out**) to hand out, pay.

shuffle-cap *n* the game of jingle-the-bonnet (qv).

shuffle-the-brogue *n* the game of hunt the slipper

shug[1] *int* a call to a horse to come to the hand.

shug[2] *same as* **shog**.

shug-bog *same as* **shog-bog**.

shuggie *same as* **shoggie**.

shuggie-shou, ~-shue *n* **1** a swing. **2** a seesaw.

shuggle *same as* **shoggle**.

shug-shug *same as* **shog-shog**.

shuil, shule *same as* **shool**[1].

shuir *v* shore.

shuit[1] *v* to shoot.

shuit[2] *same as* **shoot**[2].

shuk *v* shook.

shukkie-mill *n* the deathwatch, an omen of death.

shul *same as* **shool**[1].

shull[1] *same as* **shool**[1].

shull[2] *n* a shoal.

shullie *n* a small shoal.

shulock *v* to sweep the stakes in a game.

shulocker *n* one who sweeps the stakes.

shun *v* **1** to move aside. **2** to make room for.

shune *n* shoes.

shunner, shuner *n* a cinder.

shunner stick *n* charcoal.

shure *v* did shear.

shurf *n* **1** a puny, insignificant person. **2** a dwarf.

shurl[1] *v* to cut with shears.

shurl[2] *n* **1** snow slipping from a roof. **2** the noise it makes.

shurlin *same as* **shorling**.

shurlin skin *n* the skin of a sheep taken off after the wool has been shorn.

shurral *same as* **shirrel**.

shushlach *n* an untidy, slovenly woman.

shusy *n* a dead body taken from the grave.

shusy-lifter *n* a resurrectionist.

shut[1] *n* **1** a shutter. **2** riddance. **3** a close, an end. **4** *in phr* **shut of day**, the twilight.—*adj* (*with* **of** *or* **on**) rid of.

shut[2], **shute** *v* to shoot.

shute *n* soot.

shuten *v*, *adj* shot.

shuther[1] *same as* **shouther**.

shuther[2] *v* (*used of loose earth, etc*) to fall down in a heap, to slip.

shutted, shutten *adj* shut.

shuttle *n* **1** a hollow in the stock of a spinning wheel in which the first filled bobbin is kept till the other is ready to be reeled with it. **2** a small drawer or box in a press, chest or escritoire. **3** a shop till.—*v* **1** to weave. **2** to dart backwards and forwards. **3** to thrust, push. **4** to eject forcibly.

shuttle-airm *n* the arm with which the weaver throws the shuttle.

shuttlecock *v* to play at battledore and shuttlecock.

shuttle-gabbit *adj* having a misshapen mouth.

shuttle of ice *n* **1** a miniature glacier. **2** a sloping slide on which children can toboggan.

shuttle-ploy *n* weaving.

shuttler *n* a weaver.

shy *adj* averse, unwilling.—*v* to shun.

shyauve, shyaave *sam as* **shave**[2].

shyle *same as* **sheyle**.

shyre *same as* **shire**[2].

shyrie *same as* **shirie**.

sib *adj* **1** closely related. **2** akin. **3** of the same blood. **4** friendly, intimate. **5** bound by ties of affection. **6** like, having similar qualities. **7** being in like circumstances. **8**

having right or title to. **9** improperly intimate.—*n* kindred, relations.

sibba *same as* **sybo**.

sibbens *same as* **sivven**.

sib-like *adj* friendly.

sibly *adv* **1** closely. **2** affectionately.

sibman *n* a relation, kinsman.

sibness *n* **1** nearness of blood, relationship. **2** friendliness.

sibow *same as* **sybo**.

sic[1] *v* to sigh. **2** to sob.

sic[2] *adj* such.—*n* a similar person or thing.—*adv* so.

sicca, siccan *adj* such a, such an.

siccar *same as* **sicker**.

siccart secured, firmly settled.

sicen, sicin *adj* such an.

sich *v* to sigh.—*n* a sigh.

sicher *v* to sigh and sob.

sichin-like *adj* like one in trouble.

sicht *n* **1** sight. **2** a great number or quantity. **3** the pupil of the eye.—*v* to inspect.

sichter *n* a great quantity of small objects seen at once.

sichtly *adj* personable.

sicht-seeing *adj* seeing ghosts.

sichty *adj* striking-looking.

sick[1], **sicken** *adj* such, such an.

sick[2] *n* sickness.

sicken-like *adj* such-like.

sicker *adj* **1** secure, safe. **2** firm. **3** sure, certain. **4** steady, unyielding, to be relied on. **5** prudent, cautious in money matters, grasping. **6** severe, harsh. **7** (*of a bargain*) hard, stiff.—*adv* **1** securely, firmly, safely. **2** certainly, assuredly.—*v* **1** to make sure. **2** to fasten firmly. **3** to make certain.

sickerly *adv* **1** securely, safely, firmly. **2** surely, certainly. **3** assuredly. **4** severely.

sickerness *n* **1** security. **2** firmness. **3** assurance. **4** severity. **5** custody. **6** prison.

sick-fu' *adj* full to bursting.

sick house *n* a hospital.

sickie *int* a sheep call.

sick-laith *adj* very unwilling.

sickle *v* to reap with a sickle.

sickle-sweep *n* a curve like that of a sickle.

sicklike *adj* of the same kind.—*adv* in the same manner.

sickly-looking *adj* (*used of the moon*) hazy, watery.

sickness *n* blackwater or braxy (qv) in sheep.

sickrife *adj* **1** sickly. **2** slightly sick.

sick-saired *adj* satiated to loathing, thoroughly sated.

sick-sorry *adj* **1** very sorry. **2** extremely unwilling.

sick-tired *adj* **1** very weary of. **2** weary to nausea. **3** utterly disgusted.

sickwise *adv* in such a manner.

siclike *adj* **1** like such a person or thing. **2** such-like.

sicsae *adv* just so.

sicsame *adj* just the same, self-same.

sid[1] *v* should.

sid[2] *n* **1** the inner covering of grain. **2** a fragment.

sidderwood *same as* **sithernwood**.

siddie *same as* **seedy**.

siddle-siddle *adv* with sidelong movement.

side[1] *n* **1** a district, region. **2** the side of.

side[2] *n* time.—*adj* **1** (*of a traveller*) too late. **2** overtaken by night.

side[3] *adj* **1** wide, long. **2** hanging low down. **3** trailing.

side[4] *adj* **1** hard, severe. **2** strong. **3** rough.

side[5] *prep* beside.

side[6] *same as* **seed**.

side and wide *adj* large in every way.

side-board *n* a movable board for heightening the side of a cart.

side-coat *n* **1** a long coat, a greatcoat. **2** a long waistcoat.

side dish *n* a person invited to an entertainment to make game of one or more of the guests.

side-dykes *n in phr* **to rin side-dykes with one** to keep company or be on friendly terms with one.

side for-side *adv* alongside, in the same line, at the same place.

side-ill *n* a disease affecting cows and sheep in the side.

side-langel *v* to tie the fore- and hindleg of an animal on the same side to prevent straying.

side legs *adv* **1** side-saddle. **2** with legs on one side, as women ride.

side-lichts *n* side whiskers.

sideling[1] *adj* **1** having a declivity. **2** sidelong. **3** oblique.—*adv* sideways, obliquely.

sideling[2], **sidelans** *adv* **1** sideways. **2** with legs on one side. **3** alongside. **4** aside. **5** furtively.—*adj* slanting, sidelong.—*n* a declivity.

sider *adj* hanging down more. *See* **side**[3].

side-sark *n* a long shirt.

side-school *n* a school auxiliary to the principal one in a parish.

side's-man *n* an umpire, referee.

side-springs *n* elastic-sided boots.

side-stap *n* a false step causing a wrench to a limb.

side-tailed *adj* long-tailed.

side-wipe *n* **1** an indirect censure or sarcasm. **2** a blow on the side. **3** a covert blow.

sideyways *same as* **sidyways**.

sid-fast *same as* **sitfast**.

sidieways *same as* **sidyways**

sidle *v* (*with* **off**) to slip off.

sidlin *same as* **sideling**[1].

sids *n in phr* **never to say sids** never to mention the subject, never to say anything, though expected to say something.

sidy-for-sidy, sidie-for-sidie *same as* **side-for-side**.

sidyways *adv* **1** to one side. **2** sideways.

sie[1] *same as* **sye**.

sie[2] *same as* **sey**[1].

siecan *adj* such an.

sieffer *n* **1** an impudent, empty-headed rascal. **2** a worthless, lazy or drunken loafer. **3** a cipher. **4** a playful term of endearment applied to children. —*adj* diminutive.

siege *n* a chase with a view to chastisement.

sieging *n* a scolding.

siep *same as* **seip**.

siepher *same as* **sieffer**.

sier *v* **1** to salve. **2** to apply a salve, balm, etc.

sieve *v* **1** to pass through a sieve. **2** to become full of holes like a sieve.

sieve and sheers *n* a method of divination with a riddle and scissors.

siever *n* **1** a miller's man. **2** anyone who sifts grain.

sievewricht *n* a maker of sieves.

sievins *n* fine particles that have passed through a sieve.

sifflication *n* a supplication, petition.

sift *v* **1** (*of snow*) to fall in fine flakes as through a sieve. **2** to bandy words. **3** (*with* **out**) to find out a secret.

sifting *n* a sprinkling.

sigg *n* a callus on the skin.

sigh *n* a seer, one who is said to predict the future.

sight *n* a station on a river for observing the movements of salmon.—*v* **1** to spy from a station the movements of salmon in order to direct the casting of the net. **2** to inspect, examine.

sightman *n* the fisherman who observes the movements of salmon.

signbrod *n* a signboard.

signers *n* subscribers for a book.

sik[1] *same as* **sic**[1]

sik[2] *v* to seek.

sike[1] *same as* **sic**.

sike[2] *n* **1** a small rill. **2** a marshy bottom or hollow with one or more small streams.

sike[3] *adj* such.

sike[4] *n in phr* **to flay the sikes from one** to give one a good beating.

siken, sikken *adj* such an.
siker, sikker *same as* **sicker**.
sikie *adj* full of rills.
sikkle *n* a bicycle.
silder *n and adj* silver.
sile[1] *n* **1** a beam, a rafter. **2** the lower part of a rafter. **3** an iron bar inserted across the centre of the eye of a handmill.
sile[2] *n* soil.
sile[3] *same as* **sill**[2].
sile[4] *same as* **seil**[1].
sile-blade *n* **1** one of the upright beams of a sile. **2** the side of a sile. *See* **sile**[1].
siler *same as* **seiler**.
silit *adj* fallen behind, at a distance.
silkey, silkie *same as* **sealch**[2].
sill[1] *same as* **sile**.
sill[2] *n* **1** milt. **2** herring fry.
sillabe *n* a syllable.
siller *n* **1** silver. **2** money. **3** payment. **4** price.—*adj* of silver.—*v* **1** to pay. **2** to bribe with money.
siller bag *n* a moneybag.
siller-blind *adj* blinded by wealth.
siller-buckie *n* the grey, purple-streaked pyramid shell.
siller day *n* payday.
siller-dodge *v* to cheat out of money, to embezzle.
siller-duty *n* rent or dues paid in money alone.
siller-gatherer *n* a money-gatherer, a miser.
siller-ginglers *n* the quaking grass.
siller-grip *n* a miser, a money-grubber.
siller-hair grass *n* the mouse grass.
siller-holes *n* excavations made in working minerals, etc.
sillerie *adj* rich in money.
sillerieness *n* richness in money.
sillerless *n* poor, impecunious.
siller maill *n* rent paid in money alone.
siller marriage *n* a marriage to which the guests contributed money.
siller-owl *n* the barn owl.
siller-plover *n* the knot.
siller pock *n* a moneybag.
siller poun' *n* a pound in silver.
siller rent *n* rent paid in money alone.
siller Saturday *n* payday.
siller-savrnie *n* **1** the pearly top. **2** the periwinkle.
siller-shakers, ~-shakle *n* the quaking grass.
sill-fish *n* a male fish, a miller.
sillist *adj* laying aside work in the meantime.
sillup *n* a syllable.
silly *adj* **1** good, worthy. **2** pure, innocent, young. **3** a term of endearment or compassion. **4** weak, feeble, frail. **5** sickly, delicate. **6** lean, meagre. **7** timid, spiritless. **8** fatuous, imbecile.—*v* to show weakness, act foolishly.
silly-how, ~-hoo *same as* **seelie-hoo**.
silly man *n* a term of compassion, 'poor fellow'.
silly-willy *n* a foolish person.
sillywise *adj* somewhat weakened in mind or body.
silvendy *same as* **sevendle**.
silver-work *n* silver plate.
sim *n* **1** a hint. **2** a slight notice or warning.
simie, symie *n* **1** a name of the devil. **2** *in phr* **like simie or symie** used of two things that are quite like each other.
similar *adj in phr* **similar the same** exactly or nearly the same.
simmer[1] *v* to cool, subside.
simmer[2] *n* **1** the principal beam in the roof of a building. **2** one of the supports laid across a kiln.
simmer[3] *n* summer.—*v* **1** to bask. **2** to enjoy the warmth and brightness of summer. **3** to pasture cattle in the open in summer.
simmer and winter *v* **1** to harp on the same string. **2** to be minute and prolix in narration. **3** to ponder, ruminate. **4** to adhere to permanently.
simmer-lift *n* the summer sky.

simmerscale *v* (*of beer, etc*) to cast up scales in summer, when it begins to sour.—*n* (*in pl*) the scales thus cast up.
simmit *same as* **semmit**.
simper-faced *adj* having a simpering face.
simple *adj* of humble birth.—*n* (*in weaving*) that part of a weaver's harness to which the figure intended to be wrought is committed.—*v* to feed on herbs.
simulate *adj* **1** dissembling. **2** insincere. **3** pretended. **4** unreal.
simulatlie *adv* **1** under false pretences. **2** hypocritically.
sin[1] *n* the sun.
sin[2] *n* a son.
sin[3] *same as* **syne**[3].
sin[4] *n* blame.—*v* **1** to make to sin. **2** to injure by sin.
sinacle *n* **1** a sign. **2** the slightest trace. **3** a particle, grain.
sinal *same as* **seenil**.
since *adv* **1** afterwards. **2** then.
sinceder *n* a seceder from the Established Church. *See* **seceder**.
sincere *adj* **1** grave. **2** apparently serious.
since syne *adv* since then.
sind, sinde *same as* **synd**.
sinder *v* to sunder, part.
sindering-day *n* the day of parting after a merrymaking.
sindill, sindle *adv* seldom.
sindle-times *adv* seldom.
sindoon *n* sundown.
sindry *adj* sundry, several.—*adv* **1** asunder. **2** in pieces.
sine[1] *same as* **synd**.
sine[2] *same as* **syne**[3].
sin-eater *n* a person called in, when anyone died, to eat the sins of the deceased, which would have kept him haunting his relatives.
sin-eating *n* the custom of placing a bit of bread on the plate of salt laid on the breast of a corpse, by the sin-eater (qv), who, for money, at the same time partook of it, thereby, as it was believed, absorbing all the sins of the deceased.
sinen *same as* **shinnen**.
sing[1] *v* **1** (*of animals*) to hum, buzz, to purr. **2** to wheeze. **3** (*with* **out**) to call aloud, shout.
sing[2] *v* to singe.—*n* (*of food*) the point of burning.
singeing-dust *n* the dust from stuff goods quickly passed over a flame.
singing cake *n* a cake given to carol-singers at Hogmanay.
singing e'en *n* the last night of the year, Hogmanay.
singing-glasses *n* musical glasses.
singing lines *n* popular secular lines used for teaching psalm tunes.
singing schule *n* a singing class for the practice of psalmody.
singit *adj* **1** singed. **2** evil-smelling. **3** puny, shrivelled. **4** *in phr* **a singit hair** next to nothing.
single *adj* **1** few, slight. **2** small. **3** (*of letters of the alphabet*) not capital. **4** (*of liquor*) weak, under proof, without addition or accompaniment. **5** (*of a waistcoat*) one without a lining. **6** (*of a man*) one without means of defence. **7** (*of the shorter Catechism*) a copy without scripture proofs. **8** singular, not plural.—*adv* **1** alone. **2** singly.—*n* (*in pl*) **1** a handful or a few ears of gleaned corn. **2** the talons of a hawk.—*v* **1** (*of turnips, etc*) to thin out with the hand. **2** (*of flax*) to prepare it for making thread.
Single book *n* the shorter Catechism without proof texts.
single-en', single-end *n* a house of one apartment.
single-flooring *n* a kind of nail.
single-horse-tree *n* **1** the swingletree (qv) or stretcher of a plough, by which one horse draws. **2** a £1 banknote.
singler *n* one who singles turnips, etc. *See* **single**.
single sailor *n* a man before the mast.
single-sided *adj* widowed.
single soldier *n* a private soldier.
singles questions *n* the shorter Catechism without proof texts.

single-straw *n* straw gleaned as singles. *See* **single**.

single-tongued *adj* truthful.

singular combat *n* single combat.

sinile *same as* **seenil**.

sink *v* **1** to lose sight of a landmark on the horizon. **2** to overpower with liquor. **3** to excavate a pit shaft. **4** to cut the die used for coining money. **5** to curse, swear, used in imprecations.—*n* **1** a place where superabundant moisture stagnates in the ground. **2** the shaft of a mine. **3** a waste, a throwing away of money. **4** a weight, the weight of a clock.

sinkation *n* cursing.

sinker *n* **1** a miner. **2** a stone attached to each lower corner of a drift net. **3** a weight attached to the rope of a horse's stall collar.

sinking rope *n* a drift line to which smuggled kegs of spirits were attached and weighted.

sinkler *adj* (*used of codfish*) thin, with large head and thin body.

sinky *adj* yielding, given to sinking.

sinle, sinnle *same as* **seenil**.

sinn *same as* **synd**.

sinna[1] *v neg* shall not.

sinna[2]**, sinnan** *same as* **shinnen**.

sinnacle *n* a viciously disposed person.

sinnen, sinnin *same as* **shinnen**.

sinnery, sinnry *same as* **sindry**.

sinnet *n* merry-plait.

sinnie *n* senna.

sinnie-fynnie *n* the black guillemot.

sinno, sinnon, sinon *n* a sinew.

sinny *adj* sunny.

sinry *adj* sundry.

sinsheen *n* sunshine.

sinsyne *adv* ago, since then.

sint, sinter *n* **1** a small quantity. **2** a morsel.

sinteen *adj* seventeen.

sinwart *adv* towards the sun.

sip[1] *v* **1** to sup fluid food with a spoon. **2** to drink, not necessarily in small mouthfuls.

sip[2] *same as* **seip**.

sipage *n* a leakage.

sipe, sip *same as* **seip**.

siping *adj* soaking.—*n* (*in pl*) oozings, leakings from an insufficient cask, etc.

sipit *adj* drained of moisture, dried up.

siplin *n* a sapling.

sipper *n* supper.

sipple *same as* **sirple**.

sir *n* **1** a term of address by Highlanders to a lady. **2** (*in pl*) applied to people of both sexes.—*int* an exclamation of astonishment, without regard to the number or sex of those addressed.

sirce, sircy *int* an exclamation of surprise, as above, 'sirs'.

sirdon, sirdoun *n* a low, plaintive, bird-like cry.—*v* to emit such a cry.

sirdoning *n* the singing of birds.

sire *n* a sewer, gutter.

siree *n* sir.

Sir-John *n* a close stool.

sirken *adj* **1** tender of one's body. **2** tender of one's credit.

sirkenton *n* **1** one afraid of pain or cold. **2** one who keeps near the fire.

sirple *v* to sip often.—*n* **1** a sip. **2** a small quantity of liquid.

sirree *n* a soiree, a social gathering.

sirse *same as* **sirce**.

siskie *int* seest thou!

sist *v* **1** (*a legal term*) to stop procedure. **2** to cite, summon. **3** to stay.—*n* **1** a delay of legal procedure. **2** a summons, citation.

sistance *n* the smallest possible quantity of food, etc.

sister-bairn *n* **1** a sister's child. **2** a cousin on the mother's side.

sister-part *n* **1** a daughter's portion. **2** less than one's right. **3** nothing at all.

sistren *n* sisters.

sit[1]**, sitt** *v* **1** to lie. **2** to remain in the same position. **3** to continue in a house or farm during a lease. **4** to cease to grow. **5** to become stunted. **6** (*of a wall, etc*) to sink, settle. **7** to seat. **8** to set. **9** to ignore, disregard, refuse disobey. **10** to suit, fit, become.—*n* **1** the state of sinking. **2** continuance in a place.

sit[2] *v* sat.

sit doun *v* **1** to become settled, established. **2** to continue. **3** to settle on the lungs. **4** to become bankrupt.—*n* **1** a settlement in marriage, down-sitting.

site *n* **1** anxious care. **2** suffering. **3** punishment.

site o' claise *n* a suit of clothes.

sitfast *n* **1** a large stone fast in the earth. **2** the creeping crowfoot. **3** the restharrow.

sith[1] *conj* **1** seeing that. **2** because. **3** although.

sith[2] *adj* true.—*n* truth.—*v* **1** to make one believe. **2** to impose on one by flattery.

sith[3] *n in phr* **oh sith!** an exclamation of sorrow.

sithe[1] *v* **1** to strain through a sieve. **2** to strain milk. —*n* **1** a sieve. **2** a milk strainer.

sithe[2] *n* a scythe.

sithe[3] *n* satisfaction for injury.—*v* to give legal compensation.

sithement *n* **1** legal compensation. **2** satisfaction for injury.

sithence *adv* since that time.—*conj* seeing that.

sitherwood *n* southernwood.

sithes *n* chives.

sithe-sned *n* the handle of a scythe.

sithe-straick *n* a piece of hardwood greased and sprinkled with flinty sand for sharpening a scythe.

sit house *n* a dwelling house, as distinguished from a house used for any other purpose.

sit in *v* to sit to the table, draw in or near.

sit on *v* **1** to remain in a place or house. **2** (*used of food*) to stick to the pan, burn in cooking.

sit-on-ma-thoom *n* a contemptuous term for a diminutive person.

sitooterie *n* **1** a place to sit when not dancing. **2** a sheltered spot for sitting in out of doors.

sit-sicker *n* **1** the upright crowfoot. **2** the cornfield crowfoot.

sit still *v* to continue in a tenancy of house, farm, etc.

sitten *adj* **1** (*used of eggs*) being hatched. **2** stunted in growth. **3** not thriving.

sitten-doun *adj* **1** (*of weather*) settled. **2** (*of a cold, etc*) having taken hold, difficult to get rid of.

sitten-like *adj* ill-thriven in appearance.

sitten-on *adj* **1** stunted, small. **2** burnt and stuck to the pan in cooking.

sitten-up *adj* careless, neglectful, especially as to religious duties.

sitter *n* a rebuff, settler.

sittet *v* sat.

sittie-fittie *n* the ladybird.

sittin' *n* a situation, berth.

sittin' board *n* the seat of a pew.

sittin'-down *n* **1** a resting place. **2** a settlement in marriage. **3** bankruptcy.—*adj* **1** settled, chronic, continued. **2** (*used of a meal*) partaken of by the company seated at table.

sitting-drink *n* a drink of long duration taken in company.

sit to *v* **1** to settle down to, set in for. **2** (*used of food*) to stick to the pan in cooking.

sittrel *same as* **satteral**.

sit under *v* to attend regularly the ministry of any particular preacher.

sit up *v* **1** to watch over a dead body at night. **2** to become careless as to one's religious profession or duties.

sit upon *v* **1** to draw near to, sit near to. **2** to fit, become, suit.

sit with *v* to disregard, endure, put up with.
siv *n* a sieve.
sive *v* to drain.
siver *n* an open drain, a gutter.
sives *n* chives, small onions.
sivven *n* **1** the raspberry. **2** (*in pl*) a venereal disease resembling a raspberry.
sixpence *adj* sixpenny.—*n in phr* **to spit sixpences** to be very thirsty from hard drinking.
six-quarter cattle *n* cattle from eighteen months to two years old.
sixteen-hundred *n* very fine linen.
sixty-pence *n* a crown piece.
size[1] *v* to estimate the value of a thing or the character of a person.—*n* **1** importance. **2** estimation.
size[2] *n* an assize.
size[3] *n* chives.
sizer *n* a juryman.
sizzen, sizzon *n* a season.
sizzle *v* **1** to make a hissing sound like water on hot iron. **2** to fizz.—*n* a hissing sound as in frying.
sk *for sk words see also* **sc**.
skaal *v* to scold.
skad *same as* **scad**[4].
skadderized *same as* **scadderized**.
skaddin, skadden *adj* dry, shrivelled.—*n* **1** anything dry and shrivelled. **2** a thin, shrivelled person. **3** a very lean animal.
skaddow *same as* **scaddaw**.
skae[1] *v* **1** to aim with. **2** to direct to.
skae[2] *same as* **skee**.
skaeny *n* packthread, twine.
skaetch *v* to skate.—*n* a skate.
skaetcher *n* **1** a skater. **2** a skate.
skafe *n* **1** a merry, frolicsome person. **2** a wag.
skaff *same as* **scaff**[1].
skaffing *n* any kind of food.
skafrie *n* the contents of a larder.
skaicher[1] *same as* **skaigher**.
skaicher[2] *n* a gentle scolding term applied to a child.
skaif *n* **1** a shabby person. **2** a worthless fellow.
skaig *v* **1** to stride along clumsily. **2** to walk briskly, scud along.—*n* **1** a quick motion. **2** a scudding along. **3** an unpleasant person. **4** a woman of uncertain temper.—*adv* **1** with force. **2** flat.
skaigh *v* **1** to obtain by craft or wiles. **2** to obtain by any means. **3** to pilfer, steal. **4** to sponge for food. **5** to roam idly and foolishly.—*n* **1** a disappointment. **2** a search. **3** an outlook.
skaigher *n* **1** one who goes about seeking food. **2** a sponger. **3** one who obtains by artful means.
skaik *v* **1** to bedaub. **2** to separate awkwardly or dirtily one thing from another or part of a thing from the rest. **3** to spread.
skail, skaill *v* **1** to unrip. **2** to tear asunder. **3** to dismiss or disperse a meeting. **4** to scatter, spread about. **5** to spill. **6** to upset. **7** to fire a gun. **8** (*of a meeting*) to break up, disperse. **9** to depart from a place. **10** (*of a wall*) to jut outwards. **11** (*of a house*) to dismantle it, give up housekeeping. **12** to pass over. **13** to retreat.—*n* **1** a dispersion, dismission. **2** the noise of waves breaking on the shore. **3** a hurricane, a scattering wind or storm. **4** anything scattered or separated from its fellows. **5** a thin, shallow vessel for skimming milk.
skailach *same as* **skelloch**.
skail dish *n* a thin, shallow dish for skimming.
skail-drake *n* the sheldrake.
skailer *n* a scatterer, disperser.
skailin' *n* dispersion, dismission.
skallin'-time *n* **1** the time of dismission. **2** the hour when a congregation, school or meeting breaks up.
skailit *same as* **skellat**.
skaillie *n* **1** blue slate. **2** slate pencil.
skaillie-burd *n* a writing slate.

skaillie-pen *n* a slate pencil.
skailment *n* a scattering, dispersion.
skailaet *v* to separate, scatter, disperse.
skail-water *n* the superfluous water let off by a sluice before it reaches the mill.
skail-wind *n* a hurricane.
skailyie *n* slate pencil.
skaim *v* to scheme.
skainya *same as* **skaeny**.
skaip *same as* **skep**[1].
skair[1] *same as* **scar**.
skair[2] *v* to splice.—*n* **1** a splice. **2** the joining of a fishing rod's parts. **3** a joint in carpentry.
skair[3] *v* to share.—*n* a share, portion.
skair[4] *v* **1** to scare. **2** to frighten off. **3** to be scared. —*n* a scare, a fright.—*adj* timid, shy, affectedly modest.
Skair Furisday *n* Maundy Thursday.
skairgifdock *same as* **scargivenet**.
skairm *n* a share.
skair-like, ~-looking *adj* of wild or frightened looks.
skair-scon *n* a pancake baked and eaten on Shrove Tuesday.
skairt *adj* scared.
skait *same as* **skate**[1].
skait bird *n* Richardson's skua.
skaitch *v* to skate.
skaith *v* **1** to injure, damage. **2** to defame.—*n* **1** injury, damage, loss. **2** danger, expense.
skaithfu' *adj* hurtful, injurious.
skaithie *n* a fence of stakes or bunches of straw placed before the outer door or a wall of stone, turf or boards at the outside of a door, as a shelter from wind.
skaithless *adj* **1** unhurt. **2** harmless.
skaithly *adj* hurtful.—*n* a young romp.
skaith-seeker *n* one who seeks to harm others.
skaitie-purse *n* the ovarium of the skate.
skaive *v* **1** to calumniate. **2** to spread abroad a matter.
skaivie, skaivy *n* **1** a trick, prank. **2** the result of a mad prank. **3** a disappointment. **4** a mishap. **5** an affront.—*adj* **1** harebrained, silly. **2** delirious, on the verge of insanity.—*v* **1** to play pranks. **2** to wander idly, aimlessly or foolishly.
skaivle *v* **1** to put out of shape, wear to one side. **2** to twist. **3** to totter in walking. **4** to walk affectedly.—*adj* twisted, out of shape.
skaldocks *same as* **skelldick**.
skale *same as* **skail**.
skale-stairs *n* a straight or square staircase.
skaley *same as* **skelly**[4].
skalk *same as* **scalch**.
skall *n* the right to the next turn of the mill in grinding.
skallag *n* a bondservant who carried kelp and did the hard work.
skalrag *adj* shabby in appearance.—*n* a tatterdemalion.
skam *same as* **scaum**.
skambler, skamler *n* **1** a visitor at mealtimes. **2** a sponger.
skammit *adj* scorched, singed.
skance[1] *same as* **scance**[1].
skance[2], **skanse** *same as* **scance**[2].
skanes *n* dandruff showing in the hair of the head.
skantack *same as* **scantack**.
skap *n* **1** the scalp. **2** the head.
skar[1], **skare** *same as* **scar**[1].
skar[2] *v* to frighten.—*n* a fright.—*adj* timid, shy.
skar[3] *adj* left.
skare[1] *v* to scare.—*n* a scare.—*adj* scared.
skare[2], **skare**[3] *same as* **skair**[2], **skair**[3].
skar-gait *adj* (*used of a horse*) easily scared.
skar-handit *adj* left-handed.
skarin *n* a share.
skarnoch *same as* **scarnoch**.
skarrach *n* **1** a flying shower. **2** a squall with rain. **3** a large quantity of drink.
skarrow *same as* **scarrow**.

skart[1], **skart**[2] *same as* **scart**[1], **scart**[2].

skart[3] *adj* scared.

skart free *adj* safe and sound.

skartle *v* **1** to scrape money together by many small economies. **2** to scrape together by many little strokes. **3** to scatter.—*n* an iron dung scraper.

skashie *n* a wrangle.—*v* to wrangle.

skashle *v* **1** to quarrel. **2** to twist. **3** to tread on the side of the foot. **4** to shuffle in walking.—*n* **1** a squabble. **2** a twist, wrench. **3** a shuffling walk and the noise of it.—*adv* with a waddling or shuffling gait.

skatch *v* to skate.

skatcher *n* **1** a skater. **2** a skate.

skate[1] *n* a paper kite.

skate[2] *n* **1** the ovarium of the skate. **2** a term of contempt. **3** a boy or girl of little worth.

skate bree *n* the water in which a skate has been boiled.

skate-rings *n* jellyfish.

skate-rumple *n* **1** the hinder part of a skate. **2** a thin, awkward-looking person.

skate-sheers *n* appendages on the lower part of the male skate's body, resembling a pair of scissors.

skath *same as* **skaith**.

skathie *same as* **skaithie**.

skatie-goo *n* Richardson's skua.

skau *same as* **skew**[1].

skaud[1] *same as* **scad**[4].

skaud[2] *same as* **sca'd**.

skaul *v* to scold.

skaum *same as* **scaum**.

skaur-wrang *adj* **1** quite wrong. **2** totally out of the way morally.

skavie *same as* **skaivie**.

skavle *same as* **skaivle**.

skean, skean dhu *n* **1** a dirk. **2** a short sword. **3** a knife. **4** a dirk stuck in the stocking when the Highland costume is worn.

skear *v* to scare, frighten.—*n* a fright.—*adj* **1** timid. **2** wildly excited. **3** rousing.

skearie *adj* frightened, nervous, restive.—*n* a madcap.

skebel, skebal *same as* **skybal**.

skeblous *adj* rascally, evil-disposed.

skech *same as* **skaich**.

skedaddle *v* to spill.

skee *n* excrement, solid or liquid.—to void excrement.

skeeb *v* **1** to go about carelessly in a vain manner, flourishing a knife or other sharp instrument. **2** to carry anything about carelessly.—*n* **1** a large knife, a cutting instrument. **2** a staff or stick.—*adv* with vain parade.

skeebrie *same as* **skibbrie**.

skeebroch *n* very lean meat.

skeech, skeegh *same as* **skeigh**[2].

skeechan *n* treacle beer.

skeeg[1] *n* **1** the smallest portion of anything. **2** a drop.

skeeg[2] *v* **1** to lash. **2** to strike with the open palm.—*n* **1** a blow, a slap. **2** a blow with the open palm on the breech. **3** *in phr* **to play skeeg** to become suddenly bankrupt.

skeegat, skeegit *n* a stroke on the naked breech.

skeegers *n* **1** a whip made of sedges for whipping tops. **2** a whip.

skeel[1] *n* **1** a tub. **2** a bucket. **3** a wooden drinking vessel with a handle.

skeel[2] *same as* **scool**[1].

skeel[3] *v* to shelter, screen.—*n* a screen, shelter.

skeel[4] *v* **1** to prove, test. **2** to matter, avail.—*n* **1** skill. **2** knowledge, experience. **3** medical advice. **4** approbation, liking for. **5** confidence in. **6** a proof, trial.

skeel-duck, ~-goose *n* the common sheldrake.

skeelie, skeelie-pen *same as* **skaillie**.

skeeliegolee *n* **1** weak gruel. **2** thin broth.

skeeling goose *n* the common sheldrake.

skeel-like *adj* like a tub or water barrel.

skeelly *n* **1** weak gruel. **2** thin broth. **3** skilly.

skeely *adj* **1** skilful, clever. **2** wise, knowing. **3** skilled in the healing art.

skeelygallee *n* weak tea. *See* **skeeliegolee**.

skeely-wife *n* **1** a midwife. **2** a woman expert in nursing, healing, etc.

skeen, skeen-dhu *same as* **skean**.

skeengie, skeenzie, skeeny *n* packthread, twine.

skeenk *same as* **skink**[1].

skeenkle *same as* **skinkle**.

skeep[1] *n* **1** a scoop. **2** a baling scoop.

skeep[2] *n* scope.

skeer[1] *same as* **skear**.

skeer[2] *adj* sheer, utter.—*adv* quite, utterly.

skeer-eyed *adj* squinting.

skeerie *adj* **1** foolish, silly. **2** flighty. **3** skittish

skeer-wittit *adj* quite silly, foolish.

skeer-wud *adj* sheer mad.

skeet *same as* **skite**[3].

skeetack, skeetick *n* the cuttlefish.

skeeter *n* the cuttlefish.

skeetle *v* to drop.

skeetlich, skeetlichie *n* **1** a drop. **2** a small shower.

skeetlie *n* **1** a drop. **2** a small shower.

skeevers *same as* **skivers**.

skeg *same as* **skeeg**[2].

skegh[1] *same as* **skee**.

skegh[2] *same as* **skaigh**.

skeibalt *same as* **skybal**.

skeich *same as* **skeigh**[2].

skeigh[1] *n* a round, movable piece of wood put on the spindle of the large wheel of a spinning wheel to prevent the worsted from slipping off.

skeigh[2], **skeich** *adj* **1** timid, given to starting. **2** spirited, mettlesome. **3** skittish. **4** excited. **5** coy, shy. **6** prudish. **7** disdainful, proud. **8** fierce-looking. **9** (*used of drugs*) unpleasant to taste. **10** reserved, keeping aloof.—*adv* **1** timidly. **2** briskly. **3** skittishly. **4** coyly, shyly. **5** proudly, loftily.—*n* haughtiness.

skeigh bill *n* a wild, skittish, bull.

skeighish *adj* rather skittish.

skeighness *n* **1** timidity. **2** skittishness. **3** coyness. **4** pride, disdain.

skeil[1], **skeil**[2] *same as* **skeel**[1], **skeel**[2].

skeill *same as* **skail**.

skeillie *n* a scattering.—*v* to scatter. *See* **skail**.

skeilly, skeily *same as* **skaillie**.

skeily *same as* **skeelly**.

skein, skein-durk *same as* **skean**.

skein-ochil *n* a small dirk, a concealed one.

skeir *same as* **skear**.

skeitch *same as* **skatch**.

skelb *same as* **skelf**.

skelbin *n* **1** a splinter. **2** a thin piece. **3** a small, thin person.

skelby *adj* full of splinters. **2** tending to splinters.

skeldick, skeldock *n* **1** the wild mustard. **2** the wild radish.

skeldrake, skelldrake, skelduck *n* **1** the common sheldrake. **2** the oystercatcher.

skeldroch *n* hoarfrost.

skelet *n* **1** a skeleton. **2** form, appearance.

skelf *n* **1** a shelf. **2** a frame containing shelves. **3** a ledge on a cliff. **4** a splinter.—*v* **1** to splinter. **2** to peel off in flakes.

skelfy *adj* **1** laminated. **2** tending to splinters. **3** full of splinters. **4** shelving.

skell[1], **skel** *same as* **skail**.

skell[2] *same as* **skall**.

skellach *n* a hubbub.

skellachin *n* a shrill laughter.

skellad, skellat *same as* **skellet**.

skellag, skellach *same as* **skellock**.

skellat[1], **skellit** *n* **1** a bell. **2** a handbell.

skellat[2] *n* an imaginary spirit.

skellet *n* **1** a skillet. **2** cast metal.—*adj* made of tinned iron.

skell-faced *adj* **1** having a wry, distorted face. **2** squinting.
skellie¹ *same as* **skellock**.
skellie² *same as* **skellat**.
skellie, skellied *adj* squinting
skellie-man *n* **1** a bellman. **2** a public crier.
skellihewit *n* a rumpus.
skelloch *n* **1** a scream, shriek, yell. **2** a blow, what provokes a scream.—*v* to scream, shriek, yell.
skelloch bell *n* **1** a small bell. **2** a handbell.
skellock, skellack *n* **1** the wild mustard. **2** the wild radish.
skellop *v* **1** to beat. **2** to run fast. *See* **skelp**¹.
skellum *n* a rascal, scamp, scoundrel.
skelly¹ *n* the chub.
skelly² *same as* **skaillie**.
skelly³ *n* **1** a rock. **2** a skerry.
skelly⁴ *v* **1** to squint. **2** to look sideways. **3** to do anything crookedly. **4** to throw or shoot be side the mark. **5** to digress. **6** to exaggerate, narrate incorrectly.—*n* **1** a squint. **2** a cast in the eye.—*adj* **1** squinting. **2** having a squint.
skelly-coat *same as* **shelly-coat**.
skelly-ee *n* a squint eye.
skelly-ee'd *adj* cross-eyed, having a squint.
skelp¹ *v* **1** to strike with the open hand or a flat surface. **2** to whip, beat, drub. **3** to hammer iron, leather, etc. **4** to throb, pulsate. **5** (*of a clock*) to tick. **6** to drive with blows. **7** to drive hard. **8** to cause a rapid movement. **9** to write hastily. **10** to move quickly, run, dash. **11** to act with energy spirit, suddenness or violence.—*n* **1** a stroke with the open hand. **2** a smack, blow. **3** a dash, splash. **4** a dash of liquid. **5** a stride, leap.—*adv* with violence, energy or spirit.
skelp² *same as* **skelf**.
skelp-doup *n* a contemptuous designation of a schoolmaster.
skelper *n* **1** one who skelps with the open hand. **2** a quick walker. *See* **skelp**.
skelpie, skelpy *adj* deserving to be whipped.—*n* **1** a worthless person. **2** a mischief-maker. **3** a mischievous girl.
skelpie-limmer *n* an opprobrious term applied to a girl.
skelpin' *adj* **1** making a noise. **2** (*of a kiss*) smacking. **3** vigorous. **4** clever, agile.—*n* a beating with the open hand.
skelp-the-dub *n* a contemptuous name for one accustomed to do dirty work.—*v* to act like a footboy.
skelt *v* spilt. *See* **skail**.
skelter *v* to hurry off.—*adv* **1** rapidly. **2** at headlong speed.
skelve *n* a thin slice.—*v* to separate in laminae. *See* **skelf**.
skelvy *adj* **1** having various laminae. **2** shelving.
skemmel¹, **skemmil** *v* to kill and skin animals in the shambles.—*n* **1** (*in pl*) the shambles. **2** a butchers' market.
skemmel², **skemmil, skemmle** *v* **1** to throw the legs out awkwardly as if one had not proper command of them in walking. **2** to walk or climb over slight obstructions. **3** to scramble over rocks, walls, etc. **4** to wander. **5** to go astray. **6** to scramble. **7** to romp. **8** to throw things about in a careless and slovenly way.—*adj* having the feet thrown outwards.—*n* a tall, thin, ungainly person.
skemmil *same as* **skemmel**.
skemming *n* a foolish way of throwing the legs.
skemmle *same as* **skemmel**¹.
skemp *n* **1** a scamp. **2** a worthless fellow.
skene-occle *same as* **skein-ochil**.
skenk *same as* **skink**¹.
skenkle *same as* **skinkle**¹.
skeoch *n* **1** a very small cave. **2** a large chink in a cliff.
skep¹, **skepp** *n* **1** a large basket. **2** a bowl-shaped vessel with a handle for ladling. **3** a straw beehive. **4** the contents of a beehive.—*v* **1** to knock one's hat over the eyes. **2** to enclose in a hive. **3** to go to rest for the night. **4** (*with* **in**) to make acquaintance with.
skep² *v* to escape.
skeplet *adj* mean, tattered, ragged.—*n* a hat out of shape.
skep-moo *n* the mouth of a beehive.
skeppack *n* the game of tig.

skeppit *adj* having the hat tilted over the eyes and nose from behind.
sker¹ *adj* left.
sker² *same as* **skear**.
sker-handit *adj* left-handed.
skene *adj* **1** somewhat restive. **2** easily startled.
skerr *same as* **scar**¹.
skerregifnot *same as* **scargivenet**.
skerry, skerry-blue *n* a variety of potato.
skerry *same as* **scairy**.
sketch *same as* **skatch**.
sketcher *same as* **sketcher**.
sketchers *n* two wooden legs with a crossbar for supporting a tree during sawing.
skeu *same as* **skew**¹
skeuch, skeugh *same as* **skew**¹.
skeut *v* **1** to twist, distort. **2** to walk awkwardly, putting down the feet with force. **3** to throw or fall flat.—*n* **1** a twist. **2** anything clumsy and misshapen. **3** a broad, flat hand or foot. **4** an ill-fitting, clumsy shoe. **5** an untidy, cross-tempered woman. **6** a skate.—*adv* **1** with awkward, heavy step. **2** flatly, heavily. **3** aslant.
skeut-fittit *adj* having flat, turned-out feet.
skevl *same as* **skaivle**.
skevrel *v* to move unsteadily in a circular way.
skew¹ *adv* **1** in a distorted manner. **2** with a waddling, affected gait.—*n* **1** anything crooked. **2** a twist, turn. **3** the oblique part of a gable on which the roof rests. **4** a shade, shadow. **5** a wooden chimney cowl. **6** a state of ruin.—*v* **1** to slant. **2** to twist about. **2** to walk in an affected manner. **3** to distort. **4** to build obliquely. **5** to cover the gables of a thatched roof with sods.
skew² *n* a skewer.
skew³ *v* **1** to eschew. **2** to seek shelter from.
skewed *adj* **1** demented. **2** bemused with drink. **3** distorted.
skew-fittit *adj* splay-footed.
skewl *v* **1** to twist, distort. **2** to deflect from the plumbline. **3** to squint. **4** to waddle, walk affectedly.—*n* a twist.—*adv* **1** in a twisted manner. **2** with a waddling gait. **3** with dirty, dragging steps.
skew mouth *n* a crooked mouth.
skew-mouth plane *n* a kind of joiner's plane.
skey *same as* **skeigh**².
skeyb-horn't *adj* having the horns far asunder.
skeybil *same as* **skybald**.
skeyf *n* a shrivelled dwarf.
skeyg *same as* **skaig**.
skeyg for skeyg *adv* at full speed.
skeys *v* to run off quickly.
skeytch *same as* **skatch**.
ski *v* to slide.
skiach *n* the hawthorn fruit.
skian *same as* **skean**.
skib *n* a stroke, blow.
skibbie *n* the game of tig.
skibbrie, skibrie *n* **1** thin, light soil. **2** any worthless stuff.—*adj* worthless.
skibby *n* a left-handed person.
skibe *same as* **skype**¹.
skibel *same as* **skybal**.
skice *same as* **skeys**.
skichen *n* a disgust at food from over-nicety in taste.—*v* **1** to disgust. **2** to become disgusted.—*adj* **1** haughty. **2** showing contempt and disgust.
skick, skich *v* (*of cattle*) to frisk about.—*adj* frisky.
skid *v* **1** to slide, slip. **2** to look squint at an object.
skiddaw *n* the common guillemot.
skiddie *adj* **1** oblique. **2** squint.
skiddie-look *n* a squint look.
skiddle *n* a contemptuous name for tea or any insipid liquid.
skiech *same as* **skeigh**.
skiel *n* a tub.
skieldrake *n* the sheldrake.

skien *same as* **skean**.

skier *same as* **skeer**[2].

skiff *v* **1** to skim lightly along the ground. **2** to move or dance lightly and easily. **3** to fly lightly and airily. **4** to blow over. **5** to brush or graze or wipe off gently. **6** to cause a thin, flat stone to skim along the surface of water. **7** to rain or snow slightly. **8** to work carelessly and superficially.—*n* **1** a skip. **2** a slight whizzing sound by a body skiffing. **3** a slight movement. **4** a slight graze. **5** a light touch. **6** a sketchy description. **7** art or facility in operation. **8** a slight or flying shower.

skiffer *v* to rain, snow or hail gently.—*n* a slight shower.

skiffie *n* the tub used for bringing up coals from the pit.

skiffle *v* to scuffle.

skift, skifft *same as* **skiff**.

skifter *v* to rain, snow or hail very gently.—*n* a slight shower.

skifting *n* **1** a skimming. **2** a thin shaving from a larger piece.

skig[1], **skig**[2] *same as* **skeeg**[1], **skeeg**[2].

skiggle *v* **1** to sprinkle, scatter. **2** to spill in small quantities.

skight *same as* **skite**.

skiken *same as* **skichen**.

skile *same as* **skail**.

skill *same as* **skeel**.

skillat, skillet *same as* **skellat**.

skiller *v* to warp.

skillock *same as* **skellock**.

skilly[1] *same as* **skeely**.

skilly[2] *same as* **skaillie**.

skilly-wife *n* a midwife.

skilp *same as* **skelp**[1].

skilt[1] *v* to drink copiously, to swill.—*n* a draught, drink.

skilt[2] *v* **1** to move quickly and lightly. **2** to skip.—*n* a contemptuous name for a girl.

skim *v* **1** to evade. **2** to shirk the truth.

skime *v* **1** to gleam with reflected light. **2** to give a side-glance.—*n* **1** the glance of reflected light. **2** a glance of the eye.

skimmer, skimmar *v* **1** (*used of light*) to flicker. **2** to shimmer, glitter. **3** to have a flaunting appearance, as when women are lightly and showily dressed. **4** to dust lightly or quickly over the surface of anything. **5** to fall in a light, drizzling shower. **6** to glide rapidly. **7** to act or move quickly. **8** to flutter lightly. **9** to frisk. **10** (*used of swallows*) to skim the surface of smooth water.—*n* **1** the flickering rays of light. **2** a slight sprinkling of any powdery substance. **3** a low flight of birds.

skimmerin *n* **1** a low flight. **2** a sprinkling.

skimmering look *n* the characteristic look of an idiot or lunatic.

skimp *v* to stint, curtail, scrimp.—*adj* **1** small, scanty. **2** (*used of weight or measure*) short, scant.

skin[1], **skine** *n* **1** a parchment deed. **2** a particle, grain.—*v* **1** to exact to the full. **2** to hide, represent under a false appearance. **3** (*with* **up**) to put the best face on a story or a bare-faced lie.—*adj* skin-deep, superficial.

skin[2] *n* a term of extreme contempt.

skin-bane *adj* **1** naked. **2** very poor.

skincheon *n* (*used of drink*) a hearty pull.

skin-claes *n* **1** oilskins. **2** waterproof overalls.

skin-flype *v* to flay.

skinfu' *n* a bellyful of drink or food.

skinie, skiny *n* packthread.

skink[1] *n* **1** a shin or knuckle of beef. **2** a bad piece of flesh. **3** soup made from the shin of beef. **4** soup in general.

skink[2] *v* **1** to pour out for drinking. **2** to decant. **3** to serve with drink. **4** to drink, tipple. **5** to charge glasses and drink healths. **6** (*with* **over**) to drink together in ratifying a bargain, etc.—*n* **1** liquor, drink. **2** a draught. **3** a drinking bout.

skink[3] *v* **1** to scatter, disperse, separate, split. **2** to pour from vessel to vessel in order to mix thoroughly. **3** to crush to pieces. **4** to break by crushing the sides of anything together.—*n* **1** a small portion. **2** a chip, shred. **3** a crush, smash. **4** the sudden pressure or blow that causes a smash.

skink broth *n* soup made from the skink. *See* **skink**[1].

skinker *n* **1** a server of drink. **2** a butler. **3** a drinker, tippler.

skink hoch *n* the shin of beef.

skinking *adj* thin, liquid.

skinkle[1] *v* **1** to sparkle, twinkle, shine. **2** to make a showy appearance.—*n* lustre, glitter, sparkle.—*adj* glittering, sparkling.

skinkle[2] *v* **1** to sprinkle. **2** to spill in small quantities. **3** to sow thinly.—*n* **1** a sprinkling, scattering. **2** a very small quantity.

skinklin[1] *n* the sparkling of a bright irradiation.

skinklin[2] *n* **1** a sprinkling. **2** a small portion or quantity.

skinkling *n* meat that is nearly cold.—*adj* **1** (*of meat*) out of season. **2** tainted. **3** unpleasant to the taste.

skinny *n* a roll of bread.

skinymalink *n* an extremely thin person

skint[1] *n* **1** a drop of liquid thrown. **2** a very small quantity of liquid.—*v* **1** to splash with mud, etc. **2** to throw drops of liquid on anything.

skint[2] *v, adj* skinned.

skin-the-louse *n* a contemptuous name for a miser.

skin-whole *adj* unharmed, sound of body.

skiollag *same as* **skellock**.

skip[1] *v* **1** to make a stone skim along the surface of water. **2** to leap lightly across.

skip[2] *v* (*used in curling*) to act as captain of a rink. —*n* the captain of a rink.

skip[3] *v* to slide on ice.

skip[4] *n* the peak of a cap.

skip[5] *same as* **skep**[1].

skipjack *adj* nimble, sportive.

skipped *adj* (*used of a cap*) peaked.

skipper *n* **1** the skip (qv) or captain of a curling rink. **2** the head man on board a fishing boat.—*v* to act as captain of a boat. *See* **skip**[2].

skip rape *n* a skipping rope.

skip rig *n* an article of women's dress.

skir *n* **1** a rock in the sea. **2** a small rocky islet. **3** a cluster of rocks.

skirdoch *adj* **1** flirting. **2** easily scared.

skire[1] *adj* **1** mad. **2** eccentric.

skire[2] *same as* **skeer**[2].

skire[3] *same as* **skyre**[1].

skirg *v* to romp about.

skirge *n* **1** a termagant. **2** a brawling woman. **3** a scourge.

skirge *v* to pour liquor backwards and forwards from one vessel to another to mellow it.—*n* a dash of hot water.

skirgiffin *same as* **scargivenet**.

skirin *same as* **skyrin**.

Skirisfurisday *n* Maundy Thursday.

skirl *v* **1** to scream. **2** to sing shrilly. **3** to give forth any discordant, shrill sound. **4** to fry. **5** to frizzle, as in frying.—*n* **1** a shriek, scream, shrill sound. **2** a squall of wind with rain or snow. **3** a blow producing a scream.

skirlag *n* a long, thin leaf, as of corn, held stretched between the thumbs held parallel, which, when blown upon, emits a musical sound.

skirl-crake *n* the turnstone.

skirlie[1] *n* (*used of snow*) a slight shower.

skirlie[2] *n* a dish of meal, suet or dripping, pepper, salt and chopped onions, cooked and eaten generally with mashed potatoes.

skirling pan *n* a frying pan.

skirl-in-the-pan *n* **1** the frizzling sound made by butter frying in a pan. **2** anything fried in butter in a pan. **3** a drink composed of oatmeal, whisky and ale, mixed and heated in a pan and given to gossips at at in-lying (qv).

skirllie-weeack *v* to cry with a shrill voice.—*n* **1** a shrill cry. **2** a little person with a shrill voice.

skirl-naked *adj* stark naked.

skirl o' wind *n* a stiff breeze.

skirl up *v* to sing high notes forcibly.

skirly *same as* **skirlie**[2].

skirp *v* **1** to splash, bespatter. **2** to rain slightly. **3** to besprinkle.—*n* **1** a splash. **2** a drop of rain. **3** a small clot. **4** a sprinkling. **5** a slight shower.

skirpin *n* the gore, or strip of thin cloth, on the hinder part of breeches.

skirr *v* **1** to scurry. **2** to rush. **3** to scour, hunt.

skirrivaig *same as* **scurryvaig**.

skirry-whirry *same as* **scurrie-whurrie**.

skirt[1] *n* **1** a large overall petticoat used in riding by women. **2** a shortgown (qv). **3** the slope of a hill. **4** the close, end.

skirt[2] *v* **1** to run rapidly. **2** to hurry off. **3** to elude, run away stealthily.

skirvin' *n* a thin coating of snow, earth, etc.

skist *n* a chest, box. *See* **kist**.

skit[1] *n* **1** a taunt, sneer. **2** a practical joke. **3** a trick. **4** a humorous story or picture. **5** a foolish action. **6** a piece of silly ostentation.—*v* **1** to asperse by oblique taunts. **2** to make game of.

skit[2] *v* **1** to caper like a skittish horse. **2** to flounce. —*n* **1** a capering, restive horse. **2** one who skips about. **3** a vain, empty creature. **4** a woman of frivolous or immoral character. **5** a disagreeable woman. **6** a sharp, passing shower.

skit[3] *same as* **skite**[3].

skit[4] *v* to steal.

skitch *same as* **skatch**.

skite[1] *n* **1** a trick. **2** an ill-turn. **3** a spree, jollification. **4** a nasty person. **5** a meagre, starved-looking person. **6** a strange-looking, ugly person.

skite[2] *n* the yellowhammer.

skite[3] *v* **1** to move in leaps and bounds. **2** to fly off quickly. **3** to run swiftly and lightly. **4** to slip or slide suddenly on a smooth or frozen surface. **5** to rebound, as hail. **6** to fly off at a tangent. **7** to fly off in a slanting direction. **8** to make a flat, thin stone skim the surface of water. **9** to squirt. **10** to spit. **11** to eject liquid forcibly. **12** to project with force. **13** to have diarrhoea. **14** to splash. **15** to rain slightly.—*n* **1** the act of sliding or slipping. **2** a turn in skating, curling, etc. **3** a skate. **4** the act of squirting or spitting forcibly or through the teeth. **5** a squirt, syringe. **6** a sharp, passing shower. **7** a small quantity of any liquid. **8** a mouthful of spirits. **9** diarrhoea in animals. **10** the dung of a fowl. **11** a dash. **12** a sudden fall. **13** a sudden blow delivered sideways and causing a slanting rebound. **14** an accident, a misadventure. **15** (*with* **ill**) an unfortunate event.—*adj* fleet, active.—*adv* with sharp force.

skiter[1] *n* **1** skater. **2** a squirt. **3** a sea bather.

skiter[2] *v* **1** to go quickly from place to place. **2** to travel hither and thither.

skites *n* hemlock, from being used to make skiters or squirts as toys. *See* **skite**[3].

skitten *adj* **1** pampered. **2** over-nice as to food.

skitter[1] *n* a thief.

skitter[2] *v* **1** to have diarrhoea. **2** to potter about, waste time.—*n* **1** liquid excrement. **2** diarrhoea. **3** anything impure or incongruous, which, when mixed with what is valuable, renders the whole useless.

skitterfu' *adj* afflicted with diarrhoea.

skittery deacon *n* the common sandpiper.

skittle *same as* **skiddle**.

skiuldr *n* the jellyfish, Medusa.

skive[1] *v* **1** to cut longitudinally into equal slices. **2** to slit leather.

skive[2] *v* to move quickly.

skiver *n* a skewer.—*v* **1** to fasten with a skewer. **2** to disperse.

skivers *n* the leather used for binding schoolbooks, which is sliced into two.

skivet[1], **skivat** *n* a sharp blow.

skivet[2] *n* a blacksmith's fire shovel.

skivie *same as* **skaivie**.

sklaeve, sklaive *same as* **sclave**.

sklaff *same as* **sclaff**.

sklaffard, sklaffirt *n* **1** a blow with the flat hand on the side of the head. **2** anything thin and tough. **3** a thin, light shoe. **4** a horizontal rock lying in thin beds.—*v* to shuffle along, as with loose slippers.

sklaffer *same as* **sclaffer**.

sklafford-hole *n* a ventilating hole in a barn wall.

sklaik *same as* **slaik**[1].

sklaikie *adj* smeary.

sklait *same as* **sclate**.

sklammer *v* **1** to clamber. **2** to scramble. **3** to wander idly.

sklap *v* to slap. **2** to go slap.—*n* a slap.

sklap-dunt *n* a slapdash blow.

sklash *v* **1** to dash. **2** to strike with anything wet. **3** to splash. **4** to lick. **5** to give a slobbering kiss. —*n* **1** a heavy shower. **2** a dash of anything wet. **3** a violent dash. **4** a loud crash. **5** a wet kiss. **6** a lick. **7** a sloven.—*adv* forcibly.

sklatch *same as* **sclatch**.

sklatching *n* **1** an unseemly mass. **2** a large clot of mud, etc.

sklate *same as* **sclate**.

sklater *n* **1** a slater. **2** a woodlouse.

sklave *same as* **sclave**.

skleeny *same as* **sklenie**.

skleet[1] *v* **1** to glide rapidly. **2** to slide. **3** to wear down shoes on one side or as one splay-footed. —*adj* sleek, smooth.

skleet[2] *v* **1** to throw forcibly. **2** to empty out in a mass. **3** to walk with a stumping step.—*n* **1** a heavy fall or dash. **2** a heavy, stumping gait.—*adv* forcibly.

skleeting-fittit *adj* **1** splay-footed. **2** wearing down one side of the shoes.

skleff *adj* **1** thin and flat. **2** shallow. **3** flat-footed. —*n* a thin slice.

sklefferie *adj* separated into laminae.

skleff-fittit *adj* flat-footed.

sklender *adj* thin, slender.

sklendene, sklendry *adj* **1** thin, slender, lank. **2** faint, slight.

sklenie *adj* thin, slender.

sklent[1] *same as* **sclent**.

sklent[2] *v* **1** to tear, rend. **2** to split. **3** to splinter.—*n* a tear, a rent.

skleush *v* **1** to dash or fall softly. **2** to drag one's steps.—*n* **1** a soft dash or fall. **2** the act of dragging one's steps. **3** the sound of such a fall or dragging. **4** a misshapen, worn shoe. **5** a slatternly woman.

skleushing *adj* slatternly.

skleut *same as* **sclute**.

skleutch *v* **1** to slouch. **2** to walk in a dirty, slovenly manner.—*n* **1** a sloven. **2** an untidy woman.

skleuter *v* **1** to flow through a narrow orifice with a spluttering sound. **2** to walk in a careless, awkward way. **3** to work in slovenly fashion.—*n* **1** an untidy mass of liquid or semiliquid matter. **2** the noise of the projection of liquids or semiliquids through a narrow orifice. **3** messing among liquids or semiliquids in a slatternly way. **4** a woman of filthy habits.—*adv* **1** with a spluttering noise. **2** with a splashing step.

skleuterie, skleutrie *adj* wet and dirty.

skley *same as* **scly**.

sklice *v* to slice.—*n* a slice.

sklidder *same as* **slidder**.

skliff *same as* **scliff**.

skliffer *same as* **skliff**.

sklifferie *same as* **sklefferie**.

sklim *same as* **sclimb**.

sklinner *same as* **sklinter**.

sklint[1] *same as* **sclent**.

sklint[2] *same as* **sklent**[2].

sklinter *v* **1** to splinter. **2** to break off in laminæ.—*n* a splinter.—*adj* slender.—*adv* **1** in splinters. **2** with speed.

sklire *same as* **sklyre**.

sklite *same as* **sclyte**.

sklitter[1] *same as* **sklyter**.

sklitter[2] *v* to walk or work in slovenly fashion.

sklone *v* to squeeze a plastic substance flat.—*n* **1** a mass of plastic substance. **2** a mass of snow or sleet. **3** a big snowflake. **4** an easy-going person.

sklouff, skloof *v* **1** to strike a dull, heavy blow. **2** to strike sideways or in passing with a flat surface. **3** to rub against. **4** to walk with dull, heavy step. **5** to drag the feet.—*n* **1** a blow with the open hand or with a flat surface. **2** the noise of a rub or blow. **3** the act of walking with dull, heavy step or with dragging feet. **4** the sound so produced. **5** an old, worn shoe or slipper. **6** a big, clumsy shoe or boot. **7** an easy-going, untidy person.—*adv* with a dull, heavy sound. **8** with a shuffling, trailing motion.

sklouffer *same as* **sklouff**.

sklout, skloutsr *n* cow dung in a thin state.

skloy *same as* **scly**.

sklufe *same as* **sklouff**.

skluff *n* anything large.

sklush, sklugsh *same as* **slush**.

sklute *same as* **sclute**.

skly *same as* **scly**.

sklyde *v* to slide.—*n* a slide.

sklypach *same as* **sklype**.

sklype *v* **1** to dash down violently. **2** to fall flat and heavily. **3** to walk with heavy, splashing step. **4** to tear, rend. **5** to strip off in thin shreds or flakes. **6** to flype (qv) a stocking.—*n* **1** a heavy blow with the open hand on a flat surface. **2** a slap. **3** a box on the ears. **4** a heavy fall. **5** the noise of such blow or fall. **6** a large clot or spot. **7** a large, thin piece of anything. **8** a clumsy hand or foot. **9** a misshapen shoe, glove or bonnet. **10** a person of lazy or dirty habits.—*adv* with force.

sklyre *v* to slide.—*n* **1** a slide. **2** the act of sliding.

sklytach *same as* **sclytach**.

sklyte *same as* **sclyte**.

sklyter *v* **1** to throw down or pour out with force and a sharp sound. **2** to fall heavily.—*n* **1** a thin, semiliquid mass. **2** a heavy fall. **3** the sharp sound of this. **4** a worn-out shoe. **5** a large, clumsy foot. **6** a clumsy, untidy fellow. **7** a term of reproach.—*adv* **1** flatly. **2** suddenly, as with a fall.

sklyterach *same as* **sklyter**.

skoddy *adj* shady, verging on dishonesty.

skodgie *same as* **scodgie**.

skoffrie *n* scoffing, mockery.

skole, skolt *same as* **scoll**.

skon[1]**, skon**[2] *same as* **scon**[1]**, scon**[2].

skonce *same as* **sconce**.

skone *same as* **scon**[2].

skonke *n* part of a fishing net.

skonner same as **scunner**.

skooder *same as* **scowder**.

skoog *same as* **scog**.

skook *same as* **scouk**.

skookin-like *adj* **1** ill-looking. **2** furtive. **3** sullen.

skool *n* a shoal of fish.

skoom *same as* **scum**[1].

skoor *same as* **scour**[1].

skoosh *same as* **scoosh**.

skoot[1]**, skoot**[2] *same as* **scoot**[2], **scoot**[4].

skoot[3] *same as* **skute**[1].

skord *same as* **score**.

skore *same as* **score**.

skouder *same as* **scouther**[1].

skough *same as* **scog**.

skoup *n* a scoop.

skouper *same as* **scouper**.

skour *same as* **scoor**[1].

skourick *n* **1** a thing of no value. **2** a particle.

skout *same as* **scoot**[1].

skouth *same as* **scouth**.

skouther *same as* **scouther**[1].

skouther *same as* **scowder**.

skoutt *same as* **scout**[1].

skow[1] *n* barrel staves after the barrel has been broken up.

skow[2] *n* **1** a small boat made of willows, etc, and covered with skins. **2** a flat-bottomed boat used as a lighter.

skowder-doup *same as* **scowder-doup**.

skowel, skowl *same as* **skewl**.

skowff *same as* **scuff**[5].

skowrie *same as* **scoury**[1].

skowther[1] *same as* **scouther**.

skowther[2] *same as* **scowder**.

skoyl *v* to squeal.—*n* a squeal.

skrach *same as* **scraich**.

skrae[1] *same as* **scrae**.

skrae[2] *n* a wire sieve for sifting grain.

skrae fish *n* sun-dried, unsalted fish.

skrae-shankit *adj* having long, thin legs.

skraich, skraigh *same as* **scraich**.

skraik, skrake *same as* **scraich**.

skran *same as* **scran**.

skrank *adj* **1** lank. **2** (*used of writing*) sprawling.—*n* **1** a lean person. **2** sprawling, bad writing.—*v* to write in a scrawling hand.

skranky *same as* **scranky**.

skran-pock *n* a beggar's wallet.

skrat, skratt *same as* **scart**[1].

skrauch, skraugh *v* **1** (*of birds*) to scream. **2** to bawl.

skrauchle *same as* **scrauchle**.

skrea *n* a post or prop for a clay or wattled wall.

skreagh *same as* **scraich**.

skree *same as* **skrae**[2].

skreech, skreegh *same as* **scraich**.

skreed *same as* **screed**.

skreef *same as* **screef**.

skreek *same as* **skraik**.

skreek o' day *n* **1** cockcrow. **2** daybreak.

skreemage *same as* **scrimmage**.

skreen *same as* **screen**.

skreenge *same as* **scringe**.

skreenger *n* **1** a vigorous, energetic person. **2** anything large of its kind. **3** one who pokes about for trifles.

skreenings *n* gleanings.

skregh, skrech *same as* **scraich**.

skreich, screigh *same as* **scraich**.

skreigh[1] *same as* **scraich**.

skreigh[2] *n* whisky.

skreigh o' day *n* **1** daybreak. **2** cockcrow.

skreik *same as* **scraich**.

skrew *n* the shrewmouse.

skriech, skriegh *same as* **scraich**.

skriek *same as* **scraich**.

skriet *v* **1** to shriek. **2** to cry. **3** to proclaim.

skrieve[1] *same as* **screeve**[1].

skrieve[2] *same as* **scrive**[1].

skriever *n* **1** a smart worker. **2** a clever fellow.

skriever *n* **1** an inferior writer. **2** a poor scribe.

skriff[1] *same as* **screef**.

skriff[2] *n* a scrap of writing.

skriffin *same as* **scriffin**.

skrift *same as* **scrift**.

skrille *same as* **skirl**.

skrim *same as* **scrim**[1].

skrimmage *same as* **scrimmage**.

skrimp *same as* **scrimp**[1].

skrine *n* unboiled sowens (qv).

skringe *same as* **scringe**.

skrinkie, skrinkit *adj* **1** lank. **2** slender. **3** wrinkled. **4** shrivelled.

skrinkie-faced *adj* having wrinkles on the face.

skrow[1] *same as* **screw**[2].

skrow[2] *n* a scroll.

skrow[3], skrow[4], skrow[5] *same as* **scrow**.
skrucken *v* **1** to shrivel. **2** to cause to shrivel.—*n* anything dry or shrivelled.—*adj* shrivelled, shrunken.
skruff[1], **skruff**[2] *same as* **scruff**[1], **scruff**[2].
skrummage *same as* **scrimmage**.
skrumple *same as* **scrumple**[1].
skrumplie *adj* crisp.
skrmnplit *adj* **1** shrunk. **2** shrivelled by means of fire.
skrunge *same as* **scringe**[1].
skrunk *v* **1** to shrink. **2** to crumple. **3** to become withered or dry.
skrunkilt *adj* pinched, scanty.
skrunkit *adj* pinched, scanty.
skrunkle *v* **1** to shrink. **2** to crumple. **3** to skrunk (qv).
skrunt[1] *same as* **scrunt**[1].
skrunt[2] *v* **1** to start for. **2** to walk off.
skrunt[3] *same as* **scrunt**[2].
skruntin *n* a continuous, harsh, grating sound.
skruntiness *n* scrubbiness.
skruntit *adj* **1** stunted, dwarfed. **2** meagre, thin.
skrunty *same as* **scrunty**.
skry *same as* **scry**[2].
skube[1] *n* a hearty drink.
skube[2] *n* anything hollowed out.
skud *v* **1** to run quickly. **2** to rain slightly. **3** to drink copiously.—*n* **1** a blow. **2** (*in pl*) ale, porter.
skuddievaig *same as* **scurryvaig**.
skuddler *n* a youngster.
skudge *v* to buffet, box the ears.
skudge, skudgy *same as* **scodgie**.
skue *same as* **skew**.
skuff[1], **skuff**[2] *same as* **scuff**[1], **scuff**[2].
skug[1] *v* to flog.
skug[2] *same as* **scug**[2].
skug[3] *v* to expiate.—*n* a blow.
skugging-faced, ~-looking *adj* of gloomy face.
skuggy *adj* shady.
skug-ways, ~-wise *adv* clandestinely.
skuik *same as* **scouk**.
skuil[1] *n* a school.
skuil[2] *same as* **school**[2].
skuill *same as* **scool**[1].
Skuir Fuirsday *same as* **Skirisfurisday**.
skul *n* a scullion.
skulduddery *same as* **sculduddery**.
skule[1] *n* school.
skule[2] *same as* **school**[2].
skule[3] *same as* **scool**[1].
skuler *n* a storyteller, narrator.
skules *n* feeding stalls for cattle.
skull[1] *n* a tightly fitting cap or hat.
skull[2] *same as* **school**[1].
skull[3] *n* **1** a shallow, wicker basket. **2** a wickerwork cradle.
skull[4] *v* **1** to wander. **2** to zigzag.
skulldavie *n* **1** a kind of woman's hat. **2** any large-sized hat.
skult *same as* **scult**.
skultie *adj* naked, nude.
skumfish, skunfis *same as* **scumfish**.
skunge *same as* **scunge**.
skunkle *v* to glitter.
skunner *same as* **scunner**.
skup *n* a scoop-shaped bonnet.
skur, skurr *same as* **scurr**.
skurl *same as* **scurl**.
skurr *same as* **skirr**.
skurrie[1] *same as* **scurrie**[3].
skurrie[2] *same as* **scurry**.
skurrieman *n* **1** a wandering fellow. **2** a vagrant.
skurroch, skurrock *n* **1** a cant term for cash. **2** a particle.
skurryvaig, skurivaig, skurrievarg *same as* **scurryvaig**.
skushle *same as* **scushel**.
skute[1] *n* sour or dead liquor.
skute[2] *v* to walk awkwardly from being flat-soled.

skute[3] *same as* **scoot**[4].
skutie[1] *same as* **scootie**[2].
skutie, skutock, skuttock *same as* **scoot**[1].
skutter *same as* **scutter**.
skweel *n* a school.
skweelin' days *n* schooldays.
skwype *v* to tear, rend.—*n* a tear, rent.
sky *n* **1** twilight, dawn. **2** the red light in the sky before or after sunset. **3** the ridge or summit of a hill.—*v* **1** to skim along the horizon. **2** to hurry along. **3** (*used of the weather*) to clear up.
skyb *same as* **skybal**.
skybal, skybald, skybil, skyble *n* **1** a low, worthless fellow. **2** a scoundrel. **3** a lazy, useless ne'er-do-well. **4** a tatterdemalion. **5** a ragged urchin. **6** a lean person or animal. **7** a worn-out horse. **8** a lazy horse. **9** a gelded goat. **10** thin, poor land.—*adj* **1** mean, low. **2** ragged. **3** (*of the legs*) poor, long, bare and thin.
skybaleer *v* to rail against, abuse.
skybrie *same as* **skibbrie**.
Skyeman's puzzle *n* a most difficult question.
skyeow *same as* **skew**.
sky-goat *n* the bittern.
sky-high *v* to throw up into the air.
Skyir Thurisday *n* Maundy Thursday.
sky-laverock *n* the skylark.
skyle *same as* **skail**.
skylights *n* **1** a half-filled wine-glass. **2** the space between the wine and the rim.
skyllie, skylie *same as* **skaillie**.
skyme *same as* **skime**.
skynk *same as* **skink**[2].
skyow *same as* **skew**.
skyowl *same as* **skewl**.
skyowt *same as* **skewed**.
skypal[1] *same as* **skybal**.
skypal[2] *adj* short, lacking, deficient.
skype[1] *n* **1** a mean, worthless fellow. **2** a lean person of disagreeable manner and temper.
skype[2] *v* to wander idly from place to place.
skypel *same as* **skybal**.
skyr *same as* **skir**.
sky-racket *n* **1** an uproar. **2** a great noise.
skyre[1] *v* **1** to shine, glitter. **2** to make a foolish display of gaudy dress. **3** to look in a silly, amazed manner.—*n* **1** anything brightly coloured or gaudy. **2** a brightly coloured, tawdry piece of dress. **3** a person with a foolish, amazed look.
skyre[2] *same as* **skeer**[2].
skyre[3] *v* **1** to scare. **2** to startle. **3** to be shy.
skyre-leukin *adj* **1** shining. **2** brilliant, showy. **3** of bright, gaudy colour. **4** having a vacant, foolish look.
skyrie *adj* **1** bright. **2** glaring. **3** glowing.
skyrin *adj* **1** shining. **2** making a great show. **3** gaudy.
skyt *same as* **skite**[3].
skytch *same as* **skatch**.
skytchers *n* **1** skates. **2** skaters.
skyte[1], **skyte**[2] *same as* **skite**[3], **skite**[1].
skyter *n* **1** a squirt. **2** a sea bather. **3** a skater.
skytes *n* hemlock, from being used as toy skyters.
skytie *n* a slight, passing shower.
skyltie *v* to move from side to side, applied to the movement of liquid when carried in a vessel and shaken.
sla *same as* **slae**[1].
slab[1] *n* **1** a thick slice. **2** a large piece. **3** a tall, thin person. **4** a lubberly fellow.
slab[2] *n* to sup eagerly and greedily.
slabber *v* **1** to slobber. **2** to swallow one's words in speaking.—*n* **1** mud, slush. **2** a slovenly, dirty fellow.
slabbergash *n* a slovenly, drivelling fellow.
slabbergaucie *n* a slabbergash (qv).
slabbery *adj* **1** rainy. **2** sloppy. **3** muddy.
slab-step *n* a flat doorstep.
slachter *v* to slaughter.

slack[1] *adj* **1** slow. **2** short of work. **3** thinly occupied, not filled. **4** not trustworthy. **5** loose in conduct. **6** reluctant to pay a debt. **7** (*used of money*) slowly paid.—*n* **1** a loose, baggy part of anything, as of trousers. **2** a ewe that has missed a lamb. **3** (*in pl*) trousers.—*v* **1** to become flaccid, cease to be distended. **2** to cease, pause. **3** to slacken. **4** to grow remiss, become neglectful. **5** (*used of business*) to become less busy.

slack[2] *v* to cover up a fire with dross or slack to lessen consumption.

slack[3] *n* **1** an opening between hills. **2** a pass. **3** a hollow. **4** a dip in the ground. **5** a glade. **6** a hollow, boggy place. **7** a morass. **8** a gully in a rocky coast. **9** the narrowest part of an animal's ribs. **10** (*used of the throat*) the narrowest part.

slack[4] *v* to slake, quench the thirst.

slacked *adj* spent.

slacken[1] *v* **1** to slake. **2** to quench thirst.

slacken[2] *v* to enfeeble.

slack ewe, ~ yowe *n* a ewe past bearing.

slackie *n* a kind of sling, made of an elastic rod split at the end.

slackjaw *n* **1** impudent speech. **2** loose, frivolous talk. **3** rude, uncivil, coarse language.

slade[1] *n* a hollow between rising grounds, one with a streamlet flowing in it.

slade[2] *same as* **slaid**.

slade[3] *v* slid, did slide.

sladge *n* **1** a sloven. **2** one who muddies clothes in walking. **3** a dirty, coarse woman.—*v* **1** to walk through mire and dirt in a lounging, slovenly way. **2** to work in a slovenly way so as to soil one's clothes.

slae[1] *n* **1** the sloe. **2** the fruit of the whitethorn.

slae[2] *n* a weaver's reed.

slae-berry bloom *n* the flower of the blackthorn.

slae-black *adj* black as a slae.

slae-board *n* the board to which the slae of a weaver is affixed. *See* **slae**[2].

slaeie *adj* abounding in sloes or sloe bushes.

slae-stick *n* a blackthorn staff.

slae-thorn *n* the blackthorn. **2** a blackthorn staff. —*adj* bent, twisted, crooked.

slag, slagg *adj* **1** moist, wet, soft. **2** thawing.—*n* **1** a lump of any soft substance. **2** a portion, mess. **3** a quagmire, slough.—*v* **1** to soften. **2** to moisten. **3** to besmear. **4** (*with* **up**) to lift in large spoonfuls. **5** to gobble up greedily.

slag-day *n* a curler's designation of a day of thaw.

slagger *same as* **slaiger**.

slaggie *n* **1** an unseemly mess of anything wet or soft. **2** food dirtily mixed. **3** slatternly work. **4** the act of working in a slatternly manner.—*adj* **1** thawing. **2** soft. **3** miry. **4** wet, drizzling.

slaich *v* **1** to bedaub, besmear. **2** to paint carelessly. **3** to spit mucus. **4** to eat liquid food in a dirty, disgusting manner. **5** to wash or scour in a slatternly fashion.—*n* **1** slime. **2** anything wet and muddy or soft and disgusting. **3** the act of eating in a dirty, disgusting manner.

slaichie *adj* **1** slimy, wet, moist. **2** disgusting.

slaid[1] *v* to walk with long steps and lounging gait. —*n* **1** an indolent sloven. **2** a procrastination. **3** a heavy, inactive, unwieldy person. **4** a rather disagreeable person.—*adj* slovenly, dirty, disagreeable.

slaid[2] *same as* **slade**[1].

slaid[3] *v* did slide.

slaig *same as* **slag**.

slaiger *v* **1** to besmear with mud, bedaub. **2** to beslobber. **3** to waddle in mud. **4** to eat slowly and carelessly. **5** to make a gurgling noise in the throat. **6** to walk slowly and carelessly.—*n* **1** the act of bedaubing. **2** slatternly work. **3** a quantity of some soft substance. **4** a nasty mess of anything wet or soft. **5** the act of taking food in a slovenly way. **6** food dirtily mixed. **7** the act of making a gurgling sound in the throat. **8** the growl of a dog.

slaigerer *n* **1** one who bedaubs. **2** a dirty walker.

slaigerin *n* a bedaubing.

slaigersom *adj* dirty or slovenly in taking food, walking or working.

slaigh *same as* **slaich**.

slaik[1] *v* **1** to lick with the tongue, to lick up or eat greedily and noisily. **2** to kiss in a slabbering manner. **3** to bedaub, smirch. **4** to lounge, hang about. **5** to carry off and eat sweetmeats, etc, secretly.—*n* **1** a lick with the tongue. **2** a slabbering or wet kiss. **3** anything laid hold of secretly in small portions. **4** a small quantity of anything soft, semiliquid or viscous that smears. **5** such a quantity of such a substance applied to anything. **6** a daub, smear, dirty mark. **7** a slight wipe or brush-over or bedaubing. **8** a careless wash. **9** the act of bedaubing or smearing. **10** a slight stroke. **11** a pat, slap. **12** a low, mean sneak.

slaik[2] *n* vegetable, oozy stuff in river beds.

slaiker *n* **1** a dauber. **2** a sneak.

slaiky *adj* **1** streaked with dirt. **2** used of thick mucus in the mouth, as in great thirst.

slain *n* a wooded cleugh (qv) or precipice.

slaines *n in phr* **letter of slaines** letters subscribed, in the case of slaughter, by the wife or executors of the one slain, acknowledging that satisfaction has been given or otherwise soliciting the pardon of the offender.

slainge *n* one who clandestinely carries off anything that seems palatable.

slaipie *n* **1** a mean fellow. **2** a plate-licker.—*adj* indolent, slovenly.

slair *v* **1** to lick up in a slatternly manner. **2** to eat greedily and noisily. **3** to gobble one's food. **4** to outstrip in eating.

slairg *n* a quantity of any semifluid substance.—*adj* slimy, viscous, adhesive.—*v* **1** to bedaub. **2** to plaster. **3** to besmear with mud. **4** to beslobber. **5** to take food in a slovenly or careless manner. **6** to walk slowly and carelessly.

slairgie *adj* **1** unctuous. **2** slimy, adhesive.

slairk *v* **1** to lick with the tongue. **2** to lick up greedily. **3** to wet. **4** to smear.—*n* **1** a lick with the tongue. **2** a pat. **3** a slap. **4** a daub. **5** a slaik (qv).

slairp *v* **1** to lick up in a slatternly manner. **2** to eat greedily and noisily. **3** to slairg (qv).—*n* a slovenly woman.—*adj* **1** slovenly. **2** handless.

slairt *v* **1** to lick up in a slatternly manner. **2** to gobble. **3** to outdo in eating. **4** to outdo. **5** to go about sluggishly.—*n* a silly, dastardly fellow.—*adj* **1** slovenly. **2** handless.

slairy *v* **1** to dedaub through carelessness. **2** food, etc, taken so as to bedaub one's clothes.

slaister *v* **1** to be engaged in wet, dirty work. **2** to bedaub, bespatter. **3** to make a wet, sloppy or dirty mess. **4** to move clumsily through a muddy road. **5** to do anything in a dirty, slovenly, careless or awkward way.—*n* **1** a dirty, disgusting mess. **2** working in a mess. **3** the act of bedaubing. **4** a miscellaneous mixture. **5** slovenly work. **6** a lazy, untidy worker. **7** a sloven.

slaistering *n* liquid spilt by carelessness.

slaister-kyte *n* **1** a foul feeder. **2** a gormandizer.

slaisters *n* **1** a slovenly, dirty person. **2** one who bedaubs himself.

slaistry, slaistery *adj* **1** wet, dirty, messy. **2** apt to spill. **3** slovenly, careless, untidy.—*n* **1** dirty work. **2** drudgery. **3** kitchen refuse.

slait[1] *n* the track of cattle through standing corn.

slait[2] *v* **1** to level. **2** to disparage. **3** to depreciate. **4** to abuse grossly, maltreat. **5** to wipe.

slait[3] *v* pret did slit.

slait[4] *n* a dirty, slovenly person.—*adj* **1** dirty slovenly. **2** careless in dress.

slaither *v* to flatter.

slaiver *same as* **slaver**.

slake[1], **slake**[2] *same as* **slaik**[1], **slaik**[2].

slake[3] *same as* **slack**[3].

slake[4] *n* **1** a rocky hill. **2** wasteland near the shore, covered at high tide.

slakken *n in phr* **slakkens o' night** night watches.
slaky *same as* **slaiky**.
slam *v* **1** to beat, bang. **2** to do anything violently. —*n* the sound of a bang.
slam *n* a portion of anything acquired by force or craft.
slamach, slammach *v* **1** to slobber. **2** to eat hastily and in a slovenly manner. **3** to eat stolen food. **4** to seize unfairly.—*n* **1** a large quantity of soft food swallowed hastily and in slovenly fashion. **2** food gained by force or craft.
slammachs *n* gossamer.
slammikin *n* **1** a drab. **2** a slut. **3** an untidy person.
slamp *adj* **1** pliant, supple, flexible. **2** plump, taut.
slander *n* scandal.
slane *same as* **slain**.
slang¹ *n* talk, chat.
slang² *v* slung.
slanger *v* to linger, go slowly.
slank¹ *adj* thin, lanky.
slank² *v* did slink.
slanlas, slanlus *n* the greater plantain.
slant *n* opportunity.
slap¹ *v* **1** to slam a gate, etc. **2** to excel, beat.—*n* a large quantity.—*adv* with sudden force.
slap² *v* to separate threshed grain from broken straw by means of a riddle.—*n* a riddle for separating grain from broken straw before winnowing.
slap³ *n* **1** a narrow pass between two hills. **2** a gap or temporary opening in a hedge, fence, etc. **3** a notch in the edge of a sword.—*v* to break into gaps.
slap-bang *adj* **1** loud. **2** forcible.
slapie *same as* **slaipie**.
slaping *n* the making of a gap.
slapper *n* anything large of its kind.
slapping *adj* **1** tall and strong. **2** stalwart. **3** strapping.
slap-riddle *n* a riddle for separating threshed grain from straw, chaff, etc.
slaps *n* **1** slops. **2** liquor or liquid food of poor quality.
slarg *same as* **slairg**.
slargie *same as* **slairgie**.
slary, slarie *same as* **slairy**.
slash *v* **1** to dash liquid, splash, bespatter. **2** to rush, dash. **3** to walk violently on a wet and muddy road. **4** to lick. **5** to give a slabbering kiss. **6** to work in what is wet and flaccid.—*n* **1** a quantity of anything wet or semiliquid thrown with violence. **2** a heavy shower. **3** a great quantity of broth or other food that may be supped. **4** a violent dash. **5** the act of walking violently through mud or water. **6** a loud, crashing noise. **7** a lick. **8** a slabbering kiss. **9** a light brushing-over. **10** a sloven.—*adv* with violence.
slashy *adj* wet, sloppy, dirty.—*n* a slatternly woman.
slatch *v* **1** to dabble among mire. **2** to move heavily, as in a miry road.—*n* **1** a heavy fall or crash. **2** a sloven, slattern.
slate¹ *v* did slit.
slate² *n* **1** a flat rock. **2** a thin piece of wood nailed to the shank of an oar to prevent it from chafing.
slate³ *adj* slovenly, dirty, careless as to dress.—*n* a dirty sloven.
slate⁴ *same as* **slait²**.
slate ban' *n* **1** a stratum of slate among bands of rock. **2** schist.
slater *n* a woodlouse.
slating *n* **1** a roof. **2** a covering, not necessarily of slates.
slauch, slaugh *n* **1** slime. **2** expectoration. **3** the act of expectorating. **4** a wet covering. **5** a thin film. **6** a haze. **7** mire. **8** the eating of slimy food. **9** the working in a viscous substance.—*v* **1** to bedaub. **2** to do slimy work. **3** to eat slimy food. **4** to expectorate.
slauchie *adj* **1** slimy. **2** flaccid. **3** unctous. **4** slow in speech or motion.
slauchter *n* the destruction of springing grain by grubs.
slauchter-bucht *n* a bucht (qv) or pen in which sheep were killed.

slauke *same as* **slaik²**.
slaukie *same as* **slauchie**.
slaukie-spoken' *adj* drawling in speech.
slaum *v* **1** to slobber. **2** to blubber. **3** to smear.
slaunt *same as* **slant**.
slaupie *same as* **slaipie**.
slaurie *v* **1** to splash with mud. **2** to slander. **3** to scold.—*n* **1** mud. **2** anything gelatinous or viscous, like jelly.
slaver *v* **1** to slobber. **2** to talk fast. **3** to flatter.—*n* **1** slobber. **2** fulsome flattery. **3** plausible speech.
slaver-brewing *adj* causing the saliva to flow.
slavermagullion *n* a foolish, lubberly person.
slavery *adj* **1** slobbering. **2** (*of the weather*) damp, wet.
slaw *adj* slow.
slaw-fittit *adj* slow-footed.
slaw-gaun *adj* slow-going.
slawk *same as* **slaik²**.
slawlie *adj* slowly.
slawm *v* to slobber.
slawmach *same as* **slamach**.
slawmin *n* blubbering.
slawness *n* slowness.
slawpie *same as* **slaipie**.
slay *n* the hand board of a loom.
slay *v* to pulverize soil too much by harrowing.
slayworm *n* the slowworm.
slead *n* a sledge.
sleak, sleake *same as* **slaik¹**.
sleath *same as* **sleeth²**.
sleck *v* to groan when overcharged with food.
sled¹ *v* did slide.
sled² *n* a low cart or framework without wheels for carrying heavy loads.—*v* to slip, miss one's footing.
sled³ *adv* aslant.
sledder *n* one who drives goods on a sled (qv).
slederie *adj* slippery.
sled-full *n* a cartload.
sledge *n* a sledgehammer.
sledging mill *n* a sledgehammer.
sled-saddle *n* a saddle for a horse yoked in a cart.
slee *same as* **sly**.
sleeband *n* an iron band going round the beam of a plough to strengthen it where the coulter is inserted.
sleech *n* **1** silt. **2** sea wrack. **3** the oozy, vegetable substance found in river beds. **4** slime. **5** designing flattery. **6** (*in pl*) foreshores on which silt is deposited by the tide.—*v* to coax, cajole.
sleechy *adj* slimy.
sleegh *same as* **sleech**.
sleek¹ *adj* **1** (*of the ground*) smooth, slippery. **2** sly, cunning. **3** plausible.—*adv* slyly, stealthily.—*v* **1** to smooth the hair. **2** to fill a measure level at the top. **3** to fill to overflowing. **4** to lay out carefully. **5** to slip neatly under cover. **6** to flatter, soothe, propitiate. **7** to work or walk in a sly manner.
sleek² *same as* **slick³**.
sleek³ *n* **1** sleet. **2** snow and rain mixed.
sleek⁴ *same as* **sleech**.
sleeked-ful *n* a level measureful.
sleeken *v* to make sleek.
sleeker *n* an instrument for smoothing and stretching leather.
sleek-gabbit *adj* **1** smooth-tongued. **2** flattering.
sleekie¹, sleeky *adj* **1** sly, crafty, insinuating. **2** deceitful.—*n* **1** a person of sly, fawning disposition. **2** a term of endearment for a child.
sleekie² *adj* sleety.
sleekit *adj* **1** smooth and glossy. **2** unruffled. **3** smooth-tongued. **4** plausible. **5** cunning, sly. **6** hypocritical.
sleekit-gabbit *adj* smooth-tongued.
sleekit-like *adj* **1** sly. **2** cunning.
sleekitly *adv* **1** artfully. **2** cajolingly. **3** slyly.
sleekitness *n* **1** fair show. **2** wheedling.
sleekly *adv* **1** smoothly, easily. **2** slyly.

sleek-warm *adj* sleek and warm.
sleeky-tongued *adj* of plausible speech.
sleely *adv* 1 cleverly, skilfully. 2 slyly.
sleeness *n* slyness.
slee-nested *adj* (*used of birds' eggs*) laid or hatched in a cunningly hidden nest.
sleenge *same as* **slounge**[1].
sleenger *n* an idle lounger.
sleenie *n* a guinea.
sleep *v* 1 (*used of a limb*) to be benumbed through cold or want of circulation. 2 (*of a top*) to spin so fast and smoothly that no movement is visible. 3 (*in law*) to be dormant or in abeyance. 4 (*with* in) to oversleep oneself.
sleep-drink *n* a sleeping draught.
sleeper *n* the dunlin.
sleep-hungry *adj* sleepy, craving for sleep.
sleepies *n* 1 field brome grass. 2 wild oats.
sleepin'-fou *adj* dead-drunk.
Sleepin' Maggie *n* 1 a top. 2 a kind of humming top.
sleepin' room *n* a bedroom.
sleepit *v* slept.
sleepry *adj* sleepy.
sleep-sang *n* a lullaby.
sleepy-dose *n* the ragwort.
sleepy-fivvers *n* 1 a disease affecting a patient with a strong tendency to sleep. 2 laziness at work.
sleepy-heid, -heidit *adj* sleepy. 2 stupid.
Sleepy Maggy *same as* **Sleepin' Maggie**.
sleesh *n* a slice.
sleet *n* a load.
sleetch *same as* **sleech**.
sleeth[1] *adj* sly, cunning.
sleeth[2] *adj* slothful.—*n* 1 a sloven. 2 a sluggard.
sleeth-like *adj* 1 idiotic. 2 sottish.
sleethy *adj* slovenly.
sleeve-button *v* to put on sleeve buttons.
slegger *n* 1 a janker. 2 a pole fixed to the axle of two high wheels, used for carrying trees.
slegie *adj* smooth.
sleicht *same as* **slight**[1].
sleik[1] *same as* **sleech**.
sleik[2] *same as* **slick**[1].
sleik worm *n* a worm bred in the ooze of river beds.
sleip-eyed *adj* 1 with the inside turned out. 2 disdainfully rejected.
sleipit *v* slept.
sleitchock *n* a flattering woman. *See* **sleech**.
slekit *same as* **sleekit**.
slenk *v* slunk.
slerg *same as* **slairg**.
slerk *same as* **slairk**.
slerp *same as* **slairp**.
slester *same as* **slaister**.
slesterin' *adj* 1 untidy. 2 besmeared with food.
sletch *same as* **sleech**.
sleug *n* 1 a queer-looking person. 2 an ill-behaved fellow.
sleugh-hound *n* a sleuthhound.
sleumin *adj* 1 backbiting. 2 gossipy. 3 given to raising or spreading reports.—*n* 1 a faint rumour. 2 hearsay.
sleutch *v* 1 to slouch. 2 to lounge about. 3 to shirk work or danger.
sleuth[1] *adj* 1 hungry. 2 voracious. 3 keen.
sleuth[2] *v* 1 to act slothfully. 2 to work carelessly. 3 to neglect.
sleuthan, sleuthun *n* a lazy, good-for-nothing person.
slever *same as* **slaiver**.
slevery *same as* **slavery**.
slew[1] *v* to edge round, avoid.
slew[2] *n* a moor.
slewie *v* to walk with a heavy, swinging gait.—*n* the act of walking with such a gait.
slib, slibbie *adj* slippery.
slibber *n* 1 slipperiness. 2 a cause of slipperiness.

slibberkin, slibrikin *adj* sleek, glossy.—*n* a term of endearment.
slicht[1], **slicht**[2] *same as* **slight**[1], **slight**[2].
slicht[3] *n* 1 sleight. 2 a trick. 3 the knack of doing anything.
slicht-me-not *adj* not to be slighted.
slick[1] *same as* **sleek**[1].
slick[2] *same as* **sleech**.
slick[3] *n* a measure of fruit, etc, containing 40 pounds.
slickit *same as* **sleekit**.
slick-tongued *adj* 1 smooth-tongued. 2 plausible.
slick worm *n* a worm bred in the ooze of rivers.
slid *adj* 1 slippery. 2 sly, cunning. 3 smooth-tongued. 4 wheedling.
slidder, slider *v* 1 to slide, slip. 2 to make slippery. 3 to slip away quietly. 4 to walk with a lazy, slouching gait. 5 to pronounce indistinctly from rapid speaking, to slur one's words. 6 to delay without reason.—*n* 1 ice. 2 the slide of a scale. 3 loose stones in large numbers lying on a hillside. 4 the place where such stones lie.—*adj* 1 slippery. 2 unstable.
slidderin' *adj* 1 slippery. 2 unstable.
sliddery, sliddry *adj* 1 (*used of food*) loose and flaccid, easily eaten. 2 slippery, smooth. 3 sly, deceitful, not trustworthy. 4 squandering, spendthrift. 5 mutable, fleeting, uncertain.
slide *v* 1 to go quickly or unobserved. 2 to steal away, slip off. 3 to pass quietly. 4 to sneak. 5 to carry stealthily. 6 to fib.—*n* 1 passage, passing away unnoticed. 2 a fib, a deviation from truth.
slider[1] *n* 1 a skate. 2 a round case or stand for a decanter, which can be passed along an uncovered table.
slider[2] a prtion of ice cream between two wafers.
slide-thrift *n* the game of 'first off the board' at draughts.
slidin' *adj* given to fibbing.
slidness *n* 1 slipperiness. 2 smoothness of metre.
slieck *same as* **slick**[3].
sliek *same as* **sleech**.
sliep *v* to slip.
slieth *n* 1 a sloven. 2 a sluggard.—*adj* slothful.
slieth-like *adj* 1 idiotic. 2 sottish.
slieve fish *n* the cuttlefish.
sliggy *adj* 1 deceitful, sly. 2 loquacious.
slight[1] *v* 1 to dismantle, demolish. 2 to forsake, neglect, jilt. 3 (*used of time*) to while away.—*n* the act of one who jilts a woman.
slight *adj* 1 smooth, slippery. 2 worthless in character, unscrupulous.
slightly *adv* slightingly.
slike *same as* **sleech**.
slim *adj* 1 insufficient. 2 naughty, worthless. 3 sly. —*n* a careless workmen.—*v* 1 to scamp work. 3 to slur over. 4 to trifle.
slime *v* 1 to idle when not watched. 2 to render eye-service.
slimer *n* 1 an eye-servant. 2 one who cannot be trusted to work unwatched.
slimly *adv* 1 slightly, thinly. 2 superficially. 3 hastily.
slimmer *adj* 1 delicate. 2 easily hurt. 3 slender.
slim-o'er *n* work carelessly done.
sling *v* 1 to strike. 2 to walk with a long stride.—*n* 1 a throw, cast. 2 a blow. 3 a long, striding step. —*adv* 1 with a long, quick step. 2 like a stone from a sling.
slinge *same as* **slounge**[1].
slinger *v* 1 to move unevenly. 2 to reel. 3 to be in danger of upsetting.
slink[1] *v* to cheat, gull, deceive.—*n* 1 a cheat. 2 a greedy starveling, one that would slyly purloin and devour everything. 3 a sneak.—*adj* (*used of coin*) false, forged.
slink[2] *n* 1 the flesh of an animal prematurely born. 2 ill-fed veal. 3 inferior meat.
slink[3] *adj* 1 lank, slender. 2 not fed. 3 poor, insolvent. 4 of no account.—*n* 1 a tall, limber person. 2 a weak, starved creature. 3 anything poor and weak of its kind.
slink[4] *n* 1 greasy mud. 2 sludge.
slink-beast *n* a weak or worthless animal.

slinken *v* to grow long and thin.
slinkin *n* deceit.— *adj* deceitful.
slink-kid *n* an aborted kid.
slink o' veal *n* **1** veal from an aborted calf. **2** a term of reproach for a person.
slinky *adj* **1** tall and slender. **2** lank.
slink-veal *n* the flesh of a very young calf.
slint *n* a slovenly, untidy, awkward man.
slinter *n* a slint (qv).
slip[1] *v* **1** to let slip. **2** to convey by stealth. **3** to slit. **4** to open with a sharp point.—*n* **1** a trick. **2** an upper petticoat. **3** a loose frock. **4** a stripling. **5** a growing girl. **6** a delicate, slender person. **7** a slit, incision. **8** a wooden frame on the top of a cart to enlarge its capacity. **9** a certain quantity of yarn as it comes from the reel, containing twelve cuts.
slip[2] *adj* glib.
slip-airn *n* an oval ring connecting the plough with the swingletrees.
slip awe' *v* to die.
slip-body *n* a loose bodice.
slip-by *n* **1** a careless performance. **2** a pretence at anything. **3** a makeshift.
slip coffin *n* a coffin with a hinged bottom, allowing the corpse to fall out when lowered into the grave.
slip-ma-labour, ~-lawber *n* **1** a careless worker. **2** an unreliable servant.—*adj* careless in working, perfunctory.
slipper *n* slippery ice.
slippery *same as* **sleepry**.
slippit *adj* **1** slipped. **2** escaped from restraint. **3** aborted.
slippy *adj* **1** slippery. **2** sly. **3** untrustworthy. **4** quick, sharp, prompt.
slipshod *adj* wearing shoes but not stockings.
slip-slaps *n* thin liquid food, slops.
slister *same as* **slaister**.
slit[1] *n* **1** a splinter. **2** a splinter of rotten timber.
slit[2] *n* a particular sheep mark.
slite *v* to rip up anything sewed.—*n* the act of ripping up.
slither *same as* **slidder**.
slithery *same as* **sliddery**.
slithy *adj* slippery.
slitter[1] *n* a sloven, slattern.
slitter[2] *n* a break in cloth where the woof has given way and only the warp is left.
slittery *adj* sluttish.
slittie *n* a small slit.
slive *n* a slice.
sliver[1] *n* a large, thin slice of beef, etc, cut off.
sliver, slivver *n* slaver, saliva dribbling from the mouth.— *v* **1** to slobber. **2** to give wet kisses. **3** to eat untidily.
slivery *adj* slavering.
slo *n* the porous bone inside the horns of cattle.
sloak[1] *n* **1** a bog. **2** a slough.
sloak[2], **sloak**[3] *same as* **slack**[2], **slack**[4].
sloaking *n* a drenching.
sloan *n* a greedy, covetous person.
sloan *n* a scolding match.
sloap *n* a lazy, tawdry woman.
sloat *v* to drink plentifully.—*n* a voracious fellow.
sloatch *same as* **slotch**.
slobber[1] *v* **1** to work untidily. **2** to muddle. **3** to fit loosely.
slobber[2] *same as* **slubber**.
slobbery *adj* viscous, sticky.
sloblands *n* flat, muddy foreshores.
sloch[1] *v* **1** to expectorate. **2** to take food in a slovenly, disgusting manner. **3** to work in a viscid substance.—*n* **1** mucus, phlegm, slime. **2** the act of expectorating. **3** the working carelessly in any sticky stuff.
sloch[2] *v* to do anything carelessly.
sloch[3] *n* **1** the core of a horn. **2** the sheath of a straw, pea, bean, etc.
sloch[4], **sloch**[5], **sloch**[6] *same as* **slack**[2], **slack**[3], **slack**[4].
slochan *n* a lubberly fellow.
slocher *v* **1** to suffer from cold, asthma bronchitis, etc. **2** to take liquid food in a slobbering manner. **3** to be slovenly

in dress and gait. **4** (*used of a pig*) to wallow in mud.—*n* **1** difficult breathing from asthma. **2** the noise of breathing through mucus. **3** the taking food in a slobbering manner. **4** one who breathes with difficulty. **5** a slovenly eater. **6** an untidy, slovenly person.
slochie *adj* slimy, dirty, disgusting.
slock[1], **slock**[2], **slock**[3] *same as* **slack**[2], **slack**[3], **slack**[4].
slock[4] *same as* **sloch**[1].
slocken *v* **1** to slake. **2** to drench. **3** to quench thirst. **4** to quench a fire.
slockener, slockening *n* a thirst-quencher.
slocker *same as* **slocher**.
slocking *n* **1** a drenching. **2** a quenching of thirst.
slodge *same as* **sladge**.
sloe *same as* **slo**.
slogan *n* a to-name used to distinguish a person from others of the same name.
slogg *same as* **slag**.
slogger *v* **1** to go about in a slovenly way or with stockings hanging down about the ankles. **2** to eat in a greedy or slovenly manner.—*n* a dirty sloven.
sloggerin *adj* slovenly.
sloggorne *same as* **slughorne**.
slogie *n* a loose nightgown hanging down to the knees.
slogy, sogy-riddle *n* a wide-meshed riddle, used for potatoes, onions, etc.
sloit *n* **1** a lazy, stupid, dirty fellow. **2** a sloven.—*v* (*with* **awa'**) to pass on carelessly.
sloiter *v* **1** to engage in any wet and dirty work. **2** to eat in a slovenly, dirty way. **3** to breathe through nasal mucus. **4** to work or walk in a slovenly, loitering manner. **5** to over-nurse.—*n* **1** a wet, dirty mess. **2** nasal mucus. **3** a sloven, one dirty in person or at food. **4** the taking of food in a slovenly manner. **5** the noise made in eating thus. **6** the doing of anything, or walking, in a slovenly fashion. **7** over-nursing.
slok, sloke *v* to slake.
sloke *same as* **sleech**.
sloken, slokin *same as* **slocken**.
slomie *same as* **sloomy**.
slong *same as* **slung**[1].
slonk *n* **1** a mire. **2** a ditch. **3** the noise made by wading or sinking in a miry bog and when walking with shoes full of water.—*v* **1** to wade through a mire. **2** to sink in mud.
slooch *n* a term of contempt.—*v* to slouch.
slooie *v* **1** to fleece one by a trick or fraud. **2** to take advantage of one in a bargain.
sloom[1] *n* a report. *See* **slooming**.
sloom[2] *n* **1** a slumber. **2** a light doze. **3** an unsettled sleep.—*v* **1** to slumber. **2** to doze lightly. **3** to become powerless through fear, etc. **4** to move slowly and silently. **5** to wander aimlessly or sneakingly. **6** (*used of plants*) to become flaccid and droop through frost. **7** to waste, decay.
sloomin' *adj* **1** slinking. **2** sneaking.
slooming *adj* **1** backbiting. **2** gossipy. **3** given to raising reports.—*n* **1** a faint rumour. **2** a report, hearsay.
sloomit *adj* **1** sullen, evil-looking. **2** with a hang-dog air. **3** wily, sly.
sloomy *adj* **1** sleepy, sluggish. **2** (*used of animals*) relaxed, enfeebled. **3** (*of vegetables*) damp, beginning to putrefy.
sloomy corn *n* grain not well filled.
sloon *n* a suppressed rumour.
sloonge *same as* **slounge**[1].
sloop *v* (*with* **doun**) to descend obliquely.
sloos *n* **1** a sluice. **2** a dash of water.—*v* to dash water from a vessel.
sloot *same as* **slute**.
slooter *same as* **slutter**.
sloottery *same as* **sluttery**.
slop[1] *same as* **slap**[3].
slop[2] *v* to slap.—*n* a slap, blow.
slop[3], **slop**[4] *same as* **slope**[1], **slope**[2].
slope[1], **slop** *v* **1** to cheat, defraud. **2** to evade payment of debts, rent, etc.

slope², **slop** *n* **1** a smart, tight-fitting article of dress, made of white or striped unbleached linen, in shape a cross between a sleeved waistcoat and a common jacket. **2** a cotton smock-frock.

sloped yaw *n* an open drain.

slopin *n* a flight from creditors. *See* **slope**¹.

slopping *adj* sloping.

slorach *v* **1** to work in a semiliquid substance in an untidy way. **2** to eat in a dirty, slovenly way. **3** to expectorate.— *n* **1** work dirtily done. **2** the eating of food in a disgusting way. **3** a dirty, disgusting mess.

slorg *same as* **slork**.

slork *v* **1** to make a disagreeable noise in eating. **2** to eat up in large mouthfuls. **3** to walk through slush with wet shoes that regorge the water in them.

slorp *v* **1** to swallow ungracefully and noisily. **2** to draw in the breath convulsively. **3** to bungle. **4** to do anything in a noisy, slatternly way.—*n* **1** a sop. **2** a mess of food. **3** a spoonful of food. **4** a spoonful of food taken ungracefully. **5** a sloven. **6** an uncouth person.

slorpie *adj* slovenly, tawdry.

slorping *adj* slovenly, tawdry.

slorrich *same as* **slorach**.

slort *n* a lazy, stupid, slovenly fellow.

slot¹ *n* **1** a sum of money. **2** a windfall of money unlooked for.

slot² *n* a hollow in a hill or in the human body.

slot³ *n* the track or trail of a traveller.

slot⁴, **slott** *n* **1** a crossbar. **2** a wooden bar or support in a cart.—*v* to bolt, bar, fasten securely.

slotch *n* **1** an idle, lounging, slovenly fellow. **2** a glutton, a greedy, slovenly eater.—*v* to lounge about in a lazy, slovenly fashion.

slote *n* the bolt or bar of a door.

sloth *same as* **sleuth**².

slott *same as* **sloit**.

slotter *same as* **sloiter**.

slotter-hodge *n* a dirty, slovenly fellow in person and at food.

slottry *adj* **1** slumbering, drowsy. **2** inactive.

slouan *same as* **slowan**.

slouch¹ *v* (*with* **away**) to slip away from a place where there is anything to do or to fear.

slouch² *v* to wet, drench.

slouch³ *same as* **slough**³.

slouching *n* a wetting, drenching.

sloug, slough *n* **1** a slow, idle, lounging person. **2** a lazy, awkward fellow.

slough¹ *n* **1** a husk, the skin of a berry. **2** a coat. **3** a petticoat. **4** a warm wrapper.

slough² *n* **1** a voracious eater and drinker. **2** a lean, hungry person or animal. **2** a mean, selfish person.

slough³ *n* a deep ravine.

slough⁴ *same as* **sloug**.

slough-dog, ~-hound *same as* **sleugh-hound**.

slouk *n* **1** various species of algae. **2** the oozy vegetable substance in river beds.

sloum¹ *same as* **sloom**².

sloum² *n* the green scum that gathers on stagnant pools.

sloun *same as* **slowan**.

sloung *same as* **slung**¹.

slounge¹ *v* **1** to lounge, idle about, walk with a slovenly gait. **2** to go from place to place catering for a meal. **3** to hang the ears, look sour.—*n* **1** an idler. **2** a skulking, sneaking, vagabond fellow. **3** a glutton. **4** a stupid, dull-looking fellow. **5** a dog that goes about with hanging ears, prying for food.

slounge² *v* **1** to plunge. **2** to splash, dash water. **3** to make a plunging noise.—*n* **1** a plunge, splash. **2** its sound. **3** a great fall of rain. **4** a complete drenching.

slounge o' weet *n* a heavy fall of rain.

slounger *n* **1** a loafer. **2** an idle sneak. **3** one who goes about sponging for food.

sloungin'-like *adj* having a downcast, tired appearance or

gait.

sloupe *n* a stupid, silly person.

slouper *n* **1** a sloven. **2** a knave who tries to slip off stealthily.

slouster *same as* **slaister**.

slouter *v* to eat up greedily and untidily.

slouth *same as* **sleuth**².

slouthfu' *adj* inactive, idle.

slouth-hound *n* a sleuthhound.

slowan *n* **1** a sloven. **2** a disreputable character. **3** a sleuthhound.—*v* to idle one's time.

slow-belly *n* a louse.

slow-hound *n* a sleuthhound.

slow-thumbs *n* one who dawdles at work.

sloy *n* a slide.

sloyt *same as* **sloit**.

sluan *same as* **slowan**.

slub *n* slime.

slubber¹ *v* **1** to swallow with a gurgling noise. **2** to work carelessly. **3** to idle.—*n* **1** mire, mud slush. **2** the act of swallowing with a gurgling noise. **3** food overboiled or of a flaccid nature.

slubber² *n* half-twined or ill-twined woollen thread.

slubber-de-gullion *n* a mean, dirty fellow.

slubbery *adj* **1** slimy. **2** flaccid. **3** (*of food*) overboiled.

slubby *adj* slimy.

sluch *same as* **slutch**.

slucken *same as* **slunken**.

sludder *n* **1** a liquid or semiliquid mess. **2** a quagmire. **3** dirty, slatternly work.—*v* **1** to eat in a slovenly way. **2** to eat noisily. **3** to articulate indistinctly. **4** to slur over. **5** to work in a careless or dirty way.

sluddery *adj* **1** soft. **2** flaccid. **3** slimy. **4** muddy.

sludge *same as* **sladge**.

slue *v* **1** to twist. **2** to slew.

slug¹ *n* a loose wrapper or upper covering worn for dirty work.

slug², **slug road** *n* a road through a narrow defile between two hills.

slug³ *n* **1** a sluggard. **2** a short sleep.—*v* to move slowly.

slug⁴ *n* in *phr* **a slug for the drink** one who drinks continually but never becomes drunk.

sluggy *v* to swallow greedily.

slugh *same as* **sloug**.

slughan *n* a lazy, good-for-nothing person.

slughorne, sloggorne *n* a hereditary feature or characteristic of a family or race. *See* **slogan**.

sluice, sluich *n* **1** the flow of water from a sluice. **2** a dash of water. **3** an outburst.—*v* to dash water out of a vessel or over a person or thing.

sluich-board *n* a sluice gate.

sluip *same as* **slype**.

sluist *n* **1** a large, heavy person. **2** a sluggish person. **3** an ungraceful person.

sluit *same as* **slute**.

sluiter *same as* **slutter**.

slum *same as* **sloom**².

slammish *v* to trifle away one's time.

slump¹ *n* **1** a marsh. **2** a swamp. **3** a dull noise of something falling into a hole.—*v* **1** to sink or stick in a wet, miry place. **2** to fall suddenly into anything wet or miry. **3** to plump in.—*adv* plump.

slump² *n* **1** a large quantity. **2** a lump sum.

slump³ *n* a remnant.

slumpert *n* **1** a large quantity. **2** what is not measured.

slumpie *adj* marshy, swampy.

slump number *n* the whole number.

slump-wise *adv* **1** in the lump or mass. **2** without measure.

slump-work *n* work taken in the lump.

sluneoch, sluneuch *n* a brutal, mischievous person.—*v* to lounge idly about.

slung¹ *n* a sling.—*v* **1** to sling. **2** to walk with long steps and a swinging gait.

slung[2] *same as* **slounge**[2].

slunge[1], **slunge**[2] *same as* **slounge**[1], **slounge**[2].

slunk[1] *same as* **slonk**.

slunk[2] *n* 1 a lazy shirker of work or duty. 2 a sneak.

slunk[3] *same as* **slink**[2].

slunk[4] *n* a tall, thin, awkward person.

slunken *adj* lank, lean, empty in appearance, like a tired horse not fed fully on its journey.

slunker *v* to slink, go off stealthily.

slunkie *same as* **slinky**.

slunyoch *same as* **sluneoch**.

slupe *same as* **slype**.

slur *v* to sneer, make fun of.—*n* scorn.

slure *v* 1 to swallow ungracefully. 2 to pour. 3 to pour dirty water on one.

slurich *same as* **slorach**.

slush *n* 1 a wet, muddy place, plashy ground. 2 a pool. 3 dirty water. 4 slops. 5 sloppy food. 6 weak liquor. 7 a flow of water. 8 a large body of water. 9 any liquid or semiliquid stuff dashed or thrown. 10 an indefinite quantity of anything. 11 a dirty sloven, a drudge. 12 the act of walking with slatternly, trailing steps or through soft mud or water. 13 the noise of such walking. 14 the doing of drudgery or dirty work. 15 misshapen, worn shoes.—*v* 1 to dash water. 2 to splash. 3 to fall in a soft, wet mass. 4 to walk through mud or water. 5 to walk with a slovenly gait. 6 to do rough, dirty work. 7 to drudge. 8 to 'toil and moil'.—*adv* with violence.

slushie *adj* 1 abounding in melting snow. 2 weak, sloppy, wishy-washy.

slushit *adj* 1 slovenly. 2 untidy in dress.

slushitness *n* 1 slovenliness. 2 untidiness.

slust *same as* **sluist**.

slutch *n* a1 sloppy mess. 2 a hanger-on. 3 a parasite.—*v* to move heavily, as in a deep, soft road.

slute *n* 1 a very contemptuous term. 2 a slow, lazy animal. 3 a lazy, clumsy person. 4 a sloven. 5 a glutton. 6 a drunkard. 7 a low, greedy fellow.

sluther *same as* **sludder**.

sluthery *same as* **sluddery**.

slutter *v* 1 to spill or slobber in cooking or eating food. 2 to work in a slovenly manner. 3 to loiter, dawdle at work. 4 to loung about lazily. 5 to snore. 6 to make a noise through the nostrils when half asleep.—*n* 1 a big, clumsy sloven. 2 a glutton. 3 a noisy splash.

sluttery, sluttrie *adj* slovenly.

sly *v* 1 to go or come silently or stealthily. 2 to look in a sly manner. 3 to place or remove slyly. 4 to escape from a task.

slyaag *same as* **slag**.

slyaager *same as* **slaiger**.

slycht *same as* **slight**[1].

sly-goose *n* the common sheldrake.

slylins *adv* slyly.

slyp *n* 1 a sledge. 2 a whetstone.—*v* to whet a scythe.

slype[1] *v* 1 to strip off, peel. 2 to press gently downwards. 3 to move freely, as a weighty body drawn through mud. 4 to fall over, as a wet furrow from the plough. 5 (*of a plough*) to turn over a furrow.—*n* 1 a sledge used in agriculture. 2 a coarse, worthless fellow. 3 a term of contempt.

slype[2] *adv* aslant, aslope.

slype-eyed *adj* cross-eyed.

slyper *n* 1 one who seemingly wishes to sneak away, from fear of detection. 2 one who is tawdry and slovenly in dress.

slyple *n* a lazy person, a slype (qv).

slyppies *n* roasted peas, eaten with butter.

slyre-lawn *n* a species of lawn.

slyster *same as* **slaister**.

slyte *v* 1 to move easily or smoothly. 2 to sharpen an edged tool.

sma' *adj* 1 small. 2 young.—*n* 1 a small thing. 2 a small sum of money. 3 a small quantity.

sma'-bouket *adj* 1 of small bulk. 2 shrunken.

smacher *n* 1 a large number. 2 a confused crowd. 3 a mess, a mixture. 4 confusion. 5 trash. 6 a fondling term for a child.—*v* 1 to collect in a crowd. 2 to crowd. 3 to eat stealthily or in small pieces what is pleasant to the taste.

smachrie, smachirie *n* 1 a great number. 2 a confused gathering. 3 a miscellaneous collection. 4 a jumble. 5 trash. 6 a hodgepodge of eatables. 7 confectionery.—*adj* trashy, worthless.

smack[1] *n* style, fashion.—*v* to drink with enjoyment.

smack[2] *n* 1 a loud kiss. 2 an instant.—*v* 1 (*of guns*) to give a loud report. 2 to speed.—*adv* with force.

smackie *n* a little kiss.

smacle *n* as much.

smad *v* 1 to stain. 2 to discolour.—*n* 1 a stain. 2 a spot of mud or grease on clothes.

sma' drink *n* very weak beer.

sma' evens *n* a very small quantity.

sma' fairns *n* the intestines, the guts.

sma' folk *n* people of low rank.

smag *n* 1 a small piece. 2 a titbit. 3 anything small and nice.

smagrie, smaggrie *same as* **smachrie**.

sma' oors *n* the very early hours of the morning.

smaicher *same as* **smacher**.

smaichery *same as* **smachrie**.

smaik *n* 1 a mean, scurvy fellow. 2 a sneak. 3 a rascal.

smair, smairie *v* 1 to smear. 2 to besmear.

smair-caryin *same as* **smergh-kerien**.

smair-docken *same as* **smear-docken**.

smairg *v* 1 to bedaub. 2 (*used of sheep*) to smear or salve. See **smear**[1].

smalie *same as* **smally**.

small *same as* **sma'**.

small blue-hawk *n* the merlin.

small doucker *n* the little grebe.

small waters *n* two or three small lochs lying near each other.

small-write *n* small-text in handwriting.

smally *adj* 1 small. 2 puny. 3 undersized.

sma'-maw *n* the common gull.

smarrich *v* 1 to crowd in a confused, secret or underhand way. 2 to work weakly and unskilfully. 3 to eat, talk or work clandestinely. 4 to eat dainties secretly.—*n* 1 a confused crowd. 2 a group of persons engaged in secret work or talk. 3 an untidy heap.

smart *v* 1 to smarten, urge on. 2 to punish.

smash *v* 1 to shiver. 2 to beat down in battle. 3 to beat severely. 4 to hurl with a crash. 5 to push forward vigorously or recklessly.—*n* 1 a heavy, dashing blow. 2 the shreds of anything broken. 3 the sound of breaking.

smashables *n* things liable to be broken, breakages.

sma' sheen *n* fine shoes, dress-shoes.

smasherie *n* 1 the act of smashing. 2 a smash. 3 (*used of an epidemic*) great loss of life.

smashing *adj* 1 big. 2 burly, strapping.

sma' still, sma' still whisky *n* whisky distilled in small stills and thought superior to the product of a large still.

smatchard, smatchart, smatcher, smatchert *n* 1 a pert, impudent child. 2 a scurvy fellow. 3 a small, contemptible person.

smatchet, smatched, smatchit *same as* **smatchard**.

smatter, smathir *v* 1 to break in bits, to smash. 2 (*of children and small objects*) to swarm, crowd or move confusedly. 3 to be busily engaged with trifles. 4 to pretend to work. 5 to work or speak in a slow, hesitating, confused way. 6 to deal in smallwares. 7 (*with* **awa'**) to spend in a trifling way. 8 to consume food by eating often and little at a time.—*n* 1 a heap of small objects in confusion or motion. 2 confusion. 3 the doing of anything awkwardly or confusedly. 4 a little person weak and unskilful at work. 5 a trifle, scrap, a thing of small value. 6 a small sum of money.

smatterie *n* **1** a quantity of small objects. **2** a family of young children. **3** a flock.

smawly *same as* **smally**.

smeadum *same as* **smeddum**.

smeak *same as* **smeek**[1].

smear[1] *v* to rub sheep with a mixture of tar and train oil or butter.—*n* an ointment for smearing sheep.

smear[2] *same as* **smergh**.

smear-docken *n* (*Used in making a salve for stings, sores, etc.*) **1** the dock. **2** the good King Henry.

smearing house *n* a hut for smearing sheep. *See* **smear**[1].

smearing stool *n* a stool with a spoked bottom so as to admit the legs of a sheep and keep it steady during smearing. *See* **smear**[1].

smearless *same as* **smerghless**.

smeary *n* **1** a sheep that has been smeared. **2** a person all besmeared.—*adj* greasy, viscid. *See* **smear**[1].

smechle *v* to fumble.

smeddum *n* **1** the powder of ground malt. **2** dust. **3** powder. **4** force of character. **5** mettle, spirit. **6** liveliness. **7** sagacity, good sense, intelligence.

smeddumfu' *adj* **1** intelligent. **2** full of spins or sagacity.

smeddumless *adj* lacking intelligence, spirit or sagacity.

smeeg *n* a kiss.

smeek[1] *v* **1** to smoke. **2** to dry in smoke. **3** to fumigate. **4** to kill with smoke.—*n* **1** smoke. **2** tobacco smoke. **3** fumes. **4** a pungent, foul smell. **5** a stuffy, close atmosphere. **6** a quarrel, high words between husband and wife.

smeek[2] *v* **1** to infect. **2** to smite.

smeeky *adj* **1** smoky. **2** giving out a foul, pungent smell.

smeer[1] *same as* **smear**[1].

smeer[2] *same as* **smergh**.

smeerikin *n* **1** a hearty kiss. **2** a stolen kiss.

smeerlese *same as* **smerghless**.

smeeth *adj* smooth.—*adv* smoothly.

smeethly *adv* smoothly.

smeethness *n* smoothness.

smelk *same as* **smeek**[1].

smell *v* **1** to feel. **2** to impart a smell.—*n* **1** a small quantity. **2** a small amount of liquor.

smeller *n* a small quantity of drink.

smelt[1] *n* **1** salmon fry. **2** a term of contempt, applied generally to a child.

smelt[2] *n* a smooth spot on the sea.

smeltering *adj* applied to the roaring sound of devouring flames.

smerg *same as* **smairg**.

smergh, smer *n* **1** marrow. **2** pith. **3** vigour of mind or body. **4** sense.

smergh-kerien *n* the spinal marrow.

smerghless *adj* **1** pithless. **2** untidy. **3** insipid. **4** languid. **5** senseless.

smert *same as* **smart**.

smertish *adj* rather smart.

smertry *adj* **1** savoury. **2** fat, marrowy.

smeth *same as* **smeeth**.

smeu *same as* **smeuth**.

smeuch *v* **1** to smoke fiercely. **2** to emit fumes. **3** to drizzle thickly.—*n* **1** smoke. **2** fumes. **3** smell. **4** thick, drizzling rain.

smeuchie *adj* **1** smoky. **2** drizzly.

smeuchter *v* **1** to burn slowly with much smoke. **2** to drizzle. **3** to work slowly and unskilfully. **4** to eat slowly and sparingly. **5** to consume or waste slowly.—*n* **1** a fire buming slowly with much smoke. **2** a drizzling shower or wetting mist. **3** the doing of work slowly and unskilfully. **4** slow and sparing eating. **5** a slow wasting.

smeuth *n* the willow warbler.

smewlikin *adj* sly.

smewy *adj* **1** savoury. **2** marrowy. **3** fat.

smiach *n* sagacity, smeddum (qv).

smiaggered *adj* besmeared.

smick[1] *n* **1** a dainty. **2** anything somewhat old and worthless.

smick[2] *n* **1** a spot. **2** a tincture.

smicker *v* **1** to smirk. **2** to smile fawningly. **3** to grin.

smick-smick-smack *n* the sound of continuous kissing.

smiddle *v* **1** to smuggle. **2** to hide. **3** to work stealthily.

smiddy *n* **1** a blacksmith's workshop. **2** a brisk conversational gathering such as takes place in a smiddy.

smiddy boll *n* payment in grain made to a blacksmith.

smiddy coom, ~ gum *n* small coal used in a smithy.

smiddy seat *n* a croft attached to a smithy.

smiddy sparks *n* sparks from a smith's anvil.

smid meal *n* a coarse meal. *See* **smeddum**.

smikker *same as* **smicker**.

smill *n* **1** fragments. **2** leavings.—*v* to fall in pieces.

smiok *n* a dish of good food.—*v* to feed on the best.

smir *same as* **smirr**.

smircle *same as* **smirkle**.

smird[1] *v* to gibe, jeer.

smird[2] *n* a smart tap on the knuckles or on any other part of the body with the fingertips or with the tip of a tawse (qv).

smirikin *same as* **smeerikin**.

smirk *v* to smile pleasantly.—*n* a pleasant smile.—*adj* **1** pleasant. **2** smiling.

smirkingly *adv* smilingly.

smirkle *v* **1** to smile. **2** to giggle. **3** to laugh in a suppressed way.—*n* **1** a smile. **2** a suppressed laugh.

smirky *adj* **1** smiling. **2** good-natured-looking. **3** cheerful. **4** in good health.

smirky-faced *adj* good-natured-looking.

smirl *n* **1** a roguish trick. **2** a mocking smile. **3** a sneering laugh.—*v* **1** to smirk. **2** to smile or laugh in a mischievous, mocking mood.

smirn *same as* **smirr**.

smirr *n* **1** a drizzle. **2** fine rain.—*v* to drizzle.

smirtle *v* **1** to smile. **2** to giggle. **3** to laugh in a suppressed manner. **4** to smile bashfully.—*n* **1** a smile. **2** a suppressed laugh.

smit[1] *n* a clashing noise.

smit[2] *n* **1** a spot. **2** a stain. **3** infection, contagion. **4** disease. **5** potato disease or blight. **6** a moral stain.—*v* **1** to infect by contagion. **2** to stain, pollute, contaminate. **3** to attack, smite.

smitch[1] *n* **1** a stain, a speck. **2** a spot on the skin, blemish. **3** a moral stain. **4** a slur.

smitch[2] *n* **1** an impudent boy. **2** a chit.

smitchcock *n* a grilled or broiled chicken.

smite[1] *n* **1** a blow. **2** a hit.

smite[2] *n* **1** a mite. **2** an atom. **3** a small portion. **4** a puny, insignificant person.

smith-body *n* a contemptuous term for a blacksmith.

smithereens *n* **1** bits. **2** splinters. **3** shivers.

smithers *n* smithereens (qv).

smithy chat *n* gossip among frequenters of a smithy.

smitsome *adj* infectious.

smittable *adj* infectious.

smittal *same as* **smittle**.

smit-thumbs *n* a pledge for the fulfilment of a bargain by licking and pressing the thumbs.

smittin *adj* infectious.

smittin'-sickness *n* **1** any infectious disease. **2** infection.

smittle *v* to infect by contagion.—*adj* **1** infectious. **2** contagious.

smittleness *n* **1** infection. **2** contagion.

smittlish *adj* **1** infectious. **2** contagious.

smittral *adj* **1** infectious. **2** contagious.

smitty *adj* **1** dirty, smutty. **2** impure.

smoar *same as* **smoor**[1].

smoch *n* the smoke of burning wet, rotten wood. —*v* to burn and smoke like rotten wood.

smocher *v* to breathe with difficulty from cold.

smock-faced *adj* **1** smooth-faced. **2** pale-faced.

smod *same as* **smud**[1].

smoghie *adj* **1** close, stuffy, smoky. **2** sultry.

smoik *same as* **smiok**.

smoir *same as* **smoor**[1].
smoit *n* a foolish or obscene chatterer.
smoke, smok *same as* **smeek**[1].
smoky[1] *n* a chemise.
smoky[2] *n* **1** a smoked haddock. **2** one unsplit and smoked.
smolder *v* to smother.
smollicher *n in phr* **a black smollicher** a person with very dark features.
smolt[1] *adj* **1** (*of the weather*) fair. **2** clear. **3** mild.
smolt[2] *n* a contemptuous name for a child.
smoo[1] *v* **1** to smile placidly or benignantly. **2** to smile, smirk. **3** to laugh in one's sleeve. **4** to suppress a laugh.— *n* a placid or benignant smile.
smoo[2] *v* to sneak off.
smoochter *same as* **smeuchter**.
smoodge, smoog *same as* **smudge**.
smoogle *same as* **smuggle**.
smooin' *adj* **1** sly. **2** sneaking.
smook[1] *v* **1** to put away, hide. **2** to draw on or off, as a stocking. **3** (*with* **about**) to go about clandestinely. **4** to pilfer.
smook[2] *n* a drizzling rain, driving before the wind.
smook[3] *v* to suffocate bees, etc, by burning sulphur.—*n* such suffocation.
smook[4] *adj* thievish, pilfering.
smookie[1] *n* a bird of prey.
smookie[2] *adj* pilfering.
smookit[1] *adj* smoked.
smookit[2] *adj* cunning, artful.
smool[1] *v* to look sulky.—*n* a scowl, a sulky look.
smool[2] *same as* **smuil**.
smoolachan *n* a kiss.
smoolet-like *adj* sulky-looking.
smoor[1] *v* **1** to smother, suffocate, stifle. **3** to oppress by heat. **3** to drown. **4** to suppress. **5** to conceal. **6** to obscure. **7** to extinguish a light.—*n* **1** a stifling smoke. **2** a stuffy atmosphere. **3** a smothering.
smoor[2] *same as* **smirr**.
smoorich[1] *v* **1** to hide, conceal. **2** to kiss.—*n* **1** a stolen kiss. **2** a hearty kiss.
smoorich[2] *n* a cloud of dust, smoke or driving snow, like to choke one.
smoorikin *same as* **smeerikin**.
smoor-thow *n* heavy snow with strong wind threatening to suffocate one.
smoory *adj* **1** close, stifling. **2** hot.
smooshter *same as* **smuist**.
smoost *same as* **smuist**.
smoot[1] *v* **1** to shuffle off. **2** to hide stealthily.
smoot[2] *v* to smother.
smoot[3] *same as* **smout**[1].
smooth[1] *same as* **smeeth**.
smooth[2] *same as* **smeuth**.
smootrikin *adj* tiny and active.—*n* **1** a puny person or animal. **2** a fondling term.
smooze *v* to smoulder.
smore *same as* **smoor**[1].
smorie *same as* **smirr**.
smot, smott, smote *n* **1** a stain. **2** a sheep mark. **3** a number of sheep bearing the same mark. **4** mouldiness gathering on what is kept in a damp place. **5** moral pollution. **6** a slur or stain on character.—*v* **1** to stain. **2** to mark sheep with tar, ruddle, etc.
smote *v*, *adj* smitten.
smotter *v* **1** to besmear. **2** to bespatter.
smoukie[1] *n* **1** a little, cunning, fawning child. **2** a playful epithet applied to a child.
smoukie[2] *n* a species of bird of prey.
smoupsie *n* a stripling.
smourock *same as* **smoorich**[1].
smouster *v* to eat clandestinely.
smout[1] *n* **1** salmon fry. **2** a smolt. **3** a small speckled trout. **4** a small person or animal. **5** a fondling term for a child. **6** a small child. **7** a very small person

smout[2] *adj* (*used of the weather*) clear, fair, mild.
smoutter *v* to eat often and little at a time.
smouty *adj* obscene, smutty.
smow *same as* **smoo**.
smowe *v* to stink.
smucht *n* a smouldering.
smuchty *adj* smoky.
smud[1] *n* **1** a dirty speck. **2** any stain.—*v* to stain, blacken.
smud[2] *n* a stench.
smuddoch *n* a smouldering fire with much smoke.
smudge *v* **1** to laugh quietly or in a suppressed manner. **2** to laugh in one's sleeve.—*n* a suppressed laugh or smile.
smue[1] *same as* **smoo**.
smue[2] *v* **1** to smoke. **2** to drizzle thickly.—*n* **1** thick, stifling smoke. **2** thick, drizzling rain.
smueie *adj* drizzling thickly.
smug[1] *v* **1** to hide, conceal. **2** to go about stealthily. **2** to toy amorously in secret.
smug[2] *v* to dress well.
smug[3] *v* to laugh in one's sleeve.
smuggart *n* a puny and disagreeable person.
smuggle *v* (*with* **up**) to conceal, hide.
smuggle-boots *n* a boys' game.
smuggle-the-gig, ~-gag, ~-keg *n* a boys' game.
smuggling *adv* by means of smuggling.
smuggy *adj* muggy, foggy, drizzling.
smugly *adj* **1** amorous. **2** sly and well-dressed.
smuik *same as* **smook**[3].
smuil *v* **1** to sneak. **2** to slip through one's fingers. **3** (*with* **in**) to wheedle, curry favour. **4** to crumble. **5** to fall in pieces. **6** to cajole. **7** to slip away. —*n* **1** small pieces. **2** fragments. **3** leavings.
smuin *adj* **1** sly. **2** sneaking.
smuir *same as* **smoor**[1].
smuirach *n* very small coal.
smuist *v* **1** to smoulder. **2** to emit smoke.—*n* **1** the act of burning in a smouldering, smoky way. **2** disagreeable smoke. **3** a smouldering, suffocating smell, as of burning sulphur, etc.
smuister[1] *v* (*used of the air*) to smother.
smuister[2] *same as* **smyster**.
smuisty *adj* smoky.
smuke *v* to suffocate with burning sulphur.—*n* such suffocation.
smulachin *adj* puny, looking poorly.
smule *same as* **smuil**.
smult *v* to crop very short.
smurach, smuroch *same as* **smoorich**.
smurachin *same as* **smeerikin**.
smurack, smuragh *n* **1** a slight drizzle. **2** a summer shower. **3** peat dust. **4** a slight smoke.
smure *same as* **smoor**[1].
smurl[1] *same as* **smirl**.
smurl[2] *v* **1** to eat little and slowly. **2** to eat secretly. **3** to waste imperceptibly.
smurlin' *adj* fond of dainties and of eating them secretly.
smurr *same as* **smirr**.
smurtle *same as* **smirtle**.
smusch *n* a short, dark person with abundant hair.
smuschle *same as* **smushle**.
smush[1] *n* **1** smoke. **2** dirt. **3** a disagreeable, sulphurous smell from smoke and dust.—*adj* **1** dirty. **2** stinking.
smush[2] *v* **1** to bruise. **2** to grind to powder. **3** to eat secretly anything got improperly. **4** to waste or decay slowly.—*n* **1** a bruised, crushed mass. **2** anything reduced to pulp or powder. **3** refuse, scraps. **4** refuse hay or straw. **5** a slight, drizzling rain.—*adj* broken, fragmentary.
smushach, smuschach *v* **1** to eat slowly. **2** to decay slowly.—*n* what is small or in fragments. **3** a dainty person, small in stature and dark in complexion.—*adj* **1** small. **2** dark.
smushagh *n* a suffocating smell caused by a smothered fire.

smushlach *n* **1** a bruised, broken, crumbled state. **2** fragments, scraps, leavings.
smushle *v* **1** to eat slowly. **2** to eat in secret. **3** to use slowly. **4** to waste slowly. **5** to drizzle.—*n* **1** eating slowly or secretly. **2** a lot of titbits. **3** a dainty meal or titbit. **4** a person fond of dainties and of secret eating. **5** a small person of dark complexion. **6** a slow wasting. **7** fragments, leavings. **8** a slight, drizzling rain.
smushlin *adj* fond of dainty fare.
smushter *n* dross.
smushy *adj* **1** foul, dirty. **2** stinking.
smuster *n* a large cluster of things.
smutchack *n* a contemptuous name for a child.
smutchless *adj* stainless, spotless.
smyaager *same as* **smiaggered**.
smyach *same as* **smiach**.
smyle *same as* **smuil**.
smyout *same as* **smout**.
smysle *v* to sear.
smyster *v* **1** to work lazily and feebly. **2** to idle sitting over a fire. **3** to talk or laugh to oneself, as in a daydream.—*n* **1** working lazily and feebly. **2** an idle, dreamy state. **3** a weak and unskilful worker. **4** an idler. **5** a listless person.
smytch *n* **1** a puny, pert fellow. **2** an impudent boy. **3** a term of contempt, anger, etc.
smytcher *same as* **smytch**.
smyte *n* **1** a small bit. **2** a particle.
smyteral *n* a collection of small objects.
smytrie, smytterie *n* a collection of small individuals, children, etc.
sna, snaa *n* snow.
snab¹ *n* **1** the projecting part of a hill or rock. **2** the bank, rock or hill that projects. **3** a steep ascent.
snab² *n* **1** a shoemaker. **2** a cobbler. **3** a shoemaking or cobbling apprentice or boy.
snabbie *n* the chaffinch.
snachel *n* a puny, contemptible bantling.
snack¹ *n* a snap.—*v* **1** to snap, bite. **2** to snatch. **3** to break with a snap.
snack² *adj* **1** quick, sharp, alert. **2** smart, clever or cute.—*adv* **1** quickly, cleverly. **2** exactly, to the moment.—*n* **1** a keen, active person. **2** a good bargainer. **3** a person of short stature.
snackel *same as* **snachel**.
snackit *n* a small person of keen, active disposition.
snackly *adv* **1** cleverly, adroitly. **2** intelligently.
snackus *n* a fillip.
snacky *adj* **1** clever, acute. **2** tricky, quirky.
snaff *v* **1** to sniff in a surly, jeering manner. **2** to find fault in a surly manner.
snag¹ *n* **1** a protuberance. **2** the bolt of a door.—*v* to cut off branches with an axe, etc.
snag² *v* **1** to snap, bite. **2** to chide and taunt. **3** to scold severely. **4** to snarl. **5** to banter. **6** to nag.—*n* **1** a snap, bite. **2** a quarrel. **3** a snarl. **4** a violent scolding. **5** a slight repast, snack. **6** a dainty. **7** any kind of confectionery. **8** (*in pl*) shares, very small things.
snagger *v* **1** to snore loudly and gruntingly. **2** to snarl.—*n* **1** a snore. **2** a snoring. **3** a growl with an attempt to bite. **4** a bite.
snaggerel *same as* **snachel**.
snagger-snee *n* a large knife, originally from Germany.
snaggery *n* **1** trashy, indigestible food. **2** trashy sweet stuff.
snaggy¹ *n* raillery.
snaggy² *adj* **1** sarcastic. **2** morose. **3** cross, ill-tempered. **4** snappish.
snaid *same as* **snood**.
snaig *n* **1** a worthless fellow. **2** the obtaining of money by fair or foul means.
snaik¹ *n* a black or grey slug.
snaik² *v* **1** to sneak. **2** to walk or move furtively and secretly. **3** to walk or work slowly and indolently.—*n* **1** an indolent person. **2** the working or walking indolently.
snaikach *adj* creeping, crawling.

snaiker *n* an indolent person.
snail *v* to go slowly, loiter.
snail-caup-e'en *n* eyes like a snail's.
snail-slaw *adj* very slow.
snak *same as* **snack**².
snake *same as* **snaik**².
snakin' *adj* exulting and sneering.
snam *v* to snap at anything greedily.
snang *v* to twang.
snap *v* **1** to seize an opportunity. **2** to take advantage of. **3** to overcharge. **4** to get the advantage in argument. **5** to toy. **6** to eat hastily or greedily. **7** to make a sharp, cracking noise with the fingers. **8** (*of a gun*) to go off accidentally. **9** to stumble, trip suddenly. **10** to snub, cut anyone short. —*n* **1** a quick movement. **2** a small portion of food, a snack, a morsel. **3** a bit. **4** a fragment. **5** a small, crisp gingerbread cake, a brandy snap. **6** a brief, sudden interval. **7** a moment. **8** an angry dispute. **9** a sharp blow. **10** a sudden stumble.—*adj* **1** brittle, crisp. **2** quick, active. **3** smart, acute. **4** short-tempered, snappish. **5** eager to find fault.
snap-dyke *n* a stone fence from four to six feet high, suitable for enclosing sheep.
snapgun *n* a firelock as contrasted with a matchlock.
snap-haunce *n* **1** the spring of the lock of a gun or pistol. **2** the whole gun or pistol.
snaply *adv* hastily, quickly.
snapmaker *n* a maker of pistols and guns with triggers.
snapper¹ *v* **1** to stumble, trip. **2** to fall suddenly. **3** to fall into a scrape.—*n* **1** a false step, a stumble. **2** a failure in morals. **3** a perplexity, entanglement. **4** a misfortune. **5** an unforeseen accident.
snapper², **snappert** *adj* **1** tart. **2** hasty. **3** curt.
snappering stone *n* a stumbling stone.
snappous, snappus *adj* **1** testy. **2** hasty in temper.
snappy *adj* **1** keen in business. **2** disposed to take advantage of another. **3** cross, ill-tempered.
snapsy *adj* tart, surly, snappish.
snap-the-louse *n* a cant name for a tailor.
snapur *n* **1** a foolish and impudent person. **2** one reckless in his speaking.
snap-wark *n* a firelock.
snap-wife *n* a woman who sells gingerbread snaps.
snar, snare *adj* **1** severe. **2** ill-tempered, surly. **3** prudent, diligent, managing. **4** keen in bargaining, disposed to overreach. **5** rigid. **6** firm to the grasp.
snarbled *adj* pinched, shrivelled.
snar-gab *n* abusive language.
snark *v* **1** to snore. **2** to grumble, fret, find fault.
snarl *n* a broil, quarrel, wrangle.
snarle *n* a ravel, tangle.
snarlinger *adj* more quarrelsome.
snarly *adj* snappish, surly.
snarre *same as* **snar**.
snash *v* **1** to snap, bite. **2** to vituperate. **3** to sneer. **4** to gibe.—*n* **1** abusive language. **2** impudence. **3** sneers. **4** gibes.—*adv* **1** snappishly. **2** pertly.—*adj* pert, saucy.
snash-gab *n* **1** prating. **2** petulant talking. **3** a prattling, forward boy or girl.
snashter *n* trifles.
snashtrie *n* **1** trash. **2** trifles. **3** low chat.
snath *v* to prune timber trees.
snauchle *v* **1** to walk slowly with lingering steps. **2** to saunter.—*n* **1** a weakling. **2** a dwarf.
snaur *same as* **snar**.
snaw *n* snow.—*v* to be snowed up.
snaw-ba' *n* **1** a snowball. **2** a joke, sarcasm.
snaw bird *n* **1** the snow bunting. **2** any winter bird.
snaw-brack *n* a quick thaw.
snaw-breakers *n* sheep scraping the hardened surface of the snow to find food.
snaw bree, ~ broo, ~ broth *n* melted snow.
snaw-drift *n* fine, driving snow.
snaw-flaigh, ~-flake, ~-fleck *n* the snow bunting.

snaw flight, ~-fowl *n* the snow bunting.
snaw-hoord *n* an accumulation of snow.
snawie *adj* snowy.
snawie ba' *n* a snowball.
snawie-fowl *n* the snow bunting.
snawie heads *n* large masses of white clouds.
snaw-o'-the-rink *n* snow on the sides of a curling rink.
snaw-powther *n* fine, driving snow.
snaw-rink *n* a snow-covered track.
snaw-shurl *n* **1** snow slipping from the roof of a house. **2** the noise it makes.
snaw-tooried *adj* snow-capped.
snaw-wreath *n* a snowdrift.
snaw-wreathed *adj* blocked by snowdrifts.
snaw wride *n* a snowdrift.
snayaavie *adj* snowy.
sneaker *n* a small bowl of punch.
snear *same as* **sneer**.
sneb *same as* **snib**.
sneck¹ *n* **1** a door latch. **2** a small bolt.—*v* **1** to fasten the latch of a door. **2** to secure by a latch or catch.—*adv* with a sudden snap or catch.
sneck² *v* to snap, bite.—*n* a snatch of food, a snack.
sneck³ *v* **1** to cut sharply, incise. **2** to strike smartly. **3** to close, fill up. **4** to stop an incision or gap. **5** to drink off. **6** to finish up.—*n* **1** the act or power of cutting. **2** a slight cut or incision. **3** a cut suddenly given. **4** a portion of a wall built with single stones or stones that go from side to side.
sneck⁴ *v* **1** to sneak. **2** to pilfer. **3** to grab at.
sneck-draw *n* **1** an intruder. **2** a crafty, artful person. **3** a sly person. **4** a covetous person. **5** one who from long practice has acquired facility.
sneck-drawer *n* a sneck-draw (qv).
sneck-drawin' *adj* crafty, sly.—*n* craft, cunning.
snecker *n* a sharper.
sneck-harl *v* to harl (qv) or roughcast a wall with mortar.
sneck-pin *v* to put in small stones between the larger ones in a wall and daub the seams with mortar.
sneck-trap *n* a spring rat trap.
sned¹ *n* a branch pruned off.—*v* **1** to prune. **2** to lop off. **3** to hew or polish stones with a chisel. **4** to remove excrescences. **5** to emasculate.
sned² *n* the shaft or pole of a scythe.
sned³ *same* as **snood**.
snedder *n* one who lops off branches or turnip tops.
sneddins *n* the prunings of trees.
sned-kail *n* colewort or cabbages, of which the old stalks, after they have begun to sprout, are divided by a knife and planted.
sneed *same as* **snood**.
sneeg *v* **1** to neigh. **2** to snort.
sneel¹ *v* **1** to be lazy. **2** to lack energy. **3** to remain idle. **4** to go about stealthily.—*n* **1** the doing of anything lazily. **2** an indolent person. **3** an inactive person.
sneel² *v* **1** to snivel. **2** to speak through the nose.
sneep *same as* **snip**².
sneer *v* **1** to snort. **2** to snore. **3** to inhale by the nostrils. **4** to hiss. **5** to give forth a hissing sound.—*n* **1** a snort, inhalation by the nostrils. **2** an adder's hiss. **3** the act of a horse with a cold in throwing mucus from its nostrils.
sneerag *n* a child's toy, made of the larger bone of a pig's foot and two worsted strings and worked so as to give a snoring sound.
sneesh *n* **1** snuff. **2** a pinch of snuff.—*v* to take snuff.
sneesher *n* one who takes snuff.
sneeshin, sneeshen, sneeshan *n* **1** snuff. **2** a pinch of snuff. **3** anything of little value. **4** anything that gives comfort or pleasure.
sneeshin box *n* a snuffbox.
sneeshin-horn *n* a small horn used as a snuffbox.
sneeshinie *adj* snuffy.
sneeshin mill, ~ mull *n* a snuffbox.

sneeshin pen *n* a small bone spoon or quill used in taking snuff.
sneest *n* **1** an air of disdain. **2** impertinence. **3** a snarl. **4** a taunt.—*v* **1** to treat with scorn or contempt. **2** to sneer, sniff. **3** to snarl. **4** to taunt.
sneesty *adj* **1** scornful. **2** sneering. **3** contemptuous.
sneet¹ *v* **1** to loiter. **2** to walk slowly and stupidly. **3** to work lazily or unskilfully. **4** to remain idly. —*n* **1** the walking or working lazily. **2** a stupid, indolent person.
sneet² *n* sleet.
sneeter *v* **1** to sneet (qv). **2** to sleep a light, short sleep. **3** to weep, blubber.—*n* **1** a sneet (qv). **2** a short sleep.
sneety *adj* sleety.
sneevel, sneevle, sneevil *same as* **snivel**.
sneevlin' *adj* **1** whining. **2** cringing. **3** snivelling, used in contempt.
sneeze *v* **1** to take snuff. **2** (*with* **upon**) to sneer at, despise.
sneezing *same as* **sneeshin**.
sneezing mill *n* a snuffbox.
sneezing tobacco *n* snuff.
sneg¹ *n* a low term for gain.
sneg² *v* **1** to neigh. **2** to snort.—*n* the neigh of a horse.
sneg *v* **1** to cut with a sharp instrument. **2** to cut off or short. **3** to interrupt. **4** to check. **5** to invite a broil.—*n* a sudden cut. **2** an incision.
snegger *n* **1** a horse. **2** the neigh of a horse.
sneill *same as* **sneel**¹.
sneish *same as* **sneesh**.
sneishter *same as* **sniester**.
sneist *same as* **sneest**.
sneisty *same as* **sneesty**.
sneith *adj* **1** smooth. **2** polished. **3** refined.
snell *adj* **1** quick, sharp. **2** keen, eager. **3** fierce. **4** severe. **5** painful. **6** cold, piercing, bracing. **7** pungent. **8** acrimonious, tart. **9** sarcastic. **10** austere. **11** clear-sounding. **12** firm, resolute.—*adv* **1** quickly. **2** pungently. **3** very, exceedingly.
snell-gabbit, ~-tongued *adj* **1** sharp-tongued. **2** caustic in speech.
snelly *adj* spell (qv), keen, chilly.—*adv* **1** coldly, bitterly, keenly. **2** tartly. **3** severely.
sneuker *same as* **snooker**.
sneukit *adj* artful.
sneut *same as* **sneet**¹.
sneuter *same as* **sneet**¹.
snew *v* did snow.
snewn *v* snowed.
sneyster¹ *same as* **sniester**.
sneyster² *same as* **snister**.
sniauve *v* to snow.—*n* snow.
snib *n* **1** to check. **2** to snub. **3** to bolt, bar, fasten. **4** to trap. **5** to cut, cut short. **6** to shape, point. **7** to cut short as to money. **8** to castrate. **9** to snuff a candle.—*n* **1** a check, a snub. **2** a cut. **3** a smart stroke. **4** a small bolt for fastening a door. **5** a fastening, catch. **6** a button.
snibb *adj* **1** chastised. **2** frightened.
snibbelt *n* a small piece of wood at the end of a tether that is slipped through an eye at the other end to fasten it.
snibbert¹ *v* **1** to loiter. **2** to work stupidly.—*n* a person of sharp, hard features and little force of character.
snibbert² *same as* **snubbert**.
snibbertick, snibbertickie *n* a snibbert (qv).
snibbit *n* **1** a snibbert (qv). **2** anything curtailed of its proper proportions.—*adj* curtailed of its proper proportions.
snibble, sniblet *n* a snibbert (qv).
sniblich *n* a collar of plaited straw or rushes, formerly used to bind a cow to the stake.
snichen *same as* **sneeshin**.
snicher *same as* **snicker**.
snichter *v* to sniff, snuffle.
snick¹, **snick**², **snick**³ *same as* **sneck**¹, **sneck**³, **sneck**⁴.
snick-drawin' *same as* **sneck-drawin'**.

snicker *v* to snigger.—*n* **1** a derisive, sneering laugh. **2** a snigger.

snid *same as* **snood**.

sniest *same as* **sneest**.

sniester *v* to cauterize.

sniesty *adj* taunting.

sniff *n* **1** a trifle. **2** a very small piece.

sniffle *v* **1** to sniff, snuffle. **2** to be slow in motion or action. **3** to trifle.—*n* **1** a sniff. **2** slowness of motion or action. **3** trifling delay. **4** a slow person. **5** a trifler. **6** a driveller. **7** (*in pl*) difficulty of breathing through the nostrils caused by cold.

sniffle-bit *n* a snaffle.

sniffler *n* **1** a trifler. **2** a driveller.

sniffltie-foot *n* the green crab.

snifle *n* a snaffle.

snift *v* (*of hail*) to whiz, rattle briskly in falling.

snifter *v* **1** to sniff, snuffle. **2** to inhale sharply through the nose. **3** to scent a smell. **4** to sob.—*n* **1** a sniff, snuffle. **2** a quick inhalation by the nose. **3** a suppressed laugh or sob. **4** a sneering laugh. **5** a cutting repartee. **6** the effect of a strong purgative. **7** a severe blast, storm. **8** a reverse. **9** a defeat. **10** (*in pl*) a severe cold in the head. **11** a disease of animals and fowls causing stoppage of the nostrils.

snifterin' *n* a severe exposure to stormy weather.

snig *v* **1** to cut, chop off. **2** to pull suddenly. **3** to jerk.—*n* a sudden, sharp pull.

sniggert *n* one chargeable with wilful malversation.

sniggle *v* **1** to snigger. **2** to laugh sneeringly. **3** to giggle.

sniggle *v* to poach fish by snaring them in a mean way.

snip[1] *n* **1** a scrap. **2** a fragment. **3** a share. **4** a narrow stripe down the face of a horse. **5** a spell, snap. **6** a tailor.—*v* **1** to run with short steps. **2** to slip off quickly or suddenly. **3** to stumble slightly.

snip[2] *adj* **1** glittering. **2** of a bright colour. **3** white. —*n* the dazzling of something white.

snipe[1] *n* a thin, hard-featured person with a prominent nose.

snipe[2] *n* **1** a snub. **2** a sarcasm. **3** a muzzle on a pig's snout. **4** a smart blow. **5** a fillip. **6** a loss, a reverse of fortune. **7** a cheat, fraud. **8** one who cheats, defrauds. **9** a contemptuous designation for anyone. **10** a mean, insignificant person. **11** a scolding. **12** a sharp-tongued woman. **13** a tailor.—*v* **1** to snub. **2** to give a smart blow. **3** to scold. **4** to muzzle a pig. **5** to cheat. **6** to bring loss to one.

snipie-nebbit *adj* having a long, sharp nose.

snipper *n* a small, insignificant person.

snippert, snippart *n* **1** a crumb, a very small bit of anything. **2** a small person of sharp disposition. —*adj* quick, tart in speech. **3** addicted to giving short weight or measure.

snippiltin' *adj* **1** roaming. **2** hunting after.

snippin *adj* dazzling.

snippit *adj* (*used of a horse*) having a white stripe down the face.

snippit *adj* **1** (*used of the nose*) snub. **2** scanty. **3** niggardly, pinching.

snippy[1] *adj* **1** tart in speech, sharp-tongued. **2** speaking with a sharp accent. **3** used of one who gives scant measure in cutting cloth.—*n* **1** a sharp-tongued person. **2** a scold.

snippy[2] *n* a horse with a white-striped face.

snip-white *adj* dazzling white.

snirk *v* to draw up the nose in contempt or displeasure.

snirl[1] *v* **1** to sneeze. **2** to laugh involuntarily and in a suppressed manner.

snirl[2] *v* **1** to tangle. **2** to contract like hand-twisted yarn. **3** to ruffle or wrinkle.—*n* a knot, tangle.

snirt[1] *n* an insignificant, diminutive person.

snirt[2] *v* **1** to laugh in a suppressed manner. **2** to breathe sharply and in a jerking way through the nostrils. **3** to sneer.—*n* **1** a suppressed laugh. **2** nasal mucus. **3** a snort.

snirtle *v* **1** to laugh in a suppressed manner. **2** to sneer.—*n* **1** a suppressed laugh. **2** a sneer.

snish *same as* **sneesh**.

snishin *same as* **sneeshin**.

snisle *v* **1** to singe. **2** to burn partially. **3** to harden by heat.

snister *n* a severe blast in the face.

snisty *same as* **sneesty**.

snitan, snitern *adj* **1** loitering. **2** putting off time.

snitch *n* a noose, a loop.

snitchers *n* handcuffs.

snite[1] *n* a small, insignificant person or thing.

snite[2] *v* **1** to blow the nose with finger and thumb. **2** to wring the nose. **3** to snuff a candle. **4** to taunt, gibe.—*n* a smart blow.

snitian *same as* **sneeshin**.

snitter *n* a biting blast.

snivel *v* **1** to breathe hard through the nose. **2** to speak through the nose.—*n* **1** a snuffle. **2** a heavy breathing through the nose. **3** speaking through the nose, a nasal twang. **4** (*in pl*) a disease affecting animals.

snivelling *adj* **1** mean-spirited. **2** whining.

sneak *same as* **snook**.

snob *same as* **snab**[2].

snocher, snocker *v* **1** to breathe heavily and noisily through the nose. **2** to slobber with the nose like a pig in a trough. **3** to snort, snore.—*n* **1** a snort. **2** a loud snore. **3** difficult breathing through the nose owing to mucus. **4** (*in pl*) stoppage of the nostrils from cold.

snock *v* **1** to snort contemptuously. **2** to turn over with the nose, as a dog or pig. **3** to poke into.

snod[1] *adj* **1** smooth, level. **2** neat, trim, tidy. **3** snug, comfortable.—*v* **1** to trim, prune, lop. **2** to put in order. **3** to make neat and tidy. **4** to castrate. **5** (*with* **off**) to finish off.

snod[2] *v* did prune. *See* **sned**[1].

snoddie[1] *n* a neatly dressed person.

snoddie[2] *n* a ninny, a stupid fellow.

snoddy *adj* neat, trim.—*adv* deftly, neatly.

snodge *v* to walk deliberately.

snodit *adj* **1** dressed. **2** tidied.

snodless *adj* untidy.

snodly *adv* **1** evenly, smoothly. **2** neatly, tidily. **3** snugly.

snog[1] *same as* **snug**.

snog[2] *v* to jeer, flout.

snoick *adj* **1** virgin, chaste. **2** (*of ships, etc*) watertight.

snoid *same as* **snood**.

snoit[1] *n* **1** a young, conceited person who speaks little. **2** an upstart, a swaggerer. **3** an intruder.

snoit[2] *same as* **snite**[2].

snoiter *v* to breathe strongly through the nose.

snoity *adj* having the nose dirty with mucus.

snoke *same as* **snook**.

snoker[1] *same as* **snocher**.

snoker[2] *same as* **snooker**.

snoo *v* snowed.

snood *n* **1** a ribbon or band for confining the hair. **2** a short hairline. **3** the thin line by which hooks are attached to a fishing line. **4** a coil, a twist. **5** a twisted line or rope. **6** a twist of temper. **7** a threatening twist of the head.—*v* **1** to confine the hair with a snood. **2** to tie a hairline on a fishing hook. **3** to coil, twist. **4** to tangle. **5** (*used of cattle*) to threaten with the head.

snooded folks *n* virgins, unmarried maidens.

snoodless *adj* without a snood (qv), used of a maid who has lost her virginity.

snoofmadrune *n* a lazy, inactive person.

snook *v* **1** to smell with a loud inhalation. **2** to sniff. **3** to scent as a dog. **4** to scent. **5** to pry about. **6** to sneak.—*n* **1** a smell. **2** a sniff.

snooker *n* **1** one who smells at objects like a dog. **2** a rake, a profligate fellow. **3** an irritating smell.

snool *n* **1** an abject. **2** a cringing person. **3** one easily overborne. **4** a weak fool. **5** anything mean or paltry. **6** a tyrant. **7** one who frightens or overbears.—*v* **1** to submit tamely and weakly. **2** to act meanly and without spirit. **3** to give in, cringe, sneak. **4** to overbear, frighten, subdue. **5** to dispirit. **6** to snub. **7** to walk warily or stealthily.

snool-~, snool'd-like *adj* **1** craven. **2** weak. **3** subdued. **4** dispirited.

snoot *n* **1** the snout. **2** the nose. **3** the face. **4** the mind, head. **5** a point, a projection. **6** the point of an anvil. **7** the peak of a cap. **8** the muzzle of a gun.

snootit *adj* (*used of a cap or bonnet*) peaked.

snoove *v* **1** to move smoothly and steadily. **2** to glide. **3** to walk with a steady step. **4** to sneak. **5** to move looking to the earth. **6** to walk carelessly. **7** to move like a top.

snoovle *v* **1** to move slowly. **2** to walk in a slow, lazy way.

snooze-snoove *v* **1** to glide. **2** to move steadily along.

snooze *v* to sleep, doze.—*n* a nap.

snoozle *v* **1** to sleep, doze. **2** (*used of a dog*) to sniff and poke with the nose. **3** to nestle into.

snore *v* **1** to snort. **2** to roar. **3** to make a loud noise. **4** to rush with a roaring sound. **5** (*used of an engine*) to puff.—*n* **1** a snort, roar. **2** a loud, roaring noise. **3** a disease affecting animals.

snorick *same as* **sneerag**.

snork *v* **1** to snort. **2** to clear the throat noisily.—*n* the snort of a frightened horse.

snorl *same as* **snirl**[2].

snort *n* **1** a twist, kink. **2** a tangle.

snory-bane a sneerag (qv)

snosh *adj* **1** fat and contented. **2** comfortable.

snoshie *n* a fat, comfortable man.

snot *n* **1** the snuff of a candle or lamp. **2** a small lump of soot. **3** a mean, dirty person. **4** a despicable person. **5** a dolt, dunce. **6** a fool.—*v* **1** to blow the nose with finger and thumb. **2** to snivel.

snotter *n* **1** nasal mucus, snot. **2** the red membraneous portion of a turkey cock's beak. **3** a sniggering laugh. **3** anything of little weight or value.—*v* **1** to let mucus run from the nose. **2** to snuffle, snore, snort. **3** to cry, weep, blubber. **4** to snivel.

snotter box *n* **1** the nose. **2** a term of contempt.

snotter cap *n* a dull, stupid, boorish fellow.

snottery *adj* **1** running with nasal mucus. **2** speaking through mucus.

snotties *n* the nostrils.

snottit *adj* smeared with nasal mucus.

snotty *adj* **1** having the nose dirty with mucus. **2** peevish, snappish. **3** rude, impudent. **4** high and mighty.—*n* a dolt.

snouff *n* the snuffing sound made by a dog.

snouk, snouck *same as* **snook**.

snout *same as* **snoot**.

snouter *n* a peaked cap.

snouthie *adj* **1** drizzly, rainy. **2** dark.

snow *same as* **snaw**.

snowflake *n* the snow bunting.

snowk *same as* **snook**.

snow-tappit *adj* covered with snow.

snubbert *n* **1** a loose knot or lump. **2** a contemptuous name for the nose. **3** the snout.

snude *same as* **snood**.

snuff *v* **1** to breathe. **2** to inhale sharply. **3** to sniff in contempt or displeasure.—*n* **1** a short, quick, contemptuous inhalation. **2** a breath of fresh air. **3** anger. **4** scorn. **5** a very small quantity. **6** anything of very little value. **7** (*in pl*) an exclamation of contempt.

snuff-bean *n* a bean kept in a snuffbox to scent the snuff.

snuff-girnel *n* a snuff jar.

snuff-hauder *n* the nose.

snuff-horn *n* the tip of a horn used as a snuffbox.

snuffie *adj* **1** snuff-coloured. **2** sulky. **3** displeased.

snuffilie *adv* sulkily.

snuffiness *n* sulkiness.

snuff-man *n* a tobacconist.

snuff mill, ~ mull *n* a snuffbox.

snuff pen *n* a small bone spoon or quill for taking snuff.

snuff tankard *n* a snuff jar.

snuffy-like *adj* **1** snappish. **2** huffy.

snug[1] *adj* **1** secret, quiet. **2** convenient. **3** neat.—*v* **1** to put in order. **2** to make tight, trim.—*n* the snuggery in a tavern.

snug[2] *v* **1** to strike, push, butt. **2** to scold. **3** to reprimand severely.—*n* **1** a stroke. **2** a thrust or push with the head.

snug[3] *n* a small branch lopped off a tree.

snuggit *adj* (*used of houses*) built snugly and compactly together.

snuie *v* (*of horned cattle*) to toss the head as if angry.

snuifie *adj* awkward, sheepish.

snuift *v* went stealthily. *See* **snoove**.

snuist *same as* **sneest**.

snuister[1] *v* to laugh in a suppressed manner through the nose.—*n* a suppressed laugh.

snuister[2] *n* a sweet.

snuit *v* to move carelessly, inactively and in a stupefied manner.

snuiter *same as* **snuit**.

snuitter *v* to laugh in a suppressed manner through the nose.—*n* a suppressed laugh.

snuittit *adj* having the foolish, dazed look of one half-drunk.

snuive *same as* **snoove**.

snule *same as* **snool**[2].

snurkle *v* to run into knots, as a hard twisted thread.

snurl, snurrl *same as* **snirl**[2].

snurley, snurlie *adj* **1** twisted. **2** knotty.

snurt *same as* **snirt**[2].

snurtle *same as* **snirtle**.

snush *same as* **sneesh**.

snush *same as* **snosh**.

snut *v* to curl the nose disdainfully.

snuve *same as* **snoove**.

snyaave, sayauve *same as* **sniauve**.

snyaavie *adj* snowy.

snyb *same as* **snib**.

snype *same as* **snipe**[2].

snyte[1] *same as* **snite**[2].

snyte[2] *v* **1** to walk feebly or slowly and stupidly. **2** to loiter. **3** to work stupidly and lazily.—*n* a stupid, lazy person.

snyter *v* to loiter.—*n* a stupid, lazy person.

so *same as* **sae**[1].

soak *v* to drink hard.

soaken *v* to soak.

soakie *adj* **1** plump. **2** of full habit.—*n* a fat woman.

soal *same as* **sole**[1].

soal tree *same as* **sole tree**.

soam[1] *same as* **saim**.

soam[2] *n* the air bladder of a fish.

soam[3] *n* the rope or chain by which horses or oxen are yoked to the plough.—*v* to drive the plough.

soap bell *n* a soap bubble.

soapy-blotts *n* soapsuds.

soaper *n* a soap-boiler.

soaperie *n* a soapwork.

soap-man *n* a soap-boiler.

soap-sapples *n* soapsuds.

soapy blots, ~ sapples, ~ duds *n* soapsuds.

sob *same as* **sab**[1].

sober *adj* **1** steady. **2** poor, mean, indifferent. **3** diminutive, slender, weakly. **4** fairly well.

soberly *adv* sparingly, frugally.

sobersides *n* a person of sober habits.

soch *same as* **sooch**.

socher *v* **1** to make much of oneself. **2** to live delicately. **3** to be overcareful as to one's food and drink.—*adj* **1** lazy, effeminate. **2** inactive from delicate living.

socherer *n* a lazy, effeminate person.

socht *v* sought.

society-people *n* the sect of the Cameronians.

sock[1] *n* a schoolboys' term for sweetmeats or dainties.

sock[2] *n* a ploughshare.

sock[3] *same as* **sog**.

sock[4] *n* a frame, rest, support.

sock[5] *n* a socket.

sock[6] *n* the right of a baron to hold a court within his own domains.

sockie *n* a person who walks with a manly air.—*v* to walk with a manly air.

sockin hour *n* **1** the time between daylight and candlelight. **2** time for ceasing to work. **3** a rest time.

sockin of the tide *n* the last of a tide, either of the ebb or of the flood.

sockman *n* a tenant bound by certain restrictions and to certain services by his lease.

sock-mandrill *n* a facsimile of a plough head cast in metal.

sock-neb *n* the point of the ploughshare.

socy *same as* **sockie**.

sod[1] *adj* sad.

sod[2], **sodd** *n* **1** a rough saddle of coarse cloth or skin stuffed with straw. **2** a heavy person. **3** a dead weight.—*adj* **1** firm, steady. **2** sedate, respectable. **3** careful.—*v* **1** to cover with sods. **2** to make solid.—*adv* securely.

sod[3] *n* a roll or bap (qv) made of coarse flour.

sod[4] *n* the rock dove.

sod[5] *n* a sudden and singular sound made in a pot or pan while used in cooking, regarded as a portent of death.—*adj* singular, unaccountable.

soda *n* **1** bicarbonate of soda or baking soda. **2** carbonate of soda or washing soda.

soda drink *n* aerated water.

soda scone *n* a scone made with bicarbonate of soda.

soday *n* **1** a dirty woman. **2** a gross person.

sodd *same as* **sod**[2].

soddie *n* a seat made of sods.

sodger, sodjer *n* **1** a soldier. **2** the ribwort plantain. **3** (*in pl*) a game played with the stems of the plantain. **4** the small fiery sparks on the bottom of a pot just taken from the fire.—*v* **1** to be a soldier. **2** (*used of turnips*) to have the leaves turn red and stop growing.

sodger-blade, ~-body *n* a soldier.

sodger-folk *n* soldiers.

sodgerize *v* **1** to act as a soldier. **2** to be drilled.

sodgerly *adj* soldierly.

sodger's bite *n* a large bite.

sodger's buttons *n* the white burnet rose.

sodger's feather *n* the plant honesty.

sodger-thee'd *adj* soldier-thighed or having little or no money in one's pocket.

sodlies *adv* **1** sadly. **2** to a great degree.

sod-like, ~-looking *adj* having a singular appearance.

sod-seat *n* a seat of sods or turfs.

sod track *n* a sad state.

sody *same as* **soda**.

soft *adj* **1** muddy. **2** wet, rainy. **3** silly. **4** amorous.

soft-dud *n* **1** a weakling. **2** one without bodily stamina.

soften *v* to thaw.

softness *n* **1** weakness of character. **2** amourousness.

softy *n* a simpleton.

sog *same as* **sugg**.

soger, sojer *same as* **sodger**.

so'h *same as* **souch**.

sok *n* surety.—*v* to guarantee.

soil, soilyie *n* **1** dirt, ashes, house refuse. **2** the manure collected from the streets of a town.—*adj* soiled, dirtied.

sol *same as* **sole**[1].

solate *same as* **solid**.

solatious, solacious *adj* **1** cheerful. **2** comforting.

soldier *same as* **sodger**.

sole[1] *n* **1** the under-surface of a curling stone. **2** a windowsill. **3** a bottom shelf. **4** subsoil.—*n in phr* **to sole one's boots** to make a profit.

sole[2] *n* a potato basket.

sole[3] *n* a swivel.

sole-ale *n* ale given at the finishing of the windowsills.

sole clout, ~ shoe *n* an iron plate fastened to the part of the plough that runs on the ground to save the wooden heel from being worn.

sole-fleuk *n* the sole.

solemncholy *adj* **1** solemn. **2** sober.

solemn-leaguing *adj* **1** covenanting. **2** adhering to the Solemn League and Covenant.

sole tree *n* a beam reaching from one wall of a cow house to the opposite, into which the under-end of each stake or post is mortised, forming the crib or manger.

solicit, sollisit *adj* **1** solicitous. **2** anxious.

solid *adj* **1** sedate, staid. **2** capable. **3** sane, sober, compos mentis. **4** thorough, utter, whole.—*n* (*in pl*) solidity of character, moral worth, gravity.

solidness *n* solidity of character, steadiness, gravity.

solist *v* to solicit.—*adj* solicitous, careful, anxious.

solistar *n* one who solicits anything.

soliatation *n* solicitation, interest, influence.

solistnes *n* anxiety.

solute *adj* **1** general, not close. **2** declamatory, diffuse.

solutive *adj* laxative.

solvé *n* that member of a college who exacts the fines.

solvendie, solvendo *same as* **sevendle**.

solvendiness *n* a state of trustworthiness.

somat *adv* somewhat.

some *adv* **1** in some degree. **2** somewhat. **3** rather. **4** *in phr* **and some** much more so, used to denote pre-eminence in what has been mentioned before.

somebody *n* **1** a lover. **2** a sweetheart.

somedeal *adv* in some measure.—*n* a fairly large amount.

somegate *adv* **1** somehow. **2** in some way. **3** somewhere.

somepairt *adv* **1** somehow. **2** somewhere.

something *adv* somewhat.

son *n* a familiar term of kindly address without implying sonship.

son-afore-the-father *n* **1** the common colt's-foot. **2** the cudweed.

sonce *same as* **sonse**.

soncy *same as* **sonsy**.

sones *n* sowens. *See* **sowen**.

song *same as* **sang**[3].

sonk[1] *n* **1** a seat. **2** a couch. **3** a bag of straw. **4** a pad of straw used as a saddle or cushion.

sonk[2] *v* **1** to drivel. **2** to loiter. **3** to be in a dejected state.

sonk dyke *n* a wall or dyke built with stone or sods on one side and filled with earth on the other.

sonkie *n* **1** a low stool. **2** a man like a sackful of straw.

sonk-pocks *n* the bags tied to the sonks on the back of a tinker's ass in which children, baggage, goods, etc, were carried. *See* **sonk**.

sonnet *n* **1** a song. **2** a verse. **3** nonsensical talk or writing.

sons *n* sowens (qv).

sonse *n* **1** luck. **2** prosperity. **3** used in good wishes.

sonsy, sonsie *adj* **1** lucky, fortunate, happy. **2** thriving. **3** plump, buxom, stout. **4** jolly. **5** comely, good-looking. **6** cheerful, pleasant. **7** sensible. **8** placid. **9** tractable, good-tempered. **10** comfortable. **11** plentiful. **12** cordial.

sonsy-faced, ~-looking *adj* of buxom, pleasant or jolly appearance.

sonsy-folk *n* lucky first-foots on New Year's Day. *See* **first-foot**.

sonyie *n* an excuse.

soo[1] *v* **1** to smart. **2** to tingle. **3** to throb.—*n* an ache, a throb.

soo[2] *n* a sow, pig.

soo[3] *same as* **sow**[2].

sooans, sooins *n* sowens (qv).

sooback *same as* **sow-back**.

sooch[1] *v* **1** to swill. **2** to swig off.—*n* a copious draught.—*adj* drunken, swigging.

sooch[2], **soogh** *same as* **souch**.

sood *v* should.

soodie *same as* **soudie**.

sooh *same as* **sooch**[1].

sook *v* **1** to suck. **2** to pull at a pipe. **3** to drink leisurely. **4** to dry up by the action of the wind. **5** to drain, exhaust by overcropping. **6** (*with* **in**) to flow in slowly and quietly. **7** to ingratiate oneself.—*n* **1** a sip, drink. **2** a whirlpool. **3**

wet, boggy ground. **4** loose straw rubbish. **5** a rapid drying of the ground or atmosphere. **6** drought. **7** a stupid fellow, a duffer. **8** (*in pl*) the flowers of the red clover, sucked by children.

sookag *n* a head of clover.

sooker[1] *n* the sucker of a tree.

sooker[2] *n* **1** a horseleech. **2** the young of the cod and other fish. **3** a boy's toy, consisting of a disc of wet leather with a string through the centre, used for suction.

sookie *n* **1** the flower of the red clover. **2** a call-word for a calf, a pet name for a calf.—*adj* **1** spongy. **2** oozy. **3** untidy.

sookie-soo *n* the flower of red clover.

sookie-soorach *n* the common wood sorrel and other acid plants.

sookin' bairn *n* a sucking child.

sookin' bottle *n* a baby's feeding bottle.

sookin' stirk *n* **1** an unweaned steer. **2** one who depends on others longer than is necessary.

sookin' turkey *n* **1** a fool, ninny. **2** a childish, peevish person.

sookit *adj* **1** (*used of fish*) partially dried, semiputrescent. **2** fatigued, exhausted.

sool *same as* **sole**[3].

soolyie *n* used as a most disrespectful term for tribe, race, lot, crew.

soom[1] *v* to hum, buzz.

soom[2] *v* **1** to swim. **2** to float. **3** to cause to float.—*n* **1** a state of great wetness. **2** a flooding. **3** a pool. **4** a swim.

soom[3] *n* a state of swoon, giddiness, faintness.—*v* **1** to turn giddy. **2** to swoon. **3** to spin as a top. **4** to cause to spin.

soom[4] *same as* **soum**[1].

soomer *n* a swimmer.

soommence *n* a legal summons.

soon[1] *adj* (*used of distance*) quick, near, direct.

soon[2], **soond** *same as* **sound**.

soon[3], **soond** *v* **1** to sound. **2** to test the acoustics of a building. **3** to pronounce, utter. **4** to scold.—*n* **1** a sound. **2** a rumour.

soon[4], **soond** *adj* **1** sound. **2** orthodox. **3** sound asleep. **4** (*used of a period of time*) whole, uninterrupted. **5** smooth, unwrinked.

soond[5], **soond**[6], **soond**[7] *same as* **soon**[1], **soon**[2], **soon**[3].

soonie *adj* **1** made of the husks and siftings of oatmeal. **2** (*used of butter*) containing, or adulterated with, sowens (qv).

soons *n* sowens (qv).

soony *same as* **sound**.

soop *v* **1** to sweep. **2** to quicken the speed of a curling stone by sweeping the path clear in front of it. **3** to work or walk energetically.—*n* **1** a sweep. **2** the acceleration of a curling stone by sweeping.

sooper *n* a whisk or bunch of feathers for dusting, etc.

sooping *n* **1** the act of sweeping. **2** what is swept up.

soopit swept.

soople[1] *v* to wash, soak.—*n* **1** a soaking, washing. **2** the act of soaking, washing.

soople[2] *adj* **1** supple. **2** limp, soft. **3** quick, nimble. **4** glib. **5** swaying from side to side, as with drink. **6** tractable, agreeable, affable. **7** clever, cunning. —*v* **1** to make supple. **2** to soften dry ground with rain.

soople[3] *n* **1** the striking part of a flail. **2** a cudgel.—*v* to cudgel, beat severely.

soopled *adj* (*of a flail*) furnished with a soople (qv).

soople-neckit *adj* **1** having a supple neck. **2** cringing.

soopleness *n* **1** nimbleness. **2** craftiness, cunning.

soople Tam *n* **1** a top. **2** a child's toy pulled by a string so as to cause it to shake and seem to dance.

soor *adj* **1** sour. **2** bitter, pungent. **3** surly, cross. **4** sullen, forbidding. **5** (*used of the weather*) cold, wet, inclement. **6** (*of land*) cold, wet, unfertile.—*n* anything unpleasant or bitter.

soorag, soorak *same as* **sourock**.

soor bread *n* oatcake baked at Christmas with sour leaven.

soor cake *n* **1** soor bread (qv). **2** a kind of oatcake baked for St Luke's Fair at Rutherglen.

soor cogus *n* a preparation of milk eaten with sugar and cream.

soord *n* a sword.

soor dook *n* buttermilk.

soor draps *n* acid drops.

soor-faced, ~-faced-like *adj* surly-looking.

soor fish *n* fish kept till it is high.

soor grass *n* sedge grass.

soorick *same as* **sourock**.

soorin *n* a disappointment.

soorish *adj* **1** rather sour. **2** somewhat surly or sullen.

soor-leek, ~-lick *n* the common sorrel.

soor-like *adj* ill-tempered, cross.

soor-like-faced *adj* surly-looking.

soor-like-moo'd *adj* surly-looking.

soor-lookit *adj* surly-looking.

soor milk *n* buttermilk.

soor-moo'd *adj* surly-looking.

soorness *n* sullenness, ill-temper, surliness.

soorock *same as* **sourock**.

soorock-faced *adj* sour-faced.

soor plooms *n* bright green hard sweets with a sour flavour.

soose[1], **soose**[2] *same as* **souse**[1], **souse**[2].

soosh[1] *v* **1** to beat severely. **2** to flog. **3** to taunt, upbraid teasingly. **4** to sue at law. **5** to punish. **6** to fine.—*n* a heavy blow.

soosh[2] *v* **1** to work or walk energetically. **2** to drink off at once. **2** to keep intoxicated.

sooshin *n* **1** a beating. **2** abusive language.

soosler *n* **1** a thin fish of any of the larger sorts. **2** a debilitated animal.

sooslin *n* a soosler (qv).

soo-stack *n* a rectangular stack.

sootar, sooter *same as* **souter**.

sooth[1] *adj* true, faithful, loyal.—*int* truth!.—*v* **1** to make one believe. **2** to flatter.

sooth[2] *v* to swoon.

sooth[3] *adj* south.

sooth-aboot *adj* **1** southern. **2** belonging to the south.

soother *v* **1** to coax, flatter. **2** to soothe.

soothfast *adj* **1** trustworthy. **2** honest. **3** true.

soothfow *adj* soothfast (qv).

soothlan' *adj* **1** southern. **2** from the south. **3** belonging to the south.—*n* **1** the south. **2** one who comes from the south.

soothlin *adj* southern.

soothlins *adv* towards the south.

soothly *adv* **1** truly. **2** softly, gently.

sooth-ower *adv* southwards.

sooth side *n* the bright, the sunny side.

sooth-thro' *adj* southern.

sootiman *n* a sweep.

sootipillies, sootpillies *n* the bulrush.

soot-stour *n* soot, sooty dust.

soot-water *n* sooty water.

sooty, sootie *n* **1** a sweep. **2** a name for the devil.

sooty-scon *n* a cake baked with soot to be used on Fastern's Eve in superstitious ceremonies.

sop *same as* **sap**[1].

sord[1] *n* a sword.

sord[2] *n* the oblique crossbar in a reclining gate.

sordes, sords *n* **1** filth. **2** washings. **3** off-scourings. **4** refuse.

sore *same as* **sair**[1].

sore head *n* **1** a headache. **2** a time of possible future need, a rainy day.

sore heady *n* a small cylindrical cake wrapped in buttered paper, resembling a person with a headache, who seeks relief by wearing a bandage round the head.

sorie *v* to sorrow.

soret *adj* of a sorrel colour.

sorn, sorne *v* **1** to take food or lodging by force or threats. **2** to sponge. **3** to live at free quarters. **4** to idle, loaf about.

sorner *n* **1** one who sponges upon another. **2** an idle fellow. **3** a sturdy or threatening beggar.

sornie *n* the fireplace of a kiln and the opening beyond by which the heat enters.

sorning *n* the exacting of free board and lodgings.

sorple *v* to scrub with soap and water.

sorplins *n* soapsuds.

sorrow, sorra *n* **1** a euphemism for the devil, etc, in imprecations. **2** (*with a noun or pronoun*) an expression of the utter absence of the thing or person mentioned. **3** a troublesome child. **4** a plague, pest. **5** a fellow.

sorrowful *adj* troublesome.

sorrow rape *n* a rope or strap slung across the shoulders of persons carrying a handbarrow and attached to the steels or trams of it to relieve the arms of the bearers.

sorry *same as* **sairie**.

sorry man *n* a kindly designation of a dog.

sort *n* **1** a moderate number or quantity. **2** (*in pl*) payment.— *v* **1** to tidy oneself. **2** to dress. **3** (*with* **by**) to put away. **4** to mend. **5** to put to rights. **6** to feed and litter cows, horses, etc. **7** to supply one's requirements satisfactorily. **8** to agree, harmonize. **9** to come to an understanding. **10** (*used of animals*) to serve the female with the male. **11** to punish, scold, put to rights morally. **12** (*with* **with**) to consort with.

sorting *n* **1** a scolding. **2** a punishment.

sorting stell *n* an enclosure into which sheep are driven in order to be separated from each other.

sortless *adj* useless, good-for-nothing.

sorts *n in phr* **that's your sorts** an expression of high satisfaction with an action or thing.

sosh[1] *n* a co-operative store.

sosh[2] *adj* **1** addicted to company and the bottle. **2** frank, free, affable. **3** quiet, contented. **4** cheerful. **5** snug, comfortable. **6** lazy, indolent. **7** plump, broad-faced.

sosherie *n* social intercourse. **2** boon companionship. **2** a convivial club.

soshie *n* the manager of a co-operative store.

soshul *n* a social meeting, a soiree.

soss[1] *v* to boil or cook slowly.

soss[2] *n* **1** an incongruous or badly cooked mixture of foods. **2** liquid food. **3** liquor. **4** a mess, slop. **5** a wet, dirty substance. **6** a state of dirt and mess. **7** a muddle. **8** muddled work. **9** a dirty, lazy woman. **10** a slattern. **11** over-tender nursing.—*v* **1** to mix anything incongruously. **2** to work in dirt and disorder. **3** to nurse over-tenderly. **4** to remain idly in a place.

soss[3], **sosse** *v* **1** to sit or fall down heavily or as a dead weight. **2** to swill like a hog.—*n* **1** a heavy fall. **2** the sound of a heavy, soft body falling or squatting down.

sosserie *n* a bad mess, a soss. *See* **soss**[2].

sossing *n* an incongruous mixing of foods or medcines.

soss-poke *n* the stomach.

sot[1] *n* **1** an idiot. **2** a stupid person.—*v* to drink sottishly.

sot[2] *adv* used in assertion, contradicting a previous negation.

sott *n* the start of a plough when it meets a large stone.

sotten *v, adj* set.

sotter[1] *v* **1** to boil or cook slowly. **2** to simmer. **3** to bubble, sputter, crackle in boiling or frying. **4** to scorch any part of the body. **5** to burn with hot iron in a foundry.—*n* **1** a slow boiling. **2** a scorch or burn. **3** the noise made in boiling or frying.

sotter[2] *n* **1** an indefinite number of insects or other small animals collected together. **2** things mixed up in a heterogeneous mass.—*v* to cluster closely in cutaneous eruptions.

sotter[3] *v* **1** to saturate. **2** to work dirtily or unskilfully. **3** to nurse disgustingly. **4** to potter about. **5** to remain idly in a place.—*n* **1** a state of utter wetness. **2** a filthy, disgusting mass. **3** a large festering sore. **4** a dirty, clumsy person.

sotter[4] *n* in shinty, the first thwack at the ball.

sottle *v* to sound as porridge, broth, etc, in boiling.

sou[1] *n* a sow.

sou[2] *same as* **sow**[2].

sou[3] *same as* **soo**[1].

soucan *n* a single-ply straw rope.

souce[1], **souce**[2] *same as* **souse**[1], **souse**[2].

souch *n* **1** a hollow, murmuring sound. **2** the moaning of the wind. **3** a gentle hum. **4** a deep sigh. **5** the sound of heavy breathing. **6** a slumber, restless sleep. **7** a whining style of preaching or praying. **8** a strain, way of speaking. **9** feeling, opinion. **10** a rumour. **11** a story. **12** a scandal. **13** talk. **14** the sound of a blow or a missile in the air. **15** a stroke, blow.—*phr* **a calm souch** silence, a quiet tongue.—*adj* silent, quiet, tranquil.—*v* **1** to make a hollow, murmuring sound. **2** (*used of the wind*) to sigh. **3** to make a rushing sound, whir, whiz. **4** to breathe heavily, especially in sleep. **5** (*with* **awa'**) to breathe one's last. **6** to slumber, sleep restlessly. **7** to sing softly. **8** to hum over a tune. **9** to whine. **10** to speak in a whining voice. **11** to swoop. **12** to whisk. **13** to strike. **14** to beat severely. **15** to work or walk with great briskness.

soucht *v* sought.

soucye *n* the heliotrope.

soud[1] *n* **1** a sum. **2** a hoard. **3** a quantity. **4** a large sum or quantity. **5** a small quantity of liquor.

soud[2] *v* should.

souder *v* **1** to solder. **2** to melt with heat. **3** to burn. **4** to fasten together. **5** to repair, put to rights. **6** to unite. **7** to agree, suit. **8** to compose a quarrel. **9** to reconcile.—*n* solder.

soudie *n* **1** a heterogeneous mixture. **2** hodgepodge. **3** broth. **4** sheep's-head broth. **5** milk and meal boiled together. **6** a gross, heavy person. **7** a big, clumsy person. **8** a dirty woman.

soudlan' *same as* **soothlan'**.

soue *v* (*used of the wind*) to sigh, moan.

souf[1] *same as* **souch**.

souf[2] *same as* **souft**.

souff[1] *same as* **souch**.

souff[2], **souffe** *same as* **sooch**[1].

souffle[1] *n* **1** a blow. **2** a box on the ear.

souffle[2] *n* a stupid, lazy, drunken fellow.—*v* to drink.

souftet *n* a stroke, a blow.

souft *adj* exhausted.

sough[1] *n* **1** a sigh. **2** the sound of wind. **3** a rumour. —*v* to make a whizzing sound.

sough[2] *same as* **sheugh**[2].

soughless *adj* noiseless.

souk *same as* **sook**.

soukie-clover *same as* **sookie**.

soul[1] *same as* **saul**[1].

soul[2] *same as* **sole**[3].

soul-couper *n* one who sells his soul.

souldart *n* a soldier.

soul-heezin' *adj* uplifting the soul.

soult *same as* **sault**.

soum[1], **soume** *n* **1** twenty sheep. **2** the number of sheep or cattle proportioned to a pasture.—*v* to fix the number of animals to be kept on land occupied by more than one proprietor or tenant.

soum[2] *v* to surmise.

soum[3] *same as* **soom**[2].

soum[4] *same as* **soam**[3].

soum[5] *n* the air bladder of a fish.

soum and roum *n* pasture in summer and fodder in winter.

soun'[1] *adj* **1** sound. **2** orthodox. **3** sound asleep. **4** (*of a period of time*) whole, unbroken. **5** level, smooth.

soun'[2] *v* **1** to sound. **2** to test the acoustics of a building. **3** to utter, pronounce. **4** to scold.

sound *v* **1** to swoon. **2** to stun. **3** to spin a top. **4** to spin as a top.—*n* a swoon, faint.
soundly *adv* **1** properly. **2** regularly.
soup[1] *v* **1** to soak, drench. **2** to drink copiously.—*n* **1** a soaking, washing. **2** a state of wetness. **3** a big draught. **4** a piece of ground always wet or muddy.
soup[2] *same as* **soop**.
soup[3] *same as* **sup**.
soupet[1] *adj* water-logged.
soupet[2] *adj* **1** wearied, spent. **2** emaciated.
soupie *n* a sling.
souping-wet *adj* soaking.
soupit swept.
souple[1], **souple**[2] *same as* **soople**[2], **soople**[3].
soup-meagre *n* a thin soup.
soup-tatties *n* potato soup.
soup-the-causey *n* **1** a scrub, niggard. **2** one who would do the meanest thing for money.
sour *same as* **soor**.
sourock, sourack, sourick *n* the sorrel.
sourock-faced *adj* sour-faced.
sous, souse *n* a sou, a halfpenny.
souse[1] *n* a plunge into water.—*adv* with a sudden splash.
souse[2] *v* **1** to thump, cuff. **2** to box the ears. **3** to fall of a heap. **4** to sit down suddenly with a bump. **5** to let fall heavily, drop.—*n* **1** a blow on the head. **2** a box on the ear. **3** a heavy fall or its sound. **4** a load. **5** a dirty, mixed mass of food, etc.—*adv* with sudden violence.
soust feet *n* pickled cow heel.
souter, soutar, soutor *n* a shoemaker, cobbler.—*v* **1** to botch, spoil utterly. **2** to give up, yield. **3** to get the better of, worst.
souter's brandy *n* buttermilk.
souter's clod *n* a kind of coarse wheaten bread sold for a halfpenny a roll.
souter's deevil *n* a shoemaker's awl.
souter's ends *n* a kind of twine.
souter's grace *n* a mock appeal to St Crispin, the patron saint of shoemakers.
souter's howlet *n* an opprobrious term of address.
southen *adj* southern.
souther *same as* **souder**.
southland, southlin *adj* southern.
southlins *adj* southwards.
southron *adj* **1** southern. **2** English as distinguished from Scottish.—*n* **1** a southerner. **2** an Englishman.
soutrie *n* a miscooked liquid dish.
soutt, sout *n* **1** a leap, bounce. **2** the start or bounce of a plough when it meets a stone.
soutt, sout *v* to sob.
soutter *same as* **souter**.
sove *v in phr* **to sove awe' hame** to go home quickly.
soverty *n* surety.
sow[1] *n* **1** a dirty, swinish person. **2** a game played by a number of persons with shinties. **3** the small piece of wood or bone used in the game of sow. **4** a small heap of cherry stones in a children's game.
sow[2], **sowe** *n* **1** a large rectangular stack. **2** a cluster of objects. **3** anything in a state of disorder. **4** a bride's outfit.—*v* to stack hay or straw in a sow.
sow[3] *v* (*with* **on**) to sow for grass.
sowback *n* a woman's cap with a raised fold running lengthways from the brow to the back of the head.
sowback ~, sowbackit mutch *n* a sowback (qv).
sow-~, soo-brock *n* a badger.
sowce[1] *n* **1** flummery. **2** brose. **3** sowens. **4** porridge, etc. *See* **sowen**.
sowce[2] *same as* **souse**[2].
sow-crae *n* a pigsty, piggery.
sowd *same as* **soud**.
sowder *same as* **souder**.
sowdie *same as* **soudie**.
sow-driver *n* the player who tries to drive the sow into the hole in the game of sow. *See* **sow**.

sowe *n* a winding sheet.
sowen, sowan, sowin *v* to smear with sowens.—*n* **1** weavers' paste. **2** (*in pl*) sowens (qv).—*adj* **1** made of sowens. **2** containing sowens.
sowen boat, ~ bowie *n* a small barrel used in preparing sowens (qv).
sowen brod *n* the board used by weavers for laying their paste on the web.
sowen cog *n* a wooden vessel for holding weavers' paste.
sowen crock *n* a jar for holding weavers' paste.
sowenie mug *n* a contemptuous name for a weaver.
sowening *n* the custom of smearing neighbours' doors with sowens (qv).
sowen kit *n* a vessel in which sowens (qv) are made.
sowen mug *n* a dish for holding sowens (qv) when made.
sowen pot *n* a sowen kit (qv).
sowens *n* a dish made by steeping and fermenting the husks, seeds or siftings of oats in water and then boiling.
sowens breakfast *n* a breakfast of sowens (qv).
sowen seeds, ~ aids *n* the husks of oats used for making sowens.
sowen sieve *n* a sieve for straining sowens (qv) and freeing them from the husks used in making them.
sowens-nicht *n* Christmas Eve, OS, when parties were held for sharing sowens (qv), bread, cheese and ale and when it was the practice to besmear the doors of neighbours with sowens.
sowens pan *n* a sowen kit (qv).
sowen-splatter *n* weavers' paste.
sowens porridge *n* porridge made of cold sowens (qv) by mixing them with oatmeal while on the fire.
sowens-say, ~-sey *n* a sowens sieve, a strainer affixed to the sowen tub (qv).
sowen suds *n* weavers' paste.
sowen tub *n* a sowen kit (qv).
sower *same as* **souder**.
sower-bread *n* a flitch of bacon.
sowf[1] *same as* **sooch**[1].
sowf[2] *same as* **souch**.
sowgh *same as* **souch**.
sowie *n* a small heap of cherry stones used in a children's game. *See* **sow**[1].
sowings *n* sowens (qv).
sow-in-the-kirk *n* the game of sow. *See* **sow**[1].
sowk *v* to drench.—*n* a sot, tippler.
sow-kill *n* a lime kiln dug out of the earth.
sowl *v* to pull by the ears.
sowle *n* a swivel.
sow-libber *n* a castrator or spayer of swine.
sowloch *v* to wallow like a sow.
sow-luggit *adj* with hanging ears, with ears like a sow.
sowm[1], **sowmp** *same as* **soam**[3].
sowm[2] *same as* **soom**[2].
sowm[3], **sowme** *same as* **soum**[1].
sownack *n* a Hallowe'en bonfire.
sowns sowens (qv).
sowp[1] *same as* **soup**[1].
sowp[2] *same as* **sup**.
sowr *same as* **soor**.
sowroo *n* sorrow, used in imprecations.
sow's coach *n* the game of hot cockles.
sowse *same as* **souse**[1].
sow siller *n* **1** hush money. **2** a bribe to pervert justice.
sow's mou *n* a piece of paper rolled on the hand and twisted at one end, to hold small quantities of groceries.
sow's tail *n* a spoiled knot in binding sheaves.
sowster *n* a sempstress.
sowter *same as* **souter**.
sowth[1] *same as* **souch**.
sowth[2] *same as* **sooth**[1].
sowther *same as* **souder**.
soy *n* silk, silken material.
spa *n* drink, liquor.
spaad *n* a spade.

space *n* a pace.—*v* **1** to measure by paces. **2** to pace.
spacier *v* **1** to walk. **2** to march.
spack *v* spoke, spake.
spade'l *n* a spadeful.
spade-peat *n* a large surface turf for placing at the back of the hearth on which a peat fire burns.
spading *n* **1** a trench of a spade in depth. **2** the depth of soil raised at one time by a spade.
spae[1] *v* to foretell. **2** to tell fortunes. **3** to prophesy. **4** to forebode.
spae[2] *n* the opening or slit in a gown, petticoat, etc.
spae book *n* a book of necromancy or witch spells.
spaecraft *n* the art of fortune-telling.
spaedom *n* **1** witchcraft. **2** prognostication.
spaeg *same as* **spaig**[2].
spaeman *n* **1** a diviner, soothsayer. **2** a male fortune-teller.
späer *n* a fortune-teller, soothsayer.
spae-trade *n* the art of fortune-telling.
spaewife, spaewoman *n* a female fortune-teller.
spaework *n* spaecraft (qv).
spaig[1] *n* **1** a hand. **2** a paw. **3** a limb.
spaig[2] *n* **1** a skeleton. **2** a tall, lanky person. **3** a person with long, ill-shaped legs.
spaigin *n* a tall, lanky person.
spaik[1] *n* **1** a spoke. **2** the spoke of a wheel. **3** a bar of wood. **4** a branch or slip of a tree planted to grow. **5** (*in pl*) the spokes on which a coffin is borne to the grave.
spaik[2] *v* to speak.
spail[1], **spaill** *v* to work or walk with energy.—*n* **1** the act of so working. **2** a quantity. **3** an amount of work. **4** anything long.
spail[2] *n* **1** a splinter, chip or shaving of wood. **2** a lath of wood. **3** a lath or thin plank used in wooden houses for filling up the interstices of the beams. **4** the guttering of a candle
spain *v* to wean.
spaining brash *n* **1** milk fever. **2** the illness of infants resulting from their being weaned.
spaining time *n* **1** the season for weaning lambs. **2** weaning time.
Spainyie *adj* Spanish.—*n* **1** a West Indian cane sometimes smoked by boys. **2** used also for weavers' reeds and the reeds of bagpipes.
Spainyie flee *n* cantharides or Spanish fly.
Spainyie-flee blister *n* a fly blister.
spair[1] *adj* spare, thin.
spair[2] *same as* **spare**[1].
spairge *v* **1** to sprinkle, bespatter, scatter: **2** to slander. **3** to roughcast a wall. **4** to whitewash.—*n* a dash, a sprinkling. **5** what is sprinkled. **6** a dram of spirits. **7** a dash of contumely.
spairk *same as* **spark**.
spait *same as* **spate**.
spaive *same as* **spave**.
spaiver[1], **spaiver**[2] *same as* **spaver**[1], **spaver**[2].
spaivie *same as* **spavie**.
spaiviet *adj* spavined.
spak *v* spoke.—*v, adj* spoken.
spake *n* a spoke.
spald[1] *same as* **spaul**.
spald[2] *same as* **speld**.
spalder *same as* **spelder**[1].
spalding *same as* **spelding**.
spale[1], **spale**[2] *same as* **spail**[1], **spail**[2].
spale-board *n* a thin plank.
spale box *n* a box made of very thin wood for holding ointments, etc.
spale-horned *adj* (*of cattle*) having thin, broad horns.
spallard *n* **1** an espalier. **2** a trained fruit tree.
spaller *v* **1** to split open. **2** to injure the body in striding. **3** to sprawl.
spalliel *n* a cattle disease.
spalsh *n* a splash of colour, dirt, etc.
spalter *same as* **spaller**.

spalyin *adj* flat-footed.
span *v* to yoke horses to any sort of carriage.
spane[1] *v* **1** to grasp with both hands together. **2** (*of life*) to spend, pass.—*n* **1** the span of life, threescore and ten. **2** a grasp. **3** the act of grasping. **4** a definite portion.
spane[2] *same as* **spain**.
spang[1] *v* **1** to grasp. **2** to span.—*n* the act of grasping.
spang[2] *v* **1** to leap with elastic force. **2** to spring. **3** to cause to leap. **4** to stride along, walk quickly. —*n* **1** a leap, bound, spring. **2** a long stride. **3** a bang, a smart blow. **4** a fillip.
spang-cockle *n* a game, played with marbles, nuts, etc, placed on the second joint of the forefinger and smartly spun off by the application of the thumb.
spang-fire-new *adj* quite new.
spanghew, spanghue *v* **1** to jerk anything violently into the air by placing it on one end of a board, the middle of which rests on a wall, etc, and striking the other end smartly. **2** to torture frogs, yellowhammers, etc, thus. **3** to bend back one end of a bough and suddenly release it so as to strike a person.
spangie[1] *n* an animal fond of leaping.
spangie[2] *n* a boys' game, the game of boss and span.
spangiehewit *n* a barbarous sport of boys with young yellowhammers, frogs, etc.
spanging *adj* nimble, active.
spang-new *adj* quite new, span-new.
spang-tade, -taid *n* a barbarous sport of children with frogs and toads. *See* **spanghew**.
spanhew *same as* **spanghew**.
spank[1] *v* to stride, run.—*n* a leap, bound, speed.
spank[2] *v* **1** to sparkle. **2** to shine.
spank[3] *same as* **spunk**.
spanker *n* **1** an active, tall, well-made person. **2** one who moves rapidly. **3** (*in pl*) long, thin legs.
spankering *adj* nimble, agile and tall.
spanker-new *adj* quite new, span-new.
spanking *adj* **1** smart. **2** active. **3** showy. **4** sprightly.
spankingly *adv* **1** smartly. **2** rapidly. **3** in dashing style.
spanky *adj* **1** sprightly, frisky. **2** smart, well-dressed.—*n* one who moves rapidly.
spar[1] *v* **1** to shut. **2** to bar a door with a wooden bolt.
spar[2] *same as* **sparr**.
spare[1] *n* the slit in a gown, petticoat or front of a pair of trousers.
spare[2] *adj* **1** deficient, lacking. **2** meagre.
spare[3] *v* **1** to save, retrench. **2** to save from. **3** to do without.
sparely *adv* scantily, poorly.
spareness *n* scantiness, poverty.
sparge *same as* **spairge**.
sparginer, spargiter *n* a plasterer.
spar-hawk *n* the sparrow hawk.
spark *n* **1** a speck, spot. **2** an atom. **3** a spirt, jet of boiling water, mud, etc. **4** a spot of dirt, etc. **5** a small quantity of liquor, a nip of whisky.—*v* **1** to strike a light or match. **2** to fall or strike in drops. **3** to fly off in bits. **4** to scatter seeds thinly. **5** to bespatter with spots. **6** to rain slightly. **7** to sparkle.
spark in the hawse *or* **throat** *n* a craving for liquor.
spark in the wick *or* **candle** *n* an omen indicating the arrival of a letter.
sparkle *n* **1** a spark. **2** a gleam of light. **3** (*in pl*) large flying sparks of fire or burning wood, straw, etc.
sparklit *adj* speckled.
sparling *n* the smelt.
sparple, sparpel *v* **1** to scatter. **2** to sprinkle. **3** to spread abroad.
sparr *v* to place the legs and arms so as to resist a strain.—*adv* in a state of opposition.
sparrible *n* a sparable.
sparrow *n* the corn bunting.
sparrow-blastit *adj* dumfounded.
sparrow drift, ~ hail *n* very small shot for small birds.

sparrow hawk *n* the merlin.
sparry *adj* sharp-pointed, like a sparable.
sparrygrass *n* asparagus.
sparse *adj* (*of writing*) widely spread, far apart.
spart[1] *same as* **sprat**.
spart[2] *v* to scatter dung with a muck hack (qv).
spartle *v* **1** to leap, spring. **2** to paw. **3** (*used of a child*) to sprawl, kick about.
sparty *adj* abounding in rushes.
spash *n* the foot.
spat[1] *n* a spot, a place.
spat[2] *n* a quarrel, tiff.
spat[3] *n* a gaiter, legging.
spatch *n* **1** a large spot. **2** a patch. **3** a plaster.
spate *n* **1** a flood. **2** a sudden flood in a river. **3** a sudden, heavy downfall of rain.—*v* **1** to flood. **2** to rain heavily. **3** to overwhelm. **4** to punish severely.
spate-ridden *adj* carried along by a flood.
spathie *n* a spotted river trout.
spatril *n* **1** a kind of shoe. **2** a gaiter. **3** (*in pl*) the notes in music.
spatterdashes *n* gaiters, leggings.
spattle[1] *n* **1** a spatula. **2** a pattle (qv) or plough spade.
spattle[2] *n* a slight inundation, a little spate (qv).
spaud[1] *n* a spade.
spaud[2] *v* to hasten, go quickly.
spaul *n* **1** the shoulder or forequarter of an animal. **2** a leg, limb. **3** a feeble stretching of the limbs.—*v* to push out the limbs feebly.
spauld[1] *same as* **speld**.
spauld[2] *same as* **spaul**.
spauldrochie *adj* long-legged.—*n* a long-legged fellow.
spauly *adj* **1** leggy. **2** having long thin legs. **3** having too much leg for beauty.
spave *v* to spay.
spaver[1] *n* one who spays cattle.
spaver[2] *n* a slit in front of the trousers.
spavie *n* the spavin in horses.—*v* to walk as if having the spavin.
spavy-fittit *adj* having feet that make one walk as if spavined.
spawer *same as* **spaver**[2].
spawl *same as* **spaul**.
spawly *same as* **spauly**.
spawn *n* a span in the game of spawnie (qv).
spawnie *n* a boys' game with buttons, in which one player throws his button to a distance and another throws his as near as possible, winning the button if he reaches within a spawn of it.
spay *same as* **spae**[1].
speak *v* **1** to bespeak. **2** to be on friendly terms. **3** to attend, hearken to. **4** to come and hear what one has to say.—*n* **1** a speech. **2** talk, gossip. **3** a conversation. **4** a subject of talk or of gossip.
speakable *adj* affable.
speak-a-word room *n* a small waiting room or parlour in a large house.
speak for *v* to bespeak, engage.
speak hame *v* to answer.
speak ill *v* to scold.
speak in *v* to make a short call on one in passing.
speak to *v* **1** to rebuke. **2** to threaten. **3** to chastise. **4** to ask in marriage. **5** to bear witness to.
speal[1], **speal**[2] *same as* **speel**[1], **speel**[2].
speal[3] *same as* **spaul**.
speal[4], **speall** *same as* **spail**[2].
speal bone *n* the shoulder bone of mutton.
spean *same as* **spain**.
speaning-brash *n* illness affecting infants on being weaned.
spear[1] *v* to taper, rise to a point.
spear[2] *same as* **speer**[1].
spearmen *n* the ancient city guard, or city officers, attending the authorities.

spearwind *n* **1** a gust of rage. **2** a violent passion.
speat *same as* **spate**.
speated *adj* (*used of a river*) in flood.
speave *same as* **spave**.
speavie *same as* **spavie**.
special *n* a type of keg beer.
specialies *adv* especially.
speck-glass *n* a spectacle glass.
speckilation *same as* **speculation**.
speckits *n* spectacles.
speckle *n* kind, quality.
specks, spects *n* spectacles.
spectacle *v* to examine through a pair of spectacles.—*n* (*in pl*) the merrythought of a fowl.
speculation *n* **1** the power of vision. **2** a spectacle. **3** a subject of remark or gossip. **4** an object of contempt. **5** a fanciful rumour. **6** a romance.
speddart *n* **1** a spider. **2** a tough old creature, tight as a wire.
spedlin *n* a child just beginning to walk.
speech-crier *n* a street seller of speeches, etc.
speechman *n* a speech-crier (qv).
speed *n* a state of excitement, a quarrel.—*v* to give success.
speedard, speeder *same as* **speddart**.
speedy, speedy-fit *n* a child that can run alone.
speeho *n* **1** a rumpus. **2** outburst. **3** uproar.
speel[1] *v* **1** to climb, to ascend. **2** to climb vertically upwards by hands and feet.—*n* a climb, ascent.
speel[2] *v* **1** to play, sport, amuse oneself. **2** to slide on ice.—*n* a game, play, match.
speelick *n* **1** a smart blow or tap. **2** a hard blow.
speeliewally *n* **1** a tall, thin, delicate-looking person. **2** a tall, thin, young shoot or plant.
speen[1] *n* a spoon.
speen[2] *same as* **spain**.
speendrift *n* **1** snow driven by the wind from the ground. **2** spindrift. **3** spray.
speengie rose *n* the peony.
speeock *n* a stake or log of wood.
speer[1] *v* **1** to ask, inquire, question. **2** to ask in marriage, pop the question.—*n* **1** a search, investigation. **2** an inquisitive person.
speer[2] *v* **1** to spirt. **2** to squirt.
speere *n* an opening in a house wall through which inquiries were made and answered in the case of strange visitors.
speerings *n* **1** inquiry, investigation, interrogation. **2** news, tidings. **3** prying inspection.
speerin' word *n* the right to ask in marriage.
speerit *n* spirit.
speerity *adj* spirited.
speer-wundit *adj* out of breath with exertion.
speet[1] *same as* **spit**[2].
speet[2] *n* **1** spite. **2** a cause of grief. **3** a disappointment.
speg *n* a pin or peg of wood.
speikintare *n* the common tern.
speil[1], **speil**[2] *same as* **speel**[1], **speel**[2].
speinty *n* a spawned fish.
speir[1] *same as* **speere**.
speir[2] *same as* **speer**[1].
spek *v* to speak.
spel *same as* **speel**[2].
spelch *same as* **spelsh**.
speld *v* **1** to split open. **2** to spread open. **3** to expand.
spelder[1] *v* **1** to split, cut up. **2** to tear open. **3** to draw asunder. **4** to toss the limbs in walking. **5** to stretch out the legs. **6** to sprawl. **7** to rack the limbs in striding.
spelder[2] *n* one who splits fish for curing.
speldin, speldane *n* a small fish, split open, salted and dried in the sun.
spelding *adj* **1** broken. **2** awkward. **3** halting.
speldrin *same as* **speldin**.

speldron *n* **1** an awkward, sprawling, loose-limbed person. **2** a term of contempt.

spele *same as* **speel**¹.

spelk *n* **1** a splinter. **2** a thin piece of wood. **3** a sharp splinter of iron flying from the mass to which it belongs. **4** a splint for a broken limb. **5** a very thin person or thing. **6** a young, slender boy or girl.—*v* **1** to splinter. **2** to put in splints. **3** to set a broken limb.

spelked *adj* (*used of wood*) ragged.

spell¹ *same as* **spail**¹.

spell² *n* **1** spelling. **2** a spelling lesson.—*v* **1** to tell, narrate. **2** to discourse. **3** to asseverate falsely. **4** to exaggerate. **5** to decipher.

spell³ *same as* **spill**¹.

spellan *same as* **speldin**.

spellbook *n* a spelling book.

spell-wind *n* **1** a gust of rage. **2** a violent outburst.

spell-woman *n* a female fortune-teller.

spelsh *v* **1** to dash a liquid or semiliquid substance. **2** to splash, bespatter. **3** to dash or fall heavily into a liquid or semiliquid substance. **4** to splash through mud or water.—*n* **1** any liquid or semiliquid thrown violently. **2** the act of throwing it so. **3** a fall into mud, water, etc. **4** the sound of such fall.

spen¹ *v* to spend.

spen² *same as* **spain**.

spence *n* **1** a spare room on the same flat as the kitchen. **2** a country parlour. **3** a larder. **4** a room containing a loom.—*v* to put into the inner or spare room of a house.

spence-door *n* a door between the kitchen and the pantry or the inner room.

spend¹ *v* **1** (*used of time*) to pass. **2** to waste.—*n* wasting, expense.

spend² *v* **1** to spring. **2** to gallop.—*n* **1** a spring, bound. **2** an elastic motion.

spend³ *same as* **spain**.

spendrife *adj* **1** prodigal. **2** extravagant.—*n* a spendthrift.

Spengyie, Spengie *adj* Spanish.—*n* a West Indian cane.

spenn *v* to button or lace one's clothes.

spens, spense *same as* **spence**.

spentacles, spenticles *n* spectacles.

speochan *same as* **speuchan**.

sper¹ *same as* **spar**¹.

sper² *same as* **speer**¹.

spere¹ *same as* **speere**.

spere² *same as* **speer**¹.

sperfle *same as* **sparple**.

sperk *same as* **spark**.

sperling *same as* **sparling**.

sperple *same as* **sparple**.

spert *n* the dwarf rush.

sperthe *n* a battle-axe.

spes hie *n* species.

speuchan *n* a tobacco pouch.

speug *same as* **spyug**.

speugle *n* anything extremely slender.

speul *same as* **spaul**.

spew *v* **1** to pour forth contents. **2** to pour forth smoke, etc. **3** (*of corn*) to have the ear firm. **4** (*of snow*) to drive strongly in a blizzard.—*n* an outpouring of smoke, etc.

spewing *adj* **1** giving out smoke. **2** (*of sores*) exuding, running.

spewing-fou *adj* disgustingly drunk.

spey *same as* **spae**¹.

spey-codlin *n* a salmon.

speyk *same as* **speak**.

spice *n* **1** a small quantity. **2** a sample. **3** a specimen. **4** pepper. **5** pride. **6** a blow, thwack.—*v* **1** to pepper, as with shot. **2** to beat, thwack.

spice box, ~ buist *n* a pepper box.

spicerie *n* **1** a specimen. **2** (*in pl*) groceries.

spicket *n* **1** a spigot. **2** a wooden tap.

spicy *adj* **1** smart, showy, neat. **2** peppered. **3** peppery, testy, proud.

spidarroch *n* **1** a day's work with a spade. **2** the ground that can be dug with a spade in a day.

spider-legs *n* **1** long, thin legs. **2** a person with long, thin legs.

spidert *same as* **speddart**.

spider-webster *n* a spider.

spiel *same as* **speel**².

spier *same as* **speer**¹.

spiffer *n* **1** anything very fine or showy. **2** a smartly dressed person.

spiffin *adj* fine, capital.

spig *n* a spigot.

spike-natl *n* a long nail.

spilder *same as* **spelder**.

spile tree *n* a long pole supported horizontally on which fishermen hung their lines in order to clean the hooks.

spilgie *adj* long and slender.—*n* **1** a tall meagre person. **2** a long limb.

spilk¹ *same as* **spelk**.

spilk² *v* **1** to shell peas. **2** to beat smartly.—*n* a smart blow.

spilkins *n* split peas.

spill *v* **1** to spoil, ruin, destroy. **2** to pour forth, overflow.—*n* **1** a ruin, wreck. **2** a sum of money.

spilth *n* **1** what is spilled. **2** overflow. **3** waste.

spin¹ *n* a spoon.

spin² *v* **1** (*of the heart*) to beat quickly. **2** (*of the blood*) to course rapidly. **3** to prosper quickly, succeed. —*n* a drinking bout.

spindle *n* **1** four hanks of yarn. **2** a tall, thin person.—*adj* tall and slender.—*v* **1** (*of plants*) to grow tall and lanky with great rapidity. **2** (*of grain*) to shoot out.

spindle-shanks *n* **1** long, thin legs. **2** a person having such legs.

spindlewood *n* splinters.

spindly *adj* **1** tall and thin. **2** overgrown.

spink¹ *n* the goldfinch.

spink² *n* a diminutive person.

spink³ *n* **1** the pink, in general. **2** the primrose. **3** the polyanthus.

spink *adj* (*used of ale*) brisk, strong, good.

spinkie *n* a dram or glass of spirits.

spinkie *adj* slender and active.

spin'le *same as* **spindle**.

spin'le-neb, ~-nib *n in phr* **at the spin'le-neb wi'** at the end of one's resources or exertions.

spinly *same as* **spindly**.

Spin Maggie, ~ Mary *n* a daddy-longlegs.

spinnel *same as* **spindle**.

spinner¹ *n* a daddy-longlegs.

spinner² *v* **1** to run or fly swiftly. **2** to move in a spiral form.—*n* **1** a smart rate of speed. **2** a smart, swift rush or dash.

spinnie *n* a wheel.

spinning boy *n* a weaver.

spinning day *n* a day formerly given by tenants' daughters to spinning for the laird's wife.

spinning genny *n* **1** a spinning wheel. **2** a daddy-longlegs.

Spinning Maggie, ~ Meg *n* a daddy-longlegs.

spinnle *same as* **spindle**.

spintie *adj* **1** lean. **2** thin.

spiog *same as* **spoig**.

spire¹ *n* a small, tapering tree, generally a fir tree, of a size fit for paling.—*v* **1** to soar upwards. **2** to aspire.

spire² *n* **1** the stem of an earthfast couple (qv), reaching from the floor to the top of a cottage wall, partly inserted in and partly standing out of the wall. **2** a wall between the fire and the door, with a seat in it. **3** the lower part of a couple (qv).

spire³ *n* spray.

spire⁴ *v* **1** to wither. **2** to cause to fade.

spires *n* small particles of spittle projected from the mouth.

spirewind *same as* **spearwind**.

spirg *n* as much liquid as will moisten the lips.

spirie[1] *adj* **1** tall, slender. **2** (*used of growing plants*) tall and weak.

spirie[2] *adj* warm, parching with drought.

spiring *adj* aspiring, soaring.

spirit *v* to inspire, inspirit.

spirity *adj* **1** spirited. **2** lively. **3** full of life.

spirk *same as* **spark**.

spirl[1] *v* to run about in a light, lively way.

spirl[2] *adj* slender. *See* **spirlie**.

spirlicket *n* **1** a particle. **2** an atom.

spirlie *adj* slender, thin, spindly.—*n* **1** a slender spiral column of smoke, vapour, etc. **2** a slender person.

spirlie-legget *adj* having thin legs.

spirling[1] *n* a commotion, broil.

spirling[2] *same as* **sparling**.

spirnling *n* a spirling (qv).

spirran *n* **1** a spider. **2** a horrid old woman. **3** a hag.

spirt *same as* **sprat**[1].

spirtle *same as* **spurtle**.

spiry[1], **spiry**[2] *same as* **spirie**[1], **spirie**[2].

spit[1] *v* **1** to rain slightly. **2** to be very angry with one. —*n* **1** the spitting of a consumptive patient. **2** an outburst. **3** a slight disputation. **4** a small, hot-tempered person, a spitfire. **5** a slight shower.

spit[2] *n* a stick or skewer on which fish are hung to dry.—*v* to put fish on a skewer to dry.

spit[3] *n* the depth of a spade in digging.

spital, spittal *n* **1** a hospital. **2** the site of an old, demolished hospital.

spit-deep *adj* of the depth of a spade in digging.

spite *n* **1** provocation. **2** a disappointment.—*v* **1** to provoke, vex. **2** to exasperate. **3** to scorn, despise.

spither *n* foam, spume, froth.

spit in one's face *v* **1** to reproach. **2** to take revenge on one.

spit-stick *n* **1** a pointed piece of wood or iron prong on which meat is roasted. **2** used contemptuously of a small sword or rapier.

spitten[1] *same as* **spittin**.

spitten[2] *n* **1** a puny, mischievous creature. **2** a little person of hot temper. **3** a mettlesome, little animal. **4** a person of low rank.—*adj* of lowly birth.

spitter *n* **1** a very slight shower. **2** (*in pl*) small drops of snow or rain wind-driven.—*v* to rain or snow slightly.

spitterie *adj* spurting or flying out irregularly without connection of parts.

spittin *n* a spit, spittle.

spittle *n* **1** the act of spitting. **2** a thing of no account or value.

spitty, spittie *n* a horse.

splacher *v* **1** to splash. **2** to fall with a splash.

splae[1], **splae**[2] *same as* **splay**[1], **splay**[2].

splae seam *n* a hem seam, one side of which only is sewn down.

splairge, splarge *v* **1** to splash, sprinkle with liquid mud, etc. **2** to bespatter, besmear. **3** to fall in fragments or scattered splinters.—*n* **1** a splash of mud, etc. **2** anything spattered or splashed.

splart *v* **1** to chatter. **2** to quarrel.

splash[1] *n* a patch of colour.

splash[2] *adj* splay.

splash feet *n* splay feet.

splash fluke *n* the plaice.

splat *v* did split.

splatch *n* **1** a splash. **2** a bespattering of mud, etc. **3** anything so broad or full as to exhibit an awkward appearance, as a clumsy seal on a letter.—*v* to splash, bedaub.

splatchin *v* to bedaub.—*n* a splash or patch of dirt.

splatter *v* **1** to splash with water, mud, etc. **2** to besprinkle, bespatter. **3** to dash or splash hastily through water, mud, etc. **4** to splutter. **5** to come out in spirts or in a rush, to scatter. **6** to walk or run with a rattling noise.—*n* **1** a splash, splutter. **2** a sharp, rattling noise, the causing of such a noise. **3** a rush, dash. **4** a sudden stir or bustle. **5**

an outcry, hubbub. **6** a wrangle. **7** (*in pl*) uproarious mirth.—*adv* with a splashing noise.

splatterdash *n* **1** an uproar. **2** a splutter. **3** the sound as of racing among mud, etc.

splay[1] *n* **1** a great display or show. **2** a quarrel. **3** a stroke.

splay[2] *v* **1** to fasten down the edges of a seam. **2** to mend a tear in cloth by sewing the edges together without adding a patch.—*n* the hem made in fastening down the edges of a seam.

splay[3] *v* **1** to skin. **2** to flay.

splechrie *n* **1** furniture. **2** an unmarried woman's clothes and furniture. **3** what a bride brings with her to her husband's house. **4** the executory of a defunct person or his or her movable goods left to his or her heirs.

splee-fitted *adj* splay-footed.

spleet *v* to split.—*v*, *adj* split.—*n* a chip.

spleeted on *phr* departed from.

spleet-new *same as* **split-new**.

spleetrin *v*, *adj* spilling.

spleit *v* to split.

splender *same as* **splinder**.

splender-new *adj* quite new.

splenner *same as* **splinner**[2].

splent *same as* **splint**[1].

splerg *same as* **splairge**.

splerrie *v* to splash in or with mud.

splet *v*, *adj* split.

spleuchan *same as* **speuchan**.

spleut *v* **1** to burst forth with a spluttering noise. **2** to fall flat into mud, etc. **3** to walk in an ungainly and splashing manner.—*n* **1** a sudden spluttering gush or rush. **2** the noise of such a rush. **3** any weak or watery drink. **3** a quantity of liquid or semiliquid substance spilled in an unseemly mass.—*adv* **1** with a spluttering gush. **2** with an unbecoming, splashing step.

spleutter *same as* **spleut**.

spleutterie *adj* **1** weak and watery. **2** (*used of the weather*) very rainy.—*n* **1** weak, watery, dirty food. **2** an unseemly, dirty mess.

splew *v* to spit out, spew.

spley *same as* **splay**[2].

splinder *n* **1** a splinter. **2** a fragment.—*v* **1** to splinter. **2** to be shivered into fragments.

splinder-new *adj* quite new.

splinkey *adj* **1** tall and lank. **2** spindly.

splinner[1] *n* speed, force.—*adv* with speed.

splinner[2] *same as* **splinder**.

splint[1] *n* a hard, laminated variety of bituminous coal.

splint[2] *n* armour worn on the legs and arms.

splinter-new *adj* quite new.

splirt *v* **1** to eject liquid forcibly. **2** to spit out.

splish-splash *adv* in a splashing manner.

split[1] *n* **1** (*in weaving*) a single thread in plain linen work. **2** (*in pl*) the divisions of a weaver's reed.

split[2] *v* **1** (*used in curling*) to separate two stones lying closely together. **2** (*in ploughing*) to lay the furrows on each side off from the line at which the ploughing of the part is to be finished.

split an oath *v* to swear.

split-new *adj* quite new.

split-nut *n* a beechnut.

splitten *adj* split.

splitter[1] *v* **1** to splutter. **2** to make a spluttering noise.

splitter[2] *n* one who splits fish in order to take out the backbone.

splittie *n* a split, disagreement, division.

splitting-full *adj* full to bursting.

spliung *same as* **splung**.

sploit[1] *v* **1** to spout, squirt. **2** to splash.—*n* **1** a squirt. **2** an expectoration. **3** a little liquid.

sploit[2] *n* **1** an exploit. **2** a trick, joke.

sploiter *same as* **sploit**[1].

splore *n* **1** a frolic, a spree. **2** a revel. **3** an outing. **4** a game, romp, play. **5** an escapade. **6** a drinking bout. **7** a debauch. **8** a quarrel. **9** a scrimmage. **10** an outbreak. **11** a disturbance, rumpus, fuss. **12** a sudden movement.—*v* **1** to frolic. **2** to riot. **3** to show off. **4** to let a thing be known with startling results. **5** to boast, brag.

splore² *v* to explore.

splore³ *adj in phr* **little splore pearls** spittle, drops of saliva ejected in speaking.

splorroch *n* the sound made by walking in wet or mud.

sploy *n* **1** a frolic. **2** a frolicsome or funny story. **2** a ploy.

spluchan *same as* **speuchan**.

splung *v* **1** to carry off by stealth. **2** to filch. **3** to walk with striding, swinging, stealthy gait.—*n* a mean, disagreeable person.

splunt *v* to court under cloud of night.—*n* such courting.

splunting *adj* amorous.—*n* the running after girls at night.

splurt *n* **1** a spurt. **2** a splutter. **3** a sudden movement.

splute *v* to exaggerate in narration.—*n* an exaggerator.

splutter *v* **1** to splash, besprinkle. **2** to gush out noisily. **3** to spill awkwardly and dirtily. **4** to ramble about noisily. **5** to walk with a dirty, splashing step.—*n* **1** weak, watery liquid. **2** an unseemly mess of spilt liquid or semiliquid stuff. **3** a fuss, disturbance. **4** rain.—*adv* **1** with a sharp, spluttering noise. **2** with a dirty, splashing step.

spluttery *adj* **1** weak and watery. **2** rainy.—*n* a nasty, dirty mess.

splytten *v*, *adj* split.

splynchan *same as* **speuchan**.

spoach, spoatch *v* **1** to poach, to pick up trifles. **2** to search for anything. **3** to lounge about for meat or drink.—*n* **1** a poacher. **2** a picker-up of trifles.

spoacher *n* **1** a poacher. **2** one who lounges about in search of a meal, etc.

spodlin *same as* **spedlin**.

spog *n* the spoke of a wheel.

spogshave *n* a spokeshave.

spoig *n* **1** a paw, hand, foot. **2** a limb.

spoilzie, spoilyie *same as* **spulyie**.

spoke¹ *v*, *adj* spoken.

spoke² *same as* **spaik**².

sponga *same as* **spunga**.

sponge *n* **1** a baker's mop. **2** putrid moisture issuing from the mouth, eyes, etc, after death. **3** a low, sneaking person on the lookout for food. **4** a wandering dog. **5** a person inclined to steal.—*v* **1** to ooze. **2** (*used of a dead body*) to exude putrid moisture. **3** to prowl about in search of food.

sponk *same as* **spunk**.

sponsefu' *adj* responsible, respectable.

sponsibility *n* responsibility.

sponsible *adj* **1** respectable, trustworthy, honourable. **2** of good standing and repute. **3** substantial, well-to-do.

sponsible-looking *adj* of respectable appearance.

spool¹ *n* a weaver's shuttle.

spool² *same as* **spulyie**.

spool-fittit *adj* **1** splay-footed. **2** having the feet twisted outwards like a weaver's shuttle.

spoolie *same as* **spulyie**.

spoom *v* **1** to swoop. **2** (*of a hawk*) to dart after prey.

spoon *n* part of the breast.—*v* to attempt to feed with a spoon.

spoonbill duck *n* the scaup.

spoonge *same as* **sponge**.

spoon-hale *adj* **1** able to enjoy one's food. **2** in capital health.

spoon mouth *n* the hollow part of a spoon.

spoon shaft, ~ shank *n* the handle of a spoon.

spoot¹, **spoot**² *same as* **spout**¹, **spout**².

spootcher *same as* **spoucher**.

spooter *n* **1** a squirt, syringe. **2** a tin tube for shooting peas.

spootragh *same as* **spoutroch**.

sporge *same as* **spairge**.

sporne *v* spared.

spot *n* any person or thing remarkable or that attracts attention.

spotch *same as* **spoach**.

spot-preen *n* a kind of pin used in playing with the teetotum.

spottie *v* to run with great speed.—*n* a will-o'-the-wisp.

spotly *n* a designation of a fox.

spoucher *n* a long-handled wooden ladle, used to bale a boat or lift fish out.

spounge *same as* **sponge**.

spousal *adj* betrothed.

spouse, spouss *v* to put one's fortune out to nurse.

spout¹ *v* **1** to spurt. **2** to come with a rush. **3** to dart forth. **4** to run forth briskly. **5** to run in a frisky way. **6** to press rapidly through a narrow gap. **7** to spue. **8** to recite, give a recitation, to orate.—*n* **1** a spurt. **2** a sudden rush. **3** a frisky run. **4** a boggy part of a road. **5** a boggy spring. **6** a runner of water. **7** a waterfall. **8** a large coal shoot. **9** a horn, trumpet. **10** a squirt, syringe. **11** a shotgun.

spout², **spout fish** *n* the razorfish.

spouter *same as* **spooter**.

spout gun *n* a popgun.

spoutie *adj* **1** vain. **2** foppish.

spoutiness *n* the state of having many boggy springs.

spoutroch *n* **1** any kind of drink. **2** weak, wishy-washy drink.

spout well *n* a well with a pump or spout.

spout whale *n* a porpoise.

spouty *adj* **1** marshy. **2** abounding in springs.

sprach *same as* **spraich**.

sprachle, sprachel *same as* **sprauchle**.

sprack¹ *adj* **1** lively, animated. **2** brisk, smart, nimble.

sprack² *n* a spark.—*v* to throw off sparks.

sprackle *same as* **sprauchle**.

sprag *n* a piece of wood or iron inserted in the spokes of a wheel to arrest progress.—*v* **1** to insert a sprag in the spokes of a wheel. **2** to check one's progress.

spraghle *same as* i**sprauchle**.

spraich *v* **1** to cry shrilly or peevishly. **2** to scream. **3** to wail.—*n* **1** a cry. **2** a shriek. **3** a wail. **4** a child's scream. **5** a crowd, swarm. **6** cockcrow.

spraichle *same as* **sprauchle**.

spraich o' day *n* daybreak.

spraichrie *n* **1** cattle-lifting. **2** stolen goods.

spraickle *same as* **sprauchle**.

spraigherie *n* stolen goods.

spraickle *same as* **spreckle**.

spraing, sprain *n* **1** a long stripe or streak. **2** a variegated streak. **3** a streamer. **4** a shade of colour. —*v* **1** to streak. **2** to stripe. **3** to variegate. **4** to tint. **5** to embroider with sprays on silk.

spraint *v* **1** to run or spring forward. **2** to sprint.

spraith *n* **1** a crowd. **2** a quantity, large number.

sprallich¹ *v* to sprawl.

sprallich² *v* to shriek.—*n* a loud, shrill cry.

sprangle *v* **1** to struggle. **2** to spring in order to get free. **3** to struggle.

sprangled *adj* (*used of hens*) speckled.

sprat, spratt *same as* **sprot**.

spratoon *n* the red-throated diver.

sprattle, spratle *v* **1** to scramble. **2** to struggle. **3** to sprawl.—*n* **1** a scramble. **2** a struggle. **3** a sprawl.

sprauch¹ *n* **1** a sparrow. **2** the house sparrow.

sprauch² *v* to sprawl.

sprauchle, spraughle, sprawchle *v* **1** to climb, clamber. **2** to scramble. **3** to struggle towards. **4** to sprawl.—*n* **1** a struggle. **2** a scramble. **3** a sprawl.

sprauge *n* a long, lean, clumsy finger, toe, hand or foot.

sprawls *n* **1** limbs. **2** pieces, shreds. **3** tatters.

spread *v in phr* **to spread a piece** to butter bread.

spreading drink *n* an old trade drinking custom.

spreagh *n* **1** cattle-lifting. **2** plunder, spoil.

spreagherie *n* **1** cattle-lifting. **2** small booty, movables of an inferior kind. **3** stolen goods.

spreat *same as* **sprot**.

spreath *same as* **spreagh**.

sprech *same as* **spraich**.
sprecherie *same as* **spreagherie**.
spreckle *v* **1** to speckle. **2** to become speckled.—*n* **1** a speckle. **2** a freckle.
spreckly *adj* speckled, spotted.
spree[1] *n* **1** a frolic. **2** merrymaking. **3** a jollification. **4** a quarrel, fight, disturbance.—*v* **1** to frolic. **2** to make merry. **3** to spend money in a spree. **4** to indulge in drunken, noisy or riotous mirth.
spree[2] *adj* **1** brisk, lively, spry. **2** neat, trim, gaudy, spruce.—*v* **1** to smarten up. **2** to make spruce.
spreet *n* a mischievous young person.
spreeth *n in phr* **a great spreeth o' fowk** a crowd of people much scattered.
spreich[1] *same as* **spraich**.
spreich[2] *same as* **spreagh**.
spreicherie *same as* **spreagherie**.
spreid, spreed *v* to spread.
spreiden *v* spread.
spreidit *v* did spread.
spreit *same as* **sprat**.
spreith-hunting *n* the search for, and salving of, the wreckage and cargo of timber-laden ships.
sprend *same as* **sprent**[3].
sprent[1] *n* **1** an opening. **2** a hole.
sprent[2] *v* to sprinkle.—*v, adj* sprinkled.
sprent[3] *v* **1** to spring suddenly forward. **2** to sprint.—*n* **1** the spring at the back of a pocketknife. **2** the spring or elastic force of anything. **3** any elastic body. **4** the spine. **5** the iron clasp that fastens down the lid of a chest or trunk.
sprentacles, sprenticles *n* spectacles.
spret, sprett *same as* **sprot**.
spretty *adj* full of rushes.
sprety *adj* sprightly.
sprewl, spreul *v* to sprawl, scramble, struggle.—*n* **1** a struggle. **2** one who struggles hard against difficulties, implying a diminutive person.
spried *v* did spread.
sprig[1] *same as* **sprug**.
sprig[2] *n* a tune, piece of music.
sprig[3] *adj* brisk, active.
sprightful *adj* sprightly.
sprightfulness *n* **1** sprightliness. **2** sparkle.
sprighty *adj* sprightly.
spring[1] *n* a quick, lively tune.
spring[2] *v* to work briskly and rapidly.
springald, springal *n* a stripling.
springer *n* a trout, so called from its leaping.
spring head *n* **1** a fountainhead. **2** a source, origin.
spring juices *n* the name of a nauseous medicinal potion compounded of brooklime, scurvy grass and other ingredients.
springle, springlin *same as* **springald**.
sprint *same as* **sprent**[3].
sprit[1] *same as* **sprot**.
sprit[2] *adv* quite.
sprithy *same as* **spritty**[2].
sprit-new *adj* quite new.
spritt *v* to run off suddenly.
sprittl't *same as* **spruttled**.
spritty[1] *same as* **spirity**.
spritty[2] *adj* **1** full of rushes. **2** full of tough roots.
sproag *v* to court under cloud of night.
sproaging *n* courting under cloud of night.
sprog[1] *same as* **sprauge**.
sprog[2] *same as* **sprug**.
sprog[3] *same as* **sproag**.
sprone *n* seabirds' liquid dung.—*v (used of birds)* to eject liquid dung.
sproo *n* a disease, other than the thrush, affecting the mouths of infants.
sprool *n* **1** a handline for deep-sea fishing. **2** a wire or piece of whalebone fixed crosswise at the end of a line, carrying a snood and a hook at each end.

sproot *v* to sprout.—*n* a child.
sproot *v* to spirt from the mouth.
sprootens *n* the sproutings of potato eyes.
sprootsail *n* a spritsail.
sproozle, sproosle *v* to struggle.—*n* **1** an anxious bustle. **2** a hurried exertion.
sprose *v* **1** to boast, brag. **2** to swagger, make a great show. **3** to commend oneself ostentatiously. **4** to magnify in narration.—*n* **1** brag, bravado. **2** ostentatious appearance, swagger. **3** a byword.
sproser *n* a braggart, boaster.
sprosie *adj* **1** ostentatious in language. **2** much given to self-praise.
sprot, sprote *n* **1** a coarse kind of grass. **2** the jointed-leaved rush. **3** the withered stem of any plant, broken and lying on the ground. **4** refuse of plants gathered for fuel. **5** a chip of wood flying from a carpenter's tool. **6** the end of a stalk of grain or branch of a tree blown off by a high wind.
sprotten *adj* made of sprots. *See* **sprot**.
sproug *same as* **sprug**.
sproulsie *n* **1** a fierce conflict. **2** a sharp skirmish.
sprouse *same as* **sprose**.
sprouser *same as* **sproser**.
sprout[1] *v* to rub off the sprouts of potatoes.—*n* **1** a child. **2** offspring.
sprout[2] *v* to spirt from the mouth.
sprowee *v* to brag.
spruch *same as* **sprush**.
sprud *n* a spud for removing limpets from a rock.
sprug *n* the house sparrow.
sprung *adj* tipsy.
sprunt *v* **1** to run quickly. **2** to run among the stacks after the girls at night.
sprunting *n* running among the stacks after the girls at night.
sprush *adj* spruce, neat, smart.—*v* **1** to deck, smarten up. **2** *(used of birds)* to raise up the feathers. **3** to dress up finely. **4** to set in order.—*n* **1** a decking out. **2** a setting in order.
sprushle *same as* **sproozle**.
spruttings *n* sproutings.
spruttled *adj* speckled, spotted.
spry *adj* **1** brisk, nimble. **2** sprightly, lively. **3** spruce. **4** smartly dressed.
spryauch *same as* **spraich**.
spryly *adv* quickly, briskly.
spryness *n* sprightliness, liveliness.
spud *n* **1** a potato. **2** a potato set. **3** a fondling name for a small boy.
spuddy *n* a fondling name for a small boy.
spudyoch *n* **1** any sputtering produced by ignition. **2** a small cone of moistened gunpowder set fire to at the apex. **3** a diminutive person who speaks or acts rapidly.
spue *same as* **spew**.
spug *same as* **spyug**.
spuilzie, spuilie, spuilyie, spoilly *same as* **spulyie**.
spule[1] *n* a thin, flat piece of wood.
spule[2] *same as* **spool**.
spule[3] *same as* **spaul**.
spule bane, ~ blade *n* the shoulder bone or blade.
spule-fittit *adj* **1** splay-footed. **2** with the feet turned outwards.
spulie *same as* **spool**.
spulp *v* **1** to collect and retail scandal. **2** to be a busybody or eavesdropper.
spulper *n* **1** a busybody, an eavesdropper. **2** a collector of scandal.
spulyie, spulzie *v* **1** to plunder, sack. **2** to spoil, lay waste. **3** to romp.—*n* **1** depredation. **2** a plundering raid. **3** the act of spoiling. **4** spoil, booty, plunder. **5** illegal meddling with movable goods.
spulyiement *n* spoil, booty.

spulyie-play *n* **1** a plundering raid. **2** a popular outbreak of destructiveness.

spulyier *n* a plunderer.

spun *n* tobacco twist.

spune *n* a spoon.

spune-drift *n* snow drifted from the ground by a whirling wind.

spune-hale *adj* able to take one's usual food.

spung[1] *n* a heavy blow.

spung[2] *v* to stride.

spung[3] *v* to broach a cask of wine, etc.

spung[4] *n* **1** a purse that closes with a spring. **2** a fob.—*v* **1** to rob. **2** to pick one's pocket.

spung[5] *n* the leg of a fowl, a drumstick.

spunga *n* a flecked cow.

spung and rung *n* the stick or board on which boys spang-hewed a toad. *See* **spang-hew**.

spunge[1] *same as* **sponge**.

spunge[2] *same as* **spung**[4].

spungit *adj* flecked, mottled.

spunk *n* **1** a spark of fire. **2** a very small fire. **3** the spark of life. **4** an old-fashioned match tipped with sulphur, used for kindling purposes. **5** a lucifer match. **6** spirit, pluck, vivacity. **7** a person of quick temper. **8** a person who has more spirit than bodily strength. **9** a small portion of any principle of intelligence or action.—*v* **1** to sparkle, twinkle. **2** (*with* **out**) to come to light, become known. **3** (*with* **up**) to fire up, flash forth.

spunk-backet *adj* having a slender back.

spunk basket *n* a basket for holding spunks. *See* **spunk**.

spunk box *n* **1** a matchbox. **2** a tinderbox.

spunk flask *n* a powder flask.

spunkie *n* **1** a small fire. **2** a will-o'-the-wisp. **3** a lively young fellow. **4** a false teacher. **5** an irritable person. **6** phosphorescence of the sea. **7** liquor, whisky.—*adj* **1** haunted by will o'-the-wisps. **2** irritable, fiery. **3** lively, spirited. **4** plucky, mettlesome.

spunkie clootie *n* the devil.

spunkie-haunted *adj* haunted by will-o'-the-wisps.

spunkie howe *n* a hollow haunted by will-o'-the-wisps.

spunkis piece *n* a fowling piece.

spunk-maker, ~-man *n* a maker of matches.

spunk-seller *n* one who sells matches.

spunkwood *n* **1** matchwood. **2** small splinters.

spur[1] *n* a spirituous stimulant.—*v* **1** to run fast. **2** to kick about, sprawl. **3** to scrape, as a cock or hen on a dung-hill.

spur[2], **lipurr** *n* **1** the sparrow. **2** a little person of lively disposition. **3** a tall, thin person.

spur[3], **spure** *same as* **speer**[1].

spur[4] *n* a disease in rye.

spur-bauk *n* a crossbeam in the roof of a house.

spurd *n* **1** the house sparrow. **2** a little person of lively disposition.

spurdie *n* **1** the house sparrow. **2** any thin object nearly worn out.

spure *v* did ask. *See* **speer**.

spur-faang *n* **1** a person of a sour, dogged disposition. **2** an atom. **3** a very small piece.

spurg *n* the house-sparrow.

spurgaw *v* **1** to apply spurs. **2** to gall with spurs. **3** to irritate.

spurgie *n* **1** the house sparrow. **2** a nickname for one whose step is like the hop of a sparrow.

spur-hawk *n* **1** the sparrowhawk. **2** a little person of lively disposition.

spurkle *same as* **spurtle**.

spurl *v* to sprawl, kick about.

spur leathers *n* people of no importance.

spurmuick *n* **1** an atom. **2** a particle.

spurrie-how *n* the sparrowhawk.—*v* to run as fast as a sparrowhawk flies.

spurtle[1] *v* **1** to move the feet restlessly. **2** to kick with the feet.

spurtle[2], **spurtil** *n* **1** a wooden rod for stirring porridge, etc., when boiling. **2** a wooden or iron spattle (qv) for turning bread in firing. **3** a ludicrous name for a sword.

spurtle blade *n* a sword.

spurtle braid *n* **1** a wooden spattle (qv) for turning bread in firing. **2** a wooden stirring rod.

spurtle-leggit *adj* having spurtle-legs (qv).

spurtle legs *n* thin, spindly legs.

spurtle stick *n* a spurtle braid (qv).

spurtlit *same as* **sprutlled**.

spur whang *n* **1** a leather strap or thong spur. **2** a thing of little or no worth.

sputten *v* spat.

sputter *v* to splutter.—*n* a splutter, outcry, fuss.

spyaller *same as* **spaller**.

spy-ann *n* a variety of hide-and-seek.

spyauck *n* an example, guide.

spyglass *n* an eyeglass.

spyke *v* to speak.

spy knowe *n* a hill on which a watch is set.

spyle *v* to sample cheese with a scoop.

spyler *n* a cheese scoop.

spyle tree *same as* **spile tree**.

spyndle *same as* **spindle**.

spyniel *same as* **spyndle**.

spynner *same as* **spinner**[2].

spyo *n* the game of hide-and-seek.

spyogg *sam as* **spoig**.

spyug *n* the house sparrow.

spyung *v* **1** to carry off clandestinely. **2** to filch. **3** to walk with long, quick steps. **4** to stride along stealthily.—*n* **1** a person of disagreeable temper and manners. **2** a worthless fellow.

spywife *n* an inquisitive woman.

squaach *same as* **squaich**.

squaar *adj* square.

squabash *n* a splutter.

squach *same as* **squaich**.

squack *v* **1** to cry out. **2** to cry as a child.

squad *n* **1** a number of people. **2** a crew. **3** a squadron.

squade *n* a squadron.

squagh *same as* **squaich**.

squaich, squaigh *n* **1** a loud scream. **2** the cry of a bird or beast when being caught.—*v* **1** (*used of a fowl*) to scream. **2** to squall.

squaint *adj* squinting.

squair *n* a gentle depression between two hills.

squall, squal *n* **1** a row. **2** a disturbance. **3** a wrangle. **4** a burst of temper.

squalloch, squallach, squalach *v* to scream, squeal, squall.—*n* a loud cry.

squalloching *adj* noisy in manners and shrill in voice.

squander *v* to disperse, scatter.

square *v* to assume a fighting or pugilistic forward attitude.—*n* an equal game in golf.—*adv* exactly, properly.

square-man *n* a carpenter.

squares *n* the game of hopscotch.

square sausage *n* sausage meat cut from a large block in square-shaped slices.

square-wricht *n* a joiner who works in the finer kinds of furniture.

squash *v* **1** to splash. **2** to dash water. **3** to fall heavily into water.—*n* **1** the act of splashing. **2** a dash of water. **3** the sound of a heavy fall into water. —*adv* **1** slapdash. **2** with a sudden fall.

squat[1] *n* a contemptuous movement of the nose.

squat[2] *v* to strike with the open hand.—*n* a blow thus given.

squatter[1], **squater** *v* **1** to crouch, squat. **2** to flap or flutter in the water, as a duck. **3** to move quickly. **4** to scatter. **5** to squander.

squatter[2] *n* **1** a large collection of small objects. **2** a swarm.

squattle[1] *v* **1** to squat, settle down. **2** to sprawl.

squattle[2] *v* to swill, drink deeply.

squaw-hole *n* a broad, shallow, muddy pool.

squeal v **1** to grumble, scold. **2** (with **on**) to inform against.—n **1** an outcry. **2** a broil. **3** a debauch, spree.

squech same as **squaich**.

squeeb same as **squib**.

squeef n **1** a mean, disreputable person. **2** one shabby in appearance and conduct.

squeefy adj disreputable, mean-looking.

squeegee adj **1** askew. **2** squint.

squeek-squaakin adj (of shoes or boots) creaking.

squeeky adj squeaking.

squeel[1] n a school.—v to educate.

squeel[2] n too great sourness of buttermilk for use.

squeel[3] n a great number of people.

squeel[4] same as **squeal**.

squeem n the motion of a fish as observed by its effect on the surface of the water, including the idea of the shadow made by the fish.

squeengy, squeergy v to wander, as a dog, from place to place.

squeery same as **squeengy**.

squeesh v **1** to squeeze. **2** to squash. **3** (used of water, etc) to squirt, gush out.—n the sound of water suddenly poured out.

squeeter v **1** to scatter. **2** to work weakly and unskilfully.—n **1** weak, unskilful work. **2** a confused mess. **3** a weak, careless or unskilful worker.

squeeterer n a squeeter (qv).

squeetering, squeetrin adj **1** weak and unskilful. **2** scattering.

squeever n a squall of wind.

squelch v to make a noise, as when walking in wet boots.

squelching n a drenching.

squent adv diagonally.

squib n **1** (used of lightning) a flash. **2** a name given to an obnoxious person.

squibe v (used of a top) to run off to the side when it ceases to spin.

squigged adj crooked.

squile v to squeal.—n a squeal.

squinacy n a quinsy.

squint v **1** to look slyly. **2** to go in a slanting direction. **3** to slant.—n a passing glance.—adj squinting.

squinty, squiny n a woman's cap.

squinty-mutch n a squinty (qv).

squirbile adj **1** ingenious. **2** versatile.

squirl n an ornamental twist, tail or flourish in writing.

squirr v **1** to throw with a whirling motion. **2** to make a thin stone skim along the water or the surface of the land. **3** to go off quickly. **4** to whirl.

squirrly-wirly n an ornamental appendage to clothes, etc.

squirt adv with a bang.

squish same as **squeesh**.

squiss v to beat up an egg.

squodgie-wark same as **scodgy**.

squoil v to squeal.—n a squeal.

squrbuile same as **squirbile**.

sramullion same as **stramuilion**.

sruffle v **1** to scrape the surface of anything. **2** to scuffle the surface of ground and kill weeds.

ss n the S-shaped openings in a fiddle.

st int a call to a dog by way of inciting it.

sta[1] same as **staw**.

sta[2] v stole.

stab same as **stob**.

stab and stow adv completely.

stab callant n a short, thick fellow.

stab gaud n a set line for fishing, fixed to a small stake thrust into the bank to preserve the line from being carried off.

stable n a marsh or bog in which a horse has foundered.

stabled adj (of a horse) foundered in a marsh or bog.

stable meal n the liquor drunk in an inn by farmers in return for stabling for their horses.

stabler n a stable-keeper.

stab-munted adj (used of a gap in a hedge) repaired with stakes.

stacher v to stagger, totter.—n a stagger, reel.

stachie[1] adj stiff, lazy, not energetic.

stachie[2] same as **stashie**.

stack[1] v stuck.

stack[2] v, adj stabbed, butchered.

stack[3] n **1** (in pl) a game of hide-and-seek among stacks in a stackyard. **2** barley bracks (qv).

stacker same as **stacher**.

stacket n a palisade, stockade.—v to palisade.

stack-meels, ~-mools n peat dust and broken peat found at peat stacks.

stack-mou' n the end of a peat stack at which peats are taken away.

stacky n **1** a stack. **2** a stackyard.

staddle[1] n **1** the lower part of a corn stack as far as the sides are upright. **2** a small temporary stack.

staddle[2] n a mark made by one thing lying on another.

staddling[1] n a surface blemish.

staddling[2] n **1** the foundation of a stack. **2** the materials of it.

stadge n **1** a fit of ill-humour. **2** a pet, huff.

staffage adj **1** dry in the mouth. **2** not easily swallowed.

staff and baton n a symbol of the resignation of property or feudal right into the hands of another.

staff and burdon with one n an open rupture with one.

staff end n a proper distance, arm's-length.

staffman n a baton man.

staff swerd n a swordstick.

staffy-nevel n **1** a staff in hand. **2** a cudgelling.—adj in phr **a staffy-nevel job** a fight with cudgels.

stag[1] n **1** a young horse. **2** a stallion.

stag[2] n a stake, pile.—v **1** to stake. **2** to drive stakes into the ground.

stag[3] adj (used of skins) dried simply in the open air.

stage[1] n **1** an informal trial. **2** the bar.—v **1** to accuse without formal trial. **2** to put on trial.

stage[2] same as **staig**.

staggering-bob n a very young calf or its veal.

staggie adj (used of grain) thin.

staggrel n one who staggers in walking.

stagher same as **stacher**.

staidle same as **staddle**[1].

staig[1] v **1** to stalk with a slow, stately step. **2** to walk where one should not be found.—n a slow, stately step.

staig[2] same as **stag**[1].

staigh same as **stech**.

staik[1] n butcher's meat.

staik[2] v **1** to walk with a slow, stately step. **2** to stalk where one should not be found.—n **1** a slow, stately step. **2** the act of walking so.

staik[3] v **1** to accommodate, supply. **2** to suit, satisfy.

stail[1] n **1** the foundation or under-part of a stack. **2** the mother hive of bees.—v to lay properly the bottom sheaves of a stack.

stail[2] n a gathering of urine.—v (used of horses and cattle) to urinate.

staill, staille same as **stail**[1].

stail-sheaf n a bottom sheaf of a stack.

stainch same as **stanch**.

staincher n a stanchion.

staincher-fittit adj (perhaps) with feet like stanchions, owing to stiff fetlock joints.

staing same as **stang**[2].

stainzie v **1** to stain. **2** to fade in colour.

stair n a flight of stairs.

stair-fit n the bottom of a flight of stairs.

stairge v **1** to walk very magisterially. **2** to prance.

stair-heid n the top of a flight of stairs.

stair-heid manawge n **1** a sort of fireside accommodation. **2** bank for the housewives in a tenement, with weekly contributions and draws. See **manadge**.

stair-pit n a coal pit in which the miners could descend or ascend by a ladder erected from top to bottom in short lengths.

staithle *same as* **staddle**¹.

staive *same as* **stave**¹.

staivelt *n* a stupid person.

staiver *same as* **staver**.

stake¹ *same as* **staik**³.

stake² *v* to stalk.

stake and rice, rise *or* **ryse** *n* **1** a fence of upright stakes interlaced with boughs, wattles, etc. **2** a partition or wall of brushwood or lath. **3** anything incomplete, sketchy or in outline or skeleton.

stakey *n* a game at marbles in which stakes are played for.

stakker *same as* **stacher**.

stale¹ *same as* **stail**¹.

stale² *adj* barren.—*v* to disgust.

stale³ *v* stole.

stale-fishing *n* fishing with a stall net.

stale-sheaf *n* a sheaf laid at the bottom of a stack.

stalk¹ *n* **1** a handle. **2** a pipe stem.

stalk² *n* a quantity.

stall¹ *same as* **staw**¹.

stall² *same as* **stail**².

stallange, stallinge *n* rent paid for a market stall.

stallanger, stallinger *n* **1** one who pays rent for a market stall. **2** a person, not a freeman, who, for a consideration to his corporation, is allowed to carry on business for a year.

stalliard *adj* **1** stout, vigorous, valiant. **2** stately, gallant.

stallworthe *adj* **1** brave and strong. **2** stalwart.

stallyoch *n* a thick stalk of grain standing by itself.

stalward *adj* **1** (*used of persons*) valiant. **2** stalliard (qv). **3** (*of things*) stout, strong. **4** hard, severe. **5** stormy, tempestuous.

stalyard *n* a steelyard.

stam *v* to strike down the feet violently in walking.

stamach, stamack, stamick *n* the stomach.

stamachet *adj* stomached.

stamchless *adj* without appetite.

stamfish *adj* **1** strong, robust. **2** coarse, rank. **3** unruly.

stammacker, stammager *n* **1** a stomacher. **2** a busk. **3** a slip of staywood used by women.

stammackie *n* a child's stomach.

stammagust, stammagast *n* **1** a disgust at food. **2** a disagreeable surprise.

stammel *n* a coarse kind of red.

stammel, stammle *same as* **stample**.

stammer *v* **1** to stagger, stumble. **2** to blunder. **3** to hesitate, falter.—*n* a stumble, stagger.

stammeral *n* **1** an awkward blunderer. **2** a blockhead. **3** a stammerer. **4** one who falters in speech. —*adj* half-witted.

stammerel *n* friable stone.

stammerers *n* detached pieces of limestone.

stammering *adj* **1** rude, noisy. **2** awkward, blundering.

stamp¹ *n* **1** a trap. **2** a snare.

stamp² *n* **1** the cramp. **2** a qualm of conscience. **3** remorse.

stamp cole *n* a small rick of corn or hay erected in the field.

stamphish *same as* **stamfish**.

stampin irons *n* branding irons.

stample *v* **1** to stumble, stagger, totter. **2** to stumble in upon.

stam-ram *v* **1** to go into a thing recklessly. **2** to walk roughly and noisily.—*adj* noisy, rough walking.—*n* a noisy, rude person.—*adv* rudely, noisily, recklessly. *See* **ramstam**.

stan¹ *same as* **stand**.

stan² *same as* **stane**.

stanart *same as* **standart**.

stan-blin *adj* quite blind.

stance *n* **1** a standing place, station. **2** the line from which marbles are played. **3** a standstill. **4** a site. **5** a building area. **6** a stall. **7** a separate place for each animal in a stable or byre (qv). **8** the field, etc, in which a fair or cattle market is held.—*v* to station.

stanch *adj* **1** staunch. **2** in good health. **3** resolute. —*n*

satisfaction, surfeit.—*v* **1** to satisfy with food or drink. **2** to stanch blood. **3** to desist, stay. **4** to recall a dog from pursuit.

stanchel¹ *n* **1** a stanchion. **2** a wooden or iron window bar.—*v* to supply with stanchions.

stanchel² *n* the kestrel.

stancher *n* **1** a stanchion. **2** an iron window bar.

stanch-girss *n* the yarrow or milfoil.

stancie *n* a stance (qv).

stancle *n* **1** the wheatear. **2** the stonechat.

stand *v* **1** to place, set, make to stand. **2** (*used of a clock, etc*) to stop. **3** to rise up. **4** to continue, last. **5** to hesitate, scruple, refrain. **6** to object. **7** to cost. **8** to continue solvent. **9** to play in a game of cards. **10** to treat to.—*n* **1** a stall at fair or market. **2** the goods exposed thereon for sale. **3** a barrel set on end. **4** a water bucket. **5** a standstill. **6** a place to make a halt at. **7** a complete suit of clothes or of single articles forming a set. **8** cost, outlay.—*int* a call to horses to halt or stand still.

standart *n* **1** stature. **2** an old inhabitant. **3** one with a long residence.

stand at *v* to feel great disgust at food, so as to be unable to swallow or to retain it.

stander *n* **1** a pillar. **2** an animal's leg. **3** a barrel set on end.

stand for *v* **1** to be surety for. **2** to sail towards.

stand good *v* **1** to be surety for. **2** to hold good, be settled.

standie *n* a small or shabby stall at a fair.

stand in *v* to cost.

stand in for *v* to be surety for.

standing *adj* **1** able to stand. **2** healthy. **3** (*used of colour*) fast.

standing bands *n* tethers for cows standing in a byre (qv).

standing bed *n* a bed with posts, one that cannot be folded up.

standing drink *n* a hasty drink, one taken standing.

standing graith, ~ gear *n* the fixtures in the machinery of a mill.

standing stone *n* an upright gravestone.

stand one hard *v* to vex, grieve one.

stand owre *v* to remain unpaid or undetermined.

stand the session *v* to appear before the kirk session for discipline.

stand up *v* **1** to hesitate, stickle, be irresolute. **2** to spend time idly.

stand upon *v* to insist on.

stand-yont, ~-yon *v* **1** to stand aside. **2** to get out of the way.

stane *n* **1** a stone. **2** a curling stone. **3** the rocky seashore.— *v* **1** to set with stones. **2** to place a heavy stone on a cheese.—*adv* (*as used intensively*) utterly, completely.

stane-bark *n* liverwort, a lichen yielding a purple dye.

stane-blin *adj* stone-blind, quite blind.

stane-cast *n* a stone's-throw.

stane-chack, ~-checker *n* **1** the stonechat. **2** the whinchat. **3** the wheatear.

stane-chapper *n* **1** a stone-breaker. **2** a contemptuous name for a geologist.

stanecher *same as* **stancher**.

stane clod *n* a stone's throw.

stane couples *n* stone arches instead of timber, across which rough spars were laid for supporting thatch.

stane crib *n* a gaol.

stane-dead *adj* quite dead.

stane-dumb *adj* **1** quite dumb. **2** totally silent.

stane-dunder *n* **1** an explosion of firearms. **2** the sound of a heap of stones falling.

stane dyke *n* a stone wall.

stane-falcon *n* the merlin.

stanefish *n* the spotted blenny.

stane-gall *n* the kestrel.

stane-graze *n* a bruise from a stone.

stane-hertit *adj* stony-hearted.

stane-horse *n* a stallion.

stane-knot *n* a very tight knot.

stanel *same as* **stane-gall**.

stane-loppen, ~-loupin *adj* 1 bruised. 2 crushed, as by a stone.

stane-naig *n* a stallion.

stane-pecker *n* 1 the purple sandpiper. 2 the turnstone. 3 the stonechat.

staneraw *n* the rock liverwort, a lichen producing a purple dye.

staners *n* small stones and gravel on the margin of a river or lake.

stane-still *adj* 1 still as a stone. 2 utterly without motion.

stanewark *n* 1 masonry. 2 building of stone.

stans-wod, ~-wud *adj* stark mad.

stang[1] *v* 1 to sting. 2 to pierce, prick. 3 to shoot with pain.— *n* 1 a sting. 2 the act of piercing or stinging. 3 a sudden, sharp pain. 4 a dart. 5 the beard of barley. 6 the needlefish. 7 (*in pl*) a fit of passion.

stang[2] *n* 1 a pole, post. 2 a long wooden bar. 3 an iron-shod pole used in floating rafts of wood down a river, like a large punting pole. 4 the mast of a boat. 5 a boat pole.—*v* to cause to ride the stang, to subject a wife-beater or an unfaithful husband to punishment by carry-ing him from place to place astride a pole borne on the shoulders of others, accompanied by a noisy and con-temptuous crowd.

stangie *n* a tailor.

stang o' the trump *n* 1 the chief actor. 2 the best of the lot. 3 the most attractive of a company.

stangrill *n* an instrument for pushing in the straw in thatch-ing.

stanie *n* a small stone marble.

stanieraw *same as* **staneraw**.

stank[1] *n* 1 a pool, a pond. 2 a stagnant or slow-flowing ditch. 3 a moat. 4 a very wet, marshy piece of ground. 5 an open drain. 6 a street gutter. 7 a surfeit.—*v* 1 to drain land by open ditches. 2 to protect by a ditch, moat, etc. 3 to entrench. 4 to bank up, strengthen the bank of a stream. 5 to fill up. 6 to satisfy, sate, surfeit. 7 to stag-nate.

stank[2] *v* 1 to prick, sting. 2 to thrill with pain.—*n* 1 a sting. 2 a sharp, shooting pain.

stank[3] *v* 1 to gasp for breath. 2 to breathe.

stank-bree, ~-broo *n* 1 the edge of a pool. 2 the brow of a ditch.

stank-hen *n* the moorhen.

stankie *n* the moorhen.

stankit *adj* 1 moated. 2 surrounded by a ditch.

stank-lochen *n* a stagnant pool or lakelet.

stank-up *v* to render stagnant.

stanlock *n* 1 the grey lord or coalfish in its first year. 2 an overgrown coalfish.

stannel *same as* **stane-gall**.

stanner[1] *n* small stones and gravel in the bed or by the margin of a stream.

stanner[2] *same as* **stander**.

stanner-bed *n* a bed of gravel.

stannerie *same as* **staneraw**.

stanner steps *n* stepping stones placed across the bed of a stream.

stannery *adj* gravelly.

stannin *same as* **standing**.

stannyel *n* a stallion.

stanse *same as* **stance**.

stant[1], **stant**[2] *same as* **stent**[1], **stent**[3].

stany *same as* **stony**.

stanyel[1] *n* a stallion.

stanyel[2] *same as* **stane-gall**.

stap[1] *n* the stave of a cask, tub, wooden bicker, etc. —*phr* **to fa' a' staps** 1 to become extremely debilitated. 2 to fall to pieces.

stap[2] *v* 1 to step. 2 (*with* awa') to die. *See* **step**.

stap[3] *v* 1 to stop. 2 to stuff.

stapmither *n* a stepmother.

stapmither year *n* a year of great scarcity and of high prices for food, etc.

stappack *n* a mixture of oatmeal and cold water.

stapper *n* a stopper, anything that stuffs.

stappie *n* a game of marbles in which the player takes a step forward before firing at a number of marbles placed within a fixed area.

stappil *same as* **stapple**[2].

stappin *n* stuffing for filling fishes' heads.

stappin stane *n* a stepping stone.

stappit *adj* completely full

stappit heads *n* haddocks' heads stuffed with a mixture of oatmeal, suet, onions and pepper.

stapple[1] *n* 1 a staple for fixing wire to posts. 2 an eye in a gatepost for holding a hook to fasten the gate.

stapple[2] *n* 1 a stopple, stopper, plug. 2 a pipe stem. 3 a handful of straw tied at one end, used for thatching.

stapplick[1] *n* 1 a stopper. 2 a catch or fastening for a bar or bolt.

stapplick[2] *n* 1 a pipe stem. 2 a handful of straw tied at one end, used for thatching.

star *n* 1 the pupil of the eye. 2 a speck in the eye. 3 cata-ract.

stare[1] *v* 1 to face. 2 (*used of a horse's or cow's coat*) to stand out when roughened by cold, etc.

stare[2] *same as* **stour**[2].

starglint *n* a shooting star.

staring-mad *adj* very mad.

stark *adj* 1 (*used of liquor*) potent, intoxicating. 2 stiff, unbending. 3 rigid in death. 4 quite naked. 5 sheer. 6 arrant, utter.—*adv* 1 utterly, altogether. 2 strenuously.

starn[1] *adj* stern.

starn[2] *n* the stern of a ship, etc.

starn[3] *n* 1 a star. 2 the eye. 3 the pupil of the eye.

starn[4], **starne** *n* 1 a grain, a particle. 2 a very small quan-tity. 3 the outermost point of a needle.

starn[5] *n* the starling.

starned *adj* starred.

starn-fall *n* the fungus, *Nostoc commune*.

starnie *n* a very small quantity.

starn-keeper *n* 1 an astronomer. 2 a stargazer.

starnless *adj* starless.

starn-licht *n* 1 starlight. 2 the flash of light seen when the eye receives a slight blow.

starny *adj* starry.

starr, star *n* 1 various species of sedges. 2 the lesser tufted sedge. 3 the moss rush.

starrach *adj* 1 (*used of the weather*) cold. 2 disagreeable. 3 boisterous.

star-sheen *n* starlight.

starshie *same as* **stashie**.

start[1] *v* to shrink asunder, spring asunder.—*n* a short space of time.

start[2] *n* 1 an upright post mortised into the shafts of a cart, into which the boards of the side are nailed. 2 one of the pieces of wood that support the awes of a millwheel.

startle *v* 1 to take fright. 2 (*used of cattle*) to run about wildly in hot weather. 3 to bustle about.—*n* a scare.

startle-o'-stovie *n* undulating exhalations seen rising from the ground in very hot weather.

startling, startling-fit *n* (*used of a woman*) a desire for matrimony.

start-up *n* 1 an upstart. 2 an interloper.

starty *adj* 1 apt to start. 2 (*used of a horse*) skittish, nerv-ous.

starve *n* a fit of abstinence.

starwart, starwort *n* stitchwort.

stash *n* 1 an uproar. 2 a frolic.

stashie, stashy *n* 1 an uproar. 2 a disturbance, row. 3 a frolic. 4 banter.—*v* 1 to frolic. 2 to banter.

stassel *n* 1 a support for a stack to raise it above the ground. 2 the corn that is undermost in a stack. —*v* to build small, temporary stacks.

state *n* a state of excitement, fuss, temper, etc.—*v* **1** to set up, establish. **2** to endure. **3** to instate, invest.

stated *adj* situated.

stathel, stathle *n* **1** a support for a stack. **2** the sheaves at the foundation of a stack. **2** a small, temporary rick.—*v* to build in small, temporary ricks.

sta' tree *n* the stake in a cow house to which a cow is bound.

statute *v* **1** to ordain. **2** to decree by statute.

staucher *same as* **stacher**.

stauchie *same as* **stoich**.

stauf *n* a staff.

staug *same as* **staig**[1].

stauk[1] *n* a stalk.

stauk[2] *v* to stalk.

staul[1] *v* to squint.—*n* a squint.

staul[2] *v* stole.

staumer *same as* **stammer**.

staumrel *n* **1** a blockhead. **2** an awkward blunderer.—*adj* half-witted.

staun, staund *same as* **stand**.

staunder *same as* **stander**.

staup[1] *same as* **stap**[1].

staup[2] *v* **1** to stride, stalk. **2** to take long, awkward steps. **3** to walk uncertainly, as in darkness.—*n* **1** a long, clumsy stride. **2** an awkward step. **3** a tall, awkward person.

staup[3] *v* stepped.

staupen *adj* **1** awkwardly tall. **2** stalking awkwardly.

stav *same as* **staw**[1].

stave[1] *v* **1** to push, drive. **2** to beat against. **3** to thump vigorously. **4** to consolidate iron instruments by striking them perpendicularly on the anvil when they are half-cooled. **5** to sprain. **6** to walk quickly. **7** to walk awkwardly. **8** to walk aimlessly or as in a reverie. **9** to totter.—*n* **1** a heavy blow. **2** a push, dash. **3** a sprain.

stave[2] *n* a short song.

stave-aff *n* **1** an excuse, evasion. **2** a delay.

stavel *v* **1** to stumble. **2** to wander aimlessly.—*n* a stumble.

staver *v* **1** to saunter, walk listlessly. **2** to totter. **3** to stagger. **4** to stumble. **5** to wander.—*n* **1** a saunter. **2** an easygoing, pleasant person. **3** (*in pl*) pieces, ruin.

staverall *n* a blundering, awkward, foolish person.

stane *v* **1** to saunter. **2** to dawdle.

staw[1] *v* **1** to surfeit, satiate. **2** to disgust. **3** to cloy. **4** to weary, tire.—*n* **1** a surfeit, disrelish. **2** a dislike, aversion. **3** a nuisance, annoyance. **4** a stall, a stall in a stable.

staw[2] *v* stole.

stawmer *same as* **stammer**.

stawn *v, adj* stolen.

stawn *same as* **stand**.

stawp[1] *same as* **stap**[1].

stawp *same as* **staup**[2].

stawsome *adj* disgusting, nauseous, surfeiting.

stay[1] *adj* **1** steep, ascending. **2** stiff to climb.

stay[2] *v* **1** (*of a servant*) to remain to the end of his or her term. **2** to renew an engagement for a new term of service. **3** to reside, have one's permanent home. **4** to put to the bar.—*n* a fixed abode.

stayband *n* **1** a horizontal plank in a door. **2** a narrow linen band brought through the tie of an infant's cap and fastened to its frock to keep the head from being thrown too far back. **3** a band for keeping the brim of a hat fast to the top.

stayedly *adv* deliberately.

stay in *v* **1** to adhere to a party, church, etc. **2** not to separate or go forth from it.

stay-measure *n* the size of corsets.

stead *n* **1** a site. **2** a place, situation. **3** the bottom or foundation of anything. **4** a track, mark, impress, print. **5** a farmhouse and buildings. **6** a mass. **7** a large number or quantity. **8** a stone used to sink deep-sea fishing lines.—*v* **1** to bestead, help. **2** to lay a foundation. **3** to gather, collect.—*adv* instead.

steadable *adj* **1** necessary. **2** serviceable. **3** standing in good stead.

stead hook *n* the hook next to the stone used to sink deep-sea fishing lines.

steading *n* **1** a site. **2** building land. **3** a farmhouse and buildings. **4** the buildings as distinguished from the farmhouse.

stead sheaf *n* a sheaf at the bottom of a stack.

steak *same as* **steek**.

steak raid *n* that portion of the livestock taken in a predatory raid which was supposed to belong to any proprietor through whose lands the prey was driven.

steal[1] *n* **1** a theft. **2** anything stolen.—*v* (*used in golfing*) to hole an unlikely put from a distance.

steal[2] *n* the shaft of a barrow or plough.

steal-bonnets *n* a romping game played with hats or bonnets laid down at opposite ends of a field, like 'Scotch and English'.

steal-corn *n* a nursery name for the forefinger.

steal't *v* stole.—*v, adj* stolen.

steal-the-pigs *n* a game representing the stealing and recovery of a woman's children.

steal-wads *n* the game of steal-bonnets (qv).

steamie *n* a public laundry where people washed their clothes themselves.

steamin' *adj* extremely drunk.

steam mill *n* a travelling steam threshing mill.

stear *n* a starling.

steave *same as* **steeve**.

stech *v* **1** to stuff, cram. **2** to fill to repletion. **3** to gorge, gormandize. **4** to stuff oneself. **5** to smell unpleasantly, stink. **6** to groan, pant. **7** to have a great many clothes on the body. **8** to loiter. **9** to confine oneself to a very warm room.—*n* **1** a greedy manner of eating, guzzling. **2** cramming in food. **3** a groan. **4** a heap, crowd. **5** a confused mass. **6** a great number crowded in little space. **7** heat.

stechie *n* an over-feeder, gormandizer, glutton.—*adj* heavy, stiff in the joints, lazy.

stechle *v* **1** to rustle. **2** to emit a whistling, snoring sound through the nose.

sted, stedd *same as* **stead**.

stedding *same as* **steading**.

steddy *v* to make or keep steady.

stede, stedt *same as* **stead**.

stey *same as* **stay**[1].

steech *n* something obnoxious.

steed *v* stood.

steed *same as* **stead**.

steedge *v* to walk with slow, heavy step.—*n* **1** a slow, heavy walk. **2** a big person of slow, quiet disposition.

steeding *same as* **steading**.

steek *v* **1** to push. **2** to butt with the horns. **3** to shut, fasten. **4** to clench. **5** to stitch, sew.—*n* **1** a stitch. **2** a loop in knitting. **3** an article of clothing. **4** a fragment, the least bit. **5** a stitch in the side. **6** a sharp, painful blow. **7** a quick pace.

steek-and-hide *n* a game like hide-and-seek.

steeker *n* a bootlace, shoe tie.

steekie-nevvle *n* a clenched fist.

steekin-slap *n* a gap with a gate opening and shutting.

steekit *adj* (*used of a fog*) thick, enveloping.

steel[1] *n* **1** a needle. **2** a steelyard.—*v* to rough horseshoes.

steel[2] *n* **1** a wooded precipice. **2** the lower part of a ridge projecting from a hill where the ground declines on each side.

steel[3] *same as* **steel**[2].

steel[4] *n* a covering for a sore finger.

steel[5] *n* a stool.

steel bow *n* goods on a farm that are the property of the landlord and may not be removed by an outgoing tenant.

steel-bowed *adj* **1** set apart for a special purpose. **2** guaranteed, inviolate.

steel-rife *adj* overbearing.

steel-wamit *adj* (*perhaps*) having a wizened podex.

steely *adj* **1** covered with steel. **2** steel-tipped.

steen[1] *n* a stone.

steen[2] *v* to spring.—*n* a spring.

steenie[1] *adj* stony.—*n.* a little stone.

steenie[2] *n* **1** a gold coin. **2** a guinea.

steenie[3] *same as* **stony**.

steenie-pouter *n* the sandpiper.

steep *v* **1** to drench with rain or wet. **2** to curdle milk for cheese. **3** *in phr* **to steep the withies** to get ready.—*n* **1** a tub. **2** the small spearmint. **3** the quantity of malt steeped at a time.

steep grass *n* butterwort.

steepin *n* **1** a stipend, minister's salary. **2** (*in pl*) contributions to a stipend.

steepin' *n* a drenching with rain.

steeple[1] *n* **1** a very tall, thin person. **2** a small, square heap of partially dried fish. **3** a large stack of such fish.

steeple[2], **steepil** *n* a staple for fixing wire on posts.

steeple[3] *same as* **stapple**[2].

steeple-root *n* the base of anything.

steepy *adj* steep.

steer[1] *v* **1** to stir. **2** to bestir oneself. **3** to go, depart. **4** to bustle about, be in a stir. **5** to work confusedly. **6** to stir, poke, mix. **7** to cause to move. **8** to disturb. **9** to injure. **10** to plough slightly. **11** to plough the ground a second time when it has to be ploughed thrice.—*n* **1** a stir. **2** a poke. **3** a disturbance, commotion, fuss. **4** (*with* **cauld**) a mixture of oatmeal and cold water.

steer[2] *same as* **stour**[2].

steerabout *n* **1** a restless, stirring person. **2** stirabout.

steerach *v* **1** to crowd in disorder. **2** to fill to excess in a disorderly manner. **3** to work dirtily and confusedly.—*n* **1** a disorderly crowd. **2** domestic disorder. **3** dirty, disorderly working. **4** a quantity of ill-cooked food.

steerin' *adj* (*of children*) restless, lively, troublesome.

steerin-fur *n* a slight ploughing.

steerless *adj* lifeless, lacking energy.

steerman *n* a steersman.

steerpin *n* a pin in the stilt of the old Orkney plough.

steer tree *n* the stilt in the beam of a plough, regulating its motion.

steerum *n* **1** a stir. **2** excitement.

steer water *n* the wake of a boat.

steery *n* **1** a stir, disturbance, commotion. **2** a tumultuous assembly.—*adj* **1** stirring. **2** in commotion.

steery-fyke *n* bustle, commotion with confusion.

steet *n* **1** a prop. **2** a shore for a boat.—*v* to prop, support with pillars.

steeth *n* **1** the bottom, foundation. **2** a stone attached to a busy-rope, serving as an anchor to deep-sea fishing lines.

steethe stone *n* the first of the stones let down as an anchor to deep-sea fishing lines.

steeval *adj* (*used of food*) firm, substantial, made with little water.

steeve *adj* **1** stiff, firm. **2** strong, sturdy. **3** (*of food*) thick, substantial, stiff in substance. **4** steep, inaccessible. **5** staunch to principle, true, trusty. **6** obstinate, stubborn.—*v* to stuff, cram.

steevely *adv* firmly.

steevie *n* a quantity of thick, stodgy food.

steevin' *adj* strong, stiff.

steg[1], **stegg** *n* a gander.—*v* to stalk about.

steg[2] *v* to bring to a standstill.

stegh *same as* **stech**.

steich *same as* **stech**.

steichle, steichel *v* **1** to stifle, suffocate. **2** to be in a state of suffocation. **3** to crowd to suffocation.—*n* **1** a close, stifling air. **2** a state of suffocation. **3** a crowd of people or animals packed together to suffocation.

steichly *adj* (*used of air*) close, foul, suffocating.

steick *same as* **steek**.

steid *same as* **stead**.

steigh[1] *same as* **stech**.

steigh[2] *same as* **stay**[1].

steigh[3] *v* to look big.

steighle *same as* **steichle**.

steik *same as* **steek**.

steil[1] *same as* **steel**[4].

steil[2] *n* a shaft, handle.

steil[3] *same as* **stell**[3].

steilbow *same as* **steelbow**.

steill'd *v* stole.

stein *n* a stone.

steing *same as* **stang**[2].

steinie[1], **steinie**[2] *same as* **steenie**[1], **steenie**[2].

steinie gate *n* the place where stones gathered from a field are collected.

steinkle *n* **1** the stonechat. **2** the wheatear.

steir *same as* **steer**[1].

steit[1], **steit**[2] *same as* **stite**[1], **stite**[2].

steiter *same as* **styter**.

steith *same as* **stead**.

steive *same as* **steeve**

stell[1] *same as* **stail**[2].

stell[2] *n* a still.

stell[3] *n* **1** a prop, support. **2** a stack prop. **3** a supporting framework. **4** an enclosure for sheep. **5** a plantation or clump of trees for shelter. **6** a deep pool in a river where net fishing for salmon can be carried on. **7** (*in pl*) indentations in ice to steady the feet in curling.—*v* **1** to place, set, fix. **2** to plant firmly. **3** to point. **4** to prop. **5** to stop. **6** to bring to a stand. **7** to stand. **8** *in phr* **to stell a gun** to take aim with it.

stell[4] *adj* **1** steep. **2** precipitous.

stellage *n* the ground on which a market is held.

stell-dyke *n* the wall of an enclosure for sheep.

stell-fishing, ~-fishery *n* **1** fishing with a stell net (qv). **2** the place of such fishing.

stellfitch *adj* (*of rank flax or grain*) dry, coarse.

stell net *n* a net, fixed by stakes in or across a river, for catching salmon.

stell pat *n* **1** a pot still. **2** a small, illegal still.

stell shot *n* a shot fired from a gun resting on some object to secure accuracy of aim.

stellvitch *same as* **stellfitch**.

stelt *same as* **stilt**.

stem[1] *n* the peak of a cap.

stem[2] *v* **1** to stanch. **2** (*in quarrying*) to ram a blasting charge home.—*n* **1** a check. **2** the utmost extent of anything. **3** a dam in a stream or ditch.

stem[3] *same as* **stime**.

stembod *n* a symbol of citation, as a staff, arrow, axe or cross.

stem bonnet *n* a peaked cap.

stemple *n* a plug used by lead miners.

sten' *same as* **stend**.

stench *same as* **stanch**.

stenchel *same as* **stanchel**.

stencher *same as* **stancher**.

stend *v* **1** to stretch. **2** to bound, spring up, rear. **3** to walk with long stride, hasten. **4** to turn, twist, bend.—*n* **1** a bound, leap. **2** a long stride. **3** a sudden movement in the wrong direction.

steng, stengy *same as* **stang**[2].

stenloch, stenlock *same as* **stanlock**.

stenloch-hooks *n* hooks for catching coalfish.

stenn *same as* **stend**.

stenner *same as* **stanner**.

stennis *n* a sprain.—*v* to sprain slightly.

stensil *same as* **stanchel**.

stent[1] *v* **1** to stint. **2** to leave off, cease, stop. **3** to straiten, restrict. **4** to allot. **5** to prescribe a fixed task. **6** to measure out.—*n* **1** a fixed task. **2** an allotted portion of work. **3** a limited allowance of pasturage.

stent[2] *v* to extend, stretch out.—*n* **1** an utmost stretch, extent. **2** a bound, limit.—*adj* **1** outstretched. **2** tight. **3** stretched to the utmost. **4** taut.

stent[3] *v* **1** to assess, rate, tax. **2** to confiscate.—*n* an assessment, rate, tax.

stent[4] *v* to place.

stented[1] *adj* limited.

stented *adj* hired, engaged.

stenter,[2] **stentor** *n* an assessor, an imposer of a tax.

stentless *adj* unlimited.

stent-master *n* an assessor of a town or parish.

stent net *n* a net stretched across a river and fixed by stakes.

stent-roll *n* an assessment roll.

stenye *v* to sting.

stenyie, stenzie *v* to stretch, extend.

stenzie[1] *same as* **stenyie**

stenzie[2] *same as* **stainzie**.

step[1] *v* **1** to go away, depart. **2** to pass over, omit, neglect.—*n* **1** a distance. **2** a way. **3** a walk, stroll. **4** (*in pl*) stepping stones.

step[2] *same as* **stap**[1].

step aside *v* **1** to act in an underhand manner. **2** to go wrong.

step awa' *v* to depart, die.

stepbairn *n* a stepchild.

step ben, ~ **in**, ~ **in by** *v* to come or go into a room or house.

stepdame *n* a stepmother.

stepminnie *n* a stepmother.

stepmother-year *n* a cold, unfavourable year.

step on *v* to advance, grow old.

step-over *n* **1** a footbridge. **2** a short distance across.

steppe *same as* **stap**[1].

stepping *n* a way, path.

steppit *v* stepped.

step-stanes *n* stepping stones.

stere *same as* **stour**[2].

sterk[1] *same as* **stark**.

sterk[2] *same as* **stirk**.

sterling *n* a smelt.

stern, sterne *n* a star.

stern-licht *n* starlight.

sterny *adj* starry.

stert *same as* **start**[1].

stertle *same as* **startle**.

stertlin'-fit *same as* **startling**.

sterve *same as* **starve**.

stethel *same as* **staddle**[1].

steuch *same as* **stew**[1].

steug *n* **1** a thorn, prickle. **2** a spike. **3** anything sharp-pointed. **4** an arrow. **5** a rusty dart. **6** a stab, prick. **7** a hasty stitch with a needle. **8** light, coarse stitching.—*v* **1** to stab. **2** to prick. **3** to stitch. **4** to sew lightly and coarsely.

steur *same as* **stour**[2].

steut *n* **1** anything long and pointed or large and sharp-edged. **2** a big, stupid person.—*v* to go about in a silly, stupid way.

steutal *n* a steut (qv).—*v* to steut (qv).

steve *same as* **steeve**.

stevel[1] *v* **1** to stagger into a place into which one ought not to go. **2** to stumble.—*n* a stumble.

stevel[2] *same as* **steeval**.

steven, stevin *n* **1** a loud voice. **2** a ranting. **3** an uproar.

stew[1] *n* **1** dust, a cloud of dust. **2** vapour. **3** smoke. **4** spray. **5** an offensive smell.—*v* **1** to smell unpleasantly. **2** to rain slightly.

stew[2] *n* **1** a commotion. **2** a state of fright, perplexity, excitement.

stew[3] *v* to burn.—*n* a state of heat or great perspiration.

stew[4] *same as* **stow**[2].

steward, stewart *n* the sheriff of a stewartry (qv)

Stewartry *n* now the county of Kirkcudbright.

stewartry *n* **1** the jurisdiction over an extent of territory nearly equivalent to that of a regality. **2** the territory over which such jurisdiction extends.

stewg *same as* **steug**.

stewle *n* the foundation of a rick or haystack.

stewrn *v* to besprinkle lightly with a powder.—*n* a small quantity of anything powdered.

stewrnin *n* a very small quantity of anything powdered.

stey[1] *same as* **stay**[1].

stey[2] *v* **1** to stay. **2** to dwell. **3** to check.

steyme *same as* **stime**.

stibble[1] *n* stubble.

stibble[2] *v* to stumble.

stibble butter *n* butter from the milk of cows fed on the stubble after harvest, considered the best for salting.

stibbled lea *n* a stubble field.

stibble field, ~ **land** *n* a stubble field.

stibbler *n* **1** a horse turned loose after harvest into the stubble. **2** a labourer in harvest who goes from ridge to ridge, cutting and gathering the handfuls left by those who in their reaping go regularly forward. **3** a probationer of the Church without a settled charge.

stibble rig *n* **1** a stubble field. **2** the leading reaper on a ridge.

stibblert, stibblart *n* **1** a young fellow. **2** a stripling. —*adj* well-grown, plump.

stibble-win *v* to cut down a ridge of corn before another, the one cut down being between that other and the standing corn.

stibbly *adj* **1** covered with stubble. **2** (*used of hair*) short and stiff, stubbly.

stich *same as* **steech**.

stichle *same as* **stechle**.

stichles *n* the hot embers of the fuel of a kiln.

stichlie *adj* filled with fibres.

stick[1] *n* (*in pl*) **1** furniture. **2** lumber in a house. **3** *in phr* **nae great sticks** no great shakes.

stick[2] *v* **1** to butcher. **2** to gore, butt with horns. **3** to stake peas, etc. **4** to stitch.—*n* **1** a pedestal. **2** a stitch. **3** a loop in knitting. **4** the least article of clothing. **5** a term of disparagement for a person.

stick[3] *v* **1** to hesitate. **2** to break down. **3** to fail in one's profession or examinations. **4** to bungle. **5** to spoil in the execution.—*n* **1** a stoppage, halt, standstill. **2** a breakdown. **3** a bungle. **4** a state of hesitation.

stickamstam, stickamstan *n* **1** a thing of no value. **2** supposed to signify a halfpenny Scots, the twenty-fourth of an English penny.

stick and stow *adv* completely.—*n* the whole of a thing.

stick-armed *adj* armed with drumsticks.

stick by *v* to adhere to.

sticker[1] *n* a fish spear.

sticker[2] *n* **1** a difficulty. **2** a poser.

stick fast *v* to take firm hold.

stick in *v* to persevere.

sticking *adj* **1** stiff. **2** disobliging. **3** obstinate. **4** unwilling.

sticking-bull *n* a horned bull in the habit of attacking people.

sticking-piece *n* that part of an animal's neck where the knife is inserted to kill it.

stick into *v* **1** to devote oneself to. **2** to attack.

stick in with *v* to devote oneself to.

stick it *v with pron* **1** to remain. **2** to halt.

stickit[1] *v, adj* stabbed, gored.

stickit[2] *v* stuck.—*adj* **1** unsuccessful or failing in one's profession or business from want of ability or means. **2** dwarfed. **3** stunted in growth. **4** unfinished.

stickit coat *n* a coat that is a misfit.

stickit job *n* a bungled or unfinished job.

stickit-minister *n* a probationer who fails to obtain a settled charge.

stickit stibbler *n* a stickit minister (qv). *See* **stibbler**.

stickle[1] *n* **1** bustle, haste. **2** confusion.

stickle[2] *n* **1** stubble. **2** a spar of a kiln for supporting the haircloth or straw on which the grain was laid. **3** the trigger of a gun or pistol.

sticklie *n* the stickleback.

stickly *adj* **1** rough. **2** bristly, prickly. **3** stubbly. **4** (*of soil*) intermixed with the stems of trees.

stickly *adj* stickling.

stick out *v* to hold out.

sticks and staves *n* wreck and ruin.

stickumstam *same as* **stickamstam.**

stick up to *v* **1** to begin to court, to pay one's addresses to. **2** to ingratiate oneself with. **3** to prepare to fight.

stick with *v* **1** to displease. **2** to be objectionable to.

sticky-fingered *adj* thievish, given to stealing.

stid *same as* **stead.**

stiddie *n* **1** an anvil. **2** a blacksmith's forge. **3** a smithy.

stiddle *v* to straddle.

stied *same as* **stead.**

stiek *same as* **steek.**

stieve *same as* **steeve.**

stieve-hertit *adj* stout of heart.

stife *n* **1** a sulphurous smell. **2** a close, stifling atmosphere. **3** the bad smell from a chimney. **4** a smoky smell.

stiff *adj* **1** sturdy, strong. **2** obstinate. **3** self-willed. **4** unyielding. **5** supercilious, starchy. **6** burdensome. **7** difficult. **8** rich, wealthy.—*v* to stiffen.

stiff-back *n* a game resembling swear tree (qv) in a trial of strength.

stiffen, stiffin *v* to starch clothes.—*n* starch.

stiffener, stiffner *n* **1** a starched cravat. **2** an article used to stiffen a neckcloth.

stiffening *n* starch, for clear-starching.

stiffing *n* starch.

stiffle[1] *v* to stifle.

stiffle[2] *same as* **stevel**[1].

stifler *n* the gallows.

stiggy *n* a stile or passage over a wall or fence by means of steps.

stigil *n* a clownish fellow.

stigmatize *v* to brand with red-hot irons.

stike criech *n* a steak-raid (qv).

stike-raid *same as* **steak-raid.**

stilch *n* a fat, unwieldy young man.

stile[1] *n* **1** a gate. **2** a sparred gate. **3** a passage over a wall.

stile[2] *same as* **stell**[3].

still[1] *adj* taciturn, reserved, somewhat morose.—*n* the interval between ebb and flood tide.—*v* **1** to be at rest, cease. **2** to be quiet.—*int* a command to horses to stand still.

still[2] *adv* always.

still[3] *same as* **stell**[3].

still and on *adv* nevertheless, yet.

still as a step *adj* quite still.

still-stand *n* **1** a standstill. **2** a cessation of hostilities.

stilp *v* **1** to step, stalk. **2** to walk with long strides. **3** to go on crutches or on stilts.

stilper[1] *n* **1** a stalker. **2** one who has long legs. **3** (*in pl*) crutches, stilts.

stilper[2] *v* to walk with long, awkward strides, lifting the feet high.—*n* awkward walking with high steps by a long-legged person.

stilpert, stilpart *n* **1** a long-legged, lanky person or animal. **2** a stilt. **3** the act of walking with long legs, lifting the feet high. **4** (*in pl*) stilts.—*v* to walk in tints awkward fashion.

stilp-stilpin *adj* sauntering, stumping.

stilt *n* **1** a crutch. **2** (*in pl*) poles with rests for the feet, about 24 inches from the ground, used for crossing a river at a ford. **3** a shaft. **4** the handle of a plough.—*v* **1** to halt, limp. **2** to go on crutches. **3** to walk stiffly and awkwardly. **4** to hop. **5** to cross a river on stilts or poles.

stiltit *adj* (*used of heels*) high.

stime *v* **1** to look as one whose vision is indistinct. **2** to move awkwardly from defective vision. **3** to open the eyes partially. **4** to peer.—*n* **1** the faintest form of any object. **2** a glimpse, gleam of light. **3** the least particle, atom. **4** a look. **5** a glance. **6** a disease of the eye.

stimel *n* a reproachful term for one who does not see what another wishes him or her to see.

stimey *n* **1** one who is clumsy through defective vision. **2** one who sees indistinctly.

stimmer *v* to go about in a confused manner.

stimpart, stimpert *n* **1** quarter of a peck. **2** (*used of ground*) as much as will produce a quarter of a peck of flax seed. **3** a young person who can barely shear out the fourth part of a ridge. **4** an unskilful shearer. *See* **shear.**

stimy *n* the predicament of a golf-player whose opponent's ball lies in the line of his put.

sting[1] *n* **1** a forked instrument used in thatching. **2** the pipefish.—*v* **1** to feel a tingling, smarting sensation. **2** to thatch or repair thatch with a sting.

sting[2] *same as* **stang**[2].

sting and ring *phrs* **1 to carry sting and ring** to carry with a long pole resting on the shoulders of two people. **2 sting and ring 1** entirely, bodily. **2** by force. **3** the use of both pole and rope in managing unruly animals.

stinge *adj* stiff, austere, forbidding. **2** hard, difficult.

stinger *n* **1** a mender of thatched roofs. **2** an insect's mandible.

stingin' spurtle *n* an instrument used in thatching for pushing in the straw. *See* **sting**[1].

stingy *adj* **1** bad-tempered, irritable. **2** of poor appetite.

stink *v* **1** to disgust by smell. **2** to capture a prisoner in the game of Scots and English.—*n* a prisoner in such a game.

stinkard *n* **1** a dirty, disagreeable person. **2** a prisoner in the game of Scots and English.

stinker *n* a prisoner in the game of Scots and English.

stinkin' *adj* saucy, haughty.

stinking Danes *n* the common ragwort.

stinking Elshander *n* the common tansy.

stinking-ill *n* a disease of sheep, causing a strong, sulphurous smell when the dead body is opened.

stinking Roger *n* figwort.

stinking weed *n* the common ragwort.

stinking Willie *n* **1** the common ragwort. **2** the water ragwort. **3** the common tansy.

stinkle *same as* **steinkle.**

stint *same as* **stent.**

stipend, stipen *n* **1** a minister's salary. **2** a benefice.

stippety-stap *n* a short, mincing gait.

stir[1] *same as* **steer**[1].

stir[2] *n* sir.

stirabout *n* **1** a porridge stick. **2** meal and water without salt. *See* **steerabout.**

stirdy *n in phr* **to steer one's stirdy** to trouble one's head. *See* **sturdy.**

stirk *n* **1** a steer. **2** a stupid fellow. **3** a stout man.—*v* to be with calf.

stirkie *n* a little stirk (qv).

stirk-like *adj* stolid.

stirk's ~, stirkie's sta' *n* **1** the place in a cow house appropriated to a stirk (qv). **2** the place, generally the father's bosom, assigned to a child when the mother has a younger baby.

stirra, stirrah *n* **1** sirrah. **2** a sturdy boy. **3** a stripling. **4** a man.

stirring *adj* **1** in good health. **2** active after an illness.—*n* a slight or second ploughing.

stirring-furrow *n* **1** the second ploughing across the first. **2** the seed furrow.

stirrow *same as* **stirra.**

stirrup dram *n* a parting glass of spirits or ale from a host to his departing guest after he has mounted.

stirrup stockings *n* woollen riding gaiters.

stirve *v* to starve.

stishie *same as* **stashie.**

stitch *n* **1** an article of clothing. **2** a nickname for a tailor. **3** a furrow or drill of turnips, potatoes, etc.

stitch-through *adv* **1** straight through. **2** without delay.

stitchum *n* a nickname for a tailor.

stite[1] *n* **1** nonsense. **2** one who talks nonsense.

stite² *same as* **stot**¹.

stith *adj* **1** (*of a rope*) taut. **2** strong, lusty. **2** dead, stiff in death.

stithe *same as* **stead**.

stivage, stivvage *adj* **1** stout. **2** fit for work.

stive *same as* **steeve**.

stivel *same as* **stevel**¹.

stively *adv* **1** firmly. **2** stoutly.

stiveron *n* any very fat food, as a haggis.

stivet *n* **1** a short, stout man. **2** a stubborn, wilful person.

stivey *same as* **steevie**.

stivvage *same as* **stivage**.

stivven, stiven *v* **1** to stiffen with cold. **2** to freeze to death.—*n* freezing weather.

stoan *v* (*of trees, etc*) to send out suckers from the roots.—*n* a quantity of suckers from the roots.

stoar *same as* **stour**².

stoat *same as* **stot**.

stoater *n* **1** something outstanding, something of excellence. **2** a very good-looking person.

stoatin *same as* **stottin**.

stob *n* **1** a stake, post. **2** a spike. **3** a fencing post. **4** the stump of a tree. **5** a thorn, prickle. **6** a small, sharp pointed splinter. **7** the puncture made by a prickle, etc. **8** a small boring instrument, a bradawl. **9** a coarse nail. **10** that part of a rainbow that seems to rest on the horizon when no more of it is seen.—*v* **1** to stab. **2** to prick, pierce. **3** to dress a corn stack by driving in the ends of the sheaves with a pitchfork. **4** to uncover a peat bank by cutting off the rough surface. **5** to push or hurt the foot accidentally against a stone, etc, projecting from the ground.

stob-bairn *n* an unprovided-for child.

stobbans *n* broken pieces of straw after threshing.

stobbed *adj* (*used of a bird*) unfledged.

stobby *adj* **1** rough, stubbly. **2** bristly, unshaven. **3** beset with posts.

stob-feather *n* **1** a short, unfledged feather on a plucked fowl. **2** such a feather as appears first on a young fowl.—*v* **1** to feather one's nest. **2** to provide furniture, etc, for a young couple.

stob-feathered *adj* **1** unfledged. **2** (*used of a young couple*) having provision or furniture.

stob-spade *n* an instrument for pushing in straw in thatching.

stob-thack *v* to thatch with stobs or stakes to keep down the thatch.—*adj* thatched with stobs.

stob-thacker *n* one who stob-thacks.

stock *n* **1** the stem of a cabbage plant or kail plant. **2** the front part of a bed. **3** the part of a spinning wheel to which the wheel is attached. **4** a strong, thickset, well-built person. **5** a term of pity or contempt for an old, feeble or useless person or for a child. **6** one whose joints are stiffened by age or disease. **7** a pack of cards.—*v* **1** to amass money. **2** (*used of plants*) to branch out into various shoots immediately above ground. **3** to become stiff. **4** to be benumbed.

stock and brock *n* the whole of one's property.

stock-and-horn *n* a toast given by farmers, referring to sheep stock and cattle.

stock-and-horn *n* a musical instrument composed of (1) the stock, which is the hinder thighbone of a sheep or a piece of elder with stops in the middle; (2) the horn or smaller end of a cow's horn, cut so as to admit the stock; (3) an oaten reed held by the lips and playing loose in the smaller end of the stock.

stock annet *n* the common sheldrake.

stock duck *n* the wild duck.

stocket *adj* **1** trimmed. **2** stiffened.

stock hawk *n* the peregrine falcon.

stockie *n* a piece of cheese, or of fish, between two pieces of bread.

stocking¹ *n* farm stock and implements, in contradistinction from the crop.

stocking² *n* the sending forth of various stems.

stocking³, **stocken** *n* **1** an old stocking used as a purse. **2** savings. **3** a hoard of money.

stocking feet *n* the feet clothed in stockings without shoes.

stocking foot, ~ leg *n* **1** an old stocking used as a purse. **2** savings. **3** a banking account.

stocking needle *n* a darning needle.

stocking seamer *n* a woman who sews the seams of stockings.

stockit *adj* hard, stubborn of disposition.

stockit siller *n* amassed money.

stock owl *n* the eagle owl.

stock purse *n* a purse held in common.

stock saint *n* a graven image of a saint.

stock storm *n* snow continuing to lie on the ground.

stock whaup *n* the curlew.

stocky *adv* plainly and respectably.—*n* **1** a person of respectable, simple habits. **2** an ordinary, stay-at-home person.

stoddart, stoddert *n* a grassy hollow among hills.

stoddy *v* **1** to study. **2** to guard against. **3** to keep firm.

stodge¹ *n* **1** thick, satisfying food. **2** repletion. **3** a fat, thickset person. **4** one deformed.—*v* **1** to eat to repletion. **2** to walk with short, heavy steps.

stodge² *n* **1** a fit of ill-humour. **2** a pet.

stodger *n* one who walks with short, heavy steps.

stodgie *adj* **1** ill-humoured. **2** pettish. **3** sulky.

stodgy *adj* **1** (*of food*) stiff and substantial. **2** fat, short and stout.

stoer-mackrel *n* the tunny.

stog¹ *v* **1** to stab, pierce. **2** to drive in a tool too deeply in working with wood. **3** to probe with a stick or pole. **4** to cut or reap unevenly. **5** to jag. —*n* **1** a stab, thrust. **2** a sharp-pointed instrument. **3** a thorn, prickle. **4** a small, sharp splinter in the flesh. **5** a piece of decayed tree standing out of the ground. **6** stubble too high or uneven. **7** a short, irregular horn or one bent backwards.

stog² *v* **1** to walk heavily or awkwardly. **2** to plod on.—*n* **1** a stamp. **2** a heavy pressure of the foot. **3** a person with awkward gait.

stoggie *adj* **1** rough. **2** (*of cloth*) coarse and rough. **3** (*of stubble*) uneven in height. **4** (*of a comb*) having some of the teeth broken.

stoich *n* **1** foul, bad, suffocating air. **2** a close, sulphurous smell.—*v* to fill with bad or suffocating air.

stoichert *adj* **1** overloaded with clothes. **2** overpowered with fatigue. **3** suffocated, overpowered by fumes, etc.

stoif¹ *same as* **stife**.

stoif² *n* a stove.

stoit¹ *same as* **stot**¹.

stoit² *same as* **stite**¹.

stoit³ *n* an awkward, blundering or foolish person.

stoiter *same as* **stotter**².

stoitle *v* **1** to stagger. **2** to fall gently from weakness.—*n* the act of staggering.

stoitlin' *adj* of unsteady gait.

stoke *n* **1** a foolish person. **2** a blockhead.

stole¹ *v, adj* stolen.

stole² *n* **1** a stool. **2** the stool of repentance (qv).

stole³ *n* a single stalk of corn.

stoll *n* **1** a place of safety. **2** a covert, shelter.

stolum, stolm, stoltum *n* **1** a large piece of anything broken off another piece. **2** a large quantity of anything. **3** a good slice, as of bread or cheese. **4** a supply or store. **5** as much ink as a pen takes up at a time.

stomach *n* **1** desire. **2** power to brook.—*v* **1** to retain on the stomach. **3** to tolerate, put up with.

stomatick *n* **1** a medicine good for the stomach.

ston *same as* **stound**³.

stonach *same as* **stony**.

stondy *same as* **stony**.

stone *n* a curling stone.—*v* to set a ring with stones.

stoned horse *n* a stallion.

stone lands *n* tenement houses built of stone.

stoner *n* a stone marble.

stonern *adj* made or built of stone.
stone-thrust *n* a small pier or projecting quay.
stong *same as* **stang**².
stonk *same as* **stunk**¹.
stonkerd *same as* **stunkard**.
stony *n* **1** a stone marble. **2** a boys' game, with a large stone set up in an open place and a smaller stone set on its top.
stoo¹ *same as* **stow**².
stoo² *v* **1** to stun. **2** to astound.
stoo³ *v* to tingle, throb, smart.—*n* an ache, twinge.
stood *n* **1** a mark on a sheep's ear. **2** half the ear cut across.
stoog *n* the central matter in a boil.
stooin *n* the tender sprout of a cabbage, etc.
stook¹ *v* (*used of corn*) to bulk in the stook.
stook² *n* a kind of wedge formerly used in sinking coal and lead mines.
stook³ *n* **1** a small horn. **2** a horn pointing backwards.
stook and stour *adv* wholly, altogether.
stooker *n* one who arranges the sheaves in a stook.
stookie¹ *n* a small stook of corn.
stookie² *n* a bullock with horns turned backwards.
stookie³, **stookey** *n* **1** plaster of Paris. **2** a plaster cast for a broken limb. **3** a plaster statue. **4** a foolish person. **5** a blockhead.—*adj* **1** bashful. **2** awkward.
stookie⁴ *n* a boy's red clay marble.
stookit *adj* having irregular horns or horns turning backwards.
stook o' rags *n* one whose clothing is ragged.
stookways *adv* after the manner in which stooks of corn are set up.
stooky *adj* having stooks of corn.
Stooky Sunday *n* the Sunday in harvest on which the greatest number of stooks is seen in the fields.
stool¹ *n* **1** a small trestle used to support a coffin, etc. **2** a seat in church on which offenders formerly did public penance.
stool² *n* **1** a place where wood springs up spontaneously after having been cut down. **2** a single stalk.—*v* **1** (*used of a tree*) to shoot out after being cut down. **2** (*of corn*) to ramify, shoot out stems from the same root.
stool-bent *n* moss or heath rush.
stool of a beard *n* a bushy beard.
stool of repentance *n* the seat in a church on which offenders had to do public penance.
stoom *v* **1** to frown. **2** to look sulky.
stoon, stoond *same as* **stound**.
stoonie *adj* moody and capricious.
stoop *n* **1** a pillar. **2** a post. **3** an animal's limb. **4** a supporter. **5** a staunch adherent. **6** (*in coal mining*) a massive pillar of coal, left to support the roof. **7** a piece of the shaft of a cart projecting behind. **8** a wooden bench beside a cottage door.—*v* to leave pillars of coal to support the roof in a mine.
stoop-and-room *n* the old method of working out coal, leaving pillars to support the roof.
stoop and roop *n* the whole.—*adv* wholly.
stoop-bed *n* **1** a bed with posts. **2** one with very short posts and no tester.
stoopie *same as* **stoupie**.
stooping *n* a place where the coal has been worked out except for the pillars left to support the roof.
stoopit¹ *adj* furnished with posts.
stoopit² *adj* bent, stooping.
stoopit bed *n* a bed with posts.
stoop-shouldered, ~-shouthered *adj* round-shouldered.
stoor¹, **stoor**² *same as* **stour**¹, **stour**².
stoor³ *int* get away!
stoordie *int* a call to a dog.—*n* a dog.
stoore *same as* **stour**².
stoorie-woorie *adj* restless, excitable, bustling.
stoorock *n* **1** a warm drink. **2** gruel.
stoorum, stooram *same as* **stourum**.
stooshie *same as* **stushie**.

stoob *adj* **1** stout. **2** healthy, strong. **3** well-grown. **4** (*used of liquor*) strong. **5** plucky. **6** stubborn.—*adv* **1** sturdily. **2** strenuously.
stoot¹ *same as* **steet**.
stoot² *same as* **stute**.
stooter¹ *v* to stumble.
stooter² *n* nonsense.
stooth *v* to lath and plaster a wall.
stoot-hertit *adj* stout of heart.
stoothin, stoothing *n* **1** lathing and plastering. **2** the surface stoothed. *See* **stooth**.
stoove *v* to stumble.
stop *same as* **stap**³.
stopple *same as* **stapple**².
store¹ *v* to win all a boy's marbles in a game.
store² *v* to enable, equip.—*n* **1** sheep or cattle. **2** lean stock bought for fattening.
store farm *n* a farm consisting chiefly of a walk for sheep.
store farmer *n* one who works a store farm (qv) as tenant or owner.
storeman *n* the storekeeper at a colliery village.
store-master *n* the tenant of a sheep farm.
storey *n* the grub of the daddy-longlegs.
storg *n* a large pin.
storging *n* the noise a large pin makes in going through flesh.
storm¹ *n* a fall of snow.—*v* (*used of the weather*) to be stormy.
storm² *n* as much ink as a pen takes up at a dip.
storm-cock *n* the fieldfare.
storm-finch *n* the stormy petrel.
storming *n* stormy weather.
storm-steddit, ~-sted *adj* storm-stayed.
storm water *n* surface water.
storm window *n* a window raised from the roof and slated above and on each side.
story¹ *n in phr* **a bonny story** a fine state of matters.
story² *n* the grub of the daddy-longlegs.
story-tell *v* to tell lies, fib.
story worm *n* **1** a grub. **2** a slug.
stot¹, **stott** *v* **1** to stagger, totter. **2** to walk with uneven, unsteady step. **3** to rebound, bounce. **4** to cause to rebound. **5** to bounce or spring in walking. **6** to walk ungracefully. **7** to stutter, stammer. —*n* **1** a stagger. **2** a stumble. **3** the gait of a cripple. **4** the act of rebounding. **5** a rebound. **6** a rebounding blow. **7** sudden motion. **8** a bouncing gait. **9** a leap or step in dancing. **10** the swing of a tune. **11** the go or trick of a thing. **12** a stutter, stammer. **13** jerky speech. **14** a standstill. **15** a hindrance.—*adv* **1** bouncingly. **2** with a rebound.
stot², **stott** *n* **1** a young bull or ox. **2** a bull of any age. **3** one that has been castrated. **4** a stupid, clumsy fellow.—*v* to take the bull.
stot-ba' *n* a game of ball.
stot-calf *n* a castrated bull calf.
stot's milk *n* unboiled flummery, used as a substitute for milk when that is scarce.
stot-sticker *n* a butcher.
stott¹, **stott**² *same as* **stot**¹, **stot**².
stotter¹ *n* a ball that stots. *See* **stot**¹.
stotter² *v* **1** to stagger, stumble. **2** to totter. **3** to walk clumsily. **4** to rebound.—*n* **1** a stumble, stagger. **2** the act of stumbling or tottering.
stottin *adj* **1** staggering. **2** very drunk. *See* **stot**.
stou¹ *same as* **stow**².
stou², **stou**³ *same as* **stound**¹, **stound**³.
stouchy *same as* **stoushie**.
stouff¹ *same as* **stuff**¹.
stouff² *v* to walk lazily and heavily.—*n* **1** the act of walking with such a step. **2** the sound of such a step. **3** a slow, stupid person.—*adv* with a lazy, heavy step.
stouin *adj* stolen.
stouins *n* croppings of cabbage or colewort.
stouk *n* a stook, a shock of corn.

stound[1], **stoun** v **1** to ache. **2** to throb. **3** to tingle, smart. **4** to thrill with glee.—n **1** an intermittent, throbbing pain. **2** a sharp, sudden pang. **3** a twinge. **4** an ache. **5** a thrilling sensation. **6** a throb, wave. **7** a whim.

stound[2], **stoun** n **1** a moment. **2** a portion of time.

stound[3], **stoun** v **1** to stun with a blow or loud noise. **2** to sound, resound. **3** to clang. **4** to astonish. **5** to astound. **6** to baffle, perplex.—n **1** a heavy blow. **2** a resounding noise.

stoup[1] n **1** a deep, narrow vessel for holding liquids. **2** a flagon of wood. **3** a jug with a handle. **4** a liquid measure. **5** a measure of liquor. **6** a wooden water pail.

stoup[2], **stoupe** same as **stoop**[2].

stoup[3] same as **stupe**.

stoup and roup adv completely.

stoupfu' n **1** as much liquor as fills a stoup. **2** a bucketful. See **stoup**[1].

stoupie n a small liquid measure.

stour[1], **stoure** v **1** to stir. **2** to move or run quickly. **3** to pour or gush out. **4** to pour leisurely from a vessel held on high. **5** to sprinkle. **6** to rise in a cloud, as of dust, spray, smoke, etc. **7** to raise a dust. **8** to drive, as snow.—n **1** a quarrel, strife. **2** a bustle. **3** a state of perturbation. **4** vexation. **5** excitement. **6** severe reproof. **7** a stiff breeze. **8** a storm. **9** dust, dust in motion. **10** fine-driven snow. **11** chaff. **12** any powdered substance. **13** flour. **14** a cloud of spray. **15** a smoke-like fog. —adv in a gush.

stour[2], **stoure** adj **1** tall, large, stout. **2** robust, sturdy, strong, stiff, stubborn, unyielding. **3** rough in manner. **4** austere, stern. **5** ill-tempered. **6** (used of the voice) rough, hoarse, harsh.—adv severely, strongly.—to be in a bad humour.

stour[3], **stoure** n **1** a stake. **2** a long pole.

stourage n direction, management.

stourdie n a dog.—int a call to a dog.

stourfu' adj stirring, exciting.

stourie[1], **stoury** n bustle, stir.—adj **1** restless, bustling, excitable. **2** dusty. **3** (used of the weather) marked by driving dust or snow.

stourie[2] adj **1** long and slender. **2** gaunt.

stourin n a slight sprinkling of any powdery substance.

stour-looking adj stern-looking, of austere looks.

stourly adv **1** strongly, sturdily. **2** sternly, austerely.

stour-mackerel n the scad.

stourness n largeness, bigness.

stour-o'-words n a wordy discourse.

stourum, stourreen n **1** thin porridge or gruel. **2** a warm drink containing oatmeal and milk, with boiling water poured over the mixture.

stoushie, stousie, stoussie adj **1** squat. **2** strong and healthy.—n a stout and healthy child.

stout same as **steet**.

stouter v **1** to stumble. **2** to trip in walking.

stouth[1] n **1** theft, robbery. **2** stealth.

stouth[2] n plenty.

stouth and rief n robbery with violence. See **stouthrief**.

stouth and routh n plenty, abundance.

stouthrie[1] n provision, furniture.

stouthrie[2], **stoutherie** n **1** theft. **2** stolen or smuggled goods.

stouthrief, stouthreaf, stouthreif, stouthrife n robbery with violence.

stove[1] n **1** a feverish illness. **2** a ground mist. **3** food that has been stewed.—v **1** to stew in a pot. **2** to bleach blankets with sulphur.

stove[2] same as **staive**.

stovies n **1** mashed potatoes. **2** stewed potatoes. **3** Irish stew. **4** a dish of sliced potatoes, fat and onions cooked together.

stovins same as **stooin**.

stow[1] v **1** to store, furnish. **2** to stuff.

stow[2] v **1** to crop, lop off. **2** to mark sheep by cutting out a piece of the ear.—n **1** an incision. **2** a cut. **3** a piece.

stow[3] v to steal.

stowan[1], **stowen** adj stolen.

stowan[2], **stowin** same as **stooin**.

stowed[1] adj stolen.

stowed adj very full.

stowen[1] same as **stowan**[1].

stowen[2] adj stowed.

stowen[3] n a greedy fellow.

stowenlins adv stealthily.

stower same as **stour**[1].

stowf v **1** to steam. **2** to rise up as steam.

stowff, stowffin n a slow and measured gait in walking.

stowfie adj short and thick.—n a short thickset person or child.

stowin n silence.

stowk n a stook, a shock of corn.

stowl same as **stool**[2].

stowlins adv stealthily.

stown adj stolen.

stownlins adv stealthily.

stown-wyes adv by stealth.

stowp[1] same as **stoop**.

stowp[2] same as **stoup**[1].

stowre same as **stour**[1].

stowsie same as **stoushie**.

Stow struntin n a kind of coarse garter made at Stow.

stowth same as **stouth**.

stoy v **1** to saunter. **2** to loiter.—n a saunter.

stoyte same as **stot**[1].

stoyter same as **stotter**[2].

stra n straw.

straa in phr **to say straa to one** to find fault with one, to lay anything to one's charge.

strab n **1** anything hanging or lying loosely or adhering to a person's clothes. **2** a shred a tatter. **3** a loose straw sticking out from a sheaf or stack. **4** an end of thread. **5** a withered leaf.

strabble n **1** anything hanging loosely, a shred, tatter. **2** a long, withered stalk of grass. **3** a piece of straw, thread, etc.—v to hang in long tatters.

strabblie adj full of strabbles or long fibres or strips. See **strabble**.

strabush, strabash n tumult, uproar.

strachle same as **strauchle**.

stracht adj straight.

strack adj strict.

strack v struck.

stracummage n uproar, tumult.

straddle v **1** to stroll. **2** to wander about aimlessly. —n the small saddle on the back of a cart or carriage horse for supporting the backband (qv) and the shafts.

strade v strode.

strae n **1** straw. **2** a thing of nought.

strae boots n wisps of straw tied round the feet and legs.

strae breadth n the breadth of a straw.

strae-dead adj quite dead.

strae death n **1** a death in bed in contrast to a violent one. **2** a natural death.

strae-drawn n **1** a sheep mark. **2** a thin slice cut from the top to the bottom of an animal's ear.

strae-headit adj yellow- or flaxen-haired.

strae hoose n a house or shed for holding straw.

straein same as **straen**.

strae kiln n a kiln dug in the face of a hillock and roofed with pieces of trees covered with drawn straw on which corn was put, a fire being lighted in front with openings at the back to draw the heat.

straemash same as **stramash**.

sträen adj **1** made of straw. **2** of wattled straw.

strae sonks n a wreath of straw used as a cushion or load saddle.

strae-wisp n one easily swayed or influenced.

strag, stragg n **1** an irregular person of ill-defined purpose. **2** a tramp. **3** a thin-growing, straggly crop.

straggelt adj (used of a child) stray, forsaken.

stragger *n* a straggler.
straggly *adj* sparse, straggling.
straicht *adj* straight.
straid *v* strode.
straidle *same as* **straddle**.
straiffin *same as* **striffin**.
straight *adv* **1** frankly. **2** seriously.—*v* **1** to put to rights. **2** to tidy. **3** to lay out a dead body.—*n* a straight line.
straight-tongued *adj* plain-speaking, outspoken, honest.
straik¹ *n* a scythe-sharpener.
straik² *n* **1** whisky. **2** *in phr* **cauld straik** raw whisky.
straik³ *n* **1** a tract of country. **2** ground traversed. **3** the strip of ground passed over at one turn in harrowing. **4** the act of travelling over a tract of ground. **5** an excursion.—*v* **1** to traverse a tract of land. **2** to take an excursion.
straik⁴ *v* **1** to stroke. **2** to smooth. **3** to comb, smooth with a comb. **4** to render even or smooth what tends to overflow. **5** to level down grain in measuring it. **6** to tune a fiddle, to draw the bow over the fiddle strings. **7** to anoint or spread with any unctuous or viscous substance. **8** (*used of birds*) to preen the feathers.—*n* **1** a stroke, buffet. **2** a pat, caress. **3** a stroking or smoothing. **4** the act of anointing or spreading with an unctuous or viscous substance. **5** a flat piece of wood or a small rolling pin, used for levelling grain, etc, heaped up in the measure. **6** the grain so rubbed off the top of the measure. **7** a very small quantity. **8** a mere handful.
straik⁵ *n* a stroke, a blow.
straik⁶, **straike** *n* **1** a bushel. **2** a measure of corn, etc.
straik⁷ *n* **1** a streak. **2** a stripe. **3** a ray of the sun. **4** (*in pl*) the narrow boards or planking forming the sides and bottom of a boat.—*v* **1** to streak. **2** to stripe.
straik⁸ *same as* **streek**¹.
straik⁹ *n* a small roll or bundle of flax when dressed.—*v same as* **strick**¹.
straiked *v* struck.
straiked *adj* levelled to the brim of the measure.
straiker *n* that with which corn, etc, is levelled to the brim of the measure.
straikin¹ *n in phr* **straikin o' daylicht** daybreak.
straikin² *n* **1** coarse linen used for shirts. **2** (*in pl*) the refuse of flax.
straikin stick *n* a stick for marking sheep with tar.
straikit measure *n* exact measure.
straik o' day *n* daybreak.
strain¹ *same as* **streind**¹.
strain² *v* **1** to sprain. **2** to extort. **3** to squeeze.—*n* a sprain.
strait¹ *adj* straight.—*v* to straighten.
strait² *adj* **1** (*used of an article of clothing*) too small, tight. **2** (*of a bargain*) hard, close. **3** hard at driving a bargain. **4** straitened, in want of. **5** steep.—*v* **1** to tighten, to stretch tight. **2** to take a good, hearty meal.
strait bields *n* a shelter formed by a steep hill.
straith *n* a strath.
straitie *n* the shank of the leg.
straitnedness *n* **1** straitness. **2** the being straitened.
straak *same as* **streek**¹.
strak *v* struck.
strake¹, **strake**², **strake**³ *same as* **straik**¹, **straik**⁴, **straik**⁷.
strake⁴ *same as* **strick**¹.
strake⁵ *v* struck.—*n* a blow, stroke.
stram *n* a big person.—*v* to walk in a rude noisy manner.
stram *adj* stupid.—*n* a stupid person.
stramash *n* **1** an uproar. **2** a tumult. **3** a disturbance. **4** fuss. **5** a smash, crash. **6** wreck and ruin. —*v* to break in pieces, wreck.
strammel *n* straw.
stramp *v* **1** to tread or stamp on. **2** to trample. **3** to tread under foot. **4** to tramp, walk.—*n* **1** a stamp, tread. **2** a walk, step, tramp.
stramper *n* one who tramples.
stramulleugh *adj* cross, sour, ill-natured.
stramullion *n* **1** a strong, masculine woman, a virago. **2** a

row, broil. **3** a fit of bad temper. **4** a display of pettishness.
stramullyoch *same as* **stramulleugh**.
stramulyert *adj* **1** aghast. **2** panic-stricken.
stramyolloch *n* **1** a broil, battle. **2** a disturbance, tumult.
strand, stran' *n* **1** a stream, rivulet. **2** a gutter. **3** a channel or drain for water.
strand-scouring *n* clearing out the gutters.
strang¹ *n* **1** urine. **2** human urine formerly preserved as a lye.
strang² *adj* strong.—*n* strong ale.
strang³ *v, adj* strung.
strange *adj* aloof.—*v* **1** to think strange. **2** to wonder.—*n in phr* **strange be here!** an exclamation of surprise.
stranger *n* **1** a small bit of tea leaf in a cup of tea, supposed to indicate the arrival of a stranger. **2** a moth fluttering towards one, supposed to indicate the arrival of a stranger or a letter.
strang pig, ~ tub *n* a vessel for preserving urine as a lye.
strang-thewed *adj* having strong thews.
strap¹ *n* **1** a band for a sheaf of corn. **2** a bunch.—*v* to be hanged.
strap² *n* treacle.
strap³ *n* a fellow, a chap.
strap⁴ *n* an end of thread.
strap-oil *n* a castigation.
strapper *n* the man on a farm who has charge of the farmer's horse and gig.
strapping *adj* tall and handsome.
strath *n* a valley or plain through which a river runs.
strathspey *n* **1** a Highland dance, like a reel, but slower. **2** the music for this dance.
stratlin *n* **1** a step. **2** a straddling, striding step.
strauchen *same as* **strauchten**.
strauchle *v* **1** to struggle. **2** to toil, strive.
straucht, straught *adj* straight.—*v* **1** to make straight. **2** to stretch. **3** to smooth out. **4** to lay out a dead body.—*n* a straight line.—*adv* straightway.
strauchten, straughten *v* **1** to straighten. **2** to lay out the dead.
straucht-forrit, ~-for'at *adj* straightforward.—*adv* forthwith.
straucht-gaun *adj* straightforward.
strauchting brod *n* a board on which the dead are laid out.
strauchtly *adv* **1** straightforward. **2** forthwith.
straucht-oot-the-gate *adj* straightforward, upright.
strauchtway *adv* straightway.
strauchty-squinty *adj* **1** winding, zigzag. **2** not straight.
straun *same as* **strand**.
stravaig, stravag, stravague, stravaug *v* **1** to saunter, stroll. **2** to go about aimlessly and idly.—*n* **1** a stroll, saunter. **2** aimless walking.
stravaiger *n* **1** a saunterer. **2** a wanderer. **3** a vagabond. **4** a seceder from a religious community.
strave *v* strove.
straw¹ *n* childbed. *See* **strae**.
straw² *v* to strew, spread.
strawage *n* what is strewn.
strawn¹ *n* a string, as of beads.
strawn² *same as* **strand**.
straw-theekit, ~-thackit *adj* thatched with straw.
stray¹ *adj* lost, not at home, strange.—*n* a lost child or animal.
stray² *same as* **strae**.
streach *same as* **stretch**.
streah *n* a round, used to denote a mode of drinking practised by the chief men of the Western Islands, who sat in a circle until they became drunk.
streak *same as* **streek**¹.
streamer *n* (*in pl*) the aurora borealis or northern lights.—*v* **1** to streak. **2** to cover with straggling flashes of light, like the aurora borealis.
streamie *n* a streamlet.

streamoury *adj* having streams of light from the aurora borealis.

stream tide *n* a flowing tide.

streap *same as* **stripe**².

streauw *n* straw.

streaw *n* the shrewmouse.

strechen *v* to straighten.

strecht *adj* straight.

streck¹ *same as* **streek**¹.

streck² *same as* **strick**⁵.

streck³ *v* to strike.

streek¹ *v* **1** to stretch. **2** to stretch oneself. **3** to bear stretching without breaking. **4** to lie down at full length. **5** to lay out a dead body. **6** to draw the first furrow in autumn or spring. **7** to plough. **8** to exert oneself. **9** to set to work. **10** to engage in work. **11** to go quickly or at full speed. **12** to hasten. **13** to walk along. **14** to saunter. **15** to smooth out.—*n* **1** a stretch. **2** full length. **3** the longitudinal direction of a stratum of coal in a mine. **4** one's course, way, opinion. **5** speed, rapid progress. **6** any kind of exertion. **7** bustle, tumultuous noise, disturbance. **8** dawn, daybreak.

streek² *same as* **straik**⁴.

streek, streek o' lint *same as* **strick**¹.

streeker *n* a very tall person.

streeking *n* (*used of ploughing*) the drawing of the first furrow at the beginning of spring.

streeking buird *n* the board on which a dead body is laid out.

streeking o' day *n* dawn.

streekit claith *n* an umbrella.

streek o' day *n* dawn.

streel *same as* **strule**.

streen *n* last night, yesterday evening, *in phr* **the streen**. *See* **yestreen**.

streend *same as* **streind**².

streenge *v* to beat, scourge.—*n* a stroke.

streenzie *v* **1** to sprain. **2** to extort. **3** to distrain. **4** to squeeze.—*n* a sprain.

streetch *v* to stretch.

streeve *v* strove.

streffin *same as* **striffin**.

streik¹ *same as* **streek**¹.

streik² *same as* **strick**¹.

streikin *adj* tall and active.

streiking buird, ~ buird *n* a board for laying out a dead body.

strein *same as* **streen**.

streind¹ *n* **1** a peculiar cast or disposition of a person. **2** strain. **3** temperament.

streind² *v* to sprain, strain.—*n* a sprain, strain.

streive *v* strove.

strek¹ *same as* **streek**¹.

strek² *same as* **strick**¹.

strekin *n* (*used of ploughing*) drawing the first furrows at the beginning of spring.

strength, stren'th *n* **1** a stronghold. **2** an ample supply.

strenie *adj* lazy, sluggish.

strenkel, strenkle *same as* **strinkle**.

strenthie *adj* strong, powerful.

stress *v* **1** to incommode. **2** to overtax. **3** to strain at the swingletree.—*n* **1** an effort. **2** a pressing demand. **3** distraint. **4** a forced duty, fine, etc.

stret, strett *same as* **strait**².

stretan *n* a good, hearty meal.

stretch *v* **1** to lay out a dead body. **2** to walk with dignity. **3** to walk a long distance. **4** to take a walk.—*n* **1** a quibble. **2** a straining of law, equity, evidence, etc. **3** a walk. **4** a distance.

stretcher *n* an implement for stretching shetland shawls, drying washed flannels, etc.

streten *v* **1** to tighten. **2** to straiten. **3** to eat heartily.

streyck, streyk *v* to strike.

strib *v* **1** to milk neatly. **2** to drain the last drops from a cow's udder. *See* **strip**.

stribbings *n* the last drops of milk drawn from a cow's udder.

strick¹ *n* a handful of flax that is being dressed.—*v* to tie up flax in handfuls or small rolls for milling.

strick² *v* to dress barley.

strick³ *adj* rapid, swift.—*n* (*used of a river*) the most rapid part.

strick⁴ *v* to strike.

strick⁵ *adj* strict, rigid, in principles and in practice.—*adv* strictly.

stricken *adj* fought.

stricken hour *n* a whole hour.

stricklie *adv* strictly.

strickness *n* **1** austereness. **2** strictness.

strict¹ *v* to stroke.

strict² *n* **1** a strict way. **2** (*in pl*) formalities, ceremonies. **3** strict terms.

strict³ *same as* **strick**³.

striddle *v* **1** to straddle. **2** to sit astride. **3** to stride. —*n* **1** a stride. **2** the gait of a man with bent legs.

striddle-legs *adv* astride.

stride *n* **1** walking power. **2** the legs. **3** the fork of the legs.

strided *v* strode.

stride-legs *adv* astride, with legs apart.

stridelins, stridlins *adv* astride, with legs apart.

striek *same as* **streek**¹.

strieking *same as* **streikin**.

strif *n* a struggle for a livelihood.

striferiggs *n* **1** patches of common land. **2** debatable land.

striffen¹ *same as* **stiffen**.

striffen² *same as* **striffin**.

striffin, striffen *n* **1** a thin, membranous film. **2** a thin skin. **3** the thin, filmy substance made of the afterbirth of a cow and used for covering the mouths of bottles, etc.

striffle *v* **1** to move in a fiddling or shuffling way. **2** to assume an air of importance.—*n* a shuffling motion.

strik *v* to tie up what is reaped.

strike¹ *v* **1** (*in curling*) to dislodge a stone by striking it forcibly with another. **2** (*of a horse*) to kick out behind. **3** to start a tune. **4** to smooth, level.

strike² *same as* **streek**¹.

strike³ *same as* **strick**¹.

striken *adj* struck.

striking-teck *n* the cutting of heather with a short scythe.

strin¹, **strinn** *n* **1** a thin, narrow stream of water, etc. **2** the channel of a river. **3** (*of a pipe*) a short smoke.—*v* to flow in a thin, narrow stream.

strin² *n* the milk drawn from a cow's teat by one motion.

string¹ *n* **1** meaning, drift. **2** the thread of an argument, etc. **3** a lineal measure of 24 ells. **4** a cord for making watches and clocks act as repeaters by pulling. **5** (*in pl*) the root fibres of a plant.

string² *v* **1** to feel a passion for. **2** to feel the stirrings of animal desire.

string³ *n* a tide, current.

string⁴ *v* **1** to move or fly in a long line. **2** to walk, run or fly in single file. **3** to hang by the neck. **4** to be hanged. **5** (*used of turnips*) to spring regularly in the drills.

stringie *adj* **1** stiff, affected. **2** narrow. **3** dour. **4** discontented.

stringin' *n* **1** tape. **2** a kind of narrow web used for trouser braces. **3** strings for knee breeches.

string-of-tide *n* a rapid tideway.

strings *n* inflammation of the intestines of calves.

strink *v* **1** to dole out in small quantities. **2** (*with* **it**) to pine away.

strinkle *v* **1** to sprinkle. **2** to strew.

strinkling *n* a sprinkling.

strinnent *v, adj* measuring out very carefully into a scale anything that is to be weighed, such as dangerous drugs. *See* **strink**.

strintle, strinnle *v* **1** to trickle. **2** to flow in a small stream.—*n* **1** a very small stream. **2** a narrow channel or groove.

strip[1], **stripe** *v* **1** to draw the last milk from a cow. **2** to cleanse or wipe by drawing between the finger and thumb compressed or drawing the fingers or hand along the surface. **3** to walk, stride. **4** to draw the feet along the ground. **5** to walk or send one off.—*n* **1** a stripe. **2** a stripling.

strip[2] *n* a stirrup.

strip[3] *same as* **stripe**[3].

stripe[1] *same as* **strip**[1].

stripe[2] *n* a narrow piece of ground.—*v* **1** to thrust. **2** to whip.

stripe[3], **strip** *n* **1** a rill. **2** a small stream. **3** a small, open drain. **4** a long, narrow plantation.

stripey *n* a red-and-yellow worm, used for bait.

striphin *same as* **striffin**.

strip irons *n* stirrup irons.

strip leathers *n* stirrup leathers.

stripped, strippit *adj* striped.

strippings *n* the last and richest milk from a cow.

strippit *adj* clean milked.

stritchie *adj* lazy, sluggish.

strive *v* **1** to be restive. **2** to find fault with, object to.—*n* an effort, struggle.

strived *v* strove.

striven *adj* **1** at variance. **2** on bad terms. **3** not friendly.

stroak *same as* **stroke**[2].

stroakings *same as* **strippings**

stroan *same as* **strone**[3].

stroap *same as* **strap**[2].

strobble *v* **1** to slouch, shamble in walking. **2** to walk awkwardly.

strodd, strod *v* **1** to stride along. **2** to strut. **3** to walk fast without speaking.

stroddle *n* anything very small or worthless, a straw.

strodge *same as* **strodd**.

strods *n* **1** a pet. **2** a sulky fit. **3** one of ill-humour.

strok annet *same as* **stock-annet**.

stroke[1], **strok** *n* **1** a streak or line. **2** the least possible. **3** the point of striking in a clock.

stroke[2] *v* **1** to lay out a dead body. **2** to draw the last milk from a cow.

stroke[3] *v* did strike.

strokings *n* the last milk drawn from a cow.

strokit *adj* striped, in lines or streaks.

stroller *n* a strolling player or showman.

strommel *v* to stumble.

stronachie *n* the fifteen-spined stickleback.

strone[1], **stron** *n* a hill terminating a range, the end of a ridge of hills.

strone[2] *v* to walk about in a sulky mood.

strone[3], **stron** *v* **1** to urinate. **2** to stream. **3** to pour. **4** to milk into. **5** to spout forth as from a water pipe.—*n* **1** the act of urinating copiously. **2** a streamlet.

strong *same as* **strang**[2].

stronge *same as* **strounge**.

strong waters *n* ardent spirits.

strood[1] *n* **1** a suit of clothes. **2** a complete set of anything. **3** a worn-out shoe.

strood[2] *same as* **strowd**[1].

stroods *n* the sails of a boat.

strool[1] *same as* **strule**.

strool[2] *same as* **stroul**.

stroonge *same as* **strounge**.

stroop *n* the spout of a pump, kettle, teapot, etc.

stroopit *adj* having a spout.

stroopless *adj* without a spout.

stroosh *n* a heavy blow on anything soft or yielding.

strooshie *n* a squabble, a hurly-burly. *See* **strush**.

stroot *same as* **strute**.

stroosle *same as* **struissle**.

strop *same as* **strap**[2].

strops *n* braces.

stroud[1], **stroud**[2] *same as* **strowd**[1], **strowd**[2].

stroud[3] *same as* **strood**[1].

stroul *n* **1** any stringy substance found among food. **2** a long piece of anything.

strounge *adj* **1** harsh to the taste. **2** morose. **3** of forbidding aspect or manner.—*v* **1** to go into a mood. **2** to sulk.

stroungely *adv* harshly, forbiddingly.

stroungey *adj* quarrelsome, sulky.

stroup *same as* **stroop**.

stroupie *n* a teapot.

stroussie *same as* **strooshie**.

strouth *n* force, violence.—*v* **1** to compel. **2** to use violence.

strouthy *adj* strong.

strow[1] *n* **1** a turmoil. **2** a bustle. **3** a quarrel. **4** variance. **5** strife. **6** a pet, sulky fit. **7** a short illness. —*adj* hard to deal with.

strow[2] *n* the shrewmouse.

strowd[1] *n* a senseless, silly song.—*v* to sing in a stupid, bad style.

strowd[2] *same as* **strodd**.

strowd[3] *n* **1** a disturbance. **2** a quarrel. *See* **strow**.

strowl *same as* **stroul**.

strow mouse *n* the shrewmouse.

strown *same as* **strone**[3].

stroy *v* to destroy.

struble *v* to trouble, vex.

strublens *n* disturbance.

struchle *same as* **strushel**.

strucken *adj* **1** struck. **2** stricken.

strucken hour *n* a whole hour.

strucken-up *adj* metamorphosed into stone by the agency of evil spirits.

struckle *n* a pet, sulky fit.

struie *v* **1** (*in threshing with the flail*) to strike so that the straw is moved to the end of the threshing floor. **2** to squander. **3** to scatter things about.

struissle, struisle, struishle *v* to struggle.—*n* **1** a struggle, tussle. **2** a brawl, squabble.

struit *same as* **strute**[1].

strule *v* **1** to urinate forcibly. **2** to pour from vessel to vessel. **3** to emit liquid in a stream.—*n* a stream.

strum[1] *n* a pet, sullenness.—*adj* pettish, sullen.—*v* **1** to be pettish, sullen. **2** to gloom, take offence.

strum[2] *n* **1** the first draught of the bow over the fiddle strings. **2** the sound of a bagpipe.

strumash *same as* **stramash**.

strummel *n* the remainder of tobacco, left with the ashes, in a tobacco pipe.

strumming *n* **1** a loud, murmuring noise. **2** a thrilling sensation, sometimes implying giddiness. **3** confusion.

strummy *adj* pettish, sullen.

strump *n* a broken bit of straw.

strune *same as* **strone**[3].

strung[3] *same as* **strounge**.

strunge *same as* **strounge**.

strungely *same as* **stroungely**.

strungie *same as* **stroungey**.

strunk *v* to sulk.

strunt[1] *n* **1** a pet, pique. **2** a sulky fit. **3** a person of sulky disposition.—*v* to affront, offend, insult.

strunt[2] *n* anything long and narrow.

strunt[3] *v* **1** to walk sturdily. **2** to strut. **3** to walk with dignity. **4** to walk about in a sullen mood.

strunt[4] *n* any kind of spirituous liquor.

strunt[5] *v* to cut short.

struntain, struntin *same as* **stow-struntin**.

struntum *n* the name of a fiddler's tune.

strunty *adj* **1** short, contracted. **2** stumpy. **3** stunted. **4** short-tempered. **5** easily offended. **6** out of humour.

strush *n* **1** a disturbance, quarrel. **2** tumult. **3** a state of disorder.—*v* to go about in a lazy, careless, slovenly manner.

strushan *n* a disturbance, tumult.

strushel, strushal *adj* **1** untidy, disorderly. **2** slovenly.—*v* to go about in a lazy, careless, slovenly manner.

strushelness *n* **1** untidiness in dress. **2** slovenliness.

strushil *same as* **struissle**.

strushlach *n* an untidy, slovenly woman.

strussel, strussle *same as* **struissle**.

strute[1] *n* stubbornness, obstinacy.

strute[2] *adj* **1** stuffed full. **2** drunk. **3** vainglorious.

struve *v* strove.

struy *same as* **struie**.

stryke *same as* **streek**[1].

strynd, stryne *same as* **streind**[1].

stryne *v* to strain, sprain.

strypal *v* **1** to hang in loose, unwieldy folds or tatters. **2** to walk with long, unsteady steps or with wavering gait, like tall persons.—*n* **1** anything long and rather flexible. **2** a tall, slender person. **3** a good-looking, tall person.

strype *same as* **stripe**[2].

strypie *n* a very small stream, a rill.

stryth *n* the labouring animals on a farm.

stuan *same as* **stooin**.

stub, stubb *n* **1** a bristle. **2** a short, stumpy hair.

stubble-butter *n* butter from the milk of cows grazing in stubble land.

stubble-end *n* the posteriors.

stubble goose *n* the greylag or greylag goose.

stubble-rig *n* a stubble field.

stubblin *adj* short and thickset.

stubbly *adj* stubble-clad.

stubbly *adj* **1** strong, sturdy. **2** healthy.

stubie *n* **1** a large bucket or pitcher, narrower at the top than at the bottom, with an iron handle, for carrying water. **2** a water stoup. *See* **stoup**.

stucken[1], **stuchin, stuckin** *n* a stake driven into the ground to support a paling or sheep net.

stucken[2] *v* stuck.

studderts *same as* **stoddart**.

studdie, study, studdy *same as* **stiddie**.

stude *v* stood.

studgel *adj* stout, sturdy.

stue[1] *same as* **stew**[1].

stue[2] *same as* **stow**[2].

stuff[1] *n* dust.

stuff[2] *v* to garrison.

stuff[3] *n* **1** luggage, baggage, belongings. **2** corn, grain. **3** produce. **4** liquor, whisky. **5** physic. **6** vigour. **7** (*in pl*) provisions.

stuffen *same as* **stiffen**.

stuffily *adv* toughly, perseveringly.

stuffiness *n* ability to endure fatigue.

stuffing *n* **1** croup. **2** difficult breathing from accumulated phlegm.

stuffrie *n* **1** stuff. **2** material. **3** an article of any kind.

stuffy, stuffie *adj* **1** stout and firm. **2** sturdy. **3** mettlesome. **4** able to endure.—*n* a sturdy, persevering fellow.

stug[1] *n* a masculine woman, one who is stout and raw-boned.

stug[2] *same as* **stog**[1].

stuggen *n* **1** a post, stake. **2** an obstinate person.

stugger *n* a big, ungainly woman.

stuggy *same as* **stoggie**.

stughie *n* **1** anything that fills to repletion. **2** satisfying food.

stughrie *n* great repletion.

stuir *same as* **stour**[2].

stuit *same as* **stute**.

stule *n* a stool.

stult *n* a crutch.

stultie *n* one who uses a crutch.

stumfish *same as* **stamfish**.

stummle *v* to stumble.

stump *n* **1** an old person. **2** a fragment of a rainbow appearing on the horizon. **3** a man with a wooden leg. **4** a blockhead, a stupid person. **5** (*in pl*) legs.—*v* **1** to walk with a wooden leg. **2** to hobble. **3** to walk briskly. **4** to walk heavily. **5** to halt.

stumpart *n* **1** a person of awkward or stumbling gait. **2** such a gait.—*v* to walk with such a gait.

stumper *v* to stumpart (qv).—*n* a stumpar (qv).—*adv* with an awkward gait.

stumpers *n* legs.

stumpie *n* **1** a nickname for a person with a wooden leg. **2** a short, squat bottle. **3** a hen with short lets and a round body.

stumpish *adj* stupid, blockish.

stumpit *adj* stumpy, short.

stumple *v* **1** to walk with a stiff, hobbling motion. **2** to stump off.

stumpy *adj* **1** thickset, short and stout. **2** (*used of a leg*) amputated, mutilated. **3** (*of a pen, pencil, etc*) worn to a stump, blunted.—*n* **1** a short, thickset person. **2** a small, good-natured person. **3** an endearing name for a child. **4** anything mutilated. **5** an amputated leg. **6** a short, much worn quill pen. **7** the stump of a tooth showing above the gum. **8** a bottle. **9** a man with a wooden leg.

stumral *adj* (*used of a horse*) given to stumbling.

stun *v* to astonish, startle.—*n* a start, surprise.

stunch *n* a lump of food, as of bread and beef.

stund *same as* **stound**[1].

stungle *v* **1** to sprain a joint or limb. **2** to sprain slightly.

stunk[1] *v* **1** to be silent or sullen. **2** to sulk.—*n* (*in pl*) a sulky fit.

stunk[2] *n* a stake in a game.

stunkard *adj* **1** sullen, silent. **2** obstinate.

stunkardy *adj* stunkard (qv).

stunkle, stunkel *n* **1** a sullen or pettish fit. **2** the sulks.

stunkus *n* a stubborn girl.

stunner *n* a big, foolish man.

stunt *v* **1** to cut off from. **2** to curtail.—*n* a stunted tree, etc.

stunt *v* **1** to stamp. **2** to walk smartly.

stuog *same as* **stug**[1].

stup *same as* **stoop**.

stupe *n* a stupid person, a dullard, a fool.

stupid-fou *adj* stupid with drink.

stuppie *same as* **stoupie**.

stur[1] *same as* **stour**[2].

stur[2] *v* to stir.—*n* a stir.

sturdied *adj* afflicted with the sturdy (qv).

sturdy *adj* **1** stupid. **2** giddy-headed.—*n* **1** vertigo, a disease affecting the brain of sheep and other animals. **2** a sheep affected with sturdy. **3** the darnel and its seed. **4** giddiness caused by eating or drinking anything with which darnel seed has been mixed. **5** the head. **6** a fit of obstinacy or giddiness.

sturdy *n* a sturdy leg.

sture[1] *same as* **sture**.

sture[2] *same as* **stour**[2].

sturken *v* **1** to become stout after an illness or after childbirth. **2** to coagulate, congeal.—*adj* of sour disposition and cold manners.

sturnill *n* **1** an ill turn. **2** a relapse.

sturoch, sturroch *n* oatmeal stirred into milk or water.

sturt *v* **1** to startle. **2** to stir. **3** to vex, trouble.—*n* **1** strife, discussion. **2** trouble, vexation. **3** wrath. —*adj* turbulent, contentious.

sturten *adj* of a sour disposition and cold manners.

sturtin *adj* frightened.

sturtin-straigin *n* coarse thread, formed of blue and red worsted.

sturtle *same as* **startle**.

sturty *adj* causing trouble.

stushagh, stushach *n* a suffocating smell arising from a smothered fire.

stushie, stushy *n* an uproar, disturbance, row.

stut *v* to prop, support with stakes or pillars.—*n* a prop, support.

stute, stutt *v* to stammer, stutter.

stuter *n* a stammerer.
stutherie *n* a confused mass.
stuthy *same as* **stiddie**.
stutter *same as* **stotter**[2].
sty *v* to put a pig into a sty.
stychie *n* **1** an unseemly mass. **2** great confusion. **3** a confused crowd.
stychle *same as* **steichle**.
stychly *adj* foul, suffocating.
styen *n* a sty on the eyelid.
style[1] *v* to give a person his or her proper name in speaking or writing.
style[2] *same as* **stile**[1].
styme, stym *same as* **stime**.
stymel *same as* **stimel**.
stymie *same as* **stimey**.
styoo *n* dust.
styte[1] *same as* **stite**[1].
styte[2] *same as* **stot**.
styter[1] *n* the smallest bit.
styter[2] *same as* **stotter**[2].
styth, stythe *adj* **1** firm, steady. **2** strong. **3** lusty. **4** stiff. **5** stiff in death, rigid. **6** dead.
stythe *same as* **stead**.
styther *same as* **stotter**[2].
sualter *same as* **swatter**[1].
sub *same as* **sib**.
subcustomer *n* an under custom-house officer.
subfeu *n* a feu granted by one who himself or herself holds the property as subject to a superior.—*v* to grant a right to heritable property on condition of the payment of a certain duty to one who is himself or herself subject to a superior.
subite *adj* sudden.
subject, subjeck *n* (*in pl*) property, effects.—*v* to submit, become subject to.
submisse *adj* **1** submissive. **2** moderate. **3** gentle.
subscrive, subscryve, subscrieve *v* to subscribe, sign one's name.
subscriver *n* one who subscribes his or her name.
subservant *n* an underservant.
subsist *v* **1** to stop, cease, desist. **2** to support, maintain.—*n* a subsistence.
substancious, substantious *adj* **1** powerful. **2** possessing ability. **3** substantial. **4** effectual.
substrack, substract *v* **1** to subtract. **2** to withdraw from.
subtack *n* a sublease.
succar, succour, succre *n* sugar.
succar saps *n* pap abundantly sweetened with sugar.
succeed *v* to cause to prosper.
succles *n* stonecrop.
succre-ale *same as* **sugarallie**.
succumb *v* **1** to lose one's cause. **2** to fail in an action at law.
such *adv* so.
suck *same as* **sook**.
sucken[1] *adj* sunk.
sucken[2] *n* **1** a territory subjected to a certain jurisdiction. **2** the privilege or obligation of tenants to grind at a certain mill. **3** the jurisdiction attached to a mill. **4** the miller's dues.—*adj* **1** legally astricted to grind at a certain mill. **2** under obligation to employ any tradesman, shopkeeper, etc.—*v* to astrict the grinding of com.
suckener *n* one who is bound to grind at a certain mill.
suckens *n* a grapple used by fishermen to recover lost lines.
sucker[1] *same as* **sooker**[2].
sucker[2] *n* **1** sugar. **2** a term of endearment.—*v* to sugar.
suckered, suckert *adj* (*used of a child*) pampered, spoilt, fondled.
suckler *n* a lamb nursed by hand.
sucky *same as* **sookie**.
sud[1] *v* should.
sud[2] *n* the south.
sud[3] *n* seed.

sudart, suddart *n* a soldier.
suddard, suddart *adv* southward.
suddent *adj* sudden.—*adv* suddenly.—*n in phr* **on a sudden** on the spur of the moment.
suddent-like *adv* suddenly.
suddenty *n* **1** suddenness. **2** a mishap, harm, mischief.
suddle, suddil *v* to soil, sully, defile.—*n* **1** a stain. **2** a much worn article of dress.
Sudereys *n* the southern Hebrides.
sudge, sudgess *adj* subject to.
sudroun *adj* **1** southern. **2** English.—*n* **1** an English person. **2** the English language.
suffer *v* to suffer capital punishment.
sufflet *same as* **souflet**.
sug[1] *v* to saturate.
sug[2] *same as* **sugg**.
sugarallie, sugarelly, sugar-ally *n* **1** liquorice. **2** a policeman.
sugarallie-button *n* a sweetmeat made of liquorice, a Pomfret cake.
sugarallie-water *n* a solution of liquorice and water, made by children.
sugar-boola *n* round sugarplums.
sugar-peas *n* sweet peas.
sugar-piece *n* a slice of bread buttered and sprinkled with sugar.
sugar-tap *n* a kind of sweetmeat.
sugg *v* **1** to sink. **2** to press down. **3** to move heavily or in a rocking manner.—*n* **1** a sow. **2** a stout person. **3** an easy-going woman or child.
suggan *n* **1** a thick coverlet. **2** a saddle of straw or rushes.
suggie *n* **1** a young sow. **2** a young cow. **3** a fat person.
suggy *adj* wet, marshy, boggy.
sugh[1] *same as* **souch**.
sugh[2] *same as* **seuch**.
suh *int* a call to dogs to seek.
suill *same as* **sole**[3].
suit[1] *v* **1** (*of clothes*) to fit close. **2** to provide oneself.
suit[2] *v* to sue for.
suit[3] *v* to look attractive or becoming in.
suit[4] *v* did set.
suitten *v, adj* set.
suld *v* should.
sule[1] *v* to soil, sully.
sule[2] *same as* **sole**[3].
sulfitch *adj* (*used of a smell*) suffocating.
sulk down *v* (*used of the brows*) to droop sulkily.
sullige *n* **1** dung. **2** sediment, refuse conveyed by water.
sulyie *n* soil.
sum *adj* some.—*adv* somewhat.
sumf, sumff *same as* **sumph**.
summar *adj* summary.
summer *same as* **simmer**[3].
summer blink *n* a passing gleam of sunshine.
summer cloks *n* sunbeams dancing in the atmosphere on a fine summer day.
summer cout *n* **1** the quivering appearance of the atmosphere on a warm day. **2** a swarm of gnats dancing in the air. **3** a lively young fellow.
summer flaws *n* **1** the quivering appearance of the atmosphere on a warm day. **2** a swarm of gnats dancing in the air.
summer growth *n* **1** various species of *Sertulariae, Flustrae*, etc, attached to small stones or shells. **2** sea growth.
summer haar *n* a slight breeze from the east which often rises after the sun has passed the meridian.
summering *n* (*in pl*) cattle a year old.
summering ground *n* pasture kept for summer feeding.
summer lift *n* the summer sky.
summer preachings *n* preparatory services for the Communion, when it was formerly held once a year in country parishes during summer.

summer scale *n* (*in pl*) the scales that rise on the top of beer beginning to sour.—*v* to cast up such scales.

summer snipe *n* the common sandpiper.

summer sob *n* **1** a summer storm. **2** frequent slight rains in summer.

summons *v* **1** to summon. **2** to summon to a superior law court.

summonser *n* a server of a summons.

sump *n* **1** the pit of a mine. **2** the well of a mine below the working level, where water collects before being pumped to the surface. **3** drainage. **4** a drain. **5** mud. **6** a sudden, heavy fall of rain. —*v* **1** to be wet. **2** to soak, drench.

sumped *adj* drenched.

sumph *n* **1** a soft, blunt fellow. **2** a simpleton, stupid blockhead, fool. **3** a surly, sulky person.—*v* **1** to be stupid and dottish. **2** to remain in a state of stupor. **3** to be of a sullen, sulky temper. **4** to look sullen.

sumphie *adj* **1** stupid, foolish. **2** sulky, sullen.

sumphion *n* a musical instrument, a kind of drum.

sumphish *adj* **1** stupid, foolish. **2** sulky, sullen.

sumple *adj* pliable, easily imposed on.—*n* a simpleton, fool.

sun *n* a son.

sun-birsled *adj* sunburnt.

sunblink *n* **1** a sunbeam. **2** a gleam of sunlight.—*adj* **1** bright, gleaming at intervals. **2** having frequent gleams of sunshine.

sun-broch *n* a halo round the sun.

Sunday blacks *n* black clothes worn by men at church.

Sunday claise *n* dress for going to church.

Sunday name *n* a full baptismal name.

Sunday sark *n* a clean or finer shirt worn on Sunday.

Sunday's face *n* a solemn face, a serious look.

Sunday's morning *n* Sunday morning.

Sunday squeel, ~ schule *n* a Sunday school.

sunder *with v* **1** to part from. **2** to part with.

sundew-web *n* the gossamer.

sundry *adj* separate, distinct.—*adv* apart, asunder.

sune *adv* soon.

sunfish *n* the basking shark.

sun-flaucht *n* **1** a gleam of sunshine. **2** a sunbeam.

sung *adj* singed.

sun-gates *adv* with the sun, from east to west.

sun-glaff *n* a passing sunbeam.

sungle *adj* single.—*v* (*used of lint*) to separate flax from the core.

sun-glint *n* **1** a sunbeam. **2** a gleam of light.

sun-go-down *n* sundown, sunset.

sunk *n* the back of the fire.

sunk², sunk³ *same as* **sonk¹, sonk²**.

sunkan, sunken *adj* **1** sullen, sour. **2** ill-natured. **3** splenetic.

sun-kep *n* a sunbonnet.

sunket¹ *n* a lazy person.

sunket², sunkit *n* (*in pl*) provisions of any kind.—*adv* somewhat, slightly.

sunkie *same as* **sonkie**.

sunkit ~, sunket time *n* mealtime.

sunkots *n* something.

sunk-pocks *n* the bags tied to the sunks on the back of a tinker's ass in which goods, baggage, children, etc, were carried. *See* **sonk¹**.

sunny half, ~ side *n* **1** the south side of anything. **2** land with a southern exposure.

sun-saut *n* salt made from sea water.

sunsheen *n* sunshine.

sunsheeny *adj* bright with sunshine.

sunshines *n* a children's singing game.

sunside *n* **1** the sunny side of anything. **2** (*used of the heart*) the good side.

sun-singit *adj* sunburnt.

sun-sittin *adj* (*of eggs*) injured by the heat of the sun.

sunways *adv* with the sun, from east to west.

sunyie, sunzie *n* an excuse, an objection.

sup *v* **1** to drink. **2** to feed and give bedding to horses, cattle, etc, for the night.—*n* **1** a mouthful. **2** a small quantity of liquid, porridge, etc. **3** an indefinite quantity of liquid. **4** (*used of whisky*) a drink. **5** (*of spoon meat*) a spoonful. **6** *in phr* **bit and sup** food and drink.

supe *same as* **soop**.

super *n* a superintendent.

superior *n* the landlord to whom feu duties were payable.

superiority *n* **1** ownership of land by a superior (qv). **2** the ground rents payable to a superior (qv).

supernumerary *adj* (*of votes*) constituting the difference in number between majority and minority.

superplus *n* the surplus.

supersault *n* a somersault.

superscription *n* a subscription.

superscryve *v* to subscribe.

suple *same as* **soople²**.

suppable *adj* that may be supped.

supper *v* **1** to provide a person with supper. **2** to feed horses, cattle, etc, with food for the night.

suppie-mae *n* a pet sheep.

supping sowens *n* sowens (qv) supped with a spoon, in contrast to drinking sowens.

supple¹, supple² *same as* **soople², soople³**.

supplee *v* to supply.

supplicant *n* one in deep distress, an object of pity.

supplication well *n* a holy well.

supply *n* a locum tenens, especially for a minister.

suppone *v* **1** to suppose. **2** to hope, expect.

suppose *v* to substitute in a supposititious way.—*conj* although.

suppost *n* **1** a supporter. **2** a scholar in a college.—*v* to put one in the room of another.

surce *n* a common mode of addressing a number of people of both sexes.—*int* an exclamation of surprise, etc.

surcoat *n* **1** an under-waistcoat. **2** a knitted semmit worn over the shirt by old men.

sure¹ *adj* sour.

sure² *adv* surely.

surely *adj* certain, true.—*n* **1** certainty. **2** truth.

surfaceman *n* a labourer in charge of roads.

surf duck *n* the common scoter.

surfeit, surfeid, surfet *adj* **1** excessively painful or cruel. **2** arrogant.

surfle, surfel *v* **1** to overcast. **2** to gather or spread a wider edge over a narrower. **3** to ornament with edging, embroidery, etc.—*n* **1** an overcast. **2** a trimming. **3** an edging, embroidery. **4** a border of fur. **5** the hem of a gown.

surfy *v* **1** to satisfy. **2** to avail.

surly¹ *adv* surely.—*n* a certainty.

surly² *adj* **1** rough, boisterous. **2** stormy.

surprise *v* **1** to be surprised. **2** to wonder.

surree *n* a social gathering, with tea, music, speeches, etc.

surrender *n* speed, haste, a great rate.

surrock *same as* **sourock**.

survivance *n* survival.

sush¹ *same as* **soosh**.

sush², sushing *n* (*used of the wind*) a rushing sound.

sushie *v* to shrink.

susket *n* **1** a shot. **2** the report of a shot.

suskit *adj* (*used of clothes*) threadbare, much worn.

suspeck *v* to suspect.

suspection *n* suspicion.

suspender *n* (*a law term*) one who brings in a suit of suspension.

suspense *v* to suspend.

suspension *n* a suit seeking a stay of execution of a judgment or a charge.

sussie, sussy *n* **1** care. **2** hesitation.—*v* **1** to hesitate. **2** to be careful. **3** to care. **4** to trouble.—*adj* careful, attentive to.

sussnin *n* a very small quantity.

sustain *v* **1** (*a legal and ecclesiastical term*) to admit as valid. **2** to approve of. **3** to confirm.

sustainer *n* one who entertains another at bed and board.

sustaintnent *n* sustenance, nourishment.

susy *same as* **shusy**.

susy-lifter *n* a resurrectionist.

sut *same as* **sot**².

sute *v* to shoot.

suth *same as* **sooth**¹.

suthart *adj* southward, southern.

sutieman *n* a sweep.

sutor, sutter *same as* **souter**.

sutten *adj* **1** sat. **2** *in phr* **sutten on** stunted in growth.

suwarrow, suwaawra wursit *n* a particular kind of yarn used in knitting petticoats.

swaadge *same as* **swage**.

swaagin *same as* **swagging**.

swaat *same as* **swat**².

swab¹ *v* **1** to wipe, mop. **2** to go about in a loose, idle fashion.—*n* **1** a term of contempt for a drunkard. **2** a loose, idle fellow.

swab² *n* the pod of a pea.

swabbish *adj* mean, despicable.

swabble *v* to beat with a long, supple stick.—*n* **1** a supple, pliant rod. **2** a tall, thin, overgrown person.

swabblin' *n* a drubbing.

swabblin' stick *n* a cudgel.

swabing *n* a beating, drubbing.

swable *same as* **swabble**.

swack¹ *n* **1** a hard blow. **2** a violent fall. **3** a sudden gust. **4** a severe blast of wind.—*v* **1** to throw with force. **2** to strike violently sword against sword. **3** (*used of wind*) to blow suddenly and violently.

swack² *n* **1** a large quantity, a collection. **2** a share. **3** a deep draught of liquor.—*v* **1** to drink deeply and in haste. **2** to drink greedily, swill.—*adj* abundant and good.

swack³ *adj* **1** limber, supple, pliant. **2** nimble, agile. **3** active, clever. **4** elastic. **5** (*used of a slight bar of iron or piece of wood, etc*) slender, weak, fragile.

swacken *v* **1** to make supple or pliant. **2** to become supple. **3** to grease an axle.

swacken *v* to beat very severely.

swacking, swackan *adj* **1** clever. **2** tall. **3** active. **4** of a large size.

swad *n* a soldier.

swad, swaddie *n* the swedish turnip.

swaddle *v* to twist about, as for ease on a saddle.

swaddlins *n* **1** long-clothes. **2** baby linen.

swadge *same as* **swage**.

swaf *n* a gust, blast, swirl of wind.

swag¹ *v* **1** to move backwards and forwards. **2** to swing to and fro.—*n* **1** motion. **2** inclination from the perpendicular. **3** a leaning to. **4** a swinging motion. **5** a swaying gait. **6** a depression in the ground caused by mining. **7** a bag, a wallet, a schoolboy's pocket. **8** a festoon used as an ornament to beds, etc.

swag² *same as* **swack**².

swage *v* **1** to assuage. **2** (*used of the full stomach*) to grow empty by digestion. **3** to digest food. **4** to quiet. **5** to still.

swagger *v* **1** to stagger, reel. **2** to feel as if intoxicated.—*n* **1** an inclination to one side. **2** a stagger.

swaggie *n* the act of swinging.

swagging, swaging *adj* **1** bulging. **2** pendulous. **3** fluttering as a bird's wing. **4** wavering. **5** wagging.

swaif¹ *same as* **swaf**.

swaif² *same as* **swarf**.

swail *n* a gentle rising in the ground with a corresponding declivity.

swailsh *n* a part of a mountain or hill that slopes more than the rest.

swain *n* a shepherd.

swaip *v* to sweep.

swaip *adj* slanting.

swaipelt *n* a piece of wood, like the head of a crosier, put loosely round the fore fetlock of a horse to impede its progress.

swaird *n* sward.

swairf *same as* **swarf**.

swaish *adj* (*used of the face*) full, suave and benign.

swaith *n* **1** a wreath of mist. **2** a lock of hair.

swaits *same as* **swat**².

swak¹ *same as* **swack**¹.

swak² *v* **1** to throw with force. **2** to wield a sword.

swakken *same as* **swacken**¹.

swal, swall *v* to swell.

swald¹**, swalled, swalt** *v* did swell.

swald²**, swalled, swallen** *adj* swelled.

swall *v* **1** to devour. **2** to swallow. **3** used in imprecations.

swallin *n* a swelling.

swallow *n* **1** the martin. **2** the stormy petrel.

swally *v* to swallow.—*n* the throat.

swam *n* a large quantity.

swamp *adj* **1** thin, not gross. **2** not swelled.—*v* to become thin.

swamped *adj* a slang word for imprisoned.

swampie *n* a tall, thin fellow.

swander *v* **1** to be seized with giddiness. **2** to fall into a wavering or insensible state. **3** to lack resolution or determination.—*n* a fit of giddiness that comes on at a sudden emergency or surprise and may induce apoplexy.

swane *n* a young man, a swain.

swank¹ *adj* slender, thin, not corpulent.—*n* a tall, thin man.

swank² *adj* **1** supple, pliant. **2** active. **3** stately. **4** jolly. —*n* a clever young fellow.—*v* to be supple.

swankie, swanky *n* **1** a smart, active, strapping young fellow or girl. **2** anything large of its kind. —*adj* supple, active, agile.

swanking *adj* **1** supple, agile, active. **2** moving quickly. **3** stout and healthy-looking. **4** (*of a blow*) heavy.

swankit *v* toiled, worked hard. *See* **swink**.

swanky *adj* **1** tall and thin. **2** loosely put together.

swanky-like *adj* active-looking.

swap¹ *n* **1** the cast of countenance. **2** the general appearance.—*v* to resemble in appearance or temperament. **3** (*of a young, growing animal*) to form or shape.

swap² *n* an immature and a partially formed pod. —*v* (*used of peas, etc*) to form into pods.

swap³ *v* **1** to exchange. **2** to lose. **3** to excel, outvalue. **4** to vouch.—*n* **1** the thing exchanged. **2** an exchange.

swap⁴ *v* **1** to strike violently. **2** to wield a sword vigorously. **3** to thrash. **4** to set down with a bang. **5** to throw with a sudden, swinging motion. **6** to cast a fishing line. **7** (*with off*) to knock off, dispose of.—*n* **1** a heavy blow. **2** a sudden stroke. **2** a slap.—*adv* with sudden force. **2** quickly, smartly.

swap⁵ *v* **1** to roll tightly round. **2** to gird. **3** to twist over. **4** to put straw ropes over the thatch of a rick or house by throwing a large ball of rope.—*n* a twist, turn.

swapper *n* the person with whom one exchanges.

swappert *adj* nimble, agile.

swappet beast *n* an animal exchanged for another.

swarch *same as* **swarrach**.

sward *n* a sod for burning.—*v* to cover with grass.

sware *same as* **swire**.

swarf, swarff *v* **1** to swoon, faint. **2** (*of the breath*) to stop, as in a swoon. **3** to cause to swoon. **4** to exhaust. **5** to stupefy.—*n* **1** a swoon, fainting fit. **2** stupor.

swarfish *n* the spotted blenny.

swargh *same as* **swarrach**.

swarl *v* to swirl.

swarrach, swarrack, swarrich *n* **1** a large, untidy heap. **2** a confused mass. **3** a quantity of liquid. **4** a closely packed crowd.—*v* to crowd together in confusion.

swarricking *n* a confused crowd.

swarth¹ *n* **1** sward. **2** the surface of the ground.

swarth² *n* exchange, excambion.

swarth³ *same as* **swarf**.

swarth⁴ *v* to darken.

swarth-broo'd *adj* black-browed.

swart head *n* the edible part of the head of the large tangle.

swart tangle *n* the large red tangle.

swarve *same as* **swarf**.

swarve *v* 1 to swerve. 2 to incline to one side.

swash *v* 1 to beat. 2 to dash violently. 3 to slash. 4 (*of a tail*) to swish. 5 to walk haughtily. 6 to swagger, bounce.—*n* 1 a splash, a dash of water. 2 a rush, dash. 3 a heavy blow. 4 a fall. 5 the sound of a blow, fall, etc. 6 a large quantity. 7 a corpulent person. 8 ostentation, a swaggering gait. 9 a swaggerer, a fop.—*adj* 1 of a broad make, corpulent. 2 fuddled. 3 showy, gaudy, ostentatious. 4 haughty.

swasher *n* 1 a tall person of ostentatious manners, a swaggerer. 2 anything large and showy.

swashing *adj* striking, startling.

swashy *adj* 1 showy, gaudy. 2 swaggering. 3 soft-spoken. 4 of a broad make. 5 fuddled. 6 soft, squashy. 7 damp.

swat[1] *v* 1 to sweat. 2 did sweat. 3 sweated.

swat[2] *n* 1 (*in pl*) drink. 2 new ale. 3 small-beer. 4 the thin part of sowens (qv) fermented into a weak beer.—*v* to tipple.

swat-a-day *int* an exclamation of surprise, etc.

swatch[1] *n* 1 a sample, pattern. 2 a piece cut off as a pattern.—*v* 1 to match. 2 to make or supply according to pattern.

swatch[2] *n* a look, a glance.

swate *v* 1 did sweat. 2 sweated.

swathe *n* 1 a wreath of mist. 2 a lock of hair.

swathel *n* a strong man. 2 a hero.

swatle *same as* **swattle**.

swatroch *same as* **swattroch**.

swatt *same as* **swat**[2].

swatter[1], **swather** *v* 1 to flutter and splash in water, as a duck. 2 to move quickly and awkwardly.

swatter[2] *n* 1 a large collection, especially of small objects in quick motion. 2 a confused mass. 3 an untidy heap.

swattle[1] *v* 1 to swallow greedily and noisily. 2 to swill.—*n* 1 the act of swallowing greedily. 2 thin soup or other liquid.

swattle[2] *v* to beat soundly with a stick or wand.

swattlin *n* a drubbing.

swattroch *n* 1 substantial food. 2 strong liquor.

swauge, swanje *same as* **swage**.

swauger[1] *n* a large draught.

swauger[2] *same as* **swagger**.

swauk *same as* **swack**[1].

swaukin *adj* hesitating.

swaul *v* 1 to swell. 2 to increase in bulk.—*n* a swelling.

swauled *adj* swelled.

swaultie *n* a fat animal.

swaunder *same as* **swander**.

swaup[1] *v* to cool a spoonful of food by putting it into one s own mouth before giving it to a child.

swaup[2] *adj* strapping.

swaup[3], **swaup**[4], **swaup**[5] *same as* **swap**[1], **swap**[2], **swap**[3].

swauve, swave *same as* **swarf**.

swaver *v* 1 to stagger, totter, walk feebly. 2 to hesitate. 3 to be undecided.—*n* 1 a stagger. 2 an inclination to one side.

swaw *v* 1 to produce waves. 2 to ruffle the surface of the water, as by the movements of a fish. 3 to swing.—*n* 1 a wave. 2 an undulation of the water or slight movement of the surface by a fish swimming near the surface or by any body thrown into the water.

swawin *n* (*used of water*) the rolling of a body of water under the impression of the wind.

sway[1], **sway**[2] *same as* **swee**[1], **swee**[2].

sway-boat *n* a swingboat.

sway chain *same as* **swee chain**.

sway crook *same as* **swee crook**.

swayed *adj* (*of growing grass, etc*) waved by the wind.

swayl *same as* **sweel**[1].

sway-swaw, ~-sway *same as* **swee-sway**.

sweal[1] *v* 1 (*of a candle*) to flare and gutter. 2 to melt away. 3 to carry a candle so as to make it blaze away.

sweal[2], **sweal**[3] *same as* **sweel**[1], **sweel**[2].

sweal[4] *same as* **swill**[1].

sweap *same as* **sweep**[2].

swear[1] *v* to put on oath.—*n* an oath.

swear[2] *same as* **sweer**[3].

swearer *n* one who administers an oath.

sweart *same as* **sweert**.

sweat *v* (*of cheese*) to exude oily matter in ripening. —*n* a state of great anxiety or exciting effort.

swebar *n* the iron bar or swee in a chimney, for hanging pots, etc. *See* **swee**[1].

swech *v* (*used of rushing water*) to sound.

sweching, swechan *n* 1 a rushing sound, as of a waterfall. 2 a hollow, whistling sound, as of the wind.

swecht *n* 1 the force of a moving body. 2 violence. 3 a burden. 4 weight. 5 force. 6 a multitude. 7 a great quantity.

sweckery *same as* **swick**.

swedge *n* an iron chisel with bevelled edge for making a groove round the edge of a horseshoe. —*v* to groove a horseshoe for receiving nails.

swee[1] *v* 1 to swing. 2 to weigh down. 3 to be undecided. 4 to turn aside.—*n* 1 a swing. 2 a movement or inclination to one side. 3 a lever. 4 a pivoted iron rod suspended in a chimney from which pots, etc, are hung above the fire by a chain.

swee[2] *n* the line of grass cut down by the mower.

swee bauk *n* a balance beam.

swee chain *n* the chain hanging from the swee. *See* **swee**[1].

swee crook *n* the swee chain (qv) and its hook.

sweeg *n* a poor home-made candle.

sweege *v* to ooze between the staves of a tub.

sweek *same as* **swick**.

sweel[1] *v* 1 to swaddle. 2 to wrap round. 3 to wrap in a winding sheet.—*n* 1 the act of swathing. 2 as much cloth as goes round a person's body.

sweel[2] *v* 1 to whirl round. 2 to swing anything round with the hands. 3 to make water in a vessel eddy.—*n* 1 a circular motion, an eddy. 2 the act of turning rapidly round. 3 anything with a circular motion. 4 the rippling sound of a streamlet.

sweel[3] *same as* **swill**[1].

sweel[4] *n* a swivel.

sweeler *n* 1 a bandage. 2 a swaddling band.

sweem *v* 1 to swim. 2 to float.

sweeng *v* to swing.

sweens *n* sowens (qv).

sweep[1] *v* 1 to quicken the speed of a curling stone by sweeping the path before it. 2 to do anything briskly.—*n* 1 the rope by which stones are tied to the corners of a herring net. 2 a stretch of land. 3 sweepings. 4 a scamp, rascal.

sweep[2] *v* 1 to whip. 2 to scourge. 3 to strike with a club.

sweeped *v* swept.

sweeper *n* 1 a bunch of feathers for dusting. 2 one who sweeps before a curling stone.

sweepie *n* a sweep.

sweepit *v* swept.

sweep stone *n* the stone tied to the corner of a herring net to sink it.

sweep-the-causey *n* one who would do the meanest thing for money.

sweer[1] *v* 1 to swear. 2 to put on oath.—*n* an oath.

sweer[2] *v* swore.

sweer[3], **sweers** *adj* 1 slow, lazy, reluctant. 2 not liberal or ready to spend or give.—*n* 1 a lazy time. 2 a short rest during working hours in field labour. 3 darkness.—*v* 1 to be lazy. 2 to rest for a short time during working hours.

sweer-arse *n* a children's game, played by two seated on the ground, feet to feet, holding a stick by their hands and trying which shall raise the other up by main strength.

sweerd *same as* **sweert**.

sweer-draun *adj* reluctant.

sweered *v* swore.

sweer Jenny, ~ Kitty *n* an instrument for winding yarn.

sweerman's lift, ~ load *n* **1** an undue burden borne by a lazy person to save a double journey. **2** more than one can accomplish.

sweerness *n* laziness.

sweerock *n* a lazy girl.

sweer-out *adj* **1** unwilling to turn out. **2** hard to draw.

sweert *adj* **1** reluctant. **2** slow. **3** lazy.

sweerts, sweerty *n* **1** laziness, sloth. **2** a fit of laziness.

sweer tree *n* **1** an instrument for winding yarn. **2** a youths' game resembling sweer-arse (qv). **3** the stick used in the game.

sweer-up *adj* unwilling to get up in the morning.

sweer will *n* reluctance.

sweery *adj* **1** lazy. **2** slow. **3** unwilling.

sweesh *v* **1** to swish. **2** to move with a swishing motion.

swee-sway *adj* **1** in suspense. **2** hesitating.

swee-swee *v* to make a chirping noise.

sweet[1] *adj* (*used of butter*) not salted, fresh.

sweet[2] *v* to sweat.

sweet-breeds *n* the diaphragm of an animal.

sweet-cicely *n* the great chervil.

sweeten *v* **1** to bribe. **2** to bid at a sale without intending to buy.

sweet-gale *n* the bog myrtle.

sweet-heap *n* (*a home-brewing term*) the heap into which the malt was gathered after it had been spread long enough evenly on the barn floor.

sweetheart *v* to court, to act as a lover.

sweethearting day *n* courting time.

sweet-heat *n* (*a home-brewing term*) the proper point of heat at which malt was removed from the sweet-heap (qv) to be kiln-dried at once.

sweetie *n* **1** a sweetmeat, goody. **2** a sweetheart. **3** a considerable sum of money.

sweetie bench *n* a sweet stall.

sweetie bun *n* a large cake, made about Christmas, of flour, raisins, currants, orange peel, almonds and spices.

sweetiecook *n* **1** a sweetmeat. **2** a sugar-coated bun.

sweetie laif *n* a sweetie bun (qv).

sweetie-man *n* a retailer of sweets.

sweetie scon *n* a sweetie bun (qv).

sweetie shop *n* a confectioner's or sweet shop.

sweetie stand *n* a sweet stall.

sweetie-wife *n* **1** a woman who sells sweets. **2** a gossipy person.

sweetie-wiggy *n* a sweet cake or roll, baked with butter and currants. *See* **wig**[5].

sweet-lippit *adj* fond of sweet things.

sweet Mary *n* the rosemary.

sweet-milk cheese *n* cheese made of unskimmed milk.

sweet-milker *n* the day on which sweet-milk cheese is made.

sweet-William *n* the common tope.

sweevil *n* **1** a swirl. **2** an eddying movement.

sweg *n* **1** a copious draught, swig. **2** a quantity. **3** a large number.

sweig *n* a very bad home-made candle.

sweigh *same as* **swee**[1].

sweil[1]**, sweil**[2] *same as* **sweel**[2]**, sweel**[4].

sweill *same as* **sweel**[2].

sweir *v* to swear.

sweir *same as* **sweer**[3].

sweired, sweirt *same as* **sweert**.

sweirts, sweirtie *same as* **sweerts**.

sweit *v* to sweat.

sweited *v* **1** did sweat. **2** sweated.

swelchie[1] *n* a seal.

swelchie[2]**, swelchee** *n* a whirlpool.

swell[1] *v* **1** to swagger. **2** to play the swell.—*n* a sensation, excitement, figure.

swell[2] *n* a bog, a mire.

swelled kye *n* cattle swelled by flatulence.

swelt[1] *v* to melt, broil with heat.

swelt[2] *v, adj* melted, suffocated with heat.

swelting cod *n* a cod in poor condition.

sweltry *adj* sultry.

swerd *n* a sword.

swerd-slipper *n* a sword cutler.

swere *same as* **sweer**[3].

swerf, swerve *same as* **swarf**.

swesh *adj* (*used of the face*) full, suave, benignant.

swey *same as* **swee**[1].

swick *v* **1** to cheat. **2** to win by cheating. **3** to deceive. **4** to blame.—*n* **1** fraud, deceit. **2** any kind of trick. **3** a cheat. **4** a swindler. **5** the knack of doing a thing properly. **6** ability, knowledge. **7** approbation, good opinion. **8** blame. **9** responsibility in the sense of blame. **10** worthiness.—*adj* clear of anything.

swick an' trick *adj* unscrupulous and tricky.

swicker *n* a deceiver.

swickful *adj* deceitful.

swicky *adj* **1** deceitful. **2** sportively tricky. **3** roguish.

swidder *same as* **swither**[2].

swidderin, swiddern *v, adj* trying to make up one's mind.

swiel *same as* **sweel**[2].

swieth *same as* **swith**.

swiff *n* **1** a rapid motion and the whirring or whizzing sound it produces. **2** a soughing, sound. **3** a whiff, a puff, breath, a short interval, a snatch of sleep, etc.—*v* **1** to move with a rushing sound. **2** to whiz.

swiff a sleep *v* to have a short, disturbed sleep.

swiff awa' *v* to swoon, faint.

swift *n* a reeling machine used by weavers.

swig[1] *n* **1** a quantity. **2** a considerable number.

swig[2] *n* **1** art. **2** skill. **3** knowledge. **4** manner.

swig[3] *v* **1** to sway. **2** to move from side to side. **3** to walk with a rocking motion. **4** to turn suddenly. **5** to walk quickly. **6** to work energetically.—*n* the act of turning suddenly.

swil *same as* **sweel**[4].

swile *n* a bog in a meadow.

swilie *adj* full of bogs.

swilkie *n* a large whirlpool in the sea.

swill[1] *v* **1** to rinse, wash out. **2** to souse. **3** (*with* **away** *or* **down**) to wash down. **4** (*with* **up**) to wash up.—*n* a washing, rinse.

swill[2]**, swill**[3] *same as* **sweel**[1]**, sweel**[2].

swilter *v* **1** to agitate water or any liquid. **2** to undulate in a pail, etc.

swim[1] *n* **1** a state of great wetness. **2** a flooding.

swim[2] *n* **1** a swoon. **2** a giddiness, faintness.—*v* **1** to swoon, turn giddy. **2** to spin, as a top. **3** to cause to spin.

swimmed *v* swam.

swine arnot *n* the marsh betony or clown's all-heal.

swine bread *n* the pignut.

swine fish *n* the wolf fish.

swine-gotten *adj* used as an opprobrious epithet.

swine meat *n* pigs' wash.

swine pig *n* a pig.

swine pot *n* a large pot or caldron for boiling pigs' food.

swine ree *n* an enclosure where pigs are reared, the pigsty within it.

swine's arnuts *n* the tall oat grass with tuberous roots.

swine's cresses *n* the fool's cress.

swine shott *n* a young pig.

swine's maskert, ~ mosscroft *n* the marsh betony.

swine's murricks *n* the tuberous roots of the tall oat grass.

swine's saim, ~ saem *n* hog's lard.

swine sty *n* a pigsty.

swine thistle *n* the sow thistle.

swing *n* the hawser of a fishing boat.

swinge *v* to walk with a heavy, swinging gait.—*n* **1** a blow. **2** a heavy, swinging gait.—*adv* with such a gait.

swingeing, swinging *adj* **1** large, extremely big. **2** excellent.—*n* a whipping, a beating.

swingeour, swinger *n* **1** a sluggard, drone. **2** a rogue, rascal. **3** a bankrupt.

swinging tree *n* a flail.

swingle *v* to separate flax or hemp from the stalk or pith by beating it.—*n* the striking part of a flail.

swingler *n* an instrument used for beating flax.

swingler *n* a swindler.

swingletree *n* **1** the stock over which flax is scutched. **2** the movable part of a flail that strikes the grain.

swingle wand *n* an instrument for beating flax.

swingling hand *n* a wooden lath for dressing flax.

swingling post *n* a sloping post fixed in the barn floor over which flax was held to be dressed.

swingling stock *n* an upright board, three feet long, mortised into a foot or stock, over which the flax was held in order to be beaten.

swing lint, ~ lind *n* an instrument for breaking flax.

swing tree *n* the swingletree of a plough.

swink *v* to work hard.—*n* labour, toil.

swipe[1] *n* **1** a heavy driving stroke. **2** a heavy blow. **3** a circular motion.—*v* to move circularly, as in using a scythe.

swipe[2] *v* to drink hastily and greedily, to gulp.—*n* a copious draught.

swipe[3] *v* to sweep.

swipper, swippert *adj* **1** quick, nimble. **2** sudden. **3** hasty, tart.—*adv* suddenly, quickly.

swipper-like *adv* hastily, with ill-temper.

swippertly *adv* swiftly, suddenly.

swippit *v* swept.

swipple *same as* **soople**[3].

swire *n* **1** a level spot or steep pass between mountains. **2** the descent of a hill. **3** a declivity near the top of a hill.

swirl, swirel *v* **1** to turn or wheel round. **2** to unroll. **3** to turn out verses or rhymes. **4** to brandish. **5** to be seized with giddiness. **6** to carry off, as by a whirlwind.—*n* **1** a facial contortion. **2** a twist in the grain of wood. **3** a twist. **4** a curl. **5** a sweep, curve. **6** a tuft of hair on tbe head that refuses to lie flat, a cowlick. **7** a state of confusion. **8** the vestiges left by a whirling motion of any kind.

swirlin', swirlon *adj* (*of the human body*) distorted.

swirling *n* giddiness, vertigo.

swirly *adj* **1** curly. **2** (*used of wood*) full of twists or knots, contorted, gnarled. **3** (*of grass*) twisted, entangled and difficult to cut. **4** inconstant, fluctuating, ever in rotation.

swish *v* **1** (*used of water*) to rush noisily. **2** (*of the wind*) to blow loudly and fiercely.—*n* **1** a rush of water and its sound. **2** a slight fall or sprinkling of water.—*int* an exclamation indicating the sound of a swift, sudden stroke.

switch *n* **1** a slight blow, as with a switch. **2** a fillip. —*v* to thresh with a thin stick.

swite *v* to sweat.

swith, swithe *adv* quickly, suddenly.—*adj* swift, instant. **2** eager.—*v* to hasten, to get away.—*int* begone! quick!

swither[1] *v* **1** to dry up, wither. **2** to parch with heat.

swither[2] *v* **1** to doubt, hesitate. **2** to be undecided or in perplexity. **3** to cause doubt or apprehension. **4** to shake one's resolution.—*n* **1** doubt, hesitation. **2** a dilemma. **3** a flurry. **4** a panic, funk.

swither[3] *v* **1** to overpower forcibly. **2** to rush. **3** to whiz. **4** to put forth all one's strength. **5** to assert oneself, assume a superior dignity or merit. **6** to swagger. **7** to hector.—*n* **1** a severe blow, such as makes one stagger or become giddy. **2** a trial of strength in exerting mind or tongue.

swithly *adv* swiftly, eagerly.

switter *v* to work confusedly.—*n* **1** entanglement, confusion. **2** confused working. **3** excitement, fluster, panic.

swoaping *adj* (*used of the tail of a horse*) swishing, sweeping.

swoich *same as* **souch**[1].

swole *v*, *adj* swollen, swelled.

swoo *n* **1** a heavy sound. **2** a whizzing sound.

swoof *same as* **swuff**.

swoom *v* to swim.

swoon *n in phr* **in the swoon** said of corn, the seed of which has lost strength before the plant is fairly rooted.

swoop *same as* **soop**.

swooper *same as* **sweeper**.

swoople *same as* **soople**[3].

swoor *v* **1** swore. **2** sworn.

swoorn *v*, *adj* sworn.

sword *n* **1** the leaf of the common yellow iris. **2** a crossbar in a door or gate.

sword-claught *n* a sword thrust.

sword-slipper, ~-sliper *n* a sword cutler.

sword-straik *n* a sword stroke.

swound *v* to swoon, faint.—*n* **1** a swoon. **2** a fainting fit.

swow *n* a dull, murmuring sound.—*v* to emit such a sound.

swown *adj* swollen.

swuff *v* **1** to swoop. **2** to move with a whizzing sound. **3** to breathe loudly in sleep. **4** to whistle or hum a tune in a low key or under the breath, to sowf. **5** to faint, swoon.—*n* the act of whizzing.

swuffs *n* an implement for winding yarn.

swunged *v*, *adj* beaten. *See* **swinge**.

swuppert *adj* **1** nimble, agile. **2** quickly gliding.

swure, swuir *v* swore.

swurl *same as* **swirl**.

swurn *v*, *adj* sworn.

swuther *same as* **swither**[1].

swutten *v* sweated.

swye *same as* **swee**[1].

swyke *same as* **swick**.

swyl *same as* **sweel**[1].

swyle *same as* **swile**.

swylie *same as* **swilie**.

swype[1] *n* knowledge, art, skill.

swype[2] *v* to sweep.

swype[3] *n* the exact image or likeness.

swype[4], **swype**[5] *same as* **swipe**[1], **swipe**[2].

swyppirt *same as* **swipper**.

swyre *same as* **swire**.

swyte *v* to sweat.

swyth, swythe *same as* **swith**.

sy[1], **sy**[2] *same as* **sey**[1], **sey**[7].

sy[3] *n* a scythe.

sybo, sybie, syboe, sybow *n* **1** a young onion. **2** a shallot.

sybor *same as* **siver**.

sybo-short *adj* of short temper.

sybo tail *n* the tail of an onion.

syde[1] *v* to side with, support.

syde[2] *adj* **1** wide and long. **2** hanging low down.

sye[1] *n* a scythe.

sye[2] *same as* **sives**.

sye[3] *same as* **saithe**.

sye[4] *v* to strain a liquid.

sye dish *same as* **sey dish**.

sye milk *n* a sey dish (qv).

syer *n* a strainer.

sye sones, ~ sowens *n* a sieve for straining sowens (qv).

syke *same as* **sike**[1].

syle[1] *v* **1** to betray. **2** to circumvent.

syle[2] *same as* **seil**[1].

syle[3] *same as* **sile**[1].

syllab, syllap, sylib *n* a syllable.—*v* to divide into syllables.

syllable *v* to read very carefully.

sylling *n* ceiling.

symar *same as* **seymar**.

symie *n* the devil.

symion-brodie *n* **1** a cross-stick. **2** a children's toy.

syn *same as* **syne**[3].

synd, synde *v* **1** to rinse. **2** to wash down with drink. **3** to draw through water.—*n* **1** a rinsing. **2** a drink. **3** a drink taken with or just after food. **4** a deluge.

syndins *n* water for washing out a dish.
syndry *adj* sundry.—*adv* asunder.
syne[1] *v* to synd (qv).
syne[2] *n* a small quantity of anything.
syne[3] *adv* **1** ago, since. **2** from that time. **3** then, at that time. **4** afterwards. **5** next in time. **6** in that case. **7** late.—*prep* since.—*conj* **1** since. **2** then, thereupon, therefore.
syneteen *adj* seventeen.
syning glass *n* a looking glass.
synle *same as* **seenil**.
synn *same as* **synd**.
synner *same as* **sinder**.
synod *n* a Presbyterian church court ranking higher than a presbytery.
syp *same as* **sip**[1].

sype *same as* **seip**.
syple *n* a saucy, big-bellied person.
syre *same as* **siver**.
syse *same as* **size**[2].
syser *n* a juryman.
syte[1] *n* compensation.
syte[2] *same as* **site**.
syth[1] *n* compensation, satisfaction. **2** atonement.
syth[2], **sythe** *v* to strain through a sieve.—*n* **1** a sieve. **2** a milk strainer.
sythe[1] *n* a scythe.
sythe[2] *same as* **syth**[2].
sythment *n* compensation, damages.
syver, syror *same as* **siver**.
syzzie *v* to shake.

T

ta, taa[1] *n* a sucker or stolon of sedge, couch grass, etc.
taa[1] *same as* **ta**.
taa[2] *n* a marble, a taw.
taaie *adj* fibrous.
taanle *same as* **tawnle**.
taapie *same as* **tawpie**.
taat *same as* **taut**.
taatie *same as* **tatie**.
taave[1], **taave**[2], **taave**[3] *same as* **tyaave**[1], **tyaave**[2], **tyaave**[3].
taave-taes *n* pit fir split into fibres and twisted for ropes.
taavin-skate *n* skate separated into filaments.
tab[1] *adj* **1** (*used of a cat*) brindled, striped.—*n* a male cat. **2** a pet name for a cat.
tab[2] *n* a loop for hanging a coat, etc.
tabacca *n* tobacco.
tabbet, tabbit[1] *n* opportunity of advantage occurring.
tabbit[1] *adj* (*of a cap*) having the corners folded up.
tabbit[2] *same as* **tabbet**.
tab-cat *n* a pet cat.
tabernacle *n* **1** the bodily frame. **2** a full habit of body.
taberin *n* a beating.
tabet *n* **1** bodily sensation, feeling. **2** strength.
tabetless *adj* **1** numb, without sensation. **2** heedless, foolish.
table *n* **1** the Communion table. **2** a watercourse at the side of a road to carry off water. **3** a map, chart.—*v* to board.
table cloot *n* a tablecloth.
table seat *n* **1** a square church pew containing a table. **2** (*in pl*) seats set apart for communicants.
tablet *n* a kind of sweetmeat made from sugar, butter, flavouring and sometimes condensed milk, sold in oblongs or small squares.
table tombstane *n* a flat gravestone.
tabling *n* **1** the stone coping of a wall or gable. **2** a ledge on a slope in which a hedge may be planted.
tabour *v* to drub, thrash.—*n* (*in pl*) a drubbing.
tabrach, tabragh *n* animal food nearly in a state of carrion.
ta-brig *n* a drawbridge.
taby *n* watered silk or other stuff.
tach[1] *v* **1** to drive a nail so as to give it a slight hold. **2** to fasten on slightly.—*n* **1** fringe. **2** a shoulder knot.
tach[2], **tache** *same as* **tash**.
tacht *adj* **1** tight, tense. **2** strict, severe.
tack[1] *v* **1** to fasten. **2** to keep together. **3** to nail.—*n* **1** a stitch. **2** a slight fastening. **3** the membrane attaching the tongue to the lower part of the mouth. **4** a time, spell. **5** a manoeuvre, expedient.
tack[2] *n* a hobnail.
tack[3] *same as* **tak**[2].
tackad *n* a hobnail.
tack-duty *n* rent.

tacket[1], **tackit** *n* **1** a hobnail. **2** (*used of whisky*) a pimple caused by drink.—*v* to drive tackets into boots, etc.
tacket[2] *n* a restless, unruly boy.
tacket[3] *n* a contemptuous name for an old, toothless person
tacket-boot *n* a hobnailed boot.
tacket-soled *adj* hobnailed.
tackety *adj* hobnailed.
tackety-shoed *adj* wearing hobnailed shoes.
tackie *n* **1** a children's game in which one chases his or her playmates. **2** the one who chases.
tackit *adj* tongue-tied.
tackle[1], **tackel** *n* an arrow.
tackle[2] *v* **1** to catch with fishing tackle. **2** to punish. **3** to take to task. **4** to accost. **5** (*with* **to**) to set vigorously to work.
tack on *v* to buy on credit.
tacksman *n* **1** a leaseholder. **2** a tenant farmer. **3** a tollkeeper.
tack the gate *v* to set off, depart.
tack wi' *v* to acknowledge.
tacle *n* an arrow.
taddy *n* a snuff bearing the name of its maker.
taddy powder, ~ snuff *same as* **taddy**.
tade[1] *n* **1** a toad. **2** a term of contempt, disgust, etc. **3** a term of endearment for a child. **4** a child.
tade[2] *n* the tick, sheep louse.
tae[1] *prep* to.
tae[2] *n* **1** a toe. **2** the branch of a drain. **3** the prong of a fork.
tae[3] *n adj* the one, contrasted with the other.
tae-bit *n* a toe plate for a shoe.
taebit *same as* **tabet**.
tae-breeth *n* the smallest possible distance.
tae'd *adj* pronged.
taed *same as* **tade**[1].
taedie *n* a fondling name for a child.
tae-ee *n* a pet, fondling.
tael duck *n* the teal.
taen[1] *adj* the one, contrasted with the other.
taen[2] *v* **1** took. **2** taken.
taen[3] *v* to lay hands on the head of one caught in games.
taen-awa *n* a changeling.
taening *n* the act by which one taens another in games. *See* **taen**[3].
tae-shod *n* an iron toe piece on boot or shoe.
tae's length *n* the shortest distance possible.
tae stane *n* the stone at the foot of a grave.
taesty *same as* **tasty**.
taet *same as* **tait**.
taff *n* turf.
taff dyke *n* a turf fence.
taffel, taffil *n* a small table.
tafferel *adj* **1** giddy, thoughtless. **2** ill-dressed.

taffle[1] *n* a sweetmeat of boiled treacle and flour, eaten only at Hallowe'en.

taffle[2] *v* **1** to tire. **2** to wear out with fatigue. **3** to ravel, ruffle.

taft[1] *n* the thwart of a boat.

taft[2] *same as* **toft**.

taftan *same as* **toftin**.

taft-hoose *same as* **toft house**.

tag[1] *adj* tag-rag.

tag[2] *n* **1** any small, nasty thing adhering to a larger. **2** the white hair at the tip of the tail of an ox or cow. **3** a disease of sheep, scab on the tail.—*v* **1** to have the tip of the tail white. **2** (*with* **after**) to follow closely at the heels.

tag[3] *n* **1** anything used for tying, binding, etc. **2** a strap. **3** a shoe tie. **4** a thong. **5** a long, thin slice. **6** a piece. **7** a schoolmaster's tawse (qv).—*v* **1** to bind, fasten. **2** to punish with the tawse.

tag[4] *v* (*used of the moon*) to wane.

tag[5], **tagg** *n* **1** fatigue. **2** a burden. **3** *in phr* **in the tag** always kept hard at work.—*v* **1** to exhaust. **2** to tire. **3** to oppress with toil.

tag and rag *n* every bit, the whole.

taggie *n* a cow whose tail is white at the tip.

taggit[1] *adj* (*of a woman*) wearing a frock shorter than the petticoat underneath.

taggit[2] *adj* (*of cattle*) having the tip of the tail white.

taggle, taggil *same as* **taigle**.

tagh *same as* **tauch**.

taghairm *n* a mode of divination formerly used in the Highlands.

taght *same as* **tacht**.

tag-tailed *adj* (*used of a woman*) wearing a frock shorter than the petticoat underneath.

tah *same as* **tauch**.

tahie *adj* **1** greasy. **2** (*of the weather*) warm and moist.

taiblet *same as* **tablet**.

taid[1] *n* droppings of cattle or sheep.—*v* to dung land with taid in pasturing or folding cattle, etc.

taid[2] *same as* **tade**[1].

taidie *n* a pet designation for a little child.

taidstule *n* a mushroom.

taifle *same as* **taffel**.

taigle *v* **1** to entangle. **2** to harass. **3** to weary. **4** to detain, delay, hinder. **5** to occupy one's time. **6** to tarry, loiter, dawdle.—*n* a hindrance, cause of delay.

taiglesum *adj* causing hindrance.

taigsum *same as* **taiglesum**.

taigy *same as* **taggie**.

taik *n* a stroll, saunter.

taiken *n* **1** a token. **2** evidence. **3** a small quantity, pinch.

taikin *n* a kind of cloth, ticking.

taikle *n* tackle.

tail *n* **1** the posterior, the train of a robe, the bottom of a skirt at the back. **2** a retinue or following. **3** the pendulum of a clock. **4** the hind part of a cart or plough. **5** the stern of a boat or ship. **6** a fish. **7** a horse leech. **8** the end of a portion of time. **9** the lower end of a field. **10** (*used in weaving*) a number of cords stretching over pulleys in the harness box and connecting the simple (qv) with the yarn. **11** the taproot of a turnip. **12** (*in pl*) inferior sheep drafted out of the fat or young stock. **13** (*in pl*) onion leaves. **14** (*in pl*) the lighter grains or refuse grains from threshing.

tailboard *n* the door of a close cart.

tailer *n* a tool for cutting off the taproots of turnips.

tailie *same as* **tailyie**.

tail-ill *n* an inflammatory disease of a cow's tail.

taillyer *n* a tailor.

tail meal *n* meal made from the lighter part of grain.

tail net *n* the herring net first shot and farthest from the boat.

tailor-body *n* a tailor, used contemptuously.

tailor-man *same as* **tailor-body**.

tailors-gartens *n* the ribbon grass.

tailors-nip *n* a pinch given to a boy wearing new clothes for the first time.

tail pocks *n* bags or covers for horses' tails.

tail-pressed *adj* closely pressed.

tail rot, ~ slip *same as* **tail-ill**.

tail-toddle *n* conjugal rights.

tail-tynt *n in phrs* **1 ride tail-tynt** to stake one horse against another in a race, so that the losing horse is lost to its owner. **2 play tail-tynt** to make a fair exchange.

tail-win *n* the last band of reapers.

tail-wind *n in phr* **shear wi' a tailwind** to cut grain not straight across the ridge but diagonally.

tailworm *same as* **tail-ill**.

tail-wyrin *n* the finish of anything to be gathered up, as the end of a bout (qv) in a cornfield.

tailyie, tailzie *n* **1** a cut or slice of meat. **2** a large piece of meat. **3** an entail.—*v* to entail.

tailyour *n* a tailor.

taing *same as* **tang**.

taings *n* tongs.

tainty *same as* **tenty**.

taipet *same as* **tabet**.

taipetless *same as* **tabetless**.

taird *n* **1** a term of gross contempt, used of men and animals. **2** a gibe, taunt, sarcasm.

tairdie *adj* **1** satirical. **2** peevish, sulky.

tairge *v* **1** to beat, thrash. **2** to keep under discipline. **3** to scold vigorously. **4** to cross-examine, question closely.—*n* a scold.

tairger *n* **1** a scold, virago. **2** a quarrelsome woman.

tairgin *n* a severe scolding or cross-examination.

tairin *adj* **1** excessive. **2** boisterous. **3** strenuous. **4** violent.

tais *same as* **tass**.

taisch *n* **1** the voice of a person about to die. **2** second sight.

taise *same as* **tease**.

taisie *same as* **tass**.

taissle, taisle *v* **1** to entangle, twist. **2** to toss. **3** to disorder, jumble. **4** to handle too much. **5** to puzzle a person in an examination. **6** to confuse, perplex. **7** to tease, irritate.—*n* **1** the act of mixing or jumbling. **2** disorder caused by wind. **3** too much handling. **4** a puzzle, a puzzling. **5** a vexing, a teasing. **6** a severe tussle.

taiste *same as* **teistie**.

taistril, taistrill *n* **1** a dirty, gawkish, feckless woman. **2** a careless girl regardless of her dress.

tait *n* **1** a lock of hair, wool, etc. **2** anything like hair, wool, hay, straw, etc, plucked. **3** a small sheaf. **4** a small quantity of anything.—*v* to pluck any fibrous stuff in small quantities.

taith *n* **1** the dung of pastured sheep or cattle. **2** a tuft of grass growing where dung has been dropped in a field.—*v* to manure land by pasturing or feeding sheep or cattle on it.

tait-lock *n* a small matted lock of hair, wool, etc.

taiver *v* **1** to wander. **2** to delay. **3** to rave or talk wildly or foolishly.—*n* (*in pl*) **1** wild, raving words. **2** tatters, rags.

taiversum *adj* tiresome, tedious.

taivert *adj* **1** wandering. **2** foolish, senseless, raving. **3** stupid with drink. **4** boiled to rags. **5** fatigued.

taizie *same as* **tass**.

tak[1] *v* to sew, stitch.

tak[2], **take** *v* **1** to marry. **2** to cost time and trouble. **3** (*used of fish*) to take the bait readily. **4** to strike, deliver a blow. **5** to catch in, strike against. **6** to seize, as with pain, sickness, panic, etc. **7** to happen to, affect. **8** to take fire, burn brightly. **9** to betake oneself to. **10** to haunt. **11** to contract for work. **12** to acknowledge. **13** to understand, to take for granted. **14** to cause to come, bring.—*n* **1** a catch of fish. **2** a lease. **3** a situation. **4** a state of excitement, etc.

tak-aff *n* a mimic. **2** a jester.—*v* to go off, betake oneself.

tak-bannets *n* a game in which bonnets are generally the pledges and in which the side that carries off most of these one by one is the winner.

taken *n* a token.

take-in *n* a cheat.

take on *v* **1** to undertake. **2** to engage for.

take up *v* to register.

take-up *n* a tuck.

take with *v* to acknowledge, admit.

takie *adj* (*used of victuals*) lasting.

taking *n* **1** a state of excitement. **2** a capture. **3** a pinch of snuff.

takingest *adj* most taking.

tal *int* an expletive.

tale *n* one's own account or story.

tale-pyet, ~-pies, ~-py't *n* **1** a tale-bearer. **2** a telltale.

taler, talor *n* state, condition.

tale's man *n* **1** one who gives or originates a piece of news. **2** the authority for a statement.

taliation *n* adjustment of one thing to another.

talking *n* a scolding.—*adj* talkative, blathering.

tallan, tallin *same as* **tallon**.

talliwap *n* a blow, a stroke.

tallon, tallown *n* tallow.—*v* to grease with tallow.

tallow-leaf *n* the fat covering the entrails of animals.

tallowny-faced *adj* sallow.

tallow-powk *n* a bag through which melted tallow is strained in refining.

tally-ho-the-hounds *n* a boys' game.

taltie *n* a wig.

talyee *same as* **tailyie**.

tambourer *n* an embroiderer of silk, etc, stretched on a circular frame.

tambour major *n* a drum major.

tamer *n* **1** the sharp-nosed eel. **2** the broad-nosed eel.

tammachless *adj* **1** (*used of a child*) not eating with appetite. **2** tasteless, insipid.

tammas *n* the puffin.

Tammasmas *n* the feast of St Thomas, 21 December.

tammie *n* a loaf of bread.

tammie-cheekie *n* the puffin.

tammie-harper *n* the crab, Cancer araneus.

tammie-herl *n* the heron.

tammie-louper *n* a child's toy made of black tangle.

tammie-noddie-heid *n* the butterfly chrysalis.

tammie-noddy *n* the puffin.

tammie-norie, ~-nome *n* **1** the puffin. **2** the razorbill. **3** a simpleton.

tammie-reekie *n* a cabbage stalk hollowed out and filled with lighted tow.

tammie-toddy *n* a kind of spindle.

tammie-wake *n* the cock sparrow.

tammil *v* to scatter from carelessness, or from design, as money in a crowd by candidates at an election.

tammock *n* **1** a hillock. **2** a little knoll.

tam o' cheeks *n* the puffin.

tam o' shanter *n* a round woollen bonnet with a flat top, often decorated in the middle with a pompon called a toorie.

tam o' tae end *n* a ludicrous designation for the larger end of a pudding.

tamper away *v* to find or take one's way.

Tamson's bairns *or* **man** *n in phr* **to be John Tamson's bairns** *or* **man** to be of one stock, on an equality.

Tamson's mear *n* walking.

tam-taigle *n* a rope fastening a hindleg to a foreleg of a horse or cow to prevent straying.

tam-tary, tamtarrie *n* **1** detention under frivolous pretences. **2** the state of being hindered.

tamteen *n* a tontine.

tam-tram *v* **1** to play. **2** to play fast and loose.

tam-trot *n* a kind of toffee.

tan¹ *v* **1** to rebuke. **2** to keep one steadily at work.

tan² *n* a temporary hut.

tandle *same as* **tawnle**.

tane¹ *v* **1** taken. **2** taken aback.

tane² *num adj* the one.

tane-awa *n* **1** a decayed, unhealthy, puny child. **2** a suspected changeling substituted by the fairies.

tane coon *adj* **1** enfeebled by illness. **2** reduced in circumstances. **3** diluted.

tang¹ *n* a species of seaweed, a tangle.

tang² *n* **1** a prong. **2** a pike. **3** a sting. **4** a piece of iron used for fencing anything else. **5** a low tongue of land projecting into the sea. **6** the tongue of a jew's-harp.

tang³ *same as* **tong**.

tang⁴ *n* a strong or unpleasant flavour.

tang⁵ *adj* straight, tight.

tanghal *same as* **toighal**.

tangie *n* **1** a sea sprite appearing sometimes as a small horse, sometimes as an old man. **2** a young seal.

tangle *v* to entangle.—*adj* **1** tall and feeble. **2** loose in the joints. **3** relaxed through fatigue, too tired to stand up.— *n* **1** a tall, lank person. **2** an icicle. **3** a species of seaweed. **4** a state of perplexity. **5** (*in pl*) the knots of scroll-work cut on Celtic crosses.

tangle-backit *adj* long and lean in the back, lanky.

tangleness *n* **1** indecision, fluctuation. **2** pliability of opinion.

tangle-wise *adj* long and slender, lanky.

tangly *adj* long and slender.

tang o' the trump *n* **1** the tongue of a jew's-harp. **2** the chief personage or actor in a company.

tangs *n* tongs.

tang sparrow *n* the shore pipit.

tang whaup *n* the whimbrel.

tanker¹, tankor *n* a tankard.

tanker² *n* a large, ugly person, or lean animal.

tanker-backit *adj* hunch-backed, round-shouldered, having an ungainly back.

tanker-mouthed *adj* (*used of dogs*) having large, forbidding mouths.

tankle *n* an icicle.

tannage *n* a tannery.

tanner *n* **1** the small root of a tree. **2** the root of a tooth, corn or boil. **3** the part that is fitted into a mortise.

tanneree *n* a tannery.

tanny *adj* tawny, dark-complexioned.—*n* **1** a mulatto. **2** a dark-complexioned person.

tansy *n in phr* **my delight's in tansies** a children's singing game.

tant¹ *v* **1** to argue captiously, wrangle. **2** to rage.

tant² *v* to upset one's digestion.

tantaleeze *v* **1** to tantalize. **2** to aggravate. **3** to taunt.

tantallon, tantallan *n in phr* **ding doun tantallon** to exceed all bounds, to attempt the impossible.

tanter *v* **1** to quarrel. **2** to dispute captiously. **3** to rage.

tanterlick *n* a severe blow.

tantin' *adj* **1** raging. **2** squally, stormy.

tantivy *adv* quickly.

tantrum *n* **1** a whimsy, whim, vagary. **2** a fluster. **3** ill-temper. **4** (*in pl*) high airs, affected airs.

tantrum-fit *n* a fit of ill-temper.

tanty-ranty *n* fornication.

tan yaird *n* the poorhouse, as if old people were sent there to be got rid of, like old horses to the tannery.

tap¹ *n* a child's top.

tap² *n* **1** the top. **2** the head. **3** the tip. **4** a tuft on the head of a bird. **5** a tuft of hair. **6** the woollen knob on the top of a bonnet. **7** a fir cone. **8** a hill. **9** a heap. **10** the quantity of flax put on the distaff. **11** cream, the surface of milk. **12** (*in pl*) the best sheep or lambs in a flock.—*v* **1** to snuff a candle. **2** to lead off in a dance, etc. **3** to parade, walk in stately fashion.—*adj* excellent.

tap-an-teerie *same as* **tap-salteerie**.

tap bird *n in phr* **the tap bird of the nest** the best of a family.

tap-castle *n* the upper part of a weaver's loom.

tap-dressed *adj* **1** smartly beaten. **2** manured on the surface.

tape *v* **1** to use sparingly. **2** to stint.

tapee *n* **1** the forepart of the hair when put up with pins. **2** a small cushion worn by old women at the 'opening' of the head, to keep up the hair.

tapered *adj* (*used of a building*) high and frail.

taper-tail *adv* topsy-turvy.

tapet[1] *same as* **tabet**.

tapet[2] *v* tapped.

tapetless *adj* heedless.

tap-flude *n* high flood.

tapie *same as* **tawpie**.

tapis *n* a topcoat.

tapisht *adj* lurking.

tapi-toorie *same as* **tappie-toorie**.

tap-knot *n* **1** the human head. **2** a knot of ribbons on a woman's cap.

taplash *n* **1** bad small beer. **2** the dregs of liquor.

taploch *same as* **tawpie**.

tapmaist *adj* uppermost.

tapman *n* a ship with tops.

tap o' lint *n* the quantity of flax put on a distaff.

tapone staff *n* the stave in which the bunghole of a cask is.

tap o' tow *n* **1** tap o' lint (qv). **2** an irascible person. **3** a shaggy-headed child.

tapoun *same as* **tappin**.

tappenie *int* a term used in calling a hen.

tapper *n* one who taps a cask.

tappie *n* a crested hen.

tap-piece *n* a hat, a cap.

tap-pickle *n* the uppermost grain in a stalk of oats.

tappie-toorie, ~-tourie *n* **1** anything raised very high to a point. **2** the knob of pastry on the top of a covered pie. **3** a tappiloorie (qv).

tappie-tourock *same as* **tappie-tourie**.

tappie-tousie *n* **1** a children's game in which one holds another by the hair of the head and asks questions. **2** a shaggy head of hair.

tappiloorie *n* anything raised high on a slight or tottering foundation.

tappin[1] *n* **1** the root of a tree. **2** the taproot of a turnip, etc. **3** a long, thin person.

tappin[2] *n* **1** a crest. **2** the tuft of feathers on the head of a cock or hen. **3** the woollen knob on the top of a bonnet. **4** the top of the head. **5** the head. **6** the noddle.

tappin'd, tappent *adj* crested, tufted.

tappinless *adj* without a tassel or knob.

tappit *adj* crested, having a top.

tappit hen *n* **1** a crested hen. **2** a Scottish quart measure of ale or claret, having a knob on its lid. **3** a measure containing three English quarts. **4** a large bottle of claret, holding three magnums or Scots pints.

tappity *adj* tufted, crested.

tapple *v* to topple.

tappy[1] *same as* **tawpie**.

tappy[2] *n* the crown of a child's head.

tap-rooted *adj* deeply rooted.

tap-rung *n* the highest point, summit.

tapsalteerie, tapselterrie *adv* **1** topsy-turvy, upside-down.—*n* **1** a state of disorder. **2** a topsy-turvy manner.

tapsie-teerie, tapsill-teerie *adv* topsy-turvy.

tapanan *n* **1** the principal servant in charge. **2** the man in charge of a drove.

tap swarm *n* **1** the first swarm from a hive of bees. **2** a body of people who are the first to leave their former connection.

tap sweat *n* a profuse perspiration.

tap, tail and mane *n* neither head nor tail of a matter.

taptee *same as* **taptoo**.

tap-thrawn *adj* **1** perverse. **2** headstrong. **3** disputatious.

taptoo *n* **1** a gaudy ornament on the head. **2** a violent passion. **3** a state of eager desire.

taptree *n* a solid and rounded piece of wood used as a bung in a brewing vat or cask.

tap wark *n* part of a weaver's mounting.

tarans *n* the souls of unbaptised children.

tar buist *n* the box holding tar for marking sheep.

tard *n* a dirty person.

tardie *same as* **tairdie**.

tards *n* a schoolmaster's tawse (qv).

tare *v* to tear.

taretathers *n* what is torn in shreds.

targat, target *n* **1** a tassel. **2** an ornament for the hat. **3** a shred, a tatter. **4** a long, thin slice of dried fish.

targe *same as* **tairge**.

targed *adj* **1** tattered. **2** shabby in appearance.

targer *same as* **tairger**.

target *same as* **targat**.

targing *same as* **tairgin**.

taring *n* the common tern.

tarj *n* a dirty person.

tarle, tarl *v* **1** to work lazily. **2** to be lazily disposed. **3** to labour under disease.—*n* **1** a weak, puny person or animal. **2** a dirty person.

tar-leather *n* a strong slip of leather, salted and hung, used for coupling the staves of a flail.

tarloch, tarlack, tarlich, tarlogh *n* **1** a mean fellow. **2** a sturdy, brawling woman. **3** a dirty female tatterdemalion. **4** a silly, inactive girl. **5** any creature or thing puny, weak and worthless. **6** a horse restive at the plough, etc.—*v* **1** to go about lazily. **2** to labour under disease.—*adj* **1** weak, peevish. **2** squeamish, not caring for food. **3** restive. **4** fussy, particular, pernicketty.

tar mop *n* a mop for tarring with.

tarnation *n* damnation.—*adj, adv and int* used as expletive and as intensive.

tarnish *n* anything that tarnishes.

tarnty *n* trinity.

tar pig *n* a jar of tar for marking sheep.

tarpit *v* to interpret.

tarragat *v* to interrogate.

tarragatin *n* **1** a strict examination. **2** the act of examining strictly.

tarran *same as* **tirran**.

tarras *n* a terrace.

tarret *same as* **tarrock**.

tarrie[1] *n* trouble.

tarrie[2] *n* a terrier dog.

tarrock *n* **1** the common tern. **2** the Arctic tern. **3** the kittiwake.

tarrow *v* **1** to tarry, linger. **2** to loathe. **3** to find fault with food, to refuse food peevishly. **4** to complain. **5** to be sick and weakly. **6** (*of springing corn*) not to thrive.—*n* **1** a slight illness. **2** (*of grain springing*) exhaustion of strength, inability to draw nourishment from the soil. **3** a loathing.

tarrower *n* one who finds fault with food.

tarry *adj* (*of the hands*) adhesive, light-fingered.

tarry-breeks *n* a sailor.

tarry-fingered *adj* light-fingered, pilfering.

tarry-fingers *n* **1** dishonest fingers. **2** a dishonest person.

tarry-handit, ~-haun'd *adj* dishonest, pilfering.

tarrymichie-clay *n* a fine kind of clay.

tarry-neives *n* tarry-fingers (qv).

tarry-trick *n* cheating, pilfering.

tarsie-versie *adv* **1** walking backwards. **2** in confusion.

tart *adj* (*used of gossip*) stinging, painful.

tartan *n* **1** the Scottish Lowland dialect. **2** the Highland dialect. **3** Highland manners or customs. **4** tartan-purry (qv). **5** a kind of woollen cloth woven from cloth of several colours and in such a way as to produce a pattern of lines, bands and squares.

tartan purry *n* a pudding of red cabbage and oatmeal.

tarter *n* noise made by scrambling about.

tartle[1] *v* **1** to hesitate. **2** to hesitate in recognizing a person. **3** to boggle, scruple. **4** (*of a horse*) to shy, jib. **5** to recognize.—*n* hesitation in recognizing.

tartle[2] *v* to rend, tatter.

tartuffish *adj* sour, sulky, stubborn.

tarveal *v* **1** to fatigue. **2** to vex. **3** to travail.—*n* fatigue.—*adj* fretful, ill-tempered.

tascal money *n* money formerly given in the Highlands for information as to raided cattle.

tash *v* **1** to soil, tarnish, to bespatter. **2** to cast a stain on a person, injure by calumny. **3** to upbraid. **4** to weary out. **5** (*with* **about**) to throw things carelessly about so as to damage them.—*n* **1** a stain, spot, flaw. **2** an affront, reproach. **3** disgrace.

tashellie *adj* (*of animals*) having the hair or wool matted with dirt, dung, etc.

tasht *adj* **1** well-worn. **2** frayed.

task[1] *v* to impose a task or lesson.

task[2] *n* the angel or spirit of any person.

tasker *n* a labourer at piecework.

taskit *adj* over-fatigued with work.

taskit-like *adj* appearing to be greatly fatigued.

tass[1], **tas** *n* **1** a small heap of earth. **2** a large bunch. **3** a cluster of flowers.

tass[2], **tasse** *n* **1** a cup, glass. **2** a goblet, bowl.

tassel stane *n* the projecting stone above the door of a castle or keep, from which evildoers, etc, were hanged.

tassie *n* a small cup or glass.

tassle, tassell *same as* **taissle**.

taste *v* **1** to partake of refreshments. **2** to take a dram. **3** to give relish or appetite to. **4** to please the palate. **5** to quench hunger or thirst. **6** to appreciate mentally.—*n* (*used of drink*) a dram, a sip. **2** (*of any liquid*) a small quantity.

taster[1] *n* **1** a dram. **2** a mouthful of spirits.

taster[2] *n* a sea fowl.

tasting *n* **1** a small quantity of anything. **2** a mouthful of food or drink.

tasty *adj* **1** savoury. **2** appetizing. **3** neat, dainty. **4** attractive.

tat *n* a tuft of hair, wool, etc.—*v* to mat, to be in tufts.

ta-ta *int* goodbye!

tatch *same as* **tach**[1].

tate *same as* **tait**.

tatelock *n* a small lock of hair.

tathe, tath *same as* **taith**.

tathe faud *n* a field on which cattle, etc, are shut up at night to manure the ground with their droppings.

tathil *n* a small table.

tathing *n* the raising of rank grass by manure.

tatie, tattie *n* **1** a potato. **2** the head. **3** a term of contempt.

tatie beetle *n* a potato masher.

tatie bing *n* a potato heap.

tatie blots *n* water in which potatoes have been boiled.

tatie-bogie, ~-bogle *n* a scarecrow among growing potatoes.

tatie-boodie *n* a tatie-bogie (qv).

tatie broo *n* potato soup.

tatie-chapper *n* a potato masher.

tatie-doolie *n* a scarecrow in a potato field.

tatie dreel *n* a potato drill.

tatie-grab *n* a way of grabbing and eating potatoes from the dish.

tatie graip *n* a flat-pronged fork for digging potatoes.

tatie-grun' *n* a potato field or patch.

tatie-head *n* a stupid head.

tatie-howker *n* a potato-digger.

tatie kro *n* a corner in a house boarded to keep potatoes from frost.

tatie-liftin *n* potato digging.

tatie-like, ~-laek *adj* (*used of ground*) looking fit to grow potatoes.

tatie müld *n* a potato field or patch.

tatie pairer *n* a potato peeler.

tatie peck *n* a peck measure for potatoes.

tatie peels *n* potato skins.

tatie pat *n* a potato pot.

tatie pit *n* a potato heap protected to preserve potatoes from frost.

tatie pourins *n* water in which potatoes have been boiled.

taties and dab *n* potatoes boiled in skins, dipped in salt and eaten.

taties and point *n* potatoes eaten, with a small bit of beef or fish, which is not, however, eaten, but is pointed to with the potato.

tatie scon *n* a scone made of flour and mashed potatoes.

tatie settin' *n* potato planting.

tatie shaws *n* potato stems.

tatie soup *n* **1** potato soup. **2** *in phr* **the ticket for tatie soup** an expression of the highest praise.

tatie trap *n* the human mouth.

tatie walin' *n* sorting out potatoes.

tatie warks *n* farina or starch mills dealing with potatoes.

tatie washins *n* water in which potatoes have been washed.

tatshie *adj* dressed in slovenly manner.

tatter[1] *v* **1** to tear, rend in pieces. **2** to rave, talk in delirium.

tatter[2] *v* to hurry, go at great speed.

tatter-wallop *n* **1** a woman who does not mend her clothes. **2** (*in pl*) fluttering rags. **3** hanging rags. —*v* to hang in rags.

tattery *adj* tattered, ragged.

tattie *same as* **tatie**.

tattle *n* a clot of dirt adhering to the tail of a cow or sheep.

tattrel *n* a rag.

tatty *adj* **1** matted. **2** rough and shaggy.

tauch[1], **taugh**[1] *n* **1** tallow. **2** grease.—*v* to grease.

tauch[2], **taugh**[2] *n* the threads of large ropes.

tauchey, taughie *adj* **1** greasy, clammy. **2** (*used of the weather*) warm, moist or misty.

tauchey-faced *adj* greasy-faced.

taucht[1] *v* **1** did teach. **2** taught.

taucht[2] *n* tallow that has been melted.

taud *same as* **tade**[1].

taudy[1] *n* a child.

taudy[2] *n* the breech, buttocks.

taudy fee *n* a fine imposed for having an illegitimate child.

tauk *n* talk.—*v* to talk.

taul', tauld *v* told.

taum[1] *n* **1** a rope. **2** a line. **3** a fishing line, one made of horsehair. **4** a long thread of any viscous or glutinous substance. **5** gossamer.—*v* to draw out any viscous substance into a line.

taum[2] *v* **1** to fall gently asleep. **2** to swoon.—*n* **1** a fit of drowsiness. **2** a fit of faintness or sickness. **3** an ungovernable fit of ill-humour.

taums *adj* **1** ropy. **2** glutinous.

taun *v* to urge one on with taunts.

taundle, taunel *same as* **tawnle**.

taunt[1] *v* *with* **at**, to mock at.

taunt[2] *v* to upset the digestion.

taupie *same as* **tawpie**.

taupiet *adj* **1** foolish. **2** inactive and slovenly.

taupin *same as* **tappin**[1].

tauploch *n* a giddy, flighty girl.

taupsaleery *same as* **tapsalteerie**.

taur *n* tar.

taurd *n* a large piece.

taurie *same as* **tarrie**[2].

taury, taurrie *adj* tarry.

taut[1] *v* **1** to mat. **2** to entangle. **3** to run into tufts. **4** to make rugs of thick worsted yarn.—*n* **1** a mat. **2** matting. **3** a tuft of hair, wool, etc. **4** (*in pl*) thick worsted yarn for making rugs.

taut[2] *v* **1** to drag or dash to the ground. **2** to drag to and fro.—*n* **1** a heavy dash. **2** abuse by dragging or dashing about.

tauther *v* to abuse by dragging to and fro.—*n* such abuse.

tauthereeze *v* to tauther (qv).

tautie *same as* **tatie**.

tautie-bogle *n* a scarecrow.

tautit *adj* **1** (*used of the hair*) matted. **2** shaggy, ragged.

tautit rug n a thick bedcoverlet.
tauty adj (used of the hair) matted, shaggy.
tauty-headit adj shaggy-headed.
tauven adj tired.
tavar, taver same as **taiver**.
tavernry n tavern expenses.
tavert adj 1 stupid. 2 doted.
taw[1] v 1 to knead. 2 to work in mortar. 3 to tumble about. 4 to spoil by too much handling. 5 to pull, lay hold of. 6 to whip.—n 1 a whip. 2 the point of a whip. 3 a difficulty. 4 a great to-do. 5 hesitation, reluctance.
taw[2] v to suck greedily and continuously like a hungry child.
taw[3] n a streak of light.
tawdy[1] same as **taudy**[1].
tawdy[2] same as **taudy**[2].
taweal same as **tarveal**.
tawen, tawan v 1 to disfigure by overhandling. 2 to pull, lay hold of. 3 to tumble about. 4 to knead.—n 1 a difficulty, a great ado. 2 hesitation. 3 reluctance.
tawie adj 1 tame. 2 tractable. 3 allowing to be handled. 4 quiet. 5 gentle.
tawm[1] v 1 to fall asleep gently. 2 to swoon.—n 1 a drowsy fit. 2 a fit of sickness or fainting. 3 an ungovernable temper.
tawm[2] n 1 a fishing line. 2 a long thread of viscous matter. 3 gossamer.—v to draw out a viscous substance into
tawn v to tan with the sun.
tawnle, tawnel n a bonfire, a large fire.
tawny same as **tanny**.
tawnymichie clay same as **tarrymichie clay**.
tawpie, tawpa n 1 a foolish, awkward, giddy, idle or slovenly girl. 2 a foolish fellow. 3 a blockhead. —adj 1 foolish, awkward, slovenly, ill-conditioned. 2 tawdry.
tawpie-headit adj having a silly, stupid head.
tawploch same as **tawpie**.
tawrds same as **tards**.
tawse, taws n a leather strap cut into thongs at one end for the use of school teachers to punish with. —v to whip, scourge, belabour.
tawse-swasher n one who uses the tawse (qv).
tawse-taes n the thongs at the end of a tawse (qv).
tawt[1], **tawt**[2] same as **taut**[1], **taut**[2].
tawthrie adj 1 disordered. 2 confused. 3 slovenly.
tawtie[1] same as **tatie**.
tawtie[2] adj 1 matted. 2 shaggy.
tax v 1 to find fault with. 2 to scold.
taxative adj (a forensic term) having the power of reduction from the force of an argument or plea, as enfeebling it.
taxed-ward n (a forensic term) the wardship of a minor, in which a limited sum is accepted in lieu of the whole casualties. See **casualty**.
taxman n a tax collector.
tax master n a taskmaster.
tay n tea.
taythe same as **taith**.
taz n a tawse (qv) of a schoolmaster.—v to whip, scourge.
tazie n 1 a romping, foolish girl. 2 a mischievous child.
t'chach int an exclamation of wonder, disgust, etc.
t'cheuch int tush!
t'chuchet n the peewit or lapwing.
tea v to take tea with one.
tea and eating n a rough (qv) or high tea (qv).
teach v to preach.
teached v taught.
tea-chit-chat n cakes, etc, eaten at tea.
tead[1] v to ted hay, etc.
tead[2] same as **tade**[1].
tea-doins n a tea party.
teae num adj the one.
tea-fight n a tea party.
teagie n a cow with tail tipped with whist.
teagle same as **taigle**.
tea-haun n a tea drinker.

tea-kitchen n a tea urn.
teal[1] n a busybody. 2 a mean fellow.
teal[2] v to wheedle. 2 to inveigle by flattery, to entice.
teal[3] n 1 a tail. 2 the posteriors.
teal-duck n the common teal.
tealer n one who wheedles or entices.
tealie adj 1 encouraging. 2 offering inducements.
tea-man n a tea-drinker.
tean[1], **teane** adj the one.
tean[2] same as **teen**[1].
tear[1] v to stir the colours for dyeing in block calico printing.
tear[2] v 1 to tease. 2 to hurry along. 3 to bustle about. 4 to work hard and with speed. 5 to rage. —n 1 a great hurry. 2 a raging storm. 3 (in pl) cracks, rents, tatters.
tear[3] v to shed tears.
tearancy n 1 a rage, violence. 2 outrageous haste.
tear-blob n a teardrop.
tearboy n a boy employed to stir the colours in block calico printing.
tearer n a virago,shrew.
tearer n a tearboy (qv).
tearing adj 1 excessive, very great, used intensively. 2 boisterous, blustering. 3 energetic, strenuous. 4 passionate, violent.
tear-in-twa adj savage, violent.
teartatherr same as **taretathers**.
teary adj tearful.
tease, teaze v 1 to disentangle. 2 to open up matted wool for carding. 3 to tear in pieces. 4 to toss about in gossip. 5 to drive. 6 to stir up meal so as to make it look bulkier in the measure.
tea shine n a tea party.
tea skittle n a tea party.
teasle, teazle v 1 to entangle, twist. 2 to tease, vex. —n 1 disorder. 2 a severe tussle. 3 a puzzle.
teat same as **tait**.
teathe same as **taith**.
teather same as **tether**.
tea twine n twine with which a parcel of tea is tied up.
teauve same as **tyaave**[1].
tea water n water for making tea.
teez v to prop a golf ball.—n the prop of earth on which the golf ball is placed when first struck off.
tebbit same as **tabet**.
tebbitless same as **tabetless**.
teck n a tack, change of direction.
teckle v to tackle.—n tackle.
teckle same as **tackle**[1].
ted[1] v 1 to scatter. 2 to spill. 3 to spread out to dry. 4 to arrange in order. 5 to tidy.—n the act of tidying.
ted[2] n 1 a toad. 2 a term of contempt or disgust. 3 a child. 4 a diminutive person.
tedd adj ravelled, entangled.
tedder same as **tether**.
teddie same as **taidie**.
teddy adj (used of corn) winnowed, ready for carting to the stackyard.
tedisum, tediousome adj 1 tedious. 2 wearisome.
tedy adj peevish, fretful, cross.
tee[1] adv too, also.
tee[2] n a buckle attached to the collar or saddle of a horse.
tee[3] prep to.
tee[4] num adj the one.
tee[5] n a tittle, a T.
tee[6] n 1 the mark set up to aim at in certain games. 2 a small cone of earth, etc, from which a golf ball is driven.—v to place a golf ball on such a cone.
teed adj (used of a cow) in full milk.
teedle v to sing a song without words.
teedy adj peevish, cross.
tee-fa' same as **to-fall**.
teeger n 1 a tiger. 2 a virago.—v to look fierce.
tee head n the circle round the tee at the end of each

rink, within which curling stones must lie to count in the game.

tee-hee, te-he *n* **1** loud, derisive laughter. **2** silly laughter. **3** giggling.—*v* **1** to laugh in a silly way. **2** to giggle. **3** to laugh loudly.—*int* an exclamation of derisive laughter.

teel[1] *n* a tool.

teel[2] *v* **1** to till. **2** to toil, work at.

teel[3] *same as* **teal**[2].

tee-leuk *n* **1** a look to, attention to. **2** a prospect.

teelie[1] *adj* encouraging.

teelie[2] *n* a small job or piece of farm work.

teelie[3] *n* any agricultural implement.

teely *v* (*with* **back**) **1** to recover, restore. **2** to coax back.

teem[1] *same as* **toom**[1].

teem[2] *v* to overflow.

teem on *v* **1** to beat severely. **2** to work energetically and with speed.—*n* a severe beating.

teems *n* **1** a piece of fine crepe or muslin tightened on a circular rim of wood, for dressing flour for pastry, etc. **2** a fine hair sieve.—*v* to sift.

teen[1] *n* **1** sorrow, grief. **2** wrath, rage. **3** revenge. **4** vexation.—*v* **1** to trouble. **2** to tease, vex.

teen[2] *same as* **teind**[1].

teen[3] *v* taken.

teen[4] *same as* **tune**.

teen[5] *adv* at even.

teen[6] *num adj* the one.

tee name *n* **1** a nickname. **2** an additional name to distinguish persons of the same name.

teenfu' *adj* wrathful.

teenge *n* colic in horses.

teeock *n* the lapwing.

teep[1] *n* a type.

teep[2] *n* a tup, ram.

teep[3] *same as* **tape**.

teepical *adj* typical.

teeple *n* a slight stroke or touch.—*v* to touch or strike lightly.

teer[1] *v* to stir colours for block calico printing.

teer[2] *v* to tear.

teeribus and teri odin *n* the war cry of Hawick. *See* **teribus**.

teers *n* tares, vetches.

tee-shot *n* a curling stone played so as to rest on the tee (qv).

teesick *n* a spell of illness.

teesie *n* a gust of passion.

teessit *n* **1** the line first shot from a fishing boat. **2** the man whose line is first shot.

teet *v* **1** to peep. **2** to peep or pry clandestinely.—*n* **1** a peep. **2** a stolen glance. **3** a chirp. **4** the slightest sound. **5** the least word.

teet-bo, teetie-bo *int* peep-bo!—*n* the game of peep-bo.

tee-tee, TT *n* a teetotaller. *Same as* **tee-tot**.

teeth[1] *n* a tooth.

teeth[2] *same as* **teth**[1].

teeth[3] *n* the fragment of a rainbow appearing on the horizon.

teethache *n* toothache.

teethe, teeth *v* **1** to fix teeth in a spiked instrument. **2** to impress, indent. **3** to indent a wall with mortar on the outside.

teethed *adj* having or furnished with teeth.

teethfu' *n* **1** a toothful. **2** a small quantity of liquid.

teething bannock, ~ plaster *n* an oatmeal cake given to a child when first teething.

teethless *adj* toothless.

teethrife *adj* toothsome, palatable.

teethy *adj* **1** testy. **2** crabbed. **3** tait. **4** (*used of dogs*) showing the teeth.

teetle *n* title.

teetlin *n* **1** the meadow pipit. **2** the rock pipit.

tee-tot *n* a teetotaler. *Same as* **tee-tee**.

teetotal *n* **1** teetotalism. **2** a teetotal society.

teetotally *adv* totally, quite.

teeuck *same as* **teeock**.

teevoo *n* a male flirt.

teewheep, teewhoap *n* the lapwing.

teewheet, teewit *n* the lapwing or peewit.

teicher *v* **1** to ooze from the skin. **2** to distil almost imperceptibly.—*n* the appearance of a fretted sore.

teidsome *same as* **tedisum**.

teight *adj* fatigued.

teil *same as* **teal**[1].

teil, teill *same as* **teel**[2].

tein[1] *same as* **teen**[1].

tein[2] *same as* **teind**.

teind[1], **tein**[3] *v* to tithe. **2** to draw tithes.—*n* a tithe. **2** a church tithe.

teind[2] *same as* **tine**[1].

teind[3] *n* **1** the prong of a fork, a tine. **2** the act of harrowing.

Teind Court *n* the court of law dealing with the tithes of the Established Church of Scotland.

teind-free *adj* exempt from tithe-paying.

teind lamb *n* a tithe lamb.

teind sheaves *n* sheaves payable as tithes.

teind siller *n* tithe money.

teind skate *n* a skate or fish payable as tithe.

teist *n* a handful.

teistie *n* the black guillemot.

tek *n* **1** a dog. **2** an otter.

telegraft *n* a telegram.

tell *v* **1** to recognize. **2** to distinguish. **3** to pay. **4** to count.

tellable *adj* fit to be told.

tell'd, telt *v* told.

telling *adj* **1** to the advantage of. **2** having effect.—*n* **1** a story. **2** talk. **3** what is worth telling. **4** advice, warning. **5** a scolding, reprimand.

telyie *same as* **tailyie**.

temarare *adj* rash.

temming *n* a very coarse, thin woollen cloth.

temp *v* to tempt.

temper *v* to regulate or adjust machinery or the rate of its movement.

temperament *n* (*a legal term*) the qualifying of a confession.

temper pin *n* **1** a wooden screw for tightening the band of a spinning wheel. **2** a fiddle peg. **3** temper, disposition.

temper-thrawing *adj* souring the temper.

temples *n* long thin rods that stretch the web on the loom.

temptashious *adj* tempting, inviting.

temptsome *adj* tempting, inviting.

tenandry *n* **1** tenure. **2** tenancy. **3** the collective tenants on an estate, tenantry.

tenant-sted *adj* occupied by a tenant.

tend[1] *same as* **tent**[2].

tend[2] *v* to intend.

tender *adj* **1** delicate, ailing. **2** circumspect, scrupulous. **3** pathetic. **4** akin, closely related.—*v* **1** to make tender, delicate, soft. **2** to have regard for, care for.

tenderly *adj* poorly, unwell.

tenderness *n* **1** delicacy of health. **2** regard, consideration. **3** scrupulousness.

tendle *n* **1** firewood. **2** brushwood used for fuel.

tendle knife *n* a knife or billhook for cutting firewood.

tene *same as* **teen**[1].

tenement *n* a building of three or more storeys that is divided into flats occupied by a different tenant or owner.

tenendrie *same as* **tenandry**.

tenfauld *adj* tenfold.

tengs *same as* **taings**.

ten-hours *n* **1** ten o'clock. **2** a slight feed to horses in the yoke in the forenoon.

ten-hours' bite *n* the slight feed given to horses in the yoke in the forenoon.

tennel, tennle *same as* **tendle**.

tennendrie *same as* **tenandry**.

tenorills *n* **1** dry twigs. **2** tendrils.

tenon *n* a tendon.

tenony hough *n* the joint of a beast's hindleg.

tenor *n* the crossbar between the legs of a chair.

tenor saw *n* **1** a tenon saw. **2** a thin back saw.

tenpenny nail *n* a large, strong nail.

tensome, tensum *n* a company of ten.

tent[1] *n* an open-air pulpit of wood with a projecting roof.

tent[2] *v* **1** to attend to, look after. **2** to herd animals. **3** to notice. **4** to heed. **5** to listen to. **6** to beware, take care. **7** to incline.—*n* **1** care, heed. **2** a look. **3** notice, attention. **4** time, patience.—*adj* **1** watchful. **2** keen, intent, observant.

tentie, tenty *adj* careful, heedful, cautious, watchful.—*adv* carefully, attentively, cautiously.

tentily *adv* carefully, cautiously, heedfully.

tentive *adj* attentive, careful.

tentless *adj* careless, heedless, inattentive uncared for, unattended.

tentlessly *adv* incautiously, carelessly.

tently *adv* carefully.

tent-preaching *n* preaching from a tent (qv).

tent-reader *n* one who read the lessons from a tent (qv).

teppit *same as* **tabet**.

teppitless *adj* **1** benumbed. **2** without sensation or sense.

terbuck *v* **1** to make a false move in play. **2** to check an opponent's false move in play.—*n* **1** a false move in play, a slip. **2** a check in a game of skill.

terce *n* a widow's right to a life rent of one-third of her deceased husband's heritage.

terced *adj* divided into three parts.

tercer *n* a widow who enjoys a terce (qv).

terd *same as* **taird**.

tergat *same as* **targat**.

tergiverse *v* to use subterfuge.

teri *n* a native of Hawick.

teribus ye teri odin *n* the war cry of Hawick.

terlis *same as* **tirlass**.

termagant *n* a ptarmigan.

termin life *adv* forever, finally.

term-time *n* **1** Whitsunday. **2** Martinmas.

terr *same as* **tirr**[1].

terrible *adj* **1** great. **2** tremendous. **3** extraordinary. —*adv* extremely.

terrie *same as* **tarrie**.

terrier *n* **1** a man of bad temper and character. **2** a pugnacious fellow.

terrification *n* **1** terror. **2** any thing or person causing terror.

terrifick *adj* terrified.

terry *int* used as an expletive or oath.

terse *v* to dispute, debate.—*n* a dispute, contention.

tersy-verasy *adv* topsy-turvy.

tert *adj* tart.

tertian *n* a third year's student in arts at Aberdeen University.

tertle *same as* **tartle**[1].

teryvee *same as* **tirrivee**.

tesment, tesmont, testment *n* **1** a last will. **2** a legacy.

test[1] *n* a will, testament.—*v* to bequeath by will.

test[2] *n* a small cylindrical piece of wood, formerly kept in a school, in an aperture near the door and in the master's sight, without which being in its place no boy was allowed to get outside.

testament *n* **1** a legacy. **2** the New Testament as distinguished from the Old.—*v* to leave by will.

testamentar *adj* testamentary.

testament-man *n* a Protestant.

testie *same as* **teistie**.

testificate, testificat *n* **1** a passport. **2** a certificate, testimonial.

testification *n* a certificate, testimonial.

testoon, testan, teston *n* silver coin varying in value.

tet *same as* **tait**.

teth[1] *n* **1** temper, disposition. **2** spirit, mettle.

teth[2] *int* **1** an expletive. **2** a euphemism for 'faith!'

tether *n* **1** a hangman's halter or rope. **2** a towrope. —*v* **1** to moor a vessel. **2** to confine. **3** to bind. **4** to restrain. **5** to marry, get married.

tether chack *n* a spike of iron or wood for fixing a tether in the ground.

tether en' *n* **1** a rope's end. **2** the end of one's fortune.

tether-faced *adj* ill-natured in looks.

tether length *n* **1** the length of a tether. **2** a long distance. **3** calamity at the end of a reckless career.

tether-safe *n* a tether that holds fast.

tether's end *n* **1** extremity. **2** the farthest possible length.

tether stake *n* **1** a tether chack (qv). **2** the upright post in a stall to which a cow is tethered.

tether stick *n* a tether chack (qv).

tether string *n* a rope, halter.

tether tow *n* a cable, hawser.

tets *same as* **tits**.

tett *same as* **tait**.

tetter *same as* **tether**.

tetty *same as* **titty**[2].

tetuz *n* **1** anything tender. **2** a delicate person.

teu[1], **teu**[2] *same as* **tew**[1], **tew**[2].

teuch[1] *n* a draught of any kind of liquor.

teuch[2] *adj* **1** tough. **2** (*used of the heart*) hard, not easily broken. **3** (*of a contest*) keen, pertinacious. **4** tedious, protracted.—*adv* stoutly, sturdily.

teuchatie *n* a young or little lapwing.

teuchin' *v* (*used in relation to tough phlegm*) clearing the throat of it, hawking.

teuchit, teuchat *n* the lapwing or peewit.

teuchit-storm *n* the gale popularly associated with the arrival of the green plover or lapwing.

teuchly *adv* **1** toughly. **2** tenaciously.

teuchter *n* **1** a Lowland name for a Highlander, especially a Gaelic-speaking one. **2** a person from a country area.

teuckie *n* **1** a hen. **2** a chicken. **3** used as a nickname.—*int* a call to fowls.

teud *n* a tooth.

teudle *n* the tooth of a rake or harrow, a tine.—*v* **1** to insert teeth. **2** to renovate the teeth of a reaping hook, etc.

teudless *adj* toothless.

teug *same as* **tug**.

teugh[1] *int* an exclamation of disgust, impatience, contempt.

teugh[2] *same as* **teuch**[2].

teugs *n* **1** trousers. **2** the thighs of a pair of breeches. **3** clothes, togs.

teuk[1] *v* took.

teuk[2] *n* a disagreeable taste, a by-taste.

teukin *adj* **1** quarrelsome, troublesome. **2** (*used of the wind*) shifting, variable.

teum *same as* **toom**[1].

teurd *same as* **turd**.

teut-mout *same as* **toot-moot**.

teuve *v* wrought hard. *See* **tyaave**.

tevel, tevvel *v* **1** to confuse. **2** to put into disorder.

tew[1] *n* **1** the nozzle of the bellows of a forge, etc. **2** a blacksmith's long pincers. **3** iron hardened with a piece of cast iron. **4** (*in pl*) the leather catches of a drum by which the cords are tightened. **5** the cords of a drum.

tew[2] *v* **1** to knead. **2** to exhaust, fatigue. **3** to overpower. **4** to fidget. **5** to toil, labour. **6** to work constantly. **7** to work hard. **8** to be eagerly employed about anything. **9** to struggle, strive.—*v* toiled.—*n* **1** a struggle, difficulty. **2** hard work, toil.—*adj* fatigued.

tew[3] *v* (*of grain*) to become damp and acquire a bad taste.—*n* a bad taste occasioned by dampness.

tew[4], **tew**[5] *same as* **teuch**[1], **teugh**[2].

tew[6] *v* did amble. *See* **tiawe**.

tewel, tewl *n* **1** a tool. **2** a ship.

tewhit, tewit *same as* **teewheet**.

tew iron *n* **1** the nozzle of the bellows of a forge. **2** the long pincers of a blacksmith. **3** one of the stones at the bottom of a furnace that receives the metal.

tew-iron, ~-arne bore *n* iron hardened with cast iron to make it stand the fire in a forge.

tewkie *same as* **teuckie**.

teynd *same as* **teind**¹.

teypard *adj* (*used of a building*) high and frail.

thaar *same as* **thar**.

t'hach *int* an exclamation of disgust, contempt.

thack¹ *v* to thwack.

thack² *v* to thatch, cover, roof.—*n* **1** thatch. **2** a thatching. **3** a roof or covering of straw. **4** materials for thatching. **5** the hair of the head.—*adj* **1** thatched. **2** used for thatching.

thack and rape *n* **1** cover for stacks against wind and rain. **2** home comforts.

thack-bunch *n* a bunch of straw drawn for thatching.

thack-covered *adj* thatched.

thacker *n* a thatcher.

thack-gate *n* the sloping edge of the gable tops of a house, when the thatch covers them.

thackit-stick *n* an umbrella.

thack-lead *n* leaden roofing.

thackless *adj* **1** not roofed. **2** without thatch. **3** uncovered, hatless.

thack nail, ~ pin *n* a peg for fastening down thatch.

thack rape, ~ ram *n* a rope of straw or coir for securing thatch.

thack spurkle, ~ spurtle *n* a tool used in thatching.

thackstones *n* square slabs of sandstone used for slates.

thack strae *n* straw prepared for thatch.

thack threid *n* a coarse, strong thread for tying down thatch.

thae *pron and adj* those, these.

thaft *n* a rower's bench in a boat.

thaimsels *pron* themselves.

thain *same as* **thane**².

thair¹ *adv* there.

thair² *pron* their.

thair³ *same as* **thar**.

thairf *adj* sad.

thairfish *adj* **1** of heavy countenance. **2** lumpish.

thairm *n* **1** the belly or intestines of man or beast. **2** the gut of a beast. **3** the intestines twisted. **4** catgut. **5** a fiddle string. **6** (*in pl*) bonds.—*v* to play on a stringed instrument.

thairm band *n* a catgut cord for turning a spinning wheel.

thairsels *pron* themselves.

thait *same as* **theat**.

thaivil *n* **1** a stirring rod, a spurtle. **2** a cudgel.

thak *same as* **thack**².

than¹ *adv* then.

than² *conj* (*used to express a wish*) would that.—*adv* **1** else. **2** elsewhere.

than a days *adv* in those days.

thane¹ *n* a vane.

thane² *adj* **1** (*of meat*) underdone, raw. **2** (*of meal*) moist or made of oats not thoroughly kiln-dried.

thank *v* to suffice.—*n* **1** obligation to a person. **2** something to be thankful for.

thankful *adj* (*of payment*) sufficient, satisfactory.

thanse *adv* else, otherwise.

thar *v* to need.

that *pron* **1** this. **2** used to avoid repeating a previous word or statement. **3** also in emphatic reiteration of an assertion. **4** who.—*adj* **1** this. **2** those. **3** such.—*adv* **1** so, to such a degree. **2** very.—*conj* **1** because, seeing that. **2** alas! that, in apology for an oath, etc.

thatch-gate *same as* **thack-gate**.

thaten *adj* that.

thaur *same as* **thar**.

thaut *same as* **thout**.

thawart *same as* **thrawart**.

thaw wind *n* a wind bringing a thaw.

the *adj* (*used as a poss pron*) **1** indefinitely with some words, as 'church', 'school', 'wife'. **2** before certain diseases, as 'cold', 'measles', 'fever'. **3** before certain languages or sciences. **4** used for 'a' or 'an' before weights and measures distributively. **5** for 'to' or 'this' with 'day', 'morn', 'night', etc.

theak *same as* **thack**².

theaker *n* a thatcher.

theaking *n* **1** thatch. **2** thatching. **3** a roof. **4** clothing.

theat *n* **1** a leather band fastened round a horse, to which long chains are attached and then fixed to a plough or harrow. **2** a rope, trace, chain for drawing. **3** a liking, inclination for. **4** *in phr* **oot o' theat** **1** unreasonable, extortionate as to price. **2** out of practice. **3** out of order.

theck *same as* **thack**².

thee¹ *same as* **theigh**.

thee² *v* to thrive, prosper.

theedle *n* a porridge stirrer, a spurtle.

theef *n* **1** an escape of flatulence. **2** a bad smell.

theegh *n* the thigh.

theek *same as* **thack**².

theel *n* a porridge stirrer, a spurtle.

theet *same as* **theat**.

theevelese *same as* **thieveless**.

theevil *same as* **thaivil**.

theft-boot *n* the securing of a thief against the punishment due by law.

theftdom *n* thieving.

theftuous, theftous *adj* thievish.

theftuously *adv* thievishly.

the furth *adv* **1** out-of-doors. **2** abroad.

theg *same as* **thig**.

thegidder, thegither *adv* together.

theigh *n* the thigh.

theik, theick *same as* **theck**².

theil *same as* **theel**.

theim *same as* **thairm**.

theirsels *pron* themselves.

theivil *same as* **thaivil**.

theivil-ill, ~-shot *n* a pain in the side.

them *n* Providence, the Powers above.—*pron* those.—*adj* those.

them-lane *adv* by themselves alone.

themsel' *pron* **1** himself, herself. **2** themselves.

then *conj* than.

then-a-days *adv* **1** in former days. **2** some time ago.

the now, the noo *adv* just now.

theort *n* a large, double-necked lute with two sets of tuning pegs.

thepes *n* **1** the fruit of the gooseberry. **2** the fruit of the gorse. **3** the fruit of the thorn.

the piece *adv* apiece.

ther *same as* **thar**.

thereanent *adv* concerning that.

thereawa' *adv* **1** thereabouts. **2** in that quarter. **3** about that time. **4** that way, to that purpose.

there-ben *adv* there in a ben room (qv).

there-but *adv* there in a but room (qv).

thereby *adv* thereabouts as to time, quantity, quality.

therebye *adv* past there or that way.

there-east *adv* **1** in the east. **2** eastward.

thereckly *adv* directly.

there-fra *adv* from that place, thence.

therein *adv* within doors, at home.

thereout, thereoot *adv* **1** outside, out-of-doors. **2** out.

theretill, theretull *adv* **1** thither. **2** thereto. **3** in addition to.

there-up *adv* upwards.

therm *same as* **thairm**.

thesaurer *n* a treasurer.

thesaury *n* the treasury.

these *pron and adj* those.

theself *pron* itself.

thestreen *n* last night, yester-even.

thet, thete *same as* **theat**.

thewless *same as* **thowless**.

they'se *pron and v* they shall.

thick[1] *adj* **1** thickset. **2** stupid. **3** numerous. **4** frequent. **5** friendly, intimate. **6** criminally familiar. —*n* a crowd.

thick[2] *same as* **thack**[2].

thickness *n* **1** fog, mist. **2** intimacy, familiar friendship.

thickset *n* **1** strong, thick cloth. **2** (*in pl*) clothes made of thickset.

thick-thrang *adv* thickly crowded.

thie *same as* **theigh**.

thief[1] *n* a term of vituperation not implying dishonesty, a rascal.

thief[2] *same as* **theef**.

thief-animal *n* a thievish person.

thief-bute, ~-bote *n* the crime of taking money or goods from a thief to shelter him from justice.

thiefer-like *adj* more thief-like.

thief-like *adj* **1** having the appearance of a blackguard. **2** giving grounds for an unfavourable impression as to conduct or design. **3** plain, ugly, hard-looking. **4** (*used of dress*) unbecoming, not handsome.

thief-loon *n* a thief, thievish rascal.

thief-riever *n* **1** a thief. **2** a cattle-stealer.

thiefy *adv* thievish.

thieval *same as* **thaivil**.

thieveless *adv* **1** listless, spiritless. **2** lacking energy. **3** useless. **4** tasteless. **5** cold, bleak. **6** shy, reserved. **7** frigid, forbidding.

thieveless-like *adj* indifferent, unconcerned.

thievelessly *adv* **1** feebly. **2** aimlessly. **3** without energy or force.

thiever *n* a thief.

thieves' hole *n* **1** jail. **2** a bad dungeon reserved for thieves.

thieve-thrum'd *adj* made of stolen thrums. *See* **thrum**[1].

thig *v* **1** to beg, to borrow. **2** to solicit gifts on certain occasions. **3** to be a genteel beggar. **4** to entice. **5** to entreat. **6** to tease.—*n* begging, borrowing.

thigger *n* **1** a mendicant. **2** a genteel beggar.

thigging *n* **1** the grain, etc. collected by begging. **2** the act or practice of begging.

thigging-bit *n* an article got by thigging. *See* **thig**.

thigster *n* a beggar.

thill *n* a coarse subsoil of gravel and clay.

thilse *adv* else, otherwise.

thimba-fu' *n* a thimbleful.

thimber *adj* **1** gross. **2** heavy. **3** massive.

thimble, thimmel *n* the harebell.

thimble-ha' *n* a tailor's workshop.

thin *adj* **1** thin-skinned, touchy. **2** easily jealous. **3** scantily provided with. **4** few, scarce.—*n* a thin or slender part.— *v* **1** to lessen in numbers. **2** to pick out the bones of a fish's head and collect the fleshy parts.

thine's *pron* thine.

thing *n* **1** a state of affairs. **2** a depreciatory designation of a person. **3** a term of endearment for a child, a girl or a sweetheart. **4** (*with def art and preceding neg*) a term of disapprobation. **5** (*without the neg*) a term of great approbation. **6** (*before rel pron*) that. **7** those. **8** (*with intensive adj*) an amount, quantity, number.

thingiment *n* a thing, the name of which is unknown or forgotten.

thingum *n* a person or thing whose name is unknown or forgotten.

thingumbob *n* **1** a thing, the name of which is unknown or forgotten. **2** a useless article.

thingum-dairie *n* a thingumbob (qv).

think *v* **1** to feel. **2** to experience. **3** to expect. **4** to wonder. **5** (*with on*) to recollect.—*n* thought, opinion.

think long *v* **1** to become weary for. **2** to be long expecting.

think shame *v* to feel ashamed.

think sorry *v* to feel sorry.

thinter *same as* **thrinter**.

thir, thirs *pron and adj* **1** these. **2** those.

thir-ben *adv* there in the ben room (qv).

thirds *n* brewers' grains.

thirdsman *n* an arbiter between two.

thirdy *n* a penny loaf of inferior flour.

thirl[1], **thirle** *v* **1** to perforate, drill. **2** to pierce, penetrate. **3** to thrill, cause to vibrate. **4** to tingle.—*n* **1** a hole. **2** a thrill.

thirl[2] *v* **1** to come under legal obligation. **2** to bind a tenant by lease to grind his grain at a certain mill. **3** to subject to. **4** to be dependent on.—*n* **1** the obligation to grind at a certain mill. **2** the land held under this obligation. **3** the tenant so bound.

thirlage *n* **1** thraldom. **2** servitude to a particular mill. **3** the miller's multure. **4** a mortgage.

thirlage man *n* a man bound to grind at a certain mill.

thirl-hole *n* the hole into which the coulter of a plough is fixed.

thirlin' *adj* piercingly cold.

thirling mill *n* the mill at which tenants are bound to grind.

thirl pin *n* a pivot on which doors without hinges turned.

thirsels *pron* themselves.

thirssle *n* the song thrush.

thirssle-cock-lairag *n* the song thrush.

thirsty *adj* causing thirst.

this *n* this time.—*adj* these.

thissilago *n* the tussilago or colt's-foot.

thissle *n* a thistle.

thistle cock *n* the corn bunting.

thistle finch *n* the goldfinch.

thistle tap *n* thistledown.

thivel *same as* **thaivil**.

thiveless *same as* **thieveless**.

thoch-been *n* the collarbone of a fowl, the merry-thought.

thocht *same as* **thought**.

thochted *adj* anxious, concerned.

thochtie *n* a very little.

thochtiness, thoghtiness thought, anxiety.

thoft *same as* **toft**.

thoftin *n* **1** a toft (qv), the house built upon a toft. **2** the using and right of such house.

thole *v* **1** to bear, suffer, tolerate. **2** to allow, grant, permit. **3** to require. **4** to advantage. **5** to admit of. **6** to wait, hold out.

tholeable *adj* tolerable, bearable.

thole an assize *v* to stand one's trial.

tholemoody *adj* patient.

thole-pin *n* a peg fastening a double door.

tholesum *adj* bearable.

thole-weel *n* patient endurance.

thon *pron* that, yon (qv).—*adj* yonder.

thonder, thonner *adj and adv* yonder.

thong *n* a shoe tie.

thongs *n* tongs.

thoom *n* the thumb.—*v* **1** to handle, spread or clean with the thumb. **2** to compress with the thumb.

thoomack *n* a violin peg.

thoom licking *n* a mode of confirming a bargain.

thoom raip *n* a rope of hay or straw twisted round the thumb.

thoom simmon *n* a thoom raip (qv).

thoom syme *n* an instrument for twisting ropes of straw, etc.

thoor *poss adj* your.

thoo's *poss adj* thy.

thoosan *adj* thousand.

thoosan-leaved-clover *n* yarrow.

thoosan-taes *n* the centipede.

thor *n* durance, confinement.

thorle, thorl *n* **1** the fly of a spindle or spinning wheel, the pivot on which a wheel revolves. **2** the whorl of a wooden clock. **3** the loop or tag by which a button is sewn on.

thorle-pippin *n* a species of apple in form like the fly of a spindle.

thorn[1] *n* **1** the hawthorn. **2** a sharp, prickly spine on certain fish.

thorn[2] *v* to eat heartily.

thorny-back *n* the thornback.

thorough[1], **thorow** *adj* wise, sane.

thorough[2] *prep and adv* through.

thorough-go-nimble *n* **1** small beer. **2** diarrhoea,.

thorow, thorrow *prep and adv* through.

thorter *adj* (*used of wood*) cross-grained.—*prep* across, athwart.—*v* **1** to thwart, oppose. **2** to plough or harrow crosswise. **3** to go backwards and forwards on anything, as in sewing. **4** (*used of an argument*) to sift or try it thoroughly.

thorter-ill *same as* **thwarter-ill**.

thorter-knot *n* a knot in wood.

thorter-ower *prep* across, athwart.

thorter-ploughing *n* cross-ploughing.

thorter-throw *v* to pass an object backwards and forwards.

though *conj* nevertheless.

thought *n* **1** a source of grief or trouble. **2** a small quantity of anything. **3** a short time. **4** a short distance, a nicety.

thought bane *n* the merrythought of a fowl.

thoughty *adj* thoughtful.

thouless *same as* **thowless**.

thoum *same as* **thoom**.

thoumart *n* **1** the polecat. **2** a contemptuous term for a curious or eccentric person.

thou's *pron and v* thou art.

thout *v* to sob.—*n* a sob.

thow, thowe *v* **1** to thaw. **2** (*used of hardened blood*) to wash off.—*n* **1** a thaw. **2** a profuse sweat.

thow-hole *n* the south.

thowless *adj* **1** lacking energy, spirit, mettle. **2** useless. **3** tasteless.

thowlessness *n* **1** lack of energy. **2** laziness. **3** listlessness.

thowlie *adj* **1** lazy. **2** listless.

thow-lousin *n* a thaw.

thow-wind *n* a wind bringing a thaw.

thraa, thra *same as* **thraw**[5].

thrae[1] *prep* from.

thrae[2] *same as* **thraw**[3].

thraep *same as* **threap**.

thraif *same as* **thrave**[1].

thraim *v* to dwell or harp on.

thrain *same as* **threne**.

thraip *same as* **threap**.

thraldom *n* **1** servitude, as to property. **2** trouble.

thrall *v* to oppress.—*n* **1** oppression. **2** restraint. **3** worry.

thram[1] *same as* **thrum**[1].

thram[2] *v* **1** to prosper, thrive. **2** used also in malediction.

thramle, thrammle[1] *v* **1** to wind. **2** to reel.

thrammel[1], **thrammle**[2] *n* a rope to fasten cattle in a stall.

thrammel[2] *n* a little oatmeal put into the mouth of a sack at a mill, with a little water or ale and stirred about.

thrammle[1] *same as* **thramle**.

thrammle[2] *same as* **thrammel**.

thrang *v* **1** to throng. **2** to crowd towards a place. **3** to become crowded.—*adj* **1** pressed for space. **2** crowded. **3** numerous, thick. **4** intimate, familiar. **5** busy, absorbed in work. **6** (*used of work*) pressing.—*adv* **1** in plenty. **2** busily.—*n* **1** a large quantity. **2** intimacy. **3** business. **4** pressure of work. **5** a busy time. **6** bustle. **7** confusion. **8** a throng, crowd. **9** constant employment.

thrangerie *n* **1** a bustle, stir. **2** a busy time.

thrangetty, thrangatie, thrangity *n* **1** a press of work, pressure. **2** the state of being busy. **3** great intimacy.

thrape *same as* **threap**.

thrapple *n* the windpipe, throat, neck.—*v* **1** to throttle. **2** to seize by the throat. **3** to entangle with cords. **4** (*with* **up**) to gobble up, devour in eating.

thrapple-deep *adj* up to the throat.

thrapple girth *n* a collar or cravat.

thrapple-hearse *adv* hoarse.

thrapple plough *n* the old wooden plough with one stilt.

thrash[1] *n* a rush.

thrash[2] *v* to thresh.—*n* **1** a beating. **2** a threshing. **3** threshed grain. **4** a dashing noise, as of rain.—*phr* **wi' a thrash** immediately.

thrashel *same as* **threshel**.

thrashen *v* threshed.

thrasher *n* the striking part of a flail.

thrashin' mull *n* a threshing mill.

thrashintree *n* a flail.

thratch *v* to gasp convulsively, as in the death throes.—*n* the oppressed and violent respiration of one in the death throes.

thrave[1] *n* **1** 24 sheaves of grain. **2** a large number or quantity. **3** a crowd.—*v* to work by thraves in harvest and be paid accordingly.

thrave[2] *v* throve.

thraver *n* a reaper paid according to the thraves he cuts down. *See* **thrave**[1].

thraving *n* paying according to the thraves cut. *See* **thrave**[2].

thraw[1] *n* a throe.—*v* to suffer pain, writhe.

thraw[2] *v* (*used of young people*) to grow rapidly.

thraw[3] *adj* **1** awry. **2** stubborn. **3** unyielding. **4** cross. **5** adverse.

thraw[4] *same as* **thrall**.

thraw[5] *v* **1** to throw, cast. **2** to vomit. **3** to twist. **4** to wreathe. **5** to wrench, sprain. **6** to wring the neck. **7** to torture by twisting. **8** to turn a key. **9** to distort, pervert. **10** to oppose, thwart. **11** to warp. **12** to provoke to anger. **13** to contend, argue, contradict. **14** to carry a measure with a strong hand.—*n* **1** a twist, wrench. **2** a sprain. **3** wriggling. **4** one turn of the hand in twisting. **5** anger, ill-humour. **6** perversity. **7** a fit of stubbornness. **8** a quarrel. **9** a wrangle. **10** a reverse of fortune. **11** trouble. **12** pressure. **13** a crowd. **14** a rush.

thrawart, thrawort *adj* **1** twisted, crooked. **2** perverse, stubborn. **3** ill-tempered, cross. **4** adverse, unfavourable.—*adv* in confusion, pell-mell.

thrawart-like *adj* seemingly cross or reluctant.

thrawartness *n* frowardness, perverseness.

thraw cock *n* an instrument for twisting straw ropes.

thraw cruik, ~ crook *n* an instrument for twisting straw ropes.

thraw-gabbit *adj* peevish.

thrawin *same as* **thrawn**.

thrawmouse *n* the shrewmouse.

thrawn, thrawin *adj* **1** thrown. **2** twisted, distorted, misshapen. **3** uneven, crooked. **4** cross-grained, ill-tempered. **5** perverse, stubborn. **6** disobedient. **7** (*of the weather*) disagreeable, bitter.—*adv* crossly.

thrawn-body *n* a cross, perverse person.

thrawn-days *n* a petted child.

thraw-neckit *adj* having the neck twisted by hanging.

thrawn-faced *adj* with distorted features, surly-faced.

thrawn-gabbit *adj* **1** with a twisted mouth. **2** peevish, quarrelsome, contradictory.

thrawn-headed *adj* perverse.

thrawnly *adv* crossly.

thrawn-mou'd *adj* twisted in the mouth.

thrawn-muggent, ~-natured *adj* perverse.

thrawnness *n* perverseness, stubbornness.

thrawn-rumplet *adj* with twisted rump.

thrawn stick *n* an obstinate, ill-tempered fellow.

thraw rape *n* an instrument for twisting ropes of straw.

thraw-sitten *adj* lazy, stupefied.

thraw spang *n* an iron rod so fastened to a plough as to prevent it being straightened by the draught.

thraw wark *n* work for twisting ropes.

thread *n* the thread of life.—*v* **1** to draw in, as upon a thread. **2** to pay out a rope slowly.

thread-dry *adv* quite dry.

thread-lapper *n* a spinner of thread.

thread of blue *n* anything smutty in talk or writing.

thread pirn *n* a reel for thread.

thread the needle e'e *n* a young people's game.

threap *v* 1 to assert firmly, insist on. 2 to reiterate pertinaciously. 3 to urge, press. 4 to haggle over a bargain. 5 to argue. 6 to wrangle. 7 to complain. —*n* 1 a pertinacious assertion. 2 an indictment. 3 a statement of facts. 4 an argument. 5 a wrangle. 6 a quarrel. 7 a tradition. 8 a saying often repeated.

threaper *n* a pertinacious asserter.

threap knot *n* a groundless assertion made in order to find out truth or to prevent what is dreaded.

threat *v* to threaten.

threatful *adj* 1 threatening. 2 threatening-looking.

threave[1] *same as* **thrave**[1].

threave[2] *v* throve.

threaver *same as* **thraver**.

threaving *same as* **thraving**.

three-cockit *n* a three-cornered hat.

three-cord *adv* three-ply.

threed *n* thread.

three faces in a hood *n* the pansy.

threefauld *adj* threefold.

three-fold *n* the bogbean.

three-four *adj* three or four.

three-girr'd *adj* girded with three hoops.

threen *same as* **threne**.

three-neukit *adj* three-cornered.

threep *same as* **threap**.

threepenny *n* a first reading book.

threeple *adj* treble.

three-plet *adj* 1 three-ply. 2 threefold.

threeptree *n* the beam of a plough.

threesh *v* thrashed.

threesht *v* thrashed.

threesome *n* 1 three together. 2 a reel that is danced by three alone.

three-stand *adv* in three portions.

three sweeps *n* a girls' singing game.

three-taed *adj* three-pronged.

threeten *v* to threaten.

three threads and thrums *n* a cat's purring.

three thrums *n* a cat's purring.

threeve[1] *v* throve.

threeve[2] *same as* **thrave**[1].

three-yirl'd *adj* three years old.—*n* an animal three years old.

threft *same as* **thairf**.

threin *v, adj* thriven.

threip *same as* **threap**.

threish *same as* **treesh**.

threishin *same as* **treeshin**.

thremmel *v* 1 to squeeze, wring. 2 to extort.

thren *same as* **threne**

threne, thren *n* 1 a refrain. 2 a constant repetition, a song. 3 a ghost story, a superstitious tradition. 4 a vulgar adage.—*v* 1 to harp constantly on one subject. 2 to tell ghost stories,

thresh[1], **thresh**[2] *same as* **thrash**[1], **thrash**[2].

threshen *v, adj* thrashed.

threshie *n* a rush.

threshie coat *n* an old working coat.

threshing tree *n* a flail.

threshwart, threshwort *n* a threshold.

threshy mill *n* a threshing mill.

threshy-wick *n* a rush wick.

thresum *n* three together.

thresury *n* the treasury.

thretten *adj* thirteen.

thretty *adj* thirty.

threuch, threuchstane *same as* **throughstone**.

threush *v* thrashed, beat.

thrid[1] *adj* third.

thrid[2] *n* thread.

thriep *same as* **threap**.

thriest *n* constraint.

thrieve *same as* **thrave**[1].

thrieveless *adj* 1 thriftless. 2 not promising success.

thrift *n* 1 prosperity. 2 luck. 3 success. 4 work, employment, business. 5 industry.

thriftin *n* 1 luck. 2 success.

thriftless *adj* 1 unprofitable. 2 unsuccessful.

thrifty *adj* 1 thoughtful, considerate. 2 saving time or trouble.

thrim *same as* **thrum**[1].

thrimble, thrimle, thrimmle, thrimal *v* 1 to finger anything as if unwilling to part with it. 2 to crowd, press. 3 to wrestle. 4 to fumble. 5 to press, squeeze through.

thrime *n* a triplet in verse.

thrimp *v* 1 to press, squeeze. 2 to press or push in a crowd. 3 to push. 4 (*used of schoolboys on a bench*) to push all before them from end to end.—*n* schoolboys' pushing.

thrim-thram *n* 1 a term of ridicule or contempt. 2 used in evasive answers.

thring *v* to press, squeeze, to push one's way in.

thrinter *n* a sheep of three winters.

thrip *same as* **threap**.

thriplin' kame *n* a comb for separating the seed of flax from the stalks.

thrissel, thrissle, thrisle *n* a thistle.

thrissly *adv* 1 abounding in thistles. 2 testy.

thrist[1] *n* thirst.—*v* to cause thirst.

thrist[2] *v* to thrust. 2 to squeeze, hug. 3 to wring.—*n* 1 a thrust, push. 2 a squeeze, hug. 3 the action of the jaws in squeezing the juice of a quid of tobacco.

thrist[3] *v* to spin.

thristle *n* a thistle.

thristle ~, thrissel cock *n* the song thrush.

thristle-cock lairag *n* the common bunting.

thristled *adj* (*used of banners*) bearing the emblem of the thistle.

thristly *adv* 1 abounding in thistles. 2 bristly. 3 testy, snappish.

thriv[1] *same as* **thrave**[1].

thriv[2] *v* throve.

thrivance *n* 1 prosperity, success. 2 prosperous industry.

thrive *n* the way to prosperity.

thriven *adj* 1 thriving. 2 prosperous. 3 well-nourished.

thriver[1] *n* a thriving animal.

thriver[2] *same as* **thraver**.

throat *n* a narrow entrance.

throat-cutter *n* a cutthroat.

throch[1] *prep* through.—*v* to carry through, accomplish.

throch[2] *n* 1 a sheet of paper. 2 a small literary work.

throch-and-through, ~-throw *adv* completely through, through and through.

throchstane *n* a flat tombstone.

throck[1] *n* 1 the lower part of a plough to which the share is attached. 2 a term given to certain pairs of oxen in a twelve-ox plough.

throck[2] *v* to crowd, throng.—*n* a throng, a crowd.

throng *same as* **thrang**.

throngness *n* a crowded state.

throoch, throochstane *same as* **throughstane**[1].

throok *n* an instrument for twisting ropes of straw, etc.

throosh[1] *v* thrashed.

throosh[2] *v* to play truant.

throosh-the-schule *n* a truant.

throost *v* 1 did thrust. 2 thrust.

throother *same as* **throughither**.

thropit *v* to go.

thropple, throple *same as* **thrapple**.

thropple-deep *adj* up to the throat.

thropple-girth *n* 1 a collar. 2 a neckcloth.

thropple-hearse *adv* hoarse.

throssil *n* the song thrush.

throstle *v* to warble.

throther *same as* **throughither**.

throuch *same as* **through**.

throu'-come *n* a trying experience through which one passes.

throu'-'dder *adj* unmethodical.

througal *adj* frugal, thrifty.

througallity *n* frugality.

througang *n* a passage through.

througawn *adj* persevering.

through[1], **throwe** *prep* **1** across. **2** on the other side of. **3** during.—*adv* **1** up and down. **2** thoroughly. —*adj* **1** finished. **2** going through, penetrating. **3** active, expeditious.—*n* a grazing range.—*v* **1** to advance, to go through with. **2** to perfect, make thorough. **3** to prove.

through[2] *same as* **throughstane**[1].

through-art *n* a narrow passage or close between the barn and the cowshed of a farmstead.

through-band *n* a long binding stone that goes the whole breadth of a wall.

through-bear *v* **1** to sustain, support, provide. **2** to bear through to the end of a work or difficulty.

through-bearin' *n* **1** a livelihood. **2** means of sustenance. **3** support through work, difficulty or danger until the end.

through-coming *n* **1** a livelihood. **2** a coming through.

through-gain, ~-gaen, ~-going *adj* **1** active, pushing. **2** prodigal, wasteful. **3** passing through.—*n* **1** a severe examination. **2** a thorough reprimand. **3** a thorough overhaul. **4** a passage through. **5** a thoroughfare. **6** transit. **7** a livelihood. **8** support under difficulties to their end.

through-gain close *n* an open narrow passage from one street to another.

through-gain entry *n* a passage from the front to the back of a house.

through-gang *n* **1** a thoroughfare. **2** a passage. **3** a close scrutiny. **4** labour. **5** perseverance. **6** energy.

through-gang close *n* an open passage from one street to another.

through-ganging *adj* **1** active. **2** having a great deal of action.

through-gaun, through-gawn *same as* **through-gain**.

through-hands *adv* **1** under consideration. **2** under reprimand.—*adj* (*used of work, etc*) undertaken or finished.

throughither *adv* **1** in confusion. **2** pell-mell. **3** among each other. **4** unmethodically.—*adj* **1** confused, disorderly, unmethodical, disorganized. **2** harum-scarum. **3** careless in working. **4** mentally confused. **5** intimate. **6** living in close proximity.—*n* **1** a confusion, disturbance. **2** (*in pl*) mixed sweets.

throughitherness *n* want of method, confusion.

throughither-witted *adj* weak or confused mentally.

through-pit, ~-put *n* activity, expedition.

through-pittin *adj* active, expeditious.—*n* **1** a bare subsistence. **2** a rough handling. **3** a severe examination.

throughstane[1] *n* a flat tombstone.

throughstane[2] *n* **1** a stone going through a wall. **2** a throughband (qv).

through-the-bows *n* **1** a severe scolding. **2** a thorough dealing. **3** a strict examination.

through-the-muir, ~-meer *n* **1** a quarrel, wrangle. **2** a fault-finding.

through-the-needle-e'e *n* a young people's game.

through-the-wad-laddle *n* **1** a wrangle. **2** a fault-finding.

through time *adv* **1** gradually. **2** in the course of time.

throut *same as* **thereout**.

throu'ther *same as* **throughither**.

throw[1] *same as* **thraw**[5].

throw[2], **throwe** *prep and adv* through.

throwder *same as* **throughither**.

throwe *same as* **throw**[2].

throw-gang *adj* affording a thoroughfare.

throwlie *adv* thoroughly.

throwther *same as* **throughither**.

thruch, thrugh *same as* **through-stane**.

thruish *v* threshed.

thrum[1] *n* **1** a loose end of any kind. **2** a particle. **3** a tangle, mess. **4** the debts a man, leaving a place, leaves unpaid.

5 close and loving intercourse. **6** an engagement to marry. **7** courting with a view to marriage. **8** a fit of ill-humour. **9** a foolish whim. **10** (*in pl*) threads needed from the yarn in beginning to weave.—*v* **1** to raise a tufted pile on knitted or woollen stuffs. **2** to enwrap in a careless fashion. **3** to entangle. **4** to act on a foolish whim, to sulk. **5** to twirl the fingers in a shy, awkward manner.

thrum[2] *v* **1** to strum. **2** to hum, croon. **3** to repeat over again. **4** (*used of a cat*) to purr.—*n* **1** a drumming noise. **2** a strain, a hum. **3** the purring of a cat. **4** a theme. **5** a narrow passage for water between rocks.

thrumble *same as* **thrummil**.

thrum-cutter *n* a weaver.

thrum in the graith *n* a hitch in an undertaking.

thrummer *n* **1** an itinerant minstrel. **2** a contemptible musician.

thrummil, thrummle *v* **1** to fumble, grope. **2** to handle awkwardly or overmuch. **3** (*with out or up*) to deal out cash in small quantities. **4** to bring forth after a confused search. **5** to throng. **6** to press into or through a crowd with effort.—*n* the act of fumbling, groping or handling overmuch.

thrummle *v* to tremble.—*n* a tremor.

thrummy *n* a very coarse woollen cloth with a rough, tufted surface.—*adj* **1** shabbily dressed. **2** wearing old, worn-out clothes.

thrummy cap *n* a cap made of thrums or weavers' ends.

thrummy mittens *n* mittens woven from thrums. *See* **thrum**.

thrummy-tailed *adj* (*used of a woman*) wearing fringed gowns or petticoats.

thrummy wheelin *n* coarse worsted spun on the large wheel.

thrump *v* **1** to press. **2** to press, as in a crowd. **3** to push.—*n* the act of pushing.

thrunter *same as* **thrinter**.

thrush *same as* **thresh**[1].

thrush buss *n* a clump of rushes.

thrushe *v* threshed.

thrushen *v* **1** threshed. **2** thrashed.

thrusle *same as* **thristle**.

thrust *v* **1** to thirst. **2** to cause to thirst.—*n* thirst.

thrustle *same as* **thristle**.

thrustle-cock *n* the song thrush.

thrusty *adj* thirsty.

thry *adj* cross, contrary.

thryne *adj* **1** thriving, prosperous. **2** well-nourished.

thryst *same as* **tryst**.

thud[1] *v* **1** to fall heavily. **2** to make a noise in falling. **3** to move or drive quickly. **4** (*used of wind*) to blow in gusts, to rush with a hollow sound. **5** to beat, thump. **6** to beat hard and with a noise. —*n* **1** a buffet, thump. **2** a blow with the fist. **3** a gust of wind.

thud[2] *v* **1** to wheedle. **2** to flatter.—*n* the act of wheedling or flattering.

thuddering *adj* (*used of the wind*) blowing in gusts.

thulmart *same as* **thoumart**.

thumb *same as* **thoom**.

thumbikins *n* thumbkins, an instrument of torture applied as a screw to the thumbs.

thumble[1], **thummle** *n* a whip for driving a top.

thumble[2], **thummle** *n* **1** a thimble. **2** (*in pl*) round-leaved bellflowers, harebells.

thummart, thummert *same as* **thoumart**.

thummikins *same as* **thumbikins**.

thump *v* **1** to walk or dance with energy. **2** to work vigorously.—*n* **1** a lump. **2** anything big of its kind.

thumper *n* a gross lie.

thumpers *n* the hammers of a fulling mill.

thumping *adj* large, big, stout.

thum steil, ~ stule *n* a covering for a sore thumb, as the finger of a glove.

thunder *n* **1** a hailstorm. **2** a thundering noise. **3** a heavy blow. **4** a thunderbolt.

thunder-and-lightning *n* the common lungwort.
thunderbolt *n* **1** a stone hatchet. **2** a fossil belemnite.
thunder flower *n* the common red poppy.
thundering-drouth *n* a strong drought.
thunder-plump *n* a heavy thunder shower.
thunder-slain *adj* struck by lightning.
thunder speal, ~ spale *n* a thin piece of wood, two or three inches wide and six inches long, with notched sides, tied to twine and whirled round the head by boys to mimic thunder.
thunder speat, ~ spate *n* a heavy thunder shower, storm.
thunner *n* thunder.
thur *pron and adj* these.
thurst *v* to thrust.—*n* a thrust, stab.
thurst, thurt *v* needed. *See* **thar**.
thus-gates *adv* in this way or manner.
thwang *n* **1** a leather thong. **2** a shoe tie.
thwankin *adj* (*used of clouds*) mingling in thick and gloomy succession.
thwart *adv* crosswise.
thwart bawk *n* a crossbeam in a roof.
thwarter *same as* **thorter**.
thwarter-ill *n* a paralysis affecting sheep.
thwartlins *adv* crosswise.
thwartour *adv* athwart.
thwricken *v* to choke with thick, smouldering smoke.
thysel' *pron* thyself.
tiacheraum *adj* ill-disposed.
tial *n* **1** a latchet. **2** anything used for tying. **3** a tying.
tiawe *v* to amble.
tib *n* a tub.
tibbet *same as* **tippet**[1].
tibbie-thiefie *n* the cry of the sandpiper.
tibbit, tibet *same as* **tabet**[1].
tibb's eve *n* a time that never comes.
tibeethe *n* the tolbooth, jail. *See* **tolbooth**.
tic *same as* **tick**[1].
tice *v* **1** to entice. **2** to coax. **3** to move slowly and cautiously. **4** to attract, allure. **5** to treat kindly. —*n* **1** kind treatment. **2** a coaxing manner of treating.
tich *v* to touch.
tichel, tichil, tichle *n* **1** a number, band, troop. **2** anything attached to another. **3** any article kept secretly.—*v* to join hands in children's games.
tich'en, tichten *v* to tighten.
ticher[1] *v* **1** to laugh in a suppressed manner. **2** to titter.—*n* a titter.
ticher[2] *n* **1** a small fiery pimple. **2** an eruption on the face. **3** a dot of any kind.
ticher[3] *same as* **teicher**.
ticht *v* to tighten.—*adv* tight.
tichtly *adv* **1** tightly. **2** firmly. **3** assuredly.
ticht-trag *n* a low, mean person.
ticht wecht *n* barely the exact weight.
tick[1] *v* **1** to buy on credit. **2** to give credit.
tick[2] *n* **1** a children's game of tig. **2** a state of activity. **3** a small speck or spot on the skin.
ticker *same as* **ticher**.
ticket[1] *n* **1** a bill given for money lent on promise to pay. **2** a pat, a slight stroke. **3** a smart blow. **4** a drubbing.
ticket[2] *n* **1** the correct thing. **2** an oddity, a queer fish.
tickle[1] *v* to puzzle.
tickle[2] *adj* **1** difficult. **2** nice. **3** delicate.
tickler *n* **1** anything very puzzling or difficult. **2** a person difficult to deal with.
tickles *n* spectacles.
tickle-tails *adv* applied to any children's game in which they hold each other by the hand. *See* **tichel**.
tickly *adj* **1** easily tickled, touchy. **2** puzzling.
ticksie *n* **1** a quarrel, wrangle. **2** a scolding.
tick-tack *n* **1** the ticking sound of a clock. **2** an instant.
tick-tack-toe, tic-tac-toe *n* a children's game played on a slate, like noughts and crosses.
ticky-molie *n* a boy's pram.

ticquet *same as* **ticket**[1].
tid[1] *n* **1** the proper time or season for agricultural operations. **2** season, tide. **3** the suitable condition of soil for cultivation. **4** mood, humour, temper. **5** a fit of ill-humour.—*v* to choose the proper time.
tid[2] *same as* **tade**[1].
tid and quid *n* a term used by old farmers to denote a farm in a state of thriving rotation.
tidder *same as* **tither**.
tiddie *adj* **1** cross in temper. **2** (*used of land*) difficult to catch the proper season for ploughing, because of its quality. **3** uncertain. **4** eccentric.
tiddler *n* a small trout.
tiddy *n* **1** tidy. **2** smart, expeditious.
tide *n* **1** the sea, ocean. **2** the water in a dock. **3** the seashore. **4** the quantity of fish taken ashore at one time.
tide race *n* a strong tidal current.
tidy *adj* **1** plump and thriving. **2** lucky, favourable. **3** pregnant.
tie *v* **1** to marry. **2** to bind by moral obligation.—*n* **1** a tie-wig. **2** obligation. **3** a trick, deception.
tie-hie *same as* **tee-heel**.
tiend *same as* **teind**[1].
tiercer *n* a widow claiming her third of her husband's property.
tiff[1] *n* **1** a fit of anger or bad temper. **2** a wanton or dallying struggle.—*v* **1** to scold. **2** to show strong feelings of offence. **3** to delay. **4** to struggle against.
tiff[2] *v* to quaff.—*n* a small draught.
tiff[3] *n* **1** order. **2** condition, plight. **3** mood, humour. **4** mood of the moment. **5** a period of time, with the notion of tediousness.
tiff[4] *v* **1** to put in order. **2** to adjust.
tiff[5] *v* to eject anything from the mouth.—*n* **1** a sudden gust of wind. **2** afflatus, inspiration. **3** a whiff, sniff. **4** a sudden flight. **5** a great haste.
tiffle *n* a slight breeze or ripple of wind.
tiffy[1] *adj* of uncertain temper.
tiffy[2] *adj* **1** in good condition. **2** healthy, well. **3** smart.
tift[1], **tift**[2], **tift**[3], **tift**[4], **tift**[5] *same as* **tiff**[3], **tiff**[4], **tiff**[5], **tiff**[2], **tiff**[1].
tift[6] to throb, tinkle with pain.
tiftan *n* the act of decking.
tifter[1] *n* **1** a quandary. **2** a stiff breeze with a stormy sea.
tifter[2] *n* a quarrel.
tiftie *adj* uplifted, inspired.
tiftin *n* **1** a scolding. **2** a quarrelling bout.
tift o' tow *n* a sudden blaze of kindled flax.
tifty[1] *adj* **1** petulant. **2** touchy. **3** quarrelsome.
tifty[2] *adv* **1** in good condition. **2** healthy.
tig *v* **1** to tap. **2** to touch lightly. **3** to play the game of touch. **4** to dally. **5** to caress. **6** to treat scornfully. **7** to trifle with. **8** to work carelessly. **9** (*used of cattle*) to run hither and thither, irritated by flies or boys. **10** to go off in a pet. **11** to take a sudden whim.—*n* **1** a twitch, tap, pat. **2** a light touch in the game of touch. **3** the game of touch. **4** the player in the game who tries to touch the others, the one who is touched. **5** a sharp blow. **6** a stroke causing a wound. **7** a hard bargain. **8** a pet, fit of ill-humour.
tig-an'-tie *phr* 'touch and go'.
tig-biz *n* the cry of boys to incite cattle to run to and fro.
tig'd *adj* tired, wearied.
tiger *same as* **teeger**.
tiger-tarran *n* a waspish child.
tiggel *v* **1** to undermine. **2** to tamper with.
tigger[1] *n* the toucher in the games of tig and hie-spy.
tigger[2] *same as* **teeger**.
tiggle-taggle *same as* **tig-tag**.
tiggy *adv* pettish.
tigher[1] *same as* **teicher**.
tigher[2] *same as* **ticher**[1].
tight *adj* **1** neat, trim. **2** well-shaped. **3** good-looking. **4** tidy, in good order. **5** sound, whole, healthy. **6** dexterous, skilful. **7** ready for action. **8** (*used of ale, etc*) good, strong, pleasing. **9** stingy. **10** hard up. **11** (*used of money*) scarce.

12 tipsy.—*adv* **1** tightly. **13** strenuously.—*v* **1** to tighten. **2** to stretch. **3** (*with* up) to tidy, put in order.—*n* a setting in order.

tight-bound *adv* strong, well-made, strapping.

tight-locked *adj* (*used of comrades*) close-bound.

tightly *adv* **1** cleverly. **2** deftly. **3** promptly. **4** actively. **5** thoroughly. **6** minutely. **7** severely, sharply.

tigmateeze *v* to pull one about.

tig-me-if-you-can *n* the game of tig or touch.

tigsam, tigsum *same as* **taigsum**.

tig-tag *v* **1** to trifle. **2** to be busy while doing nothing. **3** to shilly-shally. **4** to be tedious in bargaining, to haggle.

tig-tailed *same as* **tag-tailed**.

tig-tire *v* **1** to keep in. **2** to annoy. **3** to make sport by teasing.—*n* a practical joke.

tig-tow *n* **1** the game of tig. **2** dallying.—*v* **1** to play at tig. **2** to play fast and loose. **3** to act capriciously. **4** to dally with. **5** to be off and on. **6** to pat mutually. **7** to stroke gently backwards and forwards.

ti-hi *same as* **tee-hee**.

tike[1] *n* **1** a dog, hound, cur. **2** a churl, a currish fellow, a boor. **3** a mischievous, tiresome child. **4** a playful term of reproach for a child. **5** a Yorkshireman. **6** an overgrown man or beast. **7** the common otter.

tike[2] *n* **1** ticking for covering a bed or bolster, etc. **2** the bed or bolster itself.

tike-and-tryke *adv* higgledy-piggledy.

tike-auld *adj* very old.

tiked *adj* currish.

tike-hungry *adv* ravenous as a dog.

tiken *same as* **tike**[2].

tike's-testament *n* nothing left as a legacy.

tike-tire, ~-tyrit *adj* dog-tired.

tike-tulyie *n* **1** a dogs' quarrel. **2** a coarse scolding match.

til *same as* **till**[4].

tilavie *same as* **tirrivie**.

tile *n* **1** a drainpipe. **2** a hat.

tiled *adj* (*used of fish*) dried.

tile-stone *n* a brick.

till[1] *n* **1** hard, unproductive, gravelly clay. **2** hard or soft shale.

till[2] *n* **1** stuff. **2** drink.

till[3] *same as* **teal**[2].

till[4], **til** *conj* **1** before, until. **2** to such a degree that. —*prep* **1** to. **2** at. **3** by. **4** for. **5** of. **6** after. **7** about.

tillage *v* to till, cultivate.

till band *n* pudding stone.

tiller *n* **1** a till. **2** a moneybox.

tillie-lick, ~-licket *n* **1** an unexpected blow. **2** an unexpected calamity or reverse of fortune. **3** (*in pl*) taunts and sneers.

tillie soul *n* a place to which a gentleman sent the horses and servants of his guests when he did not choose to entertain the former at his own cost.

tilliwillie *n* the curlew.

tillowie *int* tally-ho! a cry to encourage hounds on to the chase.—*n* (*used of drink*) as much as urges the drinker on.

tilly *adj* of the nature of till, or unproductive clay soil.

tilly-clay *n* **1** cold clay, unproductive soil. **2** coldness of heart.

tilly-pan *n* **1** a skillet. **2** a pan for lifting water.

tilt[1] *n* **1** a high-minded state. **2** trouble, annoyance.

tilt[2] *n* **1** filth. **2** plight, condition.

tilter *n* the man who delivered the sheaves from a reaping machine with a rake.

tilting machine *n* a reaping machine requiring a man to knock off the sheaves with a rake.

tilyer *n* a tailor.

tim *same as* **toom**[1].

timber *same as* **timmer**[2].

timber-man *n* a timber merchant.

timber mare, ~ horse *n* the wooden horse formerly used as a military punishment.

time[1] *n* thyme.

time[2] *n* **1** life. **2** lifetime. **3** the time of parturition. **4** the death hour. **5** the duration of apprenticeship or contract of service. **6** the act of once harrowing a field.

time mark *n* an epoch.

timeous, timous *adj* **1** opportune. **2** keeping time. **3** keeping proper hours.—*adv* betimes.

timeously *adv* **1** opportunely. **2** in good or proper time.

timersome *adj* timorous.

time-taker *n* one who lies in wait for an opportunity of effecting his purpose, used in a bad sense.

timmer[1] *v* to act strenuously, continuously and successfully in any work requiring exertion.

timmer[2] *n* **1** timber, wood. **2** a wooden dish or cup. **3** a stick, cudgel. **4** a leg, limb. **5** a piece of furniture.—*v* to beat, cudgel.—*adv* **1** wooden, made of wood. **2** unmusical, tuneless, without an ear for music.

timmer[3] *n* a legal quantity of forty or fifty skins packed within boards.

timmer-breeks *n* a coffin.

timmer goods *n* wooden articles.

timmerin *n* a cudgelling, thrashing.

timmerman *n* a timber merchant.

Timmer market *n* an ancient fair held in Aberdeen on the last Wednesday of August for the sale of small fruits, timber articles, toys, etc.

timmer tune *n* a poor, unmusical voice.

timmer-tuned *adj* having no ear or voice for music.

timming *n* a coarse, thin, woollen cloth.

timothy[1] *n* the cat's-tail grass.

timothy[2] *n* **1** haste, bustle. **2** an agitated state. **3** a jorum of drink.

timoursome *adj* timorous.

timpany, timpan *n* the middle part of the front of a house raised above the level of the rest, so as to resemble a gable and give an attic in the roof.

timpany gable *n* a timpany (qv).

timpany window *n* a window in the timpany gable (qv).

tim'pin *adj* tempting.

timse *same as* **teems**.

timty *n* a method of digging the ground and covering it with sea ware in the Isle of Lewis.

tin[1] *n* any article made of tin, a tin mug, etc.

tin[2] *same as* **teind**[3].

tinchel, tinchill, tinckell *n* **1** a circle formed by sportsmen to encircle deer. **2** a gin, trap, snare.

tinclarian *adj* **1** tinker-like. **2** composed of tinkers.

tindel *n* tinder

tine[1] *v* to kindle.—*n* **1** a spark of fire. **2** a spark on the side of the wick of a candle.

tine[2] *v* **1** to lose. **2** to forfeit. **3** to lose a cause in a court of justice. **4** to be lost, perish.

tin-egin *n* forced fire, as an antidote to murrain.

tineless *adj* (*used of a harrow*) without tines.

Tineman *n* an appellation given to one of the lords of Douglas, who lost almost all his sons in battle.

tinesel *n* **1** loss. **2** forfeiture.

tining *n in phr* **at the fining and the winning** at a critical point between loss or gain or ruin or safety.

ting[1] *n* a tongue of land jutting into the sea.—*v* (*of cattle*) to swell up through eating clover, etc.

ting[2] *v* **1** to ring, jingle. **2** to resound.—*n* **1** a ringing sound, a tinkle. **2** the sound of a clock striking or of a small bell.

ting-a-ling *n* **1** the sound of a small bell. **2** the imitation of such. **3** a ringing sound. **4** a clock that strikes.

tingle *v* **1** to tinkle. **2** to jingle. **3** to ring a bell.

ting-tang *n* **1** the sound of a bell. **2** a monotonous repetition. **3** an oft-told tale.

tink[1] *n* a tinker.—*v* to rivet with a tinkling sound.

tink[2] *v* to tinkle.—*n* **1** a tinkle, ring. **2** the sound of a small bell.

tinker *n* a gipsy, a randy-beggar (qv).

tinker-bairn *n* a tinker's child.

tinker-tongue *n* an abusive tongue.

tinkle[1] *v* **1** to trifle. **2** to work carelessly and lazily.

tinkle[2] *v* (*with* **on**) to ring chimes about one or to praise one unduly.

tinkler *n* **1** a tinker. **2** a gipsy, vagabond. **3** an opprobrious term. **4** a virago.—*adj* like a tinkler.

tinkler-bairn *n* a tinker's child.

tinkler gipsy *n* a wandering gipsy.

tinklerjaw *n* **1** a loud, scolding tongue. **2** coarse, abusive language.

tinkler-lass *n* a gipsy girl. **2** a tinker's daughter.

tinkler's-curse, ~-tippence, ~-whussel *n* **1** anything utterly worthless. **2** a jot, atom.

tinkler-tongue *n* a tinklerjaw (qv).

tinkler-trumpet tongue *n* a loud, abusive tongue.

tinkler-wife *n* **1** a term of contempt for a woman. **2** a woman of low character and companions. **3** a virago.

tinkle-sweetie *n* a bell formerly rung in Edinburgh at eight o'clock p.m., when shops were closed for the night.

tinkling-tool *n* a tinker's tool.

tink-wife *n* a tinker's wife.

tinner *n* a tinsmith.

tinnie *n* **1** any small tin vessel. **2** a tin canister. **3** a tinsmith.

tinnikin *n* a small tin vessel.

tinnykit *n* a tinnikin (qv).

tinsel, tinsall *same as* **tinesel**.

tinsey, tinsy *n* tinsel.

tinsey-tailed *adj* having a bright, shining tail.

tint[1] *v* to lose.

tint[2] *v, adj* lost.

tint[3] *n* **1** a taste. **2** a foretaste. **3** evidence, indication. **4** tidings, information.

tint[4] *adj* (*used of a child*) spoilt, petted.

tinte *n* loss.

tintoe *n* the pin used in turning the cloth beam of a loom.

tip[1] *n* a tup, ram.—*v* **1** to take the ram. **2** to serve with the ram.

tip[2] *n* **1** a term marking great excellence in a person or thing. **2** the belle of a ball or party. **3** the best of anything. **4** an overdressed person, a swell. **5** a match, an equal.—*v* **1** to go on tiptoe. **2** to equal, match. **3** to excel, exceed. **4** to overcome.

tip[3] *v* **1** to tap. **2** to kick in football. **3** to empty by tipping. **4** to drink off. **5** to milk a cow with a small yield. **6** to pull down the teats preparatory to milking a cow. **7** to put to silence. **8** to disappoint, nettle, mortify.—*n* **1** a tap. **2** a notch. **3** a place where rubbish is thrown down, a rubbish heap. **4** a small quantity of liquid. **5** anything that silences a person, a settler.

tip[4] *same as* **tippenny**.

tipie *adj* **1** trim, tidy. **2** neatly dressed.

tipney *same as* **tippenny**.

tippanize, tippenize *v* to tipple small beer.

tippen *same as* **tippet**[2].

tippence *same as* **tuppens**.

tippenny *n* **1** small beer sold for twopence a pint. **2** a child's first reading book, at one time costing twopence.

tippenny hoose *n* an alehouse.

tipper[1] *n* a horse used for the tipping of wagons in making a railway, etc.

tipper[2] *n* a well-dressed person of either sex.

tipper[3] *v* **1** to walk on tiptoe, or unsteadily. **2** to totter. **3** to place in an unsteady position.

tipper-taiper *v* to totter.

tippertin *n* a bit of card with a pin passed through it, resembling a teetotum.

tipperty *adj* **1** unstable. **2** walking stiffly, with mincing gait or in a flighty, ridiculous manner.

tipperty-like *adv* mincingly, in a flighty, ridiculous gait.

tippet[1] *n* **1** one length of twisted hair or gut in a fishing line. **2** a handful of straw bound together at one end, used in thatching.

tippet[2] *n in phr* **St Johnstone's tippet** a hangman's halter.

tippet stane *n* a round stone with a hook in its centre for twisting tippets.

tippet up *adj* nicely dressed.

tippy *n* the height of fashion.—*adj* dressed in the highest fashion.

tipsie *n* drink, liquor.

tiptoo *same as* **taptoo**.

tir *same as* **tirr**[1].

tiravie *same as* **tirrivee**.

tirbad *n* **1** the turbot. **2** the halibut.

tird *same as* **tirr**[1].

tire[1] *n* **1** a snood or narrow band for the hair of women. **2** an ornamental edging used by cabinet-makers and upholsterers. **3** the metal edging or ornaments of coffins.

tire[2] *n* **1** fatigue, stiffness. **2** tiredness, the feeling of tiredness.

tirivee, tiryvee *same as* **tirrivee**.

tirl, tirle *v* **1** to vibrate, quiver. **2** to thrill. **3** to make a thrilling sound. **4** to make a rattling or scraping sound so as to attract attention at a door. **5** to whirl. **6** to rotate rapidly. **7** to twist. **8** (*used of the wind*) to veer. **9** to cause to vibrate. **10** (*of the sun*) to drive its course. **11** to touch the strings of an instrument and produce vibrations of sound. **12** to cause to twirl, roll, or whirl. **13** to turn over. **14** to strip, denude. **15** to unroof. **16** to strip off thatch or slates. **17** to uncover a house. **18** to pare the surface of a peat moss.—*n* **1** a thrill. **2** a vibration. **3** a tremor. **4** a twirl, whirl. **5** a fall over and over. **6** the act of rotating. **7** a bout, a short spell at anything, as of drinking, dancing. **8** a gentle breeze. **9** a substitute for the trundle of an old Shetland mill.

tirlass, tirless, tirlies *n* **1** a trellis. **2** the lattice of a window. **3** a latticed grating or rail. **4** a wicket, a small gate. **5** a woven wire frame.—*v* to lattice.

tirless-yett *n* a turnstile.

tirle *same as* **tirl**.

tirlest *adj* trellised.

tirl-grind *n* a turnstile, a revolving gate.

tirlies *same as* **tirlass**.

tirling pin *n* a bar of iron, notched or twisted like a rope, placed vertically on a door with a ring of iron slung to it, formerly used as a knocker. The description generally given is properly that of the risp and ring (*see* **risp**). The real tirling pin was probably a different device, connected with the latch of a door, which was tirled (*see* **tirl**) to attract attention by a person seeking admittance.

tirling ring *n* the ring that was tirled round the tirling pin to make a rattling noise at the door. *See* **tirl**.

tirl-mill *n* a primitive grinding mill of Shetland.

tirl-o'-win *n* a good winnowing wind.

tirly *n* **1** an ornamental waving line in scrollwork or carving. **2** the ornament itself. **3** a winding in a footpath.

tirly-toy *n* **1** a trifle, a toy. **2** a tirly (qv).

tirly-wirly, tirly-wirl, tirly-whirly *n* **1** a flourish. **2** a fanciful ornament. **3** any figure or decoration. **4** the clock of a stocking. **5** a whirligig. **6** an ingenious contrivance.—*adj* intricate, winding, intertwisted.—*adv* round and round like a whirligig.

tirma *n* the sea pie or oystercatcher.

tirr[1] *v* **1** to strip, denude. **2** to uncover with force. **3** to unroof. **4** to tear off a covering, thatch, slates, etc. **5** to remove the surface or subsoil in quarrying. **6** to pare the surface of a peat moss before cutting peats. **7** to despoil one of property. **8** to undress, pull off one's clothes.—*n* what is removed from the bed of a quarry.

tirr[2] *v* **1** to snarl. **2** to speak in ill-temper.—*n* **1** a cross, bad-tempered child. **2** an angry or excited condition.—*adj* crabbed, quarrelsome, in an ill-temper.

tirracke, tirrik, tirrock *same as* **tarrock**.

tirran, tirrane *n* **1** a tyrant. **2** a perverse, ill-tempered person.

tirrivee, tirreveoch, tirravie, tirrievie *n* **1** a passion, rage. **2** a fit of temper. **3** a commotion, bustle. **4** excitement.

tirrle *same as* **tirl**.

tirr-wirr *n* **1** a quarrel, wrangle. **2** a contest. **3** a complaint. **4** a scolding.—*v* to wrangle.—*adj* growling, quarrelsome.

tirr-wirrin' *adj* **1** growling, quarrelsome. **2** fault-finding.

tirry *adj* **1** angry. **2** cross, ill-tempered.

tirry-mirry *n* **1** a fit of passion. **2** wild, excited mirth.

tirryvie tirrivee.

tirry-wirry *n* **1** a wrangle. **2** a fit of passion. **3** a contest. **4** a scolding fit.

tirse *v* **1** to pull with a jerk. **2** to tear.—*n* **1** a tug, a jerk. **2** a sudden gale.

tirve *n* a turf.

tirvin *n* sod taken from the top of peat.

tir-wir *adj* growling.

tiryvee *same as* **tirrivee.**

tise *v* to entice.

tisha *n* **1** a sneeze. **2** the sound of sneezing.

tissle[1] *same as* **taissle.**

tissle[2] *n* a gewgaw, a trifle, tinsel.

tit[1] *n* a teat, the nipple of the breast.

tit[2] *n* **1** a mood, humour. **2** a fit of temper.

tit[3] *v* **1** to jerk. **2** to snatch. **3** to twitch. **4** to tap. **5** to pull.—*n* **1** a sudden jerk or pull. **2** a tug. **3** a snatch. **4** a twitch. **5** a tap. **6** (*in pl*) a disease of horses causing their legs to be spasmodically contracted.

tita *same as* **titter**[1].

tit-an'-taum *n* a fit of ill-humour.

titbo-tatbo *n* the game of teet-bo (qv).

tite[1] *v* **1** to totter. **2** to fall over. **3** to walk with short, unsteady, or jerking steps.—*n* such walking. **4** a little person.—*adv* with short or jerking steps.

tite[2] *same as* **tyte.**

tithand *n* tidings, news.

tither *adj* the other.

tithy *same as* **tidy.**

titing *n* the titlark or meadow pipit.

title[1] *same as* **tittle.**

title[2] *v* to tug repeatedly at one's coat-tails.

titlene, titlin *n* **1** the meadow pipit or titlark. **2** the hedge sparrow.

tits *int* tuts! toots!

titsam *adv* **1** short-tempered. **2** touchy.

titt *same as* **tit**[3].

tit-ta *n* a child's name for father.

titter[1] *adv* rather, sooner.

titter[2] *v* **1** to totter. **2** to walk with weak or faltering steps. **3** to shiver. **4** to tremble. **5** to quiver. **6** to twitter. **7** to work in a weak, trifling manner. **8** to gossip.—*n* **1** a sorry plight. **2** a weak, unsteady gait. **3** work done in a weak, trifling manner. **4** silly gossip. **5** one who gossips.

tittersome *adv* **1** (*of the weather*) fickle, unsettled. **2** backward. **3** (*of a horse*) restless, nervous.

titter-totter *n* a seesaw.

tittie *same as* **titty**[1].

tittish *adj* captious, testy.

tittivate *v* **1** to dress up, make oneself smart. **2** to flatter, tickle.

tittivation *n* a smartening, making spruce.

tittle[1] *v* to tickle.

tittle[2] *v* **1** to tattle. **2** to prate idly. **3** to whisper.—*n* **1** gossip, idle talk. **2** a whisper.

tittle[3] *same as* **tattle.**

tittle[4] *n* anything small.

tittlin *same as* **titlene.**

tittlins *adv* in the way of whispering, tattling, etc.

titty[1] *n* **1** a child's word for sister. **2** a young girl.

titty[2] *adj* **1** captious, testy. **2** ill-tempered. **3** (*used of the wind*) gusty, boisterous.

titty-billy *n* **1** an equal. **2** a match. **3** the strongest marks of resemblance, as of sister and brother.

titular *n* **1** a layman who after the Reformation had a donation of church lands. **2** a person having a legal title to the parsonage teinds of such parishes as had been 'mortified' to the monasteries. *See* **mortify.**

titup *v* to canter, gallop.

tiv *prep* to.

tivee *same as* **tirrivee.**

tize[1] *same as* **tice.**

tize[2] *same as* **tease.**

tizzle *v* **1** to stir up or turn over. **2** to ted hay.

t'nead *v* **1** to exhaust, fatigue. **2** to dislike, annoy.

to *prep* **1** at. **2** by. **3** for. **4** on, upon. **5** towards. **6** with. **7** in comparison with. **8** in response to. **9** belonging to.—*adv* **1** (*with a verb of motion*) understood. **2** shut, close, in place. **3** down.

toachie *int* a call to a cow.

toad[1] *same as* **tade**[1].

toad[2] *same as* **tod**[6].

toad red, ~ end, ~ rud *n* the spawn of toads or frogs.

toad's-e'e *n* jealousy.

toad-spue *n* toad red (qv).

toad-stane *n* a stone formerly thought to be formed within a toad and used with a certain formula for stanching the flow of blood.

toad-stool *n* a mushroom.

to-airn *n* a piece of iron with a perforation wide enough to admit the pipe of the smith's bellows, built into the wall of his forge to preserve the pipe from being consumed by the fire.

toalie *n* a small, round cake of any kind of bread.

toam *same as* **tome**[2].

to-an'-fro *n* indecision, wavering.

toast *v* **1** to tease. **2** to vex. **3** to toss.

toaster *n* an iron frame for toasting oatcakes before a fire.

toath *same as* **taith.**

tobacco flour, ~ meal *n* snuff.

tobacco night *n* an irreverent name for a lyke-wake.

tobacco snipe *n* a boy worker under a tobacco spinner.

to'booth *same as* **tolbooth.**

to-bread *n* a biscuit given by a baker in addition to a shilling's worth or so purchased from him.

to-brig *n* a drawbridge.

tocher *n* the dowry brought by a woman at marriage.—*v* to dower.

tocher band *n* the deed signed regarding a bride's dowry.

tocher fee, ~ gear, ~ guid *n* a marriage dowry.

tocherless *adj* without a dowry.

tocherodarach *n* **1** a sergeant of court. **2** a thief-taker.

tocher purse *n* a woman's dowry.

tod[1] *int* a corruption of the word God, used as exclamation of surprise,

tod[2] *n* a disparaging term applied to a child.

tod[3] *n* a small species of crab.

tod[4] *n* a small, round cake of any kind of bread, given to pacify or please children.

tod[5] *n* a fit of the sulks.

tod[6] *n* a fox.

tod[7] *n* a glass of toddy.

tod-and-lambs *n* a game played with wooden pins on a perforated board.

tod-brod *n* the board on which the game of tod-and-lambs is played.

toddie *n* the tod (qv), or small round cake, given to children.

toddle[1] *n* a small cake or scone.

toddle[2] *v* **1** to walk with feeble, uncertain steps. **2** to waddle. **3** to stagger under the influence of drink. **4** to saunter. **5** (*used of a stream*) to purl, to move with gentle sound. **6** to make a murmuring sound in boiling.—*n* **1** a child just beginning to walk. **2** a neat little person.

toddler *n* **1** one who walks with short steps. **2** a child learning to walk.

toddy *n* a glass of toddy.

todgie *n* a small, round, flat cake.

tod-hunting *n* fox-hunting.

todie[1] *same as* **toddie.**

todie[2] *same as* **taudy**[1].

tod-i'-the-fauld *n* a boys' game.

todle *same as* **toddle**[2].

todlen *n* a rolling, short step.

todler-tyke *n* a kind of bumblebee.

todlich *n* a child beginning to walk.

tod-like *adj* fox-like, crafty.

tod-lowrie *n* **1** the fox. **2** a children's game.

to-draw *n* **1** a resource, refuge. **2** something to which one can draw in danger or threatening circumstances.

tod's bairns, ~ birds *n* **1** an evil brood. **2** a froward young generation.

tod's-hole *n* **1** a fox's hole. **2** a secret hiding place. **3** the grave.

tod's-tail, tod-tail *n* **1** a children's game in which they chase each other in single file. **2** Alpine club moss.

tod's-turn *n* **1** a sly trick. **2** a base, crafty trick.

tod-tonzing *n* a method of fox-hunting by shooting, bustling, guarding, etc.

tod-track *n* the traces of a fox's feet in snow.

tod-tyke *n* a mongrel between a fox and a dog.

toe *same as* **tae**².

to-fall, to-fa *n* **1** the close of day or night. **2** a building annexed to a larger, against which the roof rests. **3** a lean-to. **4** a porch. **5** a support. **6** a burden.

toft *n* **1** a bed for plants of cabbage, etc. **2** land once tilled but now abandoned. **3** a homestead.

toft field *n* a field belonging to a toft or messuage.

toft house *n* the house attached to a toft or messuage.

toftin *n* **1** a toft. **2** a messuage, the house built on a toft. **3** the holding of this house. **4** the right to hold it.

to-gang *n* **1** encounter. **2** meeting. **3** access.

to-gaun *n* a drubbing.

togersum *adj* **1** tedious. **2** tiresome.

to-hooch *same as* **t'chach**.

toighal *n* **1** a parcel. **2** a budget. **3** luggage. **4** any troublesome appendage.

toiled *adj* hard-wrought.

toilman *n* a toiler, a labouring man.

toil-sprent *adj* toil-worn.

toist *same as* **teistie**.

toit *v* **1** to totter from age. **2** to walk feebly. **3** to saunter. **4** to dawdle. **5** to tease.—*n* **1** a sudden attack of illness. **2** a fit of bad temper.

toited *adj* **1** feeble. **2** tottering.

toiter *v* **1** to walk about feebly. **2** to totter.

toity *adj* **1** testy, snappish. **2** easily offended.

token *n* **1** *same as* **taken**. **2** a metal ticket given as a mark of admission to the Communion.

tokie¹ *n* an old woman's headdress, resembling a monk's cowl.

tokie² *n* a child's pet name.

tolbooth, tolbuith *n* **1** the town jail. **2** the town hall.

tolerance *n* leave, permission.

tolie *same as* **toalie**.

toll *n* **1** a turnpike. **2** a taker of tolls. **3** a turnpike keeper.—*v* to take multure (qv) for grinding corn.

toll-bar *n* a turnpike.

toll-free *adj* without payment.

tollie¹ *n* a turnpike-keeper.

tollie² *n* **1** excrement. **2** (*in pl*) horse dung.

tolling *n* the sound made by bees before they swarm.

toll road *n* a turnpike road.

toll roup *n* the sale by auction of the right to take tolls at a turnpike.

toll tax *n* the toll paid at a turnpike.

toll ticket *n* a square scrap of printed paper, available for the day of issue, stating that it cleared certain neighbouring turnpikes.

to-look *n* **1** a look to. **2** an outlook. **3** matter of expectation. **4** a prospect. **5** something laid up for the future. **6** a marriage portion.

tolor *same as* **taler**.

tolsey *n* a place where toll was paid.

tolter *v* **1** to totter, hobble. **2** to move unequally. **3** to be unstable.—*n* an insecure erection.—*adj* unstable, out of the perpendicular.

toltery *adj* **1** insecure, unstable, shaky. **2** not perpendicular.

to-luck *n* a luck-penny, something given in above a bargain for luck to the buyer.

tom *same as* **taum**.

tomack *same as* **tammock**.

toman¹ *same as* **towmond**.

toman² *n* **1** a hillock. **2** a mound. **3** a thicket.

tombe *same as* **taum**¹.

tome¹ *same as* **toom**¹.

tome² *same as* **taum**¹.

tömekins *n* an implement for twisting three strands into a rope.

tomerall *n* a horse two years old.

tomes *adv* **1** ropy. **2** drawing out like toasted cheese.

tome-spinner *n* a whorl used for twisting hairlines.

tommack *same as* **tammock**.

tommie-wake *n* the cock sparrow.

tomminaul *n* an ox or heifer a year old.

tommy *same as* **tammie**.

tommy book *n* a book for entering goods bought on credit.

tom-noddy, ~-norry *n* the puffin.

tomon *same as* **towmond**.

tomontal *n* a yearling cow or colt.

tomorrow *adv* (*used of past time*) the next day.

tomorrow morning *adv* (*of past time*) next morning.

tom o' tee end *n* a haggis.

tomshee *n* **1** a fairy hillock. **2** a horse or cow.

tom-thumb *n* the willow warbler.

tom-trot *n* a kind of toffee.

to-name *same as* **tee-name**.

tong *v* **1** to ring, toll a bell. **2** (*of a bell*) to sound loudly or harshly.—*n* a twang in speaking.

tongablaa *n* a continuous gabble.

tongue *n* **1** dialect. **2** manner of speaking. **3** abuse, violent language.—*v* **1** to talk immoderately. **2** to scold, abuse.

tongue-betroosht, ~-betrusht *adj* outspoken, too ready with the tongue.

tongue-deavin' *adj* **1** voluble. **2** deafening with a loud tongue.

tongue ~, tongue's end *n* the tip of the tongue.

tongue-ferdy *adv* loquacious, glib-tongued.

tongue o' butter *n* a flattering, smooth tongue.

tongue of the trump *n* **1** the person of most importance. **2** the chief or best performer.

tongue raik *n* **1** elocution. **2** fluency.

tongue roots *n* the tip of one's tongue.

tongue strabush *n* strife of tongues.

tongue-tack *v* **1** to silence. **2** to hinder freedom of speech.

tongue-tackit *adj* **1** tongue-tied, having an impediment in speech because of the tongue being fastened to a membrane. **2** slow of speech. **3** suddenly or unusually silent. **4** mealy-mouthed, not outspoken. **5** mumbling from drink.

tongue-thief *n* a slanderer.

tonguey *adv* **1** able to speak up for oneself. **2** loquacious, in a bad sense.

tonnoch'd *adj* covered with a plaid. *See* **tunag**.

too *same as* **to**.

toober *same as* **tabour**.

tooberin *same as* **taberin**.

toofall *same as* **to-fall**.

toog *n* a small hillock.

too-hoo *n* **1** a hullabaloo. **2** an outcry of pleasure or of pain. **3** a spiritless person.

took¹ *same as* **teuk**.

took² *n* **1** the beat of a drum. **2** the sound of a trumpet.—*v* (*of drums or trumpets*) to beat or sound.

took³ *v* to pull, jerk.—*n* **1** a pull, jerk. **2** a blow, slap.

tool *n* a towel.

toolie, toolzie, tooly *same as* **tuilyie**.

tool skep *n* a tool basket.

toolter *same as* **tolter**.

toom¹ *adj* **1** empty. **2** thin, lean. **3** lacking understanding. **4** shallow, empty-sounding, vain.—*v* **1** to empty, pour out. **2** (*used of rain*) to pour down. **3** to discharge.—*n* a place into which rubbish is emptied.

toom[2] *same as* **taum**[1].

toom-brained *adj* empty-headed.

toom-clung *adv* empty from want of food.

toomed *adj* (*used of a woman*) delivered of a child.

toom-halter *n* the end of one's resources.

toom-handed *adj* empty-handed.

toom-held *n* an empty-headed person.

toom-heidit *adj* empty-headed.

toom-like *adj* **1** empty. **2** (*used of clothes hanging loosely on one*) empty-looking.

toom-looking *adj* empty-looking.

toomly *adv* emptily.

toom of rain *n* a heavy torrent of rain.

toom-skinned *adv* hungry, hungry-looking.

toom-spoon *n* **1** an empty spoon. **2** applied to an unedifying preacher.

toom-tail *adj* **1** (*of a plough*) coming back without making a furrow. **2** (*of a cart*) going with a load and returning empty.

toom-the-stoup *n* a drunken fellow.

toom-the-timmer *v* to empty the wooden cog or drinking vessel.

toon *n* **1** a town. **2** a village. **3** a hamlet. **4** a farmstead. **5** a country seat. **6** the farm people. **7** the household.

toon bodies *n* townspeople, townsfolk.

toon-born *adj* born in a town.

toon dyke *n* the dyke (qv) or wall enclosing a township.

toon end *n* **1** the end of a road leading to a farm. **2** the end of the main street of a village or town.

toon foot, ~ fit *n* the lower end of a village or village street.

toon gate *n* the chief thoroughfare of a town or village.

toon guard *n* **1** a civic watchman. **2** the men composing a guard company.

toon heid *n* the upper part of a town or village or of its main street.

toon hoose *n* **1** the town hall. **2** the courthouse of a town.

toon-keeper *n* the person in charge of a farmstead on Sunday.

toon land *n* cleared land near a township.

toon loan *n* **1** an open, uncultivated piece of land near a village or farmstead. **2** the wider area beyond the narrow strip in front of a farmhouse.

toon loon *n* a boy of the town.

toon neighbours *n* tenants of adjacent farms.

toon-rot *n* a soldier of the city guard.

toon-row *n* the privileges enjoyed by a village or community.

toon's bairn *n* a native of the same town.

toon's bodies *n* townspeople.

toon's lad *n* a townsboy, a toon's-bairn (qv).

toon's piper *n* the piper employed to make civic proclamations.

toon's talk *n* common report, the talk of the town.

toon-wife *n* a woman born and bred in a town.

toop *same as* **tup**.

toopick, toopichan, toopichen *n* **1** a pinnacle. **2** a summit. **3** a cupola. **4** a turret. **5** a steeple. **6** a narrow pile raised so high as to be in danger of falling. **7** the top that finishes off the thatch of a stack.

toopikin *n* a toopick (qv).—*v* **1** to build high without stability. **2** to place high.

toop lamb *n* a young ram.

toor[1] *same as* **turr**.

toor[2] *n* **1** a tower. **2** a small heap. **3** a knot of hair. **4** a short worsted knob on the top of a man's woollen cap.—*v* (*used of hay*) to rise on the rake in raking. **5** (*of a fire*) to blaze freely.

toor[3] *n* a weed.

toor[4] ad wearisome, difficult.

toor battle *n* a boys' fight with bits of peat.

toor ~, tour dyke *n* a fence of turf or peat.

toore *v* tore.

toorie[1] *n* a small peat or turf.

toorie[2] *n* **1** a very small heap. **2** a knot of hair. **3** a worsted knob on a man's bonnet.

toorie-top *n* a worsted knob for a bonnet or cap.

toorish *int* a dairymaid's call to a cow to stand still, or to come to be milked.

toorock *n* **1** a small tower. **2** a small heap.

toosh[1] *n* a nasty person.

toosh[2] *n* a woman's short gown.

tooshlach *same as* **tushloch**[1].

toosht *v* **1** to dash about. **2** to toss about. **3** to roll or heap up carelessly.—*n* **1** a heavy toss or dash. **2** an untidy heap of straw, litter, etc. **3** a dirty, slovenly woman. **4** a person whose conduct is under reproach.

tooshtie *n* a small quantity.

tooskie *n* a tuft of hair on each cheek below the ear.

toosle *same as* **touzle**.

toosy, toosey *same as* **tousy**.

toosying *adj* dishevelling.

toot[1] *v* **1** (*of a bird*) to whistle, sing. **2** to trumpet abroad, spread a report. **3** to whine. **4** to express dissatisfaction or contempt.—*n* **1** a boast, brag. **2** a puff.—*int* an exclamation of contempt, tut!

toot[2] *v* **1** to jut out. **2** to project.—*n* **1** a projection. **2** a jutting out.

toot[3] *v* **1** to tipple. **2** to drink copiously.—*n* **1** a drinking bout. **2** a copious draught.

toot[4] *same as* **tout**[2].

tooter[1] *v* to babble, gossip.—*n* **1** a horn, trumpet, a tin or wooden whistle. **2** silly gossip. **3** a humbug. **4** a gossip, babbler.

tooter[2] *same as* **tootter**[2].

tooteroo[1] *n* **1** a bungle. **2** a bad job.

tooteroo[2] *n* a warning signal, as of a motorcar.

toothfu' *n* a moderate quantity of strong liquor.—*v* **1** to tipple. **2** to drink in small quantities.

toothrife *adj* palatable.

toothsome *adj* **1** easily chewed. **2** having a sweet tooth.

toothy *adj* **1** having many or large teeth. **2** given to biting. **3** belonging to a tooth. **4** crabbed. **5** sarcastic. **6** hungry.

tootie[1], **tooty** *n* **1** a drunkard. **2** a dram.

tootie[2] *same as* **toutie**[1].

tootin *n* a reproachful term for a woman.

tootin' *v* tippling from a bottle at short intervals.

tooting horn *n* an ox horn for blowing.

tooting trumpet *n* a pitch pipe.

tootle[1] *v* **1** to chirp. **2** to play on a horn or other wind instrument. **3** to mutter. **4** to talk foolishly. **5** to gossip.—*n* silly gossip. **6** a silly, gossiping person.

tootle[2] *v* **1** to drink. **2** to tipple.

tootlie *adj* unsteady.

toot-moot *n* **1** a low, muttered conversation. **2** the muttering at the beginning of a quarrel. **3** a dispute.—*v* **1** to whisper. **2** to converse in low, muttering tones.—*adv* in a whisper.

toot-mootre *n* talk of the nature of hints, insinuations, etc.

toot-mouit *adj* having a projecting jaw.

toot net *n* a large fishing net anchored.

tootoroo *same as* **tooteroo**[2].

toots *int* tuts! tush!

toot's-man *n* one who warns by a cry to haul the toot net (qv).

tootter[1] *same as* **tooter**.

tootter[2] *v* to work in a weak, trifling way.—*n* **1** ruin. **2** a weak and trifling worker.

toot-too'in' *n* the blowing of a horn.

tooty *same as* **tootie**[1].

toozle *same as* **touzle**.

toozy *same as* **tousy**.

toozy-looking *adj* shaggy-looking.

top *v* to set aside by a superior authority, real or pretended.

tope, top *v* to oppose, contend.—*n* opposition.

topp *adj* excellent.

toppen *v* to surpass.

topperer *n* a term of admiration, a topper.

toppin same as **tappin**.

topping adj **1** leading, being at the head of affairs. **2** managing. **3** prominent.

to-put v **1** to affix. **2** to set or put one to work.—n **1** anything needlessly or incongruously added. **2** a fictitious addition.

to-putter n **1** one who holds another to work. **2** a taskmaster.

toque n a cushion worn on the forepart of the head, over which a woman's hair was combed.

tor[1], **tore**[1] same as **torr**[1].

tor[2] same as **tore**[2].

torchel v **1** to pine away. **2** to die. **3** to relapse into disease. **4** to draw back from a design or purpose.

tore[1] same as **tor**.

tore[2], **tor** n **1** the pommel of a saddle. **2** the knob at the corner of a cradle.

torfel, torfle v **1** to pine away. **2** to decline in health. **3** to relapse into disease or illness. **4** to toss about. **5** to draw back from a design or undertaking.—n **1** the state of being unwell. **2** declining health.

torie n the grub of the daddy-longlegs, an insect that consumes germinating grain.—v to be eaten by the torie.

torie-eat v (of the torie (qv)) to eat springing grain.

torie-eaten adj **1** (of land) poor, moorish soil, exhausted by cropping, very bare and bearing only scattered tufts of sheep's fescue. **2** eaten by the torie (qv).

torie worm n **1** the hairy caterpillar. **2** the grubworm, the torie (qv).

tork v to torture or pain by continuous puncturing, pinching, nipping or scratching.

torment n a severe pain.

tormentatious adj troublesome.

tormentors n an instrument for toasting bannocks, oatcakes, etc.

tornbelly n a herring having its belly torn open.

torn-doun adj reduced in circumstances.

torne n a tower.

torpit n turpentine.

torque same as **tork**.

torr[1] n **1** a high rock. **2** a hill. **3** wet, rocky land.

torr same as **tore**[2].

torran, torrie int a call to a bull.

torrie[1] n peas roasted in the sheaf.

torrie[2] same as **torie**.

torry n a lugsail boat.

tort adj taut.

torwooddie n an iron draught chain for a harrow.

tory[1] same as **torie**.

tory[2] n **1** a term of contempt and dislike, applied to a child or grown person. **2** a disreputable or deceitful person. **3** a tyrannical person. **4** a term of endearment for a child.

tosh[1], **tosch** adj **1** neat, trim, tidy. **2** tight. **3** comfortable. **4** happy. **5** familiar, friendly.—n a small, neat, tidy person or thing.—v **1** to tidy. **2** to touch up, smarten.—adv **1** neatly. **2** tightly. **3** smoothly.

tosh[2] same as **toosh**[2].

tosheoderoch same as **tocherodarach**.

toshings n additions to a person's means and comfort.

toshly adv neatly, snugly.

toshoch n **1** a comfortable-looking young person. **2** a neat, tidy-looking girl.

toshod, toschod n a small, trim person or thing.

tosht up adj very tidily or finely dressed.

toshy adj neat, tidy.

tosie[1] adj **1** tipsy. **2** slightly intoxicated. **3** intoxicating. **4** cosy, snug. **5** cheerful, pleasant.—n **1** a cheerful glow on the face. **2** a fire.

tosie[2] n the mark at which curling stones are aimed.

tosie-mosie adj slightly intoxicated.

tosily adv costly, snugly.

tosiness n cosiness, snugness, warmth.

tosk n the torsk.

toss[1] v **1** to toss off. **2** to discuss, debate.

toss[2] v to toast, drink to the health of.—n **1** a toast. **2** a beauty. **3** a belle frequently toasted.

toasie same as **tosie**[1].

tossil n a tassel.

tossle same as **touzle**.

tost v **1** to tease. **2** to vex. **3** to toss.

tostit adj **1** severely afflicted. **2** troubled with difficulties and opposition. **3** tossed.

tot[1] n **1** anything very small. **2** a small child. **3** a dram. **4** a term of endearment for a child.

tot[2] v **1** to move with short or feeble steps, like a child or infirm person. **2** to toddle. **3** to totter.

tot[3] n the total, the sum.

total adj teetotal.

totaller n a teetotaller.

totch v **1** to toss about. **2** to rock a cradle with the foot. **3** to move with short, quick steps.—n a sudden jerk.

tote[1], **tote**[2] same as **tot**[2], **tot**[3].

tothe, toth same as **taith**.

to the fore adj **1** still remaining. **2** coming to the front.

toth ~, tothed fold n an enclosure in a field for cattle, etc, to manure land. See **taith**.

tother[1] same as **tither**.

tother[2], **tothir** n **1** rough handling. **2** putting into disorder.—v **1** to throw into disorder. **2** to handle roughly. **3** to dash.

tott same as **tot**[1].

tottery adj changeable, fickle.

tottie[1] v **1** to move with short steps. **2** to cause to move, drive.

tottie[2] n a term of endearment for a little child.

tottie[3] adj **1** snug. **2** warm.

tottin adj walking with short steps, tottering.

tottle[1] v **1** to walk feebly or with short steps. **2** to toddle. **3** to totter. **4** (of a stream) to purl. **5** to boil, simmer. **6** to make a noise in boiling.—n **1** a little, toddling child. **2** the noise made by boiling liquid.

tottle[2] adj warm, snug.

tot-totterin adj tottering for a while.

tottum[1], **tottum**[2] same as **totum**[1], **totum**[2].

totty[1] adj small, wee.

totty[2] adj **1** shaky. **2** dizzy.

totum[1] n **1** a term of endearment for a little child or one beginning to walk. **2** a neat, little or undersized person or animal.

totum[2] n **1** a teetotum. **2** the game of teetotum.

toty adj small, puny, tiny.

toubooth same as **tolbooth**.

touch v **1** to hurt. **2** to punish. **3** to equal. **4** to come up to. **5** to play upon the fiddle. **6** to preach with vigour. **7** (with up) to animadvert on one. **8** (with with) to meddle with.—n **1** an attack of illness. **2** touchwood, tinder. **3** a very small portion of time. **4** a sensible impression. **5** a feeling of interest.

touchbell n the earwig.

touched adj slightly intoxicated.

touchet, touchit same as **teuchit**.

touchie n a very short space of time.

touch-spale n the earwig.

touck same as **took**[3].

toudie n a hen that has never laid eggs. See **how-towdie**.

tough same as **teuch**[2].

touk[1] n an embankment to hinder water from washing away the soil.—v **1** to shorten. **2** to eat greedily.

touk[2] same as **took**[2].

toulzie same as **tuilyie**.

toum[1] same as **taum**[1].

toum[2] same as **toom**[1].

touman, toumon same as **towmond**.

toums same as **tomes**.

toun same as **toon**.

tounit n **1** knitting. **2** the manufacturing of wool.

toup same as **tawpie**.

toupee n a topknot.

toupican *same as* **toopick**.

tour[1] *n* **1** one's way, one's steps. **2** an expedition.—*v* to speed.

tour[2] *n* **1** a turn. **2** alternation.

tour[3] *same as* **toor**[2].

tour[4] *same as* **toor**[3].

tour[5], **toure** *same as* **turr**.

tourbillion *n* a whirlwind.

toure-battle *n* a boys' fight with bits of peat.

tourin ppl towering.

tourkin calf, ~ lamb *n* a calf or lamb covered with the skin of another for suckling purposes. *See* **tulchan**.

tourock *same as* **toorock**.

touse *v* **1** to dishevel, ruffle up. **2** to pull about roughly. **3** to thrash.—*n* an untidy or shaggy head of hair.

tousel, tousle *same as* **touzle**.

touselled-looking *adj* dishevelled.

toush *same as* **toosh**[1].

tousily *adv* roughly.

tousle *same as* **touzle**.

touss, tousse *same as* **touzle**.

toussie *same as* **tousy**.

toustie *adj* testy, irritable.

tousy *adj* **1** disordered, dishevelled. **2** rough, shaggy. **3** unkempt. **4** rollicking. **5** (*of the weather*) rough. **6** (*of a fight*) rough, stubborn. **7** (*of food*) roughly abundant.—*adv* rudely, roughly.

tousy-faced *adj* hairy-faced.

tousy-headed *adj* having a shaggy head.

tousy-like *adj* **1** ruffled, shaggy. **2** rough-looking.

tousy-pousie *adj* rough, shaggy.

tousy-tailed *adj* having a shaggy tail.

tousy tea *n* a high tea (qv).

tout[1] *n* **1** a slight and passing attack of illness. **2** a pet, fit of temper.—*v* **1** to attack suddenly. **2** to have a sudden illness. **3** to have a fit of temper. **4** to irritate. **5** to twit.

tout[2] *v* **1** to toss about. **2** to disorder. **3** to disorder by quibbling or litigation. **4** to disturb, harm.

tout[3], **toot**[4] *same as* **toot**[1], **toot**[3].

touter[1] *n* a friendly glass.

touter[2] *n* one who banters, teases and annoys.

touther *same as* **towther**.

toutherie *adj* **1** disordered. **2** confused, slovenly.

toutie[1] *adj* irritable.—*n* **1** a person easily vexed. **2** an irritable person. **3** one subject to frequent ailments.

toutie[2], **touttie** *adj* throwing into disorder.

toutie[3] *n* a humorous term for a child.

toutit *adj* **1** disordered. **2** blown about by the wind.

toutle[1] *v* to put clothes in disorder.

toutle[2] *v* to tipple.

tout-mout *same as* **toot-moot**.

toutom *same as* **totum**[2].

touts *int* tuts!

touttie *same as* **toutie**[2].

touttie-wind *n* a boisterous wind.

touze *same as* **touse**.

touzle, touzzle *v* **1** to ruffle, dishevel, disarrange. **2** to toss hay, etc. **3** to embrace roughly. **4** to grapple indecorously with a woman. **5** to romp rudely. **6** to wrestle.—*n* **1** a struggle, tussle. **2** a shake. **3** a rough dalliance. **4** a troublesome effort.

touzlie *same as* **tousy**.

touzy *same as* **tousy**.

tove[1] *v* **1** to talk familiarly, cheerfully and at length. **2** to chat. **3** to sound cheerfully. **4** to flaunt about with girls. **5** to keep company, as lovers. **6** to flatter. **7** to praise.—*n* a chat, a friendly gossip.

tove[2] *v* **1** to cause to swell. **2** to rise in a mass. **3** to make a dense smoke. **4** to smell strongly in burning. **5** to fly back. **6** to return.

tovie *adj* **1** babbling. **2** talking incoherently. **3** garrulous in liquor. **4** fuddled. **5** pleasant, warm, comfortable.

tovize *v* **1** to flatter. **2** to cajole.

tow[1] *n* **1** flax or hemp in a prepared state. **2** what specially occupies one's attention.

tow[2] *v* (*with* **down**) to let one down with a rope.—*n* **1** a clock chain. **2** a rope. **3** a bellrope. **4** a ship's cable. **5** a coil of hair. **6** a hangman's halter. **7** a line for deep-sea fishing.

tow[3] *v* **1** to give way. **2** to fail. **3** to perish, die.

towairds *prep* towards.

towal *n* a horseleech.

tow-band-tether *n* a hempen tether.

towbeeth, towbuith *same as* **tolbooth**.

tow card *n* a card for carding flax.

towdent *adj* **1** tidied, tidy. **2** *in phr* **ill-towdent hair** unkempt locks.

towder *same as* **towther**.

towdie *n* **1** a hen that never laid. **2** a young unmarried woman. *See* **how-towdie**.

towdy[1], **towdy**[2] *same as* **taudy**[1], **taudy**[2].

towen, towin *v* **1** to maul. **2** to subdue by severity. **3** to tame. **4** to tire.

tower *same as* **toor**[2].

towerick *n* **1** a summit. **2** anything elevated.

towey-headit *adj* flaxen-haired.

towfad *n* an opprobrious term.

tow-gravat *n* a hangman's halter.

tow gun *n* a popgun, for which pellets of pob or refuse flax are used.

towie *n* a small coil or twist of hair.

towin *same as* **towen**.

towk[1] *n* **1** a bustle. **2** a set-to.

towk[2] *same as* **took**[2].

towk[3] *v* **1** to tuck. **2** to shorten.—*n* a tuck.

towl *n* **1** a toll. **2** a turnpike. **3** a tollman.—*v* to collect tolls.

towlie *same as* **tollie**.

towling *same as* **tolling**.

towm *same as* **taum**[1].

towman *n* the man who holds the halyards and controls the sail of a boat.

towmond, towmont, towmonth *n* a twelve-month, year.

towmondall, towmontill, towmontell *n* **1** a yearling cow or colt. **2** a yearling.

town[1] *n* a farmstead.

town[2] *same as* **towen**.

townin' *n* a drubbing.

township *n* **1** a farm occupied by two or more farmers of the same hamlet, in common or separately. **2** in the Highlands and islands a small crofting community.

tow-plucker *n* a heckler of flax.

tow-raip *n* a hempen rope or halter.

towre *n* a turn in rotation.

towrickie *same as* **towerick**.

tow-rock *n* the flax distaff.

tow-row *n* **1** a hubbub. **2** a romp.

towse *same as* **touzle**.

towsing *n* a ruffling.

towsie *same as* **touzle**.

towsy *same as* **tousy**.

towt[1], **towt**[2] *same as* **tout**[1], **tout**[2].

tow-tap *n* the portion of flax in the distaff.

towther *n* **1** a state of disorder. **2** a tussle. **3** an untidy, slovenly person. **4** a tousling.—*v* to put in disorder.

towzie, towzy *same as* **tousy**.

towzle *same as* **touzle**.

toxie, toxy *adj* tipsy.

toxified *adj* tipsy.

toy *n* a fancy, a conceit.

toy, toy-mutch *n* a woman's linen or woollen cap, with a deep fall hanging down on the shoulders.

toyt *n* a freshwater mussel found in the River Tay.

toyt, toyte *same as* **toit**.

tozee *same as* **tosie**[2].

tozie, tozy *same as* **tosie**[1].

tozy-mozy *adj* slightly tipsy.

traap *n* a slut.

traapach *adj* slattern.

traboond *n* **1** a rebound. **2** a blow removing out of its place. **3** the thing struck.

trabuck *same as* **trebuck**.

trace[1] *v* **1** to follow up. **2** to obey. **3** to search by travel.

trace[2] *n* a trestle for scaffolding.

trace[3] *n* **1** a trice. **2** a short, sudden movement.

traced *adj* **1** laced. **2** bound with gold lace.

tracer *n* an extra horse placed before one in the shafts.

trachle, trachel *v* **1** to draggle. **2** to trail. **3** to drag one's feet, trudge. **4** to spoil through carelessness or slovenliness. **5** to drudge. **6** to overtoil. **7** to burden. **8** to fatigue. **9** to trouble. **10** to hinder. **11** to injure corn or grass by treading on it.—*n* **1** a long, tiring exertion. **2** drudgery. **3** struggle, toil. **4** trouble. **5** a trudge, tramp. **6** a drag, burden, hindrance. **7** a sloven. **8** an incompetent person.

trachler *n* **1** one who grows weary in walking. **2** one who drags himself or trails along.

trachlie *adj* **1** dirty, slovenly, wet. **2** apt to entangle. **3** fatiguing, exhausting. **4** drudging. **5** burdensome.

track[1] *v* **1** (*of tea*) to draw, to infuse. **2** to train an animal to go in traces or harness.—*n* **1** a feature, lineament. **2** an ugly or unusual spectacle, oddity. **3** any person or thing presenting a remarkable appearance. **4** (*used of an untidy person*) a sight. **5** an earthenware teapot.

track[2] *n* **1** a tract. **2** a tractate.

track[3] *same as* **troke**.

track[4] *v* to search.

track[5] *n* **1** a period, spell. **2** course of time. **3** a tract.

track-boat *n* a canal boat drawn by horses.

tracker *same as* **tracter**.

trackie *n* an earthenware teapot.

trackie-pottie *n* a trackie (qv).

trackle *same as* **trachle**.

track pot *n* a trackie (qv).

track pot-ware *n* earthenware teapots, cups, saucers, etc.

tract *n* **1** a track. **2** a path.

tractable *adj* **1** (*used of land*) cultivable, in good order. **2** properly treated.

tracter *n* a funnel for pouring liquids into bottles, casks, etc.

trade *n* **1** fuss, ado. **2** material, stuff. **3** (*in pl*) bodies of craftsmen in burghs.

trades lad *n* a journeyman, or an apprentice to a tradesman.

tradesman *n* an artisan, handicraftsman.

trading-body *n* a trader, merchant.

tradition *n* the delivery of goods to a customer.

trad-waddie *same as* **tread-widdie**.

trae *same as* **thraw**[3].

traeddit *v* trod.

traesh *same as* **treesh**.

traese *same as* **trace**[2].

traeve *same as* **thrave**[1].

trafeck, trafeque *n* **1** intercourse, communication. **2** dealing. **3** stir.—*v* (*used of bees*) to be busy searching flowers.

traffical *adj* with much traffic.

traffick, traffeck, traffike, traffique *n* **1** discussion. **2** intercourse, communication. **2** familiarity. **3** small things, light, useless articles.—*v* **1** to have dealings with. **2** to hold familiar intercourse. **3** to conspire secretly with a person.

trafficker, traffiquer *n* **1** one who has dealings or intercourse. **2** a trader. **3** a secret agent.

trafike *same as* **traffick**.

trag *n* **1** trash, rubbish. **2** dregs. **3** anything useless or worthless. **4** a low, mean person. **5** something unpleasant to handle.

tragle *v* to bemire, wet.

tragullion *n* **1** an assortment, a collection. **2** a company of not very respectable persons.

traich *same as* **traik**.

traichle *adj* slimy, ropy.

traichin *adj* **1** of sickly constitution. **2** lazy, dirty, disgusting.

traicle[1] *n* an idler, gadabout.

traicle[2] *n* treacle.

traik *v* **1** to wander idly to and fro. **2** to stroll, saunter. **3** to gad about. **4** to wander. **5** to use circumlocution. **6** to lose oneself. **7** (*used of poultry*) to stray. **8** to follow lazily. **9** to dangle after. **10** to court. **11** to walk with difficulty. **12** to trudge. **13** to track, trace. **14** to waste away. **15** to decline in health. **16** to draw out any sticky, ropy substance. **17** to nurse over-daintily.—*n* **1** idle lounging. **2** a stroll. **3** wandering to and fro aimlessly. **4** a long, tiring tramp. **5** difficult walking. **6** weakness, declining health. **7** weariness. **8** loss, disaster, bad fortune. **9** the drawing out of any viscous substance, dirty, slovenly working. **10** the working in liquid or semiliquid material. **11** too dainty nursing. **12** a dirty, slovenly person. **13** an illness. **14** a weakly person. **15** the loss of sheep by death from whatever cause. **16** the flesh of sheep that have died from disease or accident. **17** the worst portion of a flock of sheep.—*adj* **1** weak. **2** in a declining state. **3** languid,.

traikie *adj* **1** slimy, ropy. **2** in poor health. **3** delicate-looking. **4** drooping.

traikieness *n* leanness.

traikin *adj* **1** straggling, having a sickly constitution. **2** lazy, dirty, disgusting.

traikit *adj* **1** weary, fatigued. **2** consumptive-looking. **3** in poor circumstances. **4** (*used of birds*) wet, drooping, having dirty, disordered feathers. **5** draggled, disordered in dress.

traikit-like *adj* **1** draggled and tired from trudging or ranging about. **2** (*used of birds*) having wet, dirty, disordered feathers.

traikit tyke *n* a tired or lounging dog.

traikle[1] *n* treacle.

traikle[2] *n* **1** an idler, loungir. **2** a gadabout.

trail[1] *n* **1** a trudge. **2** a long, tedious walk. **3** a lazy, dirty person. **4** a sloven. **5** a well-worn or shabby article of clothing. **6** a rag.—*v* **1** to drag forcibly, to haul along. **2** to walk slowly, lazily, in a slovenly fashion. **3** to loiter, saunter idly. **4** to gad about. **5** to drag one's feet from weariness.

trail[2] *n* **1** a part, portion. **2** a quantity.

trailach, trailoch *v* **1** to draw. **2** to go about in a lazy, slovenly fashion. **3** to work in a slovenly fashion. **4** to over-nurse in a slovenly or disgusting fashion.—*n* **1** a long, dirty piece of rope, dress, etc. **2** idle wandering to and fro. **3** dirty, lazy working. **4** one of slovenly habits. **5** a wearer of dirty or shabby clothes. **6** a person given to idle wandering. **7** a gossip.—*adj* lazy, slovenly.

trailachin' *adj* **1** slovenly. **2** always drudging.

trail cart *n* a box made with shafts like a carriage, but without wheels, mounted on a mass of brushwood.

trailer *n* (*in fly-fishing*) the hook at the end of the line.

trail hunt *n* a dog race in which dogs follow a trail dragged over the ground by hand.

trailing *adj* slovenly, slatternly, untidy.

traily, traillie *n* **1** a person who trails about in shabby clothes. **2** one who wanders idly gossiping here and there.

train *n* **1** a rope used for drawing harrows, etc. **2** a small cone of moistened gunpowder, serving to prime a toy gun.—*v* to tamper with, work upon, draw on.

traishur *v* to go about in a lazy, slovenly manner. —*n* **1** a dull, stupid person. **2** a big, ugly, or old and lean animal.

traissle, traissel *v* to tread or trample down.

traist *n* trust.

traivel *same as* **travel**[2].

traivellin' man *n* a tramp, a vagrant.

traiviss *same as* **traverse**.

trake *same as* **traik**.

trallop *same as* **trollop**.

tram *n* **1** a beam. **2** a bar. **3** a shaft of a barrow, cart, carriage, etc. **4** a prop, pillar. **5** a supporter. **6** a limb. **7** a leg. **8** a tall, ungainly person, one with long limbs.

tramble net *n* a trammel net.

tramless *adj* without shafts.

trammals *n* luggage used in travelling.

tramp *v* **1** to wash blankets in soap suds by tramping on them in a tub. **2** to trudge. **3** to dance clumsily, or heavily, or vigorously. **4** to catch flounders by stamping with bare feet on the sand until they rise.—*n* **1** a stamp with the feet. **2** a trudge. **3** a mechanic travelling in search of work. **4** the part of the spade on which the foot rests in digging. **5** a plate of iron worn in the centre of a ditcher's boot in digging. **6** a perforated and slightly spiked piece of sheet iron on which a curler stands when playing a stone. **7** a piece of spiked iron fastened to a curler's boot by a leather strap to prevent him or her slipping during play.

tramp coll *n* a hayrick compressed by tramping.

tramped-pike *n* a tramp-coll (qv).

tramper *n* **1** a travelling hawker. **2** a tinker. **3** one who travels in search of work.

trampers *n* **1** feet. **2** heavy boots.

trampet *n* a tramp (qv) or crampet (qv) on a curler's boot.

trampilfeyst *adj* unmanageable.

tramping *adj* vagrant.

tramp pick *n* a narrow kind of spade or pick used for turning up very hard soils, with a projection for the foot to rest on.—*v* to use a tramp-pick.

tramsach *n* **1** a tall, ungainly person. **2** a large, lean, ugly horse or other animal.

trance, transe *n* **1** a passage within a house. **2** a lobby. **3** an entrance hall. **4** an alley, a close. **5** a passage, a crossing over. **6** a narrow space.

trance door *n* **1** a passage door. **2** the door leading to the kitchen.

trance window *n* a passage window.

trancing, transing *adj* (*used of a middle wall*) passing across a house from wall to wall.

trangam *n* **1** a trinket. **2** a toy.

trankie *n* a small hayrick.

tranklum *same as* **trantlum**.

transack, transeck *v* **1** to transact. **2** to dispose of, finish. **3** not to decide, but pass from a decision. —*n* **1** a transaction. **2** dealing. **3** trade.

transcrive *v* to transcribe.

transires *n* goods sent for exportation.

transirie *n* **1** a custom-house permit. **2** a transiré.

translate *v* (*an ecclesiastical term*) to transfer a minister from one charge to another.

transmew, transmue *v* to transmute, transform, change.

transmugrify *v* **1** to metamorphose. **2** to transform.

transpire *v* (*used of smoke*) to issue from a chimney.

transport *v* to transfer a minister from one charge to another.—*n* **1** a minister so transferred. **2** excitement, indignation.

transportable *adj* (*of a minister*) entitled to or capable of transference from one charge to another.

transportation *n* **1** transference from one ministerial charge to another. **2** the carrying of a corpse from house to grave.

transum *n* a transom.

transume *v* to copy, transcribe.

transum plait *n* an iron plate or bar for a transom.

transumpt *n* a copy.

trantalum *same as* **trantlum**.

trantle, trantel *n* **1** a trundle. **2** the sound made by trundling. **3** a deep rut made by a wheel.—*v* **1** to trundle. **2** to roll along. **3** to make a noise by rolling along.

trantle bole, ~ hole *n* a hole for the reception of odds and ends.

trantles *n* **1** trifling or superstitious ceremonies. **2** movables of little use or value. **3** odds and ends. **4** children's toys. **5** a workman's various tools.

trantlins *n* articles of little value.

trantlum, trantloom *n* **1** a useless or worthless article. **2** a trifle. **3** a trinket. **4** a toy. **5** (*in pl*) odds and ends. **6** gear. **7** old tools.

trap[1] *n* a movable flight of stairs up to a loft.

trap[2] *n* **1** a trap door. **2** a hatch. **3** any vehicle on springs.—*v* **1** (*in games*) to catch. **2** (*in finding things*) to seize and claim. **3** (*in school life*) to take another's place in a class by answering a question when he or she failed.

trap[3] *v* to deck.—*n* (*in pl*) personal belongings, baggage.

trapane *same as* **trepan**.

trap creel *n* **1** a wicker lobster trap. **2** a creel for keeping crabs alive.

trapes, trapez *v* **1** to trudge. **2** to walk untidily, as with a trailing dress. **3** to wander aimlessly. **4** to gad about.

traping, trappan *same as* **trapping**.

trapper *n* one who answers where another fails in school and takes his or her place.

trapping *n* **1** tape. **2** small wares. **3** trimmings. **4** frippery.

trapping lesson *n* a school lesson in which children gain or lose places in the class according to their answers.

trap-pit *n* a pit in which animals are caught.

trapse *v* to seize and claim an article found.

trash[1] *n* **1** low, disreputable people. **2** riffraff. **3** a worthless person. **4** a mischievous girl.

trash[2] *v* **1** to trudge wearily through wet and dirt. **2** to jade, to overheat or override a horse. **3** to maltreat.

trash[3] *v* **1** to thrash. **2** (*used of rain*) to dash, pour.—*n* a heavy fall.

trashery *n* trash, rubbish.

trash-like *adj* good-for-nothing.

trashtrie *n* **1** trashy food or drink. **2** pap, sops.

trashy *adj* **1** rainy. **2** very wet. **3** stormy.

trattle[1] *same as* **trottle**[3].

trattle[2], **trattil** *v* to prattle, chatter.—*n* (*in pl*) tattle, idle talk.

trattler, tratler *n* **1** a prattler. **2** a chatterer.

trauchle, traughle *same as* **trachle**.

trave *same as* **thrave**[1].

travel[1], **travail** *n* **1** exertion, work. **2** trouble.—*v* **1** to labour. **2** to work soil. **3** to fatigue.

travel[2] *v* **1** to walk, journey on foot. **2** to go about begging or peddling small wares. **3** to lead about a stallion.—*n* a journey on foot.

travelled *adj* **1** (*used of soil*) worked. **2** fatigued.

traveller *n* **1** a pedestrian. **2** a tramp. **3** a travelling beggar. **4** a travelling pedlar, a packman.

travellyie *same as* **trevally**.

traverse, travesee *n* **1** a journey across. **2** a reverse of fortune. **3** a partition between two stalls in a stable. **4** a stall in a stable. **5** a smith's shoeing shed or framework for shoeing horses. **6** a retired seat in a church or chapel, with a screen across. **7** a shop counter or desk.—*v* to fit up into stalls.

travish *v* **1** to sail backwards and forwards. **2** to carry in procession. **3** to trail.

trawlie *n* a ring through which the chain or rope passes between the two horses or oxen in a plough to prevent it from trailing on the ground.

tray *adj* stiff, stubborn.

treacle ale, ~ beer *n* a thin, light beer made with treacle.

treacle peerie *n* treacle ale (qv).

treacle piece *n* a piece of bread or oatcake spread with treacle.

treacle scone *n* a scone baked with treacle.

treacley *adj* **1** pleasing. **2** flattering.

treader *n* **1** a cock. **2** a male bird.

treadle *v* **1** to go frequently and with difficulty. **2** to tramp, trudge.

tread widdie, ~ wuddy *n* the iron hook and swivel connecting a swingletree with a plough or harrow.

treasonrie *n* treachery.

treat *v* **1** to entreat, urge. **2** urged.

treave *n* twenty-four sheaves of grain.

treb *n* a long earthen rampart.

treble *n* a particular dance tune.

trebuchet *n* a military engine for throwing stones.

trebuck *v* **1** to make a false move in play. **2** to catch one doing so. **3** to check him or her for doing so. —*n* **1** a slip or false move in play. **2** a check or trip in a game of skill.

treck[1] *same as* **traik**.

treck[2] *int* an expletive, as 'troth!'

treck[3] *same as* **track**[1].

treck[4] *same as* **traik**.

treckle *n* treacle.

treck pot *n* a trackie (qv).

tred *v* to tread.

tredden *v, adj* trodden.

tredder *same as* **treader**.

tred-widdie *same as* **tread-widdie**.

tree *n* **1** wood. **2** a staff, cudgel. **3** a stirring rod for porridge, etc. **4** a pole or bar of wood. **5** an axletree. **6** a swingletree. **7** a barrel. **8** an archery bow.

tree and trantel *n* a piece of wood going behind a horse's tail, used as a crupper to keep the horse from being tickled under the tail.

tree clout *n* a piece of wood formerly put on the heels of shoes.—*adj* having wooden heels.

tree-clout shoon *n* shoes with wooden heels.

tree creeper *n* the common Certhia or creeper.

tree goose *n* the barnacle goose.

treein *same as* **treen**[2].

tree ladle *n* a wooden ladle.

tree leg *n* a wooden leg.

tree-leggit *adj* having a wooden leg.

treen[1] *n* trees.

treen[2] *adj* wooden, made of wood.

treen mare *n* a wooden horse used as an instrument of military punishment.

tree plate *n* a wooden plate or trencher.

treeple[1] *adj* triple.

treeple[2] *same as* **tripple**.

treeplet *n* a triplet.

treesh, treesch *v* **1** to entreat in a kindly and flattering way. **2** to cajole. **3** to court. **4** to call to cattle.—*n* **1** enticement. **2** cajolery, flattery.—*int* a call to cattle.

treeshin *n* courting.

tree-speeler *n* the common Certhia or creeper.

treetle *v* **1** to trickle in drops or very small quantities. **2** to work at anything weakly and unskilfully.—*n* **1** a trickle. **2** a very small quantity of liquid.—*adv* in drops.

treevolle *same as* **trevally**.

trefold *n* **1** the trefoil. **2** the water trefoil.

tregallion, tregullion *n* **1** a collection. **2** a miscellaneous assortment. **3** a company not thought respectable.

treggs *int* 'troth!' used as an oath.

trein *same as* **treen**[2].

treissle *same as* **traissle**.

treit *same as* **treat**.

trek *same as* **traik**.

tremble *n* **1** a fit of trembling. **2** a tremor, shiver. **3** (*in pl*) ague. **4** palsy or ague in sheep.

trembling axies, ~ exies, ~ fevers *n* the ague.

trembling-ill *n* a disease of sheep, the leaping-ill (qv).

tremendious *adv* exceedingly.

tremmle, tremel *v* to tremble.

trencher *n* **1** one who trenches ground or drains land by making open drains. **2** a drainer.

trencher bread *n* bread not of the first quality.

trenching *adj* trenchant.

trenchman *n* a support for the head of one learning to swim.

trendle *same as* **trindle**.

trene *same as* **treen**[2].

trenk *same as* **trink**.

trenket *n* an iron heelpiece.

trenle *same as* **trindle**.

trepan *v* **1** to seduce. **2** to cheat, trick.—*n* **1** a trick. **3** a plot. **4** a scheme.

treple *same as* **treble**.

tres-ace *n* a catching game, played by six players generally.

tress, trest *n* **1** a frame of wood. **2** a trestle. **3** a beam. **4** the support of a table.

trestarig *n* a very strong spirit, thrice distilled from grain.

tret *v* **1** treated. **2** entreated.

treuless *adj* **1** faithless. **2** truthless, false. *See* **trew**.

trevally, trevaillie *n* **1** a disturbance. **2** a catastrophe. **3** a scolding. **4** a quarrelling.

trevallyie *n* a mean retinue or train.

trevis, trevesse, trevise *same as* **traverse**.

trew *same as* **trow**[8].

trewan[1] *n* a trowel.

trewan[2] *n* a truant. *See* **troo**.

trews *n* **1** trousers, especially tartan ones. **2** the short trousers worn under a kilt. **3** stockings and breeches all of a piece.

trewsers *n* trousers.

trewsman *n* a Highlander, a wearer of trews or the kilt.

treykle, triacle *n* treacle.

trial *n* **1** a difficulty. **2** a trouble. **3** drudgery. **4** affliction. **5** effort. **6** proof, evidence. **7** (*in pl*) examinations and discourses prescribed by presbyteries for licensing preachers and ordaining ministers.

tribble *same as* **trouble**.

tribe *n* a contemptuous designation for a set or crowd of people.

tricker *n* **1** a trigger. **2** a latch, spring. **3** a wooden leg. **4** a piece of spiked iron to fix on the ice for steadying a curler when he or she his playing a shot.

trickit, tricked *adj* tricky, wicked.

tricky *adj* mischievous, playful, waggish.

triddle *same as* **treadle**.

triffle *n* **1** a trifle. **2** a small sum.

trig *adj* **1** smart. **2** active. **3** quick, clever. **4** brisk, nimble. **5** neat, tidy, trim, spruce. **6** tight.—*v* **1** to tidy up. **2** to make neat. **3** to settle. **4** to dress smartly and finely. **5** to bedeck.

trigger *same as* **tricker**.

triggin *n* **1** finery. **2** decking out.

triggs *n* plough traces made of twisted strips of horse hide and dried.

triggy *adj* neat, orderly.

trigly *adv* **1** quickly, briskly. **2** neatly, smartly, sprucely.

trig-made *adj* neatly made.

trigness *n* **1** neatness. **2** orderliness.

trig up *v* to set in order, tidy up.

trig-up *n* a tidying up.

trikle *n* treacle.

trilapser *n* one who falls into the same sin thrice.

trill *n* treble.

trillichan *n* the oystercatcher.

trim[1] *v* **1** to beat, thrash, castigate. **2** to scold, chide.—*n* **1** temper, disposition, mood. **2** haste, speed.

trim[2] *n* a poor kind of ale.

trimle *v* to tremble.

trimmer *n* **1** anything of superior quality, fine. **2** pleasing to the eye. **3** a scold, a virago. **4** a loose woman.

trimmie *n* a disrespectful term applied to a young girl. **2** a name for the devil.

trimming *n* **1** a beating. **2** a scolding.

trimmle *same as* **tremble**.

trim-tram *n* a term expressing ridicule or contempt.

trincat *same as* **trinquet**.

trinch *v* to trench.

trindle *n* **1** a wheel. **2** the felloe of a wheel, a trundle. **3** the cradle of a millwheel. **4** a small wheel for a trundle bed. **5** a whirlwind.—*v* **1** to trundle, roll. **2** to move with a rolling gait. **3** to bowl along.

tring *n* **1** a series, a succession of things. **2** a string. *See* **string**[1].

tringal *n* **1** anything long and ugly. **2** a tall uncomely person.—*v* to walk in a loose, slovenly fashion.—*adj* with loose, slovenly gait.

tringum *n* **1** anything ugly and worthless. **2** a person of loose character.—*adj* worthless, loose.

trink, trinck *n* **1** a trench. **2** a narrow, open drain for the passage of water. **3** a narrow channel between rocks on a sea coast. **4** the bed of a river or stream. **5** the water flowing in a trink. **6** a rut. **7** (*used in flag quarries*) a long, narrow stone.—*v* to become filled with ruts.

trink-about *n* a trinket, gewgaw, ornament.

trinkar *n* one who does not pay his share of a tavern bill.

trinket[1] *n* **1** a trifle. **2** a small article of any kind.

trinket[2] *v* **1** to lie indirectly. **2** to correspond clandestinely with an opposite party. **3** to tamper with. **4** to have dealings with.

trinketing *n* clandestine correspondence with an opposite party.

trinkie *n* a narrow channel between rocks on the sea coast.—*adj* filled with ruts.

trinkit *adj* having trenches, ditches or drains.

trinkle[1] *v* **1** to trickle. **2** to fall slowly in drops or in a tiny stream. **3** to sprinkle.—*n* **1** a trickle. **2** a succession of drops, a drip. **3** the sound of trickling water.—*adv* drop by drop.

trinkle[2] *v* **1** to tingle. **2** to thrill.

trinklems *n* **1** trinkets, gewgaws. **2** knick-knacks. **3** odds and ends.

trinkum *n* **1** a trinket. **2** a knick-knack.

trinkum-trankums *n* **1** trinkets, gewgaws. **2** fallals.

trinle *same as* **trindle**.

trinnel[1] *n* the entrails of a calf.

trinnel[2] *same as* **trinkle**[1].

trinnie[1] *same as* **trindle**.

trinnie[2], **trinnel** *same as* **trinkle**[1].

trinquet *same as* **trinket**[2].

trintle[1] *same as* **trinkle**[1].

trintle[2] *same as* **trindle**.

trintle aff *v* to drop off or away.

trip *v* **1** to hurry. **2** to go off quickly.—*n* a short dance.

tripe *same as* **trype**.

tripes *n* **1** the entrails. **2** the stomach.

triping *n* coal brought to the bank of a mine before it is screened.

triple *same as* **tripple**.

triply *v* to make a rejoinder to a duply (qv).—*n* a reply to a duply or rejoinder.

tripple *v* **1** to dance, trip. **2** to beat time with the feet in dancing.

trip-trout *n* a game of shuttlecock in which a ball is used instead of a cork and feathers.

trist[1] *v* **1** to squeeze. **2** to thrust.

trist[2], **triste** *same as* **tryst**[2].

trittle-trattles, tritle-tranties *n* **1** children's toys. **2** trifles. *See* **trantle**.

triv *v* **1** to push. **2** to drive.

trivage *same as* **traverse**.

trixie *n* the tune 'Hey trix, trim go trix, under the greenwood tree', an old popular melody.

troak *same as* **troke**.

troaker *same as* **troker**.

troap[1] *n* a boys' game.

troch[2] *n* **1** an extraordinary fellow. **2** a rough customer. **3** anything of little value.

troch[3] *same as* **through-stane**[1].

troch[4] *same as* **trough**.

trock *same as* **troke**.

trocker *same as* **troker**.

trockery *n* odds and ends.

trockie a trackie (qv).

trod[1] *n* **1** a tread. **2** a footstep. **3** a track, pursuit.—*v* to trace, track by the footsteps.

trod[2] *v* **1** to trot. **2** to half-run and half-walk.

troddle, trodle *v* **1** to toddle. **2** to walk with short steps like a little child. **3** to go. **4** to slip. **5** to tumble. **6** (*used of a stream*) to purl. **7** to glide gently.

trodge *v* **1** to trudge. **2** to saunter.

trod-widdie *same as* **tread-widdie**.

trogg, trog *same as* **troke**.

trogger *n* **1** a pedlar. **2** one who barters or exchanges. **3** a collector of old clothes. **4** an Irish vagrant. **5** a vagrant.

troggin *n* pedlars' wares.

trogs *int* 'troth!' as an oath.

trogue *n* a young horse.

troistry *n* **1** the entrails of a beast. **2** offal.

troitle *v* to gossip.

trojan *n* **1** a big, overgrown person, a giant. **2** an active, sturdy person.

troke, trok *v* **1** to barter, exchange. **2** to deal, bargain, in a small way. **3** to have dealings with. **4** (*used of an underhand or improper character*) to associate, be on friendly terms with. **5** (*with* **in**) to tamper with. **6** to work for money. **7** to potter. **8** to be busy about trifles. **9** to spread abroad news.—*n* **1** barter. **2** a bargain. **3** goods. **4** small articles or wares. **5** lumber. **6** trash. **7** dealings, business. **8** negotiation. **9** intercourse, communication. **10** illicit intercourse. **11** fondling, dalliance, toying. **12** a matter of business. **13** an odd job. **14** an errand.

troker *n* **1** one who exchanges goods. **2** a dealer, pedlar. **3** a low trader. **4** a secret agent.

trokery *n* **1** articles of small value. **2** a miscellaneous collection of odds and ends.

trokings *n* **1** dealings. **2** friendly terms.

trolie[1] *n* **1** any long, unshapely thing that trails on the ground. **2** a slovenly girl or woman.

trolie[2] *n* **1** any object that has length disproportionate to its breadth. **2** the dung of cows, horses or persons. **3** (*in pl*) entrails.

troll[1] *n* **1** a slovenly person. **2** a bull. **3** a long, unshapely thing trailing on the ground.—*v* **1** to walk, work or dress in a slovenly fashion. **2** to trail. **3** to carry about in a slovenly fashion.

troll[2] *same as* **trolie**[2].

trollbags, trolliebags *n* **1** the paunch of a slaughtered animal. **2** tripe.

trollop, trollope *v* **1** to hang in a wet or loose state. **2** to work in a dirty, slovenly fashion. **3** to walk in a slovenly way. **4** to slouch. **5** to lead a loose life.—*n* **1** a large, loose, hanging rag, a tatter. **2** a large, straggling mass of anything. **3** a dirty, idle sloven. **4** a woman of loose life.

trolloping *adj* slatternly, untidy.

trollops *n* a slattern, a dirty, idle, slovenly woman.

trollopy *adj* slovenly.

troliy[1], **trolly**[2] *same as* **trolie**[1], **trolie**[2].

trolollay *int* a term occurring in a rhyme used by children at Hogmanay.

troly *n* a ring through which the chain or rope passes between the two horses or oxen in a plough, preventing it from trailing on the ground.

tron *same as* **trone**.

tronach *n* the crupper used with a packsaddle, formed of a piece of wood and connected with the saddle by a cord at each end.

trone[1] *n* **1** a steelyard. **2** a weighing machine. **3** a market. **4** a marketplace. **5** a pillory. **6** the standard of weight used at the public steelyard.

trone[2] *n* a truant.—*v* to play truant.

trone[3] *n* a trowel.

troneman *same as* **tronman**.

troner *n* the person in charge of the trone (qv), the weighman.

tronie[1], **tronnie** *n* a truant.

tronie[2] *n* **1** a traditional rhyming saw. **2** anything often repeated. **3** a long story. **4** trifling conversation. **5** a darling.

tron kirk *n* a church near the trone (qv).

tron lord, trone lord *n* a sweep who was stationed at the trone (qv).

tronman *n* **1** a sweep. **2** a trone lord (qv).

tron-~, trone-weight *n* the standard weight used at the trone (qv).

troo[1], **troo**[2] *same as* **trow**[4], **trow**[8].
trood *n* wood for fences.
trooen *same as* **trone**[3].
trooie *n* a truant.
trooker *same as* **trucker**[2].
troolian *n* the common cuttlefish.
troon *same as* **trone**[3].
troop *n* a loose woman.
troos *same as* **trouss**.
troosh *same as* **treesh**.
trooshlach, trooshloch *n* **1** rubbish. **2** anything worthless.
trooshter *n* **1** a thing. **2** anything worthless.
troost *n* (*used in playing marbles*) a sort of lien (qv) that the winner has on the loser for his favourite marble or pitcher (qv) when it is the last to be lost.
troot *n* a trout.
trootie *n* **1** a small trout. **2** a fondling term for a child.
trootle *v* **1** to walk with quick, short steps. **2** to move slowly. **3** used by nurses of children beginning to walk.
trooy *int* a call to cattle.
troque *same as* **troke**.
trosk *n* a stupid fellow.
tross *same as* **trouss**.
trot *v* **1** (*used of a stream*) to flow briskly, to run with noise. **2** to play truant. **3** to tease jestingly. **4** to make sport of, or ridiculous.—*n* a raid or expedition by horsemen.
trot-cosie, ~-cozy *n* a woollen hap, covering the back of the neck, the shoulders and the breast, for keeping the throat warm.
troth *int* in truth! verily!—*n* truth.—*v* to betroth.
troth-plight, ~-plighted *adj* affianced, betrothed.
trottee *n* a person who is made sport of.
trotter *n* **1** one who makes sport of another. **2** a truant. **3** (*in pl*) a sheep's feet.
trotter board *n* the treadle of a spinning wheel.
trotter-speed *n* great celerity.
trottie[1] *n* a bad humour.
trottie[2] *n* a child who has learned to walk or run about the floor.
trottle[1], **trottel** *same as* **trattle**[2].
trottle[2] a small round pellet of sheep dung.
trottlick *n* a hard pellet of dung.
trou[1] *same as* **trow**[8].
trou[2] *n* a wretched hole of a lodging.
troublance *n* pain, trouble.
trouble *v* **1** to go to, attend. **2** to clutch, finger, like a dying person.—*n* **1** an ailment, complaint. **2** a fault or hitch in coal strata.
trouch *n* a trough.
trouff-gate *n* a right of way for carrying peats from a common or moss.
trough *n* **1** the wooden conduit conveying water to a millwheel. **2** a long wooden dish used in common by a family. **3** a vale, valley, the lower ground through which a river runs.
trough-stane *n* a stone trough.
trouk *n* a slight but teasing complaint.
troulins, troulis *adv* truly.
trounce[1] *v* **1** to hustle about. **2** to drive off.
trounce[2] *v* **1** to trudge. **2** to travel fast.
trouse *same as* **trews**.
troush *int* a call to cattle.
trousing *n* a combination of trousers and stockings in one.
trouss *v* **1** to tuck up. **2** to shorten.—*n* a tuck or fold sewn in a garment to shorten it.
trouster *n* a tuck to shorten a garment.
trout *v* to fish for trout.
trouter *n* a trout fisher.
trouth, troutha *same as* **troth**.
troutie burn *n* a trout streamlet.
troutsho *n* **1** a term of contempt. **2** a ludicrous term for a Highlander.—*int* an exclamation of contempt.
trove *n* a turf.

trow[1] *n* a double boat, used in salmon spearing.
trow[2] *n* a short fit of sickness.—*v* to have a short fit of sickness.
trow[3] *same as* **trough**.
trow[4] *v* to play truant.
trow[5] *n* **1** a fairy. **2** a goblin. **3** the devil.
trow[6] *v* **1** to troll. **2** to roll over. **3** to roll over and down. **4** to put in rotatory motion. **5** to cause to roll or spin. **6** to toss up a liquid with a spoon, etc. **7** to season a cask by rinsing it with wort before it is used. **8** to nurse carefully.—*n* **1** a continued tossing up of a liquid by a spoon, etc. **2** careful nursing.
trow[7] *int* a call to cattle.
trow[8] *v* **1** to feel sure. **2** to trust, believe. **3** to make one believe.
trowen, trowan *same as* **trewan**.
trower *n* a truant.
trowie *adj* sickly.
trowl *v* to draw gently upwards a line with hooks stretched across a stream and fastened to a rod on each side.
trowse *same as* **trouss**.
trowse, trows *same as* **trough**.
trowth *same as* **troth**.
troyt *n* an inactive person.
tru *same as* **trow**[8].
trua *same as* **trow**[4].
trual *n* a trowel.
truan *same as* **trewan**[1].
truant *v* to play truant.
truce[1] *v* **1** to keep quiet. **2** to hush up.
truce[2] *same as* **trouss**.
truck[1] *n* **1** odds and ends. **2** trash.—*v* **1** to barter. **2** to traffic.
truck[2] *same as* **track**[1].
trucker *n* **1** a term of contempt for one who has offended or is deceitful. **2** a waggish or tricky person.
truckery *n* **1** odds and ends. **2** miscellaneous articles. **3** crockery.
truckle *n* a truckle bed.
truckler *n* **1** an underhand person. **2** one who scamps his or her work.
truck-pot *n* a trackie (qv).
trudder *n* **1** lumber. **2** trumpery. **3** confusion.
trudge-back *n* a humpback.
trudget[1] *n* **1** a trick. **2** a mischievous prank.
trudget[2] *n* a paste of barley meal and water, used by tinkers to prevent a newly soldered vessel from leaking.
true[1], **true**[2] *same as* **trow**[4], **trow**[8].
true[3] *adj* (*used of ice*) perfectly smooth and level.
true-blue *n* **1** a rigid Presbyterian. **2** a person of integrity and steadiness.
trueline, trulines *adv* **1** truly. **2** indeed.—*n* truth.
true-love *n* **1** one whose love is pledged to another. **2** the herb Paris.
truey *same as* **trooy**.
truff[1] *n* **1** a turf. **2** a sod. **3** a peat.
truff[2] *v* to pilfer, steal.
truggs *n* **1** a lazy worker. **2** used as a nickname.
trugs *int* 'troth!' used as an oath.
trui *same as* **trooy**.
truiker *same as* **trucker**.
truint *same as* **trewan**[1].
truish[1] *same as* **treesh**.
truish[2] *same as* **trews**.
trukier *same as* **trucker**.
trulie *same as* **truly**.
trull *n* **1** a foolish or silly person. **2** a slattern.
trullion[1] *n* **1** a low, dirty fellow. **2** a foolish or silly person.
trullion[2] *n* a sort of crupper.
truly, trulie *adj* not false or fictitious.—*n* one's word of honour, used in mild oaths.—*int* an exclamation of surprise.
trum *n* a thread, a weaver's thrum.
trumf *same as* **trumph**[1].

trummle, trumle *v* to tremble.—*n* a tremor.
trump[1] *n* a jew's-harp.—*v* to play on the jew's-harp.
trump[2] *v* to deceive, cheat.
trump[3] *v* to go off in consequence of disgrace or necessity.
trump-about *n* a game at cards. *See* **trumph-about**.
trumper *n* 1 a deceiver. 2 a term of contempt.
trumph[1] *n* a trifle.
trumph[2], **trumf, trumph card** *n* a trump, trump card.
trumph-about *n in phr* to **play trumph-about** 1 to be on an equality or footing with. 2 to retaliate. 3 to do equal deeds of valour.
trumphery, trumphy *adj* trumpery.—*n* 1 rubbish. 2 a disreputable woman. 2 odds and ends.
trumphy *n* a stupid woman or girl. *See* **tumfie**.
trumpie *n* Richardson's skua.
trumpket *n* a spiral or turnpike stair.
trumplefeyst *n* a qualm or fit of sickness.
trumposie *adj* 1 guileful. 2 cross-tempered, perverse.
truncher *n* a wooden platter, a trencher.
trunchered *v, adj* borne in a trencher.
truncher-spear *n* a pointless spear.
trundle[1], **trunle** *same as* **trindle**.
trundle[2] *same as* **trinnel**[1].
trundle[3] *n* a small trunk.
truntle *same as* **trindle**.
truse *same as* **truce**[1].
trushel *n* 1 a sloven. 2 a person untidy in dress. 3 a confused mass of things lying carelessly together.
trushter *same as* **trooshter**.
truss *n* a large bundle.—*v* (*with* **up**) to pack up.
trust *v* to buy on credit or trust.—*n* 1 credit. 2 the charge or care of a turnpike. 3 the body formerly in charge of the district roads or turnpikes.
trustful *adj* trustworthy.
trustman *n* a creditor.
trustre *n* butter.
trust road *n* 1 a turnpike road. 2 one under the charge of the road trustees of a district.
trutchie *n* a fondling term for a cow.—*int* a call to a cow.
truthful *adj* 1 honest. 2 upright.
trutle *same as* **trootle**.
truyll *n* 1 a bull. 2 a sloven.
try *v* to taste.—*n* a trace of anything lost.
trying trotty *n* a trot to test the paces of a horse.
trykle *n* treacle.
trypal *n* a tall, lanky, ill-shaped person.—*v* to walk or work in a slovenly fashion.—*adj* 1 tall, ill-made. 2 slovenly.—*adv* in a slovenly manner.
trype *n* 1 a long, lanky person. 2 a term of contempt.—*v* to walk in a slovenly manner.—*adv* in a slovenly manner.
trysht *v* 1 to coax. 2 to wheedle. 3 to entice.—*n* 1 coaxing. 2 wheedling.
tryst, tryste *n* 1 an appointment to meet. 2 an appointed meeting. 3 a rendezvous. 4 a fixed cattle market or fair. 5 a meeting or concourse. 6 a merrymaking. 7 a betrothal, engagement to marry. 8 a journey taken by a company pledged to travel together. 9 trouble, annoyance. 10 difficulty. 11 affliction.—*v* 1 to engage to meet. 2 to agree to bargain. 3 to appoint a meeting. 4 to fix a time for, to appoint, arrange. 5 to bespeak, order in advance. 6 to betroth. 7 to engage to marry. 8 to fit in with, agree. 9 to deal with, come to terms. 10 to visit. 11 to afflict, try. 12 to invite, induce, entice. 13 to decoy.
tryst-breaker *n* one who breaks an appointment or engagement.
trysted-hour *n* an hour appointed for meeting.
tryster *n* one who convenes others, fixing the time and place of meeting.
tryster time *n* the courting time.
trysting *n* 1 a meeting by appointment. 2 an engagement to meet.
trysting place, ~ spot *n* the appointed place for meeting.
trysting style *n* a stile at which lovers meet.
trysting time *n* the time appointed for meeting.

trysting tree *n* a tree at which lovers meet by agreement.
tryst nicht *n* the night on which it is agreed to meet.
tryst-stane *n* a stone anciently erected, marking a rendezvous.
tryst-word *n* a password.
trytle *v* 1 to lag. 2 to act perfunctorily,.
tuachim *n* 1 a token. 2 *in phr* **their ain tuachim bett** an expression of a wish to escape evils that have befallen others.
tuag *same as* **toog**.
tuam *same as* **tew-iron**.
tub *n* a smuggler's keg containing four gallons.—*v* to line a fault in a pit with a wood or iron casing so that it will hold or keep back water.
tucht *n* vigour.
tuchtless *adj* 1 pithless, feeble. 2 inactive.
tuck[1], **tuck**[2] *same as* **took**[2], **took**[3].
tuck[3] *same as* **touk**[1].
tuck[4] *int* a call to poultry.
tuckie *int* a call to poultry.
tucky *adj* 1 mean, shabby. 2 contemptible.
tue[1] *same as* **tew**[1].
tue[2] *v* 1 to toil hard. 2 did struggle or toil.— *adj* fatigued.
tued *adj* 1 fatigued. 2 killed. 3 destroyed.
tufa *same as* **to-fall**.
tuff *n* a tuft of feathers or ribbons.
tuffle *v* 1 to ruffle. 2 to disorder by frequent handling.
tuffle-pack *n* a nickname for a pedlar.
tug *v* (*used of a door*) to prevent it from being opened from the inside by placing a stout sapling across the outside and fastening it to the latch.—*n* 1 raw hide, of which plough traces were formerly made. 2 a plough trace.
tug and rug *v* to haggle over a bargain.
tuggin *n* the beech or stone marten.
tuggle *v* 1 to pull by repeated jerks. 2 to contend about by pulling. 3 to handle roughly. 4 to toss backwards and forwards. 5 to fatigue with travelling or toil. 6 to overwork. 7 to keep under.—*n* a contention by pulling.
tught *same as* **tucht**.
tug-the-tow *n* a church bellman.
tug-whiting *n* a species of whiting, a whiting caught by handline.
tu-hu *same as* **too-hoo**.
tuick *same as* **took**[2].
tuik[1] *n* 1 a spell. 2 a turn.
tuik[2] *n* a cook.
tuik[3] *same as* **teuk**.
tuik[4] *v* took, did take.
tuilyie, tuilzie *n* 1 a quarrel, broil, fight. 2 a scrimmage, battle. 3 toil, labour, trouble. 4 a wrangle. 5 a wordy dispute.—*v* 1 to quarrel, scuffle, fight. 2 to wrangle, dispute. 3 to toil, work hard. 4 (*used of lovers*) to struggle or play together.
tuilyiement *n* toil, exertion, great struggle.
tuilyie-muilyie, ~-mulie *n* a tuilyie (qv).
tuilyisum *adj* quarrelsome.
tuilyie-wap *n* a boys' game, in which they clasp one another's hands, press together and end in falling all together in a mass.
tuim *same as* **toom**[1].
tuin *same as* **tune**.
tuir *v* tore.
tuish *n* a flabby infant.
tuive *v* 1 to swell or rise, as the effect of leaven. 2 to operate as yeast. 3 to fly back.
tuke *same as* **took**[3].
tukie *same as* **teuckie**.
tukie-hen *n* a hen.
tulcan *same as* **tulchan**.
tulch *n* a stout person of sulky, stubborn temper.
tulchan, tulchain, tulchin *n* 1 a calfskin stuffed with straw, used to induce a cow to give her milk. 2 a bag generally made of the skin of a calf. 3 a chubby, dwarfish child.
tulchan-bishop *n* the name given in the beginning of the

17th century to a bishop who accepted a bishopric with the condition of assigning the temporalities to a secular person.

tulchan-calf *n* a tulchan (qv).

tulie-mulie *n* a squabble.

tull *prep* till, until.

tullihoo *n* a disturbance.

tullisaul *same as* **tillie-soul**.

tulloch[1] *n* **1** a hillock. **2** a fortune, legacy. **3** a great deal of of money.

tulloch[2] *n* **1** a well-known Scotch reel. **2** its tune. **3** a noisy tune.

tullochgorum *n* a dance, the reel of Tulloch or 'Tulloch's rant'.

tully *same as* **tuilyie**.

tullyat *n* a contemptuous term for a bundle.

tulshie *same as* **tulch**.

tulshoch *n* **1** a carelessly arranged bundle. **2** a heap. **3** applied contemptuously to a person.

tuilyie, tulzie *same as* **tuilyie**.

tum *n* a cant name for a tumbler or glass.

tumble *v* **1** to toss. **2** to wander about.

tumble cart *n* **1** a box or sledge set on wooden wheels fixed on a wooden axle, which tumbled or turned together. **2** a tumbrel.

tumbler *n* **1** the porpoise. **2** a small, lightly made cart.

tumbler cart *n* a tumble cart (qv).

tumble yell *v* (*used of cows*) suddenly to cease to give milk.

tumbling-car *n* a tumble cart (qv).

tumbling-tam *n* a large, thick penny piece of copper.

tumbling-tam *n* a sieve for riddling coals.

tumbling trees *n* wheels in which wheel and axle formed one piece and revolved together.

tumbous, tumbus *n* **1** anything large. **2** a big, lazy person.—*adj* large and slovenly.

tume *same as* **toom**[1].

tumfie *n* a dull, stupid, slow, awkward person.—*adj* dull and stupid.

tumick, tummock *n* **1** a hillock, a small mound. **2** a small spot of elevated ground. **3** a grassy knoll. —*v* to build up to a high point dangerous to stability.

tummle, tumle *same as* **tumble**.

tummlers *n* part of a weaver's loom.

tummle the wullcat *v* to tumble heels over head.

tummock *same as* **tumick**.

tump *n* a small mound or hillock.

tumph, tumphy *same as* **tumfie**.

tumple *v* **1** to tumble. **2** to roll over.—*n* **1** a tumble. **2** a roll

tumult *n* the land attached to a cottar's house.

tumshie *n* a turnip.

tunag *n* a sort of shawl or short mantle worn by Highland women.

tunch *v* to push or jog with the elbow.—*n* a jog with the elbow.

tundle *n* tinder.

tundle box *n* a tinderbox.

tune *n* **1** the tone of a dialect. **2** mood, temper. **3** trim, order.—*v* **1** to hum or sing a tune. **2** (*with* up) to induce one to do something silly or wrong.

tune lines *n* popular rhymes sung to Psalm tunes instead of verses of the Psalms, in teaching children psalmody.

tun'er *n* tinder.

tunie *adj* of uncertain temper or changeable moods.

tnnnel *n* the throat.

tup, tupe *n* **1** a ram. **2** a foolish fellow. **3** an unpolished person.

tup-head *adj* (*used of a sword*) having the handle ending in a miniature figure of a ram's head.

tup-headed *adj* stupid, foolish.

tup-hog *n* a male ram, after weaning, until the first shearing.

tup-horn *n* a ram's horn, often used as a drinking cup or as a snuffbox.

tup-i'-the-wind *n in phr* **to rin like a blind tup-i-the-wind** said of a woman who haunts the company of men in her eagerness to be married.

tup-lamb *n* a male lamb.

tuppens *n* twopence.

tup yeld, ~ eild *n* a ewe that proves barren.

tuquheit *same as* **teuchit**.

turbot, turbet *n* the halibut.

turbot reeklins *n* strips of halibut dried in peat smoke.

turchie *adj* squat, short and thick.

turd *n* **1** excrement. **2** a lump of excrement. **3** a very contemptuous term for a person.

ture[1] *v* tore.

ture[2] *same as* **turr**.

turf farm *n* a farm of which the tenant pays so much to the proprietor for the peats he cuts.

turk *adj* angry, annoyed.—*n* **1** a savage, violent man. **2** a tiresome, mischievous child.

turkas, turkesse, turkis *n* **1** a pair of pincers. **2** a griping, oppressive man.

turken *v* **1** (*used of a young foal*) to harden. **2** to wax stout.

turkey *n* **1** a term of contempt. **2** a pouch, purse or pocketbook made of turkey leather.

turkey hide *n* a wallet, or a pocketbook, of turkey leather.

turkey Jock *n* a turkey cock.

turkie *n* a small bottle of straw.

turlie-whurlie *same as* **tirry-wirry**.

turmet, turmut *n* a turnip.

turmoil *v* **1** to work hard. **2** to toil.

turmour *n* turmeric.

turn[1] *n* **1** an attack of illness or faintness. **2** a surprise, a fright. **3** a piece of work, a job. **4** a service, help. **5** a trick. **6** an escapade, a whim. **7** an appearance before a court of law. **8** a check, rebuff. **9** disposition, manner. **10** style. **11** bent, liking. **12** time, season. **13** (*used of milk, etc*) the beginning to sour. **14** the change in the shortening or lengthening of the day. **15** a short stroll.

turn[2] *v* **1** to turn a corner. **2** to drive animals into a field, stable or other place. **3** to turn from one's purpose. **4** to change. **5** to grow, become. **6** (*used of milk*) to curdle.

turner[1] *n* an old copper coin worth two pennies Scots.

turner[2] *n* the man who holds and turns the instrument that twists straw ropes.

turner-aside *n* one who deviates from a particular course.

turnie *n* **1** a slight turn. **2** a short walk.

turnie box *n* a box turning on a pivot in a door, used for passing food into a cell or room.

turning *n* **1** a qualm. **2** nausea. **3** the calf of the leg. **4** the space between the ankle and the calf.

turning-lay, --loom *n* a turning lathe.

turning tree *n* a wooden stirring rod, a spurtle (qv).

turnip *n* a thick, clumsy, old-fashioned watch with cases.

turnip-heid *n* a blockhead.

turnip lantern *n* a hollowed turnip used to hold a candle at Hallowe'en, etc.

turnip oats *n* oats sown after turnips.

turnip shaw *n* a turnip top.

turnip-shawer *n* one who cuts off turnip tops.

turnip-singler *n* one who thins out young turnips by hand.

turnout *n* **1** a stroll. **2** a gathering of people. **2** an outfit.

turnpike, turnpike stair *n* a narrow, spiral, staircase.

turnscrew *n* a screwdriver.

turntail *n* a fugitive.

turr *n* a turf, sod, peat.—*v* **1** to remove the turf from wasteland. **2** to pare the surface of a moss before cutting peats.

turriefax day *n* never.

turris *n* turfs.

turrish *v* (*used of a cow*) to stand still, to be quiet. —*int* a call to a cow to stand still.

turry *same as* **turr**.

turrying spade *n* the spade with which the surface of a moss is pared off to get at the peat below.

turryvee *same as* **tirrivee**.

turry-wurry *same as* **tirry-wirry**.

turs *same as* **turse**.

tursable *adj* 1 portable. 2 capable of being packed up.

turse *v* 1 to truss. 2 to bundle or pack up. 3 to adjust one's clothes. 4 to take an infant from the cradle and dress it. 5 to send away. 6 to take oneself off. 7 to walk. 8 to set to work. 9 to carry partly and drag partly a burden with difficulty.—*n* 1 a truss, bundle. 2 a load. 3 the dressing of an infant. 4 labour or difficulty in carrying. 5 an amount, a quantity.

tursin *n* 1 a bundle. 2 baggage.

tursk *same as* **tusk**[1].

turskil *same as* **tuskar**.

turss *same as* **turse**.

turven *n* 1 peats. 2 sods.

turze *same as* **turse**.

tuse[1] *n* potato soup.

tuse[2] *int* an exclamation used to incite a bull.

tush[1] *n* 1 a tusk. 2 an animal's tooth.

tush[2] *v* to express displeasure.

tushalagy *n* the tussilago or coltsfoot.

tushkar *same as* **tuskar**.

tushloch[1], **tuschlich** *n* 1 a small bundle or truss. 2 a small cock of hay, straw, etc.

tushloch[2], **tuschlach** *n* a cake of cow dung so dry that it may be burned.

tushy-lucky-gowan *n* the coltsfoot.

tusk[1] *n* the torsk.

tusk[2] *v* to cut peat from above.

tusk[3] *v* 1 to change the contents of one bag into another. 2 to pluck or pull roughly, as a horse tears hay from a stack.

tuskar, tuskar spade *n* a peat spade.

tuskin *n* the act of turning a man upside-down so that money, etc, drops from his pockets.

tusk spade *n* a peat spade.

tusky *adj* having tusks.

tussle *v* 1 to embrace roughly. 2 to ruffle.

tussock *n* 1 a tuft of hair. 2 a tuft of heather or coarse grass.

tute *same as* **toot**[2].

tutie *n* 1 a woman tippler. 2 a child who drinks a great deal.

tutie-ta, tutie-tatie *same as* **tutti-taiti**.

tut-mute *same as* **toot-moot**.

tutor *n* the legal guardian of a boy under fourteen or a girl under twelve.

tutory *n* 1 tutorship, teaching. 2 guardianship. 3 tutelage. 4 the period of life under tutorship.

tuts *int* an exclamation of impatience.

tutti-taiti, ~-tatti *n* 1 the sound of a trumpet. 2 a child's name for a trumpet.—*int* 1 an exclamation of impatience. 2 *in phr* **hey tutti-tatti** *or* **taiti** the name of an old Scottish tune.

twa, twae *adj* 1 two. 2 few.—*n* 1 a pair. 2 a couple.

twa-beast tree *n* the swingletree of a two-horse plough.

twa-cord *adj* two-ply, having two strands.

'twad *pron* with *v* it would.

twae'rie *adj* 1 two or three. 2 few.

twa-faced *adj* hypocritical, insincere.

twa-facedness *n* 1 duplicity. 2 insincerity.

twa-fald, ~-fauld *adj* 1 twofold. 2 double. 3 bent double from age or infirmity.

twa-hand barrow *n* a barrow propelled by two persons.

twa-handit *adj* double.

twa-handit crack, twa-hand crack *n* 1 a familiar conversation between two persons. 2 a tête-à-tête.

twa-handit wark *n* work so badly done as to require to be done over again.

twa-horse farm *n* a farm requiring two horses to work it.

twa-horse tree *n* a swingletree stretcher of a plough that two horses draw.

twa-horse wark *n* a twa-horse farm (qv).

twal, twall *adj* twelve.

twal-at-e'en *n* midnight.

twal-cup *n* a midday cup of tea.

twal-hoors *n* 1 twelve o'clock. 2 noon. 3 lunch or liquor taken at noon.

twal-hoors' bell *n* 1 midnight. 2 a public clock striking at midnight.

twal-hundred *adj* (*used of linen*) fine, good.

twall *same as* **twal**.

twalmonth a year.

twa-lofted *adj* two-storeyed.

twal-o'-nicht *n* midnight.

twal-oxen plough *n* a heavy wooden plough that was drawn by twelve oxen.

twal-pence *n* one shilling sterling.

twal-pennies *n* 1 one shilling Scots. 2 one penny sterling.

twal-penny *adj* costing a shilling.

twal-pennyworth *n* the value of a penny sterling.

twal-pint hawkie *n* a cow yielding twelve pints at a milking.

twalsome *adj* consisting of twelve.—*n* a company of twelve.

twalt *adj* twelfth.

twang[1] *n* 1 a dialect accent, a brogue. 2 the vernacular speech of a district spoken by the natives.

twang[2] *n* a tinge, a spice, a little, a touch.

twang[3] *n* 1 a twinge. 2 a sudden, acute pain.

twa-part *n* two-thirds.

twa-pennies *n* a copper coin of the value of an English halfpenny.

twa-penny *same as* **tuppenny**.

twa-shear *n* a sheep that has been twice shorn.

twa-skippit *adj* (*of a man's cap*) having two peaks.

twasome, twaesum *n* a company or family of two, a couple, pair.—*adv* doubly.—*adj* 1 double, twofold. 2 performed by two persons.

twa-storeyed *adj* (*used of a chin*) double.

twa-three, twar-three *adj* 1 two or three. 2 few.

twaum *n* a pet, a temper.

tway *adj* two.

twa-year-auld *n* an animal two years old.

tweddle *v* to work cloth so that the woof seems to cross the warp vertically.

tweedie[1], **tweedle**[2] *same as* **twiddle**[1], **twiddle**[2].

tweedle-dee *n* 1 a sorry fiddler. 2 careless or indifferent singing.

tweedle-dee and tweedle-dum *v* to strum, play at random.

tweedle-dum-tweedle-dee *n* clumsy fiddling.

tweedlin' oot an' in *n* the swerving to right and left of a learner on a bicycle.

tweel[1] *adv and int* truly, indeed.

tweel[2] *v* 1 to twill. 2 to weave cloth diagonally.—*n* 1 twill. 2 the texture of literary composition.

twee-licht *n* twilight.

tweelie, tweelsie *same as* **tuilyie**.

tweelin *adj* pertaining to cloth that is tweeled. *See* **tweel**[2].

tweemay *int* a call to calves to come for their portion of milk.

'tween *prep* between.

tweesh, tweesht, tweest *prep* betwixt, between.

tweet *v* to whittle.

tweetins *n* chips cut from wood with a knife.

tweetle *n* a public assembly attended by young people who each paid a halfpenny for each dance they took part in.

tweeze *v* to pinch.

tweezelick, tweezelock *n* an implement for twisting ropes.

tweillie, twellie *same as* **tuilyie**.

twenty *adj* 1 numerous. 2 plentiful.

twet *n* a fatiguing spell of work.

tweyt *v* to whittle.

tweytins *same as* **tweetins**.

twice't *adv* twice.

twiddle[1] *v* 1 to twirl. 2 to twist. 3 to be busy about trifles. 4 to circumvent, cozen.—*n* (*used of the sea*) a succession of small waves caused by a light breeze.

twiddle[2] *v* **1** to play the bagpipes. **2** to play the fiddle carelessly or clumsily. **3** to sing.

twiddle-dee *n* useless ornaments on a woman's dress, frippery.

twiddle-twaddle *adj* trifling, idle.

twig[1] *v* **1** to glance at. **2** to see through a dodge, etc. —*n* a glance.

twig[2] *v* **1** to pull with a jerk or quickly. **2** to twitch. **3** to turn. **4** to wound the skin of a sheep in shearing.—*n* a quick pull.

twig[3] *v* to contain, hold in.

twig[4] *v* to put cross-ropes on the thatch of a house.

twig-rape *n* a cross-rope for the thatch of a house.

twilt *n* a quilt.—*v* to quilt.

twime *n* a couplet.

twin[1] *v* **1** to be a twin. **2** to resemble closely.

twin[2] *v* **1** to separate from one another. **2** to part, sever. **3** to divide. **4** to part with. **5** to deprive. **6** to extract by stratagem or importunity.

twin-bairns *n* twins.

twine[1] *v* to chastise.

twine[2] *n* **1** a tie, bond. **2** a contortion. **3** a twist, turn. **4** an intricate vicissitude.—*v* **1** to turn. **2** to wriggle. **3** to wind, meander. **4** to deviate. **5** to fasten, bind. **6** (*used of cheese*) to become leathery or tough. **7** to join. **8** to join in marriage. **9** to spin, weave. **10** to stretch out, prolong. **11** to represent, state or put a case.

twine[3] *n* **1** a short attack of illness. **2** a twinge of pain. **3** weakness resulting from disease.

twine[4] *v* **1** to put one to the utmost stretch of one's power in working. **2** to labour to the utmost of one's powers. **3** to toil. **4** to walk with great difficulty.—*n* **1** hard labour. **2** a difficult task.—*adv* with great difficulty.

twine[5] *same as* **twin**[2].

twiner *n* one who separates or teds hay by tossing.

twine-spinner *n* a rope-maker.

twingle *v* **1** to twine round. **2** to turn, twist.

twingle-twangle *v* to twang.

twink[1] *v* to twitch, jerk.

twink[2] *n* **1** a twinkling. **2** an instant.

twinkling *n* a tingling.

twinkling of a bedpost, ~ of a cat's tail *n* an instant.

twinter *n* **1** a beast two years old, especially a sheep. **2** a sheep from fifteen months up to four years old.

twinter-ewe *n* a ewe three times shorn.

twinty *adj* **1** twenty. **2** numerous.

twirk *n* a twitch.

twirl *n* **1** a grace note in singing. **2** a flourish of words. **3** a twinge.

twish *same as* **tweesh**.

twisle, twissle, twistle *v* **1** to twist. **2** to fold. **3** to wrench.—*n* **1** a shaking, tossing. **2** a grip. **3** a wrestling. **4** a twist.

twist *v* to twist yarn for weaving.—*n* **1** the peculiar screwing of the arms known as the frog's march. **2** a bond, a tie.

twister *n* **1** one who twists yarn for weaving. **2** an implement for twisting straw ropes.

twisting *n* thread.

twisty-thraws *n* colic.

twit[1] *n* (*used in weaving*) anything that entangles or gives resisting power to the thread.

twit[2] *v* to chirp, twitter.—*n* a bird's short, occasional chirp.

twitch[1] *v* **1** to draw tightly together. **2** to twinge.—*n* an instrument made of a stick and loop of cord for the nose of a restive horse.

twitch[2] *v* to touch.—*n* an instant of time, a touch.

twitching *n* a twinge.

twite *v* to whittle wood.

twitter[1] *v* **1** to tremble. **2** to quiver. **3** to flicker. **4** to sparkle. **5** (*used of lightning*) to gleam fitfully.—*n* a fluster, flurry.

twitter[2] *n* **1** the thin part of unevenly spun thread. **2** anything very thin or feeble.

twittery *adj* **1** spun very small. **2** slender. **3** without strength or substance.

twit-twitter *v* to twitter.

two *same as* **twa**.

twolt *same as* **twilt**.

two-part *n* two-thirds.

two-penny *same as* **tippenny**.

twosome *n* two together.

two-three *same as* **twa-three**.

twull *same as* **twall**.

twullsome *same as* **twalsome**.

twunty *adj* twenty.

twussle *same as* **twisle**.

twyne *same as* **twin**[2].

tyaave[1] *v* **1** to struggle, wrestle. **2** to strive, toil. **3** to struggle on. **4** to wade. **5** to labour under disease. —*n* **1** difficulty, struggle, pinch. **2** toil, toiling. **3** a hurry, stir.

tyaave[2] *v* **1** to tease out. **2** to ravel. **3** to caulk.

tyaave[3] *v* **1** to knead dough. **2** to work up anything sticky. **3** to roughen a thing by working it with the hands. **4** to meddle.

tyach *same as* **tyauch**.

tyakin *n* **1** a token. **2** *in phr* **their ain tyakin be't** an expression of a desire to escape evils that have befallen others.

tyal *n* **1** a latchet. **2** anything used for tying.

tyang *same as* **tang**[2].

tyangs *same as* **tangs**.

tyaou[1], **tyaou**[2] *same as* **tyaave**[1], **tyaave**[2].

tyauch *v* **1** to besmear with grease or viscous stuff. **2** to chew much. **3** to swallow reluctantly from disgust. **4** to be weak in health.—*n* a short fit of illness.—*int* an exclamation of disgust, impatience, etc.

tyauchie *adj* **1** greasy. **2** viscous. **3** of weak health.

tyave *same as* **tyaave**[2].

tyauve[1], **tyauve**[2], **tyauve**[3] *same as* **tyaave**[1], **tyaave**[2], **tyaave**[3].

tyawen-skate *same as* **taavin-skate**.

tyburn top *n* (*used of the hair*) a close crop.

tyce[1] *v* to move slowly and carefully.

tyce[2] *same as* **tice**.

tydie *same as* **tidy**.

tye[1] *same as* **tie**.

tye[2] *n* a pigtail.

Tyesday *n* Tuesday.

tyeuve *v* struggled. *See* **tyaave**[1].

tygie *same as* **taggie**.

tyke[1], **tyke**[2] *same as* **tike**[1], **tike**[2].

tyke and tryke *adv* higgledy-piggledy.

tyken, tykan *n* ticking.

tyken-weaver *n* a weaver of ticking.

tyle[1] *v* to cover.

tyle[2] *v* to close the door of a mason lodge.

tyler *n* the doorkeeper of a mason lodge.

tylie *same as* **tailyie**.

tymmer *n* timber.

tympany, tympany-gavel *same as* **timpany**.

tynd[1] *same as* **teind**[3].

tynd[2] *same as* **teen**[1].

tynde *same as* **tine**[1].

tyne[1] *n* the prong of a fork.

tyne[2] *same as* **tine**[2].

tynin' *n* a grubbing, harrowing.

tynin' *n* the losing.

tynsell *same as* **tinesel**.

type[1] *n* a sign, picture.

type[2] *v* **1** to trail about in weakness or weariness. **2** to struggle, labour hard.—*n* **1** hard labour accompanied by much walking. **2** a weak, hard-working woman.

typin' job *n* any employment that makes serious inroads on the constitution or physical strength.

typit *adj* exhausted by toil.

tyraneese *v* to overwork.

tyre *same as* **tire**[1].

tysee *same as* **tice**.
tyst *v* **1** to entice. **2** to stir up.
tyste, tystie *same as* **teistie**.
tystril *same as* **taistril**.
tyte[1] *same as* **tit**[2].
tyte[2] *adv* straight, directly.
tyte[3] *same as* **tite**[1].

tytle[1] *v* to walk with short steps.—*n* the act of walking so.
tytle[2] *same as* **tittle**[2].
tytter[3] *same as* **titter**[2].
tyly *n* a grandfather.
tyu *v* kneaded.
tyuchle *n* a tough morsel.—*v* to chew something tough.
tyuts *same as* **tuts**.

U

ubit[1] *adj* dwarfish.
ubit[2] *n* a hairy caterpillar.
ubitous *adj* very small, useless.
uccle *n* the image of anyone.
udder-clap *n* a tumour on the udder of ewes caused by the return of milk after being yeld (qv).
udderlock *v* to pluck the wool from a ewe's udder for cleanliness or free access of the lambs to the teats.—*n* a lock of wool from the udder of a ewe.
ug, ugg *v* **1** to feel disgust or abhorrence. **2** to loathe. **3** to cause disgust, nauseate. **4** to vomit.—*n* **1** a feeling of repulsion, disgust, nausea. **2** an object of disgust. **3** a person of disagreeable, disgusting manners.
ugertfow *adj* **1** nice. **2** squeamish.
ugfou *adj* **1** disgusting. **2** scornful.
uggin *adj* **1** disgusting, loathsome. **2** frightful.—*n* a loathing.
ugly *adj* **1** ill-tempered. **2** nasty.—*n* a collapsible shade formerly worn in front of a woman's bonnet.
ugsome, ugsum, uggsum *adj* **1** disgusting. **2** frightful. **3** ghastly. **4** horrible.
ugsomelike *adj* ghostly-looking.
ugsumness *n* **1** loathsomeness, repulsiveness. **2** frightfulness. **3** horror.
uhu, uh-uh *int* an exclamation of affirmation or approbation, used especially by children.
ui *n* an isthmus or neck of land.
ukiname *n* a nickname.
uily *n* oil.—*adj* **1** oily. **2** greasy.
uily pig *n* an oil jar.
uim *n* steam, vapour.
uke *n* a week.
ulie *same as* **uily**.
ulky *adj* every.
ull *adj* ill.
ull-eesin' *n* ill-usage.
ull-wull *n* ill-will.
ulzie, ulyie, uly *same as* **uily**.
umbersorrow *adj* **1** hardy. **2** resisting disease or the effects of bad weather. **3** rugged. **4** of a surly disposition. **5** rude, uncultivated. **6** delicate, weakly.
umbrell *n* **1** an umbrella. **2** (*in pl*) honour paid to a person by drinking his or her health and then inverting the glasses.
umcast *v* to bind or splice by wrapping round.
umist, umast *adj* uppermost, highest.
umman, uman *n* woman.
umph, umph'm, umphum *int* **1** an exclamation of doubt, disapproval or contempt. **2** a murmur of assent, used by children especially.
umquhile, umqubill, umwhile *adj* **1** former. **2** whilom. **3** of old. **4** late, deceased.—*adv* formerly, some time ago.
umrage *n* **1** spite, ill-feeling. **2** umbrage.
umshy *n* a lump from a blow on the head.
un negative particle in composition.
unable *adj* infirm.
unacquaint, unacquant *adj* **1** ignorant. **2** not familiar. **3** having no acquaintance.
unacquaintedness *n* ignorance.
unacquantit *adj* ignorant, unwitting.—*adv* unwittingly.
unafeard *adj* unafraid.

unamendable *adj* irremediable, irreparable.
unapproven *adj* not approved.
unassoilzied *adj* unpurged from sin.
unbauld *adj* humble, self-abased.
unbeast *n* the toothache.
unbeen *adj* not thoroughly closed in or made tight.
unbekent *adj* unknown.
unbeknown *adj* unknown, unperceived.
unbeknownst *adj* unknown.
unbethought *v* not bethought.
unbiddable *adj* **1** perverse. **2** intractable. **3** not to be counselled.
unbiggit *adj* unbuilt.
unboding *adj* **1** unpropitious. **2** unpromising.
unbonnet *v* (*used of a man*) to take off his cap.
unbonny *adj* **1** ugly, not bonny, unattractive. **2** unhealthy.
unbowsome, unbousome *adj* **1** unbending, unyielding. **2** unable to bend. **3** stiff, obstinate.
unbristle *v* to shave a bristly beard.
unbrizzed *adj* unbruised.
unbrunt *adj* unburnt.
unbusket *adj* unadorned.
unca *same as* **unco**.
unca'd *adj* uninvited.
uncannily *adv* **1** carelessly. **2** weirdly. **3** dangerously.
uncanny *adj* **1** awkward, inexpert. **2** imprudent. **3** unearthly, ghostly. **4** dangerous from supernatural causes. **5** ominous. **6** weird. **7** unlucky. **8** possessing supernatural powers. **9** dangerous. **10** mischievous. **11** open to suspicion of evil. **12** severe. **13** rude. **14** very hurtful.
uncapable *adj* incapable.
uncaring *adj* **1** free from care. **2** heedless, careless.
uncassable *adj* **1** unbreakable. **2** that cannot be annulled.
uncawket *adj* **1** unchalked. **2** without an account being sent.
unce *n* an ounce.
uncessant *adj* incessant.
unchance *n* **1** a misfortune, calamity. **2** a mischance.
unchancy *adj* **1** unlucky. **2** ill-omened, ill-fated. **3** unfortunate. **4** mischievous. **5** risky. **6** not safe to meddle with.
unclear *adj* undecided.
Uncle Tom is very sick *n* a singing game.
uncloured, unclowred *adj* **1** unbeaten. **2** unwounded.
unco *adj* **1** unknown. **2** strange, foreign. **3** hardly recognizable. **4** uncouth. **5** weird, uncanny. **6** terrible. **7** reserved in manner. **8** uncommon. **9** extraordinary, very great.—*adv* extremely, unusually, very.—*n* **1** a novelty. **2** a curiosity. **3** anything strange. **4** wonder. **5** stir. **6** a stranger. **7** (*in pl*) news. **8** strange tidings.
unco body *n* **1** a stranger. **2** a simple, unpretending, unimportant person.
unco fowk *n* strangers.
uncoft *adj* unbought.
unco-guid *n* an ironical designation of such persons as make a great profession of piety and are strait-laced in their religion.
uncolie, uncolies, uncoly *adv* **1** strangely. **2** very much. **3** extremely.
uncolike *adj* **1** strange. **2** strange-looking.
uncolins *adv* in a strange or odd fashion or manner.
unco-looking *adj* having a strange, wild look.

unco man *n* a stranger.
uncome *adj* not come, not arrived.
uncommon *adv* uncommonly.
uncompulsed *adj* unforced.
unconess *n* strangeness, reserve.
unconstancy *n* a lack of constancy.
unconstant *n* not constant.
uncorn *n* wild oats.
uncounselfow *adj* unadvisable.
uncouth *adj* **1** peculiar in dress, appearance, looks. **2** strange, unfamiliar.
uncouthness *n* want of acquaintance.
uncouthy *adj* **1** eerie. **2** under the influence of superstitious fears. **3** dreary. **4** causing fear. **5** unseemly. **6** unfriendly.
uncover *v* to drive a fox out of cover.
uncraized *adj* **1** unshattered. **2** unshaken.
unction *n* an auction.
unctioneer, uncshoneer *n* an auctioneer.
uncustomed *adj* smuggled, not having paid duty.
undainty *adj* unbecoming, improper.
undecent *adj* **1** indecent. **2** unbecoming.
undeemint *adj* countless, incalculable.
undeemis, undeemas, undumous *adj* **1** extraordinary, incredible. **2** immense, incalculable. **3** that cannot be reckoned.
undeemoualy *adv* excessively.
undegrate *adj* ungrateful.
undemns, undeimis *same as* **undeemis**.
undeniable *adj* unexceptionable.
under, un'er *prep* elliptically for under pretence of.
underbod *n* the swelling of the sea under a floating object.
undercoat, undercote, undercot *v* (*used of a sore*) to fester under a superficial scurf brought over it by improper treatment.
undercotie *n* a petticoat.
underfit *adj* (*used of peat*) dug beneath the feet instead of laterally.
under-fur-sowing *n* sowing in a shallow furrow.
undergang *v* to undergo, endure.
undergore *adj* in a state of leprous eruption.
underly *v* **1** to endure, undergo. **2** to be subjected to.
undermind *v* to undermine.
undermine *v* **1** to work secretly upon one. **2** to threaten, alarm.
undermoor *n* in a deep peat moss where two persons cut peats, the part cut by the second below the first cutter.
undernight *adv* under cloud of night, by night.
underside *n* the under surface.
undersook *n* an undercurrent flowing against that on the surface.
understane *n* **1** the nether millstone. **2** a foundation, beginning.
under-subscriber *n* one who subscribes a written statement.
underthoom *adv* **1** secretly. **2** in an underhand manner.
underwater *n* water about the foundations of a house.
undicht, undight *adj* **1** undressed. **2** undecked. **3** unwiped.
undichtit *adj* unwiped.
undoch, undocht *n* **1** a weak, puny creature. **2** a coward. **3** a silly, incapable, worthless person.—*adj* sickly, puny, weak, contemptable.
undoomis *same as* **undeemis**.
undought *same as* **undoch**.
undraikit *adj* not drenched.
une *n* **1** an oven. **2** the oppressive air of a room long shut up.
unease *n* an uneasy state.
uneasy *adj* troublesome, causing uneasiness.
unedicat *adj* uneducated.
uneirdly *adj* unearthly.
uneith *adj* not easy.—*adv* hardly.
unequal *adj* unfair, unjust.

uneven *adj* out of sorts.
unever *adv* never.
unevitable *adj* inevitable.
unfaceable *adj* ugly, not fit to be seen.
unfain *adj* **1** unwilling. **2** not fond.
unfandrum *adj* **1** bulky. **2** unmanageable.
unfankle *v* to unwind, disentangle.
unfarrant *adj* **1** ill-informed, senseless. **2** slow of apprehension. **3** rude, unmannerly.
unfashion *n* unfashionableness.
unfauld *v* to unfold.
unfavourable *adj* (*of persons*) unfavourably placed.
unfeil *adj* **1** uncomfortable, unpleasant. **2** rough, coarse. **3** not smooth.
unfeiroch *adj* **1** feeble, frail. **2** unwieldy.
unfeued *adj* not disposed of in feu (qv).
unflerdy *adj* **1** feeble, infirm. **2** unfit for action. **3** overgrown, unwieldy.
unflery *adj* **1** feeble, weak. **2** unwieldy.
unfleggit *adj* not frightened, unalarmed.
unfond *adj* not fond.
unforbidden *adj* unruly, disobedient.
unforlattit *adj* **1** unforsaken. **2** (*used of wine*) new, fresh.
unformal *adj* **1** irregular. **2** not according to form.
unforsained *adj* undeserved.
unfothersum *same as* **unfurthersome**.
unfree *adj* **1** not enjoying the liberties of a burgess. **2** liable to custom duty.
unfreelie *adv* very.—*adj* **1** heavy, unwieldy. **2** frail, feeble.
unfriend, unfreen *n* **1** an opponent. **2** an enemy.
unfriendship *n* unfriendly terms, enmity, ill-will.
unfrugal *adj* lavish, given to expense.
unfurthersome *adj* **1** (*of the weather*) unfavourable to vegetation. **2** unpropitious. **3** difficult.
unfylt *adj* undefiled, unsoiled.
unganed *adj* inappropriate.
ungang *v* to deceive, to lead to mistake.
ungear, ungeir *v* **1** to unclothe. **2** to unharness. **3** to castrate.
ungentilely *adv* rudely, impolitely.
ungifted *adj* not given.
ungirth *v* to take off a hoop.
unglaured *adj* unsoiled.
ungraithe *v* to unharness.
ungrate *adj* ungrateful.
unguiled *adj* not beguiled or caught by guile.
unhabile *adj* (*of witnesses*) legally incompetent.
unhalesome *adj* unwholesome.
unhalsed *adj* unsaluted.
unhandsome *adj* **1** shabby. **2** knavish.
unhanty, unhaunty *adj* **1** inconvenient. **2** overlarge. **3** very fat. **4** unwieldy, clumsy.
unhappit *adj* **1** without warm clothes. **2** uncovered.
unheartsome *adj* **1** melancholy, cheerless. **2** (*of the weather*) bad, uncomfortable. **3** slightly ailing.
unhearty *adj* **1** disheartened. **2** cheerless. **3** wretched, sad. **4** slightly ailing. **5** feeling cold. **6** (*of the weather*) cold and damp, uncomfortable.
unhine, unhyne *adj* **1** extraordinary, unparalleled in a bad sense. **2** immense, excessive in a bad sense.
unhive *v* to deprive of cover or shelter.
unhonest *adj* dishonest.
unhonesty *n* dishonesty.
unhousened *adj* unburied.
unicorn fish *n* the narwhal.
unintenet *adj* unintended, unintentional.
university *n* **1** an entire community. **2** an incorporation.
unkaimed, unkamed *adj* **1** unkempt. **2** uncombed.
unken *v* **1** to fail to recognize. **2** to be ignorant or unwitting.
unkennable *adj* **1** innumerable. **2** unknowable.
unkenned, unkent *adj* unknown, strange, unfamiliar.
unkensome *adj* unknowable, unknown.
unkilt *v* to let down a tuck or what was kilted up.

unkin *adj* unkind.
unkipple *v* to uncouple.
unkirs'en *adj* 1 unchristian. 2 unfit for human food.
unkirsen'd, unkirstened *adj* unbaptised.
unko, unka *same as* **unco**.
unlaw *n* 1 a breach of law. 2 an unjust act. 3 an injury. 4 a
fine fixed by law. 5 a law without real authority.—*v* 1 to
fine. 2 to pay a fine.
unleared *adj* uneducated, untaught.
unleeze *v* to disentangle.
unleisum *adj* unlawful.
unless *prep* except.
unlibbet *adj* not gelded.
unlickit *adj* unpunished.
unlife-like *adj* 1 likely to die. 2 not having the appearance
of living or recovering from disease.
unlife-rented *adj* not life-rented.
unlink *v* to rise up from a stooping position.
unlo'esome, unloosome, unluesome, unlusum *adj* 1
unlovely. 2 disgusting, repulsive.
unlo'esom-, unluesom-like *adj* unattractive, unpleasant-
looking.
unmackly *adj* deformed, unshapely.
unmelled, unmeled *adj* not meddled with.
unmensefu', unmencefu' *adj* 1 disorderly. 2 unmannerly.
3 unbecoming. 4 indiscreet. 5 ungenerous. 6 (*used of
the weather*) rough, unseasonable.
unnaturality *n* imbecility.
unnest *v* to dislodge.
unorderlie *adv* irregularly.
unpaid *adj* without having paid.
unpalliable *adj* that cannot be palliated.
unpassible *adj* impassable.
unpatient *adj* impatient.
unpaunded *adj* unpledged.
unperfeit *adj* imperfect.
unpignorate *v* to pledge.
unpossible *adj* impossible.
unproper *adj* improper.
unpurpose *adj* 1 awkward. 2 untidy. 3 inexact.
unpurpose-like *adj* seemingly awkward or not adapted to
the purpose to which a thing is applied.
unpurposeness *n* slovenliness.
unquarrelable *adj* unchallengeable.
unquit *adj* unrequited.
unream *v* (*used of milk*) not to skim the cream off.
unreason *n* disorder.
unreave *v* to unravel, unwind.
unreddable *adj* that cannot be disentangled or cleared up.
unregular *adj* irregular.
unremeadfu' *adj* irremediable. *See* **remeid**.
unrest *n* 1 a troublesome person. 2 one who causes disquietude.
unreverentlie *adv* irreverently.
unricht *adj* 1 dishonourable, unjust. 2 wrong.
unrid *adj* entangled.
unrig *v* to unroof.
unrigged *adj* without a roof, unroofed.
unringed *adj* (*of pigs*) without a ring in the nose.
unriped *adj* unexplored, unsearched, not investigated.
unrude *adj* 1 rude. 2 hideous. 3 diabolical, vile. 4 base.
unruleful *adj* 1 unruly. 2 ungovernable. 3 lawless.
unsaucht *n* trouble, disquietude.
unscabbit *adj* (*used of potatoes*) not scabbed.
unscaured *adj* unscared, undaunted.
unscrapit *adj* (*used of the tongue*) foul, abusive.
unseal, unsell, unseel *n* 1 a wicked, worthless person. 2
a self-willed, naughty child.
unseally, unseely *adj* 1 worthless, wretched. 2 unlucky.
unsensible *adj* 1 insensible. 2 imperceptible. 3 destitute
of sense or reasoning power.
unseyed *adj* untried, unproved.
unshappen *adj* misshapen.
unsicker *adj* 1 insecure. 2 not to be depended upon.

unskaithed *adj* uninjured.
unslockenable *adj* 1 unquenchable. 2 inextinguishable.
unslot *v* to unfasten a door, etc, by drawing back the bolt
or slot (qv).
unsnarre *adj* blunt, not sharp.
unsneck *v* to lift a latch. *See* **sneck**.
unsned *adj* not pruned or cut. *See* **sned**.
unsnib *v* to unbolt, unfasten. *See* **snib**.
unsnick *same as* **unsneck**.
unsnod *adj* untidy, in disorder. *See* **snod**.
unsocht *adj* not sought.
unsonsy *adj* 1 unlucky. 2 ominous. 3 causing ill-luck. 4
mischievous. 5 disagreeable. 6 plain, ill-looking, thin. 7
slovenly, untidy. *See* **sonsy**.
unspairket *adj* not bespattered.
unspeaned *adj* unweaned.
unspoilyied *adj* not despoiled.
unspoken water *n* water from under a bridge, over which
the living pass and the dead are carried, brought in the
dawn or twilight to the house of a sick person, without
the bearer's speaking either going or returning, used in
various ways as a powerful charm by the superstitious
for healing the sick.
unstint *adj* 1 unstinted. 2 unchecked. 3 without limit.
unstout *adj* not stubborn.
unstraighted, unstrauchted, unstreekit *adj* (*used of a
dead body*) not laid out for burial.
unsure *adj* 1 insecure, unsafe. 2 uncertain, unreliable.
unsuspect *adj* not open to suspicion.
unswack *adj* 1 stiff. 2 not nimble or agile. *See* **swack**.
unawackened *adj* (*used of an axle*) ungreased, without
oil.
unsweel *v* 1 to unwind. 2 to unwrap.
untasty *adj* without good taste.
untauld *adj* untold.
untellable *adj* 1 unfit to be told. 2 impossible to tell.
untelling *adj* 1 impossible to tell. 2 past words or reckoning.
untender *adj* 1 inconsiderate. 2 not circumspect.
untented *adj* 1 uncared for. 2 careless. 3 unconsidered.
untentie *adj* careless.—*adv*. 1 heedlessly. 2 incautiously.
3 noisily.
untested *adj* (*used of a deed, will, etc*) without the testing
clause.
unthack, untheek *v* 1 to take off thatch. 2 to uncover.
unthinkingness *n* thoughtlessness.
unthocht *adj* unthought.
unthochtfu' *adj* thoughtless, inconsiderate.
unthocht-lang *adj* without feeling ennui.
unthocht o' *adj* carelessly done.
untholeable *adj* 1 unbearable. 2 intolerable. *See* **thole**.
unthraw *v* 1 to untwist. 2 to unlock. *See* **thraw**.
unthreshen *adj* not threshed.
unticht *adj* (*used of the mind*) wandering, weak.
untochered *adj* without a dowry. *See* **tocher**.
untolerable *adj* intolerable.
untrig *adj* 1 untidy. 2 slovenly.
untrim *adj* 1 not trim. 2 dishevelled.
untrusty *adj* not trustworthy.
unwarly *adj* 1 unworldly. 2 supernatural. 3 uncouth. 4
clumsy. 5 unwieldy.
unwaukit *adj* ubwatched.
unweel *adj* 1 unwell. 2 of an ailing constitution.
unweelness *n* 1 ill-health. 2 an ailment.
unwillie *adj* illiberal.
unwinnable *adj* invincible, impregnable.
unwitten, unweetin *adj* 1 unknowing, involuntary. 2 unknown.
unwittins *adv* 1 unconsciously. 2 with no knowledge.
unwitty *adj* lacking wit.
unwordily *adv* unworthily.
unwordy *adj* unworthy.
unyerthly *adj* unearthly.
unyokit *adj* 1 unyoked. 2 finished.

up *adv* above.—*adj* **1** open. **2** grown up. **3** excited, irritated.—*v* to stand, rise or jump up.

up-again *adv* over again.

up-a-land *adj* at a distance from the sea.

upbang *v* **1** to force to rise by beating. **2** to rise up with a bang.

upbear *v* to confirm, bear out.

upbig[1] *v* to build up.

upbig[2] *adj* **1** conceited. **2** having a high opinion of oneself.

upbirl *v* to rise quickly.

upbow *n* a fiddler's action in striking an opening chord.

up-brak *n* the breaking up.

upbring *v* **1** to bring up. **2** to educate, train. **3** to maintain during youth.—*n* **1** education, training. **2** maintenance in youth.

upbuckle *v* to buckle or fasten up.

upbuller *v* to boil, bubble or throw up.

upbye *adv* **1** up yonder. **2** up the way. **3** upstairs.

up by yonder *adv* **1** up yonder. **2** a little farther up.

upcast *v* **1** to raise up, elevate. **2** to turn over. **3** to reckon, calculate. **4** (*used of clouds*) to gather. **5** to reproach, cast in the teeth, upbraid.—*n* **1** an upset. **2** a reproach. **3** a taunt. **4** an occasion of reproach.

upcasting *n* the rising of clouds above the horizon, threatening rain.

upchokit *adj* choked up.

upcoil *n* a kind of game with balls.

upcome *n* **1** promising appearance. **2** upshot. **3** bodily growth. **5** ascent.

upcoming *n* **1** ascent. **2** adolescence.

updraw *v* **1** to overtake, come up with. **2** to pick and draw a sheep from a flock. **3** to understand.

updrinking *n* an entertainment given to her gossips (*see* **gossip**) by a woman on her recovery from childbearing.

upend *v* to set upright on end.

upfam'd *adj* (*used of a turkey's tail*) spread out like a fan.

upfeshin, ~fees, ~fessin *n* training, education, upbringing.

upfuirdays *adv* up before sunrise.

upgabble *v* to gobble up.

upgae *n* an upward break in a mineral stratum.

upgaen *adj* **1** (*of a market*) rising. **2** wild, reckless.

upgang *n* **1** the act of ascending, ascent. **2** a sudden rise of wind and sea.

upget *v* to rise up.

upgive *v* **1** to give up, surrender. **2** to avow, own up.

upgiver *n* (*a legal term*) one who delivers up to another.

upgiving *n* the act of delivering up.

upgrowing *adj* growing, adolescent.

upgrown *adj* grown-up.

uphadd, uphald, uphaud *v* **1** to uphold. **2** to support, maintain. **3** to defend. **4** to provide for, furnish. **5** to keep in repair or good condition. **6** to raise, hold aloft. **7** to affirm, maintain in argument. **8** to warrant, vouch for. **9** to believe in, accept as true. **10** (*used of the weather*) to clear.—*n* **1** support, maintenance. **2** a prop. **3** one who maintains another. **4** the act or obligation of keeping in good repair. **5** chief delight. **6** ruling desire.

uphand *adv* with uplifted hand.

uphauder *n* an upholder.

upheese *v* to lift or hoist up.

uphunt *v* to hunt up.

up-ings *n* new or mended clothes, etc.

up-i'-the-buckle *adj* ambitious, intent on rising in the social scale.

upjumlet *adj* jumbled up.

upland *adj* **1** on high or hilly ground. **2** inland. **3** rustic.

uplayer *n* the person who loads ponies with peats at a peat hill.

uplift *v* **1** to take up, to collect. **2** to cheer. **3** to collect rates, dues, etc.

upliftable *adj* leviable.

uplifted *adj* **1** elated. **2** excited. **3** rendered proud.

uplifter *n* **1** a collector. **2** a tax-gatherer.

uplifting *adj* **1** elevating. **2** inspiring.—*n* **1** elation. **2** pride. **3** collection. **4** exaction.

uplight, uplicht *n* brightening after a shower.

uplins *adv* upwards.

uploppin *adj* **1** easily excited. **2** jumping hurriedly at conclusions.

uplos, uppleuse *v* to disclose, discover.

upmak *v* **1** to make up. **2** to compensate. **3** to enrich. **4** to supply a deficiency. **5** to elate.—*n* **1** style, making. **2** a fabrication, invention. **3** a contrivance.

upmaker *n* one who makes up an untrue story or false rumour.

upmost *adj* having the highest score in a game or match.

upo, upon *prep* **1** on. **2** to. **3** with. **4** at. **5** in.

uppal *n* **1** support. **2** chief delight or pursuit, hobby. **3** what gives one a good start in life and leads to prosperity.—*v* **1** (*of the weather*) to clear. **2** to build up in health.—*adj* fine, clearing up.

upper *n* the uppermost.

upper end *n* the head.

upper mes *n* those who sat at table at the aristocratic end 'above the salt'.

upper-moor *n* the one who cuts on the top where a moss is deep and two persons cut, the one below the other.

uppil *same as* **uppal**.

uppil aboon *adj* clear overhead.

uppins *adv* a little way upwards.

uppish *adj* **1** aspiring, ambitious. **2** bold, audacious.

up-pit, ~-put *v* to erect.—*n* **1** lodging, entertainment. **2** the power of secreting to prevent discovery.

uppie *v* (*used of the weather*) to clear.

up-putter *n* **1** an erector, a builder. **2** an instigator.

up-putting, ~-pitting *n* **1** accommodation. **2** lodging. **3** entertainment for man and beast. **4** erection, building.

upred *adj* tidied, put in order.

upredd *adj* (*used of doubts, etc*) cleared up.

upride *v* to cause to ride-a-cock-horse.

upright, upricht *n* a golf club the head of which is at nearly right angles to the shaft.—*adj* pure, genuine, as opposed to what is false or adulterated.

upright bur *n* the fir moss, *Lycopodium selago*.

uprin *v* to come up to running.

uprising *n* a removal from a house, farm, etc.

upseed time *n* seed time.

upset *v* to recover from an illness, wound, calamity, etc.—*adj* **1** pointing upwards. **2** tip-tilted.

upset price *n* the minimum price acceptable for an article for sale, such as a house

upsetting *adj* **1** forward, ambitious. **2** stuck-up, proud, vehement.—*n* **1** assumption of right or superiority. **2** aspiring or ambitious behaviour. **3** a fitting up.

upsetting-like *adj* appearing to have a spirit of assumption and self-elevation.

upsides *adv* **1** quits. **2** on an equal footing.

upsides wi' *adj* revenged on.

upsitten *adj* **1** callous. **2** listless. **2** indifferent.

upsitting *n* **1** an entertainment given after the recovery of a woman from childbirth. **2** indifference, callousness. **3** listlessness.

upsitting time *n* the time when a woman gets up after childbirth.

upskail *v* to scatter upwards.

upspeak *v* to speak up.

upspiel *v* to climb up.

upstack *v* to put up in stacks.

upstanding *adj* **1** standing, on one's feet. **2** tall, erect, well made. **3** upright, honourable. **4** determined.—*n* (*used of crops*) pith, substance.

upstart *n* a stick set upon the top of a wall, but not reaching the summit, in forming the woodwork of a thatch roof.

upstikket *adj* **1** stuck-up. **2** too particular.

upstirrer *n* **1** an inciter. **2** a raiser of strife or rebellion.

upstirring *n* quickening of the mind or spirit.

upstrut *v* to strut proudly.

uptail *v* to turn tail, run off.

uptak, uptack, uptake *v* **1** (*used of oneself*) to reform. **2** (*of a psalm, etc*) to start the tune. **3** to levy fines, collect money, dues, etc. **4** to make out an inventory or list. **5** to understand.—*n* **1** comprehension, understanding, intelligence. **2** (*used of weather*) a gale of wind. **3** a storm.

uptaker *n* a collector.

uptaking *n* **1** understanding, comprehension. **2** the act of collecting.

up-through *adv* **1** in the upper part of the country. **2** upwards through to the other side.—*adj* living or situated in, or belonging to, the upper part of the country.

upthrowing *n* puking, vomiting.

up-to *adj* **1** skilled in. **2** equal to.

up-ty *v* to put in bonds.

upwart *adj* **1** upward. **2** elevated.

upwauken *v* to wake up.

upwith *n* an ascent, a rising ground.—*adj* **1** taking a direction upwards. **2** uphill. **3** on an equal or superior footing. **4** equal to.—*adv* upwards.

upwreil *v* to wriggle up.

ur *v* are.

urchin *n* a hedgehog.

ure[1] *n* **1** soil. **2** barren, ferruginous soil. **3** mud, clay.

ure[2] *n* **1** colour, tinge. **2** a stain on linen caused by iron. **3** the fur adhering to iron vessels in which water is kept.

ure[3] *n* **1** a haze in the air. **2** a coloured haze that sunbeams cause in summer in passing through the air. **3** sweat, perspiration. **4** a slow heat from embers. **5** a suffocating heat.

ure[4] *n* the udder of a sheep or cow.

ureie *adj* coloured, stained.

ure-lock *n* a lock of wool pulled from a ewe's udder.

ure-red *n* small reddish stones in muddy clay.

urey *adj* **1** hazy. **2** filled with moisture or haze. **3** clammy, covered with perspiration.

urf *n* **1** a stunted, ill-grown person or child. **2** a crabbed or peevish little person. **3** a dirty, insignificant person. **4** a dwarf. **5** a fairy.

urf-like *adj* stunted, puny in appearance.

urie *adj* furred, encrusted with metallic scum.

unak *n* a Highland name for a satyr.

urisum *adj* **1** frightful. **2** terrifying.

urling *n* a dwarfish person or child.

urluch, urlich *adj* **1** cloudy, dull. **2** stupid, silly-looking, dazed.

urn[1] *n* a grave, tomb.

urn[2] *v* **1** to cause pain to. **2** to pain. **3** to torture.

urp *v* to become pettish.

ury[1] *same as* **urey**.

ury[2] *same as* **urie**.

us *pron* me.

use[1] *n* interest in relation to money.

use[2] *v* **1** to frequent. **2** to familiarize. **3** to grow accustomed to a place.

used *adj* **1** accustomed. **2** tried. **3** expert.

useless *n* the crab's claw or lady's thumb.

ush[1] *v* **1** to usher. **2** to escort. **3** to lead, guide.

ush[2]**, usch** *v* **1** to issue. **2** to flow out copiously. **3** to empty. **4** to cleanse.—*n* the entrails of a slaughtered animal.

usque *n* whisky.

usqueba, usquebae, usquebagh, usquebah, usquabae, usquebey, usquibae *n* whisky.

usual *n* usual health or circutnstances.

utgie, utgien *n* outlay, expenditure.

uther *n* an udder.

utherlock *same as* **udderlock**.

utole *n* a symbol for the infeftment (qv) or the resignation of an annual rent.

utterance *n* **1** outrance. **2** extremity of distress, etc.

Utter House *n* the Outer House in the Court of Session.

utteridge *n* utterance, power of speech.

utwith *adv* beyond.

V

vacance, vacans *n* **1** a vacation. **2** holidays. **3** a vacancy.

vacillancy *n* vacillation.

vacillant *adj* vacillating.

vady *same as* **vaudy**.

vaedge, vaege *same as* **vage**[1].

vagabond-money *n* a tax levied, half from landlords and half from tenants, according to their means and substance, to meet the weekly charges that might arise to sustain the poor.

vagabone *n* a vagabond.

vage[1] *n* **1** a voyage. **2** a journey by land. **3** a short journey to fetch or carry. **4** an expedition.—*v* to go on an expedition.

vage[2] *same as* **vaig**.

vaging *n* loafing about.

vagral *adj* vagrant.

vague *same as* **vaig**.

vaicance *same as* **vacance**.

vaig, vaige *v* **1** to roam, stroll, wander. **2** to loaf about. **3** to be discursive.—*n* **1** a wanderer. **2** a vagabond, an idler.—*adv*-**1** wandering. **2** easily swept away.

vaiger *n* **1** a wanderer. **2** a vagrant.

vaigie *n* a romp.

vaiging *n* idle strolling, loafing about.

vaigrie *n* **1** a whim. **2** a freak. **3** a piece of folly. **4** a vagary.

vaik *v* **1** to be vacant. **2** to vacate. **3** to scatter so as to empty. **4** to be dismissed. **5** to be unoccupied. **6** to be at leisure.

vailye *v* to value.—*n* value, worth.

vaiper *same as* **vapour**.

vairie *same as* **vary**.

vairtie *adj* **1** early up. **2** wide-awake. **3** cautious. **4** industrious.

vaishle *n* **1** a vassal. **2** a maidservant.

vake *same as* **vaik**.

valawish *adj* **1** profuse. **2** lavish.

valentine's deal, ~ dealing *n* a method in company, using notes with names written on them, by which a person whose name was written became the drawer's valentine from one 14 February to the next.

valetudinariness *n* weak health.

validate *adj* validated.

valises *n* saddlebags.

valour *n* worth, value.

valuedom *n* value.

vamp *v* **1** to improve, set off. **2** to mend.

vamper *v* **1** to present an ostentatious appearance. **2** to pose.

vandie *same as* **vaunty**.

vane *int* a call to a horse to come near.

vankish *v* to entwine, twist.

vanquish *n* a wasting disease of sheep, caused by the pernicious quality of a certain grass.

vantie *same as* **vaunty**.

vapour *v* **1** to bully. **2** to threaten violence. **3** to frisk about, caper. **4** to stroll, saunter.

vare *same as* **voar**.

vaziorum *n* **1** a constant change. **2** a medley. **3** variation. **4** diversion. **5** a long rigmarole. **6** a repeating psalm tune. **7** (*in pl*) odds and ends.

varlet *n* a wizard, warlock.

varsak *adj* universal.

vary *v* to show symptoms of delirium in illness.—*n* a quandary, uncertainty, loss.

vassal *n* a tenant paying for land to the superior an annual feu duty.

vassalage *n* **1** an exploit. **2** a brave deed.
vast *n* a great number or quantity.
vastage *n* waste ground.
vaudy, vaudie *adj* **1** great, strong. **2** uncommon. **3** showy, gay. **4** proud, vain. **5** conceited. **6** elated. **7** forward. **8** merry.
vaunty *adj* **1** boastful, proud. **2** vain. **3** exultant. **4** ostentatious. **5** merry. **6** wanton. **7** showy.—*n* a vain, boastful person, a braggadocio.
yaw *int* a call to a horse to come to one.
veadge, veage *same as* **vage**[1].
veak *same as* **vaik**.
veal *n* **1** a calf. **2** the carcass of a calf.
veand *adj* superannuated.
veef *same as* **vive**.
veem *n* **1** a close heat over the body with redness of face and some perspiration. **2** a state of elation, exaltation or excitement of spirit.
veeper *n* a viper.
veeperate, veeperit *adj* **1** venomous, vicious. **2** sharp-tempered. **3** bitterly abusive.
veesion *n* **1** a vision. **2** a thin, meagre person or animal.
veesit *v* **1** to visit. **2** to punish. **3** to inspect.
veesy, veesie *same as* **vizy**.
veev, veeve *adj* brisk, lively.—*adv* **1** briskly. **2** vividly.
veevera *same as* **vivers**.
veill *n* a calf.
venall *same as* **vennel**.
vendue *n* an auction.
vendue warehouse *n* an auction room.
venge *v* to avenge.
vengeable *adj* cruel, destructive.—*adv* excessively.
vengeance *n* used as an oath.
venim *n* **1** venom. **2** malice. **3** a spiteful person.
venison *n* goat's flesh.
vennel *n* an alley, a narrow lane.
vent[1] *n* **1** a hole. **2** the anus of a fowl. **3** a chimney. —*v* **1** (*used of a chimney*) to draw. **2** to smoke. **3** to issue false coin.
vent[2] *n* **1** progress, speed. **2** a sale.—*v* to sell.
venter *v* to venture.—*n* anything driven ashore by tide or wind.
venterer *n* one who looks for articles driven ashore by tide or wind.
ventoner *n* a vintner.
venus *adj* impure, immoral.
vera *adv* very.
verge *n* a belt or strip of planting.
vergus *n* verjuice.
verilies *adv* verily.
vermin *n* a term applied playfully to a child.
versant *adj* versed in, conversant.
version *n* an exercise in translating a piece of English into Latin.
verter *n* **1** virtue. **2** a charm for curing certain diseases.
verter water *n* water found in the hollows of tombstones and rocks, a charm for warts.
verter-well *n* a well possessing medicinal virtue.
vertie *adj* **1** cautious, prudent. **2** industrious. **3** eager. **4** wide-awake. **5** early up, early at business.
verties, vertise *v* **1** to advertise. **2** to warn.
vertue *n* thrift, industry.
vertuous *adj* thrifty, industrious.
verylies *adv* verily.
veshell *n* a vessel.
vesie *same as* **vizy**.
vessel *n* a cow's udder.
vetcher *n* a man of a very suspicious appearance.
veve *adj* alive.
vex *v* to fret, grieve, be sorry.—*n* **1** a trouble. **2** vexation. **3** a cause of vexation or worry.
vexome *adj* grievous, sad.
veyage, viage *same as* **vage**[1].
vicinity *n* close resemblance.

vicious *same as* **vitious**.
victual *n* **1** grain of any kind. **2** standing corn.
victualler *n* **1** a grain dealer. **2** a corn factor.
vievers *same as* **vivers**.
vile *same as* **vyld**.
villanious *adj* villainous.
vincus *v* to conquer.
vindicat *v* to relieve, deliver.
vinel *n* an alley.
vintiner *n* a vintner.
violent *v* **1** to act violently. **2** to bring very strong pressure to bear.—*adj* extremely strong.
violer *n* a fiddler.
violing *n* fiddling.
viparously *adv* malignantly.
viperean *adj* viperous, venomous.
viporeus *adj* venomous.
vir, virr *n* **1** force, vigour, go. **2** activity, impetus.—*v* to move or walk with energy.—*adv* by force.
virgin honey *n* honey from the hive of the second swarm from the parent stock.
virgus *n* verjuice.
virl, virle, virrel *n* **1** a ferrule. **2** an encircling band or ring put round any body to keep it firm.—*v* to ring round.
virr *same as* **vir**.
virtue *same as* **vertue**.
virtuous *adj* thrifty.
vise *n* the indication of the direction that a mineral stratum has taken when interrupted in its course.
visie *same as* **vizy**.
vision *n* a thin, meagre person or animal.
visit *v* **1** to punish. **2** to inspect ecclesiastical records, etc.
visitation *n* the public yearly visit of magistrates, etc, to a burgh grammar school to distribute prizes, etc.
visitation acquaintance *n* a visiting acquaintance.
vienomy *n* physiognomy.
vissy *same as* **vizy**.
vital[1] *adj* having vitality.
vital[2] *n* grain.
vitcher *n* a visitor.
vitiate, vitiat *adj* vitiated.
vitiosity *n* what vitiates an animal or article.
vitious *adj* **1** unauthorized. **2** legally informal, irregular. **3** fierce, fiery.
vitioueness *n* **1** fierceness. **2** unmanageableness.
vittle *n* **1** grain. **2** standing corn. **3** (*in pl*) victuals. —*v* to support or supply with victuals.
vittler *n* a corn merchant.
vivacity *n* the degree of life in a newborn child.
vive *adj* **1** vivid. **2** life-like. **3** clear. **4** living. **5** lively. **6** brisk, vigorous. **7** fresh.
vively *adv* **1** clearly, vividly. **2** to the life.
vive-prent *n* print easily read.
vivers, vivres *n* provisions, food.
vivual *adj* **1** alive. **2** identical, self-same.
vivuallie *adv* **1** in life. **2** identically.
vizy, vizzy *n* **1** a look. **2** a scrutinizing gaze. **3** the sight of a gun.—*v* **1** to look. **2** to scrutinize. **3** to visit for inspection. **4** to aim at.
vizzie drap *n* the sight of a gun.
vizzy *same as* **vizy**.
vizzy hole *n* a peephole or small wicket in the door or gate of a castle or fort for spying.
vizzying-port *n* the door or gate of a castle or fort having a vizzy hole (qv).
vizzyless, visyless *adj* (*used of a gun*) not sighted.
voar, vor *n* **1** the spring. **2** seed time.
voar-fee *n* wages for work done in seed time.
voar-time *n* springtime.
vocable *n* (*in pl*) a vocabulary.
voce *n* voice.
vogerous *adj* boastful, vaunting.
vogie, voggie *adj* **1** vain. **2** merry, cheerful. **3** vaunting. **4** fondly, kindly. **5** caressing.

vogue *n* **1** reputation. **2** humour, mood. **3** a strong inclination.

voice *n* a vote.—*v* to vote.

voicer *n* a voter.

vokie *same as* **vogie**.

volage *adj* **1** giddy. **2** inconsiderate. **3** profuse, lavish, prodigal.—*v* to talk ostentatiously.

volageous *adj* **1** very giddy and light. **2** very boastful.

volanting *adj* **1** paying a flying visit. **2** flying from one's creditors.

vole mouse *n* the short-tailed mouse or fieldmouse.

voler *n* a thief.

volish *same as* **volage**.

volisher *n* an ostentatious talker.

voluntar *adj* voluntary.

voluptuous *adj* (*used of repairs on a house*) unnecessarily luxurious or convenient.

vomiter *n* an emetic.

voost *same as* **voust**.

vougis *same as* **vogie**.

vour *same as* **voar**.

vouss *n* the liquor of hay and chaff boiled.

voust *v* to boast, brag.—*n* **1** a boast. **2** vaunting.

vouster *n* a braggart, a boaster.

voustin *n* boasting.

vousty *adj* given to vain boasting.

vout *n* **1** a vault. **2** a deep hole.

vow *int* an exclamation of surprise, admiration, sorrow, etc.

vowbit *n* **1** a hairy worm. **2** the caterpillar of the tiger moth. **3** a puny creature.

vowgie *same as* **vogie**.

vowhy *same as* **vogie**.

vowl *v* (*used in card-playing*) to draw all the tricks. —*n* a deal that draws all the tricks, a vole.

vowst *v* to boast.—*n* a boast.

vowater *n* a boaster.

vowt *n* a vault.

vrack[1] *n* wreck, ruin.

vrack[2] *n* wrack, sea ware.

vracket *adj* shattered, dismembered.

vraith *n* an apparition.

vran *n* the wren.

vrang *adj* wrong.

vrap *v* to wrap.

vrapper *n* **1** a wrapper. **2** a women's loose jacket or blouse.

vrat *v* wrote.

vratch *n* a wretch.

vrath *n* wrath.

vreath *n* a snow-wreath.

vreet *v* to write.

vreetin' *n* writing.

vricht *n* a wright.

vrite *v* to write.

vriter *n* an attorney.

vrocht *v* wrought.

vrutten *v* written.

vung *v* to move swiftly with a buzzing sound.—*n* a buzzing or humming sound.

vyaachle *n* a vehicle.

vyaag, vyaug *n* a woman of rude manners.—*adj* incorrigible.

vyld *adj* **1** dirty, filthy. **2** worthless.

vyldness *n* dirt, filth.

vyokie *same as* **vogie**.

W

wa'[1] *n* a wall.

wa'[2] *n* a way.

wa'[3] *int* an exclamation of contempt.

wa'[4] *v* to choose.—*adj* **1** chosen. **2** strongest. **3** best. *See* **wale**[3].

wa, waah *same as* **waw**[3].

waajer *v* to wager.

waak *v* **1** to wake. **2** to watch.

waal *v* **1** to weld. **2** to comply with.

waalaquyte *n* an undervest.

waalin heat *n* the heat at which iron will weld.

waalipend, waalipenn *v* **1** to slight, undervalue. **2** to vilipend.

waan *same as* **wan**[4].

waanly *adj* hopeful.

waap *same as* **wap**[3].

waapon *n* a weapon.

waar[1] *same as* **ware**[2].

waar[2] *n* sea wrack.—*v* to manure with sea wrack.

waar-blade *n* a blade of sea wrack.

waarcaist *n* a heap of sea wrack.

waariebowg *n* a bladder of the yellow tangle.

waariebug *n* **1** a tumour on cattle caused by the larva of the gadfly. **2** a warble.

waarsche *same as* **wairsh**.

waar strand *n* a beach on which seaweed is cast up.

waat *n* **1** a welt. **2** a fissure. **3** a weal or mark made by a blow.

waav *v* to signal by a wave of the hand.

waavle *same as* **wavel**[1].

wab *n* **1** a web. **2** the omentum.—*v* to weave.

wa'baw *n* a handball for playing against a wall.

wabbit *adj* fatigued, exhausted.

wabble, wable *v* to wobble, hobble.—*n* hobbling.

waberan ~, wabert leaf *n* the great plantain.

wab-fittit *adj* web-footed.

wabran ~, wabron leaf *n* the great plantain.

wabster *n* **1** a weaver. **2** a spider.

wa-cast *n* **1** a castaway. **2** anything worthless or to be despised. **3** a piece of extravagance.

wace *n* wax.

wach *same as* **wack**.

wachie *adj* **1** wet. **2** foggy. **3** swampy.

wachle, wachel *same as* **wauchle**.

wacht[1] *n* a guard, a watch.

wacht[2] *same as* **waught**[1].

wack *adj* **1** damp. **2** clammy. **3** swampy. **4** foggy. **5** rainy.

wackness *n* moisture, humidity.

wad[1] *v* would.

wad[2] *n* **1** a pawn. **2** a pledge. **3** a forfeit. **4** a wager. —*v* **1** to pledge. **2** to engage oneself. **3** to wager.

wad[3] *v* to marry, wed.

wad[4] *adj* married.

wa'd *adj* chosen, choice

wad-be *adj* would-be.

wad-be-at *n* one who aspires above his or her station.

wadd[1] *same as* **wad**[2].

wadd[2] *n* **1** black lead. **2** a lead pencil.

wadder[1] *n* weather.

wadder[2] *n* a wether.

waddie *n* a twig with smaller shoots branching from it, which, being plaited together, becomes a kind of whip.

waddin *adj* strong, like two pieces of iron welded into one.

waddin' *n* a wedding.

waddin' ba'a, ~ baws *n* money scattered at a wedding.

waddin' braws *n* wedding clothes, a trousseau.

waddin' coat *n* the coat a bridegroom wears at his marriage.

waddin' day *n* the wedding day.

waddin' o' craws *n* a large flock of crows.

waddin' sark *n* a shirt made by the bride for the bridegroom before the wedding.

waddin' store *n* the wedding feast.

waddin' treat *n* a feast given on the fourth day of the marriage festivities by the young men at their own expense as a compliment to the newly married and as a return for the liberality of their entertaiment.

waddler *n* one who would keep house or act properly but does not.

wadds *n* **1** various games of forfeits, played within doors and in the open air. **2** the game of Scots and English.

wadds and weare *n* a rhyming game of forfeits, formerly common in Galloway farm kitchens.

waddy *adj* **1** great, strong. **2** uncommon. **3** gay, showy. **4** proud, vain. **5** forward. **6** merry.

wade[1] *v* to wager.

wade[2] *v* **1** (*used of the sun or moon*) to gleam at intervals through clouds or mists. **2** to ford a river.

wadeable *adj* fordable.

waden *adj* young and supple.

wader *n* the heron.

wadge[1] *n* a wedge.

wadge[2] *v* to brandish threateningly.—*n* the act of so brandishing.

wadie, wady *adj* **1** strong. **2** showy. **3** plucky. **4** merry, gay.

wad-keeper *n* one who takes charge of forfeits or pledges.

wadna *v neg* would not.

wa'-drap *n* water dropping from the eaves of a house, wall drop.

wadset *n* **1** a mortgage. **2** a deed from a debtor to a creditor assigning the rents of land until the debt is paid. **3** a pledge.—*v* **1** to mortgage. **2** to pawn. **3** to alienate land, etc, under reversion.

wadset o' an aith *n* a bet.

wadsetter *n* one who holds another's property in wadset (qv).

wad-shootin *n* shooting at a mark for a prize.

wae *n* woe.—*adj* **1** woeful, sorrowful. **2** vexed.

waeak *same as* **weak**[2].

wae-begane *adj* woebegone.

wae-days *n* days of adversity.

waefleed *n* the water of a millstream after passing the mill.

waefu' *adj* woeful, sad, miserable.

waefu'some *adj* **1** sad. **2** sorry. **3** wretched.

waeg *n* the kittiwake.

wae-hearted *adj* **1** sad-hearted. **2** sad.

waelike *adj* sorrowful, sad-looking.

waely *adv* sadly.

waen *same as* **wean**.

waeness *n* **1** sadness, sorrow. **2** vexation.

waeock *same as* **weak**[2].

waese *n* **1** a small bundle of hay or straw, larger than a wisp. **2** a bundle of wheat straw used for thatching. **3** a bundle of sticks or brushwood placed on the wind side of a cottage door to ward off the blast. **4** a circular pad of straw placed on the head for carrying a tub, basket, etc. **5** a straw collar for oxen. **6** a bulky necktie.

wae' s-heart *int* alas for you!

wae's me *int* woe is me!

waes my craws *int* an exclamation of sorrow, pity, etc.

waes my fell *int* an exclamation of mingled sadness and astonishment.

waesome *adj* sorrowful, sad.

waesomelike *adj* sad.

waesomely *adv* sadly.

waesuck, waesucks *int* alas!

wae wags ye *int* an exclamation of imprecation.

wae-wan *adj* pale with grief.

wae-weirdit *adj* doomed to woe.

wae-worn *adj* grief-stricken.

wae worth *int* woe betide! woe worth!

waey *n* way.

waff[1] *v* **1** to wave. **2** to flap. **3** to fan. **4** to flutter. **5** to excel in vigorous dancing.—*n* **1** a flapping. **2** a wave of the hand. **3** a flag, signal. **4** a puff of wind. **5** a current or gust of wind caused by the swift passage of a moving body. **6** a whiff. **7** an odour assailing the nostrils. **8** a slight touch from a soft body in passing. **9** a slight, sudden ailment. **10** a touch of cold. **11** a passing glimpse. **12** a good or bad influence. **13** a wraith.—*adj* brief, fleeting.

waff[2] *adj* **1** strayed, wandering alone. **2** solitary. **3** woebegone. **4** vagabond-like. **5** unprincipled. **6** wild. **7** immoral. **8** shabby. **9** of poor quality. **10** feeble, paltry. **11** worn-out, weak in mind. **12** lowborn. **13** hard, difficult.—*n* **1** a waif, vagrant. **2** a rascal. **3** a low, idle fellow. **4** one who keeps bad company.—*v* to wander idly.

waffel *same as* **waffle**[2].

waffer *n* **1** (*used in mining*) a break or dip. **2** a fault.

waffer *adj* strayed, wandering.

waffie *n* **1** a worthless fellow. **2** one given to idleness or low company.

waffil *same as* **waffle**[1].

waffinger *n* **1** a vagabond. **2** a good-for-nothing fellow.

waffish *adj* **1** (*used of persons*) disreputable, immoral. **2** (*of things*) worthless.

waffle[1] *same as* **wuffle**.

waffle[2] *v* **1** to wave about. **2** to flap in the wind.—*adj* flexible, pliant.

waffleness *n* pliability, limberness.

waffler *n* a weak, undecided person.

waff-like *adj* **1** of disreputable appearance. **2** shabby-looking. **3** weak.

wafflin *adj* hesitating, tmsteadied, vacillatory.

waff-looking *adj* of disreputable, suspicious appearance.

waffly *adj* hesitating, undecided.

waffness *n* a shabby appearance.

waft[1] *n* **1** a puff of wind. **2** a whiff. **3** a passing smell or taste. **4** a passing glimpse. **5** a benevolent or favourable influence. **6** one who, under the appearance of friendship, holds a person up to ridicule.

waft[2] *n* woft, woof.

waft and warp *v* to weave.

wafters *n* pinions.

wag, wagg *v* **1** to move about. **2** to keep going. **3** to shake. **4** to wave. **5** to beckon with hand or head. **6** (*used of the tongue*) to chatter.—*n* **1** a waving motion. **2** a signal with the hand. **3** a flag. **4** a contemptuous designation of a fellow. **5** (*in pl*) tricks, conduct.

wa-gaen, wa-gang *same as* **way-gang**.

wa-gaen ~, wa-gang crap *same as* **way-gang crop**.

wag along *int* a driver's call to his oxen.

waganging *n* going or passing along.

wa'gate *same as* **waygate**.

wag-at-the-wa *n* **1** a cheap clock, hanging on a wall, with pendulum and weights exposed. **2** a spectre supposed to haunt the kitchen and to wag backwards and forwards on the crook before a death in the house.

wage[1] *n* wages.

wage[2] *v* to wager.

waggary *n* a wagging movement.

waggie *same as* **wag-at-the-wa**.

waggity, waggit-wa *same as* **wag-at-the-wa**.

waggle *v* **1** to waddle. **2** to walk along unsteadily. —*n* a bog, quagmire, marsh.—*adv* swaying from side to side.

waggle-waggle *adv* swaying from side to side.

waggly *adj* waggling, unsteady.

waggy *n* the pied wagtail.

wagh *same as* **waugh**[2].

waghorn *n* **1** a fabulous personage, supposed to be a far greater liar than the devil and therefore the king of liars. **2** a name for the devil.

wag-o'-the-pen *n* **1** a scrap of writing. **2** the least bit of a letter.

wag-string *n* one who is hanged.

wag-tawse *n* a schoolmaster.

wag-wits *n* a waggish person.

wa' head *n* the empty space at the head of a cottage wall, that is not beam-filled, where articles are deposited.

waible *v* to walk unsteadily from feebleness.

waichle *same as* **wauchle**².

waicht *n* a hoop with a skin stretched over it, used for winnowing or carrying corn.—*v* to winnow.

waiden *same as* **waden**.

waidge *same as* **wadge**².

waif¹ *n* a stray animal.—*adj* **1** solitary. **2** in a strange place. **3** paltry, weak, inferior. **4** worn-out.

waif² *same as* **waff**¹.

waif-beast *n* a stray animal the owner of which is unknown.

waif-woman *n* a woman without property or connections.

waigle *same as* **waggle**.

waik¹ *v* to watch.—*n* **1** a watch. **2** a company of musicians who serenade on the street early in the morning.

waik² *adj* weak.—*v* to weaken.

waik-leggit *adj* weak in the legs.

waikly *adj* weakly.

waikness *n* weakness.

wail, waile *same as* **wale**².

wail-a-wins *int* an exclamation of surprise, pity or sorrow.

wailed *adj* mourned, lamented.

wailow *v* **1** to fade. **2** to wither. **3** to dwindle.

waim *same as* **wame**.

wain¹ *v* to remove, convey.

wain² *same as* **wean**.

waingle *same as* **wingle**.

wainisht *adj* **1** vanished. **2** pinched, thin.

wainness *n* **1** childishness. **2** feebleness.

wainscot *n* oak.—*adj* oaken.

waint¹ *n* **1** a glimpse, a passing view. **2** a moment.

waint² *n* **1** an alley. **2** the bend of a fishing line not cast at a stretch.—*v* **1** (*of liquids*) to turn sour. **2** to become flavourless.

waip *same as* **wap**².

waipon *n* a weapon.

waipon-shaw *same of* **wapenshaw**.

wair¹ *n* a pillowslip.

wair² *n* the spring.

wair³ *same as* **ware**².

wair⁴ *n* sea wrack.—*v* to manure with sea wrack.

wair⁵ *n* wire.

wairawons *int* well-a-day!

waird¹, **waird**² *same as* **ward**¹, **ward**².

waird³ *same as* **weird**¹.

wairder *n* one who mortises joints with pins.

wairdhouse *n* the guardhouse.

wairdless *same as* **weirdless**.

wairin *n* the strip of wood forming the top of the gunwale of a boat.

wairin' *same as* **waring**.

wairn *same as* **warn**¹.

wairsh *adj* **1** rather saltless. **2** tasteless. **3** squeamish. **4** insipid to the mind. **5** delicate. **6** faint. **7** easily affected. **8** raw. **9** having no fixed principles.

wairsh crap *n* the third crop from the outfield (qv).

wairshless *adj* insipid.

wairsh-like *adj* sickly-looking, sorry-looking.

wairsh-looking *same as* **wairsh-like**.

wairshly *adj* sickly, feebly.

wairshness *n* insipidity.

wairsh-stamack'd *adj* squeamish.

waister *n* a spendthrift.

waistin *n* **1** wasting. **2** consumption.

waist-leather *n* a leather belt for the waist.

waistrel *same as* **wastrel**.

waistry *n* prodigality, waste, extravagance.

wait¹ *n* the watercourse from a mill.

wait² *v* to happen, befall.

wait³ *v* (*with* on) **1** to wait for. **2** to watch beside those near death.—*n* arrangement to lie in wait.

wait⁴ *same as* **wat**².

waite *same as* **wite**.

waiter¹ *n* **1** a person charged with guarding the gates of Edinburgh. **2** a tray.

waiter² *adj* water.

waiter³ *n* a token.

waiter-wench *n* a maidservant.

waith¹ *n* **1** cloth made into clothes. **2** a woman's plaid.

waith² *adj* strong-spirited.

waith³ *v* to stray.—*n* **1** what strays and is unclaimed. **2** flotsam and jetsam. **3** a straying.—*adj* wandering, roaming, straying.

waithman *n* a hunter.

waive *v* **1** to wield. **2** (*with* up) to raise up.

wak *same as* **wack**.

wa'k *v* to walk.

wake¹ *v* to wander.

wake² *v* **1** to watch. **2** to keep watch. **3** to keep watch over a corpse.—*n* **1** the watch held over the dead between death and burial. **2** an annual fair.

wake³ *same as* **waik**².

wake⁴ *same as* **walk**².

waken⁵ *adj* awake.

waken⁶ *v* **1** to become excited. **2** to grow violent in language. **3** to revive a dormant legal action. **4** to watch over.

wakening *n* **1** the revival of a dormant legal action. **2** a severe scolding.

wakerife, wakrife *adj* **1** wakeful, sleepless. **2** easily wakened. **3** watchful.

wakerifely *adv* wakefully.

wakerifeness *n* **1** wakefulness. **2** sleeplessness.

wakness *n* humidity.

wal¹ *n* a well.

wal² *same as* **wale**³.

wal³ *same as* **wall**⁴.

wal-a-day *int* alas! well-a-day!

walaquyte *same as* **waalaquyte**.

walaway, walaways *int* an exclamation of sorrow. —*n* **1** a lamentation. **2** an object of pity or contempt. **3** a name for the devil.

walawaying *n* a lamentation.

walcome *adj* welcome.

wald¹ *same as* **wall**⁴.

wald² *v* **1** to wield. **2** to manage. **3** to govern. **4** to possess.

wald³ *v* would.

walder *n* one who would act but fails to do so.

walding heat *n* **1** the right degree of heat for welding iron. **2** fitness for a particular object or design being carried out.

waldritch *adj* unearthly.

wale¹ *same as* **wall**⁴.

wale² *v* to thrash.—*n* **1** a weal. **2** the verge of a mountain.

wale³ *v* **1** to choose, select, pick out. **2** to woo. **3** to look out for.—*n* **1** choice. **2** choosing. **3** the choicest. **4** the pick. **5** the equal, match.—*adj* choice, select, picked.

waled *adj* the best and bravest, the strongest.

wale-wight *adj* chosen, strongest, best and bravest.

walgan, walgon *n* **1** a wallet. **2** a pouch. **3** something large and roomy. **4** an ill-made or dirty article of dress.—*v* to go about ill-dressed in an idle and slovenly fashion.

walgie *n* **1** a woolsack made of leather. **2** a calfskin bag.

walise *n* a portmanteau.

walk¹ *v* **1** to leave or be dismissed from a situation. **2** (*used of a shoe*) to be loose at the heel.—*n* a procession.

walk² *v* **1** to full cloth. **2** to render hard and callous, as by hard work. **3** (*used of flannel, etc*) to shrink after wetting. **4** to beat, thrash.

walk³ *same as* **wauk**¹.

walken *same as* **wauken**¹.

walker *n* a fuller.

walking rod *n* a walking stick.

walking song *n* a song with a regular beat sung while walking cloth, especially in the Outer Hebrides. *See* **walk**².

walkit *adj* (*used of the hand*) rendered hard by toil.

walkitness *n* callousness.

walk-mill *n* a mill for fulling cloth.

walk-miller *n* a fuller.

walkrife *same as* **wakerife**.

walkster *n* a fuller.

wall[1] *same as* **wale**[2].

wall[2] *n* the crust of cheese round the width.

wall[3] *n* **1** a well. **2** a spring of water. **3** a whirlpool in the sea.—*v* to well up, as water.

wall[4] *v* to weld.

wallach[1], **walloch** *v* **1** to cry, as a peevish child. **2** to scream. **3** to wail. **4** to use many circumlocutions.—*n* **1** a wail. **2** a howl. **3** a scream. **4** a noisy blusterer. **5** the lapwing.

wallach[2] *v* **1** to wallow. **2** to walk with difficulty. —*n* **1** the act of wallowing and of walking with difficulty. **2** a noisy step, thump or fall.—*adv* with heavy, labouring step.

wallachie-weit *n* the lapwing.

wallachin' *adj* noisy, demonstrative in manner.

wall-away *int* alas! well-a-day!

wallagoo *n* a silly person.

wallan *v* to wither, fade.—*adj* withered, faded.

wallap *n* the lapwing.

wallawae, wallyway *same as* **walaway**.

wallcarses *n* watercress.

walle *same as* **wale**[3].

wallee *n* **1** a spring in a quagmire. **2** a spring or pool of water. **3** the orifice of a well. **4** a source.

wallees *n* **1** saddlebags. **2** pockets to an under-waistcoat.

waller[1] *n* a confused crowd in quick motion.

waller[2] *v* **1** to wallow. **2** to roll on the ground. **3** to toss about, as a fish on dry land.

wallet *n* **1** a small, neatly made person. **2** a fondling term. **3** a valet.

wallflower *n* a children's singing and dancing game.

wall-girse *same as* **wallcarses**.

wall-girse kail *n* the watercress.

walli-drag, walli-dreg *same as* **wally-draigle**.

wallies[1] *n* the intestines.

wallies[2] *n* saddlebags.

wallies[3] *n* **1** finery. **2** toys.

wallies[4] *n* false teeth.

wallie-tragle *same as* **wallydraigle**.

wallifou fa' *int* 'bad luck to!'

walling *n* a cementing, a close alliance with.

wallink *n* the brooklime.

wallipend *v* **1** to undervalue. **2** to vilipend.

walloch[1] *same as* **wallach**[1].

walloch[2], **wallock** *n* a Highland dance, the Highland fling.

walloch-goul[1] *n* a noisy, blustering, demonstrative person.

walloch-goul[2] *n* a woman of slovenly appearance.

wallop[1] *n* the lapwing.

wallop[2] *v* **1** to dance. **2** to gallop. **3** to move fast, shaking the body or clothes. **4** to flounder. **5** to tumble over. **6** to kick about. **7** to move heavily. **8** to waddle. **9** (*used of the heart*) to go pit-a-pat. **10** to flutter. **11** to dangle loosely. **12** to chatter. **13** to scold. **14** to talk volubly. **15** to dash with a swinging force.—*n* **1** a gallop. **2** a dance. **3** a quick movement agitating one's clothes. **4** a sudden, heavy plunge. **5** a leap. **6** the act of dangling loose. **7** a fluttering. **8** a fluttering rag, a dangling tatter. **9** a beat of the heart.—*adv* with a lurch, plunge or jump.

wallop[3] *v* to boil violently and with a bubbling sound.

wallop[4] *v* **1** to beat, thrash. **2** to knock.—*n* **1** a blow. **2** a thrashing.

wallopy-week, ~-weep, ~-weet *n* the lapwing.

wallow[1] *v* to walk or run in a helpless, lumbering fashion.

wallow[2] *v* **1** to fade, wither. **2** to dwindle.

wallowwa, wallowae *same as* **walaway**.

wall-pepper *n* ginger.

wall-rae *n* **1** the green growth on damp walls. **2** freshwater algae.

walls of Troy *n* a labyrinth.

wall tea *n* a tea at which the guests sit round the walls and not at the table.

wall water[1] *n* water that penetrates a wall or runs down its surface.

wall-water[2] *n* water from a well.

wall-wight *same as* **wale-wight**.

wallwood *adj* wildwood.

wallwort *n* the dwarf elder.

wally[1] *adj* **1** beautiful, excellent. **2** fine, thriving. **3** jolly, pleasant. **4** ample, large. **5** made of porcelain or china.— *n* **1** a toy. **2** a gewgaw. **3** a choice ornament. **4** good luck.

wally[2] *same as* **wallow**[2].

wally[3], **wally**[4] *same as* **waly**[1],

wally[4] *same as* **waly**[3].

wally-draig *same as* **wally-draigle**.

wally-draigle *n* **1** a feeble, ill-grown person or animal. **2** the youngest bird in a nest. **3** a young child. **4** the youngest daughter. **5** a sloven. **6** a worthless woman. **7** a wastrel. **8** a vagrant. **9** three sheaves set up without the hood sheaf (qv) to dry speedily.

wally-draiglin *adj* **1** weak and worthless. **2** dirty.

wally-dye[1] *n* a toy.

wally-dye[2] *int* well-a-day! alas!

wally-fa' ye *int* 'good luck to you!'

wally-flower *n* wallflower.

wally-gowdie *n* a term of endearment.

wally-kwite *same as* **wyliecoat**.

wally-stane *n* a nodule of quartz used as a plaything by children.

wally-waeing *same as* **walawaying**.

wally-wallying *n* lamentation.

wa-look *same as* **waylook**.

walsh *adj* insipid.

walshness *n* insipidity.

walshoch *adj* insipid.

walt *n* **1** a welt. **2** a crust of cheese. **3** a weal caused by a blow. **4** a blow. **5** anything large of its kind. —*v* to beat.

waltams *n* straps to keep trousers from mud.

walter *v* **1** to welter. **2** to wallow. **3** to roll and twist about. **4** to swell, surge. **5** to overturn.—*n* **1** an upset. **2** confusion. **3** a change causing confusion.

walth *n* **1** wealth. **2** plenty, abundance.

walthy *adj* **1** wealthy. **2** plentiful, abundant.

walt-sheep *n* a fallen sheep.

waly[1] *n* a small flower.

waly[2] *adj* **1** goodly. **2** beautiful. **3** jolly.

waly[3] *int* an exclamation of woe.—*n* a lamentation.

waly-coat *same as* **wylie-coat**.

waly-draigle *same as* **wally-draigle**.

waly-draiglin *same as* **wally-draiglin**.

waly sprig *n* a small flower, a daisy.

wamb *same as* **wame**.

wamble *v* **1** (*used of the intestines*) to rumble, roll or stir uneasily. **2** to quiver, shake, undulate. **3** to turn over and over. **4** to revolve. **5** to wriggle, writhe. **6** to twist about the body. **7** to stagger. **8** to walk clumsily or unsteadily. **9** to wallow.—*n* **1** an undulating motion. **2** a wriggle. **3** the movement of the stomach in digesting food.—*adv* with an undulating or writhing motion.

wamblin *n* **1** a puny child with a big belly. **2** a weak, restless child.

wambly *adj* insecure, shaky, unsteady.

wame *n* **1** the belly. **2** the stomach. **3** the womb. **4** a hollow. **5** room, capacity of holding.—*v* to fill the belly.

wamefu' *n* a bellyful.

wame-gird *n* a horse's bellyband.

wame-ill *n* stomach ache.

wamel, wamle *same as* **wamble**.

wamelin, wanlin *n* a big-bellied, puny child.

wame-tow *n* a horse's bellyband.

wamfil *adj* **1** weak. **2** useless. **3** helpless. **4** limp.

wamfle *v* **1** to flap. **2** to flutter. **3** to sully.

wamflet *n* the water of a millstream after passing the mill.

wamflin *n* **1** a big-bellied, puny child. **2** a weak, restless child.

wamie *adj* **1** big-bellied. **2** corpulent.

wamil *same as* **wamble**.

waminess *n* corpulence.

wammle *same as* **wamble**.

wammlin *n* a restless child.

wampasin *n* a winding street or lane.

wampish, -wampes *v* 1 to fluctuate. 2 to move backwards and forwards. 3 to move like an eel or adder. 4 to brandish, flourish. 5 to make curvilinear dashes, like a large fish in the water.—*n* the motion of an adder.

wample, wamphle *v* 1 to wriggle. 2 to writhe. 3 to intertwine. 4 to twist. 5 to wind, as a stream.—*n* 1 an undulating motion. 2 a wriggling motion, like that of an eel.—*adj* slender, easily bent.

wampler *n* a rake, a wencher.

wampuz *v* 1 to toss about in a threatening, boasting manner. 2 to fluctuate. 3 to go backwards and forwards.

wan[1] *adj* (*used of water*) black, gloomy.

wan[2] *v* dwelt. *See* **won**.

wan[3] *adj* not fully round or plump.

wan[4] *n* 1 hope. 2 a prospect of success. 3 a liking for anything.

wan[5] *n* a direction.—*adv* in the direction of.

wan[6] *v* won. *See* **win**[1].

wan[7] *v* wound. *See* **wind**[2].

wan[8] a negative prefix corresponding to 'un'.

wan' *adj* one.

wancanny *adj* 1 uncanny. 2 unlucky.

wance *adv* one.

wanchance *n* 1 a mishap. 2 misfortune.

wanchancy, wanchancie *adj* 1 unlucky. 2 boding evil. 3 wicked. 4 dangerous.

wan-cheekit *adj* having thin cheeks.

wancheerie *adj* 1 cheerless. 2 sad.

wancouth *adj* 1 uncouth. 2 strange.

wand[1] *n* 1 a switch. 2 a stick. 3 a willow wand. 4 wicker. 5 a fishing rod. 6 a sheriff officer's rod, the symbol of his authority.—*adj* 1 made of willow. 2 wicker.

wand[2] *v* wound. *See* **wind**[2].

wand-bed *n* a wicker bed.

wand-birn *n* a straight burn on the face of a sheep.

wand-hair *n* a wicker chair.

wandeedy *adj* mischievous.

wander *v* 1 to travel begging, hawking, etc. 2 to lose oneself or one's way. 3 to confuse, perplex. —*n* confusion.

wandered *adj* 1 strayed. 2 lost. 3 confused.

wanderer *n* a fugitive Covenanter.

wandering-folks *n* 1 beggars. 2 hawkers. 3 vagrants.

wandering-cailor *n* the ivy-leaved toadflax.

wandocht, wandough, wandout *adj* 1 weak. 2 puny. 3 silly. 4 contemptible.—*n* 1 a weak, puny creature. 2 a silly and inactive person. 3 a worthless person.

wand of peace *n* the wand of an officer of justice, with which he touched a rebel to make him prisoner.

wane[1] *n* 1 a dwelling. 2 a habitation.

wane[2] *same as* **wean**.

wanearthly, wanerthly *adj* 1 unearthly. 2 supernatural. 3 ghostly.

wanease, waneis *n* 1 uneasiness. 2 vexation.—*v* to put oneself about.

wan'er *same as* **wander**.

wanfortune *n* misfortune.

wanfortunate *adj* unfortunate.

wangle *v* 1 to wag. 2 to dangle.

wangrace, wangrease *n* oatmeal gruel with a little butter and honey.

wangrace *n* 1 wickedness. 2 lack of grace. 3 a blackguard, scamp.

wangracefu' *adj* 1 wicked. 2 graceless. 3 ungraceful.

wangracie *adj* 1 blackguardly. 2 ill-behaved.

wanhap *n* 1 misfortune. 2 a mishap.

wanhappie *adj* unlucky, unfortunate.

wanhelt *n* ill-health, sickness.

wanhope *n* despair.

wanion *n* 1 bad luck. 2 mischief. 3 used as an imprecation.

wanjoy *n* 1 misery. 2 sorrow.

wankill *adj* unstable.

wankish *v* to twist, entwine.

wanlas *n* a surprise.

wanle *adj* 1 agile, lithe, nimble. 2 strong, healthy.

wanless *adj* hopeless. *See* **wan**[4].

wanlie *adj* 1 auspicious, hopeful. 2 agreeable. 3 comfortable.

wanliesum *adj* unlovely.

wanlit *adj* unlit, darkened.

wanluck *n* 1 misfortune. 2 bad luck.

wannel[1], **wannle** *same as* **wanle**.

wannel[2] *v* to stagger, be unsteady.

wanner *v* to wander.

wanny *adj* pale, ill-looking.

wanown't *adj* 1 unclaimed. 2 not acknowledged.

waureck *n* 1 mischance. 2 ruin.

wanrest *n* 1 unrest, inquietude. 2 the cause of inquietude. 2 the pendulum of a clock.

wanrestfu' *adj* restless.

wanrestie *adj* restless.

wanruly *adj* unruly.

Wansday *n* Wednesday.

wanshaiken *adj* deformed.

wansonsy *adj* 1 mischievous. 2 unlucky,.

want *n* 1 a mental defect, a weakness of intellect. 2 a search for anything missing.—*v* 1 (*with* **for**) to need. 2 to do without. 3 to search, seek. 4 to ask. 5 to seek a wife. 6 to be unmarried. 7 to deserve.

wanter *n* a bachelor seeking a wife.

wanthriven *adj* 1 not thriving. 2 stunted. 3 in a state of decline.

wantin' *adj* deficient in intellect.—*prep* without.

wanton *n* 1 a girth. 2 a horse's bellyband.

wanton-meat *n* an entertainment of spirits, sweetmeats, etc, given to those in a house at the birth of a child.

wanton-yeuk *n* a disease of horses of the nature of the itch.

wanty *n* a horse's bellyband.

wanuse *n* a misuse, abuse, waste.

wanut *n* a walnut.

wanweird *n* misfortune, ill-luck, ill-fate.

wanwordy *adj* unworthy, worthless.

wanworth, wanwuth[1] *adj* 1 unworthy. 2 useless, valueless.—*n* 1 an undervaluation. 2 a very low price. 3 a cheap bargain. 4 anything worthless or of little value, a mere nothing. 5 a worthless person.

wanwuth[1] *same as* **wanworth**.

wanwuth[2] *n* a surprise.

wanyoch *adj* pale, wan.

wap[1] *v* 1 to wrap, fold up. 2 to make a loose bundle. 3 to bind with thread, twine, etc. 4 to splice with cord. 5 to swaddle.—*n* 1 a wrappage. 2 a roll or tie. 3 a thread for tying. 4 cord for splicing. 5 turns of string twisted round a rope or other string. 6 a bundle of straw.

wap[2] *v* 1 to strut. 2 to walk haughtily or with a bustling air.—*n* 1 a vain, bustling style of walking. 2 vain, showy, vulgar conduct. 3 a vain person, one with showy manners, with a vain, silly manner.

wap[3] *v* 1 to strike smartly. 2 to strike with a swing. 3 to flog, thrash. 4 to thresh with a flail. 5 to flap. 6 to seize quickly. 7 to thrust. 8 to 'whip'. 9 to throw. 10 to cast. 11 to dash violently. 12 to pitch. 13 to excel, surpass. 14 to riot. 15 to quarrel. 16 to wrestle.—*n* 1 a sweeping or swinging movement. 2 a stroke of an oar. 3 a knock. 4 a smart stroke. 5 the sound of a smart blow. 6 a disturbance. 7 a riot. 8 a round, fall or throw in wrestling. 9 (*in pl*) a large amount, plenty.—*adv* with a flop. 2 violently.

wapenshaw, wapinschaw *n* 1 an exhibition of arms formerly made at certain times in every district. 2 a competition in rifle-shooting on a large scale.

wapin *n* a loose dress worn by a fisherman at work.

wa-pit *same as* **wayput**.

wappan, wapping *adj* 1 exceptionally large or fine. 2 strapping, huge, stout. 3 (*used of persons*) vain, showy, vulgar.

wapper[1] *n* **1** anything exceptionally large or fine. **2** a great falsehood. **3** a big, fat or strapping person.

wapper[2] *n* **1** a showy, vain, vulgar person. **2** a beau. **3** a belle.

wappin' *n* a flapping of wings.

wapping *same as* **wapin**.

wappon *n* a weapon.

wappy *adj* **1** neat, natty. **2** dressing fashionably. **3** careful as to dress and appearance.

war[1] *v* were.

war[2] *n* goods, stuff.

war[3] *same as* **wear**[5].

war[4] *adj* **1** cautious, wary. **2** aware, conscious.

war[5] *adj* worse.—*adv* the worse.—*n* **1** a defeat. **2** something rather bad.—*v* **1** to put to the worse. **2** to overcome. **3** to excel. **4** to get the better of. **5** to requite for an injury. **6** to injure.

warba-blade *n* the greater plantain.

warbie, warback *n* **1** a maggot bred in the backs of cattle. **2** a warble.

warble[1] *n* **1** a bump, a swelling. **2** a lean, scraggy person.

warble[2] *v* to play the quicker measures of a piece of bagpipe music in which there are many grace notes.

warble[3] *v* to swing. **2** to reel. **3** to wriggle. **4** to worm one's way.

warbler *n* a combination of five or more grace notes in a piece of bagpipe music.

war-brook *n* a large heap of seaweed cast ashore.

ward[1] *v* to award, assign.—*n* **1** an award. **2** what one thoroughly deserves.

ward[2] *v* **1** to watch for. **2** to keep off, guard against. **3** to confine. **4** to go to prison. **5** to fasten a mortised joint by driving a pin through it.—*n* **1** a division of a county. **2** a piece of pasture. **3** land enclosed on all sides for young animals. **4** a beacon hill, a signal hill. **5** confinement.

ward[3] *n* the world.

ward and warsel *n* **1** security. **2** a pledge.

warden *n* a particular kind of pear. *See* **wash-warden**.

ward fire *n* a beacon fire.

ward hill *n* a beacon hill.

wardle *n* **1** the world. **2** (*in pl*) times.

wardle's-make *n* an earthly mate or spouse.

wardle's winner *n* a world's wonder, in a bad sense.

wardly *adj* worldly.

wardly-wary *adj* worldly-wise.

wardroper *n* a wardrobe woman.

ware[1] *v* worn. *See* **wear**[1].

ware[2] *n* **1** stuff. **2** goods. **3** rhymes. **4** money for spending.—*v* **1** to spend. **2** to bestow upon. **3** to squander. **4** to wager.

ware[3] *same as* **waar**[2].

ware[4] *n* the spring.

ware[5], **war**[6] *same as* **war**[5], **war**[4].

ware[7] *n* wire.

ware bear *n* barley manured with seaweed.

wareblade *n* the blade of seaweed.

ware-caist *n* a heap of seaweed.

ware-cock *n* the blackcock.

ware-strand *n* the part of the beach on to which the seaweed is washed.

ware-time *n* **1** spring. **2** the early time of youth.

warf *n* **1** a puny, contemptible creature. **2** a dwarfish person. **3** a fairy.

war-far'd, ~-faured *adj* worse-looking.

war-gang *n* a pennon.

war-hawk *int* beware! take care!

waridrag *same as* **wally-draigle**.

waring *n* leisure.

warison *n* the note of assault.

wark[1] *v* **1** to ache. **2** to throb.

wark[2] *n* **1** work. **2** a fuss. **3** a show of affection. **4** a structure. **5** works. **6** a religious revival.—*v* **1** to knit. **2** to net. **3** (*used of material, etc*) to lend itself easily to work. **4** (*of a pipe*) to draw. **5** to manage, control. **6** to struggle

convulsively. **7** to purge. **8** to ferment. **9** to cause pain. **10** to retaliate. **11** to sprain.

wark-a-day *adj* working, everyday.

wark-claes *n* working clothes.

wark-day *n* **1** a workday. **2** a weekday.

wark-fit *adj* fit for work.

wark-folk *n* working people, labourers.

wark-leem, ~-loom, ~-lume *n* a tool, implement.

warkless *adj* unable to work.

wark-like *adj* industrious.

wark-little *adj* lazy.

warkly *adj* **1** given to work. **2** industrious.

wark machine *n* any machine or contrivance.

warkman *n* **1** a jobber. **2** a porter. **3** an Aberdeen shore porter.

warkrife *adj* **1** industrious. **2** fond of work. **3** hard-working.

wark-stot *n* a work ox, an ox used for ploughing.

wark-worn *adj* toil-worn.

warl[1] *v* to whirl.

warl[2], **warld** *n* **1** the world. **2** worldly goods. **3** a large number.

warldlie *adj* **1** worldly. **2** parsimonious.

warld-like *adj* **1** like the rest of the world. **2** not unnatural.

warld's gear *n* **1** worldly substance. **2** (*with a negative*) nothing at all.

warld's-make *n* an earthly mate or spouse.

warld's waster *n* a spendthrift.

warld's worm *n* a miser, niggard.

warld's wunner *n* **1** a spectacle for all beholders. **2** a person of notorious or surprising conduct.

warl-gear *n* worldly substance.

warlin *n* a worldling.

warlock, warlick *n* a wizard.

warlock breef *n* **1** enchantment. **2** a wizard's spell.

warlock craigie *n* a wizard's rock.

warlock fecket *n* a magic jacket woven from the skins of water snakes at a certain period of a March moon.

warlockin *n* **1** a mischievous imp. **2** an imp of darkness.

warlock knowe *n* a hill where wizards were thought to meet.

warlockry *n* **1** wizardry. **2** magical skill.

warly *same as* **warldlie**.

warm *n* the act of warming.—*v* to thrash.

warm-wise *adj* rather warm, sultry.

warn[1] *v* **1** to cite, summon. **2** to invite verbally to a meeting, funeral, etc. **3** to give verbal intimation. **4** (*used of a clock*) to click before striking.

warn[2] *same as* **warran**.

warna *v neg* were not.

warney *n* a boys' game.

warniement *n* warning, notice.

warning *n* **1** the clicking sound of a clock before striking. **2** a death omen, a portent. **3** a notice. **4** a citation. **5** a verbal invitation to attend a funeral, etc.

warnish, warnice, warnis *v* to warn.

warnishment *n* warning.

warnisin *n* warning.

warp *v* **1** to make an embankment with piles and brushwood. **2** (*used of bees*) to take flight. **3** to make a bleating sound.—*n* **1** the number four, used by fishwives in counting oysters. **2** a smart blow. **3** a stroke of the oar in rowing.

warp and waft *n* every bit.—*adv* completely.

warping-dinner *n* a dinner or food given to a weaver by those who brought their own yarn to his hand loom.

warping-pins *n* the machine in which threads are arranged into warps.

warping wheel *n* a machine for arranging threads into warps.

warple, warpel *v* **1** to entangle. **2** to intertwine. **3** to twist or wind round. **4** to wriggle. **5** to twist the limbs about in the tumbling and tossing of children. **6** to confuse or be confused in any business. **7** to struggle.

warr *same as* **war**[5].

warrach, warrack *n* **1** a knotted stick. **2** a stubborn, ill-tempered person. **3** a stunted, ill-grown person. **4** a puny child. **5** a worthless fellow.—*v* **1** to scold. **2** to vituperate. **3** to blackguard.

warrachie *adj* rough and knotty, gnarled, like the trunk of a tree.

warran, warrand *v* **1** to warrant. **2** to assure. **3** to be bound or go bail.—*n* **1** a security. **2** a surety.

warrandice, warrandise *n* **1** a surety. **2** security for the fulfilment of a bargain or that goods are as they are represented. **3** a warranty. **4** a legal warrant.

warrant sale a compulsory sale of property in order to pay off the owner's debts.

warrer *adj* more wary.

warricoe *same as* **worricow**.

warroch[1] *v* **1** to wallow. **2** to struggle in mud.

warroch[2] *same as* **warrach**.

warry, in take heed! look out!—*adj* wary, heedful.

warry *adj* pertaining to seaweed.

warse *adj* worse.

warsh, warsche *same as* **wairsh**.

warsle, warstle, warsal, warsel, warsell *v* **1** to wrestle. **2** to strive. **3** to struggle. **4** to grapple with difficulties. **5** (*used of time*) to pass, bringing toil and sorrow. **6** (*with* **through**) to come out successful, overcome difficulties, etc.—*n* **1** a wrestle. **2** a struggle. **3** a tussle. **4** a grapple with a difficulty.

warsler *n* a wrestler.

warst *adj* worst.

warstan *adj* worst.

warstling-herrings *n* 'herrings all alive!' an Edinburgh fishwife's cry.

wart[1] *v with pron* were it.

wart[2] *n* **1** a beacon hill. **2** an elevated signalling station. **3** the beacon kindled on a wart.

warth *n* the apparition of a living person, a wraith.

wart hill *same as* **ward hill**.

wart nor *v with pron and neg* **1** had it not been for. **2** were it not for.

wartweil *n* the skin at the base of the fingernail when loose or fretted.

warwoof, warwooph *n* **1** a puny child. **2** an undergrown person. **3** a werewolf.

wary *same as* **warry**[1].

wary-draggle *same as* **wally-draigle**.

wa'a *n* **1** ways. **2** *in phr* **come your wa's** come away.

wash *n* **1** liquid mud. **2** weak, washy drink. **3** stale urine, formerly used for washing clothes.

wash bine, ~ boyne *n* a wash tub.

washen *adj* washed.

washer *n* a washerwoman.

washer-wife *n* a washerwoman, laundress.

washing boyne, ~ boin *n* a wash tub.

washing hoose *n* a washhouse.

washing say *n* a wash tub.

wash mug *n* a chamber pot.

wash tub *n* a large tub or cask for storing urine for washing clothes.

wash-up *n* a ducking.

wash-warden *n* a coarse, sour winter pear.

wash words *v* to converse.

washy-waulker *n* a cloth fuller.

wasie *adj* **1** sagacious. **2** of quick apprehension. **3** merry, playful, lively.

wasp bike, ~ bink *n* a wasps' nest.

wasper *n* a fish spear, a leister.

waspet *adj* thin about the loins.

wassel[1] *same as* **wastel**.

wassel[2] *adv* westwards.

wassie *n* a horse collar.

wassock *n* **1** a pad worn by milkmaids to relieve the pressure of their pails on their heads. **2** a kind of bunch put on a boring jumper to prevent the water

used in boring from leaping up into the quarrier's eyes.

wast *adj* west.

wastage *n* **1** a waste. **2** a place of desolation.

wast-bye *adv* westward.

wastcoat *n* a waistcoat.

waste[1] *adj* wasted.—*n* **1** disused workings in a coal mine. **2** coal-mining refuse. **3** remnants of weft, broken threads, etc, in weaving. **4** consumption, phthisis.

waste[2] *v* to spoil or damage.

waste-heart *same as* **wae's-heart**.

wastel, wastel bread *n* thin oatcake baked with yeast.

wastell *n in phr* **willy wastell** a children's rhyming game.

wasteness *n* waste.

waster[1] *n* **1** an extravagant person. **2** an idler. **3** an imperfection in the wick of a candle causing guttering.—*v* **1** to waste. **2** to spend needlessly.

waster[2] *same as* **wasper**.

waster[3] *adj* western.—*v* to go or drift westwards.

wasterfu' *adj* **1** wasteful. **2** extravagant. **3** lavish.

wasterfully *adv* **1** extravagantly. **2** wastefully.

wasterfulness *n* **1** extravagance. **2** lavishness.

wasterie *n* **1** waste. **2** wastefulness.

wasterous *adj* wasteful.

wasting *n* consumption, a decline.

wastland *adj* western.—*n* the west country.

wastle *adv* westward.

wastlin *adj* western.—*n* the west country.

wastlins *adv* westward.

wast-ower *adv* westward.

wastrel, wastril *n* **1** a spendthrift. **2** a ne'er-do-well. **3** a vagrant. **4** a thin, unhealthy-looking person.—*adj* **1** vagabond. **2** wasteful. **3** thin, wasted.

wastrey, wastrie *n* **1** a waste. **2** extravagance. **3** wastefulness.

wastrife *adj* **1** extravagant. **2** wasteful.—*n* **1** extravagance. **2** wastefulness.

wat[1] *n* an outer garment.

wat[2] *v* **1** to know. **2** to inform. **3** to assure. **4** to be sensible of.

wat[3] *same as* **wad**[2].

wat[4] *same as* **waat**.

wat[5] *same as* **wet**[2].

wa'taking *n* carrying off by theft or violence.

watch *n* **1** a watchdog. **2** an outpost. **3** a hill of a certain height.

watchglass *n* an hourglass.

watch house *n* a police station.

watchie *n* a watchmaker.

watchlight *n* a rush light.

watchmail *n* a duty imposed for maintaining a garrison.

watchman *n* the uppermost grain in a stalk of corn.

watch money *n* blackmail.

watchword *n* **1** a note of warning. **2** a hint to be on one's guard.

wate[1] *same as* **wait**[1].

wate[2] *same as* **wat**[2].

water, watter *n* **1** a river, a good-sized stream. **2** a lake. **3** a pool in a river. **4** a wave. **5** a heavy sea. **6** a disease of sheep, shell-sickness (qv). **7** the banks of a river. **8** the district bordering a river.—*v* **1** to wash down any food. **2** (*used of the mouth*) to make it water.

water berry *n* water gruel.

water betony *n* the water figwort.

water blackbird *n* the dipper.

water blinks *n* the water chickweed.

water brash *n* watery acid belches.

water brod *n* a bench or board on which water pails rest.

water broo *n* water gruel.

water brose *n* oatmeal stirred into boiling water until the mixture is thick and rather stiff.

waterburn *n* the phosphorescence of the sea.

water calf *n* the placenta of a cow.

water corn *n* the grain paid by farmers for the maintenance of the dams and races of the mills to which they are astricted.

water cow¹ *n* a water sprite inhabiting a lake.

water cow² *n* a water beetle.

water craw *n* **1** the water ouzel or dipper. **2** the coot. **3** the great northern diver.

water custom *n* the custom of going to a well near midnight of 31 December to draw the first water of the New Year, a custom supposed to bring good luck for the year.

water deevil *n* a water sprite, a kelpie.

waterdog *n* the water rat.

water draucht *n* the outlet of water from a loch.

water droger *n* the last-born of a litter.

water dyke *n* a wall or embarkment to keep a river or stream in flood from overflowing the adjoining lands.

water eagle *n* the osprey.

water elder *n* the guelder rose.

waterfall *n* a watershed.

waterfast *adj* **1** watertight. **2** capable of resisting the force of rain.

water fishings *n* river fishings.

waterfit *n* **1** the mouth of a river. **2** a village or hamlet at the mouth of a river or stream.

water fur *n* a furrow made to drain off surface water.—*v* to form furrows in ploughed land for draining off the water.

watergang *n* **1** a millrace. **2** a watercourse. **3** a right to draw water along a neighbour's ground to water one's own.

watergate *n* **1** a road leading to a watering place. **2** the act of voiding urine. **2** an advantage over a man.

watergaw *n* **1** the fragment of a rainbow appearing in the horizon. **2** seen in the north or east, a sign of bad weather.

water-gled *n* a revenue officer, a preventive officer.

water hole *n* a pond.

water horse *n* a water goblin, a kelpie.

water-ill *n* a disease of cows affecting their water.

watering *n* drink for a horse.

watering pan *n* a watering pot.

water kail *n* broth made without meat and only with vegetables.

water kelpie *n* **1** a mischievous water sprite. **2** a river horse.

water kit *n* a wooden bucket for holding water, narrower at the top than at the bottom and having a wooden handle fixed across the top.

water kyle *n* meadowland that is possessed by the tenants of an estate in common or individually by rotation.

water lamp *n* marine phosphorescence.

water laverock *n* the common sandpiper.

waterloo *v* **1** to overcome. **2** to overcome by strong drink.

watermouse *n* a water rat.

water mouth, ~ mow *n* the mouth of a river.

water neb *n* the mouth of a river.

Water-of-Ayr stone *n* a stone highly valued for hones and boys' marbles.

water peggie *n* the water ouzel or dipper.

water purple, ~ purple *n* the common brooklime.

water pyet *n* the water ouzel or dipper.

water run *n* a waterspout or gutter under the eaves of a house.

water saps *n* invalids' food.

water sapwort *n* the hemlock dropwort.

waterside *n* a river bank.

water-skater *n* an insect that glides or skates or darts along the surface of stagnant pools.

water-slain-moss *n* peat earth carried off by water and then deposited.

waterstane *n* a pebble from a brook.

water stoup 1 *same as* **water kit**. **2** the common periwinkle, from its resemblance to a pitcher.

water table *n* the ditch or gutter on each side of a road for carrying off water.

water-tabling *n* the work of making or cleaning water tables (qv).

water tath *n* luxuriant grass owing to excess of moisture.

water thraw *same as* **water brash**.

water tiger *n* a swimming water beetle.

water twist *n* a particular kind of yarn.

water wader *n* a home-made candle of the worst kind.

water-wag, ~-waggie *n* the wagtail.

water wan *n* part of a watermill, the axle.

water-water *n* water obtained from a stream, as contrasted with water drawn from a well.

water-weak, ~-weik *n* a frail, delicate person.

water-weikit *adj* frail, delicate.

water wraith, ~ waith *n* a water sprite.

watery *n* the pied wagtail.

watery-braxy *n* inflammation of a sheep's bladder through over-distention.

watery-nebbit, ~-nibbit *adj* **1** of a pale and sickly countenance. **2** having a watery nose.

watery-pleeps *n* **1** the common sandpiper. **2** the redshank.

watery-pox *n* the chickenpox.

watery-wagtail *n* the yellow wagtail.

wat-finger *n* little effort.

wath *n* a ford.

wather *n* weather.

wat-lookin' *adj* threatening rain.

watreck *int* an exclamation of surprise or pity.

watshod *adj* (*used of the eyes*) brimful of tears.

Watsunday *n* Whitsunday term.

watten *v* to wet.

watter *n* water.

watter vraith *n* a water sprite.

wattie *n* a blow.

wattin *n* a wetting.

wattle *n* **1** a twig. **2** a switch. **3** a billet of wood. **4** an entanglement of a line, thread or twine. **5** (*in pl*) the rods laid on the framework of a roof to lay the thatch on.—*v* to strike with a switch, cane, etc, repeatedly.

watty *n* **1** an eel. **2** the pied wagtail. **3** the white-throat.

wauble *v* **1** to wobble. **2** to swing. **3** to reel. **4** to undulate. **5** to walk unsteadily from weakness.—*n* **1** the act of so walking. **2** weak, watery food or drink.—*adj* **1** slender, easily shaken. **2** of a weak, watery flavour.—*adv* **1** tremulously. **2** with weak, faltering steps.

wauch¹ *same as* **wack**.

wauch² *same as* **waugh²**.

wauch³ *same as* **waught¹**.

wauch⁴, wauck *v* to full cloth.

wauchie¹ *adj* clammy.

wauchie² *adj* **1** of a sallow and greasy face. **2** feeble, weak.

wauchie, wauchile *v* **1** to move backwards and forwards. **2** to waggle. **3** to waddle. **4** to stagger. **5** to walk as fatigued. **6** to fatigue greatly. **7** to struggle, strive with difficulties. **8** to puzzle.—*n* **1** an unsteady movement. **2** a struggle. **3** a difficulty. **4** weary work.

waucht¹ *same as* **waught¹**.

waucht² *n* weight.

wauchty *adj* **1** weighty. **2** corpulent. **3** valiant.

waud¹ *same as* **wadd²**.

waud² *v* to wade.

wauf¹, wauf² *same as* **waff¹, waff²**.

waufish *same as* **waffish**.

waufie *v* to waver in the air, as snow, chaff or any light substance.—*n* a slight fall of snow.

wauge, wanje *v* (*used with* **nieve**) to shake one's fist at a person.

waugh¹ *same as* **waught¹**.

waugh² *adj* **1** insipid. **2** nauseous to the taste or smell. **3** musty, stale. **4** smelling of damp. **5** wan and pale. **6** sallow and greasy. **7** debased, worthless.

waugh² *same as* **wack**.

waughie *same as* **wauchie¹**.

waughle *same as* **wauchle**.

waughorn *same as* **waghorn**.

waught¹ *v* **1** to drink deeply. **2** to quaff.—*n* **1** a copious draught. **2** a big drink.

waught[2] *n* weight.
waughy *same as* **wauchie**[2].
wauk[1] *v* **1** to wake. **2** to watch. **3** to watch over.
wauk[2] *v* to walk.
wauk[3] *same as* **wack**.
wauk[4], **wauck** *same as* **walk**[2].
wauken[1] *v* **1** to awake. **2** to become animated. **3** to use violent language. **4** to awaken. **5** to revive a dormant legal process. **6** to watch over.
wauken[2] *adj* **1** awake. **2** disinclined for sleep.
wauken[3] *v* to chastise.
waukening *n* **1** the act of awaking or of awakening. **2** outrageous scolding.
wauker[1] *n* **1** a watcher. **2** one who watches clothes during the night.
wauker[2] *n* a fuller.
waukerife *same as* **wakerife**.
waukfere *adj* able to go about. *See* **fere**.
wauking, waukan *n* **1** the act of watching. **2** the night watch kept over an unburied corpse or of one buried in resurrectionist times or over clothes or over the fauld or sheepfold.
waukit *adj* (*used of the hands*) hardened, rendered callous by hard work.
waukitness *n* callousness of skin.
waukmill *n* a fulling mill.
waukmiller *n* a fuller.
waukrife *adj* wakeful.
waukster *n* a fuller.
waul[1] *v* **1** to roll the eyes. **2** to gaze wildly. **3** to gaze drowsily.
waul[2] *adj* nimble, agile.
waul[3] *int* an exclamation of sorrow.
waul[4] *n* a well.
waul[5] *v* **1** to weld. **2** to comply. **3** to consent.
waul[6], **waule** *same as* **wale**[3].
wauld[1] *v* **1** to wield. **2** to possess. **3** to manage.
wauld[2] *n* the plain open country, without wood.
waulie *same as* **waul**[2].
waulie *same as* **waly**[2].
wauliesum *adj* causing sorrow.
wauling heat *n* the proper temperature for welding iron.
waulk *same as* **walk**[2].
waulking wicker *n* a basket used in fulling cloth.
waumish *adj* **1** uneasy. **2** squeamish.
waumle *v* **1** to rumble. **2** to roll. **3** to move awkwardly.
waund *same as* **wand**[1].
wauner *v* to wander.
waup[1] *same as* **wap**[3].
waup[2] *n* an outcry.
waur[1] *v* **1** to defeat. **2** to beat off. **3** to ward off.
waur[2] *n* the spring.
waur[3], **waure** *same as* **war**[4].
waur[4] *same as* **war**[5].—*n in phr* **ten waurs** a great misfortune, a great pity.
waur[5] *same as* **ware**[2].
waurn *same as* **warran**.
waurst *adj* worst.
wausie *adj* **1** weary, tired and sore. **2** bored.
wausper *same as* **wasper**.
waut *same as* **walt**.
wauts *n* the harness resting on a pony's hips.
wauw *same as* **waw**[4].
wave *v* to signal by a wave of the hand.
wavel[1] *v* **1** to move backwards and forwards. **2** to stagger. **3** to wave.
wavel[2] *n* a weevil.
wavelock *n* an implement for twisting ropes of hay, straw, etc.
waver *v* to be slightly delirious.
wavy *adj* voyaging by sea.
waw[1] *n* a wall.
waw[2] *int* **1** an exclamation of sorrow. **2** of pleasure, admiration.

waw[3] *int* well! why! pshaw! an exclamation of expostulation, contempt or encouragement.
waw[4] *v* **1** to mew as a cat, caterwaul. **2** to wail.—*n* **1** the mew of a cat. **2** the wail of an infant.
wawf *same as* **waff**[2].
wawl[1] *same as* **waul**[1].
wawl[2] *v* **1** to howl. **2** to whine. **3** to mew as a cat.
waws *n* (*used of cheese*) the crust round the width.
wawsper *same as* **wasper**.
waxen ~, wax kernel *n* a glandular swelling in the neck.
way[1] *n* **1** a state of anxiety, anger, perturbation, etc. **2** the direction of. **3** a tradition, saw. **4** cause, reason. **5** *in phr* **to make way of oneself** to commit suicide.—*adv* away.
way[2] *int* a call to a horse to stop.
way-bread *n* the greater plantain.
way-burn leaf *n* the greater plantain.
waygang *n* **1** departure. **2** death. **3** a leave-taking or farewell social meeting. **4** a flavour. **5** a disagreeable taste. **6** a whiff. **7** a whisper. **8** a faint sound. **9** the channel of water running from a mill.
waygang crop *n* the last crop belonging to a tenant before he leaves his farm.
wayganging, waygoing *n* a waygang (qv).—*adj* departing, outgoing.
wayganging crop *same as* **waygang crop**.
waygate, wayget *n* **1** room, space. **2** the tailrace of a mill. **3** progress, speed.
waygaun *adj* outgoing.—*n* **1** a departure. **2** death.
waygoe *n* a place where a body of water breaks out.
way-kenning *n* the knowledge of one's way from a place.
waylay *v* **1** to hide. **2** to lay aside.
wayleave *n* right of way, privilege of passage.
waylook *n* a suspicious, downcast look away from the person one addresses.
wayput *v* **1** to put away. **2** to make away with.
wayputting *n* **1** execution. **2** murder. **3** burial.
waywart *adj* **1** preparatory, preliminary. **2** warning.
waz *n* **1** a small bundle of straw, etc. **2** a bulky necktie. **3** a straw collar for oxen.
wazban *n* a waistband.
wazie *same as* **wasie**.
wazzan *n* the windpipe, the weasand.
we *same as* **wee**.
weagh *v* to waggle.
weak *same as* **waik**[2].
wĕak *v* **1** to squeak. **2** to whine, whimper. **3** to scream. **4** to utter loud cries, as an animal. **5** to whistle at intervals.—*n* **1** a squeak. **2** a chirp. **3** a little, thin person with a squeaky voice.
weal *same as* **wale**[3].
wealth *same as* **walth**.
wealth and worle *n* abundance to choose from.
weam *same as* **wame**.
weam-ill *n* belly-ache.
wean *n* **1** a child. **2** an infant.
weanie *n* a little child.
weanly *adj* **1** childish. **2** feeble. **3** slender. **4** ill-grown.
weanock *n* a little child.
weapon-shaw *same as* **wapenshaw**.
wear[1] *v* **1** to last. **2** to retain vigour. **3** to serve for wearing. **4** to use. **5** to grow, become. **6** to cause to become. **7** to make gradually. **8** to waste away. **9** to live in wedlock with a person. **10** to walk quietly, go slowly. **11** to pass on.—*n* **1** clothing. **2** fashion in dress.
wear[2] *v* to long for, desire earnestly.
wear[3] *v* wore.
wear[4] *same as* **ware**[2].
wear[5] *v* **1** to watch, guard. **2** to stop. **3** to turn aside. **4** to cause to veer. **5** to lead cattle, sheep, etc, gently to an enclosure. **6** to guide, help on. **7** to incite.—*n* **1** a defence. **2** a hedge. **3** a guard. **4** a guard in fencing. **5** force, restraint.
wearables *n* clothes.

wear awa v **1** to pass away slowly. **2** to fade away. **3** to draw near to death. **4** to make time pass.

wear-a-wins int an exclamation of sorrow.

wear by v to pass by.

weard same as **weird**[1].

weardie n the youngest or feeblest bird in a nest.

wear down v **1** to descend slowly and surely. **2** to grow old.

weared v **1** wore. **2** worn.

wearifu' adj **1** tedious. **2** dismal, dreary. **3** tiresome, vexatious.

wear in v **1** (used of time) to pass slowly. **2** to while away. **3** to bring to a close. **4** to move slowly and cautiously to a place. **5** to lead carefully, or drive slowly, cattle, sheep, etc.

wear in by v to move cautiously towards a place.

wearing adj **1** tedious. **2** tiresome, trying.

wear in o' or in til v to acquire by degrees.

wear off[1] v to ward off.

wear off[2] v to pay off gradually.

wear on v **1** to near slowly. **2** to introduce gradually.

wear out v **1** to decline. **2** to apostatize. **3** to exhaust.

wear round v **1** to recover health. **2** to prevail in. **3** to gain one's favour.

wear through v **1** to waste. **2** to get through. **3** to endure. **4** to while away time.

wear up v **1** to grow up. **2** to grow old. **3** to waste away.

weary, wearie adj **1** wearisome. **2** monotonous, tedious. **3** sad, sorrowful. **4** disastrous. **5** vexatious. **6** troublesome. **7** bad. **8** feeble, puny, sickly.—n **1** a feeling of weariness. **2** a girls' singing game.—v to long for, desire earnestly.—adv sadly.

weary, wearie n **1** the deuce. **2** a nuisance, trouble.

weary-fa' int as an imprecation, a curse.

weary-wae adj weary with woe.

weasan, weason n **1** the gullet. **2** windpipe.

wease same as **waese**.

weased adj uneasy, anxious.

weasel-body n an inquisitive, prying person.

weasses n a species of breeching for the necks of horses.

weather[1] n a wether.

weather[2] n **1** a storm. **2** rough weather. **3** the weather side. **4** a season, a condition of things. **5** means, method.—v **1** to keep clear of. **2** to make way with difficulty.

weather-brack n a break or change in the weather.

weather-cock n in phr **aneth the weathercock** imprisoned in the church steeple, in which offenders formerly were confined.

weather-dame n a weather prophetess.

weather-days n the time for sheepshearing.

weather-fender n protection from the weather.

weather-fu' adj boisterous, stormy.

weather-gaw n **1** the lower part of a rainbow left visible above the horizon. **2** a fine day during much bad weather. **3** brightness before a storm. **4** a gleam of sunshine between storms. **5** anything so favourable as to seem to indicate the reverse.

weather-gleam n **1** a clear sky near a dark horizon. **2** (used of objects seen in the twilight or dusk) near the horizon. **3** a place exposed to the wind.

weather-gloom same as **weather-gleam**.

weather-wear n the severity or wearing influence of the weather.

weather-wiseacre n **1** a weather prophet. **2** one who is weather-wise.

weathery adj stormy, unsettled.

weave v **1** to knit. **2** to wind in pursuit.

weaven, weavin n a moment.

weaver n **1** a knitter of stockings. **2** a spider.

weaver-kneed adj knock-kneed.

weaverty-waverty n a contemptuous name for a weaver.

weezle-blawing n a disease of the roots of the fingers.

weazon, weazen same as **weasan**.

weaz't same as **weezet**.

web same as **wab**.

web-glass n a magnifying glass for examining a web of cloth.

webis same as **weebo**.

web-o'-the-body n the omentum.

web's end n the last moment.

webster same as **wabster**.

webster-craft n the art of weaving.

wecht[1] n **1** a weight. **2** the standard by which a thing is weighed. **3** a great amount. **4** a bundle of fishing lines. **5** (in pl) a pair of scales.—v **1** to weigh. **2** to feel the weight of. **3** to depress, dispirit.

wecht[2] n **1** an unperforated sheepskin or calfskin stretched over a hoop for winnowing or carrying corn. **2** a sort of tambourine.—v to winnow, fan.

wechtfu' n as much as a wecht (qv) will contain.

wechtsman n a winnower who uses a wecht (qv).

wechty adj weighty.

wechty-fittit adj advanced in pregnancy.

wechty-tochered adj well-dowered.

wed[1] same as **wad**[2].

wed[2] same as **wad**[3].

wed[3] v weeded.

wed[4] adj faded, vanished.

wedder[1] n a wether.

wedder[2] n weather.

weddinger n **1** a wedding guest. **2** (in pl) the whole marriage party.

weddin-sou n a trousseau.

wede, wede-away v **1** to die out. **2** to cause to vanish. **3** to destroy.—adj faded, vanished, removed by death.

wedless adj unmarried.

wedset same as **wadset**.

wee[1] adj **1** little. **2** young. **3** of low station, humble. **4** on a small scale. **5** close-fisted. **6** mean, despicable.—n **1** a short time. **2** a while.

wee[2] v to weigh.—n (in pl) a balance beam and scales.

weeack, weeak same as **weak**[2].

wee-ane same as **wean**.

wee-bauk n a small crossbeam nearest the angle of a roof.

weebis, weebie same as **weebo**.

wee bit adj little, puny.—n **1** a small bit of anything. **2** used often contemptuously of persons of small stature.

weebo n **1** the common ragwort. **2** the tansy.

wee-boukit adj **1** small-bodied. **2** in small compass.

wee cheese, wee butter n a children's play in which two children, back to back with linked arms, lift each other alternately, the one crying 'wee [weigh] cheese', the other 'wee butter', when their turns come to lift.

weed[1] n a worthless person.—v **1** to thin out plants. **2** to single turnips.

weed[2] n **1** a garment. **2** dress. **3** a winding sheet. **4** grave clothes.

weed[3] n **1** a chill causing inflammation of milk ducts in a woman's breasts after confinement. **2** a disease of horses and cattle. **3** pains of labour.

weed[4] adj faded.

weeder n one who thins out plants.

weeder-clips n an instrument for pulling up weeds growing among grain.

weedins n plants weeded out or cut out in thinning trees, turnips, etc.

weedit ppl adj (used of the hair) thin, sparse.

weedock[1] n a weed hook for grubbing up weeds.

weedock[2] n a little weed.

weedow, weeda, weedy n **1** a widow. **2** a widower.

wee drap n **1** whisky. **2** a little whisky.

weefil n a contemptuous designation of an extravagant person.

Wee Free adj belonging to the Free Church of Scotland.— n a member of the Free Church of Scotland.

weegilty-waggiltie adj unstable, wavering.

weegle v **1** to waggle. **2** to wiggle.

weegler n one who waddles.

weeglie *adj* having a wriggling motion in walking.
wee-hauf *n* a half-glass of whisky.
week[1] *same as* **weak**[2].
week[2] *same as* **wick**[2].
week teeth *n* a canine tooth.
weel[1] *n* **1** an eddy. **2** a pool. **3** a deep, still part in a river.
weel[2] *same as* **wale**[3].
weel[3] *n* happiness, prosperity, weal.
weel[4] *adj* **1** well. **2** healthy. **3** (*of food*) well cooked.—*adv* well, very, quite.—*int* an exclamation of contentment, resignation, impatience, surprise, etc.
weel-a-day *int* alas! well-a-day!
weel-aff *adj* well off.
weel-a-wat *int* assuredly!
weel-a-weel *int* an exclamation of resignation, well, well!
weel-a-wins, weel-a-wons *int* an exclamation of pity, sorrow, etc.
weel-awyte *int* assuredly!
weel-bred *adj* polite, civil.
weel-comed *adj* **1** come of good family or stock. **2** legitimate.
weel-countit *adj* counted correctly or to the full amount.
weel-creeshed *adj* (*used of a pig*) well-fattened.
weeld *v* **1** to gain over. **2** to subdue.
weel-doin' *adj* **1** prosperous, well-to-do. **2** well-behaved. **3** of good character.
weel done to *adj* well cared for.
weel-ees't *adj* well-treated.
weel-faced *adj* of comely face.
weel-faird *same as* **weel-farrand**.
weel-fardy *same as* **weel-farrand**.
weelfare *n* welfare.
weel-farrand *adj* good-looking, comely.
weel-faured, ~-faurt *same as* **weel-farrand**.
weel-faurtly *adv* **1** handsomely. **2** with good grace. **3** distinctly. **4** openly.
weel-faurtness *n* comeliness.
weel-favoured *adj* good-looking.
weel-fished *adj* **1** with a good supply of fish. **2** a whale-fishing term.
weel-flittin *adj* a sarcastic word applied to one who scolds another and himself or herself deserves a scolding. *See* **flite**.
weel-foggit *adj* used of one who has earned or saved plenty of money.
weel-gain, -gaun *adj* **1** (*of a horse*) spirited. **2** (*of machinery, etc*) going or working smoothly.
weel-gaited *adj* (*of a horse*) thoroughly broken in.
weel-geizened, ~-gizzened *adj* very thirsty.
weel-girst *adj* well-fed on good grass.
weel-hain't *adj* **1** well-kept. **2** saved to good purpose. **3** not wasted. **4** saved by frugality.
weel-handit *adj* **1** clever with the hands. **2** expert.
weel-hauden in *same as* **weel-hain't**.
weel head *n* **1** an eddy. **2** the centre of an eddy.
weel-heartit *adj* **1** kind-hearted. **2** hopeful, not cast down.
weel-hung *adj* (*of the tongue*) ready, fluent, glib.
weelins *n* power over oneself to keep one's feet after a paralytic shock, etc.
weel-kent, ~-kenned *adj* **1** well-known. **2** conspicuous. **3** familiar.
weel-leared, ~-learnit *adj* **1** well-informed. **2** well-educated.
weel-leggit *adj* having good, strong, shapely legs.
weel-lickit *adj* (*used of speech*) careful, plausible. **2** well-whipped.
weel-like *adj* **1** good-looking. **2** looking in good health.
weel-likit *adj* much liked.
weel-lo'ed *adj* dearly loved.
weel-lookin', ~-lookit *adj* **1** good-looking. **2** looking well.
weel man *int* a common form of address.
weel-meatit *adj* **1** (*used of grain*) full in the ear. **2** well-fed.
weel-mindit, ~-min't *adj* well brought to recollection.

weel-natured *adj* good-natured.
weelness *n* good health.
weel-on *adj* far gone in drink.
weel-paid *adj* **1** well-satisfied. **2** well-punished.
weel-pang't *adj* well-stuffed or crammed.
weel-pitten on, ~-putten on *adj* well-dressed.
weel-raxed *adj* widely stretched.
weel-redd-up *adj* **1** tidy. **2** made thoroughly tidy. *See* **redd**.
weel sae *adv* **1** very. **2** too.
weel-saired *adj* **1** well-served. **2** feasted. **3** deservedly punished.
weel-set *adj* **1** well-disposed. **2** partial. **3** sharpset. **4** very hungry.
weel-set-on *adj* **1** (*used of a stack, etc*) well-built. **2** well-provided.
weel-settin' *adj* **1** good-looking. **2** well set up.
weel-sleekit *adj* well-beaten.
weel's-me-on *int* blessings on! happy am I with! an exclamation expressive of very great pleasure.
weel-socht *adj* greatly exhausted.
weel-sookit *adj* almost exhausted.
weel-standing *adj* (*used of a house*) well-furnished.
weel-thrashen *adj* well-whipped.
weel-tochered *adj* having a large dowry.
weel-to-do *adj* nearly drunk, tipsy.
weel-to-leeve, ~-to-live *adj* **1** in easy circumstances. **2** half-drunk.
weel-to-pass *adj* prosperous, well-to-do.
weel-to-see *adj* good-looking.
weel-wal'd *adj* well-chosen. *See* **wale**[3].
weel-war *adj* much the worse.
weel-wared, ~-waurt *adj* **1** well-spent. **2** well-laid-out. **3** well-earned, well-deserved. **4** well done, properly awarded.
weel-warst *adj* the very worst.
weel-willed *adj* **1** kindly disposed. **2** generous. **3** very willing.
weel-willer *n* **1** a friend. **2** a well-wisher.
weel-willie, -willied *adj* **1** well-disposed towards one. **2** liberal. **2** very willing.
weel-willin *adj* **1** kindly disposed. **2** favourable. **3** complacent. **4** well-meaning.
weel-wintered *adj* (*of cattle*) well-fed in winter.
weel-wish *n* a good wish.—*v* to wish well.
weel-wished *adj* given with goodwill.
weel-won *adj* well-earned.
weem *n* **1** a natural cave. **2** an artificial cave. **3** an underground passage. **4** an underground building.
weemen, weemen-bodies *n* women.
ween[1] *v* to boast.—*n* **1** a boast. **2** a boaster.
ween[2] *same as* **wean**.
weeness *n* **1** smallness. **2** meanness of spirit.
weeoch *n* a little while.
weeock, wesok *same as* **weak**[2].
wee oor *n* one o'clock a.m.
weep *v* **1** (*used of cheese*) to exude. **2** to ooze.
weepers *n* **1** strips of muslin or cambric stitched on the cuffs of a coat or gown as a sign of mourning, often covered with crepe. **2** mourners for the dead.
weer[1] *v* **1** to turn away, or back, an animal.
weer[2] *n* **1** doubt. **2** fear.
weer[3] *n* wire.
weer[4] *v* to wear.
weerd *same as* **weird**[1].
weerdie *n* a queer, uncanny, weird person.
weerigills *n* **1** quarrels. **2** the act of quarrelling.
weerit *n* **1** the young of the guillemot. **2** a peevish child.
weerock *same as* **whirrock**.
weers *n* *in phr* **on the weers o'** on the point of.
weer-stanes *adv* in a state of hesitation. *See* **weer**[2].
wees *n* a balance beam and scales.
wee-saul't *adj* having a little soul.
wee-schule *n* an infant school.
weese[1] *same as* **waese**.

weese² *same as* weeze¹.
weesh¹ *same as* weest².
weesh² *v* washed.
weeshen *adj* washed.
weeshie *adj* 1 delicate. 2 watery.—*v* to hesitate.
weesht *same as* wheesht.
weesp *n* 1 a measure of fish. 2 a small quantity.
weest¹ *adj* depressed with dullness.
weest² *int* a call to a horse to go to the right.
weet¹ *same as* wet².
weet² *n* the cry of the chaffinch.
weet³ *v* to know.
wee-taws *n* a small taws (qv) used for slight offences.
wee thing *n* 1 a child. 2 a darling. 3 a trifle.
wee-thocht *n* 1 a very little thing. 2 a trifle. 3 a particle.
weetie *adj* 1 rainy. 2 wet.
weetit *v* wetted.
weet-my-fit *n* the quail.
weetness *n* 1 wet. 2 rainy weather. 3 anything drinkable.
weeuk *same as* weak².
wee way *n* 1 a small trade or business. 2 a retail trade.
weeze¹ *v* to ooze.
weeze² *same as* waese.
weezen *same as* wizzen.
weezet *adj* excited over some new possession or over the prospect of it.
weff *adj* of a musty smell.
weffil, weffle *same as* waffle².
weffilness *n* limberness, pliancy.
wefflin, wefflum *same as* waefleed.
weght¹, wecht² *same as* wecht¹, wecht².
wehaw *int* a cry that displeases or alarms horses.
weibis *same as* weebo.
weicht¹ *n* weight.
weicht² *same as* wecht².
weid¹, weid² *same as* weed², weed³.
weidinonfa *n* a chill, fever, the onset of a weed (qv).
weigh *n* a weight or measure of dry goods.
weigh-bauk *n* 1 a balance. 2 (*in pl*) scales. 3 a state of indecision.
weigh-beam *n* a balance.
weigh-brods *n* the boards used as scales in a large balance.
weigh-scale *n* 1 a pair of scales. 2 a steelyard.
weight¹, wecht² *same as* wecht¹,
weightsman *same as* wechtsman.
weighty *adj* 1 heavy, corpulent. 2 valiant, doughty.
weighty-fitted *adj* advanced in pregnancy.
weik¹ *same as* wick³.
weik² *n* a rush wick.
weil¹ *same as* wale³.
weil², weil³, weil⁴ *same as* weel¹, weel³, weel⁴.
weild *same as* wield.
weil'd *adj* chosen, choice. *See* wale³.
weil'd-wight *same as* wall-wight.
weill¹, weill² *same as* weel³, weel⁴.
weilycoat *same as* wylie-coat.
weind *n* thought.—*v* to ween.
weint¹, weint² *same as* waint¹, waint².
weir¹ *n* war.
weir² *same as* wear⁵.
weir³ *n* cows and ewes giving milk.
weir⁴ *same as* weer².
weir-buist, ~-buse *n* a partition between cows in a byre.
weird¹ *n* 1 a fateful being. 2 a dealer in the supernatural. 3 disaster. 4 a fateful story. 5 a prediction, prophecy.—*v* 1 to doom to. 2 to adjure by the knowledge of impending fate. 3 to predict. 4 to waft kind wishes. 5 to make liable to. 6 to expose to evil.
weird² *n* the world.
weird³ *same as* wierd¹.
weird⁴, weirded *adj* 1 fated. 2 destined. 3 predicted. 4 determined.
weird-fixed *adj* 1 fateful. 2 destined.

weird-fu' *adj* fateful.
weirdin *adj* employed for the purpose of divination.
weirdless *adj* 1 ill-fated. 2 unprosperous. 3 improvident. 4 purposeless. 5 worthless.
weirdleseness *n* 1 wastefulness. 2 mismanagement. 3 improvidence.
weird-light *n* the light of one's destiny.
weird-like *adj* ominous.
weirdly *adj* 1 ghastly. 2 fate-bringing. 3 eerie. 4 happy, prosperous.
weirdly cake *n* a cake broken at Christmas so as to portend the future.
weirdman *n* a seer.
weird-set *adj* 1 fateful. 2 destined.
weirdy *adj* fateful.
weirfu' *adj* warlike.
weir-glove *n* a war glove or gauntlet.
weir-harness *n* armour.
weir-horse *n* a stallion.
weiriegills *same as* weerigills.
weir-men *n* armed men, warriors.
weirs *n in phr* on weirs 1 in danger of. 2 on the point of.
weir-saddle *n* a war-saddle.
weise, weisse *v* 1 to direct. 2 to lead. 3 to use policy for attaining an object. 4 to turn by art rather than strength. 5 to manoeuvre. 6 to advise. 7 to lure. 8 to persuade. 9 to beguile. 10 to wheedle. 11 to draw or let out anything cautiously, so as to prevent it from breaking. 12 to spend. 13 to use. 14 to withdraw. 15 to incline, slip away.
weish *adj* washed.
weit *same as* wet².
weize *same as* weise.
weke *same as* wick⁴.
welcome-hame *n* 1 the repast presented to a bride as she enters the bridegroom's house. 2 a festivity on the day after a newly married pair have made their first appearance at church. 3 a welcome given to a newly engaged ploughman.
wel'd *adj* welded.
weld *same as* wield.
wele¹ *same as* weel¹.
wele² *same as* wale³.
wele³ *same as* weel³.
welk *v* to wither.
well¹ *same as* weel¹.
well² *n* the hollow centre of an Irish car, used as a receptacle for luggage.
well³ *same as* weel³.
well⁴ *same as* wall⁴.
well⁵ *same as* weel⁴.
well-a, well-a-day *int* alas!
well-a-wins *int* an exclamation of sorrow.
well-ee, ~-ey *n* 1 a spring in a quagmire. 2 a spring of water. 3 the orifice of a well.
weller *v* 1 to crave. 2 to call for.
well-fired *adj* (*of bread, rolls, etc*) baked for a longer time so that the top or crust is dark brown and crisp.
well head *n* the spring from which a marsh is supplied.
wellicot *same as* wylie-coat.
well-shanker *n* a well-digger.
well-sitting *adj* favourably disposed.
well's-me *int* an exclamation of pleasure.
well-strand *n* a stream flowing from a well.
well-stripe *n* a well-strand (qv).
well-warst *adj* the very worst.
well-wight *same as* wall-wight.
welt *n* 1 a seam. 2 the crust of cheese. 3 a weal made by a blow. 4 a blow. 5 anything large of its kind.
welter *v* 1 to overturn, upset. 2 to reel, stagger, stumble.—*n* a confused noise.
welth *same as* walth.
wench *n* a female servant.
wene *same as* wane¹.
weng *n* a penny.

went[1], **went**[2] *same as* **waint**[1], **waint**[2].
wer[1] *poss adj* our.
wer[2] *same as* **war**[4].
werd[1] *same as* **ward**[1].
werd[2] *same as* **weird**[1].
werdie *n* the youngest bird in a nest.
werk[1], **werk**[2] *same as* **wark**[1], **wark**[2].
wer-nain *poss adj* our own.
wer nainsels *refl pron* our ownselves.
wersels *refl pron* ourselves.
wersh *same as* **wairsh**.
wery[1], **wery**[2] *same as* **weary**[1], **weary**[2].
we'se *pron with v* we shall.
weslin *adj* western.
wesp *n* a wasp.
west-bye *same as* **wast-bye**.
wester *same as* **waster**.
westlin *n* the west country.—*adj* western.
westlins *adv* westward.
wet[1] *v* waited.
wet[2] *adj* given to drink.—*n* **1** moisture. **2** a drizzling rain. **3** wet weather. **4** a small quantity of liquid. **5** water. **6** a wetting. **7** wet clothes.—*v* **1** to rain. **2** to drizzle. **3** (*used of a river*) to water, irrigate.
wet bird *n* the chaffinch.
wete *n* hope.
wet finger *n* an effort.
wet fish *n* fresh fish.
wether bell *n* the bell worn by the bellwether.
wether-bleat *n* the snipe.
wether-gammon *n* a leg of mutton.
wether-haggis *n* a haggis boiled in a sheep's stomach.
wether-hog *n* a male sheep of the second season.
wether-lamb *n* a male lamb.
wet-looking *adj* threatening rain.
wetness *n* **1** rainy weather. **2** anything drinkable.
wet-shod *adj* **1** wet-footed. **2** brimful of tears.
wet-shoe ford *n* a ford that just wets the feet of the forclers.
wetting *n* **1** a small quantity of liquor. **2** a convivial feast.
wetty *adj* wet.
wevil *v* to wriggle.
wew *v* to mew as a kitten.
wewleck, wewlock *n* an instrument for twisting ropes of straw.
wey[1] *n* a way.
wey[2] *pron* we.
wey[3] *same as* **wee**[1].
weyke *same as* **waik**[1].
weykness *n* weakness.
weynt[1], **weynt**[2] *same as* **waint**[1], **waint**[2].
weyse[1] *same as* **waese**.
weyse[2] *same as* **weise**.
weysh *same as* **weest**[2].
weyve *v* to weave.
weyver *n* **1** a weaver. **2** a knitter.
wez *pron* **1** us. **2** we.
wha *pron* who.
whaal *n* **1** a whale. **2** a long, unbroken wave.
whaap[1] *same as* **whaup**.
whaap[2] *n* the sheltered part of a hill.
whaap-neb *same as* **whaup-neb**.
whaarl *v* to whirl.
whack[1] *v* **1** to cut in large slices. **2** to pull out smartly. **3** to surpass.—*n* **1** a cut. **2** a slice. **3** a large portion of food or drink. **4** a great number.
whack[2] *v* **1** to quack. **2** to drink copiously or with gulping noise.
whacker *n* **1** anything large of its kind. **2** a great lie.
whacking *adj* big, very great.
whackle *v* to fish with fly.
whae *pron* who.
whaff *same as* **waff**[1].
whaile *same as* **wale**[2].
whaingle *v* to whine.

whaish *v* to wheeze as one that has taken cold.
whaishle *v* to wheeze.
whaisk *v* **1** to speak huskily or with difficulty because of a throat affection. **2** to hawk. **3** to clear one's throat. **4** to gasp violently for breath.
whaisle, whaisle *same as* **wheezle**.
whaky *n* whisky.
whale[1] *same as* **wale**[2].
whale[2] *adj* whole.
whale[3] *n* **1** a large species of cuttlefish, the whale skate. **2** (*in pl*) long, unbroken waves.
whale-blubs *n* the sea jelly.
whale money *n* money paid to whalers for blubber, etc.
whale-ruck *n* the whole collection of things.
whale skate *n* a large species of cuttlefish.
whalm *v* **1** to whelm. **2** to turn a vessel upside-down. **3** to come in large numbers. **4** (*used of a crowd*) to surge.
whalp *v* to bring forth whelps.—*n* **1** a whelp. **2** a term of contempt.
whalpin *n* a whipping.
wham[1] *n* **1** a swamp. **2** a hollow in a field. **3** a wide, flat glen through which a brook runs. **4** a corrie.
wham[2] *pron* whom.
wham[3] *n* **1** a blow. **2** a bend.
whamble, whamal, whamel, whammel, whammle *v* **1** to upset. **2** to turn upside-down. **3** to capsize. **4** to invert a vessel. **5** to cover over with a vessel. **6** to toss to and fro. **7** to tumble about. **8** to move quickly. **9** to overcome. **10** to throng off. **11** to pour over, swallow liquor. **12** to turn round.—*n* **1** a violent overturn. **2** a capsize. **3** a tumble. **4** a toss. **5** a turn. **6** a rocking. **7** a state of confusion or of being overturned.
whame *same as* **wame**.
whample *n* **1** a stroke, blow. **2** a cut. **3** a chip.
whan *adv* when.
whan-a-be *adv* **1** notwithstanding. **2** however.
whand *same as* **wand**[1].
whand-cage *n* a wicker cage.
whang[1] *n* **1** a thong. **2** a long strip of leather. **3** a leather lace for boot or shoe. **4** a whiplash. **5** a rope. **6** a band. **7** anything long and supple. **8** a long narrow stretch of road.
whang[2] *v* **1** to beat, thrash. **2** to lash. **3** to cut in large lumps. **4** to slice.—*n* **1** a blow or lash with a whip. **2** a lump. **3** a large piece or slice.
whang-bit *n* a leather bridle.
whanger *n* one who wields a lash.
whangkin *n* **1** a lump. **2** a portion.
whank *v* **1** to beat, flog. **2** to cut off large portions. —*n* **1** a stroke, a violent blow with the fist. **2** the act of striking.
whanker *n* anything larger than common of its kind.
whankin *same as* **whangkin**.
whap[1] *same as* **wap**[3].
whap[2] *same as* **whaup**.
whapie *n* a little whelp, a young puppy.
whapper *n* **1** anything excessive in its kind or beyond expectation. **2** a great lie, a whopper.
whapping *adj* stout, lusty, exceptionally big, fine, good.
whar *adv* **1** where. **2** whither.
wharin' *adv* wherewith.
wharle *v* to roll the letter R.
wha's *pron with v* who is.
wha's, whase *pron* whose.
whasle *same as* **wheezle**[3].
whassl-whiezl *v* to wheeze in breathing.
whate *v* did whittle. *See* **white**[1].
whaten, whatten, whatens *adj* what kind of.
whatever *adv* **1** in any circumstances. **2** at all, on any account.
what-for *n* punishment, retribution.
what-like *adj* resembling what.
whatna *adj* what kind of.
wha-to-be-married-first *n* the name of a card game.
whatrack, whatreck, whatrecks *int* **1** an exclamation of

surprise, indifference, contempt. **2** what matters it? no matter!

whatreck *conj* nevertheless.

whatrick *n* a weasel.

what's-comin'-next? *adj* uncertain what is to happen next.

whatsomever, whatsomer *adj* whatsoever.—*adv* whenever.—*n* anything of importance.

whatt *v* cut, whittled. *See* **white**.

whattie *same as* **watty**.

whaubert *same as* **wheebert**.

whaugh *int* an exclamation of surprise or disapproval.

whauk *v* to thwack.—*n* a heavy blow.

whauk, whauky *same as* **whawkie**.

whaum¹, whaum² *same as* **wham¹, wham³**.

whaumle, whaumil *same as* **whamble**.

whaund *same as* **wand¹**.

whaup¹ *n* a curlew.—*v* **1** to make an unpleasant noise. **2** to tootle clumsily on a flute.

whaup² *n* **1** a pod in its earliest stage. **2** a capsule. **3** an empty pod. **4** a term of contempt for a disagreeable person. **5** a lout. **6** a lazy person. **7** a scamp.—*v* to form into pods.

whaup³ *v* to wheeze.

whaup⁴ *n* **1** an outcry. **2** a fuss.

whaup⁵ *n in phr* **a whaup in the raip 1** something wrong, a hitch somewhere. **2** a fraudulent trick. **3** a spoke in one's wheel.

whaupie-mou'd *adj* having a mouth like the curlew.

whaupin *same as* **whapping**.

whaup-neb *n* **1** a curlew's beak. **2** (*with* **auld**) a name for the devil.

whaup-nebbit *adj* having a long, sharp nose.

whaup-neckit *adj* (*used of a bottle*) long-necked.

whaur *adv* **1** where. **2** whither.

whaurie *n* **1** a misgrown or a mischievous child. **2** a fondling term, or a jocular, reproachful term, addressed to a child.

whaurtee *adv* **1** whereto. **2** whither.

whauzle *same as* **wheezle**.

whawbert *same as* **wheebert**.

whawk *v* to thwack.

whawkie *n* whisky.

whawmle *same as* **whamble**.

whawp¹, whawp² *same as* **whaup¹, whaup²**.

whaxle *same as* **wheezle**.

whëak *same as* **weak²**.

whesale *same as* **wheezle**.

wheat *same as* **white²**.

wheck *v* to thwack.

wheeber *v* to whistle a tune.

wheeber, wheebre *v* **1** to beat severely. **2** to dash. **3** to walk hurriedly and clumsily.—*n* a tall, ungainly person.

wheebert¹ *n* a lean, tall, ungainly person.

wheebert² *v* to whistle.

wheebring *adj* hurried and clumsy in manner.

wheech¹ *n* a stench.—*int* an exclamation of disgust with a stench.

wheech² *v* **1** to move quickly. **2** to move or remove something quickly.

wheef¹ *same as* **whiff¹**.

wheef² *n* a fife, a flute.—*v* to play the fife or the flute.

wheefer *n* **1** a fifer. **2** a flute-player.

wheefle *v* to play on the flute or the fife.—*n* a shrill, intermittent note with little variation of tone.

wheefle² *v* **1** to puff. **2** to blow away. **3** (*of the wind*) to blow in puffs, to drive before it. **4** to veer.

wheefer *n* **1** a fifer. **2** a flute-player.

wheegee, wheejee *n* **1** a whim, fancy. **2** (*in pl*) superfluous ornaments in dress.—*v* to beat about the bush, to be long-winded in speech.

wheegil *n* a piece of wood for pushing in the end of the straw rope with which a sheaf is bound.

wheegle *v* to wheedle, coax, flatter.—*n* a wheedling.

wheel¹ *same as* **weel¹**.

wheel² *v* **1** to drive in a wheeled vehicle. **2** to whirl in dancing. **3** to hurry. **4** to bid at an auction simply to raise the price.—*n* a wheel round. **5** a spinning wheel.

wheel-abouts *n* (*used of horses*) paces.

wheelband *n* **1** a band passing round a wheel and causing it to revolve. **2** what keeps any business going.

wheel bird *n* the nightjar.

wheel-chargeman *n* one who wheels pig iron to the smelting furnace.

wheeler *n* **1** one who bids at an auction simply to raise the price. **2** one who wheels peats in a moss.

wheelin *n* coarse worsted spun on the large wheel from wool that has been only carded.

wheelmagic *n* anything whirling rapidly along.

wheel treck *n* the part of a spinning wheel armed with teeth.

wheel-wricht *n in phr* **to make a wheel-wricht of a woman** to seduce her.

wheem¹ *n* a whim.

wheem² *adj* **1** gentle. **2** smooth. **3** calm. **4** neat, tidy. **5** close, tight.

wheemer *v* to whimper. **2** to go about muttering complaints.

wheen *n* **1** a number. **2** a quantity. **3** a party, group. **4** a division. **5** somewhat. **6** a few.

wheenge *same as* **whinge**.

wheeoin *n* the whistling of a steam engine.

wheep¹ *v* **1** to give a sharp, intermittent, whistling sound. **2** to squeak. **3** to whistle.—*n* a sharp, shrill sound, cry or whistle.

wheep² *same as* **whip²**.

wheep³ *n* (*used with* **penny**) **1** small beer at a penny a bottle. **2** whisky at a penny a quartern.

wheeper *n* a jocular name for a tuning fork.

wheeple *v* **1** to utter short, sharp, melancholy cries, like a curlew or plover. **2** to whistle. **3** to try to whistle. **4** to whistle in an almost inaudible tone. —*n* **1** a shrill, intermittent cry of certain birds. **2** a whistle. **3** an unsuccessful attempt to whistle.

wheepler *n* a whistler.

wheeps *n* an instrument for raising the bridgeheads of a mill.

wheeriemigo *n* **1** a gimcrack. **2** an insignificant person.—*v* **1** to work in a trifling, insignificant manner. **2** to play fast and loose.

wheerikins *n* the hips.

wheerim, wheeram, wheerum *n* **1** anything insignificant. **2** a toy. **3** a plaything. **4** a trifling excuse. **5** a trifling peculiarity. **6** an insignificant, trifling person. **7** the act of working in a trifling, imperfect way.—*v* to turn. **2** to work in a trifling way. **3** to play fast and loose.

wheerip *same as* **whyripe**.

wheese *same as* **wheeze¹**.

wheesh¹ *same as* **weest²**.

wheesh² *adv* with a whizz or swish.

wheesht *int* hush!—*n* **1** silence. **2** a hush.

wheesk *v* to creak gently.—*n* a creaking sound.

wheest *int* hush!—*n* silence.

wheet¹ *n* a whit.

wheet², wheetie *int* a call to poultry, especially ducks.—*v* (*used of young birds*) to twitter, chirp or cheep.—*n* **1** a very young bird. **2** a duck.

wheet-ah *n* the cry of the tern.

wheetie¹ *n* the white-throat.

wheetie² *adj* low, mean, shabby.

wheetie-like *adj* having the appearance of meanness.

wheetie-wheet *n* a very young bird.

wheetie-whitebeard *n* the whitethroat.

wheetle¹ *v* to wheedle.

wheetle² *int* a call to ducks.—*v* (*used of birds*) to cheep.—*n* a young duck.

wheetle-wheetie *n* a very young bird.

wheetle-wheetle *n* the cheep of a young bird.

wheetlie *int* a call to ducks.—*v* to cheep as a young bird.

wheety *same as* **wheet²**.

wheety-what *same as* **whittie-whattie**.

wheezan *n* the noise carriage wheels make when moving fast.

wheeze[1] *v* 1 to coax. 2 to flatter. 3 to urge.—*n* 1 flattery. 2 a deception.

wheeze[2] *same as* **whizz**.

wheezie[1] *v* to blaze with a hissing sound.—*n* a blaze making such a sound.

wheezie[2] *v* to steal fruit, peas and vegetables.—*n* such theft.

wheezle *v* 1 to breathe with difficulty. 2 to wheeze. 3 (*of the wind*) to whistle.—*n* 1 a wheeze. 2 the act of wheezing. 3 the difficult breathing of asthma.

wheezle-rung *n* a strong stick used by country people for lifting a large boiling pot off the fire.

wheezloch *n* 1 the state of being short-winded. 2 a disease of horses affecting their wind.

whegle *same as* **wheegle**.

wheich[1] *n* fine wheaten bread.

wheich[2] *n* whisky.

whelm *v* 1 to turn a vessel upside-down so as to be a cover. 2 to come in overwhelming numbers.

whelp *n* 1 a silly, stupid fellow. 2 a foolish braggart.

wheme *same as* **wheem**.

when-a-be, when-a-by *adv* 1 however. 2 nevertheless.

whenever *conj* as soon as.

where *n* a place.

whereas *n* a warrant of apprehension, of which it is the opening word.

whereawa' *adv* 1 where. 2 whereabouts.

wherefrae *adv* whence.

where-out *adv* whence, out of which.

whereto *adv* 1 whither. 2 why, wherefore.

whesk *v* 1 to speak huskily. 2 to gasp violently.

whet *n* a small dram of spirits.

whether or no *adv* 1 in any case. 2 willingly or unwillingly.

whew, whe-ew *n* 1 the shrill cry of a bird, as the plover. 2 a whistle.—*v* 1 to whistle. 2 (*used of a plover*) to cry.

whey beard *n* the whitethroat.

whey bird *n* the woodlark.

whey blots *n* the scum of boiling whey.

whey brose *n* brose (qv) made with whey.

whey cream *n* the cream left in the whey after the removal of the curd.

whey drap *n* a hole from which whey has not been pressed out of the cheese and in which it putrefies.

whey ee *n* a whey drap (qv).

whey-faced *adj* 1 pale-faced. 2 beardless.

whey parritch *n* porridge made with whey.

whey sey *n* a tub in which milk is curdled.

whey spring *n* a whey drap (qv).

whey-white *adj* 1 white as whey. 2 very pale.

whey rullions *n* a dish for dinner, formerly common among peasants, consisting of the porridge left at breakfast beaten down with fresh whey, with an addition of oatmeal.

whezle *n* a weasel.

whick *v* to dash or rush with a soft, whizzing sound.—*n* 1 a soft, whizzing sound. 2 a blow accompanied by such a noise. 3 the hiss of an adder when angered.—*adv* with a soft, whizzing sound.

whicker *same as* **whihher**.

whickie *adj* crafty. 2 knavish.

whid[1] *n* 1 a light, nimble, noiseless movement. 2 a start, a spring. 3 a whisk. 4 a quick run. 5 a hare's hasty flight. 6 an instant.—*v* 1 to move nimbly and noiselessly. 2 to run or fly quickly. 3 to frisk. 4 to whisk or scamper as a hare.—*adv* nimbly.

whid[2] *v* 1 to fib. 2 to exaggerate. 3 to equivocate. 4 to deceive.—*n* 1 an exaggerated statement. 2 a fib, lie.

whidder[1] *pron, adj, adv and conj* whether.

whidder[2] *adv* whither.

whidder[3] *same as* **whither**[1].

whiddle *v* 1 to flutter about, as birds at pairing time. 2 to move with quick, short flight. 3 to go lightly and quickly.

whiddy *n* a hare.—*adj* unsettled, unsteady.

whiff[1] *n* 1 a glimpse. 2 a transient view. 3 a short time, a jiffy. 4 a slight or passing touch.—*v* to smoke a pipe.

whiff[2] *same as* **wheef**[2].

whiflinger *n* a vagabond.

whiffle[1], **whiffle**[2] *same as* **wheefle**[1], **wheefle**[2].

whiffler *n* 1 a fifer. 2 a flute-player.

Whig *n* an old name for a Covenanter, a Presbyterian or a dissenter from the Established Church of Scotland, used contemptuously.

whig[1], **whigg** *n* 1 the sour part of cream, spontaneously separated from the rest. 2 the thin part of a liquid mixture.—*v* (*used of stale churned milk*) to throw off a sediment.

whig[2] *v* 1 to go quickly. 2 to move at a steady, easy pace. 3 to jog along. 4 to work nimbly and heartily. 5 to drink copiously.—*n* a copious draught.

whig[3] *n* 1 fine wheaten bread. 2 a small, oblong roll, baked with butter and currants.

whigg *same as* **whig**[1].

Whigamore *n* a Whig (qv), a Presbyterian covenanter.

Whiggery *n* the practices and tenets of the Presbyterian Covenanters.

whiggle *v* 1 to waddle. 2 to move loosely. 3 to wriggle. 4 to trifle. 5 to idle. 6 to work listlessly. —*n* 1 the act of waddling. 2 a swing in the gait. 3 a trifle. 4 a gimcrack, toy. 5 anything more ornamental than useful.

Whiggonite *n* a Whig (qv).

Whigling *n* a contemptuous name for a Whig.

whigmaleerie, whigmeleerie *n* 1 a game played with pins for drink at a drinking club. 2 a gimcrack. 3 a fantastic, useless ornament. 4 a whim, crotchet. 5 a foolish fancy.—*adj* whimsical, odd.

whig-mig-morum *same as* **whip-meg-morum**.

whihher *v* 1 to move through the air with a whizzing noise. 2 to flutter quickly, as a bird. 3 to titter, giggle. 4 to laugh in a suppressed manner.—*n* a giggle.

whike *same as* **whick**.

whil *same as* **while**.

while *conj* until.—*prep* 1 since. 2 from.

whileag *n* a little while.

while as *adv* as long as.

whileoms *adv* at times.

whiles *adv* 1 sometimes. 2 at other times. 3 now and then.

while-sin, ~-syne *adv* 1 a while ago. 2 some time back.

whilesome *adj* former, whilom.

whilie *n* a short time.

whilk *pron* which.

whilkever *pron* whichever.

whilking *adj* complaining.

whill[1] *n* a small skiff.

whill[2] *same as* **while**.

whillie-billow, whillabaloo *same as* **hullie-bullie**.

whilliegoleerie *n* 1 a hypocritical fellow. 2 a wheedler. 3 a selfish flatterer.

whillie-lu, whilli-lu, whilly-lou *n* 1 an air in music. 2 a prolonged strain of melancholy music. 3 an outcry. 4 a hubbub.

whillie-whallie *v* 1 to coax. 2 to wheedle. 3 to dally. 4 to loiter.

whilly *v* 1 to cheat. 2 to wheedle. 3 to gull.

whillybaloo *n* an uproar.

whillywha, whillywhae, whillywhaw *adj* 1 not to be depended on. 2 wheedling. 3 flattering.—*n* 1 a flatterer. 2 one not to be depended on. 3 a deceitful, wheedling person. 4 a cheat. 5 cajolery, flattery.—*v* 1 to flatter. 2 to cajole. 3 to wheedle. 4 to delay. 5 to be undecided.

whilock, whileock *n* 1 a short space of time. 2 a little while.

whilockie *n* a very little while.

whilom *conj* while, whilst.

whiloms *adv* sometimes.

whilper *n* anything large of its kind.

whilt *n* **1** a blow, a stroke. **2** perturbation. **3** a pit-a-pat condition.

whiltie-whaltie *n* a state of palpitation.—*v* **1** to palpitate. **2** to dally. **3** to loiter.—*adj* in a state of palpitation, pit-a-pat.

whim *v* to carry one's point by humouring another's whims.

whim-ma-gary *adj* whimsical, fanciful.

whimmer *v* **1** to cry feebly, like a child. **2** to whimper.

whimper *v* **1** to grumble. **2** to make complaints. **3** to sound as running water.—*n* **1** the cry of a dog at the sight of game. **2** a whisper.

whimple *same as* **whumple**.

whimsey, whimsy *n* **1** a capricious liking. **2** a fanciful device.

whim-wham *n* **1** a whim, fancy, fad. **2** a kickshaw.

whin[1] *n* whinstone, ragstone.

whin[2] *same as* **wheen**.

whin[3] *n* furze.

whin bloom *n* furze blossom.

whin buss *n* a furze bush.

whin-chacker *n* the whinchat.

whin-clad *adj* furze-covered.

whin-clocharet *n* the whinchat.

whin cowe, ~ kow *n* **1** a furze bush. **2** a branch of furze.

whinge *v* **1** to whine. **2** to cry fretfully and peevishly. **3** to whimper as a dog.—*n* **1** a whine, moan. **2** a low, complaining cry.

whinger[1] *n* one who whinges.

whinger[2] *n* **1** a short dagger, used as a knife at meals and also as a weapon. **2** a sword.

whin hoe *n* an adze-shaped hoe for stubbing up furze.

whinil *same as* **winnel**.

whinilstrae *n* a stalk of withered grass.

whink *v* to bark, as an untrained collie dog in pursuit of game, when, breathless and impatient, he loses sight of a hare.—*n* **1** the suppressed bark of a sheepdog. **2** a whine.

whinkens *n* flummery.

whinlet *n* young furze.

whin-linnet *n* the linnet.

whin-lintie *n* the whinchat.

whin-mull *n* a rude kind of mill for crushing young furze for fodder.

whinner[1] *v* to neigh.

whinner[2] *v* **1** to pass swiftly with a humming sound. **2** to thunder or whizz along. **3** to strike with force and loud noise. **4** (*used of corn, etc*) to rustle to the touch through severe drought.—*n* **1** the whizzing sound of rapid flight or motion. **2** a thundering sound. **3** a thundering or resounding blow.

whinnering drouth *n* a severe drought, followed by a sifting wind.

whinny[1] *adj* **1** producing whins or furze. **2** furze-clad.

whinny[2] *v* to cry as a snipe or a lapwing.

whinny buss, ~ cowe *n* a furze bush.

whinny knowe *n* a furze-clad knoll.

whin pod *n* the seed vessel of the furze.

whinsie *adj* whimsical.

whin-sparrow *n* the hedge sparrow.

whinstane *n* a name given to a curling stone.

whip[1] *v* to warp, splice.

whip[2] *v* **1** to run quickly, rush. **2** to jerk. **3** to drink off.—*n* **1** a sudden movement. **2** a single swift blow. **3** a moment. **4** an attack or touch of illness. **5** a sip. **6** a hurried drink of liquor. **7** (*in pl*) punishment.—*adv* smartly, suddenly.

whip-col *n* a drink composed of rum, whipped eggs and cream.

whip-licker *n* one who has a horse and cart to hire.

whip-ma-denty *n* **1** a fop. **2** a conceited dandy.

whipman *n* a carter.

whip-meg-morum *n* **1** the name of a tune. **2** party politics, whiggery.

whipper-snapper *n* **1** a cheat. **2** a trick.

whippert *adj* hasty, tart, irritable.

whipper-like *adj* showing irritation in speech or manner.

whipper-tooties *n* **1** silly scruples. **2** frivolous difficulties.

whipple *same as* **wheeple**.

whippy *n* a term of contempt applied to a young girl.—*adj* **1** clever. **2** agile.

whipshard *v* to whip, scourge.

whip-the-cat *n* an itinerant tailor.—*v* to itinerate as a tailor from house to house plying his trade.

whip-together *n* food, the ingredients of which are coarse, hastily mixed and badly cooked.

whir *same as* **whirr**.

whirken *v* **1** to strangle. **2** to choke.

whirkins *n* the posteriors.

whirky *v* to fly with a whizzing sound, like a startled partridge.

whirl *v* **1** (*used of the eyes*) to roll. **2** to wheel. **3** to drive. **4** to speak with the uvular utterance of the letter r.—*n* **1** an eddy, whirlpool. **2** a drive. **3** a very small wheel or whorl. **4** the flywheel of a spindle. **5** a kind of apple shaped like the flywheel of a spindle. **6** a fanciful ornament.

whirlbarrow *n* a wheelbarrow.

whirlbone *n* the knee-pan.

whirligig *n* **1** any rapidly revolving object. **2** a turning of fortune. **3** a trifle, whim. **4** a fanciful ornament. **5** a child's toy, consisting of four cross-arms with paper sails attached that spin round in the wind. **6** a whimsical notion. **7** an untrustworthy person. **8** a light-headed girl.

whirligigum, whirliegigin *n* a whirligig (qv), fanciful ornament.

whirlimagig *n* **1** a strange fancy. **2** a sudden whim.

whirliwhaw, whirliwha, whirly-wha *n* **1** a useless ornament. **2** a gimcrack. **3** a trifle. **4** a high and difficult trill in singing.—*v* **1** to gull, cheat. **2** to mystify.

whirlmagee *n* an unnecessary ornament.

whirly[1] *adj* like an adder-bead (qv).—*n* **1** an eddy. **2** a whirlpool. **3** a small wheel. **4** a castor. **5** a wheelbarrow. **6** a two-wheeled barrow with two legs. **7** a truckle bed. **8** a colliery hutch.

whirly[2] *adj* weak, delicate.

whirly-bed *n* a truckle bed.

whirly-birlie *n* **1** a rapid, circular motion. **2** anything that whirls round. **3** a child's toy.

whirly-mill *n* a toy waterwheel or mill.

whirly-stane *n* an adder-bead (qv).

whirmel *v* to upset.

whirr *v* **1** to purr as a cat. **2** to spear. **3** with the uvular utterance of the letter r. **4** to whirl a thing round so fast as to make a whizzing sound. **5** to move or drive along with great speed.—*n* **1** a smart blow. **2** haste, hurry.

whirret *n* a blow.

whirrock *n* **1** a knot in wood caused by the growth of a branch from the place. **2** a corn or bunion on the foot. **3** a pimple on the sole of the foot. **4** a boil.

whirry *v* **1** to hurry off. **2** to whirl away.

whiscar *same as* **whisker**.

whish[1] *n* **1** a rushing or whizzing sound. **2** a swish. **3** a slight sound, as of falling water. **4** the least whisper. **5** a rumour, noise.—*v* **1** to whizz. **2** to rush with a whizzing noise. **3** to whistle, as the wind.

whish[2] *int* hush!—*v* **1** to hush. **2** to be or remain silent. **3** to soothe.—*n* **1** the sound made by saying 'which'. **2** the slightest sound. **3** a whisper.—*adj* quiet, silent.

whish[3] *int* a cry to scare away fowls, etc.—*v* to scare away fowls by saying 'whish!'.

whishie[1] *n* **1** the slightest sound. **2** a whisper.

whishie[2] *n* the whitethroat.

whisht *int* hush!—*v* **1** to hush, quiet, silence. **2** to be silent.—*n* **1** one's tongue as 'held' or kept silent. **2** the slightest sound. **3** a whisper. **4** a faint rumour.—*adj* hushed, silent, quiet.

whisk[1] *n* **1** a one-horse conveyance. **2** a blow. **3** a slight cleaning. **4** (*in pl*) a machine for winding yarn on a quill (qv) or clue (qv).—*v* **1** to curry a horse. **2** to lash, switch.

whisk[2] *n* whisky.

whisker *n* **1** a bunch of feathers for dusting with. **2** a beard, moustache and whiskers. **3** a knitting sheath. **4** a blustering wind.

whiskie *n* a kind of gig or one-horse chaise.

whiskied *adj* tipsy, drunk with whisky.

whisking *adj* great, sweeping.—*n* palpitation of the heart.

whiskit *adj* (*used of a horse*) **1** curried. **2** having a switched tail.

whiskybae *n* whisky.

whisky-bukky *n* a compound of oatmeal and whisky rolled together into a ball of two or three pounds weight.

whisky-can *n* **1** any vessel from which whisky can be drunk. **2** drinking, the intemperate use of whisky.

whisky-fair *n* **1** a gathering to drink whisky. **2** a drunken revel.

whisky house *n* a public house with no bar.

whisky maker *n* a distiller.

whisky pig *n* a whisky jar.

whisky pistol *n* a spirit flask.

whisky plash *n* a liberal supply of whisky, a drinking bout.

whisky splore *n* a drunken revel, a drinking bout.

whisky tacket *n* a pimple supposed to be caused by intemperance.

whisky-wife *n* a woman who sells whisky.

whissel[1] *same as* **wissel**.

whissel[2] *same as* **whistle**[1].

whissle[1] *same as* **wissel**.

whissle[2] *same as* **whistle**[1].

Whissuntide *n* Whitsunday.

whist *same as* **whisht**.

whistle[1] *v* to play on a reed, pipe, fife or flute.—*n* **1** a pipe, fife. **2** a flute. **3** a smart blow. **4** (*in pl*) organ pipes.

whistle[2] *same as* **wissel**.

whistleband *n* a fife band.

whistle-binkie *n* one who attends a penny wedding without paying anything and has no right to share in the festivities and who may sit on a bink or bench by himself and whistle for his own amusement or that of the company.

whistle kirk *n* **1** a church with an organ in it. **2** an Episcopal church.

whistle-kirk minister *n* an Episcopal clergyman.

whistle-kist *n* an organ, a kist o' whistles (qv).

whistle over *v* to swill liquor.

whistler *n* **1** a small, grey waterbird haunting Loch Leven, called also a Loch-learock. **2** anything exceptionally large. **3** (*in pl*) the farmers on a large estate who inform the landlord as to rent and value of their neighbours' farms when he is about to raise his rents.

whistle-the-whaup *n* one who is supposed to be making fun of another.

whistle-whistle *v* to go on whistling.

whistlewood *n* **1** a smooth wood used by boys for making whistles. **2** the willow. **3** the plane tree.

whistling duck *n* the coot.

whistling plover *n* the golden plover.

whit[1] *n* **1** a bit. **2** an action. **3** a deed.

whit[2] *v* **1** to milk closely. **2** to draw off the dregs.

whit[3] *adj* what.

whit[4] *same as* **white**[2].

white[1] *n* wheat.

white[2] *v* **1** to whittle. **2** to shave off portions of wood, etc, with a knife.—*n* **1** a cut. **2** a whittling.

white[3] *adj* (*used of coin*) silver.—*n* **1** silver coin. **2** the ling, a fish. **3** a good action. **4** (*in pl*) white clothes.—*v* to flatter.

white aboon-gled *n* the hen harrier.

white airn *n* sheet iron coated with tin, white iron.

white-bonnet *n* one who bids at a sale only to raise the price.

white bread, ~ breid *n* wheaten bread from a baker's shop.

white-chaff't *adj* white-checked.

white corn *n* wheat, barley and oats alone.

white crap *n* white corn (qv).

white drap *n* snow.

white fish *n* seafish, as haddock, cod, ling, tusk, etc.

white-fisher *n* one who fishes for white fish in the sea.

white-fish-in-the-net *n* a sport in which two persons hold a plaid pretty high, over which the rest of the company leap and he who is entangled loses the game.

white folk *n* flatterers, wheedlers.

white geordie *n* a shilling.

white hare *n* an alpine hare.

white hass, ~ hawse *n* **1** a sheep's gullet. **2** a favourite meat pudding.

white-horned owl *n* the long-eared owl.

white-horse *n* the fish, fuller ray.

white-iron smith *n* a tinsmith.

white-land *n* land that is not moss or peat.

white-legs *n* the smaller wood, branches, etc, of a cutting.

white-lintie *n* the whitethroat.

white-lip *n* a flatterer, a wheedler.

white-liver *n* a flatterer.

whitely *adj* **1** white, pallid. **2** delicate-looking.—*adv* **1** pallidly. **2** with a white appearance.

whitely-faced *adj* white-faced.

white maw *n* the herring gull.

white meal *n* oatmeal, as distinguished from barley meal.

white money *n* silver coin.

whiten *same as* **whitie**.

whitening *n* pulverized chalk, freed from impurities, used for whitewashing, cleaning plate, making putty, etc.

white-pow'd *adj* white-headed.

white pudding *n* a pudding of oatmeal, suet and onions, stuffed in one of the intestines of a sheep and tied tightly into sections.

whiter *n* **1** one that whittles. **2** a knife for whittling.

whiteret *n* a weasel.

white sark *n* a surplice.

white-sarkit *adj* surpliced.

white-seam *n* plain needlework.—*v* to do plain needlework.

white shilling *n* a shilling in silver.

white shower *n* a snow shower.

white siller *n* **1** silver coin. **2** small change in silver.

white-siller shilling *n* a shilling in silver.

white-skin blankets *n* blankets to be used without sheets.

white spate *n* a flood in which the water is not muddy.

white victual *n* wheat, barley and oats alone.

white-washen *adj* (*of the complexion*) pale, pallid.

white wind *n* **1** flattery. **2** wheedling.

white wood *n* the outermost circles of oak trees found in peat bogs.

white wren *n* the willow warbler.

whitey-brown thread *n* strong, unbleached thread.

whither[1] *v* **1** to flutter. **2** (*used of the wind*) to bluster, rage. **3** (*of an arrow, bullet or other missile*) to whizz by in its flight. **4** to rush along. **5** to whirl along with a booming sound. **6** to beat, belabour. —*n* **1** a shaking. **2** a slight attack of illness. **3** a gust of wind. **4** the sound of a rushing, violent movement. **5** a stroke. **6** a smart blow. **7** the noise of a hare starting from its den.

whither[2] *n* a direction.

whither[3] *conj* whether.

whither and beyont *adv* where and how far.

whither-spale *n* **1** a child's toy of a piece of notched lath to which a cord is attached to swing it round and cause mimic thunder. **2** a thin, lathy person. **3** a versatile person who is easily turned from his or her opinion or purpose.

whitie[1] *n* a species of sea trout, probably the salmon trout.

whitie[2] *n* a flatterer.

whitie[3] *n* a name given to a white cow.

whitie-whatie *same as* **whittie-whattie**.

whiting[1] *n* the young of the salmon trout.

whiting[2] *n* the language of flattery.

whitings *n* **1** wood shavings. **2** thin slices cut off with a knife.

whitlie *same as* **whitely**.

whitling *n* **1** a species of sea trout. **2** the bull trout in its first year.

whitling stone *n* a whetstone.

whitna *same as* **whatna**.

whitrack, whitreck, whitruck *n* a weasel.

whitrack skin *n* a purse made of a weasel's skin.

whitred, whitrat, whitrit *n* a weasel.

whitter[1] *n* **1** a hearty draught of liquor, whisky, etc. **2** a social glass.

whitter[2] *n* **1** any weak stuff. **2** anything weak in growth.

whitter[3] *v* **1** to chirp, warble, twitter. **2** to speak low and rapidly. **3** to chatter, prattle.—*n* loquacity, chatter.

whitter[4] *v* **1** to lessen by taking away small portions. **2** to fritter.

whitter[5] *same as* **witter**.

whitter[6] *v* **1** to move with lightness and speed. **2** to scamper. **3** to patter along. **4** to shuffle about.

whitteret, whitterit, whittrit *same as* **whitrack**.

whitterick, whitterock, whittrick *n* the curlew.

whitter-whatter *v* to converse in a low tone of voice.—*n* **1** trifling conversation. **2** chattering. **3** tittle-tattle. **4** a garrulous woman.

whittery *same as* **whitter**[2].

whittie *adj* low, mean.

whittie-whattie *v* **1** to shillyshally. **2** to make frivolous excuses. **3** to talk frivolously. **4** to whisper.—*n* **1** an idle pretence. **2** a vague, shuffling or coaxing speech. **3** a frivolous excuse. **4** one who employs every means to gain his or her end.

whittins *n* the last milk drawn from a cow, and the richest.

whittle[1] *n* **1** a butcher's knife. **2** a carving knife, a gully (qv). **3** a reaping hook. **4** a steel for sharpening knives. **5** a state of uneasiness or of being on the edge or fidgety.—*v* **1** to trim wood by paring it. **2** to sharpen.

whittle[2] *n* a whitlow.

whittle-case *n* a sheath for a knife.

whitty, whittie *n* the whitethroat.

whitty-whaws *n* silly pretences.

whiver *v* to quiver.

whiz *v* **1** to move rapidly. **2** (*used of water, etc*) to hiss on hot iron, stones, etc.—*n* the hissing sound of hot iron in water.

whizz *v* to inquire, cross-question, quiz.

whizzle *v* to make a hissing sound.

whoa *int* an interjectional sound used by a speaker in a hurry to introduce a sentence.

whoick *int* a call to dogs.

whole *adj* **1** healthy. **2** well in health. **3** (*with a pl n*) all.

whole-bodied cart *n* a cart with fixed shafts.

whole hypothec *n* the whole collection, number, etc.

whole ruck *n* the whole collection, number, etc.

whole water *n* very heavy rain.

whollup *same as* **whullup**.

whomble, whomel, whomil, whoml, whomle *same as* **whamble**.

whombel, whommil, whommle *same as* **whamble**.

whon *n* a worthless person.

whoogh *int* an exclamation of surprise, delight, etc, used by dancers for mutual excitation.

whoorle *n* **1** a very small wheel. **2** the flywheel of a spindle.

whoosh *int* an exclamation expressive of a swift, sudden, rushing motion.

whop *same as* **whap**[1].

whopin *adj* big.

whopper *same as* **whapper**.

whopper-snapper *n* **1** a little, presumptuous person. **2** a cheat, a fraudulent trick.

whorl-bane *same as* **whirlbone**.

whorlie *same as* **whirly**[1].

whosle *same as* **whozle**.

whow *int* an exclamation of admiration or pleasure.

who-yauds *int* a call to dogs to pursue horses.

whozle, whozzle *v* **1** to wheeze. **2** to breathe hard. —*n* a difficulty in breathing.

whripe *same as* **whyripe**.

whud[1] *same as.* **whid**[1].

whud[2] *n* a fib, a lie.—*v* to fib.

whudder *v* to make a whizzing or rushing sound. —*n* such a sound.

whuff *same as* **whiff**[1].

whuffle *same as* **wuffle**.

whuffy *n* an instant, a jiffy.

whulk *same as* **whilk**.

whulli-goleerie *same as* **whillie-goleerie**.

whullilow *same as* **whillie-lu**.

whullup *v* **1** to fawn, wheedle. **2** to curry favour.

whully *same as* **whilly**.

whully-wha *same as* **whilly-wha**.

whulper *same as* **whilper**.

wholt *n* **1** a blow from a fall. **2** a blow with a stick. **3** the noise of such a fall. **4** anything very large of its kind. **5** a large piece.

whulter *n* **1** anything large of its kind. **2** a large potato. **3** a large trout.

whulting *adj* **1** thumping, sounding. **2** large.

whumble, whumel, whumil, whumle *same as* **whamble**.

whumgee *n* **1** a vexatious whispering. **2** a trivial trick.

whummils *n* a whip for a top.

whummle, whummel, whummil *same as* **whamble**.

whummle *n* a wimble (qv).

whummle-bore *n* a hole bored by a wimble (qv).

whumpie *n* a wooden dish containing liquid food enough for two persons.

whumple *v* **1** to wrap. **2** to cover. **3** to wind. **4** to squirm.

whun[1], **whun**[2] *same as* **whin**[1], **whin**[2].

whun[3] *same as* **whon**.

whunce *n* **1** a heavy blow. **2** the sound of such a blow.

whunge *same as* **whinge**.

whun-lintie *n* the red linnet.

whunn *same as* **whin**[2].

whunner *same as* **whinner**.

whup *v* to whip.

whupers, whuppers *n* a family of itinerant drivers.

whupper *same as* **whapper**.

whuppie *same as* **whippy**.

whuppin *same as* **whapping**.

whuppity-stourie *n* the name of a certain brownie (qv).

whuppy *same as* **whippy**.

whuram *n* **1** grace notes or slurs in singing. **2** any ornamental piece of dress.

whur-cocks *int* a call given when game birds rise.

whurken *same as* **whirken**.

whurl[1] *n* a fawning, cunning child.

whurl[2] *same as* **whirl**.

whurl-barrow *n* a wheelbarrow.

whurlie-bed *n* a truckle bed.

whurlie-birlie *n* **1** anything that whirls round. **2** any toy that a child spins.

whurlie-girkie *n* a fanciful or untrue tale.

whurlie-wha' *same as* **whirliwhaw**.

whurligig *same as* **whirligig**.

whurly[1], **whurlie** *same as* **whurl**[1].

whurly, whurlie *same as* **whirly**.

whurr, whur *same as* **whirr**.

whurroo *int* a cry to draw attention.

whush[1], **whush**[2], **whush**[3] *same as* **whish**[1], **whish**[2], **whish**[3].

whusher *v* to whisper.—*n* a whisper.

whush-hoo *int* a cry used to scare away cats or birds.

whushie *v* to soothe, to lull.—*int* hush!

whusker *n* **1** a whisker. **2** the hair on one's face.

whussle[1] *v* to rustle.

whussle[2], **whustle, whus'le** *same as* **whistle**[1].
whusslewud *same as* **whistlewood**.
whut[1] *n* 1 a morning dram. 2 an appetizer.
whut[2] *adj* what.
whuten *same as* **whaten**.
whuther *same as* **whither**[1].
whuther-spale *same as* **whither-spale**.
whutter *same as* **witter**[1].
whutterick *n* a weasel.
whutterick-faced *adj* having a weasel-like face.
whutterick-fuffing *n* a gathering of weasels.
whut-throat *n* a weasel.
whutting *n* (*used of spirits*) a small draught.
whuther *same as* **whither**[1].
whuttle *same as* **whittle**[1].
whuttle grass *n* the melilot, a species of trefoil.
whuttling *n* 1 a whispering. 2 a quickening.
whuttorock *same as* **whutterick**.
why[1] *n* a reason.
why[2] *int* a call to a carthorse to keep to the left.
whyles *same as* **whiles**.
whylock, whyleock *same as* **whilock**.
whynger *same as* **whinger**[2].
whyripe *v* 1 to whimper, whine. 2 to torment with mourning.
whyte[1] *same as* **white**[2].
whyte[2] *n* wheat.
whyten *n* the whiting.
wi' *prep* with.
wic *same as* **wick**[2].
wice *same as* **wise**[3].
wicht[1] *n* 1 a creature, person, fellow. 2 the shrew-mouse.
wicht[2] *adj* 1 strong. 2 stout. 3 brisk, nimble. 4 clever.
wichtfu' *adj* strong, vigorous.
wichtly *adj* 1 vigorously. 2 briskly. 3 swiftly.
wichty *adj* powerful.
wick[1] *n* a farmstead.
wick[2], **wic** *n* 1 a creek. 2 a small bay or inlet of the sea. 3 an open bay.
wick[3] *n* 1 a corner, angle. 2 a corner of the eye or mouth.
wick[4] *n* (*used in curling*) 1 a narrow passage in the rink flanked by the stones of previous players. 2 a shot to remove a stone by striking it at an angle.—*v* 1 to drive a stone through an opening. 2 to cannon a stone.
wicker[1] *v* 1 to whizz through the air. 2 to flutter, as a bird. *same as* **whither**[1].
wicker[2] *n* 1 a pliant twig. 2 a switch. 3 an erection of wickerwork.
wicker[3] *n in phr* **wicker o' a shower** a quick, sharp shower.
wicker[4] *n* an old, cross-grained woman.
wicker[5] *v* 1 to twist a thread very tightly. 2 to become knotted from being too tightly twisted.
wicker[6] *n* the barb of a hoof.
wickerton *n* an old, cross-grained woman.
wicket *adj* 1 wicked. 2 vicious, savage. 3 angry, bitter.—*adv* very, exceedingly.
wicket *n* 1 the back door of a barn. 2 a sparred opening on either side of an old-fashioned barn for the purpose of winnowing.
wid[1] *n* wood.
wid[2] *v* would.
wid[3] *same as* **wood**[2].
widbin *n* woodbine.
widda *n* a widow.
widden[1] waded. *See* **wide**.
widden[2] *adj* wooden, stiff.
widden-dreme *n* 1 a wild dream. 2 a state of madness or confusion. 3 a state of sudden perturbation.
widder *n* weather.
widder-gaw, ga *same as* **weather-gaw**.
widder-gleam *same as* **weather-gleam**.
widdershins, widdersins, widdersones *same as* **withershins**.
widdershins-grow *same as* **withershins-grow**.

widdie[1], **widdy** *n* 1 a withy. 2 a hangman's noose, the gallows. 3 a band or hoop of twisted willow. 4 a twig with several smaller shoots branching out from it, which, being plaited, is used as a whip, the single grain serving for a handle. 5 a person who has been hanged or deserves hanging.
widdie[2] *n in phr* **at the knag and the widdie thegither** at loggerheads.
widdie[3] *n* a haddock dried without being split.
widdie-waan *n* 1 a willow wand. 2 a band of twisted willow twigs.
widdifow, widdiefu *n* 1 a small, ill-tempered person. 2 a romp. 3 a scamp. 4 a gallows bird.—*adj* 1 ill-tempered, wrathful. 2 worthless. 3 deserving to be hanged. 4 romping.
widdle, widdil *v* 1 to walk slowly about. 2 to waddle. 3 to wriggle. 4 to attain an end by short, noiseless or apparently feeble but prolonged exertions. 5 to struggle. 6 to deceive, beguile. 7 to introduce by shifting motion, also by circuitous courses.—*n* 1 a wriggling motion. 2 a contention, a struggle. 3 a bustle, a crowd. 4 the space occupied by a crowd.
widdle-waddle *v* to waddle.
widdrim, wid-dreme *same as* **widden-dreme**.
widdy, widdie *same as* **widdie**[1].
wide *v* to wade.
wide-gab *n* the dogfish.
wide-waken *adj* wide-awake.
widi *same as* **widdie**[1].
widow *n* 1 a widower. 2 a children's singing game.
widow-body *n* a widow.
widowerhood *n* the state of being a widower.
widow-man *n* a widower.
widow-wife, --woman *n* a widow.
wie *same as* **wee**[1].
wiel *same as* **weel**[1].
wield *v* 1 to manage successfully. 2 to exert. 3 to exercise. 4 to possess.
wieldiness *n* 1 easiness of management. 2 nimbleness.
wieldy *adj* 1 manageable. 2 nimble, easy.
wier *same as* **wear**[5].
wierd[1] *adj* 1 troublesome. 2 mischievous.
wierd[2] *same as* **weird**[1].
wiers *same as* **weirs**.
wife *n* 1 a woman. 2 a landlady.
wife-body *n* a woman.
wife-carle *n* a man who takes on himself a woman's household duties.
wifely *adj* womanish, feminine.
wifie, wifey *n* 1 a term of endearment used to a wife. 2 a little woman. 3 used endearingly, familiarly or contemptuottsly of a woman.—*adj* matronly.
wifiekie, wifikie *n* 1 a little wife. 2 a little woman. 3 a term of endearment.
wifie-like *adj* like a little wife.
wiffin *n* a moment.
wifock, wifockie *same as* **wifiekie**.
wig[1] *n* 1 a piece of paper for holding small groceries, confections, etc, rolled upon the hand and twisted at one end, called also **sow's-mou**. 2 a sharp stroke. 3 a whim, caprice.—*v* 1 to beat, strike sharply. 2 to scold severely.
wig[2], **wyg** *n in phr* **from wig to we** from pillar to post.
wig[3], **wigg** *n* whey.
wig[4] *same as* **whig**[2].
wig[5], **wigg** *same as* **whig**[3].
wig[6], **wigg** *v* 1 to wag, shake. 2 to move.
wig[7] *n* a penny.
wigg[1], **wigg**[2], **wigg**[3] *same as* **wig**[3], **wig**[5], **wig**[6].
wiggam tree *n* the mountain ash.
wiggie[1] *adj* loose, shaky, waggly.
wiggie[2], **wiggy** *n* 1 a barber. 2 a name for the devil. 3 any judge who wears a wig on the bench.
wiggle *v* 1 to waggle, shake, move loosely. 2 to swing in walking. 3 to wriggle. 4 to waddle, reel, stagger. 5 to

work listlessly and without heart. **6** to trifle.—*n* **1** a waggle. **2** a shaking motion. **3** a waddling gait. **4** a swing in the gait. **5** a trifle, toy, gimcrack. **6** anything more ornamental than useful.

wigglety-wagglety *adj* **1** swinging from side to side. **2** unstable.—*adv* (*used of a rider who does not move with the motion of his horse*) from side to side, unsteadily.

wiggle-waggle *v* **1** to shake or move from side to side, to sway. **2** to wriggle.—*n* waggling, quivering.—*adv* zigzag.

wiggle-waggly *adj* very unstable.

wiggly *adj* waggling, unstable.

wiggly-waggly *adj* waggling, shaking.

wiggy *same as* **whig**³.

wight¹, **wight**² *same as* **wicht**¹, **wicht**².

wight³ *same as* **wite**.

wightdom *n* weight.

wightly *adv* vigorously, strongly.

wightman *n* a strong man.

wightness *n* power, strength.

wight-warping *n* nimble-throwing at the loom.

wigle *same as* **wiggle**.

wigle-wagle *same as* **wiggle-waggle**.

wig-wag *v* to swing backwards and forwards.—*n* vicissitude.

wig-waggle *v* to swing backwards and forwards.

wig-wag-slow *adj* slow as the swing of a pendulum.

wike *same as* **wick**³.

wil *same as* **wild**¹.

wilcat, wild-cat *n* **1** the polecat. **2** an ill-natured person.—*adj* wild, stormy, raging.

wild¹ *adj* **1** mad with anger. **2** cross.—*adv* extremely.

wild² *same as* **will**¹.

wild-bear *n in phr* **shoein' the wild-bear** a game in which a person sits cross-legged on a swinging beam or pole and with a switch he whips the beam as if riding and if he keeps his balance, he is victor over those who fail to do so.

wild birds *n in phr* **all the wild birds in the air** a naming and carrying game in which the person who fails is switched on the back.

wild cotton *n* the tassel cotton grass.

wilder, wildar *v* **1** to lose one's way. **2** to go astray.

wildering *adj* **1** bewildered. **2** gone astray.

wildert, wilderit *adj* gone astray.

wildfire *n* **1** the phosphorescence of decaying vegetation, etc. **2** summer lightning. **3** erysipelas. **4** a will-o'-the-wisp. **5** the small spearmint. **6** the marsh marigold. **7** false zeal.

wildie *n* a wild, restless child.

wild-like *adj* **1** wild. **2** (*used of weather*) threatening storm.—*adv* wildly.

wild-liquorice *n* the sweet milk vetch.

wild mustard *n* **1** the charlock. **2** the wild radish.

wild pink *n* the maiden pink.

wildrif, wildruff *adj* **1** wild, boisterous, unruly. **2** wild-looking.

wile¹ *n* an instrument for twisting straw ropes.

wile² *same as* **wale**².

wile³ *same as* **will**¹.

wile⁴ *adj* wild.

wile⁵ *adj* vile.

wilerie *n* **1** wiling. **2** seductiveness.

wilesome *adj* wilful.

wiley-coat *same as* **wylie-coat**.

wil fire *same as* **wildfire**.

wilful *adj* willing, eager to work.

wilk *n* a periwinkle, an edible shellfish.

will¹ *adj* **1** bewildered. **2** lost in error. **3** uncertain how to proceed.—*adv* astray.—*v* **1** to lose one's way. **2** to wander about.—*n* the state of having lost one's way.

will² *n* **1** a wish. **2** a desire. **3** inclination. **4** hope. **5** liking for.—*v* **1** to bequeath. **2** to impose one's will on another.

will³ *v* **1** to be accustomed to. **2** shall. **3** to be bent upon. **4** to be under necessity. **5** (*with* **be**) indicates the simple

present in estimating distances and time.

willan *n* a willow.

willawackits *int* alas.

will-a-waes *int* an exclamation of sorrow, alas.

willawaun *int* an exclamation of sorrow, etc.

will-a-wins *int* an exclamation of pity, sorrow, etc.

willa-woo *same as* **willa-waes**.

will-be *n* **1** a guess. **2** a conjecture.

willcorn *n* **1** wild oats. **2** oats growing without culture.

willed *adj* wilful.

willess *adj* **1** aimless, purposeless. **2** mechanical.

will-gate *n* **1** an erroneous course. **2** an improper course.

will he, nill he *adv* perforce. **2** willy-nilly.

willick *n* **1** the common guillemot. **2** the puffin. **3** the razorbill. **4** a young heron.

willie *n* a willow.

willie-and-the-wisp *n* a will-o'-the-wisp.

Willie Arnot *n* a slang name for good whisky.

Willie Cossar *n* **1** a large pin of brass, two or three inches long, for pinning shawls or plaids, called after its maker. **2** an expression of bigness, applied to a turnip, animal or woman.

willie-dragel *adj* dirty, draggled.

Willie Fisher *n* a notorious liar.

willie fisher *n* **1** the comnon tern. **2** a waterfowl. **3** the little grebe.

willie-goat *n* a goat, a billy goat.

willie-gow *n* the herring gull.

Willie-Jack *n* a go-between in a love affair.

willie- miln *n* a door latch worked by a string.

willie-muflie *n* the willow warbler.

willie-o'-the-wisp *n* a will-o'-the-wisp, ignis fatuus.

willie-pourit *n* **1** the spawn of the frog. **2** a tadpole.

willie-powret *n* a child's name for the seal.

willie-run-hedge *n* the goosegrass.

willies *n* clippings of cloth.

willie's-wisp *n* a will-o'-the-wisp.

willie-wagtail *n* **1** a name given to various species of wagtail. **2** the pied wagtail.

williewaick *n* a loud shout.—*v* to shout loudly.

willie-wanbeard *n* the fifteen-spined stickleback.

willie-wand, ~-wain, ~-wairn *same as* **willow wand**.

willie-wastell, ~-wassie *n* a children's game.

willie-waught, ~-waucht *n* a hearty drink of any strong liquor.

willie-whae *v* to make the cry of the curlew.

willie-whaup *n* the curlew.

willie-whip-the-wind *n* the kestrel.

willie-winkie *n* a fondling name for a small child.

willie-with-a-wisp *n* a will-o'-the-wisp.

willie-wogie *n* a small piece of wood burning at one end, which is twirled quickly and continuously round.

willin-sweert *adj* **1** coy. **2** partly willing, partly unwilling.

willint *adj* willing.

willintly *adv* **1** willingly. **2** readily.

williwa *int* an exclamation of sorrow.

will-kail *n* wild mustard or charlock.

willness *n* dizziness.

willow-boost *n* a rustic basket for holding meal, etc.

willow wand *n* **1** a willow rod or twig. **2** a willow rod, which, when peeled and placed against the door of a Highland house, indicated that the inmates wished no visitors to enter. **3** a thin, lanky person.

willy *adj* **1** wilful. **2** self-willed.

willyard, willyart *same as* **wilyart**¹.

willyart¹ *same as* **wilyart**².

willy-wa *same as* **whilly-wha**.

willy-wacht *same as* **willie-waught**.

willy-wally *int* an exclamation of sorrow.

willy-wambles *n* a complaint of the bowels attended with a rumbling noise.

wilshoch *adj* **1** perverse. **2** changeable.—*n* a timid courter.

wilsum, wilsome *adj* bewildered, wandering, lonely, dreary.

wilsum, willsome *adj* wilful.

wilt[1] *same as* **whilt**.

wilt[2] *v* to wither, fade.—*n* a state of feebleness or despondency.

wiltu, wilto *v and pron* wilt thou?

wiltuna *v, pron and neg* wilt thou not?

wilyart[1], **wilyard** *adj* 1 obstinate. 2 unmanageable. 3 self-willed.

wilyart[2] *adj* 1 shy, bashful. 2 awkward. 3 bewildered. 4 lonely. 5 wild. 6 shunning human habitations and society.—*n* a timid, faint-hearted fellow.

wimble *n* a twist.

wimble-bore *n* 1 a hole bored by a wimble. 2 a defect in the throat causing indistinct speech.

wime *same as* **wame**.

wimmel *n* the windpipe.

wimmelbree, winmelbreis *n* a thin soup made of the same constituents as a haggis.

wimple, wimpil *v* 1 to wrap, cover. 2 (*of a river, stream*) to wind, meander, ripple. 3 (*of love*) to glance forth shyly from the eye. 4 to wriggle, squirm, writhe. 5 (*of growing corn*) to toss, wave. 6 (*of a boat*) to move unsteadily, to be top-heavy. 7 to perplex. 8 to use circumlocution with intent to deceive.—*n* 1 a winding. 2 a curve. 3 a meandering movement. 4 a curl. 5 an intricate turn. 6 a wile. 7 a piece of craft. 8 a fit of perversity. 9 a sulky temper.

wimpled *adj* 1 indirect, involved, intricate. 2 circumlocutory, perplexed.

wimplefeyst *n* a sulky humour.—*adj* unmanageable, untoward.

wimpler *n* a waving lock of hair.

win[1] *v* 1 to earn. 2 to quarry stone. 3 to find and dig out coal. 4 to attain or reach by effort or with difficulty. 5 to succeed. 6 to succeed in reaching a place. 7 to go. 8 to come. 9 to have power or liberty to go. 10 to arrive at. 11 to work, labour. 12 to deliver a blow.—*n* earnings, wages.

win[2] *n* 1 the quantity of standing corn that a band of reapers could cut. 2 the group of three reapers, generally a man and two women, who worked on the same rig (qv).

win[3] *v* 1 to dry hay, corn, peat, etc, by exposure to the air. 2 to dry or season by the heat of the fire. 3 to winnow.

win[4] *same as* **won**[1].

win[5] *n* 1 wind. 2 a boasting, empty bravado.

win[6] *v* 1 to wind. 2 wound.

win aboon *v* to get above.

win about *v* to circumvent.

winach *v* to winnow.

win and loss *n* a game at marbles in which marbles are won or lost by the players.

win awa *v* 1 to get away. 2 to die.

wine *v* (*used of a horse*) to prance, kick out behind.

winch[1] *n* a wench.—*v* to court a person of the opposite sex.

winch[2] *v* to wince.—*n* 1 a wince. 2 the act of wincing.

winchancie *adj* unlucky.

winchie *n* a young woman.

wincock *n* 1 a toy windmill. 2 a person of unstable disposition.

wind[1] *n* 1 talk, foolish talk. 2 mood, spirits. 3 a children's singing game.—*v* 1 to boast. 2 to talk long and loudly. 3 to outtalk a person. 4 to taint. 5 to become tainted or sour.

wind[2] *v* 1 to wrap a corpse in grave clothes. 2 to twist.

wind[3] *same as* **wynd**[1].

wind, winde *same as* **wynd**[2].

windasses *n* fanners for winnowing grain.

wind-ba', ~-ball *n* 1 a balloon. 2 wind broken behind.

windband *n* an iron band wound round anything broken or spliced.

wind bill *n* an accommodation bill.

wind-broken *adj* broken-winded.

wind-buff't *adj* driven and buffeted by wind.

wind-craw *n* a large potato, stuck full of a gull's wing feathers, which will drive and jump before a strong breeze

and which boys considered it a feat to be able to catch.

wind-cuffer *n* the kestrel.

winder *n* one who deals in the marvellous in storytelling.—*v* to wonder.

wind-feed *n* occasional showers that increase the force of the wind.

wind-flaucht, ~-flaught *adv* with impetuous force, as if driven by the wind.

windin *n* the smallest matter.

windin' *n* 1 outtalking. 2 silencing by loud, long talking.

winding *n* a gathering of tallow rising up against the wick of a candle, deemed an omen of death in the family.

windings *n* what is wound in spinning.

windisome *adj* 1 producing flatulence. 2 long-winded.

windle[1] *same as* **winnel**.

windle[2], **windles** *n* an instrument used for winding yarn.

windle[3] *v* to walk wearily in the wind.—*n* a measure of straw, corn, etc.

windlen *same as* **winnel**.

windless *adj* breathless. 2 exhausted.

windlestrae *n* 1 smooth-crested grass. 2 a stalk of withered grass. 3 a thin, unhealthy person. 4 a vacillating fellow. 5 anything weak and slender. 6 a trifling obstacle.

windlin, windling *same as* **winnel**.

windock *n* a window.

window[1] *v* to winnow.

window[2] *n* 1 any opening in a room other than the door. 2 a recess in the wall of a room for small articles.

window bole *n* a small opening in a wall for light and air, covered with a wooden shutter.

window brod *n* a shutter.

window sole *n* a windowsill.

windraw *n* a windrow.—*v* to put hay, peats, etc, into windrows.

windrem *same as* **widden-dreme**.

windskew *n* a broad piece of wood attached to a long handle which is placed within the chimney top and is movable with changing winds to prevent smoke.

wind-sucker *n* a horse that draws air into its stomach by sucking the manger or biting the crib.

wind-warks *n* the lungs.

wind-waved *adj* (*used of plants, etc*) having the stem whirled about by the wind so that the roots become loosened in the earth.

wind-wacht *n* a hoop covered with skin, for winnowing grain.

windy *adj* 1 having plenty of breath. 2 flatulent. 3 causing flatulence. 4 noisy, talkative, garrulous. 5 boastful. 6 vain, ostentatious.

Windy Saturday *n* a peculiarly windy day, which became a traditional era from which subsequent events were dated.

windysome *adj* 1 causing flatulence. 2 long-winded.

windy-wallets *n* 1 one given to fibbing or exaggeration. 2 a person given to breaking wind behind.

wine *same as* **wynd**[2].

wine-berry *n* the common redcurrant.

wine tree *n* the blackthorn.

win-free *v* 1 to liberate, set free. 2 to obtain release. 3 to raise from the ground. 4 to disentangle.

wing *n* 1 an arm. 2 the side of a cart. 3 (*in pl*) the mudguards of gig wheels.—*v* (*used in curling*) to strike the side of an unguarded stone.

winged chair *n* an easy chair with projecting sides.

winged-row *n* a halfpenny roll baked with flat sides like wings.

wingel *n* 1 a tumour. 2 a soft blister from walking in tight shoes.

wingle *v* 1 to flutter, wave. 2 to hang or dangle loosely. 3 to flap, wag. 4 to bend and twist. 5 to walk feebly. 6 to wriggle. 7 to carry in a dangling way. 8 to move with difficulty under a load.

wingle strae *same as* **windlestrae**.

winglit-looking *adj* very slender.
wink *n* **1** a nap. **2** a sleep. **3** a moment.
winker *n* **1** an eye. **2** an eyelash. **3** an eyelid.
winkie *n* **1** the twinkling of an eye. **2** a nursery word for sleep.
win-kill *n* a hollow in a stack of oats, etc, for ventilation and the prevention of heating.
winkish *v* **1** to deceive. **2** to cajole.
winkit *adj* (*used of milk*) slightly turned.
winkle *v* **1** to sparkle. **2** to twinkle.
winklot *n* **1** a wench. **2** a young woman.
wink o' a wintle *n* a very short time.
winle *same as* **winnel**.
winless *adj* breathless.
winlin *same as* **winnel**.
winn[1], **winn**[2] *same as* **win**[1], **win**[3].
winna, winnae *v neg* will not.
winned *v* winnowed.
winnel, winnle a bottle of straw or hay.—*v* to put up hay or straw in bottles.
winnel-skewed *adj* under optical illusion.
winnel strae *same as* **windlestrae**.
winner[1] *v* to wonder.
winner[2] *n* (*used in curling*) the stone lying nearest the tee, the winning shot.
winnerfu' *adj* **1** wonderful. **2** wonderfully well or recovered from an illness.
winnes *n* **1** misuse. **2** abuse. **3** waste.
winnie[1] *adj* windy.
winnie[2] *n* a game of marbles in which the stakes are lost and won.
winning *n* **1** earnings. **2** wages.
winning-ring *n* the game of winnie (qv).
winnister *same as* **winnowster**.
winnle[1] *same as* **winnel**.
winnle[2] *same as* **windle**[2].
winnlen *same as* **winnel**.
winnles *same as* **windle**[2].
winnle strae *same as* **windlestrae**.
winnock[1], **winnoc** *n* a window.
winnock[2] *n* **1** a wind-egg.
winnock bole *n* a small aperture for a window, usually closed with a wooden shutter instead of glass.
winnock brod *n* a window shutter.
winnock bunker *n* a window seat forming a chest.
winnock cheek, ~ lug *n* the side of a window.
winnock glass *n* **1** window glass. **2** a glazed window.
winnock neuk *n* a window corner.
winnock sole *n* a windowsill.
winnow *v* **1** to fan. **2** to wave. **3** to wave wings.
winnow claith *n* a winnowing sheet.
winnowster *n* a winnowing fan.
winny[1] *adj* windy.
winny[2] *v* to winnow.
winraa, winraw *same as* **windraw**.
winrame's birde *n in phr* **like winrame's birds** used of a tedious tale.
-wins *suffix* **1** towards. **2** in the direction of.
win's *n* rheumatism.
Winsday *n* Wednesday.
winsome *adj* **1** large. **2** comely.
winsomelie *adv* **1** pleasantly. **2** winningly. **3** in an engaging way.
winsomeness *n* cheerfulness.
wint[1] *v* **1** to want. **2** to wish.
wint[2] *v* to befall.
wint[3] *n* **1** a glimpse. **2** an instant. **3** a hint as to the whereabouts of a person or thing.
winter[1] *same as* **wanter**.
winter[2] *n* **1** the last load of corn brought home from the harvest field. **2** the person who brought it. **3** the state of having all the harvest ingathered. **4** the feast of the ingathering.—*v* to keep and feed cattle through the winter.

winter *n* an iron frame or loose bar made to fit on to the bars of a grate to hold anything that has to be heated.
winter downfall *n* the descent of sheep in winter from the hills to lower adjacent ground.
winter-dykes *n* **1** a clotheshorse. **2** a wooden frame for drying clothes out-of-doors.
winterer *n* **1** an animal kept to feed in a particular place during winter. **2** an animal taken to be kept during winter.
winter fish *n* ling salted for winter use.
winter-haining *n* pasture or common enclosed in winter in order to get hay from it.
winter-hap *n* winter covering.
winterin *n* an ox or cow of one year.
winterish *adj* wintry.
winterling *same as* **winterin**
Winter Saturday *n* the last Saturday of October, on which the winter half-year begins.
winter-shadit *adj* sheltered from the north, facing the south.
winter-slap *n* a gap in a fence allowing cattle to roam from field to field in winter.
winter-sour *n* **1** curds and butter mixed and eaten with bread. **2** curds, made of soured milk, mixed with butter.
Winter Sunday *n* the last Sunday in October.
wintin *same as* **wantin'**.
wintle[1] *v* **1** to stagger. **2** to reel. **3** to tumble. **4** to struggle. **5** to wriggle. **6** to wave to and fro hanging on a gallows. **7** to writhe. **8** to wind round.—*n* a staggering motion.
wintle[2] *same as* **windlestrae**.
winton money *n* money given to a herd to induce carefulness of the cattle under his charge while grazing.
winze *v* to curse.—*n* **1** an oath. **2** a curse.
winzie *adj* winsome, pleasant.
wi'outen *same as* **withouten**.
wip, wipp *v* **1** to wrap or bind round tightly. **2** to overlay with cord, etc. **3** to tie.—*n* **1** a tight twist of a rope, etc. **2** a coil. **3** a wrapping.
wipe *v* to whip, strike, beat.—*n* **1** a blow, stroke. **2** a sarcastic remark. **3** a large amount, degree or extent.
wiper *n* **1** a severe blow. **2** a severe taunt or retort.
wippen *n* that with which the handle of a golf club is overlaid.
wipple *v* **1** to wind, twist. **2** to intertwine. **3** to roll or bundle up.
wir *pron* our.
wird *same as* **word**[1].
wirdie *n* **1** a little word. **2** a word or two. **3** a short speech.
wirdy *adj* wordy, full of words.
wire *n* a knitting needle.—*v* to work vigorously.
wire-scraper *n* a fiddler.
wirk *same as* **wark**.
wirl *n* **1** a small, rickety child. **2** a small, harsh-featured person. **3** a stunted animal.
wir lane, wirlens *n* ourselves alone.
wirlie[1] *n* a puny, rickety child.
wirlie[2] *same as* **whirly**[1].
wirling *n* a puny, feeble child or animal.
wirly *adj* **1** puny. **2** small.
wirr[1] *n* **1** a dog's growl. **2** an angry answer. **3** a fit of bad temper. **4** wrath. **5** roughness. **6** a crabbed fellow. **7** a diminutive, peevish person.—*v* **1** to growl as a dog. **2** to fret. **3** to whine.—*int* a call to dogs, inciting them to fight.
wirr[2] *v* to fly like a startled partridge.
wirrablaa *n* a violent but short exertion.
wirricow *same as* **worricow**.
wirring *adj* crabbed.
wirry *same as* **worry**.
wirry carl *n* a bugbear.
wirrycow *same as* **worricow**.
wirsat, wirsit *same as* **worset**.
wirsels *refl pron* ourselves.
wirsle *same as* **warsle**.

wirsle-warsle *n* a hard, continuous struggle.—*v* to struggle hard and continuously.

wirth *n* importance, worth.—*adj* **1** worthy. **2** deserving. **3** of use. **4** of value.

wirthless *adj* worthless.

wis[1] *v* to wish.

wis[2] *v* knew.

wisdom *n* a wise or prudent action.

wise[1] *v* **1** to direct, guide, lead. **2** to counsel, advise. **3** to be cautious or use policy in reaching one's end. **4** to get by skill or craft. **5** to manoeuvre. **6** to entice, lure, persuade. **7** to beguile. **8** to induce. **9** to let out or draw anything so as to prevent it from breaking. **10** to spend. **11** to use. **12** to withdraw, take away. **13** to incline. **14** to slip away.

wise[2] *n* guise.

wise[3] *adj* **1** knowing, well-informed. **2** sane. **3** possessing or pretending to possess powers of magic or witchcraft.

wisehorn *same as* **weasan**.

wiselike *adj* **1** sagacious. **2** proper. **3** seemly. **4** respectable. **5** becoming, befitting. **6** good- or nice-looking.— *adv* **1** properly, sensibly. **2** decently. **3** becomingly.

wise-looking *adj* **1** prudent. **2** sensible. **3** proper. **4** respectable. **5** seemly.

wisen *same as* **wizzen**.

wise-spoken *adj* wise or prudent of speech.

wise-wife *n* **1** a witch. **2** a fortune-teller.

wise-woman *n* a woman who professed to cure ailments by skill or by charms, a wise-wife (qv).

wish[1] *v* **1** to hope. **2** to trust.

wish[2] *int* hush!

wishie[1] *same as* **wishy**.

wishie[2] *n in phr* **neither hishie nor wishie** profound silence.

wisht *same as* **whisht**.

wish-wash *n* worthless stuff.

wishy, wishie *adj* **1** delicate. **2** watery, weak.—*v* **1** to hesitate. **2** to make trifling excuses.

wishy-washy *adj* **1** delicate. **2** of weak constitution. —*n* any weak, watery drink. **3** (*in pl*) shuffling language. **4** prevarications. **5** fanciful evasions. **6** slowness in coming to the point.—*v* to make trifling excuses.

wisk[1] *n* a bulky, untidy wrapping about the neck.

wisk[2] *v* **1** to give a light brushing stroke with anything pliant. **2** to hurry away.—*n* a slight brushing stroke with anything pliant.

wiskar *same as* **whisker**.

wisle *same as* **wissel**.

wislie *adj* **1** thin, shrivelled. **2** stunted.

wisn'd *adj* **1** parched. **2** dried up. *See* **wizzen**.

wisock *n* a wise person.

wisp[1] *n* **1** a bunch of twigs. **2** a bush, as a tavern sign. **3** a candle. **4** the nest of a certain kind of wild bee, made on the surface of the ground.—*v* **1** to rub down a horse with a wisp of straw, hay, etc. **2** (*used of shoes or clogs*) to put a wisp of straw in them in order to keep the feet warm and dry.

wisp[2] *n* **1** a wasp. **2** an ill-natured person.

wiss[1] *same as* **wish**[1].

wiss[2] *same as* **wise**[1].

wiss[3] *n* the moisture exuding from bark in preparing it for tanning.

wiss[4] *same as* **wis**[2].

wissel, wissle *n* (*used of money*) the change.—*v* **1** to exchange. **2** to change money. **3** (*with* **words**) to talk. **4** to hold discourse. **5** to exchange angry words, to quarrel. **6** to club in payment of drink. **7** to wager, bet.

wissen *same as* **wizzen**.

wissler *n* a moneychanger.

wist *n* a wisp.

wist[2] *v* wished.

wistel *same as* **wissel**.

wister *v* **1** to scuffle. **2** to mix in a broil.—*n* a broil, a noisy scuffle, accompanied by high words.

wit[1] *n* **1** intelligence. **2** information, knowledge. **3** sense. **4** wisdom.

wit[2] *same as* **wat**[2].

witch *n* **1** a wizard. **2** a moth.

witch-bead *n* a kind of fossil of the class of Entrochi.

witch bell *n* the harebell.

witch book *n* a book of spells, charms, etc.

witch bracken *n* a species of bracken.

witch bridle *n* an iron collar or frame with prongs fixed on a witch's neck and head and fastened to a wall.

witch cake *n* an uncanny and virulent cake prepared for purposes of incantation at witches' meetings.

witch carline *n* a witch.

witch charming *n* witchcraft.

witch doctor *n* **1** one who claims to cure by charming. **2** one who cures the bewitched.

witchery *n* **1** witchcraft. **2** a tale of witchcraft.

witches *n* round, red, clay marbles.

witches' butterfly *n* a large, thick-bodied moth of drab or light-brown colour.

witches' hazel *n* the mountain ash.

witches' knots *n* **1** a bundle of matted twigs formed on branches of birch and blackthorn and resembling birds' nests. **2** a disease supposed to arise from the stoppage of the juices. **3** a sort of charm applied to a woman's hair.

witches' ride *n* a riding of witches at midnight of Hallowe'en.

witches' thimmles, ~ thummles *n* the flowers of the foxglove.

witch-gathering *n* a gathering of witches for a witches' ride (qv).

witch-gowan *n* the dandelion.

witch-hag *n* the swallow.

witching *n* witchcraft.

witching-docken *n* an old woman's name for tobacco.

witch-knots *n* a charm applied to a woman's hair.

witch mark *n* a mark supposed to exist on the body of a witch.

witch-pricker *n* a witch-finder who discovered witches by pricking them for the witch mark (qv).

Witch Sabbath *n* a gathering of all the witches in Scotland on the evening between the first Friday and Saturday in April.

witch score *n* the mark made with a sharp instrument on the forehead of a supposed witch to render her harmless.

witch's milk *n* the juice of the witch-gowan (qv).

witchuk *n* the sand martin.

witch-wean *n* a changeling substituted by fairies, etc, for a newborn child.

witch-wife, ~-woman *n* a witch.

witchy *adj* **1** witch-like. **2** bewitching.

wite *v* **1** to blame. **2** to accuse. **3** to twit with. **4** to bear the blame.—*n* **1** blame. **2** accusation. **3** the fault of. **4** the cause of any ill. **5** a wrong. **6** an injury.

witeless *adj* blameless.

witer *n* **1** one who blames. **2** a fault-finder.

witewordy *adj* blameworthy.

with *prep* **1** against. **2** upsides with. **3** according to. **4** in agreement with. **5** expressing tolerance of. **6** by. **7** owing to. **8** in consequence of. **9** for. **10** in exchange for. **11** of. **12** to.

withe *n* a rod.

wither[1] *v* **1** to fret. **2** to whine, whimper.

wither[2] *n* weather.

wither[3] *prefix* indicating contrary direction.

wither[4] *n* a wether.

wither[5] *v* **1** to tremble. **2** to bluster.

wither[6] *n* the barb of an arrowhead, fishing hook, etc, *same as* **witter**[1].

withergates *adv* **1** in a contrary direction. **2** against the sun's course.

withergloom *n* the clear sky near the horizon.

witherips *n* the sweet woodruff.

witherlands *adv* **1** in a contrary direction. **2** against the sun's course.

witherlock *n* the lock of hair in a horse's mane, grasped by a rider in mounting.

withershins, withershines *adv* **1** against the sun's course. **2** topsy-turvily. **3** unluckily. **4** contrarily. —*adj* **1** at enmity with. **2** opposed to.—*n* contrariness.

withershins-grow *n* anything growing contrary to the sun's course.

witherspail *n* the goosegrass.

witherspale *same as* **whitherspale**.

witherty-weep *n* the plover.

wither-wecht *n* the weight allowed to counterbalance the paper, vessel, etc, in which the goods are weighed.

witherwise *adv* against the course of the sun.

withgate *n* the advantage, the better of a person, by overreaching.

withinside *prep* inside, within.

wi' this *adv* hereupon.

without *prep* outside.—*conj* unless.

withouten, withooten *prep* without.

witling *n* **1** a simpleton. **2** a fool.

witness *n* a sponsor at a baptism.—*v* **1** to see. **2** to be present at.

witrat *same as* **whitrack**.

witten, wittan *n* **1** knowledge. **2** (*in pl*) news.

witten *v* waited.

witter[1] *n* the barb of an arrowhead, fish hook, etc.

witter[2] *v* **1** to be peevish. **2** to growl.—*n* a peevish person, one always growling.

witter[3] *n* **1** a token, sign. **2** a mark. **3** a tree reserved in cutting timber. **4** a pennon. **5** a standard. **6** (*used in curling*) the tee.—*v* **1** to inform. **2** to guide. **3** to prognosticate.

witter[4] *v* **1** to struggle for a livelihood. **2** to fight. **3** to fall foul of. **4** to take by the throat.—*n* the throat.

wittered *adj* **1** barbed. **2** mixed.

wittered-heuks *n* barbed hooks.

witterel *n* a peevish, waspish person.

witteret *same as* **whitrack**.

wittering *n* **1** knowledge, information. **2** a hint. **3** a rumour.

witter-length *n* (*in curling*) as far as the tee.

witterly *adv* wittingly, knowingly.

witterous[1] *adj* barbed.

witterous[2] *adj* **1** crabbed. **2** determined.

witters *same as* **witter**[4].

witter-stone *n* a stone placed as a mark.

wittert *adj* barbed.

wittin, wittins *n* **1** knowledge. **2** information. **3** tidings.

witty *adj* **1** wise. **2** knowing. **3** shrewd. **4** well-informed. **5** sensible.—*n* **1** cleverness. **2** skill.

wize *same as* **wise**[1].

wizen *same as* **weasan**.

wizz *same as* **wise**[1].

wizzards *n* couch grass and other weeds dried on fallow fields.

wizzen[1] *v* **1** to wither. **2** to shrivel. **3** to become dry, parched. **4** to be wrinkled. **5** to bake.—*adj* withered, dried up, shrivelled.

wizzen[2] *same as* **weasan**.

wizzen-faced *adj* with withered, pinched, wrinkled features.

wizzon *same as* **weasan**.

wo *same as* **wae**.

wo, woa *int* a call to a horse to stand still.

wob *same as* **wab**.

wo-back *int* a call to a horse to back.

wobart *adj* **1** weak, feeble. **2** decayed.

wobat-like *adj* used of a faded, withered appearance.

wobat[1] *same as* **wobart**.

wobat[2] *same as* **woubit**.

wobble *v* to sell drink without a licence.

wobbling-shop *n* an unlicensed drinking shop.

wobster *same as* **wabster**.

wochle *same as* **wauchle**.

wod *same as* **wood**[1].

wod *n* a wood.

wodat *adj* weak, feeble, decayed.

wodder *same as* **wither**[3].

woddie *same as* **widdie**[1].

woddram *same as* **woodrum**.

wode[1] *n* a corruption of the word God, used as an expletive.

wode[2] *same as* **wood**[1].

wodeness *n* madness.

Wodensday *n* Wednesday.

wodershins *same as* **withershins**.

wodge *same as* **wadge**[3].

wodroam, wodrome *same as* **woodrum**.

wodset *same as* **wadset**.

wodspur *n* a forward, unsettled, fiery person.

wog[1] *v* **1** to wag. **2** to twitch.

wog[2] *n* vogue, a fashion.

wogh *same as* **waugh**[2].

wolron, wolroun *n* a poor, miserable creature.

wolter *same as* **walter**.

woman *n* **1** a familiar term of address. **2** a contemptuous designation. **3** a maidservant.

woman-big *adj* grown to womanhood.

woman-body *n* **1** a woman. **2** a female.

woman-folk *n* women.

woman-grown *adj* grown to womanhood.

woman-house *n* a laundry.

woman-muckle *adj* grown to womanhood.

woman-scared *adj* shy in the presence of women.

woman-school *n* a dame's school.

woman's wark *n* what takes up a woman's whole time.

woman-wark *n* work a woman may do.

womb *n* the belly.

womble *same as* **wamble**.

womell, womill, wommle *n* a wimble.

wommal *n* a warble in the skin of cattle caused by the larva of the gadfly.

wommle *same as* **wamble**.

won[1] *v* to dwell, reside, live.—*n* a dwelling, an abode.

won[2] *v* to dry by exposure to air.—*adj* dried.

won[3] *v* quarried, dug from a mine. *See* **win**.

won[4] *v* to have in one's power.

wonding sheet *n* a winding sheet.

wone *same as* **won**[1].

won'er *v* to wonder.

wonlyne *same as* **winnel**.

wonna *v neg* will not.

wonne *same as* **won**[1].

wonnels *same as* **windle**[2].

wonner *v* to wonder.—*n* **1** a wonder. **2** a prodigy. **3** a term of contempt.—*adv* **1** wonderfully. **2** extremely.

wonnerfu *adj* great, large.—*adv* extremely.

wonnerfully *adv* very, extremely.

wonnersome *adv* **1** wonderfully. **2** very.

wonning *n* **1** a dwelling. **2** the chief house on a farm.

wonning house *n* a dwelling house.

wonnles *same as* **windle**[2].

wonnle ~, wondle sheet *n* a winding sheet for the dead.

wont *v* to accustom.

wont-to-be *n* a custom or practice that prevailed in former times.

woo' *n* wool.

woocreel *n* a wicker basket for holding wool.

wood[1] *adj* **1** mad. **2** furious with rage. **3** eager. **4** excited. **5** keen.—*adv* **1** madly. **2** wildly.

wood[2] *n* a blue dye, woad.

wood-body *n* a person of very violent temper.

wood-doo *n* the stock dove.

wooden *adj* **1** clumsy. **2** stiff.

wooden breeks, ~ sark, ~ surtout, ~ surtoo *n* a coffin.

wooden turnpike *n* the treadmill.

wooder *n* the dust of cotton or flax.

woodersones *same as* **withershins**.

woodie[1] *same as* **widdie**[1].

woodie[2] *n* a mad person or animal.

woodie-~, woodee-~, woody-carl *n* a particular kind of pear.

wood-ill *n* a disease of cattle causing bloody urine, etc.

woodlins *adv* very eagerly.

woodlouse *n* the bookworm.

woodly *adv* madly.

woodness *n* madness.

woodpecker *n* the tree-creeper, *Certhia*.

wood-rasp *n* the wild raspberry.

woodrip *n* woodruff.

woodrum *n* **1** furious madness, especially causing cattle to run about madly. **2** a fit of obstinacy or wildness. **3** a state of confusion unexpectedly created.

wood-scud *n* a mad, romping boy or girl.

woodspurs *n* a fiery, unsettled person.

wood-thrush *n* the missal-thrush.

woodwise *n* the dyer's broom, *Genista tinctoria*.

wood-wrang *adj* thoroughly in the wrong.

wood-wroth *adj* madly angry.

woody[1] *same as* **widdie**[1].

woody[2] *n* a child's wooden plaything.—*adj* (*used of vegetables*) stringy.

wooer-bab *n* **1** a lover's knot. **2** the garter knot below the knee with a couple of knots, formerly worn by sheepish wooers. **3** a neckcloth fastened in a lover's knot so as to show the ends or babs.

woof[1] *same as* **wowff**.

woof[2] *n* the grey gurnard.

wooin-swabs *n* **1** cupboard love. **2** a bellyful.

wook *n* a week.

wool *n* **1** (*with* **the**) blankets. **2** thistledown.

woo'-leddy *n* a woman who gathers wool left by sheep on bushes, hedges, etc.

wool-gather *v* to gather wool left by sheep on bushes, etc.

wool-gleaner *n* one who gathers wool left by sheep on bushes, etc.

woolly *adj* (*of pasture*) thick with sheep feeding.

woolly-bear *n* the large hairy caterpillar.

woolly-soft grass *n* the meadow soft-grass.

wool-shears *n* shears for clipping sheep.

woolster *n* a wool-stapler.

woon *adj* woollen.

woor *v* wore.

woosh *v* washed.

wooster *n* **1** a lover. **2** a wooer.

wooster-tryst *n* a lovers' meeting.

woo' wheel *n* a large wheel for spinning wool.

wooy *adj* woolly.

wooze *v* **1** to ooze. **2** to distil.

woozlie *adj* **1** thin. **2** shrivelled. **3** stunted. **4** unhealthy-looking.

wop *same as* **wap**[1].

word[1] *n* **1** a saying. **2** a proverb. **3** an order, command. **4** news. **5** a rumour, report. **6** the voice. **7** (*in pl with* **the**) the baptismal formula.—*v* **1** to be credited with by report. **2** (*with* **over**) to reprove. **3** (*with refl pron*) to express oneself.

word[2] *v* to become.

wordld *same as* **wardle**.

wordy *adj* worthy.

wore *adj* worn.

work *n* **1** a structure. **2** a stately building. **3** a fuss, disturbance. **4** a religious revival.—*v* **1** to knit. **2** to net. **3** (*used of material*) to lend itself easily to work. **4** (*of a pipe*) to draw, smoke easily. **5** to manage, influence. **6** to struggle convulsively. **7** (*used of physic*) to purge, operate. **8** to ferment. **9** to irritate, trouble, harass. **10** to sprain.

working body *n* an industrious, active person.

workingsome *adj* fit for work working steadily.

worl *same as* **wirl**.

worlin *same as* **wirling**.

worm *n* **1** a serpent. **2** a snake-like dragon. **3** a term of contempt. **4** a gimlet. **5** toothache. **6** the gnawings of hunger. **7** the craving for liquor. **8** sour water from the stomach.

wormful *n* as much whisky as fills a distilling tube.

worming *n* a gnawing pain.

worm month *n* **1** the month of July. **2** the last half of July and the first half of August.

worm-web *n* a cobweb.

worn-wab *n* a thin or ill-spun web of cloth.

worping-dinner *same as* **warping-dinner**.

worricow, woriecow, woricow, worrycow *n* **1** a bugbear. **2** a hobgoblin. **3** a frightful object. **4** an awkward-looking person. **5** a scarecrow. **6** (*with* **the**) the devil.

worriecraw *same as* **worricow**.

worriganger *n* a sturdy beggar.

worry *v* **1** to choke. **2** to strangle. **3** to suffocate. **4** to devour. **5** to eat voraciously. **6** to dispute angrily. **7** to snarl and gibe.—*n* an altercation, a wrangle.

worry-baldie *n* an artichoke.

worry-carl *n* **1** a snarling, ill-natured person. **2** a bugbear. **3** a coarse winter pear.

worrycow, worrycraw *same as* **worricow**.

worser *adj* worse.

worset, worsat, worsit, worsad *n* worsted.

worship *n* family prayers.

worsted *adj* worse off, poorer.

worst one *n* the devil.

wort[1] *v* to waste food.—*n* (*in pl*) refuse.

wort[2] *v* **1** to become. **2** to befall. **3** worth (as in **wae worth**).

worth *adj* **1** worthy, deserving. **2** of use. **3** of value. —*n* importance.

worthy *adj* prudent.

woslie *same as* **woozlie**.

woster *n* a struggle, a scrimmage.

wot[1] *same as* **wort**[2].

wot[2] *same as* **wat**[2].

wot[3] *same as* **wit**[1].

wother *prefix* indicating contrary direction.

wother-weight *same as* **wither-wecht**.

wottin *adj* aware, informed.

wou' *same as* **woo'**.

woubit *n* a hairy caterpillar.

wouch *v* to bark.—*n* a dog's bark.

wouf[1] *n* a wolf.

wouf[2] *same as* **waff**[2].

wouff, wouf[3] *v* to bark as a dog.—*n* a dog's bark.

wough *same as* **wouch**.

woulder *n* one who would.

would I, nould I *adv* **1** willy-nilly. **2** perforce.

woun *adj* woollen.

woundily *adv* exceedingly.

woursum *same as* **wursum**.

woust *v* to boast.—*n* a boast.

wouster *n* a boaster.

wouy *adj* woolly.

wow[1] *same as* **waw**[4].

wow[2] *v* **1** to wave. **2** to beckon. **3** to wag.

wow[3] *int* an exclamation of wonder, surprise, grief or gratification.

wowbat *same as* **wobart**[1].

wowf[1] *same as* **waff**[2].

wowf[2] *n* a wolf.

wowff, wowf[3] *same as* **wouff**.

wowfish *adj* approaching mental derangement.

wowfness *n* the condition of being somewhat deranged, madness.

wowg *same as* **wow**[2].

wowgie *adj* **1** vain. **2** lively. **3** dashing. **4** moving so as to draw attention.

wowt *n* **1** an arch. **2** a deep well, pond or hole of any kind.— *v* to arch, vault.

wozlie *same as* **woozlie**.

wrack[1] *n* **1** any kind of rubbish. **2** field weeds. **3** vegetable rubbish found on land. **4** anything worthless. **5** a broken-down person or animal. **6** scum, sediment. **7** destruction.—*v* **1** to break. **2** to destroy, ruin.

wrack[2] *v* **1** to wreak. **2** to execute vengeance. **3** to avenge.

wrack[3] *v* **1** to worry. **2** to tease. **3** to torment.

wrack[4] *v* (*used of the sky*) to clear.—*n* flying clouds.

wrack[5] *n* couch grass.

wrack boxes *n* vesicles or air bladders found on certain seaweeds.

wrack's grass *n* a kind of rye-grass.

wrack-ship *n* a wrecked ship.

wrack-wid *n* wood cast up by the sea.

wraik, wrak *same as* **wrack**[1].

wraith[1] *n* **1** an apparition. **2** the spectral apparition of a living person. **3** a water sprite.

wraith[2] *n* a quarter of a year.

wraith[3] *n* wrath.

wraith[4] *n* **1** a wreath. **2** a drift. **3** a mass of drifted snow.

wraith bell *n* **1** a bell supposed to sound before a death. **2** a ghostly, solemn passing bell.

wraith-like *adj* ghost-like.

wramp *v* to wrench, twist, sprain.—*n* a wrench, sprain.

wran *n* the wren.

wrang[1] *v* wrung.

wrang[2] *adj* **1** wrong. **2** injured. **3** deranged in intellect. **4** unjust. **5** injurious.—*n* **1** a mistake. **2** a fault. **3** an untruth.—*v* **1** to disorder. **2** to hurt, injure. **3** (*with* **self**) to be guilty of perjury or falsehood.

wrang-gaites *adv* **1** in a wrong direction. **2** against the course of the sun.

wrang-like *adj* apparently wrong.

wrang-nail *n* a sore condition of the skin at the base of the fingernails.

wrangous *adj* **1** wrongful. **2** unjust. **3** (*used of a move at play*) bad, false.

wrangously *adv* wrongfully, unjustly.

wrangwise *adv* **1** in a wrong direction. **2** backwards.

wrannie, wrannock *n* the wren.

wrap *v* to knock smartly.

wraple *v* **1** to entangle. **2** to warp.

wrapper *n* a working apron or overall.

wrassel, wrassle, wrastle *same as* **warsle**.

wrat *n* a wart.

wratack *n* a dwarf.

wratch[1] *v* **1** to overstrain by exertion. **2** to fatigue oneself.

wratch[2] *n* a wretch. **2** a niggard, miser. **3** a covetous person.—*v* to become niggardly or avaricious.

wrate *v* wrote.

wrathily *adv* angrily.

wrathsome *adj* **1** wrathful. **2** angry.

wrathy *adj* **1** wrathful. **2** angry.

wrattle *adj* warty.

wrattieness *n* the condition of being warty.

wratwel *same as* **wartweil**.

wraught *same as* **wrat**.

wraul *same as* **wroul**.

wrawt *same as* **wrat**.

wrax *v* **1** to stretch, extend. **2** to overstrain. **3** to hand.—*n* a wrench, a sprain.

wray *adj* wry.—*v* **1** to distort. **2** to writhe.

wread[1], **wread**[2] *same as* **wreath**[1], **wreath**[2].

wreat *v* to write.

wreath[1] *n* **1** a drift. **2** a mass of any substance, especially of snow, drifted together.—*v* **1** to twist, twine, curl. **2** (*used of snow*) to drift, eddy, swirl. **3** to bank up with drift.

wreath[2] *n* an enclosure for cattle.

wreathe *v* to writhe.

wreck *same as* **wrack**[1].

wrede *same as* **wreath**[1].

wree[1] *same as* **wry**.

wree[2] *v* to riddle corn.

wregling *n* **1** the youngest or smallest of a brood or litter. **2** the weakest and youngest of a family. **3** a weakling.

wreist *same as* **wrest**.

wrek *same as* **wrack**[1].

wrest *v* **1** to twist. **2** to sprain.—*n* **1** a sprain. **2** a wrench.

wrested thread *n* a thread wound round a sprain.

wresting string, ~ thread *n* a thread wound round a sprain.

wret *v* wrote.

wretch *same as* **wratch**[2].

wreuch *n* wretchedness.

wricht *n* a wright, a carpenter.—*v* to follow the trade of a wright.

wrichtin' *n* the trade of a carpenter.

wride *same as* **wreath**[1].

wridy *adj* covered with snow wreaths. *See* **wreath**[1].

wrig *n* **1** the smallest or weakest of a brood or litter. **2** the youngest or weakest of a family. **3** a weak, puny child.

wriggle *v* **1** to wrestle. **2** to struggle.—*n* an instrument for preventing smoke, a wind skew.

wring *v* **1** (*used of a sword*) to cut. **2** to sweep.

wringit *v* wrung.

wringle *v* **1** to writhe. **2** to wriggle.—*n* a writhing motion.

wrinkle *n* a hint.—*v* (*used of paper*) to crumple.

wrinkle-frichtin' *adj* smoothing or banishing wrinkles.

wrisk *n* a brownie (qv).

wrist *same as* **wrest**.

writ, write *n* **1** writing. **2** anything written. **3** handwriting. **4** the size of handwriting. **5** a lawyer.

writer *n* **1** a lawyer, solicitor, law agent. **2** an agent or man of business.

writer-body *n* a contemptuous designation of a lawyer.

writhen *v* writhed.

writing *n* **1** law business. **2** the profession of a lawyer. **3** a written agreement. **4** a legal document.

writing-pen *n* a goose quill.

wro *n* an enclosure in a grass field for penning up cattle at night.

wroch *same as* **wruch**.

wrocht *v* **1** worked, laboured, struggled. **2** (*with* **for**) deserved, earned. **3** (*with* **about**) happened. —*adj* **1** knitted. **2** woven. **3** made with the hands. **4** brought about. **5** troubled. **6** annoyed. **7** frightened. **8** sprained.

wrocht-bane *n* a sprained joint.

wroo *same as* **wroo**.

wrothily *adv* wrathfully, angrily.

wrothy *same as* **wrathy**.

wroucht *same as* **wrocht**.

wrought *n* a manufactory, works.

wroul *n* **1** an ill-grown person. **2** a puny child. **3** a changeling. **4** a dwarf.

wruch *adj* **1** rough. **2** reckless.—*n* the larger part of anything.

wrunch *n* **1** a winch. **2** a windlass.

wrunkle *v* to wrinkle.—*n* a wrinkle.

wry *v* **1** to twist. **2** to writhe. **3** to distort.

wrythe *n* **1** a wreath. **2** a snow wreath.

wub *same as* **wab**.

wubbit *same as* **woubit**.

wud[1] *v* would.

wud[2], **wuddy** *same as* **wood**[1].

wud[3] *n* a wood.

wud[4] *same as* **wood**[2].

wuddie *same as* **widdie**[1].

wuddiefu *same as* **widdifow**.

wuddie-tow *n* a hangman's rope.

wuddle *same as* **widdle**.

wuddrum *same as* **woodrum**.

wuddy *same as* **woodie**[2].

wude *same as* **wood**[1].

wudlins *adj* most eagerly.

wud-muffled *adj* (*used of sounds, voices, etc*) muffled by woods.

wudscud *same as* **woodscud**.

wudwise *same as* **woodwise**.

wudy *same as* **widdie**[1].

wuff[1] *n* a flighty, fiery person.

wuff[2] *same as* **waff**[2].

wuffle *v* 1 to turn over anything lightly. 2 to rumple. 3 to knit loosely.

wuggle *same as* **waggle**.

wugrum *n* water running down the inside of a wall from leakage about the eaves.

wuif *n* woof, weft.

wuir *v* wore.

wuish *v* washed.

wuive *v* wove.

wul *n* a well.

wul *adj* ind *adv* well.

wul, wull *adj* wild.—*adv* extremely.

wulbeast *n* 1 a maddened horse or ox.

wulcat *n* 1 a wild-cat. 2 *in phr* **to tumble the wulcat** to whirl heels overhead.

wuld[1] *adj* wild.

wuld[2] *adj* 1 bewildered. 2 roving.—*adv* astray.

wulee *same as* **wull-ee**.

wulfire *same as* **wildfire**.

wulk *same as* **wilk**.

wull[1] *n* 1 will, wish. 2 choice.

wull[2] *v* will.

wull[3] *adv* astray.

wull-a-wean *int* an exclamation of sorrow.

wull-a-wins, ~-wona, ~-wuns *int* weel-a-wins! (qv).

wullcat *same as* **wulcat**.

wull-ee *n* 1 the orifice of a well. 2 a spring in a quagmire. 3 a pool.

wullees *n* saddlebags.

wullet *n* 1 a wallet. 2 a budget of news.

wull-gate *same as* **will-gate**.

wullie-wagtail *same as* **willie-wagtail**.

wullie-waucht, ~-waught *same as* **willie-waught**.

wullin', wullint *adj* willing.

wull-like *adj* wild-like.

wullshoch, wulshoch *same as* **wilshoch**.

wullsome *adj* 1 wild. 2 lonely, dreary.

wullyart *same as* **wilyart**[2].

wully-wambles, ~-wamles *same as* **willy-wambles**.

wul-wierd *n* an evil prediction.

wumble *same as* **whamble**.

wumble, wumle, wummle *n* a wimble.

wummilton, wummilton's mutch *n* (*used in whist*) the four of spades.

wummle[1] *same as* **wamble**.

wummle[2] *same as* **whamble**.

wummle-bore *n* a hole bored by a wimble.

wumple, wumpel *same as* **wimple**.

wun[1] *v* 1 to win. 2 won.

wun[2] *n* wind.—*v* to dry in the wind.

wun[3] *v* did wind, wound.

wun[4] *same as* **won**[1].

wund[1] *v* to wind.

wund[2] *n* 1 wind. 2 boastful talk.

wund band *n* an iron band round anything weak, broken or spliced.

wundy[1] *adj* 1 boastful. 2 windy.

wundy[2] *n* a window.

wungall *same as* **wingel**.

wunna *v neg* will not.

wunnel, wunnle *same as* **windle**[1].

wunnel strae *same as* **windlestrae**.

wunner *same as* **wonner**.

wunnock *same as* **winnock**[1].

wunt *v* to want.—*n* a mental deficiency.

wuntle *same as* **wintle**[1].

wuntlin *n* the writhing in a passion.

wup *same as* **wip**.

wupple *same as* **wipple**.

wur *v* were.

wurble[1] *v* 1 to wriggle. 2 to crawl. 3 to stagger, stumble. 4 to move like a worm.

wurble[2] *v* 1 (*in weaving*) to tie a broken thread. 2 to twist.

3 to twine with the fingers. 4 to crush by friction between the thumb and finger.—*n* 1 a twist. 2 a twine. 3 a rub between the thumb and finger.

wurd *n* a word.

wurdle *v* to work hard with little prospect of success.

wurdy *same as* **wordy**.

wure *v* wore.

wurf *n* 1 an ill-grown, stunted person. 2 a fairy.

wurf-like *adj* having a stunted and puny appearance.

wurgill *n* a narrow-minded worldling.

wurk *same as* **wark**[2].

wurl *same as* **wirl**.

wurlie[1], **wurly** *adj* 1 rough, knotted. 2 wrinkled.

wurlie[2] *same as* **wirlie**[1].

wurlin, wurlyon *same as* **wirling**.

wurn *v* to be peevish and complaining.

wurna *v neg* were not.

wurp *v* to be fretful.—*n* a fretful, peevish person.

wurpit *adj* fretful, peevish.

wurr *same as* **wirr**[1].

wurrico, wurrycow *same as* **worricow**.

wurset *n* worsted.

wursum *n* pus, purulent matter.

wurtle *v* to writhe like a worm.—*n* a writhe.

wurts *n* 1 herbs. 2 worts.

wush[1] *v* to wish.—*n* a wish.

wush[2] *v* washed.

wushen *v, adj* washed.

wusp *n* a wisp.

wuss[1] *v* to wish.

wuss[2] *n* 1 juice. 2 moisture.

wust *v* knew.

wuster *same as* **woster**.

wut[1], **wut**[2] *same as* **wit**[1], **wit**[2].

wutch *n* a witch.—*v* to bewitch.

wuth *n* anger, wrath.

wutless *adj* senseless, thoughtless.

wutter[1], **wutter**[2], **wutter**[3] *same as* **witter**[1], **witter**[2], **witter**[3].

wutterel *same as* **witterel**.

wutterick *same as* **whitrack**.

wutterin' *same as* **wittering**.

wutter-length *n* the distance of the player from the tee in curling.

wutter-shot *n* a stone played in curling so as to rest on the tee.

wuzlie *same as* **woozlie**.

wuzlie-like *adj* woozlie (qv) in appearance.

wy *v* to weigh.

w'y *n* way.

wybis *same as* **weebo**.

wybister *same as* **wabster**.

wyde[1] *v* to wade.

wyde[2] *n* a weed.

wye[1] *n* way.

wye[2] *v* to weigh.

wyelay *v* to waylay.

wyfock, wyfockie *n* 1 a wife. 2 a term of endearment addressed to a wife.

wyg[1] *n* (*perhaps*) a wall.

wyg[2] *same as* **whig**[3].

wyise *n* 1 a wisp. 2 a truss of hay or straw.

wyke *same as* **waik**[2].

wyl *adj* bewildered.

wylart[1], **wylart**[2] *same as* **wilyart**[1], **wilyart**[2].

wyle[1] *same as* **wale**[3].

wyle[2] *adj* wicked. 2 vile.

wyle[3] *adj* wild.

wyle[4] *same as* **wile**[1].

wyle *v* to wile, lure.

wylecot *same as* **wylie-coat**.

wylie[1] *n* an instrument for twisting straw ropes.

wylie[2] *n* a kind of flannel used for vests and petticoats.

wylie-coat *n* 1 an undervest. 2 an under-petticoat. 3 a flannel shirt. 4 a child's nightdress.

wylly *adj* wily.

wyme *same as* **wame**.

wyn[1] *same as* **win**[1].

wyn[2] *same as* **wynd**[2].

wynan *n* the half of a field.

wynd[1] *n* **1** a narrow lane or street. **2** an alley. **3** a small court.

wynd[2], **wyne** *v* (*used of horses*) to turn to the left.—*int* a call to a horse or ox to turn to the left.—*n* **1** the call of wynd. **2** a turn. **3** a winding. **4** an end, a termination.

wyndel-stray *same as* **windlestrae**.

wyne and on wyne *adv* **1** to the right and left. **2** everywhere.

wyner *n* **1** the foremost ox on the right hand in a team of oxen. **2** (*in pl*) the foremost pair of oxen.

wynis *v* **1** to decay. **2** to pine away.

wynish'd *adj* pinched, thin.

wynnie *n* an alley.

wynt *v* (*used of milk, butter, etc*) to become tainted or sour.

wyntit *adj* tainted.

wype *n* **1** a blow given accidentally or carelessly. **2** a gibe.

wyringing *n* fretting, carking.

wyrock *same as* **weerock**.

wyse[1] *same as* **wise**[1].

wyse[2] *adj* wise.

wysh, wyshe *int* a call to a horse to turn to the right.—*n* wysh, the call.

wyson *same as* **weasan**.

wyss, wysse *adj* wise.

wyster *same as* **wister**.

wyt[1] *same as* **wat**[1].

wyt[2] *same as* **wite**.

wyte[1] *v* to wait.

wyte[2] *same as* **wat**[2].

wyte[3] *same as* **wite**.

wyteless *adj* blameless, innocent.

wytenonfa *n* **1** a chill. **2** a fever.

wyth *n* width.

wyttle *n* a big knife.

wynchlet *n* a thin, spare person or thing.

wyve *v* to weave.

wyven-kwite *n* a knitted petticoat.

wyver *n* **1** a weaver. **2** a spider.

wyvers' wobs *n* cobwebs.

wyze *same as* **wise**[1].

wyzeron, wyzon *same as* **weasan**.

Y

ya[1] *int* an exclamation of contempt or derision.

ya[2], **yaa**[1] *adv* yes.

yaa[1] *same as* **ya**[2].

yaa[2] *same as* **yaw**[1].

yaab *same as* **yab**.

yaaber *n* an incessant talker.

yaad *same as* **yad**[1].

yaag *same as* **yag**.

yaager[1] *n* one given to gossip.

yaager[2] *n* **1** a pedlar, hawker. **2** a clandestine buyer of things unfairly disposed of.

yaal[1] *v* to howl, cry.

yaal[2] *int* an exclamation of defiance, contempt, etc.

yaalta *int* an exclamation used to prevent a person from doing a thing.

yaam *same as* **yam**.

yaap *v* **1** to bawl, shout. **2** to talk loudly.

yaar *same as* **yair**.

yaavel *same as* **yaval**.

yab *v* **1** to talk incessantly. **2** to harp on a subject.

yabble[1] *v* to bark rapidly.—*n* **1** a dog's rapid barking. **2** a wrangling.

yabble[2] *v* **1** to gabble. **2** to scold. **3** to be querulous. **4** to mutter. **5** to speak incoherently.

yabblock *n* **1** a chatterer. **2** a talkative person.

yabbock *same as* **yabblock**.

yable *adj* able.

yachis *same as* **yassich**.

yachle *v* to shamble, to shuffle in walking.

yachlin *n* one who shambles.

yacht[1] *v* to own.—*v* owned, was owner.

yacht[2] *n* a big drink.

yack[1] *n* **1** perplexity. **2** perturbation.—*v* to be in perturbation.

yack[2] *v* to talk thickly.

yackie *n* perturbation.

yackuz *n* one who talks thickly.

yad[1] *n* **1** an old mare. **2** a mare. **3** an old cow. **4** a contemptuous term for a slovenly or vicious woman. **5** a jade.

yad[2] *n* a piece of bad coal that becomes a white, ashy lump when burned.

yad[3] *n* a thread which, in reeling, has been let over one of the reel spokes.

yaddle *v* to contend.

yade *n* **1** a mare, horse. **2** a worthless woman.

yae[1] *adj* one.

yae[2] *int* an exclamation of interrogatory surprise.

yae[3], **yae** *adj* one only.

yaff[1] *v* **1** to bark, as a small dog. **2** to yelp. **3** to scold. **4** to nag.—*n* the bark of a dog.

yaff[2] *v* **1** to talk nonsense. **2** to prate. **3** to talk pertly.

yaffing *n* the act of barking.

yag *v* **1** to make a noise. **2** to talk angrily. **3** to importune. **4** to irritate. **5** to gossip.—*n* gossip, a gossiper.

yagger *n* a travelling pedlar, a trader.

yaghies *n* the sound of a soft, heavy body falling.

yagiment *n* a state of great excitement or anxiety to get at anything.

yah *int* an exclamation of contempt, etc.

yaid *same as* **yad**.

yaik[1] *v* to ache.

yaik[2] *same as* **yack**[1].

yaike, yaik *n* a stroke, a blow.

yaikert *adj* (*used of grain*) eared.

yail *same as* **yaal**[2].

yaip *adj* **1** hungry. **2** keen. **3** forward.

yair, yaire *n* a small enclosure built in a curve near the shore for catching salmon.

yaird[1] *n* a yard in length, etc.

yaird[2] *n* **1** a garden. **2** an enclosure or court near a house. **3** a churchyard.

yaird-dyke *n* a garden wall.

yaird-fit *n* the lower end of a garden.

yaird-heid *n* the upper end of a garden.

yairdin *n* a garden.

yaire *same as* **yair**.

yair-fishing *n* fishing by yairs. *See* **yair**.

yair-haugh *n* a haugh (qv) on which a yair (qv) is built.

yair net *n* a net extending into the bed of a river, inclining upwards and fixed by poles.

yald[1], **yal** *same as* **yauld**.

yald[2] *v* yielded.

yald[3] *adj* niggardly, close-fisted.

yalder *v* to bark noisily and rapidly.—*n* the noisy barking of a dog in chase or bringing an animal to bay.

yaldie *n* the yellowhammer.

yaldran, yaldrin *n* the yellowhammer.

yalala *adj* yellow.

yallackie *same as* **yallock**.

yaller[1] *v* **1** to bawl, yell. **2** to speak indistinctly through passion.

yaller[2] *v* to bark noisily and rapidly, as a dog in chase.

yallieckie *n* the yellowhammer.

yalloch *same as* **yelloch**.

yallock *n* the yellowhammer.

yallow *adj* yellow.

yallowchy *adj* yellowish.

yalp *same as* **yelp**[1].

yalp-yulp *v* to whine.

yaltie *adv* slowly.—*int* take time! take leisure!

yalto, yaltoco *int* an expression of surprise or defiance.

yam *n* a large potato.

yamer *same as* **yammer**.

yamf[1] *same as* **yamph**[1].

yamf[2], **yamff** *same as* **yamph**[2].

yammer, yammir *v* **1** to lament. **2** to cry aloud fretfully. **3** to fret, complain. **4** to grumble. **5** to make a great outcry or a loud, disagreeable noise. **6** to talk loudly and continuously. **7** to shout. **8** to utter a shrill cry, as a bird. **9** to sing loudly. **10** to talk or hum indistinctly. **11** to stammer.—*n* **1** a lamentation, whimpering. **2** continuous loud talking or complaining. **3** a great outcry. **4** a loud, disagreeable noise. **5** loud, incessant or rambling talk. **6** the cry of a bird.

yammerer *n* a loud, incessant talker.

yammering *n* a continued whining.

yamner, yamour *same as* **yammer**.

yamp *adj* noisy.

yamph[1] *v* **1** to bark. **2** to yelp. **3** to yap. **4** to rampage. **5** to career.—*n* **1** a bark. **2** a yelp.

yamph[2] *adj* **1** hungry. **2** ravenous.

yamps *n* garlic.

yan *adj* **1** small. **2** puny.—*n* a small thing.

yance *adv* once.

yane *adj* one.

yank *v* **1** to move nimbly and quickly. **2** to push on smartly. **3** to pull suddenly. **4** to jerk. **5** to pass quickly.—*n* a sudden, severe blow.

yanker *n* **1** a smart stroke. **2** a yank (qv). **3** a great falsehood. **4** a tall, agile girl. **5** a clever girl. **6** an incessant talker.

yankie *n* a sharp, clever, forward woman.

yanking *adj* **1** active. **2** forward, pushing.

yanky *adj* **1** agile. **2** nimble. **3** active.

yant *same as* **yan**.

yap[1] *same as* **yaup**[1].

yap[2], **yape** *adj* **1** quick, apt. **2** eager, keen. **3** desirous. **4** forward. **5** very hungry.—*v* to be hungry.

yap[3] *n* a cant name for an apple.

yapish *adj* **1** somewhat keen. **2** hungry.

yaply *adv* hungrily.

yapness *n* **1** hunger. **2** keenness for food.

yappish *adj* hungry.

yapps *n* apples stolen by boys from a garden.

yappy *adj* **1** hungry-looking. **2** thin.

yarbin-carblin *n* **1** a wordy fight. **2** an ill-natured argument.

yard[1] *same as* **yaird**[2].

yard[2] *n* **1** a rod, staff. **2** a sceptre. **3** a yardstick.

yardie *n* a small garden.

yare[1] *adj* **1** desirous, eager. **2** alert, nimble. **3** ready. —*int* quick!.

yare[2] *same as* **yair**.

yare[3] *n* yore.

yarely *adv* **1** eagerly. **2** quickly.

yark *v* **1** to jerk. **2** to seize and pull forcibly. **3** to wrench. **4** to throw with a jerk. **5** to throw violently. **6** to dig out smartly. **7** to push. **8** to slam. **9** to strike hard with a cane, to thrash. **10** (*of a blacksmith*) to hammer smartly. **11** to stab. **12** to chop, split. **13** (*of the sun's rays*) to beat strongly. **14** to start a tune. **15** to strike up, reel off. **16** to move on quickly. **17** to push on with work. **18** (*of beer*) to 'work', ferment. **19** to think hard, cudgel one's brains. **20** to be busy. **21** to get excited. **22** to bind tightly and smartly. **23** to pack tightly. **24** (*with* on) to growl incessantly. **25** to ram in full. **26** (*of fish*) to bite greedily. **27** to drink.—*n* **1** a smart stroke. **2** a stab. **3** a heavy blow. **4** any quick movement. **5** a long drink. **6** a greedy bite. **7** an indefinite quantity.

yarker *n* a sudden, severe blow.

yarkin *adj* severe.

yarking[1] *same as* **yerkin**.

yarking[2] *n* continual fault-finding.

yarking-elshin, ~-allishen *n* an out-seam awl.

yarlin *n* the yellowhammer.

yarn beam *n* (*in weaving*) the beam on which the warp is wrapped.

yarn clue *n* a ball of worsted for knitting.

yarnets *n* an instrument for winding wool.

yarn-nag *n* a stock of worsted.

yarnut *n* the pignut, earthnut.

yarn-washer *n* a woman who washes yarn in a dye house.

yarn windles, ~-winules *n* an instrument for winding yarn.

yarn winds, ~ wins *n* a yarn windles (qv).

yarp *v* **1** to harp on fretfully. **2** to grumble. **3** to carp. **4** whine.—*n* **1** a fretting, a whine. **2** a carping.

yarr[1] *n* spurrey.

yarr[2] *same as* **yirr**.

yarring *adj* **1** snarling. **2** captious. **3** troublesome.

yarrow *v* **1** to earn. **2** to gain by industry.

yassich *adv* with violence.

yatch *n* a yacht.

yate *same as* **yett**[2].

yater *same as* **yatter**[1].

yatter[1] *v* **1** to chatter. **2** to speak loudly or angrily. **3** to carp, fret, grumble. **4** to rattle. **5** to rustle.—*n* **1** chatter. **2** a chattering sound. **3** noisy or angry talk. **4** brawling, scolding. **5** grumbling. **6** confused talk. **7** an incessant talker.

yatter[2] *n* a confused mass of small objects.

yatter[3] *adj* fretful.

yattle[1] *n* **1** an endeavour. **2** strength of mind.

yattle[2] *n* a quantity of small stones on the land.—*adj* (*used of ground*) covered with small stones.

yauchle[1] *same as* **yachle**.

yauchle[2] *n* a Highlander.

yaucht *v* to owe.

yaud[1] *int* a call to a dog to go after sheep.

yaud[2] *n* **1** an old horse. **2** an old cow. **3** a jade.

yaud[3] *same as* **yad**[3].

yauff *same as* **youff**.

yaught *n* **1** a yacht. **2** a transport, ship.

yauk *same as* **yaik**[1].

yaul[1] *same as* **yauld**.

yaul[2] *n in phr* **drunk as a yaul** dead drunk.

yaul[3] *same as* **yawl**[1].

yaul-cuted *adj* having the ankles formed for quick motion.

yauld *adj* **1** alert, sprightly. **2** nimble, agile. **3** able-bodied. **4** strong, powerful. **5** (*used of an elderly person*) vigorous. **6** sharp, cold, frosty.

yaumer, yaummer, yaumour *same as* **yammer**.

yaup[1] *v* **1** to shout. **2** to cry aloud, bawl. **3** to talk boisterously. **4** to whine. **5** to bark, to yelp. **6** (*of birds*) to scream, utter cries of distress. **7** to cough. —*n* **1** a shout, yell. **2** a loud cry. **3** a short, sharp bark. **4** the cry of a sickly or distressed bird. **5** a cough.

yaup[2] *n* the blue titmouse.

yaup[3] *same as* **yap**[2].

yauping *adj* **1** peevish. **2** ill-natured.

yaupish-looking *adj* hungry-looking.

yaupit *n* the blue titmouse.

yauprie *n* the refuse of grain blown away by the wind.

yaur *n* the name given by Newhaven fishermen to a species of fucus, which children used for painting their faces.

yauvins *n* the awns of barley.

yauw[1] *n* the sail of a windmill.

yauw[2] *same as* **yaw**[2].

yaux *n* an axe.
yaval, yavil *n* a second crop of grain afer lea.
yave *v* **1** to keep in subjection. **2** to impress most earnestly.—*n* **1** the power of keeping in subjection. **2** the act of impressing very earnestly, awe.
yavil, yaval, yavel *adj* **1** prostrate and unable to rise. **2** prone, flat.
yavil-bachelor *n* a widower.
yaw[1] *n* a child's name for an eel.
yaw[2] *v* **1** to mew as a cat. **2** to whine.
yaw[3] *v* to yawn.
yaw[4] *v* to own, possess.
yawd *same as* **yad**[1].
yawe *v* to own, possess.
yawfu' *adj* awful.—*adv* awfully.
yawin' *v* owing.
yawk, yawok *v* **1** to speak quickly and thickly. **2** to shout. **3** to hoot.
yawkie *n* the yellowhammer.
yawl[1] *v* **1** to howl. **2** to bawl, shout.—*n* **1** a howl. **2** a cry.
yawl[2] *same as* **yauld**.
yawmer *same as* **yammer**.
yawn *v* to own.
yawp[1] *same as* **yap**[2].
yawp[2] *v* to help.—*n* the cry of a sickly bird.
yawpish *adj* rather hungry.
yawr *same as* **yarr**[1].
yaws *n* syphilis.
yaxe *n* an axe.
ye *pron* **1** yourself. **2** yourselves.
yea[1] *adj* one.
yea[2] *adv* **1** yes. **2** (*before a vb*) again, again and again.
yeables *adv* perhaps.
yeadies'-race, ~-sons *n* the human race, Adam's sons.
yeal, yeald *same as* **yeld**.
yealie *v* to disappear gradually.
yealins *n* equals in age.—*adj* born in the same year.
yealtou, yealto *int* yea, wilt thou? used as an exclamation of surprise and as a noun in expletives.
yean *int* a call to a horse.
yeanling *adj* newborn.
year *n* years.
yearack *n* a hen a year old.
year-auld *n* an animal a year old.
yeard[1] *same as* **yerd**[3].
yeard[2] *same as* **yaird**[2].
yearl *n* an earl.
yearn[1] *n* an errand.
yearn[2] *v* **1** to coagulate. **2** to cause to coagulate. **3** to curdle.—*n* rennet.
yearn[3] *n* an eagle.
yearned milk *n* **1** curdled milk. **2** curds.
yearnin' bag *n* the stomach of a calf, used for curdling, milk.
yearning *n* **1** rennet used in cheese-making. **2** a calf's stomach. **3** the human stomach.
yearnin' gress *n* the common butterwort.
yearock *n* a hen a year old.
year's bairns *n* children born in the same year.
year's-mate *n* a companion of the same age.
yearth *n* earth.
yearthen *adj* earthen.
yeather *same as* **yether**.
yeattle *v* **1** to snarl. **2** to grumble.
yeck *v* **1** to retch. **2** to hiccup.
ye'd[1] *pron and v* ye would.
ye'd[2] *pron and v* ye had.
yed[1] *v* **1** to fib. **2** to exaggerate in narration.—*n* a fib.
yed[2], **yedd** *v* **1** to contend. **2** to wrangle.—*n* **1** strife. **2** contention.
yeddle *adj* (*used of water*) thick, muddy, putrid.—*n* dunghill drainage.
yeddlie *adj* (*used of water*) thick, muddy.
yede, yeed *v* went.

yedicate *v* to educate.
yeekie-yakie *same as* **yickie-yawkie**.
Yeel *same as* **Yule**.
yeel, yeeld *same as* **yeld**.
yeeld *n* old age.
Yeel-day *n* Christmas Day.
yeelin, yeelins *adj* of the same age, equal in age.
Yeel kebbuck *n* a kind of cheese eaten at Christmas.
Yeel mart *n* an ox killed at Christmas for home use.
Yeel play *n* Christmas holidays.
yeel-preens *n* pins used for playing with the teetotum for sweets at Christmas.
yeenoo *adv* **1** even now. **2** at present.
yeerie, yeery *adj* **1** afraid of goblins. **2** dismal. **3** weird.
yeesk, yeisk *same as* **yesk**.
yeild *same as* **yeld**.
yeildins *n* equals in age.
yeld *adj* **1** childless. **2** (*used of an animal*) barren, having aborted, ceasing to have young, not old enough to have young, ceasing to give milk. **3** (*of birds*) unmated. **4** (*of broth*) made without meat. —*n* a barren cow or ewe.—*v* to keep from breeding.
yelder-e'ed *adj* having evil or unlucky eyes.
yeld ewe *n* a ewe from which the lamb has been weaned.
yeld-gimmer *n* a ewe once or twice shorn, without having ever been served by a ram.
yeld-kittiwake *n* the kittiwake, *Larus corvus*.
yeldness *n* the cessation of milk in cows.
yeldrick, yeldrin, yeldrock *n* the yellowhammer.
ye'll *pron and v* you will.
yell[1] *v* **1** to bawl. **2** to quarrel noisily.—*n* **1** a shout, roar. **2** a spree. **3** a brawl.
yell[2] *n* an echo.
yell[3] *same as* **yeld**.
yell[4] *int* yea will, an expression of defiance.
yello *same as* **yelloch**.
yelloch, yellough *v* to scream, yell, bawl.—*n* **1** a yell. **2** a shrill cry.
yellop *v* to yelp.
yellow *n* a gold guinea.
yellow beak *n* a bejan (qv), a first year's student at Aberdeen University.
yellow boy *n* a gold coin.
yellowch *same as* **yelloch**.
yellowchin' *n* yelling.
yellow fin *n* a trout with yellow fins.
yellow-gowan *n* **1** various species of buttercup. **2** the corn marigold. **2** the marsh marigold.
yellowing grass *n* a grass yielding a yellow dye.
yellow July flower *n* a double garden variety of the common winter cress.
yellowman *n* a kind of candy.
yellow plover *n* the golden plover.
yellow queen *n* a sovereign of Queen Victoria's reign.
yellow rattle *n* the penny grass.
yellow-rocket *n* **1** the yellow July flower (qv). **2** the dyer's rocket.
yellow tang *n* the knotty fucus, a seaweed.
yellow wagtail *n* the grey wagtail.
yellow wymed *adj* yellow-bellied.
yellow-yarlin, -yerlin *n* the yellowhammer.
yellow-yeldering, ~-yeldrick, ~-yeldrin *n* the yellowhammer.
yellow-yite, ~-yoit *n* **1** the yellowhammer. **2** the fieldfare.
yellow-yoldrin, ~-yorlin *n* the yellowhammer.
yellow-yout, ~-yowley *n* the yellowhammer.
yelly *int* yea, will you? an exclamation of defiance.
yelly-hooing, *n* yelling, screaming.
yelp[1] *n* **1** a buffet. **2** a blow.
yelp[2] *v* **1** (*used of a person*) to call loudly and shrilly. **2** to whine.—*n* a whine.
yelta, yaltow *ints* exclamations of surprise.
yence *adv* once.
yenoo *adv* **1** just now. **2** presently.

yeorling *n* the yellowhammer.

yepie *n* a blow, as with a sword.

yer *poss adj, pron* your.

yerbs *n* herbs.

yerd[1] *same as* **yard**[2].

yerd[2] *same as* **yaird**[2].

yerd[3] *n* 1 earth. 2 the grave.—*v* 1 to bury, inter. 2 to cover with earth. 3 to knock violently on the ground.—*adj* buried.

yerd-fast *adj* firmly fastened in the ground.

yerd-hunger *n* 1 a keen desire for food sometimes shown by dying persons and viewed as a presage of the grave. 2 voraciousness.

yerd-hungry *adj* 1 voraciously hungry. 2 having an unnatural appetite before death.

yerd meal *n* 1 earth mould. 2 churchyard dust.

yerd-swine *n* a mysterious, dreaded animal supposed to burrow among graves and devour their contents.

ye're *v and pron* you are.

yere *same as* **yirr**.

yerestrene *n* the night before last.

yerk *same as* **yark**.

yerker *n* a sudden, severe blow.

yerkin', yerking *n* the seam by which the hinder part of the upper of a shoe is joined to the forepart.

yerksome *adj* irksome.

yerl *n* 1 an earl. 2 *in comb* **the long-necked yerl** the red-breasted merganser.

yerlin *n* the yellowhammer.

yerm *same as* **yirm**.

yern[1] *v* to desire, yearn.

yern[2] *same as* **yern**[2].

yern[3] *n* the heron.

yern-bliter *n* the snipe.

yerp[1] *v* 1 to yelp. 2 to fret, grumble.—*n* the act of fretting.

yerp[2] *v* to dwell constantly on one subject, to harp on.

yerran *n* an errand.

yerre *same as* **yirr**.

yersel' *pron* yourself.

yesday *n* yesterday.

ye'se *pron and v* you shall.

yesk *v* 1 to hiccup. 2 to retch. 3 to heave at the stomach.—*n* a hiccup.

yester *v* 1 to discompose. 2 to disturb.

yestere'en *n* last night, yester-even.

yester-tale *n* a thing of yesterday, what happened recently.

yestreen *n* yestere'en (qv).

yet *same as* **yett**[2].

yeterie *adj* 1 severe, tormenting. 2 excessive.

yether, yethar *n* 1 a willow. 2 a switch. 3 a wand. 4 a smart blow with a switch, etc. 5 the mark of tight binding.—*v* 1 to bind firmly. 2 to flog with a pliant rod or lash with a whip.

yethering *n* a thrashing, whipping.

yethert *adj* heather-clad.

yetin, yeten *n* a giant.

yetlin, yetlan, yetland *n* 1 cast iron. 2 a small pot or boiler. 3 a girdle (qv) on which cakes are baked. 4 an iron ball used in games in Fife.—*adj* made of cast iron.

yetrie *same as* **yeterie**.

yett[1] *v* 1 to rivet. 2 to fasten in the firmest way.

yett[2] *n* a gate.

yett-cheek *n* the side or post of a gate.

yetter *same as* **yatter**[1].

yettis *adv* 1 yet. 2 as yet.

yettlin-soles *n* iron toepieces, heelpieces, etc, for boots, etc.

yeubit *n* the caterpillar of the tiger moth.

yeuk, yeuck *v* to itch.—*n* 1 the itch. 2 itchiness.

yeukie bane *n* the funny bone, the elbow joint.

yeukieness *n* 1 itchiness. 2 itching.

yeuky *adj* itching.

yeul *same as* **yowl**.

yeuns *n* the refuse of grain blown away by fanners.

ye've *pron and v* you have.

yevey *adj* 1 voracious. 2 clamorous for food.

yevrisome *adj* having a habitually craving appetite.

yewest *adj* 1 nearest. 2 most contiguous.

yewk *same as* **yeuk**.

yewns *same as* **yeuns**.

yickie-yawkie, ~-yakie *n* a wooden tool, blunted like a wedge, with which shoemakers polished the edges and bottoms of soles.

yield[1] *n* the influence of the sun on frost.

yield[2] *v* to admit, confess.

yieldins *n* persons of the same age.

yieldy *adj* yielding, giving way.

yield-yow *n* a violent pressure of the thumb under the lobe of the ear.

yiff-yaff *n* a small person who talks a great deal to little purpose.

yill[1], **yild** *n* ale.—*v* to treat to ale.

yill[2] *same as* **yeld**.

yill-boat *n* 1 an ale barrel. 2 a brewing tub.

yill-caup, ~-cap *n* a horn or wooden cup from which ale is drunk.

yill-caup een *n* large or saucer eyes.

yill house *n* an alehouse.

yilloch *same as* **yelloch**.

yill-seasoned *adj* seasoned with ale.

yill-seller *n* one who sells ale.

yill-shop *n* an alehouse.

yill-wife *n* the landlady of an alehouse.

yillyart *adj* 1 stubborn. 2 ill-conditioned. 3 froward.

yim *n* 1 a particle, an atom. 2 the smallest portion of anything. 3 a very thin film of fat or of condensed vapour.—*v* 1 to break into fragments. 2 to become covered with a thin film.

yimmet *n* a lunch, a packed lunch, a snack.

yimost *adj* uppermost.

yin[1] *num adj* one.—*n* one o'clock.

yin[2] *adj* yon.

yince *adv* once.

yinst *adv* once.

yinterrup *v* to interrupt.

yip *n* 1 a pert, forward girl. 2 a shrew.

yirbs *same as* **yerbs**.

yirb-wife, *n* a woman skilled in the virtues of herbs.

yird *same as* **yerd**[3].

yird-drift *n* snow lifted from the earth and driven by the wind.

yird-eldin *n* fuel of peat or turf.

yird-fast *n* a stone firmly fixed in the ground.

yirdie-bee *n* a bee that burrows in the ground.

yirdin *n* 1 thunder. 2 an earthquake.—*adj* earthen.

yirditams, yirdie-tams *n* small heaps of earth spread over a field.

yird-laigh *adj* as low as earth.

yirdlins *adv* to the earth, earthwards.

yirdy *adj* earthy.

yirk *same as* **yark**.

yirl *n* an earl.

yirlich *adj* wild, unnatural, eldritch.

yirlichly *adv* wildly.

yirlin *n* the yellowhammer.

yirlish *same as* **yirlich**.

yirlishly *adv* wildly.

yirm *v* 1 to whine, complain. 2 to utter low cries. 3 to ask in a querulous tone. 4 to chirp as a bird. —*n* the rattle in the throat of the dying.

yirmin *n* a grumbling, complaining.

yirms *n* small-sized fruit.

yirn[1] *v* 1 to whine. 2 to grumble. 3 to girn (qv). 4 to distort the face. 5 to grimace.—*n* a complaint, whine.

yirn[2] *v* 1 to twist. 2 to entwine.

yirn[3], **yirn**[4] *same as* **yearn**[2], **yearn**[3].

yirnin *n* 1 rennet. 2 a rennet bag.

yirp *same as* **yerp**[1].

yirr v **1** to snarl or growl as a dog. **2** to yell.—n the growl of a dog.

yirth n earth.

yirze adj not acquainted.

yis[1], **yiss** adv yes.

yis[2] n use.

yisk same as **yesk**.

yisky adj given to hiccups.

yisless adj useless.

yister adj yester, last, past.

yistrene same as **yestreen**.

yit adv at present.—conj yet.

yite n the yellowhammer.

yite-hub, ~-hup int a call to a horse.

yite-wo int a call to a horse.

yits n oats.

yivvering adj eager for, hungering.

ymmer v to break into fragments.

yoak v to look.

yoam n **1** steam, vapour. **2** a blast of warm air.—v to blow with a warm, close air.

yochel, yocho n **1** a yokel. **2** a stupid, clumsy person.

yock same as **yoke**[2].

yode v went. See **yede**.

yof same as **youff**.

yoir adj **1** ready. **2** alert.

yoit same as **yite**.

yok same as **yoke**[2].

yoke[1] n **1** yolk. **2** the natural grease of wool.

yoke[2] n **1** harness. **2** a wooden frame or pole borne on the shoulders for carrying pails, etc. **3** the quantity of water carried by means of a yoke on the shoulders at a time. **4** the load carried by a cart at a yoking. **5** the time during which ploughmen and carters with their teams work at a stretch. **6** a bout, game. **7** a trial of strength or skill. **8** a grasp. **9** a quarrel.—v **1** to attach a horse to a plough, cart or gig, etc. **2** to plough the ridges of a field in pairs. **3** to join, match, marry. **4** to burden. **5** to fasten. **6** to bind down. **7** to oppress. **8** to clear or meddle with. **9** to set to with vigour. **10** to begin. **11** to attack, grip, fight. **12** to tackle with.

yoke-sticks n the crossbeams of a plough at right angles to the pole.

yokie same as **yewky**.

yoking n **1** the period during which a ploughman and his team work at a stretch. **2** any long stretch of work. **3** a fight. **4** a mauling. **5** a bout, turn. **6** (in pl) harness.

yoking time n the time to begin or resume farm work.

yokit-tuilyie n a winter game in which a group of lads sit on ice, holding each other by their clothes, and are dragged along by two or three others.

yoldrin n the yellowhammer.

yole n a yawl.

yolk n **1** a pane of glass taken from the thick central parts of cylindrical sheets of glass with a sort of bull's-eye in the middle. **2** the natural greasiness of wool.

yolky stane n plum-pudding stone.

yoll v **1** to strike. **2** to strike with an axe.

yoller v **1** to speak in a loud, passionate and inarticulate manner. **2** to bellow, bawl. **3** to yell discordantly. **4** to bark noisily.

yollerin n confused or convulsed noise.

yolling n the yellowhammer.

yolpin n **1** an unfledged bird. **2** a child.

yome same as **youm**.

yomer same as **yammer**.

yomf n a blow.—v **1** to strike. **2** to thrust.

yon adj **1** that. **2** those.—adv thither.

yond same as **yont**.

yonder same as **yonter**.

yondmost n the uttermost.

yong, yongue adj young.

yonker n a youngster.

yonner, yon'er adv **1** yonder. **2** in that place. **3** over there.—adj **1** that. **2** yon.

yonner-abouts adv in that place.

yont adv **1** yonder. **2** thither. **3** farther. **4** away.—adj **1** distant. **2** removed. **3** that. **4** those.—prep **1** beyond, past. **2** along.

yonter adj more distant.

yontermost adj most distant.

yook same as **yeuk**.

yool same as **yowl**

Yool same as **Yule**.

yooll n **1** a yawl. **2** a small coasting vessel.

yoolughan n yelling.

yoons same as **yeuns**.

yoorn v to move lazily.

yoornt adj **1** inured. **1** (used of a horse) broken into work. **2** (of a postman) going on his round easily and without being tired, because seasoned.

yore adj **1** ready. **2** alert.

Yorkshire fog n the meadow soft-grass.

yorlin, yorlyn n the yellowhammer.

youch v to bark.

youd n youth.

youden v **1** to move. **2** to agitate. **3** to tremble.—n **1** the act of moving. **2** inconvenience. **3** agitation. **4** yielded.—adj wearied.

youden drift n snow driven by the wind.

youdfu' adj youthful.

youdith, youdeth n youth.

youdlin n **1** a youth. **2** a stripling.

youf[1], **youff** same as **yowff**.

youf[2] same as **youff**[2].

youfat adj puny, diminutive.

youff[1] same as **yowff**[1].

youff[2], **youf** v **1** to bark as a dog. **2** to bark in a suppressed manner.—n a bark.

youk same as **yeuk**.

youkfit n the snipe.

youky same as **yeuky**.

youl, youle same as **yowl**.

youldrin, youlring n the yellowhammer.

youllie same as **yowlie**.

youm n **1** aroma. **2** steam, vapour. **3** the odour of brewing.—v to smell strongly of drink.

yound same as **yont**.

young adj **1** youngest. **2** (used of time) early.

young fowk n a newly married pair.

young guidman n a newly married man.

young guidwife n a newly married wife.

young laird n the eldest son or heir of a laird.

young-like adj as if young again.

youngsome adj youthful.

young tide n a tide just beginning to flow.

younklin n **1** a youngster. **2** a youngling.—adj **1** young. **2** youthful.

youp same as **yaup**[1].

youph same as **youff**[2].

yourn same as **yoorn**.

youse pron you (used when referring to more than one person).

youst v to talk idly and loosely, with volubility and noise.—n conversation of this kind.

yout same as **yowt**.

youtheid, youthied n the state of youth.

youther n **1** a strong, disagreeable smell or odour. **2** the steam or vapour arising from anything boiling or burning. **3** dust. **4** a collection of small particles. **5** the dust of flax. **6** a haze. **7** flickering ground exhalations in heat.

youthhood n youtheid (qv).

youthiness n youthfulness.

youthir n the red ashes of peat or turf.

youth-time n youthful days.

youth-wort n the common sundew.

youthy *adj* **1** youthful. **2** affecting youthful habits, dress, etc.

youtt *same as* **yowt**.

yove *v* **1** to talk in a free, familiar and jocular way. **2** to go at a round pace.

yow[1] *v* to caterwaul.

yow[2] *n* **1** a ewe. **2** a larch or pine cone used as a plaything.

yowch *v* to bark.

yowden[1] *same as* **youden**.

yowden[2] *adj* wearied.

yowden-drift *same as* **youden-drift**.

yowdlin *adj* **1** dilatory. **2** wearied.

yowe[1] *pron* you.

yowe[2] *n* **1** a ewe. **2** a contemptuous term for a man.

yowe-brose *n* ewe-milk brose.

yowff[1], **yowf** *n* a smart, swinging blow.—*v* **1** to beat. **2** to drive or send forcibly.—*adv* with a heavy fall.

yowff[2], **yowf** *same as* **youff**[2].

yowie *n* a little ewe.

yowl, yowll *v* **1** to howl. **2** to cry loudly or piteously. **3** to yelp as a dog.—*n* **1** a howl, yell, a loud cry. **2** the sound made in yelling or barking.

yowl for yowl *n* continuous howling.

yowlie *n* a policeman.

yowm *n* **1** steam. **2** vapour.

yown-drift *n* wind-driven snow.

yowp *same as* **yaup**[1].

yowt, yowte *v* **1** to howl, roar, cry. **2** to scream. **3** to bark. **4** to yelp.—*n* a cry, yell, bellow.

yowther[1] *v* **1** to push anything heavy. **2** to move by a lever. **3** to walk heavily with a lumbering step. —*n* **1** a push. **2** a lever. **3** the act of walking heavily. **4** a tall, heavy, awkward person.—*adv* with a heavy, lumbering step.

yowther[2] *same as* **youther**.

yrlin *n* **1** a puny, sickly, stunted creature. **2** a dwarf.

yuck *same as* **yeuk**.

yuckfit, yucfit *n* the snipe.

yucky *adj* itching.

yudith *same as* **youdith**.

yuff *same as* **youff**.

yuik *same as* **yeuk**.

yuill *same as* **yill**[1].

yuke *same as* **yeuk**.

yukie *adj* itching, itchy.

Yule *n* **1** Christmas. **2** Hogmanay, 31 December. **3** an entertainment given by a farmer to his servants on 31 December and repeated on the first Monday morning of the New Year.—*v* to keep Christmas.

yule[1] *same as* **yeld**.

yule[2] *same as* **yowl**.

Yule blinker *n* the Christmas star.

Yule boys *n* Christmas guisers.

Yule brose *n* rich Christmas beef brose in which a ring was placed, the winner of which was to be first married.

Yule candles *n* the remains of specially large candles burned at Yule and extinguished at the close of the day, what was left being carefully preserved and locked away to be burned at the owner's lykewake (qv).

Yule-day *n* Christmas Day.

Yule-e'en *n* Christmas Eve.

Yule feast *n* a Christmas feast.

Yule guse *n* a Christmas goose.

Yule hole *n* the last hole to which a man could stretch his belt at a Christmas feast.

Yule-kebbuck *n* a special cheese prepared for Christmas.

Yule mairt *n* an ox or sheep killed at Christmas for home use.

Yule morning *n* Christmas morning.

Yule night *n* Christmas night, as a merry, festive night.

Yule pins *n* pins for playing at Christmas with the teetotum.

Yule play *n* the Christmas holidays.

Yule preens *same as* **Yule pins**.

Yule sowens *n* flummery made at Christmas.

Yule steek *n* a very wide stitch in sewing.

Yuletime *n* Christmastime.

Yule toy *n* a Christmas plaything.

Yule yowe *n* a sheep killed and eaten at Christmas.

yurlin *n* **1** a puny, sickly, stunted creature. **2** a dwarf.

yurm *same as* **yirm**.

yurn[1] *same as* **yearn**.

yurn[2] *same as* **yirn**.

yyte *same as* **yite**.

Z

zeenty-teenty *n* a children's counting-out game.

zickety, zickerty *n* a children's counting-out game.

zill *n* a child.